RELATED TITLES FOR COLLEGE-BOUND STUDENTS

SAT Comprehensive Program 2006
SAT Premier Program 2006
New SAT Strategies for Super Busy Students
Inside the SAT: 10 Strategies to Help You Score Higher
SAT 2400
NEW SAT Critical Reading Workbook
NEW SAT Math Workbook
NEW SAT Writing Workbook
SAT Vocabulary Flashcards Flip-O-Matic
Extreme SAT Vocabulary Flashcards Flip-O-Matic
The Ring of McAllister: A Score-Raising Mystery Featuring 1,046 Must-Know SAT Vocabulary Words
Frankenstein: A Kaplan New SAT Score-Raising Classic
The Tales of Edgar Allan Poe: A Kaplan New SAT Score-Raising Classic
Dr. Jekyll and Mr. Hyde: A Kaplan New SAT Score-Raising Classic
Wuthering Heights: A Kaplan New SAT Score-Raising Classic
Domina El SAT: Prepárate para Tomar el Examen para Ingresar a la Universidad

AP Biology
AP Calculus AB/BC
AP Chemistry
AP English Language & Composition
AP English Literature & Composition
AP Macroeconomics/Microeconomics
AP Physics B & C
AP Psychology
AP Statistics
AP U.S. Government & Politics
AP U.S. History
AP World History

SAT Subject Test: Biology E/M
SAT Subject Test: Chemistry
SAT Subject Test: Literature
SAT Subject Test: Mathematics Level 1
SAT Subject Test: Mathematics Level 2
SAT Subject Test: Physics
SAT Subject Test: Spanish
SAT Subject Test: U.S. History
SAT Subject Test: World History

Test Prep and Admissions

12 Practice Tests for the SAT

By the Staff of Kaplan Test Prep and Admissions

Simon & Schuster

NEW YORK · LONDON · SYDNEY · TORONTO

Kaplan Publishing
Published by Simon & Schuster
1230 Avenue of the Americas
New York, NY 10020

Contributing Editor: Jon Zeitlin
Editorial Director: Jennifer Farthing
Project Editor: Sheryl Gordon
Production Manager: Michael Shevlin
Interior Page Layout: Renée Mitchell, Dave Chipps, Baldur Gudbjornsson, Jan Gladish
Cover Design: Cheung Tai and Mark Weaver

July 2005
10 9 8 7 6 5 4 3 2

Manufactured in the United States of America
Published simultaneously in Canada

ISBN-13: 978-0-7432-7337-4
ISBN-10:   0-7432-7337-0

Table of Contents

Practice, Times 12

Recently, the SAT changed format. It's now longer, tougher, and includes an essay. But don't be scared—be relieved. Why? Because we know what's on the new SAT, and we know exactly how you should prepare for it. Kaplan has been teaching kids how to succeed on the SAT for over 65 years— longer than anyone else, period.

This book contains 12 practice exams that mirror the SAT you will face on Test Day—more SAT practice than can be found between the covers of any other book. Practice is one of the keys to mastery, and these 12 exams give you plenty of practice to assess your strengths and weaknesses before you take the actual exam. Detailed answer explanations not only tell you the correct answers, but why they are correct and why the wrong answers are not the best choices.

Every practice question and answer explanation in this book is geared toward one thing—to get you more points on the SAT. So don't stress out over the SAT—Kaplan's got you covered.

HOW TO USE THIS BOOK

This book is filled with over 2,000 practice questions to help you master the SAT. Follow these steps to get the most out of these 12 practice tests.

1. Read about the SAT structure in the next section. This way, you'll know what to expect—not only as you work through the book, but more important, on Test Day.

2. Begin your practice! Buying this book has given you an advantage—after you've worked your way through the exams, the format and timing of the SAT will be second nature to you. All you will have to concentrate on is improving your skills in the areas that need work.

3. Keep track. Turn to the Score Tracker on page xvi, where you can track your score as you take each exam. Keep a record of your scores, and watch how much you improve from test to test.

4. Assess your strengths and weaknesses. After you finish each test, carefully read the detailed answer explanations— pay attention to the questions you got wrong, but don't forget to read about the ones you got right. It's important to note your areas of strength as well as weakness. Take your own personal inventory of the skills you've mastered and the skills you need to work on.

5. Watch your scores improve! After you've made your way halfway through the book, compare your scores on Test 1 and Test 6. You've made progress, haven't you? See if your strengths and weaknesses have changed. Then, work your way through the remaining tests, building skills and SAT competency along the way.

After making your way through these steps, we guarantee that you will have the test expertise and improved skills to tackle the SAT with confidence.

WHAT'S CHANGED ON THE SAT

- Writing Section Added
- Changes to the Critical Reading Section
- Changes to the Math Section
- Changes to Your Score

Beginning with the March 2005 administration, the SAT became a little longer, a little harder, and a lot different. There are changes in the content tested and the types of questions used.

HOW THE SAT IS STRUCTURED

The SAT is 3 hours and 45 minutes long. It's primarily a multiple-choice exam, with a written essay and some student-produced math as the exceptions. It's divided into ten sections: three Math, three Critical Reading, and two Writing sections in addition to the essay and the experimental section. The essay always comes first; the other sections can appear in any order on test day. There are two ten-minute breaks.

The sections are broken down like this:

Section	Length	Content
1. Writing	25 minutes	Essay
2. Critical Reading	25 minutes	Multiple Choice Sentence Completion and Multiple-Choice Reading Comprehension
3. Math	25 minutes	Multiple-Choice Math
4. Writing	25 minutes	Multiple-Choice Identifying Sentence Errors, Improving Sentences, and Identifying Paragraph Errors
5. Math	25 minutes	Multiple-Choice Math and Grid-Ins (student produced responses)
6. Critical Reading	25 minutes	Multiple Choice Sentence Completion and Multiple-Choice Reading Comprehension
7. Experimental Section*	25 minutes	Math, Writing, or Critical Reading
8. Math	20 minutes	Multiple-Choice
9. Critical Reading	20 minutes	Multiple-Choice Sentence Completion and Multiple-Choice Reading Comprehension
10. Writing	10 minutes	Multiple Choice Improving Sentences

*Note: The experimental section can come at any time after the essay.

KAPLAN
Test Prep and Admissions

The Writing Section

The biggest change to the SAT is the addition of a writing section. The writing test has two parts: a multiple-choice section and a written essay. The multiple-choice questions test your ability to identify sentence errors and to make improvements in sentences and paragraphs. The essay section tests your writing ability and reasoning skills as you agree or disagree with a statement, marshalling evidence from your reading, studies, and/or experience to make your case.

The Critical Reading Section

For years and years, the SAT had a part called the Verbal section. Not anymore. Now it's called the Critical Reading section. How is it different? In place of the analogies are new, very short reading passages followed by sets of two to four multiple-choice questions. The longer reading passages and question sets are still on the test, and so are the sentence completion questions.

Sentence Completion Questions

Sentence Completion questions are multiple-choice questions that test your ability to see how the parts of a sentence relate. About half of the sentence completion questions on the SAT have one word missing from a sentence; the other half have two words missing. Both types test vocabulary and reasoning skills. Sentence Completion questions are arranged by order of difficulty on the SAT. The first few questions in a set are meant to be fairly easy. The middle few questions will be a little harder, and the last few are the most difficult. Keep this in mind as you work.

Reading Comprehension Questions

These questions test your ability to understand a piece of writing. The passages are short (about 100–150 words) and long (about 400–850 words), and at least one item will contain a set of paired passages on related topics. Most Reading Comprehension questions test how well you understand the passage, some ask you to draw conclusions, and some test your vocabulary. After a short passage, you can expect about two to four questions, depending on the length of the passage; after a short paired passage you can expect about four questions; after a long passage you can expect about 12 questions; and after a long paired passage you can expect about 13 questions.

Reading Comprehension questions are not arranged by difficulty. Whenever you find yourself spending too much time on a Reading Comprehension question, you should skip it and return to it later.

The Math Section

Some harder questions have been added to the SAT Math section. These questions cover the math usually taught in high school algebra II classes. In addition, the old Quantitative Comparison questions have been replaced with multiple-choice questions and Grid-in questions (a.k.a. "student-produced responses") that test the more difficult math.

Most questions are straightforward multiple-choice math questions, with five answer choices. The math section also features Grid-ins. Grid-ins are not multiple-choice questions. Instead of picking an answer choice, you write your response in a little grid. Both question types cover the same math concepts. Either one can ask you a geometry, algebra, or statistics question. The only difference is that one asks you to write your answer; the other asks you to fill in a bubble.

Some of the concepts likely to be tested on the new SAT include:

Basic Math	**Advanced Math**	
Remainders	Sequences	Quadratic functions—equations and graphs
Averages	Sets	Geometric notation
Ratios	Absolute value	Problems in which trigonometry can be used as an alternative method of solution
Rates	Rational equations and inequalities	
Percents	Radical equations	
Combinations	Integers and rational exponents	Properties of tangent lines
Simultaneous equations	Direct and inverse variation	Coordinate geometry
Symbols	Function notation and evaluation	Qualitative behavior of graphs and functions
Special triangles	Domain and range	Transformations and their effect on graphs and functions
Multiple and strange figures	Functions as models	
	Linear functions—equations and graphs	Data interpretation, scatterplots, and matrices
		Geometric probability

The Experimental Section

Every SAT has an experimental section. The experimental section is used by the test makers to try out new questions before they use them in upcoming SATs. The experimental section does not count in your score. It can show up anywhere on the exam and will look like just like a normal section. *Do not* try to figure out which SAT section is experimental. You will fail to do so. Treat all the sections as if they count.

SCORING THE TEST

The Writing multiple-choice section is scored on a scale of 200–800, as are the Math and Critical Reading sections. So the composite scores on the new test are 600–2400. The essay is scored on a scale of 1–6, with 6 being the highest score. Your total Writing section score is a combination of your multiple choice raw score and your score on the essay converted into a standard score by the testmaker. The totals for the Writing, Critical Reading, and Math sections are added up to produce three raw scores. These raw scores are then converted into scaled scores, with 200 as the lowest score and 800 the highest.

You gain one point for each correct answer on the SAT, and lose 1/4 of a point for each wrong answer. You do not gain or lose any points for questions you leave blank. The only exception is with Grid-ins, where you lose nothing for a wrong answer. That's why you must always fill in an answer on the Grid-ins—you have nothing to lose and a potential point to gain.

Remember…

The SAT is divided into ten sections:
- 3 Critical Reading sections
- 3 Math sections
- 2 Writing sections
- 1 Experimental section
- Essay

Some sections (but not all) arrange their questions from easiest to hardest.

You gain 1 point for every question you get right; you lose no points for leaving a blank.

You lose $\frac{1}{4}$ of a point for every question you get wrong (except for Grid-ins).

Scoring information and conversion charts are found from pages xiii–xvi.

SAT TEST DATES

As a general rule, it's important to get one SAT score under your belt by the end of your junior year. This way you know where you stand as you plan your college choices. Plus, it's likely that you'll improve your score by taking the exam again, since it will be familiar to you.

The SAT is administered on select Saturdays during the school year. Sunday testing is available for students who cannot take the Saturday test because of religious observances. Here are the upcoming test dates for 2005 and 2006:

Test Date	Registration Deadlines	U.S. Late Registration	International Deadlines
October 8, 2005	September 7, 2005	September 14, 2005	September 7, 2005
November 5, 2005	September 30, 2005	October 12, 2005	September 30, 2005
December 3, 2005	October 28, 2005	November 9, 2005	October 28, 2005
January 28, 2005	December 22, 2005	January 4, 2006	December 22, 2005
April 1, 2006	February 24, 2006	March 8, 2008	N/A
May 6, 2006	April 3, 2006	April 12, 2006	April 3, 2006
June 3, 2006	April 28, 2006	May 10, 2006	April 28, 2006

SAT REGISTRATION

Check the College Board website at www.collegeboard.com for complete information about registering for the SAT. Here are some important highlights.

- To register for the SAT by mail, you'll need to get a Registration Bulletin from your high school guidance counselor.
- You can register online at www.collegeboard.com/sat/html/satform.html. Important: Not all students are eligible to register online, so read the instructions and requirements carefully.
- Register early to secure the time you want at the test center of your choice and to avoid late registration fees.
- Students with Disabilities can call (609) 771-7137 (TTY: (609) 882-4118) for more information.
- At press time, the basic fee is about $40 in the United States. This price includes reports for you, your high school, and up to four colleges and scholarship programs.
- You may reregister by telephone if you've previously registered for the SAT and you require no special forms (like a fee waiver). If you have a touch-tone phone and a major credit card, you can reregister by calling (800) SAT-SCORE.
- You will receive an admission ticket at least a week before the test. The ticket confirms your registration at a specified date, at a specified test center. Make sure to bring it, and proper identification, with you to the test center. Some acceptable forms of identification include photo IDs such as a driver's license, a school identification card, or a valid passport. (Unacceptable forms of identification include a social security card, credit card, and birth certificate.)
- Your SAT scores will be available online approximately three weeks after the test. If you can't wait that long, you can get your scores eight days earlier with Scores by Web or Scores by Phone. Please visit www.collegeboard.com for more information.
- Remember to check with the College Board for all the latest information on the new SAT. Every effort has been made to keep the information in this book as up-to-date as possible, but changes may occur after the book is published.
- Finally, bookmark the College Board's website: www.collegeboard.com.

Start your practice!

Test Prep and Admissions

ESSAY SCORING CHART

Score	Competence	Organization	Language
6	clear and consistent competence, though it may have errors	is well organized and fully developed with supporting examples	displays consistent language facility, varied sentence structure, and range of vocabulary
5	reasonable competence, with occasional errors or lapses in quality	is generally organized and well developed with appropriate examples	displays language facility, with syntactic variety and a range of vocabulary
4	adequate competence with occasional errors and lapses in quality	is organized and adequately developed with examples	displays adequate but inconsistent language facility
3	developing competence, with weaknesses	inadequate organization or development	many errors in grammar or diction; little variety
2	some incompetence with one or more weaknesses	poor organization, thin development	frequent errors in grammar and diction; no variety
1	incompetence, with serious flaws	no organization, no development	severe grammar and diction errors obscure meaning

CONVERT YOUR RAW SCORE TO A SCALED SCORE.

For each subject area in the practice test, convert your raw score to your scaled score using the table below.

RAW	Critical Reading	Math	Writing 0	Writing 1	Writing 2	Writing 3	Writing 4	Writing 5	Writing 6
67	800								
66	800								
65	790								
64	770								
63	750								
62	740								
61	730								
60	720								
59	700								
58	690								
57	690								
56	680								
55	670								
54	660	800							
53	650	790							
52	650	760							
51	640	740							
50	630	720							
49	620	710	670	700	720	740	780	790	800
48	620	700	660	680	700	730	760	780	790
47	610	680	650	670	690	720	750	770	780
46	600	670	640	660	680	710	740	750	770
45	600	660	630	650	670	700	740	750	770
44	590	650	620	640	660	690	730	750	760
43	590	640	600	630	650	680	710	740	750
42	580	630	600	620	640	670	700	730	750
41	570	620	590	610	630	660	690	730	740
40	570	620	580	600	620	650	690	720	740
39	560	610	570	590	610	640	680	710	740
38	550	600	560	590	610	630	670	700	730
37	550	590	550	580	600	630	660	690	720
36	540	580	540	570	590	620	650	680	710
35	540	580	540	560	580	610	640	680	710
34	530	570	530	550	570	600	640	670	700
33	520	560	520	540	560	590	630	660	690
32	520	550	510	540	560	580	620	650	680
31	520	550	500	530	550	580	610	640	670
30	510	550	490	520	540	570	600	630	660
29	510	540	490	510	530	560	590	630	650

*These are not official College Board scores. They are rough estimates to help you get an idea of your performance.

RAW	Critical Reading	Math	Writing 0	Writing 1	Writing 2	Writing 3	Writing 4	Writing 5	Writing 6
28	500	540	480	500	520	550	590	620	640
27	490	530	470	490	510	540	580	610	640
26	480	520	460	490	500	530	570	600	630
25	470	510	450	480	500	520	560	590	620
24	460	500	440	470	490	510	550	580	610
23	460	500	430	460	480	510	540	570	600
22	450	490	430	450	470	500	530	570	590
21	450	490	430	450	470	500	530	570	590
20	440	480	420	440	460	490	520	560	580
19	430	470	410	430	450	480	520	550	570
18	420	460	400	420	440	470	510	540	570
17	410	460	390	420	430	460	500	530	560
16	400	450	380	410	430	450	490	520	550
15	390	440	370	400	420	450	480	510	540
14	380	430	360	390	410	440	470	500	530
13	360	420	360	380	400	430	460	500	520
12	340	400	340	370	390	420	450	490	510
11	330	390	340	360	380	410	450	480	510
10	320	380	330	350	370	400	440	470	500
9	310	370	320	350	360	390	430	460	490
8	300	360	310	340	360	390	420	450	480
7	290	350	300	330	350	380	410	440	470
6	270	340	290	320	340	370	400	430	460
5	270	330	290	310	330	360	390	430	450
4	260	300	280	300	320	350	390	420	450
3	240	280	270	290	310	340	380	410	440
2	230	260	260	280	300	330	370	400	430
1	210	240	250	270	290	320	340	380	410
0	200	220	250	260	280	310	340	370	400
neg 1	200	200	240	260	270	290	320	360	380
neg 2	200	200	230	250	260	270	310	340	370
neg 3	200	200	220	240	250	260	300	330	360
neg 4	200	200	220	230	240	250	290	320	350
neg 5	200	200	200	220	230	240	280	310	340
neg 6	200	200	200	210	220	240	280	310	340
neg 7	200	200	200	210	220	230	270	300	330
neg 8	200	200	200	210	220	230	270	300	330
neg 9	200	200	200	210	220	230	270	300	330
neg 10	200	200	200	210	220	230	270	300	330

SCORE TRACKER

After you take each test, refer to the scoring conversion chart on the pages directly following each Answers and Explanations section. Then translate your raw score into a scaled score of 200-800 for each section on page xiv. Write your results in the chart below. As you take more and more practice tests, watch as your scores in each section begin to go up!

	Math	Critical Reading	Writing	Total
Test 1				
Test 2				
Test 3				
Test 4				
Test 5				
Test 6				
Test 7				
Test 8				
Test 9				
Test 10				
Test 11				
Test 12				

Practice Tests and Explanations

Before taking this practice test, find a quiet room where you can work uninterrupted for 4 hours. Make sure you have a comfortable desk and several No. 2 pencils. Use the answer sheet on the following page to record your answers. (You can tear it out or photocopy it.)

Once you start this practice test, do not stop until you have finished. Remember, you may review any questions within a section, but you may not go back or forward a section.

When you have finished taking your practice test, you can go on to the section that follows Practice Test One to calculate your score.

Good luck!

SAT PRACTICE TEST ONE ANSWER SHEET

Remove (or photocopy) the answer sheet, and use it to complete the practice test.

How to Take the Practice Tests

Each Practice Test includes eight scored multiple-choice sections and one essay. Keep in mind that on the actual SAT, there will be an additional multiple-choice section—the experimental section—that will not contribute to your score.

Once you start a Practice Test, don't stop until you've gone through all nine sections. Remember, you can review any questions within a section, but you may not go back or forward a section.

Good luck!

Start with number 1 for each section. If a section has fewer questions than answer spaces, leave the extra spaces blank.

Section One

Section One is the writing section's essay component.
Lined pages on which you will write your essay can be found in that section.

Section Two

1. Ⓐ Ⓑ Ⓒ Ⓓ Ⓔ	9. Ⓐ Ⓑ Ⓒ Ⓓ Ⓔ	17. Ⓐ Ⓑ Ⓒ Ⓓ Ⓔ	25. Ⓐ Ⓑ Ⓒ Ⓓ Ⓔ
2. Ⓐ Ⓑ Ⓒ Ⓓ Ⓔ	10. Ⓐ Ⓑ Ⓒ Ⓓ Ⓔ	18. Ⓐ Ⓑ Ⓒ Ⓓ Ⓔ
3. Ⓐ Ⓑ Ⓒ Ⓓ Ⓔ	11. Ⓐ Ⓑ Ⓒ Ⓓ Ⓔ	19. Ⓐ Ⓑ Ⓒ Ⓓ Ⓔ
4. Ⓐ Ⓑ Ⓒ Ⓓ Ⓔ	12. Ⓐ Ⓑ Ⓒ Ⓓ Ⓔ	20. Ⓐ Ⓑ Ⓒ Ⓓ Ⓔ
5. Ⓐ Ⓑ Ⓒ Ⓓ Ⓔ	13. Ⓐ Ⓑ Ⓒ Ⓓ Ⓔ	21. Ⓐ Ⓑ Ⓒ Ⓓ Ⓔ
6. Ⓐ Ⓑ Ⓒ Ⓓ Ⓔ	14. Ⓐ Ⓑ Ⓒ Ⓓ Ⓔ	22. Ⓐ Ⓑ Ⓒ Ⓓ Ⓔ
7. Ⓐ Ⓑ Ⓒ Ⓓ Ⓔ	15. Ⓐ Ⓑ Ⓒ Ⓓ Ⓔ	23. Ⓐ Ⓑ Ⓒ Ⓓ Ⓔ
8. Ⓐ Ⓑ Ⓒ Ⓓ Ⓔ	16. Ⓐ Ⓑ Ⓒ Ⓓ Ⓔ	24. Ⓐ Ⓑ Ⓒ Ⓓ Ⓔ

☐ # right in Section Two

☐ # wrong in Section Two

Section Three

1. Ⓐ Ⓑ Ⓒ Ⓓ Ⓔ	9. Ⓐ Ⓑ Ⓒ Ⓓ Ⓔ	17. Ⓐ Ⓑ Ⓒ Ⓓ Ⓔ
2. Ⓐ Ⓑ Ⓒ Ⓓ Ⓔ	10. Ⓐ Ⓑ Ⓒ Ⓓ Ⓔ	18. Ⓐ Ⓑ Ⓒ Ⓓ Ⓔ
3. Ⓐ Ⓑ Ⓒ Ⓓ Ⓔ	11. Ⓐ Ⓑ Ⓒ Ⓓ Ⓔ	19. Ⓐ Ⓑ Ⓒ Ⓓ Ⓔ
4. Ⓐ Ⓑ Ⓒ Ⓓ Ⓔ	12. Ⓐ Ⓑ Ⓒ Ⓓ Ⓔ	20. Ⓐ Ⓑ Ⓒ Ⓓ Ⓔ
5. Ⓐ Ⓑ Ⓒ Ⓓ Ⓔ	13. Ⓐ Ⓑ Ⓒ Ⓓ Ⓔ
6. Ⓐ Ⓑ Ⓒ Ⓓ Ⓔ	14. Ⓐ Ⓑ Ⓒ Ⓓ Ⓔ
7. Ⓐ Ⓑ Ⓒ Ⓓ Ⓔ	15. Ⓐ Ⓑ Ⓒ Ⓓ Ⓔ
8. Ⓐ Ⓑ Ⓒ Ⓓ Ⓔ	16. Ⓐ Ⓑ Ⓒ Ⓓ Ⓔ

☐ # right in Section Three

☐ # wrong in Section Three

Remove (or photocopy) this answer sheet, and use it to complete the practice test.

Start with number 1 for each section. If a section has fewer questions than answer spaces, leave the extra spaces blank.

Section Four

1. Ⓐ Ⓑ Ⓒ Ⓓ Ⓔ   9. Ⓐ Ⓑ Ⓒ Ⓓ Ⓔ   17. Ⓐ Ⓑ Ⓒ Ⓓ Ⓔ
2. Ⓐ Ⓑ Ⓒ Ⓓ Ⓔ   10. Ⓐ Ⓑ Ⓒ Ⓓ Ⓔ   18. Ⓐ Ⓑ Ⓒ Ⓓ Ⓔ
3. Ⓐ Ⓑ Ⓒ Ⓓ Ⓔ   11. Ⓐ Ⓑ Ⓒ Ⓓ Ⓔ   19. Ⓐ Ⓑ Ⓒ Ⓓ Ⓔ
4. Ⓐ Ⓑ Ⓒ Ⓓ Ⓔ   12. Ⓐ Ⓑ Ⓒ Ⓓ Ⓔ   20. Ⓐ Ⓑ Ⓒ Ⓓ Ⓔ
5. Ⓐ Ⓑ Ⓒ Ⓓ Ⓔ   13. Ⓐ Ⓑ Ⓒ Ⓓ Ⓔ   21. Ⓐ Ⓑ Ⓒ Ⓓ Ⓔ
6. Ⓐ Ⓑ Ⓒ Ⓓ Ⓔ   14. Ⓐ Ⓑ Ⓒ Ⓓ Ⓔ   22. Ⓐ Ⓑ Ⓒ Ⓓ Ⓔ
7. Ⓐ Ⓑ Ⓒ Ⓓ Ⓔ   15. Ⓐ Ⓑ Ⓒ Ⓓ Ⓔ   23. Ⓐ Ⓑ Ⓒ Ⓓ Ⓔ
8. Ⓐ Ⓑ Ⓒ Ⓓ Ⓔ   16. Ⓐ Ⓑ Ⓒ Ⓓ Ⓔ   24. Ⓐ Ⓑ Ⓒ Ⓓ Ⓔ

☐ # right in Section Four

☐ # wrong in Section Four

Section Five

1. Ⓐ Ⓑ Ⓒ Ⓓ Ⓔ   9. Ⓐ Ⓑ Ⓒ Ⓓ Ⓔ   17. Ⓐ Ⓑ Ⓒ Ⓓ Ⓔ
2. Ⓐ Ⓑ Ⓒ Ⓓ Ⓔ   10. Ⓐ Ⓑ Ⓒ Ⓓ Ⓔ   18. Ⓐ Ⓑ Ⓒ Ⓓ Ⓔ
3. Ⓐ Ⓑ Ⓒ Ⓓ Ⓔ   11. Ⓐ Ⓑ Ⓒ Ⓓ Ⓔ
4. Ⓐ Ⓑ Ⓒ Ⓓ Ⓔ   12. Ⓐ Ⓑ Ⓒ Ⓓ Ⓔ
5. Ⓐ Ⓑ Ⓒ Ⓓ Ⓔ   13. Ⓐ Ⓑ Ⓒ Ⓓ Ⓔ
6. Ⓐ Ⓑ Ⓒ Ⓓ Ⓔ   14. Ⓐ Ⓑ Ⓒ Ⓓ Ⓔ
7. Ⓐ Ⓑ Ⓒ Ⓓ Ⓔ   15. Ⓐ Ⓑ Ⓒ Ⓓ Ⓔ
8. Ⓐ Ⓑ Ⓒ Ⓓ Ⓔ   16. Ⓐ Ⓑ Ⓒ Ⓓ Ⓔ

☐ # right in Section Five

☐ # wrong in Section Five

If section 5 of your test book contains math questions that are not multiple choice, continue to item 9 below. Otherwise, continue to item 9 above.

9. 10. 11. 12. 13.

14. 15. 16. 17. 18.

Remove (or photocopy) this answer sheet, and use it to complete the practice test.

Start with number 1 for each section. If a section has fewer questions than answer spaces, leave the extra spaces blank.

Section Six

#		#		#		#	
1. Ⓐ Ⓑ Ⓒ Ⓓ Ⓔ		10. Ⓐ Ⓑ Ⓒ Ⓓ Ⓔ		19. Ⓐ Ⓑ Ⓒ Ⓓ Ⓔ		28. Ⓐ Ⓑ Ⓒ Ⓓ Ⓔ	
2. Ⓐ Ⓑ Ⓒ Ⓓ Ⓔ		11. Ⓐ Ⓑ Ⓒ Ⓓ Ⓔ		20. Ⓐ Ⓑ Ⓒ Ⓓ Ⓔ		29. Ⓐ Ⓑ Ⓒ Ⓓ Ⓔ	
3. Ⓐ Ⓑ Ⓒ Ⓓ Ⓔ		12. Ⓐ Ⓑ Ⓒ Ⓓ Ⓔ		21. Ⓐ Ⓑ Ⓒ Ⓓ Ⓔ		30. Ⓐ Ⓑ Ⓒ Ⓓ Ⓔ	
4. Ⓐ Ⓑ Ⓒ Ⓓ Ⓔ		13. Ⓐ Ⓑ Ⓒ Ⓓ Ⓔ		22. Ⓐ Ⓑ Ⓒ Ⓓ Ⓔ		31. Ⓐ Ⓑ Ⓒ Ⓓ Ⓔ	
5. Ⓐ Ⓑ Ⓒ Ⓓ Ⓔ		14. Ⓐ Ⓑ Ⓒ Ⓓ Ⓔ		23. Ⓐ Ⓑ Ⓒ Ⓓ Ⓔ		32. Ⓐ Ⓑ Ⓒ Ⓓ Ⓔ	
6. Ⓐ Ⓑ Ⓒ Ⓓ Ⓔ		15. Ⓐ Ⓑ Ⓒ Ⓓ Ⓔ		24. Ⓐ Ⓑ Ⓒ Ⓓ Ⓔ		33. Ⓐ Ⓑ Ⓒ Ⓓ Ⓔ	
7. Ⓐ Ⓑ Ⓒ Ⓓ Ⓔ		16. Ⓐ Ⓑ Ⓒ Ⓓ Ⓔ		25. Ⓐ Ⓑ Ⓒ Ⓓ Ⓔ		34. Ⓐ Ⓑ Ⓒ Ⓓ Ⓔ	
8. Ⓐ Ⓑ Ⓒ Ⓓ Ⓔ		17. Ⓐ Ⓑ Ⓒ Ⓓ Ⓔ		26. Ⓐ Ⓑ Ⓒ Ⓓ Ⓔ		35. Ⓐ Ⓑ Ⓒ Ⓓ Ⓔ	
9. Ⓐ Ⓑ Ⓒ Ⓓ Ⓔ		18. Ⓐ Ⓑ Ⓒ Ⓓ Ⓔ		27. Ⓐ Ⓑ Ⓒ Ⓓ Ⓔ			

☐ # right in Section Six

☐ # wrong in Section Six

Section Seven

#		#		#	
1. Ⓐ Ⓑ Ⓒ Ⓓ Ⓔ		9. Ⓐ Ⓑ Ⓒ Ⓓ Ⓔ		17. Ⓐ Ⓑ Ⓒ Ⓓ Ⓔ	
2. Ⓐ Ⓑ Ⓒ Ⓓ Ⓔ		10. Ⓐ Ⓑ Ⓒ Ⓓ Ⓔ		18. Ⓐ Ⓑ Ⓒ Ⓓ Ⓔ	
3. Ⓐ Ⓑ Ⓒ Ⓓ Ⓔ		11. Ⓐ Ⓑ Ⓒ Ⓓ Ⓔ			
4. Ⓐ Ⓑ Ⓒ Ⓓ Ⓔ		12. Ⓐ Ⓑ Ⓒ Ⓓ Ⓔ			
5. Ⓐ Ⓑ Ⓒ Ⓓ Ⓔ		13. Ⓐ Ⓑ Ⓒ Ⓓ Ⓔ			
6. Ⓐ Ⓑ Ⓒ Ⓓ Ⓔ		14. Ⓐ Ⓑ Ⓒ Ⓓ Ⓔ			
7. Ⓐ Ⓑ Ⓒ Ⓓ Ⓔ		15. Ⓐ Ⓑ Ⓒ Ⓓ Ⓔ			
8. Ⓐ Ⓑ Ⓒ Ⓓ Ⓔ		16. Ⓐ Ⓑ Ⓒ Ⓓ Ⓔ			

☐ # right in Section Seven

☐ # wrong in Section Seven

Section Eight

#		#	
1. Ⓐ Ⓑ Ⓒ Ⓓ Ⓔ		9. Ⓐ Ⓑ Ⓒ Ⓓ Ⓔ	
2. Ⓐ Ⓑ Ⓒ Ⓓ Ⓔ		10. Ⓐ Ⓑ Ⓒ Ⓓ Ⓔ	
3. Ⓐ Ⓑ Ⓒ Ⓓ Ⓔ		11. Ⓐ Ⓑ Ⓒ Ⓓ Ⓔ	
4. Ⓐ Ⓑ Ⓒ Ⓓ Ⓔ		12. Ⓐ Ⓑ Ⓒ Ⓓ Ⓔ	
5. Ⓐ Ⓑ Ⓒ Ⓓ Ⓔ		13. Ⓐ Ⓑ Ⓒ Ⓓ Ⓔ	
6. Ⓐ Ⓑ Ⓒ Ⓓ Ⓔ		14. Ⓐ Ⓑ Ⓒ Ⓓ Ⓔ	
7. Ⓐ Ⓑ Ⓒ Ⓓ Ⓔ		15. Ⓐ Ⓑ Ⓒ Ⓓ Ⓔ	
8. Ⓐ Ⓑ Ⓒ Ⓓ Ⓔ		16. Ⓐ Ⓑ Ⓒ Ⓓ Ⓔ	

☐ # right in Section Eight

☐ # wrong in Section Eight

Section Nine

#		#	
1. Ⓐ Ⓑ Ⓒ Ⓓ Ⓔ		9. Ⓐ Ⓑ Ⓒ Ⓓ Ⓔ	
2. Ⓐ Ⓑ Ⓒ Ⓓ Ⓔ		10. Ⓐ Ⓑ Ⓒ Ⓓ Ⓔ	
3. Ⓐ Ⓑ Ⓒ Ⓓ Ⓔ		11. Ⓐ Ⓑ Ⓒ Ⓓ Ⓔ	
4. Ⓐ Ⓑ Ⓒ Ⓓ Ⓔ		12. Ⓐ Ⓑ Ⓒ Ⓓ Ⓔ	
5. Ⓐ Ⓑ Ⓒ Ⓓ Ⓔ		13. Ⓐ Ⓑ Ⓒ Ⓓ Ⓔ	
6. Ⓐ Ⓑ Ⓒ Ⓓ Ⓔ		14. Ⓐ Ⓑ Ⓒ Ⓓ Ⓔ	
7. Ⓐ Ⓑ Ⓒ Ⓓ Ⓔ			
8. Ⓐ Ⓑ Ⓒ Ⓓ Ⓔ			

☐ # right in Section Nine

☐ # wrong in Section Nine

Practice Test One

SECTION 1
Time—25 Minutes
ESSAY

The essay gives you an opportunity to show how effectively you can develop and express ideas. You should, therefore, take care to develop your point of view, present your ideas logically and clearly, and use language precisely.

Your essay must be written in your Answer Grid Booklet—you will receive no other paper on which to write. You will have enough space if you write on every line, avoid wide margins, and keep your handwriting to a reasonable size. Remember that people who are not familiar with your handwriting will read what you write. Try to write or print so that what you are writing is legible to those readers.

You have twenty-five minutes to write an essay on the topic assigned below.

DO NOT WRITE ON ANOTHER TOPIC. AN OFF-TOPIC ESSAY WILL RECEIVE A SCORE OF ZERO.

Think carefully about the issue presented in the following excerpt and the assignment below.

> "No one is contented in this world, I believe. There is always some-thing left to desire, and the last thing longed for always seems the most necessary to happiness."
>
> –Marie Corelli, *A Romance of Two Worlds*

Assignment: Do you think that people are capable of finding happiness or are they always searching for something beyond what they have? Plan and write an essay in which you develop your point of view on this issue. Support your position with reasoning and examples taken from your reading, studies, experience, or observations.

DO NOT WRITE YOUR ESSAY IN YOUR TEST BOOK.
You will receive credit only for what you write in your Answer Grid Booklet.

_____

_____

_____

_____

_____

_____

_____

_____

_____

_____

_____

_____

_____

_____

_____

_____

_____

_____

_____

_____

_____

IF YOU FINISH BEFORE TIME IS CALLED, YOU MAY CHECK YOUR WORK ON THIS SECTION ONLY. DO NOT TURN TO ANY OTHER SECTION IN THE TEST.

SECTION 2

Time—25 Minutes
25 Questions

Directions: For each of the following questions, choose the best answer and darken the corresponding oval on the answer sheet.

Each sentence below has one or two blanks, each blank indicating that something has been omitted. Beneath the sentence are five words or sets of words labeled (A) through (E). Choose the word or set of words that, when inserted in the sentence, best fits the meaning of the sentence as a whole.

EXAMPLE:

Today's small, portable computers contrast markedly with the earliest electronic computers, which were ----.

(A) effective
(B) invented
(C) useful
(D) destructive
(E) enormous   Ⓐ Ⓑ Ⓒ Ⓓ ●

1. The parents, hoping to ---- the dispute between her and her younger brother, proposed a compromise that they thought might be ---- to both children.

(A) enforce . . useful
(B) end . . divisive
(C) overcome . . unattractive
(D) extend . . satisfactory
(E) resolve . . acceptable

2. Whether Nathan Lane is performing on Broadway, acting in a film, or discussing the techniques of acting, the actor's animated disposition ---- his passion for his profession.

(A) misrepresents
(B) exaggerates
(C) satisfies
(D) reflects
(E) disguises

3. When the principal addresses the students he is very powerful and often has more ---- than do the teachers.

(A) influence
(B) pretense
(C) discrimination
(D) restraint
(E) integrity

4. Trying to ---- about post-modern literature is not only ---- but also foolish, because it is a movement that encompasses many different styles and elements.

(A) brag . . necessary
(B) generalize . . difficult
(C) complain . . important
(D) rhapsodize . . fair
(E) learn . . unproductive

GO ON TO THE NEXT PAGE ▷

KAPLAN
Test Prep and Admissions

5. My brother is always ---- in doing his homework, waiting until the night before it's due to start it.

    (A) incompetent
    (B) obtrusive
    (C) dilatory
    (D) surreptitious
    (E) extroverted

6. Even though the FBI agent's attempts to uncover an outlandish alien conspiracy were ----, he was still ---- by the severe reprimand he received from his superiors.

    (A) obstinate . . elated
    (B) insightful . . impenitent
    (C) persuasive . . exultant
    (D) thwarted . . discomfited
    (E) successful . . satisfied

7. Alex is so ---- that it is nearly impossible to offer him constructive criticism without him taking it personally and acting defensive.

    (A) cerebral
    (B) obdurate
    (C) sensitive
    (D) pretentious
    (E) enervated

8. Many artists seem to be seeking to express what they consider to be ----, or incommunicable by any other means.

    (A) ineffable
    (B) mundane
    (C) onerous
    (D) incisive
    (E) auspicious

GO ON TO THE NEXT PAGE

Directions: The passages below are followed by questions based on their content; questions following a pair of related passages may also be based on the relationship between the paired passages. Answer the questions on the basis of what is <u>stated</u> or <u>implied</u> in the passages and in any introductory material that may be provided.

Questions 9–10 are based on the following passage.

Cryptozoology is the study of still unknown animals, or of creatures, like the Loch Ness Monster, whose existence hasn't been proven. Cryptozoology, however, doesn't just refer to the

(5) discovery of animals that may exist only in the minds of the over-imaginative. It also refers to animals that may live in areas of the world that are so remote or parts of the ocean that are so deep that no one has discovered them. In fact, there is a

(10) whole host of animals, called cryptids, whom reputable scientists believe may one day be discovered. A great example of a cryptid is the coelacanth. This fish was thought to have been extinct for 70 million years, but it was rediscovered in the

(15) Indian Ocean in 1938.

9. The author most likely believes that the Loch Ness Monster

(A) will be discovered one day

(B) is mythological

(C) lives so deep in Loch Ness that its existence will never be proven

(D) dwells in a remote part of the world

(E) is ignored by reputable scientists

10. In line 10, the word "host" most nearly means

(A) network

(B) blend

(C) unit

(D) den

(E) multitude

Questions 11–13 are based on the following passage.

For thousands of years money, whether paper or coins, was a tangible object that people could keep in their pockets or purses, or safely tucked under their mattresses. The late 20th century saw the

(5) birth of intangible wealth, from e-money to Bowie Bonds. Bowie Bonds are named after the rock musician, David Bowie, who in 1997 used his future music as security for bonds. The bonds were the brain-child of banker David Pullman.

(10) Pullman's innovation caught fire and many well-known entertainers, such as Ashford & Simpson, James Brown, and the Isley Brothers followed in Bowie's pioneering footsteps. Today asset-backed security is becoming the norm.

11. It's possible to infer from the passage that Bowie Bonds (line 6) are

(A) not as popular today as they were when they were first offered

(B) used only by entertainers

(C) a form of asset-backed security

(D) available only to the very wealthy

(E) a type of tangible wealth

12. In line 9, "brain-child" means

(A) offspring

(B) unspoken thought

(C) unclaimed property

(D) original idea

(E) avocation

13. In line 10, which of the following could replace the phrase "caught fire" without changing the meaning of the sentence?

(A) was destroyed

(B) became popular

(C) sunk into oblivion

(D) was highly publicized

(E) belied its early promise

GO ON TO THE NEXT PAGE

Questions 14–25 are based on the following passage.

The following passage is from an essay that discusses the criticisms of lip-synching in popular music.

Very public examples of lip-synching—the act of pretending to sing in synchronization with recorded sound—can be traced as far back as the Beatles, who faked many so-called live performances
(5) on television. Lip-synching, however, will forever be associated with the German pop duo Milli Vanilli, who in 1991 admitted to mouthing the words to songs sung by performers other than themselves. While much of the popular music-lov-
(10) ing world was seemingly scandalized by this revelation—to the point where a United States court ruled that anyone who had bought the Milli Vanilli album was entitled to a refund—this episode was hardly as duplicitous as the media
(15) portrayed it to be. Those who would categorically accuse Milli Vanilli of being guilty of dishonesty do have a point, but these accusers are guilty themselves of making the naïve assumption that anything in pop music is the sole creation of the
(20) artist on the stage, television, or the radio. They simply do not comprehend the bigger, more complex picture.

Everyday people are often taken aback when they glimpse a striking supermodel from the pages
(25) of *Vogue* or *Cosmopolitan* walking around in real life. Removed from the glossy realm of the magazine, many of these models are often revealed to be surprisingly plain. A model's transformation into the alluring image on the cover page that
(30) helps to sell magazines begins with a photographer's vision and requires numerous photo and wardrobe assistants, make-up artists and hairdressers, set dressers, stylists, expensive equipment, and elaborate lighting. The finished product
(35) of this complex ensemble's collaboration is an illusion that is decidedly more eye-catching and wholly more appealing than anything one might find in the frames of reality. All record company executives understand this concept implicitly; they
(40) simply apply it to pop stars.

Back in 1981, the first music video MTV ever aired was the fittingly titled "Video Killed the Radio Star," by the Buggles. From that day forth, popular culture would be forever altered—images
(45) and songs would be eternally linked. After that date, an artist's hairstyle, clothes, attitude, and dance moves have been just as important as the songs they have performed. Music has officially become a product. And it is this idea that brings
(50) us to the heart of my argument. Let us consider a hypothetical young pop star's rise to stardom. A pretty girl with a great voice and exceptional dance skills is hand-picked by a record company and given a recording contract. This singer is
(55) immediately sent to a stylist who changes her entire image. She is given a strict regimen of one-on-one vocal and dance lessons. When it is time to record her album, talented writers are hired to pen the songs, one of the most gifted producers in the
(60) industry is brought on board, and a group of accomplished professional musicians serves to create the instrumental support. In the recording studio, the singer's vocals are layered with numerous supporting tracks distorted and softened by studio
(65) effects to add depth and range that the young woman does not naturally possess. Take after take of each song is meticulously edited until the best possible version of the song is ready for mass consumption. Then the video is produced, where
(70) everything right down to the nail polish is laboriously styled to create the desired effect—a hit, which it is. But, halfway through the pop star's first tour it is revealed that she sometimes lip-synchs on stage, the better to reproduce the dis-
(75) tinct sound that her fans love. In the ensuing media criticism, her true level of talent is brought into question.

When an audience sees its pop idols perform live, it expects to see something similar to what
(80) they see in the music video—stars ethereally beautiful, able to pull off tightly choreographed dance moves on the stage, all the while maintaining perfect vocal pitch and not losing a breath while they perform songs that took hours, if not days, to pro-
(85) duce in a studio. An entire generation has grown into adulthood accustomed to and desiring these illusions, fueling the market to keep producing more of them. The pop star is not to blame when these illusions are broken; it is the fault of those
(90) who believe in the illusion in the first place.

GO ON TO THE NEXT PAGE ▷

14. According to the author, the scandal involving Milli Vanilli was

    (A) an insignificant event that was quickly forgotten
    (B) similar to a scandal involving the Beatles
    (C) the result of a court ruling
    (D) based on rumors, not evidence
    (E) overblown by the media

15. In the second paragraph of the passage, the author suggests that fashion magazines and pop music

    (A) distort reality to appeal to consumers
    (B) are shallow mediums of expression
    (C) are declining in popularity
    (D) fail to address important societal issues
    (E) are maliciously deceitful

16. The author describes the entire process that goes into a "model's transformation" (lines 28–34) mainly to

    (A) demonstrate how demanding a model's job can be
    (B) teach a lesson about fashion photography
    (C) compare fashion photographers to music video directors
    (D) illustrate a point about the fashion and pop music industries
    (E) relate the importance of make-up artists

17. In line 31, "vision" most nearly means

    (A) exceptional beauty
    (B) image
    (C) eyesight
    (D) idea
    (E) apparition

18. In line 38, "the frames of reality" describe

    (A) extraordinary life events
    (B) the photographer's snapshots
    (C) normal, day-to-day living
    (D) the pages of a fashion magazine
    (E) a technical photography method

19. In line 42, the author mentions the name of the first video ever aired on MTV because

    (A) the Buggles will forever occupy a place in American history
    (B) the song's name is symbolic of the impact MTV would have upon pop music
    (C) it went on to become a smash hit
    (D) the video never aired on MTV again
    (E) the Buggles were lip-synching in the video

20. Lines 51–62 ("A pretty girl … support") portray a performer who is

    (A) struggling
    (B) being mishandled by her record company
    (C) undeserving of stardom
    (D) being groomed for stardom
    (E) unable to appreciate her opportunity

GO ON TO THE NEXT PAGE

21. The author's description of the recording process in lines 62–69 ("In the recording ... consumption") serves primarily to illustrate

   (A) that, with the right equipment, anyone can sound good in a studio
   (B) how difficult artists can be
   (C) the many steps involved in crafting a pop song
   (D) the importance of having good recording equipment
   (E) the difference between recording live on stage and in a studio

22. The author would characterize the consequence of the pop star's lip-synching (lines 75–77) as

   (A) completely reasonable
   (B) totally ridiculous
   (C) shocking
   (D) unprecedented
   (E) somewhat unfair

23. In lines 78–85, the expectations of the audience can best be described as

   (A) absurd
   (B) unrealistic
   (C) overwhelming
   (D) disheartening
   (E) optimistic

24. The final paragraph suggests that the author believes lip-synching pop stars

   (A) are forced by record company executives to lip-synch
   (B) should never perform live
   (C) are only guilty of giving the public what it wants
   (D) are a trivial matter in the grand scheme of things
   (E) will soon be a thing of the past

25. The passage's primary purpose is to

   (A) suggest a solution to a problem
   (B) offer one side of an argument
   (C) draw a comparison between fashion and pop music
   (D) relate the history of lip-synching
   (E) revive an old issue

IF YOU FINISH BEFORE TIME IS CALLED, YOU MAY CHECK YOUR WORK ON THIS SECTION ONLY. DO NOT TURN TO ANY OTHER SECTION IN THE TEST.   STOP

SECTION 3

Time—25 Minutes

20 Questions

Directions: For this section, solve each problem and decide which is the best of the choices given. Fill in the corresponding oval on the answer sheet. You may use any available space for scratchwork.

Notes:

(1) Calculator use is permitted.

(2) All numbers used are real numbers.

(3) Figures are provided for some problems. All figures are drawn to scale and lie in a plane UNLESS otherwise indicated.

(4) Unless otherwise specified, the domain of any function f is assumed to be the set of all real numbers x for which $f(x)$ is a real number.

Information

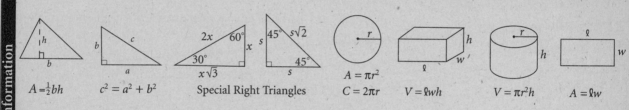

$A = \frac{1}{2}bh$ $c^2 = a^2 + b^2$ Special Right Triangles $A = \pi r^2$ $C = 2\pi r$ $V = \ell w h$ $V = \pi r^2 h$ $A = \ell w$

The sum of the degree measures of the angles in a triangle is 180.

The number of degrees of arc in a circle is 360.

A straight angle has a degree measure of 180.

1. If $2\sqrt{4n^2} + 7 = 39$, what is the value of n?

   (A) 8
   (B) 4
   (C) $2\sqrt{2}$
   (D) 2
   (E) $\sqrt{2}$

2. If $x^2 = k$, where x and k are integers, which of the following could be the value of k?

   (A) 13
   (B) 14
   (C) 15
   (D) 16
   (E) 17

3. Which of the following numbers is between 1 and 2?

   (A) $\dfrac{7}{9}$
   (B) $\dfrac{7}{3}$
   (C) $\dfrac{9}{4}$
   (D) $\dfrac{10}{7}$
   (E) $\dfrac{12}{5}$

4. If $2x + 4 = b$, then $6x + 12 = ?$

   (A) $b + 3$
   (B) $b + 12$
   (C) $3b$
   (D) $3b + 3$
   (E) $3b + 12$

GO ON TO THE NEXT PAGE

KAPLAN

Test Prep and Admissions

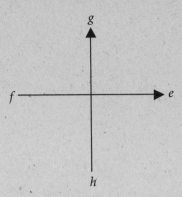

Note: Figure not drawn to scale.

5. If the figure above represents the facts that $g > h$ and $e > f$, which of the following is true?

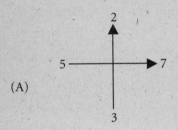

(A)

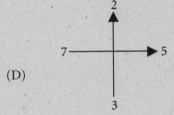

(D)

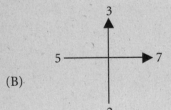

(B)

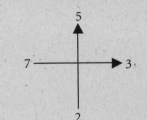

(E)

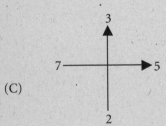

(C)

GO ON TO THE NEXT PAGE

KAPLAN

Test Prep and Admissions

6. John has y to spend on some new CDs from Music Plus, an online record store. He can buy any CDs at the members' price of x each. To be a member, John has to pay a one-time fee of $19. Which of the following expressions represents the number of CDs John can purchase from Music Plus?

   (A) $\dfrac{xy}{19}$

   (B) $\dfrac{(y + 19)}{x}$

   (C) $\dfrac{(2y - x)}{19}$

   (D) $\dfrac{(y - 19)}{x}$

   (E) $\dfrac{(19 - x)}{y}$

7. Which of the following expressions must be negative if $x < 0$?

   (A) $x^4 + x^2 + 4$

   (B) $x^5 - 1$

   (C) $x^6 - 1$

   (D) $x^6 + x^2 + 1$

   (E) $x^2 + 10$

8. In an airport security line, every 20th person has their bag searched and every 10th person is asked to put their shoes through a special x-ray machine. Of 100 passengers, what is the probability that a passenger will be asked to put his shoes through the x-ray and have their bag searched?

   (A) $\dfrac{1}{100}$

   (B) $\dfrac{1}{50}$

   (C) $\dfrac{1}{20}$

   (D) $\dfrac{1}{10}$

   (E) $\dfrac{1}{5}$

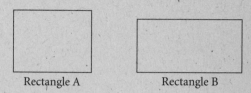

Rectangle A   Rectangle B

9. The width of Rectangle B in the figure above is 30 percent less than that of Rectangle A. The length of Rectangle B is 30 percent greater than that of Rectangle A. The area of rectangle B is

   (A) 30 percent greater than that of Rectangle A

   (B) 9 percent greater than that of Rectangle A

   (C) equal to that of Rectangle A

   (D) 9 percent less than that of Rectangle A

   (E) 30 percent less than that of Rectangle A

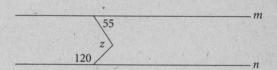

10. In the figure above, lines m and n are parallel. What is the value of z?

   (A) 65

   (B) 115

   (C) 125

   (D) 145

   (E) 170

GO ON TO THE NEXT PAGE

KAPLAN
Test Prep and Admissions

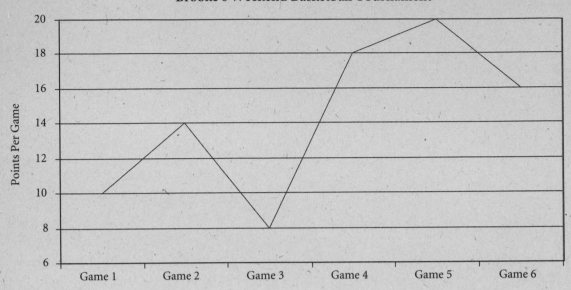

11. The figure above shows Brooke's points per game in a weekend basketball tournament. What is the average (arithmetic mean) number of points Brooke scored per game for the entire basketball tournament?

(A) 11.66
(B) 12.67
(C) 13.00
(D) 14.33
(E) 15.33

12. If $x^{-2/3} = \dfrac{1}{36}$, then what does x equal?

(A) −6
(B) $\dfrac{1}{6}$
(C) 6
(D) 18
(E) 216

13. If $\dfrac{14x}{\sqrt{2x+2}} = 7$, what is one possible value of x?

(A) −7
(B) −1
(C) $\dfrac{1}{2}$
(D) 1
(E) 7

GO ON TO THE NEXT PAGE

14. If $|2r - 2| = 8$ and $|3r + 2| = 17$, then what is the value of r?

   (A) -5
   (B) $\dfrac{-19}{6}$
   (C) -3
   (D) 5
   (E) 15

Questions 15–17 refer to the following sequence of steps.

   1. Choose a number between 0 and 9.9.
   2. Multiply the number from the previous step by 100.
   3. Determine the smallest integer greater than or equal to the number obtained from the previous step.
   4. Add 12 to the number found in the previous step.
   5. Print the resulting number.

15. If 6.127 is the number chosen in step 1, what is the number printed in step 5?

   (A) 12
   (B) 74
   (C) 624
   (D) 624.7
   (E) 625

16. Which of the following could be a number printed in step 5 after steps 1 through 4 are performed?

   (A) -1
   (B) 10
   (C) 27.3
   (D) 674
   (E) 1050

17. Which change, if any, could be made in the order of the steps without changing the number printed in step 5?

   (A) Only steps 2 and 3 could be switched
   (B) Only steps 2 and 4 could be switched
   (C) Only steps 3 and 4 could be switched
   (D) Steps 2, 3 and 4 can be done in any order
   (E) None of the above changes can be made

18. If $a = 3(2c^2 + 3c + 4)$ and $b = -c + 4$ what is a in terms of b?

   (A) $6b^2 - 48b + 96$
   (B) $6b^2 - 57b + 132$
   (C) $6b^2 - 57b + 144$
   (D) $6b^2 - 9b - 132$
   (E) $6b^2 - 9b + 144$

GO ON TO THE NEXT PAGE

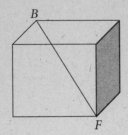

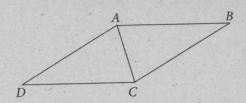

Note: Figure not drawn to scale

19. A square cube has a side length of 3. What is the length of a diagonal which cuts through the center of the cube?

(A) 3

(B) $3\sqrt{2}$

(C) $3\sqrt{3}$

(D) 18

(E) 27

20. In the figure above, two identical isosceles triangles with side length of 5 are joined at their bases, which have a length of 6. What is the area of quadrilateral *ABCD*?

(A) 9

(B) 18

(C) 24

(D) 48

(E) 52

IF YOU FINISH BEFORE TIME IS CALLED, YOU MAY CHECK YOUR WORK ON THIS SECTION ONLY. DO NOT TURN TO ANY OTHER SECTION IN THE TEST.

STOP

KAPLAN

Test Prep and Admissions

SECTION 4

Time—25 Minutes
24 Questions

Directions: For each of the following questions, choose the best answer and darken the corresponding oval on the answer sheet.

Each sentence below has one or two blanks, each blank indicating that something has been omitted. Beneath the sentence are five words or sets of words labeled (A) through (E). Choose the word or set of words that, when inserted in the sentence, best fits the meaning of the sentence as a whole.

EXAMPLE:

Today's small, portable computers contrast markedly with the earliest electronic computers, which were ----.

(A) effective
(B) invented
(C) useful
(D) destructive
(E) enormous   Ⓐ Ⓑ Ⓒ Ⓓ ●

---

1. The ability to walk is acquired very early in life through observation: infants become ---- by ---- their parents.

    (A) socialized . . overcoming
    (B) dominant . . obeying
    (C) vocal . . mimicking
    (D) adept . . imitating
    (E) agile . . following

2. The chanting crowds of angry protestors turned the dedication ceremony of the controversial new building into a ---- rather than a celebration.

    (A) colossus
    (B) milestone
    (C) debacle
    (D) consecration
    (E) fabrication

3. The damage caused by the rampant corruption was ----: the company's reputation was nearly ---- before anyone realized it was having an effect.

    (A) manifest . . eradicated
    (B) nefarious . . polarized
    (C) insidious . . destroyed
    (D) methodical . . amalgamated
    (E) obvious . . stagnated

4. To be able to ---- more smoothly the individual facts of the case, the prosecutor spent a great deal of time simply ---- them, instead of analyzing their importance to his argument.

    (A) synthesize . . regurgitating
    (B) recite . . memorizing
    (C) denounce . . falsifying
    (D) acquire . . misinterpreting
    (E) disregard . . recalling

5. Because Ben had been known for being ---- in college, his former classmates were surprised to hear that his colleagues at work found him rather lazy.

    (A) indiscriminate
    (B) enigmatic
    (C) vicarious
    (D) rancorous
    (E) assiduous

GO ON TO THE NEXT PAGE

Directions: The passages below are followed by questions based on their content; questions following a pair of related passages may also be based on the relationship between the paired passages. Answer the questions on the basis of what is <u>stated</u> or <u>implied</u> in the passages and in any introductory material that may be provided.

Questions 6–7 are based on he following passage.

Efforts to understand how prehistoric animals interacted with one another inevitably focus on predatory relationships. Given this concentration, it is not surprising that paleontologists—those
(5) who study prehistoric life using fossil evidence—often rely upon teeth to describe animals that lived in the distant past and to determine their behaviors. Through the evolutionary process, an animal's teeth become precisely adapted for the
(10) acquisition and initial processing of the specific types of foods consumed by that animal. In addition, because teeth are one of the hardest structures of the body, they can remain in the environment for centuries after an animal has
(15) died. Both of these qualities make teeth quite serviceable as prehistoric clues.

6. In line 16, "serviceable" most nearly means

   (A) durable
   (B) useful
   (C) precious
   (D) fixable
   (E) reliable

7. In the context of this passage, it can be inferred from the use of the words "not surprising" (line 4) that the author thinks

   (A) paleontologists are rarely surprised by the fossils they find
   (B) most people understand the importance of fossilized teeth to paleontology
   (C) the focus of paleontologists on predatory relationships is quite understandable
   (D) the connection between predatory behavior and teeth has been thoroughly explored
   (E) it is quite apparent that predatory relationships often involve the use of teeth

Questions 8–9 are based on he following passage.

As I walk, alone and lonely, on the streets around my small apartment, I feel a bond with virtually everyone I see: the elderly man struggling to walk up the stoop (a man who finds even the
(5) most basic tasks challenging), the child playing with a soccer ball (a blithe boy, experiencing easy joy), and even the wrinkled woman stationed behind the cash register of the convenience store, where she seems to be eight days a week (a hard
(10) worker facing a daily struggle to make a living). My own identity feels lost, wrapped up in the lives of others. And yet I realize that as I struggle to identify myself, I feel closer to the world around me and less alone.

8. The author mentions that the woman in the convenience store seems to be there "eight days a week" (line 9) in order to

   (A) suggest that she makes her home at the store
   (B) indicate that she is merely part of the author's imagination
   (C) provide an anecdote about the challenges of accomplishing basic tasks
   (D) argue that convenience store workers have easy lives
   (E) highlight how hard she must work to earn a living

9. In the passage, the word "blithe" (line 6) most nearly means

   (A) flexible
   (B) nervous
   (C) carefree
   (D) young
   (E) envious

GO ON TO THE NEXT PAGE ⟶

Questions 10–19 are based on the following passage.

The following excerpt discusses the contributions of Susan B. Anthony (1820–1906), a political advocate for temperance, education reform, the abolition of slavery, and most famously for women's civil rights.

When Susan B. Anthony, a tireless worker for temperance, was refused the right to speak at an 1853 Sons of Temperance convention because she was a woman, she left the meeting and called her
(5) own. A lifetime of accumulated frustration at not being listened to simply because of her gender had come to a head. She and Elizabeth Cady Stanton founded the Women's State Temperance Association that year, and delivered a petition
(10) containing over 28,000 signatures to the New York State Legislature in order to pass a law limiting the sale of alcohol. The Legislature rejected it because most of the signatures were from women and children. Anthony knew that women needed the
(15) power to vote in order for their views ever to be taken seriously by politicians.

Anthony had been introduced in a significant way to the women's suffrage movement in 1851. She wrote pro-temperance articles for the nation's
(20) first woman-owned periodical, the *Lily*, and became aquainted with the paper's editor, Amelia Bloomer. Bloomer introduced her to Elizabeth Stanton, and the two women formed a friendship and political alliance that lasted the rest of their
(25) lives. From this point on, Anthony and Stanton worked ceaselessly together in support of women's rights. Anthony lectured, traveled, and organized conventions on the topic, while Stanton wrote speeches and articles and generated ideas for the
(30) two of them to promote. They collected signatures for a petition to grant women the right to vote and own property, and in 1860 their work was rewarded in the New York Legislature with the Married Women's Property Act, which allowed
(35) some women to own property and enter into legal contracts.

Throughout this work, Anthony became widely recognized as the face of the women's rights movement. She also began to receive unwelcome
(40) attention. Male columnists from anti-suffrage papers mocked her cruelly. She was confronted by armed mobs, and received threats of physical harm from those whose politics were threatened by her own. The prevailing tactic of her oppo-
(45) nents was to ridicule her unladylike attempts at insisting that the minds of women and men were no different. Political cartoons from the day put Anthony and Stanton side by side with George Washington, or showed members of the women's
(50) suffrage movement crossing the Delaware in grandiose fashion, in order to make fun of their supposed self-importance. (Ironically, of course, modern viewers looking at these cartoons can't figure out what the joke is. In this century's per-
(55) ception, putting Susan B. Anthony next to a great figure like George Washington seems hardly inap-propriate.) Despite all her enemies, though, Anthony had a fair complement of influential allies in civil rights circles, and managed to win
(60) the respect and admiration of some, if not a majority, of the public. With the support of such like-minded folks as Stanton, Bloomer, and Frederick Douglass (an escaped slave who became a publisher and campaigned vociferously and suc-
(65) cessfully for the abolition of slavery), Anthony managed to advocate for women's rights on a larg-er and larger scale.

In 1868, the Fourteenth Amendment was adopt-ed, which asserted that all people born in the
(70) United States were citizens and that no legal privi-leges could be denied to any citizen. Anthony claimed that since the language of the amendment did not specify gender, it meant that women were citizens and could therefore legally vote. She regis-
(75) tered to vote in New York in 1872. On Election Day, she and fifteen other women voted in the presidential election. Three weeks later, they were all arrested, and Anthony was brought to trial.

The presiding judge opposed women's suffrage.
(80) He had written his decision before the trial began and, refusing to allow Anthony to testify, ordered the jury to find her guilty. She was fined $100 plus court fees. When she refused to pay, though, the judge did not imprison her, thus denying her
(85) the opportunity to appeal and send the case to a higher court where it might have gotten more national attention.

GO ON TO THE NEXT PAGE ⇨

Before and during the Civil War, Anthony and most of the rest of the women's movement allied (90) themselves with the abolitionist movement. "All rights for all!," the subtitle of Frederick Douglass' pro-abolitionist paper, became the unofficial motto of every facet of civil rights work. It was Anthony's hope that if she used the influence she (95) had created in the women's movement to support black emancipation and suffrage, that the Republican Party would support women's suffrage in return. She was surprised and disappointed when, in 1870, the Fifteenth Amendment was (100) adopted to extend the vote specifically to black men only. It was the first time the word "male" had been written into the constitution, and Anthony felt abandoned and betrayed by the people she had worked so hard to support. This (105) event spawned some regrettably racist commentary by Anthony, who bitterly wrote that educated white women would make better voters than "ignorant" black men.

Despite her disillusionment and disappoint-(110) ment, she and Stanton continued to work for the female vote, this time without abolitionist support. Together they formed the National Woman Suffrage Association and later the National American Woman Suffrage Association (NAWSA). (115) Though by the time of her death in 1906, she had not seen a federal amendment granting women the right to vote, her work was not in vain. In 1920, one hundred years after Susan B. Anthony's birth, the Nineteenth Amendment finally gave (125) adult American women the right to vote.

10. The passage provides the most information about Anthony's

   (A) enduring friendships
   (B) racism
   (C) ineffectiveness as a speaker
   (D) advocacy for female suffrage
   (E) work for temperance

11. The passage suggests that the New York State Legislature did not accept the petition to limit the sale of alcohol (lines 12–14) because

   (A) they did not think that women and children were wise enough to propose legislation
   (B) it was too politically unpopular to restrict the sale of alcohol
   (C) they were out of touch with their constituency
   (D) the opinions of nonvoters are of less interest to elected officials
   (E) petitions were generally ignored in state governments in those days

12. The discussion of political cartoons featuring Susan B. Anthony (lines 47–52) suggests that Anthony

   (A) had a reputation equivalent to that of George Washington during her lifetime
   (B) grew in importance in the public eye in the decades after her death
   (C) knew George Washington personally
   (D) was considered much more important when she was alive than she is today
   (E) was a failure as a political activist

13. In context, the word "complement" (line 58) most nearly means

   (A) praise
   (B) assistance
   (C) contribution
   (D) dearth
   (E) number

14. In lines 63–65, the passage mainly suggests which of the following about Frederick Douglass?

(A) He was interested in more than one political cause.

(B) He had little in common with Anthony politically.

(C) He cared only about abolition.

(D) He thought that black men, but not women, should be allowed to vote.

(E) He was an advocate of temperance.

15. The discussion of Anthony's refusal to pay her court fees (lines 82–87) suggests that Anthony was

(A) a tightwad who wouldn't let go of money

(B) more committed to court reform than to women's rights

(C) supportive of civil disobedience as her most effective political tactic

(D) a political tactician who tried attract as much notice to her cause as possible

(E) not very well-off financially

16. Anthony probably believed that her support of the abolitionists would have the effect of

(A) making the abolition movement much stronger

(B) exposing her own hidden racism

(C) hurting the Republican Party

(D) making politicians pay attention to the views of women

(E) furthering the cause of women's suffrage

17. In context, the phrase "in vain" (line 117) most nearly means

(A) conceited

(B) relating to blood

(C) for nothing

(D) effective

(E) handy

18. As presented in the passage, Susan B. Anthony's politics most closely coincided with those of

(A) Frederick Douglass

(B) Amelia Bloomer

(C) George Washington

(D) the Sons of Temperance

(E) Elizabeth Cady Stanton

19. According to the passage, Anthony most fervently supported

(A) abolishing slavery

(B) temperance, or restricting the sale of alcohol

(C) the Republican Party

(D) giving the vote to all women born in the United States

(E) an end to female suffering in the United States

GO ON TO THE NEXT PAGE

Questions 20–24 are based on the following passage.

This passage, about infant language acquisition, was adapted from a research paper that explores early childhood development.

For an infant just beginning to interact with the surrounding world, it is imperative that he quickly become proficient in his native language. While developing a vocabulary and the ability to com-
(5) municate using it are obviously important steps in this process, an infant must first be able to learn from the various streams of audible communication around him. To that end, during the course of even the first few months of development, an
(10) infant will begin to absorb the rhythmic patterns and sequences of sounds that characterize his language, and will begin to differentiate between the meanings of various pitch and stress changes.

However, it is important to recognize that such
(15) learning does not take place in a vacuum. Infants must confront these language acquisition challenges in an environment where, quite frequently, several streams of communication or noise are occurring simultaneously. In other words, infants
(20) must not only learn how to segment individual speech streams into their component words, but they must also be able to distinguish between concurrent streams of sound.

Consider, for example, an infant being spoken
(25) to by his mother. Before he can learn from the nuances of his mother's speech, he must first separate that speech from the sounds of the dishwasher, the family dog, the bus stopping on the street outside, and, quite possibly, background noise in
(30) the form of speech: a newscaster on the television down the hall or siblings playing in an adjacent room.

How exactly do infants wade through such a murky conglomeration of audible stimuli? While
(35) most infants are capable of separating out two different voices despite the presence of additional, competing streams of sound, this capability is predicated upon several specific conditions.

First, infants are better able to learn from a par-
(40) ticular speech stream when that voice is louder than any of the competing streams of background speech; when two voices are of equal amplitude,

infants typically demonstrate little preference towards one stream or the other. Most likely,
(45) equally loud competing voice streams, for the infant, become combined into a single stream that necessarily contains unfamiliar patterns and sounds that can quite easily induce confusion. Secondly, an infant is more likely to attend to a
(50) particular voice stream if it is perceived as more familiar than another stream. When an infant, for example, is presented with a voice stream spoken by his mother and a background stream delivered by an unfamiliar voice, usually he can easily sepa-
(55) rate out her voice from the distraction of the background stream. By using these simple yet important cues an infant can become quite adept at concentrating on a single stream of communication and, therefore, capable of more quickly
(60) learning the invaluable characteristics and rules of his native language.

20. In line 10, the word "absorb" most nearly refers to

(A) environmental awareness

(B) language aptitude

(C) acquisition of knowledge

(D) intent perception

(E) speech differentiation

21. The phrase "predicated upon several specific conditions" (line 38) is used by the author to suggest that

(A) most infants have trouble separating out simultaneous streams of speech

(B) infants can only learn when they are comfortable in their surroundings

(C) only in rare instances do these required conditions occur

(D) an infant's language acquisition ability is entirely dependent upon his environment

(E) infants are not always able to learn from their surrounding environment

GO ON TO THE NEXT PAGE ⇒

22. The author uses the word "necessarily" (line 47) in order to suggest that

    (A) it is inevitable that two streams of speech are more confusing than one

    (B) even adults can have trouble distinguishing between streams of equal volume

    (C) infants always combine separate streams into a single sound

    (D) an individual stream understandably changes character when mixed with another

    (E) the diversity of audible stimuli makes an infant's confusion quite understandable

23. The example in the last paragraph suggests that in the situation described in lines 25–32 ("Before he can learn...adjacent room.") an infant would most likely

    (A) understand his mother's communication stream

    (B) absorb many of the nuances of his mother's speech

    (C) be able to distinguish between his mother's voice from that of the newscaster

    (D) not learn anything about his language from the television voice

    (E) separate out his mother's speech from most of the background noises

24. The example in the last paragraph is used to illustrate how

    (A) an infant who spends little time with his parents would probably have trouble with language acquisition

    (B) an infant in constant vocal interaction with his parents could experience accelerated language acquisition

    (C) the complexity of an infant's native language is not a factor in determining whether that language will be easily acquired

    (D) infants with particularly attentive parents are more likely to acquire language skills more quickly

    (E) eliminating unfamiliar voices from an infant's environment can facilitate language acquisition

Test Prep and Admissions

SECTION 5

Time—25 Minutes

18 Questions

Directions: For this section, solve each problem and decide which is the best of the choices given. Fill in the corresponding oval on the answer sheet. You may use any available space for scratchwork.

Notes:

(1) Calculator use is permitted.

(2) All numbers used are real numbers.

(3) Figures are provided for some problems. All figures are drawn to scale and lie in a plane UNLESS otherwise indicated.

(4) Unless otherwise specified, the domain of any function f is assumed to be the set of all real numbers x for which $f(x)$ is a real number.

Information

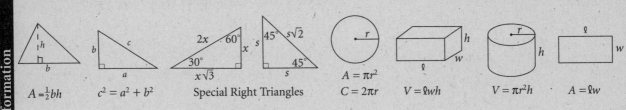

$A = \frac{1}{2}bh$ $c^2 = a^2 + b^2$ Special Right Triangles $A = \pi r^2$ $V = \ell wh$ $V = \pi r^2 h$ $A = \ell w$
$C = 2\pi r$

The sum of the degree measures of the angles in a triangle is 180.
The number of degrees of arc in a circle is 360.
A straight angle has a degree measure of 180.

1. If t is 5 more than s, and s is 3 less than r, what is t when $r = 3$?

   (A) −5
   (B) −2
   (C) 1
   (D) 5
   (E) 8

2. If $\dfrac{y}{y-3} = \dfrac{42}{39}$, then what does y equal?

   (A) 39
   (B) 41
   (C) 42
   (D) 45
   (E) 81

GO ON TO THE NEXT PAGE

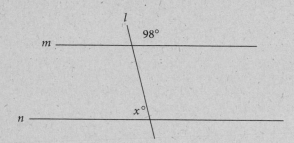

Note: Figure not drawn to scale.

3. In the figure above, lines *m* and *n* are <u>not</u> parallel. Which of the following CANNOT be the value of *x*?

(A) 80

(B) 81

(C) 82

(D) 83

(E) 84

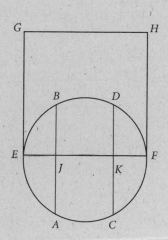

4. In the figure above lines $\overline{BA}$ and $\overline{DC}$ have equal length, and are perpendicular to $\overline{EF}$, which passes through the center of the circle. If the area of square *GEFH* is 81, and *JK* = 5, what is the length of $\overline{EJ}$?

(A) 2

(B) 3

(C) 4

(D) 6

(E) 9

5. If *a* and *b* are multiples of 3, which of the following CANNOT also be a multiple of 3?

(A) $a + b$

(B) $a - b$

(C) $a + b + 1$

(D) ab

(E) $ab + 3$

6. Which of the following represents the statement "When the sum of the squares of 2*a* and 3*b* are added to the difference between 8*c* and 7*d*, the result is 3 more than *e*"?

(A) $(2a)^2 + (3b)^2 + (8c - 7d) = e + 3$

(B) $(2a)^2 + (3b)^2 + (8c - 7d) + 3 = e$

(C) $(2a + 3b)^2 + (8c - 7d) + 3 = e$

(D) $(2a + 3b)^2 + (8c - 7d) = e + 3$

(E) $2a^2 + 3b^2 + (8c - 7d) + 3 = e$

7. After 21 kids were added to a class, there were 4 times as many students as before. How many kids were in the class before the addition?

(A) 3

(B) 7

(C) 11

(D) 14

(E) 17

8. If $\frac{a}{b} = 4$, $a = 8c$, and $c = 9$, what is the value of *b*?

(A) 2

(B) 8

(C) 18

(D) 36

(E) 72

GO ON TO THE NEXT PAGE

Directions: For Student-Produced Response questions 9–18, use the grids at the bottom of the answer sheet page on which you have answered questions 1–8.

Each of the remaining 10 questions requires you to solve the problem and enter your answer by marking the ovals in the special grid, as shown in the example below. You may use any available space for scratch work.

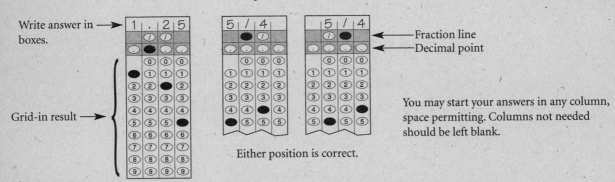

Answer: 1.25 or $\frac{5}{4}$ or 5/4

Write answer in → boxes.

Grid-in result →

Fraction line
Decimal point

Either position is correct.

You may start your answers in any column, space permitting. Columns not needed should be left blank.

• It is recommended, though not required, that you write your answer in the boxes at the top of the columns. However, you will receive credit only for darkening the ovals correctly.

• Grid only one answer to a question, even though some problems have more than one correct answer.

• Darken no more than one oval in a column.

• No answers are negative.

• Mixed numbers cannot be gridded. For example: the number $1\frac{1}{4}$ must be gridded as 1.25 or 5/4.

(If [1 | 1 | / | 4] is gridded, it will be interpreted as $\frac{11}{4}$ not $1\frac{1}{4}$.)

• Decimal Accuracy: Decimal answers must be entered as accurately as possible. For example, if you obtain an answer such as 0.1666…, you should record the result as .166 or .167. **Less accurate values such as .16 or .17 are not acceptable.**

Acceptable ways to grid $\frac{1}{6}$ = .1666…

9. If $3d + ed = f - e$, what is the value of d when $e = 2$ and $f = 9$?

10. If $3(x - 2) = 8$, what is the value of x?

11. If, $\dfrac{z + 2}{5} = 2$, what does $\dfrac{z + 2}{z - 6}$ equal?

12. In a rectangular coordinate system, the center of a circle has coordinates $(8, 3)$, and the circle touches the y-axis at only one point. What is the radius of the circle?

13. For all numbers a and b,

$$a \triangleright b = \frac{1}{3}a + \frac{2}{3}b$$

$$a \triangleleft b = \frac{2}{3}a + \frac{1}{3}b$$

What is the value of $(3 \triangleright 2) \triangleleft 6$?

14. If $x(x - 6) = -9$, what is the value of $x^2 + x - 2$?

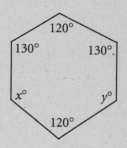

Note: Figure not drawn to scale.

16. In the figure above, what is the sum of x and y?

17. If $9^r = 27^{r-1}$, then $r =$

18. Let «x« be defined for all positive integer values of x as the product of all odd factors of $3x$. For example, «5« $= 15 \times 5 \times 3 \times 1 = 225$. What is the value of «$7$«?

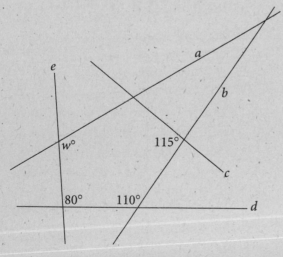

Note: Figure not drawn to scale.

15. In the figure above, if the angle where lines a and b intersect is twice as large as the angle (not shown) where lines e and b intersect, what is the value of w?

IF YOU FINISH BEFORE TIME IS CALLED, YOU MAY CHECK YOUR WORK ON THIS SECTION ONLY. DO NOT TURN TO ANY OTHER SECTION IN THE TEST.

STOP

SECTION 6

Time—25 Minutes
35 Questions

Directions: For each question in this section, select the best answer from among the choices given and fill in the corresponding oval on the answer sheet.

The following sentences test correctness and effectiveness of expression. Part of each sentence or the entire sentence is underlined; beneath each sentence are five ways of phrasing the underlined material. Choice (A) repeats the original phrasing; the other four choices are different. If you think the original phrasing produces a better sentence than any of the alternatives, select choice (A); if not, select one of the other choices.

In making your selection, follow the requirements of standard written English; that is, pay attention to grammar, choice of words, sentence construction, and punctuation. Your selection should result in the most effective sentence—clear and precise, without awkwardness or ambiguity.

EXAMPLE:

Every apple in the baskets <u>are ripe and labeled according to the date it was picked</u>.

(A) are ripe and labeled according to the date it was picked
(B) is ripe and labeled according to the date it was picked
(C) are ripe and labeled according to the date they were picked
(D) is ripe and labeled according to the date they were picked
(E) are ripe and labeled as to the date it was picked

ANSWER:

(A) ● (C) (D) (E)

1. Among the students of Highland Park Middle School, art, plays, and songs are used to introduce complex ideas <u>that might otherwise be misunderstood by young adults</u>.

   (A) that might otherwise be misunderstood by young adults
   (B) that otherwise, to young adults, were misunderstood by them
   (C) and they are otherwise misunderstood by young adults
   (D) by which young adults were otherwise being misunderstood
   (E) whereby young adults that might otherwise misunderstand are not

2. <u>The lost car keys having finally been found</u>, the frustrated couple rushed out the door to catch the second half of the play.

   (A) The lost car keys having finally been found
   (B) The car's lost keys finally being found
   (C) At finding the lost car keys, finally
   (D) When they finally found the lost car keys
   (E) When having finally found the lost car keys

3. Many Irish citizens were frightened by the 1922 Civil Authorities Act, which gave the government discretionary power to determine <u>about procuring warrants</u> before a search or arrest.

   (A) about procuring warrants
   (B) whether he or she ought to procure warrants
   (C) whether warrants should be procured
   (D) if he or she should procure warrants
   (E) the procuring of warrants, if they wish,

GO ON TO THE NEXT PAGE

4. One of the most frequently published and hardworking professors at the law school <u>were available so frequently to lunch with students that the faculty thought something was</u> amiss with his research.

   (A) were available so frequently to lunch with students that the faculty thought something was

   (B) was available so frequently to lunch with students that the faculty thought something were

   (C) was available so frequently to lunch with students that the faculty thought something has gone

   (D) was available so frequently to lunch with students that the faculty thought something was

   (E) was available with great frequency to lunch with students, so the faculty thought of it as something was

5. The host flitted about her party, pouring drinks, offering hors d'oeuvres, and <u>guests were greeted</u>.

   (A) guests were greeted

   (B) guests greeting

   (C) greeting guests

   (D) greeted guests

   (E) guests having been greeted

6. As I climbed the steps of the Eiffel Tower, an architectural triumph admired all around the world, my friend <u>is turning to me to announce</u> that the landmark of Paris, initially considered ugly, was almost destroyed at the end of the World's Fair for which it was built.

   (A) is turning to me to announce

   (B) turned to me and announced

   (C) turns to me and is announcing

   (D) turns and also announces to me

   (E) would turn and announce to me

7. No one is <u>more happier than me</u> that you were elected class president.

   (A) more happier than me

   (B) happier than I

   (C) more happy like myself

   (D) as happy like I am

   (E) happier but me

8. <u>Whether Stalin actually murdered Kirov, his popular second in command, or did not</u> remains a mystery, but Stalin's Great Purges prove the ruler had the power to do so.

   (A) Whether Stalin actually murdered Kirov, his popular second in command, or did not

   (B) Whether in actuality Stalin murdered Kirov, his popular second in command, or did not

   (C) The actuality of Stalin murdering Kirov, his popular second in command,

   (D) That Stalin actually murdered Kirov, his popular second in command,

   (E) Stalin, his actual murdering of Kirov, his popular second in command,

9. In 1984, the United States defeated rival countries to win its first Olympic all-around gold medal in <u>gymnastics, even so, they</u> did not win again until 2004.

   (A) gymnastics, even so, they

   (B) gymnastics, so they

   (C) gymnastics, they

   (D) gymnastics; as a result, it

   (E) gymnastics, but it

GO ON TO THE NEXT PAGE

10. Ahead of his time, the English painter James Turner <u>had created impressionist landscapes</u> long before the works of artists like Claude Monet popularized the movement.

    (A) had created impressionist landscapes
    (B) had created impressionist landscapes and he painted them
    (C) having created impressionist landscapes
    (D) has painted impressionist landscapes, he created
    (E) has painted impressionist landscapes; creation was

11. Although dismissed by *Salon* attendees for its subject matter, <u>most artists viewed Manet's *Olympia* as a groundbreaking work</u>.

    (A) most artists viewed Manet's *Olympia* as a groundbreaking work
    (B) most artists viewed Manet's *Olympia* to be a groundbreaking work
    (C) a groundbreaking work was what most artists viewed Manet's *Olympia* as
    (D) Manet's *Olympia* was viewed by most artists as a groundbreaking work
    (E) Manet's *Olympia*, a groundbreaking work in the view of most artists

GO ON TO THE NEXT PAGE ⟹

> **Directions:** The following sentences test your ability to recognize grammar and usage errors. Each sentence contains either a single error or no error at all. No sentence contains more than one error. The error, if there is one, is underlined and lettered. If the sentence contains an error, select the one underlined part that must be changed to make the sentence correct. If the sentence is correct, select choice (E). In choosing answers, follow the requirements of standard written English.
>
> EXAMPLE:
>
> <u>Whenever</u> one is driving late at night, <u>you</u> must take extra precautions <u>against</u>
>   A   B   C
>
> falling asleep <u>at the wheel</u>. <u>No error</u>
>   D   E
>
>

12. The director wanted Delia <u>for portraying</u> her
                             A

    character with <u>more conviction</u>, so he suggested
                   B

    <u>that she remember</u> an actual experience that <u>had</u>
        C   D

    <u>saddened</u> her. <u>No error</u>
      D   E

13. My parents, my younger sister, and <u>me</u> <u>were</u>
                               A   B

    delighted to see how much my cousin had grown

    <u>since</u> we last visited his family <u>in the summer</u>.
     C   D
    <u>No error</u>
     E

14. <u>If you want</u> <u>to buy</u> a house <u>in the future</u>, you must
     A   B   C
    <u>to establish</u> and maintain good credit now.
      D
    <u>No error</u>
     E

15. As Jerry and Ming argued about the many possible

    tile colors for <u>the floor of</u> the new ice-cream parlor,
                 A

    Maria <u>thinking</u> about whether <u>to paint</u> the walls or
         B   C

    wallpaper <u>them</u>. <u>No error</u>
          D   E

16. Tino was upset when Mai carelessly <u>cracks</u> his
                            A

    favorite mug <u>against the counter</u>, <u>but</u> he brightened
               B   C

    when he realized he could still use it to hold pencils

    <u>on his desk</u>. <u>No error</u>
      D   E

17. The chef herself <u>will be creating</u> the grand finale
               A

    <u>of the celebration</u>: an extraordinary cake
        B

    smothered in strawberries and <u>being topped</u> with
                             C

    <u>freshly</u> whipped cream. <u>No error</u>
     D   E

18. We spent a <u>most enjoyable</u> afternoon lounging
            A

    <u>on the grass</u>, <u>watching for</u> <u>unusual</u> shaped cloud
       B   C   D

    formations. <u>No error</u>
         E

19. <u>Beside the dusty road</u> <u>sets</u> a pond, which serves
     A   B

    <u>as a breeding ground</u> for several species of <u>the</u>
         C   D

    <u>noisiest</u> amphibians. <u>No error</u>
     D   E

GO ON TO THE NEXT PAGE ➡

20. Doctors <u>researching</u> diseases affecting the liver <u>find</u>
     A   B
that the consumption of alcohol was <u>generally</u> an
                                      C
<u>indicator of</u> susceptibility to the disease. <u>No error</u>
     D   E

21. The other students and <u>her</u> felt <u>unprepared</u> <u>when</u>
                             A   B   C
tested <u>on facts</u> not learned in class. <u>No error</u>
        D   E

22. Permanent loss of eyesight <u>if</u> <u>they stare</u> <u>too long</u> at
                                A   B   C
the sun is a common problem <u>during</u> eclipses.
                              D

<u>No error</u>
  E

23. The voters <u>who elected</u> the new members
                A
<u>of the school board</u> <u>includes</u> several hundred
        B   C
who were voting <u>for the first time</u>. <u>No error</u>
                     D   E

24. The essayist <u>writing</u> on art in America was less
                  A
concerned with why funding was decreasing

<u>than with</u> whether <u>it was</u> becoming <u>less popular</u>
  B   C   D
with the public. <u>No error</u>
                   E

25. Working two jobs is common <u>among</u> struggling
                                A
actors, the majority <u>of them wait</u> tables in
                       B
restaurants that <u>allow them</u> flexible hours <u>to</u>
                  C
<u>audition</u> for acting roles. <u>No error</u>
  D   E

26. As the concert drew to a close, I realized <u>once more</u>
                                                A
that I usually respond <u>most</u> enthusiastically to
                        B
Beethoven's harmonic language because <u>it</u> seems
                                        C
far more dramatic to me than <u>other composers</u>.
                               D

<u>No error</u>
  E

27. Organic production of food for sale in the U.S.

could affect people's health because food <u>produced</u>
                                            A
without pesticides <u>poses less danger</u> and promotes
                     B
easier digestion <u>than</u> <u>traditional agriculture</u>. <u>No</u>
                   C   D   E
<u>error</u>.
  E

28. <u>That</u> the grade point average of the student <u>who</u>
     A   B
paid the most attention in class increased

<u>dramatically</u> during the semester <u>came</u> as no
  C   D
surprise to the teacher. <u>No error</u>
                           E

29. After <u>exhaustively</u> <u>researching</u> his new work of
           A   B
historical fiction, the novelist grew

<u>less interested in</u> the modern repercussions of the
  C
Apollo moonmission than in how <u>they affected</u>
                                 D
international relations at the time. <u>No error</u>
                                      E

<u>GO ON TO THE NEXT PAGE</u> ⟩

Directions: The passages below are followed by questions based on their content; questions following a pair of related passages may also be based on the relationship between the paired passages. Answer the questions on the basis of what is <u>stated</u> or <u>implied</u> in the passages and in any introductory material that may be provided.

Questions 30–35 are based on the following passage.

(1) There was one simple thing from my recent trip to the Mohave Desert that amazed me. (2) At night, millions of stars were clearly visible in a way they never are at home. (3) When brilliant city lights shine into the sky, they obstruct our view of the galaxy. (4) Scientists have given this phenomenon a name, they call it "light pollution."

(5) I am concerned about light pollution because I think stargazing is an important intellectual and historical pastime. (6) Looking at the night sky helps us remember that we all inhabit the same planet in space. (7) I have also enjoyed many evenings studying the constellations, like so many humans throughout history, talking with my friends about ancient Greek myths. (8) I hope people will be willing to improve the situation, because light pollution is truly a growing concern.

(9) The Internet lists some excellent solutions to light pollution. (10) For example, individuals can simply turn off lights when they weren't using them. (11) In some cities, local ordinances require people to install lights that are directed down towards the ground. (12) Lights around malls and used car lots don't need to light up the whole sky just to advertise their products.

(13) I think that anyone who views the brilliant night sky in a remote rural area will understand my point.

30. The sentence that best states the main idea of the passage is:

(A) sentence 1

(B) sentence 3

(C) sentence 5

(D) sentence 12

(E) sentence 13

31. Of the following, which is the best version of sentence 1, (reproduced below)?

There was one simple thing from my recent trip to the Mohave Desert that amazed me.

(A) (As it is now)

(B) It was simply amazing in the Mohave Desert during my recent trip.

(C) There was one thing from my recent trip to the Mohave Desert that amazed me.

(D) I recently traveled to the Mohave Desert and was amazed by one simple thing.

(E) One simple thing from my recent trip to the Mohave Desert that amazed me.

GO ON TO THE NEXT PAGE

32. In context, what is the best version of sentence 4 (reproduced below)?

    Scientists have given this phenomenon a name, they call it "light pollution."

    (A) (As it is now)

    (B) Scientists have given this phenomenon a name; they call it "light pollution."

    (C) Scientists have given this phenomenon a name, because they call it "light pollution."

    (D) This phenomenon has been given a name by scientists; they call it "light pollution."

    (E) Scientists naming this phenomenon "light pollution."

33. Sentence 8 would make the most sense if placed after which sentence?

    (A) sentence 3

    (B) sentence 4

    (C) sentence 9

    (D) sentence 12

    (E) sentence 13

34. In the context, what revision is needed in sentence 10?

    (A) No revision is necessary

    (B) Change "individuals" to "an individual"

    (C) Change "simply" to "simple"

    (D) Change "when" to "if"

    (E) Change "weren't" to "aren't"

35. In context, which is the best version of sentence 12 (reproduced below)?

    Lights around malls and used car lots don't need to light up the whole sky just to advertise their products.

    (A) (As it is now)

    (B) You don't need to light up the whole sky around malls and used car lots just to advertise their products.

    (C) Advertising the products of malls and used car lots doesn't require the lighting up of the whole sky.

    (D) Lights around malls and used car lots not needing to light up the whole sky just to advertise their products.

    (E) Mall owners and used car dealers don't need to light up the whole sky just to advertise their products.

SECTION 7

Time—20 Minutes
18 Questions

Directions: For each of the following questions, choose the best answer and darken the corresponding oval on the answer sheet.

Each sentence below has one or two blanks, each blank indicating that something has been omitted. Beneath the sentence are five words or sets of words labeled (A) through (E). Choose the word or set of words that, when inserted in the sentence, **best** fits the meaning of the sentence as a whole.

EXAMPLE:

Today's small, portable computers contrast markedly with the earliest electronic computers, which were ----.

(A) effective
(B) invented
(C) useful
(D) destructive
(E) enormous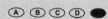

---

1. There are a small number of people in third world countries who live ---- but most people have no hope of ---- even the basic amenities of life.

   (A) poorly . . enjoying
   (B) responsibly . . acquiring
   (C) pretentiously . . yielding
   (D) simply . . missing
   (E) lavishly . . attaining

2. Most cultures throughout history have their own creation myth, indicating that the origin of life is a ---- interest.

   (A) distant
   (B) universal
   (C) mythical
   (D) superficial
   (E) debatable

3. While the servants quarters exemplified a simple and austere style of décor, the other rooms in the palace of Versailles were ---- and opulent.

   (A) basic
   (B) severe
   (C) florid
   (D) efficient
   (E) straightforward

4. The teacher tried to negotiate an agreement between the quarreling students but felt ---- about the outcome because the students refused to compromise.

   (A) cordial
   (B) dubious
   (C) benevolent
   (D) biased
   (E) prophetic

5. While the musician's biography mostly reiterates stories that many readers will find familiar, several chapters about his childhood may even be ---- to experts.

   (A) surprising
   (B) trivial
   (C) boring
   (D) unclear
   (E) irrelevant

6. Since the mid-eighteenth century, there has been much ---- between the cultures of France and Germany despite the frequent ---- between those two countries.

   (A) communication .. alliances
   (B) hatred .. opposition
   (C) interaction .. enmity
   (D) antagonism . .misunderstandings
   (E) hostility .. alienation

GO ON TO THE NEXT PAGE

Directions: The passages below are followed by questions based on their content; questions following a pair of related passages may also be based on the relationship between the paired passages. Answer the questions on the basis of what is <u>stated</u> or <u>implied</u> in the passages and in any introductory material that may be provided.

Questions 7–18 are based on the following passages.

The following two passages discuss the unreleased movie "45 Minutes from Denver" by student filmmaker Oscar Grey. Passage 1 describes some early critiques of the film's preview. Passage 2 is an excerpt from a magazine article in which Grey talks about his film.

Passage 1

At four hours and forty-five minutes, it is the longest feature film in motion picture history. Its budget of over 150 million dollars has led many pundits to speculate that it may end up being the
(5) biggest flop of all time. One reviewer opened her column by likening *45 Minutes from Denver* to *Titanic*, then quickly clarified she was speaking of the ship, not the Oscar-winning film. Another critic wailed that at times during the film he felt as
(10) if he was "drowning in the director's woeful self-indulgence."

The film was written and directed by Oscar Grey, who also stars as the main (and basically only) character. This is his second effort, his debut
(15) work was 2002's quiet hit *Revisited*, which earned him a Best Director nomination. *45 Minutes from Denver* is Grey's loose interpretation of the life story of the mysterious and reclusive American author, Alexander Roth. The actual known details
(20) of Roth's life are spotty at best, and the liberties Mr. Grey takes while attempting to fill in the many blanks have sparked outrage in the literary community in which the author is revered. Most who have reviewed the film are suitably impressed by
(25) the talented director's extraordinary eye and acting ability, but it is the film's questionable content and complete lack of story structure that has left the majority of movie critics predicting this film's quick death.
(30) There are a few Hollywood insiders, however, who feel the reports of the film's early demise have been greatly exaggerated. The quirky *Revisited* was also a critical failure, yet since its release it has managed, by word of mouth, to generate legions
(35) of fans fiercely loyal to Grey. What's more, just last year countless admirers of Alexander Roth braved the New York winter to stand in line just to be the first to buy his posthumously published book of short stories. But whether the fans of the film-
(40) maker or the subject will be able to deal with the apparent lack of a plot and characters, nonexistent story structure, or the unprecedented running time remains to be seen. According to film critic Michael Reynolds, "*45 Minutes* is an art film with
(45) an action film's budget and expectations. Every scene, though uniquely appealing visually, is disconnected from the next, seemingly ordered in no particular manner. There is only one character with significant dialog (Grey as Roth), no hint of
(50) the traditional three-act story form, hence no drama, and there is a constant, lingering sense of confusion that is not at all cleared up when the credits mercifully roll. The only thread that keeps the story from complete disintegration are the
(55) Rockies, beautifully imposing themselves upon each of Grey's shots like an antagonist plucked from a silent film."

While *45 Minutes from Denver* apparently contains enough fodder to keep the coffeehouse
(60) crowds in deep conversation for at least a couple of weeks, the average "summer blockbuster" fan who spends his or her hard-earned dollars on this hype machine may find themselves walking out of their local multiplex very disappointed (long
(65) before the movie is over).

GO ON TO THE NEXT PAGE ⟩

Passage 2

True beauty and experimentation in art have long been the domain of painters and poets. After the panning by the critics of *Revisited* and then its subsequent, unexpected success, I arrived at the

(70) conclusion that in the mainstream there is an appetite for cinematic art of the highest form. For too long Hollywood has been force-feeding the American audience the same old recycled formula, and we have been mindlessly ingesting it over and

(75) over again, for the simple lack of a better option. To say "regular" filmgoers are not ready for my movie is an insult to them and their intelligence. They have yet to be given an alternative—until now.

(80)   Trying to get this movie off the ground was a lesson in the prejudices and small-mindedness of Hollywood. Though I'd received numerous offers to direct and star in others' movies after the success of my first film, finding a studio to produce

(85) *45 Minutes from Denver* was an exercise in futility. Everyone had an opinion on how to make it more "accessible": add more characters to the movie's script, include more dialogue, reshape the story; basically completely rewrite it because it did not

(90) fit into the cookie-cutter mold. Finally, after almost a year of begging and pleading on the steps of seemingly every major studio, I found it took only a simple quote by Francis Bacon to open one very rich, very wise investor's eyes: "There is no

(95) excellent beauty that hath not some strangeness in the proportion."

As for the script, attempting to structure and interpret Alexander Roth's life into the classic three acts not only immediately struck me as awk-

(100) ward, but also as an injustice to the great writer himself. Roth did not attempt to put a traditionalized order to his life or his art and therefore neither could I, the Aristotles and Robert Mckees of the world be damned. The underlying theme in all

(105) of Roth's books is the idea that only from the seemingly random disconnected events of a long arduous journey can true enlightenment spawn. I strove to accomplish this in my film, and I believe I succeeded.

(110)   Sure, there will be those who, clinging to a meaningless set of rules, will not embrace the unconventionality of my film, but these are the descendants of those same men who ravaged Picasso. And like that great painter, I do not listen

(115) to the keys of the critic's typewriter or the applause of the audience; I listen only to my instinct as an artist.

7. In the first paragraph of Passage 1, the reviewer compares *45 Minutes from Denver* to the *Titanic* because she believes that like the *Titanic*, the film

   (A) will capture the world's imagination
   (B) is guaranteed to be an attraction because of its sheer magnitude
   (C) will be one of the greatest box office hits of all time
   (D) is doomed to be a disaster, but will revolutionize its industry
   (E) is over-hyped, oversized, and doomed to disaster.

8. "Quiet" as it used in line 15 of Passage 1, most closely means

   (A) barely audible
   (B) lacking action
   (C) placid in tone
   (D) without fanfare
   (E) financially unsuccessful

9. In lines 19–23 in Passage 1, the author describes the film's portrayal of Alexander Roth's life as

   (A) an admixture of truth and dramatic license
   (B) a complete fabrication
   (C) a mild embellishment
   (D) a faithful representation of the facts
   (E) undisguised idolatry

GO ON TO THE NEXT PAGE

10. Lines 30–39 in Passage 1 ("There are … stories")
imply that the critics who are predicting that *45
Minutes from Denver* will be a colossal failure

    (A) are correct, its bad reviews have all but sealed
    the film's fate.

    (B) are not taking into account of the true
    numbers of both Grey's and Roth's devoted
    fans

    (C) were wrong about *Revisited*, and will be
    wrong about this film

    (D) are surprisingly ignorant to the tastes of the
    average moviegoer

    (E) are unfairly biased against both Grey and
    Roth

11. Which of the following best summarizes Author 1's
and Reynold's criticisms of the film?

    (A) it is cinematically unattractive

    (B) it is much too long

    (C) Alexander Roth is not worthy of being the
    basis of a film

    (D) it is too artistic for its own good

    (E) it is surprisingly unoriginal

12. The first paragraph of Passage 2 indicates that
Oscar Grey believes

    (A) he is the greatest director of all time

    (B) *45 Minutes from Denver* will be ground-
    breaking

    (C) many filmgoers will not appreciate his film

    (D) Experimentation belongs in painting, poetry,
    and cinema.

    (E) Hollywoood keeps recycling the same movie
    formula for economic reasons

13. From the Francis Bacon quote Grey mentions in
line 94, "some strangeness in the proportion" is a
reference to

    (A) the unconventional aspects of the film's script

    (B) the amount of cash the producer wants to
    invest

    (C) the investor's eyes

    (D) Grey's desire to have his film produced

    (E) the number of studios that rejected him

14. According to Passage 2, Grey gave *45 Minutes from
Denver* an unconventional structure in order to

    (A) entice a studio to produce the film

    (B) please the coffeehouse crowds

    (C) reflect the nature of the film's subject

    (D) mock the critics who disparage him

    (E) emulate the paintings of Picasso

15. Based on Passage 2, which of the following best
describes how Grey would respond to the Passage 1
author's statements about "the average 'summer
blockbuster'" fans in line 61?

    (A) in this particular case, the author may be
    correct

    (B) the author is guilty of underestimating the
    audience

    (C) he might edit the movie down a bit

    (D) a moviegoer is entitled to his or her opinion

    (E) the average critic and the average moviegoer
    are both fools

GO ON TO THE NEXT PAGE

16. Which specific aspect of the film is of great concern to the critics in Passage 1, but does not warrant a mention from Oscar Grey in Passage 2?

    (A) Grey's interpretation of Alexander Roth's life
    (B) the lack of characters and dialog
    (C) the film's large budget
    (D) the length of the film
    (E) competition from other films

17. Both the author and critics in Passage 1 and most of the major film studios in Passage 2 would probably say that

    (A) Oscar Grey does not belong in Hollywood.
    (B) Oscar Grey is a better actor than he is a director.
    (C) The film has no redeeming qualities.
    (D) Oscar Grey is a better director than he is a screenwriter.
    (E) *Revisited* was an extraordinary film.

18. Based on Passage 2's final paragraph, Oscar Gray would probably most agree with which of the following statements about critics, such as those in Passage 1?

    (A) Critics are just strongly opinionated movie-goers.
    (B) Critics are never right or justified in their reviews.
    (C) Most critics are too close-minded to appreciate something revolutionary.
    (D) The audience's reaction is more important than a critic's
    (E) Negative reviews can damage an artist's confidence.

IF YOU FINISH BEFORE TIME IS CALLED, YOU MAY CHECK YOUR WORK ON THIS SECTION ONLY. DO NOT TURN TO ANY OTHER SECTION IN THE TEST. **STOP**

KAPLAN
Test Prep and Admissions

SECTION 8
Time—20 Minutes
16 Questions

Directions: For this section, solve each problem and decide which is the best of the choices given. Fill in the corresponding oval on the answer sheet. You may use any available space for scratchwork.

Notes:

(1) Calculator use is permitted.

(2) All numbers used are real numbers.

(3) Figures are provided for some problems. All figures are drawn to scale and lie in a plane UNLESS otherwise indicated.

(4) Unless otherwise specified, the domain of any function f is assumed to be the set of all real numbers x for which $f(x)$ is a real number.

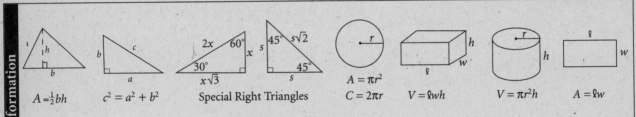

$A = \frac{1}{2}bh$ $\quad$ $c^2 = a^2 + b^2$ $\quad$ Special Right Triangles $\quad$ $A = \pi r^2$ $\quad$ $C = 2\pi r$ $\quad$ $V = \ell wh$ $\quad$ $V = \pi r^2 h$ $\quad$ $A = \ell w$

The sum of the degree measures of the angles in a triangle is 180.
The number of degrees of arc in a circle is 360.
A straight angle has a degree measure of 180.

Department	Number of Teams	Employees per Team
Development	1	4
Marketing	2	3
Accounting	3	2
Public Relations	5	5

1. The chart above shows the distribution of employees at a company into different teams in different departments. According to the chart, how many total employees are there?

(A) 14
(B) 25
(C) 41
(D) 84
(E) 154

2. If $-a^3 + b^2 = -a^3 + 9$, then b could equal which of the following?

(A) -9
(B) $-\sqrt[3]{9}$
(C) $\sqrt[3]{9}$
(D) 3
(E) 9

GO ON TO THE NEXT PAGE

3. A long distance runner takes between 5 and 7 minutes to run one mile during the first half of a cross country race. During the second half, she starts to get tired and adds 1 to 2 minutes to the time it takes her to run a mile. What are the minimum and maximum number of minutes it would take the runner to run one mile during the second half of the race?

(A) 5 and 7 minutes

(B) 6 and 8 minutes

(C) 6 and 9 minutes

(D) 7 and 8 minutes

(E) 7 and 9 minutes

4. Carmel is spinning a basketball on his finger so that it turns around completely every 1.5 seconds. How many degrees does the logo on the ball turn in 10 seconds, assuming it is not on the spinning axis?

(A) 54°

(B) 240°

(C) 720°

(D) 2160°

(E) 2400°

5. A certain fraction is equal to $\frac{1}{3}$. If one is subtracted from the numerator and the denominator is divided by two, the resulting fraction is equivalent to $\frac{1}{2}$. What is the denominator of the original fraction?

(A) 3

(B) 4

(C) 6

(D) 9

(E) 12

6. A new airplane can travel at speeds up to 4,680 miles per hour. How many miles can the airplane travel in 10 seconds?

(A) 1.3

(B) 7.8

(C) 13

(D) 78

(E) 130

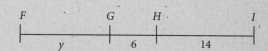

7. In the diagram above, line segment $\overline{FI}$ has a length of 32. What is the length of the line segment whose endpoints are H and the midpoint of line segment $\overline{FG}$?

(A) 7

(B) 12

(C) 13

(D) 18

(E) 20

8. If $\dfrac{2x+4}{x-3} = \dfrac{4}{3}$ then what is the value of x?

(A) −12

(B) −3

(C) −2

(D)   3

(E) 12

9. The percent increase from 6 to 16 is equal to the percent increase from 12 to what number?

(A) 16

(B) 22

(C) 23

(D) 32

(E) 36

GO ON TO THE NEXT PAGE

10. If $b > a > 0$, which of the following is less than $\frac{a}{b}$?

    (A) 2

    (B) $\frac{b}{a}$

    (C) $\frac{\frac{1}{a}}{b}$

    (D) $\frac{a}{2b}$

    (E) $\frac{2a}{b}$

11. A class of 30 students had an average (arithmetic mean) of 92 points on a geography test out of a possible 100. If 10 of the students had a perfect score, what was the average score for the remaining students?

    (A) 58

    (B) 87

    (C) 88

    (D) 90

    (E) 92

12. By noon, $\frac{1}{4}$ of Company X's employees had arrived to work. An hour later, 30 more employees had arrived, raising total attendance to $\frac{1}{2}$ of the total staff. How many employees work for Company X?

    (A)   30

    (B)   45

    (C)   60

    (D) 120

    (E) 135

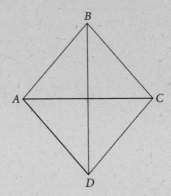

13. In the figure above, line segment $\overline{BD}$ and $\overline{AC}$ bisect each other. If $\overline{BD} = 12$ and $\overline{AC} = 16$, what is the area of $\triangle ACD$?

    (A)   48

    (B)   54

    (C)   96

    (D) 112

    (E) 192

14. If $q = \frac{5}{4}st$, what is the value of t when $s = 2$ and $q = 50$?

    (A) 2.5

    (B) 20

    (C) 35

    (D) 40

    (E) 70

GO ON TO THE NEXT PAGE

15. Lines *l* and *m* and two circles lie in a plane. If *l* passes through the center of the two circles and *m* is perpendicular to *l*, which of the following could NOT be the number of points at which *m* intersects the circles?

(A) 0
(B) 1
(C) 2
(D) 4
(E) 5

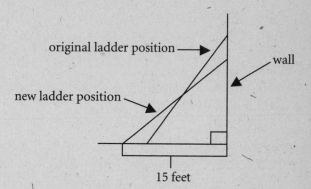

original ladder position →

wall

new ladder position →

15 feet

16. A 25 foot ladder is propped against a wall as shown in the figure above. If the ladder slips down 4 feet along the wall so that the bottom of the ladder is now 15 feet away from the base of the wall, how far away from the wall was the bottom of the ladder originally?

(A) 5
(B) 7
(C) 9
(D) 20
(E) 24

IF YOU FINISH BEFORE TIME IS CALLED, YOU MAY CHECK YOUR WORK ON THIS SECTION ONLY. DO NOT TURN TO ANY OTHER SECTION IN THE TEST.

STOP

SECTION 9

Time—10 Minutes
14 Questions

Directions: For each question in this section, select the best answer from among the choices given and fill in the corresponding oval on the answer sheet.

The following sentences test correctness and effectiveness of expression. Part of each sentence or the entire sentence is underlined; beneath each sentence are five ways of phrasing the underlined material. Choice (A) repeats the original phrasing; the other four choices are different. If you think the original phrasing produces a better sentence than any of the alternatives, select choice (A); if not, select one of the other choices.

In making your selection, follow the requirements of standard written English; that is, pay attention to grammar, choice of words, sentence construction, and punctuation. Your selection should result in the most effective sentence—clear and precise, without awkwardness or ambiguity.

EXAMPLE:

Every apple in the baskets <u>are ripe and labeled according to the date it was picked</u>.

(A) are ripe and labeled according to the date it was picked
(B) is ripe and labeled according to the date it was picked
(C) are ripe and labeled according to the date they were picked
(D) is ripe and labeled according to the date they were picked
(E) are ripe and labeled as to the date it was picked

ANSWER:

Ⓐ ● Ⓒ Ⓓ Ⓔ

---

1. <u>The mule refused to eat the oats, he</u> kicked over the bucket to show his displeasure.

   (A) The mule refused to eat the oats, he
   (B) The mule, having refused to eat the oats, he
   (C) In addition to refusing to eat the oats, the mule
   (D) The oats, which the mule refused to eat, were
   (E) The oats were initially refused by the mule, then

2. An industrial spy is <u>where one company steals products or designs from another company</u> in the same field.

   (A) where one company steals products or designs from another company
   (B) stealing of products or designs from one company by another
   (C) when one company steals products or designs from another company
   (D) how products or designs stolen by one company from another company
   (E) someone who steals products or designs from one company for another company

---

GO ON TO THE NEXT PAGE ▷

3. Some speedometers register <u>high speeds as</u> two hundred miles per hour, even though few cars will ever go faster than one hundred.

   (A) high speeds as

   (B) speeds as high as

   (C) speeds that are high

   (D) high speeds that are capable of exceeding

   (E) a speed as

4. <u>Having the same strength but much less weight when compared with metal</u>, carbon fibre plastic composites are ideal materials for prostheses to replace lost limbs.

   (A) Having the same strength but much less weight when compared with metal

   (B) By being stronger and having much less weight than metal

   (C) Stronger and less weightier than metal

   (D) With the same strength but much less weighty when compared with metal

   (E) Stronger and lighter than metal

5. At holidays, my uncle was the relative who told me the stories <u>that I had heard every year throughout my childhood and also the years of my adolescence</u>.

   (A) had heard every year throughout my child-hood and also the years of my adolescence

   (B) had heard every year throughout my child-hood and my adolescence

   (C) have heard repeatedly throughout my child-hood and my adolescence alike

   (D) have, every year, had told to me both in my childhood as well as my adolescence

   (E) every year have had told to me throughout my childhood and my adolescent years alike

6. Although still constrained by gravity, <u>the idea might strike astronauts on the International Space Station that they are flying</u>.

   (A) the idea might strike astronauts on the International Space Station that they are flying

   (B) that they are flying is an idea that might strike astronauts on the International Space Station

   (C) astronauts on the International Space Station might be struck by the idea that they are flying

   (D) astronauts on the International Space Station are flying and might be struck by the idea

   (E) astronauts on the International Space Station might be flying as the idea might strike them

7. According to Greek myth, <u>Zeus's inability to control his lust, this made his wife,</u> Hera, extremely angry.

   (A) Zeus's inability to control his lust, this made his wife,

   (B) when out of Zeus's control, his lust made his wife,

   (C) Zeus's inability at controlling his lust was making his wife,

   (D) Zeus's inability to control his lust made his wife,

   (E) the lack of control over his lust that Zeus exhibited made his wife,

GO ON TO THE NEXT PAGE

8. Marathoners train for years <u>to turn their bodies into a highly efficient machine</u>.

   (A) to turn their bodies into a highly efficient machine
   (B) to turn his or her body into highly efficient machines
   (C) in turning their bodies into a highly efficient machine
   (D) turning their bodies into what could be called a highly efficient machine
   (E) to turn their bodies into highly efficient machines

9. Renaissance sculptures were often placed in elevated positions, so artists made adjustments <u>to account for one's position and your resulting perspective</u>.

   (A) to account for one's position and your resulting perspective
   (B) which were accounting for one's position and resulting perspective
   (C) to account for one's position and resulting perspective
   (D) to account for their position and your resulting perspective
   (E) accounting for your position and thus, consequently your resulting perspective

10. During the power outage, machines malfunctioned throughout the <u>factory, and it therefore prevented all production</u>.

    (A) factory, and it therefore prevented all production
    (B) factory and thereby preventing it from all production
    (C) factory, by which all production was thereby prevented
    (D) factory, and thereby this had all production prevented
    (E) factory, preventing all production

11. Having lived away from home for many years, <u>that his parents did not visit him disappointed James extremely</u>.

    (A) that his parents did not visit him disappointed James extremely
    (B) James's extreme disappointment resulted from his parent's not visiting him
    (C) James was extremely disappointed that his parents did not visit him
    (D) James's extreme disappointment at his parent's failing to visit
    (E) his parent's failing to visit was an extreme disappointment to James

12. Analysts say that the companies projected annual profit, <u>which is $10 million less than expected and $15 million less than</u> the previous year, is a severe disappointment to stock holders.

    (A) which is $10 million less than expected and $15 million less than
    (B) estimated $10 million lower than expected while having fallen $15 million from
    (C) with an amount $10 million less than expected as well as $15 million less than that of
    (D) $10 million less than expected, and it amounts to $15 million less than
    (E) being $10 million less than expected and $15 million less than measured from

GO ON TO THE NEXT PAGE

KAPLAN
Test Prep and Admissions

13. Though strongly dependent on the Moscow
government for regulations and <u>laws while former
Soviet countries supply Kaliningrad with business,
as a city it remains</u> geographically independent of
both.

  (A) laws while former Soviet countries supply
  Kaliningrad with business, as a city it remains

  (B) laws and on business by former Soviet
  countries, Kaliningrad, a city

  (C) laws and on former Soviet countries for
  business, Kaliningrad is a city

  (D) laws, former Soviet countries supply
  Kaliningrad with business, but it is a city

  (E) laws, former Soviet countries supply
  Kaliningrad with business, while it remains a
  city

14. <u>The Secretary of State's speech, detailing foreign
policy in this hemisphere and beyond and setting
out a plan for peace in the region,</u> became a classic
of modern statesmanship.

  (A) The Secretary of State's speech, detailing foreign policy in this hemisphere and beyond
  and setting out a plan for peace in the region,

  (B) Detailing foreign policy in this hemisphere
  and beyond, the Secretary of State's speech
  setting out a plan for peace in the region, it
  also

  (C) With details of foreign policy in this hemisphere and beyond and setting out a plan for
  peace in the region the Secretary of State's
  speech

  (D) The Secretary of State's speech with its
  detailing of foreign policy in this hemisphere
  and beyond and setting out a plan for peace
  in the region,

  (E) Although the Secretary of State's speech
  detailed foreign policy in this hemisphere and
  beyond and also set out a plan for peace in
  the region,

IF YOU FINISH BEFORE TIME IS CALLED, YOU MAY CHECK YOUR WORK ON
THIS SECTION ONLY. DO NOT TURN TO ANY OTHER SECTION IN THE TEST.

STOP

Practice Test One: **Answer Key**

SECTION 1	SECTION 3	15. D	SECTION 6	SECTION 7	SECTION 9
Essay	1. A	16. E	1. A	1. E	1. C
	2. D	17. C	2. D	2. B	2. E
SECTION 2	3. D	18. E	3. C	3. C	3. B
	4. C	19. D	4. D	4. B	4. E
1. E	5. B	20. C	5. C	5. A	5. B
2. D	6. D	21. E	6. B	6. C	6. C
3. A	7. B	22. D	7. B	7. E	7. D
4. B	8. C	23. C	8. D	8. D	8. E
5. C	9. D	24. B	9. E	9. A	9. C
6. D	10. B		10. A	10. B	10. E
7. C	11. D	SECTION 5	11. D	11. D	11. C
8. A	12. E		12. A	12. B	12. A
9. B	13. D	1. D	13. A	13. A	13. C
10. E	14. D	2. C	14. D	14. C	14. A
11. C	15. E	3. C	15. B	15. B	
12. D	16. D	4. A	16. A	16. D	
13. B	17. C	5. C	17. C	17. D	
14. E	18. C	6. A	18. D	18. C	
15. A	19. C	7. B	19. B		
16. D	20. C	8. C	20. B	SECTION 8	
17. D		9. 7/5	21. A		
18. C	SECTION 4	10. 14/3 or	22. B	1. C	
19. B		4.67	23. C	2. D	
20. D	1. D	11. 5	24. C	3. C	
21. C	2. C	12. 8	25. B	4. E	
22. E	3. C	13. 32/9	26. D	5. E	
23. B	4. B	14. 10	27. D	6. C	
24. C	5. E	15. 150	28. E	7. B	
25. B	6. B	16. 220	29. D	8. A	
	7. E	17. 3	30. C	9. D	
	8. E	18. 441	31. D	10. D	
	9. C		32. B	11. C	
	10. D		33. E	12. D	
	11. D		34. E	13. A	
	12. B		35. E	14. B	
	13. E			15. E	
	14. A			16. B	

PRACTICE TEST ONE

Critical Reading

	Number Right	Number Wrong	Raw Score
Section 2:	☐	− (.25 × ☐)	= ☐
Section 4:	☐	− (.25 × ☐)	= ☐
Section 7:	☐	− (.25 × ☐)	= ☐
	Critical Reading Raw Score	=	☐ (rounded up)

Writing

	Number Right	Number Wrong	Raw Score
Section 1:	☐ (ESSAY GRADE)	× 3.17	= ☐
Section 6:	☐	− (.25 × ☐)	= ☐
Section 9:	☐	− (.25 × ☐)	= ☐
	Writing Raw Score	=	☐ (rounded up)

Math

	Number Right	Number Wrong	Raw Score
Section 3:	☐	− (.25 × ☐)	= ☐
Section 5A: (QUESTIONS 1–8)	☐	− (.25 × ☐)	= ☐
Section 5B: (QUESTIONS 9–18)	☐	(no wrong answer penalty)	= ☐
Section 8:	☐	− (.25 × ☐)	= ☐
	Math Raw Score	=	☐ (rounded up)

Turn to page xiv to convert your raw score to a scaled score.

Answers and Explanations

SECTION 1

6 Score Essay

Happiness means different things to different people. My sister is happiest when she performs onstage in a play. My best friend is happiest when he's pitching a perfect game on the baseball field. People find happiness in all sorts of ways, but that doesn't mean they stop searching for something more. Finding happiness and continuing to pursue other goals are not mutually exclusive propositions. Instead, both of these activities can work together to motivate you, as I've learned from my own experience.

When I was in middle school, my favorite class was art and I was disappointed that the class period was so short and only twice a week. Although I was happy during those times, I really missed art during the rest of the week. However, knowing that art class was approaching helped motivate me to pay attention in the rest of my classes because I knew that my "reward" would soon follow. Once we were in the art room and I was immersed in painting or sculpting or drawing, I found incredible happiness in the creative process and carried this feeling with me throughout the remainder of the day. Yet I wasn't fully satisfied with this small amount of exposure and I wanted more. I could and did appreciate the happiness I had, but at the same time I was looking for something beyond that.

So I begged my parents to let me take art classes after school and on the weekend. I managed to convince them I'd be happier if I could have this additional creative time, and I was right. Taking more and different art classes outside of school exposed me to a variety of different techniques and media that I never had time to explore in school, like metal-working, wood-carving, and print-making. I grew even more enthusiastic about the visual arts and found even more happiness than I could have imagined thanks to these additional classes. By wanting something more, I was able to find additional contentment and inspiration and I truly was happy with the results.

Yet I didn't stop reaching for other goals. I really wanted to have my artwork displayed for the public, so I worked very hard for several years to develop a portfolio and I achieved my goal last year with my first solo show at a local gallery. This success gave me much happiness, and I'm already planning additional shows. Being content with my art makes me happy on a regular basis, but this doesn't keep me from wanting something more at the same time. For me, striving for additional goals adds to my happiness, so I don't see the two actions as contradictory at all. Instead, searching for something beyond what you have can help you to appreciate and enhance whatever it is that makes you truly happy.

6 Score Critique

All essays are evaluated on four basic criteria: Topic, Support, Organization, and Language. This essay begins with the author's interpretation of the topic, showing that the author understood the prompt. The introductory paragraph clearly states the author's opinion and introduces the personal example that the author develops throughout the essay. Although the author uses a single example, she fully develops this example to support her opinion as she narrates a personal experience that illustrates her perspective on the prompt.

The organization of this essay is consistent and coherent, with transitional phrases and keywords ("but," "instead," "although," "however," "once," "yet," "so," "such as") to link ideas and paragraphs. The essay's clear introduction leads logically into its body paragraphs, which in turn link to a strong conclusion. The excellent support and organization of this essay indicate that the author spent sufficient time planning her essay and that she followed her plan as she wrote.

Finally, the author's vocabulary and sentence structure are both sophisticated and varied, showing a high level of language facility and above-average written expression. The lack of grammatical or spelling errors suggests that the author remembered to proofread her essay, giving her writing that final polish that helps lead to a high score.

4 Score Essay

My Mom's favorite expression is "The grass is always greener on the other side." She says this if I ask for something new because she wants me to be content with what I do have instead of always wanting something else. In my opinion, though, its hard to be happy with what you have because there are always more things to acquire or other goals to reach, and each new thing you want seems to be the most important for being happy.

Look at the Boston Red Sox, they have a long rivalry with the New York Yankees but were able to beat them with an amazing come-from-behind victory in the ALCS. What they did was historic, but they weren't happy with that upset victory because they still had to deal with the World Series. They wanted more than an ALCS title, they wanted a World Series championship. And for the first time in almost a century, they won the World Series and rejoiced for days. But then the moment and the emotions started to fade, so their happiness didn't last. Now they have to figure out what else to pursue in order to regain that happiness.

A similar thing happened to me last year when I wanted to be exempt from my final exams. All I needed was less than 5 absences and an A- average in each class. I worked really hard all year to achieve this goal and I was really happy during exam week when most of my friends were still in school but I wasn't. This happiness didn't last long, though, because the event that inspired it didn't last long. So after a week or so, my focus turned to my summer job and my happiness died out because my job as a sales clerk was so miserable. At that point, all I wanted was to find something else so that I could be happy again.

It's pretty clear that happiness can be achieved but its usually fleeting. What makes you happy at one moment doesn't last forever, and you start to wonder what other activities or goals might make you happy again. We all hope the grass will be greener on the other side, and sometimes it is.

4 Score Critique

All essays are evaluated on four basic criteria: Topic, Support, Organization, and Language. The author begins this essay with another common phrase that relates to the quotation provided in the prompt. By explaining this phrase, the author shows that he understood the prompt. The introductory paragraph ends with a clear statement of the author's opinion but does not mention what examples the author will use and lacks a transition to the next paragraph.

The two examples provided are fairly well-developed and provide adequate support for the author's argument. The organization of the essay, however, could be improved with transitional words or phrases between paragraphs to help the reader navigate the essay. Although the essay is structured appropriately, with a clear introduction and conclusion surrounding two body paragraphs, the different parts of the essay are not strongly linked in a logical manner, suggesting that the author didn't spend enough time planning his essay before he began to write.

Another weakness of this essay is the author's language. Vague vocabulary ("something," "thing," "things"), unclear pronouns ("they" in the second paragraph), a few grammatical errors ("its" instead of "it's" in the first and fourth paragraphs, sentences beginning with "But," "So," "And" in the second and third paragraphs, "less" instead of "fewer" in the third paragraph), and run-on sentences (second paragraph) indicate that the author needs to leave time to proofread to correct any basic errors that detract from the overall message of his essay.

2 Score Essay

I used to think that being happy was the easiest thing in the world because I was always happy when I was little. Everything I wanted was given to me, since my parents took care of everything. But then when I got older, I realized that life wasn't so simple and being happy doesn't always happen easily. The main thing that made me realize this was when my parents got divorced. I know now that divorce is a pretty common thing since lots of my friends have parents who are divorced. But when it happened to my family I couldn't believe it. I didn't understand how my parents could have seemed so happy when actually they were both pretty miserable. At the time they couldn't really explain it to my sister and brother and me so we were all pretty confused about what was going on. But then I got older and talked to my mom and dad more about what happened, and they were able to explain that they just didn't make each other happy any more so they decided it was better for them to separate than to try to make things work out in an unhappy situation. Luckily for both of them, they've found more happiness apart with new partners than when they were together.

So I think people actually are capable of finding happiness even if they aren't aware of it at the time. Sometimes people think they're happy and may even be happy for a little while. But then something might change so that they're not happy any more. The main thing to remember is that since we all have choices in life we can make decisions to do things to make ourselves happier, like my parents did. They made the tough choice to get a divorce and they each found happiness in another way.

2 Score Critique

All essays are evaluated on four basic criteria: Topic, Support, Organization, and Language. This essay discusses the topic but doesn't immediately address the given prompt. In fact, the author doesn't make a clear statement of his opinion of the prompt until the first sentence of the final paragraph, which makes his essay difficult to follow, since the reader doesn't know what point the author is trying to make.

The author provides a single example to support his opinion, but this example is vague and not well-developed. Likewise, the organization of the essay is extremely weak, since the author doesn't provide a clear introduction, conclusion, or transitions between paragraphs. The author needs to spend time brainstorming his examples and planning his essay to make sure that he has an outline to follow while he's writing.

Finally, the author's language is generic and repetitive ("everything," "happen," "thing," "people," "something"). In addition, his sentence structure is simplistic and unrefined, and several sentences are fragments beginning with conjunctions such as "so" and "but." This author must practice writing SAT essays, and leave enough time to proofread and correct any obvious mistakes if he hopes to get a higher score on the essay part of his SAT.

SECTION 2

1.   E

Difficulty: Low

What's the best way to end an argument? *Compromise.* Obviously the parents want to end the argument between their children, so they might try to suggest a compromise that would satisfy both children. Look for alternative words for "end" and "satisfy."

In (A), they certainly wouldn't want to *enforce* the argument. In (B), though the word *end* could be exactly what you're looking for, a *divisive* solution won't end the argument. In (C), the parents might want the kids to *overcome* the argument, but a solution that's *unattractive* to both kids hardly seems helpful. In (D), again, it wouldn't make sense for the parents to want to *extend* the argument. Choice (E) works well. It makes sense that the parents would hope to *resolve* the argument, and offering a solution that's *acceptable* to both kids seems like a good move.

2.   D

Difficulty: Low

His animated disposition is doing something (good) for his passion. Wouldn't you want your excitement for the thing you love most to ooze out of you when you talk about it? Can you come up with a more eloquent way of expressing how Nathan Lane's animated disposition gives away his passion?

In (A), his excitement definitely wouldn't *misrepresent* his passion. In (B), if he feels really excited and passionate, acting excited and animated wouldn't *exaggerate* anything. In (C), how could his animated disposition *satisfy* his passion? Choice (D) is a good fit. It is more than likely that his animated disposition *reflects* his passion. In (E), being animated wouldn't *disguise* passion.

3.   A

Difficulty: Low

The key word is "powerful." Powerful people can often possess inexplicable powers of persuasion. Find a word that agrees with "powerful" and is similar to "persuasion."

Choice (A) is perfect. Powerful people are renowned for exerting a strong *influence* on others. In (B), the principal's powerful nature has nothing to do with *pretense*. In (C), *discrimination* does not imply power. In (D), addressing the students with *restraint* would not indicate that he's a powerful person. In (E), though *integrity* is a good quality, it is not indicative of power.

4.   B

Difficulty: Medium

Only one choice really makes sense. Look for words that make sense together. The movement encompasses many different styles and elements, so it must be diverse and hard to pin down. Out of all the answer choices, only one expresses that sentiment.

In (A), it's unlikely that *bragging* about post-modern literature is *necessary* for any reason. In (B), trying to *generalize* about a diverse topic is definitely *difficult*, and probably foolish. This choice seems to work. In (C), though many people like to *complain* about post-modern literature, its diversity hardly makes complaining *important*. In (D), why would *rhapsodizing* about post-modern literature be viewed as particularly *fair*? In (E), trying to *learn* is never *unproductive*.

5.   C

Difficulty: Medium

The second half of the sentence is a big hint toward the meaning of the missing word. Fill in the blank in your head with a word you know, perhaps "procrastinating," and then look for a word that is a synonym.

In (A), though many of us may think of our little brothers as *incompetent*, it doesn't mean the same thing as "procrastinating." In (B), if he is *obtrusive* in doing his homework, he might be getting in the way or brash about doing his homework, but he's not procrastinating doing the work. If he's *dilatory* in doing his homework, then he's putting it off, or "procrastinating." Choice (C) fits well. In (D), being *surreptitious* or sneaky is not the same as procrastinating. In (E), how can someone be *extroverted* or outgoing in doing his homework?

6.   D

Difficulty: Medium

The phrase "he was still" indicates that even though his superiors reacted a certain way, he was surprised by the outcome. Seeing how the alien conspiracy is referred to as "outlandish," it's likely the agent's superiors have stopped the investigation. Still, the agent seemed surprised and uncomfortable by the kind of reprimand he was given. What two words fit this scenario?

In (A), his attempts would only have been *obstinate* if he was told prior to his investigation that it was not allowed.

Furthermore, we doubt the agent would be *elated* by a severe reprimand. In (B), though the investigation might be viewed by some as *insightful*, *impenitent* certainly doesn't work in this sentence. In (C), it's not indicated anywhere in the sentence that the agent's efforts were *persuasive*. Again, we doubt that the agent would be *exultant* by a severe reprimand. In (D), it would make sense that his attempts were *thwarted* if his superiors wanted to stop the investigation. It also makes sense that if the agent wasn't expecting a severe reprimand, he might feel *discomfited* by it. This choice works well. In (E), if his attempts to uncover the alien conspiracy were *successful*, then his superiors certainly didn't stop him.

7.   C

Difficulty: High

What kind of person takes things personally too often? The last part of the sentence describes Alex's reaction, and the blank is asking for a word that will sum or fit with that description.

In (A), if Alex were *cerebral* he'd probably think about the criticism, not take it personally. In (B), *obdurate* people are usually hardened and unfeeling, so they don't take too much personally. Choice (C) fits. *Sensitive* people often take things personally. In (D), someone who is *pretentious* wouldn't necessarily react that way. In (E), Alex might become *enervated* if he continues to take things personally, but for now this is not the best fit.

8.   A

Difficulty: High

The key word is "or." The word "or" tells you that you are looking for a synonym for "incommunicable."

Choice (A) is the right choice. *Ineffable* is the synonym you're looking for. In (B), *mundane* means average or boring. In (C), *onerous* seems off the bat to have too negative a charge, and if you got that feeling you're right. It means "burdensome." In (D), if the artist thought it was *incisive* when expressed plainly, he wouldn't feel it was hard to communicate. In (E), *auspicious* means "prosperous" which is not a synonym for incommunicable.

9. B

Difficulty: High

Even with high difficulty Inference questions, you find support for your answer in the passage. It just may take a little longer to find it. Here, the author mentions the Loch Ness Monster in the first sentence. Read that sentence and a little further to get the full context. Note, in sentence 2, that the author talks about *animals that may exist only in the minds of the over-imaginative*. She is using the Loch Ness Monster as an example of such an animal, even though she doesn't use key words such as *for example*. The lack of key words, in fact, is one of the things that makes this a high difficulty question. So, the author thinks that the Loch Ness Monster doesn't exist, or is *mythological*, as in (B).

The answer certainly can't be (A), (C), or (D) as all of these answers assume that the Monster exists. Choice (E) is out as well; the author doesn't offer an opinion about how reputable scientists regard the Loch Ness Monster.

10. E

Difficulty: Medium

Sometimes the context is of limited help to you and you need to rely on a strong vocabulary to get you to the right answer. If you're not sure what *host* means in this context, you may be able to eliminate some answers:

(A) *network* = complex or interconnected group. It's hard to imagine an interconnected group of undiscovered animals. Eliminate this one. (B) *blend* = uniform mixture. This doesn't make much sense in context. A uniform mixture of animals? Eliminate. (C) *unit* = a single thing. Since the paragraph talks about *animals* (plural), this is illogical. Eliminate it. (D) *den* = a shelter for wild animals. Some cryptids could live in dens, but not all of them (the coelacanth, e.g.) do, so this can't be the meaning of *host*. (E) *multitude* = great number, mass. This is the meaning of *host* that the author had in mind when she wrote the sentence.

11. C

Difficulty: Medium

Finding the answer may often involve more than just reading the line reference; you may have to research more of the paragraph. Luckily, with one paragraph CR there's not a lot of text to read. The answer to this question comes from the last sentence of the paragraph. It's clear that the author is including Bowie Bonds in the group that he calls *asset-backed security*.

Choice (A) is out-of-scope. You have no way of knowing from the passage if this is true or not, although it seems more likely that it isn't true, given the last sentence. In any case, it's not the correct answer. Choice (B) is also out-of-scope. While the author uses only entertainers as examples, you can't infer that only entertainers use Bowie Bonds. Choice (C) is the correct answer. Choice (D) is also out-of-scope. The author uses entertainers, whom you may regard as very wealthy, as examples of people who buy Bowie Bonds, but as in (B) you can't infer that only the wealthy use Bowie Bonds. Choice (E) is an opposite. In the beginning of the paragraph, the author says Bowie Bonds are an example of intangible money.

12. D

Difficulty: Medium

The definition of a vocab-in-context word may be right in the passage. *The bonds were the brain-child of banker David Pullman. Pullman's innovation. . .* Here you have the exact definition of *brain-child*; it's *an innovation*. All you have to do is find the answer that matches the definition. And that's (C), *original idea*. (A) *offspring* = child, descendant. (E) *avocation* = hobby.

13. B

Difficulty: Medium

Reading the choices back into the sentence is a good way to narrow down your choices. It's clear from the context of the paragraph, that *caught fire* has a positive meaning. After all, once the idea caught fire, many other people bought Bowie Bonds and now they're the norm. So, at the very least, you can eliminate negative answers then read the remaining answers into the sentence. Negative answers (A), (C), and (E) are out. Choice (B) is the better choice, since it means *to become the subject of great interest and widespread enthusiasm*. Choice (D) doesn't work because just because the bonds were publicized doesn't mean that they became popular and were bought by others. Many things can be publicized and not become popular.

14. E

Difficulty: Low

"According to the author" usually indicates a Detail question, meaning the answer is in the passage. The author offers his personal views of the Milli Vanilli lip-synching scandal in the first paragraph. Look for the answer choice that best sums up his feelings on the subject.

Choice (A) is an opposite; in the second sentence of the paragraph, the author states that lip-synching "will forever be associated with" Milli Vanilli. Choice (B) is distortion; the author does mention that the Beatles were known to have lip-synched on television, but never suggests there was any scandal involved. Choice (C) is distortion; the court ruling was a result of the scandal, not the other way around. Choice (D) is an opposite; the author states in line 7 that Milli Vanilli "admitted" to lip-synching. Choice (E) best sums up the prediction.

15. A

Difficulty: Medium

First find the reference and understand it; then you can draw your inference. The author refers to the "image on the cover page that helps to sell magazines" (line 29) as "an illusion" that is "more appealing than one might find in the frames of reality." This fits with the tone of the prior paragraph's discussion of music. Look for an answer that focuses on the illusionary aspect of the two vehicles.

Choice (A) is a good fit. Choice (B) is out of scope; nowhere in the paragraph does the author suggest that fashion magazines and pop music are *shallow mediums of expression*. Choice (C) is out of scope; declining *popularity* is never referred to in the passage. Choice (D) is out of scope; *important societal issues* are never referred to in the passage. Choice (E) is distortion; while the author's reference to the word "illusion" definitely suggests a form of deception, he never implies that there is anything inherently *malicious* about it.

16. D

Difficulty: Medium

Determine how the description of the "transformation" serves to support the author's opinion as presented in the passage. In line 38, the author connects the "concept" of transforming a model into a beautiful image that helps to sell magazines to the thinking of record company executives. Look for a choice that matches this idea.

Choice (A) is out of scope; the demands of a model's job are never mentioned in the paragraph. Choice (B) is distortion; although the author's description of all that goes into creating the images for a magazine may teach the reader about fashion photography, this is not the function of the description in the passage. Choice (C) is out of scope; a comparison can be made between fashion photographers and music video directors, but the author does not specifically make any such comparison. Choice (D) is a good match for your prediction. Choice (E) is distortion; the author does state that the transformation "requires" a make-up artist (line 31), but this reference is a detail of the author's description, not the main reason for it.

17. D

Difficulty: Low

Read the sentence and restate it in your own words to get a predicted answer. Lines 30-34 state that the "photographer's vision" is the first step in a creative collaboration that culminates into a "finished product," so look for the answer choice that offers the best definition of what is a required first step for any creative process—a *main concept* or *idea*.

Choice (A) is distortion; this definition of vision describes what the photographer hopes to create, but it does not fit in the context of the sentence. Choice (B) is distortion; this does not fit in context. Choice (C) is distortion; this literal definition of "vision" makes no sense in context. Choice (D) fits nicely. Choice (E) is out of scope; *apparition* does not fit in context.

18. C

Difficulty: Medium

Read the cited sentence and restate it in your own words to help form a prediction. In the second paragraph, the author describes how the "glossy realm of the magazine" is an "illusion"—a creation that is more "eye-catching" and "appealing" than anything that exists in reality. Think about a definition of that reality in comparison to the illusion, and look for the choice that best matches that definition.

Choice (A) is out of scope; *extraordinary life events* are not mentioned. Choice (B) is a misused detail; the "frames of reality" exist outside the camera's eye, not inside of it. Choice (C) matches your prediction. Choice (D) is an opposite; the "frames of reality" are described as what exists off *the pages of a fashion magazine*. Choice (E) is out of scope; methods of *technical photography* are not mentioned anywhere in the passage.

19. B

Difficulty: Medium

Read the cited sentence closely; the correct inference will not stray far from it. In lines 41-48, the author refers to "Video Killed the Radio Star" as "fittingly titled" to be MTV's first song, and then goes on to state that the network changed popular culture forever. The title fits because video soon trumped audio as the medium of musical expression. Look for something close to this among the choices.

Choice (A) is extreme; the Buggles are not as important as was the selection of their video. Choice (B) is a good match. Choice (C) is out of scope; the author never mentions whether or not the song was a *smash hit*. Choice (D) is out of scope; this is never mentioned in the passage. Choice (E) is distortion; although lip-synching is the subject of the passage, nowhere is it implied that the Buggles were lip-synching in their video.

20. D

Difficulty: Low

Predicting an answer will keep you from falling for trap answer choices. This a Detail question, so the answer should be quickly discernible from the given text. Which choice would best describe a singer who is "hand-picked," sent to a stylist, given vocal and dance lessons, and surrounded by other top industry talent by her record company? Predict something like *positioned for success.*

Choice (A) is out of scope; the artist may not yet be a star, but nothing indicates that she is *struggling*. Choice (B) is an opposite; the text portrays the artist as being handled very well by her record company. Choice (C) is distortion; the fact that the singer is sent to a stylist and is given vocal and dance lessons does not necessarily imply that she is *undeserving of stardom*. Choice (D) is a good match for your prediction. Choice (E) is out of scope; nothing in the passage suggests that she is *unable to appreciate her opportunity.*

21. C

Difficulty: Medium

Consult your notes for this paragraph and ask yourself what role this excerpt plays in it. The author's description of the recording processing reveals the patience and technical skill required to record a pop song in a studio. The answer choice that best reflects this statement should contain your answer.

Choice (A) is distortion; the studio equipment adds "depth and range" to the singer's vocals that she "does not naturally possess," but that does not mean it can make *anyone* sound good. Choice (B) is out of scope; nowhere in the passage does it mention *how difficult artists can be*. Choice (C) best reflects your prediction. Choice (D) is distortion; although the author probably agrees with this statement, it does not reflect the primary function of the description in the passage. Choice (E) is out of scope; the author's description is concerned with recording in a studio only.

22. E

Difficulty: High

The correct answer should also match the author's tone in the passage. Consider the attitude of the author up until this point in the passage regarding lip-synching. While in the first paragraph he did not defend Milli Vanilli's lip-synching, he did state that those who would accuse them of gross wrongdoing "simply do not comprehend the bigger, more complex picture." That "more complex picture" is his argument that pop music is a product that appeals to the masses because it is based in illusion, not reality. Look for the answer that best matches up with this argument.

Choice (A) is an opposite; based on the author's argument, you can infer that he would not consider the media questioning the singer's talent to be *completely reasonable*. Choice (B) is extreme; in line 17, the author admits that the people who criticize Milli Vanilli "do have a point," so it can be assumed that he would never characterize the consequence of the singer's lip-synching as something so extreme as *totally ridiculous*. Choice (C) is out of scope; the passage mentioned earlier cases of lip-synching in popular music. There should be nothing particularly *shocking* about it. Choice (D) is an opposite; in fact, there is a precedent mentioned in the passage, and the consequence of Milli Vanilli's lip-synching was much more severe than the singer's. Choice (E) fits your prediction.

23. B

Difficulty: Medium

Make a prediction before looking at the choices. The easiest way to answer this Detail question is to come up with your own word that best sums up the audience's expectations, and then find the answer choice that most closely matches it. The sentence states that an audience expects pop stars to be "able to pull off tightly choreographed dance moves on the stage, all the while maintaining perfect vocal pitch and not losing a breath while they perform songs that took hours, if not days, to produce in a studio." Predict something like *overly demanding.*

Choice (A) is extreme; while the expectations may be unreasonable; they aren't *absurd.* Choice (B) matches the prediction nicely. Choice (C) is out of scope; the expectations may indeed be *overwhelming* for the pop star, but they are not described as such in the passage. Choice (D) is out of scope; this choice is not supported by any detail from the passage. Choice (E) is out of scope; *optimism* is another sentiment not supported by any detail from the passage.

24. C

Difficulty: Medium

Scan the paragraph for remarks that sound like a conclusion. Note the author's concluding statement in the final sentence of the paragraph: "the pop star is not to blame when these illusions are broken; it is the fault of those who believe in the illusion in the first place." This sums up the main idea of the paragraph (and the passage as well). Predict something like *doing what is required of them.*

Choice (A) is distortion; the power of record company executives is depicted in the passage, but nowhere is it suggested that they *force* pop stars to lip-synch. Choice (B) is distortion; the author does discuss live performances, but he doesn't suggest that pop stars should *never perform live.* Choice (C) matches your prediction. Choice (D) is out of scope; the passage never suggests that lip-synching pop stars *are a trivial matter in the grand scheme of things.* Choice (E) is an opposite; in line 87, the author states that the public is "fueling the market to keep producing more" such artists.

25. B

Difficulty: Medium

You should be able to predict an answer to this question after every passage you read; be sure to practice it This Global question asks for the "primary purpose" of the passage, which means it addresses the entire passage, not just individual details. To best answer this question, think about the author's reasons for writing the passage. In the very first paragraph, he offers his opinion on the criticism of lip-synching in pop music, saying that the critics "simply do not comprehend the bigger, more complex picture." He then spends the rest of the passage trying to explain his position, using facts and details to prove his points. Predict something like *advance a position on a controversial topic.*

Choice (A) is out of scope; the author never offers a solution, nor does he necessarily consider lip-synching a problem. Choice (B) fits well. Choice (C) is distortion; the author does *draw a comparison between fashion and pop music* in the second paragraph, but it is a supporting detail in the passage, not the purpose of it. Choice (D) is distortion; again, this is just a supporting detail of the passage. Choice (E) is out of scope; it is never mentioned anywhere in the passage that the author's argument is a *revival* of an old one.

SECTION 3

1. A

Difficulty: Low

Strategic Advice: The algebra here isn't too difficult; you just need to be careful about bringing values outside the radical. Isolate the radical expression on one side of the equation, then square both sides. Backsolving, or plugging the answers into the question, would also work well.

Getting to the Answer:

$$2\sqrt{4n^2} + 7 = 39$$
$$2\sqrt{4n^2} = 32$$
$$\sqrt{4n^2} = 16$$
$$2n = 16$$
$$n = 8$$

2. D

Difficulty: Low

Strategic Advice: An integer is any positive or negative whole number. Make sure you understand the definition of an integer on Test Day.

Getting to the Answer:

Since x must be an integer, k must be a perfect square. Eliminate (A), (B), (C), and (E) because they are not perfect squares. If you're not sure which answer choices are perfect squares, take the square root of each answer choice to see if it is an integer.

3. D

Difficulty: Low

Strategic Advice: Convert the improper fractions to decimals or mixed fractions. Notice that in this question the answer choices are not ordered from least to greatest or greatest to least.

Getting to the Answer:

(A) $\frac{7}{9} < 1$

(B) $\frac{7}{3} = 2\frac{1}{3} > 2$

(C) $\frac{9}{4} = 2\frac{1}{4} > 2$

(D) $\frac{10}{7} = 1\frac{3}{7}$. This is between 1 and 2, so (D) is correct.

(E) $\frac{12}{5} = 2\frac{2}{5} > 2$

4. C

Difficulty: Low

Strategic Advice: When a problem asks about an expression, look for a shortcut. You could solve the first equation for x in terms of b, then plug that into the second equation, but you'll solve the problem faster if you can find a way to relate $2x + 4$ and $6x + 12$ directly.

Getting to the Answer:

$2x + 4 = b$

$3(2x + 4) = 3(b)$

$6x + 12 = 3b$

5. B

Difficulty: Low

Strategic Advice: Look for a pattern in the figure. What will help you figure out where the numbers need to go?

Getting to the Answer:

From the figure the larger numbers are on the side of the line with the arrow head. Look for this in your answer. Only (B) fits.

6. D

Difficulty: Low

Strategic Advice: Do not be intimidated by the multiple variables. If you don't see how to turn the word problem into an equation, try picking your own values for x and y.

Getting to the Answer:

Remember, John has to pay the $19 first before spending any leftover money on CDs, so he has $y - 19$ dollars to buy CDs with. Since each CD costs x dollars, he can buy $\frac{y - 19}{x}$ CDs.

7. B

Difficulty: Medium

Strategic Advice: Make this abstract problem more concrete by picking simple numbers. You'll find that this problem isn't so difficult with real numbers in place of the variables. You can also solve it by applying your knowledge of number properties.

You can eliminate choices (A), (C), (D), and (E) by noticing that they contain even exponents, which will produce positive numbers no matter what x is. The only answer choice that will always be negative is choice (B).

8. C

Difficulty: Medium

Strategic Advice: Keep in mind that probability is defined by:

$$\frac{\text{total favorable outcomes}}{\text{total possible outcomes}} = \text{probability}$$

Getting to the Answer:

If every 10th person puts his shoes through a machine, then person 10, person 20, person 30, and so on will put his shoes through the machine. If every 20th person has his bag searched, then person 20, person 40, person 60, and so on will have his bags searched. Since all the people who have their bags searched also have their shoes checked, you just need to find the number of people who will have their bags searched and divide that by the total number of people. People 20, 40, 60, 80, and 100 will have their bags searched, so the probability that a randomly selected passenger will have his or her bags searched is $\frac{5}{100} = \frac{1}{20}$.

9. D

Difficulty: Medium

Strategic Advice: Pick numbers. To make your work as easy as possible, make A a 10-by-10 square.

Getting to the Answer:

The area of A is 100. So the width of B is 7 and the length of B is 13. The area of B is $13 \times 7 = 91$, which is 9 percent less than that of A.

10. B

Difficulty: Medium

Strategic Advice: Sometimes the figure as drawn doesn't contain enough information. Feel free to add to it. Remember that the interior angles of a triangle add up to $180°$ and that straight angles add up to $180°$.

Getting to the Answer:

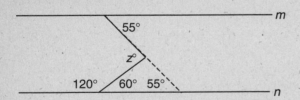

Extend one of the interior line segments to meet line n. This creates a triangle in which one angle is $180° - 120° = 60°$, one angle is $55°$ since it is formed by a transversal meeting a parallel line, and one angle is $180° - z°$.

$$60 + 55 + 180 - z = 180$$
$$115 = z$$

11. D

Difficulty: Medium

Strategic Advice: On graph problems, all of the information you need to solve the problem has been presented to you! Take a minute to identify the labels on the x and y axis and find the information you need. Remember that average (arithmetic mean) $= \frac{\text{sum of terms}}{\text{number of terms}}$.

Getting to the Answer:

Take the average of the points per game as determined from the graph:

$$\frac{10 + 14 + 8 + 18 + 20 + 16}{6} = 14.33$$

12. E

Difficulty: Medium

Strategic Advice: Don't feel intimidated by negative or fractional exponents. Convert negative exponents into fractions. Express any fractional exponents as the product of two exponents so that it is easier to reduce the equation. Backsolving, or plugging the answers into the question stem, also works well for this type of question.

Getting to the Answer:

$$x^{\frac{-2}{3}} = \frac{1}{36}$$

$$\frac{1}{x^{\frac{2}{3}}} = \frac{1}{36}$$

$$x^{\frac{2}{3}} = 36$$

$$(x^{\frac{1}{3}})^2 = 36$$

$$x^{\frac{1}{3}} = 6$$

$$(x^{\frac{1}{3}})^3 = 6^3$$

$$x = 216$$

13. D

Difficulty: Medium

Strategic Advice: Don't be intimidated by radicals in the denominator. Cross-multiply to remove the radical from the denominator and square both sides. This converts the problem into a familiar form, the quadratic equation.

Backsolving, or plugging the answers into the question stem, would also work well.

Getting to the Answer:

$$\frac{14x}{\sqrt{2x + 2}} = 7$$

$$14x = 7\sqrt{2x + 2}$$

$$2x = \sqrt{2x + 2}$$

$$4x^2 = 2x + 2$$

$$4x^2 - 2x - 2 = 0$$

$$(4x + 2)(x - 1) = 0$$

$$4x = -2 \text{ or } x = 1$$

$$x = \frac{-2}{4} = \frac{-1}{2}$$

14. D

Difficulty: Medium

Strategic Advice: Remember that there are always two possibilities when solving absolute value equations. If you get stuck, try Backsolving, or plugging the answers into the question stem.

Getting to the Answer:

$$|2r - 2| = 8$$

$$2r - 2 = 8 \text{ or } -(2r - 2) = 8$$

$$r - 1 = 4 \text{ or } -2r + 2 = 8$$

$$-2r = 6$$

$$r = -3$$

$$r = 5 \text{ or } r = -3$$

$$|3r + 2| = 17 \text{ or } -(3r + 2) = 17$$

$$3r = 15 \text{ or } 3r = -19$$

$$r = 5 \text{ or } r = \frac{-19}{3}$$

The only value that fits both equations is $r = 5$.

15. E

Difficulty: Medium

Strategic Advice: This problem is designed to let you try out this procedure. Don't worry about having major insights—just plug in the given number and see what happens. This will help you gain the insight you need for the next two questions.

Getting to the Answer:

1. Choose 6.127
2. $6.127 * 100 = 612.7$
3. The smallest integer greater than or equal to 612.7 is 613 (just round up)
4. $613 + 12 = 625$
5. Print 625

16. D

Difficulty: Medium

Strategic Advice: You can attack this by either trying to work backwards with each of the answers, or thinking about what kinds of results you can get from the procedure.

Getting to the Answer:

1. Choose a number 0 – 9.9
2. Result is between 0 and 990
3. Round up to nearest integer—now number is an integer between 0 and 990
4. Add 12—now number is an integer between 12 and 1002
5. Print the number from step 4
   (A) Doesn't work because it's too small
   (B) Doesn't work because it's too small
   (C) Not an integer
   (D) Correct
   (E) Too large

17. C

Difficulty: Medium

Strategic Advice: Try plugging in a number into the reordered steps to see if you still get the same answer.

Getting to the Answer:

We can try 6.127 again (the number doesn't change in 5, so we'll only show 1-4)

(A) step 1: 6.127

   step 3: 7

   step 2: 700

   step 4: 712

This does not match with what we found in #15, so it does not work.

(B) step 1: 6.127

step 4: 18.127

step 3: 19

step 2: 1900

This does not match with what we found in #15, so it does not work.

(C) step 1: 6.127

step 2: 612.7

step 3: 624.7

step 4: 625

This seems to work. Notice that since we're adding an integer, it doesn't matter whether we add first or round first.

(D) Doesn't work since (A) and (B) don't work

(E) Not true, since (C) works

18. C

Difficulty: High

Strategic Advice: In a substitution problem like this, look for the common term that will help you express one equation in terms of another. Substitute carefully!

Getting to the Answer:

Start with the smallest equation. Express it in terms of c.

$$b = -c + 4$$
$$-b + 4 = c$$

Substitute this into the other equation:

$a = 3(2c^2 + 3c + 4)$

$a = 3[2(-b + 4)^2 + 3(-b + 4) + 4]$

$a = 3[2(b^2 - 8b + 16) + -3b + 12 + 4]$

$a = 3[2b^2 - 16b + 32 + -3b + 12 + 4]$

$a = 3[2b^2 - 19b + 48]$

$a = 6b^2 - 57b + 144$

19. C

Difficulty: High

Strategic Advice: Visualizing a three dimensional diagram can be difficult. Redraw this diagram if necessary. Be sure to label what you know as you work through the problem.

Getting to the Answer:

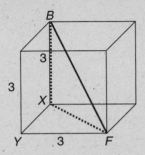

We're essentially trying to work out two Pythagorean Theorems, once for the $\overline{XF}$ base of the cube, and once again for $\overline{BF}$. Looking at the base of the cube, since $\overline{XY}$ and $\overline{YF}$ are both 3, the base forms a 45–45–90 right triangle with sides in the ratio of $x : x : x\sqrt{2}$. Therefore, the hypotenuse is $3\sqrt{2}$.

Now let's find BF. This diagonal is a hypotenuse of a right triangle with legs of 3 and $3\sqrt{2}$, so let's apply the Pythagorean Theorem:

$3^2 + (3\sqrt{2})^2 = (\overline{BF})^2$

$9 + (9)(2) = (\overline{BF})^2$

$9 + 18 = (\overline{BF})^2$

$27 = (\overline{BF})^2$

$BF = \sqrt{27} = \sqrt{9}\sqrt{3} = 3\sqrt{3}$

20. C

Difficulty: High

Strategic Advice: When extra information is given in the question stem, fill in what you know and work from there.

Getting to the Answer:

Fill in the information for one triangle. One half of the triangle forms a 3:4:5 triangle. Thus, the height is 4 and the area of one triangle $= \frac{1}{2} \times 4 \times 6 = 12$

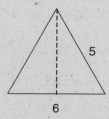

Since the parallelogram is made up of two triangles, the total area is $2 \times 12 = 24$

SECTION 4

1. D

Difficulty: Low

How would "observation" help an infant to walk? Because the opening of the sentence refers to "the ability to walk", then the first blank must also refer to this ability, such as to "become" *able* or *skilled*, both great predictions for the first blank. If infants become able through observation, then they must watch their parents walk and attempt to *copy* or *replicate* those movements. In choice (A), the sentence is referring to the "ability to walk," not *socialize*. In choice (B), again, the sentence is clearly referring to the "ability to walk," not how a baby controls or *dominates* his or her parents. In choice (C), while an infant might become *vocal* by *mimicking* his or her parents, this has nothing to do with the "ability to walk." Choice (D) is a great fit for your prediction. Choice (E) is very tempting, but the sentence is only referring to the "ability to walk," not necessarily the ability to walk quickly or nimbly.

2. C

Difficulty: Low

The words "rather than" signal a contrast to "a celebration". How might "chanting crowds of angry protestors" affect a dedication ceremony that was supposed to be "a celebration"? Most likely negatively, so look for a word that describes how the ceremony, instead of being celebratory, became a *failure* or *disaster*, both great fits for the blank.

In choice (A), an enormously large or *colossal* ceremony would not necessarily be unfortunate. In choice (B), a ceremony that became a *milestone* or significant event could have been celebratory. Choice (C) is a great match for your prediction. In choice (D), a dedication ceremony is a *consecration*. In choice (E), angry protestors would not necessarily make a ceremony that was supposed to be celebratory into a *fabrication*, or a lie or falsehood.

3. C

Difficulty: Medium

How might damage caused by "rampant corruption" effect a company's reputation?

Start with the first blank; you know from the words "damage" and "rampant corruption" that it must refer to something bad that happened to the company's reputation, such as it becoming *weakened* or even *ruined*. If this bad effect happened "before anyone realized," then it must have been *subtlety* damaging. Ruined and subtle make great predictions for the blanks.

In choice (A), if the damage caused by the corruption had been *manifest*, or easy to understand, then it would not have happened without anyone noticing. In choice (B), despicable or *nefarious* damage would not necessarily create a *polarized* reputation. Choice (C) matches your prediction nicely. In choice (D), *methodical* or systematic damage would not necessarily *amalgamate* or compound a company's reputation. In choice (E), damage caused by corruption, even if it were *obvious*, would not necessarily *stagnate* or make motionless a company's reputation.

4. B

Difficulty: Medium

"To be able to" signals that the two blanks agree with one another. The words "instead of" indicate that the two blanks represent a contrast to "analyzing their importance to his argument." Look for two words that would allow someone to deal "more smoothly" with the "individual facts of the case," something that would take a "great deal of time" but that also require something less, or more simple, than analysis. A word like *list* or *reel off* would be a good prediction for the first blank, making a word that means *commit to memory* a good fit for the second blank.

In choice (A), "simply" *regurgitating* facts would not necessarily make them easier to *synthesize*. Choice (B) is a good match for your prediction. In choice (C), "simply" *falsifying* the facts of a case would not necessarily *denounce* them. In choice (D), these words form a contrast, as *misinterpreting* the facts would not help one *acquire* them. In choice (E), if the prosecutor wanted to *disregard* the facts, he probably wouldn't have spent a lot of time *recalling* them.

5. E

Difficulty: High

If Ben's former classmates were "surprised to hear" he was "lazy" at work, what type of reputation might he have had before? The words "surprised to hear" indicate that the blank must contrast with "lazy" behavior, so look for a word that means *hard* working or *diligent*, both great predictions for the blank.

In choice (A), if Ben were known for being *indiscriminate* or making random and confused choices, he would not necessarily be surprisingly lazy. In choice (B), if Ben had been *enigmatic* or difficult to understand it would not necessarily have been surprising to learn he had become lazy. In choice (C), having a reputation for being *vicarious* would also not necessarily make one surprisingly lazy. In choice (D), once again, having a reputation for being *rancorous*, bitter, or unforgiving would not necessarily make one surprisingly lazy. Choice (E) is a good fit for your prediction.

6. B

Difficulty: Low

Notice that the word is used to describe "both" qualities discussed in the passage. What are the two qualities, and what do they have in common?

You know that paleontologists are interested in studying "prehistoric life using fossil evidence," and that teeth can be used to "describe animals that lived in the distant past." The two qualities of teeth mentioned toward the end of the passage—their adaptation to processing specific foods and

their ability to survive for centuries—only add to their *usefulness* to paleontologists.

In choice (A), the durability of teeth is *one* of the two qualities discussed in the passage, but this choice does not fit the context of the sentence, which is about *both* qualities. Choice (B) is a great match for your prediction. In choice (C), the passage does not suggest that fossilized teeth are rare, unique, or especially valuable. In choice (D), while this definition appears to match the cited word, nothing in the passage indicates that teeth are easily repaired. Choice (E) is close, but the passage does not suggest that teeth are trustworthy or dependable, just that they're useful to paleontologists.

7. E

Difficulty: Medium

Often, incorrect choices in Inference questions can tempt you by fitting in with the general focus and topic of the passage; however, you can usually eliminate choices that make assumptions not actually supported by the text. The cited content follows the words "given this concentration," a direct reference to the opening sentence, where the author says that studies of prehistoric animal interactions "inevitably focus on predatory relationships." In other words, the author is stating that this focus on predatory relationships makes paleontologists' study of teeth "not surprising," or understandable and obvious.

Choice (A) is out of scope; the cited words are not being used to describe the discovery of fossils. Choice (B) is out of scope; the author does not describe what most people know about the importance of fossilized teeth. Choice (C) is distortion; this is tempting, but it fails to recognize that the cited words are used to suggest that paleontologists' *reliance on teeth* is understandable, not that their focus on predatory relationships is understandable. Choice (D) is out of scope; the author does not say how thoroughly this connection has been investigated. Choice (E) is a nice match for your prediction.

8. E

Difficulty: Low

When an author repeats a certain stylistic device or structural feature, think about how that structure helps convey the author's point. The author describes a series of three scenes involving three different people, and each description is followed by a parenthetical reference indicating what the author finds significant about the person described. The description of the woman working at the store is followed by a parenthetical reference to her "daily struggle to make a living," suggesting that the author finds her seemingly-endless hard work significant. Look for a choice that refers to this struggle.

Choice (A) is out of scope; the author never suggests that the woman lives in the store. Choice (B) is distortion; while the author exaggerates the number of days in a week, the passage does not suggest that the woman herself is imaginary. Choice (C) is an irrelevant detail; challenges of accomplishing daily tasks are mentioned when discussing the elderly man, not the woman in the convenience store. Choice (D) is an opposite; the author says that the convenience store worker struggles to make a living. Choice (E) is a good match for your prediction.

9. C

Difficulty: Medium

Don't panic if you're not sure what the word means! Look for other descriptions associated with the same person that can help you infer its meaning in this context. The child playing with the soccer ball is described as "a blithe boy" who is "experiencing easy joy." Even if you don't know what "blithe" means, you can infer from the context that it involves being lighthearted, joyous, merry, or carefree. Look for a choice that reflects this feeling.

In choice (A), the boy playing with a soccer ball may be flexible, but this choice does not capture his joyous nature. Choice (B) is an opposite; since the boy is "experiencing easy joy," you can infer that he is not nervous. Choice (C) is a nice match for your prediction. In choice (D), the boy may be young, but this is not a meaning of "blithe." Choice (E) is not a meaning of "blithe," and nothing in the passage suggests that the boy is envious.

10. D

Difficulty: Low

When a question asks about the passage as a whole, be sure your prediction reflects everything in the passage, not just a detail here or there. The passage describes Susan B. Anthony's political activism, and though it mentions other work, it spends the greatest amount of time talking about her efforts to grant women the vote.

Choice (A) is a misused detail; only one *friendship* is mentioned in the passage. Choice (B) is a misused detail; the author mentions her supposed *racism* in only one sentence. Choice (C) is out of scope; the passage mentions that Anthony is a speaker, but does not say how effective her speaking was. Choice (D) matches your prediction nicely. Choice (E) is a misused detail; Anthony did *work for temperance*, but it is not the focus of the passage.

11. D

Difficulty: Medium

The correct answer to an Inference question is always strongly based on clues to be found nearby in the passage. The passage says that the legislature rejected the petition because the signatures were mostly from women and children. It also says that this made Anthony determined to win the vote for women. We can infer that the legislature rejected the petition because the people who signed it could not vote and therefore had little influence over the politicians.

Choice (A) is extreme; there is nothing in the passage to suggest that the Legislature as a whole thought that women and children were not *wise*. Choice (B) is out of scope; the political popularity of temperance is not addressed in this passage. Choice (C) is an opposite; the whole problem was that there were no women or children in the constituency that the politicians depended on, not that the politicians were out of touch with voters. Choice (D) matches your prediction nicely. Choice (E) is out of scope; the passage only gives us information about one petition, and so we can't know how they were generally treated.

12. B

Difficulty: Medium

When answering Inference questions, remember that the answer will not be stated directly in the passage, but it will be close to something the passage says. The passage says that cartoonists made Anthony look ridiculous by putting her next to great figures like George Washington. It also says that modern viewers don't get the joke, because today it seems reasonable to equate Anthony with greatness. Predict that this implies that Anthony's reputation has significantly improved from the time she was alive to now.

Choice (A) is an opposite; the cartoonists were making fun of her by putting her next to Washington. Choice (B) matches your prediction. Choice (C) is out of scope; there is no suggestion in the passage that Anthony and Washington ever met. The dates of Anthony's life also make that rather unlikely. Choice (D) is an opposite; she is considered more important today than she was when she was alive. Choice (E) is extreme; just because some people made fun of Anthony doesn't mean she failed.

13. E

Difficulty: Medium

Be sure to make a prediction before looking at the choices, so you won't be tempted by a primary definition of the word. The relevant sentence says: "Despite all her enemies, though, Anthony had a fair complement of influential allies." Since having allies would counteract having enemies, the sentence is probably saying that she did have some allies. Predict something like a fair *number* of influential allies.

Choice (A) is an opposite; besides its not matching the prediction, if you read this definition back into the sentence, it simply doesn't make sense. Choice (B) is out of scope; while they may have rendered her assistance, this doesn't make sufficient sense in context. Choice (C) is out of scope; while these people may have made different forms of contributions to Anthony's cause, this doesn't make sufficient sense in context. Choice (D) is an opposite; a *dearth* is a lack, and it is clear that she must have had some allies. Choice (E) works with your prediction and makes sense in the original sentence.

14. A

Difficulty: Medium

When asked to make inferences about a person, find everything in the relevant lines about the person and sum it up. In the cited lines, all the passage says about Frederick Douglass is that he was a supporter of Anthony's and that he campaigned successfully to abolish slavery. You know, therefore, he was involved in at least two political causes, and also that he was successful in one of them. Look for an answer that reflects any of this.

Choice (A) matches your prediction beautifully. Choice (B) is an opposite; the passage says he supports her. Choice (C) is an opposite; it is clear from the passage that he believed in at least one other cause. Choice (D) is out of scope; the passage makes no such indication. Choice (E) is a misused detail; the passage does not mention whether or not Douglass cared about *temperance*, only that Anthony did.

15. D

Difficulty: Medium

Every question, no matter how hard, is essentially about what the author was trying to say. An answer that seems accurate but has little to do with the purpose of the passage is probably not correct. The discussion of Anthony's refusal to pay the fees assigned her in court concludes with the sentence "When she refused to pay, though, the judge did not imprison her, thus denying her the opportunity to appeal and send the case to a higher court where it might have gotten more national attention" (lines 83–87). The relevant opportunity for Anthony was having another trial and getting national attention for her cause. This suggests that Anthony was thinking strategically about her political actions, trying to get more media coverage.

Choice (A) is out of scope; there would need to be more evidence before Anthony could be declared a *tightwad*. Choice (B) is out of scope; nothing in the passage even suggests that Anthony was interested in *court reform*. Choice (C) is extreme; *civil disobedience* is definitely a tactic of Anthony's, but we have no information to indicate that it is her *most effective*, especially since in this example it did not achieve what she wanted it to. Choice (D) matches your prediction nicely. Choice (E) is out of scope; there is no information in the passage as to Anthony's economic status.

16. E

Difficulty: Medium

Restrict your prediction to things specifically supported in the passage. Anthony hoped that the Republican Party would support women's rights if she brought her influence to bear on the slavery question. But she was "surprised and disappointed" (line 98) when she did not receive that support. Infer that she had expected that supporting the abolitionist movement would aid her own cause.

Choice (A) is out of scope; the passage does not discuss how much help she expected to be to the abolition movement. Choice (B) is a misused detail; it was not Anthony's goal to expose any *racism* on her part. Choice (C) is an opposite; Anthony wanted to help the Republican Party, in order to gain their help in return. Choice (D) is a misused detail; it is getting women the right to vote that Anthony thinks will make politicians pay attention to women. Choice (E) works with your prediction.

17. C

Difficulty: Low

If you're having trouble making a prediction for what a word means, try rephrasing the whole sentence in your own words—the definition might become clear that way. The passage says that Anthony's work "was not in vain" and then says that her work became successful years after her death. Predict that "in vain" means *unsuccessful*.

Choice (A) is out of scope; whether or not Anthony's work reflected an exaggerated love of self is not addressed in the passage at all. Choice (B) is out of scope; *blood* or heredity is not mentioned in the passage. Choice (C) works well with your prediction. Choice (D) is an opposite; the passage says her work *was* effective (remember the "not" in front of "in vain"). Choice (E) is out of scope; how convenient Anthony's work was is not discussed in the passage

18. E

Difficulty: Medium

Names are easy to scan for in a passage because they begin with capital letters. The passage mentions that Anthony's "friends" included Douglass, Bloomer and Stanton. However, in line 22 it says that "Bloomer introduced her to Elizabeth Stanton, and the two women formed a friendship and political alliance that lasted the rest of their lives." Stanton, then, would be the one whose politics most closely aligned with Anthony.

Choice (A) is a misused detail; Douglass is cited as a supporter of hers, but worked mainly for the abolition of slavery, which was not a primary motivation for Anthony. Choice (B) is a misused detail; Bloomer is cited as a friend of Anthony's, but did not work with her as much as Stanton did. Choice (C) is a misused detail; there is nothing in the passage about Washington's politics. Choice (D) is a misused detail; the Sons of Temperance had the cause of temperance in common with Anthony, but the author indicates nothing about other causes. Choice (E) matches your prediction.

19. D

Difficulty: Low

Use your notes to get a sense of what is most important in the passage. Anthony supported many things that the passage describes, but the one referred to most often is women's suffrage, or giving women the vote.

Choice (A) is a misused detail; Anthony supported the abolitionists primarily to win political allies for her own cause. Choice (B) is a misused detail; Anthony was a supporter of this cause, but the passage spends more time discussing her efforts to win the vote for women. Choice (C) is a misused detail; the passage does not mention any particular affiliation with the Republican Party, except that she hopes they will support her cause. Choice (D) matches your prediction. Choice (E) is extreme; this is a bit more ambitious than what Anthony was shooting for.

20. C

Difficulty: Medium

Never answer a detail question from memory. Instead, go back to the text and pay close attention to the cited content. In this case, the cited word comes in a sentence that begins with the phrase "to that end" which immediately links it to the previous sentence, which focuses on how an infant *learns* from the streams of audible communication around him in order to acquire language skills. As "absorb" is used in reference to "rhythmic patterns" and other nuances of language, it is likely that "absorb" is being used as a synonym of learning or language acquisition.

Choice (A) is distortion; this choice is too vague, as here the author is describing how infants *take in* information from their environment, not that they are just aware of their surroundings. Choice (B) is distortion; this is close, but again all that is being described here is the *acquisition* of language skills, not necessarily a natural talent. Choice (C) is correct; "absorbing" patterns of speech can be considered equivalent to acquiring knowledge. Choice (D) is out of scope; this choice also comes close, but nothing in the paragraph actually indicates that infants *deliberately* attempt to learn from streams of speech. Choice (E) is an irrelevant detail; while infants must be able to differentiate between streams of speech, the sentence here is describing the learning that takes place after this has been accomplished.

21. E

Difficulty: Medium

Always reexamine the relevant portion of the paragraph and use evidence found there to support your answer choice.

The word "while" at the beginning of the sentence indicates that in spite of the fact "infants are capable of separating out" voice streams, their ability to do so is based on certain factors. In other words, while they are quite capable, infants are not always able to separate streams.

Choice (A) is an opposite; the sentence clearly states that most infants *are* capable of separating out different voice streams. Choice (B) is out of scope; the paragraph does not discuss the comfort level of infants. Choice (C) is out of scope; the paragraph does not describe the frequency of these conditions. Choice (D) is out of scope; nowhere is it stated that an infant is wholly dependent upon his environment for language acquisition. Choice (E) is correct; the paragraph that contains these lines discusses stimuli of the surrounding environment.

22. D

Difficulty: Medium

To determine how a particular word or phrase is being used by the author, first identify that its meaning, and then go back and re-familiarize yourself with its context. In this case, as "necessarily" refers to an inevitable or unavoidable consequence and the referenced sentence is referring to "competing voice streams" becoming "combined into a single stream," then the author is stating that the consequences of this occurrence, the resulting "unfamiliar patterns and sounds" and the infant's confusion, are inevitable.

Choice (A) is distortion; the author is not simply discussing two streams of speech, but two streams of *equal volume* mixing and becoming confusing. Choice (B) is out of scope; nothing in the paragraph refers to an adult's ability to distinguish between streams of speech. Choice (C) is distortion; again, the author is only referring to separate streams of equal volume, not just any two streams. Choice (D) is correct; an inevitable confusion would also be understandable. Choice (E) is out of scope; the author, at least in this sentence, does not explore how the diversity of audible stimuli could add to an infant's confusion.

23. C

Difficulty: Medium

This question asks you to use information from one portion of the paragraph in the context of another. Start by finding the exact information needed from the first portion referenced and then apply it to the second piece of cited content. In this case, by beginning with a look at the "example" in the final paragraph, you learn that an infant "presented with a voice stream spoken by his mother" will be able to "easily separate out her voice from the distraction of the background stream" because her voice is more

familiar to him. This information applies almost directly to the cited content in paragraph three, which also refers to "an infant being spoken to by his mother." Here, the competing speech comes from "a newscaster on the television" or "siblings playing" nearby, so look for an answer choice that describes how the infant would be able to separate out his mother's voice from these competing speech streams.

Choice (A) is distortion; nothing in the paragraph indicates that infants necessarily understand these speech streams, only that they can begin to learn their language from them. Choice (B) is distortion; this statement also goes too far, as the paragraph only mentions that in this case an infant would be able to "separate out" his mother's voice. Choice (C) is correct; his mother's voice would be the most familiar stream to the infant, and he would "push" the newscaster's voice to the background. Choice (D) is out of scope; the paragraph does not explore whether or not the infant would learn anything from the television voice. Choice (E) is distortion; the example in the final paragraph only describes an infant's ability to separate out his mother's voice from other competing streams of speech, but not necessarily the background noises described in the second paragraph

24. B

Difficulty: High

It is sometimes helpful to step back from the details and consider the scope and purpose of the paragraph as a whole. It's likely that the cited content is being used to advance this purpose. Notice that in the last sentence of the paragraph, which provides something of a summary of the author's main idea, the example referred to in the question stem is described as an important cue that enables an infant to be "capable of more quickly learning the invaluable characteristics and rules of his native language". In other words, being spoken to by the familiar voice of his mother speeds up the infant's language acquisition process.

Choice (A) is distortion; the author's argument involves *vocal* interaction, not necessarily interaction in general, which need not be vocal. Choice (B) is correct; by interacting more frequently with their child, parents can help that child to more quickly distinguish their voices and therefore help them to acquire language skills earlier than other children. Choice (C) is out of scope; nothing in the paragraph refers to the *complexity* of any given language. Choice (D) is distortion; the example in question only refers to familiar *voice* streams and a parent speaking to an infant, not necessarily parents who pay close attention to an infant. Choice (E) is distortion; as the paragraph indicates that most infants can separate out unfamiliar voices, then removing such sounds seems unnecessary.

SECTION 5

1. D

Difficulty: Low

Strategic Advice: Read the stem carefully to translate the sentence into the correct equations.

Getting to the Answer:

$t = s + 5$

$s = r - 3$

When $r = 3$,

$s = 0$

So,

$t = 0 + 5$

$t = 5$

2. C

Difficulty: Low

Strategic Advice: Early questions like this one are not trying to trick you or test your ability to think critically, but rather just to follow directions carefully. Remember this, and you can rack up easy points on Test Day.

Getting to the Answer:

If you happen to notice that the difference between the numerator and denominator is the same for both fractions, then you can tell that $y = 42$ and $y - 3 = 39$. If you don't see that right away, you can either Backsolve or cross-multiply and solve for y.

3. C

Difficulty: Low

Strategic Advice: Angles along a straight line add up to 180°. When a line intersects two parallel lines, corresponding angles are equal. If the lines are not parallel, the corresponding angles cannot be equal.

Getting to the Answer: You know that the lines are not parallel, so adding angle x to the 98° angle cannot equal 180°. Therefore, x cannot equal 82.

4. A

Difficulty: Medium

Strategic Advice: If two chords have equal length, they are the same distance from the center of the circle. Remember to add all the information from the question stem to the figure.

Getting to the Answer:

Since *EFGH* is a square, its area is equal to the length of a side squared:

$81 = (EF)^2$

$9 = EF$

Since the chords are the same distance from the center of the circle, $EJ = KF$.

$EF = EJ + JK + KF$

$9 = 5 + 2(EJ)$

$4 = 2(EJ)$

$2 = EJ$

5. C

Difficulty: Medium

Strategic Advice: You can use concrete numbers to get a handle on the situation.

Getting to the Answer:

Try $a = 6$ and $b = 3$

(A) $a + b = 9$, eliminate

(B) $a - b = 3$, eliminate

(C) $a + b + 1 = 10$

(D) $ab = 18$, eliminate

(E) $ab + 3 = 21$, eliminate

6. A

Difficulty: Medium

Strategic Advice: If you're stuck, focus on the differences between the answers; anything that's clearly wrong can be eliminated.

Getting to the Answer:

Squares of $2a$ and $3b$: $(2a)^2$ and $(3b)^2$

Sum of those squares: $(2a)^2 + (3b)^2$

Difference between $8c$ and $7d$: $(8c - 7d)$

Sum of squares added to the difference: $(2a)^2 + (9b)^2 + (8c - 7d)$

3 more than e: $e + 3$

Sum is 3 more than e: $(2a)^2 + (3b)^2 + (8c - 7d) = e + 3$

7. B

Difficulty: Medium

Translate the words into algebra, and then let your algebra skills take you home!

Getting to the Answer:

Let x be the number of students at the beginning.

After the addition there are $x + 21$ students, which is 4 times x.

So
$$x + 21 = 4x$$
$$21 = 3x$$
$$x = 7$$

8. C

Difficulty: Medium

Strategic Advice: Systematically solve for the variables until you have what you're looking for. Start with c, since it's defined in the question stem. Use c to find a, then a to find b.

Getting to the Answer:

$$a = 8c = 8 * 9 = 72$$
$$\frac{72}{b} = 4$$
$$72 = 4b$$
$$18 = b$$

9. $\dfrac{7}{5}$

Difficulty: Low

Strategic Advice: Plug in the given values and solve for d. As long as you work carefully, this type of problem should be easy to solve.

Getting to the Answer:

$$3d + 2d = 9 - 2$$
$$5d = 7$$
$$d = \frac{7}{5}$$

10. $\dfrac{14}{3}$ or 4.67

Difficulty: Low

Strategic Advice: Questions like this one are not trying to trick you or test your ability to think, but rather to just follow procedures carefully.

Getting to the Answer:

$$3(x - 2) = 8$$
$$x - 2 = \frac{8}{3}$$
$$x = \frac{14}{3}$$

11. 5

Difficulty: Low

Strategic Advice: The writers of the SAT tend to make grid-in algebra problems slightly easier. You have the skills to solve these algebraically, so use them.

Getting to the Answer:

First, solve for z:

$$\frac{z + 2}{5} = 2$$
$$z + 2 = 10$$
$$z = 8$$

Then evaluate: $\dfrac{z + 2}{z - 6}$:

$$\frac{8 + 2}{z - 6} = \frac{10}{2} = 5$$

12. 8

Difficulty: Medium

Strategic Advice: Draw a quick sketch to help you find the solution to this problem. Also, remember that if a circle touches an axis at one and only one point then the distance from that point to the center of the circle is the radius.

Getting to the Answer:

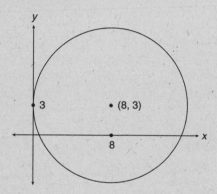

Once you draw a sketch, it is easy to see that the radius is equal to the x coordinate of the center of the circle, 8.

13. $\frac{32}{9}$

Difficulty: Medium

Strategic Advice: Plug in carefully—don't confuse the two functions!

Getting to the Answer:

$$3 \triangleright 2 = \frac{1}{3} * 3 + \frac{2}{3} * 2 = 1 + \frac{4}{3} = \frac{7}{3}$$

$$\frac{7}{3} \triangleleft 6 = \frac{2}{3} * \frac{7}{3} + \frac{1}{3} * \frac{6}{1} = \frac{14}{9} + 2 = \frac{14}{9} + \frac{18}{9} = \frac{32}{9}$$

14. 10

Difficulty: High

Strategic Advice: First, solve for the variable. Then, carefully plug in that information to answer the question that is asked.

Getting to the Answer: Solve for the first equation. After distributing the x, the equation reads:

$$x^2 - 6x = -9$$
$$x^2 - 6x + 9 = 0$$
$$(x - 3)(x - 3) = 0$$
$$x = 3$$

Plug 3 in for x in the second equation: $3^2 + 3 - 2 = 10$.

15. 150

Difficulty: Medium

Strategic Advice: Sketch in the information that isn't included in the diagram and work from there. Don't let the polygon fool you. This is a *triangle* problem.

Getting to the Answer:

Re-sketch the figure:

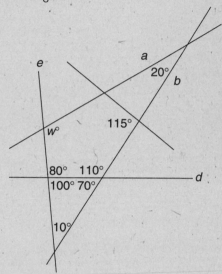

Add the information you know to the figure:

The triangle on the bottom tells lets you find the angle between e and b: $180 - (100 + 70) = 10$.

If the angle formed by lines a and b is twice the angle formed by lines b and e, then that angle is 20°.

$$w = 180 - (10 + 20)$$
$$w = 150$$

16. 220

Difficulty: High

Strategic Advice: You know that a triangle's interior angles add up to 180°. Every time you add a side to a figure, you add 180° to the sum of the interior angles. Since this figure has six sides, its interior angles sum to 720°.

Getting to the Answer:

$$120 + 120 + 130 + 130 + x + y = 720$$
$$500 + x + y = 720$$
$$x + y = 220$$

17. 3

Difficulty: High

Strategic Advice: One of the keys to success on Test Day will be making all parts of the question look like each other. Try to rewrite the question using the same bases on the both sides of the question.

Getting to the Answer:

$$9^r = 27^{r-1}$$
$$(3^2)^r = (3^3)^{r-1}$$
$$2r = 3r - 3$$
$$0 = r - 3$$
$$3 = r$$

18. 441

Difficulty: High

Strategic Advice: Don't be thrown off by new symbols. Try not to miss any potential factors for this problem.

Getting to the Answer:

$$«7« = 21 \times 7 \times 3 \times 1 = 441$$

SECTION 6

1. A

Difficulty: Low

If you don't spot an error, don't be afraid to choose (A). The sentence is correct as written. (B) is awkward and unnecessarily wordy. (C), (D) and (E) all incorrectly express the relationship between the underlined phrase and the rest of the sentence.

2. D

Difficulty: Low

Although the passive voice will not always be wrong on the SAT, if a sentence can easily be put into the active voice, the correct answer choice will do so. In this sentence, the passive voice is unnecessary. (D) puts the sentence into the active voice without introducing any additional errors. (B) does not address the error. (C) is awkwardly worded. *When having…found* in (E) is incorrect grammatical structure.

3. C

Difficulty: Low

Sometimes a sentence can be too concise; what is it *about procuring warrants* that the Act provides for? *Determine about* is idiomatically incorrect, and the sentence as written is not very clear. (C), although it's slightly longer than the original, corrects the idiom and clarifies the meaning. (This is one of those instances where a passive structure—*warrants should be procured*—cannot easily and clearly be made active.)

(B) and (D) use the personal pronouns *he* and *she* to refer back to *government.* (E) is awkward and unnecessarily wordy.

4. D

Difficulty: Low

Always make sure that underlined verbs are in agreement with their subjects. The plural verb *were* isn't correct with the singular subject *One of the…professors.* (D) corrects this error. The plural verb *were* in (B) is incorrect with the singular subject *faculty.* (D) introduces an inconsistent verb tense. (E) is awkward and unnecessarily wordy.

5. C

Difficulty: Medium

Items in a list must always be in parallel form. As written, this sentence violates the rules of parallel structure. (E) corrects the error. (B), (C), and (D) do not address the error.

6. B

Difficulty: Medium

Make sure verb tense properly express the time frames referred to. As written, the underlined phrase uses an inconsistent verb tense. *Is turning* should be in the past tense to be consistent with *climbed* and *admired.* (B) corrects this error. (C), (D), and (E) do not correct the error.

7. B

Difficulty: Medium

Not sure which pronoun form is correct? Rewording the sentence sometimes helps. As written, the sentence uses the incorrect pronoun case (you wouldn't say "No one is…happier than me am) and *more* is redundant with *happier*. (B) corrects both errors. (C) is incorrect grammatical structure. (D) fails to correctly complete the comparative construction *as…as*. (E) changes the meaning of the original selection.

8. D

Difficulty: Medium

If you don't spot a grammatical error, look for errors in style. The sentence as written is unnecessarily wordy. (D) is concise and contains no additional errors. (B) is even wordier than the original. (C) is awkwardly structured. (E) changes the meaning of the sentence by suggesting that *Stalin*, not the murder, is the *mystery*.

9. E

Difficulty: Medium

There are a number of ways to correct a run-on sentence, but only one answer choice will do so without introducing additional errors. As written, this is a run-on sentence. Additionally, the plural pronoun *they* is used to refer to *the United States* which is grammatically singular when used to refer to the country as a whole. (E) corrects both errors. (B) does not address the pronoun error and uses a transition word that is inappropriate in context. (C) does not address either error. (D) also inappropriately uses a cause-and-effect transition.

10. A

Difficulty: Medium

Expect to encounter between five and eight sentences without errors on your SAT. This sentence is correct as written.

(B) is unnecessarily wordy. (C) is a sentence fragment. (D) and (E) use verb tenses that are inappropriate in context; additionally, (D) creates a run-on sentence.

11. D

Difficulty: High

Make sure the correct noun is placed after a modifying phrase. As written, this sentence tells us that *most artists,* rather than *Manet's Olympia,* were *dismissed by Salon attendees.* Only (D) corrects this error without introducing any additional issues. (B) does not address the error. In (C), *groundbreaking work* is the noun modified by the initial clause. (E) is a sentence fragment.

12. A

Difficulty: Low

Some idiomatic phrases may be grammatically correct, but inappropriate in context. Although someone could be "wanted for" questioning, in this context, the verb *wanted* requires the infinitive verb form. The error is in (A), which should read "to portray."

(B) correctly uses an adjective to modify a noun. (C) properly uses *that* as a conjunction, and uses the correct verb tense in context. In (D), the past *had saddened* is correctly used to describe an action completed prior to another stated past action (*The director wanted*).

13. A

Difficulty: Low

In a compound subject containing a pronoun, read the sentence with the pronoun as the subject to make sure it is in the subjective case. Since you wouldn't say "Me was delighted…," *me* is incorrect as part of the compound subject; "I" would be correct in (A). The plural verb *were* in (B) is used correctly to agree with its compound (and therefore, plural) subject. In (C), *since* correctly establishes the relationship between the ideas in the sentence. (D) is a properly used prepositional phrase.

14. D

Difficulty: Low

In a compound verb construction, the verbs must be parallel in form. In (D), the two verb forms *to establish* and *maintain* are not parallel; the first verb should simply be "establish." (A) properly sets up the relationship between the two clauses, and the verb agrees with its subject. In (B), the infinitive verb form is used correctly. (C) is a correct prepositional phrase.

15. B

Difficulty: Low

A sentence can have numerous nouns and verbs and still be a fragment. As written, this sentence is a fragment, since it has no independent clause. Changing (B) to "thought" would make the second clause independent, correcting the error. (A) uses the correct preposition in context. (C) is correct usage of the infinitive. The pronoun in (D) agrees with its plural antecedent *walls*.

16. A

Difficulty: Low

All verbs within a sentence must agree in tense, unless a verb is included in a phrase that implies a different time from the rest of the sentence. In (A), the present tense is incorrect for an action that has already taken place; "cracked" would be the correct form here. In (B) and (D), the prepositional phrases are correctly written and properly used.

17. C

Difficulty: Medium

In a compound structure, verb forms must be in parallel form. In the second clause of this sentence, the verb forms *smothered...and being topped* violate the rules of parallel structure. (C) contains the error; it should read simply "topped." (A) is the proper tense for an action that will occur in the future. (B) is a correctly structured the prepositional phrase. (D) uses an adverb to modify a verb form.

18. D

Difficulty: Medium

Adjectives can only modify nouns or pronouns; to modify any other part of speech, an adverb is needed. Although the phrase *unusual shaped* is intended to modify the noun *cloud formations*, within the phrase, the adjective *unusual* is used to modify the verb form *shaped*. (D) should read "unusually." (A) is correct idiomatic usage. (B) and (C) use the proper prepositions in context.

19. B

Difficulty: Medium

The verb *set* requires an object; the verb *sit* does not. *A pond* cannot "set," since "set" is an action. "Sits" is the correct verb in (B). The preposition *beside*, in (A), is appropriate in context, and the adjective *dusty* properly modifies the noun *road*. (C) correctly uses *as* as a preposition. (D) uses a comparative adjective correctly.

20. B

Difficulty: Medium

Make sure verb tenses accurately represent the sequence of events in the sentence. Here, the verbs *find* and *was* are in different tenses. Since *was* is not underlined, *find* must be changed to the past tense; the error is in (B). (A) correctly

uses the gerund verb form as an adjective. In (C), the adverb *generally* correctly modifies *was*. (D) uses the proper preposition in context.

21. A

Difficulty: Medium

When a pronoun is part of a compound subject, read the sentence with the pronoun alone to make sure it's in the proper case. Since you wouldn't say *her felt unprepared*, (A) should be "she." (B) is the proper verb form in context. (C) correctly uses *when* in reference to time, which is the only use of *when* that will be correct on the SAT. (D) is correct idiomatic usage.

22. B

Difficulty: Medium

Pronouns must have clear, unambiguous antecedents. The pronoun *they* doesn't clearly refer to anything in the sentence; a noun would be needed to clarify (B). (A) properly conveys the cause-and-effect relationship of the ideas in the sentence. (C) is correct idiomatic usage. (D) is an appropriate preposition in context.

23. C

Difficulty: Medium

Note that there is an intervening phrase between the subject and the verb; read the sentence without it to check for agreement. The plural subject *voters* does not agree with the singular verb form *includes*; the error is in (C). (A) uses the correct relative pronoun referring to *voters*, and the past tense verb is appropriate in context. (B) and (D) are proper prepositional phrases.

24. C

Difficulty: Medium

Make sure all pronouns have clear, unambiguous antecedents. The pronoun *it* in (C) could refer to either *art* or *funding*; it would have to be replaced by the appropriate noun for clarity. (A) is correct use of the gerund verb form to describe *essayist. Than with*, in (B), correctly completes the comparative construction beginning with *less concerned with*. (D) correctly uses the adverb *less* to modify the adjective *popular*.

25. B

Difficulty: Medium

There are a number of ways to correct a run-on sentence, but only one underlined segment will allow you to do so correctly. This sentence is a run-on: two independent clauses joined by a comma splice. Since the comma is not underlined, one of these clauses will have to be made subordinate. Changing *them* to "whom" in (B) accomplishes this. (A) is correct when referring to more than two people. The verb in (C) agrees with its plural subject *restaurants,* and the pronoun *them* clearly refers back to *actors*. (D) properly uses the infinitive verb form.

26. D

Difficulty: High

When dealing with comparisons, always ask yourself what is being compared. The writer meant to compare *Beethoven's harmonic language* with that of other composers but in fact, she compares *Beethoven's harmonic language* with the composers themselves; the error is in (D). (A) is correct idiomatic usage. (B) properly uses one adverb (*most*) to modify another (*enthusiastically*). In (C), the singular pronoun correctly refers back to a singular antecedent—*language*.

27. D

Difficulty: High

This sentence presents an illogical comparison: *organic...food* is compared to *traditional agriculture*. (D) should read "food produced through traditional agriculture," or something to that effect. (A) is an appropriate verb tense in context. The verb *poses* in (B) agrees with its singular subject *food,* and *less danger* is an idiomatically correct phrase. (B) agrees with the subject *food*. (C) correctly completes the comparison *less...than.*

28. E

Difficulty: High

Don't mistake complex or unusual sentence structure for grammatical error; this sentence is correct as written. (A) correctly uses *that* as a conjunction. (B) is the correct relative pronoun referring to *student.* (C) correctly modifies the verb *increased*. (D) is the appropriate verb tense in context.

29. D

Difficulty: High

Logically, the sentence draws a comparison between the moon mission's current effects and the effects it had at the time. The plural pronoun *they* does not agree with the singular noun *moon mission*. (D) should read "it affected." (A) correctly uses an adverb to modify the verb form *researching*. (B) is the appropriate verb form in context. (C) correctly sets up the comparative structure *less interested in...than in*.

30. C

Difficulty: Medium

You might want to sum up each paragraph to help yourself arrive at the main idea of the passage. Sentence 5 correctly names the topic sentence. It expresses the writer's opinion about light pollution and the reason for her concern. None of the other choices is broad enough to encompass the main idea of the entire passage.

31. D

Difficulty: Medium

The passive voice will not always be incorrect on the SAT, but always look for an active version of a passive construction. This sentence is unnecessarily in the passive voice. (D) makes the author, rather than her observation, the subject of the sentence. (B) and (C) do not address the error; additionally, each introduces a pronoun without an antecedent. (E) is a sentence fragment.

32. B

Difficulty: Low

There may be more than one answer choice that addresses the initial error; if so, some will introduce new issues. As written, this is a run-on sentence. By replacing the comma with a semicolon, (B) corrects the error. (C) introduces a transition word that inappropriately relates the two clauses. (D) corrects the run-on error, but is unnecessarily in the passive voice. (E) is a sentence fragment.

33. E

Difficulty: High

Use your Reading Comp skills to determine the best flow of ideas in the passage. Sentence 8 sums up the author's hopes for a solution to the problem of light pollution, so its best position is after sentence 13, as a conclusion to the passage. (E) is the correct choice. Since light pollution isn't mentioned until the end of the first paragraph, placing it where (A) suggests would not make sense. (B) puts the author's hopes that people will work to solve this problem before any information that the problem can be solved. (C) interrupts the flow of sentences 9 and 10, as evidenced by the transition keywords "For example." Placing the sentence where (D) suggests does not lead into the concluding paragraph.

34. E

Difficulty: Low

Make sure that verb tenses accurately represent the sequence of events in the passage. The past tense verb "weren't" here is inconsistent; (E) is correct. None of the other choices addresses the error. Additionally, (B) is inconsistent with the plural pronoun "they," and (C) uses an adjective to modify the verb phrase "turn off."

35. E

Difficulty: Medium

On the SAT, a pronoun will be incorrect if its antecedent is not clear and unambiguous. Here, the possessive pronoun "their" is meant to refer to "malls and used car lots" but, as the sentence is written, it actually refers to "lights." (E) clarifies the pronouns antecedent. (B) does not address the error; additionally, the pronoun *you* is introduced with no antecedent. (C) is unnecessarily in the passive voice. (D) is a sentence fragment.

SECTION 7

1. E

Difficulty: Low

The word "but" let's you know that the sentence is creating a contrast. Think about the sentence and translate it in your head into something simpler. The sentence is saying that some people are able to live a certain way, but other people are forced to live differently.

In choice (A), if other people aren't even *enjoying* the basic amenities of life, chances are they're probably living *poorly* as well. In choice (B), living *responsibly* doesn't necessarily have anything to do with the ability to *acquire* basic

amenities. In choice (C), living *pretentiously* certainly isn't any kind of investment on which one can expect to *yield* any kind of return. In choice (D), why would anyone hope to *miss* out on the basic amenities of life? Choice (E) works. Some people live *lavishly* while others live poorly and can barely *attain* basic amenities.

2. B

Difficulty: Low

If most cultures have a creation myth, it must be something a lot of people are interested in. What's a more concise way of saying that the subject of the origin of life is a common interest among people of many cultures?

In choice (A), a *distant* interest doesn't mean it's necessarily common to many people. Choice (B), *universal,* fits. In choice (C), just because many cultures have what we call "creation myths" doesn't mean the origin of life is a *mythical* interest. It's a common interest often expressed in myths. In choice (D), nothing in this sentence indicates that the interest is *superficial*. In choice (E), though many people would say that the origin of life is a *debatable* subject, this sentence is asking for a word that means "similar" or "common."

3. C

Difficulty: Medium

The words "while" and "and" let you know there are contrasting *and* complimentary words in the sentence. The word "while" lets you know that the blank and "opulent" contrast in meaning with "simple" and "austere." The word "and" let's you know the blank is a compliment to "opulent." Which word contrasts with "simple" and "austere," and is a similar word to "opulent"?

In choice (A), *basic* is complimentary to "simple" and "austere" and contrary to "opulent." In choice (B), a style that is "opulent" generally isn't viewed as *severe*. In choice (C), *florid* goes well with "opulent" and is the opposite of "simple" and "austere." This choice is perfect. In choice (D), *efficient* doesn't match with any of the key words. In choice (E), something that is "simple" can often be *straightforward*, but we're looking for a contrasting word, or a word that compliments "opulent," which *straightforward* doesn't do.

4. B

Difficulty: High

This is a cause and effect question. One event causes a particular feeling. If the teacher is trying to negotiate a compromise, but the students refuse to cooperate, the teacher might feel doubtful that a compromise could be reached. What word means the same thing as doubtful?

In choice (A), *cordial* does not express any sort of doubtful feelings. In choice (B), it seems likely that the teacher would feel *dubious*, or fraught with doubt, over the outcome of the argument if the students were refusing to compromise. This choice makes sense. In choice (C), though the teacher was performing a *benevolent* action, the students' refusal to compromise wouldn't have made her feel that way. In choice (D), hopefully the teacher wasn't feeling *biased* about the argument at all. In choice (E), *prophetic* doesn't make any sense at all in this context.

5. A

Difficulty: Medium

The structure of the sentence sets up a contrast; while the biography mostly covers familiar events, we're told, several chapters may well be ---- even to experts. So you're looking for a word that means "unfamiliar"—making choice (A), *surprising,* the best choice. Notice how the clue word *even* reinforces the contrast—even the experts, we're told, are not going to be familiar with parts of the musician's early life.

6. C

Difficulty: High

The word "despite" indicates that there is a contrast between how France and Germany relate to one another politically and how they relate to one another culturally. Choice (C), *interaction* and *enmity,* ("the quality of being enemies") best expresses this contrast. The other choices don't reflect the contrast you need; the two words are either both positive or both negative.

Questions 7–18

Passage 1 is an expanded critique of a film that not only discusses the content of the motion picture itself, but also questions the artistic choices and vision of the film's writer, director, and main star Oscar Grey, who justifies those choices and his vision in Passage 2. The author of the first passage, who seems to be a film critic, wastes no time in introducing the idea that she believes the film will be colossal failure, which she expands upon in the remainder of the passage. With few exceptions, her tone is consistently negative, and she quotes several other critics who share and support her opinion.

In Passage 2 Oscar Grey never references one specific critic from Passage 1; however, the descriptions of his inspirations, the film's subject, the choices he made as an artist to convey his vision, as well as how he went about getting the movie financed, address most of Passage 1's criticisms, and offer a unique, alternative point of view. While Passage 1 painted the film as disorganized and boring, Oscar Grey convincingly offers that the film is groundbreaking and captivating. Both passages illustrate how a single subject may produce points of view that are starkly in contrast with one another.

7. E

Difficulty: Low

What is the reviewer implying about *45 Minutes* by comparing it to a ship famous for sinking?

45 Minutes from Denver is the longest film of all time, and one of the most expensive. The *Titanic*, which in her day was the largest and most expensive ship afloat, famously sank in the Atlantic on her maiden voyage. By comparing the movie to the ill-fated ship, what is the reviewer suggesting about the film's own fate?

Choice (A) is out of scope; the overall attitude of the author and reviewers in the first paragraph is negative, this choice has a positive spin on it. Choice (B) is distortion; this will probably be true of *45 Minutes* and was true for the ship, however, it does not take acknowledge the *Titanic*'s fate, and is therefore not the best choice. Choice (C) is a misused detail; the choice is a distracter for those who did not read or understand the passage correctly; the reviewer specifically compares *45 Minutes* to ill-fated ship *Titanic*, not the successful film based upon it. Choice (D) is distortion; the "doomed" part of this choice is correct, but there is no indication that the author believes the film will "will revolutionize its industry." Choice (E) meets your prediction.

8. D

Difficulty: Low

The passage states that *Revisited* managed to become a success "through word of mouth." In terms of movies that are heavily promoted, how would you characterize this type of advertising? The best context clue to help you answer this vocabulary question is found in the third paragraph of Passage 1, where the author states that "by word of mouth" (line 34) *Revisited* managed to become a success. Look for the answer choice that best describes what this clue implies about the type of hit the movie was.

Choice (A) is distortion; this particular definition of "quiet" makes no sense in context. Choice (B) is out of scope; there is nothing in the passage that indicates *Revisited* lacked action. Choice (C) is distortion; *Revisited* is only described as "quirky" (line 32); the tone of the film is not offered. Choice (D) is a good match. Choice (E) is an opposite; here, "quiet" is modifying the noun "hit"—a film that enjoys monetary success.

9. A

Difficulty: Medium

What does the author Passage 1 state that Oscar Grey does in piecing together the events of Roth's life for the film? Passage 1 states that the film is a "loose interpretation" of the details of Alexander's Roth's life, which "are spotty at best," and that Oscar Grey takes "liberties … while attempting to fill in the many blanks." These "blanks" of course, are the unknown details of the author's life. Look for the choice that best summarizes this information.

Choice (A) is a good match for your prediction. Choice (B) is extreme; a "loose interpretation" implies that the portrayal was based on some fact, therefore to label it as a *complete fabrication* is incorrect. Choice (C) is distortion; a *mild embellishment* is to be expected in a film, and would probably not spark an outrage. Choice (D) is out of scope; the passage specifically states that Grey "took liberties." Choice (E) is out of scope; there is nothing in the passage to suggest that the film's portrayal of Roth is idolatrous; in fact the outrage of Roth's fans might even suggest the opposite.

10. B

Difficulty: Medium

There are a few "Hollywood insiders" who are not convinced the movie will be a complete failure. What reasons do they offer for their conviction? The "Hollywood insiders" suggest that the critics predicting the film's quick death may be exaggerating things a bit. These "insiders" then go on to inform us of the large numbers of both Grey and Roth admirers, and their fierce loyalty to the artists. It can be assumed that these fans will fill more than a few seats in the theater. Look for the choice that best sums this up.

Choice (A) is an opposite; on the contrary, the "Hollywood insiders" in fact suggest that the bad reviews may not seriously affect the turnout for the movie. Choice (B) is a good match for your prediction. Choice (C) is distortion; the critics were wrong about *Revisited*, but the author mentions this fact only to accentuate how many fans of Oscar Grey the film generated. Choice (D) is an opposite; the "Hollywood insiders" are referring to fans with a particular in interest in Grey and Roth, they do not discuss the "average moviegoer." Choice (E) is out of scope; there is nothing in passage that indicates a bias against Grey or Roth.

11. D

Difficulty: Medium

Which of the choices best rewords Reynold's description, "an art film with an action film's budget and expectations"? The passage is full of criticisms of the film, and this question asks you to find the choice that sums all of them up. Both the author and the critic Reynolds offer clues to help you: In line 44, Reynolds calls *45 Minutes* an "art film with an action film's budget and expectations;" in addition, in the concluding paragraph the author says the film will please the "coffeehouse crowds," but disappoint the average filmgoer. Look for the choice that best describes what can be gleaned from these two examples.

Choice (A) is an opposite; though Reynolds dislikes the film, he does say that it is "uniquely appealing visually" (line 46) Choice (B) is distortion; this is a particular criticism of the film—you are looking for a choice that lumps them all together. Choice (C) is distortion; it is indicated that there may not be enough known about Roth to base a film upon him, but the author never suggests Roth is *not worthy*. Choice (D) is a good match for your prediction. Choice (E) is an opposite; the criticisms, though mostly negative, in fact suggest that the film is perhaps *too* original.

12. B

Difficulty: High

In the first paragraph Oscar Grey suggests his film is going to break the established Hollywood mold. What words come to mind when you think of such a feat? In the paragraph, Oscar Grey talks about how Hollywood keeps recycling the same old formulas and we as an audience keep accepting them, not because we want to, but because "until now" there has a been lack of a better option or alternative. The "until now" Grey is referring to is the impending release of his film. Which choice best expresses what he is alluding to here?

Choice (A) is extreme; Grey is certainly self-assured, but he does not make the extreme suggestion that he is the *greatest director of all time*. Choice (B) should match your prediction. Choice (C) is an opposite; Grey concludes that, "in the mainstream there is an appetite for cinematic art of the highest form." Choice (D) is distortion; in first two sentences, Grey suggests that *Revisited*'s success showed him that cinema does belong in the "domain of painters and poets." Choice (E) is out of scope; Grey may believe this, but he never indicates it in the first paragraph.

13. A

Difficulty: High

What was it about the film's script that probably made most of the studios want to rewrite it? In the second paragraph of Passage 2, Grey discusses how every studio wanted to rewrite his script "because it did not fit into the cookie-cutter mold." The script was different than what the studios were used to; in other words, in the studios' eyes it could be said there was "some strangeness in the proportion." Look for the choice that best expresses this conclusion.

Choice (A) is a fine match for your prediction. Choice (B) is out of scope; Grey never discusses specific amounts of cash invested in his film. Choice (C) is distortion; the quote helped to open "one very rich, very wise investor's eyes" to producing the film; it was not a reference to the investor's eyes. Choice (D) is distortion; Grey's desire to have his film produced is very evident, but it makes no sense in the context of the quote. Choice (E) is a misused detail; this makes no sense as a choice.

14. C

Difficulty: Medium

Why did attempting to structure the film into the traditional three-act structure seem "awkward" to Grey? Oscar Grey spends a great deal of Passage 2 discussing the unconventional nature of his script, but it is in the third paragraph where he offers the important detail that "Roth did not attempt to put a traditionalized order to his life or his art and therefore neither could I." Choose the answer that best expresses this.

Choice (A) is an opposite; the unconventional structure of the film made it difficult to entice a major studio. Choice (B) is a misused detail; this is a detail offered from Passage 1 that Grey never indicates to be true. Choice (C) matches your prediction. Choice (D) is distortion; in the final paragraph of the passage, Grey indicates that he does not pay attention to critics. Choice (E) is distortion; Grey compares himself to Picasso in terms of ignoring the critics, but he never indicates that he emulates the painter's work.

15. B

Difficulty: High

What does Grey say about the "mainstream" American film viewer in the first paragraph of Passage 1? In lines 76–79 of the first paragraph of Passage 2, Oscar Grey somewhat addresses the author's statement by proclaiming that that those who believe that the "regular" filmgoer won't enjoy or understand *45 Minutes from Denver* are insulting that filmgoers intelligence. Look for the choice that expresses this statement.

Choice (A) is an opposite; Oscar Grey feels the average filmgoer is waiting for a film that deviates from the norm. Choice (B) matches your prediction. Choice (C) is an opposite; Grey would not change the screenplay of his movie for the major studios; he certainly would not edit his film based on the remarks of a critic. Choice (D) is a misused detail; Grey probably believes this, but there is no detail in the passage that indicates he would make such a response. Choice (E) is an opposite; Grey probably does believe some film critics are fools, but the first paragraph of Passage 1 indicates that he respects his audience.

16. D

Difficulty: Medium

What specific aspect of *45 Minutes from Denver* mentioned in Passage 1 makes it particularly unique in terms of previous films?

This is a simple detail question that only requires that you pay attention to the details of both passages while you are reading. However, the wording here is important, because the question asks for a *specific* aspect of the film, which you should keep in mind as you are making your choice. Look for the choice that contains that specific aspect.

Choice (A) is an opposite; Grey mentions his interpretation in the first sentence of the third paragraph. Choice (B) is an opposite; these details are mention when Grey speaks of the studios wanting to rewrite his script (lines 86–90). Choice (C) is an opposite; Grey's reference to the "very rich" investor (line 94) eliminates this choice. Choice (D) is a match. Choice (E) is out of scope; there is no reference to competition from other films in Passage 1 or 2.

17. D

Difficulty: Medium

What aspect of Oscar Grey's multifaceted artistic abilities do both the critics and the studios seem to appreciate the least? The author and critics in Passage 1 and most of the major studios Oscar Grey mentions in Passage 2 all agreed that Grey was a talented director and actor, but 45 *Minutes from Denver*, which he wrote, was seriously flawed. Look for the choice that contains the best conclusion that can be drawn from this information.

Choice (A) is distortion; in Passage 1 the author mentions that many critics were "impressed by the talented director's extraordinary eye and acting ability," and in Passage 2 Grey states that he received many acting and directing offers, so this choice is not supported Choice (B) is distortion; neither passage offers anything to suggest this. Choice (C) is distortion; in Passage 1, the Reynolds calls the film "uniquely appealing visually," and it can be assumed in Passage 2 that if the film had no redeeming qualities, the studios would not even care to rewrite it. Choice (D) is a good match for your prediction. Choice (E) is an opposite; *Revisited* may have been a hit, but it was a "critical failure," and as stated in line 33 of Passage 1, the film did not really help Grey to get his second film produced.

18. C

Difficulty: Medium

In line 110–111, Grey references those who cling to the rules. How would you describe a person who person breaks the rules to make a difference? In the final paragraph, Grey's mention of those "clinging to a meaningless set of rules" is a reference to critics who he believes are not open minded enough to understand work that challenges the norm. He punctuates this by comparing the critics of today to those in the past who discounted the work of Picasso, a painter who is universally regarded as a groundbreaking genius. Look for the statement that is in accord with what is suggested by Grey's statement.

Choice (A) is out of scope; its possible Grey may agree with this, but he never suggests it. Choice (B) is extreme; to suggest that Grey would agree that critics are never right or justified is too extreme to be correct. Choice (C) is a good match for your prediction. Choice (D) is distortion; in the final sentence of the passage, Grey states that he pays attention to the reaction of nobody but himself. Choice (E) is distortion; again, in the final sentence Grey suggests that reviews have no effect on him.

SECTION 8

1. C

Difficulty: Low

Strategic Advice: If a problem at the beginning of a section seems easy, it probably is. All you have to do is be careful that you don't make a silly arithmetic error.

Getting to the Answer:

Employees by division:

Development $= 1 * 4 = 4$

Marketing $= 2 * 3 = 6$

Accounting $= 3 * 2 = 6$

Public Relations $= 5 * 5 = 25$

Overall total: $4 + 6 + 6 + 25 = 41$

2. D

Difficulty: Low

Strategic Advice: Simplify the equation by getting rid of the like terms. Sometimes problems that seem complicated have a very straightforward solution, particularly if they appear early in the section.

Getting to the Answer:

$$-a^3 + b^2 = a^3 + 9$$
$$b^2 = 9$$
$$b = 3 \text{ or } -3$$

3. C

Difficulty: Low

Strategic Advice: You may think this problem is complicated because it is lengthy. The trick, as with all word problems, is to read carefully and get to the heart of the question.

Getting to the Answer:

Add the lowest original mile time to the lowest additional time: $5 + 1 = 6$

Add the highest original mile time to the highest additional time: $7 + 2 = 9$

Minimum and maximum mile time: 6 minutes and 9 minutes

4. E

Difficulty: Medium

Strategic Advice: We know that one revolution is $360°$. Since this happens every 1.5 seconds, (A) and (B) are definitely too low.

Getting to the Answer: The ball goes around $\frac{10}{1.5} = \frac{100}{15}$

$= \frac{20}{3}$ times, for a total of $\frac{20}{3}(360°) = 2400°$

5. E

Difficulty: Medium

Strategic Advice: You can either Backsolve or set up an equation and solve algebraically.

Getting to the Answer: Backsolving works well here since there are numbers in the answer choices.

(A) original fraction $= \frac{1}{3}$, new fraction $= \frac{0}{1.5} \neq \frac{1}{2}$, so (A) is wrong.

(B) original fraction $= \frac{\left(\frac{4}{3}\right)}{4}$, new fraction $= \frac{\left(\frac{1}{3}\right)}{2} \neq \frac{1}{2}$, so (B) is wrong.

(C) original fraction $= \frac{2}{6}$, new fraction $= \frac{1}{3} \neq \frac{1}{2}$, so (C) is wrong.

(D) original fraction $= \frac{3}{9}$, new fraction $= \frac{2}{4.5} \neq \frac{1}{2}$, so (D) is wrong.

(E) original fraction $= \frac{4}{12}$, new fraction $= \frac{3}{6} = \frac{1}{2}$, so (E) is correct.

To solve the problem algebraically, first translate each sentence into an equation:

$$\frac{x}{y} = \frac{1}{3} \text{ and } \frac{x-1}{y} \text{ divided by } 2 = \frac{1}{2}$$

Solve the first equation for x in terms of y, then plug this into the second equation and solve for y (the denominator of the original fraction).

$$3x = y$$
$$x = \frac{y}{3}$$
$$\frac{\frac{y}{3} - 1}{\frac{y}{2}} = \frac{1}{2}$$
$$\frac{y}{3} - 1 = \frac{y}{4}$$
$$4y - 12 = 3y$$
$$y = 12$$

6. C

Difficulty: Medium

Strategic Advice: When the SAT presents measurements in different units, convert everything to the same unit of measure and pay attention to the question that is asked.

Getting to the Answer: First, convert miles per hour to miles per minute: to do this, divide by 60.

$\frac{4,680}{60} = 78$, so the plane can travel 78 miles per minute.

Ten seconds is one sixth of a minute, so divide 78 by 6 to find the number of miles the plane can travel in 10 seconds: $\frac{78}{6} = 13$.

7.   B

Difficulty: Medium

Strategic Advice: Be sure to read the question carefully, and draw the extra points on the diagram. This will help you prevent careless errors on test day.

Getting to the Answer: First, find FG. $FI = FG + GH + HI = 32$, so $FG = 32 - 6 - 14 = 12$. One endpoint of the new line is the midpoint of FG. The distance from this endpoint to G is 6. The distance from G to H is 6. The total length of the new line segment is $6 + 6 = 12$.

8.   A

Difficulty: Medium

Strategic Advice: Don't be intimidated by algebraic expressions with fractions in them. You can always cross multiply to get rid of the fractions. It is important to know how to make the problem as simple to calculate as possible.

Getting to the Answer:

If you have fractions on both sides of the equation you can cross multiply to get them out of fractional form.

$$\frac{2x + 4}{x - 3} = \frac{4}{3}$$
$$3(2x + 4) = 4(x - 3)$$
$$6x + 12 = 4x - 12$$
$$2x = -24$$
$$x = -12$$

9.   D

Difficulty: Medium

Strategic Advice: Even though this question uses the word "percent," you are never asked to find the actual percent itself. Set this problem up as a ratio to get the answer more quickly.

Getting to the Answer:

$$\frac{16 - 6}{6} = \frac{x - 12}{12}$$
$$\frac{10}{6} = \frac{x - 12}{12}$$
$$120 = 6(x - 12)$$
$$120 = 6x - 72$$
$$192 = 6x$$
$$32 = x$$

10.   D

Difficulty: Medium

Strategic Advice: A question involving variables in both the stem and answer choices is a perfect candidate for Picking Numbers.

Getting to the Answer:

Let $a = 2$ and $b = 3$. So, $\frac{a}{b} = \frac{2}{3}$

(A) $2 > \frac{2}{3}$

(B) $\frac{3}{2} > \frac{2}{3}$

(C) $\frac{\frac{1}{3}}{2} = \frac{2}{3}$

(D) $\frac{2}{6} < \frac{2}{3}$

(E) $\frac{4}{3} > \frac{2}{3}$

11.   C

Difficulty: Medium

Strategic Advice: Use the formula for averages to find the missing pieces of an averages question.

Getting to the Answer: The average is the sum of the terms divided by the number of terms. So 10 students got 100, leaving 20 to get y scores each (we can assume each will have the same score) so we set up:

$$\frac{100(10) + 20y}{30} = 92$$
$$1000 + 20y = 2760$$
$$20y = 1760$$
$$y = 88$$

12.   D

Difficulty: Medium

Strategic Advice: You've got variables in the question, and only numbers in the answer choices, so Backsolving would be a great strategy for this question. Start with (C), then work your way through the problem backwards.

Getting to the Answer:

Start with (C) and assume that there are 60 employees in Company X. $\frac{1}{2}$ of the total staff would 30, so when the 30 more employees arrived at 1PM, that would mean that there were 0 employees at work at noon. That doesn't make sense. We need more total employees in the company, so now choose between (D) and (E).

Work with (D) and assume that there are 120 employees at Company X. That would make $\frac{1}{2}$ of the total staff 60. When the 30 more employees arrived at 1PM, that would mean that there were 30 employees to start off with at noon $(60 - 30 = 30)$. 30 equals $\frac{1}{4}$ of Company X's total employees, so (D) works.

13. A

Difficulty: Medium

Strategic Advice: A bisecting line cuts another line in half. For this problem, take the information you know and fill in the diagram. We know that $\overline{BD}$ and $\overline{AC}$ bisect each other, so we know the base of $\overline{ACD}$ is 16, and since the height of $\overline{ACD}$ is half of $\overline{AC}$, the height is 6.

Getting to the Answer:

$A = \frac{1}{2}bh$

$A = \frac{1}{2}(16)(6)$

$A = 48$

14. B

Difficulty: Medium

Strategic Advice: When solving a question with multiple variables, plug in for the values you know and then solve as you would a single–variable equation.

Getting to the Answer:

$$50 = \frac{5}{4}(2)t$$

$$50 = \frac{10}{4}t$$

$$50 \div \frac{10}{4} = 50 * \frac{4}{10} = 20$$

$$t = 20$$

15. E

Difficulty: Medium

Strategic Advice: For geometry problems that do not provide a figure, take the time to sketch a figure. This will help you visualize the problem.

Getting to the Answer:

Test the answer choices by sketching m in different positions.

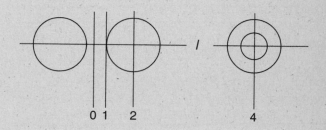

Since all of the answer choices other than (E) are possible, (E) is the correct answer.

16. B

Difficulty: High

Strategic Advice: Use your knowledge of special triangles and the Pythagorean Theorem to find the length of the sides of right triangles.

Getting to the Answer: In the new position, the ladder is 15 feet away from the wall, and the ladder is 25 feet long. Therefore, the sides of the triangle that the ladder forms are $15, x, 25$. This fits the pattern of the 3-4-5 special triangle (namely, 3, 4, and 5 are all multiplied by 5 to get the sides of our triangle). The missing side x is therefore 20, so the ladder in the new position touches the wall 20 feet above the ground. In the original position, the ladder was 4 feet higher, or 24. The triangle formed by the original position has sides measuring $(y, 24, 25)$. Use the Pythagorean Theorem to find the missing base:

$$y^2 + 24^2 = 25^2$$

$$y^2 + 576 = 625$$

$$y^2 = 49$$

$$y = 7, \text{ which is choice (B).}$$

SECTION 9

1. C

Difficulty: Low

Make sure that sentences use conjunctions to connect ideas and avoid run-ons. The two parts of this sentence describe the same subject, the mule. (C) is the only answer choice that fixes the run-on without resorting to the passive voice. (B) is grammatically incorrect. Both (D) and (E) change the subject of the sentence from the *mule* to the *oats*. This leads both to use the passive voice unnecessarily.

2. E

Difficulty: Low

Any time a word refers back to the subject, it needs to agree with the subject. In this sentence, *where* is referring to the subject of the sentence, *An industrial spy*. This is incorrect because "where" can only refer to places, while an industrial spy is a person. (E) correctly refers to the subject as *someone*. (B) is idiomatically incorrect. (C) and (D) are wrong for the same reason as (A): they mischaracterize the subject, using *when* and *how* respectively.

3. B

Difficulty: Low

Certain idioms appear regularly on the SAT; learn their proper structure. This question tests your knowledge of the idiom that compares two nouns using *as*; the correct construction is "as (adjective) as." Only (B) correctly completes the construction. (C) is grammatically incorrect, (D) is unnecessarily wordy, and (E) does not correct the error.

4. E

Difficulty: Low

If the original sentence seems unnecessarily wordy, look for an Answer choice that says the same thing more concisely. The opening of this sentence uses far too many words to get its point across. (E) is a concise and accurate way to say the same thing. (B) and (D) phrase the opening differently, but both are still wordier than they need to be. "Less weightier" in (C) is grammatically incorrect.

5. B

Difficulty: Medium

When you have a set of objects in a list, series, or compound structure, they should all be parallel in structure. Here, the object of the preposition *throughout* is the compound *childhood and...adolescence*; adding additional words violates the necessary parallel structure. (B) makes the correction. None of the other answer choices correct the error; additionally, (C) introduces an inappropriate verb tense in context, (D) unnecessarily uses the passive voice, and (E) is overly wordy.

6. C

Difficulty: Medium

Descriptive phrases, just like adjectives, have to refer to a noun. Make sure that they refer to the right noun and that they agree with that noun. The opening of this sentence describes something that is *constrained by gravity*, but then incorrectly applies that description to an *idea*. (C) correctly applies the description to the *astronauts*. (B) is wordy and still applies the description to the *idea*. (D) and (E) fix the original problem, but (D) is awkward and (E) is grammatically incorrect.

7. D

Difficulty: Medium

When two clauses refer to the same subject, a second pronoun subject is unnecessary. The sentence as written is grammatically incorrect; the pronoun *this* is an unnecessary restatement of the subject. (D) eliminates the unnecessary pronoun. (B) is awkwardly structured. (C) is wordy and changes the tense of the verb unnecessarily. (E) is unnecessarily wordy and introduces the passive voice unnecessarily.

8. E

Difficulty: Medium

When you describe an object, make sure the object and the description agree in number. Because the first part of this sentence discusses the plural *bodies*, the second part must also be plural. (E) does exactly this, replacing *a highly efficient machine* with *highly efficient machines*. (B) is incorrect because, although it replaces the singular *machine* with the plural form, it also changes *bodies* to *body*, mirroring the original error. (C) and (D) don't address the error; additionally, (C) is idiomatically incorrect and (D) is unnecessarily wordy

9. C
Difficulty: Medium

Be consistent when you use pronouns like *you* and *one*. The artists made adjustments to accommodate the viewers of the sculptures. When referring to a general person like a viewer, you have to be consistent in the pronoun you use. (C) solves this problem by eliminating the second. (B) and (E) are consistent in the pronoun they use, but they are unnecessarily wordy. (D) uses *their* instead of *one's*, but is still inconsistent.

10. E
Difficulty: Medium

Ambiguous pronouns will always be wrong on the SAT; pronouns must refer to specific antecedents. The pronouns *it* is incorrect here because it has no antecedent. (E) corrects this error by eliminating the pronoun, while also making the sentence more concise. (B) does not address the error. (C) is awkward and unnecessarily wordy. *This,* in (D), is ambiguous, and the sentence is overly wordy.

11. C
Difficulty: Medium

The passive voice will not always be incorrect on the SAT, but if the sentence can easily be put into the active voice, the correct answer choice will do so. The passive voice here is unnecessary. (C) puts the sentence into the active voice without introducing any additional errors. (B) is unnecessarily wordy. (D) is a sentence fragment. (E) does not address the error.

12. A
Difficulty: High

Expect to encounter between five and eight sentences without errors on your SAT. This sentence is correct as written. *Which is* is the correct transition between the modifying phrase and *$10 million,* and the comparative phrase *less than* is used correctly. (B), (C), (D), and (E) are awkward and unnecessarily wordy.

13. C
Difficulty: High

Look for the most concise answer that correctly expresses the relationship between clauses. As written, this sentence is overly wordy, and *While* does not express the correct relationship between the ideas. The *former Soviet countries* are an addition to the idea of the *Moscow government.* (C) correctly express this with the conjunction *and.* (B) fixes the transition, but is a sentence fragment. (D) and (E) are awkward and unnecessarily wordy.

14. A
Difficulty: High

When a question seems best as written, don't be afraid to choose (A) as your answer. This sentence is correct as written. (B) is grammatically incorrect. (C) and (D) are unnecessarily wordy. (E) begins with "although," a conjunction that does not make sense in the context of the sentence.

SAT PRACTICE TEST TWO ANSWER SHEET

Remove (or photocopy) the answer sheet, and use it to complete the practice test.

How to Take the Practice Tests

Each Practice Test includes eight scored multiple-choice sections and one essay. Keep in mind that on the actual SAT, there will be an additional multiple-choice section—the experimental section—that will not contribute to your score.

Once you start a Practice Test, don't stop until you've gone through all nine sections. Remember, you can review any questions within a section, but you may not go back or forward a section.

Good luck!

Start with number 1 for each section. If a section has fewer questions than answer spaces, leave the extra spaces blank.

Section One

Section One is the writing section's essay component.
Lined pages on which you will write your essay can be found in that section.

Section Two

1. Ⓐ Ⓑ Ⓒ Ⓓ Ⓔ   9. Ⓐ Ⓑ Ⓒ Ⓓ Ⓔ   17. Ⓐ Ⓑ Ⓒ Ⓓ Ⓔ   25. Ⓐ Ⓑ Ⓒ Ⓓ Ⓔ
2. Ⓐ Ⓑ Ⓒ Ⓓ Ⓔ   10. Ⓐ Ⓑ Ⓒ Ⓓ Ⓔ   18. Ⓐ Ⓑ Ⓒ Ⓓ Ⓔ
3. Ⓐ Ⓑ Ⓒ Ⓓ Ⓔ   11. Ⓐ Ⓑ Ⓒ Ⓓ Ⓔ   19. Ⓐ Ⓑ Ⓒ Ⓓ Ⓔ
4. Ⓐ Ⓑ Ⓒ Ⓓ Ⓔ   12. Ⓐ Ⓑ Ⓒ Ⓓ Ⓔ   20. Ⓐ Ⓑ Ⓒ Ⓓ Ⓔ
5. Ⓐ Ⓑ Ⓒ Ⓓ Ⓔ   13. Ⓐ Ⓑ Ⓒ Ⓓ Ⓔ   21. Ⓐ Ⓑ Ⓒ Ⓓ Ⓔ
6. Ⓐ Ⓑ Ⓒ Ⓓ Ⓔ   14. Ⓐ Ⓑ Ⓒ Ⓓ Ⓔ   22. Ⓐ Ⓑ Ⓒ Ⓓ Ⓔ
7. Ⓐ Ⓑ Ⓒ Ⓓ Ⓔ   15. Ⓐ Ⓑ Ⓒ Ⓓ Ⓔ   23. Ⓐ Ⓑ Ⓒ Ⓓ Ⓔ
8. Ⓐ Ⓑ Ⓒ Ⓓ Ⓔ   16. Ⓐ Ⓑ Ⓒ Ⓓ Ⓔ   24. Ⓐ Ⓑ Ⓒ Ⓓ Ⓔ

☐ # right in Section Two

☐ # wrong in Section Two

Section Three

1. Ⓐ Ⓑ Ⓒ Ⓓ Ⓔ   9. Ⓐ Ⓑ Ⓒ Ⓓ Ⓔ   17. Ⓐ Ⓑ Ⓒ Ⓓ Ⓔ
2. Ⓐ Ⓑ Ⓒ Ⓓ Ⓔ   10. Ⓐ Ⓑ Ⓒ Ⓓ Ⓔ   18. Ⓐ Ⓑ Ⓒ Ⓓ Ⓔ
3. Ⓐ Ⓑ Ⓒ Ⓓ Ⓔ   11. Ⓐ Ⓑ Ⓒ Ⓓ Ⓔ   19. Ⓐ Ⓑ Ⓒ Ⓓ Ⓔ
4. Ⓐ Ⓑ Ⓒ Ⓓ Ⓔ   12. Ⓐ Ⓑ Ⓒ Ⓓ Ⓔ   20. Ⓐ Ⓑ Ⓒ Ⓓ Ⓔ
5. Ⓐ Ⓑ Ⓒ Ⓓ Ⓔ   13. Ⓐ Ⓑ Ⓒ Ⓓ Ⓔ
6. Ⓐ Ⓑ Ⓒ Ⓓ Ⓔ   14. Ⓐ Ⓑ Ⓒ Ⓓ Ⓔ
7. Ⓐ Ⓑ Ⓒ Ⓓ Ⓔ   15. Ⓐ Ⓑ Ⓒ Ⓓ Ⓔ
8. Ⓐ Ⓑ Ⓒ Ⓓ Ⓔ   16. Ⓐ Ⓑ Ⓒ Ⓓ Ⓔ

☐ # right in Section Three

☐ # wrong in Section Three

Section Four

1. Ⓐ Ⓑ Ⓒ Ⓓ Ⓔ   10. Ⓐ Ⓑ Ⓒ Ⓓ Ⓔ   19. Ⓐ Ⓑ Ⓒ Ⓓ Ⓔ   28. Ⓐ Ⓑ Ⓒ Ⓓ Ⓔ
2. Ⓐ Ⓑ Ⓒ Ⓓ Ⓔ   11. Ⓐ Ⓑ Ⓒ Ⓓ Ⓔ   20. Ⓐ Ⓑ Ⓒ Ⓓ Ⓔ   29. Ⓐ Ⓑ Ⓒ Ⓓ Ⓔ
3. Ⓐ Ⓑ Ⓒ Ⓓ Ⓔ   12. Ⓐ Ⓑ Ⓒ Ⓓ Ⓔ   21. Ⓐ Ⓑ Ⓒ Ⓓ Ⓔ   30. Ⓐ Ⓑ Ⓒ Ⓓ Ⓔ
4. Ⓐ Ⓑ Ⓒ Ⓓ Ⓔ   13. Ⓐ Ⓑ Ⓒ Ⓓ Ⓔ   22. Ⓐ Ⓑ Ⓒ Ⓓ Ⓔ   31. Ⓐ Ⓑ Ⓒ Ⓓ Ⓔ
5. Ⓐ Ⓑ Ⓒ Ⓓ Ⓔ   14. Ⓐ Ⓑ Ⓒ Ⓓ Ⓔ   23. Ⓐ Ⓑ Ⓒ Ⓓ Ⓔ   32. Ⓐ Ⓑ Ⓒ Ⓓ Ⓔ
6. Ⓐ Ⓑ Ⓒ Ⓓ Ⓔ   15. Ⓐ Ⓑ Ⓒ Ⓓ Ⓔ   24. Ⓐ Ⓑ Ⓒ Ⓓ Ⓔ   33. Ⓐ Ⓑ Ⓒ Ⓓ Ⓔ
7. Ⓐ Ⓑ Ⓒ Ⓓ Ⓔ   16. Ⓐ Ⓑ Ⓒ Ⓓ Ⓔ   25. Ⓐ Ⓑ Ⓒ Ⓓ Ⓔ   34. Ⓐ Ⓑ Ⓒ Ⓓ Ⓔ
8. Ⓐ Ⓑ Ⓒ Ⓓ Ⓔ   17. Ⓐ Ⓑ Ⓒ Ⓓ Ⓔ   26. Ⓐ Ⓑ Ⓒ Ⓓ Ⓔ   35. Ⓐ Ⓑ Ⓒ Ⓓ Ⓔ
9. Ⓐ Ⓑ Ⓒ Ⓓ Ⓔ   18. Ⓐ Ⓑ Ⓒ Ⓓ Ⓔ   27. Ⓐ Ⓑ Ⓒ Ⓓ Ⓔ

☐ # right in Section Four

☐ # wrong in Section Four

Section Five

1. Ⓐ Ⓑ Ⓒ Ⓓ Ⓔ   ➤9. Ⓐ Ⓑ Ⓒ Ⓓ Ⓔ   17. Ⓐ Ⓑ Ⓒ Ⓓ Ⓔ
2. Ⓐ Ⓑ Ⓒ Ⓓ Ⓔ   10. Ⓐ Ⓑ Ⓒ Ⓓ Ⓔ   18. Ⓐ Ⓑ Ⓒ Ⓓ Ⓔ
3. Ⓐ Ⓑ Ⓒ Ⓓ Ⓔ   11. Ⓐ Ⓑ Ⓒ Ⓓ Ⓔ
4. Ⓐ Ⓑ Ⓒ Ⓓ Ⓔ   12. Ⓐ Ⓑ Ⓒ Ⓓ Ⓔ
5. Ⓐ Ⓑ Ⓒ Ⓓ Ⓔ   13. Ⓐ Ⓑ Ⓒ Ⓓ Ⓔ
6. Ⓐ Ⓑ Ⓒ Ⓓ Ⓔ   14. Ⓐ Ⓑ Ⓒ Ⓓ Ⓔ
7. Ⓐ Ⓑ Ⓒ Ⓓ Ⓔ   15. Ⓐ Ⓑ Ⓒ Ⓓ Ⓔ
8. Ⓐ Ⓑ Ⓒ Ⓓ Ⓔ   16. Ⓐ Ⓑ Ⓒ Ⓓ Ⓔ

☐ # right in Section Five

☐ # wrong in Section Five

If section 5 of your test book contains math questions that are not multiple choice, continue to item 9 below. Otherwise, continue to item 9 above.

9.   10.   11.   12.   13.

14.   15.   16.   17.   18.

Remove (or photocopy) this answer sheet, and use it to complete the practice test.

Start with number 1 for each section. If a section has fewer questions than answer spaces, leave the extra spaces blank.

Section Six

1. Ⓐ Ⓑ Ⓒ Ⓓ Ⓔ   9. Ⓐ Ⓑ Ⓒ Ⓓ Ⓔ   17. Ⓐ Ⓑ Ⓒ Ⓓ Ⓔ
2. Ⓐ Ⓑ Ⓒ Ⓓ Ⓔ   10. Ⓐ Ⓑ Ⓒ Ⓓ Ⓔ   18. Ⓐ Ⓑ Ⓒ Ⓓ Ⓔ
3. Ⓐ Ⓑ Ⓒ Ⓓ Ⓔ   11. Ⓐ Ⓑ Ⓒ Ⓓ Ⓔ   19. Ⓐ Ⓑ Ⓒ Ⓓ Ⓔ
4. Ⓐ Ⓑ Ⓒ Ⓓ Ⓔ   12. Ⓐ Ⓑ Ⓒ Ⓓ Ⓔ   20. Ⓐ Ⓑ Ⓒ Ⓓ Ⓔ
5. Ⓐ Ⓑ Ⓒ Ⓓ Ⓔ   13. Ⓐ Ⓑ Ⓒ Ⓓ Ⓔ   21. Ⓐ Ⓑ Ⓒ Ⓓ Ⓔ
6. Ⓐ Ⓑ Ⓒ Ⓓ Ⓔ   14. Ⓐ Ⓑ Ⓒ Ⓓ Ⓔ   22. Ⓐ Ⓑ Ⓒ Ⓓ Ⓔ
7. Ⓐ Ⓑ Ⓒ Ⓓ Ⓔ   15. Ⓐ Ⓑ Ⓒ Ⓓ Ⓔ   23. Ⓐ Ⓑ Ⓒ Ⓓ Ⓔ
8. Ⓐ Ⓑ Ⓒ Ⓓ Ⓔ   16. Ⓐ Ⓑ Ⓒ Ⓓ Ⓔ   24. Ⓐ Ⓑ Ⓒ Ⓓ Ⓔ

right in Section Six

wrong in Section Six

Section Seven

1. Ⓐ Ⓑ Ⓒ Ⓓ Ⓔ   9. Ⓐ Ⓑ Ⓒ Ⓓ Ⓔ
2. Ⓐ Ⓑ Ⓒ Ⓓ Ⓔ   10. Ⓐ Ⓑ Ⓒ Ⓓ Ⓔ
3. Ⓐ Ⓑ Ⓒ Ⓓ Ⓔ   11. Ⓐ Ⓑ Ⓒ Ⓓ Ⓔ
4. Ⓐ Ⓑ Ⓒ Ⓓ Ⓔ   12. Ⓐ Ⓑ Ⓒ Ⓓ Ⓔ
5. Ⓐ Ⓑ Ⓒ Ⓓ Ⓔ   13. Ⓐ Ⓑ Ⓒ Ⓓ Ⓔ
6. Ⓐ Ⓑ Ⓒ Ⓓ Ⓔ   14. Ⓐ Ⓑ Ⓒ Ⓓ Ⓔ
7. Ⓐ Ⓑ Ⓒ Ⓓ Ⓔ   15. Ⓐ Ⓑ Ⓒ Ⓓ Ⓔ
8. Ⓐ Ⓑ Ⓒ Ⓓ Ⓔ   16. Ⓐ Ⓑ Ⓒ Ⓓ Ⓔ

right in Section Seven

wrong in Section Seven

Section Eight

1. Ⓐ Ⓑ Ⓒ Ⓓ Ⓔ   9. Ⓐ Ⓑ Ⓒ Ⓓ Ⓔ   17. Ⓐ Ⓑ Ⓒ Ⓓ Ⓔ
2. Ⓐ Ⓑ Ⓒ Ⓓ Ⓔ   10. Ⓐ Ⓑ Ⓒ Ⓓ Ⓔ   18. Ⓐ Ⓑ Ⓒ Ⓓ Ⓔ
3. Ⓐ Ⓑ Ⓒ Ⓓ Ⓔ   11. Ⓐ Ⓑ Ⓒ Ⓓ Ⓔ
4. Ⓐ Ⓑ Ⓒ Ⓓ Ⓔ   12. Ⓐ Ⓑ Ⓒ Ⓓ Ⓔ
5. Ⓐ Ⓑ Ⓒ Ⓓ Ⓔ   13. Ⓐ Ⓑ Ⓒ Ⓓ Ⓔ
6. Ⓐ Ⓑ Ⓒ Ⓓ Ⓔ   14. Ⓐ Ⓑ Ⓒ Ⓓ Ⓔ
7. Ⓐ Ⓑ Ⓒ Ⓓ Ⓔ   15. Ⓐ Ⓑ Ⓒ Ⓓ Ⓔ
8. Ⓐ Ⓑ Ⓒ Ⓓ Ⓔ   16. Ⓐ Ⓑ Ⓒ Ⓓ Ⓔ

right in Section Eight

wrong in Section Eight

Section Nine

1. Ⓐ Ⓑ Ⓒ Ⓓ Ⓔ   9. Ⓐ Ⓑ Ⓒ Ⓓ Ⓔ
2. Ⓐ Ⓑ Ⓒ Ⓓ Ⓔ   10. Ⓐ Ⓑ Ⓒ Ⓓ Ⓔ
3. Ⓐ Ⓑ Ⓒ Ⓓ Ⓔ   11. Ⓐ Ⓑ Ⓒ Ⓓ Ⓔ
4. Ⓐ Ⓑ Ⓒ Ⓓ Ⓔ   12. Ⓐ Ⓑ Ⓒ Ⓓ Ⓔ
5. Ⓐ Ⓑ Ⓒ Ⓓ Ⓔ   13. Ⓐ Ⓑ Ⓒ Ⓓ Ⓔ
6. Ⓐ Ⓑ Ⓒ Ⓓ Ⓔ   14. Ⓐ Ⓑ Ⓒ Ⓓ Ⓔ
7. Ⓐ Ⓑ Ⓒ Ⓓ Ⓔ
8. Ⓐ Ⓑ Ⓒ Ⓓ Ⓔ

right in Section Nine

wrong in Section Nine

Practice Test Two

The essay gives you an opportunity to show how effectively you can develop and express ideas. You should, therefore, take care to develop your point of view, present your ideas logically and clearly, and use language precisely.

Your essay must be written in your Answer Grid Booklet—you will receive no other paper on which to write. You will have enough space if you write on every line, avoid wide margins, and keep your handwriting to a reasonable size. Remember that people who are not familiar with your handwriting will read what you write. Try to write or print so that what you are writing is legible to those readers.

You have twenty-five minutes to write an essay on the topic assigned below.

DO NOT WRITE ON ANOTHER TOPIC. AN OFF-TOPIC ESSAY WILL RECEIVE A SCORE OF ZERO.

Think carefully about the issue presented in the following excerpt and the assignment below.

> "Champions aren't made in gyms. Champions are made from something they have deep inside them: A desire, a dream, a vision. They have to have last-minute stamina, they have to be a little faster, they have to have the skill and the will. But the will must be stronger than the skill."
>
> –Muhammad Ali

Assignment: If you want to become an expert in a certain field, do you need to have more talent or more motivation? Plan and write an essay in which you develop your point of view on this issue. Support your position with reasoning and examples taken from your reading, studies, experience, or observations.

DO NOT WRITE YOUR ESSAY IN YOUR TEST BOOK.
You will receive credit only for what you write in your Answer Grid Booklet.

_____

_____

_____

_____

_____

_____

_____

_____

_____

_____

_____

_____

_____

_____

_____

_____

_____

_____

IF YOU FINISH BEFORE TIME IS CALLED, YOU MAY CHECK YOUR WORK ON THIS SECTION ONLY. DO NOT TURN TO ANY OTHER SECTION IN THE TEST.

KAPLAN
Test Prep and Admissions

SECTION 2

Time—25 Minutes
25 Questions

Directions: For each of the following questions, choose the best answer and darken the corresponding oval on the answer sheet.

Each sentence below has one or two blanks, each blank indicating that something has been omitted. Beneath the sentence are five words or sets of words labeled (A) through (E). Choose the word or set of words that, when inserted in the sentence, <u>best</u> fits the meaning of the sentence as a whole.

EXAMPLE:

Today's small, portable computers contrast markedly with the earliest electronic computers, which were ----.

(A) effective
(B) invented
(C) useful
(D) destructive
(E) enormous   Ⓐ Ⓑ Ⓒ Ⓓ ●

1. The usually ---- CEO shocked his employees by severely overreacting to the jocular tease made by one of his subordinates.

(A) demanding
(B) inarticulate
(C) aggressive
(D) persuasive
(E) composed

2. Although the vintage clothing store already has a large and devoted customer base among college students, the owner tries to expand her ---- by having big promotional sales.

(A) clientele
(B) investments
(C) coverage
(D) staffing
(E) liability

3. Despite their ---- backgrounds, those who fought for civil rights overcame their differences in a ---- effort.

(A) incompatible . . divisive
(B) eccentric . . prosaic
(C) distinguished . . futile
(D) disparate . . united
(E) comparable . . joint

4. Although it is not ---- , the college's student directory is a useful tool because the supply of other resources for locating students is ----.

(A) intense . . vast
(B) obsolete . . outdated
(C) ostentatious . . varied
(D) contemporary . . plentiful
(E) comprehensive . . meager

5. Developmental psychologists often cite yelling at children as ---- and a poor way to help them learn.

(A) benign
(B) diagnostic
(C) inefficacious
(D) discretionary
(E) therapeutic

GO ON TO THE NEXT PAGE

Directions: The passages below are followed by questions based on their content; questions following a pair of related passages may also be based on the relationship between the paired passages. Answer the questions on the basis of what is <u>stated</u> or <u>implied</u> in the passages and in any introductory material that may be provided.

Questions 6–9 are based on the following passages.

Passage 1

The French Revolution reverberated around the world when it happened—a telling blow was struck for the people's rights, and a step was taken toward true democracy that could not be taken
(5) back. We are indebted to renegade artists for lighting the match that set that blaze. In the eighteenth century, it was unheard of for commoners to speak out against the King. Several guerrilla theatre groups performing outside the castle,
(10) however, began doing shocking things; they mocked the royalty, burned them in effigy, and drenched them in scorn. The performances gave the downtrodden commoners the courage and license they required to form a body to rise
(15) against the monarchy.

Passage 2

The French Revolution was a powerful and inevitable occurrence. Social and economic pressures gave the peasants of France literally no choice but to fight against their oppressive govern-
(20) ment. Much has been made recently of the impact of a few ragtag theatre groups outside the palace; while they probably did a good job of reflecting the growing discontent of the people, it is certain that a family's need to eat was a more compelling
(25) argument for revolution than a funny play that Father saw on the way home from the fields. These plays provided a mirror, not a catalyst, for the mood of the populace.

6. Both authors agree that the French Revolution

    (A) was a natural outgrowth of extreme poverty and oppression

    (B) was a historically significant event

    (C) was encouraged by plays mocking the royalty

    (D) was similar to the American Revolution

    (E) was an unlikely and impressive event

7. The statement in lines 6–8 ("In the eighteenth …the King") is important to the overall argument of Passage 1 in its suggestion of

    (A) gradual development

    (B) an inhibiting obstacle

    (C) severe decorum

    (D) a false conclusion

    (E) time-honored tradition

8. Author 2 would most likely view the "shocking things" mentioned in line 10, Passage 1, as elements that

    (A) changed the course of the Revolution

    (B) were unfit for public viewing

    (C) the commoners considered unpleasant

    (D) had no relevance to the French Revolution

    (E) represented commoners' viewpoints about the royalty

9. Author 1 would most likely regard the "social and economic pressures" (lines 17–18, Passage 2) as

    (A) noncontributing factors in the French Revolution

    (B) exaggerated by Author 2

    (C) making the French Revolution less likely

    (D) insufficient to incite the French Revolution on their own

    (E) the most important contributing factors to the French Revolution

GO ON TO THE NEXT PAGE

Questions 10–15 are based on the following passage.

The passage below is excerpted from the introduction to a new book about global conflict and peace.

My introduction into the field of social history was fortuitous. I spent my early formative years in Lebanon during that country's civil war. Living through this turmoil inspired my quest to study
(5) and understand global conflict. Breaking away to America in my pre-teen years cushioned the blow, as did living in suburban Maryland. After my entry to Stanford University, I found myself reengaged by the factors that contributed to my
(10) horrific childhood living conditions. I invested myself in the study of International Relations in hopes of gaining a deeper understanding of war, conflict, and peace. Yet, once again, I too quickly lost my bearings, this time in the immersion of
(15) abstract theories of global security—theories that justify, even advocate war as a policy tool. I am still embarrassed by the fact that I went to school in order to contribute to world peace but found myself becoming a hawkish supporter of
(20) militarized solutions.

During graduate school, I met a professor who urged me to refocus my studies from the global system to the local one. He recommended that I study the people of the various regions of the
(25) world rather than the regional power balance among governments. I, of course, scoffed at the suggestion, for that type of study was the job of historians. International Relations theorists do not often examine people. I, like most others in my
(30) field, viewed the state as a black box. States and their governments were the subjects of my studies; populations were merely the objects of state action. But I eventually reached a point that high-lighted the inadequacy of such analyses. Ironically,
(35) I had first sought to study International Relations in order to help people overcome conflict, but in my focus on the politics of conflict, I had lost sight of the people.

I eventually refocused my studies by examining
(40) the history of the people in the regions I studied. Primary source documents revealed common struggles and aspirations. This examination elucidated the politics of the regions and their conflicts. By overlaying the two studies, I was
(45) eventually able to see how political motivations, calculations, and missteps affected groups and individuals who then fell into conflict.

This examination of the human aspect of inter-national politics opened my eyes to the fact that
(50) conflicts are often not endemic. Traditional views of the state and nation never addressed, for instance, how governments and demagogues spur previously coexisting populations into battle, or why. Ironically, the examination of the human
(55) level cemented the notion that groups and popu-lations seldom harbor true hatred and conflict. I learned that such conflicts originate from and remain the tools of those in power. This circle finally accorded me the comprehensive under-
(60) standing I sought. My examination of social history aided my understanding of international politics by highlighting the states of affair within the regions and countries I studied. They helped me to investigate the true origins of the world's
(65) past conflicts—and my own.

10. The primary purpose of the passage is to show how the author

(A) discovered a more effective framework of analysis for his studies

(B) became an International Relations scholar to help people in his homeland achieve social justice

(C) improved his research abilities by taking a new approach

(D) became more well-rounded thanks to the tutelage of a graduate school professor

(E) came to view local populations as a worthy subject for study

GO ON TO THE NEXT PAGE

11. The first sentence indicates that the author's "introduction into…social history" was

(A) difficult but rewarding

(B) confusing but worthwhile

(C) unsought but unavoidable

(D) accidental but pleasant

(E) surprising and controversial

12. The author initially "scoffed" at the graduate school professor's suggestion (lines 26–28) because the author

(A) knew that the graduate school professor was not tenured in the history department.

(B) believed that historians should pursue loftier goals

(C) had job offers that would present even greater opportunity

(D) rejected the idea that such a study was the job of an International Relations scholar

(E) viewed the suggestion as condescending

13. According to the passage, why did the author go to school?

(A) to escape the civil war in his own country

(B) to contribute to world peace

(C) to become a hawkish supporter of militarized policies

(D) to examine the human aspect of International Relations

(E) to improve his understanding of the people in the regions he studied

14. In line 44, "overlaying" most nearly means

(A) researching

(B) sidestepping

(C) abandoning

(D) combining

(E) exaggerating

15. The last two sentences ("My examination… my own") suggest that the author

(A) realizes global conflicts can only be examined through social history

(B) believes that social history provides information on global conflicts

(C) assumes all international conflicts have their bases in social problems

(D) believes that knowledge of social history can prevent conflicts

(E) was previously aware of the social history, but felt unqualified to write on it

GO ON TO THE NEXT PAGE

Questions 16–25 are based on the following passage.

Ask any jazz guitarist who their biggest
influences are, and odds are good you'll emerge
from the conversation with the name Django
Reinhardt. Django, a gypsy guitarist born in a
(5) caravan in a small town in Belgium in 1910, developed a style of music that blended the rhythmic
gypsy tones of a musette with American jazz and
swing. The haunting sadness of his music stood in
stark contrast to the bouncy jubilance of early
(10) jazz, as Django, against all odds, single-handedly
created a style of music that has been revered and
imitated without cease since his death in 1953.

In Django's case, "single-handedly" isn't just lip
service. He began playing banjo at the tender age
(15) of 12, picked up guitar at 13, and attained so
much skill so quickly that at 18 he was already
highly regarded for his natural skill among the
gypsies. But Django was nothing more than a very
skilled player until 1928, when the event occurred
(20) that changed his style forever and sealed his fate.
One night, Django returned home late to his
caravan, which was filled with celluloid flowers
that his wife had made to sell at the market the
next day. The wick fell out of the candle he was
(25) holding and ignited the highly flammable plastic
flowers, turning the caravan into an inferno in a
matter of seconds. Django and his wife escaped
with their lives, but Django suffered severe burns
to half his body. He nearly lost one leg, and his
(30) left hand was severely crippled—only two of his
five fingers still had full functionality. With his
fingering hand so disfigured, it seemed likely he
would never play the guitar again, and the general
recognition of his talent was already so strong, the
(35) legend goes, that the men of his tribe wept at the
tragedy.

This was the event, however, that focused and
distinguished Django Reinhardt as a musician.
Faced with the loss of the pastime he loved,
(40) Django refused to give up. At the nursing home
where he recuperated, bedridden for eighteen
months, Django practiced methodically every day,
systematically working out a way to get around
the loss of three digits. He invented an entirely
(45) new fingering system to compensate for his loss.
In the process, he found chord progressions that

no one had ever played before, and a virtuosic
technical skill that was unmatched in the world of
jazz musicians. All of his subsequent innovations
(50) in guitar technique can be traced back to his "
disability"—it set him apart and forced him to try
new things. And the sound was incredible.

Django is not the only artist who owes his
uniqueness to what most people would consider a
(55) setback. There's a fair complement of geniuses
with difficulties—Picasso and his madness,
Beethoven and his mounting deafness, and
Stephen Hawking and his confinement to a wheelchair. Certainly not every human being who
(60) achieves something great is limited by a disability,
but a surprising percentage of those who have
altered human thought forever are handicapped in
some way.

These days, it seems that it isn't quite enough to
(65) be very, very good at what you do; to have a significant impact, you must apparently do something differently from the way that anyone else in
the world has done it. A guitarist who must learn
to construct chords with only two working fingers
(70) will necessarily stumble across techniques no
musician has ever conceived of before—and why
should another musician be expected to try such a
thing? If gifted with the use of all five fingers, it is
unnecessary to learn to use just two. But without
(75) the two-fingered chords, Django's unique, impos-
sibly virtuosic style could never have existed.

It may be time to regard people who have
crippling disabilities with something besides the
pity that so frequently (and, some say, insultingly)
(80) colors the outlooks of the fully able. Those who
are different—really, substantially different—have
access to a whole world that "normal" people
can only dream of. A human being's remarkable
ability to adapt, to invent, and to mutate in
(85) response to the challenges in his environment is
the most impressive thing about our species.
Greater challenges require greater invention, and
the innovation required to do the impossible must
come most quickly when presented inflexibly with
(90) that impossibility.

GO ON TO THE NEXT PAGE

16. The passage can primarily be described as

    (A) a fictional story followed by an insightful theory

    (B) a scientific hypothesis proved with a systematic study

    (C) a personal account illustrating an argument

    (D) analytical commentary refuting a generally held belief

    (E) an anecdotal example leading to a generalization

17. The author uses the phrase "against all odds" (line 10) when referring to Django's achievements in order to

    (A) convey the ease with which Django became a great jazz guitarist

    (B) emphasize the discrimination prevalent against Gypsy musicians at the time

    (C) foreshadow the difficulties that Django had to overcome to make his mark in music

    (D) add an element of drama to the story of Django's life

    (E) explain why Django was greater than other jazz guitarists

18. In lines 34–36, the men of Django's tribe wept because

    (A) the flowers that Django's wife made were renowned for their beauty and their loss was deeply felt

    (B) the caravan had been worth a significant amount of money to the tribe

    (C) Django was universally beloved, and they felt sorry for him

    (D) they believed that Django's significant musical gifts had been taken from the world

    (E) Django's new style of music moved them deeply

19. In line 38, "distinguished" most nearly means

    (A) sophisticated

    (B) identified

    (C) sharpened

    (D) set apart

    (E) gave honors to

20. In line 44, "digits" most nearly means

    (A) numbers

    (B) amounts of money

    (C) points

    (D) fingers

    (E) electronic figures

21. The author's remark in lines 64–68 ("These days…has done it") can best be described as

    (A) speculation

    (B) explanation

    (C) narrative

    (D) inquiry

    (E) example

22. The author's remark in lines 73–74 ("If gifted…just two") reveals the assumption that

    (A) many musicians foolishly use less of their body than they are capable of

    (B) musicians are limited because they can only use two fingers on the fret board

    (C) no musician would self-impose restrictions on their technique if they didn't have to

    (D) musicians are disinclined to work hard

    (E) it is not necessary for musicians to endeavor to improve their technique

GO ON TO THE NEXT PAGE

23. The author's parenthetical aside in line 79 serves to

 (A) reveal the author's passionate sympathy for physically challenged people

 (B) elaborate on the argument that came just before it

 (C) depict the author's bruised pride

 (D) introduce the opinion of qualified experts

 (E) briefly introduce another argument against feeling pity for the physically disabled

24. Lines 80–83 primarily encourages readers to view physical disability as

 (A) an unfortunate, unmitigated tragedy

 (B) an opportunity for experimentation and innovation

 (C) not an obstacle at all

 (D) superior to physical "normalcy"

 (E) a condition to be dealt with intellectually rather than physically

25. The main point of the passage is to

 (A) describe events in Django Reinhardt's life

 (B) analyze the elements that go into a successful musician's career

 (C) assert that physical handicaps are always inspiring

 (D) compare Django Reinhardt to other physically challenged greats

 (E) explore the effect that a physical "setback" might have on an artist or thinker's career

IF YOU FINISH BEFORE TIME IS CALLED, YOU MAY CHECK YOUR WORK ON THIS SECTION ONLY. DO NOT TURN TO ANY OTHER SECTION IN THE TEST.

SECTION 3
Time—25 Minutes
20 Questions

Directions: For this section, solve each problem and decide which is the best of the choices given. Fill in the corresponding oval on the answer sheet. You may use any available space for scratchwork.

Notes:

(1) Calculator use is permitted.

(2) All numbers used are real numbers.

(3) Figures are provided for some problems. All figures are drawn to scale and lie in a plane UNLESS otherwise indicated.

(4) Unless otherwise specified, the domain of any function f is assumed to be the set of all real numbers x for which $f(x)$ is a real number.

Information

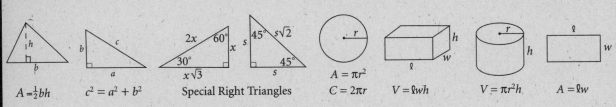

$A = \frac{1}{2}bh$ $c^2 = a^2 + b^2$ Special Right Triangles $A = \pi r^2$ $C = 2\pi r$ $V = \ell wh$ $V = \pi r^2 h$ $A = \ell w$

The sum of the degree measures of the angles in a triangle is 180.
The number of degrees of arc in a circle is 360.
A straight angle has a degree measure of 180.

1. If $\dfrac{\sqrt{x} + n}{\sqrt{x} + 9} = 1$, then $n = ?$

   (A) 1

   (B) 3

   (C) 5

   (D) 8

   (E) 9

2. When $2x$ is subtracted from 48 and the difference is divided by $x + 3$, the result is 4. What is the value of x?

   (A) 2

   (B) 5

   (C) 6

   (D) 8

   (E) 12

   $48 - 2x = ?$

   $\dfrac{?}{x+3} = 4$

3. Depending on the cycle, washing a load of clothes takes from 22 to 28 minutes. Drying takes an additional 20 to 30 minutes. What are the minimum and maximum total times to complete a load of laundry?

   (A) 22 minutes and 28 minutes

   (B) 28 minutes and 48 minutes

   (C) 28 minutes and 58 minutes

   (D) 42 minutes and 48 minutes

   (E) 42 minutes and 58 minutes

GO ON TO THE NEXT PAGE

4. If $4(n + 6) = 44$, what is the value of n?

(A) $\dfrac{25}{2}$

(B) $\dfrac{19}{2}$

(C) 11

(D) 5

(E) 50

5. The planet Caleb makes one complete rotation on its axis every 36 hours. If it turns at a constant rate, through how many degrees does any point on Caleb except the poles rotate from 9 A.M. January 14th to 9 P.M. January 17th?

(A) 480

(B) 720

(C) 840

(D) 900

(E) 1080

6. For any positive odd integer n, how many positive even integers are less than n?

(A) $\dfrac{n - 1}{2}$

(B) $\dfrac{n}{2}$

(C) $\dfrac{n + 1}{2}$

(D) $n - 1$

(E) $2n - 1$

7. If $5 = m^x$, then $5m =$

(A) $m^{x + 1}$

(B) $m^{x + 2}$

(C) $m^{x + 5}$

(D) m^{5x}

(E) m^{2x}

8. If $\dfrac{p + q}{s} = 9$, $\dfrac{q}{p} = 4$, and $\sqrt{q} = 6$, what is the value of s?

(A) $\dfrac{5}{6}$

(B) 5

(C) 9

(D) 13

(E) 36

9. What is the equation of the line that passes through the points $(3, 4)$ and $(-1, 5)$?

(A) $x + 4y = 19$

(B) $3x + 4y = 19$

(C) $3x + 4y = 20$

(D) $4x + y = 19$

(E) $4x + y = 20$

10. If $f(x) = \dfrac{x^3 - 6}{x^2 - 2x + 6}$, then what is $f(6)$?

(A) 0

(B) 3

(C) 6

(D) 7

(E) 35

11. If $3^5 = x$, which of the following expressions is equal to 3^{11}?

(A) $243x$

(B) $3x^2$

(C) $9x^4$

(D) $27x^3$

(E) x^6

GO ON TO THE NEXT PAGE

12. If the average (arithmetic mean) of 7 numbers is greater than 7 and less than 12, which of the following could be the sum of the 7 numbers?

    (A) 84
    (B) 77
    (C) 49
    (D) 42
    (E) 35

13. If k and s are positive integers and the ratio of $2k$ to $6s$ is the same as the ratio of $6k + 5$ to $18s + 10$, which of the following must be true?

    I. $k = s$
    II. $k = 1.5$
    III. $k = 1.5s$

    (A) None
    (B) I only
    (C) II only
    (D) III only
    (E) I and II

14. For all u and v, let ∇ be defined by $u \nabla v = u - v + 2$. What is the value of $(2\nabla 3)\nabla 1$?

    (A) 0
    (B) 1
    (C) 2
    (D) 3
    (E) 4

15. If $a < b < 0 < c$ which of the following must be true?

    I. $-b > -a$
    II. $a + c < b + c$
    III. $a + b < c$

    (A) I only
    (B) II only
    (C) III only
    (D) II and III only
    (E) I, II and III

16. The value of $3x + 9$ is how much more than the value of $3x - 2$?

    (A) 7
    (B) 11
    (C) $3x + 7$
    (D) $3x + 11$
    (E) $6x + 7$

17. If $r = -2$ and $s = 5$, what is the value of $r^2(2r + s)$?

    (A) −36
    (B) −28
    (C) −4
    (D) 4
    (E) 36

GO ON TO THE NEXT PAGE

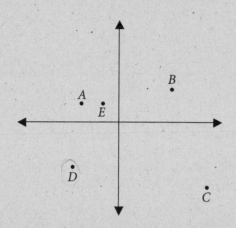

18. In the figure above, for which point is the product of its x and y coordinates the least value?

    (A) A
    (B) B
    (C) C
    (D) D
    (E) E

19. If $a = 3n + 4$ and $b = 7 + 9n^2$, what is b in terms of a?

    (A) $a^2 + 8a + 23$
    (B) $a^2 - 8a + 23$
    (C) $9a^2 - 108a + 144$
    (D) $9a^2 - 108a + 148$
    (E) $9a^2 + 108a + 148$

20. What is the greatest number of pieces that can result from slicing a spherical orange with 3 straight cuts?

    (A) 5
    (B) 6
    (C) 7
    (D) 8
    (E) 9

IF YOU FINISH BEFORE TIME IS CALLED, YOU MAY CHECK YOUR WORK ON THIS SECTION ONLY. DO NOT TURN TO ANY OTHER SECTION IN THE TEST.

STOP

SECTION 4
Time—25 Minutes
35 Questions

Directions: For each question in this section, select the best answer from among the choices given and fill in the corresponding oval on the answer sheet.

The following sentences test correctness and effectiveness of expression. Part of each sentence or the entire sentence is underlined; beneath each sentence are five ways of phrasing the underlined material. Choice (A) repeats the original phrasing; the other four choices are different. If you think the original phrasing produces a better sentence than any of the alternatives, select choice (A); if not, select one of the other choices.

In making your selection, follow the requirements of standard written English; that is, pay attention to grammar, choice of words, sentence construction, and punctuation. Your selection should result in the most effective sentence—clear and precise, without awkwardness or ambiguity.

EXAMPLE:

Every apple in the baskets <u>are ripe and labeled according to the date it was picked</u>.

ANSWER:
Ⓐ ● Ⓒ Ⓓ Ⓔ

(A) are ripe and labeled according to the date it was picked
(B) is ripe and labeled according to the date it was picked
(C) are ripe and labeled according to the date they were picked
(D) is ripe and labeled according to the date they were picked
(E) are ripe and labeled as to the date it was picked

---

1. Some speedometers register <u>high speeds as</u> two hundred miles per hour, even though few cars will ever go faster than one hundred.

   (A) high speeds as
   (B) speeds as high as
   (C) speeds that are high
   (D) high speeds that are capable of exceeding
   (E) a speed as

2. In past years, more students from Michigan attended Ann Arbor universities than <u>New York City</u>.

   (A) New York City
   (B) New York City did
   (C) compared to New York City's
   (D) New York City's ones
   (E) those in New York City

3. The Lions, a strong offensive team, compete against the <u>Cowboys, they play</u> tough defense.

   (A) Cowboys, they play
   (B) Cowboys, who play
   (C) Cowboys, having played
   (D) Cowboys; playing
   (E) Cowboys; for playing

GO ON TO THE NEXT PAGE ⟩

4. The major complaints professors have about teaching <u>is that they have challenging research to complete and must also work hard to</u> hold student interest.

   (A) is that they have challenging research to complete and must also work hard to

   (B) are challenging research and they must also work hard to

   (C) are that they have challenging research to complete and must also work hard to

   (D) is having challenging research and having also to work hard to

   (E) are challenging research, in addition to working hard to

5. <u>Returning to work after a long and relaxing vacation, the office seemed duller to Boris</u> than it had been before he left.

   (A) Returning to work after a long and relaxing vacation, the office seemed duller to Boris

   (B) Having returned to work after a long and relaxing vacation, it seemed a much duller office to Boris

   (C) When Boris returned to work after a long and relaxing vacation, the office seems much duller

   (D) Boris returned to work after a long and relaxing vacation, the office was seemingly much duller

   (E) When Boris returned to work after a long and relaxing vacation, the office seemed much duller to him

6. <u>Having achieved fame, widespread acclaim, as well as continued relevance</u>, *Doctor Strangelove* is considered to be a classic American movie.

   (A) Having achieved fame, widespread acclaim, as well as continued relevance

   (B) Having achieved fame, widespread acclaim, and its continued relevance

   (C) By achieving fame, widespread acclaim, and also continued relevance

   (D) With its achievement of fame, widespread acclaim, and being continually relevant

   (E) Having achieved fame, widespread acclaim, and continued relevance

7. Phillip Carey switched careers many times in his life, <u>switching first from accounting to painting, then eventually to medicine from that</u>.

   (A) switching first from accounting to painting, then eventually to medicine from that

   (B) he switched first from accounting to painting, then eventually to medicine

   (C) first from accounting to painting, and eventually to medicine

   (D) switching first from accounting to painting and eventually to medicine

   (E) from accounting he switched to painting and eventually ended up in medicine

GO ON TO THE NEXT PAGE

8. Efficient work is not the same as fast work, <u>for efficiency implies a level of quality that mere speed does not.</u>

    (A) for efficiency implies a level of quality that mere speed does not

    (B) since you must have a certain quality for efficient work while the same is not true about speed

    (C) for efficiency implied a level of quality that mere speed did not

    (D) for efficiency implying a level of quality that mere speed does not

    (E) for implied by efficiency is a level of quality that mere speed does not have

9. In the city, by just walking outside or taking the subway, <u>new people and events can be seen.</u>

    (A) new people and events can be seen

    (B) seeing new people and events

    (C) new people and events being seen

    (D) one can see new people and events

    (E) it is new people and events that can be seen

10. Some fans believe that in the next Olympics <u>Michael Phelps will not only win seven gold swimming medals, but also many world records will be claimed.</u>

    (A) Michael Phelps will not only win seven gold swimming medals, but also many world records will be claimed

    (B) Michael Phelps will win not only seven gold swimming medals, but will claim many world records as well

    (C) Michael Phelps will not only win seven gold swimming medals but also claim many world records

    (D) Michael Phelps will not only win seven gold swimming medals, but claim many world records in addition

    (E) Michael Phelps will not only win seven gold swimming medals, but he will claim many world records also

11. Hauling the laundry basket up the fifth flight of stairs, <u>exhaustion forced Maria to stop and sit down</u> on the landing for a moment.

    (A) exhaustion forced Maria to stop and sit down

    (B) exhaustion was what forced Maria to stop and sit down

    (C) it was exhaustion that forced Maria to stop and sit down

    (D) Maria, forced by exhaustion to stop and sit down

    (E) Maria was forced by exhaustion to stop and sit down

GO ON TO THE NEXT PAGE

Directions: The following sentences test your ability to recognize grammar and usage errors. Each sentence contains either a single error or no error at all. No sentence contains more than one error. The error, if there is one, is underlined and lettered. If the sentence contains an error, select the one underlined part that must be changed to make the sentence correct. If the sentence is correct, select choice (E). In choosing answers, follow the requirements of standard written English.

EXAMPLE:

<u>Whenever</u> one is driving late at night, <u>you</u> must take extra precautions <u>against</u>
   A   B   C

falling asleep <u>at the wheel</u>. <u>No error</u>
             D   E   Ⓐ ● Ⓒ Ⓓ Ⓔ

12. Yoni would have been able <u>to avoid</u> the <u>extreme</u>
                            A   B

    cold air of the Montana winter morning if he

    <u>had awoken</u> <u>later</u>. <u>No error</u>
       C   D   E

13. At breakfast, Dad asked <u>Hilary and I</u> if we <u>wanted</u>
                           A   B

    to attend <u>my cousin Noah's</u> university graduation
                  C

    ceremony in Nebraska <u>next spring</u>. <u>No error</u>
                       D   E

14. <u>Outside the barn,</u> a commotion <u>involving</u> three
        A   B

    hens and a rooster <u>woke</u> the twins, who were
                   C

    sleeping <u>deep</u>. <u>No error</u>
          D   E

15. Thomas <u>was</u> so proud of his <u>younger</u> brother,
          A   B

    who <u>was graduating</u> <u>from</u> college last month.
           C   D

    <u>No error</u>
      E

16. <u>When</u> we <u>looked</u> at the photograph of the
     A   B

    lightning bolt hitting the tree we noticed a

    <u>more smaller</u> bolt of electricity also <u>emanating</u>
       C   D

    from the ground. <u>No error</u>
                 E

17. <u>When Shirin Abadi <u>was awarded</u> the Nobel Peace
    A   B

    Prize many of her colleagues <u>praised</u> her
                          C

    exceptional efforts <u>about</u> democracy and human
                   D

    rights in Iran. <u>No error</u>
             E

18. Although the San Francisco Earthquake in the

    spring of 1906 <u>was leveling</u> many buildings, <u>it</u> was
        A   B   C

    the subsequent series of fires that <u>destroyed</u> most
                              D

    of the city. <u>No error</u>
            E

GO ON TO THE NEXT PAGE

KAPLAN
Test Prep and Admissions

19. The great blue heron, perhaps the most elegant

    species among birds, <u>live</u> in <u>most</u> parts of the
            A   B

    United States, <u>at home</u> in wetland habitats in <u>both</u>
            C   D

    inland and coastal regions. <u>No error</u>
                      E

20. The cake recipe <u>called for</u> sugar, <u>and</u> Chad used a
              A   B

    sugar substitute instead <u>since</u> he wanted to <u>lower</u>
                   C   D

    the cake's calorie count. <u>No error</u>
                    E

21. <u>They</u> were relieved <u>when</u> monsoons <u>carried</u> rain
     A   B   C

    from the southern seas <u>and</u> replenished India's
                   D

    drought-stricken water supply. <u>No error</u>
                      E

22. <u>Because of</u> their identical appearance and dress, the
     A

    twins <u>were</u> often mistaken for each other, <u>but</u> Mary
        B   C

    had <u>the more</u> vivacious personality. <u>No error</u>
       D   E

23. Because the tree fungus is <u>so great a</u> danger to local
                   A

    oak trees, it <u>has become</u> the concern of regional
           B

    botanists <u>to uncover</u> new ways of controlling <u>their</u>
          C   D

    growth. <u>No error</u>
         E

24. In an attempt <u>at drawing</u> a larger number
             A

    <u>of young fans</u> to the daytime games <u>at the ballpark</u>,
       B   C

    the baseball manager <u>provided</u>
                  D

    free hot dogs this season. <u>No error</u>
                      E

25. <u>Although</u> Luther Burbank <u>conducted</u> experiments
      A   B

    that led to many new or improved plants, <u>such as</u>
                              C

    the blight-resistant potato, his attempt <u>to develop</u> a
                           D

    spineless cactus was not a success. <u>No error</u>
                          E

26. The candidate, John Kallan, is of an <u>undetermined</u>
                                A

    age, <u>and</u> he <u>uses</u> this ambiguity <u>to</u> his benefit.
        B   C   D

    <u>No error</u>
      E

27. Studies indicate that the environment in schools

    <u>where</u> there are <u>less</u> adults on staff <u>is</u> often not
     A   B   C

    conducive <u>to</u> learning. <u>No error</u>
           D   E

GO ON TO THE NEXT PAGE ▷

KAPLAN
Test Prep and Admissions

28. Concerned <u>about</u> the playoff game <u>on</u> Saturday,
        A   B
    each of the team members <u>spent</u> most of the week
                                C
    practicing <u>their</u> plays. <u>No error</u>
               D   E

29. Although fair, the new law <u>requiring</u> seat belts in
                                    A
    the front and back seats <u>have</u> somewhat harsh
                                B
    <u>repercussions for</u> drivers and passengers <u>alike</u>.
         C   D
    <u>No error</u>
        E

GO ON TO THE NEXT PAGE

> **Directions:** The following passage is an early draft of an essay. Some parts of the passage need to be rewritten.
>
> Read the passage and select the best answer for each question that follows. Some questions are about particular sentences or parts of sentences and ask you to improve sentence structure or word choice. Other questions ask you to consider organization and development. In choosing answers, follow the conventions of standard written English.

Questions 30–35 are based on the following passage.

(1) Today, microwaves are used for many purposes: long distance telephone calls, television programming, even communications between Earth and objects in space. (2) But the microwave is probably most familiar to us as an energy source for cooking food. (3) Since their accidental invention fifty years ago, microwave ovens have become standard equipment in American homes.

(4) Despite their familiarity, some have claimed that microwave cooking has a negative effect on human health. (5) A Swiss researcher found that nutrients in food cooked in microwave ovens had been changed. (6) Potentially harmful changes were identified in the blood of research participants who had consumed food or drink cooked in a microwave. (7) The balance between good and bad cholesterol changes for the worse, and the number of white blood cells decreases in the short term.

(8) These claims are not only unfortunate, they frighten consumers unduly. (9) Much evidence exists to indicate that these claims are simply wrong. (10) When a microwave oven's power is switched off, microwaves cease to exist and do not remain in food after cooking. (11) Perhaps most significantly, experts in the medical community has concluded that the results of the Swiss study and others of its kind are not relevant to food cooked in microwave ovens and eaten by domestic consumers.

30. The sentence that best states the main idea of the passage is

    (A) sentence 1

    (B) sentence 4

    (C) sentence 6

    (D) sentence 9

    (E) sentence 10

31. Which of the following sentences is best inserted at the end of the first paragraph, after sentence 3?

    (A) An estimated ninety percent of American homes have them, indicating that microwaves are an indispensable tool for most cooks.

    (B) The fact that the government allows them to be sold makes it clear that microwaves are safe for cooking food for human consumption.

    (C) Families who use microwave ovens, however, tend not to use long distance and television programming services that use microwaves due to the possible negative impact of these services on health.

    (D) I'd like now to tell you the reasons users of microwave ovens for meal preparation are putting their families at risk of receiving a large dose of radiation.

    (E) Many are unaware that a microwave oven can reduce cooking time, making it possible for families to engage in other activities, such as calling faraway friends and watching television.

32. In context, which revision is needed in sentence 4?

    (A) Replace "Despite" with "Because of."

    (B) Replace "their" with "its."

    (C) Replace "have" with "has."

    (D) Replace "have" with "had."

    (E) Replace "effect" with "affect."

GO ON TO THE NEXT PAGE ⟩

33. In context, which revision is needed in sentence 7?

   (A) Insert "On the contrary" at the beginning.

   (B) Omit "the number of."

   (C) Omit "for the worse."

   (D) Change the comma to a semicolon.

   (E) Change "changes" to "changed" and "decreases" to "decreased."

34. In context, what is the best version of the underlined portion of sentence 8 (reproduced below)?

   These claims are not only <u>unfortunate, they frighten consumers unduly</u>.

   (A) (As it is now)

   (B) unfortunate; they frighten consumers unduly

   (C) unfortunate, but also frighten consumers unduly

   (D) unfortunate, they also frighten consumers unduly

   (E) unfortunate, but they frighten consumers unduly

35. In context, which revision is needed in sentence 11?

   (A) No revision is necessary.

   (B) Change "significantly" to "significant".

   (C) Change "has concluded" to "have concluded."

   (D) Change "are not relevant" to "is not relevant."

   (E) Change "eaten" to "ate."

IF YOU FINISH BEFORE TIME IS CALLED, YOU MAY CHECK YOUR WORK ON THIS SECTION ONLY. DO NOT TURN TO ANY OTHER SECTION IN THE TEST.

STOP

Test Prep and Admissions

SECTION 5
Time—25 Minutes
18 Questions

Directions: For this section, solve each problem and decide which is the best of the choices given. Fill in the corresponding oval on the answer sheet. You may use any available space for scratchwork.

Notes:

(1) Calculator use is permitted.

(2) All numbers used are real numbers.

(3) Figures are provided for some problems. All figures are drawn to scale and lie in a plane UNLESS otherwise indicated.

(4) Unless otherwise specified, the domain of any function f is assumed to be the set of all real numbers x for which $f(x)$ is a real number.

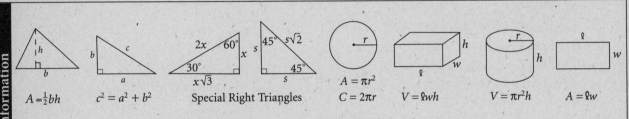

$A = \frac{1}{2}bh$ $c^2 = a^2 + b^2$ Special Right Triangles $C = 2\pi r$ $V = \ell wh$ $V = \pi r^2 h$ $A = \ell w$

The sum of the degree measures of the angles in a triangle is 180.
The number of degrees of arc in a circle is 360.
A straight angle has a degree measure of 180.

1. If $|5x + 15| = 10$, then x could equal

   (A) 1 and 5
   (B) −1 and 5
   (C) −1 and −5
   (D) −1
   (E) −5

2. If $(.0013)x = 0.013$, then $x =$

   (A) .01
   (B) .1
   (C) 1
   (D) 10
   (E) 100

3. If $\frac{a}{b} = 8$ and $\frac{a}{c} = 4$ then what does c equal if $b = 2$?

   (A) 2
   (B) 4
   (C) 8
   (D) 10
   (E) 16

4. Points J, K, and L lie on a circle whose center is point O. If $\overline{JK}$ passes through O, which of the following is true about triangle LOK?

   (A) All three angles are less than 90°
   (B) One angle measures exactly 90°
   (C) At least one angle is greater than 90°
   (D) At least two of the angles have the same measure
   (E) $KO = KL$

GO ON TO THE NEXT PAGE

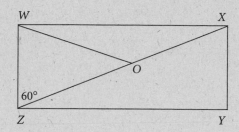

5. In the figure above, *WXYZ* is a rectangle. Point *O* is the midpoint of the diagonal $\overline{XZ}$. What is the measure of $\angle WOX$?

(A) 30°
(B) 60°
(C) 90°
(D) 120°
(E) 150°

6. Let *x* represent the average (arithmetic mean) of a list of test scores. What is the result of multiplying *x* by the number of scores?

(A) the average of the scores
(B) the highest score
(C) the number of scores
(D) the number of possible scores
(E) the sum of the scores

7. The spare change on a dresser is composed of pennies, nickels, and dimes. If the ratio of pennies to nickels is 2:3 and the ratio of pennies to dimes is 3:4, what is the ratio of nickels to dimes?

(A) 9:8
(B) 5:7
(C) 4:5
(D) 3:4
(E) 2:3

8. Set *C* is made up of a series of consecutive integers whose sum is a positive even number. If the smallest number in the set is −2, what is the least possible number of integers that could be in the set?

(A) 4
(B) 5
(C) 6
(D) 7
(E) 8

GO ON TO THE NEXT PAGE

Directions: For Student-Produced Response questions 9–18, use the grids at the bottom of the answer sheet page on which you have answered questions 1–8.

Each of the remaining 10 questions requires you to solve the problem and enter your answer by marking the ovals in the special grid, as shown in the example below. You may use any available space for scratch work.

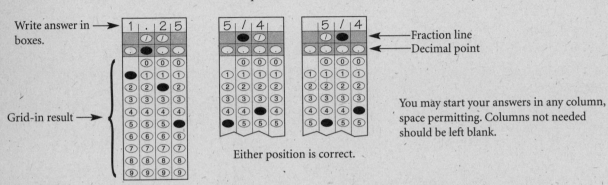

Answer: 1.25 or $\frac{5}{4}$ or 5/4

Write answer in boxes.

Grid-in result

Fraction line
Decimal point

You may start your answers in any column, space permitting. Columns not needed should be left blank.

Either position is correct.

- It is recommended, though not required, that you write your answer in the boxes at the top of the columns. However, you will receive credit only for darkening the ovals correctly.

- Grid only one answer to a question, even though some problems have more than one correct answer.

- Darken no more than one oval in a column.

- No answers are negative.

- Mixed numbers cannot be gridded. For example: the number $1\frac{1}{4}$ must be gridded as 1.25 or 5/4.

(If $1\ 1\ /\ 4$ is gridded, it will be interpreted as $\frac{11}{4}$ not $1\frac{1}{4}$.)

- Decimal Accuracy: Decimal answers must be entered as accurately as possible. For example, if you obtain an answer such as 0.1666..., you should record the result as .166 or .167. **Less accurate values such as .16 or .17 are not acceptable.**

Acceptable ways to grid $\frac{1}{6}$ = .1666...

GO ON TO THE NEXT PAGE

	Chairs with armrest	Chairs without armrests	Total
Blue	5,700		16,200
Green			3,800
Total		13,500	

9. The Comf-E Chair Corporation makes only blue and green chairs, either with or without armrests. Based on the chart above, how many green chairs with armrests did they sell in 2002?

10. If a is 30 percent of 400, b is 40 percent of a, and c is 25 percent of b, what is $a + b + c$?

11. If $\frac{q}{2} = \frac{7}{10}$, what is the value of q?

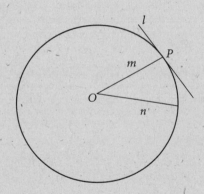

Note: Figure not drawn to scale.

12. Point O is the center of the circle in the figure above. Line l is tangent to circle O at point P. Line m intersects line l at point P. If the angle where l and n intersect (not shown) is 30°, and the distance from point O to the point where lines l and n intersect is 6, what is the radius of the circle?

13. If $\frac{2}{5}$ of $\frac{1}{2}$ is added to 5, what is the resulting value?

14. In a survey of 1,200 people, one question asked was "How many hours do you spend commuting to work?" All but 100 people surveyed responded to the question. If $n =$ the number of hours spent commuting, how many respondents have a commute greater than .5 hours?

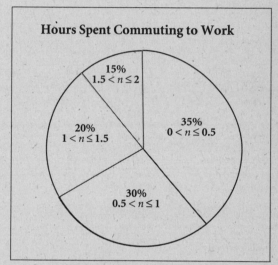

Note: Figure not drawn to scale.

GO ON TO THE NEXT PAGE

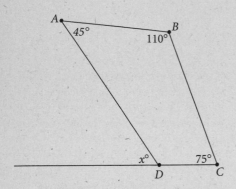

Note: Figure not drawn to scale

15. What is the value of *x* in the figure above?

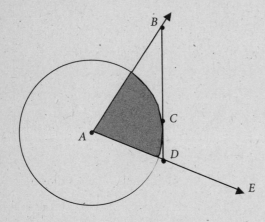

Note: Figure not drawn to scale

16. In the figure above, $\overline{BD}$ is tangent to circle *A* at point *C* and $m\angle ABD = 25°$. The area of the shaded portion is exactly $\frac{1}{4}$ the area of circle *A*. What is $\angle CDE$ in degrees?

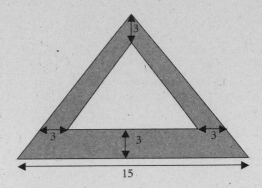

Note: Figure not drawn to scale

17. In the figure above, the area of the shaded region is 75 square units. What is the height of the smaller triangle?

18. The total cost of a car rental is the sum of

(1) A basic fixed rental charge for the car, and

(2) An additional charge for every 25 miles traveled.

If the total cost to rent a car and drive it 50 miles is $200 and the total cost to rent a car and drive it 200 miles is $245, what is the total cost, in dollars to rent a car and travel 450 miles?

(Disregard the $ sign when gridding your answer. If, for example, you answer is $1.37, grid 1.37.)

SECTION 6

Time—25 Minutes
24 Questions

Directions: For each of the following questions, choose the best answer and darken the corresponding oval on the answer sheet.

Each sentence below has one or two blanks, each blank indicating that something has been omitted. Beneath the sentence are five words or sets of words labeled (A) through (E). Choose the word or set of words that, when inserted in the sentence, <u>best</u> fits the meaning of the sentence as a whole.

EXAMPLE:

Today's small, portable computers contrast markedly with the earliest electronic computers, which were ----.

(A) effective
(B) invented
(C) useful
(D) destructive
(E) enormous

---

1. When a baby first learns to walk he will generally walk cautiously, placing one foot ---- in front of the other while trying to find his balance.

   (A) heavily
   (B) clumsily
   (C) tentatively
   (D) confidently
   (E) languidly

2. The salesman showed off his latest acquisition to the eager crowd, claiming it was an amazing kitchen gadget with a ---- purpose; it could chop and seed a tomato.

   (A) foreign
   (B) literary
   (C) false
   (D) dual
   (E) direct

3. Many astrophysicists believe that the universe is infinite in size and that it will continue to expand quickly and ---- .

   (A) conclusively
   (B) precisely
   (C) periodically
   (D) indefinitely
   (E) occasionally

4. Trying to ---- about post-modern literature is not only ---- but also foolish, because it is a movement that encompasses many different styles and elements.

   (A) brag . . necessary
   (B) generalize . . difficult
   (C) complain . . important
   (D) rhapsodize . . fair
   (E) learn . . unproductive

GO ON TO THE NEXT PAGE

5. Even though the large computer company seems to have cornered the personal computer and software market, the CEO insists that his company has no ---- the industry.

   (A) interest in
   (B) misgivings about
   (C) monopoly on
   (D) responsibility in
   (E) consensus on

6. Because the lyrics of the Beatles weren't concerned with ---- subject matter, their music seems as ---- today as it did 40 years ago.

   (A) sagacious . . wise
   (B) dated . . quaint
   (C) evanescent . . nostalgic
   (D) transient . . fresh
   (E) momentary . . derivative

7. The young professional's boss praised her ---- nature and stated that she seemed to have an unconquerable positive spirit.

   (A) morose
   (B) opulent
   (C) indomitable
   (D) lithe
   (E) ephemeral

8. A male Green Anole lizard views his territory as ---- and often instigates confrontations with any male of his species that may wander within its boundaries.

   (A) dissipated
   (B) circuitous
   (C) unparalleled
   (D) inviolable
   (E) mandated

GO ON TO THE NEXT PAGE

Questions 9–10 are based on the following passage.

Over the centuries, rice has sculpted much of Chinese culture. In countless folktales, rice is enjoyed by gods and mortals alike, and it is considered by many to be the only grain that can link
(5) the heavens with the earth. Such beliefs have inspired numerous festivals, traditions, and rituals, many of which are nearly requisite occurrences wherever rice crops are planted. The green, terraced patties that cultivate this grain often hold
(10) a spiritual significance, even among those for whom rice is an everyday sight and source of sustenance. And although its effectiveness is not scientifically proven, rice is believed by some to have powerful medicinal properties.

9. The author uses the word "sculpted" (line 1) in order to

(A) imply that rice quite suddenly altered Chinese culture when it was first planted

(B) indicate that Chinese culture was resistant to change

(C) state that it took a great deal of work to change Chinese culture

(D) emphasize just how important rice is as a source of sustenance

(E) suggest that Chinese culture was shaped over time by its relationship with rice

10. The purpose of mentioning that the medicinal properties of rice are "not scientifically proven" (line 12–13) is to

(A) criticize those who use rice for medicinal purposes

(B) imply that the medicinal properties of rice have not yet been scientifically tested

(C) reiterate the author's point that the usefulness of rice is exaggerated in China

(D) emphasize the passage's primary focus on beliefs about rice

(E) suggest that scientific proof is not always important

GO ON TO THE NEXT PAGE

Questions 11–12 are based on the following passage.

The following is adapted from an article about the increasing demand for public transportation as America's elderly population grows.

America may be facing a transportation crisis as the remarkably populous post-World War II generation begins to approach the age of 65, a milestone many transportation researchers cite as
(5) a time when it is advisable for some drivers to begin abandoning the luxury of private cars for the safety of public transportation. According to some statistics, each year hundreds of thousands of older people who have outlived their ability or
(10) willingness to drive must depend on alternative transportation systems that, outside of the nation's most urbanized communities, are usually unable to meet their needs. This gap between driving expectancy and life expectancy has placed signifi-
(15) cant and usually unforeseen economic and social burdens on many seniors.

11. In line 13–14, "driving expectancy" most nearly refers to

(A) the age at which most people decide to give up their cars

(B) the number of seniors that expect to use public transportation

(C) the number of years that a person can be expected to drive

(D) the year transportation researches believe a crisis will begin

(E) the rapidly aging post-World War II generation

12. According to the passage, which of the following is a reason why America may soon be facing a transportation crisis?

(A) Some American cities have public transportation systems that can meet the needs of the elderly

(B) The post-World War II generation is large and will increasingly rely upon public transportation as it ages

(C) Researchers are increasingly advising seniors to abandon their cars for the safety of public transportation

(D) Many seniors are burdened by social and economic problems when they depend only upon public transportation

(E) Statistics indicate that life expectancies are rising while driving expectancies are falling

GO ON TO THE NEXT PAGE

Questions 13–24 are based on the following passages.

The following passages discuss recent changes in the way that museums in America construct their exhibits. Passage 1 is from a 2004 article by a museum critic. Passage 2 is adapted from a 2003 chapter by an educational researcher.

Passage 1

Modern museums are earnestly trying everything they can to shore up declining attendance. Somehow, there always seems to be some crisis that they are valiantly struggling against—a severe

(5) funding cut or building code renovations that are exceeding budget—and in the midst of it all, the unappreciative public is drifting farther and farther away. So museums do what they can to lure the people back, and the results are occasionally

(10) wonderful and occasionally laughable.

The worst of such results occurs when some condescending curator decides that the reason the audience isn't pouring through the doors is that the content is over their heads—that the history

(15) presented is too complex and political, the art is too obscure, or the scientific explanations too indepth. What occurs then is a uniform dumbing down of the exhibits. Content is explained rather than interpreted. Text is minimized, and histori-

(20) cally significant pieces are passed over in favor of those more aesthetically pleasing. The museum becomes a place where people go to look at pretty things instead of a temple to learning and understanding and appreciating different cultures, aes-

(25) thetics, and facets of the earth. Unnecessary and inexplicable "interactive" exhibits are introduced in which the hapless viewer is instructed to press various buttons for a predetermined result—the theory apparently being that the way to engage the

(30) public is to cater to those whose attention span does not exceed five or ten seconds.

All these efforts have given rise to the concept of "edutainment"—a hybrid in which learning is supposed to be accomplished without any effort

(35) at all on the part of the visitor. Displays are constructed with an eye toward their entertainment value, with relevant facts slipped slyly in, as though learning were a bitter pill that must be sugarcoated before the average museum visitor

(40) can be induced to swallow it. But true education is an active pursuit, not something one receives like a piece of candy from an automated dispenser. It requires a proactive inquiry on the part of the visitor. The museum's job should be to inspire the

(45) visitor to look deeper, not to force-feed them predigested facts.

Ultimately, if a museum becomes indistinguishable from a theme park, it has failed. Non-profit institutions exist because, if they did not, no for-

(50) profit institution would serve their function. The grail of the successful curator is to identify the missing resource—the thing not already provided to a citizen by movies, parks, or other entertaining commercial enterprise—and provide it. If active

(55) scholarship is missing, then by all means, supply it, instead of shaping the museum to resemble the successful entertainment enterprises already extant.

Passage 2

There is a particular brand of elitist, intellectual snobbery that is currently decrying the innovations

(60) being made in museum displays nationwide. It is the kind that believes that museums ought to be reserved for those who already know a great deal about the topic, whether it be eighteenth-century engineering, the Impressionist movement, or early

(65) Paleolithic society. These people prefer museums that house a bewildering array of artifacts that cater to the specialized scholar, and they deride any attempt to broaden the appeal of these exhibits as a "dumbing down" of the museum interface.

(70) This is a mistake. To broaden the audience of a museum's exhibit and make it accessible to a wide range of the populace is a worthy goal—and does not require "dumbing down" of material at all. In fact, in an effort to help audiences appreciate

(75) the more specialized exhibits, museums are working to "write upward" for their exhibits and to bring those who may not have studied a particular subject up to speed enough to appreciate and marvel at the contents of an exhibit. New concepts

(80) are presented in a digestible format that does not require condescension at all, but does present more information than before.

GO ON TO THE NEXT PAGE

The purpose of these exhibits is not to provide the viewer with a complex and thorough understand-
(85) ing of a particular phenomenon—there are whole college courses for that—but to introduce them to an area of knowledge that they have not been exposed to before and inspire them to want to learn more. Not only that, but the exhibits are pre-
(90) sented with nested layers of knowledge, footnotes and references and further reading, so that the portion of the audience that does have a background in the topic will have something new to chew on as well.

(95)   Improved understanding of different peoples' learning styles has led to entirely new exhibit types, such as the much-maligned interactive stations where viewers can participate in the quest for knowledge in a more active way. These
(100) exhibits, far from being passive learning tools, engage a visitor's kinesthetic sense to give information another path into the brain. These tools are meant to increase the value of the museum visit by providing a variety of experiences, not just
(105) passive viewing and label-reading, along the way. One exhibit might allow a visitor to operate an antique machine by proxy or allow the visitor to choose between different aspects of the exhibit that they wish to have more information about.

(110)   It's true that there may be a shift in the mission statement of the museum as we know it. Instead of providing specialized scholars with more and more arcane knowledge about their topic, museums are encouraging laymen and the generally
(115) educated to interact and to be inspired by things their minds have not encompassed before. These public institutions are heading in the right direction: to be more and more useful to—who else?—the public.

13. What would the authors of both passages probably agree is the main purpose of a museum?

(A) to inspire visitors to learn more about the topics on display

(B) to help visitors develop a complex and thorough understanding of relevant concepts

(C) to be a fun place to visit

(D) to raise funds to complete new exhibits

(E) to provide specialized scholars with in-depth research material

14. What does the author of Passage 1 claim is the cause of "the worst of such results" (line 11)?

(A) the decline in education of the visitors

(B) entertaining interactive displays

(C) a museum curator's belief that the museum content is too difficult for visitors to understand

(D) a museum curator who fails to understand that different people have different learning styles

(E) a decline in federal funding for museums

15. In Passage 1, "interactive" exhibits (line 26) are mentioned in order to provide an example of

(A) a way that museums have broadened their exhibits to appeal to different learning styles

(B) a way that museums have "dumbed down" their content

(C) a method for raising funds to forestall the current crisis in museums

(D) a tactic museums use to cater to specialized scholars

(E) the way that visitors have influenced the evolution of museum exhibits

GO ON TO THE NEXT PAGE

16. The author of Passage 1 probably believes that the effect of the "displays" (line 35) is to

   (A) make otherwise boring topics interesting to the average museum visitor
   (B) provide visitors with inaccurate information about the featured topics
   (C) engage those who learn kinesthetically
   (D) entertain without inspiring real learning
   (E) encourage visitors to return to the museum

17. Which of the following approaches to education is most similar to the approach described in paragraph 3 of Passage 1?

   (A) a funny cartoon that incorporates Newton's Laws of Motion
   (B) a biography of Napoleon
   (C) a plot-driven comic book
   (D) a discussion about the ethics of experimentation with animals
   (E) a database containing political statistics for every country in the world

18. In context, "house" (Passage 2, line 66) most nearly means

   (A) indwell
   (B) build
   (C) contain
   (D) domesticate
   (E) nurture

19. The word "digestible" in line 80 of Passage 2 supports the viewpoint that

   (A) making snack food available to visitors is an important innovation for museums
   (B) new museum exhibits should avoid controversial topics
   (C) new museum exhibits should present only summaries of the information a visitor needs to know to understand the exhibit
   (D) a layman museum visitor may understand a concept from a new museum exhibit with more ease than from a conventional museum exhibit
   (E) a wide range of people will appreciate the new exhibits

20. What does the author of Passage 2 suggest about "passive viewing and label-reading" (line 105)?

   (A) It is an effective way to help museum visitors learn
   (B) It is the primary innovation of forward-thinking museums
   (C) It is a way to increase the value of the museum visit
   (D) It is not to be found in newer and more innovative museums
   (E) It is the dominant exhibit format of traditional museums

GO ON TO THE NEXT PAGE

21. The author of Passage 2 might defend the "unnecessary and inexplicable 'interactive' exhibits" mentioned in lines 25–26 of Passage 1 by

   (A) arguing in favor of learning passively while being entertained

   (B) analyzing the relative popularity of these exhibits versus that of more traditional presentations

   (C) pointing out how inexpensive it is for museums to construct these exhibits

   (D) mentioning how little such exhibits are actually being used anyway

   (E) presenting the results of a study on the differing needs of people with different learning styles

22. The author of Passage 1 might criticize the "worthy goal" mentioned on line 72 of Passage 2 with the argument that

   (A) museums should attempt to engage the well-educated, not the layperson

   (B) it is too ambitious in a climate of funding cuts

   (C) there are more pressing matters for museums to attend to

   (D) museums have been going about accomplishing it in regrettable ways

   (E) curators lack the training to enact it

23. The author of Passage 1 would probably interpret the statement made in lines 83–85 of Passage 2 ("The purpose...particular phenomenon") as confirmation that

   (A) museums are not encouraging higher education in their visitors

   (B) new exhibits are not doing what curators have hoped they would

   (C) museum visitors must learn a significant amount of material before they understand a museum exhibit

   (D) new exhibits are incomprehensible to the average visitor

   (E) new exhibits have set lower standards for the understanding of museum visitors

24. Both authors would agree that the primary goal for museums should be

   (A) finding new funding for museums that lack it

   (B) catering to people of different learning styles

   (C) constructing exhibits that promote active learning in their visitors

   (D) constructing exhibits that are useful to specialized scholars

   (E) designing museum exhibits to be entertaining

IF YOU FINISH BEFORE TIME IS CALLED, YOU MAY CHECK YOUR WORK ON THIS SECTION ONLY. DO NOT TURN TO ANY OTHER SECTION IN THE TEST.

SECTION 7
Time—20 Minutes
16 Questions

Directions: For this section, solve each problem and decide which is the best of the choices given. Fill in the corresponding oval on the answer sheet. You may use any available space for scratchwork.

Notes:

(1) Calculator use is permitted.

(2) All numbers used are real numbers.

(3) Figures are provided for some problems. All figures are drawn to scale and lie in a plane UNLESS otherwise indicated.

(4) Unless otherwise specified, the domain of any function f is assumed to be the set of all real numbers x for which $f(x)$ is a real number.

Information

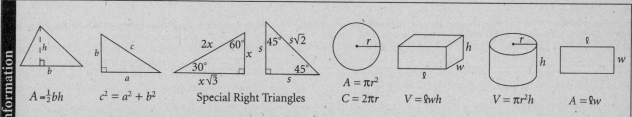

$A = \frac{1}{2}bh$ $c^2 = a^2 + b^2$ Special Right Triangles $A = \pi r^2$
$C = 2\pi r$ $V = \ell wh$ $V = \pi r^2 h$ $A = \ell w$

The sum of the degree measures of the angles in a triangle is 180.
The number of degrees of arc in a circle is 360.
A straight angle has a degree measure of 180.

1. The letter O is symmetric with respect to two different lines, as shown by the dotted lines in the figure above. Which of the following letters is symmetric with respect to at least two different lines?

(A) T
(B) S
(C) I
(D) A
(E) B

2. If you add some number j to 50, and then divide this sum by j, the result is 3. What is the value of j?

(A) 5
(B) 10
(C) 15
(D) 20
(E) 25

GO ON TO THE NEXT PAGE

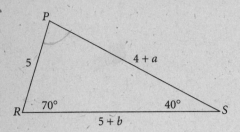

3. In the triangle above, which of the following must be true?

(A) $a = b$

(B) angle P = angle S

(C) $a < b$

(D) $a = b + 1$

(E) $a + 1 = b$

4. Which of the following represents the same value as 0.00326691?

(A) 3.26691×10^{-3}

(B) 3.26691×10^{-2}

(C) 3.26691×10^{-1}

(D) 32.6691×10^{-2}

(E) 32.6691×10^{-3}

5. If $x^{\frac{1}{2}} = 4$, then what is the value of x^2?

(A) $\frac{1}{2}$

(B) 2

(C) 4

(D) 16

(E) 256

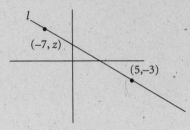

Note: Figure not drawn to scale.

6. In the figure above, the slope of line l is $-\frac{5}{12}$. What is the value of z?

(A) $\frac{1}{4}$

(B) $\frac{1}{2}$

(C) 1

(D) 2

(E) 4

7. While biking on a 50 mile path, Jerry averages 5 miles per hour for the first h hours. In terms of h, where $h < 10$, how many miles remain to be traveled?

(A) $\frac{50}{5h}$

(B) $50 - 5h$

(C) $250h$

(D) $50 - \frac{5}{h}$

(E) $5h - 50$

GO ON TO THE NEXT PAGE

8. At a certain school, if the ratio of teachers to students is 1 to 10, which of the following could be the total number of teachers and students?

   (A)   100
   (B)   121
   (C)   144
   (D)   222
   (E)   1,011

9. If $y > 0$, what is 60 percent of $20y$?

   (A) $1.2y$
   (B) $10y$
   (C) $12y$
   (D) $15y$
   (E) $120y$

10. In a certain neighborhood, the number of cats is inversely proportional to the number of dogs. At one point, there were 10 cats and 50 dogs in the neighborhood. If today there are 20 dogs in the neighborhood, how many cats are in the neighborhood?

   (A)   4
   (B)   8
   (C)   15
   (D)   20
   (E)   25

11. In a display consisting of one row of coins, there are an equal number of silver and gold coins. Which of the following must be true?

   (A) The first coin and the last coin are different types
   (B) There are two adjacent gold coins in a row
   (C) There are two adjacent silver coins in a row
   (D) If there are two adjacent silver coins, there are also two gold coins
   (E) If the last two coins are gold, there are at least two adjacent silver coins

12. If $x = -3$ and $y = 9$, what is the value of $|\sqrt[3]{xy} - y|$?

   (A) -12
   (B)   0
   (C)   6
   (D)   12
   (E)   36

GO ON TO THE NEXT PAGE

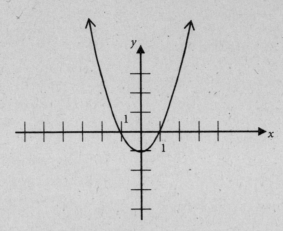

Note: Figure not drawn to scale.

13. If the figure above is the graph of $g(x)$, then which of the following is the graph of $g(x - 2)$?

(A)
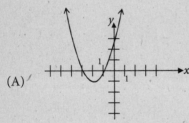

(D)
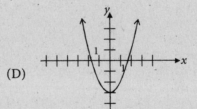

(B)

(E)
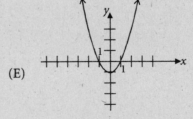

(C)
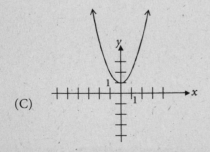

GO ON TO THE NEXT PAGE

14. After 6 new cars entered the parking lot and 2 cars left the parking lot, there were 2 times as many cars as before. How many cars were parked in the parking lot before the changes?

   (A) 2
   (B) 4
   (C) 6
   (D) 8
   (E) 10

15. Four students reach into a bag of coins. Steve grabs $\frac{1}{3}$ of the coins, Joe grabs $\frac{1}{4}$, and Kyle grabs $\frac{1}{6}$. If Ryan gets the remaining 6 coins, how many coins were originally in the bag?

   (A) 12
   (B) 18
   (C) 24
   (D) 27
   (E) 281

16. If $y = 2^{\frac{3}{4}}$, which of the following expressions is equal to 2^3?

   (A) 4
   (B) $4y$
   (C) $4y^2$
   (D) y^4
   (E) y^5

IF YOU FINISH BEFORE TIME IS CALLED, YOU MAY CHECK YOUR WORK ON THIS SECTION ONLY. DO NOT TURN TO ANY OTHER SECTION IN THE TEST.

STOP

SECTION 8

Time—20 Minutes
18 Questions

Directions: For each of the following questions, choose the best answer and darken the corresponding oval on the answer sheet.

Each sentence below has one or two blanks, each blank indicating that something has been omitted. Beneath the sentence are five words or sets of words labeled (A) through (E). Choose the word or set of words that, when inserted in the sentence, best fits the meaning of the sentence as a whole.

EXAMPLE:

Today's small, portable computers contrast markedly with the earliest electronic computers, which were ----.

(A) effective
(B) invented
(C) useful
(D) destructive
(E) enormous

---

1. The coach's clothes were ---- with water from the water cooler dumped over him by the victorious football team.

    (A) diverted
    (B) confined
    (C) scuttled
    (D) cleansed
    (E) drenched

2. As sea otters rely on air trapped in their fur to ---- warmth, oil spills can damage this fine fur and cause them to become ---- to the cold arctic waters.

    (A) insure . . inclined
    (B) maintain . . vulnerable
    (C) squander . . liable
    (D) stimulate . . resistant
    (E) retain . . immune

3. Henry David Thoreau found inspiration for his writing in the ---- woods of Walden Pond, where he immersed himself in nature rather than in the company of men.

    (A) sequestered
    (B) urbane
    (C) intrusive
    (D) luxurious
    (E) frugal

4. Despite U.S. efforts to provide the foreign country with the means to ---- the drug trade, the production and trafficking of cocaine and heroin continues to ---- as narcotics are still being smuggled across the border at an alarming rate.

    (A) cure . . flag
    (B) foster . . thrive
    (C) combat . . abate
    (D) scrutinize . . prosper
    (E) eradicate . . flourish

GO ON TO THE NEXT PAGE

5. The philosopher reasoned that paradoxically, ---- is harmonious because without dissonance there would be no learning from each other.

   (A) discord
   (B) corruption
   (C) injunction
   (D) collusion
   (E) diplomacy

6. ---- is a common theme in Greek tragedies and mythology, whose stories often featured protagonists suffering from exaggerated pride and subsequently being punished by the gods for it.

   (A) Obstinacy
   (B) Hubris
   (C) Impetuosity
   (D) Valor
   (E) Callousness

GO ON TO THE NEXT PAGE

Directions: The passages below are followed by questions based on their content; questions following a pair of related passages may also be based on the relationship between the paired passages. Answer the questions on the basis of what is <u>stated</u> or <u>implied</u> in the passages and in any introductory material that may be provided.

Questions 7–18 are based on the following passage.

In the following excerpt from an article, the author considers the new possibilities for information transfer made available by new communications technology, along with the accompanying notion that the more "virtual" interactions one has, the better.

In a culture in which email, cell phones, pagers, and Internet chat rooms have become everyday modes of communication, we are on the verge of breaking down all barriers to the complete and
(5) constant transfer of information. But if we seem to be moving toward unfettered union, we could also be seen as being more isolated as individuals than we have ever been before. As we entered what has come to be known as the "Information Age,"
(10) every new technological advance was touted as the solution to a myriad of problems. With more ways to pass along all types of information, the communications industry reasons, we will become more efficient at work, more in touch with distant
(15) family, and more likely to meet new people. With such expanded access to the world at large, we can only become more adept social animals.

Communications technology has now contributed, paradoxically but predictably (for to
(20) communicate across a distance at all first requires that there be a distance), to an actual lessening of live human contact in favor of interaction via electronics and satellite beams. Gradually but surely, a technology that was intended to bring
(25) people closer together is instead helping them drift apart, as shopping from home becomes easier than driving to the store and speaking with a clerk, as meeting people online in a chat room eliminates the need to be honest about one's
(30) physical and social flaws, and as faxing someone a blueprint gets rid of the necessity of meeting to discuss a plan. In place of real human interaction, we now have what might be called "virtual

relationships." In place of daily, neighborly com-
(35) munity building, we now have solitary convenience from the comfort—and isolation—of home.

"The right partner is waiting for you; what are you waiting for?" inquire the ads for a bumper crop of online dating services. "You state your
(40) requirements for the perfect mate, and we'll dig through our database of thousands [or hundreds of thousands] of singles to find you the ideal match." The ritual of dating, once relegated to awkward or uncertain meetings, blind dates, and
(45) vulnerable situations, is now simplified and sterilized for anyone with a high-speed Internet connection. On the platonic front services such as the widespread *Friendster* promise effortless ways to meet new friends by making electronic connec-
(50) tions with friends of friends and friends of friends of friends after viewing their picture and bare-bones "biography" online and reading "testimonials" from other friends eager to promote the people they like. It is a process not dissimilar to pur-
(55) chasing equipment from a catalogue—a picture, a brief description of the product, and quoted statements from happy customers who have found the product satisfactory.

Prevailing Internet culture shows no signs of
(60) slowing this trend toward the endless quest for human contact in a place where real human contact is actually impossible. As some people on their computers at home become more alienated from face-to-face human contact, they reach out
(65) more desperately for friendship in the only place they feel comfortable—online. Completely virtual communities gather at imaginary meeting places and have passionate debates and volatile relationships, and bits of information displayed on a
(70) screen acquire the significance necessary to elevate people to heights of emotion. Unfortunately, the fact that this communication is emanating from such distant participants has a real impact.

GO ON TO THE NEXT PAGE ⟶

There is much less social accountability
(75) demanded of one who says something awful in an
Internet chat room than of one who offends at a
party. Should one person be rude to another
online, the act seems nearly free of consequences—the offender needn't be subjected to the
(80) sight of the emotional discomfort they are causing, and since interactions online are usually
anonymous, he or she need take no responsibility
for their remark in any meaningful way. The effects
of this can be devastating, and "Internet bullies"
(85) are capable of wreaking enormous havoc among
younger, less socialized pockets of society, such as
high school students. In the wake of the first generation of Americans who have grown up knowing
the Internet, we are scrambling to redefine social
(90) behavior in a time when the meaning of "social"
has expanded to include interactions between
strangers who are potentially thousands of miles
apart in physical reality.

    We are surrounded by appeals to join the
(95) twenty-first century and high praise for new
advances in communications technology. But the
very technology that purports to make connections
and bring everyone closer together is offering only
a substitute, a false notion of tightly-knit commu-
(100) nity, that drives us out of one another's homes and
awareness. Enthusiasts of convenience overlook
these drawbacks and do not recognize the real,
human contact that is being replaced by a much
vaster and less personal network. They would have
(105) us interact more and more as virtual beings, effortlessly increasing the sheer number of interactions
without regard for their quality or duration.

7. The author's analysis of new communications
   technology supports the proposition that

   (A) only those with high-speed Internet connec-
       tions should have access to new technologies

   (B) the communications industry should be
       worried about profits, not improving
       relationships between people

   (C) today's high school students are less vulnera-
       ble than adults to the distancing effects of
       new technology

   (D) convenience is the most important criteria by
       which new technologies are judged

   (E) such technology should not be embraced
       without reservation

8. In line 3, "verge" most nearly means

   (A) joint
   (B) pinnacle
   (C) togetherness
   (D) brink
   (E) interest

9. The last sentence of the first paragraph (lines
   15–17) is intended to express the

   (A) best way of looking at the impact of new
       communications technology

   (B) belief that being social is beneficial to human
       psyches

   (C) way everybody thinks today about communi-
       cations technology

   (D) conception of new technology as endorsed by
       the communications industry

   (E) view of communications technology that
       people might take in the future

GO ON TO THE NEXT PAGE

10. Which of the following pairs best expresses the contrast between what the communications industry says is the role of new technology and what the author claims?

    (A) optimizer versus hindrance

    (B) dating revolution versus new social community

    (C) financial failure versus untapped gold mine

    (D) uniter versus divider

    (E) progress versus regression

11. The ads for online dating services (lines 37–43) are cited in order to

    (A) persuade readers to use the services

    (B) provide a positive counterexample to the author's argument

    (C) provide an example of the way new technology is changing the way we conduct social interaction

    (D) illustrate the awkwardness of dating before Internet services existed

    (E) contrast the mission of dating services with the fundamentally different service *Friendster*

12. According to the passage, one reason that there is less social accountability for comments made in an Internet chat room is that

    (A) words sent via the Internet have less impact than spoken words

    (B) the person commenting doesn't see a negative reaction from the person affected

    (C) the level of convenience achieved is perceived as more important than personal concerns

    (D) companies that host such chat rooms are only interested in profits

    (E) all chat room participants are isolated individuals

13. The author implies that "enthusiasts of convenience" (line 101) are people who

    (A) emphasize quantity over quality in their reasoning

    (B) are completely isolated

    (C) utilize online dating services

    (D) are interested in improving human interaction

    (E) disagree with the communication industry

14. The reference to "faxing someone a blueprint" (lines 30–31) is used to illustrate the

    (A) ways in which more advanced technology can reduce human interaction

    (B) increase in efficiency that new communications technologies foster

    (C) superiority of the fax machine over email

    (D) reduced social accountability of electronic interaction

    (E) importance of new technologies to the construction industry

15. The author's attitude toward the belief that new technology is bringing us closer together as human beings is one of

    (A) enthusiastic appreciation

    (B) firm opposition

    (C) snide contempt

    (D) wary disbelief

    (E) neutral analysis

GO ON TO THE NEXT PAGE

16. The author's analysis of the effects of new communications technology is most weakened by a failure to explore the

    (A) positive interactions made possible by, and not replaced by, the new technology
    (B) practical benefits of the fax machine
    (C) point of view of those who use *Friendster*
    (D) dangers of carpal tunnel and other long-term injuries stemming from use of new technology
    (E) differences between cellular and Internet communications technology

17. The author implies that the "virtual relationships" (lines 33–34) we are now forming have the effect of

    (A) decreasing peoples' need for face-to-face relationships
    (B) making people into more beneficially social animals
    (C) giving people more time for other tasks
    (D) causing psychological damage
    (E) taking time and energy away from forming face-to-face relationships

18. It can be inferred from the passage that in place of live community-building, the new communications technology is substituting

    (A) online shopping
    (B) fax machines
    (C) anonymous interaction
    (D) dating services
    (E) Internet bullies

SECTION 9

Time—10 Minutes
14 Questions

Directions: For each question in this section, select the best answer from among the choices given and fill in the corresponding oval on the answer sheet.

The following sentences test correctness and effectiveness of expression. Part of each sentence or the entire sentence is underlined; beneath each sentence are five ways of phrasing the underlined material. Choice (A) repeats the original phrasing; the other four choices are different. If you think the original phrasing produces a better sentence than any of the alternatives, select choice (A); if not, select one of the other choices.

In making your selection, follow the requirements of standard written English; that is, pay attention to grammar, choice of words, sentence construction, and punctuation. Your selection should result in the most effective sentence—clear and precise, without awkwardness or ambiguity.

EXAMPLE: ANSWER:

Every apple in the baskets <u>are ripe and labeled according to the date it was picked</u>.   Ⓐ ● Ⓒ Ⓓ Ⓔ

(A) are ripe and labeled according to the date it was picked
(B) is ripe and labeled according to the date it was picked
(C) are ripe and labeled according to the date they were picked
(D) is ripe and labeled according to the date they were picked
(E) are ripe and labeled as to the date it was picked

---

1. <u>For as many as nine months or more,</u> Thad Carthart lived in Paris.

   (A) For as many as nine months or more
   (B) For not much more than about nine months
   (C) For a little over nine months and more
   (D) For nine months and then some
   (E) For more than nine months

2. The daily responsibilities of a law student are often as strenuous <u>as a medical student</u>.

   (A) as a medical student
   (B) as those of a medical student
   (C) like a medical student
   (D) such as a medical student
   (E) like a medical student's

3. This year's high school tennis championships, held in Nebraska, were won by a Michigan team from <u>Grand Rapids, and there were six Grand Rapids triumphs and no losses</u>.

   (A) Grand Rapids, and there were six Grand Rapids triumphs and no losses
   (B) Grand Rapids, which had six triumphs and no losses
   (C) Grand Rapids, having six triumphs and with no losses
   (D) Grand Rapids, which was triumphant six times and no losses
   (E) Grand Rapids; it was won by six triumphs and no losses

GO ON TO THE NEXT PAGE

4. Like most foreigners, <u>the city's local customs baffled the Greg</u> for a few days.

    (A) the city's local customs baffled the Greg
    (B) the local customs of the city baffling Greg
    (C) Greg was baffled by the city's local customs
    (D) Greg, who found the city's local customs baffling
    (E) there were local customs in the city which confused Greg

5. D.H. Lawrence, one of the most prolific novelists of his <u>time, writing more than 40 volumes of fiction, poetry, and drama from 1911 to 1930</u>.

    (A) time, writing more than 40 volumes of fiction, poetry, and drama from 1911 to 1930
    (B) time, writing more than 40 volumes, which he wrote from 1911 to 1930 in the areas of fiction, poetry, and drama
    (C) time, and he wrote more than 40 volumes of fiction, poetry, and drama from 1911 to 1930
    (D) time, wrote more than 40 volumes of fiction, poetry, and drama from 1911 to 1930
    (E) time, his fiction, poetry, and drama amounting to more than 40 volumes from 1911 to 1930

6. <u>The more you run at high altitudes</u>, the more our bodies and lungs will acclimate to changing elevations.

    (A) The more you run at high altitudes
    (B) The more we run at high altitudes
    (C) The more high altitudes run
    (D) As the running at high altitudes increases
    (E) As people run more at high altitudes

7. Universities today offer <u>a large number of courses, and it has</u> improved the quality of education.

    (A) a large number of courses, and it has
    (B) a great deal of courses, and that is
    (C) so many courses; it is, therefore
    (D) so many courses that they have
    (E) so many courses, which they have been

8. Classic cinema, such as the French new wave films or the movies of Stanley Kubrick, remains important <u>by their speaking personally and creatively</u> to each generation of film buffs.

    (A) by their speaking personally and creatively
    (B) by its speaking personal and creative
    (C) because it speaks personally and creatively
    (D) because of speaking personal and creative
    (E) since they speak with personality and creativeness

9. A policeman was sent out to verify <u>the claiming of a witness's that</u> he had found the murder weapon on his street.

    (A) the claiming of a witness's that
    (B) a witness's claim that
    (C) the claiming of a witness
    (D) that a witness who claimed
    (E) the witness claim saying

10. Many home owners in the northern states use a window sealant, <u>for it will prevent</u> heat loss in the winter.

    (A) for it will prevent
    (B) in which it will prevent
    (C) that will prevent
    (D) for the prevention of
    (E) being able to prevent

GO ON TO THE NEXT PAGE

11. Scientists once believed that the universe was <u>decelerating, the reason was that they believed gravity would slow acceleration</u> by pulling the planets towards each other.

    (A) decelerating, the reason was that they believed gravity would slow acceleration

    (B) decelerating, it is believing gravity would slow acceleration

    (C) decelerating; believing gravity would slow acceleration

    (D) decelerating because they believed gravity would slow acceleration

    (E) decelerating because their belief had been that gravity would slow acceleration

12. People who <u>have low motivation or are not at least moderately intelligent</u> are not likely to make it as international journalists.

    (A) have low motivation or are not at least moderately intelligent

    (B) has either low motivation or not intelligence in at least moderate amounts

    (C) are not highly motivated or who don't have at least moderate intelligence instead

    (D) are not highly motivated or at least moderately intelligent

    (E) has low motivation or else at least moderate amounts of intelligence

13. Although Mike is very much interested in music, <u>he does not play an instrument and has never attended a musical</u>.

    (A) he does not play an instrument and has never attended a musical

    (B) it is without being able to play an instrument or having attended a musical

    (C) he does not play an instrument and has never seen it

    (D) he does not play an instrument nor has he ever seen it

    (E) it is without playing an instrument nor having seen it

14. <u>Having Sam Erlich as their leader</u> and the increasing athletic ability of the team helped to bring about a victorious era for track and field at Bartle High School.

    (A) Having Sam Erlich as their leader

    (B) Having the leadership of Sam Erlich's

    (D) Sam Erlich as their leader

    (D) To be led by Sam Erlich

    (E) The leadership of Sam Erlich

THE ANSWER KEY APPEARS ON THE FOLLOWING PAGE.

Practice Test Two: **Answer Key**

SECTION 1

Essay

SECTION 2

1. E
2. A
3. D
4. E
5. C
6. B
7. B
8. E
9. D
10. A
11. D
12. D
13. B
14. D
15. B
16. E
17. C
18. D
19. D
20. D
21. A
22. C
23. E
24. B
25. E

SECTION 3

1. E
2. C
3. E
4. D
5. C
6. A
7. A
8. B
9. A
10. D
11. B
12. B
13. D
14. C
15. D
16. B
17. D
18. C
19. B
20. D

SECTION 4

1. B
2. E
3. B
4. C
5. E
6. E
7. C
8. A
9. D
10. C
11. E
12. B
13. A
14. D

15. C
16. C
17. D
18. B
19. A
20. B
21. A
22. E
23. D
24. A
25. E
26. A
27. B
28. D
29. B
30. D
31. A
32. B
33. E
34. C
35. C

SECTION 5

1. C
2. D
3. B
4. D
5. D
6. E
7. A
8. E
9. 800
10. 180
11. 7/5
12. 3
13. 5.2 or 26/5

14. 715
15. 50
16. 115
17. 10
18. 320

SECTION 6

1. C
2. D
3. D
4. B
5. C
6. D
7. C
8. D
9. E
10. D
11. C
12. B
13. A
14. C
15. B
16. D
17. A
18. C
19. D
20. E
21. E
22. D
23. E
24. C

SECTION 7

1. C
2. E
3. D
4. A
5. E
6. D
7. B
8. B
9. C
10. E
11. E
12. D
13. B
14. B
15. C
16. D

SECTION 8

1. E
2. B
3. A
4. E
5. A
6. B
7. E
8. D
9. D
10. D
11. C
12. B
13. A
14. A
15. B
16. A
17. E
18. C

SECTION 9

1. E
2. B
3. B
4. C
5. D
6. B
7. D
8. C
9. B
10. C
11. D
12. D
13. A
14. E

PRACTICE TEST TWO

Critical Reading

	Number Right	Number Wrong	Raw Score
Section 2:	☐	− (.25 × ☐)	= ☐
Section 6:	☐	− (.25 × ☐)	= ☐
Section 8:	☐	− (.25 × ☐)	= ☐
	Critical Reading Raw Score		= ☐

(rounded up)

Writing

	Number Right	Number Wrong	Raw Score
Section 1:	☐ (ESSAY GRADE)	× 3.17	= ☐
Section 4:	☐	− (.25 × ☐)	= ☐
Section 9:	☐	− (.25 × ☐)	= ☐
	Writing Raw Score		= ☐

(rounded up)

Math

	Number Right	Number Wrong	Raw Score
Section 3:	☐	− (.25 × ☐)	= ☐
Section 5A: (QUESTIONS 1–8)	☐	− (.25 × ☐)	= ☐
Section 5B: (QUESTIONS 9–18)	☐	(no wrong answer penalty)	= ☐
Section 7:	☐	− (.25 × ☐)	= ☐
	Math Raw Score		= ☐

(rounded up)

Turn to page xiv to convert your raw score to a scaled score.

Answers and Explanations

SECTION 1

6 Score Essay

To me, being an expert means being successful, and achieving success requires lots of hard work, time, and practice. This is true regardless of what you pursue, from running to drawing, acting to skating, teaching to dancing. Yet expertise and success don't come from skill alone. To truly succeed, you need to have at least as much motivation as talent, because if you don't possess the desire to do something, your talent may simply wither from neglect, and people who prove this to be the case include Jewel and my sister.

Pop singer Jewel has a critically acclaimed voice and songwriting skills. She's won awards for her songs and succeeded in the music business. Yet she didn't achieve fame and fortune simply with her talent. Instead, she struggled and worked incredibly hard for many years before she ever found success. In fact, at one point she was living in her car because she didn't have enough money to support herself, but she never gave up or stopped believing in her dream to play guitar and sing. Jewel's strong motivation and drive finally paid off when she was "discovered" by a music producer and recorded albums that showed off her talent and sold well to the general public, making her a successful expert in her field.

My sister is a contrast to Jewel's effective combination of talent and motivation. When she was little, my sister showed natural talent as a dancer, and my parents enrolled her in classes to develop her talent. My sister, however, didn't care about dancing, so she never practiced or put any effort into her classes. Eventually, my parents realized that they were wasting their money to pay for her training because even though she had talent she didn't possess the motivation to support her talent. My sister's lack of will meant that her talent became useless, because she needed to work to transform her talent into true skill and expertise in order to achieve success, but she didn't have the motivation to follow through with this.

By looking at the contrasting examples of Jewel and my sister, both with natural talent but only one with the matching will to succeed, you can see that motivation is the critical factor for success or expertise in a field. You can only really make full use of your talent if you have the will to succeed.

6 Score Critique

All essays are evaluated on four basic criteria: Topic, Support, Organization, and Language. The writer begins this essay by providing her definition of the word *expert* in the assignment. By equating expertise with success, the writer clearly indicates her own interpretation of the prompt and then develops her thesis to show how talent and motivation are relevant to this interpretation.

The two contrasting examples in the body paragraphs are both well developed with sufficient details and direct integration to the author's thesis. By citing opposing examples, both of which support her thesis, the author demonstrates a high level of understanding and critical thinking about the prompt. Each paragraph flows smoothly into the next, thanks to the use of clear transitional words and phrases, such as *yet, instead, in fact, but, in contrast,* and *however.* The strong organization of this essay helps to reinforce the author's thesis by creating a clear and consistent argument for the reader to follow.

Finally, the writer's language and sentence structure are both sophisticated and varied, with no grammatical errors to detract from the overall strength of the essay. This is an excellent SAT essay.

4 Score Essay

Not many people can be called "experts" at anything. We all have certain skills and talents but that doesn't mean we're able to rise to the very top of our field because other people may be more talented or have better skills. So the real difference between the "experts" and the rest of us is that they have something extra that allows them to be just a little more or just a little better, and that's motivation or drive.

A good example of an expert is figure skater Kristi Yamaguchi. She's won Olympic medals and other world championships in her chosen field. She's got lots of talent as a skater but to become an expert athlete she also had to really want to improve her skills to reach the championship level. Without the desire to practice and practice every day, she wouldn't have become an expert skater.

But athletes aren't the only ones who become champions. Look at Kelly Clarkson, the winner of American Idol. She has a great voice and is a very talented singer, but no one really knew who she was until she won the TV competition. All of the contestants chosen for the show had talent, but only one could win, and she did it by having more motivation and desire than anyone else.

These examples show that having a little something extra to add to your talent is critical for becoming an expert in your field. You really need more motivation than talent if you want to be a champion, like Muhammad Ali says in the quote.

4 Score Critique

All essays are evaluated on four basic criteria: Topic, Support, Organization, and Language. This essay stays on topic throughout, beginning with a clear statement of the author's opinion followed by two examples and an adequate conclusion. Although both examples offer some support for the writer's thesis, neither of them is developed enough to be convincing. The author needs to show what truly differentiated Yamaguchi and Clarkson from their peers, for her inference that each had more motivation than their peers remains largely unsubstantiated by additional evidence or information.

The essay's organization is satisfactory, although the introduction lacks a clear plan of how the author will develop her argument. Likewise, the transition between examples is weak, in the form of a sentence fragment starting with *But* at the beginning of the third paragraph. The conclusion consists of a repetition of the author's declaration in the introduction but does neatly refer to the prompt to wrap up the essay.

Overall, the writer's language is satisfactory, with only a few sentence fragments as minor grammatical flaws to detract from her essay.

2 Score Essay

Anyone can really want to do something but only people who actually have a skill can be true experts. I'd love to be a famous actress but I failed my drama classes and hated being onstage. So it didn't matter how much I wanted to do

this because I just didn't have any talent. And my brother wants to be a famous writer but he always gets bad grades in English class no matter how hard he tries or how much time he spends on his homework. That's how it happens for lots of people who want something alot but fail because they don't have talent. Like the guys who got eliminated from the TV show *Manhunt*. They were all really cute but some of them just couldn't make it in the modeling business because they were too tall or had the wrong attitude or couldn't express emotion when working with famous female models or professional photographers, etc. So they didn't succeed even though they all said they really really wanted to be the next top male model. And the same thing happened to a lot of contestants on other TV shows like *Survivor* or *Big Brother*. They all wanted to win but couldn't because everyone got voted off except the final person who played the best. Only that person was really an expert and was champion because of it. In conclusion, it doesn't matter how badly you want something because just wanting it isn't enough. You need to have some talent or skill too.

2 Score Critique

All essays are evaluated on four basic criteria: Topic, Support, Organization, and Language. This essay begins with a clear statement of the writer's opinion of the topic in the assignment. To support her opinion, the writer immediately provides two personal examples, neither of which is sufficiently developed. Additional examples from several television shows comprise the bulk of the essay, but again, none of these examples are developed in detail, and they simply appear as a series of statements that are only weakly tied to the writer's main point.

The scattered organization of this essay is its most serious flaw. The introduction consists of a single sentence, and the two sentences of the conclusion merely repeat what the author has already declared earlier in her essay. The second example about the writer's brother is not clearly related to the author's thesis, and the essay contains few transitions between ideas, making the author's logic difficult to follow. In addition, the one-paragraph structure of this essay suggests that the author herself doesn't understand how to differentiate between her examples or develop them individually to provide support for her thesis.

Finally, the writer's language is simplistic and repetitive, as is her sentence structure. Several sentence fragments beginning with *So*, *And*, and *Like* further detract from the essay. Although weak grammar alone isn't sufficient cause for deducting points, the combination of poor language with poor organization and support makes this a low-scoring essay.

SECTION 2

1.   E

Difficulty: Low

If the CEO usually reacts a certain way and this particular reaction shocked his employees, the reaction is probably contrary to what his employees have come to expect. If the CEO's overreaction shocked his employees, then they're probably used to him reacting in a way that is opposite of that. Find a word that expresses the opposite of a severe over reaction.

In choice (A), if the CEO is usually *demanding* then a severe overreaction might not be that shocking. In choice (B), being *inarticulate* doesn't have anything to do with how someone would react to being teased. In choice (C), again, if the CEO is inclined toward *aggressive* behavior, then an over reaction might be expected. In choice (D), the CEO's *persuasive* nature would not dictate a severe over reaction. In choice (E), if the CEO is usually *composed* then it would make sense for his employees to be shocked at a severe over reaction. This choice works.

2.   A

Difficulty: Low

What do big sales usually draw? Big sales usually draw in a lot of people. The storeowner has a large customer base among college students, but she wants to have a customer base among other groups as well. The sentence is asking you to find another word for customer base.

In choice (A), *clientele* is the synonym you're looking for. In choice (B), she's certainly not going to expand her *investments* by having a big sale. In choice (C), this choice might work if it was clear what she was expanding her *coverage* of, but just saying that she's expanding her *coverage* doesn't work. In choice (D), expanding her *staffing* might make her life easier or improve customer

service, but having a big sale won't make people want to work at the store. In choice (E), How would a big sale expand her *liability*?

3.   D

Difficulty: Medium

The word "despite" indicates that you're looking for contrasting words. Looking at the answer choices, can you tell which word pair offers a genuine contrast? Look for a word that is similar to "differences" and then for the second blank a word that is contrasting, because the differences were overcome.

In choice (A), although *incompatible* works for the first blank, the effort wouldn't be *divisive* if they overcame their differences. In choice (B), neither of these words has anything to do with differences or overcoming them. In choice (C), why would having *distinguished* backgrounds create differences for the people to overcome? Choice (D) makes sense. *Disparate* backgrounds would create differences, and a contrast to disparity is unity. In choice (E), if the people had *comparable* backgrounds, that means their backgrounds were similar, not different.

4.   E

Difficulty: Medium

Though the directory is lacking in some way, it's still useful because of the condition of the supply of this kind of information. If the directory is lacking in some way, perhaps it doesn't contain the names of all the students, but if it's still useful, it's probably because there aren't a lot of other sources for that information.

In choice (A), even if the directory was *intense*, that doesn't indicate that it's lacking in any way. In choice (B), the directory wouldn't be useful at all if it were *obsolete*. In choice (C), a directory that is *ostentatious* is not necessarily a directory that is lacking in information. In choice (D), *contemporary* could work for the first blank, but why would an outdated directory be useful if other resources were *plentiful*? Choice (E) works. Even though the directory isn't particularly *comprehensive* people use it because the supply of other resources is *meager*.

5. C

Difficulty: High

A word that means the same as "a poor way." The sentence is saying that yelling is an ineffective way to help children learn. The word "and" indicates that the blank is going to be a word similar in meaning to "a poor way."

In choice (A), *benign* people usually don't yell, so this doesn't make sense. In choice (B), how would yelling help identify or *diagnose* a problem? Choice (C) works. Something that is *inefficacious* is ineffective and probably a poor way to go about doing something. In choice (D), though any reaction is *discretionary*, this answer is clearly not the best fit. In choice (E), yelling can be *therapeutic* in the right context, but not yelling at a child for the purpose of helping him learn.

6. B

Difficulty: Low

Be sure you can find the support in *each* passage for the answer you choose. Though they disagree about its causes, both authors certainly seem to think the French Revolution *had a significant impact* on the world.

Choice (A) is a distortion; only Author 2 supports this. Choice (B) is correct; both authors would agree with this statement. Choice (C) is a distortion; only Author 1 supports this. Choice (D) is out of scope; *the American Revolution* is not addressed in either passage. Choice (E) is an opposite; Author 2 thinks it was "inevitable," not *unlikely*.

7. B

Difficulty: High

Have a very clear idea of the author's overall purpose when answering a Function question. Author 1 mentions the fact that commoners rarely spoke out against the king in order to demonstrate how the theatre helped peasants begin the revolution—it freed them from this obstacle that had kept them so docile. It is valuable to the passage in its suggestion of *the obstacle that the peasants had to overcome*.

Choice (A) is out of scope; there is no indication whether this attitude developed gradually or not. Choice (B) matches your prediction. Choice (C) is a misused detail; this custom may seem *severe*, but that isn't why the author included the reference to it. Choice (D) is out of scope; no *conclusion* is made in this sentence that could be characterized as *false* based on the information in the

passage. Choice (E) is out of scope; this is not the purpose of the reference.

8. E

Difficulty: High

Be careful not to confuse the two authors' viewpoints. The "shocking things" are elements of the performances put on by the guerilla theatre troupes that mocked the royalty. Author 2 says that those performances reflected the "growing discontent of the people," but didn't directly cause the revolution.

Choice (A) is an opposite; this fits the opinion of Author 1. Choice (B) is out of scope; no mention is made of the appropriateness of the plays. Choice (C) is out of scope; the commoners' opinions of the performances are not addressed in either passage. Choice (D) is extreme; Author 2 would say that the plays did represent the peasants' reasons for revolting, even if it didn't cause them to do so. Choice (E) is supported by the passage.

9. D

Difficulty: High

Beware of going too far afield from what is directly stated in the text. Author 1 thinks that, while the people of France were indeed oppressed, it took the voice of the guerilla theatre to give them the courage to act. Look for a choice that says she thinks they were contributing causes, but not the primary spur for revolution.

Choice (A) is an opposite; Author 1 acknowledges that the commoners were "downtrodden." This contradicts any contention that she feels those pressures played no part. Choice (B) is out of scope; Author 1 never mentions perceived exaggeration of the pressures on the peasants. Choice (C) is an opposite; Author 1 believes that the peasants were oppressed and that they revolted, in part, because of this. Choice (D) works; the author says we are "indebted to renegade artists" for the Revolution, implying that the social injustice alone was not enough to make the people revolt. Choice (E) is an opposite; Author 1 does not dwell on these factors for any length of time, speaking instead about the theatre of the time as a prime cause.

10. A

Difficulty: Medium

In this passage, the author depicts his intellectual journey to a deeper understanding of global conflicts, like the one that scarred his childhood. He goes on to describe how he *discovered a different way to analyze international conflicts.*

Choice (A) is correct; this matches the thrust of the prediction. Choice (B) is a distortion; the author never mentions social justice. Choice (C) is out of scope; the author does not discuss this. Choice (D) is out of scope; while the author does expand his understanding, *well-rounded* is not an appropriate description of this development. Choice (E) is out of scope; the author did come to *view local populations as worthy of study*, but that is too narrow to be the purpose of the entire passage.

11. D

Difficulty: Medium

Knowledge of vocabulary can save time in finding correct answers. The author states that his "introduction into the field of social history was fortuitous." When something is fortuitous, it represents a lucky accident. If you didn't know this, you still could find the correct answer here by reading further in the paragraph for context.

Choice (A) is out of scope; nothing in the passage suggests that the author's entry into the field was *difficult*. Choice (B) is out of scope; nothing in the passage suggests that the author's entry was *confusing*. Choice (C) is out of scope; nothing in the passage suggests that the author's entry was *unavoidable*. Choice (D) is correct; this matches the prediction. Choice (E) is out of scope; nothing in the passage suggests that the author's entry was *controversial*.

12. D

Difficulty: Low

Find the relevant detail, and re-read the applicable text. Find the answer that restates that detail. In paragraph 2, the author discusses a professor who urged him to redirect his studies "from the global system to the local one. I...scoffed at the suggestion, for that type of study was the job of historians." So the author *considered that type of analysis the job of historians.*

Choice (A) is out of scope; the author never considers the professor's *tenure.* Choice (B) is out of scope; the author

never discusses or defines *loftier goals.* Choice (C) is out of scope; the author does not discuss other *job offers.* Choice (D) is correct; this matches the text. Choice (E) is a distortion; the author never makes a value judgment of the suggestion.

13. B

Difficulty: Medium

Be careful about answering a Detail question from memory. You may fall for a tempting, but wrong, choice. From a general recollection of the passage or from your notes, you should know to look at the first paragraph. Near the end, the author writes, "I am still embarrassed by the fact that I went to school in order to contribute to world peace but found myself becoming a hawkish supporter of militarized solutions." Look for a match among the choices.

Choice (A) is a misused detail; the author escaped his country's civil war as a child, years before going to school. Choice (B) is correct; this matches the detail in the text. Choice (C) is an opposite; the author states that while this was the result, it was not the reason why he went to school. Choice (D) is a distortion; the author eventually found this method superior to others, but it is not why he went to school. Choice (E) is a distortion; this happened much later.

14. D

Difficulty: Medium

Gain context from the reference, and predict before peeking at the wrong choices. The sentence in question provides strong context: "By overlaying the two studies, I was eventually able to see how political motivations, calculations, and missteps affected groups and individuals who then fell into conflict." The author was able to understand more about the interplay between governments and the people, two groups the author states have been traditionally studied separately. Predict something like *combining.*

Choice (A) is a distortion; this doesn't reflect the sense of combination that the author conveys. Choice (B) is out of scope; this doesn't make sense in context. Choice (C) is an opposite; the author is making best use of the studies rather than discarding them. Choice (D) is correct; this matches your prediction. Choice (E) is out of scope; this doesn't make sense in context.

15. B

Difficulty: Medium

Remember that a valid inference can never be more extreme than the facts upon which it is based. The author states that a knowledge of social history was helpful in understanding international conflict. Look for something in this vein.

Choice (A) is extreme; the author never goes so far as to say that global conflicts can *only* be examined through social history. Choice (B) is correct; the author states that he was able understand global conflict by studying social history. Thus, it must be true that social history provides important information on global conflict. Choice (C) is an opposite; the author never states that international conflicts have their basis in social history. Choice (D) is extreme; the author states that knowledge of social history helps to analyze global conflict, not that knowledge of social history helps to avoid global conflict. Choice (E) is a distortion; nothing in the passage indicates this.

16. E

Difficulty: Medium

Use your notes to help you form a broad overview of a passage. The passage recounts the story of Django Reinhardt's accident and recuperation and goes on to attribute his unique style to his disability. Then it takes a more general look at great contributors to human thought and how disabilities may actually provoke innovation. Look for an answer that fits this pattern.

Choice (A) is an opposite; the story of Django Reinhardt is presented as accurate and biographical. Choice (B) is out of scope; no *scientific hypothesis* or controlled study appears in the passage. Choice (C) is out of scope; the author states nothing *personal* about herself in the passage. Choice (D) is out of scope; the account of Django's life is written biographically, and there is little analysis until the final paragraphs. Choice (E) works with the structure you outlined in your prediction.

17. C

Difficulty: Low

Ask yourself what specifically in the passage a given phrase refers to. The phrase "against all odds" means that it was unlikely that Django went on to create a new style of music. The only thing in the passage that indicates why it was unlikely is the accident that Django suffered in which he lost the use of some of his fingers. With "against all odds," the author probably means to suggest the difficulties that Django faced.

Choice (A) is an opposite; it was difficult for Django to learn to play with a crippled hand. Choice (B) is out of scope; the passage does not discuss racial *discrimination* at all. Choice (C) resembles your prediction. Choice (D) is out of scope; the point of the passage is to explore the impact of handicaps on genius, not necessarily to tell a dramatic story. Choice (E) is out of scope; no *other jazz guitarists* are mentioned in the passage.

18. D

Difficulty: Low

Because usually indicates a Detail question. The passage says that "it seemed likely he would never play the guitar again, and the general recognition of his talent was already so strong...that the men of his tribe wept at the tragedy" (lines 32–36). The men apparently wept because the loss of Django's guitar playing was deeply felt.

Choice (A) is out of scope; the passage makes no mention of the artistic value of the flowers. Choice (B) is out of scope; the value of the caravan is not discussed in the passage. Choice (C) is out of scope; there is no information in the passage about whether the men in his tribe liked him personally. Choice (D) matches the prediction. Choice (E) is a misused detail; Django, at the time of losing his fingers, had not yet invented his new style of music.

19. D

Difficulty: Medium

Predictions are especially important in Vocab-in-Context questions, as many wrong answers will be tempting. The passage says that it was the accident that hurt Django's hand that "focused and distinguished" him. Later, at the end of the paragraph, the passage says that it was the thing that "set him apart and forced him to try new things" (lines 51–52). You can predict that "distinguished" means something like "set apart."

Choice (A) is out of scope; the passage doesn't address the social refinement of Django Reinhardt. Choice (B) is a distortion; this isn't strong enough in tone to match the prediction. Choice (C) is an opposite; it doesn't make sense for a musician to be "sharpened." His technique could be, but not the musician himself. Choice (D) matches your prediction perfectly. Choice (E) is out of scope; the passage does not indicate whether Django was given any honors.

20. D

Difficulty: Low

Be sure to predict first and look at the choices second. The difficulty Django faced was the disfigurement of his hand and the loss of three fingers. If he was working hard to compensate for losing three digits, you can infer that "digits" are the same thing as "fingers."

Choice (A) is an opposite; though this is a common meaning of the word "digits," it makes no sense for Django to be coping with the loss of three *numbers*. Choice (B) is out of scope; there is nothing in the passage to indicate that the accident caused Django to lose money. Choice (C) is out of scope; this doesn't make sense in context. Choice (D) matches your prediction. Choice (E) is out of scope; *electronics* are not mentioned in the passage at all.

21. A

Difficulty: High

Note the difference, in prose, between language that indicates a firm conclusion and language that is not necessarily supported by evidence. "Seems" and "apparently" suggest that the author is making a conjecture rather than drawing a conclusion based on firm evidence. She is speculating that people who are the same as everyone else have trouble making art that is very different from everyone else's.

Choice (A) matches your prediction perfectly. Choice (B) is a distortion; if this were an explanation, it would be elaborating on a point made previously. This statement, however, introduces a new idea. Choice (C) is an opposite; the phrase is a generalization, not a specific story. Choice (D) is a distortion; the author is taking a guess but not exploring the topic for support. Choice (E) is an opposite; the phrase is a generalization, not a specific example.

22. C

Difficulty: Medium

When looking for an assumption made in the text, ask yourself what has to be true for the relevant phrase to make sense. The author says that for a musician to restrict herself to two-fingered technique, if she has five working fingers, is unnecessary work. In the sentence before, she poses the

question "why should another musician be expected to try such a thing?" (lines 71–73). It seems that the author is making the assumption that most musicians wouldn't limit themselves if they didn't have to.

Choice (A) is an opposite; the assumption is that they *don't* do this. Choice (B) is an opposite; most musicians have access to a full hand of fingers. Django is the exception. Choice (C) works with your prediction. Choice (D) is out of scope; the author doesn't make any judgements on the work ethic of musicians in general. Choice (E) is extreme; the author assumes only that musicians wouldn't unnecessarily restrict themselves in order to improve their technique, not that they don't work to improve their technique at all.

23. E

Difficulty: Medium

Ask yourself what point the author is supporting with the given phrase. The notion that expressing pity for those who are physically challenged can be seen as insulting is not mentioned anywhere else in the passage. It seems that the author wants to quickly add a supplementary reason to the main argument—that it's not necessary to pity the physically challenged.

Choice (A) is an opposite; the author seems to admire, not feel inordinate sympathy toward, physically challenged people. Choice (B) is an opposite; the notion that pity might be deemed insulting has little to do with the previous argument (that such pity is unnecessary). Choice (C) is out of scope; the author does not mention that she herself is insulted. Choice (D) is out of scope; "some say" does not indicate the presence of experts, because the "some" does not identify anybody specific. Choice (E) works well with your prediction.

24. B

Difficulty: Low

Use your notes to help you determine the intent of a paragraph and zero in on the purpose of a section of it.

The cited section includes the phrase "Those who are different—really, substantially different—have access to a whole world that 'normal' people can only dream of" (lines 80–83). The view expressed here is that physical disability provides a person with the opportunity to explore things from a different point of view than that of others, and therefore find new techniques and ideas.

Choice (A) is an opposite; the author is much more positive than this in the cited lines. Choice (B) matches your prediction nicely. Choice (C) is an opposite; the author claims that the advantage of disability is that it *is* an obstacle. Choice (D) is out of scope; the author does not call one condition better than the other. Choice (E) is out of scope; whether to deal with a disability intellectually or physically is not a topic of the passage.

25. E

Difficulty: Medium

Be alert for misused details among the answer choices in a question that asks about the passage as a whole; remember that you're looking for what the *entire* passage is about, not just one piece. The passage begins with a description of Django Reinhardt's life and life-altering accident, then goes on to discuss how physical disabilities may prompt some artists to think outside the box and invent completely new ideas. Predict that the purpose of the passage is to examine a possible positive effect of a disability that initially seems indisputably negative.

Choice (A) is a distortion; only the first half of the passage is about this. Choice (B) is out of scope; there are certainly many elements of a musician's career that are not discussed in the passage. Choice (C) is extreme; the author does not claim that physical handicaps always provoke inspiration, only that they can. Choice (D) is out of scope; there is no direct comparison in the passage except for a brief mention of a few other physically impaired geniuses, which does not suffice to make it the main purpose of the passage. Choice (E) matches your prediction nicely.

SECTION 3

1. E

Difficulty: Low

Strategic Advice: Cross multiply whenever you see a rational expression. Keep an eye out for variables that appear on both sides of an equation. Remove these by doing the same thing to both sides of the equation.

Getting to the Answer:

$$\frac{\sqrt{x}+n}{\sqrt{x}+9} = 1$$
$$\sqrt{x}+n = \sqrt{x}+9$$
$$n = 9$$

2. C

Difficulty: Low

Strategic Advice: Translate carefully from English to Math.

Getting to the Answer:

$$\frac{48-2x}{x+3} = 4$$
$$48-2x = 4x + 12$$
$$36 = 6x$$
$$6 = x$$

3. E

Difficulty: Low

Strategic Advice: To find the minimum total time, add the minimum times for each part; for the maximum total time, add the maximum times for each part.

Getting to the Answer:

Minimum $= 22 + 20 = 42$

Maximum $= 28 + 30 = 58$

4. D

Difficulty: Low

Strategic Advice: This is a straightforward algebra problem. As long as you follow the order of operations, these problems should be easy points.

Getting to the Answer:

$$4(n + 6) = 44$$
$$n + 6 = 11$$
$$n = 5$$

5. C

Difficulty: Medium

Strategic Advice: Sometimes the best method of attack is a longer method than normal. Writing the entire sequence of values here will help you keep track of exactly how many degrees Caleb has rotated.

Getting to the Answer:

Caleb completes one full rotation in 36 hours. Write out the hour sequence in 12 hour increments and add carefully:

9 a.m. Jan 14 – 9 p.m. Jan 14

9 p.m. Jan 14 – 9 a.m. Jan 15

9 a.m. Jan 15 – 9 p.m. Jan 15 ←360°

9 p.m. Jan 15 – 9 a.m. Jan 16

9 a.m. Jan 16 – 9 p.m. Jan 16

9 p.m. Jan 16 – 9 a.m. Jan 17 ←360°

9 a.m. Jan 17 – 9 p.m. Jan 17 ←120°

Add all of the degrees to get 840°

6. A

Difficulty: Medium

Strategic Advice: Picking numbers works great here. Select numbers that follow all the rules in the question stem and are easy to work with.

Getting to the Answer:

Pick an odd integer: 11

How many positive even integers are less than 11? 2,4,6,8, and 10 for a total of 5

Plug 11 into the answer choices until you find the one that produces a value of 5.

7. A

Difficulty: Medium

Strategic Advice: You're given 5 and asked for $5m$—which means you want to multiple 5 by m. But remember that if you multiply the 5 on the left side of the equation by m, you must do the same to the m^x on the right side.

Getting to the Answer:

$5 = m^x$

$5m = mm^x$

$5m = m^1 m^x$

$5m = m^{1+x}$

8. B

Difficulty: Medium

Strategic Advice: A good idea for a problem like this is to create a mental roadmap that will take you to the final answer. Figure out what you're looking for, see what you need to know to find that, then work out how to get from the information in the question to the information you need. In this case, you need to start with q to get to s. Substitute carefully according to your roadmap.

Getting to the Answer:

$\sqrt{q} = 6$, so $q = 36$

$\dfrac{q}{p} = 4$, $\dfrac{36}{p} = 4$ so $p = 9$

$\dfrac{p+q}{s} = 9$

$\dfrac{9+36}{s} = 9$

$\dfrac{45}{s} = 9$, so $s = 5$

9. A

Difficulty: Medium

Strategic Advice: First find the equation of the line in slope-intercept form ($y = mx + b$). Find the slope (m) using the formula $\dfrac{y_2 - y_1}{x_2 - x_1}$, then use the slope and any point on the line to determine what the y-intercept (b) is. Once you have an equation, rearrange it into the form given in the answer choices.

Getting to the Answer:

$m = \dfrac{y_2 - y_1}{x_2 - x_1} = \dfrac{5-4}{-1-3} = \dfrac{1}{-4} = \dfrac{-1}{4}$

$4 = \dfrac{-1}{4}(3) + b$

$\dfrac{16}{4} = \dfrac{-3}{4} + b$

$\dfrac{19}{4} = b$

$y = -\dfrac{1}{4}x + \dfrac{19}{4}$

$4y = -x + 19$

$x + 4y = 19$

10. D

Difficulty: Medium

Strategic Advice: Substitute $x = 6$ into the function and simplify. Be sure to follow the correct order of operations (*PEMDAS*).

Getting to the Answer:

$$f(6) = \frac{6^3 - 6}{6^2 - 2(6) + 6} = \frac{216 - 6}{36 - 12 + 6} = \frac{210}{30} = 7$$

11. B

Difficulty: Medium

Strategic Advice: Don't waste time trying to write fancy expressions for 3^5 in terms of x—just convert the answer choices into powers of 3.

Getting to the Answer:

(A) $243x = 3^5(3^5) = 3^{10}$

(B) $3x^2 = 3(3^5)^2 = 3(3^{10}) = 3^{11}$

(C) $9x^4 = 3^2(3^5)^4 = 3^2(3^{20})\,3^{22}$

(D) $27x^3 = 3^3(3^5)^3 = 3^3(3^{15}) = 3^{18}$

(E) $x^6 = (3^5)^6 = 3^{30}$

12. B

Difficulty: Medium

Strategic Advice: You can rearrange the average formula to get whichever part you're missing. For example, sum = (average) $\times$ (number of items).

Getting to the Answer:

$$7 < \frac{sum}{7} < 12$$

$$49 < sum < 84$$

13. D

Difficulty: Medium

Strategic Advice: Your task here is to translate English into math—what does "the ratio of $2k$ to $6s$" really mean?

Getting to the Answer:

The ratios described in the question can be written as:

$$\frac{2k}{6s} = \frac{6k + 5}{18s + 10}$$

Cross-multiply and simplify to get:

$$2k(18s + 10) = 6s(6k + 5)$$

$$36ks + 20k = 36ks + 30s$$

$$20k = 30s$$

$$k = 1.5s$$

You can see that statement I is never true, statement II is not necessarily true, and statement III must be true. If you're not sure about that, you can try plugging in numbers that fit each statement to see if they make the described ratios equivalent.

14. C

Difficulty: Medium

Strategic Advice: Don't worry if you see a symbol you've never seen before — the operation will be defined in the problem. All you need to do is plug in the given values. Be sure to do anything in parentheses first.

Getting to the Answer:

$$2\nabla 3 = 2 - 3 + 2 = 1$$

$$1\nabla 1 = 1 - 1 + 2 = 2$$

15. D

Difficulty: Medium

Strategic Advice: Remember that you can always plug in numbers for the variables (being careful to follow all the rules you are given).

Getting to the Answer:

I. When you multiply by a negative, the inequality flips. If $b > a$, then $-b < -a$. So this statement is always false.

II. If $a < b$, you can add c to both sides to get $a + c < b + c$. Always true.

III. a and b are negative, so their sum will be negative, while c is positive. So this statement will be always true.

16. B

Difficulty: Medium

Strategic Advice: When you find the language confusing, try to put it in concrete terms. If you wanted to know how much more 9 was than 7, what would you do? You would subtract: $9 - 7 = 2$ more. So you need to subtract these two algebraic expressions.

Getting to the Answer:

$(3x + 9) - (3x - 2) = 3x + 9 - 3x + 2 = 11$

17. D

Difficulty: Medium

Strategic Advice: When the SAT presents a problem that only requires plugging in numbers, make sure you calculate carefully to avoid careless mistakes.

Getting to the Answer: Plug in the given values:

$(-2)^2[2(-2) + 5] = 4[-4 + 5] = 4(1) = 4$

18. C

Difficulty: High

Strategic Advice: The trick to this problem is knowing the signs of the quadrants on a Cartesian coordinate graph:

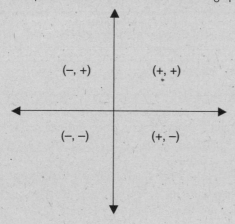

Remembering this on Test Day will help you conquer any problems similar to this one.

Getting to the Answer:

A: $(-x, +y) =$ negative product

B: $(+x, +y) =$ positive product. Eliminate (B).

C: $(+x, -y) =$ negative product

D: $(-x, -y) =$ positive product. Eliminate (D).

E: $(-x, +y) =$ negative product

Looking at the relative distance from the origin, C is very far from the origin so the absolute value of its coordinates are likely to be bigger than either A or E. Since we know that the x-coordinate is positive and the y-coordinate is negative, their product is a negative number with a high absolute value, so it is the least of the products of the coordinates of the given points.

19. B

Difficulty: High

Strategic Advice: You're looking for a way to get a and b in the same equation, without n. So solve for n in terms of a, and substitute it into the equation for b.

Getting to the Answer:

$a - 4 = 3n$

$a - 4 = 3n$

$\dfrac{a - 4}{3} = n$

$b = 7 + 9n^2 = 7 + 9\,\dfrac{(a-4)^2}{3^2} = 7 + 9\,\dfrac{(a-4)^2}{9} = 7 +$

$(a - 4)^2 = 7 + a^2 - 8a + 16 = a^2 - 8a + 23$

20. D

Difficulty: High

Strategic Advice: This one is hard to draw. Think logically and try to visualize the orange.

Getting to the Answer:

The first cut breaks the orange into 2 pieces. If you cut the orange so that you cut the 2 halves into equal pieces, you have 4 equal quarters. Your next cut can cut the quarters into 8 equal pieces. Therefore, 3 cuts can yield a maximum of 8 pieces, choice (D).

SECTION 4

1. B

Difficulty: Low

Certain idioms appear regularly on the SAT; learn their proper structure. This question tests your knowledge of the idiom that compares two nouns using *as*; the correct construction is "as (adjective) as." Only (B) correctly completes the construction. Choice (C) is grammatically incorrect, choice (D) is unnecessarily wordy, and choice (E) does not correct the error.

2. E

Difficulty: Low

Make sure that comparisons are structured to compare logical things. Here, *universities* are being compared to *New York City.* Choice (E) corrects the error. In choice (B), the preposition *in* is correctly used with *Ann Arbor,* but a parallel form is needed for the comparison to *New York City.* Choice (E) corrects this error by adding the preposition *in* preceding *New York City.* Choice (B) is ambiguous and unclear. The verb *did* incorrectly makes *New York City* a subject. The comparison in choice (C) is awkward, and incorrectly omits the possessive object (*universities*). Choice (D) uses an ambiguous pronoun *ones* that could refer to the universities or the students.

3. B

Difficulty: Low

There are several ways to correct a run-on sentence; making one of the independent clauses subordinate is one of them.

As written, this is a run-on sentence; *they* in the second clause could also refer to either the Lions or the Cowboys. Choice (B) corrects both errors by making the second clause subordinate. Choice (C) introduces an inconsistent verb tense. Choices (D) and (E) misuse the semicolon splice, which is only correct when used to combine two independent clauses.

4. C

Difficulty: Medium

Always make sure that underlined verbs are in agreement with their subjects. The singular verb *is* isn't correct with the plural subject *complaints.* Choice (C) corrects this error. Choices (B) and (E) are awkwardly worded. Choice (D) does not address the subject-verb error.

5. E

Difficulty: Medium

Make sure the correct noun is placed after a modifying phrase. Here, due to a misplaced modifier, it is *the office* and not *Boris* that is *returning to work.* Only choice (E) corrects this error without introducing additional errors. Choice (B) uses the pronoun *it* without an antecedent. Choice (C) changes the past tense verb *seemed* to the present tense *seems,* which is inappropriate in context. Choice (D) is a run-on sentence because two independent clauses can not be joined simply by a comma.

6. E

Difficulty: Medium

Items in a series, list, or compound must be in parallel form

As well as in the original breaks the parallel form of the items in the list. Only choice (E) uses correct parallel structure. Choices (B), (C), and (D) do not address the error.

7. C

Difficulty: Medium

If you don't spot a grammatical error, look for errors in style. The sentence as written is unnecessarily wordy, and *switching* is redundant, since *switched* is already used in the first part of the sentence. Choice (C) eliminates the redundant word, is concise and contains no additional errors. Choice (B) creates a run-on sentence. Choices (D) and (E) are both wordier than choice (C).

8. A

Difficulty: Medium

If you don't spot an error, don't be afraid to choose (A).

The sentence is correct as written. The transitions are correct, and the sentence is concise. Choice (B) is unnecessarily wordy and illogically compares *efficient work* to *speed.* Choice (C) introduces an inconsistent verb tense. Choice (D) leaves the meaning of the second clause incomplete. Choice (E) is wordy and unnecessarily introduces the passive voice.

9. D

Difficulty: High

The passive voice will not always be wrong on the SAT, but look for an answer choice that makes the sentence active. As written, the sentence is unnecessarily in the passive voice. Choice (D) corrects this with the pronoun subject *one.* Choices (B) and (C) create sentence fragments because a gerund (*-ing*) verb cannot be used as the main verb of a sentence. Choice (E) is unnecessarily wordy and uses the pronoun *it* with no antecedent.

10. C

Difficulty: High

In comparative structures like *not only…but also,* the items compared must be parallel in form. As written, the sentence violates the rules of parallelism. Only choice (C) corrects this error without introducing additional issues. Choices (B), (D), and (E) all fail to properly complete the idiom *not only…but also*

11. E

Difficulty: High

If a sentence begins with a modifying phrase, the word it modifies must be the subject of the sentence. *Exhaustion* was not *Hauling the laundry basket*; the opening phrase is meant to modify *Maria.* Both choices (D) and (E) make this change, but choice (D) is a sentence fragment, since it has no independent clause. Choice (B) does not address the error. In choice (C), the pronoun *it* has no antecedent and is incorrectly modified by the opening phrase.

12. B

Difficulty: Low

In the phrase *extreme cold air* an adjective is used to modify another adjective. This is incorrect. The adjective *extreme* should be an adverb, and the phrase should read "extremely cold air." In choice (A), the infinitive *to avoid* correctly completes the expression *would have been able.* In choice (C), the verb *had awoken* is in the correct tense because it happened before *he would have been able.* The word *later* choice (D) is idiomatically correct.

13. A

Difficulty: Low

Using a subjective pronoun when an objective pronoun is required is a common error on the SAT Writing section. When dealing with a compound object that contains a noun and a pronoun, a simple way to test which one you need is to eliminate the noun.

Choice (A) is a compound object using a noun, *Hilary*, and a pronoun, *I.* Read the sentence without *Hilary.* You would never say: "Dad asked I" so you need the objective pronoun, *me.* Choice (B) uses the correct simple past tense. Choice (C) uses the possessive correctly. Choice (D) is correct, since the seasons are never capitalized unless they begin a sentence.

14. D

Difficulty: Low

Modification issues show up with some frequency on the SAT Writing Section, so as you check the sentence for errors, be sure that adverbs and adjectives are used correctly. The

adjective "deep" is incorrectly used to modify "sleeping." Remember, adjectives modify nouns and adverbs modify verbs, adjectives, and other adverbs.

Choice (A) is an idiomatically correct prepositional phrase that explains where the commotion took place. In choice (B), the modifying form *involving* is correctly used to indicate that the hens and the rooster were part of an ongoing ruckus. In choice (C), the past tense verb *woke* is correct here since the sentence in explaining something that happened in the past.

15. C

Difficulty: Low

Your knowledge of verb tenses is often tested on the SAT Writing section. A quick check of the sentence to assure that all verb tenses are written correctly will get you points. You have a clear indication of time in this sentence—last month. Make sure that the verb or verbs that refer to this event, which was completed in the past, are written correctly in the simple past tense. Choice (C) is in the progressive past tense and needs to be changed to the simple past —graduated. Choice (A) uses the correct, simple past tense form of the verb. Choice (B), *younger,* is the correct comparative form of the adjective. Choice (D), *from,* is, the correct preposition to use with *graduate.*

16. C

Difficulty: Medium

Remember that comparative adjectives compare two things. They are formed either by adding the suffix *-er* to the adjective or by placing the word "more" in front of it. A general rule for forming comparatives is to use "more" if the adjective has more than one syllable and the suffix *-er* if the adjective has one syllable. In this sentence choice (C) does both things—it places *more* in front of *small and* adds the suffix *-er* to it. Since *small* has one syllable, the correct comparative form is *smaller.*

Choice (A), *when,* is an adverb that answers the question, "At what time?" It's used correctly in this sentence. Choice (B) correctly uses the past tense form of the verb *to look.* Choice (D) is a good vocabulary word (not that you need vocabulary for this section of the SAT). It means *to come forth.* Here the progressive tense is correct. It indicates that something was happening over a period of time.

17. D

Difficulty: Medium

Sometimes a sentence won't "sound" right. This might mean that it contains a idiom error. Did efforts *about* democracy sound correct when you read this sentence? Probably not, since you wouldn't use the preposition "about" in this context. What you would need is something like "efforts on behalf of" or even, a little less elegantly, "efforts for."

In choice (A), the adverb *when* answers the question, "At what time?" and is correctly used here. In choice (B), the verb tense is correct, past perfect, which indicates that something happened before something else happened. Simply put, in this sentence Abadi got the Nobel Prize before her colleagues praised her. In choice (C), the use of the simple past is the correct sequence of tenses for this sentence.

18. B

Difficulty: Medium

Be sure that the verbs in the sentence correctly express the the time of the action.

This sentence contains a clear indication of time—1906— which is in the past. Anything that happened in 1906 is done. The verb tenses should express this completeness. Choice (B) should be in the simple past tense—leveled. In choice (A), names of seasons should not be capitalized. In choice (C), the singular pronoun is correct here since it refers to the singular noun, *series*. Choice (D) uses the correct tense—the simple past.

19. A

Difficulty: Medium

It's especially important to check subject-verb agreement when a verb is separated from its subject. The subject is the singular *heron*, but the verb is the plural *live*. To correct this sentence you would have to change *live* to *lives*. In choice (B), most is the correct superlative form of the adjective *many*. Choice (C) is a common idiom which means comfortable. In choice (D), the conjunction *both* is correctly used with *and* to indicate relationship between 2 things—in this case inland and coastal regions.

20. B

Difficulty: Medium

Make sure that sentences are logically correct. This sentence wants to set up a contrast between what the recipe required and what Chad did. However, the conjunction *and* indicates an addition rather than a contrast and should be replaced with a word like "but." In choice (A), *called for* is an idiomatic expression often used in a context like this. It means "needed in the circumstances." Choice (C) sets up the right cause/effect logic required by the meaning of the sentence. In choice (D), this verb, which means to reduce, is in the correct infinitive form.

21. A

Difficulty: Medium

When there are underlined pronouns in an Identifying Sentence Errors question, check to see that they have clear antecedents. The pronoun *They* has no clear antecedent. You can guess that *They* are the people of India, but that would be only a guess since the sentence doesn't provide that information.

In choice (B), this adverb answers the question, "At what time?" It is correctly used here. In choice (C), the past tense verb is correct. In choice (D), the conjunction *and* correctly expresses a result.

22. E

Difficulty: Medium

The sentence is correct. The two transition words *because* and *but* correctly set up causal and contrasting relationships, respectively, and *of* is the correct preposition. The verb *were,* choice (C), is correctly plural and in the past tense. When two people are being compared, the superlative word "more" should be used, and so choice (D) is also correct.

23. D

Difficulty: Medium

The fungus needs to be controlled, not the local oak trees, and so the singular pronoun should be used. The pronoun *their,* (D), should be "its". The phrase *so great a* is idiomatically correct. The verbs *has become,* (B), and *to uncover,* (C), are in the correct tense and the word *uncover* correctly uses the preposition *to* (C).

KAPLAN
Test Prep and Admissions

24. A

Difficulty: Medium

The phrase *at drawing,* (A), should read "to draw." The phrases *of young fans,* (B), and *at the ballpark,* (C), use the correct prepositions. The verb *provided,* (D), is correctly in the present tense.

25. E

Difficulty: High

Read all sentences carefully looking for common errors, but remember that about 20% of Identifying Sentence Errors questions will be error-free.

In Choice (A) this is the correct word to express the contrast that the sentence sets up. In choice (B), the past tense verb is correct—Burbank's experiments are over. In choice (C), *Such as* is an adjective phrase that indicates that an example is being given, choice (D), the infinitive form of the verb is correct after the verb *attempt.* Choice (E) is the answer since this sentence is correct as written.

26. A

Difficulty: High

Although the SAT Writing test is not a direct test of your vocabulary, it occasionally requires you to know the meaning of words, especially those often confused with other words. This sentence confuses *undetermined* with *indeterminate. Undetermined* means not decided. You can see that this makes no sense—everyone's age is known or decided. The word you want is indeterminate, which means not precisely established. In other words, Kallan's age is determined but those who don't know it can't guess it. Notice how this meaning works well with the rest of the sentence—the ambiguity, or uncertainty, is a result of this lack of precision. In choice (B), the conjunction "and," which indicates additional, related information is correctly used. In choice (C), the present tense is correct since it expresses something that the candidate does regularly. Choice (D) is the correct preposition in this context.

27. B

Difficulty: High

Know the rules for less/fewer and amount/number. Use fewer for countable nouns and less for uncountable nouns. *Adults* is a countable noun, so choice (B) is incorrect. In choice (A), *where* is an adverb that answers the question,

"In what place?" It's correctly used in this sentence. In choice (C), the singular noun, *is*, agrees with the singular subject, *environment.* In choice (D), the preposition *to* is correctly used with the adjective, *conducive.*

28. D

Difficulty: High

Always make sure that pronouns agree in number and gender with the noun or pronoun to which they're referring. The pronoun *their,* which is plural, is referring to the pronoun *each,* which is singular. If you were correcting this sentence, you would have to replace *their* with *his* or *her.* Notice that the plural noun, *members* is *not* the subject of the verb but is placed in the sentence to distract the unprepared test taker.

Choice (A), *about,* is one of the prepositions that can be used with *concerned.* In choice (B), the preposition *on* is used correctly. In choice (C), the past tense verb correctly expresses the time indicated in the sentence.

29. B

Difficulty: High

The phrase *about seat belts in the front and back seats* masks the fact that the singular subject *new law* doesn't agree with the plural verb *have.* Choice (B) should read *has.* The prepositions *about,* choice (A), and *for,* choice (C), are idiomatically correct, as is the adjective *alike* choice (D).

30. D

Difficulty: High

It's tempting to assume that the main idea is always expressed early on in a passage, but that may not be the case. The first paragraph serves as an introduction to microwave ovens and explains how they became typical fixtures in American homes. The second paragraph describes a claim that food cooked in microwave ovens may have a negative effect on human health. The last paragraph provides evidence that these claims are misleading or false. Clearly, the author of the passage agrees with the viewpoint expressed in the last paragraph, and does not believe that cooking in microwave ovens is harmful. Therefore, you're looking for an answer choice that expresses skepticism about the dangers of microwave cooking.

Choice (D) is a good candidate; it states that "they" (that is, the claims that microwave ovens have a negative effect on human health) are "simply wrong." Choice (A) is too general. Choices (B) and (C) are the opposite of what you seek; both come from the second paragraph, which is critical of microwave cooking. Choice (E) appears in the third paragraph, but as a detail, not a statement of purpose.

31. A

Difficulty: Low

When asked to add a sentence to a passage, make sure your choice matches the voice and tone of the passage as a whole. Read through the first paragraph: microwaves have many purposes, the most familiar of which is in the microwave oven, an item that has become standard equipment in American homes. Choice (A) follows directly and logically from the thought begun in sentence 3. Choice (B) introduces a concept—*the government*—that appears nowhere else in the passage. Choices (C) and (E) distort references to microwave ovens, long distance, and television programming in a way that does not follow from the paragraph. Choice (D) uses the first person and adopts a narrative tone that is inconsistent with the rest of the passage.

32. B

Difficulty: High

A pronoun may appear before its antecedent in a sentence; make sure all pronouns agree with the proper antecedent noun.

In Improving Paragraphs sentences, the antecedent to a pronoun may appear in an earlier sentence and, since sentence 3 deals with "microwave ovens," you might have thought that was the antecedent for the pronoun "their." But context reveals that the plural pronoun "their" is being used here to refer to the singular noun "microwave cooking"; choice (B) corrects this error.

Choice (A) indicates an inappropriate cause-and-effect relationship between the sentence's two clauses. Choice (C) is incorrect with the singular subject "microwave cooking." Choice (D) introduces an inconsistent verb tense. Choice (E) incorrectly replaces the noun "effect" with the verb "affect."

33. E

Difficulty: Medium

For questions that raise a number of issues, a methodical check of the choices is best.

The answer choices here cover a number of issues, so it's best to check each in turn. The keywords *on the contrary* in choice (A) would have to be followed by a sentence that contrasts with the information in the previous sentence, which is not the case here. Eliminating (B) causes a grammatical error; *a number* can decrease, but *white blood cells* cannot. Without choice (C), the logic of the sentence is lost. Choice (D) makes incorrect use of the semicolon splice, which is only correct when used to combine two independent clauses. Since sentence 7 continues the discussion of a study that was completed in the past looks good, the verbs should be in the past tense; choice (E) is the correct choice here.

34. C

Difficulty: Medium

Some structures are only correct when used together. "Not only...but also" is one such construction.

Only choice (C) correctly completes the construction. Additionally, choice (A) misuses the semicolon splice; since the first clause does not express a complete thought, it's not independent.

35. C

Difficulty: Medium

A verb must agree in number with its subject noun, which may not be the noun closest to it in the sentence.

Although the singular noun "community" is closer to the verb phrase "has concluded," its subject is actually the plural "experts"; choice (C) is the needed revision. In choice (B), "significantly" modifies "has concluded," so the adverb form is correct. Choice (D) agrees with its plural subject "others." Choice (E) introduces a verb tense that is incorrect in context.

SECTION 5

1. C

Difficulty: Low

Strategic Advice: There are two solutions to an absolute value equation. Find the first by ignoring the absolute value sign and solving as normal. You can then find the second equation by multiplying everything inside the absolute value sign by (-1) and then solving the equation that results.

$$5x + 15 = 10 \quad \text{or} \quad -5x - 15 = 10$$
$$5x = -5 \quad \text{or} \quad -5x = 25$$
$$\text{so } x = -1 \quad \text{or} \quad x = -5$$

2. D

Difficulty: Low

Strategic Advice: Don't do excess math. All you need to know to solve this problem is how to get the decimal point to move.

Getting to the Answer:

$(.0013)x = 0.013$

so $x = \dfrac{0.013}{.0013} = 10$

3. B

Difficulty: Low

Strategic Advice: Use $b = 2$ to solve for a in the first equation. Then solve for c in the second equation.

Getting to the Answer:

First equation:

$$\frac{a}{2} = 8$$
$$a = 16$$

Second equation:

$$\frac{16}{c} = 4$$
$$16 = 4c$$
$$c = 4$$

4. D

Difficulty: Medium

Strategic Advice: On geometry word problems, draw a rough sketch of what the figure could look like. This will make it easier to see the answer on Test Day. If there are several possible versions of the figure, sketch a few of them.

Getting to the Answer: Draw the circle, and place point O in the middle. Place J and K on the outside of the circle so that a line drawn between them passes through O. Notice that $\overline{JK}$ is a diameter of the circle. Now, place point L anywhere on the circle.

You know that $KO = LO$ because both are radii of the circle. Because the lengths of these two lines are the same, angle LKO and angle KLO must have the same measure.

Therefore, (D) is correct. The other choices can be true, depending on where you place L, but none of them are always true.

5. D

Difficulty: Medium

Strategic Advice: On Test Day, use what you know about angles to help you find the missing information. In this case, you need to realize that each angle in a rectangle is 90°, and the angles in a triangle add up to 180°.

Getting to the Answer: Since WZ and XY are parallel, their opposite angles are equal. Angle WZX is 60° so angle ZXY is also 60°. Since angle WXY is 90°, angle $WXZ = 90° - 60° = 30°$.

Since line segments WO and XO run from a corner of the rectangle to the center, they are equal in length. This means that triangle WOX is isosceles, and angle $WXZ =$ angle $XWY = 30°$. This means that angle $WOX = 180 - 30 - 30 = 120$, or choice (D).

6. E

Difficulty: Medium

Strategic Advice: You know the formula for finding an average—divide the sum of the items by the number of items. Just don't get confused as you translate between English and math.

Getting to the Answer:

$x = \dfrac{\text{sum of scores}}{\text{number of scores}}$

x (number of scores) $=$ sum of scores

7. A

Difficulty: Medium

Strategic Advice: Don't fall into the "obvious answer" trap of just taking the number of nickels and the number of dimes from the two ratios to come up with 3:4. To find the ratio of nickels to dimes, you need to get the two ratios in proportion to one another by getting the same number of pennies in each.

Getting to the Answer: Multiplying the first ratio by 3 gives you 6:9; multiplying the second by 2 gives you 6:8. Since the number corresponding to pennies is now the same in each ratio, the ratio of nickels to dimes can now be found. The ratio of nickels to dimes is 9:8.

8. E

Difficulty: Medium

Strategic Advice: Try out the answer choices. Since you know that the smallest integer in set C is -2, and the numbers are consecutive, you can make up set C given the number of elements for that answer choice. The set containing the least possible number of integers, where the integers in the set also add up to a positive even number, will be the correct answer.

Getting to the Answer:

Choice (A): set C has 4 elements so $C = \{-2, -1, 0, 1\}$. This adds up to -2, so discard choice (A).

Choice (B): set C has 5 elements, so $C = \{-2, -1, 0, 1, 2\}$. This adds up to zero, and although zero is even, it is neither positive nor negative, so discard choice (B).

Choice (C): set C has 6 elements, so $C = \{-2, -1, 0, 1, 2, 3\}$. These add up to 3, which isn't even. Discard.

Choice (D): set C has 7 elements, so $C = \{-2, -1, 0, 1, 2, 3, 4\}$. These add up to 7, which isn't even. Discard.

Since all other answer choices have been discarded, choice (E) must be the correct answer, but let's check it anyway.

Choice (E): set C has 8 elements, so $C = \{-2, -1, 0, 1, 2, 3, 4, 5\}$. These add up to 12, which is positive and even, so again, it must be correct.

9. 800

Difficulty: Low

Strategic Advice: Use the information you have to fill in what's missing.

Getting to the Answer:

	Chairs with armrest	Chairs without armrests	Total
Blue	5,700		16,200
Green	6,500 − 5,700 = 800		3,800
Total	20,000 − 13,500 = 6,500	13,500	16,200 + 3,800 = 20,000

10. 180

Difficulty: Low

Strategic Advice: The first step to solving any math question should be to ask yourself, "What am I trying to solve for?" Asking this question here will get you a long way toward solving this problem.

Getting to the Answer:

$a = 30$ percent of $400 = 400 \times .3 = 120$

$b = 40$ percent of $a = .4 \times 120 = 48$

$c = 25$ percent of $b = .25 \times 48 = 12$

$a + b + c = 120 + 48 + 12 = 180$

11. $\dfrac{7}{5}$

Difficulty: Low

Strategic Advice: Whenever you are given two fractions which are equal to each other, think of cross multiplying.

Getting to the Answer:

$10q = 14$

$q = \dfrac{14}{10} = \dfrac{7}{5}$

12. 3

Difficulty: Medium

Strategic Advice: Figure out additional information based on what is given, and interpret the problem to understand the "question behind the question."

Getting to the Answer: Line l is tangent to the circle, and line m intersects l at the point of tangency. Therefore, l is perpendicular to m. If you extend lines l and n so that they intersect, you can form a 30-60-90 triangle, where line n extended is the hypotenuse. You are told that line n extended to the intersection with line l measures 6. In other words, the hypotenuse is 6. The measures of the sides of a 30-60-90 triangle are $(x, x\sqrt{3}, 2x)$. In this case, $6 = 2x$, so $x = 3 =$ the short side of the triangle. In this case, the short side is OP. This is also the radius of the circle, which is what the question asks for.

13. 5.2 or $\dfrac{26}{5}$

Difficulty: Medium

Strategic Advice: When the SAT puts a problem in words, try to translate it into numbers. After that, simply solve carefully.

Getting to the Answer: $\frac{2}{5}$ of $\frac{1}{2}$ is $\frac{2}{5}\left(\frac{1}{2}\right) = \frac{1}{5} = 0.2$. Add this value to 5: $5 + .0.2 = 5.2$, or $\frac{26}{5}$.

14. 715

Difficulty: Medium

Strategic Advice: With all math questions, especially percent questions, be sure you are answering the correct question.

Getting to the Answer: Total up the percentage of respondents who commute more than .5 hours, and then find the total respondents.

$$30\% + 20\% + 15\% = 65\%$$
$$1,200 - 100 = 1,100$$
$$1,100 \times .65 = 715$$

15. 50

Difficulty: Medium

Strategic Advice: Questions such as this one require you to know certain facts or formulas. In this case, you need to know that the sum of supplementary angles is 180° and that the sum of the interior angles of a quadrilateral is 360°.

Getting to the Answer:

First, find the angle supplementary to x (called x'), then use it to find x. You can find x' because every quadrilateral has 360 degrees; just sum up the other 3 angles and subtract them from 360.

$$x' = 360 - (110 + 75 + 45)$$
$$x' = 360 - 230$$
$$x' = 130$$

Since x is supplementary to x', we know that $180 - x' = x$, so:

$$180 - 130 = x$$
$$50 = x$$

16. 115

Difficulty: High

Strategic Advice: The tangent line here forms the third side of a triangle. Since the shaded portion is exactly $\frac{1}{4}$ the area of circle A, $m\angle BAD = 90°$. Use this information to find $m\angle BDA$. Find $m\angle CDE$ by using the fact that $m\angle CDE$ and $m\angle BDA$ are supplementary.

Getting to the Answer:

$$m\angle BDA = 180° - 25° - 90° = 65°$$
$$m\angle CDE = 180° - 65° = 115°$$

17. 10

Difficulty: High

Strategic Advice: The shaded region is just the area of the larger triangle minus the area of the smaller triangle. Set up an equation using this information. Before you grid in your answer, make sure you're answering the right question (*height* of *smaller* triangle).

Getting to the Answer:

Large triangle: base = 15; height = x

Small triangle: base = $15 - 6 = 9$; height = $x - 6$

Shaded area = Large area − small area =

$$\left(\frac{1}{2} \times 15 \times x\right) - \left(\frac{1}{2} \times 9 \times (x - 6)\right) = 75$$
$$\left(\frac{15}{2}x\right) - \left(\frac{9}{2}(x - 6)\right) = 75$$
$$\left(\frac{15}{2}x\right) - \left(\frac{9}{2}x - \frac{54}{2}\right) = 75$$
$$\frac{15}{2}x - \frac{9}{2}x + \frac{54}{2} = 75$$
$$\frac{6}{2}x + 27 = 75$$
$$3x = 48$$
$$x = 16$$

The height of the small triangle is

$$x - 6 = 16 - 6 = 10$$

18. 320

Difficulty: High

Strategic Advice: Take a complicated problem like this one step at a time. Keep the ultimate end point in your head, and work towards it carefully.

Getting to the Answer:

From the problem we know that it costs an extra $45 to go 200 miles when compared to 50 miles. Thus, it costs $45 to travel an extra 150 miles and the additional charge is $15 for every 50 miles.

To travel 450 miles, one needs to go 400 miles more than in the first journey. $\frac{400}{50} = 8 \times \$15 = \$120$ and $\$200 + \$120 = \$320$.

SECTION 6

1. C

Difficulty: Low

Don't' be fooled by the trap choice (B).

The key word is "cautious." A baby learning to walk is cautious because he's unsure of how to walk. His steps might be hesitant because of that. Is there a synonym for "hesitant" among the answer choices?

In choice (A), baby's don't really carry enough body weight to do anything *heavily*. Choice (B) might trap you, because although a baby learning to walk is often *clumsy*, that doesn't make him definitively hesitant. Choice (C), *tentatively,* is the synonym you're looking for. Choice (D), *confidently,* is the opposite of hesitantly. In choice (E), usually young children have lots of energy and are rarely *languid*.

2. D

Difficulty: Low

The gadget does two things: chops and seeds. The salesman is using that feature as a selling point. Look for an adjective to put before "purpose" that means "does two things."

In choice (A), a *foreign* purpose does not make the gadget more useful. In choice (B), a kitchen gadget with a *literary* purpose would be rather useless. In choice (C), if the gadget had a *false* purpose then the salesman would be pretty unethical. Choice (D) fits. The word *dual* means two, in this case that it functions in two ways. In choice (E), a gadget with a *direct* purpose would be great, though the fact that it does two things is not illustrated by this word.

3. D

Difficulty: Medium

The word "infinite" should accurately indicate the breadth of the expansion. If the universe is believed to be infinite in size, meaning it goes on forever, it's probably going to keep expanding forever too.

In choice (A), even if the universe is *conclusively* or undoubtedly expanding, that doesn't have anything to do with the key word "infinite." In choice (B), the universe's infinite size is hardly indicative of *precise* expansion. In choice (C), if the universe is expanding quickly it's probably not expanding *periodically*. Choice (D) works. The word *indefinitely* means "forever," which makes sense with the key word "infinite." In choice (E), again, a quickly expanding universe has to expand more than *occasionally*.

4. B

Difficulty: Medium

Only one choice really makes sense. Look for words that make sense together. The movement encompasses many different styles and elements, so it must be diverse and hard to pin down. Out of all the answer choices, only one expresses that sentiment.

In choice (A), it's unlikely that *bragging* about post-modern literature is *necessary* for any reason. In choice (B), trying to *generalize* about a diverse topic is definitely *difficult*, and probably foolish. This choice seems to work. In choice (C), though many people like to *complain* about post-modern literature, its diversity hardly makes complaining *important*. In choice (D), why would *rhapsodizing* about post-modern literature be viewed as particularly *fair*? In choice (E), trying to *learn* is never *unproductive*.

5. C

Difficulty: Medium

If they've cornered the market, they've got a special kind of hold on it. Think about different industries throughout history. If one company had too much control over an industry, the government would step in and make laws to prevent the company from controlling the market. You're looking for a word that means "exclusive control."

In choice (A), if the company makes personal computers and software then they definitely have a vested *interest in* the market. In choice (B), why would a company work to corner a market it has *misgivings about*? In choice (C), if the company has a *monopoly on* the personal computer and software industry, the government would have to step in, so of course the CEO would insist that there's no monopoly. This choice works. In choice (D), the company's *responsibility in* the industry hardly has anything to do with their share in the market. In choice (E), it would be very bad for business (not to mention nonsensical) if the people in the company didn't have a general *consensus on*, or general agreed opinion, on the market.

6.   D

Difficulty: Medium

If they wanted their music to stand the test of time, they might have tried to write lyrics with timeless or universal appeal. This way the songs would be as relevant today as they were when they were written. Notice that the question says "weren't concerned with," so you're looking for an antonym.

In choice (A), being unconcerned with *sagacious* or wise subject matter wouldn't make the songs timeless. In choice (B), if they intended the songs to stand the test of time, they wouldn't have tried to focus on *dated* subjects. In choice (C), if they didn't use *evanescent* subjects the music wouldn't seem *nostalgic* today. Choice (D) will work. If they weren't using *transient* subjects then they're music would be timeless and feel as *fresh* and new today as it always was. In choice (E), straying from the use of *momentary* subjects wouldn't make their music *derivative*.

7.   C

Difficulty: Hard

The key word is "unconquerable." You're looking for a positive word because it's something the young professional is being praised for. In addition it's been said that she has an "unconquerable positive sprit." Think about which word would agree with "unconquerable."

In choice (A), m*orose* is the opposite of positive. In choice (B), *opulence* has little to do with a positive spirit. In choice (C), her *indomitable* nature could certainly give way to an unconquerable positive nature. This choice fits. In choice (D), though it is good to be *lithe*, it doesn't beget an unconquerable positive spirit. In choice (E), if her spirit is *ephemeral* then it's probably not unconquerable.

8.   D

Difficulty: Hard

He doesn't want any trespassers. If the male is instigating confrontations over territory, he probably views his territory as important and doesn't want it violated. By instigating confrontations he's trying to create an impenetrable territory.

In choice (A), he certainly wouldn't fight for something he felt was *dissipated* or lost. In choice (B), if he views his territory as *circuitous* it doesn't necessarily mean he'd want to keep others out. In choice (C), why would he specifically instigate fights with other males if he merely viewed his territory as *unparalleled*? Choice (D) is a good choice. If he views his territory as *inviolable*, he views it as impenetrable, and would certainly be unhappy to find it had been penetrated. In choice (E), even if his territory was *mandated* to him (which wouldn't make sense, he's a lizard), it doesn't mean he has a stake in defending it.

9.   E

Difficulty: Low

Be sensitive to the timing discussed in the passage. Ask yourself what was sculpted and when. When a word is associated with a certain time-frame, thinking about this connection may help you identify the function of the word. It is clear from the context that the cited word is referring to some degree of influence rice has had over Chinese culture. The words "Over the centuries" suggest that this influence was not sudden, but rather that it took place over time.

Choice (A) is an opposite; the text indicates that the influence of rice developed "Over the centuries." Choice (B) is out of scope; the passage does not discuss Chinese culture's possible resistance to change. Choice (C) is a distortion; because the text is focused on how *rice* has shaped Chinese culture, the word "work" does not make much sense in this context. Choice (D) is an irrelevant detail; while sustenance is mentioned later in the passage, this is not the function of the word "sculpted." Choice (E) is a great fit for your prediction.

10.   D

Difficulty: High

Notice any keywords that emphasize or de-emphasize information in the sentence. Always keep in mind the overall purpose of the passage when answering function questions. The overall purpose of the passage is to describe how rice has influenced various aspects of Chinese culture and beliefs. By pointing out that the medicinal properties of rice are not scientifically proven, the author is advancing this overall purpose by focusing attention on beliefs rather than scientific facts. The keyword "although" in the first clause of the sentence helps de-emphasize scientific proof and focus attention on beliefs.

Choice (A) is a distortion; nothing in the passage suggests that the author is critical of these beliefs about rice. Choice (B) is out of scope; the passage does not indicate whether or not these properties have been *tested*, only that they have not been proven effective. Choice (C) is a distortion; nowhere in the passage does the author suggest that rice's usefulness has been exaggerated. Choice (D) is a nice match for your prediction. Choice (E) is out of scope; the passage does not discuss the importance of scientific proof in general.

11. C

Difficulty: Medium

Since "driving expectancy" and "life expectancy" are being compared, you can expect that they refer to similar kinds of things. Thinking about "life expectancy" can help you figure out what "driving expectancy" is. While you may not be familiar with this particular phrase, go back to its context in the passage to find out precisely how it is used by the author. Pay particular attention to the meaning of other phrases that seem similar. The author refers to a gap, or difference, between "driving expectancy and life expectancy," and the previous sentence mentions seniors who have "outlived their ability or willingness to drive." This juxtaposition of information suggests that the gap involves a difference between how long people are living and how long they are able to drive. Since the phrase "life expectancy" seems to refer to how long a person can be expected to live, "driving expectancy" most likely refers to how long a person can be expected to drive.

Choice (A) is out of scope; the passage never mentions when *most people* actually do decide to stop driving. Choice (B) is a distortion; as the word "driving" suggests, the cited phrase is not referring to the number of people who rely on *public* transportation. Choice (C) is a good match for your prediction. Choice (D) is out of scope; the passage never gives a year when researchers expect the crisis to begin. Choice (E) is a distortion; while this group is mentioned earlier in the passage, it does not fit the context surrounding the cited phrase.

12. B

Difficulty: Medium

Where is the possibility of a "transportation crisis" first mentioned? Going directly to this part of the text will save you time. Look for clues in the question stem that can save you time by pointing you to a particular part of the text. Note that the question is specifically asking why there could "soon be" a transportation crisis. These words should narrow your research to the first sentence of the passage, which describes an impending situation: the "remarkably populous" post-World War II generation is getting to be an age where people should begin using public transportation more.

Choice (A) is a misused detail; while the passage supports this statement, it is the *lack* of adequate public transportation *elsewhere* that may create the crisis. Choice (B) is a good match for your prediction. Choice (C) is a distortion; the passage does not suggest that researchers are *increasingly* advising seniors to stop driving. Choice (D) is a misused detail; while the last sentence makes this point, this information does not describe why there may soon be a *transportation* crisis. Choice (E) is out of scope; the passage does not explore changing life expectancies or driving expectancies.

Questions 13–24

In Passage 1, the author discusses ways that she believes museums have regrettably "dumbed down" their exhibits in an attempt to lure more patrons. In paragraph 1, she explains that museums are struggling and therefore are trying new things to entice visitors, with mixed results. In paragraph 2, she discusses the "worst" of such results—that exhibits are "dumbed-down." In paragraph 3, she defines "edutainment" as passive learning. In paragraph 4, she concludes with the assertion that a museum ought to provide what for-profit enterprises do not: active scholarship.

In Passage 2, the author advocates making museums accessible to the general public, rather than simply to people who have already studied a particular topic extensively. In paragraph 1, she frames the opposition argument as "snobbery." In paragraph 2, she argues that new, accessible exhibits are not "dumbed-down" at all, but include more information to increase the layperson's appreciation of the exhibit without sacrificing things of interest to the scholar. In paragraph 3, she applauds the use of interactive exhibits to appeal to people with different learning styles. In paragraph 4, she affirms that the function of a public institution is to appeal to the public.

13. A

Difficulty: Medium

When the passages appear to take opposing views, any point of agreement will be fairly broad—something that virtually anyone would agree with. The author of Passage 1 says, "The museum's job should be to inspire the visitor to look deeper, not to force-feed them pre-digested facts" (lines 44–46). The author of Passage 2 says, "The purpose of these exhibits is…to introduce [visitors] to an area of knowledge that they have not been exposed to before, and inspire them to want to learn more" (lines 83–89). The authors agree that museums should inspire a visitor to learn more about the subject.

Choice (A) matches your prediction nicely. Choice (B) is an opposite; the author of Passage 2 specifically says that this is NOT the point of a museum exhibit. Choice (C) is a distortion; the author of Passage 1 speaks negatively about modeling exhibits on "entertainment," and the author of Passage 2, while supporting these exhibits, never says that the purpose of them is to be fun. Choice (D) is a misused detail; Passage 1 briefly mentions funding cuts, but does not cast fundraising as a primary purpose of a museum. Choice (E) is an opposite; the author of Passage 2 argues specifically against this.

14. C

Difficulty: Medium

The best predictions are those that you can back up with a specific sentence from the text. The passage says, "The worst of such results occurs when some condescending curator decides that the reason the audience isn't pouring through the doors is that the content is over their heads" (lines 11–14). Predict that the cause of "the worst of such results" is that *a curator thinks the audience cannot understand the content in the museum exhibits*.

Choice (A) is out of scope; the passage does not address the education level of the visitors. Choice (B) is a misused detail; this is the result, not the cause. Choice (C) matches your prediction. Choice (D) is out of scope; Passage 1 does not address *learning styles*. Choice (E) is out of scope; it is not clear that *a decline in funding* directly causes the "worst" result.

15. B

Difficulty: Low

If you answer Passage 1 questions before you read Passage 2, then answers designed to confuse the two won't trick you. The author of Passage 1 is discussing the different ways that museums have "dumbed down" their exhibits when she mentions the interactive exhibits. She uses them as an example of *a dumbed-down exhibit*.

Choice (A) is a misused detail; this is the viewpoint of the author of Passage 2. Choice (B) matches your prediction. Choice (C) is a distortion; the need for funds is not relevant to this paragraph. Choice (D) is an opposite; this is an example of how museums have stopped *catering to specialized scholars*. Choice (E) is out of scope; there is no information in the passage about how (or whether) *visitors have influenced* the museums directly.

16. D

Difficulty: Medium

When the passage doesn't state an answer directly, try summing up in your own words what the relevant lines do say or imply—this can often get you to the right answer. The author of Passage 1 disapproves of the displays she describes. From the last sentence of paragraph 3, it is clear that she feels these displays are failing to inspire visitors to look deeper, and that are "force-feeding" facts to visitors. Look for this in the correct choice.

Choice (A) is an opposite; this is too approving. The author of Passage 1 dislikes these displays. Choice (B) is out of scope; the author does not address the accuracy of the information in the exhibits. Choice (C) is a misused detail; this is the opinion of the author of Passage 2, not the author of Passage 1. Choice (D) matches your prediction. Choice (E) is a distortion; this is not the point the author is making.

17. A

Difficulty: Medium

When a question asks you to apply a piece of reasoning from the passage to a new situation, you can still make a prediction—state the reasoning from the passage in your own words, in simple terms, so you can apply that to the answer choices. The relevant text is describing a system that is designed to be entertaining but with facts "slyly" slipped in. Look for an answer choice that fits that description.

Choice (A) works with your prediction. Choice (B) is an opposite; a *biography* is not necessarily entertaining and requires more active perusal than the passage suggests. Choice (C) is a distortion; this example does not mention any facts or concrete learning at all. Choice (D) is out of scope; there is nothing in this answer choice to indicate that someone has prepared it specifically to be entertaining. Choice (E) is out of scope; this is a research tool, not a piece of entertainment with educational components.

18. C

Difficulty: Medium

Beware, the most common definition of a word when selecting your answer—it's usually wrong. The sentence says that the museums "house" artifacts. The only relationship that makes sense here is that the artifacts are inside the museum, so the museum *contains* them.

Choices (A), (D), and (E) are out of scope; they draw on a common definition of the noun "house," but if you read them into the sentence, you'll find they make no sense. Choice (B) is a distortion; it doesn't make sense for a museum to *build* anything. Choice (C) matches your prediction.

19. D

Difficulty: Medium

Watch out for answers that support one workable interpretation of a word but have little to do with the surrounding passage. The author is discussing how new museum exhibits cater to visitors who do not have much specific background in a topic. It says that concepts are introduced in a "digestible" format. It must have something to do with how easily visitors can understand material from the new exhibits.

Choice (A) is a distortion; the word is not to be taken literally in this context. Food is not relevant to the author's point. Choice (B) is out of scope; *controversial* exhibits are not discussed in the passage. Choice (C) is out of scope; whether or not the new exhibits *present only summaries* is not addressed. Choice (D) works with your prediction. Choice (E) is a misused detail; "digestible" refers to people learning material more easily, not to the types of people who do so.

20. E

Difficulty: Medium

An effective strategy for Inference questions is simply to paraphrase the relevant material from the passage in your own words. This will help you to draw conclusions more easily. In the course of the paragraph, the author discusses the "much-maligned interactive stations" and how they are an improvement over the "passive viewing and label-reading" of other displays. The author assumes that this has been the primary mode of exhibit for museums without interactive stations.

Choice (A) is an opposite; the author of Passage 2 thinks this method can be improved upon. Choice (B) is an opposite; the interactive stations, not the label-reading exhibits, are the innovation the author discusses. Choice (C) is a misused detail; it is the interactive stations that the author says will increase the value of the museum visit. Choice (D) is extreme; the author says that innovative museums have introduced interactive exhibits, but never says that they have completely done away with exhibits that rely on "passive viewing and label-reading." Choice (E) works with your prediction.

21. E

Difficulty: High

It's worth the extra few seconds to make a prediction for questions that ask about both passages—remember to research both as well. The author of Passage 2 says that these exhibits were born out of "improved understanding of different peoples' learning styles" (lines 95–96), and that they "engage a visitor's kinesthetic sense" (line 101) to provide "a variety of experiences, not just passive viewing and label-reading" (lines 104–105). She could defend these exhibits by showing that they were effective teaching tools for people with learning styles that are not purely visual.

Choice (A) is an opposite; the author of Passage 2 is against *passive learning*. Choice (B) is out of scope; a measure of the popularity of these exhibits would not support the assertion that they are effective. Choice (C) is out of scope; the expense of these exhibits is not discussed in either passage. Choice (D) is out of scope; the number of such exhibits in use is not addressed in either passage. Choice (E) works with your prediction.

22. D

Difficulty: Medium

For these types of questions, try applying the author's main argument to the relevant portion of the other passage. The author of Passage 1 thinks that innovations made in museums are condescending and a "dumbing-down" of content. She does not have an argument with the goal of engaging more people, but she thinks that museums are going about it in the wrong way.

Choice (A) is out of scope; the author of Passage 1 never hints at this. Choice (B) is a misused detail; the author does mention funding cuts, but only as a motivation for luring people back into museums, not as a reason against broadening museums' appeal. Choice (C) is out of scope; no other *pressing* issues are addressed in either passage. Choice (D) matches your prediction. Choice (E) is out of scope; the amount of training given to curators is not discussed in either passage.

23. E

Difficulty: High

Questions like this ask you to take on one author's viewpoint and respond to something through that lens. The author of Passage 1 thinks that new exhibits are a "dumbing down" of museum content. The statement that the exhibit is not trying to give a visitor a thorough and detailed understanding of a topic would serve to confirm this idea.

Choice (A) is out of scope; the author never mentions *higher education* and whether museums should encourage it. Choice (B) is out of scope; there is not enough information about curators' hopes to draw this conclusion. Choice (C) is an opposite; the exhibits being described are designed specifically so that those who know nothing about a topic can still understand them. Choice (D) is an opposite; the author of Passage 1 thinks they are insufficiently challenging. Choice (E) matches your prediction.

24. C

Difficulty: Medium

When you finish reading the second passage, it's a good idea to check what the passages had in common, and what they agreed and disagreed on. Both passages discuss the ideal of making a museum into a place where people learn actively rather than passively. They only differ in how to accomplish this.

Choice (A) is a misused detail; only Passage 1 mentions *funding,* and it does so only briefly. Choice (B) is a misused detail; only Passage 2 is concerned with this. Choice (C) is correct; both passages advocate *active learning.* Choice (D) is an opposite; neither passage claims to desire this. Choice (E) is an opposite; Passage 1 in particular seems opposed to this.

SECTION 7

1. C

Difficulty: Low

Strategic Advice: On symmetry problems, draw a line and see if each half is perfect reflection of the other choices.

Getting the Answer: Choices (A), (D), and (E) have one line of symmetry; (B) doesn't have any.

2. E

Difficulty: Low

Strategic Advice: Since there are numbers in the answer choices, Backsolving is a good strategy for this problem. If you decide to solve it algebraically, be careful and meticulous when translating the words into an equation.

Getting the Answer: To solve the problem algebraically, first translate from English to math. "The sum of 50 and j" is $(50 + j)$.

"Divide this sum by j, the result is 3"

$$\frac{(50 + j)}{j} = 3$$
$$50 + j = 3j$$
$$50 = 2j$$
$$j = 25.$$

You could also backsolve. Start with choice (C): $\frac{15 + 50}{15} = \frac{65}{15} = \frac{13}{3} > 3$. Since the result is more than 3, you need a bigger number. Try 20 next: $\frac{20 + 50}{20} = \frac{7}{2} > 3$. Again, you need a bigger number, so you know choice (E) must be correct.

3. D

Difficulty: Medium

Strategic Advice: When faced with a geometry problem with lots of unknowns, try to establish what you *do* know. In this case, you can easily figure out the measures of all the angles. Use that to help you find the lengths of the sides.

Getting to the Answer: Angle R is 70° and angle S is 40°, so angle P is $180° - 70° - 40° = 70°$. Since angle $P =$ angle $R = 70°$, the sides opposite those angles are of equal length and $4 + a = 5 + b$. Therefore, $a = b + 1$. That matches choice (D).

4. A

Difficulty: Low

Strategic Advice: Work carefully! Negative exponents can be tricky. You may find it helpful to write out each answer choice.

Getting to the Answer:

To get from 3.26691 to 0.00326691, you must move the decimal point three places to the left. Therefore, $0.00326691 = 3.26691 \times 10^{-3}$.

5. E

Difficulty: Medium

Strategic Advice: Before you start solving each question, make sure you know what the question stem is asking for. You are not asked to solve for x in this question, something that might trip up less observant test takers.

Getting to the Answer:

$x^{\frac{1}{2}} = 4$, so $\sqrt{x} = 4$. To solve for x, just square both sides.

$x = 16$

Now plug this into the expression you are asked to find.

$x^2 = 16^2 = 256$

6. D

Difficulty: Medium

Strategic Advice: Use the slope formula to find the missing coordinate.

Getting to the Answer:

$$m = \frac{y_2 - y_1}{x_2 - x_1}$$

$$-\frac{5}{12} = \frac{z - (-3)}{-7 - 5}$$

$$-\frac{5}{12} = \frac{z + 3}{-12}$$

$$5 = z + 3$$

$$2 = z$$

7. B

Difficulty: Medium

Strategic Advice: There are variables in the question and variables in the answer choices, so pick numbers to get to the answer quickly

Getting to the Answer:

Let $h = 1$. After the first hour at 5 miles per hour, Jerry will have traveled 5 miles, leaving 45 miles to go. Plug 1 into your Answer Choices and see which one gets you 45.

(A) $\frac{50}{5(1)} = \frac{50}{5} = 10$	
(B) $50 - 5(1) = 50 - 5 = 45$	OK
(C) $250(1) = 250$	
(D) $50 - \frac{5}{1} = 50 - 5 = 45$	OK
(E) $5(1) - 50 = 5 - 45 = -40$	

Now decide between (B) and (D) using the second hour. After the second hour at 5 miles per hour, Jerry will have traveled 10 miles, leaving 40 miles to go. Plug 2 into your Answer Choices and see which one gets you 40.

(B) $50 - 5(2) = 50 - 10 = 40$
(D) $50 - \frac{5}{2} = 50 - 2.5 = 47.5$

8. B

Difficulty: Medium

Strategic Advice: You won't have to use complicated math in every problem. Sometimes using common sense and knowledge of SAT basics will be enough.

Getting to the Answer:

The ratio of teachers to students is 1 to 10. That could mean that there is 1 teacher and 10 students, 50 teachers and 500 students, or another some other numbers with that ratio. Teachers and the students can be divided into groups of 11, each of which contains 1 teacher and 10 students. The total number of teachers and students in the school, then, must be a multiple of 11. Of the answer choices, only (B) is a multiple of 11.

9. C

Difficulty: Medium

Strategic Advice: When solving percent problems, make sure you place the decimal point in the right place. You could also pick numbers if you get stuck.

Getting to the Answer:

$.60 \times 20y = 12y$

10. E

Difficulty: Medium

Strategic Advice: The number of cats, c, and the number of dogs, d, are inversely proportional to each other so the equation $c = \dfrac{k}{d}$ (where k is a constant) describes their relationship. First, solve for k. Once you have k, you can solve for either quantity given the other.

Getting to the Answer:

You are given the values $c = 10$ and $d = 50$, so

$10 \; \dfrac{k}{50}$

$k = 500$

Then when $d = 20$, $c = \dfrac{500}{20} = 25$.

11. E

Difficulty: Medium

Strategic Advice: To find the answer choice that must be true, eliminate the ones that are sometimes or always false.

Getting to the Answer: To more easily visualize the scenario, pick numbers. The easiest scenario is to pick 4 coins, 2 G and 2 S. If the last two coins are G, then the display is SSGG, and (E) is true. If there are 6 coins and the last two are G, you could have GSSSGG, SGSSGG, or SSGSGG. No matter what you do, there will be at least 2 adjacent S coins. So (E) is true. Choices (A), (B), and (C) are not true: to return to the 4-coin example, you could have GSSG, ruling out choices (A) and (B), or SGSG, ruling out choice (C). Choice (D) is a bit trickier, but if you put two S coins together in the middle and alternate the others, you do not have to have 2 adjacent G coins. With 4 coins, GSSG does this. With six, GSSGSG works as well, and so on. Therefore, (D) is incorrect as well.

12. D

Difficulty: Medium

Strategic Advice: Substitute the values given in the initial setup of the problem. Work carefully to avoid mistakes, and be sure not to stop too soon.

Getting to the Answer:

$\left| \sqrt[3]{xy} - y \right|$

$= \left| \sqrt[3]{-3*9} - 9 \right|$

$= \left| \sqrt[3]{-27} - 9 \right|$

$= \left| -3 - 9 \right|$

$= \left| -12 \right| = 12$

13. B

Difficulty: Medium

Strategic Advice: Just remember the rules for transformations of functions; the graph of $g(x - n)$ is the graph of $g(x)$ shifted n units to the right.

Getting to the Answer:

Only (B) is shifted to the right; (A), (C), and (D) are shifted in different directions, and (E) is identical to the graph in the question.

14. B

Difficulty: Medium

This is a great problem to practice your English to math translation skills. Translate each part of the word problem into an equation and then solve.

Getting to the Answer:

$x + 6 - 2 = 2x$

$\quad\quad 4 = x$

15. C

Difficulty: Medium

Strategic Advice: The SAT presents some word problems that are not what they seem. This question appears to test probability, but in reality, algebra is all that is necessary. Backsolving also works well because there are numbers in the answer choices.

Getting to the Answer: Algebraically, if x represents the total number of coins, you can solve for x using the equation $\dfrac{1}{3}x + \dfrac{1}{4}x + \dfrac{1}{6}x + 6 = x$

$\dfrac{4}{12}x + \dfrac{3}{12}x + \dfrac{2}{12}x + 6 = x$

$\dfrac{9}{12}x + 6 =$

$$6 = \frac{3}{12}x$$

$$\text{So } x = 24$$

Using Backsolving, start with (C): $\frac{1}{3}(24) + \frac{1}{4}(24) + \frac{1}{6}(24) + 6 = x$

$8 + 6 + 4 + 6 = 24$, so choice (C) is correct.

16. D

Difficulty: Medium

Strategic Advice: Remember that $(xa)^b = x^{ab}$ and solve the original equation for 2^3 or simplify each answer choice to see which one equals 2^3.

Getting to the Answer:

$$(y)^4 = (2^{\frac{3}{4}})^4$$

$$y^4 = 2^3$$

SECTION 8

1. E

Difficulty: Low

Your prediction should describe the state of the coach's clothes after being soaked with water. Look for the answer choice that matches the prediction "soaked."

In choice (A), although the coach's attention was diverted to the state of his clothes, his clothes were wet. Choice (B) does not match the prediction. In choice (C), although this word relates to water as a "scuttled" ship lets in water and sinks, this word does not fit the context of the sentence. Choice (D) is out of scope; whether or not his clothes were dirty is not mentioned in the sentence. Choice (E) is the correct answer.

2. B

Difficulty: Low

Start with a prediction for the first blank. Sea otters are mammals that rely on their fur to keep them warm. For the second blank, focus on the part of the sentence that falls after the comma. Given that the otters live in "cold arctic waters," the "damaged fur" would cause them to lose body heat. Your prediction for the first blank should be "sustain"

or "preserve." For the second blank, try "exposed" or "defenseless."

In choice (A), neither word works. The first word relates to protection through insurance; don't confuse this word with "ensure." The second choice means "influenced" and does not have the negative connotation required by the prediction. Choice (B) is the answer. Eliminate choice (C) based on the first blank; the first word is the opposite of the prediction. Choice (D) is the opposite of the prediction. Choice (E) does not match the prediction.

3. A

Difficulty: Medium

Thoreau was inspired by a life lived away from "the company of men." Nothing other than this is stated about his lifestyle. The answer choice must be related only to what is said in the sentence; not to what can be inferred from it. A good prediction is "secluded." The answer must describe his lifestyle choice to live alone.

Choice (A) is the answer. Choice (B) means "sophisticated" or "suave." In choice (C), the calmness of nature found in the woods would be anything but "intrusive." In choice (D), although Thoreau may have found the woods to be "luxurious" or magnificent in a metaphorical sense of the word, this choice does not match the prediction. In choice (E), life in the woods may be "economical" compared with life in a town, however this does not match the prediction.

4. E

Difficulty: Medium

Start with the first blank. Would efforts be made to stop or encourage the drug trade? Note the keyword "despite": it indicates contrast between the blanks. The two predictions will contrast each other. The prediction for the first blank should be a synonym to "stop." The second blank should contain a word that means "thrive" or "grow."

In choice (A), the first choice means more along the lines of "to make better" than "to stop." If the production of drugs continued to *flag* or "decline," then there would not be so much effort to stop the drug trade. Eliminate choice (B) based on the first blank; it is the opposite of the prediction. Eliminate choice (C) based on the second word; *abate* is the opposite of the prediction. In choice (D), the first word is too weak; the drug trade needs not to be merely examined but rather eliminated. Choice (E) is the answer.

5.   A

Difficulty: Medium

The word "paradoxically" indicates that there is a supposed contradiction between the word in the blank and "harmonious." The rest of the sentence goes on to argue that there is in fact a linkage between these seemingly opposite concepts. Even if you didn't know that "dissonance" means "disagreement," you would still be able to make a prediction for the blank based on the fact that the word must mean the opposite of "harmonious."

Choice (A) is the answer. In choice (B), although this word is negatively charged, *immoral* or "dishonest" does not match the prediction for "disagreement." In choice (C), an *injunction* is a "court order" and although it is meant to bring harmony to quarreling parties, the word does not fit within the context of the sentence. Choice (D) means "conspiracy" and does not match the prediction. Choice (E) means "politeness" or "skill in dealing with people" and does not match the prediction.

6.   B

Difficulty: High

Look for the hotwords. The protagonists suffered from "exaggerated pride." Your prediction should be "arrogance" or "excessive pride." Although Greek tragedies had many themes, this sentence is describing one "common theme" in particular; be sure to scan the entire sentence for hotwords!

Choice (A) is out of scope; nothing is said about protagonists being "stubborn." Choice (B) is the answer. In choice (C), this word means "impulsivity" or "spontaneity" and does not match the prediction. In choice (D), *bravery* or "courage" does not match the prediction, although it may be a common theme in Greek myths. Be careful! In choice (E), *cold-heartedness* or "insensitiveness" does not match the prediction.

7.   E

Difficulty: Medium

Use your notes to help you infer conclusions about the author's larger intentions. The author explains that new communications technologies such as the Internet, while advertised as bringing people together, seem actually to be driving people apart. She might believe that one should be cautious about using new technologies like these.

Choice (A) is a distortion; some technologies are only available to those with high-speed Internet connections, but there is no indication that the author thinks it "should" be this way. Choice (B) is an opposite; the author seems distressed that personal relationships are suffering and would not recommend that the communications industry focus merely on profit. Choice (C) is an opposite; the passage says that high school students are especially vulnerable to Internet-caused alienation. Choice (D) is an opposite; the author is not interested in convenience but in human relationships. Choice (E) works well with your prediction.

8.   D

Difficulty: Low

Try reading your choice back into the sentence—if it sounds wrong, try another. The author cites some new communications technologies and says, "we are on the verge of breaking down all barriers to the complete and constant transfer of information. But if we seem to be moving toward unfettered union…," so the "breaking down all barriers" refers to the "unfettered union" mentioned in the next sentence. Since the "unfettered union" is something we are moving towards not something already achieved, "on the verge" must mean something like "almost to the point of." Pick an answer that makes the same amount of sense in the phrase.

Choice (A) is out of scope; "on the joint" makes no sense at all. Choice (B) is out of scope; "pinnacle" means "peak" or "high point" and that doesn't quite match the sense of our prediction. Choice (C) is out of scope; "on the togetherness" is nonsensical. Choice (D) "brink," means "edge," so this matches your prediction nicely. Choice (E) is out of scope; there are no clues as to whether people are particularly interested or not in this paragraph.

9.   D

Difficulty: Medium

To answer a Function question, ask yourself "What point was the author trying to make when she wrote this statement?" The end of the first paragraph is discussing the point of view of the communications industry ("With more ways to pass along all types of information, the communications industry reasons…" lines 11–13) and the final sentence is demonstrating the continuation of the communication industry's point of view about new technology.

Choice (A) is an opposite; the author disagrees with this point of view later in the passage. She clearly doesn't think it's the "best" way of looking at new technology. Choice (B) is a misused detail; this may be true and implied in the passage, but the author was not making this point when she wrote the relevant sentence. Choice (C) is extreme; nothing says that "everybody" thinks this way, only the communications industry. Choice (D) matches your prediction nicely. Choice (E) is out of scope; there is no information in the passage about what people might think in the future.

10. D

Difficulty: High

Be able to summarize each position taken about the topic of the passage. The communications industry, as depicted in the first paragraph, claims that new technologies will put us more in touch with other people. The author claims that these same technologies, in fact, isolate us. This is the key contrast.

Choice (A) is an opposite; the author does admit that these technologies increase efficiency, so she doesn't believe that they are a "hindrance." Choice (B) is an opposite; the communications industry may believe that new technologies are revolutionizing dating, but the author says that the technologies are making us less social, not more. Choice (C) is out of scope; nowhere in the passage are finances mentioned. Choice (D) works with your prediction; the communications industry says that these technologies are bringing us closer together, and the author claims they are driving us apart. Choice (E) is out of scope; the author never indicates that this technology is a regression into some earlier phase of society.

11. C

Difficulty: Medium

Your notes can help you determine the author's intention in the relevant paragraph, and that can help you predict a function for the cited lines. The paragraph that mentions the dating services also mentions *Friendster*, and describes the purposes of the companies. The end of the previous paragraph mentions that things that used to be done with people are now done from the "comfort—and isolation—of home." (line 36) The dating services are providing an example supporting that point—one way in which the Internet has led us to do things in a more solitary way, even dating.

Choice (A) is an opposite; the author does not have a favorable opinion of these services. Choice (B) is an opposite; the author is citing these services to support a point she made, not oppose it. Choice (C) matches your prediction nicely. Choice (D) is a misused detail; though awkwardness in dating is mentioned, this is not the focus of the paragraph nor what the author is interested in exploring. Choice (E) is a distortion; the purpose is not to contrast two Internet services but to explain how they are both dehumanizing.

12. B

Difficulty: Medium

The words "According to the passage" should alert you that the right answer is plainly stated somewhere in the passage, although it may be re-worded in the answer choices. The passage says, "Should one person be rude to another online; the act seems nearly free of consequences—the offender needn't be subjected to the sight of the emotional discomfort they are causing, and since interactions online are usually anonymous, he or she need take no responsibility for their remark in any meaningful way" (lines 77–83). The two reasons given for freedom from consequences are that the offender doesn't have to witness emotional discomfort and that the remark is anonymous.

Choice (A) is out of scope; no part of the passage addresses the relative impact of spoken versus electronic words. Choice (B) matches one of the reasons from the passage, and is the correct answer. Choice (C) is out of scope; no party is ever portrayed as being more interested in convenience than "personal concerns." Choice (D) is out of scope; you are not told anything about the companies that host such chat rooms. Choice (E) is a misused detail; while it may be derived from the author's argument that chat-room patrons are isolated, this is not given as the reason that less social accountability is demanded in a chat room.

13. A

Difficulty: Low

If you find yourself really "stretching" to justify your answer for an Inference question, reevaluate the other choices. The author says that enthusiasts of convenience wish to increase the number of virtual contacts people make without regard for the quality of those contacts. Infer that they care more about quantity than quality.

Choice (A) matches your prediction nicely. Choice (B) is extreme; the author says that online communications have an isolating effect, but there is not enough evidence to state that people who use them are "completely" isolated. Choice (C) is a misused detail; we don't know for sure whether or not the "enthusiasts of convenience" mentioned are customers of the dating services referred to earlier in the passage. Choice (D) is an opposite; the author says that these people want to increase the number of virtual interactions "without regard for their quality or duration" (line 107). Choice (E) is an opposite; the views attributed to the enthusiasts of convenience fit quite nicely with what the communications industry is reported to believe.

14. A

Difficulty: Low

Be sure to read several lines above a cited bit of text to get the author's full intention for writing it. Faxing a blueprint is mentioned in a list of examples that are introduced with the words "Gradually but surely, a technology that was originally intended to bring people closer together is instead helping them drift apart…" (lines 23–26). The list is meant to provide examples of technologies that make people interact less.

Choice (A) matches your prediction nicely. Choice (B) is a misused detail; this may be the case, but it is not the author's point in this sentence. Choice (C) is out of scope; there is no discussion in the passage of which technology is superior to another. Choice (D) is a misused detail; social accountability is discussed later in the passage and is not relevant here. Choice (E) is out of scope; the construction industry is never discussed in the passage.

15. B

Difficulty: Medium

Keep watch for any words in the passage that might indicate the author's opinion. "Communications technology has now contributed,…to an actual lessening of live human contact" (lines 18–22) indicates that the author disagrees with this premise. Words like "unfortunately" indicate that the author has an unfavorable view of the use of this technology. Predict that the author opposes this stance.

Choice (A) is an opposite; the author is not appreciative of the benefits of this technology. Choice (B) matches your prediction. Choice (C) is extreme; an example of *snide contempt* might be the use of outright insults in the passage, which are not apparent here. Choice (D) is out of scope; the issue is not so much that the author disbelieves any claims she is refuting, only that she disagrees with them. Choice (E) is an opposite; the author has a very strong opinion about communications technology, which she expresses in the passage.

16. A

Difficulty: High

When stuck, eliminate answer choices that seem to come out of nowhere. One notable omission from the author's argument is that while she objects to interactions that used to take place in person that now occur electronically, she does not address or refute the possible benefit of being more in touch with people that previously one could not reach otherwise. If this doesn't come to mind, try eliminating answers that seem to come from left field.

Choice (A) matches your prediction nicely. Choice (B) is a misused detail; the use of a fax machine is overly specific and would not affect the author's argument about human contact in a meaningful way. Choice (C) is a misused detail; while *Friendster* users' opinions might be relevant, the author could probably make her point thoroughly without using their input. Choice (D) is out of scope; the author is discussing human contact, not physical well-being. Choice (E) is out of scope; the distinction between technologies is not an issue in this essay, only their cumulative effect.

17. E

Difficulty: High

Remember that the correct answer to an Inference question, while not stated directly in the passage, will be very supportable from the information in the passage. The author's main complaint is that as more and more virtual connections are made, there are fewer and fewer face-to-face interactions. Most likely, the author would say that a focus on virtual relationships is taking people away from more human connections.

Choice (A) is an opposite; though fewer face-to-face interactions are taking place, the author never says that people have less need of them. Choice (B) is a misused detail; this is given as the opinion of the communications industry, not the author. Choice (C) is out of scope; the issue of time for other tasks is never raised in the passage. Choice (D) is extreme; though the author has a negative view of these virtual interactions, she never goes so far as to say they are causing psychological damage. Choice (E) suits your prediction well.

18. C
Difficulty: Low

For questions that do not cite a line reference, use your notes to get a solid grasp on the broad points of the essay. The author points out repeatedly that electronic interaction is replacing live communication. Look for an answer that reflects this.

Choice (A) is a misused detail; this is too specific. Online shopping is not the sole thing that the author claims replaces live community. Choice (B) is a misused detail; this is also too specific. Choice (C) works well with your prediction. Choice (D) is a misused detail; this is also too specific. Choice (E) is a distortion; Internet bullies are a phenomenon arising from distant interaction, not a replacement for anything.

SECTION 9

1. E
Difficulty: Low

Look for the most concise answer choice that does not contain any grammatical errors. As written, this sentence is unnecessarily wordy. Choice (E) is concise and contains no errors. Choices (B) and (C) change the meaning of the phrase and are unnecessarily wordy. Choice (D) is also overly wordy.

2. B
Difficulty: Low

Make sure that comparisons are structured to compare logical items. Here, *responsibilities* are being compared to *a medical student.* Choice (B) corrects this error by adding the pronoun *those*, which refers to *responsibilities.* Choices (C) and (D) to not address the error. Choice (E) fails to correctly complete the comparative idiom *as…as.*

3. B
Difficulty: Low

Look for the most concise answer that does not introduce additional errors.

As written, this sentence is awkward and unnecessarily wordy. Choice (B) is concise without losing any of the meaning of the original sentence. Choices (C) and (D) do not use correct parallel structure for the compound object *triumphs and…losses.* Choice (E) uses the pronoun *it* with no clear antecedent.

4. C
Difficulty: Low

Make sure a modifying phrase is correctly placed for the noun it is meant to modify. As written, this sentence states that *the city's local customs* are *foreigners.* Both choices (C) and (D) correctly place *Greg* directly after the clause; however, choice (D) is a sentence fragment. Choice (B) does not address the error. Choice (E) is awkward and unnecessarily wordy.

5. D
Difficulty: Medium

The gerund (*-ing*) verb form can never be the main verb in a sentence.

As written, this sentence is a fragment. By changing the verb form to the past tense *wrote*, choice (D) corrects the error without introducing any additional problems. Choices (B) and (E) are awkward and overly wordy. While not technically a run-on, choice (C) strings the two clauses together without relating them.

6. B
Difficulty: Medium

Pronouns use must be consistent throughout a sentence.

This sentence starts out using the second person pronoun *you,* then switches to the first person *our.* Since only *you* is underlined, it should be changed to the first person "we." Only choice (B) does so. Choice (C) changes the meaning of the sentence; *high altitudes* can't *run.* Choice (D) is unnecessarily wordy. The subject *people* in choice (E) is still inconsistent with the pronoun *our.*

7. D

Difficulty: Medium

Beware of the pronoun *it* on the SAT. It will not always be incorrect, but it frequently figures in ambiguity and pronoun agreement errors.

Here, the pronoun *it* does not have a singular antecedent. Choice (D) corrects this error with the correct plural pronoun *they.* Choices (B) ,(C), and (E) are grammatically incorrect.

8. C

Difficulty: Medium

Pronouns must agree in number with their antecedents.

The plural pronoun *their* does not agree with its singular antecedent *cinema.* Additionally, *important by* is idiomatically incorrect in context. Choice (C) corrects both errors without introducing any new ones. Choice (B) does not address the idiom error. Choice (D) uses adjectives (*personal* and *creative*) to modify a verb form (*speaking*). Choice (E) does not address the pronoun error.

9. B

Difficulty: Medium

When you don't spot a clear grammatical error, look for a more concise way to word the underlined information. Choice (B) is a more concise version of the sentence and doesn't introduce any additional errors. Choices (C) and (E) are still wordier than they need to be. Choice (D) creates a sentence fragment.

10. C

Difficulty: Medium

Look for the most concise answer choice that does not contain additional errors. As written, this sentence is unnecessarily wordy. Choice (C) is concise and contains no error. Choice (B) uses a transition that does not make sense in context. Choice (D) is even wordier than the original. Choice (E) leaves the meaning of the second clause incomplete.

11. D

Difficulty: Medium

One way to correct a run-on sentence is to make one of the clauses subordinate. This sentence is a run-on: two independent clauses joined by a comma splice. Choice (D) corrects this by making the second clause dependent. The pronoun *it* in choice (B) has no antecedent. Choice (C) misuses the semicolon splice, which is only correct between two independent clauses. Choice (E) is even wordier than the original.

12. D

Difficulty: High

Look for the most concise correct version of the underlined selection. As written, this sentence is unnecessarily awkward and wordy. Although the shortest answer won't always be correct, it's always a good place to start, and in this case, it is correct. The singular verb forms in choices (B) and (E) do not agree with the plural subject *People.* Choice (C) is awkward and overly wordy. People who *have low motivation or are not at least moderately intelligent* are not likely to make it as international journalists.

13. A

Difficulty: High

If you don't spot an error, don't be afraid to choose choice (A). This sentence is correct as written. The pronoun *he* correctly refers to *Mike* and the two verbs (*does* and *has*) are parallel in form. The pronoun *it* in choices (B), (C), and (E) has no clear antecedent. The verb phrase *is without being able to* in choice (B) is also grammatically incorrect. Choice (E) incorrectly uses *it* to refer to *Mike.*

14. E

Difficulty: High

Items in a series, list, or compound must be in parallel form.

The subject of this sentence is a compound, so they must be parallel in form. *The leadership* in choice (E) is parallel to *the…ability* in the second part of the compound. Choices (B), (C), and (D) do not address the error; additionally, choice (B) is grammatically incorrect.

SAT PRACTICE TEST THREE ANSWER SHEET

Remove (or photocopy) the answer sheet, and use it to complete the practice test.

How to Take the Practice Tests

Each Practice Test includes eight scored multiple-choice sections and one essay. Keep in mind that on the actual SAT, there will be an additional multiple-choice section—the experimental section—that will not contribute to your score.

Once you start a Practice Test, don't stop until you've gone through all nine sections. Remember, you can review any questions within a section, but you may not go back or forward a section.

Good luck!

Start with number 1 for each section. If a section has fewer questions than answer spaces, leave the extra spaces blank.

Section One

Section One is the writing section's essay component.
Lined pages on which you will write your essay can be found in that section.

Section Two

1. Ⓐ Ⓑ Ⓒ Ⓓ Ⓔ   9. Ⓐ Ⓑ Ⓒ Ⓓ Ⓔ   17. Ⓐ Ⓑ Ⓒ Ⓓ Ⓔ
2. Ⓐ Ⓑ Ⓒ Ⓓ Ⓔ   10. Ⓐ Ⓑ Ⓒ Ⓓ Ⓔ   18. Ⓐ Ⓑ Ⓒ Ⓓ Ⓔ
3. Ⓐ Ⓑ Ⓒ Ⓓ Ⓔ   11. Ⓐ Ⓑ Ⓒ Ⓓ Ⓔ   19. Ⓐ Ⓑ Ⓒ Ⓓ Ⓔ
4. Ⓐ Ⓑ Ⓒ Ⓓ Ⓔ   12. Ⓐ Ⓑ Ⓒ Ⓓ Ⓔ   20. Ⓐ Ⓑ Ⓒ Ⓓ Ⓔ
5. Ⓐ Ⓑ Ⓒ Ⓓ Ⓔ   13. Ⓐ Ⓑ Ⓒ Ⓓ Ⓔ   21. Ⓐ Ⓑ Ⓒ Ⓓ Ⓔ
6. Ⓐ Ⓑ Ⓒ Ⓓ Ⓔ   14. Ⓐ Ⓑ Ⓒ Ⓓ Ⓔ   22. Ⓐ Ⓑ Ⓒ Ⓓ Ⓔ
7. Ⓐ Ⓑ Ⓒ Ⓓ Ⓔ   15. Ⓐ Ⓑ Ⓒ Ⓓ Ⓔ   23. Ⓐ Ⓑ Ⓒ Ⓓ Ⓔ
8. Ⓐ Ⓑ Ⓒ Ⓓ Ⓔ   16. Ⓐ Ⓑ Ⓒ Ⓓ Ⓔ   24. Ⓐ Ⓑ Ⓒ Ⓓ Ⓔ

☐ # right in Section Two

☐ # wrong in Section Two

Section Three

1. Ⓐ Ⓑ Ⓒ Ⓓ Ⓔ   9. Ⓐ Ⓑ Ⓒ Ⓓ Ⓔ   17. Ⓐ Ⓑ Ⓒ Ⓓ Ⓔ
2. Ⓐ Ⓑ Ⓒ Ⓓ Ⓔ   10. Ⓐ Ⓑ Ⓒ Ⓓ Ⓔ   18. Ⓐ Ⓑ Ⓒ Ⓓ Ⓔ
3. Ⓐ Ⓑ Ⓒ Ⓓ Ⓔ   11. Ⓐ Ⓑ Ⓒ Ⓓ Ⓔ   19. Ⓐ Ⓑ Ⓒ Ⓓ Ⓔ
4. Ⓐ Ⓑ Ⓒ Ⓓ Ⓔ   12. Ⓐ Ⓑ Ⓒ Ⓓ Ⓔ   20. Ⓐ Ⓑ Ⓒ Ⓓ Ⓔ
5. Ⓐ Ⓑ Ⓒ Ⓓ Ⓔ   13. Ⓐ Ⓑ Ⓒ Ⓓ Ⓔ
6. Ⓐ Ⓑ Ⓒ Ⓓ Ⓔ   14. Ⓐ Ⓑ Ⓒ Ⓓ Ⓔ
7. Ⓐ Ⓑ Ⓒ Ⓓ Ⓔ   15. Ⓐ Ⓑ Ⓒ Ⓓ Ⓔ
8. Ⓐ Ⓑ Ⓒ Ⓓ Ⓔ   16. Ⓐ Ⓑ Ⓒ Ⓓ Ⓔ

☐ # right in Section Three

☐ # wrong in Section Three

Remove (or photocopy) this answer sheet, and use it to complete the practice test.

Start with number 1 for each section. If a section has fewer questions than answer spaces, leave the extra spaces blank.

Section Four

1. Ⓐ Ⓑ Ⓒ Ⓓ Ⓔ   9. Ⓐ Ⓑ Ⓒ Ⓓ Ⓔ   17. Ⓐ Ⓑ Ⓒ Ⓓ Ⓔ
2. Ⓐ Ⓑ Ⓒ Ⓓ Ⓔ   10. Ⓐ Ⓑ Ⓒ Ⓓ Ⓔ   18. Ⓐ Ⓑ Ⓒ Ⓓ Ⓔ
3. Ⓐ Ⓑ Ⓒ Ⓓ Ⓔ   11. Ⓐ Ⓑ Ⓒ Ⓓ Ⓔ   19. Ⓐ Ⓑ Ⓒ Ⓓ Ⓔ
4. Ⓐ Ⓑ Ⓒ Ⓓ Ⓔ   12. Ⓐ Ⓑ Ⓒ Ⓓ Ⓔ   20. Ⓐ Ⓑ Ⓒ Ⓓ Ⓔ
5. Ⓐ Ⓑ Ⓒ Ⓓ Ⓔ   13. Ⓐ Ⓑ Ⓒ Ⓓ Ⓔ   21. Ⓐ Ⓑ Ⓒ Ⓓ Ⓔ
6. Ⓐ Ⓑ Ⓒ Ⓓ Ⓔ   14. Ⓐ Ⓑ Ⓒ Ⓓ Ⓔ   22. Ⓐ Ⓑ Ⓒ Ⓓ Ⓔ
7. Ⓐ Ⓑ Ⓒ Ⓓ Ⓔ   15. Ⓐ Ⓑ Ⓒ Ⓓ Ⓔ   23. Ⓐ Ⓑ Ⓒ Ⓓ Ⓔ
8. Ⓐ Ⓑ Ⓒ Ⓓ Ⓔ   16. Ⓐ Ⓑ Ⓒ Ⓓ Ⓔ   24. Ⓐ Ⓑ Ⓒ Ⓓ Ⓔ

☐ # right in Section Four

☐ # wrong in Section Four

Section Five

1. Ⓐ Ⓑ Ⓒ Ⓓ Ⓔ   9. Ⓐ Ⓑ Ⓒ Ⓓ Ⓔ   17. Ⓐ Ⓑ Ⓒ Ⓓ Ⓔ
2. Ⓐ Ⓑ Ⓒ Ⓓ Ⓔ   10. Ⓐ Ⓑ Ⓒ Ⓓ Ⓔ   18. Ⓐ Ⓑ Ⓒ Ⓓ Ⓔ
3. Ⓐ Ⓑ Ⓒ Ⓓ Ⓔ   11. Ⓐ Ⓑ Ⓒ Ⓓ Ⓔ
4. Ⓐ Ⓑ Ⓒ Ⓓ Ⓔ   12. Ⓐ Ⓑ Ⓒ Ⓓ Ⓔ
5. Ⓐ Ⓑ Ⓒ Ⓓ Ⓔ   13. Ⓐ Ⓑ Ⓒ Ⓓ Ⓔ
6. Ⓐ Ⓑ Ⓒ Ⓓ Ⓔ   14. Ⓐ Ⓑ Ⓒ Ⓓ Ⓔ
7. Ⓐ Ⓑ Ⓒ Ⓓ Ⓔ   15. Ⓐ Ⓑ Ⓒ Ⓓ Ⓔ
8. Ⓐ Ⓑ Ⓒ Ⓓ Ⓔ   16. Ⓐ Ⓑ Ⓒ Ⓓ Ⓔ

☐ # right in Section Five

☐ # wrong in Section Five

If section 5 of your test book contains math questions that are not multiple choice, continue to item 9 below. Otherwise, continue to item 9 above.

9. 10. 11. 12. 13.

14. 15. 16. 17. 18.

Remove (or photocopy) this answer sheet, and use it to complete the practice test.

Start with number 1 for each section. If a section has fewer questions than answer spaces, leave the extra spaces blank.

Section Six

1. Ⓐ Ⓑ Ⓒ Ⓓ Ⓔ 10. Ⓐ Ⓑ Ⓒ Ⓓ Ⓔ 19. Ⓐ Ⓑ Ⓒ Ⓓ Ⓔ 28. Ⓐ Ⓑ Ⓒ Ⓓ Ⓔ
2. Ⓐ Ⓑ Ⓒ Ⓓ Ⓔ 11. Ⓐ Ⓑ Ⓒ Ⓓ Ⓔ 20. Ⓐ Ⓑ Ⓒ Ⓓ Ⓔ 29. Ⓐ Ⓑ Ⓒ Ⓓ Ⓔ
3. Ⓐ Ⓑ Ⓒ Ⓓ Ⓔ 12. Ⓐ Ⓑ Ⓒ Ⓓ Ⓔ 21. Ⓐ Ⓑ Ⓒ Ⓓ Ⓔ 30. Ⓐ Ⓑ Ⓒ Ⓓ Ⓔ
4. Ⓐ Ⓑ Ⓒ Ⓓ Ⓔ 13. Ⓐ Ⓑ Ⓒ Ⓓ Ⓔ 22. Ⓐ Ⓑ Ⓒ Ⓓ Ⓔ 31. Ⓐ Ⓑ Ⓒ Ⓓ Ⓔ
5. Ⓐ Ⓑ Ⓒ Ⓓ Ⓔ 14. Ⓐ Ⓑ Ⓒ Ⓓ Ⓔ 23. Ⓐ Ⓑ Ⓒ Ⓓ Ⓔ 32. Ⓐ Ⓑ Ⓒ Ⓓ Ⓔ
6. Ⓐ Ⓑ Ⓒ Ⓓ Ⓔ 15. Ⓐ Ⓑ Ⓒ Ⓓ Ⓔ 24. Ⓐ Ⓑ Ⓒ Ⓓ Ⓔ 33. Ⓐ Ⓑ Ⓒ Ⓓ Ⓔ
7. Ⓐ Ⓑ Ⓒ Ⓓ Ⓔ 16. Ⓐ Ⓑ Ⓒ Ⓓ Ⓔ 25. Ⓐ Ⓑ Ⓒ Ⓓ Ⓔ 34. Ⓐ Ⓑ Ⓒ Ⓓ Ⓔ
8. Ⓐ Ⓑ Ⓒ Ⓓ Ⓔ 17. Ⓐ Ⓑ Ⓒ Ⓓ Ⓔ 26. Ⓐ Ⓑ Ⓒ Ⓓ Ⓔ 35. Ⓐ Ⓑ Ⓒ Ⓓ Ⓔ
9. Ⓐ Ⓑ Ⓒ Ⓓ Ⓔ 18. Ⓐ Ⓑ Ⓒ Ⓓ Ⓔ 27. Ⓐ Ⓑ Ⓒ Ⓓ Ⓔ

right in Section Six

wrong in Section Six

Section Seven

1. Ⓐ Ⓑ Ⓒ Ⓓ Ⓔ 9. Ⓐ Ⓑ Ⓒ Ⓓ Ⓔ 17. Ⓐ Ⓑ Ⓒ Ⓓ Ⓔ
2. Ⓐ Ⓑ Ⓒ Ⓓ Ⓔ 10. Ⓐ Ⓑ Ⓒ Ⓓ Ⓔ 18. Ⓐ Ⓑ Ⓒ Ⓓ Ⓔ
3. Ⓐ Ⓑ Ⓒ Ⓓ Ⓔ 11. Ⓐ Ⓑ Ⓒ Ⓓ Ⓔ 19. Ⓐ Ⓑ Ⓒ Ⓓ Ⓔ
4. Ⓐ Ⓑ Ⓒ Ⓓ Ⓔ 12. Ⓐ Ⓑ Ⓒ Ⓓ Ⓔ
5. Ⓐ Ⓑ Ⓒ Ⓓ Ⓔ 13. Ⓐ Ⓑ Ⓒ Ⓓ Ⓔ
6. Ⓐ Ⓑ Ⓒ Ⓓ Ⓔ 14. Ⓐ Ⓑ Ⓒ Ⓓ Ⓔ
7. Ⓐ Ⓑ Ⓒ Ⓓ Ⓔ 15. Ⓐ Ⓑ Ⓒ Ⓓ Ⓔ
8. Ⓐ Ⓑ Ⓒ Ⓓ Ⓔ 16. Ⓐ Ⓑ Ⓒ Ⓓ Ⓔ

right in Section Seven

wrong in Section Seven

Section Eight

1. Ⓐ Ⓑ Ⓒ Ⓓ Ⓔ 9. Ⓐ Ⓑ Ⓒ Ⓓ Ⓔ
2. Ⓐ Ⓑ Ⓒ Ⓓ Ⓔ 10. Ⓐ Ⓑ Ⓒ Ⓓ Ⓔ
3. Ⓐ Ⓑ Ⓒ Ⓓ Ⓔ 11. Ⓐ Ⓑ Ⓒ Ⓓ Ⓔ
4. Ⓐ Ⓑ Ⓒ Ⓓ Ⓔ 12. Ⓐ Ⓑ Ⓒ Ⓓ Ⓔ
5. Ⓐ Ⓑ Ⓒ Ⓓ Ⓔ 13. Ⓐ Ⓑ Ⓒ Ⓓ Ⓔ
6. Ⓐ Ⓑ Ⓒ Ⓓ Ⓔ 14. Ⓐ Ⓑ Ⓒ Ⓓ Ⓔ
7. Ⓐ Ⓑ Ⓒ Ⓓ Ⓔ 15. Ⓐ Ⓑ Ⓒ Ⓓ Ⓔ
8. Ⓐ Ⓑ Ⓒ Ⓓ Ⓔ 16. Ⓐ Ⓑ Ⓒ Ⓓ Ⓔ

right in Section Eight

wrong in Section Eight

Section Nine

1. Ⓐ Ⓑ Ⓒ Ⓓ Ⓔ 9. Ⓐ Ⓑ Ⓒ Ⓓ Ⓔ
2. Ⓐ Ⓑ Ⓒ Ⓓ Ⓔ 10. Ⓐ Ⓑ Ⓒ Ⓓ Ⓔ
3. Ⓐ Ⓑ Ⓒ Ⓓ Ⓔ 11. Ⓐ Ⓑ Ⓒ Ⓓ Ⓔ
4. Ⓐ Ⓑ Ⓒ Ⓓ Ⓔ 12. Ⓐ Ⓑ Ⓒ Ⓓ Ⓔ
5. Ⓐ Ⓑ Ⓒ Ⓓ Ⓔ 13. Ⓐ Ⓑ Ⓒ Ⓓ Ⓔ
6. Ⓐ Ⓑ Ⓒ Ⓓ Ⓔ 14. Ⓐ Ⓑ Ⓒ Ⓓ Ⓔ
7. Ⓐ Ⓑ Ⓒ Ⓓ Ⓔ
8. Ⓐ Ⓑ Ⓒ Ⓓ Ⓔ

right in Section Nine

wrong in Section Nine

Practice Test Three

SECTION 1
Time—25 Minutes
ESSAY

The essay gives you an opportunity to show how effectively you can develop and express ideas. You should, therefore, take care to develop your point of view, present your ideas logically and clearly, and use language precisely.

Your essay must be written in your Answer Grid Booklet—you will receive no other paper on which to write. You will have enough space if you write on every line, avoid wide margins, and keep your handwriting to a reasonable size. Remember that people who are not familiar with your handwriting will read what you write. Try to write or print so that what you are writing is legible to those readers.

You have twenty-five minutes to write an essay on the topic assigned below.

DO NOT WRITE ON ANOTHER TOPIC. AN OFF-TOPIC ESSAY WILL RECEIVE A SCORE OF ZERO.

Think carefully about the issue presented in the following excerpt and the assignment below.

> "I am more and more convinced that our happiness or unhappiness depends far more on the way we meet the events of life, than on the nature of those events themselves"
>
> —Wilhelm von Humboldt

Assignment: Which do you think contributes more to personal happiness: what happens to you or the way you respond to what happens? Plan and write an essay in which you develop your point of view on this issue. Support your position with reasoning and examples taken from your reading, studies, experience, or observations.

DO NOT WRITE YOUR ESSAY IN YOUR TEST BOOK.
You will receive credit only for what you write in your Answer Grid Booklet.

_____

_____

_____

_____

_____

_____

_____

_____

_____

_____

_____

_____

_____

_____

_____

_____

_____

_____

_____

_____

SECTION 2

Time—25 Minutes

24 Questions

Directions: For each of the following questions, choose the best answer and darken the corresponding oval on the answer sheet.

Each sentence below has one or two blanks, each blank indicating that something has been omitted. Beneath the sentence are five words or sets of words labeled (A) through (E). Choose the word or set of words that, when inserted in the sentence, <u>best</u> fits the meaning of the sentence as a whole.

EXAMPLE:

Today's small, portable computers contrast markedly with the earliest electronic computers, which were ----.

(A) effective
(B) invented
(C) useful
(D) destructive
(E) enormous   Ⓐ Ⓑ Ⓒ Ⓓ ⬤

1. Because this time he had at least ---- the culprit, the security officer was able to ---- the ridicule he usually received for his laziness.

(A) obtained . . succumb to
(B) escaped . . subvert
(C) pursued . . avoid
(D) ignored . . observe
(E) disavowed . . enjoy

2. Diane was finally able to satisfy her passion for both sports and writing when she ---- the two by becoming a sports journalist.

(A) reclaimed
(B) merged
(C) defined
(D) abandoned
(E) conveyed

3. Instead of being ---- by her oppressive boss and unfortunate working conditions, the young professional found ---- in the workplace by exhibiting her talents to higher executives and moving up the corporate ladder.

(A) discouraged . . reconciliation
(B) defeated . . prosperity
(C) elevated . . happiness
(D) aided . . opportunity
(E) delayed . . unity

4. Many pieces of ancient pottery we now consider art were originally made for purely ---- reasons, such as to carry water.

(A) utilitarian
(B) grandiose
(C) imaginative
(D) aesthetic
(E) external

GO ON TO THE NEXT PAGE

5. While the Italian dressmaker often liked to use ----
materials to make her clothing, her designs are not
---- her country or Europe; in fact, her dresses are
marketed in other countries throughout the world.

(A) ancient . . condescending
(B) modest . . concerned with
(C) native . . limited to
(D) ordinary . . lobbying for
(E) cosmopolitan . . indebted to

6. The severe structural damage caused by the
corrosion occurred in such ---- manner that the
ultimate ---- of the building came as a complete
surprise.

(A) a manifest . . eradication
(B) a nefarious . . polarization
(C) an insidious . . destruction
(D) a methodical . . amalgamation
(E) an obvious . . stagnation

7. Despite his apparent ---- lifestyle, the old man was
known to drink to excess when visited by friends.

(A) temperate
(B) laconic
(C) duplicitous
(D) aesthetic
(E) voluble

GO ON TO THE NEXT PAGE

Directions: The passages below are followed by questions based on their content; questions following a pair of related passages may also be based on the relationship between the paired passages. Answer the questions on the basis of what is <u>stated</u> or <u>implied</u> in the passages and in any introductory material that may be provided.

Questions 8–9 are based on the following passage.

The following was adapted from a biography on Hollywood screen legend Cary Grant.

Long before Cary Grant even began the acting career that would spread his image across movie screens around the world, he was already a per-former. Desperate to escape an unstable home life
(5) and the humble environs of Bristol, England, where he grew up, Grant joined a traveling acro-batic troupe. He became the show's stilt walker, an unenviable position that required much painful practice before it could be mastered. As the rigors
(10) of carnival life took their toll and the excitement of crisscrossing the fairgrounds of his native England waned, Grant abandoned the troupe for the stage. His first roles, though small, served to mark the beginnings of what would become an
(15) illustrious career.

8. In the concluding sentence of the passage, the author suggests that

    (A) Grant displayed great ability, even in the first small roles he was given

    (B) Grant was rarely given more than small roles in the early stages of his career

    (C) the small roles Grant initially played are sig-nificant as the origins of his acting career

    (D) Grant owes much of his later success to his first small acting roles

    (E) when beginning a career, most actors must initially play small roles

9. In line 10, the phrase "took their toll" accentuates how Grant

    (A) grew discouraged by his failure to get acting roles

    (B) was working hard but earning very little money

    (C) came to regret the decision to leave his home and family

    (D) was unable to truly master the stilts before he left the troupe

    (E) was worn down by the carnival life that had once excited him

Questions 10–11 are based on the following passage.

When the revolutionary American chocolate maker Milton Hershey enthusiastically opened his first candy shop in Philadelphia at the age of 18, he knew little of the business, and his inexperience
(5) caused his endeavor to fold six years later. Nonetheless, getting his feet wet in the industry proved enough to keep him hooked on it, for he went on to work as an intern for a local caramel manufacturer. There he learned that superior
(10) results could only be achieved when the freshest milk was used and thus was born a lifelong dedi-cation to quality ingredients upon which he would later build his chocolate empire.

10. As indicated in the first sentence of the passage, Milton Hershey was

    (A) quite industrious

    (B) something of a child prodigy

    (C) an untalented entrepreneur

    (D) a groundbreaking candy producer

    (E) committed to using high-quality ingredients

11. The passage implies that Hershey

    (A) was the first to make candy from quality ingredients

    (B) had a persisting interest in candy manufac-turing

    (C) tried to apply caramel-making techniques to chocolate production

    (D) was well suited for a career only in candy making

    (E) had been fascinated by making candy since early childhood

GO ON TO THE NEXT PAGE

Questions 12–24 are based on the following passages.

Author 1 describes herself in relation to her friends in high school. In Passage 2, a different narrator describes the behavior of her college roommate Jessie.

Passage 1

It was puzzling to me that my one real advantage was the agent of my "uncoolness," and yet at the time I was cowed into believing that it was perfectly just. I adored my friends; they were
(5) smart, funny, beautiful, counterculture, and—as a rule—utterly depressed. As the "happy" one, I was the butt of most of the jokes. They had devised a ranking system among themselves that meant that the more emotionally fragile one was, the higher
(10) one rose on the totem pole. I asserted my independence from them by valuing mental stability and laughing cheerfully, yet I secretly, desperately wanted something to be wrong with me so that they would see me with new eyes. I would be
(15) deep. I would be twisted. I would turn out to have been the most wounded one of all, but so stoic about it that no one would know until years later.

Unfortunately for my social aspirations, I had had a happy childhood, surrounded by the com-
(20) forts of the upper-middle class and two loving parents, the only set of parents among my friends who were not divorced or separated. I had grown up a sensible child; my parents were fairly permissive, and I repaid their trust by taking few risks. I
(25) would drift into other parts of the store while my friends shoplifted, or turn the other way while they gave themselves tiny homemade tattoos with ink and a sewing needle, but never did I condemn them or tattle; I accepted what they
(30) did, and in turn, they accepted my presence among them.

It wasn't until years after high school, traveling with another friend who had had a good bit of horror in her life already, that I was impressed by
(35) the folly of my thinking. I expressed to her, after hearing her litany of misfortune and truly awful circumstance, my strange desire to have had something terrible happen to me so that I could be more complicated. She flew into a rage. How
(40) could I treat her misfortune so lightly as to express

even a hint of longing for it? I finally realized that the only way to show true respect for the terrible things that happen to other people was to be deeply grateful for, not dismissive of, my own
(45) good fortune.

Passage 2

Jessie could never get very far into a conversation with somebody new before she would blurt out some reference to the lithium pills she was taking or the manic phase she had just been
(50) through. Her battle with bipolar disorder was simultaneously the thing she was most proud of and the thing she was most ashamed of; she would tell people about it, I think, partly to show off and partly to get the worst over with. She could never
(55) bring herself to say something as straightforward as "Just so you know, I'm manic depressive," but it was always something like "Oops! I forgot to take my pill today—better take care of that," followed immediately by a calculatedly embarrassed side-
(60) ways glance that both invited inquiry and made one feel inexpressibly awkward.

And yet I couldn't help but like her. She feigned being a wide-eyed blank slate; she would go up to our professors after class and ask "dumb" question
(65) after "dumb" question, each one betraying a sharp insight into the topic and a weirdly sophisticated analysis of what was going on. She was always the first to ask the chemistry professor a question he couldn't answer. She played her intellect the same
(70) way she played her disorder; she would pretend to be trying to hide it, all the while proudly displaying it, framed in carefully constructed "accidental" scenarios. I forgave her each time; her transparent manipulation was so clearly a product of a true
(75) discomfort with who she really was that I could not feel inferior around her.

In this way, Jessie surrounded herself with a coterie of exceptional misfits. We were all going about the process of learning how to be adults in
(80) radically different ways from those of our peers; that was the thing that held our odd group together, and Jessie was at the center of it, flattering us with her insecurity.

GO ON TO THE NEXT PAGE

KAPLAN
Test Prep and Admissions

12. The first sentence of Passage 1 implies that

   (A) the narrator has difficulty understanding personal motivations

   (B) the narrator failed to recognize the crucial difference between herself and her friends

   (C) the narrator is intolerant of her friends' depression

   (D) the narrator's perspective on the implications of her emotional nature changed over time

   (E) the narrator's friends were unaware of their effect on others

13. In line 2, "agent" most nearly means

   (A) spy

   (B) active ingredient

   (C) destroyer

   (D) secret

   (E) cause

14. In lines 14–15, the phrase "I would be deep" indicates that the narrator

   (A) was not deep during the time described in the passage, but later became so

   (B) is hiding the terrible things that happened to her in the past

   (C) thinks that being happy is more profound than being depressed

   (D) believes that developing spiritually is the most important way to grow

   (E) thinks her friends would respect her more if she had something to be depressed about

15. In line 34, "impressed by" most nearly means

   (A) admiring of

   (B) forced into

   (C) made aware of

   (D) shown the good side of

   (E) surprised by

16. In lines 41–45 of Passage 1, the narrator's perspective changes from

   (A) admiration of her friends to disapproval of them

   (B) isolation to a sense of closeness

   (C) optimism to pessimism

   (D) dissatisfaction to gratitude

   (E) self-satisfied to solicitous

17. In the context of Passage 2, "played" (line 69) suggests that

   (A) Jessie made a conscious effort to portray her illness in a particular way

   (B) Jessie did not take her disorder seriously

   (C) the narrator was fooled into thinking that Jessie was different from her

   (D) Jessie has lost the ability to distinguish between deception and reality

   (E) the narrator believes Jessie's behavior is entertaining

18. The statement in lines 73–76 ("her transparent...around her") suggests that the narrator

   (A) is uncomfortable with who she really is

   (B) is an "exceptional misfit"

   (C) looks up to Jessie

   (D) pretends that she knows more about Jessie than she really does

   (E) might not forgive Jessie if Jessie made her feel inferior

19. Passage 2 indicates that the narrator feels as she does about Jessie because

   (A) she feels confident around Jessie's apparent insecurity

   (B) she admires Jessie's skill at manipulation

   (C) Jessie makes her uncomfortable

   (D) Jessie looks up to the narrator

   (E) Jessie helps her with Chemistry homework

GO ON TO THE NEXT PAGE

20. Author 1 and Jessie in Passage 2 are similar in that both

   (A) feel a strong desire to advance socially
   (B) feel insecure about their state of emotional health
   (C) are successful in deceiving others
   (D) are determined to remain genuine despite social disapproval
   (E) have been deeply affected by the attitudes of their friends

21. Jessie differs most from Author 1 in her

   (A) degree of social influence
   (B) ability to be successful in academics
   (C) willingness to devote her time to cultivating friendships
   (D) refusal to accept the labels and judgements of others
   (E) desire to befriend people of all different intellectual and emotional types

22. The two passages differ in that, unlike Jessie, Author 1 has

   (A) reluctantly decided to stay in school
   (B) rediscovered a love of family gatherings
   (C) found that emotional change is frequently impossible to obtain
   (D) overcome a negative attitude about her own emotional state
   (E) recently stopped lying about her childhood

23. Which best characterizes how the subject of self-assurance is treated in these two passages?

   (A) Passage 1 suggests that acceptance of self is an act of maturity, while Passage 2 implies that insecurity makes others feel better.
   (B) Passage 1 emphasizes the importance of genetics to emotional health, while Passage 2 focuses mainly on external circumstances.
   (C) Both passages portray characters who are unusually comfortable with themselves.
   (D) Passage 1 argues that emotional states can be consciously controlled, while Passage 2 claims that they are out of the individual's control.
   (E) Neither Passage 1 nor Passage 2 considers the psychological effect of pretending to be something other than one is.

24. Which generalization about emotional disorders is most strongly supported by both passages?

   (A) Economic status has more to do with social position than emotional states.
   (B) Students are the primary group afflicted by emotional disorders.
   (C) It is only after going to college that young people come to understand the intricacies of emotion.
   (D) People have emotional disorders primarily because of a desire to be interesting.
   (E) Emotional disorders play a large role in the social interactions of those afflicted by them and the people they associate with.

IF YOU FINISH BEFORE TIME IS CALLED, YOU MAY CHECK YOUR WORK ON THIS SECTION ONLY. DO NOT TURN TO ANY OTHER SECTION IN THE TEST.

SECTION 3

Time—25 Minutes

20 Questions

Directions: For this section, solve each problem and decide which is the best of the choices given. Fill in the corresponding oval on the answer sheet. You may use any available space for scratchwork.

Notes:

(1) Calculator use is permitted.

(2) All numbers used are real numbers.

(3) Figures are provided for some problems. All figures are drawn to scale and lie in a plane UNLESS otherwise indicated.

(4) Unless otherwise specified, the domain of any function f is assumed to be the set of all real numbers x for which $f(x)$ is a real number.

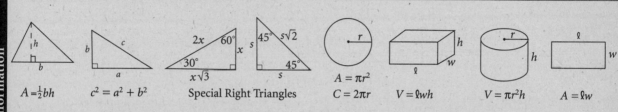

$A = \frac{1}{2}bh$ $c^2 = a^2 + b^2$ Special Right Triangles $A = \pi r^2$ $C = 2\pi r$ $V = \ell wh$ $V = \pi r^2 h$ $A = \ell w$

The sum of the degree measures of the angles in a triangle is 180.
The number of degrees of arc in a circle is 360.
A straight angle has a degree measure of 180.

---

1. If $4x + 2 = 26$, then $4x + 8 =$

    (A) 32
    (B) 34
    (C) 36
    (D) 38
    (E) 40

2. What are all the values of x for which $(x - 2)(x + 5) = 0$?

    (A) −5
    (B) −2
    (C) 2 and −5
    (D) −2 and 5
    (E) 2 and 5

3. If $a + 2 > 5$ and $a - 4 < 1$, which of the following could be a value for a?

    (A) 2
    (B) 3
    (C) 4
    (D) 5
    (E) 6

GO ON TO THE NEXT PAGE

7,X7X

4. The four-digit number above is divisible by 3 if X is replaced by which of the following digits?

(A) 4

(B) 5

(C) 6

(D) 7

(E) 9

5. If the perimeter of a regular polygon is 21, which of the following could be the length of one side of the polygon?

(A) 6

(B) 5

(C) 4

(D) 3

(E) 2

6. If Jorge earns $2,000 a month and spends $600 a month on rent, what percent of Jorge's monthly earnings does he spend on rent?

(A) 25%

(B) 30%

(C) 35%

(D) 40%

(E) 45%

7. If a is an odd negative number and b is a positive even number, which of the following must be even and positive?

(A) $a + b$

(B) $-ab$

(C) ab

(D) $\dfrac{b}{a}$

(E) $b - a$

8. Patty uses 2 gallons of paint to cover 875 square feet of surface. At this rate, how many gallons will she need to cover 4,375 square feet of surface?

(A) 4

(B) 5

(C) 8

(D) 10

(E) 15

9. A rectangular box is 24 inches long, 10 inches wide, and 15 inches high. If exactly 60 smaller identical rectangular boxes can be stored perfectly in this larger box, which of the following could be the dimensions, in inches, of these smaller boxes?

(A) 2 by 5 by 6

(B) 3 by 4 by 6

(C) 3 by 5 by 6

(D) 4 by 5 by 6

(E) 5 by 6 by 12

10. If the sum of 4 numbers is between 53 and 57, then the average (arithmetic mean) of the 4 numbers could be which of the following?

(A) $11\dfrac{1}{2}$

(B) 12

(C) $12\dfrac{1}{2}$

(D) 13

(E) 14

GO ON TO THE NEXT PAGE

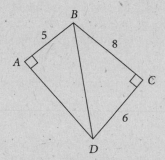

11. In quadrilateral *ABCD* above, if $CD = 6$, $BC = 8$, and $AB = 5$, what is the length of AD?

   (A) 4
   (B) $3\sqrt{5}$
   (C) $5\sqrt{3}$
   (D) 10
   (E) 15

12. In a coordinate plane, if points $C(2,5)$, $D(-1,2)$, and $E(x,y)$ lie on line l, which of the following could be the coordinates of point E?

   (A) (0,1)
   (B) (1,1)
   (C) (0,2)
   (D) (1,3)
   (E) (1,4)

13. If the fraction $\frac{1}{21}$ equals the repeating decimal .0476190476190..., what is the 51st digit after the decimal point of the repeating decimal?

   (A) 0
   (B) 1
   (C) 4
   (D) 6
   (E) 7

14. Sharon has exactly 6 quarters, 5 dimes, and 10 nickels in her pocket. She pulls out a coin at random and puts it aside since the coin is not a quarter. If she pulls out a second coin at random from her pocket, what is the probability that the second coin is a quarter?

   (A) $\frac{3}{7}$
   (B) $\frac{3}{10}$
   (C) $\frac{3}{11}$
   (D) $\frac{6}{19}$
   (E) $\frac{1}{4}$

15. If a is a nonzero integer and b is not an integer, which of the following could be an integer?

   (A) $a + b$
   (B) $a - b$
   (C) ab
   (D) $2a - b$
   (E) $\frac{b}{a}$

16. The daily cost of running a certain air conditioner is 12 cents per hour for the first 8 hours, and 10 cents per hour for each additional hour over 8 hours. Which of the following expressions represents the cost, in dollars, of running this air conditioner for h hours each day, for 90 days, if $8 < h < 24$?

   (A) $90(.12) + 9(h - 8)$
   (B) $90(.12)h + h - 8$
   (C) $90(.12)h + 9(h - 8)$
   (D) $90(.12)(8) + 9(h - 8)$
   (E) $90(.12)(8) + (h - 8)$

GO ON TO THE NEXT PAGE

17. If the lengths of the sides of a certain triangle are a, b, and c, which of the following statements could be true?

    (A) $c = b + a$
    (B) $c = b - a$
    (C) $c = 2a + b$
    (D) $c + 2 = a + b + 3$
    (E) $c + 3 = a + b + 2$

18. If $xy > 0$, $\dfrac{1}{x} + \dfrac{1}{y} = 5$, and $\dfrac{1}{xy} = 6$, then $\dfrac{x + y}{5} =$

    (A) $\dfrac{1}{25}$
    (B) $\dfrac{1}{6}$
    (C) $\dfrac{1}{5}$
    (D) 5
    (E) 6

19. At a basketball tournament involving 8 teams, each team played 4 games with each of the other teams. How many games were played at this tournament?

    (A) 64
    (B) 98
    (C) 112
    (D) 128
    (E) 224

20. The lengths of two sides of a triangle are $(x - 2)$ and $(x + 2)$, where $x > 2$. Which of the following ranges includes all and only the possible values of the third side y?

    (A) $0 < y < x$
    (B) $0 < y < 2x$
    (C) $2 < y < x$
    (D) $4 < y < x$
    (E) $4 < y < 2x$

SECTION 4

Time—25 Minutes
24 Questions

Directions: For each of the following questions, choose the best answer and darken the corresponding oval on the answer sheet.

Each sentence below has one or two blanks, each blank indicating that something has been omitted. Beneath the sentence are five words or sets of words labeled (A) through (E). Choose the word or set of words that, when inserted in the sentence, best fits the meaning of the sentence as a whole.

EXAMPLE:

Today's small, portable computers contrast markedly with the earliest electronic computers, which were ----.

(A) effective
(B) invented
(C) useful
(D) destructive
(E) enormous

1. Mr. Chandler's ostentatious tastes were clearly displayed when he was made president of the company, as the promotion caused him to ---- his new ---- with even more vigor.

(A) endure . . hardship
(B) flaunt . . prosperity
(C) undermine . . image
(D) calculate . . successes
(E) moderate . . consumption

2. Maria found it easy to ---- her meager winnings in the lottery, as her ticket was worth next to nothing.

(A) digest
(B) extol
(C) impugn
(D) forgo
(E) relish

3. Although Edward once ---- the intense publicity his more famous colleagues received, he came to appreciate his ---- and relative anonymity.

(A) envied . . privacy
(B) celebrated . . popularity
(C) imitated . . privilege
(D) regretted . . isolation
(E) refused . . generosity

4. Mrs. Smith was ---- by her son's insolence, feeling exasperated by his refusal to behave.

(A) fascinated
(B) galled
(C) uplifted
(D) soothed
(E) disoriented

5. The newly found eyewitness filled in many of the gaps in the case, providing certainty where before there had been a ---- of evidence.

(A) spate
(B) revision
(C) dearth
(D) dispersal
(E) consensus

GO ON TO THE NEXT PAGE

> **Directions:** The passages below are followed by questions based on their content; questions following a pair of related passages may also be based on the relationship between the paired passages. Answer the questions on the basis of what is <u>stated</u> or <u>implied</u> in the passages and in any introductory material that may be provided.

Questions 6–9 are based on he following passage.

Passage 1

In their heyday during the first half of the 19th century, hydroelectric schemes were regarded as a proven technology with extremely high energy-conversion efficiencies and a seemingly limitless
(5) source of low-cost power. It has been roughly 70 years since the most ambitious American implementation of hydroelectric technology resulted in the massive Hoover Dam, yet the public is only just beginning to grasp the significant tradeoffs
(10) inherent in this type of power generation. While dams add to domestic water supplies, provide employment and flood control, and create recreational water parks in the form of reservoirs, the ratio of people displaced to wattage generated is
(15) surprisingly high.

Passage 2

Hydroelectric dams have long been considered the cleanest, most environmentally-friendly source of electricity. Unlike fossil-fueled plants, hydroelectric facilities themselves do not emit harmful
(20) atmospheric pollutants, such as carbon dioxide, that have been shown to cause global warming and acid rain. However, recent studies have begun to demonstrate convincingly that hydroelectric power is not quite as benign as many once
(25) thought. While the large reservoirs and flood plains that are a direct result of damming can be valuable resources, the decaying of vegetation submerged by these watersheds creates gases largely equivalent to those generated from the burning of
(30) fossil fuels.

6. The author of Passage 1 refers to the Hoover Dam to make the point that

   (A) the construction of this particular facility failed to provide much employment

   (B) this dam is the most impressive American realization of energy-conversion technology

   (C) this project became the catalyst for reducing the use of hydroelectric power in America

   (D) it has taken decades for the public to grasp the costs of hydroelectric power

   (E) large constructions like this dam have an unexplainably high displacement to wattage ratio

7. In line 24, "benign" most nearly means

   (A) kind

   (B) gentle

   (C) harmless

   (D) useful

   (E) effective

GO ON TO THE NEXT PAGE

8. The central focus of the two passages suggests that

    (A) the environmental damage caused by hydro-electric dams is often overlooked

    (B) the proliferation of hydroelectric technology across America was unfortunate

    (C) hydroelectric dams generate power more efficiently than fossil fuel plants

    (D) the social tradeoffs presented by hydroelectric facilities must be considered

    (E) some consequences of hydroelectric technology were previously overlooked

9. The last sentence of each passage

    (A) summarizes the author's arguments

    (B) provides conclusive evidence to support the author's theory

    (C) presents positive and negative effects

    (D) introduces opposing opinions

    (E) narrows the author's statements to a single conclusion

GO ON TO THE NEXT PAGE

Questions 10–15 are based on the following passage.

The passage below is based upon an introduction to the memoirs of the grandson of Great Depression-era immigrants.

So often in America, we tend to take for granted the freedoms and liberties that we enjoy; it is only by revisiting our past and discovering the places that we are from that we are able to attain an
(5) awareness of our good fortune. I grew up in a middle-class neighborhood just outside Hartford, Connecticut, a mere two hours' journey to Ellis Island, where only 40 years earlier my grandparents had concluded their trans-Atlantic journey.
(10) Yet the sacrifices that such an endeavor necessitated were lost upon me. As a young man, I had neither the time to spend nor any interest in delving into my family's recent—and what was sure to be a very boring—history. The first college-bound
(15) member of my family, I was far too arrogant and conceited to allow that my grandparents had accomplished anything truly impressive. Had it not been for a chance discovery, I never would have realized how sorely mistaken I was.
(20) One day during the summer before I was to leave for college, I was home alone, rummaging through my father's old trunk. As I pawed through the old books and pamphlets and clothes, I uncovered an old, tattered photograph. It was of a
(25) young, handsome man sitting on the boardwalk at what appeared to be Coney Island. Though the passage of time had aged the face, I instantly recognized the figure in the picture as my grandfather. After taking a moment to scan the old black-
(30) and-white, I placed it back in the trunk, and would not have given it anymore thought except the doorbell rang, and I heard the voice of the old man himself. He had stopped by to say hello on his way home from the bakery. Such a fortuitous
(35) appearance, I thought, and with the photograph in hand, I went to greet him and show him my find.
My grandfather took the photo and looked it over for a long time, his mind's eye wandering to
(40) some far-off place. He was normally quite garrulous, so to see him silenced for so long caught me a bit off-guard. After what seemed like an age, and

a little lost for words, I asked him when the photograph was taken. I was certainly not prepared
(45) for the answer I received. He sat me down and launched into the story of the journey that had brought him and his young wife to America. From fleeing death and persecution in the pogroms of Russia, to changing his last name to secure safe
(50) passage across Eastern Europe, to the voyage across the Atlantic, to his arrival in New York City, he laid down the most mesmerizing story I had ever heard. The hardships that he, my grandmother, and untold numbers of immigrants like them
(55) had overcome had been unknown, and more significantly, unimportant to me, until that very instant. In the span of two hours, my grandfather had endowed me with a new knowledge, one that would forever alter my perspective on the privi-
(60) leges and opportunities that his actions had afforded me.

10. The primary purpose of the passage is to show how the author

(A) developed an arrogant attitude towards the rest of his family

(B) came to view the sacrifices of immigrants as mundane and mediocre

(C) discovered a new outlook on his prospects through a chance conversation with his grandfather

(D) learned to appreciate his grandfather at last

(E) overcame his shame from being the only educated individual in his family

11. In line 10, "endeavor" most nearly means

(A) pursuit

(B) effort

(C) ship

(D) goal

(E) drudgery

GO ON TO THE NEXT PAGE ▷

12. The first paragraph suggests that the author's "awareness" (line 5) initially was

    (A) very broad
    (B) very limited
    (C) misdirected
    (D) in line with that of his parents
    (E) non-existent

13. The author implies that he had adopted an arrogant attitude towards the rest of his family because he

    (A) believed that they were not intelligent
    (B) was the first person in the family to go to college
    (C) thought that anyone who left their home country must be foolish
    (D) was disappointed with his family's financial situation
    (E) was the first family member to be born in America

14. The author describes his grandfather as "normally quite garrulous" in order to

    (A) illustrate why he would be so eager to tell the story of his journey from Europe
    (B) explain his decision to talk about the photograph
    (C) show his desire to teach the author about his heritage
    (D) provide a reason for the grandfather's reticence
    (E) emphasize his reaction to the photograph

15. The author's tone throughout the passage can best be described as

    (A) appreciative and nostalgic
    (B) regretful and gloomy
    (C) angry and admonishing
    (D) patriotic and exasperated
    (E) reflective and indifferent

GO ON TO THE NEXT PAGE

Questions 16–24 are based on the following passage.

The definition of aesthetic pleasure is a popular subject for many different fields. In the following, adapted from an article found in a science journal, a physicist discusses the unique perspective that his discipline allows him.

Since time immemorial, countless scholars have asked the question: What is beauty? As philosophers engage in weighty discourses, designers update the latest fashions, and artists create their masterpieces, what is considered beautiful changes
(5) at an alarming pace. Fifty years ago, the full-figured Marilyn Monroe embodied the American aesthetic value; today, a legion of Hollywood actresses vastly different in appearance from Marilyn's have taken her place. However, aesthetic
(10) values not only differ from generation to generation, but do so along cultural lines as well. The conventions that govern painting and music vary greatly from East to West. Often, what is considered repellent to one civilization is the pinnacle of
(15) aesthetic appeal in another. Thus, when left to the sphere of human design, the search for an absolute definition of beauty remains an elusive one at best.

As fundamental physicists, my colleagues and I
(20) like to believe that we are involved in a search for a beauty that does not remain impervious to definition. The beauty that we search for is not that which is laid down through the work of people and subject to ephemeral tastes, but rather that
(25) which has been established by Nature. Those not involved with physics tend to think of it as a precise and predictive science—certainly not a field of study fit for the contemplation of the beautiful. Yet, one of physics' greatest gifts is that it allows its
(30) students to look past extrinsic appearances, into a more overwhelming beauty. As a human being, I am captivated by the visual appeal of a wave crashing on the beach. As a physicist however, I possess the ability to be captivated by the much
(35) deeper beauty of the physical laws that govern such a phenomenon. Where the non-physicist sees a lovely but inexplicable event, the well-schooled physicist is able to perceive a brilliant design.

In truth, since the day that Albert Einstein first
(40) proposed the notion that there might be one over-arching physical theory that governs the universe, aesthetics have become a driving force in modern physics. What Einstein and we, as his intellectual descendants, have discovered is this: Nature, at its
(45) most fundamental level, is beautifully constructed. The remarkable simplicity of the laws that govern the universe is, at times, nothing short of breathtaking. And at every step, as new discoveries and technologies allow us to examine the physical
(50) world on deeper and deeper levels, we find that the beauty itself becomes more profound. As Einstein himself said, it would seem more likely that we should find ourselves living in a "chaotic world, in no way graspable through thinking." Yet
(55) here we are, closer than ever to a full understanding of the universe's beautiful clockwork.

16. The reference to "Marilyn Monroe" in line 6 primarily serves to

(A) provide an example of today's standards of beauty

(B) discuss her abilities as an actress

(C) demonstrate how susceptible aesthetics are to change

(D) compare traditions of East and West

(E) illustrate that the standard definition of beauty remains constant

17. The author's assertion in lines 13–15 ("what is considered repellent… in another") suggests that

(A) cultures are naturally destined to clash

(B) many civilizations are prone to disgusting behavior

(C) different societies are tied together by an appreciation for physics

(D) it is nearly impossible to say what is truly beautiful

(E) individuals tend to disagree on what they find beautiful

GO ON TO THE NEXT PAGE

18. As used in line 23, the phrase "laid down" most nearly means

    (A) rested
    (B) slept
    (C) created
    (D) set
    (E) secured

19. The author uses the words "ephemeral" and "Nature" (lines 24 and 25) in order to

    (A) contrast the concept of impermanent beauty with the beauty for which physics searches
    (B) evaluate the effectiveness of physics as an art form
    (C) discuss how physicists visualize beauty
    (D) argue against the relevance of traditional forms of beauty
    (E) criticize people who don't understand physics

20. In the course of outlining the various gifts of physics, the author cites all of the following EXCEPT

    (A) the ability to look for a beauty that is unchanging
    (B) appreciating the visual beauty of a wave crashing
    (C) understanding both extrinsic and intrinsic beauty
    (D) a greater comprehension of Nature's ways
    (E) seeing a deeper design in natural events

21. In the third paragraph, Albert Einstein's proposal of an "overarching...theory" suggests that

    (A) the author believes that there is beauty in simplicity
    (B) the universe is infinitely complex
    (C) aesthetics has no place in physics
    (D) the physical world will never be understood rationally
    (E) the discovery of a full understanding of the universe is imminent

22. As used in line 42, "driving" most nearly means

    (A) leading
    (B) controlling
    (C) traveling
    (D) escaping
    (E) pounding

23. The author quotes Albert Einstein in lines 51–54 in order to

    (A) detail the way physical laws affect chaos
    (B) emphasize the scope of Einstein's influence
    (C) suggest that Einstein might have doubted the beauty of physics
    (D) stress just how remarkable the order of the universe really is
    (E) cast doubt upon Einstein's abilities

24. The passage is primarily concerned with

    (A) discussing the way various cultures assess beauty
    (B) explaining the beauty that is unmasked through an understanding of physics
    (C) demonstrating the way concepts of beauty change over time
    (D) recounting the achievements of Albert Einstein
    (E) finding new relevance for different physical laws

IF YOU FINISH BEFORE TIME IS CALLED, YOU MAY CHECK YOUR WORK ON THIS SECTION ONLY. DO NOT TURN TO ANY OTHER SECTION IN THE TEST.

STOP

Test Prep and Admissions

SECTION 5
Time—25 Minutes
18 Questions

Directions: For this section, solve each problem and decide which is the best of the choices given. Fill in the corresponding oval on the answer sheet. You may use any available space for scratchwork.

Notes:

(1) Calculator use is permitted.

(2) All numbers used are real numbers.

(3) Figures are provided for some problems. All figures are drawn to scale and lie in a plane UNLESS otherwise indicated.

(4) Unless otherwise specified, the domain of any function f is assumed to be the set of all real numbers x for which $f(x)$ is a real number.

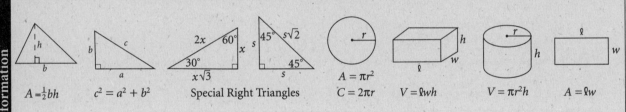

$A = \frac{1}{2}bh$ $c^2 = a^2 + b^2$ Special Right Triangles $C = 2\pi r$ $V = \ell wh$ $V = \pi r^2 h$ $A = \ell w$

The sum of the degree measures of the angles in a triangle is 180.
The number of degrees of arc in a circle is 360.
A straight angle has a degree measure of 180.

---

1. Which of the following is the equivalent of the statement that three-fourths of the cube of a plus the value of b divided by the square of c equals a?

    (A) $(-a)^3 + b - c^2 = a$

    (B) $\frac{3}{4}a^2 + \frac{b}{c} = a$

    (C) $\frac{3a^3}{4} + \frac{b}{c^2} = a$

    (D) $\frac{3}{4}a^3 + \frac{b}{c} = a$

    (E) $\frac{3}{4}a^3 + bc^2 = a$

2. A car rental agency charges $40 per day for the first 7 days, and $35 a day for each day after that. How much would Joe be charged if he rented a car for 10 days?

    (A) $375

    (B) $385

    (C) $395

    (D) $405

    (E) $415

GO ON TO THE NEXT PAGE

3. The number of tulips that Samantha grows each season varies directly with the age of her daughter Kim. If Samantha grew 16 tulips when Kim was 10 years old, how many tulips will she grow when Kim is 25 years old?

    (A) 25
    (B) 26
    (C) 30
    (D) 40
    (E) 45

g	h
2	10
4	j
j	k

4. In the table above, if $h = 3g + 4$, what is the value of k?

    (A) 12
    (B) 16
    (C) 27
    (D) 36
    (E) 52

5. Tameka cleans her house every 7 days and does laundry every 5 days. In the next 315 days, how many times will she have to clean her house <u>and</u> do laundry on the same day?

    (A) 9
    (B) 12
    (C) 26
    (D) 45
    (E) 63

6. If the length of one side of a triangle is 5, which of the following CANNOT be the lengths of the other two sides of the triangle?

    (A) 3 and 3
    (B) 3 and 5
    (C) 7 and 8
    (D) 7 and 3
    (E) 7 and 12

7. Line l has an undefined slope and contains the point $(-2, 3)$. Which of the following points is also on line l?

    (A) $(0, 3)$
    (B) $(5, 5)$
    (C) $(0, 0)$
    (D) $(3, -2)$
    (E) $(-2, 5)$

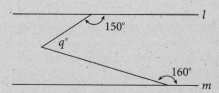

8. In the figure above, $l \parallel m$. What is the value of q?

    (A) 40°
    (B) 50°
    (C) 60°
    (D) 70°
    (E) 80°

GO ON TO THE NEXT PAGE

Directions: For Student-Produced Response questions 9–18, use the grids at the bottom of the answer sheet page on which you have answered questions 1–8.

Each of the remaining 10 questions requires you to solve the problem and enter your answer by marking the ovals in the special grid, as shown in the example below. You may use any available space for scratch work.

Answer: 1.25 or $\frac{5}{4}$ or 5/4

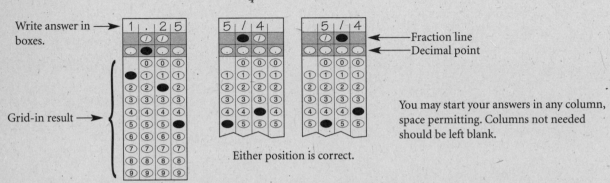

Write answer in boxes.

Grid-in result

Fraction line
Decimal point

Either position is correct.

You may start your answers in any column, space permitting. Columns not needed should be left blank.

- It is recommended, though not required, that you write your answer in the boxes at the top of the columns. However, you will receive credit only for darkening the ovals correctly.

- Grid only one answer to a question, even though some problems have more than one correct answer.

- Darken no more than one oval in a column.

- No answers are negative.

- Mixed numbers cannot be gridded. For example: the number $1\frac{1}{4}$ must be gridded as 1.25 or 5/4.

(If $\boxed{1\ |\ 1\ |\ /\ |\ 4}$ is gridded, it will be interpreted as $\frac{11}{4}$ not $1\frac{1}{4}$.)

- **Decimal Accuracy:** Decimal answers must be entered as accurately as possible. For example, if you obtain an answer such as 0.1666..., you should record the result as .166 or .167. **Less accurate values such as .16 or .17 are not acceptable.**

Acceptable ways to grid $\frac{1}{6}$ = .1666...

GO ON TO THE NEXT PAGE

9. On a cruise, 80 percent of the 3,000 passengers were married. Of these married passengers, 60 percent had been married less than a year, and 200 had been married more than 10 years. How many had been married 1–10 years?

10. In a class of 720 students, 35% are boys. How many girls are in the class?

11. To borrow a single book from a lending library, Mr. Brown was charged $2 for 2 weeks, plus a fine of $.15 per day for every day he was late returning it. If he paid a total of $4.55, how many days did he have the book?

12. If (&j) is the least prime integer greater than j, and (@j) is the greatest even integer less than j, what is the value of [&(−1.32)] − (@3.481)?

13. The perimeter of a rectangular plot of land is 300 meters. If the length of one side of the plot is 55 meters, what is the area of the plot, in square meters?

14. What is the slope of a line that passes through the points (0,1) and (−5,−1)?

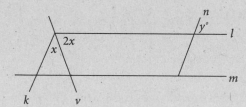

15. In the figure above, k is parallel to n and l is parallel to m. If 37° < x < 40°, what is one possible value of y?

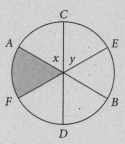

Note: Figure not drawn to scale.

16. In the figure above, $\overline{AB}$, $\overline{CD}$, and $\overline{EF}$ are diameters of the circle. If $y = 3x + 10$ and the shaded area is $\frac{1}{4}$ the area of the circle, what is the value of x?

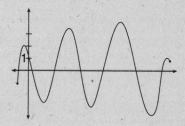

17. In the function above, for how many positive values of x does y = 3?

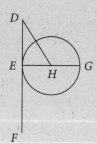

18. In the diagram above, $\overline{DF}$ is tangent to circle H at point E. EG = DH = 7. What is the length of $\overline{DE}$?

Test Prep and Admissions

SECTION 6

Time—25 Minutes
35 Questions

Directions: For each question in this section, select the best answer from among the choices given and fill in the corresponding oval on the answer sheet.

The following sentences test correctness and effectiveness of expression. Part of each sentence or the entire sentence is underlined; beneath each sentence are five ways of phrasing the underlined material. Choice (A) repeats the original phrasing; the other four choices are different. If you think the original phrasing produces a better sentence than any of the alternatives, select choice (A); if not, select one of the other choices.

In making your selection, follow the requirements of standard written English; that is, pay attention to grammar, choice of words, sentence construction, and punctuation. Your selection should result in the most effective sentence—clear and precise, without awkwardness or ambiguity.

EXAMPLE: ANSWER:

Every apple in the baskets <u>are ripe and labeled according to the date it was picked</u>.   Ⓐ ● Ⓒ Ⓓ Ⓔ

(A) are ripe and labeled according to the date it was picked
(B) is ripe and labeled according to the date it was picked
(C) are ripe and labeled according to the date they were picked
(D) is ripe and labeled according to the date they were picked
(E) are ripe and labeled as to the date it was picked

---

1. The pizzas from New York Pizza Depot <u>are better than Guido's</u>.

   (A) are better than Guido's
   (B) are better than those from Guido's
   (C) compared to Guido's
   (D) are better than like Guido's
   (E) better than those from Guido's

2. With ambition reminiscent of his idols, the already successful artist <u>hopes making</u> many great masterpieces.

   (A) hopes making
   (B) hopes to make
   (C) hopes it can make
   (D) has hope to make
   (E) is having hope of making

3. Richard Nixon, one of the only presidents impeached during his term, <u>and eventually to resign and leave office</u>.

   (A) and eventually to resign and leave office
   (B) eventually resigned and left office
   (C) he eventually resigned and left office
   (D) he eventually having resigned and left office
   (E) having eventually resigned and left his office

GO ON TO THE NEXT PAGE ⟩

4. Richard Avedon was celebrated by the *New Yorker* not only as a great photographer but also <u>he documented brilliantly decades of history</u> of America and the world.

   (A) he documented brilliantly decades of history

   (B) having documented decades of history brilliantly

   (C) documenting brilliantly decades of history

   (D) being a brilliant documenter of decades of history

   (E) as a brilliant documenter of decades of history

5. <u>Although the Chicago White Sox win more often than the Chicago Cubs, Chicago residents, who are historically avid baseball fans, prefer the Cubs.</u>

   (A) Although the Chicago White Sox win more often than the Chicago Cubs, Chicago residents, who are historically avid baseball fans, prefer the Cubs.

   (B) The Chicago White Sox winning more often than the Chicago Cubs; Chicago residents, who are historically avid baseball fans, prefer the Cubs.

   (C) Although not winning as often as the Chicago White Sox, the Chicago Cubs are preferred by Chicago residents, who are historically avid baseball fans.

   (D) Historically avid baseball fans in Chicago, who prefer the Cubs to the Chicago White Sox.

   (E) Although more games are won by the Chicago White Sox than the Chicago Cubs, Chicago residents, who are historically avid baseball fans, prefer the Cubs.

6. Because the lenses have UV <u>protection, nearly all UV rays are prevented from reaching the wearer's eyes.</u>

   (A) protection, nearly all UV rays are prevented from reaching the wearer's eyes

   (B) protection; nearly all UV rays are prevented from reaching the wearer's eyes

   (C) protection is the reason why they prevent nearly all UV rays from reaching the wearer's eyes

   (D) protection, they prevent nearly all UV rays from reaching the wearer's eyes

   (E) protection, it prevents nearly all UV rays from reaching the wearer's eyes

7. Having plenty of training, <u>my errors in judgment during my first day on the job were few.</u>

   (A) my errors in judgment during my first day on the job were few

   (B) I made few errors in judgment during my first day on the job

   (C) there were few errors in the judgment I used during my first day on the job

   (D) my first day on the job, I made few errors in judgment

   (E) the judgment I used during my first day on the job had few errors

8. Jean-Jacques is <u>so busy with work and thus</u> has no time for leisure activities.

   (A) so busy with work and thus

   (B) so busy with work and therefore

   (C) so busy with work that he

   (D) busy so much with work that he

   (E) so busy with work, and so he

GO ON TO THE NEXT PAGE

9. Despite their unanimous love of Hemingway, <u>the authors read by the members of the book club range from Danielle Steele to J.R.R. Tolkien</u>.

(A) the authors read by the members of the book club range from Danielle Steele to J.R.R. Tolkien

(B) authors ranging from Danielle Steele to J.R.R. Tolkien are read by the members of the book club

(C) authors ranging from Danielle Steele to J.R.R. Tolkien being read by the members of the book club

(D) the members of the book club read authors ranging from Danielle Steele to J.R.R. Tolkien

(E) a range of authors from Danielle Steele to J.R.R. Tolkien are read by the members of the book club

10. The issue the economists <u>considered, which was whether a tax decrease will cause an increase</u> in consumer spending or simply an increase in consumer savings.

(A) considered, which was whether a tax decrease will cause an increase

(B) considered was if they would decrease taxes would this cause an increase

(C) considered was that a decrease of taxes would result in an increased

(D) considered was will decreasing taxes mean an increase

(E) considered was whether a tax decrease would cause an increase

11. After shopping all day in crowded department stores, Kathy and Erica were as tired as <u>if running</u> a marathon.

(A) if running

(B) having run

(C) if from running

(D) if they had run

(E) if they would have run

GO ON TO THE NEXT PAGE ▷

Directions: The following sentences test your ability to recognize grammar and usage errors. Each sentence contains either a single error or no error at all. No sentence contains more than one error. The error, if there is one, is underlined and lettered. If the sentence contains an error, select the one underlined part that must be changed to make the sentence correct. If the sentence is correct, select choice (E). In choosing answers, follow the requirements of standard written English.

EXAMPLE:

<u>Whenever</u> one is driving late at night, <u>you</u> must take extra precautions <u>against</u>
    A   B   C

falling asleep <u>at the wheel</u>. <u>No error</u>
               D   E

(A) ● (C) (D) (E)

12. <u>Over the last</u> two weeks, I <u>learn</u> that all of the
     A   B

    family stories I heard throughout my childhood

    were fiction—fairy tales invented <u>to hide</u> the past I
                                          C

    was not allowed <u>to know</u>. <u>No error</u>
                   D   E

13. The <u>sickening</u> odor <u>emanating</u> <u>from</u> the bottles
          A   B   C

    <u>make</u> anyone in the general vicinity feel queasy.
    D

    <u>No error</u>
      E

14. New Jersey is now the most <u>dense populated</u> state,
                             A

    <u>while</u> Alaska <u>remains</u> the <u>most sparsely</u> populated.
     B   C   D

    <u>No error</u>
      E

15. <u>Like other archipelagos</u>, French Polynesia's culture
         A

    <u>has been</u> <u>profoundly shaped</u> by <u>its</u> geographic
      B   C   D

    isolation. <u>No error</u>
            E

16. In airplanes <u>as to</u> boats, <u>some</u> people <u>experience</u>
              A   B   C

    the feeling of nausea <u>known as,</u> motion sickness.
                       D

    <u>No error</u>
      E

17. <u>With</u> the <u>introduction of</u> inexpensive,
     A   B

    high-quality audio equipment, recording

    <u>by amateurs and hobbyists</u> <u>are becoming</u> more
              C   D

    common. <u>No error</u>
            E

18. <u>When</u> one reads Shakespeare, <u>we</u> can easily see how
     A   B

    <u>dramatically</u> the English language <u>has changed</u> in
      C   D

    the last 400 years. <u>No error</u>
                  E

19. Three of Jim's classmates who were <u>going</u> on the
                              A

    class trip <u>been</u> nervous about <u>being</u>
          B   C

    <u>away from home</u> for a whole week. <u>No error</u>
      D   E

GO ON TO THE NEXT PAGE →

20. The professor, in his flawed <u>interpretation of</u> the
                                        A
    revolutionary movement, stated that,

    <u>intense moved</u>, the revolutionaries forgot
         B

    <u>to be practical</u> and made a plan <u>only feasible in</u> a
         C   D
    different era. <u>No error</u>
                        E

21. <u>Since</u> the Kennedy Administration, fitness
         A

    standards <u>for</u> a child of eleven <u>has</u> greatly increased
                   B   C
    <u>throughout</u> the American public school system.
         D
    <u>No error</u>
         E

22. <u>Due to</u> strict confidentiality rules, which <u>have been</u>
         A   B
    in effect for years, only recently <u>has</u> the courtroom
                                            C
    statements of that witness <u>become known</u> to the
                                     D
    public. <u>No error</u>
                 E

23. <u>On the whole</u>, Steven <u>preferred driving</u> on small,
         A   B
    rural roads, which he found <u>more scenic</u>
                                     C
    <u>than the big city</u> where he lived. <u>No error</u>
         D   E

24. The soprano <u>who led</u> the opera production to its
                     A
    <u>first place finishes</u> in national and international
         B
    competitions <u>have</u> more than five costume
                      C
    changes, <u>which</u> occur in the opera's first act.
                 D
    <u>No error</u>
         E

25. <u>No matter</u> where Gwen traveled <u>or what</u> her
         A   B
    <u>experiences is</u> in the country, she was always <u>thankful</u>
         C   D
    for a kind word in her native language. <u>No error</u>
                                                  E

26. Jill and Casey <u>were convinced</u> to become <u>a member</u>
                        A   B
    of the Peace Corps <u>after seeing</u> a <u>video clip about</u>
                            C   D
    the rewards of volunteer service. <u>No error</u>
                                            E

27. Baseball was a typical American pastime <u>before</u>
                                                 A
    either basketball <u>and</u> football, its play <u>quickly</u>
                          B   C
    moving from New York and Boston to Pittsburgh,

    St. Louis, Cincinnati, <u>and then across</u> the country
                                D
    to California. <u>No error</u>
                        E

28. Heated debates between members of different

    political parties have recently <u>arose</u>, <u>causing</u> teachers
                                        A   B
    to reassess lessons <u>that encourage</u> students to
                             C
    express their opinions <u>in the classroom</u>. <u>No error</u>
                                D   E

29. The Russian language teachers <u>are convinced</u> that
                                        A
    their students' progress, coming <u>just weeks</u> after the
                                          B
    beginning of the term, <u>were caused</u> by extra efforts
                                C
    to discourage students <u>from speaking</u> English.
                                D
    <u>No error</u>
         E

GO ON TO THE NEXT PAGE

Directions: The following passage is an early draft of an essay. Some parts of the passage need to be rewritten.

Read the passage and select the best answer for each question that follows. Some questions are about particular sentences or parts of sentences and ask you to improve sentence structure or word choice. Other questions ask you to consider organization and development. In choosing answers, follow the conventions of standard written English.

Questions 30–35 are based on the following passage.

(1) The Kloss gibbon is an unusual ape species that can be found only in the rain forests of the Mentawai Islands off the western coast of Sumatra. (2) Kloss gibbons live in family "homes," as do most of us. (3) An adult male, an adult female, and their offspring sleep, eat, and enjoy one another's company within a specific territory that they have selected to be their own.

(4) If a male from another family group comes too close to the territory, the "homeowner" will view this approach as a threat, and would be fighting quite actively to defend his turf. (5) However, the use of physical force is rarely necessary, these animals have a unique way of avoiding conflicts. (6) Kloss gibbons sing to prevent a fight.

(7) Every two days or so, shortly before dawn, a male Kloss gibbon begins his "musical" performance by "whistling" for a few minutes. (8) As he gets more enthusiastic, he produces longer phrases, which can include as many as 12 notes and a trill. (9) The male stops, maybe even eats a piece of fruit, and then repeats his recital again, over and over, as he moves throughout the boundaries of his family's home territory. (10) These concerts can last anywhere from ten minutes to two hours.

(11) The beginning of the song is a male's simple way of saying "This is my house, and visitors are not welcome." (12) The rest of the complex song is not just showing off, though. (13) Unlike in many animals, the size of male Kloss gibbons does not vary much, so it is not a factor in determining strength. (14) If two males could see one another (which they can't because of the thick growth of the rain forest), they would not be able to decide, merely on sight, which one was likely to be the stronger of the two. (15) The elaborate part of the song conveys a clear message: "Don't make me hurt you!"

30. The sentence that best states the main idea of the passage is

   (A) sentence 1

   (B) sentence 3

   (C) sentence 6

   (D) sentence 11

   (E) sentence 15

31. In context, which is the best version of the underlined portion of sentence 4 (reproduced below)?

If a male from another family group comes too close to the territory, the "homeowner" will view this approach as a threat, and would be fighting quite actively to defend his turf.

   (A) and would be fighting quite actively

   (B) and might fight quite actively

   (C) and would quite actively be fighting

   (D) and will fight quite actively

   (E) and will engage in quite an active fight

GO ON TO THE NEXT PAGE ▶

32. In context, which is the best version of sentence 5 (reproduced below)?

    However, the use of physical force is rarely necessary, these animals have a unique way of avoiding conflicts.

    (A) (As it is now)

    (B) Since the use of physical force is rarely necessary, these animals have a unique way of avoiding conflicts.

    (C) However, the use of physical force is rarely necessary, this is because these animals have a unique way of avoiding conflicts.

    (D) However, the use of physical force is rarely necessary, while these animals have a unique way of avoiding conflicts.

    (E) However, the use of physical force is rarely necessary, because these animals have a unique way of avoiding conflicts.

33. In context, what revision is needed in sentence 13?

    (A) No revision is needed

    (B) Change "many animals" to "that of many animals"

    (C) Change "many animals" to "those of many animals"

    (D) Change "does not vary" to "do not vary"

    (E) Change "it is not a factor" to "they are not factors"

34. Of the following, which is the best version of sentence 14 (reproduced below)?

    If two males could see one another (which they can't because of the thick growths of the rain forest), they would not be able to decide, merely on sight, which one was likely to be the stronger of the two.

    (A) If two males could see one another (which they can't because of the thick growth of the rain forest), they would not be able to decide, merely on sight, which one was likely to be the stronger of the two.

    (B) Even if two males could see one another through the rain forest's thick growth, they probably would not be able to tell which one was stronger.

    (C) If two males happen to see one another through the thick growth of the rain forest, they will be unable to tell which one is stronger.

    (D) Even if two males could see one another, which they can't (because of the thick growths of the rain forest), they would not be able to decide merely on sight which one was the strongest.

    (E) Because of the thick growths in the rain forest, two males cannot see one another, and even if they could, they would not be able to decide which one was probably stronger.

35. Which of the following would be the most suitable sentence to insert immediately after sentence 14?

    (A) So a "homeowner" demonstrates his toughness by vocalizing.

    (B) This frequently can be a confusing situation for both the male gibbons.

    (C) Therefore, the "homeowner," realizing that he is much smaller, must sing to scare the intruder off.

    (D) For this reason, the intruding male shows how tough he is by vocalizing.

    (E) So the two males engage in a singing contest to see whose voice is louder.

IF YOU FINISH BEFORE TIME IS CALLED, YOU MAY CHECK YOUR WORK ON THIS SECTION ONLY. DO NOT TURN TO ANY OTHER SECTION IN THE TEST.

SECTION 7

Time—20 Minutes
19 Questions

Directions: For each of the following questions, choose the best answer and darken the corresponding oval on the answer sheet.

Each sentence below has one or two blanks, each blank indicating that something has been omitted. Beneath the sentence are five words or sets of words labeled (A) through (E). Choose the word or set of words that, when inserted in the sentence, <u>best</u> fits the meaning of the sentence as a whole.

EXAMPLE:

Today's small, portable computers contrast markedly with the earliest electronic computers, which were ----.

(A) effective
(B) invented
(C) useful
(D) destructive
(E) enormous ⒶⒷⒸⒹ●

---

1. Although his ---- amused his peers, his teacher found his mischief to be immature and disruptive.

   (A) anecdotes
   (B) researches
   (C) demands
   (D) pranks
   (E) debts

2. Although the thin stems of ferns appear ----, their sinewy structure actually makes them quite ---- and difficult to break.

   (A) vivid . . powerful
   (B) iridescent . . skillful
   (C) slender . . thick
   (D) beautiful . . heavy
   (E) fragile . . sturdy

3. Because he wanted to master the art of the ----, Carl worked on being able to communicate through a precise control over the muscles of his body and face, rather than his speaking skills.

   (A) mediator
   (B) ensemble
   (C) elocutionist
   (D) pantomime
   (E) troubadour

4. Although he was unsure of which activities were the ---- cause of his back pain, he knew enough to avoid running and heavy lifting, both of which could easily ---- the discomfort.

   (A) original . . alleviate
   (B) sole . . relieve
   (C) predominant . . induce
   (D) actual . . inhibit
   (E) partial . . produce

5. Ricky was such a captivating and memorable entertainer that his participation in the circus almost ---- the need for any other events.

   (A) accelerated
   (B) predetermined
   (C) substantiated
   (D) precluded
   (E) anticipated

GO ON TO THE NEXT PAGE

6. The senators decided to ---- the most contentious
   bill and focus instead on passing another law that
   was easier to reach a suitable ----.

   (A) table . . consensus on
   (B) enact . . opinion about
   (C) berate . . decision about
   (D) proclaim . . agreement on
   (E) endorse . . compromise on

7. His ---- was so limitless that it bordered on
   recklessness, for he gave more to charity than he
   could really afford.

   (A) amicability
   (B) inexorableness
   (C) frivolity
   (D) munificence
   (E) venerability

GO ON TO THE NEXT PAGE ▷

KAPLAN
Test Prep and Admissions

Questions 8–19 are based on the following passage.

The following passage is adapted from an article on the importance of bacteria to modern life.

There is a whole category of life that is fascinating, versatile, useful, and surprisingly varied and populous, and it's overlooked by a majority of people. Bacteria make up one and possibly two
(5) overarching categories of life, as biologists currently classify it. Prokaryotes, or true bacteria, are organisms without an organized cell nucleus. Archaebacteria were originally classified as prokaryotes, but recent studies have revealed dif-
(10) ferences in their cellular structure that might necessitate a whole new category to describe them. Bacteria are incredibly numerous; it may be that all the species we have ever catalogued make up only five percent of the total number of species of
(15) bacteria. They are everywhere in our world, from our dirt to our food to the very insides of our bodies. The fact that we can't see them makes them easy to ignore, but their impact on our lives is undeniable, and probably extends into more
(20) aspects of living than scientists are currently even aware of.

Perhaps the most remarkable thing about bacteria is their ability to survive in extreme environmental conditions. The oldest fossils scientists
(25) have discovered are fossilized bacteria; they were on earth when the planet was unbearably hot and carried no oxygen in its atmosphere. It was through bacteria evolving to adapt the sun's light into nutrients, and their subsequent development
(30) of the same kind of photosynthesis that plants use today, that oxygen and carbon dioxide were introduced to our atmosphere as waste products, allowing plants and animals to find a toehold on an otherwise inhospitable planet.
(35) One thing that makes bacteria such hardy survivors is their ability to alter their living DNA by exchanging their own with that in the environment around them or with that of other bacteria using methods called, respectively, transformation
(40) and conjugation. In this way, they can acquire the genes necessary to protect themselves from

extreme conditions like exceptionally hot, acidic, or airless environments; they can also acquire resistance to a particular antibiotic from another
(45) bacteria that already has the resistance. With these DNA-trading tactics, bacteria can benefit from evolutionary progress made by other species, simply by assuming it as their own.

The most common response to the word "bacte-
(50) ria" is to think of disease. While bacteria are the cause of many annoying and deadly diseases, most species are harmless, and many are actually beneficial. Bacteria is indispensable to many aspects of modern industry and production. We use bacteria
(55) to culture cheese and give each type its distinctive flavor, to treat sewage by breaking down harmful toxins into methane gas, to extract the desirable metal from other minerals in mines in a more environment-friendly alternative to smelting, and
(60) to improve the nutrient absorption and therefore the yield of food crops. Bacteria is also the basis for biotechnology; by combining bacteria with human DNA, we can use bacterial reproduction to manufacture important hormones like insulin, or
(65) antibodies that fight disease.

Despite all their beneficial uses, of course, the negative impacts of some bacteria cannot be ignored. While one strain of bacteria might give your smoked gouda its distinctive flavor, another
(70) species could very well be working on spoiling it, covering it with mold. Much of the bacteria in pre-treated sewage can cause deadly diseases. Some bacteria accelerates rusting, especially in metals containing iron. Other species will kill a
(75) farm's entire crop. If canned food during preservation is not heated to 250° Fahrenheit, it could be infected with botulism, a deadly toxin. With all their dangers, ironically enough, bacteria are supporting other industries, such as those devoted to
(80) antibacterial cleaning products, sterilization, and controlling the growth of dangerous species. Our relationship with bacteria is not a simple one, but it is an important one, and one that is highly if invisibly ingrained into our daily way of life.

GO ON TO THE NEXT PAGE

8. The author assumes that "a majority of people" (lines 3–4) are

   (A) not curious about things they can't see
   (B) infected with bacterial diseases
   (C) spreading bacteria intentionally in their everyday life
   (D) poorly educated
   (E) using antibacterial products

9. In line 18, "easy to ignore" emphasizes that bacteria are

   (A) useful
   (B) widely acknowledged
   (C) deeply misunderstood
   (D) too scarce to pay attention to
   (E) taken for granted

10. In line 19, the author uses "undeniable" to convey the

    (A) unavoidable incidence of disease caused by bacteria
    (B) necessity of using bacteria in industry
    (C) incontrovertible nature of the fact that bacteria affect us
    (D) inevitability of encountering visible bacteria
    (E) lack of solid support for the conjecture that bacteria are all around us

11. The reference to "extreme environmental conditions" in lines 23–24 primarily serves to

    (A) highlight the fact that certain environments cannot support life
    (B) exaggerate the adversity of places that bacteria live
    (C) emphasize the difficulty overcome by bacteria to live where other types of life cannot
    (D) emphasize the difficulty of conquering infectious disease
    (E) provide an example of ways to use bacteria in industry

12. In line 32, the author mentions "waste products" to illustrate that

    (A) bacteria can excrete harmful substances
    (B) plants and animals were only able to live on Earth due to bacteria's production of necessary gases
    (C) bacteria can live in extreme environments
    (D) plants and animals made Earth's environment hospitable for bacteria
    (E) bacteria are useful in treating sewage

13. The author argues that one reason bacteria are such "hardy survivors" (line 35) is that

    (A) they can adapt their own DNA
    (B) they can live inside humans
    (C) they use photosynthesis
    (D) they cause diseases
    (E) they have very long lifespans

14. In line 48, "assuming" most nearly means

    (A) jumping to conclusions
    (B) ascending
    (C) calculating
    (D) gaining
    (E) rejecting

15. The author mentions several industries in paragraph 4 (lines 53–65) in order to

    (A) illustrate all the uses of bacteria in modern industry
    (B) explain that using bacteria is good for the environment
    (C) provide examples of ways in which bacteria can be harmful
    (D) inform the reader in-depth about distinct species of bacteria
    (E) provide examples of ways in which bacteria can be beneficial

GO ON TO THE NEXT PAGE

16. Which example would be most appropriate to add to the list of bacteria's effects in paragraph 4?

    (A) bacteria contribute carbon dioxide to the atmosphere

    (B) bacteria produce enzymes used to manufacture laundry detergent

    (C) bacteria are responsible for mildew in humid places

    (D) bacteria are used to aid in digestion

    (E) bacteria coat different surfaces with a slimy substance called a "biofilm'

17. Which of the following industries are both helped and harmed by bacteria, according to the passage?

        I. agriculture
       II. cheese manufacture
      III. canning foods

    (A) I only

    (B) II only

    (C) II and III only

    (D) I and II only

    (E) I, II, and III

18. The passage indicates that which industry is supported by the actual dangers of bacteria?

    (A) mining

    (B) cheese manufacture

    (C) sewage treatment

    (D) the antibacterial industry

    (E) agriculture

19. The tone of the passage is primarily one of

    (A) scientific exhilaration

    (B) dry humor

    (C) conservative criticism

    (D) informed appreciation

    (E) mild disapproval

IF YOU FINISH BEFORE TIME IS CALLED, YOU MAY CHECK YOUR WORK ON THIS SECTION ONLY. DO NOT TURN TO ANY OTHER SECTION IN THE TEST. **STOP**

SECTION 8
Time—20 Minutes
16 Questions

Directions: For this section, solve each problem and decide which is the best of the choices given. Fill in the corresponding oval on the answer sheet. You may use any available space for scratchwork.

Notes:

(1) Calculator use is permitted.

(2) All numbers used are real numbers.

(3) Figures are provided for some problems. All figures are drawn to scale and lie in a plane UNLESS otherwise indicated.

(4) Unless otherwise specified, the domain of any function f is assumed to be the set of all real numbers x for which $f(x)$ is a real number.

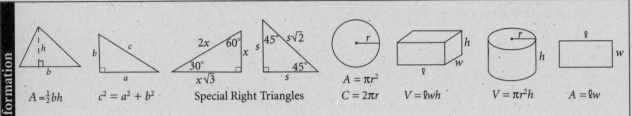

$A = \frac{1}{2}bh$ $c^2 = a^2 + b^2$ Special Right Triangles $A = \pi r^2$ $V = \ell wh$ $V = \pi r^2 h$ $A = \ell w$
$C = 2\pi r$

The sum of the degree measures of the angles in a triangle is 180.
The number of degrees of arc in a circle is 360.
A straight angle has a degree measure of 180.

1. If $8a < 3b$ and $3b < 10c$, which of the following is true?

    (A) $8a < 10c$

    (B) $10c < 8a$

    (C) $c < a$

    (D) $8a = 10c$

    (E) $8a + 1 = 10c$

2. If $g(t) = 2t - 6$, then at what value of t does the graph of $g(t)$ cross the x-axis?

    (A) -6

    (B) −3

    (C) 0

    (D) 2

    (E) 3

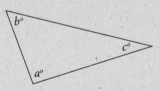

Note: Figure not drawn to scale

3. In the figure above, if $a = 7c$ and $b = 2c$, what is the value of c?

    (A) 18

    (B) 20

    (C) 28

    (D) 34

    (E) 36

GO ON TO THE NEXT PAGE

4. If $x^6 + 4 = x^6 + w$, then $w =$

   (A) -4
   (B) $-\sqrt[6]{4}$
   (C) $\sqrt[6]{4}$
   (D) 4
   (E) 4^6

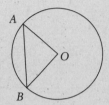

5. Point O is the center of the circle in the figure above. If angle $AOB = 70°$, what is the measure of angle ABO?

   (A) 40
   (B) 50
   (C) 55
   (D) 70
   (E) 110

6. For all positive integers f and g, let $f \# g$ be defined as $\dfrac{f + 2g}{f - 2g}$. What is the value of $1007 \# 3.5$?

   (A) 1014
   (B) 1.014
   (C) 10.14
   (D) 10,140
   (E) 101,400

Note: Diagram not drawn to scale

7. In the figure above, a square with side length 8 is divided into 16 squares. What is the area of the circle (not shown) that passes through points A, B, C, and D, which are the centers of the four corner squares?

   (A) $\sqrt{2}\pi$
   (B) $2\sqrt{2}\pi$
   (C) $3\sqrt{2}\pi$
   (D) 9π
   (E) 18π

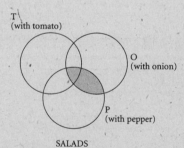

8. In the figure above, circular region O represents salads with onions, circular region P represents salads with pepper, and circular region T represents salads with tomato. What does the shaded region represent?

   (A) Salads with tomatoes, onions, and peppers.
   (B) Salads with onions and peppers, but without tomatoes.
   (C) Salads with onions and peppers (some possibly with tomatoes).
   (D) Salads with onions and tomatoes (some possibly with peppers).
   (E) Salads with peppers and tomatoes (some possibly with onions).

GO ON TO THE NEXT PAGE

9. While away at school, Eileen receives an allowance of $400 each month, 35 percent of which she uses to pay her bills. If she budgets 30 percent of the remainder for shopping, allots $130 for entertainment, and saves the rest of the money, what percentage of her allowance is she able to save each month?

(A) 2.5%

(B) 13%

(C) 20%

(D) 35%

(E) 52%

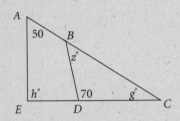

Note: Figure not drawn to scale

10. In the figure above, line $\overline{BD}$ crosses $\angle ACE$, what is the value of h in terms of z?

(A) $20 + z$

(B) $20 + 2z$

(C) $20 - 2z$

(D) $140 - z$

(E) $140 + z$

11. The lines are equally spaced on the number line above. What is the value of $p - q$?

(A) $\dfrac{1}{5}$

(B) $\dfrac{1}{4}$

(C) $\dfrac{2}{5}$

(D) $\dfrac{2}{4}$

(E) $\dfrac{3}{5}$

12. If a number is rounded to 16.8, which of the following could have been the original number?

(A) 16

(B) 16.704

(C) 16.763

(D) 16.873

(E) 17

13. If $f(x) = \sqrt{x^2 - 4}$, then $f(x)$ is undefined for which of the following values of x?

(A) −6

(B) −4

(C) −2

(D) 0

(E) 2

GO ON TO THE NEXT PAGE

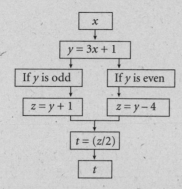

14. A person selects a positive integer x and follows the steps in the diagram above to get t. Which of the following statements must be true?

    I. $t > 0$
   II. z is even
  III. t is even

(A) I only
(B) II only
(C) I and II only
(D) II and III only
(E) I, II, and III

15. If $3a + 5b - 4c = 12$ and $a + 3b - 2c = -4$, what is the value of $a - b$?

(A) 4
(B) 8
(C) 16
(D) 20
(E) The answer can not be determined from this information.

16. If k friends contribute d dollars each, and that money is distributed equally among c number of charities, how much money is received by each charity?

(A) $\dfrac{kd}{c}$

(B) $\dfrac{c}{dk}$

(C) $dk + c$

(D) $\dfrac{dc}{k}$

(E) $(k - c)d$

IF YOU FINISH BEFORE TIME IS CALLED, YOU MAY CHECK YOUR WORK ON THIS SECTION ONLY. DO NOT TURN TO ANY OTHER SECTION IN THE TEST.

STOP

SECTION 9

Time—10 Minutes
14 Questions

Directions: For each question in this section, select the best answer from among the choices given and fill in the corresponding oval on the answer sheet.

The following sentences test correctness and effectiveness of expression. Part of each sentence or the entire sentence is underlined; beneath each sentence are five ways of phrasing the underlined material. Choice (A) repeats the original phrasing; the other four choices are different. If you think the original phrasing produces a better sentence than any of the alternatives, select choice (A); if not, select one of the other choices.

In making your selection, follow the requirements of standard written English; that is, pay attention to grammar, choice of words, sentence construction, and punctuation. Your selection should result in the most effective sentence—clear and precise, without awkwardness or ambiguity.

EXAMPLE: ANSWER:

Every apple in the baskets <u>are ripe and labeled according to the date it was picked</u>.

(A) are ripe and labeled according to the date it was picked
(B) is ripe and labeled according to the date it was picked
(C) are ripe and labeled according to the date they were picked
(D) is ripe and labeled according to the date they were picked
(E) are ripe and labeled as to the date it was picked

---

1. New Year's Day is traditionally when people make resolutions to improve themselves in the <u>future, the renewal the new year provides</u> is a natural time for self-reflection

    (A) future, the renewal the new year provides

    (B) future; the renewal the new year provides

    (C) future, the new year, and the renewal it provides

    (D) future, the new year provides renewal that

    (E) future; because the renewal the new year provides

2. The hills in Santa Barbara County, like <u>neighboring San Luis Obispo County, is</u> home to some of California's best vineyards.

    (A) neighboring San Luis Obispo County, is

    (B) the hills of neighboring San Luis Obispo County, is

    (C) the hills of neighboring San Luis Obispo County, are

    (D) those in neighboring San Luis Obispo County, is

    (E) neighboring San Luis Obispo County, are

GO ON TO THE NEXT PAGE

3. Nurses and anesthesiologists are both essential in the operating room, <u>and the anesthesiologists would keep the patient sedated while the nurses would assist and support</u> the surgeon.

   (A) and the anesthesiologists would keep the patient sedated while the nurses would assist and support

   (B) the anesthesiologists keep the patient sedated and the nurses are assisting and supporting

   (C) the anesthesiologists to keep the patient sedated and the nurses to assist and support

   (D) and the anesthesiologists keep the patient sedated while the nurses would assist and support

   (E) the anesthesiologists keeping the patient sedated while the nurses would assist and support

4. Roberto attempted to lose <u>weight, tried</u> various diets, including one which required him only to eat raw foods.

   (A) weight, tried

   (B) weight, he tried

   (C) weight; and tried

   (D) weight by trying

   (E) weight with the trying of

5. The floods displaced many people, forcing them to find new homes, <u>to find new sources of drinking water</u>, and new supplies of food.

   (A) to find new sources of drinking water

   (B) new sources of drinking water

   (C) new sources of drinking water to find

   (D) the drinking water at new sources

   (E) new sources of water that could be drunk

6. The monkeys grew agitated <u>very quickly and the havoc it wrought was nearly unbelievable</u>.

   (A) very quickly and the havoc it wrought was nearly unbelievable

   (B) very quick and the havoc they wrought was nearly unbelievable

   (C) very quickly, the havoc they wrought was nearly unbelievable

   (D) very quick and the havoc it wrought was nearly unbelievable

   (E) very quickly and the havoc they wrought was nearly unbelievable

7. The food critic from *Cuisine* magazine found <u>as to the likeability of the new chef's dishes as surprising and thorough</u>.

   (A) as to the likeability of the new chef's dishes as surprising and thorough

   (B) as to the new chef, his dishes are surprisingly and thoroughly likeable

   (C) that the new chef's surprisingly and thoroughly likeable dishes

   (D) that in regards the new chef's dishes, they are surprisingly and thoroughly likeable

   (E) that the new chef's dishes are surprisingly and thoroughly likeable

GO ON TO THE NEXT PAGE

8. The animal shelter reported fewer stray dogs than ever before this <u>year, this is because an ever-growing percentage of dogs are spayed or neutered and there are fewer unwanted puppies consequently</u>.

  (A) year, this is because an ever-growing percentage of dogs are spayed or neutered and there are fewer unwanted puppies consequently

  (B) year, an ever-growing percentage of dogs being spayed or neutered means fewer unwanted puppies consequently

  (C) year as a result of the fact that an ever-growing percentage of dogs are spayed or neutered and there are fewer unwanted puppies consequently

  (D) year because an ever-growing percentage of dogs are spayed or neutered and there are consequently fewer unwanted puppies

  (E) year because of the spaying or neutering of an ever-growing percentage of dogs and therefore fewer unwanted puppies

9. The sausage served at the end of the meal <u>was more flavorful than any of the other pastas I had tasted; probably because</u> it was roasted in its own juices.

  (A) was more flavorful than any of the other pastas I had tasted; probably because

  (B) tasting more flavorful than any of the other pastas I had; probably because

  (C) than any of the other pastas I had tasted was more flavorful, probably because

  (D) was more flavorful than any of the pastas I had tasted, as a result most likely of the fact that

  (E) was more flavorful than any of the pastas I had tasted, probably because

10. <u>Similar to William Shakespeare were the works of Christopher Marlowe, which</u> included plays, poetry, and translations of ancient works into English.

  (A) Similar to William Shakespeare were the works of Christopher Marlowe, which

  (B) Similar to William Shakespeare's works were those of Christopher Marlowe, which

  (C) Similar to William Shakespeare was Christopher Marlowe, who

  (D) Similarly to William Shakespeare's works were those of Christopher Marlowe, which

  (E) Similar to William Shakespeare's works were those of Christopher Marlowe, where they

11. <u>When a bacterial culture is handled in an environment that is not appropriately sterilized, they can be introducing new organisms, ruining</u> the culture.

  (A) When a bacterial culture is handled in an environment that is not appropriately sterilized, they can be introducing new organisms, ruining

  (B) A bacterial culture, when handled in a not appropriately sterilized environment, can introduce new organisms and this ruins

  (C) When a bacterial culture is handled in an environment that is not appropriately sterilized, new organisms can be introduced, ruining

  (D) If you handle a bacterial culture in an environment that is not appropriate sterilized, it can introduce new organisms, ruining

  (E) A bacterial culture, when handled in an environment that is not appropriately sterilized, can introduce new organisms and ruins

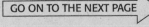
GO ON TO THE NEXT PAGE

12. The internet is becoming an indispensable part of everyday <u>life, but there is not much use in the developing world</u>.

  (A) life, but there is not much use in the developing world

  (B) life, but in the developing world there is not much use

  (C) life but is not used much in the developing world

  (D) life, but use in the developing world is not much

  (E) life, but using it is not done much in the developing world

13. The computer repair course emphasized <u>the importance of using a properly connected grounding wire to prevent a static electric charge</u> that could damage fragile computer components.

  (A) the importance of using a properly connected grounding wire to prevent a static electric charge

  (B) the importance of using a properly connected grounding wire preventing a static electric charge

  (C) to prevent a static electric charge it is important to use a properly connected grounding wire

  (D) the importance of using a properly connected grounding wire and to prevent a static electric charge

  (E) why it is important using a properly connected grounding wire to prevent a static electric charge

14. The hawks' nest, wedged into an apartment building's façade, was a rather unique sight in Chicago; <u>they became such an attraction that several books were written about them and</u> tourists came from all over the country to see them.

  (A) they became such an attraction that several books were written about them and

  (B) several books were written about them and they became such an attraction that

  (C) they had become such an attraction that several books were written about them and

  (D) it became such an attraction, writing several books, and

  (E) the hawks, after several books were written about them, became such an attraction that

IF YOU FINISH BEFORE TIME IS CALLED, YOU MAY CHECK YOUR WORK ON THIS SECTION ONLY. DO NOT TURN TO ANY OTHER SECTION IN THE TEST.

STOP

Practice Test Three: **Answer Key**

SECTION 1

Essay

SECTION 2

1. C
2. B
3. B
4. A
5. C
6. C
7. A
8. C
9. E
10. D
11. B
12. D
13. E
14. E
15. C
16. D
17. A
18. E
19. A
20. B
21. A
22. D
23. A
24. E

SECTION 3

1. A
2. C
3. C
4. B
5. D
6. B
7. B
8. D
9. A
10. E
11. C
12. E
13. E
14. B
15. C
16. D
17. E
18. B
19. C
20. E

SECTION 4

1. B
2. D
3. A
4. B
5. C
6. D
7. C
8. E
9. C
10. C
11. B
12. B
13. B
14. E

15. A
16. C
17. D
18. C
19. A
20. B
21. A
22. A
23. D
24. B

SECTION 5

1. C
2. B
3. D
4. E
5. A
6. E
7. E
8. B
9. 760
10. 468
11. 31
12. 0
13. 5,225
14. 2/5 or .4
15. $60 < y < 69$
16. 20
17. 4
18. 6.06

SECTION 6

1. B
2. B
3. B
4. E
5. A
6. D
7. B
8. C
9. D
10. E
11. D
12. B
13. D
14. A
15. A
16. A
17. D
18. B
19. B
20. B
21. C
22. C
23. D
24. C
25. C
26. B
27. B
28. A
29. C
30. C
31. D
32. E
33. B
34. B
35. A

SECTION 7

1. D
2. E
3. D
4. C
5. D
6. A
7. D
8. A
9. E
10. C
11. C
12. B
13. A
14. D
15. E
16. B
17. D
18. D
19. D

SECTION 8

1. A
2. E
3. A
4. D
5. C
6. B
7. E
8. C
9. B
10. A
11. C
12. C
13. D
14. B

15. D
16. A

SECTION 9

1. B
2. C
3. C
4. D
5. B
6. E
7. E
8. D
9. E
10. B
11. C
12. C
13. A
14. E

KAPLAN
Test Prep and Admissions

PRACTICE TEST THREE

Critical Reading

	Number Right	Number Wrong	Raw Score
Section 2:	☐	− (.25 × ☐) =	☐
Section 4:	☐	− (.25 × ☐) =	☐
Section 7:	☐	− (.25 × ☐) =	☐

Critical Reading Raw Score = ☐

(rounded up)

Writing

	Number Right	Number Wrong	Raw Score
Section 1:	☐ (ESSAY GRADE)	× 3.17 =	☐
Section 6:	☐	− (.25 × ☐) =	☐
Section 9:	☐	− (.25 × ☐) =	☐

Writing Raw Score = ☐

(rounded up)

Math

	Number Right	Number Wrong	Raw Score
Section 3:	☐	− (.25 × ☐) =	☐
Section 5A: (QUESTIONS 1–8)	☐	− (.25 × ☐) =	☐
Section 5B: (QUESTIONS 9–18)	☐	(no wrong answer penalty) =	☐
Section 8:	☐	− (.25 × ☐) =	☐

Math Raw Score = ☐

(rounded up)

Turn to page xiv to convert your raw score to a scaled score.

Answers and Explanations

SECTION 1

6 Score Essay

There's a common saying usually applied to sports: "It's not whether you win or lose, it's how you play the game." This saying, however, can easily be applied to how we live and whether or not we are able to achieve personal happiness. As the Humboldt quotation suggests, it's not the events that occur in our lives but rather the way we react to these events that most affects our happiness. Excellent representations of this can be found in Shakespeare's "Hamlet," where characters respond differently to the same situation and gain varying levels of happiness because of their respective reactions.

Gertrude, for example, responds to the death of her husband, the King, by remarrying shortly after his death. Rather than dwelling on her new role as widow and the accompanying sorrow and misfortune that have fallen upon her, she chooses to react by quickly recovering and aligning herself with her former brother-in-law. Given her situation, this is a very intelligent and rational decision, for it provides her with the security of a strong marriage as well as a continued high status as queen, since Claudius has now ascended to the throne. All of these positive attributes make Gertrude happy even though she continues to mourn and miss her dead husband. In this way, Gertrude pursues and achieves her own personal happiness by reacting positively to a negative event rather than letting that event destroy her.

In contrast, Hamlet reacts to his father's death by obsessing about what happened and by brooding over his mother's remarriage. Because of his vision of the ghost, Hamlet begins to believe that his father was murdered, but instead of acting decisively on this information and confronting his uncle directly, Hamlet ponders his vision and sinks deeper and deeper into his sorrow and depression. Allowing himself to be heavily influenced by everything that is happening around him, Hamlet eventually succumbs to his despair and dies along with several other characters in the final scene of the play. Hamlet is a prime example of someone who lets his happiness be ruled by outside forces rather than choosing how to react to events to exert some control over his own emotional state of mind.

Although Gertrude and Hamlet are fictional characters, the way Shakespeare portrays them is representative of real human behavior. Many people let themselves be influenced by what happens to them, like Hamlet, and these people have difficulty finding happiness. On the other hand, some people, like Gertrude, react in a more positive way to any event that occurs and thus achieve a certain level of personal happiness regardless of what happens. This contrast proves that our reaction to events rather than the events themselves is the critical factor for achieving happiness.

6 Score Critique

All essays are evaluated on four basic criteria: Topic, Support, Organization, and Language. The writer begins this essay with a common saying that she relates to the prompt and the assignment, demonstrating that she has clearly understood the prompt Her thesis is included in the introductory paragraph, as is her plan for the body of her essay, an early indication that the author has taken the time to outline her essay before she began to write.

The examples provided, though drawn from a single literary source, demonstrate that the writer has well-developed critical thinking skills, for she contrasts the two examples as a means of providing thorough support for her thesis. Both examples are clearly explained and related to the assignment, and the entire essay is capped off by a strong conclusion that links the fictional examples to their real-life counterparts.

The organization of this essay is consistent and easy to follow, with numerous transitional words and phrases (*usually, after all, for example, since, in contrast, because, although*) that provide a clear framework for the author's logic of the Kaplan Method. Finally, the vocabulary is varied and sophisticated (*respective, accompanying, aligning, dwelling, ascended, brooding, ponders, fallen upon, succumbs, critical*), as is the author's sentence structure, and the strong and accurate use of language suggests that the author took time to proofread, which contributes to the overall quality of this high-scoring essay.

4 Score Essay

What contributes the most to personal happiness is definitely how you respond to things that happen to you. I've seen this in my own life because of many difficult events that have happened to some close friends. What they people experienced would have been enough to make most people just give up on life, but my friends somehow managed to continue to live and even find some personal happiness of their own.

The first thing that happened was that the older brother had bad intestinal problems for several years and no doctor could figure out why he was in so much pain. He had to be in the hospital alot, take lots of medication, and even tried alternative therapies like visualization and bio-feedback. He never gave up, though, and always managed to keep his sense of humor throughout the entire thing and eventually he got better. The whole family was affected by this lingering illness but they were able to somehow keep up their spirits and maintain some happiness and hope.

The next thing that happened was that the father, a long-time smoker, got emphysema and was hospitalized. He died on Christmas Day that year which was devestating to his wife and sons. But the next year, the three of them took a trip together to celebrate the anniversary of his life by swimming with dolphins in the Caribbean Sea. Again, they managed to look at things in a positive way and find happiness even though they were sad.

Another thing that happened was that the younger brother got in a car wreck and flipped his Jeep. Then the older brother got stabbed randomly in a fast-food restaurant. It's a pretty amazing thing that they both survived these traumas and didn't get totally depressed. Instead, each time they confronted a difficult thing, they learned from the experience, grew stronger, and moved on with their lives.

My grandmother used to say, "If life gives you lemons, make lemonade." To me, this means that you have to make the best out of whatever happens to you in life and not let yourself be controlled by events. Having personal happiness means choosing to react in ways that keep you positive, despite how negative things might be. And my close family friends are an example of how you can achieve happiness in the face of tragedy and pain.

4 Score Critique

All essays are evaluated on four basic criteria: Topic, Support, Organization, and Language. The writer begins his essay with a strong statement of his thesis, showing immediately that he has understood the prompt and has a clear response to the assignment. The body paragraphs gradually develop the single example by describing a series of events and reactions to adequately support the author's main point. With several transitions to link ideas and paragraphs (*The first thing*, *The next thing*, *Another thing*), the organization of this essay is consistent and indicates that the author took time to plan his essay before writing. The conclusion uses a common generalization to reinforce the author's idea and neatly summarizes his main points to provide a strong ending to the essay.

Overall, the author's language is adequate, although some simplistic vocabulary, especially repetition of the vague terms thing and things throughout the essay, detracts from the strength of the author's writing. A few spelling errors (*alot* instead of "a lot" in the first and second paragraphs; they instead of "the" or "these" in paragraph 1; devestating instead of "devastating" in the third paragraph), some sentence fragments (phrases beginning with *But* or *And*), and inconsistent verb tenses also weaken the essay. This writer should leave enough time to proofread to catch any careless mistakes.

2 Score Essay

Each person experiences alot of different things in their life. Some good some bad. But we can't really control what happens to us all we can control is how we react to what happens to us. So we're really in control of our own happiness since we can decide how we react to different experiences.

The best example to prove this is divorce, like what happened to both me and my best friend. My parents got divorced when I was in fourth grade so I was old enough to understand what was happening and to be really upset about it at first. But then my mother and father each talked to me about why they were splitting up and I started to understand that it was better for both of them not to be together. But my best friend had a totally different situation when his parents divorced because he was totally depressed by the entire situation and couldn't really get over it for a long time. With me, I could understand why my

KAPLAN
Test Prep and Admissions

parents made their decision so I could decide
reaction wouldn't be so negative and then I c
happy unlike my friend.

So choosing how to react to events is definite
have personal happiness. If you let events ru
may be unhappy but if you take some contro
effect whether you're happy or not. And sinc
really important, you should make sure you f
always react well to whatever happens in yo

2 Score Critique

All essays are evaluated on four basic criteri
Support, Organization, and Language. Althou
begins with a clear statement of the author'
demonstrating that the author understood t
remainder of the essay provides insufficient support for the
author's main point. The single example provided in the
second paragraph is not well-developed and remains too
vague and simplistic to offer adequate support for the
author's thesis.

In addition, this essay is poorly organized with few transitions
to link paragraphs and ideas, although the writer does include
a distinct introduction and conclusion, which somewhat helps
the reader to navigate the essay. However, the essay ends
with a digression about the importance of happiness, which
is irrelevant within the context of the essay or the assignment.
This writer needs to spend more time brainstorming and
outlining his essay in order to assure that he has sufficient
and relevant supporting examples for his thesis before he
begins to write.

Finally, the biggest flaw of this essay is that the author's
language is weak and inconsistent. Numerous sentence
fragments and run-on sentences (phrases beginning with
Some, *But*, *So*) in each paragraph, several grammatical
errors (*alot* instead of *a lot* and *their* instead of *his/her* in
the first sentence; *than* instead of *then* and *effect* instead of
affect in the next-to-last sentence), and repetitive language
(*experiences*, *really*, *totally*, *control*, *things*, *situation*) all
detract from this essay and contribute to its low score.
Leaving time to proofread will help to improve this aspect of
the author's writing.

3. B

Difficulty: Medium

She made the best of a lousy situati
"instead." Instead of letting her b
young professional found so
workplace that helped her
you're looking for a wo
(A), *discouraged* wo
that she would h
the sentence
Choice (B
rose ab
pe

not likely try to *escape* from a criminal, nor can ...
actually be *subverted*. Choice (C) is great fit for your
prediction. In choice (D), these words do not make sense in
the structure of the sentence, as the words "this time" and
"at least" indicate the security officer did something good
regarding the criminal, not that he *ignored* him. In choice
(E), denying that he even knew of the criminal would not
have necessarily made the officer *enjoy* the ridicule.

2. B

Difficulty: Low

How would a "passion for both sports and writing" be
satisfied by "becoming a sports journalist"? If Diane had a
"passion for both sports and writing" that was satisfied by
her "becoming a sports journalist," a profession that
requires one to write about sports, then the blank must
describe how she *brought together* or *combined* these two
interests. Look for a word that means *combined*. In choice
(A), the sentence never suggests that Diane lost these
passions, so she could not then have *reclaimed* them.
Choice (B) is a perfect match for your prediction. In choice
(C), *defining*, or giving the precise meaning of these two
interests, would not necessarily satisfy her passion for them.
In choice (D), she could not have satisfied her passion for
sports and writing by *abandoning*, or giving up on, them. In
choice (E), Diane would not have satisfied her passion for
these interests by transporting or moving them.

...on. The key word is
...oss get her down, the
...ething positive in the
...move up. For the second blank
...d with a positive charge. In choice
...uld work, but it wouldn't make sense
...ave found *reconciliation* when nothing in
...mplies she was feeling sorry for anything.
...works. Instead of being *defeated*, or beaten, she
...ove the difficulty and found *prosperity*. In choice (C),
...ple aren't generally *elevated* by oppressive things. In
...hoice (D), again, oppressive things rarely *aid* in anything. In
choice (E), even if she was *delayed* by her oppressive boss,
how would finding *unity* in the workplace help her be
upwardly mobile?

4. A

Difficulty: Medium

The pottery had a purpose, such as to carry water. We
consider it art now, but it was originally made with a
purpose in mind. Look for a synonym for "functional."

Choice (A) works. *Utilitarian* is a synonym for "functional." In
choice (B), carrying water does not exemplify a *grandiose*
reason for making pottery. In choice (C), carrying water is an
every day function and not particularly *imaginative*. In
choice (D), if it were made originally for *aesthetic* reasons,
then it was probably art to begin with. Choice (E) doesn't
really make sense at all.

5. C

Difficulty: Medium

The keyword is "not." You're looking for two words that
make sense in a contradictory way. She likes to use
something, even though her dresses are "not" something
else. Try out each work pair in this context. In choice (A),
ancient and *condescending* do not make sense in this
sentence. In choice (B), *modest* could work, but what
would that have to do with the designs being *concerned
with* her country? Choice (C) works. Even though she uses
native materials, her designs are not *limited to* her country.
In choice (D), *ordinary* could work but *lobbying* certainly
doesn't. In choice (E), there is no correlation between
cosmopolitan materials and being *indebted* to one's
country.

6. C

Difficulty: Medium

If the damage was surprising, then it must have gone
unnoticed. Start with the second blank; the word "ultimate"
indicates that an end result for the building is being
described, and considering the damage in mention, that
end result is probably the buildings *destruction*. If this result
was surprising, then the first blank could be filled with a
word that refers to *subtle* damage. In choice (A), if the
structural damage was clear and understandable, or
manifest, then the destruction, or *eradication*, of the
building would not have been a surprise. In choice (B),
nothing in the sentence indicates that the damage was
immoral or wicked, or that the building was separated into
groups. In choice (C) is a good match for your prediction. In
choice (D) damage that occurred in a systematic or
methodical manner is wholly unrelated to the unification or
amalgamation of a building. In choice (E) a building
structure itself cannot become motionless or inactive.

7. A

Difficulty: Medium

The hot words "despite" and "apparent" clue you in to the
fact that his lifestyle was not what the word in the blank
describes. What word describes someone who does not
"drink to excess?" A good prediction would be someone
who leads an "abstinent" or "self-restrained" lifestyle.
Choice (A) is the correct answer. *Temperate* means
"disciplined" or "self-restrained." In choice (B), *laconic*
means "brief" or "concise." The fact that the man is old and
has therefore lived a long life is not what is being contrasted
by the hotwords and the word in the blank. In choice (C),
duplicitous means "deceitful;" who was the old man
deceiving? He would only be deceptive if he were trying to
hide his drinking habits. Choice (D) can mean either
"artistic" or "tasteful." Whether or not his lifestyle was
"aesthetic" is not related to his drinking habits. Someone
can drink alcohol and still be regarded as being "tasteful." In
choice (E), the man being talkative or not has nothing to do
with drinking.

8. C

Difficulty: Medium

Keywords or structural clues can help you identify the
conceptual focus of a sentence. How do structural words
contribute to the meaning in this case?

Look for structural clues or keywords that indicate the relationship of ideas in the sentence. The last sentence of the passage uses the structural clue "though" to indicate that Grant's first roles, *despite* being small, were significant because they constituted the start of a career that would later become quite celebrated. This is a good paraphrase of what you can expect in the correct answer. Choice (A) is out of scope; the author never states how well Grant performed in these roles. Choice (B) is extreme; although Grant's first roles were small, the author does not discuss how frequently Grant played small roles in the early stages of his career in general. Choice (C) matches your prediction nicely. Choice (D) is a distortion; the passage only suggests that these roles were the beginning of his illustrious career, not that they created his success. Choice (E) is out of scope; the author does not explore how most actors begin a career.

9. E

Difficulty: Medium

Why did Grant choose to leave the acrobatic troupe? You can expect the cited phrase to emphasize his reasons for leaving. Notice whether the relevant sentence has a negative or positive tone overall, and identify the reasons for this negative or positive feeling. Since the relevant sentence describes how Grant abandoned the traveling troupe, the cited phrase most likely indicates a negative feeling or a reason why he chose to leave. The sentence suggests two reasons behind his decision: the "rigors" or harshness of carnival life "took their toll" on Grant, and his excitement for traveling diminished. The combination of these negative factors most likely resulted in Grant feeling tired or worn down. Choice (A) is out of scope; at this point in the passage, the author has not indicated that Grant even *tried* to get acting roles. Choice (B) is out of scope; although the word "toll" can refer to a monetary fee, the author never mentions Grant's earnings. Choice (C) is a distortion; the author does not indicate that Grant regretted his decision to leave home, only that he was worn down by life in the troupe. Choice (D) is a distortion; the cited phrase emphasizes Grant's experience with carnival life in general, and the author does not mention how well he mastered stilts. Choice (E) is a good match for your prediction.

10. D

Difficulty: Low

Make a mental list of descriptions the author uses, and then look for a choice that matches the meaning of an item on this list. Be aware of the various adjectives and verbs that the author uses, and notice the general tone expressed by these words. In the first sentence, the author refers to Hershey as a "revolutionary" chocolate maker and suggests that he was enthusiastic, although his "inexperience" in the candy industry was the downfall of his first candy shop. You can expect the correct choice to match at least one of these characterizations. Choice (A) is out of scope; this sentence does not say whether Hershey was particularly hard-working. Choice (B) is a distortion; while the passage indicates that Hershey opened his own business when he was quite young, this information does not necessarily suggest he was exceptionally talented for his age. Choice (C) is a distortion; the passage describes Hershey as "inexperienced" but does not say that he lacked talent. Choice (D) is a good match for your prediction. "Groundbreaking" is a good synonym for "revolutionary." Choice (E) is an irrelevant detail; Hershey's commitment to using high-quality ingredients is mentioned in the last sentence, not the first.

11. B

Difficulty: Medium

Since it can be difficult to predict the answer to such broadly phrased questions, your focus should be on evaluating each choice efficiently. Go through the choices one by one, comparing each with the evidence found in the text. Choice (A) is a distortion; the passage indicates that Hershey acquired this dedication from another candy maker. Choice (B) is a good choice; the author indicates that Hershey was enthusiastic about candy making when he opened his shop at age 18 and that he was still "hooked on it" after his shop closed six years later. Choice (C) is out of scope; the passage indicates that Hershey learned to use quality ingredients from the caramel manufacturer, but it does not say that he tried to apply the *techniques* he learned there to make chocolate. Choice (D) is extreme; while the passage suggests that Hershey was successful and that he was dedicated to the candy industry from a young age, it does not imply that he could *only* have succeeded at candy making. Choice (E) is out of scope; the passage only begins describing Hershey at age 18 and does not say whether his interest in making candy originated in early childhood.

12. D

Difficulty: High

The first sentence says that her "real advantage" was the "agent of her uncoolness" and that "at the time" she believed it was just. We learn from the next few sentences that it was the narrator's emotional stability that made her uncool among her friends. From that first sentence, we can gather that though she once believed it was fair that she be uncool for being happy, "at the time" indicates that her opinion has changed since then. Choice (A) is out of scope; that first sentence doesn't cover the understanding of personal motivations. Choice (B) is an opposite; the narrator has pinpointed the difference between herself and her friends. Choice (C) is an opposite; the narrator never says a word of condemnation about her friends' depression. Choice (D) matches your prediction. Choice (E) is out of scope; we are given no information about the narrator's friends' awareness of their effect on others.

13. E

Difficulty: Medium

Be sure to plug the word you select back into the sentence in place of the unknown word to make sure it sounds right. Since it was "puzzling" that an "advantage" be the "agent" of "uncoolness," the advantage probably did something negative, like cause the uncoolness rather than defeat it. Choice (A) is out of scope; there is no *spy* in this passage. Choice (B) is out of scope; it doesn't make sense to say that something is an *active ingredient* of uncoolness. Choice (C) is an opposite; the advantage is the thing that caused the uncoolness, not destroyed it. Choice (D) is an opposite; the advantage is not a *secret*, since at least the narrator's friends knew about it. Choice (E) makes sense in the sentence.

14. E

Difficulty: High

Some Inference questions simply ask you to restate what the passage is saying in different words.

The narrator says in the previous sentence that she "secretly, desperately wanted something to be wrong" with her so that her friends would see her "with new eyes." This is what she hopes to accomplish by being "deep." Choice (A) is out of scope; the narrator does not suggest that she ever became "deep" in the way she means here—letting misfortune make her depressed. Choice (B) is an opposite; the narrator's initial frustration is with never having had

anything terrible happen. Choice (C) is an opposite; her friends have led her to believe, that being depressed is more profound than being happy. Choice (D) is out of scope; there is no reference to any spiritual matters in the passage. Choice (E) works with your prediction.

15. C

Difficulty: Medium

Beware of the trap answer that is the most common definition of a word! The author says she was impressed by the folly of her thinking, and then describes how a friend made her understand that she was thinking about it wrong. "Impressed by" must mean that she was *shown* the folly of her thinking. Choice (A) is an opposite; although this is the common definition of "impressed," in this case the narrator comes to a negative conclusion about her thinking. Choice (B) is extreme; she came to these conclusions of her own free will, not by force. Choice (C) fits your prediction and makes sense when read back into the sentence. Choice (D) is an opposite; she was shown the folly of her thinking, which is not a positive thing. Choice (E) is out of scope; whether she was surprised is not discussed.

16. D

Difficulty: Medium

The narrator says she had wanted to have something bad in her history, but she realized that instead of being unhappy about her circumstances, she needed to be grateful for her fortune. Predict something that reflects this change. Choice (A) is out of scope; though the narrator begins the passage with admiration for her friends, nothing in the passage ever suggests that she disapproves of them. Choice (B) is out of scope; you are given no information about how isolated the narrator feels, or how close. Choice (C) is an opposite; the narrator's attitude at the end of the passage changes to a more positive outlook, not a more negative one. Choice (D) works with your prediction. Choice (E) is an opposite; the narrator was not self-satisfied to begin with and does not become more solicitous than she already was.

17. A

Difficulty: Medium

Be careful not to go beyond what the passage immediately suggests. Things that only "might" be true are probably wrong answers. The passage describes how Jessie cultivates a self-conscious attitude toward both her disorder and her intellect. She tries to create a particular impression of them, and "played" suggests that she does this consciously, as a performance, as though in a play. Choice (A) matches your prediction nicely. Choice (B) is out of scope; we don't have information one way or the other about how seriously Jessie took her disorder. Choice (C) is an opposite; the narrator has a keen perception of Jessie's self-consciousness and performance. Choice (D) is extreme; there is nothing in the passage to indicate that Jessie is not aware of what is real and what is not. Choice (E) is out of scope; the narrator is drawn to Jessie, but never says anything like that she is "entertained" by Jessie's behavior.

18. E

Difficulty: Medium

The statement is the narrator's analysis of why she forgives Jessie for her manipulations—the narrator says she does not feel inferior around Jessie because Jessie is insecure. Predict that the statement implies that the narrator would not forgive Jessie if Jessie did make her feel inferior. Choice (A) is out of scope; though she does describe herself as a "misfit", there is no specific information that she is uncomfortable with herself. Choice (B) is a misused detail; while this may be true, this is not implied by the cited lines. Choice (C) is an opposite; if she does not feel inferior to Jessie, she must feel equal or superior to Jessie, which precludes being able to "look up" to her. Choice (D) is out of scope; whether or not the narrator is making the details about Jessie up, it is not clear in the passage that this is the case. Choice (E) matches your prediction.

19. A

Difficulty: Low

Always research the passage before making your prediction—the answer is often spelled out there, and something you don't recall could be the key. The narrator says "and yet I couldn't help but like her," (line 62) and that "her transparent manipulation was so clearly a product of a true discomfort with who she really was that I could not feel inferior around her," (lines 73–76). The narrator feels confident around Jessie because of this insecurity. Choice (A) matches your prediction. Choice (B) is a distortion; she notices Jessie's skill, but does not express admiration toward it. Choice (C) is an opposite; this would not explain why the narrator likes Jessie. Choice (D) is out of scope; Jessie's feelings about the narrator are not discussed. Choice (E) is a distortion; though they do have chemistry class together, there is no mention of homework.

20. B

Difficulty: Medium

Author 1 is insecure because her emotional health is regarded as "uncool" by her friends; Jessie in Passage 2 is described as insecure about who she is and her battle with bipolar disorder. Look for an answer that says they are insecure about their *respective states* of *emotional health*. Choice (A) is a misused detail; Author 1 may feel this, but there is no evidence to support that Jessie does. Choice (B) matches your prediction. Choice (C) is a misused detail; while Jessie may use deceptive manipulation, she is not particularly successful since the narrator is aware of it. And Author 1 does not attempt to practice deception. Choice (D) is an opposite; Jessie in Passage 2 is manipulative, which is nearly the opposite of being *genuine*. Choice (E) is out of scope; while this may be true of the narrator in Passage 1, there is nothing to support that this is true of Jessie in Passage 2.

21. A

Difficulty: Medium

Take a flexible approach to interpreting answer choices—ask yourself "how would this apply to this passage if it were true?" The most obvious difference between Jessie and Author 1 is that Jessie has bipolar disorder and Author 1 does not. Another important difference is that while Author 1 struggles for her friends' approval, Jessie is at the "center" of her social group. Choice (A) matches one of your predictions. Choice (B) is out of scope; we have no information about Author 1's academic success. Choice (C) is a misused detail; both Author 1 and Jessie seem to spend a significant portion of their energy on friendships. There is no identifiable difference. Choice (D) is an opposite; both are influenced by the judgement of others, as is shown by their respective insecurities. Choice (E) is out of scope; we don't have any strong information that either Jessie or Author 1 has a conscious desire to befriend an emotionally diverse group of people.

22. D

Difficulty: Low

Work through the choices, eliminating ones that do describe Jessie or don't describe Author 1. Author 1 used to believe that her happiness made her somehow inferior but no longer feels that way, as can be derived from her statement that she felt that way "at the time." Jessie, on the other hand, is described as thinking about her disorder as "simultaneously the thing she was most proud of and the thing she was most ashamed of." She also had "a true discomfort with who she really was," according to the narrator. So the difference between these two is that Author 1 has come to accept herself, while Jessie did not. Choice (A) is out of scope; nobody in either passage is considering leaving school. Choice (B) is a distortion; though Author 1 describes her family life in a positive way, there is no mention of "family gatherings." Choice (C) is extreme; Author 1 is not described as attempting to obtain an "emotional change." Choice (D) works with your prediction. Choice (E) is out of scope; there is no evidence that Author 1 ever lied about her childhood.

23. A

Difficulty: Medium

There are many possible answers for a question as broad as this. One prediction could be that Passage 1 advocates against trying to be other than you are (since at the end, the character realized that the most respectful thing she could do was to accept her own circumstances), and Passage 2 seems to imply that being insecure doesn't have to be a social drawback. Choice (A) works with both passages. Choice (B) is out of scope; genetics are never mentioned in Passage 1, only class and external social factors. Choice (C) is an opposite; both passages portray characters who are somewhat uncomfortable with themselves. Choice (D) is a distortion; though Author 1 would like to be different, she does not succeed in becoming so. Choice (E) is an opposite; both passages investigate the psychological landscapes of their characters.

24. E

Difficulty: Medium

Both passages discuss the social effects of emotional disorders; one woman longs to have one because her friends do, and another lets bipolar disorder affect all her social interactions. Look for an answer that reflects this. Choice (A) is out of scope; the effect of economic status on social position is not discussed in either passage. Choice (B) is extreme; though both passages deal with students, neither passage attempts to claim that students are the primary group affected. Choice (C) is extreme; Passage 1 does not even mention college. Choice (D) is out of scope; the causes of emotional disorders are not examined in either passage. Choice (E) matches your prediction.

SECTION 3

1. A

Difficulty: Low

Strategic Advice: You could approach this problem by solving the first equation for x and then substituting that value into the second equation, but note that both equations include $4x$. All you need is to solve for $4x$ and then substitute that value into the second equation.

Getting to the Answer:

$$4x + 2 = 26$$
$$4x = 24$$

Substitute:

$$4x + 8$$
$$= 24 + 8$$
$$= 32$$

2. C

Difficulty: Low

Strategic Advice: For the given equation to equal 0, either $(x - 2)$ or $(x + 5)$ equals 0.

Getting to the Answer:

$$x - 2 = 0$$
$$x = 2$$

or

$$x + 5 = 0$$
$$x = -5$$

Choice (C) is correct.

3. C

Difficulty: Low

Strategic Advice: Solve each inequality for a and then eliminate wrong answer choices.

Getting to the Answer:

$$a + 2 > 5$$
$$a > 3$$

and

$$a - 4 < 1$$
$$a < 5$$
$$5 > a > 3$$

Only choice (C) applies.

4. B

Difficulty: Medium

Strategic Advice: A number is divisible by 3 if its digits sum to a multiple of 3. Go through the answer choices and add the four digits.

Getting to the Answer:

$7 + X + 7 + X$

$\qquad = 14 + 2X$

(A) $X = 4$

$14 + 2(4) = 22$

This is not divisible by 3.

(B) $X = 5$

$14 + 2(5) = 24$

$\dfrac{24}{3} = 8$

This is divisible by 3. Choice (B) is correct.

(C) $X = 6$

$14 + 2(6) = 26$

This is not divisible by 3.

(D) $X = 7$

$14 + 2(7) = 28$

This is not divisible by 3.

(E) $X = 9$

$14 + 2(9) = 32$

This is not divisible by 3.

5. D

Difficulty: Medium

Strategic Advice: The perimeter is the sum of the lengths of the sides, and a polygon is a closed figure whose sides are straight-line segments (i.e. a triangle, rectangle, octagon, etc.). A regular polygon is one in which all sides are congruent.

Getting to the Answer: If the perimeter is 21, then the length of one side must be a factor of 21.

Only (D) is a factor of 3. The polygon must have 7 sides, each with the length of 3.

6. B

Difficulty: Medium

Strategic Advice: A percent is the ratio of $\dfrac{\text{part}}{\text{whole}}$.

Getting to the Answer:

$\dfrac{\text{part}}{\text{whole}} = \dfrac{\$600}{\$2000}$

$\qquad = \dfrac{3}{10}$

$\qquad = 30\%$

7. B

Difficulty: Medium

Strategic Advice: An easy way to solve this problem is to pick numbers for a and b and then test the answer choices.

Getting to the Answer:

Pick numbers:

$a = -1$

$b = 2$

(A) $a + b = -1 + 2 = 1$ — Positive but not even.

(B) $-ab = -(-1)(2) = 2$ — Positive and even.

(C) $ab = (-1)(2) = -2$ — Even but not positive.

(D) $\dfrac{b}{a} = \dfrac{2}{-1} = -2$ — Even but not positive.

(E) $b - a = 2 - (-1) = 3$ — Positive but not even.

Choice (B) is correct.

8. D

Difficulty: Medium

Strategic Advice: Set up two proportions of gallons of paint over square feet and cross multiply.

Getting to the Answer:

$\dfrac{2 \text{ gallons}}{875 \text{ ft}^2} = \dfrac{g \text{ gallons}}{4375 \text{ ft}^2}$

$2(4375) = 875g$

$8750 = 875g$

$10 = g$

9. A

Difficulty: Medium

Strategic Advice: First determine the total volume of the bigger box (volume = length × width × height). Then divide that by 60 to determine the volume of each smaller box. Go through the answer choices to see which dimensions can work.

Getting to the Answer:

Volume bigger box = (24)(10)(15) = 3600

Volume of each smaller box = $\frac{3600}{60}$ = 60

Check the answer choices:

Volume = length × width × height

(A) (2)(5)(6) = 60   (A) works.

If you have time, check the other answer choices to be sure.

(B) (3)(4)(6) = 72   Incorrect.
(C) (3)(5)(6) = 90   Incorrect.
(D) (4)(5)(6) = 120   Incorrect.
(E) (5)(6)(12) = 360   Incorrect.

10. E

Difficulty: Medium

Strategic Advice: The average is the sum of the terms divided by the number of terms. The question stem gives you a range for the sum of the terms, so all you need to do is divide the smallest and the greatest by the number of terms (4) to determine the range of the average.

Getting to the Answer:

$\frac{53}{4} = 13\frac{1}{4}$

$\frac{57}{4} = 14\frac{1}{4}$

The average is between $13\frac{1}{4}$ and $14\frac{1}{4}$. Only (E) works.

11. C

Difficulty: Medium

Strategic Advice: Use the Pythagorean theorem to determine the hypotenuse, which the triangles share, and use the theorem again to determine side AD.

Getting to the Answer:

First triangle:
$$a^2 + b^2 = c^2$$
$$(8)^2 + (6)^2 = c^2$$
$$64 + 36 = c^2$$
$$100 = c^2$$
$$10 = c$$

Second triangle:
$$a^2 + b^2 = c^2$$
$$(5)^2 + b^2 = (10)^2$$
$$25 + b^2 = 100$$
$$b^2 = 75$$
$$b = \sqrt{75}$$
$$= \sqrt{25 \times 3}$$
$$= 5\sqrt{3}$$

12. E

Difficulty: High

Strategic Advice: Use points C and D to determine the slope of the line and the y-intercept, which will give you the equation for the line. Then go through the answer choices to see which other point fits into that equation.

Getting to the Answer:

Slope = $\frac{\Delta y}{\Delta x}$

Slope = $\frac{y_2 - y_1}{x_2 - x_1}$

$= \frac{5 - 2}{2 - (-1)} = \frac{3}{3} = 1$

Find the y intercept (when x = 0):

Slope = $1 = \frac{\Delta y}{\Delta x} = \frac{2 - y}{-1 - 0} = \frac{2 - y}{-1} = -2 + y$

$1 = -2 + y$

$3 = y$

Line equation:

$y = 1(x) + 3$

$y = x + 3$

Eyeball the answer choices to see which one might fit.

(E) (1, 4)

$4 = 1 + 3$

$4 = 4$ (E) is the correct choice.

13. E

Difficulty: Medium

Strategic Advice: First determine the pattern in the repeating decimal. Then determine which of the numbers from 1 to 10 the 51st digit will equal.

Getting to the Answer:

.0476190476190476190...

The pattern repeats after every 6 digits.

So 0 begins with the 1st, 7th, 13th, 19th, 25th, 31st, 37th, 43rd, 49th.

The question is for the 51st digit. So if the 49th digit is 0, then the 51st digit is 7.

14. B

Difficulty: Medium

Strategic Advice: Probability is the ratio of the number of desired outcomes to the total number of possible outcomes. Determine each of the two numbers after Sharon takes out a coin that is not a quarter.

Getting to the Answer:

# of desired outcomes = # of quarters = 6

# of possible outcomes = # of coins

= original # − 1 = (6 + 5 + 10) − 1 = 20

Probability $\dfrac{6}{20} = \dfrac{3}{10}$

Choice (B) is correct.

15. C

Difficulty: Medium

Strategic Advice: Go through each answer choice to see if it is possible given the rules in the question stem.

Getting to the Answer:

(A) $a + b$. This could never be an integer. Only an integer plus an integer will result in an integer. An integer plus a fraction will be a fraction.

(B) $a − b$. This could never be an integer. Only an integer minus an integer will result in an integer. An integer minus a fraction will be a fraction.

(C) ab. This could be an integer.

i.e. $a = 2, b = \dfrac{1}{2}$

$$ab = 2\left(\dfrac{1}{2}\right) = 1$$

(D) $2a − b$. This could not be an integer for the same reason as (B). $2a$ is an integer because a is an integer, but b is still a noninteger.

(E) $\dfrac{b}{a}$. Again, take $a = 2$ and $b = \dfrac{1}{2}$

$\dfrac{b}{a} = \dfrac{\frac{1}{2}}{2} = \dfrac{1}{2 \times 2} = \dfrac{1}{4}$. This is not an integer.

Choice (C) is correct.

16. D

Difficulty: Medium

Strategic Advice: First determine the equation for the daily cost, and then determine the cost of running the air conditioner for 90 days.

Getting to the Answer:

daily cost = $.12(8) + .10(h − 8)$

cost for 90 days = $90[.12(8) + .10(h − 8)]$

$= 90(.12)8 + 9(h − 8)$

Choice (D)

Note: be sure to distribute the 90.

17. E

Difficulty: Medium

Strategic Advice: The sum of the lengths of any two sides of a triangle is greater than the length of the third side. Therefore $a + b > c, a + c > b$, and $c + b > a$. Look through the answer choices to determine which is possible, keeping these inequalities in mind.

Getting to the Answer:

(A) $c = b + a$ Incorrect. $c < a + b$.

(B) $c = b - a$

    $c + a = b$ Incorrect. $c + a > b$

(C) $c = 2a + b$

If this was true, then

    $c > a + b$ Incorrect. $c < a + b$

(D) $c + 2 = a + b + 3$

    $c = a + b + 1$

This could be not true because in this equation, c is greater than $a + b$.

(E) $c + 3 = a + b + 2$

    $c = a + b - 1$

This could be true because c is less than $a + b$.

18. B

Difficulty: High

Strategic Advice: This question looks complicated, but if you notice that the common denominator of $\frac{1}{x} + \frac{1}{y}$ is xy, then you can solve for $\frac{1}{xy}$, which equals 6, and then use algebra to answer the question.

Getting to the Answer:

$$\frac{1}{x} + \frac{1}{y} = 5$$

$$\frac{y}{xy} + \frac{x}{xy} = \frac{(y+x)}{xy}$$

$$= \left(\frac{1}{xy}\right)(y + x)$$

Substitute $\left(\frac{1}{xy}\right) = 6$

$$6(y + x) = 5$$

$$\frac{6(y + x)}{5} = 1$$

$$\frac{(y + x)}{5} = \frac{1}{6}$$

19. C

Difficulty: High

Strategic Advice: If each team played 4 games with each of the other teams, then each team played $(7)(4) = 28$ games. Use this number to determine how many total games were played.

Getting to the Answer:

28 games were played, and each game involved 2 teams. Therefore:

$$28\left(\frac{8}{2}\right) = 28(4) = 112 \text{ games were played.}$$

20. E

Difficulty: High

Strategic Advice: If you know the length of two sides of a triangle, then you also know something about the length of the third side; it's greater than the difference and less than the sum of the two other sides. You have $(x - 2)$ for one side and $(x + 2)$ for another side, so use this knowledge to form an inequality that represents the possible values of the third side.

Getting to the Answer:

$(x - 2) + (x + 2) > y$ $(x + 2) - (x - 2) < y$

$2x > y$ $4 < y$

$4 < y < 2x$

SECTION 4

1. B

Difficulty: Low

How could Mr. Chandler have "clearly displayed" his "ostentatious tastes"? Start with the first blank; the words "clearly displayed" indicate that when Mr. Chandler received his new promotion, he *showed off*. As for the second blank, the word "new" that precedes it indicates that it probably refers to his recent promotion, so the second blank likely means *wealth*. *Show off* and *wealth* are good predictions for the blanks. In choice (A), being "made president of the company" would not likely be considered a *hardship*. Choice (B) is a great match for your prediction. In choice (C), displaying "ostentatious tastes" would not necessarily *undermine* or harm one's *image*. In choice (D), nothing in the sentence refers to Mr. Chandler *calculating* or thinking *undermine* or harm one's *image*. In choice (D), nothing in the sentence refers to Mr. Chandler *calculating* or thinking carefully about his new *successes*. In choice (E), again, *moderating* one's *consumption* could not be referred to as displaying "ostentatious tastes".

2. D

Difficulty: Medium

If Maria's winnings in the lottery were "meager" and "worth next to nothing", what might she have found it "easy" to do?

Given that the sentence underscores the fact that Maria's winning lottery ticket was "worth next to nothing," it is likely the blank is referring to how it was easy for her to *pass up* or *decline* her "meager winnings," both great predictions for the blank. In choice (A), the fact that her ticket was "worth next to nothing" would not have necessarily made it easy for Maria to better understand or appreciate here winnings. In choice (B), if her winnings were "worth next to nothing", most likely she would not have enthusiastically praised them. In choice (C), just because her winnings were "meager" does not mean they were untrustworthy. Choice (D) matches your prediction nicely. In choice (E), if her winnings were so "meager" she most likely would not have found it easy to *relish*, or deeply appreciate the pleasure they gave her.

3. A

Difficulty: Medium

"Although" signals the sentence will present contrasting feelings about "publicity."

The word "once" is important here, as it indicates that Edward's prior feelings about the "intense publicity his more famous colleagues received" have changed. Start with the second blank; if Edward was relatively anonymous, then he must have come to appreciate his *lack* of publicity, a good prediction for the blank. Given that Edward's feelings changed, he must have *coveted* or *been jealous* of such publicity before, both great predictions for the first blank. Choice (A) is a great match for your prediction. In choice (B), these words do not present contrasting feelings. In choice (C), similarly, *imitating* publicity and appreciating *privilege* do not really contrast with one another. In choice (D), if Edward had once *regretted* the publicity his colleagues received, then he would have already appreciated his *isolation*. In choice (E), *refusing* intense publicity does not contrast with appreciating *generosity*.

4. B

Difficulty: Medium

The blank must be consistent with "feeling exasperated".

If Mrs. Smith was "feeling exasperated" by her son's insolence, then she must have also felt extremely annoyed or irritated, both great predictions for the blank. In choice (A), if Mrs. Smith felt "exasperated", she likely would not have been *fascinated* by her son's behavior. Choice (B) is a good match for your prediction. In choice (C), again, if Mrs. Smith felt "exasperated", she would not also have felt *uplifted* or encouraged by her son's behavior. In choice (D), exasperating behavior would most likely not be *soothing* or calming. In choice (E), nothing in the sentence suggests that Mrs. Smith felt *disoriented* or lost because of her son's behavior.

5. C

Difficulty: High

How much evidence would there be in a case with lots of "gaps"?

The words "where before" provide an important structural clue, as they indicate that the blank refers to something that contrasts with certainty. In other words, if the "newly found eyewitness filled in many of the gaps in the case" and provided a new sense of certainty, then there must have been a lack or scarcity of evidence before. *Scarcity* makes a great prediction for the blank.

In choice (A), if there had been a large quantity of evidence before, then there likely would also have been certainty and not many gaps in the case. In choice (B), nothing in the sentence suggests the evidence itself was changed or edited, only that more evidence was found. Choice (C) is a perfect match for your prediction. In choice (D), evidence that was spread out, or *dispersed*, would not necessarily create uncertainty. In choice (E), certainty and *consensus* agree far more than they contrast.

6. D

Difficulty: Medium

Where does the Hoover Dam fit into the timeframe discussed by the author?

Because Function questions ask you to identify how a particular detail or piece of information works in the general scheme of the passage, make sure to reexamine the overall point of the passage before selecting a choice.

The author of Passage 1 focuses on how hydroelectric power, once unquestioned, has slowly begun to generate a debate regarding the tradeoffs it presents. The Hoover Dam is mentioned by the author as a symbol marking the *starting point* of this long, slow period of public recognition of the tradeoffs. Look for a choice that reflects the author's reference to the Hoover Dam as a chronological tool.

Choice (A) is a misused detail; the author's point is that dams have drawbacks, even though they may provide employment and other benefits. Choice (B) is out of scope; the Hoover Dam is mentioned as an example of impressive hydroelectric technology, not necessarily as the most impressive example of energy-conversion technology in general. Choice (C) is a distortion; the Hoover Dam was an "ambitious" project that increased the use of hydroelectric power. Choice (D) matches your prediction. Choice (E) is a distortion; the author suggests that the high ratio is surprising, but not that it's unexplainable.

7. C

Difficulty: Low

What exactly is the contrast the author is drawing between fossil-fueled plants and hydroelectric facilities?

When the cited word has a number of common meanings that could reasonably fit into the context, be careful to select the choice that completely captures the author's meaning.

The author draws a contrast between fossil-fueled plants and hydroelectric facilities: fossil-fueled plants can clearly cause environmental harm, whereas hydroelectric facilities avoid at least some of these problems because the plants themselves don't emit "harmful atmospheric pollutants." But the author says that hydroelectric power is not really as "benign," or harmless, as it once appeared—it can cause other problems. Look for a choice that fits comfortably into this discussion of the safety or desirability of side-effects.

In choice (A), while a "benign" person may be kind, in this passage the word is used to describe hydroelectric power. Choice (B) is a primary definition of the cited word, but it does not capture the author's point about potential harm. Choice (C) is a good match for your prediction. In choice (D), the author is suggesting that hydroelectric power may be less desirable than previously realized because it has more drawbacks or side-effects, but this doesn't mean it's less *useful*. In choice (E), again, while the author is discussing environmental effects, the focus is not on whether dams work well.

8. E

Difficulty: Medium

What aspect of hydroelectric power does each passage focus on? What ideas do they have in common?

When asked to identify common ground between two passages, look for a choice that is specific enough to accurately capture the overall focus of both passages but general enough to accommodate their differences.

Passage 1 focuses on the social implications of hydroelectric power, while Passage 2 focuses on the environmental implications. In addition to their common focus on implications of hydroelectric power, both mention that it took a long time for people to recognize these implications. Look for the choice that best presents this common theme.

Choice (A) is out of scope; only Passage 2 discusses environmental damage. Choice (B) is out of scope; neither author reaches this conclusion. Choice (C) is out of scope; neither passage compares the efficiency of hydroelectric dams specifically with fossil fuel plants. Choice (D) is a distortion; only Passage 1 examines the social implications of hydroelectric power. Choice (E) is a good match for your prediction.

9. C

Difficulty: High

What clue does the word "While" give you about the content of the sentences?

Look for keywords or grammatical clues that indicate the role of the sentences.

The keyword "While" suggests that the concluding sentences contain some sort of contrast. Both sentences mention positive and negative aspects of damming, and both provide specific examples of the various effects of hydroelectric power. Look for a choice that notes one of these functions.

Choice (A) is an opposite; in both passages, the final sentences serve to narrow the author's focus with examples, rather than capturing it in more general terms. Choice (B) is out of scope; neither author defends a specific theory. Choice (C) is a good match for your prediction. Choice (D) is out of scope; both sentences are based on facts, not opinions. Choice (E) is a distortion; neither passage comes to a single, definitive conclusion in the last sentence.

10. C

Difficulty: Low

You need to determine what the author is trying to achieve in this passage.

The author tells you in the first paragraph that, "had it not been for a chance discovery," he would have always taken his freedom and liberty for granted. Your prediction should be something close to this.

Choice (A) is a misused detail; though he mentions being arrogant, it is a small detail and the focus of neither the paragraph nor the passage. Choice (B) is an opposite; the author tells you how much he came to appreciate these sacrifices. Choice (C) fits nicely. Choice (D) is out of scope; there is nothing to suggest that the author did not *appreciate his grandfather* prior to this conversation. Choice (E) is out of scope; there is nothing that suggests anything about the author feeling ashamed.

11. B

Difficulty: Medium

Read around the word and look for context, then make a prediction.

The author writes that his grandparent's "endeavor"—their journey—was marked by many "sacrifices." Predict something like *attempt*.

Choice (A) is out of scope; *pursuit* is overly specific, as if it is a hobby. Choice (B) fits the prediction well. Choice (C) is out of scope; a *ship* is involved in the journey, but this has nothing to do with the meaning of "endeavor." Choice (D) is out of scope; an endeavor may lead to a *goal*, but the two words are not synonymous. Choice (E) is out of scope; this derives from one of the meanings of the word, but doesn't make sense in this context.

12. B

Difficulty: Medium

Suggests in the question stem lets you know that this is an Inference question. Make sure you know what "awareness" is referring to, and then use the information in and around the given sentence to help make your prediction.

The first sentence tells you that the author is talking about his and others' "awareness" of the freedoms enjoyed as Americans. He then goes on to tell you that such an awareness was "lost upon me" and that he came to realize

how "sorely mistaken" he was. Look for an answer choice that reflects these sentiments.

Choice (A) is an opposite; if facts are lost upon him, than the author's awareness is not *broad*. Choice (B) fits perfectly. Choice (C) is an opposite; his awareness is limited, not askew. Choice (D) is an opposite; *his parents'* awareness of their good fortune is not addressed. Choice (E) is extreme; though the author admits to being sorely mistaken, *non-existent* is too strong to describe his awareness.

13. B

Difficulty: Low

Find the reference in question, then look for an inference fairly close to what is said in the passage.

The author tells you that he was the "first college-bound member of my family" and "far too arrogant." The correct answer will likely incorporate the detail about college.

Choice (A) is out of scope; there is nothing that suggests that he thinks the rest of his family is unintelligent. Choice (B) fits the prediction. Choice (C) is a distortion; though he initially lacks an appreciation for their sacrifice, he never implies that immigrants are *foolish*. Choice (D) is out of scope; the author never mentions *his family's financial situation*. Choice (E) is a distortion; the passage suggests that at least one of his parents could have been born in the U.S. (if the parent were born after the grandparents arrived in the country).

14. E

Difficulty: Medium

In order to in the question stem lets you know that you are looking for the function of this sentence. Use keywords in the sentence to make your prediction.

Because his grandfather was usually so "garrulous," the author tells you that his silence while looking at the photograph took him by surprise; it is the grandfather's reaction that is being highlighted here.

Choice (A) is a misused detail; though the grandfather does relate his story to the author, this doesn't address the function of the comment. Choice (B) is out of scope; the point of the reference is his hesitation. Choice (C) is out of scope; nothing suggests that his talkativeness is what makes the grandfather recount his story. Choice (D) is an opposite; if the grandfather is very talkative, this would not explain his unwillingness to talk. Choice (E) fits nicely.

15. A

Difficulty: Medium

Look for an answer that reflects the tone as a whole—focusing on word charge could be a helpful strategy here.

The author seems to stress how grateful he is that his grandfather taught him a greater understanding of his own fortunes, so *grateful* would be a good prediction. The author also takes a good deal of time reminiscing about the specifics of his encounter, so *reflective* would be another good prediction.

In choice (A), this fits splendidly. Choice (B) is a distortion; though he expresses regret at times over having been so arrogant, the overall tone is much more positive. Choice (C) is out of scope; there is nothing that suggests anger in this passage. Choice (D) is out of scope; though the tone is somewhat *patriotic*, there is nothing *exasperated* about it. Choice (E) is out of scope; the tone certainly is *reflective*, but the author seems to care very much about this material, so *indifferent* doesn't work.

Questions 16–24

In this passage, the author conveys his opinion that physicists possess an ability to see beauty wholly different from that possessed by other people. In the first paragraph, he discusses how beauty is traditionally defined and concludes that there is no absolute definition in this sense. He spends the second paragraph beginning to detail the type of beauty that is revealed by studying physics. In the final paragraph, he sums up this beauty as the "remarkable simplicity" with which the universe is constructed.

16. C

Difficulty: Medium

Pay attention to Keywords around the referenced text to help you make your prediction.

In the sentence preceding the reference, the author states, "what is considered beautiful changes at an alarming pace." This would fit into a good prediction.

Choice (A) is an opposite; the author is using Monroe to discuss past standards of beauty. Choice (B) is out of scope; the author makes no mention *of her abilities as an actress*. Choice (C) matches your prediction nicely. Choice (D) is a misused detail; the reference to *East and West* later in the paragraph is unrelated to Monroe. Choice (E) is an

opposite; the author is trying to show how much the standard definition changes.

17. D

Difficulty: Medium

Suggests that in the question stem lets you know that this is an Inference question. Find the relevant text in the paragraph and use the sentences around it to come up with a prediction.

In the sentence following the referenced text, the author tells us that a definition of beauty is "elusive…at best." This would be a good prediction.

Choice (A) is out of scope; the author never suggests anything about civilizations clashing. Choice (B) is out of scope; the author never implies this. Choice (C) is a misused detail; the author does not mention this until later. Choice (D) matches your prediction well. Choice (E) is out of scope; the author is telling us that standards of beauty differ from culture to culture—he does not talk about *individuals*.

18. C

Difficulty: Low

Look for the context surrounding the word, and be careful—the primary meaning is usually the wrong choice.

The author talks about the difference between what is "established by Nature" and what is "created through…people"; *made* would be a good prediction.

Choice (A) is out of scope; this is related to the concept of "lie down," and doesn't make sense in context. Choice (B) is out of scope; this is related to the concept of "lie down," and doesn't make sense in context. Choice (C) fits very well. Choice (D) is a distortion; this is a variation on the concept of "lying down." Choice (E) is out of scope; this doesn't make sense in context.

19. A

Difficulty: High

Return to the text and identify what the author is talking about when he mentions "ephemeral" and "Nature;" then use the surrounding sentences to assist in making a prediction.

In the preceding sentence, the author states that physicists are looking for "a beauty that does not remain impervious to definition." Since he spent the entire first paragraph talking about the type of beauty that is subject to change, we can safely assume he is now contrasting two types of beauty. Your prediction should reflect this.

Choice (A) fits well. Choice (B) is a distortion; the author talks about physics as a way to view beauty, not as a form of art. Choice (C) is a distortion; this lacks the element of contrast called for by the prediction. Also, the physicist's view involves much more than visualization. Choice (D) is out of scope; the author never says that aesthetics aren't relevant. Choice (E) is out of scope; the author never says anything negative about those who aren't trained in physics

20. B

Difficulty: Medium

Be careful—this Detail question is asking you to find the one answer choice that is NOT directly mentioned in the text.

First, find the starting point (in paragraph 2). Then find and eliminate answer choices that DO appear in the passage. You should see that the author states that appreciating a wave crashing is something that he does as a human being, not as a physicist.

Choice (A) is an opposite; the author discusses looking for a beauty that is "not...subject to ephemeral tastes." Choice (B) is correct; this is not listed as a gift peculiar to physicists. Choice (C) is an opposite; the author discusses appreciating both. Choice (D) is an opposite; the author talks about appreciating the beauty of Nature's laws in paragraph 3. Choice (E) is an opposite; the author specifically states that he "is able to perceive a brilliant design."

21. A

Difficulty: High

Suggests that in the question stem lets you know that this is an Inference question.

This sentence tells us that Einstein and his intellectual followers believe that there may be one group of laws that governs the universe, which implies a degree of simplicity. Following this sentence, the author goes on to tell us that the "remarkable simplicity" of the universe is breathtaking; your prediction should be something along these lines.

Choice (A) fits perfectly. Choice (B) is an opposite; while this may seem true at first glance, the discussion of an overarching theory implies that the universe is fundamentally more simple. Choice (C) is an opposite; the author tells us specifically that aesthetics does have a place

in physics. Choice (D) is an opposite; the author states that we are "closer than ever to a full understanding" of how the universe works. Choice (E) is extreme; though the author does believe that there is an overarching theory, he never implies that a *full understanding is imminent.*

22. A

Difficulty: Medium

Remember to make a prediction first; this will help you avoid misleading choices.

The author uses "driving" to talk about a "force" that is affecting physics, one important enough to have written this article about. *Important* would be a good prediction.

Choice (A) fits nicely. Choice (B) is extreme; nothing in the context indicates *control*. Choice (C) is out of scope; this relates to another meaning of the word. Choice (D) is out of scope; there is nothing that implies anything about an *escaping* force. Choice (E) is out of scope; this relates to another meaning of the word.

23. D

Difficulty: Medium

Locate the quote and search the relevant text around it to help in making your prediction.

In the referenced sentence, the author tells us that Einstein commented that one could reasonably expect the world to be "in no way graspable through thinking." But in the next sentence, the author states that a full understanding is achievable. Your prediction should reflect a sense of wonder at this concept.

Choice (A) is out of scope; the author does not talk about the effect of *physical laws* on *chaos*. Choice (B) is a distortion; though he discusses Einstein's influence, the author is not using this quote to do so. Choice (C) is an opposite; this quote implies that Einstein treasured the beauty of physics. Choice (D) fits well. Choice (E) is out of scope; there is nothing to imply this.

24. B

Difficulty: Medium

With any passage, your notes should include a prediction of the author's purpose or main idea. Your work on questions like these will already be mostly done.

The author spends most of his time discussing how an understanding of physics adds to his appreciation of perceiving beauty; this would be a good prediction.

Choice (A) is a misused detail; this is only discussed in the first paragraph. Choice (B) fits your prediction very well. Choice (C) is a misused detail; this is mentioned only briefly. Choice (D) is out of scope; the author never discusses *Einstein's achievements*. Choice (E) is out of scope; the author does not spend much time discussing *physical laws*.

SECTION 5

1. C

Difficulty: Low

Strategic Advice: Translate the words into an algebraic expression, paying close attention to the exponents

Getting to the Answer:

Take it step by step:

"three-fourths of the cube of *a*"

$$\frac{3}{4} * a^3$$

"plus the value of *b* divided by the square of *c*"

$$\frac{3}{4}a^3 + \frac{b}{c^2}$$

"equals *a*"

$$\frac{3}{4}a^3 + \frac{b}{c^2} = a$$

Choice (C) is correct

$$\left(\text{note that } \frac{3}{4}a^3 = \frac{3a^3}{4}\right)$$

2. B

Difficulty: Low

Strategic Advice: When a question charges different rates in a problem, figure out how much is charged at each rate and add the totals together.

Getting to the Answer: The rental would have 7 days charged at $40, and 3 days charged at $35. Therefore, the first 7 days would cost 7 × $40 = $280. The next 3 days would cost 3 × $35 = $105. The total is $280 + $105 = $385.

3. D

Difficulty: Low

Strategic Advice: If the number of tulips, *n*, varies directly with Kim's age, *a*, their relationship can be written as $n = ka$, where *k* is a constant. You can use the given set of values to find *k*, then use that to find the value of *n* when $a = 25$.

Getting to the Answer:

$$16 = k(10)$$

$$k = \frac{16}{10} = \frac{8}{5}$$

$$n = \frac{8}{5}(25) = 40$$

4. E

Difficulty: Low

With multiple unknowns, solving for one will often help you solve the unknown that the question is asking about.

$$j = 3(4) + 4 = 16$$

$$k = 3(16) + 4 = 52$$

5. A

Difficulty: Medium

Strategic Advice: She will clean the house on days 7, 14, 21…(multiples of 7) and do laundry on days 5, 10, 15…(multiples of 5). Think about what has to be true of days where both happen.

Getting to the Answer:

The least common multiple of 7 and 5 is 35. So every 35th day she will do both. This will happen $\frac{315}{35} = 9$ times.

6. E

Difficulty: Medium

Strategic Advice: Any side of a triangle must be larger than the difference between than other two sides, and less than the sum of the other two sides

Getting to the Answer:

In choice (E), 12 = 5 + 7, so the "triangle" would be totally flat.

7. E

Difficulty: Medium

Strategic Advice: Remember, slope is $\frac{rise}{run}$ or $\frac{y_2 - y_1}{x_2 - x_1}$, so a slope of zero means the line is horizontal (rise = 0), and an undefined slope means the line is vertical (run = 0).

Getting to the Answer:

This line is vertical, so the x-coordinate stays the same. The only answer choice with the same x-coordinate is choice (E).

8. B

Difficulty: Medium

Strategic Advice: Remember that you can always assume the diagram is drawn to scale, unless you're told otherwise. Use this to eliminate wrong answer choices if you get stuck.

Getting to the Answer:

Draw a third line parallel to *l* and *m*. Find the supplements of the given angles. The angle we want has been split into two angles, each of which is an alternate interior angle with one of the supplements, so $q = 30° + 20° = 50°$

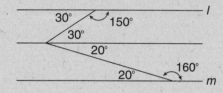

9. 760

Difficulty: Low

Strategic Advice: Be sure to read percent problems carefully. Pay particular attention to what a percent is of -- is it some percent of the total number of passengers, or of the married passengers, or of some other group?

Getting to the Answer:

80% of $3,000 = .8 \times 3,000 = 2,400$ married passengers

60% of $2,400 = .6 \times 2,400 = 1,440$ married less than a year

$2,400 - 1,440 - 200 = 760$ married 1–10 years

10. 468

Difficulty: Low

Strategic Advice: Be careful when translating the word problem into numbers. Be sure to answer the question that is asked.

Getting to the Answer: 35% of the 720 person class are boys. There are $.35 \times 720 = 252$ boys. This means that the number of girls is $720 - 252 = 468$. Alternatively, you could use the fact that if the class was 35% boys, then it was 100% - 35% = 65% girls. Therefore, there are $.65 \times 720 = 468$ girls.

11. 31

Difficulty: Low

Strategic Advice: You don't even have to turn this into algebra if you don't want to—just work backwards

Getting to the Answer:

$2 for the first 14 days

$4.55 - $2 = $2.55 for the rest of the days

$\dfrac{\$2.55}{\$.15} = 17$ additional days

$17 + 14 = 31$ days total

12. 0

Difficulty: Medium

Strategic Advice: When the SAT presents new functions, the problem often looks more confusing than it actually is. Figure out how to operate the new function, then plug in the numbers carefully.

Getting to the Answer: The & function simply instructs you to find the least prime number greater than the number given. In this case, the least prime number greater than -1.32 is 2. The @ function tells you to find the largest even integer that is less than the number given. In this case, the largest even integer below 3.481 is 2. Therefore, the final equation is $2 - 2 = 0$.

13. 5,225

Difficulty: Medium

Strategic Advice: If you are having trouble with this type of problem, draw a picture to help you decipher the information.

Getting to the Answer:

Perimeter = 300 meters

One side = 55 meters

You know that opposite sides of a rectangle are equal and that the perimeter is the sum of all four sides. You can use the perimeter to find the width:

$2w + 2(55) = 300$

$2w = 190$

$w = 95$

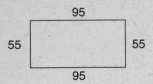

Area is length × width = 55 × 95 = 5225 square meters.

14. $\frac{2}{5}$ or .4

Difficulty: Medium

Strategic Advice: Use the slope formula to find the slope on Test Day.

Getting to the Answer: Use the slope formula to get the answer:

$$\frac{y_2 - y_1}{x_2 - x_1} = \frac{1 - (-1)}{0 - (-5)} = \frac{2}{5}$$

15. $60 < y < 69$

Difficulty: Medium

Strategic Advice: Pick a value for x and work systematically to find the other angles, until you can get to y. Remember that vertical angles are equal, that equivalent angles formed by parallel lines are equal, and that angles that make up a straight line sum to 180°.

Getting to the Answer:

Say $x = 38°$. Then $2x = 76°$ and the obtuse angle formed by k and v is $38° + 76° = 114°$. This is equivalent to the obtuse angle formed by n and l.

$$114 + y = 180$$
$$y = 66$$

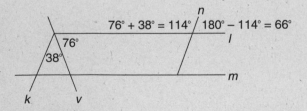

16. 20

Difficulty: High

Strategic Advice: Since $\overline{AB}$, $\overline{CD}$, and $\overline{EF}$ are diameters, the sum of x, y, and the interior angle of the shaded region is 180. The interior angle of the shaded region can be found using the fact that the ratio between the area of a sector and the area of the entire circle is the same as the ratio between the angle of the sector and 360°.

Getting to the Answer:

$$\frac{1}{4} = \frac{a°}{360°}$$
$$4a = 360$$
$$a = 90$$
$$90 + x + y = 180$$
$$90 + x + (3x + 10) = 180$$
$$4x = 80$$
$$x = 20$$

17. 4

Difficulty: High

Strategic Advice: Draw the line $y = 3$ and count how many times this line intersects the graph of the function.

Getting to the Answer:

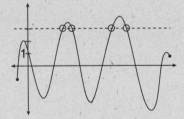

18. 6.06

Difficulty: High

Strategic Advice: A line tangent to a circle forms a right angle with a diameter of the circle at the point of tangency. Also, remember that a right triangle with short leg s and hypotenuse $2s$ has long leg $s\sqrt{3}$.

Getting to the Answer:

$\overline{DH} =$ Hypotenuse $= 7$

$\overline{EH} = \dfrac{1}{2}$ the diameter $= \dfrac{7}{2}$

$\overline{DE} =$ Long leg $= \dfrac{7\sqrt{3}}{2} \approx 6.06$

SECTION 6

1. B

Difficulty: Low

Make sure items in a comparative structure are logical.

As written, the sentence is comparing *pizzas* to *Guido's*. (B) fixes this error by adding a pronoun that refers back to *pizzas*. (C) and (E) are fragments. (D) does not address the error and introduces the idiomatically incorrect *better than like*.

2. B

Difficulty: Low

Although most idiom questions test preposition usage, some also test constructions that require the infinitive verb form.

In this context, the verb *hopes* requires the infinitive verb form. (B) makes the correction. (C) incorrectly uses the pronoun *it* to refer to a person. (D) and (E) are unnecessarily wordy.

3. B

Difficulty: Low

To be complete, a sentence must have a subject and verb in an independent clause.

As written, this sentence is a fragment. (B) corrects the error. (C) and (D) incorrectly add *he*, and (D) is unnecessarily wordy. (E) does not address the error.

4. E

Difficulty: Medium

Comparative structures such as *not only…but also* require that the subjects of the comparison be presented in parallel form.

As written, this sentence violates the rules of parallel structure. (E) corrects the error; none of the other answer choices does.

5. A

Difficulty: Medium

Don't mistake complex sentence structure for grammatical error.

This sentence is correct as written. The modifying phrase *who are historically avid baseball fans* correctly modifies *Chicago residents* and *Although* is the appropriate transition. (B) misuses the semicolon splice, which is only correct when used to connect two independent clauses. (C) and (E) introduce the passive voice unnecessarily. (D) creates a sentence fragment.

6. D

Difficulty: Medium

If a sentence in the passive voice can be easily reworded to use an active verb, the correct answer choice will do so. (D) changes the passive *UV rays are prevented* to the active *they prevent…UV rays*. (B) incorrectly uses a semicolon splice between a dependent and an independent clause. (C) awkward and unnecessarily wordy. The pronoun *it* in (E) does not agree with its plural antecedent, lenses.

7. B

Difficulty: Medium

A modifying phrase must always be closely followed by the noun it modifies.

As written, the phrase *Having plenty of training* modifies *my errors*. (B) corrects this by placed the subject I directly after the modifying phrase. (C) is unnecessarily wordy. In (D), the opening phrase is modifying *my first day on the job*. (E) does not address the error.

8. C

Difficulty: Medium

Some constructions are only correct when used in combination; "so… that" is one such phrase.

So, when used in this context, must be followed by "that" to be correct. (C) corrects this error. No other answer choice is idiomatically correct.

9. D

Difficulty: Medium

Make sure modifying phrases modify the correct noun.

As written, *the authors* are the people with the *unanimous love of Hemingway*. (D) correctly makes *the members of the book club* the first noun after the modifying phrase. (B) does not address the error and is unnecessarily in the passive voice. (C) creates a sentence fragment, since both clauses are dependent. In (E), the noun being modified is *range*.

10. E

Difficulty: High

A sentence must have a subject and a verb in an independent clause, and express a complete thought.

As written, this sentence is a fragment. (E) corrects the error without introducing any additional issues. (B) is awkward and unnecessarily wordy. (C) and (D) eliminate *whether*, which is correct when discussing an either/or proposition.

11. D

Difficulty: High

Make sure verb tenses accurately reflect the sequence of events in a sentence.

The second clause of the sentence is in the past tense: *Kathy and Erica were tired*. Therefore, the underlined verb should be in the past perfect, to indicate an action completed prior to another stated past action. (D) corrects the error; none of the other choices are appropriate in context.

12. B

Difficulty: Medium

Certain key words establish when an action took place, and therefore, which verb tense is needed.

Over the last two weeks indicates that the action took place in the past. Thus, *I learn* should be *I learned*; the error is in (B). (A) is a correctly constructed and properly used idiom. Both (C) and (D) are appropriate uses of the infinitive verb form.

13. D

Difficulty: Medium

Each verb in a sentence must agree with its subject noun, which may not be the noun closest to it in the sentence.

Here, the subject of the verb *make* is actually the singular *odor* (*bottles* is the object of the preposition *from*). (D) should be "makes." (A) and (B) are used correctly to modify *odor*. (C) is an appropriate preposition in context.

14. A

Difficulty: Low

Verbs and verb forms are always modified by adverbs.

Here, the adjective *dense* is being used to modify the verb form *populated*; the error is in (A). (B) is is an appropriate

transitional word in context. (C) agrees with its singular subject *Alaska*. (D) correctly employs the superlative *most sparsely*, since there are more than two states.

15. A

Difficulty: Medium

When a sentence presents a comparison, make sure like items are being compared.

This sentence compares *French Polynesia's culture* to *other archipelagos*. (A) should begin reference the culture of other archipelagos. (B) agrees with its singular subject *culture*. (C) properly uses an adverb to modify a verb form. (D) correctly uses a singular pronoun to refer back to *culture*.

16. A

Difficulty: Medium

An idiom may be correctly constructed and still be incorrect in context.

Although *as to* is an idiomatic expression, it is not correctly used here; (A) should read "as in." (B) properly uses an adjective to modify a noun. (C) agrees with its plural subject *people*. (D) is a correctly used idiomatic expression.

17. D

Difficulty: Medium

In complex sentences, it can be difficult to match each verb with its subject. Make sure you know which verb refers to which subject so that you can check their agreement.

In this sentence, the subject is the singular *recording*, so *are* in (D) should be "is." (A), (B), and (C) are all idiomatically correct in context.

18. B

Difficulty: Medium

Pronoun use must be consistent throughout a sentence.

This sentence begins by using the third person pronoun *one*, then switches to the first person *we*; the error is in (B). (A) appropriately relates the two clauses. (C) correctly uses an adverb to modify the verb phrase *has changed*. (D) agrees with its singular subject *language*.

19. B

Difficulty: Low

The action took place in the past, and should use the simple past tense *were* instead of the past participle of the verb "to be" (*been*).

The verbs *going,* (A), and *being,* (C), are in the correct form and the phrase *away from home,* (D), is idiomatically correct.

20. B

Difficulty: Medium

The phrase *intense moved* has an adjective (*intense*) modifying a participle (*moved*). This is incorrect.

The phrase should read "intensely moved". The phrases *interpretation of* (A), *to be practical* (C), and *only feasible in* (D) are all idiomatically correct.

21. C

Difficulty: High

The phrase *for a child of eleven, for instance* masks the fact that the plural subject *fitness standards* doesn't agree with the singular verb *has*. (C) should read *have*. The prepositions *for,* (B), and *throughout,* (D), are idiomatically correct, as is the conjunction *since,* (A).

22. C

Difficulty: High

Reversing the sentence order can help you find the error. Does it make sense to say "The courtroom statements … has become known"?

No. The plural subject *statements* takes the plural verb "have", rather than *has,* (C). The transition *due to,* (A), correctly sets up the causal relationship. (B) is in the correct tense (it takes place before the second part of the sentence) and is the correct form. Therefore, the past participle *become,* (D), is also in the correct tense (you can also reverse the order to say "statements … have become known").

23. D

Difficulty: Medium

Steven illogically compares driving on rural roads to driving on the big city. This doesn't make sense. and *preferred…than* isn't idiomatically correct.

Steven should compare driving on rural roads and big city roads. The phrase *on the whole,* (A), is an idiomatically correct introductory phrase. The verb *preferred driving,* (B), correctly uses the past tense. The phrase *more scenic,* (C), correctly compares two things.

24. C

Difficulty: Medium

The intervening clause *who led the opera production to its first places finishes in numerous competitions* interrupts the subject and verb.

The singular subject *soprano* needs a singular verb and so (C) should be "has". (A) correctly uses the past tense. The phrase *first place finishes,* (B), is idiomatically correct, as here *finishes* is a noun not a verb. The relative pronoun *which,* (D), is used correctly.

25. C

Difficulty: Low

When the subject and verb appear together in a sentence, it's easy to spot disagreement.

Here, the verb *is* does not agree in number with its plural subject *experiences,* and its tense is inconsistent. The error is in (C). (A) and (B) are correct idiomatic phrases. (D) is proper use of the adjective *thankful.*

26. B

Difficulty: Low

Always make sure underlined nouns are in agreement.

The singular noun *member* isn't correct with the compound subject *Jill and Casey.* Two convinced people would become "members." The error is in (B). (A) agrees with its plural subject. (C) and (D) are appropriate idiomatic phrases.

27. B

Difficulty: Medium

This section will test your knowledge of certain idiomatic phrases. *Either* must always be paired with *or.*

In (B), *and* is incorrectly paired with *either*. (A) is correct idiomatic usage. (C) properly uses an adverb to modify *moving*. (D) uses the appropriate transition and preposition.

28. A

Difficulty: High

This section will test your knowledge of some irregular verbs. Familiarize yourself with the most common ones before Test Day.

(A) is not the appropriate form of the irregular verb "to arise." With the auxiliary verb *have*, "arisen" is correct. (B) is correct use of the gerund verb form. (C) is in the correct plural form to agree with its subject *lessons*. (D) uses an appropriate preposition in context.

29. C

Difficulty: High

Long intervening phrases sometimes hide disagreement between a verb and its subject.

The subject of the verb *were* in (C) is the singular *progress*; the error is in (C). In (A), the verb phrase agrees with its plural subject *teachers*. (B) is a correct idiomatic phrase. (D) is a correct prepositional phrase.

30. C

Difficulty: Low

The main idea does not necessarily have to come in the first paragraph, although this is a good place to start looking for it.

The passage focuses on the Kloss gibbon's use of song to avoid physical encounters. A good statement of the main idea should therefore include a reference to song or singing; (C) states the main idea straightforwardly. (A) and (B) can be eliminated, since they don't reference the idea of singing. (D) and (E) refer only to specific parts of the gibbon's song, so they are not broad enough to cover the entire main idea.

31. D

Difficulty: Medium

In a sentence or clause with a compound verb, both verbs must be in the same tense.

The simple predicate in the independent clause here in *will view...and would be fighting.* Both (D) and (E) make the second verb parallel, but (E) is unnecessarily wordy. If

something happens (present tense), then something else will happen afterwards (future tense). (B) and (C) do not address the error.

32. E

Difficulty: Medium

Only one answer choice will correct a run-on sentence without introducing additional errors.

As written, this sentence is a run-on. (B), (D), and (E) all correct the run-on error, but only (E) correctly relates the two clauses. (B) reverses the cause-and-effect relationship between the two clauses. (C) does not address the error. (D) fails to correctly express the relationship between the ideas in the two clauses.

33. B

Difficulty: Medium

Make sure items in a comparative structure are logical.

Here, "many animals" are being compared to "the size of the male Kloss gibbons." (B) inserts the pronoun *that*, which makes the comparison between the sizes of the gibbons and other animals. *Those*, in (C), *do not* in (D), and *they* in (E) all incorrectly refer to the singular noun "size."

34. B

Difficulty: High

Expect to see several sentences that have no grammatical errors, but that could be improved in style.

As written, this sentence is unnecessarily wordy and difficult to follow. (B) contains all the information in the original, but it much more concise. (C) changes the meaning of the sentence, losing the fact that it would be impossible for two gibbons to see one another. (D) misuses the superlative form (*strongest*) in a comparison of only two items. (E) is not as concise as (B).

35. A

Difficulty: High

When asked to insert a new sentence, look for a disconnect between the sentences that will precede and follow the new sentence.

Sentence 14 discusses how two gibbons would be unable to tell by sight which was stronger. Sentence 15 discusses "the song." What's missing is the connection between the two ideas. (A) provides this. (B) does not relate sentence 14 to sentence 15. (C) is a 180; the paragraph tells us this can't be determined by the gibbons. Context tells us that the singing gibbon in sentence 15 is the "homeowner," so (D) is incorrect. (E) is out of scope; there is no information in the passage to support this idea.

SECTION 7

1. D

Difficulty: Low

What might he have been doing if his teacher "found his mischief to be immature and disruptive" but his classmates were "amused"?

If all you know is that he amused his peers, but that his teachers "found his mischief to be immature and disruptive," then you can conclude he was playing some sort of silly trick or stunt for their entertainment. A word like *trick* or *stunt* makes a great prediction for the blank.

In choice (A), an *anecdote* or a recounting of an event would not necessarily be considered mischievous, or "immature and disruptive." In choice (B), again, *researching* would probably not be considered mischievous by a teacher, nor would it be likely to amuse his peers. In choice (C), once again, simply by making *demands* he would not necessarily be able to amuse his peers or be causing mischief. Choice (D) is a perfect match for your prediction. In choice (E), having *debts*, or owing someone else money, would probably not amuse anyone, nor would it be considered mischievous.

2. E

Difficulty: Low

"Although" the two blanks will contrast with one another, or that the fern's appearance contrasts with its "sinewy structure".

Start with the second blank; the content here reveals fern stems have a "sinewy structure" and are "difficult to break", descriptions that suggest these stems are *strong* or *durable*. If the first blank must contrast with this actuality, then it must describe how fern stems "appear" *weak* or *delicate*. *Delicate* and *strong* make great predictions for the blanks.

In choice (A), a *vivid* or bright appearance does not necessarily contrast with a structure that is actually *powerful*.

In choice (B), again, these words do not contrast with one another. In choice (C), be careful here; this choice may be tempting, but something that was actually quite *thick* could not really appear to be *slender*. In choice (D), once again, the words *beautiful* and *heavy* do not contrast with one another. Choice (E) is a great fit for your prediction.

3. D

Difficulty: Medium

If Carl wanted to communicate using the "muscles of his body and face" instead of "his ability to speak", what might he have practiced?

"Because" signals that the blank must agrees with the description of Carl working on "precise control over the muscles of his body and face, rather than his speaking skills". And notice that the blank must satisfy two criteria: controlling the muscles of the body and face, and not needing to speak well. Look for a word that describes the art of communicating through gesture and facial expression, rather than speaking.

In choice (A), most likely a *mediator* would need to speak in order to work with both sides in a dispute. In choice (B), an *ensemble* is just a grouping of individual parts, a definition that does not necessarily satisfy the two criteria mentioned in the sentence. In choice (C), if Carl wanted to master the art of *elocution*, or public speaking, then he certainly would have worked on his "speaking skills". Choice (D) satisfies the criteria in your prediction perfectly. In choice (E), as a *troubadour* is a writer or singer of love poems or songs, this art does not necessarily satisfy the two criteria mentioned in the sentence.

4. C

Difficulty: Medium

How might "running and heavy lifting" effect someone with back pain?

Start with the second blank; what could "running and heavy lifting" easily do to someone with back pain? Most likely, such activities would *cause* or *bring about* the discomfort. As for the first blank, if he has back pain despite knowing enough to avoid these activities that would "easily" cause him discomfort, then he is probably "unsure" of the *principal* or *main* source of his pain. Principal and cause are great predictions for the blanks.

In choice (A), *original* could work in the first blank, but "running and heavy lifting" would probably not *alleviate* his discomfort. In choice (B), again, *sole* could work in the first blank, but "running and heavy lifting" would probably not *relieve* back pain. Choice (C) is a good fit for your prediction. In choice (D), once again, activities like "running and heavy lifting" would not *inhibit* back pain. In choice (E), be careful here; knowing the *partial* cause of his pain and knowing to avoid "running and heavy lifting" do not necessarily contrast with one another.

5. D

Difficulty: Medium

If a particular circus act were extremely "captivating and memorable", what effect might it have on the other acts?

If one particular act were extremely "captivating and memorable" it would probably lessen or somewhat excuse the "need for any other events". Look for a word that means to *lessen* or *excuse*.

In choice (A), a particularly "captivating and memorable" act would lessen, not *accelerate*, the "need for any other events". In choice (B), one successful act would not necessarily *predetermine*, or decide in advance, anything about other events. In choice (C), again, if one event were particularly "captivating and memorable" it would lessen, not *confirm*, the "need for any other events". Choice (D) is the best fit given your prediction. In choice (E), again, one successful act would not necessarily cause one to *anticipate* a need for other events.

6. A

Difficulty: High

What sort of "suitable" outcome would senators likely be hoping to achieve?

The words "focus instead" are important here, as they indicate the first blank describes how the senators turned their attention away from, or *set aside*, the more contentious bill. As for the second blank, if the words "most contentious" indicate the two bills are being compared by the degree of disagreement over them. So, if one bill was "most contentious", then the other must have been "easier to reach" *agreement on*. *Set aside* and *agreement on* make great predictions for the blanks.

Choice (A) is a good fit for your prediction. In choice (B), the word "instead" in the sentence makes this choice incorrect, as focusing on an easier bill would not occur instead of *enacting* or passing another. In choice (C), one cannot really *berate*, or vigorously scold, a bill. In choice (D),

again, moving on to an easier bill would not occur instead of *proclaiming*, or formally announcing, the more contentious bill. In choice (E), once again, the word "instead" makes this choice incorrect.

7. D

Difficulty: High

If he "gave more to charity than he could really afford," what quality would have seemed "limitless."

All you know from the sentence is that he rather recklessly "gave more to charity than he could really afford," so it must have been his *generosity* or *philanthropy* that appeared "limitless," both great predictions for the blank.

In choice (A), be careful here; "limitless" friendliness, or *amicability*, would not necessarily suggest he was charitable. In choice (B), nothing in the sentence suggests that he was particularly immovable, or *inexorable*. In choice (C), the act of giving more to charity than he could afford is not necessarily *frivolous*, or silly and trivial behavior. Choice (D) is a perfect match for your prediction. In choice (E), again, be careful here; giving more to charity than he could afford would not necessarily make his *venerability*, or respectability, seem "limitless".

8. A

Difficulty: Medium

If the answer doesn't jump out at you from the cited text, hunt around the passage for other references to the subject.

The author says that bacteria is overlooked by a majority of people; she also says that "The fact that we can't see them makes them easy to ignore," (lines 17–18). Predict that she is assuming that most people aren't that interested in finding out about things they can't see.

Choice (A) matches your prediction. Choice (B) is out of scope; there's no mention of how many people carry disease. Choice (C) is an opposite; if people are ignoring bacteria, they probably aren't using it on purpose. Choice (D) is out of scope; there is no mention of whether people are well-educated, or of whether that is relevant to bacteria. Choice (E) is a misused detail; antibacterial products are mentioned, but there is no mention of whether many people use them.

9. E

Difficulty: Medium

Find out what point is being supported with the cited information.

A sentence at the beginning of the paragraph says that bacteria are "overlooked by a majority of people" (lines 1–4) and the sentence with "easy to ignore" explains why people may overlook them. Predict that "easy to ignore" supports the point that people underestimate the effect of bacteria on their lives.

Choice (A) is a misused detail; bacteria are useful, but this doesn't make them easy to ignore. Choice (B) is an opposite; the passage says that people overlook bacteria. Choice (C) is out of scope; nothing in the passage deals specifically with how well understood bacteria are (or aren't). Choice (D) is an opposite; the passage states that bacteria are plentiful. Choice (E) is closest to your prediction.

10. C

Difficulty: Medium

Try restating a key sentence in your own words to decipher its basic meaning.

The author states "their impact on our lives is undeniable, and probably extends into more aspects of living than scientists are currently even aware of." Basically, we can't deny that bacteria have an impact on our life. Predict that "undeniable" is used to convey that the fact that bacteria influence our life is absolutely true.

Choice (A) is a distortion; bacteria do cause disease, but that isn't being discussed in this paragraph, and there's nothing in the passage that says the disease is "unavoidable" in any case. Choice (B) is a misused detail; the passage does say in paragraph 4 that bacteria is useful in industry, but that isn't being discussed here. Choice (C) matches your prediction; "incontrovertible" means "absolutely true." Choice (D) is an opposite; bacteria are invisible, as the author refers to "the fact that we can't see them" in line 17. Choice (E) is an opposite; "undeniable" is unlikely to imply a lack of solid support; in fact, there is support for the statement in the remainder of the passage.

11. C

Difficulty: Medium

Find out what concept a quoted phrase actually refers to.

The sentence in which "extreme environmental conditions" are mentioned discusses bacteria's "remarkable" ability to live in environments inhospitable to other kinds of life. Predict that the phrase "extreme environmental conditions" is describing the difficult environmental obstacles that bacteria can overcome.

Choice (A) is a distortion; bacteria can live in these conditions, so these environments are capable of supporting at least one kind of life. Choice (B) is out of scope; there is no information in the passage to indicate that "extreme environmental conditions" is an exaggeration. The passage presents it as a factual type of environment. Choice (C) is close to your prediction; check the other answers. Choice (D) is out of scope; the passage never addresses the issue of conquering disease. Choice (E) is a misused detail; uses for bacteria in industry aren't mentioned until paragraph 4.

12. B

Difficulty: High

Examine the surrounding context to find the overarching point the author was making before forming your prediction.

The "waste products" referred to are oxygen and CO_2, which made it possible for plants and animals to live on the planet. Predict that the reference to waste products is showing how bacteria made the planet livable for other organisms.

Choice (A) is an opposite; Oxygen and CO_2 are actually beneficial. Choice (B) matches your prediction. Choice (C) is a misused detail; though it is true that bacteria can live in extreme environments, the "waste products" are referring to the gases they produced. Choice (D) is an opposite; this is the reverse of the correct relationship. It is bacteria that made the planet livable for plants and animals, not the other way around. Choice (E) is a misused detail; this is true, but that's not mentioned until paragraph 4.

13. A

Difficulty: Low

You can pluck the answer to a detail question directly from the passage.

The author says that "One thing that makes bacteria such hardy survivors is their ability to actually alter their living DNA." (line 35–36) Use that sentence as your ready-made prediction.

Choice (A) matches your prediction. Choice (B) is a misused detail; this is not a reason they can survive well, only a fact mentioned in the first paragraph about how ubiquitous they are. Choice (C) is a misused detail; this is true, but not the explanation the author puts forth for why they survive so well. Choice (D) is out of scope; there is no information in the passage about whether causing disease helps bacteria survive well. Choice (E) is out of scope; there is nothing in the passage indicating the lifespan of bacteria.

14. D

Difficulty: Medium

Beware the common definition of the cited word—always return to the passage to discover the context.

The sentence is discussing how bacteria can take on evolutionary characteristics from other animals or bacteria by exchanging DNA with them. "it" refers to the evolutionary progress the bacteria is gaining, so predict "gaining" as a replacement for "assuming."

Choice (A) is out of scope; notice that this is the common definition of the word "assuming," but not the one used in the passage. Choice (B) is out of scope; "ascending" means rising, which has nothing to do with the sentence. Choice (C) is out of scope; no bacteria is doing any calculating here. Choice (D) matches your prediction. Choice (E) is an opposite; the bacteria are actually receiving the evolutionary progress, not rejecting it.

15. E

Difficulty: Medium

When asked about the author's intention, look for the point being supported by the cited details.

The author begins the paragraph with the argument that "While bacteria are the cause of many annoying and deadly diseases, most species are harmless, and many are actually beneficial." She then goes on to list the ways in which

bacteria are useful, so predict that she mentions the industries as examples of ways that bacteria can be beneficial.

Choice (A) is out of scope; only a few uses are listed, not "all" of them. Choice (B) is a misused detail; though bacteria in mining is described as an environmentally friendly alternative, that is not the point being made by the rest of the examples. Choice (C) is an opposite; this paragraph is about how bacteria can be helpful. Choice (D) is out of scope; we don't know a lot of details about these bacteria species, only a few examples of how they are useful. Choice (E) matches your prediction nicely.

16. B

Difficulty: Medium

Use your notes to determine the purpose of the relevant paragraph, and what would be appropriate to add to it.

The passage is listing ways in which bacteria are useful in industry and production; predict that a right answer will list some specific use of bacteria in industry.

Choice (A) is an opposite; this is not relevant to a human-controlled industry. Choice (B) works; it's an intentional use of bacteria in manufacture. Choice (C) is an opposite; this is a negative impact, not a useful function of bacteria. Choice (D) is an opposite; this is a natural process, not an industry. Choice (E) is an opposite; this is also a natural process rather than an industry

17. D

Difficulty: High

For Roman numeral questions, eliminate answer choices after evaluating each of the three options.

The passage says that bacteria improves "the nutrient absorption and therefore the yield of food crops" (lines 60–61) but also that it can "kill a farm's entire crop" (lines 74–75), so it can both help and harm agriculture. Eliminate answers (B) and (C), since neither of them includes agriculture. The passage says "we use bacteria to culture cheese and give each type its distinctive flavor" (lines 54–56) but also that another species of bacteria "could very well be working on spoiling it," (line 72) so cheese manufacture is another industry bacteria can both help and harm. Eliminate (A) because it doesn't include cheese manufacture. Finally, the passage says,"If canned food during preservation is not heated to 250° Fahrenheit, it could be infected with botulism," but there is no example in the passage of how canning could be helped by bacteria, so III is not going to be in the answer. Eliminate (E); the answer is (D).

18. D

Difficulty: Low

Use your notes to find the paragraph with the information that is relevant to the question.

The dangers of bacteria are discussed in paragraph 5, which states that the industry concerned with antibacterial cleaning and sterilization is supported by the fact that bacteria is dangerous. Predict something like "the antibacterial cleaning industry."

Choices (A), (B), and (C) are all uses of beneficial bacteria. Choice (D) matches your prediction. Choice (E) is an opposite; this is a use of beneficial bacteria.

19. D

Difficulty: Medium

As you read, notice any key words which might indicate the author's opinion.

The opening sentence mentions a category of life which is "fascinating, versatile, useful, and surprisingly varied and populous." From this, you can predict that the author's attitude toward her topic of bacteria is one of interest and appreciation.

Choice (A) is extreme; though the author appreciates bacteria, "exhilaration" is too strong a word. Choice (B) is out of scope; there is no humor in the passage. Choice (C) is out of scope; the author down not set out to criticize anything. Choice (D) is close to your prediction. Choice (E) is an opposite; if anything, the author seems to like bacteria.

SECTION 8

1. A

Difficulty: Low

Strategic Advice: If $a < b$ and $b < c$, then $a < c$.

Getting to the Answer:

$8a < 3b < 10c$, so $8a < 10c$

2. E

Difficulty: Low

Strategic Advice: The graph of a function crosses the x-axis when the value of the function equals zero. Find the values of t at which $g(t) = 0$ by solving the equation $2t - 6 = 0$. You could also use Backsolving, plugging each possible value of t into the function to see which ones give a value of 0.

Getting to the Answer:

$$2t - 6 = 0$$
$$2t = 6$$
$$t = 3$$

3. A

Difficulty: Medium

Strategic Advice: Whenever you see a triangle question about angles, remember that the sum of the interior angles of a triangle is 180 degrees

Getting to the Answer:

$$a + b + c = 180$$
$$7c + 2c + c = 180$$
$$10c = 180$$
$$c = 18$$

4. D

Difficulty: Low

Strategic Advice: Don't over think this one—the x^6 is on each side and can be subtracted from both sides.

Getting to the Answer:

Subtract x^6 from both sides to get $4 = w$.

5. C

Difficulty: Medium

Strategic Advice: Remember key triangle rules on test day: the sum of the interior angles total 180°, and triangles with two equal sides also have two equal angles.

Getting to the Answer: OA and OB are radii of the circle, so they are equal. This means that angles OAB and ABO are equal as well. The interior angles of the triangle total 180°, and angle AOB is 70°. Therefore, $ABO + ABO + 70° = 180°$

$$2ABO = 110°$$
$$ABO = 55°$$

6. B

Difficulty: Medium

Strategic Advice: When you are presented with a new function, it might look complicated. As long as you plug in numbers carefully and meticulously, these types of questions are easier than they appear.

Getting to the Answer: Plug in the given numbers.

$$\frac{1007 + 2(3.5)}{1007 - 2(3.5)} = \frac{1007 + 7}{1007 - 7} = \frac{1014}{1000}$$

Change to the decimal equivalent, which is 1.014, which is choice (B).

7. E

Difficulty: Medium

Strategic Advice: Be sure to draw in any information that is given in the question stem, but not included in the diagram.

Getting to the Answer:

If the whole side is 8, each smaller square has a side length of 2. The radius of the circle is formed by one and one half diagonals of the square. Each diagonal is $2\sqrt{2}$, so the entire radius is $2\sqrt{2} + \frac{2\sqrt{2}}{2} = 3\sqrt{2}$

Area of circle $= \pi(3\sqrt{2})^2 = 18\pi$

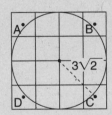

8. C

Difficulty: Medium

Strategic Advice: Be sure to distinguish between the terms *may be, possibly,* and *must be.*

Getting to the Answer: The shaded area includes all sandwiches with onions and peppers. Some of these may have tomatoes as well as the shaded region overlaps into the tomato region.

9. B

Difficulty: Medium

Strategic Advice: Take this carefully, step by step, as you translate from English to math.

Getting to the Answer:

She spends 35% of $400 to pay bills, that is

$\frac{35}{100} \times \$400 = \$140$. That leaves her with $400 - $140 =

$260. She budgets 30% of this for shopping, that is

$\frac{30}{100} \times \$260 = \$78$. That leaves $260 - $78 = $182. Of

this she allots $130 for entertainment, leaving

$182 - $130 = $52 to save. $52 as a percent of the original

$400 is $\frac{\$52}{\$400} \times 100\% = 13\%$.

10. A

Difficulty: Medium

Strategic Advice: In complex geometry problems look for parts in common between the various shapes.

Getting to the Answer: Since angles of a triangle add up to 180 degrees, then

$50 + h + g = 180$ and

$70 + z + g = 180$

so...

$$g = 130 - h$$
$$g = 110 - z$$
$$130 - h = 110 - z$$
$$h = 20 + z$$

11. C

Difficulty: Medium

Strategic Advice: Use any diagram given to your full advantage. They're usually the key to a great score.

Getting to the Answer: Therer are five tick marks between 0 and 1, so therefore

$p = \frac{1}{5}$ and $q = \frac{3}{5}$, so $p - q$ is:

$$\frac{3}{5} - \frac{1}{5} = \frac{2}{5}$$

12. C

Difficulty: Medium

Strategic Advice: Round up when the succeeding digit is 5 or above. Round down if the succeeding digit is less than 5.

Getting to the Answer:

16.763 rounds to 16.8 because 6 is greater than 5.

13. D

Difficulty: Medium

Strategic Advice: The square root of a negative number is undefined. Backsolving might let you solve this problem more quickly.

Getting to the Answer:

$0 \le x^2 - 4$

$4 \le x^2$

$2 \le x$ or $-2 \ge x$

$f(x)$ is undefined for any values of x that are not within the above range. Since 0 is not within the range, choice (D) is correct.

14. B

Difficulty: High

Strategic Advice: You are asked to Pick Numbers to plug into the function. Use the resulting information to confirm or eliminate each of the choices.

Getting to the Answer: Pick Numbers to try to eliminate choices. Choice I says $t > 0$. If you select 1 for x, then $y = 4$, $z = 0$, and $t = 0$. Therefore, I is wrong. Eliminate choices (A), (C), and (E). The only difference between the remaining choices is whether or not III is correct, so test it first. Try using 4 for x. This means that $y = 13$, $z = 14$, and $t = 7$, which is odd. So III is not correct and (B) is the correct answer.

Although you don't need to check II, it is correct because no matter what you get for y, z will always be even. If y is odd, then 1 is added to it to get z, which would always make z even. If y is even, then 4 is subtracted, and z is still even. Therefore, no matter what, z will always be even.

15. D

Difficulty: High

Strategic Advice: When you have multiple variables and multiple equations, use substitution or elimination to determine the answer. Often, one method is much easier than the other.

Getting to the Answer: You are not looking for the individual values of the variables, simply the value of $a - b$. The easiest way to do this is through elimination. Multiply the second equation by -2, then add the equations together:

$$\begin{array}{r} 3a + 5b - 4c = 12 \\ -2a - 6b + 4c = 8 \\ \hline a - b \quad\quad = 20 \end{array}$$

By eliminating the variable c, the value of $a - b$ was determined. (D) is the correct answer.

16. A

Difficulty: High

Strategic Advice: Picking Numbers is a good choice for word problems with expressions in the answer choices.

Getting to the Answer: Say there are 4 friends, each of whom contributes 10 dollars, and 5 charities. This means that there would be $4 \times 10 = \$40$ in the pot, and 5 charities to split it, so $\frac{\$40}{5} = \$8$ per charity. Find an answer choice that equals 8 when you plug in these numbers. The only one that does so is (A).

Algebraically, there are $k \times d$ dollars available. This is divided equally among c charities, so each charity receives $\frac{kd}{c}$ dollars.

SECTION 9

1. B

Difficulty: Medium

Independent clauses must be joined by a semicolon splice.

The sentence as written is a run-on. (B) fixes the problem by replacing the comma splice with a semicolon. (C) and (D) change the arrangement of the words, but neither addresses the problem of the run-on. (E) adds the semicolon, but also adds *because*, which makes the second clause dependent and thus incorrect after a semicolon.

2. C

Difficulty: Medium

In a sentence with multiple errors, make sure your answer choice addresses all of them.

This sentence has two problems: it compares *hills* to *San Luis Obispo County*, and the singular verb does not agree with its plural subject. (C) replaces is with *are* and fixes the sentence so it is the hills in both counties that are being compared. (B) and (D) don't correct the subject-verb error. (E) corrects the verb problem, but still has the incorrect comparison between *hills* and a whole county.

3. C

Difficulty: Medium

The clauses in this sentence are not properly related by the conjunction *and*. (C) properly relates the two clauses without introducing any additional errors. (B), (D), and (E) all violate the rules of parallel structure for compounds.

4. D

Difficulty: Low

Make sure verb tenses properly express the time frames referred to.

The structure of the underlined phrase is incorrect because a transition is needed after *weight*. (D) corrects this error by adding the appropriate transition *by* and changing *tried* to the participle *trying*. (B) creates a run-on sentence. (C) incorrectly joins two dependent clauses with a semi-colon. (E) is unnecessary wordy.

5. B

Difficulty: Low

Whenever you encounter a list, make sure that each element of the list is constructed in the same way.

Lists should be constructed of parallel elements. The second element of this list reiterates the verb, making it different from the other two elements. (B) fixes this by removing the second *to find*. (C) is incorrect grammatical structure. (D) and (E) eliminate *to find*, but change the phrasing so the items are no longer parallel.

6. E

Difficulty: Medium

A pronouns must agree in number with its antecedent, which may not be the noun closest to it in the sentence.

This sentence incorrectly uses the singular pronoun it to refer to a plural noun, *monkeys*. (E) uses the correct plural pronoun without introducing any new errors. (B) corrects the pronoun, but both (B) and (D) use the adjective *quick* instead of the adverb *quickly* to modify the verb *grew*. By eliminating the conjunction *and*, (C) creates a run-on sentence.

7. E

Difficulty: Low

Familiarize yourself with common idioms; they are not common as the main error in a sentence, but they frequently appear in wrong answer choices.

As to is incorrect following *claimed*. (C), (D), and (E) fix this error by replacing *as to* with *that*. However, (C) is a sentence fragment and (D) is unnecessarily wordy. (B), although it uses *as to* correctly, is also unnecessarily wordy.

8. D

Difficulty: Medium

There are a number of ways to correct a run-on sentence, but only one answer choice will do so without introducing additional errors.

This sentence is a run-on: two independent clauses joined by a comma splice. (D) uses *because* to make the second clause subordinate. (B) doesn't address the run-on error. (C) fixes the run-on but is unnecessarily wordy. (E) leaves the meaning of the final clause incomplete.

9. E

Difficulty: Medium

Some answer choices will correct one of a sentence's errors, but fail to address the others.

This sentence has two problems. *Any of the other pastas* implies that the sausage was a pasta, and a semicolon splice is incorrectly used to combine an independent and a subordinate clause. (E) corrects these problems by removing the word *other* and replacing the semicolon with a comma. (B) doesn't address either error. (C) still implies that the sausage was a pasta. (D) is unnecessarily wordy.

10. B

Difficulty: Medium

When a sentence provides a comparison, like items must be compared.

As written, this sentence compares one author, William Shakespeare, to the *works* of another author, Christopher Marlowe. (B) corrects this by making the comparison between the works of the two authors. (C) compares the two authors themselves, which is incorrect in the context of the rest of the sentence. (D) incorrectly uses the adverb *similarly* in place of the correct adjective *similar* and (E) incorrectly uses *where* which, on the SAT, will only be correct when referring to location or direction.

11. C

Difficulty: Medium

You should always be able to point to the noun that a pronoun replaces. If you can't, you may have the wrong pronoun or be missing the pronoun antecedent.

They is a pronoun and needs a plural antecedent, but there isn't one in this sentence. Also, *can be introducing* is an inappropriate verb phrase in context. (C) corrects both errors. (B) is awkward and unnecessarily wordy. (D) misuses the adjective *appropriate* when the adverb *appropriately* is needed. The compound verb *can introduce...and ruins* in (E) does not use the required parallel verb forms.

12. C

Difficulty: Medium

Some pronoun uses that are common in everyday speech will be incorrect on the SAT.

The second part of this sentence does not clearly refer back to the subject, *the internet*. (C) fixes this problem by combining the two ideas presented into one cohesive thought. (B), (D), and (E) don't specify what is not being used in the developing world. Additionally, (D) is grammatically incorrect and (E) is unnecessarily wordy.

13. A

Difficulty: Medium

Don't let the length or complexity of a sentence confuse you. The SAT frequently uses complex sentence structure to disguise a sentence with no errors.

Although this sentence is long and complex, it contains no errors. (B) has an incorrect verb form, changing *to prevent* to *preventing*. (C) and (E) are grammatically incorrect; *using...and to prevent* in (D) violates the rules of parallel structure.

14. E

Difficulty: High

Always be on the lookout for pronouns that don't match the noun they replace.

The subject of this sentence is *the hawks' nest*, not the hawks themselves. The *they* that begins the second clause doesn't agree with the antecedent. (E) fixes this problem by specifying the hawks as the subject of the second clause. (B) and (C) change the wording of the clause, but they still have the incorrect *they*. (D) uses the correct pronoun, *it*, to describe the nest, but is awkward and says that it was the nest that wrote the books.

SAT PRACTICE TEST FOUR ANSWER SHEET

Remove (or photocopy) the answer sheet, and use it to complete the practice test.

How to Take the Practice Tests

Each Practice Test includes eight scored multiple-choice sections and one essay. Keep in mind that on the actual SAT, there will be an additional multiple-choice section—the experimental section—that will not contribute to your score.

Once you start a Practice Test, don't stop until you've gone through all nine sections. Remember, you can review any questions within a section, but you may not go back or forward a section.

Good luck!

Start with number 1 for each section. If a section has fewer questions than answer spaces, leave the extra spaces blank.

Section One

Section One is the writing section's essay component.
Lined pages on which you will write your essay can be found in that section.

Section Two

1. Ⓐ Ⓑ Ⓒ Ⓓ Ⓔ
2. Ⓐ Ⓑ Ⓒ Ⓓ Ⓔ
3. Ⓐ Ⓑ Ⓒ Ⓓ Ⓔ
4. Ⓐ Ⓑ Ⓒ Ⓓ Ⓔ
5. Ⓐ Ⓑ Ⓒ Ⓓ Ⓔ
6. Ⓐ Ⓑ Ⓒ Ⓓ Ⓔ
7. Ⓐ Ⓑ Ⓒ Ⓓ Ⓔ
8. Ⓐ Ⓑ Ⓒ Ⓓ Ⓔ

9. Ⓐ Ⓑ Ⓒ Ⓓ Ⓔ
10. Ⓐ Ⓑ Ⓒ Ⓓ Ⓔ
11. Ⓐ Ⓑ Ⓒ Ⓓ Ⓔ
12. Ⓐ Ⓑ Ⓒ Ⓓ Ⓔ
13. Ⓐ Ⓑ Ⓒ Ⓓ Ⓔ
14. Ⓐ Ⓑ Ⓒ Ⓓ Ⓔ
15. Ⓐ Ⓑ Ⓒ Ⓓ Ⓔ
16. Ⓐ Ⓑ Ⓒ Ⓓ Ⓔ

17. Ⓐ Ⓑ Ⓒ Ⓓ Ⓔ
18. Ⓐ Ⓑ Ⓒ Ⓓ Ⓔ
19. Ⓐ Ⓑ Ⓒ Ⓓ Ⓔ
20. Ⓐ Ⓑ Ⓒ Ⓓ Ⓔ

right in Section Two

wrong in Section Two

Section Three

1. Ⓐ Ⓑ Ⓒ Ⓓ Ⓔ
2. Ⓐ Ⓑ Ⓒ Ⓓ Ⓔ
3. Ⓐ Ⓑ Ⓒ Ⓓ Ⓔ
4. Ⓐ Ⓑ Ⓒ Ⓓ Ⓔ
5. Ⓐ Ⓑ Ⓒ Ⓓ Ⓔ
6. Ⓐ Ⓑ Ⓒ Ⓓ Ⓔ
7. Ⓐ Ⓑ Ⓒ Ⓓ Ⓔ
8. Ⓐ Ⓑ Ⓒ Ⓓ Ⓔ

9. Ⓐ Ⓑ Ⓒ Ⓓ Ⓔ
10. Ⓐ Ⓑ Ⓒ Ⓓ Ⓔ
11. Ⓐ Ⓑ Ⓒ Ⓓ Ⓔ
12. Ⓐ Ⓑ Ⓒ Ⓓ Ⓔ
13. Ⓐ Ⓑ Ⓒ Ⓓ Ⓔ
14. Ⓐ Ⓑ Ⓒ Ⓓ Ⓔ
15. Ⓐ Ⓑ Ⓒ Ⓓ Ⓔ
16. Ⓐ Ⓑ Ⓒ Ⓓ Ⓔ

17. Ⓐ Ⓑ Ⓒ Ⓓ Ⓔ
18. Ⓐ Ⓑ Ⓒ Ⓓ Ⓔ
19. Ⓐ Ⓑ Ⓒ Ⓓ Ⓔ
20. Ⓐ Ⓑ Ⓒ Ⓓ Ⓔ
21. Ⓐ Ⓑ Ⓒ Ⓓ Ⓔ
22. Ⓐ Ⓑ Ⓒ Ⓓ Ⓔ
23. Ⓐ Ⓑ Ⓒ Ⓓ Ⓔ
24. Ⓐ Ⓑ Ⓒ Ⓓ Ⓔ

25. Ⓐ Ⓑ Ⓒ Ⓓ Ⓔ

right in Section Three

wrong in Section Three

Remove (or photocopy) this answer sheet, and use it to complete the practice test.

Start with number 1 for each section. If a section has fewer questions than answer spaces, leave the extra spaces blank.

Section Four

1. Ⓐ Ⓑ Ⓒ Ⓓ Ⓔ 9. Ⓐ Ⓑ Ⓒ Ⓓ Ⓔ 17. Ⓐ Ⓑ Ⓒ Ⓓ Ⓔ
2. Ⓐ Ⓑ Ⓒ Ⓓ Ⓔ 10. Ⓐ Ⓑ Ⓒ Ⓓ Ⓔ 18. Ⓐ Ⓑ Ⓒ Ⓓ Ⓔ
3. Ⓐ Ⓑ Ⓒ Ⓓ Ⓔ 11. Ⓐ Ⓑ Ⓒ Ⓓ Ⓔ
4. Ⓐ Ⓑ Ⓒ Ⓓ Ⓔ 12. Ⓐ Ⓑ Ⓒ Ⓓ Ⓔ
5. Ⓐ Ⓑ Ⓒ Ⓓ Ⓔ 13. Ⓐ Ⓑ Ⓒ Ⓓ Ⓔ
6. Ⓐ Ⓑ Ⓒ Ⓓ Ⓔ 14. Ⓐ Ⓑ Ⓒ Ⓓ Ⓔ
7. Ⓐ Ⓑ Ⓒ Ⓓ Ⓔ 15. Ⓐ Ⓑ Ⓒ Ⓓ Ⓔ
8. Ⓐ Ⓑ Ⓒ Ⓓ Ⓔ 16. Ⓐ Ⓑ Ⓒ Ⓓ Ⓔ

right in Section Four

wrong in Section Four

If section 4 of your test book contains math questions that are not multiple choice, continue to item 9 below. Otherwise, continue to item 9 above.

9. 10. 11. 12. 13.

14. 15. 16. 17. 18.

Section Five

1. Ⓐ Ⓑ Ⓒ Ⓓ Ⓔ 10. Ⓐ Ⓑ Ⓒ Ⓓ Ⓔ 19. Ⓐ Ⓑ Ⓒ Ⓓ Ⓔ 28. Ⓐ Ⓑ Ⓒ Ⓓ Ⓔ
2. Ⓐ Ⓑ Ⓒ Ⓓ Ⓔ 11. Ⓐ Ⓑ Ⓒ Ⓓ Ⓔ 20. Ⓐ Ⓑ Ⓒ Ⓓ Ⓔ 29. Ⓐ Ⓑ Ⓒ Ⓓ Ⓔ
3. Ⓐ Ⓑ Ⓒ Ⓓ Ⓔ 12. Ⓐ Ⓑ Ⓒ Ⓓ Ⓔ 21. Ⓐ Ⓑ Ⓒ Ⓓ Ⓔ 30. Ⓐ Ⓑ Ⓒ Ⓓ Ⓔ
4. Ⓐ Ⓑ Ⓒ Ⓓ Ⓔ 13. Ⓐ Ⓑ Ⓒ Ⓓ Ⓔ 22. Ⓐ Ⓑ Ⓒ Ⓓ Ⓔ 31. Ⓐ Ⓑ Ⓒ Ⓓ Ⓔ
5. Ⓐ Ⓑ Ⓒ Ⓓ Ⓔ 14. Ⓐ Ⓑ Ⓒ Ⓓ Ⓔ 23. Ⓐ Ⓑ Ⓒ Ⓓ Ⓔ 32. Ⓐ Ⓑ Ⓒ Ⓓ Ⓔ
6. Ⓐ Ⓑ Ⓒ Ⓓ Ⓔ 15. Ⓐ Ⓑ Ⓒ Ⓓ Ⓔ 24. Ⓐ Ⓑ Ⓒ Ⓓ Ⓔ 33. Ⓐ Ⓑ Ⓒ Ⓓ Ⓔ
7. Ⓐ Ⓑ Ⓒ Ⓓ Ⓔ 16. Ⓐ Ⓑ Ⓒ Ⓓ Ⓔ 25. Ⓐ Ⓑ Ⓒ Ⓓ Ⓔ 34 Ⓐ Ⓑ Ⓒ Ⓓ Ⓔ
8. Ⓐ Ⓑ Ⓒ Ⓓ Ⓔ 17. Ⓐ Ⓑ Ⓒ Ⓓ Ⓔ 26. Ⓐ Ⓑ Ⓒ Ⓓ Ⓔ 35. Ⓐ Ⓑ Ⓒ Ⓓ Ⓔ
9. Ⓐ Ⓑ Ⓒ Ⓓ Ⓔ 18. Ⓐ Ⓑ Ⓒ Ⓓ Ⓔ 27. Ⓐ Ⓑ Ⓒ Ⓓ Ⓔ

right in Section Five

wrong in Section Five

Remove (or photocopy) this answer sheet, and use it to complete the practice test.

Start with number 1 for each section. If a section has fewer questions than answer spaces, leave the extra spaces blank.

Section Six

1. Ⓐ Ⓑ Ⓒ Ⓓ Ⓔ   9. Ⓐ Ⓑ Ⓒ Ⓓ Ⓔ   17. Ⓐ Ⓑ Ⓒ Ⓓ Ⓔ
2. Ⓐ Ⓑ Ⓒ Ⓓ Ⓔ   10. Ⓐ Ⓑ Ⓒ Ⓓ Ⓔ   18. Ⓐ Ⓑ Ⓒ Ⓓ Ⓔ
3. Ⓐ Ⓑ Ⓒ Ⓓ Ⓔ   11. Ⓐ Ⓑ Ⓒ Ⓓ Ⓔ   19. Ⓐ Ⓑ Ⓒ Ⓓ Ⓔ
4. Ⓐ Ⓑ Ⓒ Ⓓ Ⓔ   12. Ⓐ Ⓑ Ⓒ Ⓓ Ⓔ   20. Ⓐ Ⓑ Ⓒ Ⓓ Ⓔ
5. Ⓐ Ⓑ Ⓒ Ⓓ Ⓔ   13. Ⓐ Ⓑ Ⓒ Ⓓ Ⓔ   21. Ⓐ Ⓑ Ⓒ Ⓓ Ⓔ
6. Ⓐ Ⓑ Ⓒ Ⓓ Ⓔ   14. Ⓐ Ⓑ Ⓒ Ⓓ Ⓔ   22. Ⓐ Ⓑ Ⓒ Ⓓ Ⓔ
7. Ⓐ Ⓑ Ⓒ Ⓓ Ⓔ   15. Ⓐ Ⓑ Ⓒ Ⓓ Ⓔ   23. Ⓐ Ⓑ Ⓒ Ⓓ Ⓔ
8. Ⓐ Ⓑ Ⓒ Ⓓ Ⓔ   16. Ⓐ Ⓑ Ⓒ Ⓓ Ⓔ   24. Ⓐ Ⓑ Ⓒ Ⓓ Ⓔ

☐ # right in Section Six

☐ # wrong in Section Six

Section Seven

1. Ⓐ Ⓑ Ⓒ Ⓓ Ⓔ   9. Ⓐ Ⓑ Ⓒ Ⓓ Ⓔ
2. Ⓐ Ⓑ Ⓒ Ⓓ Ⓔ   10. Ⓐ Ⓑ Ⓒ Ⓓ Ⓔ
3. Ⓐ Ⓑ Ⓒ Ⓓ Ⓔ   11. Ⓐ Ⓑ Ⓒ Ⓓ Ⓔ
4. Ⓐ Ⓑ Ⓒ Ⓓ Ⓔ   12. Ⓐ Ⓑ Ⓒ Ⓓ Ⓔ
5. Ⓐ Ⓑ Ⓒ Ⓓ Ⓔ   13. Ⓐ Ⓑ Ⓒ Ⓓ Ⓔ
6. Ⓐ Ⓑ Ⓒ Ⓓ Ⓔ   14. Ⓐ Ⓑ Ⓒ Ⓓ Ⓔ
7. Ⓐ Ⓑ Ⓒ Ⓓ Ⓔ   15. Ⓐ Ⓑ Ⓒ Ⓓ Ⓔ
8. Ⓐ Ⓑ Ⓒ Ⓓ Ⓔ   16. Ⓐ Ⓑ Ⓒ Ⓓ Ⓔ

☐ # right in Section Seven

☐ # wrong in Section Seven

Section Eight

1. Ⓐ Ⓑ Ⓒ Ⓓ Ⓔ   9. Ⓐ Ⓑ Ⓒ Ⓓ Ⓔ   17. Ⓐ Ⓑ Ⓒ Ⓓ Ⓔ
2. Ⓐ Ⓑ Ⓒ Ⓓ Ⓔ   10. Ⓐ Ⓑ Ⓒ Ⓓ Ⓔ   18. Ⓐ Ⓑ Ⓒ Ⓓ Ⓔ
3. Ⓐ Ⓑ Ⓒ Ⓓ Ⓔ   11. Ⓐ Ⓑ Ⓒ Ⓓ Ⓔ
4. Ⓐ Ⓑ Ⓒ Ⓓ Ⓔ   12. Ⓐ Ⓑ Ⓒ Ⓓ Ⓔ
5. Ⓐ Ⓑ Ⓒ Ⓓ Ⓔ   13. Ⓐ Ⓑ Ⓒ Ⓓ Ⓔ
6. Ⓐ Ⓑ Ⓒ Ⓓ Ⓔ   14. Ⓐ Ⓑ Ⓒ Ⓓ Ⓔ
7. Ⓐ Ⓑ Ⓒ Ⓓ Ⓔ   15. Ⓐ Ⓑ Ⓒ Ⓓ Ⓔ
8. Ⓐ Ⓑ Ⓒ Ⓓ Ⓔ   16. Ⓐ Ⓑ Ⓒ Ⓓ Ⓔ

☐ # right in Section Eight

☐ # wrong in Section Eight

Section Nine

1. Ⓐ Ⓑ Ⓒ Ⓓ Ⓔ   9. Ⓐ Ⓑ Ⓒ Ⓓ Ⓔ
2. Ⓐ Ⓑ Ⓒ Ⓓ Ⓔ   10. Ⓐ Ⓑ Ⓒ Ⓓ Ⓔ
3. Ⓐ Ⓑ Ⓒ Ⓓ Ⓔ   11. Ⓐ Ⓑ Ⓒ Ⓓ Ⓔ
4. Ⓐ Ⓑ Ⓒ Ⓓ Ⓔ   12. Ⓐ Ⓑ Ⓒ Ⓓ Ⓔ
5. Ⓐ Ⓑ Ⓒ Ⓓ Ⓔ   13. Ⓐ Ⓑ Ⓒ Ⓓ Ⓔ
6. Ⓐ Ⓑ Ⓒ Ⓓ Ⓔ   14. Ⓐ Ⓑ Ⓒ Ⓓ Ⓔ
7. Ⓐ Ⓑ Ⓒ Ⓓ Ⓔ
8. Ⓐ Ⓑ Ⓒ Ⓓ Ⓔ

☐ # right in Section Nine

☐ # wrong in Section Nine

Practice Test Four

SECTION 1
Time—25 Minutes
ESSAY

The essay gives you an opportunity to show how effectively you can develop and express ideas. You should, therefore, take care to develop your point of view, present your ideas logically and clearly, and use language precisely.

Your essay must be written in your Answer Grid Booklet—you will receive no other paper on which to write. You will have enough space if you write on every line, avoid wide margins, and keep your handwriting to a reasonable size. Remember that people who are not familiar with your handwriting will read what you write. Try to write or print so that what you are writing is legible to those readers.

You have twenty-five minutes to write an essay on the topic assigned below.

DO NOT WRITE ON ANOTHER TOPIC. AN OFF-TOPIC ESSAY WILL RECEIVE A SCORE OF ZERO.

Think carefully about the issue presented in the following excerpt and the assignment below.

> "Never do today what you can do tomorrow. Something may occur to make you regret your premature action."
>
> –Aaron Burr

Assignment: Do you agree with Aaron Burr that it's wisest to put things off if you can? Plan and write an essay in which you develop your point of view on this issue. Support your position with reasoning and examples taken from your reading, studies, experience, or observations.

DO NOT WRITE YOUR ESSAY IN YOUR TEST BOOK.
You will receive credit only for what you write in your Answer Grid Booklet.

_____

_____

_____

_____

_____

_____

_____

_____

_____

_____

_____

_____

_____

_____

_____

_____

_____

_____

IF YOU FINISH BEFORE TIME IS CALLED, YOU MAY CHECK YOUR WORK ON THIS SECTION ONLY. DO NOT TURN TO ANY OTHER SECTION IN THE TEST.

SECTION 2

Time—25 Minutes

20 Questions

Directions: For this section, solve each problem and decide which is the best of the choices given. Fill in the corresponding oval on the answer sheet. You may use any available space for scratchwork.

Notes:

(1) Calculator use is permitted.

(2) All numbers used are real numbers.

(3) Figures are provided for some problems. All figures are drawn to scale and lie in a plane UNLESS otherwise indicated.

(4) Unless otherwise specified, the domain of any function f is assumed to be the set of all real numbers x for which $f(x)$ is a real number.

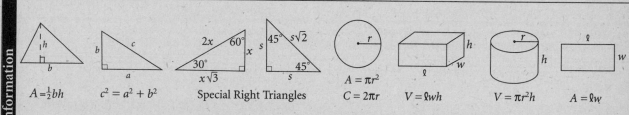

$A = \frac{1}{2}bh$ $\qquad$ $c^2 = a^2 + b^2$ $\qquad$ Special Right Triangles $\qquad$ $A = \pi r^2$ $\qquad$ $C = 2\pi r$ $\qquad$ $V = \ell wh$ $\qquad$ $V = \pi r^2 h$ $\qquad$ $A = \ell w$

The sum of the degree measures of the angles in a triangle is 180.
The number of degrees of arc in a circle is 360.
A straight angle has a degree measure of 180.

1. If $3x + 2 = 14$, what is the value of $5x - 6$?

   (A) −1
   (B) 14
   (C) 19
   (D) 26
   (E) 32

2. There are nine classrooms in a particular school. Each classroom has at least 24 students, and at most 30 students. Which of the following could be the total number of students in the school?

   (A) 90
   (B) 100
   (C) 200
   (D) 250
   (E) 300

3. The figure above shows Jane's neighborhood. Her house is located directly north of the Town Square. The distance from her house to which of the following places is the greatest?

   (A) Library
   (B) Town Square
   (C) Drugstore
   (D) Police
   (E) Hotel

GO ON TO THE NEXT PAGE

FACTORIES OPERATED BY MANUFACTURING, INC.

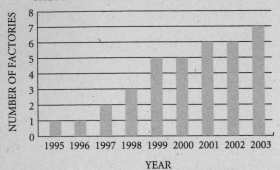

4. The graph above shows how Manufacturing, Inc. grew over an eight year period by indicating the number of factories operating at the end of each year. Manufacturing, Inc. has never closed a factory. One February they opened two factories. During what year did they do this?

(A) 1997
(B) 1998
(C) 1999
(D) 2000
(E) 2001

5. The average (arithmetic mean) of x and y is 7, and the average of x, y, and z is 10. What is the value of z?

(A) 23
(B) 17
(C) 16
(D) 11
(E) 3

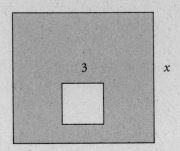

6. In the figure above, a small square is inside a larger square. What is the area, in terms of x, of the shaded region?

(A) $6 - 2x$
(B) $2x - 6$
(C) $x^2 - 6$
(D) $9 - x^2$
(E) $x^2 - 9$

7. If $abcd = 3$ and $abce = 0$, which of the following must be true?

(A) $e = 0$
(B) $c = 0$
(C) $a > 0$
(D) $b < 0$
(E) $b > 3$

8. During the 2000 fiscal year, a company made $\frac{1}{7}$ of its profits in the first quarter, $\frac{1}{3}$ of its profits in the second quarter, $\frac{1}{2}$ of its profits in the third quarter, and the remaining $2 million in the fourth quarter. What were the total profits for the fiscal year?

(A) $18 million
(B) $36 million
(C) $63 million
(D) $84 million
(E) $126 million

GO ON TO THE NEXT PAGE

9. If $4^{4x+6} = 64^{2x}$, what is the value of x?

    (A) 1
    (B) 2
    (C) 3
    (D) 4
    (E) 5

10. If 5 more than 3 times a certain number is 3 less than the number, what is the number?

    (A) -7
    (B) -4
    (C) $-\dfrac{1}{2}$
    (D) 4
    (E) 7

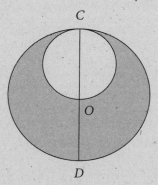

11. The larger circle above has center O and diameter CD. The smaller circle has diameter OC. If the area of the larger circle is 25π, what is the circumference of the shaded region?

    (A) 5π
    (B) 10π
    (C) 15π
    (D) 20π
    (E) 25π

12. If a linear function passes through the points $(1, a)$, $(2, b)$ and $(4, 18)$, what is the value of $\dfrac{3}{2}b - a$?

    (A) 4
    (B) 7
    (C) 9
    (D) 18
    (E) It cannot be determined from the information given

$$4, -4, -1, \ldots$$

13. The first term in the sequence above is 4. Each even-numbered term is found by multiplying the previous term by -1; each odd-numbered term is found by adding 3 to the previous term. For example, the second term is $4 \times -1 = -4$, and the third term is $-4 + 3 = -1$. What is the 37th term of the sequence?

    (A) -4
    (B) -1
    (C) 0
    (D) 1
    (E) 4

14. In the xy-plane, the equation of line l is $y = 3x + 2$. If line m is the reflection of line l in the y-axis, what is the equation of line m?

    (A) $y = -3x + 2$
    (B) $y = -3x - 2$
    (C) $y = 3x - 2$
    (D) $y = \dfrac{1}{3}x + 2$
    (E) $y = -\dfrac{1}{3}x + 2$

GO ON TO THE NEXT PAGE

KAPLAN
Test Prep and Admissions

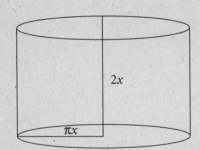

Pine tree height

100 *ft*

50 *ft*

5 6 7 8 9 10

Years of growth

15. The graph above shows a pine tree's height in feet from year 5 to year 10 of growth. What was the tree's percent increase in height from year 6 to year 9?

(A) 25%
(B) 75%
(C) 200%
(D) 300%
(E) 400%

2x

πx

16. Which of the following has the same volume as the cylinder shown above with radius $πx$ and height $2x$?

(A) a cylinder with radius $2x$ and height $πx$
(B) a cube with edge $2πx$
(C) a cylinder with radius $2πx$ and height x
(D) a rectangular solid with dimensions $2x$, $πx$, $πx$
(E) a rectangular solid with dimensions $πx$, $2πx$, $πx$

17. If $3a + 3(b + 1) = c$, what is $b + 1$ in terms of a and c?

(A) $\dfrac{c}{9a}$

(B) $\dfrac{c}{3} - a$

(C) $\dfrac{c}{3} + a$

(D) $\dfrac{c}{3} - 3a$

(E) $\dfrac{c}{3} + 3a$

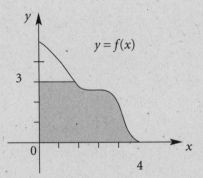

18. The shaded region in the figure above is bounded by the x-axis, the y-axis, $y = 3$ and the graph of $y = f(x)$. If the point (m, n) is in the shaded region, which of the following must be true?

   I. $m \le 3$
   II. $n \ge m$
   III. $f(m) \ge n$

(A) I only
(B) III only
(C) I and III
(D) II and III
(E) I, II, and III

GO ON TO THE NEXT PAGE

19. A lumber company producing 13 inch boards can only sell ones cut between $12\frac{15}{16}$ and $13\frac{1}{16}$. If they sell a board that is x inches long, which of the following describes all possible values of x?

   (A) $|x - 13| = \frac{1}{16}$

   (B) $|x + 13| = \frac{1}{16}$

   (C) $|x - 13| > \frac{1}{16}$

   (D) $|x + 13| < \frac{1}{16}$

   (E) $|x - 13| < \frac{1}{16}$

20. The least integer of a set of consecutive even integers is -30. If the sum of these integers is 66, how many integers are in the set?

   (A) 12

   (B) 14

   (C) 30

   (D) 33

   (E) 35

IF YOU FINISH BEFORE TIME IS CALLED, YOU MAY CHECK YOUR WORK ON THIS SECTION ONLY. DO NOT TURN TO ANY OTHER SECTION IN THE TEST.

STOP

Test Prep and Admissions

SECTION 3

Time—25 Minutes
25 Questions

Directions: For each of the following questions, choose the best answer and darken the corresponding oval on the answer sheet.

Each sentence below has one or two blanks, each blank indicating that something has been omitted. Beneath the sentence are five words or sets of words labeled (A) through (E). Choose the word or set of words that, when inserted in the sentence, best fits the meaning of the sentence as a whole.

EXAMPLE:

Today's small, portable computers contrast markedly with the earliest electronic computers, which were ----.

(A) effective
(B) invented
(C) useful
(D) destructive
(E) enormous

---

1. His discomfort was ----, coming and going regularly throughout the day.

   (A) unmediated
   (B) spontaneous
   (C) periodic
   (D) incidental
   (E) endemic

2. Despite being in the midst of angry and noisy ----, Lucinda felt surprisingly ----.

   (A) discord . . tranquil
   (B) pomp . . daunting
   (C) banality . . conventional
   (D) turmoil . . controversial
   (E) serenity . . opportune

3. The hospital's inept administration was so ---- that the doctors working there considered the facility a ----, debasing the entire medical profession.

   (A) apathetic . . victory
   (B) exacting . . spectacle
   (C) astute . . debacle
   (D) negligent . . travesty
   (E) surreptitious . . triumph

4. The new reflecting pool was ----, dazzling onlookers with its ---- in the bright sunlight.

   (A) unassuming . . audaciousness
   (B) capricious . . innocuousness
   (C) tawdry . . precociousness
   (D) vivacious . . insipidness
   (E) resplendent . . incandescence

5. The composition's ---- was impossible to miss, as the series of rhythmic drum beats dominated the other sounds.

   (A) cadence
   (B) speciousness
   (C) convolution
   (D) adulation
   (E) passion

GO ON TO THE NEXT PAGE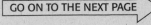

KAPLAN
Test Prep and Admissions

Directions: The passages below are followed by questions based on their content; questions following a pair of related passages may also be based on the relationship between the paired passages. Answer the questions on the basis of what is <u>stated</u> or <u>implied</u> in the passages and in any introductory material that may be provided.

Questions 6–7 are based on the following passage.

So much of human social activity revolves around eating that, especially when traveling in a foreign country, acceptance of the local foods and observance of table customs become essential
(5) steps towards fitting in. Being aware of the strict religious prohibitions practiced in many societies is particularly important. In India, for example, it is best not to ask for beef, since cows are considered by many there to be sacred animals. Table
(10) etiquette can prove to be even trickier, as breaking even *subtle* rules can quite easily offend people. In Zambia, for instance, the guest should ask to be served first because it is impolite for the host to offer food first.

6. In line 6, "practiced" is best understood as meaning

(A) repeated

(B) trained

(C) observed

(D) honed

(E) enforced

7. The author emphasizes the word "*subtle*" (line 11) in order to stress the point that

(A) despite the intricacies involved, a violation of religious customs can be quite overt

(B) understanding table etiquette is always more complicated than learning religious customs

(C) by its very nature, table etiquette is composed of indecipherable rules

(D) rules governing table etiquette can be especially hard to discern

(E) the people of Zambia are particularly guarded about their table manners

Questions 8–9 are based on the following passage.

For my 10th birthday I asked my mother to bake my favorite dish: an egg and cheese casserole spiced with long, red slices of chili peppers. I'm not sure why I asked for this dish. Perhaps it was
(5) for purely aesthetic reasons: the maroon pan she always used complemented the brilliant hues of the peppers and enhanced the more subtle yellows of the cheese. More likely, however, I was attracted by the inherent contrast of the ingredients: sweet,
(10) tame cheese dripping with fiery, intimidating pepper juice I knew would singe my tongue the moment it entered my mouth. Maybe it was simply selfishness, for the dish proved too threatening for my friends and I was left with it all to myself.

8. The author mentions the "brilliant hues of the peppers" (lins 6–7) in order to

(A) better describe the dish as pleasing to the eye

(B) accentuate the hotness of the peppers

(C) indicate a reason why it was selfish to request the dish

(D) describe the burning sensation the peppers caused in the author's mouth

(E) discount the suggestion that the dish's appearance was important

9. The author's description of the pepper juice as "intimidating" (line 10) serves to

(A) reinforce the claim that the author's favorite dish is unusual

(B) warn the reader of the dangers of eating hot peppers

(C) suggest that the narrator was unaware of the hotness of the peppers

(D) emphasize the contrast between the tastes of the peppers and cheese

(E) explain the pleasant appearance of the dish

GO ON TO THE NEXT PAGE ▷

Questions 10–19 are based on the following passage.

The following is taken from the introduction to a piece on the literary themes of the American author Kurt Vonnegut, Jr.

After World War I (which was, at the time, known simply as the "Great War"), a new era began in art and literature. The movement was called Modernism, and though we still use the word
(5) "modern" to refer to the present day, the true Modernist movement mostly took place between about 1915 and 1940. The movement was not entirely an outgrowth of the "Great War," but many of its themes can be traced back to the war and the
(10) feelings that pervaded public culture during its aftermath. Modernism took on the sense of a loss of innocence; it relays the disillusionment of those who have suddenly realized that the world is much scarier and lonelier than they had previously
(15) imagined it to be. Gone were the proper manners and happy endings of the Victorian novel. Instead, modern novels were often depressing, sometimes lewd, and often nearly incomprehensible; in forging a style that conveys the sense of being "cut
(20) off" from previous art and history, Modernists often created works so unlike their predecessors that they were inaccessible to the general public.

The next major artistic movement was also closely tied to the global climate of its time;
(25) Postmodernism, as it became known, rose from the ashes of the Second World War. In American circles particularly, Postmodernist thought was also influenced by an underlying feeling of paranoia from the mounting threat of the Cold War,
(30) and later on it absorbed the political uprisings against the continuation of the Vietnam War. Though less closely knit as a movement than Modernism, Postmodernism continued to be increasingly experimental in style and, though
(35) sometimes playful, it lacked the saccharine optimism we see in *Leave it to Beaver*, *Happy Days*, and other pop culture depictions of the decades following World War II.

Both Modernists and Postmodernists were con-
(40) cerned with the role of the artist. Although it is hard to make sweeping generalizations about either movement, it is probably fair to say that on the whole, Modernists were concerned with art for art's sake, whereas more Postmodernists were likely
(45) to consider their works as a way of commenting on the state of society. The works of one Postmodern writer, Kurt Vonnegut, Jr., reflect some aspects of both artistic movements. His style, in most of his more influential novels, is
(50) fairly unique; the writing is split up into many different fragments of prose, averaging perhaps a page or less in length. The stories he tells are often nonlinear, jumping around in time, place, and character between each chunk of text. This style is
(55) thought to be reflective of the fragmentation of society, a concept near to the hearts of Modernists and Postmodernists alike.

Though some critics may, not entirely without justification, characterize Vonnegut as a cynic, I
(60) see more optimism in his works than in some of his Postmodern contemporaries, many of whom freely acknowledge the fragmentation and seeming chaos of Postmodern existence as something to accept and, oddly enough, revel in. Vonnegut
(65) claims in his most well-known book, *Slaughterhouse-Five*, that he is writing in the style of a Tralfamadorian novel, referring to an imaginary alien species that is supposedly capable of seeing through time as well as space. According to
(70) Vonnegut, such a novel appears disjointed to human readers when read from beginning to end; a Tralfamadorian, on the other hand, is able to look through time and see all the pieces at once coming together into a single brilliant point of
(75) clarity and truth. In this way, Vonnegut seems to suggest that the appearance of fragmentation and chaos in our society is largely due to humans' failure to achieve the proper perspective, and that the role of the artist is to bring together the proper
(80) points in order to reveal the order and beauty behind it all. For such a Postmodern writer, these are in fact two very modern ideas.

GO ON TO THE NEXT PAGE ▷

10. In this excerpt, the author's main point about the writings of Kurt Vonnegut is that

   (A) they keep him from being classified as a member of any particular artistic movement

   (B) his style and content reflect aspects of both Modernism and Postmodernism

   (C) he is a mere science-fiction writer whose work is incorrectly raised to the level of "real" literature

   (D) they are cynical and depressing

   (E) they do not break any new literary ground

11. According to the passage, the "Great War" (line 2) was responsible for

   (A) virtually every single aspect of Modernist art and writing

   (B) a revolutionary change in the way nations around the world regarded one another

   (C) the pacifist sentiments of many a Postmodernist writer

   (D) feelings of cultural detachment that were reflected in the arts of the postwar era

   (E) Kurt Vonnegut's decision to enter the arts and heal the wounds war had opened

12. The quotation marks around the phrase "cut off" (lines 19–20) help serve to

   (A) introduce a term with which the reader may be unfamiliar

   (B) indicate a particular literary application separate from the common meaning of the phrase

   (C) set apart a figurative usage

   (D) highlight a note of sarcasm that might otherwise go unnoticed

   (E) suggest the author's doubts about the veracity of what he is writing

13. In the first sentence of the second paragraph, the author suggests that

   (A) even tragedies such as worldwide wars can have positive results

   (B) artistic movements are often closely tied to political and historical events

   (C) one cannot bring about intellectual change without some devastating side effects

   (D) World War II marked the end of mankind's eagerness to solve all of its problems on the battlefield

   (E) the two World Wars were so damaging that equivalent calamities will never again occur in history

14. The author's attitude towards "pop culture depictions" (line 37) can best be described as

   (A) admiring

   (B) pessimistic

   (C) revolted

   (D) curious

   (E) dismissive

15. The passage indicates that Kurt Vonnegut's uniqueness among Postmodern writers can largely be attributed to

   (A) the unequalled depth and sympathy in his characterizations

   (B) the creativity of his novels' settings and plot developments

   (C) his choppy style and nonlinear methods of storytelling

   (D) his rejection of nearly every convention of writing before his time

   (E) his vision of society as chaotic and frightening

GO ON TO THE NEXT PAGE

16. The author would probably agree with which of the following statements about "some critics" (line 58)?

    (A) They are essentially correct in their assessment of cynicism and only need to elaborate their views more completely.

    (B) Their foolish conjectures fly in the face of all respectable Vonnegut criticism.

    (C) They could be correct, but there is really not enough evidence in Vonnegut's writings to prove the issue for certain.

    (D) They are taking far too simplistic a view of literature to make any reasonable claims about it.

    (E) There is some evidence for their opinions, but underlying currents in Vonnegut's fiction ultimately reveal them to be incomplete.

17. In line 74, the word "brilliant" is used to mean

    (A) never before envisioned

    (B) difficult to comprehend

    (C) ahead of its time

    (D) shocking and enlightening

    (E) revolutionary and headstrong

18. According to the passage, Vonnegut's conception of "the role of the artist" (line 79) is

    (A) to show people that only art can lift them out of the pointlessness and drudgery of their everyday lives

    (B) to teach people about ways of improving the society of the world around them

    (C) to combat injustices and bring equality and optimism back to human culture

    (D) to reveal an underlying structure and meaning beneath the seeming chaos of modern existence

    (E) to prove that nihilism is not only a valid perspective, but the only rational way of viewing the world

19. The main flow of the argument in the passage is

    (A) an initial claim that suddenly results in a total reversal

    (B) a specific instance followed by increasingly extensive generalizations

    (C) a general artistic background followed by an extended example

    (D) a plodding reiteration of a single point with myriad supporting details

    (E) a proof that initially assumes the opposite of the author's true point

GO ON TO THE NEXT PAGE

Questions 20–25 are based on the following passage.

The swimming sky of oceanic expanse in Van Gogh's *The Starry Night*; the human figure born of marble by the careful hands of Rodin; the graceful, ethereal figure of Degas' ballerina; all communicate (5) both emotion and essence in a world where aesthetic reigns supreme. Art has forever been humankind's tool for expressing the ineffable, a form of communication when words fail or are wholly inadequate. Art challenges the artist by (10) constructing a world in which opposing forces—impulse and control, emotion and thought, ideation and actuality—must cooperate to produce a piece of art. The artist must wrestle an almost untamable creative force for control in order to (15) grant space to its expression. The process of facing and governing this force while conveying it to others makes artistic creation an especially valuable therapeutic tool for the emotionally disturbed.

The process of creation and the created product (20) are equally valuable parts of therapeutic art. Creating art requires balancing two aspects of personality that are, in the case of the emotionally disturbed person, especially irreconcilable. Like all artists, the emotionally disturbed person must (25) learn to control and harness the dangerous, unpredictable forces of creation while remaining sufficiently unrestrictive to allow its expression. Balancing these forces in a constructive way while granting full play to both is an important ability (30) to master, one that art therapy teaches particularly well.

The emotionally disturbed artist's goal is not the perfect expression of an aesthetic ideal. Yet communicating the mind's content and having it (35) recognized by others is intensely valuable to the disturbed artist's healing. Taking ideas out of the isolation imposed by the mind and reproducing them in a form that can be shared and understood by others releases those ideas from the mind and (40) removes from them some of their power. Using the brush where the pen and voice fail allows others, like the therapist, to recognize, understand, and begin to deconstruct the mind's content.

Artistic creation allows emotionally disturbed (45) people to communicate ideas they are unable to express in words, and it provides therapists with an otherwise unobtainable window into the mind. Examination of their artistic pieces reveals an inner world that the self of the disturbed person (50) cannot express another way. Art then becomes a new therapeutic medium through which to understand and address the complex issues that threaten and haunt the disturbed person, and in which to free them.

20. The primary purpose of the passage is to

(A) show that art therapy is the only effective way of dealing with disturbed individuals

(B) prove that art therapy has made significant strides in recent decades

(C) demonstrate how art therapy can transform non-functioning individuals into productive members of society

(D) show how art therapy can be beneficial for emotionally disturbed people

(E) describe the methods by which artwork can be interpreted by a therapist

21. In line 41, "the brush" primarily signifies

(A) the wide variety of artistic equipment

(B) the author's preference for art over written communication

(C) the process of painting

(D) artistic creation

(E) a powerful idea

22. The passage suggests that the main reason a therapist might use art to work with emotionally disturbed people is that art therapy can

(A) allow them to address ideas or emotions in a nonverbal way

(B) share their innermost thoughts with the public

(C) teach them to appreciate the great artists of the past

(D) broaden the scope of their social interaction

(E) encourage them to cooperate with others

GO ON TO THE NEXT PAGE

23. The author suggests that artwork functions as a "window" (line 47) because artwork

    (A) is transparent
    (B) is divided into segments
    (C) stifles communication
    (D) can be extremely fragile
    (E) allows access to thoughts

24. In line 51, "medium" most nearly means

    (A) midpoint
    (B) indication of action
    (C) mode of communication
    (D) average
    (E) psychic

25. The author's conclusion would be most directly supported by additional information proving that

    (A) art therapists are better able to evaluate the quality of art than regular therapists
    (B) individuals involved in art programs have more control over their emotions
    (C) there is a documented connection between creativity and attention span
    (D) art programs in elementary schools reduce the number of fights among children
    (E) painting relieves some symptoms of arthritis

IF YOU FINISH BEFORE TIME IS CALLED, YOU MAY CHECK YOUR WORK ON THIS SECTION ONLY. DO NOT TURN TO ANY OTHER SECTION IN THE TEST. **STOP**

SECTION 4
Time—25 Minutes
18 Questions

Directions: For this section, solve each problem and decide which is the best of the choices given. Fill in the corresponding oval on the answer sheet. You may use any available space for scratchwork.

Notes:

(1) Calculator use is permitted.

(2) All numbers used are real numbers.

(3) Figures are provided for some problems. All figures are drawn to scale and lie in a plane UNLESS otherwise indicated.

(4) Unless otherwise specified, the domain of any function f is assumed to be the set of all real numbers x for which $f(x)$ is a real number.

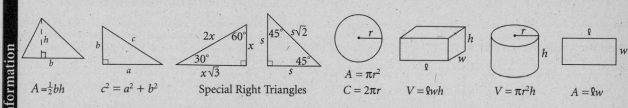

$A = \frac{1}{2}bh$ $\quad c^2 = a^2 + b^2$ $\quad$ Special Right Triangles $\quad A = \pi r^2$ $\quad C = 2\pi r$ $\quad V = \ell wh$ $\quad V = \pi r^2 h$ $\quad A = \ell w$

The sum of the degree measures of the angles in a triangle is 180.
The number of degrees of arc in a circle is 360.
A straight angle has a degree measure of 180.

1. If $\frac{3}{x} + x = 7 + \frac{3}{7}$, then x can equal which of the following?

(A) $\frac{1}{7}$

(B) $\frac{3}{7}$

(C) 1

(D) $\frac{7}{3}$

(E) 7

Note: Figure not drawn to scale

2. In the right triangle above, if $b = 5$, what is the value of a ?

(A) $\sqrt{3}$ (approximately 1.73)

(B) 3

(C) $\sqrt{13}$ (approximately 3.61)

(D) $\sqrt{21}$ (approximately 4.58)

(E) $\sqrt{29}$ (approximately 5.39)

GO ON TO THE NEXT PAGE

All numbers that are divisible by both 4 and 6
are also divisible by 8

3. Which of the following numbers can be used to
show that the above statement is FALSE?

(A) 12
(B) 24
(C) 32
(D) 40
(E) 48

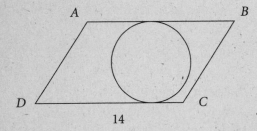

4. In the figure above, the circle is tangent to sides *AB*
and *DC* of the parallelogram *ABCD*, which has
area 168. What is the area of the circle?

(A) 12π
(B) 26π
(C) 36π
(D) 49π
(E) 144π

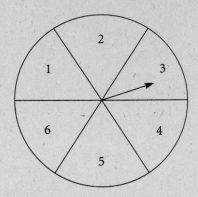

5. On the disk shown above, a player spins the arrow
twice and multiplies the numbers. On every spin,
each of the numbered sectors has an equal
probability of being the sector on which the arrow
stops. What's the probability that the product is even?

(A) $\dfrac{9}{36}$

(B) $\dfrac{12}{36}$

(C) $\dfrac{18}{36}$

(D) $\dfrac{24}{36}$

(E) $\dfrac{27}{36}$

GO ON TO THE NEXT PAGE

6. Which of the following tables shows a relationship in which *a* is inversely proportional to *b* ?

(A)

a	b
1	6
2	7
3	5

(B)

a	b
1	9
2	4
3	1

(C)

a	b
5	0
10	5
15	10

(D)

a	b
10	3
20	1.5
30	1

(E)

a	b
4	1
12	4
16	8

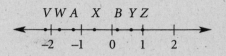

7. Which of the lettered points on the number line above could represent the result when the coordinate of point *A* is multiplied by the coordinate of point *B* ?

(A) V

(B) W

(C) X

(D) Y

(E) Z

8. A supermarket buys cartons of orange juice for *k* dollars each and then sells them for $\frac{4k}{3}$ dollars each. How many cartons do they need to sell to make a profit of $2,000?

(A) $\dfrac{2000}{k}$

(B) $\dfrac{6000}{k}$

(C) $\dfrac{k}{2000}$

(D) $\dfrac{k}{6000}$

(E) $6000k$

GO ON TO THE NEXT PAGE

Directions: For Student-Produced Response questions 9–18, use the grids at the bottom of the answer sheet page on which you have answered questions 1–8.

Each of the remaining 10 questions requires you to solve the problem and enter your answer by marking the ovals in the special grid, as shown in the example below. You may use any available space for scratch work.

Answer: 1.25 or $\frac{5}{4}$ or 5/4

Write answer in → boxes.

Grid-in result →

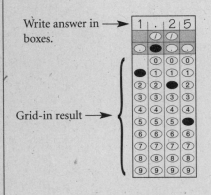

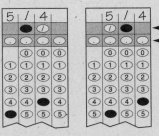

Fraction line
Decimal point

Either position is correct.

You may start your answers in any column, space permitting. Columns not needed should be left blank.

- It is recommended, though not required, that you write your answer in the boxes at the top of the columns. However, you will receive credit only for darkening the ovals correctly.

- Grid only one answer to a question, even though some problems have more than one correct answer.

- Darken no more than one oval in a column.

- No answers are negative.

- Mixed numbers cannot be gridded. For example: the number $1\frac{1}{4}$ must be gridded as 1.25 or 5/4.

(If $\boxed{1\,|\,1\,|\,/\,|\,4}$ is gridded, it will be interpreted as $\frac{11}{4}$ not $1\frac{1}{4}$.)

- Decimal Accuracy: Decimal answers must be entered as accurately as possible. For example, if you obtain an answer such as 0.1666…, you should record the result as .166 or .167. **Less accurate values such as .16 or .17 are not acceptable.**

Acceptable ways to grid $\frac{1}{6}$ = .1666…

KAPLAN
Test Prep and Admissions

9. If $4c + 3d = 37$ and $d = c + 3$, what is the value of c?

10. A family spent $500 on groceries in January. Due to price increases, they spent 25% more in February. How much did they spend on groceries in February? (disregard the $ sign when gridding your answer)

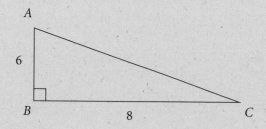

11. Each angle of $\triangle ABC$ has the same measure as an angle in $\triangle JKL$ (not shown). If the length of one side of $\triangle JKL$ is 120, what is one possible area of $\triangle JKL$?

12. The sum of 5 consecutive integers is 500. What is the value of the median of these integers?

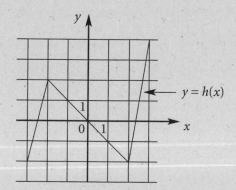

13. The figure above shows the graph of $y = h(x)$. If the function k is defined by $k(x) = h\left(\dfrac{x}{2}\right) + 3$, what is the value of $k(-2)$?

14. Five friends decide to go for a pony ride and have a choice of exactly 5 different ponies, any of which would be suitable for any friend. If each friend gets a pony, how many different assignments of ponies are possible?

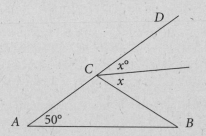

15. In the figure above, $\triangle ABC$ is isosceles with vertex ACB, and points A, C, and D are collinear. What is the value of x?

16. Let the operations $\Rightarrow$ and $\Leftarrow$ be defined for all real numbers x and y as follows.

$x \Rightarrow y = 2x + 3y$

$x \Leftarrow y = 3x + 2y$

If $4 \Rightarrow (3a) = 4 \Leftarrow (3a)$, what is the value of a?

17. In the xy-coordinate plane, the graph of $x = 2y^2 + 3$ intersects the line l at $(5, s)$ and $(11, d)$, what is the greatest possible slope of the line l?

18. Roxanne drove to the circus at an average speed of 30 miles per hour. She returned home along the same route and averaged 25 miles per hour. If her total travel time was 2 hours and 12 minutes, how many miles did she drive on her return from the circus?

IF YOU FINISH BEFORE TIME IS CALLED, YOU MAY CHECK YOUR WORK ON THIS SECTION ONLY. DO NOT TURN TO ANY OTHER SECTION IN THE TEST. STOP

Test Prep and Admissions

SECTION 5
Time—25 Minutes
35 Questions

Directions: For each question in this section, select the best answer from among the choices given and fill in the corresponding oval on the answer sheet.

The following sentences test correctness and effectiveness of expression. Part of each sentence or the entire sentence is underlined; beneath each sentence are five ways of phrasing the underlined material. Choice (A) repeats the original phrasing; the other four choices are different. If you think the original phrasing produces a better sentence than any of the alternatives, select choice (A); if not, select one of the other choices.

In making your selection, follow the requirements of standard written English; that is, pay attention to grammar, choice of words, sentence construction, and punctuation. Your selection should result in the most effective sentence—clear and precise, without awkwardness or ambiguity.

EXAMPLE: ANSWER:

Every apple in the baskets <u>are ripe and labeled according to the date it was picked</u>.   Ⓐ ● Ⓒ Ⓓ Ⓔ

(A) are ripe and labeled according to the date it was picked
(B) is ripe and labeled according to the date it was picked
(C) are ripe and labeled according to the date they were picked
(D) is ripe and labeled according to the date they were picked
(E) are ripe and labeled as to the date it was picked

---

1. Although some residents welcomed the new stadium, others <u>being adamant in their opposition to</u> the proposed project.

   (A) being adamant in their opposition to
   (B) were adamant and opposed to
   (C) adamantly opposed
   (D) adamantly opposing
   (E) are adamantly opposed to

2. The solution to global <u>warming, not completely agreed upon around the world because</u> of various political and corporate interests.

   (A) warming, not completely agreed upon around the world because
   (B) warming, not completely agreed upon around the world and
   (C) warming, not completely agreed upon around the world when
   (D) warming is not completely agreed upon around the world because
   (E) warming is not completely agreed upon around the world and

GO ON TO THE NEXT PAGE ⟶

3. <u>Having received helpful advice in the past,</u> Jason felt confident in consulting the website.

   (A) Having received helpful advice in the past,

   (B) His having received helpful advice in the past,

   (C) His having been helped by advice in the past,

   (D) Because receiving helpful advice in the past,

   (E) Because having received helpful advice in the past,

4. In the theater, <u>they have unions which ensure that actors and technicians are paid</u> fairly for their work.

   (A) they have unions which ensure that actors and technicians are paid

   (B) they have unions ensuring that actors and technicians are paid

   (C) their unions ensuring that actors and technicians are paid

   (D) unions ensure that actors and technicians are paid

   (E) unions to ensure that actors and technicians are paid

5. While taking a sightseeing tour of Paris, <u>the Eiffel Tower was the Emily's first stop</u>.

   (A) the Eiffel Tower was Emily's first stop

   (B) the Eiffel Tower was where Emily stopped first

   (C) Emily's first stop was the Eiffel Tower

   (D) Emily's first stop being the Eiffel Tower

   (E) Emily first stopped at the Eiffel Tower

6. Next to summer, spring is my favorite <u>season, the reason is that the weather is warm and</u> the flowers are beginning to bloom.

   (A) season, the reason is that the weather is warm and

   (B) season, which has warm weather and

   (C) season, the weather of which being warm and

   (D) season because the weather is warm and

   (E) season, whose weather is warm and

7. <u>Both Cinderella and Snow White being dependant on a prince to rescue them from unfortunate circumstances.</u>

   (A) Both Cinderella and Snow White being dependant on a prince to rescue them from unfortunate circumstances.

   (B) Both Cinderella and Snow White were dependant on a prince to rescue them from unfortunate circumstances.

   (C) Dependent on a prince to rescue them from unfortunate circumstances being both Cinderella and Snow White.

   (D) Unfortunate circumstances were what both Cinderella and Snow White were dependent on a prince to rescue them from.

   (E) Dependent on a prince to rescue them from unfortunate circumstances were both known Cinderella and Snow White.

8. <u>Doctors are trying to figure out how to make sure everyone at risk receives a flu shot, and they</u> are calling on federal health department authorities to launch more vigorous public awareness campaigns.

   (A) Doctors are trying to figure out how to make sure everyone at risk receives a flu shot, and they

   (B) Doctors who try to figure out how to make sure everyone at risk receives a flu shot, they

   (C) Doctors trying to figure out how to make sure everyone at risk receives a flu shot

   (D) Trying to figure out how to make sure everyone at risk receives a flu shot, doctors who

   (E) Trying to figure out how to make sure everyone at risk receives a flu shot is why doctors

GO ON TO THE NEXT PAGE

9. Psychologists believe that the way children acquire knowledge <u>is no different for girls than boys</u>.

    (A) is no different for girls than boys

    (B) are no different for girls than being boys

    (C) is no different for girls than for boys

    (D) are no different for girls than for those who are boys

    (E) are no different from those for girls than boys

10. The reason for the continued interest in Olympic athletes is <u>that it draws on</u> experiences with which people can identify.

    (A) that it draws on

    (B) that their struggle to win draws on

    (C) because the struggle to win draws on

    (D) because of them drawing from

    (E) they will draw from

11. Brought up in a small suburban town, <u>it was only when she began working in Boston that she realized how exciting life in a metropolitan area could be</u>.

    (A) it was only when she began working in Boston that she realized how exciting life in a metropolitan area could be

    (B) when she began working in Boston she then realized how exciting life in a metropolitan area could be.

    (C) going to work in Boston made her realize how exciting life in a metropolitan area could be

    (D) she did not realize how exciting life in a metropolitan area could be until she began working in Boston

    (E) exciting life in a metropolitan area was unrealized by her until she began working in Boston

GO ON TO THE NEXT PAGE

Directions: The following sentences test your ability to recognize grammar and usage errors. Each sentence contains either a single error or no error at all. No sentence contains more than one error. The error, if there is one, is underlined and lettered. If the sentence contains an error, select the one underlined part that must be changed to make the sentence correct. If the sentence is correct, select choice (E). In choosing answers, follow the requirements of standard written English.

EXAMPLE:

<u>Whenever</u> one is driving late at night, <u>you</u> must take extra precautions <u>against</u>
  A   B   C

falling asleep <u>at the wheel</u>. <u>No error</u>
          D   E

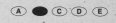

12. The new music class, <u>eagerly anticipated</u> by our
                      A
    students, <u>include</u> exercises for developing vocal
               B
    range <u>and for making</u> musical notation
              C
    <u>understandable to</u> new musicians. <u>No error</u>
          D   E

13. The extremely cold weather in the Alps <u>has</u>
                                  A
    managed <u>preventing</u> children and parents <u>alike</u>
           B   C
    from going out <u>for</u> a day of skiing. <u>No error</u>
              D   E

14. <u>Implementing</u> new procedures and eliminating
      A
    <u>outdated ones</u> <u>can be</u> difficult, <u>especially since</u>
        B   C   D
    office workers are used to a routine. <u>No error</u>
                                E

15. It <u>is likely that</u> we <u>will be able</u> <u>to purchase</u> concert
       A   B   C
    tickets <u>inexpensive</u> if we order them online.
           D
    <u>No error</u>
      E

16. Although the train schedule <u>have</u> not yet been
                               A
    posted, <u>we will probably</u> take the one <u>leaving</u>
             B   C
    closest <u>to</u> noon. <u>No error</u>
          D   E

17. Right after <u>those</u> of us who had to catch the bus left
            A
    <u>for the station</u>, the running back <u>himself</u> <u>scores</u> the
      B   C   D
    winning touchdown. <u>No error</u>
                   E

18. <u>Although</u> <u>their</u> research <u>was</u> neither original <u>or</u>
      A   B   C   D
    current, the doctors received grant money from the
    university. <u>No error</u>
             E

19. Sister Margaret <u>belongs to</u> of an order of nuns who
                A
    <u>dedicate</u> <u>their life</u> <u>to helping</u> children in
        B   C   D
    impoverished countries. <u>No error</u>
                      E

GO ON TO THE NEXT PAGE

20. After Rory graduated from college, she <u>spends</u>
                                              A
<u>most of</u> the next five years <u>working towards</u> a
  B   C
graduate degree <u>in computer science</u>. <u>No error</u>
                      D   E

21. <u>In a time that</u> tuition costs are rising <u>alarmingly</u>,
        A   B
tuition <u>itself</u> is often beyond the means of <u>most</u>
            C   D
middle-class families. <u>No error</u>
                             E

22. Jonathan asked <u>David and I</u> <u>if</u> we <u>would consider</u>
                        A   B   C
<u>going to</u> the Central Park Zoo on Saturday.
    D
<u>No error</u>
    E

23. <u>Something of</u> a history buff, my uncle has a
        A
collection <u>of</u> first edition biographies that
              B
<u>has been featured</u> in newspaper articles and
        C
magazine stories <u>alike</u>. <u>No error</u>
                        D   E

24. In the future, co-op members <u>will be responsible</u>
                                        A
for a self-managed work plan, <u>under which</u> they,
                                      B
<u>rather than</u> salaried workers, <u>figures</u> out the
    C   D
monthly duties. <u>No error</u>
                      E

25. Looking <u>to</u> the display of goods for sale, the young
            A
man realized <u>that</u> the store did not carry
                  B
everything he was <u>responsible for</u> bringing <u>to the</u>
                        C   D
office party. <u>No error</u>
                    E

26. The school principal and vice-principal <u>were given</u>
                                                  A
the same vacation week, <u>although</u> <u>she</u> came back a
                              B   C
few days early to attend a series <u>of seminars</u> on
                                        D
educational reform. <u>No error</u>
                          E

27. <u>Reaching</u> a weight of <u>up to</u> 100 tons, the great blue
        A   B
whale <u>is likely</u> the <u>largest</u> mammal currently in
          C   D
existence. <u>No error</u>
                  E

28. Though not all of us are talented as
a <u>photographer</u>, digital cameras <u>have made</u> the
    A   B
taking and printing <u>of photographs</u> <u>into</u> a viable
                          C   D
hobby. <u>No error</u>
            E

29. The <u>highly disturbing</u> news of the looming civil
            A
war <u>makes it understandable</u> that the family
        B
<u>has become</u> <u>more inclined</u> to leave the country.
    C   D
<u>No error</u>
    E

GO ON TO THE NEXT PAGE

> **Directions:** The following passage is an early draft of an essay. Some parts of the passage need to be rewritten.
>
> Read the passage and select the best answer for each question that follows. Some questions are about particular sentences or parts of sentences and ask you to improve sentence structure or word choice. Other questions ask you to consider organization and development. In choosing answers, follow the conventions of standard written English.

Questions 30–35 are based on the following passage.

(1) Scientists working in the Arctic and Antarctic have been trying to figure out if our world is getting warmer. (2) However, research on global warming could not be accomplished without the aid of a tough and reliable ice breaker, a tool which has only been around for slightly more than a hundred years. (3) Ice breakers do not "push" the thick expanses of ice, contrary to what most people believe. (4) They are instead crushed under the weight of the ship's bow, which is pushed through by powerful engines. (5) The ship then reverses, powers ahead, and runs up onto the ice again. (6) So that the vessel clears a path for itself. (7) What is time consuming about this is that the ice can be up to sixteen feet thick.

(8) Rather, their ability to break through thick ice is due to several unique design features: the bow, the hull, and the propulsion system. (9) Since a typical ice breaker may only spend 25 percent of its time in ice, it must perform well in open water, too. (10) For example, the bow of an ice breaker does not go straight down, it is sloping at a 30 degree angle.

(11) Aside from their role in helping scientists study global warming, ice breakers have other uses. (12) They are used to conduct fundamental research to understand the nature and characteristics of snow, ice, frozen ground, and other materials in cold regions.

30. In context, what is the best way to deal with sentence 4 (reproduced below)?

    They are instead crushed under the weight of the ship's bow, which is pushed through by powerful engines.

    (A) Delete it
    (B) Switch it with sentence 5
    (C) Change *they are* to "the ice is"
    (D) Change *which* to "that"
    (E) Change *is pushed* to "are pushed"

31. What is the best way to revise the underlined portion of sentences 5 and 6 (reproduced below)?

    The ship then reverses, powers ahead, and runs up onto the ice <u>again. So that the vessel clears</u> a path for itself.

    (A) again, by which the vessel clears
    (B) again, because the vessel clears
    (C) again, and the vessel, clearing
    (D) again, so that the vessel clears
    (E) ice, the vessel clears

GO ON TO THE NEXT PAGE

32. Which of the following is the best version of
    sentence 7 (reproduced below)?

    *What is time-consuming about this is that the ice can
    be up to sixteen feet thick.*

    (A) (As it is now)
    (B) Consequently, the ice can be up to sixteen
        feet thick, and this is time consuming.
    (C) The ice can be up to sixteen feet thick, mak-
        ing it time consuming.
    (D) This process is time consuming because the
        ice can be up to sixteen feet thick.
    (E) It is time consuming that the ice can be up to
        sixteen feet thick.

33. Which of the following is the best sentence to
    insert at the beginning of the second paragraph
    before sentence 8?

    (A) Icebreakers do not weigh more than other
        ships.
    (B) It's cold on an icebreaker.
    (C) How can ice breakers move through such
        thick ice?
    (D) Ice breakers may lead to decreased global
        warming.
    (E) Ice breakers are also used by the army.

34. Which of the following is the best version of the
    underlined portion of sentence 10 (reproduced
    below)?

    *For example, the bow of an ice breaker does not go
    straight down, it is sloping at a 30 degree angle.*

    (A) (As it is now)
    (B) does not go straight down because it slopes
    (C) not going straight down, but rather sloping
    (D) does not go straight down; rather sloping
    (E) does not go straight down, but rather slopes

35. Which sentence should be deleted from the essay
    because it contains unrelated information?

    (A) Sentence 1
    (B) Sentence 3
    (C) Sentence 8
    (D) Sentence 9
    (E) Sentence 12

IF YOU FINISH BEFORE TIME IS CALLED, YOU MAY CHECK YOUR WORK ON
THIS SECTION ONLY. DO NOT TURN TO ANY OTHER SECTION IN THE TEST. STOP

SECTION 6

Time—25 Minutes

24 Questions

Directions: For each of the following questions, choose the best answer and darken the corresponding oval on the answer sheet.

Each sentence below has one or two blanks, each blank indicating that something has been omitted. Beneath the sentence are five words or sets of words labeled (A) through (E). Choose the word or set of words that, when inserted in the sentence, best fits the meaning of the sentence as a whole.

EXAMPLE:

Today's small, portable computers contrast markedly with the earliest electronic computers, which were ----.

(A) effective

(B) invented

(C) useful

(D) destructive

(E) enormous

1. The contamination of groundwater by landfill leachate is a threat to public health not only because of toxic chemicals that cause disease, but also because of ---- chemicals that cause ---- physiological and psychological responses.

    (A) scurrilous . . elusive

    (B) noxious . . adverse

    (C) aggressive . . unprecedented

    (D) conciliatory . . numbing

    (E) studied . . amicable

2. Abraham Lincoln distinguished himself as a remarkable ---- and was admired most for the Gettysburg Address and his two inaugural speeches.

    (A) conformist

    (B) moralist

    (C) orator

    (D) rival

    (E) compatriot

3. Through the efforts of twenty heroic, ---- mushers, a life-saving serum was relayed by dog-sled teams across the 674 miles of frigid Alaskan wilderness from Nenana to Nome in 1925 to save a town stricken with diphtheria.

    (A) empathetic

    (B) indomitable

    (C) expeditious

    (D) idiosyncratic

    (E) astute

4. The judge reduced the sentence of those involved in the corporate scandal who chose to be honest and enter the court proceedings with a ---- not found in most of the indicted, who were more ---- and refused to talk about the offense.

    (A) serenity . . placid

    (B) forthrightness . . reserved

    (C) fairness . . dilatory

    (D) meticulousness . . accessible

    (E) peevishness . . irritable

GO ON TO THE NEXT PAGE

5. Rosalind Franklin used the technique of x-ray crystallography to elucidate the structure of DNA by mapping the basic helical structure of the tiny, ---- molecules.

   (A) comprehensive
   (B) fallacious
   (C) insuperable
   (D) parochial
   (E) infinitesimal

6. Anthropologists, psychologists, and dream workers have found common themes in dreams that have come to be known as ---- dreams as they ---- all generations and cultures.

   (A) provincial . . expand
   (B) universal . . transcend
   (C) personal . . deride
   (D) worldwide . . attain
   (E) intuitive . . describe

7. The ---- decision made by a panicked hunter lost in scrubland to start a small fire to signal for help led to an inferno that engulfed miles of San Diego County, leaving behind nothing but the skeletal remains of bushes and trees scattered on barren, ---- hills.

   (A) conscientious . . despoiled
   (B) incompetent . . sustained
   (C) shrewd . . debilitated
   (D) innovative . . fertilized
   (E) imprudent . . denuded

8. The soothing flow of the orator's words became progressively more steady and rhythmic; such ---- speaking was very mesmerizing.

   (A) cadent
   (B) specious
   (C) convoluted
   (D) adulatory
   (E) impassioned

GO ON TO THE NEXT PAGE

> **Directions:** The passages below are followed by questions based on their content; questions following a pair of related passages may also be based on the relationship between the paired passages. Answer the questions on the basis of what is <u>stated</u> or <u>implied</u> in the passages and in any introductory material that may be provided.

Questions 9–12 are based on the following passages.

Passage 1

The first Industrial Revolution, which occurred in Great Britain in the latter half of the 18th century, represented a sudden acceleration of technological and economic development that would
(5) permeate all levels of British society. Specifically, the traditional agrarian economy was supplanted by one based on manufacturing and machinery. Very much an urban movement, the revolution gave rise to a new system of social class, based pri-
(10) marily upon the relationship of the industrial capitalist to the factory worker. These changes can be attributed to a number of favorable societal circumstances—including an increasing population, which would provide both a larger work force and
(15) expanding markets, a strong middle class, and stability in both the political environment and the monetary system.

Passage 2

Though the Industrial Revolution certainly saw the transformation of many different aspects of
(20) British social and economic life, these changes were primarily effects, not to be mistaken for causes. Undoubtedly, the burgeoning population and established political system provided an apt environment for revolution. Yet the chief factors
(25) were rooted not in broad changes in society, but rather in extraordinary technological innovations within a few industries. Within the smelting industry, for example, the production of new materials, namely iron and steel, would allow for
(30) stronger, more complex machinery. Coupled with the invention of James Watt's steam engine in the 1780s, these innovations laid the groundwork for massive technological progress that would in turn pave the way for those significant social and eco-
(35) nomic changes.

9. In Passage 1, "movement" (line 8) most nearly means

(A) progress
(B) motion
(C) emigration
(D) development
(E) drift

10. The author of Passage 2 refers to James Watt's steam engine in order to

(A) show how certain innovations were major factors in the Industrial Revolution
(B) demonstrate the high level of talent among Britain's inventors
(C) illustrate how social and economic change affected technology
(D) discuss the revolutionary railroad network established in Britain
(E) exhibit his sense of admiration for Watt's ingenuity

11. Both passages support which generalization about the Industrial Revolution in Britain?

(A) It was caused primarily by social factors.
(B) It was caused primarily by technological factors.
(C) It changed British life for the worse.
(D) It was a time of rapid transformation.
(E) It brought on the demise of the traditional agrarian economy.

GO ON TO THE NEXT PAGE

12. Which statement best describes a significant difference between the authors' interpretations of population increase and its relationship to the Industrial Revolution?

(A) Author 1 maintains that a growing population was not a major factor in the revolution; Author 2 maintains that it was a prerequisite.

(B) Author 1 emphasizes that it was a main cause; Author 2 claims that it had no effect on the revolution.

(C) Author 1 states that it was one of the major factors; Author 2 claims that it was important for setting the stage, but was not the main catalyst.

(D) Author 1 contends that population growth was greatest in the more industrialized regions; Author 2 maintains that population growth was suppressed in those areas.

(E) Author 1 believes the relationship has been distorted; Author 2 believes it has been overemphasized.

Questions 13–24 are based on the following passages.

The following passages both consider the relationship between literature and film. Passage 1 is from an essay in a literary magazine; Passage 2 comes from an essay written by an independent filmmaker for a book on contemporary cinema.

Passage 1

When we sit down to read a good book, we rarely take pause to contemplate the wonder of the act we are performing. In the case of true literature, at least, reading is not simply the process of
(5) scanning a series of symbols on a page and trying to mentally encode the information they represent; it is a much more organic experience. As the words flow into our minds, we are continually piecing together a strange and unique universe
(10) that is a fusion of our own world, the characters', and the author's. Unlike the marks on the page, which appear the same to everyone, the stories that form in our minds are curiously personal concoctions; no two readers' experiences are ever
(15) quite alike.

This process is what author J.R.R. Tolkien referred to as "sub-creation," and it is a fundamental and particular property of the written word. Tolkien himself would likely have been horrified
(20) at the recent series of movies based on his *Lord of the Rings* novels, despite their success and critical acclaim; he believed that the ability to visualize characters and scenes for oneself was the right and privilege of the reader alone. I cannot help but
(25) agree, for anytime a filmmaker shares his inner vision of a book with you, he simultaneously robs you of your own. Try as you might, you'll never quite regain the pure, personal image of a story you once had; it will forever be tarnished with ves
(30) tiges of the figures you saw on the silver screen.

Now, I do not mean to say that movies are no good, nor even that it is impossible to make a good movie based on a book; I simply wish filmmakers were more aware of the way their
(35) adaptations degrade the public's enjoyment of the original works of literature. I trust that all of us

GO ON TO THE NEXT PAGE

have, at one time or another, gone to see the theatrical version of a favorite novel and declared
upon emerging, "It wasn't as good as the book."
(40) Although the film may contain all the appealing
characters, stunning action, and insightful dialogue from the written work, it will always be
missing one key ingredient: the active engagement
of a reader who adds his own ideas, reflections,
(45) and visualizations to the author's prose to create a
personally fulfilling experience, versus the passive
acceptance of an audience member whose theatrical encounter, though perhaps enjoyable in its
own right, is no different from that of all the other
(50) people seated around him.

Passage 2

I am continually amazed that there are still people who claim that film is not as legitimate an art
form as "real" (I suppose by this they mean "written") literature. Despite being relatively young to
(55) the artistic world, cinema has quickly established
itself as a form capable of delivering powerful
messages that can be just as enduring as those of
its literary predecessors; indeed, one could even
argue that film is a medium that captures the best
(60) of both worlds, combining the depth and expressiveness of written forms with the sheer aesthetic
appeal of the visual arts. Although its detractors
may try to tell you otherwise, film is a world apart
from the domain of television; like the frozen din-
(65) ners that bear its name, TV is meant to be cheap,
quickly and conveniently enjoyed, and, ultimately,
disposable. Motion pictures, on the other hand,
are many times more costly in both time and
money, can engage one's attention for hours on
(70) end, and with the recent advent of home video,
are capable of being enjoyed over and over in
much the same way that someone would read and
reread a favorite book. In fact, I look forward to
the day when the home video library will take its
(75) rightful place next to the bookshelf as a center of
intellectual enjoyment and individual expression.
Now, all this is not to say that I encourage the
death of literacy; far from it. After all, though
many forget this fact, every film begins its life as a
(80) written work in the form of a screenplay. I actually

think it's a shame that more people don't read
screenplays; a well-written movie script can be a
work of art in itself, whether or not anyone ever
decides to film it. In its essence, a screenplay is no
(85) different from a stage play, one of the oldest and
most revered of all literary forms—and just like a
stage play, a screenplay can be either enhanced or
degraded by the quality of a performance. Is the
literary reputation of William Shakespeare com-
(90) promised by the fact that he wrote his plays to be
performed as well as read on paper? I should hope
not! Thus, if you are ever tempted to question the
artistic heritage of the cinema, bear this in mind:
When a piece of brilliant writing lies before the
(95) author, his work is complete, but when it lies in
front of the filmmaker, the voyage to fulfill his
artistic vision has only just begun.

13. In contrast to the author of Passage 2, the author of
    Passage 1 is more concerned with

    (A) the extent to which literacy in our society has
        diminished
    (B) the relative lack of depth in contemporary
        television entertainment
    (C) the ways in which film has positively
        impacted the literary field
    (D) the difficult task that filmmakers have in
        front of them
    (E) the limiting effects film can have on people's
        imaginations

14. The author of Passage 1 primarily mentions the
    "marks on the page" (line 11) in order to

    (A) comment upon the universal appeal of a
        good novel
    (B) suggest that even the appearance of the words
        has an impact on the reader's impressions
    (C) provide an example of a shared perception
    (D) imply that the message of a well-written story
        will be easily understood by everyone
    (E) illustrate a common misconception

GO ON TO THE NEXT PAGE →

15. The sentence in lines 16–18 ("This...word") suggests that the author of Passage 1 believes that

   (A) the reader's imaginative process is less noble than that of the writer

   (B) writing is the only art form that truly occupies one's intellect

   (C) Tolkien would never have written his books if he knew they would be made into movies

   (D) the act of reading necessarily engages the imagination of the reader

   (E) any piece of good writing requires the reader to conjure up lifelike scenes in his mind

16. Which of the following situations would involve the same kind of "inner vision" (lines 25–26) mentioned in Passage 1?

   (A) A screenwriter pens a story inspired by deeply personal memories known only to himself.

   (B) A serious writer takes a break from her career to create lighthearted novelizations of popular films.

   (C) A publisher decides to add more diagrams to a statistics textbook in order to increase its readability.

   (D) A photographer accompanies each of his shots with a note describing the events in his life at the time it was taken.

   (E) A poem full of vivid imagery is used by an artist as the basis for a series of oil paintings.

17. In line 35, the phrase "public's enjoyment" refers to occasions when

   (A) people are free to envision the author's words without the intrusion of outside influences

   (B) difficult literary works are brought to life so anyone can understand them

   (C) viewers are able to relax with a classic film work in the privacy of their own homes

   (D) people read more because no other sources of entertainment are available

   (E) moviegoers actually prefer a film adaptation to the original book

18. Lines 36–50 ("I trust...around him") in Passage 1 mainly serve to

   (A) offer a counterexample to the discussion up to that point

   (B) re-establish and elaborate upon an argument begun in the previous paragraph

   (C) introduce a complication the author had not previously considered

   (D) point out some particularly egregious examples of inadequate film adaptations

   (E) assert that books of average quality can be turned into movies, but great literature should never be

19. The author of Passage 1 would probably characterize the "powerful messages" (lines 56–57) mentioned in Passage 2 as

   (A) potentially dangerous because they have such an impact on so many people

   (B) less powerful than messages delivered through a medium with greater audience participation

   (C) less capable of delivering key ideas clearly than messages from other forms of media

   (D) vastly superior to the quality of the messages delivered by a night of television viewing

   (E) more complex than literary messages because the visual and auditory senses are more engaged

GO ON TO THE NEXT PAGE

20. The author of Passage 2 discusses the "domain of
television" (line 64) in order to

(A) argue that film requires more sophistication
and knowledge to understand than television
does

(B) depict similarities among the various forms
of media that can be enjoyed at home

(C) suggest that watching a film in the theater is a
significantly different experience from viewing it at home

(D) insinuate that television is inferior because
television programs are rarely based on great
literature

(E) imply that one medium's apparent similarity
to another does not mean they have similar
artistic impacts

21. In lines 73–78 ("In fact… from it"), the author of
Passage 2 expresses the view that the artistic
contribution of film is

(A) irreplaceable but not unfathomable

(B) underestimated but not unrivaled

(C) transitory but not forgettable

(D) moderate but not of lasting impact

(E) paramount but not well established

22. The author of Passage 2 uses the example of the
"stage play" (line 85) in order to illustrate that

(A) neither plays nor movies can achieve quite
the same depth as novels do

(B) the role of the playwright has now been
almost entirely replaced by that of the screenwriter

(C) the best plays are often adaptations of good
novels

(D) the screenplay has its roots in a rich literary
tradition

(E) screenplays based on stage plays are often the
cheapest and easiest to produce

23. In lines 89–91, the author of Passage 2 mentions
William Shakespeare in order to

(A) suggest that the next writer of Shakespeare's
genius will probably be a screenwriter

(B) deride those who choose to watch his plays
performed instead of reading them at home

(C) argue for the literary validity of a work meant
to be both read and performed

(D) show that even someone working in the film
industry can have a thorough understanding
of great literature

(E) imply that, in years to come, movies themselves will not be as well known as their
screenplays

24. How do the examples of J.R.R. Tolkien in Passage 1
(line 16) and William Shakespeare in Passage 2
(line 89) relate to the arguments in their respective
passages?

(A) The first is used as a defense of modern writers, whereas the second is used to glorify the
great authors of older times.

(B) The first is offered as an example of fantasy
writing, whereas the second argues for works
that are more realistic.

(C) The first promotes the value of individual
imagination, whereas the second defends the
validity of public performance.

(D) The first is used as an affirmation of the value
of screenplays, whereas the second defends
the reputation of the stage play.

(E) The first illustrates the difficulties behind
successful adaptation, whereas the second
promotes the ease of writing directly for the
stage.

SECTION 7

Time—20 Minutes
16 Questions

Directions: For this section, solve each problem and decide which is the best of the choices given. Fill in the corresponding oval on the answer sheet. You may use any available space for scratchwork.

Notes:

(1). Calculator use is permitted.

(2) All numbers used are real numbers.

(3) Figures are provided for some problems. All figures are drawn to scale and lie in a plane UNLESS otherwise indicated.

(4) Unless otherwise specified, the domain of any function f is assumed to be the set of all real numbers x for which $f(x)$ is a real number.

Information

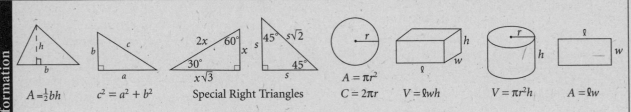

$A = \frac{1}{2}bh$ $c^2 = a^2 + b^2$ Special Right Triangles $C = 2\pi r$ $V = \ell wh$ $V = \pi r^2 h$ $A = \ell w$

The sum of the degree measures of the angles in a triangle is 180.
The number of degrees of arc in a circle is 360.
A straight angle has a degree measure of 180.

1. If $6a = 48$ and $ab = 1$, what is the value of b?

    (A) $\frac{1}{48}$

    (B) $\frac{1}{8}$

    (C) $\frac{1}{6}$

    (D) 6

    (E) 8

2. It takes 5 complete turns of the crank to raise a fishing rod hook 2 feet. At this rate, how many turns will it take to raise the hook 4.4 feet?

    (A) 4.4

    (B) 11

    (C) 22

    (D) 33

    (E) 44

GO ON TO THE NEXT PAGE

KAPLAN
Test Prep and Admissions

3. If $\frac{x}{y} = \frac{5}{7}$, what is the value of $\frac{7x}{5y}$?

(A) $\frac{2}{7}$

(B) $\frac{5}{7}$

(C) 1

(D) $\frac{7}{5}$

(E) $\frac{49}{25}$

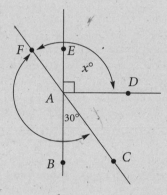

4. In the figure above, $\overline{EB}$, $\overline{AD}$, and $\overline{CF}$ intersect at point A, and $\overline{EB}$ is perpendicular to $\overline{AD}$. What is the value of $\frac{x+y}{2}$?

(A) 75°

(B) 90°

(C) 120°

(D) 135°

(E) 150°

DAILY SCHOOL SCHEDULE

	Beginning Time	Ending Time
Class 1	?	
Break		
Class 2		
Lunch		
Class 3		
Break		
Class 4		2:30

5. In the schedule above, each class period is to be 1 hour and 20 minutes, each break is to be 5 minutes, and lunch is to be 30 minutes. If 4th period is to end at 2:30, what time should the school day begin?

(A) 8:30

(B) 8:40

(C) 8:50

(D) 9:00

(E) 9:10

6. If $2x - 8$, $x + 4$, and $3x - 13$ are all integers, and $x + 4$ is the median of these integers, which of the following could be a value of x ?

(A)   6

(B)   8

(C)   11

(D)   13

(E)   15

7. A bookseller's net profit, in dollars, from the sale of b books is given by $P(b) = 2.5b - 100$. How many books must she sell in order to earn a net profit of $225?

(A) 130

(B) 225

(C) 331

(D) 463

(E) 563

GO ON TO THE NEXT PAGE

8. If $x^2 + y^2 = 153$ and $xy = 36$, what is the value of $(x - y)^2$?

(A) 81
(B) 117
(C) 153
(D) 189
(E) 225

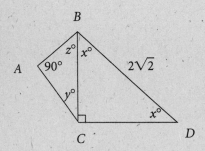

Note: Figure not drawn to scale

9. In the figure above, $AB = 1$ and $BD = 2\sqrt{2}$. What is the value of z?

(A) 40°
(B) 45°
(C) 50°
(D) 55°
(E) 60°

10. If 20 percent of 30 percent of a positive number is equal to 15 percent of h percent of the same number, what is the value of h?

(A) 30
(B) 35
(C) 40
(D) 45
(E) 60

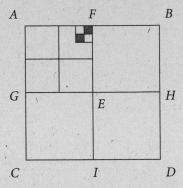

11. In the figure above, each square is split into 4 squares of the same size, starting by splitting $ABDC$ into $AFEG$, $GEIC$, $EHDI$, and $FBHE$, all of which have the same area. The total shaded area is what fraction of the area of square $ABCD$?

(A) $\dfrac{1}{256}$

(B) $\dfrac{1}{128}$

(C) $\dfrac{1}{64}$

(D) $\dfrac{1}{32}$

(E) $\dfrac{2}{13}$

12. If $3x < 0 < y$, which of the following is greatest?

(A) 0
(B) y
(C) $-3x$
(D) $-(3x + y)$
(E) $-(3x - y)$

GO ON TO THE NEXT PAGE

13. Suraj solved m Physics problems on Monday, three times as many Physics problems on Tuesday as on Monday, and three more than twice as many Physics problems on Wednesday as on Monday. What is the average (arithmetic mean) number of Physics problems he solved per day over the three days?

(A) $6m + 1$

(B) $\frac{10}{3}m + 1$

(C) $2m + 3$

(D) $2m + 1$

(E) $2m - 1$

14. If $\dfrac{1}{(a+b)^{-\frac{1}{2}}} = (a+b)^{-\frac{1}{2}}$, which of the following must be true?

(A) $a = 0$

(B) $\sqrt{a+b} = -1$

(C) $\sqrt{a+b} = 0$

(D) $a + b = 1$

(E) $(a+b)^2 = 0$

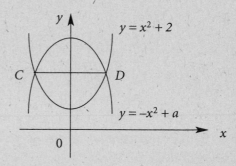

15. The figure above shows the graphs of $y = x^2 + 2$ and $y = -x^2 + a$ for some constant a. If the length of $\overline{CD}$ is equal to 4, what is the value of a?

(A) 2

(B) 4

(C) 5

(D) 8

(E) 10

16. Set X has $x + 2b$ members and set Y has $y + 3b$ members. If they have exactly b members in common, how many elements are in the union of X and Y but not in the intersection of X and Y?

(A) $x + y$

(B) $x + y + 3b$

(C) $x + y + 4b$

(D) $x + y + 5b$

(E) $x + y + 6b$

IF YOU FINISH BEFORE TIME IS CALLED, YOU MAY CHECK YOUR WORK ON THIS SECTION ONLY. DO NOT TURN TO ANY OTHER SECTION IN THE TEST. **STOP**

SECTION 8
Time—20 Minutes
18 Questions

Directions: For each of the following questions, choose the best answer and darken the corresponding oval on the answer sheet.

Each sentence below has one or two blanks, each blank indicating that something has been omitted. Beneath the sentence are five words or sets of words labeled (A) through (E). Choose the word or set of words that, when inserted in the sentence, <u>best</u> fits the meaning of the sentence as a whole.

EXAMPLE:

Today's small, portable computers contrast markedly with the earliest electronic computers, which were ----.

(A) effective
(B) invented
(C) useful
(D) destructive
(E) enormous

1. Studies indicate that most people vaccinated for smallpox may retain ---- immunity: experts have shown that protection from the vaccine ---- up to 75 years.

   (A) limited . . developed
   (B) diverse . . foundered
   (C) variable . . declined
   (D) lengthy . . lasted
   (E) sedate . . soared

2. The committee was established to help ---- undesirable traffic impacts such as air pollution and congestion by placing priority on the development of pedestrian facilities that would connect neighborhoods.

   (A) engage
   (B) alleviate
   (C) transport
   (D) regenerate
   (E) trivialize

3. Advisors warned the congressman to communicate directly and intelligibly; speech that required extensive ---- would bewilder and alienate the voters.

   (A) elucidation
   (B) mystification
   (C) recitation
   (D) alliteration
   (E) vocalization

4. The school principal considered the student's actions so reprehensible that he termed them ---- and refused to accept any excuse.

   (A) indefensible
   (B) surreptitious
   (C) indefatigable
   (D) comprehensive
   (E) corrective

GO ON TO THE NEXT PAGE

5. Convinced by critics that his play was too verbose, Johnson ---- the third act, making it more ----.

    (A) expanded…concise
    (B) curtailed…prolix
    (C) promulgated…insouciant
    (D) abbreviated…succinct
    (E) fostered…pliant

6. Investors who check their portfolios more often are more prone to lose profits due to ---- behavior; that is, they experience a narrowing of view focusing only on the most recent, short-term results even when the investment horizon is long.

    (A) irresolute
    (B) officious
    (C) rancorous
    (D) punctilious
    (E) myopic

GO ON TO THE NEXT PAGE

Directions: The passages below are followed by questions based on their content; questions following a pair of related passages may also be based on the relationship between the paired passages. Answer the questions on the basis of what is stated or implied in the passages and in any introductory material that may be provided.

Questions 7–18 are based on the following passage.

The following passage is adapted from a psychologist's discussion of the development of the human brain.

Although it comprises only two percent of the human body's average weight, the billions of neurons and trillions of synaptic connections that are the human brain constitute a truly impressive
(5) organ. In terms of what it can do, the human brain is in some ways unable to match the brain functioning of "lower" animals; in other ways, its capabilities are quite unrivaled. Salmon, caribou, and migrating birds, for example, have navigation-
(10) al abilities unparalleled in our own species, and even dogs and cats have senses of hearing and smell known only, in human form, to comic book superheroes. Yet no other animal on the planet can communicate, solve problems, or think
(15) abstractly about itself and the future as we do. While these relative strengths and weaknesses can be attributed to the unique and complex structure of the human brain, neuroscientists also have traced these characteristics to the human brain's
(20) remarkable flexibility, or what researchers call plasticity.
Encased in a hard, protective skull that by the age of two is already 80 percent of its eventual adult size, the human brain has little room for size
(25) expansion even while the rest of the body, especially during adolescence, is experiencing significant changes in physical appearance. Nevertheless, the human brain's plasticity allows for marked capacity changes because of usage, practice, and
(30) experience throughout one's entire life. This idea that the human brain continues to develop and, some might say, improve over the course of one's life is a relatively new concept. Neuroscientists, even after brain size was no longer considered a
(35) direct determiner of brain capacity, once believed that the basic structure and abilities of the adult brain are developed early in life and not subject to change. Then, several provocative experiments

dramatically complicated such thinking.
(40) One of these experiments, for example, examined the various effects an enriched environment, in this case an "amusement park" for rats, could have on brain development. Researchers kept one group of rats in an empty cage, devoid of any stim-
(45) ulus, while another group lived in a cage filled with ladders, platforms, boxes, and other toys. Over the course of the experiment, researchers used magnetic resonance imaging technology to observe the brain development of the two groups. Those rats
(50) that lived in the enriched environment full of stimuli developed heavier, thicker brains with more neurons and synaptic connections—the cellular activity by which the brain functions—than those that were deprived. Such results were then found
(55) to be even more noticeable in humans, confirming an essential point: one's life experiences and environment not only mold the brain's particular architecture but also can continue to spark the expansion of its capacity to function.

7. The author's comparisons between the human brain and those of other animals (lines 5–15) are meant to

(A) suggest that despite areas of weakness the human brain is the most sophisticated

(B) emphasize the diversity of brain types found in the animal kingdom

(C) reiterate that it is not only the human brain that displays remarkable plasticity

(D) illustrate the unique characteristics and capabilities of the human brain

(E) praise the sensory abilities of the human brain over those of other animals

GO ON TO THE NEXT PAGE ⟶

8. The reference to "comic book superheroes" in lines 12–13 primary serves to

(A) show the sensory capabilities of cats and dogs are irrelevant when evaluating brain development

(B) suggest that as humans we have always exaggerated our sensory capabilities

(C) demonstrate that the human brain is not superior to but different from those of other animals

(D) indicate that it is impossible for a single brain type to be highly capable in all areas

(E) illustrate that regardless of their remarkable sensory capabilities the brains of cats and dogs have great weaknesses

9. In lines 24–25, the author mentions the "human brain has little room for size expansion" in order to illustrate that

(A) most human brain development takes place before the age of two

(B) the human brain can change in ways other than physical size

(C) most human brain development occurs during adolescence

(D) the human brain is uniquely capable of expanding its capacity throughout one's life

(E) the skull inhibits the brain's ability to expand its capabilities

10. The author asserts that the human brain experiences "marked capacity changes" (lines 28–29) according to

(A) how its structure develops during adolescence

(B) how it is employed during one's life

(C) how challenging one's life has been

(D) one's age and body size

(E) one's ability to communicate and solve problems

11. In line 19, "traced" most nearly means

(A) connected

(B) drawn

(C) searched

(D) copied

(E) found

12. In line 32, the author uses the phrase "some might say" to suggest the word "improve" is

(A) rather inappropriate

(B) too biased

(C) certainly apt

(D) not applicable

(E) quite subjective

13. According to the passage, which of the following is true of one's brain size?

(A) It can be used to determine plasticity.

(B) It was once used to indicate brain capacity.

(C) It expands when in the presence of external stimuli.

(D) It has no correlation to one's brain capacity.

(E) It changes markedly after the age of two.

14. The two groups of rats described in the third paragraph are similar in which of the following ways?

I. Both were exposed to external stimuli.
II. Both were studied using magnetic resonance imaging.
III. Both exhibited at least some degree of change.

(A) I only

(B) II only

(C) I and III only

(D) II and III only

(E) I, II, and III

GO ON TO THE NEXT PAGE

15. In line 38, "provocative" emphasizes that the described experiment was

    (A) intended to be controversial
    (B) interesting only to neuroscientists
    (C) particularly exciting for neuroscientists
    (D) deliberately meant to excite the neuroscience community
    (E) criticized by the neuroscience community

16. Which of the following is implied in the last sentence of the passage?

    (A) Researchers tested humans in precisely the same manner as the described experiment.
    (B) Researchers were able to draw similar conclusions from the described experiment and one involving humans.
    (C) Researchers observed humans learning far more from external stimuli than the rats tested in the described experiment.
    (D) Researchers were able to conclude that brain structure determines brain capacity.
    (E) Researchers used the described experiment to test only rats and humans.

17. According to the passage, the author considers the described experiment

    (A) flawless
    (B) astounding
    (C) unquestionable
    (D) insignificant
    (E) telling

18. The tone of the passage is primarily one of

    (A) fervent interest
    (B) informed enthusiasm
    (C) guarded optimism
    (D) playful subjectivity
    (E) detached skepticism

IF YOU FINISH BEFORE TIME IS CALLED, YOU MAY CHECK YOUR WORK ON THIS SECTION ONLY. DO NOT TURN TO ANY OTHER SECTION IN THE TEST. **STOP**

SECTION 9

Time—10 Minutes

14 Questions

Directions: For each question in this section, select the best answer from among the choices given and fill in the corresponding oval on the answer sheet.

The following sentences test correctness and effectiveness of expression. Part of each sentence or the entire sentence is underlined; beneath each sentence are five ways of phrasing the underlined material. Choice (A) repeats the original phrasing; the other four choices are different. If you think the original phrasing produces a better sentence than any of the alternatives, select choice (A); if not, select one of the other choices.

In making your selection, follow the requirements of standard written English; that is, pay attention to grammar, choice of words, sentence construction, and punctuation. Your selection should result in the most effective sentence—clear and precise, without awkwardness or ambiguity.

EXAMPLE: ANSWER:

Every apple in the baskets <u>are ripe and labeled according to the date it was picked</u>.   Ⓐ ● Ⓒ Ⓓ Ⓔ

(A) are ripe and labeled according to the date it was picked
(B) is ripe and labeled according to the date it was picked
(C) are ripe and labeled according to the date they were picked
(D) is ripe and labeled according to the date they were picked
(E) are ripe and labeled as to the date it was picked

---

1. Biographers should portray their subject in a historical context but <u>they should also include a discussion of</u> the person's human failings and qualities.

   (A) they should also include a discussion of
   (B) should also discuss
   (C) discussing at the same time
   (D) also they should be trying to discuss
   (E) also discussing

2. <u>The theatergoers walked this far, they</u> wanted to get to the opera without paying for a taxi.

   (A) The theatergoers walked this far, they
   (B) Although they walked this far, the theatergoers felt they
   (C) Having walked this far, the theatergoers
   (D) To walk this far, the theatergoers
   (E) The theatergoers walked this far; so that they

3. <u>Although the celebrated cartoonist Charles Schultz never having wanted his comic strip to be titled *Peanuts*, he viewed the name</u> as an insult to his work that, despite humble beginnings, he intended to be a masterpiece.

   (A) Although the celebrated cartoonist Charles Schultz never having wanted his comic strip to be titled *Peanuts*, he viewed the name
   (B) The celebrated cartoonist Charles Schultz never wanted his comic strip to be titled *Peanuts*, he viewed the name
   (C) Never having wanted his comic strip to be titled *Peanuts*, the name was viewed by the celebrated cartoonist Charles Schultz
   (D) The celebrated cartoonist Charles Schultz never wanted his comic strip to be titled *Peanuts*; however, regarding the name
   (E) The celebrated cartoonist Charles Schultz never wanted his comic strip to be titled *Peanuts* because he viewed the name

GO ON TO THE NEXT PAGE

4. The reason newly-hired attorneys are so often given routine cases <u>is that it allows</u> them to gain the experience necessary to handle more complex matters.

   (A) is that it allows

   (B) is that these cases allow

   (C) is because of these cases allowing

   (D) is because of them allowing

   (E) is their allowing of

5. After reading about a series of local break-ins, the Levy family believed they had purchased a security system that <u>would have prevented any intrusion</u>.

   (A) would have prevented any intrusion

   (B) would prevent any intrusion

   (C) had prevented any intrusion

   (D) will prevent any intrusion

   (E) prevents any intrusion

6. The library's <u>collection, consisting of five million books, and is the largest in the country</u>.

   (A) collection, consisting of five million books, and is the largest in the country

   (B) collection is the largest in the country, it consisting of five million books

   (C) collection, consisting of five million books, is the largest in the country

   (D) collection is the largest in the country consisting of five million books

   (E) collection to consist of five million books and to be the largest in the country

7. No sooner had *Fahrenheit 9/11* been rejected by the Disney film company <u>but the director convinced Miramax to distribute</u> it instead.

   (A) but the director convinced Miramax to distribute

   (B) but the director had Miramax convinced into distributing

   (C) than Miramax was convinced by the director that they will distribute

   (D) but Miramax was convinced by the director into distributing

   (E) than the director convinced Miramax to distribute

8. Today the industries showing the most rapid growth are service and technology rather than <u>what they once did, producing manufacture goods and farming</u>.

   (A) what they once did, producing manufacture goods and farming

   (B) what they once did, which was producing manufacture goods and farming

   (C) what they once were, producing manufacture goods and farming

   (D) what they once did, manufacturing and farming

   (E) what they once were, manufacturing and farming

9. The negative consequences of eating fast food often <u>is increasingly discussed in the media</u>.

   (A) is increasingly discussed in the media

   (B) is more and more discussed in the media

   (C) are increasingly discussed in the media

   (D) are increasing in discussion in the media

   (E) has increased in discussion in the media

GO ON TO THE NEXT PAGE

10. Baseball player <u>Barry Bonds, the first man to hit 73 home runs in a single season, doing it</u> just three years after Mark McGuire hit a record 70 home runs.

(A) Barry Bonds, the first man to hit 73 home runs in a single season, doing it

(B) Barry Bonds the first man who hit 73 home runs in a single season, and who did so

(C) Barry Bonds became the first man to have hit 73 home runs in a single season and did it

(D) Barry Bonds became the first man to hit 73 home runs in a single season, reaching this milestone

(E) Barry Bonds was the first man hitting 73 home runs in a single season, the milestone was reached

11. The film's clever plot and its exciting climax <u>give the viewer satisfaction</u>.

(A) give the viewer satisfaction

(B) satisfy the one who is viewing

(C) gives satisfaction to the one who views it

(D) give one satisfaction in the viewing of it

(E) gives one satisfaction in viewing it

12. Daniel will attend a prestigious university this <u>fall, his performance in this having been stellar throughout high school</u>.

(A) fall, his performance in this having been stellar throughout high school

(B) fall; he has done stellar work throughout high school for that

(C) fall, for throughout high school he has done stellar work for that

(D) fall, for his academic work has been stellar throughout high school

(E) fall; his academic work having been stellar throughout high school

13. In baseball's early days, 20 home runs in a season was considered extraordinary, but <u>that idea had been drastically changed by Babe Ruth</u> when he hit 54 home runs in 1920.

(A) that idea had been drastically changed by Babe Ruth

(B) that idea having been drastically changed by Babe Ruth

(C) drastically changing that idea was Babe Ruth

(D) that idea was drastically changed by Babe Ruth

(E) that idea has been drastically changed by Babe Ruth

14. <u>Being as he is a talented geographer</u>, Andreas is an expert at locating cities and countries on maps.

(A) Being as he is a talented geographer

(B) In being a talented geographer

(C) A talented geographer

(D) Although he is a talented geographer

(E) Being a geographer with talent

IF YOU FINISH BEFORE TIME IS CALLED, YOU MAY CHECK YOUR WORK ON THIS SECTION ONLY. DO NOT TURN TO ANY OTHER SECTION IN THE TEST. **STOP**

Practice Test Four: **Answer Key**

SECTION 1

Essay

SECTION 2

1. B
2. D
3. A
4. C
5. C
6. E
7. A
8. D
9. C
10. B
11. C
12. C
13. E
14. A
15. D
16. E
17. B
18. B
19. E
20. D

SECTION 3

1. C
2. A
3. D
4. E
5. A
6. C
7. D
8. A
9. D
10. B
11. D
12. C
13. B
14. E
15. C
16. E
17. D
18. D
19. C
20. D
21. D
22. A
23. E
24. C
25. B

SECTION 4

1. E
2. D
3. A
4. C
5. E
6. D
7. C
8. B
9. 4
10. 625
11. 3456, 5400, 9600
12. 100
13. 4
14. 120
15. 50
16. 4/3 or 1.33
17. 1/2
18. 30

SECTION 5

1. C
2. D
3. A
4. D
5. E
6. D
7. B
8. C
9. C
10. B
11. D
12. B
13. B
14. E
15. D
16. A
17. D
18. D
19. C
20. A
21. A
22. A
23. E
24. D
25. A
26. C
27. E
28. A
29. E
30. C
31. D
32. D
33. A
34. E
35. D

SECTION 6

1. B
2. C
3. B
4. B
5. E
6. B
7. E
8. A
9. D
10. A
11. D
12. C
13. E
14. C
15. D
16. E
17. A
18. B
19. B
20. E
21. B
22. D
23. C
24. C

SECTION 7

1. B
2. B
3. C
4. D
5. A
6. C
7. A
8. A
9. E
10. C
11. B
12. E
13. D
14. D
15. E
16. B

SECTION 8

1. D
2. B
3. C
4. A
5. D
6. E
7. D
8. C
9. B
10. B
11. A
12. E
13. B
14. B
15. C
16. B
17. E
18. B

SECTION 9

1. B
2. C
3. E
4. B
5. B
6. C
7. E
8. E
9. C
10. D
11. A
12. D
13. D
14. C

PRACTICE TEST FOUR

Critical Reading

	Number Right	Number Wrong	Raw Score
Section 3:	□	− (.25 × □)	= □
Section 6:	□	− (.25 × □)	= □
Section 8:	□	− (.25 × □)	= □
	Critical Reading Raw Score	=	□
			(rounded up)

Writing

	Number Right	Number Wrong	Raw Score
Section 1:	□ (ESSAY GRADE)	× 3.17	= □
Section 5:	□	− (.25 × □)	= □
Section 9:	□	− (.25 × □)	= □
	Writing Raw Score	=	□
			(rounded up)

Math

	Number Right	Number Wrong	Raw Score
Section 2:	□	− (.25 × □)	= □
Section 4A: (QUESTIONS 1–8)	□	− (.25 × □)	= □
Section 4B: (QUESTIONS 9–18)	□	(no wrong answer penalty)	= □
Section 7:	□	− (.25 × □)	= □
	Math Raw Score	=	□
			(rounded up)

Turn to page xiv to convert your raw score to a scaled score.

Answers and Explanations

SECTION 1

6 Score Essay

My mother used to say that "procrastination" was my middle name, because I continually put off doing chores or homework until the last minute. I preferred to spend my time playing or reading, as these activities were more interesting and fun. However, leaving responsibilities unfulfilled right up to the deadline meant that I always felt very rushed and stressed when I finally got around to doing what I should have done earlier. I also discovered that I didn't always leave myself enough time. Sometimes I wasn't able to finish, and incomplete projects led to negative consequences, like bad grades or additional chores. Ultimately, I learned that it's not wise to put things off. So I disagree with Aaron Burr's statement, and one of the best literary examples to support my point of view is Shakespeare's *Hamlet*.

Hamlet is often referred to as the classic procrastinator, since he spends almost the entire play debating with himself about how or if to avenge his father's death. In the first scene, his father's ghost appears to Hamlet and implies that the new king, Claudius, may be a murderer. Hamlet is extremely upset about this, and determines to investigate the situation to learn if the ghost has told the truth or not. However, even when Hamlet is convinced of Claudius' guilt, he can't seem to take action and kill Claudius, despite having several opportunities during the course of the play. By continuing to procrastinate, Hamlet involves other characters in his plot, and several of them lose their lives, including Polonius, Ophelia, and Laertes. If Hamlet had taken action sooner, these other characters might not have died. Hamlet's procrastination, then, has mortal consequences.

Taking action in the moment tends to result in fewer regrets compared to endlessly procrastinating, as the example of Hamlet proves. For this reason, it's wisest to act when you can rather than putting things off.

6 Score Critique

All essays are evaluated on four basic criteria: Topic, Support, Organization, and Language. The writer begins this essay by discussing a personal example related to the topic, showing that she has understood the prompt. This first example comprises the majority of the introductory paragraph and leads to a clear statement of the author's opinion followed by another supporting example. In the second paragraph, the author develops her second example, providing support for her opinion. She closes her essay with a conclusion that reiterates her viewpoint.

Overall, the organization of this composition is clear and coherent, with keywords like *however, also, ultimately,* and *for this reason* to help the reader follow the logic of the essay. This suggests that the author followed the appropriate steps in the Kaplan Method of outlining a plan before writing.

In addition, the author uses sophisticated language (*procrastination, unfulfilled, consequences, ultimately, avenge, mortal*) and varied sentence structure, which contribute to her high score. Finally, the lack of grammatical or spelling errors indicates that the author left enough time to proofread her essay.

4 Score Essay

Putting things off, at least for a little while, can be a good choice. Similar to the saying "Look before you leap," meaning you should take time to consider the consequences of your actions. If you act too quick you may regret it.

My brother hasn't learned this. He's a total tech junkie and loves all the new toys he sees in Circuit City or Best Buy. He was the first person in our school to have an iPod, a picture phone, a Blackberry, etc. The problem is, he buys things on impulse without thinking about whether or not he really needs it or if it's the best thing for him to buy. For example, the iPod. He bought one when they first came out. Now you can get a smaller one with a lot more memory for about half the price. If my brother had waited, he might of ended up with a better value. But he didn't want to wait so now he regrets it.

I'm the opposite. I also have an iPod but I bought mine after all the improvements had been made. So mine is better and cheaper. I took my time and looked at other mp3 players to make sure the iPod was the best deal. Although I had to wait longer to have an iPod, I don't regret it because the result was better.

So putting off certain actions can lead to a better result. If you act too quickly, you may not think through all the consequences and you might regret that you didn't wait. So I agree with putting things off if you can.

4 Score Critique

All essays are evaluated on four basic criteria: Topic, Support, Organization, and Language. The introductory paragraph of this essay begins immediately with the author's opinion of the question in the assignment, showing that he has understood the prompt. He uses personal examples to illustrate the two sides of the issue, indicating some critical thinking skills. Both examples are relevant and fairly well developed, indicating that the author spent some time formulating a plan before beginning to produce his essay.

The essay's organization is adequate, and there are only a few minor grammatical errors (*quick* is used where "quickly" would be correct, *might of* instead of "might have," some sentence fragments). However, the language is weak and vague (*it* and *things* are used frequently, *etc.,* in the second paragraph) and there is some use of slang (*tech junky, cheaper*). This author should be sure to proofread to catch any errors.

2 Score Essay

I disagree that it's good to put things off. It just means you're avoiding something that will happen anyway or maybe missing out on something cool that will pass you by if you don't take advantage of it. On "Let's Make a Deal" the contestants could see one prize and they'd have to either just accept that prize or another door opened and then have to take whatever was there. Some people would stick with what they had, but other people gave up what they had to risk getting something better. Sometimes they got lucky and won a new car or something so it paid off for

them to put things off. They gained something good because of it. But sometimes these people also got really bad prizes so they probably regretted putting off the decision. That's always the danger of not acting right away, you never know exactly what will happen and if you delay for too long you may miss out on something good, so you shouldn't always try to put things off to another time.

2 Score Critique

All essays are evaluated on four basic criteria: Topic, Support, Organization, and Language. The writer begins this essay with a clear statement of his point of view, showing that he understood what was being asked by the prompt. However, he does not lay out a clear plan for the remainder of the essay, and there is no apparent structure or logic to his argument. This lack of organization makes the essay confusing for a reader, and suggests that the author did not spend much time planning before beginning to write.

The single example offered in the essay doesn't provide sufficient support for the author's argument. In addition, the example doesn't really address the assignment, and the author doesn't provide enough explanation to link the example to the topic.

The author's language is simplistic and repetitive (*something, sometimes, things*), as is his sentence structure. Several sentence fragments also indicate weak writing skills and suggest that the author didn't take time to proofread.

SECTION 2

1. B

Difficulty: Low

Strategic Advice: Solve for x, then plug that value into the second equation

Getting to the Answer:

$$3x + 2 = 14$$
$$3x = 12$$
$$x = 4$$
$$5x - 6 = 5(4) - 6 = 14$$

2. D

Difficulty: Low

Strategic Advice: Pretend each classroom has the minimum number of students and find the total, then do the same for the maximum number. This will give you the range of possibilities.

Getting to the Answer:

Lowest total is if each has 24 students: $24(9) = 216$

Highest total is if each has 30: $30(9) = 270$

Only (D) is between 216 and 270.

3. A

Difficulty: Low

Strategic Advice: "Directly north" means the two lines in the figure make a right angle. Since the shortest distance between two points is a straight line, try drawing in the lines from her house to the different places in her neighborhood. How could you compare the distances without computing them?

Getting to the Answer:

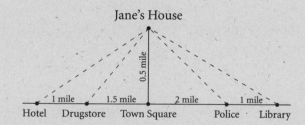

Each line to each place in the neighborhood forms a right triangle on the map. You can find the length of each hypotenuse, which is the distance from her house, by using the Pythagorean Theorem, but that would eat away at valuable time. The longer the legs, the longer the distance. The short leg is always .5 miles, so you just need to find the place the farthest distance (west or east) from the Town Square; this is the Library, which is 3 miles away.

4. C

Difficulty: Low

Strategic Advice: In what year did the number of factories increase by 2?

Getting to the Answer:

From the end of 1998 to the end of 1999, the number of factories increased from 3 to 5. This is the only time the graph jumps by 2, so those 2 factories must have been opened in February of 1999.

5. C

Difficulty: Medium

Strategic Advice: Remember that you can't always solve for all the variables. Concentrate on setting up the average equations and solving for z.

Getting to the Answer:

Write the two equations for the averages, then plug in the expression for $x + y$ from the first one into the second one:

$$\frac{x + y}{2} = 7$$
$$x + y = 14$$
$$\frac{x + y + z}{3} = 10$$
$$x + y + z = 30$$
$$(x + y) + z = 30$$
$$(14) + z = 30$$
$$z = 16$$

6. E

Difficulty: Low

Strategic Advice: Find the area of the big square and the area of the small square, then subtract.

Getting to the Answer:

Area of big square $= x \times x = x^2$

Area of small square $= 3 \times 3 = 9$

Area of shaded region $= x^2 - 9$

7. A

Difficulty: Low

Strategic Advice: If a product is 0, then one of its factors is 0. The inverse is also true: if a product is not 0, then none of its factors can be 0.

Getting to the Answer:

Since $abce = 0$, this means either $a = 0, b = 0, c = 0$ or $e = 0$

Since $abcd = 3$, this means that $a \neq 0, b \neq 0, c \neq 0$, and $d \neq 0$

By process of elimination, this means that $e = 0$

8. D

Difficulty: Low

Strategic Advice: Use your answers given to figure out how much was earned in each quarter.

Getting to the Answer:

Start with (C):

Total profits $= \$63$ million

First quarter: $\frac{1}{7}(63) = \$9$ million

Second quarter: $\frac{1}{3}(63) = \$21$ million

Third quarter: $\frac{1}{2}(63) = \$31.5$ million

This leaves $\$63m - \$9m - \$21m - \$31.5m = \$1.5$ million, which is not $\$2$ million. The number we came up with is way too low, so move to (D) and repeat the same process.

Total profits $= \$84$ million

First quarter: $\frac{1}{7}(84) = \$12$ million

Second quarter: $\frac{1}{3}(84) = \$28$ million

Third quarter: $\frac{1}{2}(84) = \$42$ million

This leaves $\$84m - \$12m - \$28m - \$42m = \$2$ million.

9. C

Difficulty: Medium

Strategic Advice: Don't reach for that calculator just yet! All that typing might waste valuable time. Rewrite the equation so that both sides have the same base number. Once you get both sides in the form of a common base, you can set the exponents equal to each other.

Getting to the Answer:

$$64 = 4^3$$

$$4^{4x+6} = 64^{2x} = (4^3)^{2x} = 4^{6x}$$

$$4x + 6 = 6x$$

$$6 = 2x$$

$$x = 3$$

Alternatively, you could try plugging in the answers, since your calculator can handle these powers. For example, in (A) $4^{4x+6} = 4^{4(1)+6} = 4^{10} = 1,048,576$, while $64^{2(1)} = 64^2 = 4096$, so (A) is incorrect.

10. B

Difficulty: Medium

Strategic Advice: Carefully translate to an equation; don't forget that "3 less than 5" means $5 - 3$, not $3 - 5$.

Getting to the Answer:

$$3x + 5 = x - 3$$

$$2x + 5 = -3$$

$$2x = -8$$

$$x = -4$$

11. C

Difficulty: Medium

Strategic Advice: The circumference of the shaded region is made up of the sum of the circumference of the bigger circle and the circumference of the smaller circle.

Getting to the Answer:

Area $= 25\pi = \pi r^2$

$r = 5$

Circumference (larger circle) $= 2\pi r = 2\pi(5) = 10\pi$

Radius (smaller circle) $= \frac{1}{2}$ radius (larger circle) $= \frac{5}{2}$

Circumference (smaller circle) $= 2\pi r = 2\pi\left(\frac{5}{2}\right) = 5\pi$

Total circumference of the shaded region $= 10\pi + 5\pi = 15\pi$

12. C

Difficulty: Medium

Strategic Advice: If the points are on a line, that means the slope between any two points must always be the same. Write the slope using two sets of points, then set one slope equation equal to the other.

Getting to the Answer:

Slope $= \dfrac{b-a}{2-1} = \dfrac{18-b}{4-2}$

$b - a = \dfrac{18-b}{2}$

$b - a = 9 - \dfrac{b}{2}$

$\dfrac{3}{2}b - a = 9$

13. E

Difficulty: Medium

Strategic Advice: Find the pattern, then figure out how often it repeats.

Getting to the Answer:

The first few terms of the series are 4, −4, −1, 1, 4, −4, −1, 1..., so the pattern repeats every 4 terms. Since $\dfrac{37}{4} = 9\,r\,1$, it will go through the cycle 9 times, and end on the 1st number of the cycle, which is 4.

14. A

Difficulty: Medium

Strategic Advice: Sketch yourself a picture, and look for how the y-intercept and slope change.

Getting to the Answer:

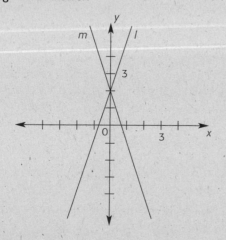

From the diagram, you can see that *m* still has y-intercept 2, but the slope now goes down 3 and over 1, which is −3. So plugging into $y = mx + b$, the equation is $y = -3x + 2$.

15. D

Difficulty: Medium

Getting to the Answer:

From year 6 to year 9, the tree increased from 25 ft to 100 ft, or 75 ft. This is $\dfrac{75}{25} = \dfrac{300}{100} = 300\%$ of the height in year 6.

16. E

Difficulty: Medium

Strategic Advice: Find the volume of the cylinder in the figure, then find the volume of each answer and compare. Start with the formula that is easier to work with: the volume of a rectangular solid.

Getting to the Answer:

Volume of cylinder $= \pi r^2 h = \pi(\pi x)^2(2x) = 2\pi^3 x^3$

(D) Volume of solid $= (2x)(\pi x)(\pi x) = 2\pi^2 x^3$ (E) Volume of solid $= (2\pi x)(\pi x)(\pi x) = 2\pi^3 x^3$

17. B

Difficulty: Medium

Strategic Advice: Don't solve for *b*! On Test Day, you will see questions that ask you to solve for expressions with variables, like $b + 1$. There's got to be an easy way to factor or rearrange the variables in the equation in order to solve for $b + 1$.

Getting to the Answer:

Remember when you're solving for a variable that you have to remove the stuff that's added and subtracted first, then get rid of what's multiplied/divided. In other words, you need to move the $3a$ before you can worry about the 3 in front of $b + 1$.

$3(b + 1) = c - 3a$

$(b + 1) = \dfrac{c - 3a}{3} = \dfrac{c}{3} - a$

18. B

Difficulty: High

Strategic Advice: Start with the easiest Roman Numeral to evaluate. If you're able to prove that Roman Numeral true, then eliminate any answer choice that does not use that Roman Numeral.

Getting to the Answer:

I. It looks like (3.5, .5) is in the shaded region. This would make $m = 3.5$, so I is false. Eliminate (A), (C), and (E).

II. (2,1) is in the shaded region, which would make $m = 2$, $n = 1$, so II is false. Eliminate (D). So all you have left is choice (B).

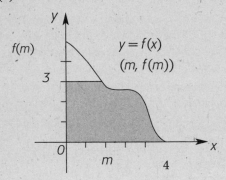

19. E

Difficulty: High

Strategic Advice: Some questions on Test Day will have answer choices that look very similar. Since you have the same variable in your question as in your answer choice, try picking numbers.

Getting to the Answer:

Pick a number like 12.99

(A) $|12.99 - 13| = \frac{1}{16}$? No.

$0.01 \neq \frac{1}{16}$

(B) $|12.99 + 13| = \frac{1}{16}$? No.

$25.99 \neq \frac{1}{16}$

(C) $|12.99 - 13| > \frac{1}{16}$? No.

$0.01 < \frac{1}{16}$

(D) $|12.99 + 13| < \frac{1}{16}$? No.

$25.99 > \frac{1}{16}$

(E) $|12.99 - 13| < \frac{1}{16}$? Yes.

$0.01 < \frac{1}{16}$

20. D

Difficulty: High

Strategic Advice: This is the last question in the section. The testmaker wants you to count out all of the integers in the set: a big timewaster! There's probably an easier way to solve the problem. What happens if you add up all the integers from −5 to 5?

Getting to the Answer:

$-30 + (-28) + (-26) + \dots + (-2) + 0 + 2 + \dots + 30 = 0$, so the first 31 numbers cancel out. Then $32 + 34 = 66$, for a total of 33 numbers.

SECTION 3

1. C

Difficulty: Low

What would you call something that comes and goes regularly?

All you know about his discomfort is that it was "coming and going regularly throughout the day," so all that can really be inferred here is that this discomfort was *recurring* or *regular*, both great predictions for the blank.

In (A), *unmediated,* discomfort would not necessarily come and go regularly. In (B), if the comfort was "coming and going regularly throughout the day," then it could not have been *spontaneous*. Choice (C) is a perfect match for your prediction. In (D), nothing in the sentence describes the importance of the discomfort. In (E), similarly, nothing in the sentence indicates whether or not the discomfort was particular to the subject or that area.

2. A

Difficulty: Low

If Lucinda was "in the midst" of something "angry and noisy," what might she be surprised to feel?

Stick to only what you know from the sentence. Beginning with the first blank, all you know is that whatever Lucinda was in the middle of, it was "angry and noisy," so a word like *disorder* or *commotion* would be a good prediction here. And if Lucinda was in such a situation, she would most likely be surprised to feel *peaceful*, or *free of disturbance or commotion*, both great predictions for the second blank.

Choice (A) is a perfect match for your prediction. In (B), if *pomp* could be "angry and noisy," Lucinda would not be surprised to feel a bit intimidated or frightened. In (C), something that is "angry and noisy" would probably not also be *banal*, but if it were one would expect to feel *conventional*. In (D), *turmoil* fits perfectly into the first blank, but one would not necessarily feel *controversial* in such a situation. In (E), *serenity*, by definition, cannot be "angry and noisy."

3. D

Difficulty: Medium

What kind of facility might an "inept administration" run?

Start with the first blank; the word "inept" is key here, as it suggests the blank must be filled with a word that has a similar meaning, such as incompetent. Moving on to the second blank, if the administration was so inept and incompetent that the hospital "debased the entire medical profession," then the hospital must have been a mockery. Incompetent and mockery are great predictions for the blanks.

In (A), if the administrators were *apathetic*, the facility likely would not have been considered a *victory*. In (B), an *exacting* or demanding administration would not necessarily lead to a facility being considered a *spectacle*, or a phenomenon. In (C), an *astute* administration would not likely head a facility considered a *debacle*. Choice (D) is a good fit for your prediction. In (E), again, a *surreptitious* or secretive administration would not necessarily make for a *triumphant* facility.

4. E

Difficulty: Medium

How might a "dazzling" reflecting pool appear in the bright sunlight? If all you know of the new reflecting pool is that "in the bright sunlight" it somehow dazzled the onlookers, then all you can really conclude is that it was shining or sparkling brightly. Look for two words that mean *dazzling* or *shining brightly*.

In (A), an *unassuming* or modest reflecting pool would not likely dazzle onlookers. In (B), a *capricious* or inconstant pool would not necessarily be *harmless*, let alone dazzling. In (C), again, a *tawdry* or inferior pool would probably not be dazzling. In (D), while a dazzling reflecting pool could be *vivacious* or lively, it could not also be dull. Choice (E) is a nice match for your prediction.

5. A

Difficulty: High

What would you call a "series of rhythmic drum beats"?

If the composition was dominated by a "series of rhythmic drum beats," then those beats, or the composition's beat or rhythm, would have been "impossible to miss." *Beat* or *rhythm* make great predictions for the blank.

Choice (A) is a good match for your prediction. In (B), while a piece of music could be superficially attractive, or *specious*, a "series of rhythmic drum beats" would not necessarily make such a quality hard to miss. In (C), nothing in the sentence indicates that the music was particularly complex, or *convoluted*. In (D), nothing indicates that the composition was particularly flattering or admiring. In (E), a "series of rhythmic drum beats" would not necessarily make a piece of music seem passionate.

6. C

Difficulty: Medium

What is it that's being "practiced"? Notice how the word contributes to the meaning of the sentence as a whole.

Since Vocab-in-Context questions usually do *not* test your understanding of the most common definition of a word, examine the context to pinpoint which meaning is relevant.

In the relevant sentence, the author is discussing "religious prohibitions," or strict rules and customs, and how these prohibitions are "particularly important" to many societies. Given this context, it is likely that the prohibitions "practiced" are those that are faithfully, dutifully, or carefully carried out or acted upon.

Choice (A) is a primary definition of the cited word, and it does not capture the author's meaning. Choice (B) matches the primary definition of "practiced" and has no support in the context of this passage. Choice (C) is a great fit for your prediction. A common meaning of "observed" involves complying with or carrying out laws or customs. In (D), the author mentions nothing about refining or improving one's ability to comply with these prohibitions, only that they are carefully adhered to. In (E), while this choice could make sense in the context of the passage, it does not match any of the meanings of the cited word.

7.   D

Difficulty: High

There's an implicit comparison in this sentence, between table etiquette and something else. What is table etiquette being compared to? Think about how the emphasis on "*subtle*" reinforces this comparison.

When a function question asks about the author's emphasis on a particular word, think about the meaning of the word before looking for the role of the emphasis.

The author says that table etiquette can be "even trickier" to learn than the strict religious prohibitions mentioned earlier in the passage. Since rules are "*subtle*" when they are not particularly obvious or apparent, you can infer that the author is emphasizing the fact that table etiquette can be harder for a foreigner to figure out than religious rules are.

Choice (A) is distortion; the cited word is used to describe table etiquette, not violations of religious customs. Choice (B) is extreme; the author only indicates that table etiquette "can" be more challenging to figure out, not that it *always* is. Choice (C) is out of scope; the author makes no mention of the "very nature" of table etiquette. Choice (D) matches your prediction nicely. Choice (E) is distortion; the author does not mention anyone's table manners being cautiously hidden or protected.

8.   A

Difficulty: Low

Notice the colon in the relevant sentence. What idea does it call particular attention to? The cited description most likely reinforces or elaborates on that idea.

Pay attention to the punctuation in the sentence, since it can serve as a structural clue to help emphasize an idea.

The cited words come in a sentence describing one possible reason why the author asked for the casserole—he liked its appearance. The colon makes it clear that "aesthetic reasons" for liking the casserole are the focus of the sentence. Since the "brilliant hues of the peppers" describe how the peppers look, you can expect that the author uses this phrase in order to explain why he finds the dish aesthetically pleasing.

Choice (A) is a good match for your prediction. Choice (B) is distortion; the author does not connect the hotness of the peppers to their appearance. Choice (C) is a misused detail; selfishness is mentioned in the last sentence, but it is not connected to this description. Choice (D) is distortion; again, the appearance of the peppers is not given as a reason for their hotness. Choice (E) is an opposite; the sentence describes why its appearance *was* potentially important to the author.

9.   D

Difficulty: Medium

What point is the author trying to make in this sentence? Think about how the description contributes to the purpose of the sentence as a whole.

In questions about the function of a particular word, think about how that word contributes to the purpose of the sentence in which it occurs.

The author mentions two possible explanations for why he is so fond of the casserole: he likes the way it looks, and he likes the contrast in tastes. Pepper juice is described as "intimidating" in the context of a discussion of contrast in tastes. Specifically, it is compared to the "tame" taste of cheese.

Choice (A) is out of scope; the dish may be unusual, but the author does not make this claim in the passage. Choice (B) is distortion; the author is discussing his own fondness for the dish, not warning the reader. Choice (C) is an opposite; the author liked the peppers precisely because he "knew" they would "singe" his tongue. Choice (D) is a nice match for your prediction. Choice (E) is a misused detail; the appearance of the dish is described in the previous sentence, not this one.

10. B

Difficulty: High

This is a global question, so you can't rely on any one part of the passage. Still, if you're unsure, you might want to skim the passage and look for anything that would confirm or deny the answer choices.

Look for the answer choice that is neutral or appreciative towards Vonnegut, doesn't contradict the passage, and is fairly general without being too vague for the contents of the passage.

Choice (A) is an opposite; in fact, half the passage is spent describing movements that fit his work. Choice (B) seems to be a fairly safe choice. Choice (C) is an opposite; actually, the author seems to have quite a bit of respect for Vonnegut's work as literature. Choice (D) is distortion; the author says that some people might find Vonnegut cynical. He does not say that he feels that way. Choice (E) is an opposite; the passage actually stresses the uniqueness of Vonnegut's style.

11. D

Difficulty: Medium

This is a fairly general question, but it still refers to a particular part of the passage. Make sure to go back and re-read that part so you don't get confused.

The passage states that many of the themes of Modernism are based on public attitudes after World War I. Look for the answer that agrees with this.

Choice (A) is extreme; the passage says the war was responsible for some of Modernism's themes, not *virtually every single aspect*. Choice (B) is out of scope; this may be true, but it is never mentioned in the passage. Choice (C) is a misused detail; remember, World War I influenced Modernism, not Postmodernism. Choice (D) seems to match your prediction well. Choice (E) is out of scope; nothing like this appears anywhere in the passage.

12. C

Difficulty: Medium

In a question like this one, you're going to have to figure out the function of the quotes from the surrounding context. You know what that means—back to the passage.

This is not a direct quote or unfamiliar terminology; instead, these quotation marks seem to have the sense of a phrase like "so to speak."

Choice (A) is a misused detail; "cut off" is actually a fairly common phrase. Choice (B) is out of scope; nothing in the passage suggests that this is a special literary usage. Choice (C) seems to fit the passage well. Choice (D) is a misused detail; nothing else in this sentence seems to convey a tone of *sarcasm*. Choice (E) is a misused detail; the author does not seem to be unsure about what he is saying here.

13. B

Difficulty: Medium

Go back and read the entire sentence surrounding this phrase—often, the correct answer choice will rely on information that comes slightly before or after the quoted material.

The author is saying here that Postmodernism was at least partly a consequence of World War II. Look for the answer choice that mirrors this.

Choice (A) is distortion; one might try to conclude this based on the passage, but this is a bit outside of the author's real point. Choice (B) matches the prediction well. Choice (C) is distortion; one can hardly consider World War II a *side effect* of Postmodernism. Choice (D) is out of scope; nothing in the passage relates to this answer choice. Choice (E) is out of scope; again, nothing that suggests this is anywhere to be found.

14. E

Difficulty: Medium

To correctly get the sense of the author's tone here, you need a little context—make sure you read at least the entire sentence containing the phrase in question.

The author seems to feel that such depictions were too optimistic and oversimplified the era. Look for the answer choice that reflects this tone.

Choice (A) is an opposite; the tone is actually a little negative, certainly not *admiring*. Choice (B) is distortion; although this is more negative, *pessimistic* doesn't really make sense in this context. Choice (C) is extreme; although this is certainly negative, *revolted* is much too strong a term for this passage. Choice (D) is a misused detail; nothing in this sentence really suggests that the author is *curious* about anything. Choice (E) fits the author's tone in the sentence well.

15. C

Difficulty: Medium

Although no specific line is referenced, remember that questions will still go in order of their place in the passage. Look around the right general area for a discussion of Vonnegut's *uniqueness*.

The passage mentions that Vonnegut's style of breaking up his prose into chunks is a unique aspect of his novels. Look for the answer choice that captures this statement.

Choice (A) is out of scope; the passage doesn't really talk about Vonnegut's *characterizations*. Choice (B) is out of scope; again, setting and specific plot elements aren't really mentioned. Choice (C) appears to parallel what the author is saying. Choice (D) is extreme; the author finds some aspects of Vonnegut unique but never says that he rejects *nearly every convention of writing*. Choice (E) is a misused detail; actually, the author would probably say that Vonnegut's vision is not as *chaotic and frightening* as other writers'.

16. E

Difficulty: High

A reasoning question like this relies on a firm grasp of what the author is saying at this point in the passage—go back and make sure you remember the content and tone correctly.

The author seems to disagree with the critics but says they are "not entirely without justification"—look for the answer choice that agrees with both attitudes.

Choice (A) is an opposite; actually, the author thinks these people are incorrect. Choice (B) is extreme; the author disagrees with the critics in question, but not so strongly as this. Choice (C) is distortion; the author actually takes quite a certain stance here. Choice (D) is out of scope; this answer choice is too general for a fairly specific question like this one. Choice (E) matches the author's opinion and tone nicely.

17. D

Difficulty: Medium

For Vocab-in-Context questions, remember that the obvious-sounding choices are frequently wrong—you need to rely on the passage rather than your gut instinct about the word itself.

The full phrase here is "a single brilliant point of clarity and truth," so look for the answer choice that reflects something clear and true.

Choice (A) is distortion; this may not be far from the author's tone, but it is a stretch as a meaning for the word "brilliant." Choice (B) is out of scope; nothing here seems to indicate that the point in question is *difficult to comprehend*. Choice (C) is a misused detail; this could be a meaning of "brilliant," but it is not really appropriate here. Choice (D) seems to fit well with the author's other word

choices in this part of the passage. Choice (E) is distortion; *revolutionary* might fit a little, but *headstrong* is inappropriate for this sentence.

18. D

Difficulty: Medium

The wording of the question sounds general, but it refers to a specific part of the passage. This is your clue that the correct answer is probably going to be found near the quoted material.

The author's own words say that Vonnegut thinks the artist should "reveal the order and beauty behind it all." Look for the answer choice that paraphrases this idea.

Choice (A) is a misused detail; *pointlessness and drudgery* seem more appropriate for writers more pessimistic than Vonnegut. Choice (B) is out of scope; nothing in the passage suggests this. Choice (C) is out of scope; this is certainly idealistic, but it's not explicitly mentioned in the passage anywhere. Choice (D) captures the author's words well. Choice (E) is an opposite; actually, the author believes that Vonnegut is against the *nihilism* of some other Postmodern authors.

19. C

Difficulty: High

This question asks about the organization of the passage, so it will probably help to quickly go over the main point of each paragraph to help summarize the author's argument.

The author spends two paragraphs discussing Modernism and Postmodernism and the following two paragraphs applying their ideas to Vonnegut. Look for the answer choice that fits this progression.

Choice (A) is a misused detail; the author doesn't ever reverse his overall opinion in this passage. Choice (B) is an opposite; actually, if anything, the author begins with general topics and then becomes more specific. Choice (C) works well—the first two paragraphs provide *artistic background*, and Vonnegut is the *extended example*. Choice (D) is distortion; this passage isn't really just the same point over and over again. Choice (E) is out of scope; this really has nothing to do with the argument in the passage.

20. D

Difficulty: Low

The passage starts out fairly broad and becomes more specific as it progresses. What idea does the author focus on by the end of the passage?

Avoid choices that describe minor points in the passage rather than the overall focus or theme.

The author portrays art therapy as a useful tool in helping emotionally disturbed people. Expect the answer to reflect this positive attitude about art therapy.

Choice (A) is extreme; art therapy is one effective way, but it may not be the *only* way to treat emotionally disturbed individuals. Choice (B) is out of scope; the author never addresses the development of art therapy across the decades. Choice (C) is distortion; making emotionally disturbed people productive is not the main focus of the passage. Choice (D) is a nice match for your prediction. Choice (E) is out of scope; the passage does not discuss *methods* by which therapists interpret art.

21. D

Difficulty: Medium

What contrast is the author suggesting between "the brush" and "the pen and voice"?

To determine what a phrase signifies, research how it is used in the passage. The context will help reveal the phrase's meaning.

Before and after the cited phrase, the author discusses the value of art in helping emotionally disturbed people communicate what's in their minds. The contrast between "the brush" and "the pen and voice" is a contrast between artistic expression and written or verbal expression. The author's suggestion is that art therapy can succeed where language-based communication fails.

Choice (A) is out of scope; the author never discusses artistic equipment. Choice (B) is out of scope; the author does not express a preferred form of communication. Choice (C) is a misused detail; art therapy is not limited to painting. Choice (D) is a good match for your prediction. Choice (E) is a misused detail; "the brush" signifies artistic creation itself, not the ideas it can be used to communicate.

22. A

Difficulty: Medium

Why does the author think art therapy can be especially valuable? Look for an idea repeated throughout the passage.

The word "main" indicates that the answer will be the reason most broadly supported by the passage. Look for a choice that corresponds to a point the author emphasizes.

The author repeatedly indicates that art therapy is effective when the individual cannot verbalize thoughts. You can expect the answer to reflect this emphasis.

Choice (A) matches your prediction nicely. Choice (B) is a misused detail; the therapeutic artwork shares ideas with select others, but not necessarily with the general public. Choice (C) is out of scope; the author does not discuss appreciation of past artists. Choice (D) is a misused detail; art removes ideas from mental isolation, but it does not necessarily remove the individual from social isolation. Choice (E) is a misused detail; the cooperation the author mentions is between opposing forces in the patient's mind, not between the patient and others.

23. E

Difficulty: High

The cited line makes an implicit comparison between artwork and windows. In what ways might the two be similar?

When a comparison is implicit in the passage, look for qualities the compared objects share.

The author suggests that artwork grants access to the mind, just as a window grants access to a building. Look for a choice that reflects this relationship.

Choice (A) is out of scope; the artwork is never described as transparent. Choice (B) is a misused detail; a disturbed mind may be divided, but the artwork does not necessarily reflect this aspect. Choice (C) is an opposite; creating artwork is a means of communicating. Choice (D) is out of scope; the author does not discuss the fragility of some artwork. Choice (E) is a nice match for your prediction.

24. C

Difficulty: Low

What *is* the "medium" being discussed? Once you've identified what the medium is, use the context to figure out what the word itself means.

Think of a word or phrase that could be used to replace or explain the cited term without changing the meaning of the sentence.

According to the passage, art is a therapeutic medium. The word "medium" is followed by the phrase "through which to understand," indicating that it is functioning as a communication tool. This interpretation is further supported by the discussion of expression in the previous sentence.

In choice (A), although this choice is related to a common meaning of "medium," the passage does not rank or order any of the topics discussed. Choice (B) is not among the meanings of "medium." Choice (C) is a nice fit given the context of the passage. Choice (D) is another meaning of the cited word, but it does not fit the context. In choice (E), artwork can be used to show the mind's content, but this does not imply that it has psychic powers.

25. B

Difficulty: Medium

What is the author's conclusion in this passage? Make sure you identify it before turning to the choices.

Make sure you identify the conclusion before looking for information to support it.

The author's conclusion is that art therapy can be especially helpful for emotionally disturbed people because it requires "facing and governing" the "creative force," and because it provides a non-verbal means of communication. Look for a choice that would strengthen either of these effects.

Choice (A) is out of scope; evaluating the quality of art is not directly relevant to the author's conclusion. Choice (B) is a good match for your prediction. Choice (C) is out of scope; attention span is not discussed in the passage. Choice (D) is a misused detail; although art therapy can help disturbed individuals, the author does not claim that art has a pacifying effect in general. Choice (E) is out of scope; the physical effects of artistic creation are not mentioned in the passage.

SECTION 4

1. E

Difficulty: Low

Strategic Advice: Try rewriting the equation to make both sides look like each other. Look for what number you can plug in to the left side to get the same thing on the right side—you shouldn't have to do any actual algebra.

Getting to the Answer:

If x were 7 then you'd have $\frac{3}{7} + 7$ on the left side as well.

2. D

Difficulty: Low

Strategic Advice: Use the Pythagorean Theorem to find a.

Getting to the Answer:

$$2^2 + a^2 = 5^2$$
$$4 + a^2 = 25$$
$$a^2 = 21$$
$$a = \sqrt{21}$$

3. A

Difficulty: Low

Strategic Advice: You want the number that fits the conditions (divisible by 4 and 6) but not the conclusion (divisible by 8)

Getting to the Answer:

	Divisible by 4	Divisible by 6	Divisible by 8
12	Y	Y	N
24	Y	Y	Y
32	Y	N	Y
40	Y	N	Y
48	Y	Y	Y

Only 12 fits what we're looking for.

4. C

Difficulty: Medium

Strategic Advice: If you can't remember the area of a parallelogram (which is the same for any quadrilateral with two sets of congruent sides), use the area of the parallelogram to guess the area of the circle, which looks to be about half of the parallelogram.

Getting to the Answer:

Area of parallelogram $= b \times h = 14 \times h = 168$

$$h = 12$$

The height of the parallelogram is also the diameter of the circle, so $r = 6$

Area of circle $= \pi r^2 = 36\pi$

5. E

Difficulty: Medium

Strategic Advice: If the first number is even, then what do you know about the product? If the first number is odd, then what has to happen for the product to be even?

Getting to the Answer:

If the first number is even, then the product will always be even. There are 3 even numbers on the first spin, and then 6 numbers on the second spin, so this is a total of $3 \times 6 = 18$ possibilities

If the first number is not even (which can happen 3 ways), the second number must be even (which can happen 3 ways), so this is a total of $3 \times 3 = 9$ possibilities

So the total number of positive products is $9 + 18 = 27$

Since we have 6 numbers on the first spin and 6 numbers on the second spin, there are $6 \times 6 = 36$ possibilities overall, so the probability of an even product is $\frac{27}{36}$

6. D

Difficulty: Medium

Strategic Advice: Remember that directly proportional means $a = kb$ (or $\frac{a}{b} = k$) and inversely proportional means $ab = k$.

Getting to the Answer:

We want the points where ab always turns out to be the same number. This is only true in (D).

7. C

Difficulty: Medium

Strategic Advice: This is a perfect chance for you to pick numbers.

Getting to the Answer:

Let $A = -1.5$

Let $B = 0.5$

$A \times B = -1.5 \times 0.5 = -0.75$

From the answer choices given, only X could be -0.75.

8. B

Difficulty: High

Strategic Advice: How much profit does the store make on each carton? Then how long will it take them to make $2,000?

Getting to the Answer:

The store makes $\frac{4k}{3} - k = \frac{k}{3}$ dollars on each carton.

So they will have to sell

$$\frac{\$2,000}{\frac{k}{3}} = \frac{\$2,000}{1} \times \frac{3}{k} = \frac{\$6,000}{k} \text{ cartons}$$

9. 4

Difficulty: Medium

Strategic Advice: Plug the second equation into the first and simplify.

Getting to the Answer:

$$4c + 3(c + 3) = 37$$
$$4c + 3c + 9 = 37$$
$$7c + 9 = 37$$
$$7c = 28$$
$$c = 4$$

10. 625

Difficulty: Low

Strategic Advice: This a straightforward percentage problem. Collect the quick points and move on!

Getting to the Answer:

In February they spent 25% of $500 = $125 more. Thus their February bill was $500 + $125 = $625.

11. 3456, 5400, or 9600

Difficulty: Medium

Strategic Advice: If two triangles have the same angles, they are similar, so their sides will be in the same ratio. $\triangle JKL$ just $\triangle ABC$ scaled up (multiplied) by a certain number. Using 3:4:5 triangles, the hypotenuse of $\triangle ABC$ must be 10.

Getting to the Answer:

We have 3 cases for which side of $\triangle ABC$ corresponds to the side of $\triangle JKL$ that's length 120:

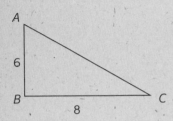

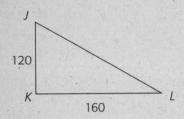

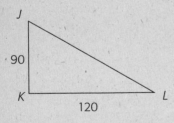

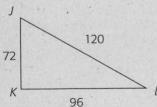

In the first case, the triangle is scaled up by a factor of 20, in the second case by a factor of 15, and in the third case by a factor of 12. Using the formula for the area of a triangle, the areas are 9600, 5400, and 3456, respectively.

12. 100

Difficulty: Medium

Strategic Advice: Remember that median means "middle number".

Getting to the Answer:

$$x + (x + 1) + (x + 2) + (x + 3) + (x + 4) = 500$$
$$5x + 10 = 500$$
$$5x = 490$$
$$x = 98$$

This is the smallest number. The median one will be $x + 2$, or 100.

13. 4

Difficulty: Medium

Strategic Advice: Use the graph to find the value of $h(x)$, then use the y-coordinate in your k function.

Getting to the Answer:

$$k(-2) = h\left(\frac{-2}{2}\right) + 3 = h(-1) + 3 = 1 + 3 = 4$$

$(h(-1) = 1$ came from the point $(-1,1)$ on the graph)

14. 120

Difficulty: High

Strategic Advice: How many choices does the first friend have? Then how many ponies does that leave for the second friend?

Getting to the Answer:

The first friend has their choice of 5 ponies, which leaves 4 for the second friend, 3 for the third friend, 2 for the fourth friend, and the last one is stuck with the last pony. So the number of possibilities is

$$5 \times 4 \times 3 \times 2 \times 1 = 120$$

15. 50

Difficulty: Medium

Strategic Advice: Try to find the other angles of $\triangle ABC$

Getting to the Answer:

Since $\triangle ABC$ is isosceles, angle B is also 50°, and angle ACB is $180° - 50° - 50° = 80°$

ACD is a line, so

$$80° + x + x = 180°$$
$$80° + 2x = 180°$$
$$2x = 100°$$
$$x = 50°$$

16. $\frac{4}{3}$ or 1.33

Difficulty: Medium

Strategic Advice: Evaluate each side of the equation by plugging into the definitions, then solve for a.

Getting to the Answer:

$$4 \Rightarrow (3a) = 2(4) + 3(3a) = 8 + 9a$$
$$4 \Leftarrow (3a) = 3(4) + 2(3a) = 12 + 6a$$

Since these are equal, $8 + 9a = 12 + 6a$

$$9a = 4 + 6a$$
$$3a = 4$$
$$a = \frac{4}{3}$$

17. $\frac{1}{2}$

Difficulty: High

Strategic Advice: Find the possible values of s and d, then determine which will give you the largest slope through the two points. Notice that x and y are not in their usual positions in the equation.

Getting to the Answer:

First, plug $(5, s)$ into the equation of the function: $5 = 2s^2 + 3$

$$2 = 2s^2$$
$$1 = s^2$$
$$s = 1, -1$$

Now do the same with $(11, d)$:

$$11 = 2d^2 + 3$$
$$8 = 2d^2$$
$$4 = d^2$$
$$d = 2, -2$$

The slope through $(5, s)$ and $(11, d)$ is $\dfrac{d - s}{11 - 5} = \dfrac{d - s}{6}$

To make this as large as possible, choose $d = 2, s = -1$, so that the slope is

$$\frac{d - s}{6} = \frac{2 - (-1)}{6} = \frac{3}{6} = \frac{1}{2}$$

18. 30

Difficulty: High

Strategic Advice: Write out a chart with rate, time, and distance and fill in what you know. Then try to use that to solve for the distance. If it took her t hours to get to the circus, and the total trip was 2.2 hours, how long (in terms of t) did she spend returning?

Getting to the Answer:

2 hours and 12 min $= 2 + \dfrac{12}{60} = 2.2$ hours

	rate	time	distance
To circus	30 mph	t	d
From circus	25 mph	$2.2 - t$	d

Now use the rate formula $r \times t = d$ for both parts of the trip:

$$30 \times t = d$$
$$25 \times (2.2 - t) = d$$

Since both are equal to d, you can set them equal and solve for t:

$$25(2.2 - t) = 30 \times t$$
$$55 - 25t = 30t$$
$$55 = 55t$$
$$t = 1$$

Now plug back in to solve for d:

$$30 \times t = d$$
$$30 \times 1 = d$$
$$d = 30$$

SECTION 5

1. C

Difficulty: Medium

To be grammatically complete, a sentence must have a subject and verb in an independent clause.

As written, this sentence is a fragment, since neither of the clauses is independent. (C) changes the gerund (*–ing*) verb form (which can never be the main verb in a sentence) to an acceptable predicate verb. (B) alters the meaning of the sentence (*adamant and opposed to* is not the same as *adamantly opposed*). (D) does not address the error. (E) introduces an inconsistent verb tense.

2. D

Difficulty: Medium

A sentence may have multiple nouns and verbs and still be a fragment.

(D) corrects the fragment error by inserting a predicate verb, *is*. (B) and (C) do not address the error. (E) eliminates the cause-and-effect relationship between the clauses that is present in the original.

3. A

Difficulty: High

In Improving Sentences questions, (A) always repeats the underlined selection, so don't waste time reading this choice on Test Day.

This sentence contains no error; the correct choice is (A). (B), (C), (D), and (E) are all incorrect grammatical structure.

4. D

Difficulty: Medium

Pronouns without clear antecedents will be incorrect on the SAT.

The pronoun *they* in this sentence has no antecedent. (C), (D), and (E) all correct this error, but (C) and (E) are sentence fragments. (B) does not address the error.

5. E

Difficulty: High

Make sure any modifying words and phrases are properly placed for the words they are intended to modify.

As written, and in (B), it is *the Eiffel Tower* that is *taking a...tour of Paris.* Only (E) places the correct noun, *Emily,* after the modifying phrase. In (C) and (D), the noun being modified is *stop* (a possessive noun acts grammatically as an adjective).

6. D

Difficulty: Medium

Although there are a number of ways to correct a run-on sentence, only one answer choice will do so without adding additional errors.

(D) corrects the run-on by making the second clause of the sentence subordinate; it also correctly expresses the cause-and-effect relationship between the clauses. (B) is incorrect grammatical structure. (C) leaves the meaning of the second clause incomplete. (E) uses the pronoun *whose,* which is only correct when used to refer to people.

7. B

Difficulty: Medium

The gerund (*–ing*) verb form can never be the predicate (main) verb in a sentence.

(B) corrects this sentence fragment by replacing the gerund form *being* with *were.* (C) does not address the error. (D)

introduces the passive voice unnecessarily. (E) is awkward and unnecessarily wordy.

8. C

Difficulty: Medium

Although conjunctions may keep a sentence from being a run-on, if they don't properly relate the sentence's clauses, they will not be correct on the SAT.

The conjunction *and* does not properly relate the ideas in these two clauses. (C) corrects the error. (B) is incorrect grammatical structure. (D) creates a sentence fragment. (E) is awkward and unnecessarily wordy.

9. C

Difficulty: High

The comparative idiom takes the following structure: *for...than for.*

(C) corrects the idiom. (B), (D), and (E) use a plural verb (*are*) with a singular subject (*way*).

10. B

Difficulty: Medium

A pronoun without a clear antecedent will be incorrect on the SAT.

The problem here is that we do not know what *it* refers to. (B) clarifies that the athletes' *struggle to win* is what people can identify with. In (C) and (D), *The reason is...because* is redundant. (E) uses an inconsistent verb tense and a plural pronoun (*they*) with a singular antecedent (*interest*).

11. D

Difficulty: High

When a sentence contains more than one error, make sure your answer choice addresses them all.

This sentence has two problems. First, the pronoun *it* is used without an antecedent. This is common usage in everyday speech, but will be incorrect on the SAT. Additionally, since *it* is the first noun or pronoun after the modifying phrase, *it* is what was *Brought up in a small suburban town.* (D) corrects both errors. (B) is grammatically incorrect structure. *Going to work* and *life* are modified by the opening phrase in (C) and (E), respectively.

12. B

Difficulty: Medium

Subjects and verbs must agree in number.

Since *class* is singular, the verb should also be in the singular form; the error is in (B). (A) correctly uses an adverb to modify a verb form. (C) parallels *for developing* and (D) uses the correct preposition with *understandable*.

13. B

Difficulty: Medium

Some constructions require specific prepositions to be correct; others must be followed by an infinitive verb form.

When used in this context, *managed* must be followed by an infinitive; (B) should read *to prevent*. (A) agrees with its singular subject *weather*. (C) and (D) are correct idiomatic usage.

14. E

Difficulty: High

Don't mistake complex sentence structure for grammatical error; between five and eight Writing section sentences will be correct as written.

(A) parallels *eliminating*. (B) correctly uses *outdated* as an adjective. (C) is an appropriate verb tense in context. (D) correctly relates the ideas in the two clauses.

15. D

Difficulty: Low

Adjectives can only modify nouns or pronouns. To modify any other part of speech, an adverb is needed.

The problem is in (D). Since *purchase* is used here as a verb, the word modifying it should be an adverb, not an adjective. The verb in (A) agrees with its singular subject and *that* is properly used as a conjunction. (B) is an appropriate verb tense in context. (C) is proper use of the infinitive.

16. A

Difficulty: Low

Subjects and verbs must agree in number.

Since *schedule* is singular, the verb in (A) should be "has," not *have*. (B) correctly uses an adverb to modify *will...take*. (C) and (D) are proper idiomatic usage.

17. D

Difficulty: Medium

Unless context makes it clear that more than one time frame is referenced, verb tenses within a sentence should be consistent.

The verb in (D) should be consistent with the past tense *left* in the first clause. (A) and (C) are appropriate pronouns in context. (B) is correct idiomatic usage.

18. D

Difficulty: Medium

A conjunction phrase that begins with *neither* must be completed with *nor*.

Since this sentence uses *neither*, (D) should read "nor." (A) correctly relates the ideas in the two clauses. (B) is the appropriate possessive pronoun with *doctors*. (C) agrees with its singular subject *research*.

19. C

Difficulty: Medium

Related nouns in a sentence must agree in number.

Orders have more than one life, so "their lives" would be correct in (C). The verb in (A) agrees with the singular *Sister Margaret*, and the idiom is correct in context. (B) agrees with its plural subject *nuns*. (D) is correct use of the infinitive.

20. A

Difficulty: Low

Use context to determine the appropriate verb tenses.

To be consistent, (A) should be the past tense *spent*. (B), (C), and (D) are correctly used idiomatic phrases.

21. A

Difficulty: Medium

Look for clues in sentence to determine if transition words are correct.

"In which," rather than *that*, would be the correct transition in (A). (B) correctly uses an adverb to modify the verb phrase *are rising*. (C) uses the pronoun *itself* for emphasis. (D) uses the superlative correctly, since there are more than two middle-class families.

22. A

Difficulty: Medium

If an underlined compound contains a pronoun, read the sentence with just the pronoun to check the case. Since you wouldn't say *Jonathan asked I…*, you've found your error.

The objective pronoun case should be used in (A); "Jonathan and me" would be correct here. (B) and (D) are correct idiomatic usage. (C) is the appropriate verb tense with *if.*

23. E

Difficulty: High

Check each answer choice methodically, but remember that between five and eight sentences are likely to have no error.

(A), (B), and (D) are correct idiomatic usage. (C) agrees with its singular subject, *collection*.

24. D

Difficulty: Medium

Most SAT sentences will have multiple nouns and verbs; make sure each verb agrees with the appropriate noun, which may not be the noun closest to it in the sentence.

The subject of *figures* is the plural pronoun *they*; (D) should be "figure." (A) uses an appropriate verb tense in context. *Which*, in (B), is correct to refer back to *plan.* (C) is correct idiomatic usage.

25. A

Difficulty: Medium

An idiom may be grammatically correct, but misused in context.

Although you can "look to" someone for advice, the correct preposition with *look* in this context is "at"; the error is in (A). (B) is appropriate use of *that* as a conjunction. (C) and (D) are correct idiomatic usage.

26. C

Difficulty: Medium

If a sentence does not make a pronoun's antecedent clear, the pronoun is incorrectly used.

Since we don't know the gender of either of the subjects, the pronoun *she* in (C) is ambiguous. The plural verb form

is correct in (A), since the subject is a compound. (B) correctly expresses the contrast between the clauses. (D) is idiomatically correct usage.

27. E

Difficulty: High

Eliminate answer choices methodically, but remember—some sentences will be correct as written.

This sentence is correct as written. (A) and (B) are idiomatically correct. (C) agrees with its singular subject. (D) is correct use of the superlative, since there are more than two *mammals…in existence.*

28. A

Difficulty: Medium

Related nouns and pronouns in a sentence must agree in number.

Since *us* is plural, the plural "photographers" would be correct in (A). (B) agrees with its plural subject *cameras.* (C) and (D) are correct idiomatic usage in context.

29. E

Difficulty: High

Eliminate answer choices methodically; choose (E) if the sentence contains no error.

(A) correctly uses an adverb to modify an adjective, and an adjective to modify a noun. (B) and (C) agree with their singular subjects, *news* and *family*, respectively. (D) properly uses *more* as an adverb.

30. C

Difficulty: High

In Improving Paragraphs, a pronoun's antecedent may appear in an earlier passage, but it should still be unambiguous and the noun and pronoun must agree in number.

The only possible plural antecedents for *They* are *ice breakers* and *people,* neither of which makes sense in context. (C) eliminates the ambiguity and corrects the agreement error. Deleting or moving the sentence would make the paragraph difficult to understand. *Which* is the correct pronoun in context, and (E) does not agree with the verb's singular subject *bow.*

31. D

Difficulty: Medium

Remember, in this section, choice (A) will not repeat the original selection. Read (A) as carefully as you do the other choices.

Here, sentence 6 is a fragment. Combining the two sentences with a comma splice is the simplest way to correct this. Neither sentence contains a logical antecedent for *which* in (A). (B) creates an illogical cause-and-effect relationship between the clauses. (C) leaves the meaning of the second clause incomplete. (E) creates a run-on sentence.

32. D

Difficulty: High

Check all pronouns for clear antecedents.

In context, the meaning of the pronoun *this* is unclear. (D) eliminates the ambiguity by adding a noun to clarify the meaning. (B) does not address the error, and uses a transition word that is inappropriate in context. (C) changes the pronoun from *this* to *it*, but there is still no clear antecedent. (E) changes the meaning of the sentence.

33. A

Difficulty: High

Use context clues to determine the proper placement of new information.

Since sentence 8 begins with *Rather*, the sentence that comes before should provide a contrast to the idea that design features are what allow ice breakers to do their job. (A) does so. (B) is out of scope and also uses a pronoun without a clear antecedent. (C) would need to be followed by a sentence that answered the question. Global warming is discussed in paragraph 1 and other uses for ice breakers in paragraph 3, which eliminates (D) and (E).

34. E

Difficulty: Medium

One way of correcting a run-on sentence is to make one of the clauses subordinate.

As written, this sentence is a run-on. (E) makes the second clause dependent without introducing any additional errors. (B) creates an inappropriate cause-and-effect relationship between the clauses. (C) is grammatically incorrect. (D)

uses the semicolon splice incorrectly; a semicolon must connect two independent clauses.

35. D

Difficulty: Medium

Your reading comprehension skills will be helpful in about half of all Improving Paragraph questions.

All of the answer choices but (D) provide information that is pertinent to the passage's topic except for (B) since sentence 4 already implies this information.

SECTION 6

1. B

Difficulty: Low

Look for the hot words that indicate what the charges of the blanked words are. Contaminated water is a "threat" to public health because of "toxic chemicals" and "also because" of what kind of chemicals? Good or bad? Would contaminated water that poses a threat to health cause positive or negative "physiological and psychological responses"?

Both blanks should be filled with a prediction that has a negative charge. For the first blank, scan the answer choices for a word that means "unpleasant." A good prediction for the second blank is "harmful."

In (A), although the first word is negatively charged, it is a little extreme. It means more along the lines of "obscenely abusive" rather than "offensive." This choice can be eliminated based on the second blank as the negative physiological and psychological responses are not "elusive" because they are indeed detectable. Choice (B) is the correct answer. In (C), the first choice doesn't quite match the prediction. The second choice is out of scope because the sentence is not discussing whether these types of responses have occurred in previous cases. In (D), the first choice means "soothing" and hence is the opposite of the prediction. For the second blank, all that can be deduced is that the responses are negative but they are not necessarily "numbing." In (E), this choice can be eliminated based on both blanks. The first word is neutral and does not match the prediction. The second choice is positively charged.

2.   C

Difficulty: Low

Although there are many things Lincoln was admired for, the hot words clue you into what the blanked word should be. Even if you didn't know that the Gettysburg Address was a famous speech, the hot words "Lincoln. . .was admired" for his two "inaugural speeches" indicate that the blank is referring to his ability to speak in public.

A good prediction is "skillful speaker." Eliminate answer choices that do not match this prediction.

In (A), Lincoln was President at a time when laws and customs were being challenged and was anything but a "conformist." In (B), whether or not Lincoln expressed moralistic opinions is not what the sentence is discussing. Choice (C) is the credited answer. In (D), "rivals" do not necessarily "admire" each other for their speeches. This choice would only be correct if the sentence mentioned an opponent. Choice (E) means "a person from one's own country" and does not match the prediction. A fellow countryman is not by definition a great speaker.

3.   B

Difficulty: Medium

The prediction must be positive as the mushers were "heroic" and relayed the serum across miles of "frigid Alaskan wilderness."

Eliminate all answer choices that do not mean "heroic" or "courageous."

Choice (A) means "understanding" and does not match the prediction. Choice (B) is the correct answer. In (C), although the mushers raced the serum as "fast" and "efficiently" as they could, the hot words indicate that the blank is describing their bravery; not their pace. In (D), *idiosyncratic* means "a behavioral characteristic peculiar to a group." It tends to refer to a peculiarity and does not match the prediction. In (E), the intelligence of the mushers did not provide the courage it took to relay the serum; brains and determination are two different characteristics.

4.   B

Difficulty: Medium

Start with the first blank. Those who chose to be "honest" entered the court proceedings with what kind of an attitude? This attitude was "not found in most" of those accused, as they "refused to talk" about the crime.

Those who were "honest" entered the proceedings with a "straightforwardness" or "honesty" not found in those who were more "reticent" or "uncommunicative."

In (A), neither choice matches the predictions. The second choice clearly does not fit with the hot words that describe the second blank. Choice (B) is the credited answer. Eliminate (C) based on the first blank. In (D), the second choice is the opposite of the prediction. In (E), neither choice matches the predictions and the first choice has a negative rather than a positive charge.

5.   E

Difficulty: Medium

The sentence mentions a technique required to map the structure of something very small.

Franklin mapped the structure of DNA, which is "tiny." Your prediction should be synonymous with "small."

In (A), *comprehensive* means "inclusive" or "extensive" and does not match the prediction. In (B), "deceptive" is not the correct word to describe molecules. Choice (C) means "overwhelming" and is not the correct choice. In choice (D), this word means "limited" and does not match the prediction. Choice (E) is the credited answer.

6.   B

Difficulty: Medium

Given that certain dreams have "common themes," look at the relationship between the blanks. If the dreams share something in common then they must ---- "generations and cultures."

Common dreams have come to be known as "widespread" dreams as they "are found across" all generations and cultures.

Eliminate (A) based on the first blank; *provincial* means "local." Choice (B) is the credited answer. In (C), the first choice is the opposite of the prediction. *Deride* means "ridicule" and does not make sense in the context of the sentence. Eliminate (D) based on the second choice; "grasp" does match the prediction. In (E), those who study dreams are not arguing that some are *intuitive* or "instinctual," only that certain dreams are common. These dreams "transcend" generations and cultures, but do not necessarily "describe" them.

7. E

Difficulty: High

Focus on the hot words that describe each blank. What kind of a decision would be made by a "panicked" hunter that caused a huge fire? For the second blank, how would you describe hills that are "barren" and consist of nothing but the remains of burnt trees?

A good prediction for the first blank is "incautious" or "unwise." For the second blank, look for a choice that is synonymous with "barren." Eliminate all answer choices that do not match both of these predictions; go through the choices and eliminate based on one blank and then eliminate based on the other blank.

Eliminate (A) based on the first blank; "conscientious" or "careful" is the opposite of the prediction. In (B), "incompetent" or "inadequate" does not match the prediction for the first blank. The second choice is the opposite of the prediction for the second blank. Eliminate (C) based on the first blank; it is the opposite of the prediction. In (D), both choices are the opposite of the predictions. Choice (E) is the credited answer.

8. A

Difficulty: High

The blank is described by the first clause.

The keyword "such" indicates that the description of the "flow of the orator's words" in the first clause also describes the blank in the second clause. If the flow became more "steady and rhythmic," then it was *modulated*. Some of the vocab words in the answer choices might not look familiar, so if you can't find one to match the prediction, eliminate those that don't fit.

Choice (A) fits your prediction; *cadent* is the adjective form of the noun "cadence," which is a rhythmic flow. In (B), the word *specious* implies deception (seeming true but actually false), which doesn't fit the context. Choice (C) is opposite to your prediction—*convoluted* speaking would be unsteady and non-rhythmic. In (D), speaking can certainly be "adulatory" (or admiring), but it is "adulatory" toward the topic of the speech, and you can't make that distinction here. In (E), again, you don't know if the speaking as "impassioned," just that it is "steady" and "rhythmic."

9. D

Difficulty: High

Look for clues in the text around the cited word, and remember that the most obvious meaning is rarely the correct answer.

The author uses the word "movement" to refer to the revolution, which is an *occurrence* or *development*. Look for an answer choice that reflects this.

Choice (A) is out of scope; the author is not using the word to talk about advancement or improvement. Choice (B) is out of scope; the author is not talking about spatial movement. Choice (C) is out of scope; the author is not using the word "movement" to talk about population movement within the country. Choice (D) fits your prediction nicely. Choice (E) is out of scope; again, the author is not discussing spatial motion.

10. A

Difficulty: Medium

The question is asking you what function the steam engine serves in the passage. Look for clues in the sentences around the mentioned text.

Two sentences before the cited text, the author states that the "chief factors" in the Industrial Revolution were technological innovations. Make an appropriate prediction based on this.

Choice (A) matches your prediction nicely. Choice (B) is out of scope; though the author may very well believe the inventors were talented, this is not the purpose of the reference. Choice (C) is an opposite; the author maintains that technology affected both society and the economy, not the other way around. Choice (D) is out of scope; the author never refers to *railroads*. Choice (E) is out of scope; though he may admire Watt, the author never expresses an opinion or any *sense of admiration*.

11. D

Difficulty: Low

The question asks for a viewpoint that both authors would agree upon. Think about the main idea of each passage, and use elimination to narrow down the answer choices if necessary.

Although the authors disagree on what changes were important—social revolution versus technological innovation—they both agree that the Industrial Revolution was a time of great change. Look for an answer choice that reflects this.

Choice (A) is distortion; only the first author maintains this point of view. Choice (B) is distortion; only the second author maintains this point of view. Choice (C) is out of scope; neither author ever mentions the revolution being a change *for the worse*. Choice (D) matches your prediction. Choice (E) is distortion; only the first author discusses the decline of the *agrarian economy*.

12. C

Difficulty: Medium

The question is asking you to spell out the difference between the two interpretations. Find where population growth is mentioned in each passage and use the text around it to make a prediction.

In Passage 1, population growth is mentioned as one of the factors responsible for the changes of the Industrial Revolution. Passage 2 states that it "provided an apt environment" but was not among the "chief factors." Make a prediction that reflects this.

Choice (A) is distortion; Passage 1 claims that the population increase was a *major factor*. Choice (B) is distortion; Passage 2 specifically mentions that population growth helped to set the stage for the Industrial Revolution. Choice (C) matches your prediction nicely. Choice (D) is out of scope; neither passage mentions where population growth occurred. Choice (E) is out of scope; while the second part may seem reasonable, nothing in Passage 1 supports the idea that the relationship between these factors *has been distorted*.

13. E

Difficulty: Medium

Although this question does not mention any specific details to point you to the correct answer choice, review the main arguments of Passage 1; the correct choice will likely agree closely with one of the author's major points.

Generally speaking, the author of Passage 1 writes much more negatively about the film industry than does the author of Passage 2. Predict that the correct choice will involve the first author's critiques of the cinema.

Choice (A) is out of scope; neither passage ever discusses the issue of literacy rates. Choice (B) is a misused detail; television is a topic only mentioned in Passage 2. Choice (C) is an opposite; Passage 1 argues that film has had a

negative impact on literature, not a positive one. Choice (D) is a misused detail; this point would be more appropriate for Passage 2. Choice (E) is the best fit for your prediction.

14. C

Difficulty: High

Pay particular attention to phrases and elaborations that occur close to the quoted material; they often contain significant clues about the author's intended meaning.

The author follows these words with the phrase "which appear the same to everyone," so you should predict that the answer has to do with the words' looking the same to all readers.

Choice (A) is out of scope; neither passage makes the argument for the novel's *universal appeal*. Choice (B) is distortion; the author is not really arguing that the appearance of the letters affects the reader's perception of the story. Choice (C) matches your prediction nicely. Choice (D) is distortion; the author is making the point that everyone understands stories slightly differently. Choice (E) is out of scope; no particular *misconception* is mentioned in this part of the passage.

15. D

Difficulty: High

Re-read and paraphrase the sentence in question, bearing in mind that you may also have to read part of the preceding paragraph in order to draw a proper inference.

This sentence refers to the contention that each reader visualizes a piece of writing somewhat differently, as mentioned in the passage's first paragraph, and suggests that this process is "fundamental" to writing. Use this paraphrase, or a similar one, as the basis of your prediction.

Choice (A) is distortion; the author is not trying to compare the imaginations of readers to those of writers. Choice (B) is extreme; although the author is arguing for a particular property of writing, he does not go so far as to say that it is the only art form that is intellectually stimulating. Choice (C) is a misused detail; this answer choice refers to a detail further on in the passage, but it draws a conclusion that is not well supported by the text. Choice (D) is a good match for your prediction. Choice (E) is extreme; the author is not necessarily suggesting that all good writing involves *lifelike* visualizations, but merely a bit of imagination.

16. E

Difficulty: Medium

Reasoning questions require you to extract the essence of an argument and apply it to a new situation. Start by paraphrasing the quoted sentence, while trying to remove the particular details specific to this passage.

This sentence is basically saying that when a person exhibits his own interpretation of a work, he keeps others from reaching their own interpretations independently. Find the choice that best captures the idea of sharing one's interpretation of a work of art.

Choice (A) is out of scope; since the memories are *known only to* the screenwriter, any viewer would be unable to develop a personal interpretation of them. Choice (B) is distortion; although this choice describes the act of writing about another work, it does not share the passage's sense of interpretation and imagination. Choice (C) is distortion; the author of the passage is talking about interpretations of artworks, not merely explanatory figures in textbooks. Choice (D) is out of scope; the passage is concerned with interpreting others' works, not describing the ideas behind one's own. Choice (E) best fits your prediction.

17. A

Difficulty: Medium

For questions like this, you simply have to discover how the author is using the quoted phrase in the context of the passage. Go back and re-read the sentence, paraphrasing the words in the question.

Here, the author is talking about people enjoying books, and how that enjoyment is lessened by the way film adaptations reduce the imaginative possibilities resulting from reading. Use this as the basis of your prediction.

Choice (A) is a good match for your prediction, just made slightly more general. Choice (B) is out of scope; ease of understanding is not brought up in Passage 1. Choice (C) is a misused detail; this would be more appropriate for Passage 2. Choice (D) is out of scope; the author of Passage 1 never specifically discusses occasions when reading is or was the only entertainment available. Choice (E) is an opposite; the author believes the ability to imagine things for oneself makes the reading experience better than that of seeing a movie.

18. B

Difficulty: Medium

Go back and scan the discussion in question again. Ask yourself what the author's argument is here, and whether it is similar to or different from the arguments that have appeared in the passage so far.

The author asserts that film adaptations are less enjoyable than the original books are because the element of imagination is missing, which is a continuation of the argument about film adaptations that began in the second paragraph. Use this as the basis of your prediction.

Choice (A) is an opposite; the argument here is well in line with the author's previously expressed point of view. Choice (B) is the best fit for your prediction. Choice (C) is an opposite; this discussion is actually well in line with the author's views. Choice (D) is out of scope; no particular *film examples* are mentioned here. Choice (E) is out of scope; the author never makes the distinction between *average books* and *great* ones.

19. B

Difficulty: Medium

This question requires both specific knowledge of the quoted material as well as general knowledge of the first author's opinions. Make sure you review both before trying to form a prediction.

The "powerful messages" being discussed are those made in films, and although the first author mentions that good films can exist, he generally prefers books because they are more engaging to the imagination. Use this as a starting point for your prediction.

Choice (A) is out of scope; the potential dangers of wide-reaching messages are never discussed. Choice (B) works well with your prediction. Choice (C) is distortion; although the author of Passage 1 is often critical of film, he never asserts that it is incapable of *delivering ideas clearly*. Choice (D) is a misused detail; this is more in line with the arguments in Passage 2. Choice (E) is out of scope; neither author makes the point that the sights and sounds of film make their messages more complex.

20. E

Difficulty: Medium

Remember that function questions build on the author's argument in the given reference, so paraphrasing the author's original sentence is usually a good start.

In this part of the passage, the author argues for the superiority of film over television, despite the argument by some that they are similar forms of cheap entertainment. Predict that the correct answer hinges on this distinction between television and film.

Choice (A) is distortion; although the author claims that film is more enduring, he never claims that it is more difficult to understand. Choice (B) is an opposite; the author is actually arguing for a difference between these media, not a similarity. Choice (C) is out of scope; the author never makes the distinction between theatrical viewing and home viewing. Choice (D) is a misused detail; the author never argues that being based on printed material is what makes film superior to television. Choice (E) matches your prediction well.

21. B

Difficulty: High

In this question you must not only understand the author's point but also muddle through some tough vocabulary. Make sure to predict your answer ahead of time so that you don't get tricked by tempting words.

In these two sentences, the author says that film's importance should be as well regarded as literature, although it should not actually replace reading. Look for an answer choice that agrees with this viewpoint.

Choice (A) is extreme; *irreplaceable* expresses too strong a sentiment. Choice (B) is the best match for your prediction. Choice (C) is an opposite; the author believes the impact of film is quite important, not *transitory*. Choice (D) is distortion; neither word captures the author's thrust in the passage. Choice (E) is extreme; *paramount* is too strong a word for film's importance, and the author never claims that film is not *well established*.

22. D

Difficulty: Low

Don't rely on your memory of the passage; you want to make sure that your prediction fits the exact sentence that is being quoted, not another argument from elsewhere in the passage. Go back and refresh your memory before doing anything else.

In this sentence, the author stresses the similarity of screenplays and stage plays, mentioning that the latter are "one of the oldest and most revered of all literary forms." Predict that the author is using the stage play to enhance the prestige of screenplays.

Choice (A) is a misused detail; the superiority of novels is an idea more appropriate to Passage 1. Choice (B) is distortion; although the author mentions that stage plays are an older form, he never claims that they have been *replaced* in some way by screenplays. Choice (C) is out of scope; the issue of plays based on novels never comes up in either passage. Choice (D) is the most appropriate fit for your prediction. Choice (E) is out of scope; expense and ease of production are never mentioned in the discussion of stage plays.

23. C

Difficulty: Medium

The correct answer choice will probably not just involve the detail in question, but also how it fits into the logic of the author's overall argument. Make sure you understand both the use of the detail and the overall context before making a prediction.

The author is using a rhetorical question to suggest that Shakespeare's reputation is not affected adversely by the fact that his plays were meant to be enjoyed either by reading them or in performance. Predict that the correct answer choice will involve a restatement of this idea.

Choice (A) is out of scope; although the author might believe this, Shakespeare is not used in the context of trying to predict from where the next writer of similar genius will arise. Choice (B) is distortion; the author never argues for the superiority of reading plays to watching them. Choice (C) is a good match for your prediction, restated in slightly more general terms. Choice (D) is out of scope; the author never has the explicit purpose of trying to prove his own knowledge of literature. Choice (E) is out of scope; the author never suggests that reading screenplays should take the place of watching films.

24. C

Difficulty: Medium

Remember that the use of two examples gives you two ways to rule out wrong answer choices; select only the choice that agrees with BOTH passages. If either part of an answer choice doesn't fit, cross it out.

Tolkien is mentioned as someone who defended the value of reading a story and imagining it for oneself, whereas Shakespeare is used as an example of someone who wrote great literature that was also meant to be performed onstage. Predict that the correct choice will involve this distinction.

Choice (A) is a misused detail; although Tolkien is a more recent writer than Shakespeare is, the issue of older versus modern writing never comes up in either passage. Choice (B) is out of scope; the value of fantasy writing versus realistic writing is never mentioned by either author. Choice (C) is the best fit for your prediction. Choice (D) is distortion; the first author never explicitly mentions screenplays, and would probably not be defending them even if he had. Choice (E) is an opposite; neither part of this choice is in keeping with the topic or views of either author.

SECTION 7

1. B

Difficulty: Low

Strategic Advice: Solve for a, then find b (which must be the reciprocal of a in order for the product to be 1).

Getting to the Answer:

$$6a = 48$$
$$a = 8$$
$$ab = 8b = 1$$
$$b = \frac{1}{8}$$

2. B

Difficulty: Low

Strategic Advice: Set up a proportion and do the arithmetic carefully.

Getting to the Answer:

$$\frac{5}{2} = \frac{x}{4.4}$$
$$2x = 5(4.4) = 22$$
$$x = 11$$

3. C

Difficulty: Low

Strategic Advice: Cross-multiply then simplify.

Getting to the Answer:

$$\frac{x}{y} = \frac{5}{7}$$
$$7x = 5y$$
$$\frac{7x}{5y} = \frac{5y}{5y}$$
$$\frac{7x}{5y} = 1$$

4. D

Difficulty: Low

Strategic Advice: Look for vertical angles and straight angles.

Getting to the Answer:

Angle FAE is a vertical angle with angle BAC, so it is also 30°

Then $x = 90° + 30° = 120°$

Angle FAB forms a straight angle with angle BAC, so $y = 180° - 30° = 150°$

$$\frac{x + y}{2} = \frac{120° + 150°}{2} = 135°$$

5. A

Difficulty: Low

Strategic Advice: Add up the total school time and subtract from 2:30 to find the starting time

Getting to the Answer:

Each class period is 1 hr and 20 minutes, or $1\frac{1}{3}$ or $\frac{4}{3}$ hours, so the 4 class periods are a total of $4\left(\frac{4}{3}\right) = \frac{16}{3} = 5\frac{1}{3}$ hours.

The breaks and lunch add up to $5 + 5 + 30 = 40$ minutes $= \frac{40}{60} = \frac{2}{3}$ of an hour. So the total school time is $5\frac{1}{3} + \frac{2}{3} = 6$ hours. Six hours before 2:30 is 8:30.

6. C

Difficulty: Medium

Strategic Advice: Try using your given answers on this one—remember that all 3 should be integers, and $x + 4$ is the median (middle) number

Getting to the Answer:

(C) $x = 11: 2x - 8 = 2(11) - 8 = 14, x + 4 = 11 + 4 = 15$, and $3x - 13 = 3(11) - 13 = 20$

7. A

Difficulty: Medium

Strategic Advice: You want to figure out what b has to be in order to get $225 out of the net profit equation.

Getting to the Answer:

$$P(b) = 2.5b - 100 = \$225$$
$$2.5b = \$325$$
$$b = 130$$

8. A

Difficulty: Medium

Strategic Advice: FOIL out $(x - y)^2$ and then try to substitute what you know

Getting to the Answer:

$$(x - y)^2 = (x - y)(x - y)$$
$$= x^2 - xy - xy + y^2$$
$$= x^2 - 2xy + y^2$$
$$= (x^2 + y^2) - 2(xy)$$
$$= (153) - 2(36)$$
$$= 81$$

9. E

Difficulty: Medium

Strategic Advice: Look for special triangles in order to speed up your arithmetic. It's rare that you'll have to use the Pythagorean Theorem more than once on any given question.

Getting to the Answer:

Triangle BCD is a 45–45–90 triangle, which means each of the legs has length 2. So $BC = 2$. Then since hypotenuse BC is twice leg AB for the left triangle, this must be a 30–60–90 triangle; $y = 30°$, so $z = 60°$.

10. C

Difficulty: Medium

Strategic Advice: Since it's percentages of the same number, you can forget about the "positive number." Just think about 20% of 30% is the same as 15% of what?

Getting to the Answer:

$$20\% \text{ of } 30\% = 15\% \text{ of } h$$
$$.2(.3) = .15h$$
$$.06 = .15h$$
$$h = .4 = 40\%$$

11. B

Difficulty: Medium

Strategic Advice: Each time the square is split, each smaller square is $\frac{1}{4}$ the size of the original square. How many such splits did we make?

Getting to the Answer: We made 4 splits, so the smallest squares are each $\frac{1}{4}$ of $\frac{1}{4}$ of $\frac{1}{4}$ of $\frac{1}{4}$ of the largest square, which is $\frac{1}{4} \times \frac{1}{4} \times \frac{1}{4} \times \frac{1}{4} = \frac{1}{256}$ of the largest square. Since two of the smallest squares are shaded, they are $\frac{2}{256} = \frac{1}{128}$ of the largest square.

12. E

Difficulty: Medium

Strategic Advice: Variables in the answer choices make this a great time to pick numbers.

Getting to the Answer:

Try $x = -1$ and $y = 2$, so that $-3 < 0 < 2$, as required.

(A) 0

(B) $y = 2$ (larger than A)

(C) $-3x = -3(-1) = 3$ (larger than B)

(D) $-(3x + y) = -(3(-1) + 2) = -(-3 + 2) = -(-1) = 1$ (smaller than C)

(E) $-(3x - y) = -(3(-1) - 2) = -(-3 - 2) = -(-5) = 5$ (larger than C)

So (E) is the largest

13. D

Difficulty: Medium

Strategic Advice: Write an expression for each day's Physics problems, then find the average

Getting to the Answer:

Monday $= m$

Tuesday $= 3m$

Wedesday $= 2m + 3$

Average $= \dfrac{m + (3m) + (2m + 3)}{3} = \dfrac{6m + 3}{3} = 2m + 1.$

14. D

Difficulty: High

Strategic Advice: In the question, the reciprocal of the expression is equal to itself. What numbers can you think of that have those properties?

Getting to the Answer:

First rewrite $(a + b)^{-\frac{1}{2}}$ as $\dfrac{1}{\sqrt{a + b}}$ to make it easier to work with.

The only possible numbers that are equal to their reciprocals are 1 and -1, so $\dfrac{1}{\sqrt{a + b}} = 1$ or $\dfrac{1}{\sqrt{a + b}} = -1$. Since the SAT doesn't cover imaginary numbers, only work with the first option.

$$\dfrac{1}{\sqrt{a + b}} = 1$$

$$\dfrac{1}{\sqrt{a + b}} = \dfrac{1}{1}$$

Cross-multiply, then square both sides.

$$\dfrac{1}{\sqrt{a + b}} = \dfrac{1}{1}$$

$$\sqrt{a + b} = 1$$

$$a + b = 1$$

$$a + b = 1$$

15. E

Difficulty: High

Strategic Advice: What is the x-coordinate at D? What do you know about the functions at that value?

Getting to the Answer:

Parabolas are symmetric, so each half of $\overline{CD}$ is 2. Therefore the x value at point D is 2. But the functions also intersect here, so plug in $x = 2$ to each equation and set the results equal.

$$y = x^2 + 2 = 2^2 + 2 = 6$$

$$y = -x^2 + a = -(2)^2 + a = -4 + a$$

$$6 = -4 + a$$

$$10 = a$$

16. B

Difficulty: High

Strategic Advice: Last question! Take a deep breath and think about what this description really means. A Venn diagram might be very helpful.

Getting to the Answer:

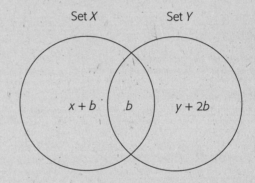

The intersection, which has b elements, is shown by the overlap of the two circles. The union is everything in both circles. We want everything in the union, but not in the intersection. This is $(x + b) + (y + 2b) = x + y + 3b$ elements.

SECTION 8

1. D

Difficulty: Low

It may be easier to start with the second blank and work backwards. Focus on the hot words at the end of the sentence: "protection . . . up to 75 years." The vaccine must have been effective for a very long time. Therefore, the "immunity" described by the first blank must have been effective for a long time.

The predictions must relate to the long amount of time the vaccine was effective for; "long" works in the first blank and "was effective for" is a good prediction for the second blank.

In (A), the first choice is the opposite of the prediction. Regarding the second choice, "protection" from a vaccine does not "develop" over time, but may actually decline over time. In (B), the first choice is outside the scope of the sentence. The sentence is not discussing whether the level of immunity was "different" for various groups of people. The second choice means "collapsed" and does not match the prediction. In (C), the sentence is not discussing whether people experienced "variable" levels of immunity. Also, protection would not decline "up to" a certain number of years, but would "decline for" those years. Choice (D) is the credited answer. In (E), the first choice does not match the prediction. The second choice is too extreme.

2. B

Difficulty: Low

Would a committee be established to increase or decrease "undesirable" traffic impacts?

Eliminate all answer choices that do not match the prediction "reduce."

In (A), this word means "guarantee" and is the opposite of the prediction. Choice (B) is the correct answer. In (C), the committee was established to reduce pollution and congestion, not move it elsewhere. Choice (D) is the opposite of the prediction. In (E), if the committee was established to *trivialize* or play down the importance of the problem, they would not put effort into solving it by planning the development of pedestrian pathways.

3. C

Difficulty: Medium

Since advisors are warning the congressman to speak directly and intelligibly, he must not be speaking very clearly. If his manner of speaking is unclear, it would require explanation or (A), *elucidation*. In choice (B), *mystification* would further bewilder voters. In choice (C), *recitation*, or repetition, would do nothing to clear up the speech. *Alliteration*, (D), and *vocalization*, (E), have nothing to do with clarifying speech for listeners.

4. A

Difficulty: Medium

How might you consider an action you thought extremely reprehensible?

All you know about the action is that it must have been bad to be considered *reprehensible*, and that if the principal "refused to accept any excuse" then he must have also considered it *inexcusable* or *unjustifiable*, both great predictions for the blank.

Choice (A) is a perfect fit given your prediction. In (B), just because the action was "reprehensible" and inexcusable does not mean it was necessarily sneaky or done *surreptitiously*. In (C), the sentence only emphasizes the inexcusable nature of the action, not that it necessarily took an *indefatigable* or tireless effort. In (D), nothing in the sentence indicates whether the action was complete or all-inclusive. In (E), the action would probably not have been reprehensible if it had been capable of fixing anything.

5. D

Difficulty: High

The cause and effect statement in the sentence is one of action and reaction. Johnson's play was criticized for being too *verbose*, too wordy. *Convinced* by the criticism, Johnson sought to make his play less verbose; he *abbreviated* it, making it shorter, or *more succinct*. In choice (A), *expanded* means increased; and *concise* means expressing much in a few words, so the two words are more nearly opposite in meaning than the allied words called for by the sentence. *Curtailed*, in choice (B), means cut short or interrupted; and *prolix* means tediously wordy, so again the words work against each other. *Promulgated*, (C), means proclaimed or announced, and *insouciant* means blithely unconcerned. In choice (E), *fostered* means nurtured or cultivated; and *pliant* means easily bent or shaped

6. E

Difficulty: High

Look at the structural clue provided by the semicolon; what follows describes the type of behavior typified by the blanked word. The words "that is" followed by a comma also indicate that a definition of the word that follows. Think of a word that means "narrowing of view."

"Short-sighted" is a good prediction. Eliminate all choices that do not match the prediction.

In (A), the behavior of someone who is "short-sighted" is not necessarily *indecisive*. In (B), this word means "bossy" and does not match the prediction. In (C), a word that means bitter is not the correct choice. Choice (D) is the opposite of the prediction; it means "careful." Choice (E) is the credited answer.

7. D

Difficulty: High

It is always important to keep in mind the general tone of the text, as incorrect answer choices can usually be eliminated for not fitting with the author's tone or meaning.

Notice that while the author mentions some of the "unrivaled" strengths of the human brain, nowhere in the text is one animal's brain described as superior to another. The sentence beginning with the words "And while these relative strengths and weaknesses..." clearly illustrates this non-judgmental tone, and indicates that the author is comparing the brain capabilities of various animals to describe how the human brain differs and can be distinguished.

Choice (A) is distortion; this choice does not match the tone of the text, which does not describe one animal's brain as more sophisticated than another. Choice (B) is a misused detail; while the author's comparisons may have this effect, nowhere is the diversity of brain types mentioned or focused on in the passage. Choice (C) is out of scope; the author only mentions the human brain as having "plasticity." Choice (D) is a great fit for your prediction. Choice (E) is distortion; the author praises the sensory abilities of both animals and humans.

8. C

Difficulty: Medium

Make sure to consider the surrounding context before making your answer selection.

Notice that the cited content here is being used as an example that supports the preceding sentence: "In terms of what it can do, the human brain is in some ways unable to match the brain functioning of 'lower' animals; in other ways, its capabilities are quite unrivaled." In other words, the cited content supports the idea that the brain capabilities of different animals vary so dramatically that it is hard to compare one to another.

Choice (A) is distortion; while the paragraph does not focus on cats and dogs nowhere is it suggested that this information is irrelevant. Choice (B) is out of scope; the paragraph does not discuss how humans have historically represented our sensory capabilities. Choice (C) is the best fit given your prediction. Choice (D) is extreme; while the cited content begins to make this point, it does not go so far as to suggest that it is impossible. Choice (E) is out of scope; the

paragraph does not mention any great weaknesses of the brains of cats and dogs.

9. B

Difficulty: Medium

When answering a function question always read the cited content in the context of the larger paragraph's focus.

As the second paragraph focuses on explaining how the plasticity of the human brain is independent of its actual physical size, it is likely that the cited content is advancing this point. The word "however" that comes in the following sentence also indicates that the cited content is being used to set up this larger point.

Choice (A) is out of scope; the paragraph does not indicate when most human brain *development* takes place, only that adult brain size is nearly achieved before the age of two. Choice (B) is a good fit for your prediction. Choice (C) is out of scope; again, the paragraph does not explore when most human brain development takes place. Choice (D) is distortion; the paragraph suggests, especially through the rat experiment, that the brains of other animals also demonstrate plasticity. Choice (E) is distortion; the paragraph only suggests that the skull inhibits size, but not capability expansion.

10. B

Difficulty: Low

Never answer a detail question from memory; instead, go back and re-familiarize yourself with the facts presented in the text.

In this case, the author states that the human brain experience such changes because of usage, practice, and experience"; in other words, due to how one's brain is used during life.

Choice (A) is out of scope; the author does not connect brain structure to capacity. Choice (B) is a perfect match for your prediction. Choice (C) is out of scope; the author only mentions experiences in general, not necessarily challenging ones. Choice (D) is out of scope; the author does not connect age and body size with brain capacity. Choice (E) is out of scope; the author only mentions these abilities as characteristics of human brain capabilities, but not as reasons for capability expansion.

11. A

Difficulty: Low

Don't worry too much about what you know of any given word and focus only on how this word fits within the sentence where it is used.

In this case, notice that earlier in the sentence the word "attributed" is used in essentially the same way as the cited word; that is, *connecting* the characteristics and capabilities of the human brain with the concept of plasticity.

Choice (A) is a great match for your prediction. Choice (B) fits with the primary definition of the cited word, but not its context in the passage. Choice (C) matches another meaning of the cited word, but the author is implying more than just the idea of a search. Choice (D) also fits with the cited word but not its specific meaning here. In choice (E), the author is not simply suggesting that these characteristics have been "found," but that the neuroscientists have attributed, or connected, them to the brain's plasticity.

12. E

Difficulty: Medium

Again, make sure to keep in mind the author's overall tone when looking at answer choices.

In this case, as the author uses a purely informational, scientific, and objective tone throughout the paragraph, so a particularly subjective word, such as "improve," might appear out of place. By adding the cited phrase, the author is acknowledging that the word "improve" is quite subjective by indicating that it is simply an opinion of some.

Choice (A) is distortion; the author is only pointing out that the word "improve" is opinionated, but not necessarily inappropriate. Choice (B) is distortion; the word "biased" suggests a degree of unfairness that would only be lessened by the use of the cited phrase. Choice (C) is distortion; by using the cited phrase, the author indicates that the word "improve" is considered suitable by others, but not necessarily by himself. Choice (D) is distortion; simply by including the word "improve", with or without the cited phrase, the author is at least suggesting that it *could* be applicable. Choice (E) is a good choice given your prediction.

13. B

Difficulty: Medium

Often incorrect answer choices will tempt you by making statements that relate to the main idea, but that are not applicable to the question itself.

In this case, while the question should point you towards the second paragraph, as it is there that the author focuses on brain size, the lack of a specific line reference indicates that you should begin by reading through the answer choices. Then, use the details found in the second paragraph to determine which choice is correct.

Choice (A) is distortion; the author never connects brain size with plasticity. (B) is a great choice; line 35 in the second paragraph suggests that brain size was once "considered a direct determiner of brain capacity." Choice (C) is distortion; it is brain *capacity* that can expand due to external stimuli, not brain size. Choice (D) is out of scope; just because the author mentions no correlation does not mean that one does not exist. Choice (E) is an opposite; the passage indicates that one's brain reaches "80% of its eventual adult size" *before* the age of two.

14. B

Difficulty: Medium

Often, even when no specific line reference is included in the question stem, the question's wording will guide you the relevant part of the text.

In this case, the question points you towards the third paragraph, specifically to the author's description of the rat experiment. While only one group is exposed to external stimuli, both are kept in cages and monitored using "magnetic resonance imaging technology."

In (A), only one group was exposed to external stimuli. In (B), this choice is the only one that matches the details of the text. In (C), again, only one group was exposed to external stimuli, and it was only this group that is described as changed. In (D), while this choice includes one correct statement, it must be eliminated because only one of the rat groups is described as changed. In (E), again, this choice must be eliminated as it includes two incorrect statements.

15. C

Difficulty: High

Function questions often require you to first find the exact meaning of the cited content, and to identify how this meaning applies to its context.

The cited word refers to something that is interesting, exciting, or even annoying. In this case, after examining its context, it is clear the cited word is being used to describe an experiment that changed how people thought of the human brain. It is probably being used to refer to something that is extremely interesting or exciting.

Choice (A) is out of scope; while something that is provocative can be controversial, nothing in the text supports this interpretation. Choice (B) is distortion; while the word "interesting" captures the author's intended meaning, nowhere it is suggesting that *only* neuroscientists appreciated the experiment. Choice (C) is a great match for your prediction. Choice (D) is distortion; the author does not suggest that the *intent* of the experiment was to arouse excitement, only that such feelings were the result. Choice (E) is out of scope; the author does not explore whether or not the experiment was criticized.

16. B

Difficulty: Medium

Although inference questions require you to draw conclusions not explicitly stated in the text, looking at the cited content is usually helpful.

Here, notice that the last sentence of the passage applies the conclusions drawn from the rat experiment to humans with the words "such results were then found to be even more noticeable in humans." This content implies, at the very least, that humans were also tested by, most likely, a similar experiment, so look for an answer choice that fits.

Choice (A) is out of scope; the passage only suggests that humans were also tested in an experiment, but not necessarily in precisely the same manner as the rat experiment. Choice (B) is a great fit for your prediction. Choice (C) is out of scope; the paragraph only suggests that the human brains changed more than those of the rats, but not necessarily that they *learned* more. Choice (D) is distortion; nowhere in the paragraph is it suggested that brain structure determines brain capacity. Choice (E) is out of scope; just because the paragraph does not mention the experiment being applied to other animals does not mean other animals were not tested.

17. E

Difficulty: Medium

Even when answering detail questions it can be helpful to step back from the passage and consider its overall purpose and focus.

In this case, as the paragraph focuses on describing the plasticity of the human brain, a characteristic that the author presents as fact, it is clear that he finds the described experiment, the only piece of evidence to back his main idea, credible and revealing.

Choice (A) is extreme; while the author considers the described experiment revealing and never mentions any criticism, he does not go so far as to describe it as flawless. Choice (B) is extreme; while the author indicates that he finds the experiment exciting, nothing in the paragraph indicates that its results were particularly shocking. Choice (C) is extreme; just because the author does not mention any doubts does not mean that the experiment is *impossible* to question. Choice (D) is an opposite; the author clearly considers the experiment quite important. Choice (E) is the best fit given your prediction.

18. B

Difficulty: Medium

Whenever a detail question asks you to identify the tone of a given text, carefully re-examine the specific adjectives and adverbs used by the author.

Words like "truly impressive organ," "remarkable flexibility," and "provocative experiments" indicate that the author is excited with this particular subject, but his apparent excitement is also tempered throughout the passage by a clear focus on the facts and information known about the plasticity of the human brain.

Choice (A) is extreme; while the author expresses excitement, to describe his enthusiasm as extremely or intensely passionate is going too far. Choice (B) is a perfect match for your prediction. Choice (C) is out of scope; as the word "optimism" suggests that one feels confident or positively about the future, this characterization does not fit the passage, which makes no statements about the future. Choice (D) is distortion; nowhere in the paragraph is the author playful, and throughout he is careful not to be too subjective. Choice (E) is distortion; neither of the words fit the paragraph, as the author is clearly taken with this subject and never expresses any doubts.

SECTION 9

1. B

Difficulty: Low

Look for the most concise answer choice that does not introduce any additional grammatical errors.

As written, this sentence is unnecessarily wordy. (B) is concise and contains no errors. (C) and (E) are grammatically incorrect. (D) is still overly wordy.

2. C

Difficulty: Low

One way to correct a run-on sentence is to make one of the independent clauses subordinate.

As written, this is a run-on sentence. (C) corrects this by making the first clause subordinate. (B) and (D) use transition words that are inappropriate in context. (E) misuses the semicolon splice.

3. E

Difficulty: Medium

Transition words must express the correct relationship between clauses.

The transition word *although* indicates contrast. In this sentence the second clause explains the first, so *although* is incorrect. (E) corrects this error with an appropriate transition word, *because*. (B) creates a run-on sentence because two independent clauses cannot be joined simply by a comma. The first clause of (C) should modify *Charles Schultz*, however, as written, it modifies *the name*; the second clause is also unnecessarily in the passive voice. (D) misuses the semicolon splice, which is only correct between two independent clauses.

4. B

Difficulty: Medium

All pronouns must have clear antecedents.

As written, the pronoun *it* does not have a clear antecedent. (B) corrects this error by replacing the ambiguous pronoun with the appropriate noun. (C) corrects the pronoun error, but is unnecessarily wordy. The pronouns *them* in (D) and *their* in (E) also lack antecedents.

5. B

Difficulty: Medium

Make sure verb tenses accurately reflect the sequence of events within a sentence.

The action in this sentence takes place in the past, as *believed* and *purchased* indicate. However, the system was purchased to prevent future intrusions. Therefore, *would have prevented* is incorrect. (B) corrects this error; none of the other choices uses an appropriate verb tense in context.

6. C

Difficulty: Low

A sentence must have a subject and verb in an independent clause to be complete.

As written, this sentence is a fragment: there is no main verb in the first clause and no subject in the second. (C) corrects this error. (B) is incorrect grammatical structure. (D) changes the meaning of the sentence by suggesting that the library is only the largest among libraries with five million books. (E) is also a sentence fragment.

7. E

Difficulty: Medium

No sooner must always be paired with *than*.

As written, *No sooner* is incorrectly paired with *but*. (E) corrects this error. (B) and (D) do not address the error; additionally, *convinced into* in (B) is idiomatically incorrect and (D) is unnecessarily in the passive voice. (C) is also unnecessarily in the passive voice and introduces an inappropriate verb tense in context.

8. E

Difficulty: High

Items in a comparison must be parallel in structure. As written, this sentence violates parallel structure. (E) changes *did* to *were* and makes *manufacturing and farming* parallel to *service and technology*. None of the other choices corrects the error.

9. C

Difficulty: Medium

A verb must agree with its subject noun, which may not be the noun closest to it in the sentence.

The subject of this sentence is plural (*consequences*), so the singular verb *is* is incorrect. (C) and (D) both correct this error. However, (D) changes the meaning of the original selection. (B) and (E) do not address the error.

10. D

Difficulty: Medium

The gerund (*-ing*) verb form can never be the main verb in a sentence.

As written, this is a sentence fragments and the pronoun *it* has no clear antecedent. (D) corrects both errors. (B) does not correct the fragment error. (C) does not address the ambiguous pronoun. (E) is a run-on sentence.

11. A

Difficulty: Medium

Expect between five and eight sentences to contain no error.

This sentence is correct as written, (A). The plural verb *give* is in agreement with the compound subject *The film's clever plot and its exciting climax*, and the sentence is concise. (B), (C), (D), and (E) all make the sentence unnecessarily wordy; additionally, *gives* in (C) and (E) does not agree with the compound subject.

12. D

Difficulty: High

Pronouns must always have clear antecedents.

The pronoun *this* does not have a clear antecedent. (D) corrects this error by specifying that *his academic work* is what was *stellar*. (B) and (C) change the pronoun to *that*, but there is still no clear antecedent. The semicolon in (E) is used incorrectly; a semicolon can only join two independent clauses.

13. D

Difficulty: High

Make sure verb tenses properly sequence events in a sentence.

The verb *had been* indicates that the event happened prior to another specific completed event. However, in this case, there is no other event referred to. (D) correctly replaces *had been* with *was*. (B) leaves the meaning of the second clause incomplete. (C) is awkwardly constructed. (E) introduces a verb tense that is incorrect in context.

14. C

Difficulty: High

Look for the most concise answer choice that doesn't violate the rules of grammar or change the meaning of the original sentence.

As written, the first clause is unnecessarily wordy. (C) makes a correct and concise modifying phrase. (B) and (E) are less concise than (C). The transition *although* in (D) incorrectly suggests that the second clause contrasts with the first clause.

SAT PRACTICE TEST FIVE ANSWER SHEET

Remove (or photocopy) the answer sheet, and use it to complete the practice test.

How to Take the Practice Tests

Each Practice Test includes eight scored multiple-choice sections and one essay. Keep in mind that on the actual SAT, there will be an additional multiple-choice section—the experimental section—that will not contribute to your score.

Once you start a Practice Test, don't stop until you've gone through all nine sections. Remember, you can review any questions within a section, but you may not go back or forward a section.

Good luck!

Start with number 1 for each section. If a section has fewer questions than answer spaces, leave the extra spaces blank.

Section One

Section One is the writing section's essay component.
Lined pages on which you will write your essay can be found in that section.

Section Two

1. Ⓐ Ⓑ Ⓒ Ⓓ Ⓔ   9. Ⓐ Ⓑ Ⓒ Ⓓ Ⓔ   17. Ⓐ Ⓑ Ⓒ Ⓓ Ⓔ
2. Ⓐ Ⓑ Ⓒ Ⓓ Ⓔ   10. Ⓐ Ⓑ Ⓒ Ⓓ Ⓔ   18. Ⓐ Ⓑ Ⓒ Ⓓ Ⓔ
3. Ⓐ Ⓑ Ⓒ Ⓓ Ⓔ   11. Ⓐ Ⓑ Ⓒ Ⓓ Ⓔ   19. Ⓐ Ⓑ Ⓒ Ⓓ Ⓔ
4. Ⓐ Ⓑ Ⓒ Ⓓ Ⓔ   12. Ⓐ Ⓑ Ⓒ Ⓓ Ⓔ   20. Ⓐ Ⓑ Ⓒ Ⓓ Ⓔ
5. Ⓐ Ⓑ Ⓒ Ⓓ Ⓔ   13. Ⓐ Ⓑ Ⓒ Ⓓ Ⓔ
6. Ⓐ Ⓑ Ⓒ Ⓓ Ⓔ   14. Ⓐ Ⓑ Ⓒ Ⓓ Ⓔ
7. Ⓐ Ⓑ Ⓒ Ⓓ Ⓔ   15. Ⓐ Ⓑ Ⓒ Ⓓ Ⓔ
8. Ⓐ Ⓑ Ⓒ Ⓓ Ⓔ   16. Ⓐ Ⓑ Ⓒ Ⓓ Ⓔ

☐ # right in Section Two

☐ # wrong in Section Two

Section Three

1. Ⓐ Ⓑ Ⓒ Ⓓ Ⓔ   9. Ⓐ Ⓑ Ⓒ Ⓓ Ⓔ   17. Ⓐ Ⓑ Ⓒ Ⓓ Ⓔ
2. Ⓐ Ⓑ Ⓒ Ⓓ Ⓔ   10. Ⓐ Ⓑ Ⓒ Ⓓ Ⓔ   18. Ⓐ Ⓑ Ⓒ Ⓓ Ⓔ
3. Ⓐ Ⓑ Ⓒ Ⓓ Ⓔ   11. Ⓐ Ⓑ Ⓒ Ⓓ Ⓔ   19. Ⓐ Ⓑ Ⓒ Ⓓ Ⓔ
4. Ⓐ Ⓑ Ⓒ Ⓓ Ⓔ   12. Ⓐ Ⓑ Ⓒ Ⓓ Ⓔ   20. Ⓐ Ⓑ Ⓒ Ⓓ Ⓔ
5. Ⓐ Ⓑ Ⓒ Ⓓ Ⓔ   13. Ⓐ Ⓑ Ⓒ Ⓓ Ⓔ   21. Ⓐ Ⓑ Ⓒ Ⓓ Ⓔ
6. Ⓐ Ⓑ Ⓒ Ⓓ Ⓔ   14. Ⓐ Ⓑ Ⓒ Ⓓ Ⓔ   22. Ⓐ Ⓑ Ⓒ Ⓓ Ⓔ
7. Ⓐ Ⓑ Ⓒ Ⓓ Ⓔ   15. Ⓐ Ⓑ Ⓒ Ⓓ Ⓔ   23. Ⓐ Ⓑ Ⓒ Ⓓ Ⓔ
8. Ⓐ Ⓑ Ⓒ Ⓓ Ⓔ   16. Ⓐ Ⓑ Ⓒ Ⓓ Ⓔ   24. Ⓐ Ⓑ Ⓒ Ⓓ Ⓔ

☐ # right in Section Three

☐ # wrong in Section Three

Section Four

1. Ⓐ Ⓑ Ⓒ Ⓓ Ⓔ   9. Ⓐ Ⓑ Ⓒ Ⓓ Ⓔ   17. Ⓐ Ⓑ Ⓒ Ⓓ Ⓔ
2. Ⓐ Ⓑ Ⓒ Ⓓ Ⓔ   10. Ⓐ Ⓑ Ⓒ Ⓓ Ⓔ   18. Ⓐ Ⓑ Ⓒ Ⓓ Ⓔ
3. Ⓐ Ⓑ Ⓒ Ⓓ Ⓔ   11. Ⓐ Ⓑ Ⓒ Ⓓ Ⓔ
4. Ⓐ Ⓑ Ⓒ Ⓓ Ⓔ   12. Ⓐ Ⓑ Ⓒ Ⓓ Ⓔ
5. Ⓐ Ⓑ Ⓒ Ⓓ Ⓔ   13. Ⓐ Ⓑ Ⓒ Ⓓ Ⓔ
6. Ⓐ Ⓑ Ⓒ Ⓓ Ⓔ   14. Ⓐ Ⓑ Ⓒ Ⓓ Ⓔ
7. Ⓐ Ⓑ Ⓒ Ⓓ Ⓔ   15. Ⓐ Ⓑ Ⓒ Ⓓ Ⓔ
8. Ⓐ Ⓑ Ⓒ Ⓓ Ⓔ   16. Ⓐ Ⓑ Ⓒ Ⓓ Ⓔ

right in Section Four

wrong in Section Four

If section 4 of your test book contains math questions that are not multiple choice, continue to item 9 below. Otherwise, continue to item 9 above.

9.   10.   11.   12.   13.

14.   15.   16.   17.   18.

(Grid-in answer boxes for items 9–18, each with digits 0–9.)

Section Five

1. Ⓐ Ⓑ Ⓒ Ⓓ Ⓔ   10. Ⓐ Ⓑ Ⓒ Ⓓ Ⓔ   19. Ⓐ Ⓑ Ⓒ Ⓓ Ⓔ   28. Ⓐ Ⓑ Ⓒ Ⓓ Ⓔ
2. Ⓐ Ⓑ Ⓒ Ⓓ Ⓔ   11. Ⓐ Ⓑ Ⓒ Ⓓ Ⓔ   20. Ⓐ Ⓑ Ⓒ Ⓓ Ⓔ   29. Ⓐ Ⓑ Ⓒ Ⓓ Ⓔ
3. Ⓐ Ⓑ Ⓒ Ⓓ Ⓔ   12. Ⓐ Ⓑ Ⓒ Ⓓ Ⓔ   21. Ⓐ Ⓑ Ⓒ Ⓓ Ⓔ   30. Ⓐ Ⓑ Ⓒ Ⓓ Ⓔ
4. Ⓐ Ⓑ Ⓒ Ⓓ Ⓔ   13. Ⓐ Ⓑ Ⓒ Ⓓ Ⓔ   22. Ⓐ Ⓑ Ⓒ Ⓓ Ⓔ   31. Ⓐ Ⓑ Ⓒ Ⓓ Ⓔ
5. Ⓐ Ⓑ Ⓒ Ⓓ Ⓔ   14. Ⓐ Ⓑ Ⓒ Ⓓ Ⓔ   23. Ⓐ Ⓑ Ⓒ Ⓓ Ⓔ   32. Ⓐ Ⓑ Ⓒ Ⓓ Ⓔ
6. Ⓐ Ⓑ Ⓒ Ⓓ Ⓔ   15. Ⓐ Ⓑ Ⓒ Ⓓ Ⓔ   24. Ⓐ Ⓑ Ⓒ Ⓓ Ⓔ   33. Ⓐ Ⓑ Ⓒ Ⓓ Ⓔ
7. Ⓐ Ⓑ Ⓒ Ⓓ Ⓔ   16. Ⓐ Ⓑ Ⓒ Ⓓ Ⓔ   25. Ⓐ Ⓑ Ⓒ Ⓓ Ⓔ   34 Ⓐ Ⓑ Ⓒ Ⓓ Ⓔ
8. Ⓐ Ⓑ Ⓒ Ⓓ Ⓔ   17. Ⓐ Ⓑ Ⓒ Ⓓ Ⓔ   26. Ⓐ Ⓑ Ⓒ Ⓓ Ⓔ   35. Ⓐ Ⓑ Ⓒ Ⓓ Ⓔ
9. Ⓐ Ⓑ Ⓒ Ⓓ Ⓔ   18. Ⓐ Ⓑ Ⓒ Ⓓ Ⓔ   27. Ⓐ Ⓑ Ⓒ Ⓓ Ⓔ

right in Section Five

wrong in Section Five

Remove (or photocopy) this answer sheet, and use it to complete the practice test.

Start with number 1 for each section. If a section has fewer questions than answer spaces, leave the extra spaces blank.

Section Six

1. Ⓐ Ⓑ Ⓒ Ⓓ Ⓔ 9. Ⓐ Ⓑ Ⓒ Ⓓ Ⓔ 17. Ⓐ Ⓑ Ⓒ Ⓓ Ⓔ
2. Ⓐ Ⓑ Ⓒ Ⓓ Ⓔ 10. Ⓐ Ⓑ Ⓒ Ⓓ Ⓔ 18. Ⓐ Ⓑ Ⓒ Ⓓ Ⓔ
3. Ⓐ Ⓑ Ⓒ Ⓓ Ⓔ 11. Ⓐ Ⓑ Ⓒ Ⓓ Ⓔ 19. Ⓐ Ⓑ Ⓒ Ⓓ Ⓔ
4. Ⓐ Ⓑ Ⓒ Ⓓ Ⓔ 12. Ⓐ Ⓑ Ⓒ Ⓓ Ⓔ 20. Ⓐ Ⓑ Ⓒ Ⓓ Ⓔ
5. Ⓐ Ⓑ Ⓒ Ⓓ Ⓔ 13. Ⓐ Ⓑ Ⓒ Ⓓ Ⓔ 21. Ⓐ Ⓑ Ⓒ Ⓓ Ⓔ
6. Ⓐ Ⓑ Ⓒ Ⓓ Ⓔ 14. Ⓐ Ⓑ Ⓒ Ⓓ Ⓔ 22. Ⓐ Ⓑ Ⓒ Ⓓ Ⓔ
7. Ⓐ Ⓑ Ⓒ Ⓓ Ⓔ 15. Ⓐ Ⓑ Ⓒ Ⓓ Ⓔ 23. Ⓐ Ⓑ Ⓒ Ⓓ Ⓔ
8. Ⓐ Ⓑ Ⓒ Ⓓ Ⓔ 16. Ⓐ Ⓑ Ⓒ Ⓓ Ⓔ 24. Ⓐ Ⓑ Ⓒ Ⓓ Ⓔ

right in Section Six

wrong in Section Six

Section Seven

1. Ⓐ Ⓑ Ⓒ Ⓓ Ⓔ 9. Ⓐ Ⓑ Ⓒ Ⓓ Ⓔ
2. Ⓐ Ⓑ Ⓒ Ⓓ Ⓔ 10. Ⓐ Ⓑ Ⓒ Ⓓ Ⓔ
3. Ⓐ Ⓑ Ⓒ Ⓓ Ⓔ 11. Ⓐ Ⓑ Ⓒ Ⓓ Ⓔ
4. Ⓐ Ⓑ Ⓒ Ⓓ Ⓔ 12. Ⓐ Ⓑ Ⓒ Ⓓ Ⓔ
5. Ⓐ Ⓑ Ⓒ Ⓓ Ⓔ 13. Ⓐ Ⓑ Ⓒ Ⓓ Ⓔ
6. Ⓐ Ⓑ Ⓒ Ⓓ Ⓔ 14. Ⓐ Ⓑ Ⓒ Ⓓ Ⓔ
7. Ⓐ Ⓑ Ⓒ Ⓓ Ⓔ 15. Ⓐ Ⓑ Ⓒ Ⓓ Ⓔ
8. Ⓐ Ⓑ Ⓒ Ⓓ Ⓔ 16. Ⓐ Ⓑ Ⓒ Ⓓ Ⓔ

right in Section Seven

wrong in Section Seven

Section Eight

1. Ⓐ Ⓑ Ⓒ Ⓓ Ⓔ 9. Ⓐ Ⓑ Ⓒ Ⓓ Ⓔ 17. Ⓐ Ⓑ Ⓒ Ⓓ Ⓔ
2. Ⓐ Ⓑ Ⓒ Ⓓ Ⓔ 10. Ⓐ Ⓑ Ⓒ Ⓓ Ⓔ 18. Ⓐ Ⓑ Ⓒ Ⓓ Ⓔ
3. Ⓐ Ⓑ Ⓒ Ⓓ Ⓔ 11. Ⓐ Ⓑ Ⓒ Ⓓ Ⓔ 19. Ⓐ Ⓑ Ⓒ Ⓓ Ⓔ
4. Ⓐ Ⓑ Ⓒ Ⓓ Ⓔ 12. Ⓐ Ⓑ Ⓒ Ⓓ Ⓔ
5. Ⓐ Ⓑ Ⓒ Ⓓ Ⓔ 13. Ⓐ Ⓑ Ⓒ Ⓓ Ⓔ
6. Ⓐ Ⓑ Ⓒ Ⓓ Ⓔ 14. Ⓐ Ⓑ Ⓒ Ⓓ Ⓔ
7. Ⓐ Ⓑ Ⓒ Ⓓ Ⓔ 15. Ⓐ Ⓑ Ⓒ Ⓓ Ⓔ
8. Ⓐ Ⓑ Ⓒ Ⓓ Ⓔ 16. Ⓐ Ⓑ Ⓒ Ⓓ Ⓔ

right in Section Eight

wrong in Section Eight

Section Nine

1. Ⓐ Ⓑ Ⓒ Ⓓ Ⓔ 9. Ⓐ Ⓑ Ⓒ Ⓓ Ⓔ
2. Ⓐ Ⓑ Ⓒ Ⓓ Ⓔ 10. Ⓐ Ⓑ Ⓒ Ⓓ Ⓔ
3. Ⓐ Ⓑ Ⓒ Ⓓ Ⓔ 11. Ⓐ Ⓑ Ⓒ Ⓓ Ⓔ
4. Ⓐ Ⓑ Ⓒ Ⓓ Ⓔ 12. Ⓐ Ⓑ Ⓒ Ⓓ Ⓔ
5. Ⓐ Ⓑ Ⓒ Ⓓ Ⓔ 13. Ⓐ Ⓑ Ⓒ Ⓓ Ⓔ
6. Ⓐ Ⓑ Ⓒ Ⓓ Ⓔ 14. Ⓐ Ⓑ Ⓒ Ⓓ Ⓔ
7. Ⓐ Ⓑ Ⓒ Ⓓ Ⓔ
8. Ⓐ Ⓑ Ⓒ Ⓓ Ⓔ

right in Section Nine

wrong in Section Nine

Practice Test Five

SECTION 1
Time—25 Minutes
ESSAY

The essay gives you an opportunity to show how effectively you can develop and express ideas. You should, therefore, take care to develop your point of view, present your ideas logically and clearly, and use language precisely.

Your essay must be written in your Answer Grid Booklet—you will receive no other paper on which to write. You will have enough space if you write on every line, avoid wide margins, and keep your handwriting to a reasonable size. Remember that people who are not familiar with your handwriting will read what you write. Try to write or print so that what you are writing is legible to those readers.

You have twenty-five minutes to write an essay on the topic assigned below.

DO NOT WRITE ON ANOTHER TOPIC. AN OFF-TOPIC ESSAY WILL RECEIVE A SCORE OF ZERO.

Think carefully about the issue presented in the following excerpt and the assignment below.

> "Things do not change; we change."
>
> –Henry David Thoreau, *Walden*

Assignment: Do we ourselves cause change in our lives by making certain decisions, or are we acted upon by events that happen around us? Plan and write an essay in which you develop your point of view on this issue. Support your position with reasoning and examples taken from your reading, studies, experience, or observations.

DO NOT WRITE YOUR ESSAY IN YOUR TEST BOOK.
You will receive credit only for what you write in your Answer Grid Booklet.

_____

_____

_____

_____

_____

_____

_____

_____

_____

_____

_____

_____

_____

_____

_____

_____

_____

_____

_____

IF YOU FINISH BEFORE TIME IS CALLED, YOU MAY CHECK YOUR WORK ON THIS SECTION ONLY. DO NOT TURN TO ANY OTHER SECTION IN THE TEST.

STOP

SECTION 2
Time—25 Minutes
20 Questions

Directions: For this section, solve each problem and decide which is the best of the choices given. Fill in the corresponding oval on the answer sheet. You may use any available space for scratchwork.

Notes:

(1) Calculator use is permitted.

(2) All numbers used are real numbers.

(3) Figures are provided for some problems. All figures are drawn to scale and lie in a plane UNLESS otherwise indicated.

(4) Unless otherwise specified, the domain of any function f is assumed to be the set of all real numbers x for which $f(x)$ is a real number.

Information

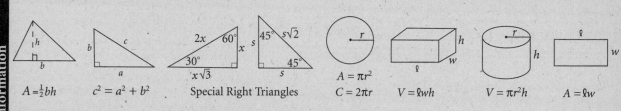

$A = \frac{1}{2}bh$ $c^2 = a^2 + b^2$ Special Right Triangles $A = \pi r^2$ $C = 2\pi r$ $V = \ell wh$ $V = \pi r^2 h$ $A = \ell w$

The sum of the degree measures of the angles in a triangle is 180.
The number of degrees of arc in a circle is 360.
A straight angle has a degree measure of 180.

1. If $x^2 - 49 = 0$, which of the following could be a value of x?

(A) −7

(B) −3

(C) 0

(D) 4

(E) 14

2. The length of the playground is 3 feet more than its width. If the length of the playground is 13 feet, what is the area of the playground in square feet?

(A) 93

(B) 130

(C) 145

(D) 153

(E) 160

GO ON TO THE NEXT PAGE

3. If $s = 3q$ and $q = 4$, what is the value of $3s$?

(A) 3

(B) 4

(C) 12

(D) 24

(E) 36

Some integers in set T are negative.

4. If the statement above is true, which of the following must also be true?

(A) If an integer is positive, it is in set T.

(B) If an integer is negative, it is in set T.

(C) All integers in set T are positive.

(D) All integers in set T are negative.

(E) Not all integers in set T are positive.

5. A triangle has a perimeter of 16 and one side of length 4. If the lengths of the other two sides are equal, what is the length of each of the other two sides?

(A) 5

(B) 6

(C) 7

(D) 8

(E) 9

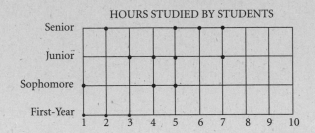

HOURS STUDIED BY STUDENTS

6. The grid above shows the number of hours spent studying last week by 14 students in various grades. Which of the following is true, according to this grid?

(A) Half of the students studied for more than 4 hours each.

(B) One student studied exactly 8 hours.

(C) One Junior studied for 2 hours.

(D) More Sophomores than First–Years studied more than 2 hours each.

(E) Most students were First–Years.

7. Squaring the product of z and 6 gives the same result as squaring the difference of z and 6. Which of the following equations could be used to find all the possible values of z?

(A) $6z^2 = (z + 6)^2$

(B) $(6z)^2 = z^2 + 6^2$

(C) $6^2z = z^2 - 6^2$

(D) $(6z)^2 = (z - 6)^2$

(E) $6z^2 = z^2 + 6^2$

GO ON TO THE NEXT PAGE

8. If as many 7–inch pieces of wire as possible are cut from a wire that is 6 feet long, what is the total length of the wire that is left over? (12 inches = 1 foot)

   (A) 2 inches
   (B) 3 inches
   (C) 4 inches
   (D) 5 inches
   (E) 8 inches

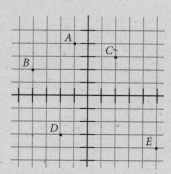

9. Which of the lettered points in the figure above has coordinates (x, y) such that $|x| + |y| = 6$?

   (A) A
   (B) B
   (C) C
   (D) D
   (E) E

$$A = \left\{ \frac{3}{5}, 2, \frac{7}{2}, 4, \frac{15}{3}, 8 \right\}$$

$$B = \left\{ \frac{3}{5}, \frac{5}{3}, 4, 8 \right\}$$

10. If n is a member of both set A and set B above, which of the following must be true?

   I. n is an integer.
   II. $5n$ is an integer.
   III. $n = 5$

   (A) II only
   (B) III only
   (C) I and II only
   (D) I and III only
   (E) I, II, and III

11. If y is directly proportional to x and if $y = 30$ when $x = 6$, what is the value of y when $x = 8$?

   (A) $\dfrac{15}{2}$
   (B) $\dfrac{75}{2}$
   (C) 32
   (D) 38
   (E) 40

12. The nth term of a sequence is defined to be $5n + 2$. The 35th term is how much greater than the 30th term?

   (A) 5
   (B) 18
   (C) 25
   (D) 36
   (E) 40

GO ON TO THE NEXT PAGE

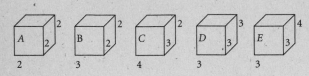

Note: Figures not drawn to scale.

13. Which of the rectangular solids shown above has a volume closest to the volume of a right circular cylinder with radius 4 and height 2?

   (A) A
   (B) B
   (C) C
   (D) D
   (E) E

$$r = n^3 - 0.61$$
$$s = n^2 - 0.61$$
$$t = (n - 0.61)^2$$

14. If n is a negative integer, what is the ordering of $r, s,$ and t from least to greatest?

   (A) $t < r < s$
   (B) $r < t < s$
   (C) $s < r < t$
   (D) $r \leqslant s < t$
   (E) $t < s < r$

15. Flour, sugar and baking soda are mixed by weight in the ratio of 6:4:2, respectively, to produce a certain type of cookie. In order to make 6 pounds of this dough, what weight of sugar, in pounds, is required?

   (A) 4
   (B) 2
   (C) $\frac{7}{6}$
   (D) $\frac{1}{2}$
   (E) $\frac{1}{4}$

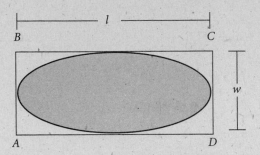

16. In the rectangle $ABCD$ above, the area of the shaded region is given by $\frac{\pi \ell w}{5}$. If the area of the shaded region is 8π, what is the total area, to the nearest whole number, of the unshaded regions of the rectangle $ABCD$?

   (A) 14
   (B) 15
   (C) 20
   (D) 22
   (E) 25

17. A local store donated some markers to Mrs. Kettz's fourth-grade class. If each student takes 2 markers, there will be 16 markers left. If 4 students do not take any markers and the rest of the students take 6 markers, there will be no markers left. How many markers were donated to the class?

   (A) 24
   (B) 30
   (C) 36
   (D) 40
   (E) 48

GO ON TO THE NEXT PAGE

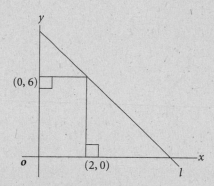

Note: Figure not drawn to scale.

18. In the figure above, if line *l* has a slope of −3, what is the *y*–intercept of *l*?

(A) 6

(B) 8

(C) 10

(D) 12

(E) 14

19. For all positive integers *r* and *q*, where *r* > *q*, let the operation & be defined by $r \& q = \dfrac{3^{r+q}}{3^{r-q}}$. For how many positive integers *r* is *r* & 1 equal to 9?

(A) none

(B) one

(C) two

(D) four

(E) more than four

20. The figure above represents six offices that will be assigned randomly to six employees, one employee per office. If Mary and Anne are two of the six employees, what is the probability that each will be assigned an office indicated with an **X**?

(A) $\dfrac{1}{6}$

(B) $\dfrac{1}{8}$

(C) $\dfrac{1}{15}$

(D) $\dfrac{2}{15}$

(E) $\dfrac{1}{30}$

IF YOU FINISH BEFORE TIME IS CALLED, YOU MAY CHECK YOUR WORK ON THIS SECTION ONLY. DO NOT TURN TO ANY OTHER SECTION IN THE TEST.

STOP

SECTION 3

Time—25 Minutes
24 Questions

Directions: For each of the following questions, choose the best answer and darken the corresponding oval on the answer sheet.

Each sentence below has one or two blanks, each blank indicating that something has been omitted. Beneath the sentence are five words or sets of words labeled (A) through (E). Choose the word or set of words that, when inserted in the sentence, best fits the meaning of the sentence as a whole.

EXAMPLE:

Today's small, portable computers contrast markedly with the earliest electronic computers, which were ----.

(A) effective
(B) invented
(C) useful
(D) destructive
(E) enormous   Ⓐ Ⓑ Ⓒ Ⓓ ●

1. Although Professor Chang's simple ---- was intended to merely gain more information, the student took it as a slight to her intelligence.

   (A) query
   (B) confession
   (C) dismissal
   (D) condemnation
   (E) credo

2. Despite her dog's ---- appearance, Stephanie spent ---- amount of money on his grooming.

   (A) orderly . . an enormous
   (B) disheveled . . an inordinate
   (C) annoyed . . an unfortunate
   (D) distracted . . an unrealistic
   (E) agitated . . a considerable

3. Although when it was first introduced to the market his invention had been the most technologically advanced of its time, less than a year later it was ---- by an even more sophisticated machine.

   (A) supplanted
   (B) redoubled
   (C) augmented
   (D) brandished
   (E) evaded

4. Because he consistently advanced arguments based on possibilities and speculation rather than proven certainties, Jonas became known as a ----.

   (A) dogmatist
   (B) consultant
   (C) prodigy
   (D) materialist
   (E) theorist

5. The ---- of the newly constructed temple was tragically violated by the vandals' offensive graffiti.

   (A) turpitude
   (B) sacrosanctity
   (C) perspicuity
   (D) verisimilitude
   (E) duplicity

GO ON TO THE NEXT PAGE

Directions: The passages below are followed by questions based on their content; questions following a pair of related passages may also be based on the relationship between the paired passages. Answer the questions on the basis of what is <u>stated</u> or <u>implied</u> in the passages and in any introductory material that may be provided.

Questions 6–9 are based on the following passages.

Passage 1

People who work closely with animals readily acknowledge that they observe emotions in, or attribute emotions to, the animals they work with. Though this idea is derided by some in the scien-
(5) tific community, it is important to note that the most successful animal trainers are the ones who understand the "mood" of an animal—who are comfortable reading the emotional state of their charges. A horse trainer had better know whether
(10) a horse will take coaxing or commanding on a given day, and any trainer will tell you that different approaches are effective with different individuals, even those from the same breed. These trainers attribute the difference to the animals'
(15) emotional tendencies.

Passage 2

The Oxford Companion to Animal Behavior advises animal behaviorists: "One is well advised to study the behavior [of an animal], rather than attempting to get at any underlying emotion."
(20) Whether or not animals experience emotions similar to those that humans do, the fact is that there is no scientific way to quantify and categorize them. If animals do experience emotion, it is certain that they do not express it in the same
(25) way we do. Accordingly, making any conclusions about emotions based on behavior amounts to nothing more than guesswork and wishful anthropomorphizing.

6. In lines 9–10, the reference to the horse trainer suggests that horses

(A) have unusually sensitive emotions
(B) do not generally cooperate with humans
(C) have a unique emotional makeup
(D) are uncommonly eager to help
(E) have emotions that affect their interactions with people

7. Author 2 would most likely respond to the second sentence of Passage 1 by

(A) arguing that animals actually feel no emotion
(B) questioning the objectivity of trainers who claim to know their charges' emotions
(C) arguing that little is actually known about animals' emotional relationships with one another
(D) suggesting other possible explanations for an animal acting differently on different days
(E) noting that training animals does not require understanding of emotional states

GO ON TO THE NEXT PAGE

8. The two passages differ in their views of animal
   emotion in that Passage 1 states that animals

   (A) show love for their trainers, while Passage 2
       contends that animals can only love their
       own kind

   (B) have emotions that are identical to those of
       humans, while Passage 2 notes that horses
       have stronger emotions than other animals

   (C) have strong emotions, while Passage 2 points
       out that they have no emotions at all

   (D) have identifiable emotions, while Passage 2
       suggests that there is not enough scientific
       data to understand animal emotions fully

   (E) anthropomorphize, while Passage 2 argues
       that it is humans who do that

9. Which generalization about animals is supported
   by both passages?

   (A) Animals display emotions.

   (B) Horses are more emotional than other
       animals.

   (C) There is no scientific evidence supporting the
       presence of emotions in animals.

   (D) Animal behavior can offer important insight
       into that animal.

   (E) Animals who work closely with humans are
       more likely to express emotions.

GO ON TO THE NEXT PAGE

Questions 10–15 are based on the following passage.

The passage below is excerpted from the introduction to a new book about global conflict and peace.

My introduction into the field of social history was fortuitous. I spent my early formative years in Lebanon during that country's civil war. Living through this turmoil inspired my quest to study
(5) and understand global conflict. Breaking away to America in my pre-teen years cushioned the blow, as did living in suburban Maryland. After my entry to Stanford University, I found myself reengaged by the factors that contributed to my
(10) horrific childhood living conditions. I invested myself in the study of International Relations in hopes of gaining a deeper understanding of war, conflict and peace. Yet, once again, I too quickly lost my bearings, this time in the immersion of
(15) abstract theories of global security—theories that justify, even advocate war as a policy tool. I am still embarrassed by the fact that I went to school in order to contribute to world peace but found myself becoming a hawkish supporter of milita-
(20) rized solutions.

During graduate school, I met a professor who urged me to refocus my studies from the global system to the local one. He recommended that I study the people of the various regions of the
(25) world rather than the regional power balance among governments. I, of course, scoffed at the suggestion, for that type of study was the job of historians. International Relations theorists do not often examine people. I, like most others in my
(30) field, viewed the state as a black box. States and their governments were the subjects of my studies; populations were merely the objects of state action. But I eventually reached a point that high-lighted the inadequacy of such analyses. Ironically,
(35) I had first sought to study International Relations in order to help people overcome conflict, but in my focus on the politics of conflict, I had lost sight of the people.

I eventually refocused my studies by examining
(40) the history of the people in the regions I studied. Primary source documents revealed common struggles and aspirations. This examination elucidated the politics of the regions and their conflicts. By overlaying the two studies, I was
(45) eventually able to see how political motivations, calculations, and missteps affected groups and individuals who then fell into conflict.

This examination of the human aspect of inter-national politics opened my eyes to the fact that
(50) conflicts are often not endemic. Traditional views of the state and nation never addressed, for instance, how governments and demagogues spur previously coexisting populations into battle, or why. Ironically, the examination of the human level
(55) cemented the notion that groups and populations seldom harbor true hatred and conflict. I learned that such conflicts originate from and remain the tools of those in power. This circle finally accorded me the comprehensive understanding I sought. My
(60) examination of social history aided my under-standing of international politics by highlighting the states of affair within the regions and countries I studied. They helped me to investigate the true origins of the world's past conflicts—and my own.

10. The primary purpose of the passage is to show how the author

(A) discovered a more effective framework of analysis for his studies

(B) became an International Relations scholar to help people in his homeland achieve social justice

(C) improved his research abilities by taking a new approach

(D) became more well-rounded thanks to the tutelage of a graduate school professor

(E) came to view local populations as a worthy subject for study

GO ON TO THE NEXT PAGE

11. The first sentence indicates that the author's "introduction into...social history" was

   (A) difficult but rewarding
   (B) confusing but worthwhile
   (C) unsought but unavoidable
   (D) accidental but pleasant
   (E) surprising and controversial

12. The author initially "scoffed" at the graduate school professor's suggestion (lines 26–28) because the author

   (A) knew that the graduate school professor was not tenured in the history department
   (B) believed that historians should pursue loftier goals
   (C) had job offers that would present even greater opportunity
   (D) rejected the idea that such a study was the job of an international relations scholar
   (E) viewed the suggestion as condescending

13. According to the passage, why did the author go to school?

   (A) to escape the civil war in his own country
   (B) to contribute to world peace
   (C) to become a hawkish supporter of militarized policies
   (D) to examine the human aspect of International Relations
   (E) to improve his understanding of the people in the regions he studied

14. In line 44, "overlaying" most nearly means

   (A) researching
   (B) sidestepping
   (C) abandoning
   (D) combining
   (E) exaggerating

15. The last two sentences ("My examination...my own") suggest that the author

   (A) realizes global conflicts can only be examined through social history
   (B) believes that social history provides information on global conflicts
   (C) assumes all international conflicts have their bases in social problems
   (D) believes that knowledge of social history can prevent conflicts
   (E) was previously aware of the social history, but felt unqualified to write on it

GO ON TO THE NEXT PAGE

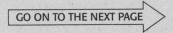

KAPLAN
Test Prep and Admissions

Questions 16–24 are based on the following passage.

The following passage below is adapted from a NASA researcher's position paper on the possibility of human colonization of Mars.

While Venus is commonly called Earth's sister planet, its proximity to the Sun causes surface temperatures of 900 degrees Fahrenheit, too hot to support life. Alternately, due to distance from the
(5) Sun, every planet past Mars is too cold. Thus, Mars is the only planet in our solar system, other than Earth, that might be able to support life. While many scientists believe that life may have existed on Mars in the past, some are now begin-
(10) ning to believe that human life may be able to exist there in the future, but not without earthly intervention.

Scientists have long envisioned human colonization of Mars in space station-like enclosed
(15) structures, but some are now beginning to believe in the possibility of altering the Martian climate and atmosphere to create an Earth-like world where humans can live unencumbered by pressurized suits or structures. These scientists point out
(20) that before it supported life, Earth was, like Mars, a desolate, uninhabitable planet devoid of oxygen. This situation only changed with the evolution of photosynthetic bacteria that absorb carbon dioxide from the atmosphere and release oxygen back
(25) into it. These scientists postulate that a similar catalyst could be used to transform the Martian atmosphere into one inhabitable by humans. Such a process, called terraforming, would take decades, if not centuries or even millennia, and involve
(30) technology not yet developed.

Warming stands as the first domino in terraforming Mars. Since Mars is about fifty percent farther from the Sun than is Earth and has only one percent as much atmospheric pressure,
(35) Martian surface temperatures average minus 81 degrees Fahrenheit. Since it is theoretically impossible to move Mars into a warmer orbit, scientists have concluded, ironically, that the same process many blame for harming Earth, global warming

(40) caused by greenhouse gasses, must be used to terraform Mars. Scientists have postulated three methods for releasing greenhouse gasses into the Martian atmosphere to begin the process of Martian warming.

(45) Large orbital mirrors can be used to reflect sunlight onto the Martian surface. NASA scientists have invested large amounts of research into the development of such mirrors for use as solar sails, which capture the Sun's radiation in order to
(50) propel a spacecraft. NASA could easily decouple solar sail technology from propulsion systems in order to use the large mirrors for terraforming Mars. Unfortunately, each mirror would need to be at least the size of West Virginia in order to
(55) reflect enough sunlight to warm even a small area of the Martian surface. Additionally, such mirrors would weigh over 200,000 tons, meaning they cannot be launched from Earth. However, such mirrors could be constructed in and from materi-
(60) als found in space. Furthermore, once constructed, the mirrors can be concentrated at the Martian polar ice caps in order to melt the ice and release the large reservoirs of native carbon dioxide that scientists believe to be trapped there.

(65) Crashing large asteroids, mostly comprised of frozen ammonia gas, onto the Martian surface would release large amounts of that gas, a powerful greenhouse agent, into the atmosphere. The engineering required for this process lies within
(70) reach. The massive thermonuclear rockets needed to push the asteroids closer to Mars before gravity pulls them into collision can and probably will be developed at some point during the 21st century. Nevertheless, astrophysical complications over-
(75) shadow the engineering. It would be far too difficult to move one of these rocks from the asteroid belt near Mars. Since objects closer to the Sun orbit faster than objects farther from the Sun, asteroids from farther orbits, near Pluto's, would
(80) have to be used. Not only would reaching these more distant objects take a long time, but it has not, as of yet, been proven that these objects exist in the outer solar system, even though most scientists think they do. Furthermore, while each of

GO ON TO THE NEXT PAGE

(85) these impacts would raise the average Martian
surface temperature by about 5 degrees
Fahrenheit, causing the melting of a trillion tons
of water, the bombardment of the planet by the
number of asteroids required to change its climate
(90) sufficiently would release the energy equivalent of
a nuclear war, delaying colonization for centuries.

The third option for Martian warming involves
constructing solar-powered green, house-gas emitting factories on the planet similar to the industri-
(95) al factories humans have been building on this
planet during the 20th and 21st centuries. Unlike
the industrial factories on this planet, which produce greenhouse gasses as waste byproducts, the
sole purpose of the network of factories on Mars
(100) would be to produce greenhouse gasses to thicken
the Martian atmosphere in order to warm the
planet. Such factories could be constructed on
Earth and transported to Mars or constructed on
the planet itself, either with materials transported
(105) from Earth or those already present on Mars.

Each of these methods of Martian warming,
which aim to produce enough greenhouse gasses
to trap sunlight and warm the planet, may seem
daunting logistically and scientifically, but once
(110) started would set in motion a chain reaction.
Once warming begins, it would lead to increased
polar melting and surface thawing, thereby releasing even more carbon dioxide, which would not
only continue but also exponentially speed the
(115) terraforming processes. As one NASA scientist
recently wrote: "The Mars atmosphere greenhouse
effect system is thus one with a built-in positive
feedback. The warmer it gets, the thicker the
atmosphere becomes; and the thicker the atmos-
(120) phere becomes the warmer it gets." The melting
ice would form oceans, lakes, rivers, and streams
that would cover over a quarter of the Martian
surface. Once bodies of water form, the last step
requires only the addition of seeds, which when
(125) watered would absorb the carbon dioxide in the
atmosphere and grow into trees that release
oxygen, thereby turning the red planet blue.

16. In line 25, "catalyst" most nearly means

   (A) an agent that brings about significant change
   (B) an agent that brings about gradual change
   (C) an agent that prematurely brings about a change
   (D) an agent that brings about rapid change
   (E) an agent that retards change

17. In line 31, the author uses "domino" to refer to

   (A) a cloak surrounding the Martian atmosphere
   (B) the division of the Martian atmosphere into two parts
   (C) Mars' expected behavior in accordance with theory
   (D) the initial step in a succession of atmospheric events
   (E) the cumulative effect produced on the Martian atmosphere by warming

18. The third paragraph of the passage ("Warming stands…warming") suggests that Martian surface temperatures

   (A) are controlled by native greenhouse gasses
   (B) are related to atmospheric pressure
   (C) will rise as the pressure of the Martian atmosphere increases
   (D) are one percent of Earth's average surface temperature
   (E) thicken the Martian atmosphere

GO ON TO THE NEXT PAGE ▷

19. According to the passage, reflective mirrors are difficult to use for terraforming because

(A) it would be impossible to decouple the technology from propulsion systems

(B) they would create the energy equivalent of a thermonuclear war, which would delay colonization of the planet for centuries

(C) they would melt the polar ice caps, thereby flooding the planet

(D) their mass makes them unwieldy

(E) the massive thermonuclear rockets needed to launch and position these mirrors have not yet been developed

20. The reference to West Virginia in line 54 primarily serves to

(A) highlight the size requirements of the mirrors

(B) indicate the orientation of the mirrors

(C) illustrate the size of the area the mirrors are capable of heating

(D) delineate the shape of the mirrors

(E) relate the orbital coordinates of the mirrors

21. What does the passage suggest about asteroids?

(A) Asteroids that orbit too fast are not useful for terraforming.

(B) Objects that orbit at faster speeds are hard to move.

(C) Ammonia gas is the essential element required for terraforming Mars.

(D) They contain nuclear elements that explode upon impact.

(E) It is impossible to land on an asteroid that orbits at such high speeds.

22. The three methods of terraforming mentioned in the passage are similar in which of the following ways?

 I. They all manufacture greenhouse gasses.
 II. They all involve manned missions to Mars.
 III. They all aim to raise the surface temperature of Mars.

(A) I only

(B) II only

(C) III only

(D) I and III only

(E) I, II, and III

23. Which of the following, if true, would most clearly strengthen the assertion by the author that, once bodies of water form, plant life would contribute more oxygen to the Martian atmosphere?

(A) Only primitive plants can survive in an atmosphere without oxygen.

(B) It would take 900 years to grow enough plants to produce enough oxygen on Mars to support human life.

(C) Advanced plant forms must absorb at least some oxygen along with their carbon dioxide.

(D) All plants absorb carbon dioxide.

(E) Plants can be genetically engineered to withstand conditions unique to Mars.

24. The tone of the passage is primarily one of

(A) passionate advocacy

(B) moderate skepticism

(C) earnest entreaty

(D) reasoned appreciation

(E) detached objectivity

IF YOU FINISH BEFORE TIME IS CALLED, YOU MAY CHECK YOUR WORK ON THIS SECTION ONLY. DO NOT TURN TO ANY OTHER SECTION IN THE TEST.

STOP

SECTION 4
Time—25 Minutes
18 Questions

Directions: For this section, solve each problem and decide which is the best of the choices given. Fill in the corresponding oval on the answer sheet. You may use any available space for scratchwork.

Notes:

(1) Calculator use is permitted.

(2) All numbers used are real numbers.

(3) Figures are provided for some problems. All figures are drawn to scale and lie in a plane UNLESS otherwise indicated.

(4) Unless otherwise specified, the domain of any function f is assumed to be the set of all real numbers x for which $f(x)$ is a real number.

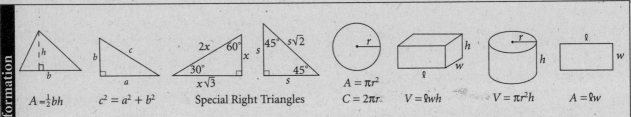

Information

$A = \frac{1}{2}bh \qquad c^2 = a^2 + b^2 \qquad$ Special Right Triangles $\qquad A = \pi r^2 \qquad V = \ell w h \qquad V = \pi r^2 h \qquad A = \ell w$
$C = 2\pi r$

The sum of the degree measures of the angles in a triangle is 180.
The number of degrees of arc in a circle is 360.
A straight angle has a degree measure of 180.

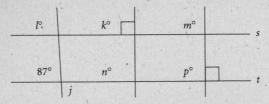

1. The figure above shows five lines. If $s \| t$, which of the following is NOT equal to 90?

(A) j

(B) k

(C) m

(D) n

(E) p

2. Which of the following is divisible by 5 and 7 but is <u>not</u> divisible by 10?

(A) 28

(B) 50

(C) 90

(D) 105

(E) 135

GO ON TO THE NEXT PAGE

w	0	1	2	3
$f(w)$	−1	2	5	8

3. The table above gives values of the linear function f for several values of w. Which of the following defines $f(w)$?

(A) $f(w) = w - 1$

(B) $f(w) = w + 1$

(C) $f(w) = 3w + 1$

(D) $f(w) = 3w - 1$

(E) $f(w) = 1 - 3w$

$P \qquad\qquad S \qquad\qquad\qquad T$

4. In the figure above, the intersection of ray PT and ray SP is

(A) Segment PT

(B) Segment PS

(C) Ray PT

(D) Ray SP

(E) Line PT

AGE DISTRIBUTION OF RESIDENTS
IN FLORA COUNTY

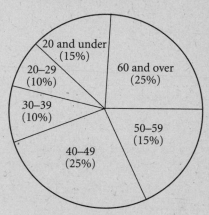

Note: Figure not drawn to scale

5. According to the graph above, if there are 9,000 residents aged 50 to 59 in Flora County, how many residents are under the age of 30?

(A)   6,000

(B)   11,000

(C)   12,000

(D)   14,000

(E)   15,000

GO ON TO THE NEXT PAGE

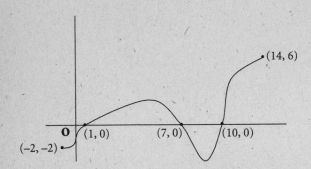

6. Based on the graph of the function f above, what are the values of x for which $f(x)$ is positive?

(A) $-2 \leq x < 1$ or $10 < x \leq 14$

(B) $-2 \leq x < 1$ or $7 < x < 10$

(C) $1 < x < 7$ or $10 < x \leq 14$

(D) $-2 \leq x \leq 10$

(E) $1 < x < 10$

7. Eduardo drives to school at an average speed of 60 miles per hour and returns along the same route at an average speed of 30 miles per hour. If his total travel time is 3 hours, what is the total number of miles in the round trip?

(A) 220

(B) 190

(C) 120

(D) 85.5

(E) 60

8. If x and y are integers such that $x^2 = 81$ and $2y^3 = 54$, which of the following could be true?

   I. $x = 9$
   II. $y = -3$
   III. $x + y = -6$

(A) I only

(B) II only

(C) I and III only

(D) II and III only

(E) I, II, and III

Directions: For Student-Produced Response questions 9–18, use the grids at the bottom of the answer sheet page on which you have answered questions 1–8.

Each of the remaining 10 questions requires you to solve the problem and enter your answer by marking the ovals in the special grid, as shown in the example below. You may use any available space for scratch work.

Answer: 1.25 or $\frac{5}{4}$ or 5/4

Write answer in → boxes.

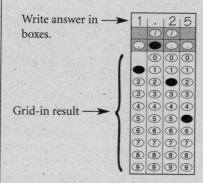

Grid-in result →

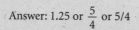

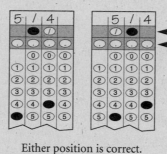

Fraction line
Decimal point

Either position is correct.

You may start your answers in any column, space permitting. Columns not needed should be left blank.

- It is recommended, though not required, that you write your answer in the boxes at the top of the columns. However, you will receive credit only for darkening the ovals correctly.

- Grid only one answer to a question, even though some problems have more than one correct answer.

- Darken no more than one oval in a column.

- No answers are negative.

- Mixed numbers cannot be gridded. For example: the number $1\frac{1}{4}$ must be gridded as 1.25 or 5/4.

(If [1 | 1 | / | 4] is gridded, it will be interpreted as $\frac{11}{4}$, not $1\frac{1}{4}$.)

- Decimal Accuracy: Decimal answers must be entered as accurately as possible. For example, if you obtain an answer such as 0.1666..., you should record the result as .166 or .167. **Less accurate values such as .16 or .17 are not acceptable.**

Acceptable ways to grid $\frac{1}{6}$ = .1666...

GO ON TO THE NEXT PAGE

9. When a certain number is multiplied by $\frac{1}{2}$ and the product is then multiplied by 24, the result is 102. What is the number?

10. What is the greatest integer value of x for which $5x - 30 < 0$?

11. An object thrown upward from a height of f feet with an initial velocity of s feet per second will reach a maximum height of $f + \frac{s^2}{64}$ feet. If the object is thrown upward from a height of 8 feet with an initial velocity of 16 feet per second, what will be its maximum height, in feet?

12. The three angles of a triangle have measures of $g°$, $3g°$, and $h°$, where $g > 40$. If g and h are integers, what is one possible value of h?

KAREY'S EXPENSES

	Food	Transportation	Total
Monday	$80		
Tuesday	$70		
Wednessday	$105		
Total			$345

13. The incomplete table above is an expense sheet for Karey's vacation. If her transportation expenses were the same each day, what were here <u>total</u> expenses for Tuesday, in dollars? (Disregard the $ sign when gridding in your answer.)

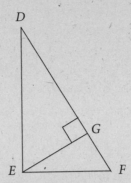

14. In $\triangle DEF$ above, $EF = 10$, $GF = 6$ and $DG = 8\sqrt{3}$. What is the length of $\overline{DE}$?

15. On Tuesday morning Mr. Brown had a certain amount of money that he planned to spend during the week. On each subsequent morning, he had one–third the amount of the previous morning. On Sunday morning, 5 days later, he had $2. How many dollars did Mr. Brown originally start with on Tuesday morning? (Disregard the $ sign when gridding in your answer.)

16. The median of a list of 97 consecutive integers is 55. What is the greatest integer in the list?

17. When the positive integer m is divided by 4, the remainder is 3. What is the remainder when $22m$ is divided by 8?

GO ON TO THE NEXT PAGE

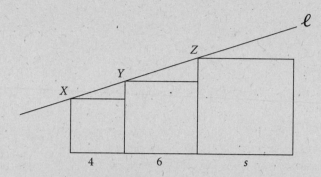

18. The figure above shows three squares with sides of
     length 4, 6, s, respectively. If X, Y, and Z lie on line
     ℓ, what is the value of s?

SECTION 5

Time—25 Minutes

35 Questions

Directions: For each question in this section, select the best answer from among the choices given and fill in the corresponding oval on the answer sheet.

The following sentences test correctness and effectiveness of expression. Part of each sentence or the entire sentence is underlined; beneath each sentence are five ways of phrasing the underlined material. Choice (A) repeats the original phrasing; the other four choices are different. If you think the original phrasing produces a better sentence than any of the alternatives, select choice (A); if not, select one of the other choices.

In making your selection, follow the requirements of standard written English; that is, pay attention to grammar, choice of words, sentence construction, and punctuation. Your selection should result in the most effective sentence—clear and precise, without awkwardness or ambiguity.

EXAMPLE: ANSWER:

Every apple in the baskets <u>are ripe and labeled according to the date it was picked</u>.   Ⓐ ● Ⓒ Ⓓ Ⓔ

(A) are ripe and labeled according to the date it was picked
(B) is ripe and labeled according to the date it was picked
(C) are ripe and labeled according to the date they were picked
(D) is ripe and labeled according to the date they were picked
(E) are ripe and labeled as to the date it was picked

---

1. While shopping for a birthday present for Anna, <u>that was when Julie remembered a clearance sale at the outlet mall</u>.

   (A) that was when Julie remembered a clearance sale at the outlet mall

   (B) Julie remembered a clearance sale at the outlet mall

   (C) then Julie's memory of the outlet mall's clearance sale took place

   (D) the outlet mall's clearance sale was what Julie remembered

   (E) a clearance sale at the outlet mall was remembered by Julie

2. The teachers agreed <u>to meet in a month's time and they would discuss</u> a number of issues affecting the school.

   (A) to meet in a month's time and they would discuss

   (B) to meet in a month's time to discuss

   (C) to meeting in a month's time, thereby discussing

   (D) with meeting in a month's time for discussing of

   (E) on the meeting in a month's time to the discussing

GO ON TO THE NEXT PAGE ⟩

3. Word has it that employees <u>using the latest version of word processing software to produce documents streamlining</u> the week's work schedule.

(A) using the latest version of word processing software to produce documents streamlining

(B) using the latest version of word processing software to produce documents and stream-line

(C) using the latest version of word processing software and producing documents, they streamlined

(D) are using the latest version of word processing software to produce documents, thus streamlining

(E) used the latest version of word processing software, so streamlining methods of

4. Last month, one of my best friends <u>were absent so often that I was afraid she might be</u> seriously ill.

(A) were absent so often that I was afraid she might be

(B) were absent so often that I were afraid she might be

(C) were absent so often; that I was afraid she might be

(D) was absent so often that I was afraid she might be

(E) was absent so often; that I was afraid she might be

5. The city's administration constantly complained of having too little money to fix roads, but actually <u>it had a greater amount of funding than</u> other cities in the state.

(A) it had a greater amount of funding than

(B) its funding was the most among

(C) it was having more funding than

(D) the amount of funds they had was the most of

(E) it had more funding than

6. Hockey fans in the 1990s saw more violence on the rink <u>than</u> the 1950s and 1960s.

(A) than

(B) than did

(C) than the hockey of

(D) than with the fans in

(E) than did fans in

7. <u>Unlike many female poets who preceded her, Emily Dickinson</u> did not find her inspiration in light verse.

(A) Unlike many female poets who preceded her, Emily Dickinson

(B) Unlike the inspiration of many female poets who preceded her, Emily Dickinson

(C) Emily Dickinson's poetry, unlike many female poets who preceded her,

(D) Different from many female poets who preceded her, Emily Dickinson's poetry

(E) Emily Dickinson's inspirations, different from many female poets who preceded her,

8. In the United States, the movement toward neo-classicism was perhaps even more pronounced in architecture than <u>either music or literature</u>.

(A) either music or literature

(B) either music or in literature

(C) either in music or literature

(D) in either music or literature

(E) in either music or in literature

GO ON TO THE NEXT PAGE

9. <u>Because environmental waste is at the root of many other problems is the reason why</u> the new government tackled industrial cleanup first.

   (A) Because environmental waste is at the root of many other problems is the reason why

   (B) Because environmental waste is at the root of many other problems,

   (C) Environmental waste causes many other problems and is the reason why

   (D) As a result of environmental waste causing many other problems,

   (E) The fact that environmental waste is the real source of many other problems is why

10. In New York's Central Park, you can still see a number <u>of birds, even though most species have already completed their migration.</u>

   (A) of birds, even though most species have already completed their migration

   (B) of birds, but most species having already completed their migration

   (C) of birds, most species having already completed their migration, however

   (D) of birds despite the migration of most species having already been completed

   (E) of birds, most species have already completed their migration

11. In New England, deer are found only in sparsely populated areas, <u>since such is the case, very few are ever seen by urban dwellers.</u>

   (A) since such is the case, very few are ever seen by urban dwellers

   (B) and very few are ever seen by urban dwellers because of that

   (C) no more than a few are ever seen by urban dwellers as a result

   (D) the number ever seen by urban dwellers is very few for this reason

   (E) and so no more than a few are ever seen by urban dwellers

GO ON TO THE NEXT PAGE

Directions: The following sentences test your ability to recognize grammar and usage errors. Each sentence contains either a single error or no error at all. No sentence contains more than one error. The error, if there is one, is underlined and lettered. If the sentence contains an error, select the one underlined part that must be changed to make the sentence correct. If the sentence is correct, select choice (E). In choosing answers, follow the requirements of standard written English.

EXAMPLE:

<u>Whenever</u> one is driving late at night, <u>you</u> must take extra precautions <u>against</u>
  A   B   C

falling asleep <u>at the wheel</u>. <u>No error</u>
            D   E

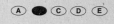

12. Although raised in Canada, Janet lived most of her

    adult life in the United States, <u>where,</u> <u>like</u> other
                                      A   B

    expatriates, she <u>had took</u> some of her
                      C

    <u>most memorable</u> vacations. <u>No error</u>
        D   E

13. In constant <u>demand as</u> a pianist, David
                A

    <u>had never been</u> <u>more richer</u> than he <u>is now</u>.
      B   C   D

    <u>No error</u>
      E

14. <u>During</u> the day, <u>there is</u> often two guards at the
    A   B

    entrance <u>to prevent</u> burglary <u>attempts</u>. <u>No error</u>
             C   D   E

15. Fans of downhill skiing respected the <u>decision by</u>
                                     A

    the judges that athletes <u>which</u> take performance-
                        B

    enhancing drugs <u>while training</u>
                   C

    <u>would be disqualified</u> from the competition.
              D

    <u>No error</u>
      E

16. <u>One would have</u> <u>difficulty determining</u>
      A   B

    <u>which factor</u> contributes <u>more</u> to the success of
        C   D

    a great writer—talent or hard work. <u>No error</u>
                                     E

17. We were surprised to find <u>volunteers from</u> the local
                              A

    high school <u>to be</u> as helpful and efficient <u>as those</u>
             B   C

    whom we <u>had trained</u> to assist in earlier
             D

    emergencies. <u>No error</u>
              E

18. <u>Although</u> rescuers found thirty people in the
    A

    wreckage, there <u>was</u> <u>no more than</u> five children
                   B   C

    <u>among them</u>. <u>No error</u>
        D   E

19. The human resources department <u>is using</u> online
                             A

    ads to recruit new employees because applicants

    can respond to <u>this</u> <u>more quickly</u> than
                  B   C

    <u>to print ones</u>. <u>No error</u>
         D   E

GO ON TO THE NEXT PAGE

20. The performers auditioning for the musical

    <u>are having to prepare</u> both a monologue and a song
           A

    <u>whereas</u> those who want <u>to be</u> in the Shakespeare
      B   C

    production can try out <u>without singing</u>. <u>No error</u>
                  D   E

21. Many countries, <u>including</u> the United States,
             A

    <u>has signed</u> treaties <u>that address</u> the problem
      B   C

    <u>of the warming of</u> the earth's atmosphere. <u>No error</u>
       D   E

22. The botanical garden program familiarizes

    children <u>with</u> names of different flowers,
          A

    <u>teaches them</u> the conventions of naming plants,
      B

    and <u>they have</u> the <u>opportunity to</u> learn skills used
         C   D

    by gardeners. <u>No error</u>
              E

23. Analysis of in-house memos <u>indicate that</u> the
                    A

    <u>most promising</u> aspects of the plan for expansion
      B

    are also <u>those which</u> are the least <u>popular with</u> the
           C   D

    company's management. <u>No error</u>
              E

24. Far <u>away from</u> having a life-threatening condition,
        A

    <u>Jason is</u>, doctors <u>have determined</u>, well enough to
      B   C

    continue his recuperation <u>at home</u>. <u>No error</u>
                    D   E

25. <u>For the past</u> few years, the abandoned building <u>was</u>
      A   B

    a kind of sanctuary <u>in which</u> feral cats have been
                  C

    eating food <u>brought to them</u> by neighbors.
              D

    <u>No error</u>
    E

26. <u>Concerned by</u> the patient's chest pains and
      A

    breathing difficulty, the nursing student was quick

    <u>to realize</u> that these symptoms were <u>consistent to</u>
      B   C

    <u>those</u> of a heart attack. <u>No error</u>
      D   E

27. <u>In many ways</u>, the Catskills and the Adirondacks
      A

    offer similar hiking trails, <u>but</u> the Adirondacks
                    B

    <u>have</u> <u>the most unobstructed</u> views. <u>No error</u>
     C   D   E

28. Between my roommate <u>and I</u> <u>exists</u>
                  A B

    <u>an exceptionally close</u> relationship; <u>neither of us</u>
            C   D

    has any desire to request a change. <u>No error</u>
                            E

29. <u>As</u> the mayor of the city, he had <u>a presence</u> that was
    A   B

    comforting <u>to</u> his constituents, who <u>had supported</u>
            C   D

    him since he first ran for city council. <u>No error</u>
                            E

GO ON TO THE NEXT PAGE ⟹

Directions: The passages below are followed by questions based on their content; questions following a pair of related passages may also be based on the relationship between the paired passages. Answer the questions on the basis of what is <u>stated</u> or <u>implied</u> in the passages and in any introductory material that may be provided.

Questions 30–35 are based on the following passage.

(**1**) Many art lovers have never heard of Dieter Roth. (**2**) Of all the Swiss artists of the past century, he is probably the least well known. (**3**) He attended school in Switzerland, where he cultivated a love of poetry and art—the Constructivist-inspired Concrete Art style espoused by Swiss artist Max Bill—and became known for his graphic work in prints and art books. (**4**) He made his living designing books, textiles, jewelry, and plywood furniture. (**5**) In 1953, Roth was involved with a group of artists and writers who published a journal called *Spirale*. (**6**) He designed the first cover in 1953.

(**7**) In 1960, Roth encountered the kinetic sculptures of Swiss artist Jean Tinguely, some of which were built to self-destruct. (**8**) Tinguely's belief that art and life were part of the same process had a profound effect on Roth. (**9**) By 1966, Roth was using bananas and sausages in his printmaking instead of metal. (**10**) From then on, his main theme was the passage of time. (**11**) It was illustrated with depictions of visible decay, chance, and mindless accumulation. (**12**) Dieter Roth being seen as an anti-art satirist because he used unconventional materials.

(**13**) Roth remained elusive to the public. (**14**) He was suspicious of galleries and dealers, and skeptical of museums and curators as interpreters of his work. (**15**) Roth spurned the art world and distrusted other artists, while managing to command their respect.

30. Which is the best version of the underlined portion of sentence 3 (reproduced below)?

    He attended school in Switzerland, where he cultivated a love of poetry and art—the Constructivist-inspired Concrete Art style espoused by Swiss artist Max Bill—and became known for his graphic arts work in prints and art books.

    (A) (As it is now)
    (B) Attending school in Switzerland, where he
    (C) At school in Switzerland, where he
    (D) Having attended school in Switzerland, he
    (E) He attended school in Switzerland, he

31. Which of the following is the best version of the underlined portion of sentences 5 and 6 (reproduced below)?

    In 1953 Roth was involved with a group of artists and writers who published a journal called Spirale. *He designed the first cover.*

    (A) In 1953 Roth was involved with a group of artists and writers who published a journal called *Spirale* and he designed
    (B) In 1953 Roth was involved with a group of artists and writers who published a journal called *Spirale*, for which he designed
    (C) So in 1953 Roth was involved with a group of artists and writers who published a journal called *Spirale*, designing
    (D) Consequently, a group of artists and writers who published a journal called *Spirale* had Roth involved in 1953 with his designing
    (E) By being involved with a group of artists and writers who published a journal called *Spirale*, he designed

GO ON TO THE NEXT PAGE →

32. Which of the following is the best version of the underlined portion of sentences 10 and 11 (reproduced below)?

From then on, his main theme was the passage of <u>*time. It was illustrated*</u> *with depictions of visible decay, chance, and mindless accumulation.*

(A) time, which he illustrated
(B) time, and it was illustrated
(C) time that was nevertheless illustrated
(D) time that would be illustrated
(E) time. It was being illustrated

33. In context, which is the best way to deal with sentence 12?

(A) Change *being* to "was."
(B) Insert "Finally" at the beginning.
(C) Change *Dieter Roth* to "he."
(D) Delete *he used*.
(E) Change *he used* to "he had used."

34. Which of the following ways to revise the underlined portion of sentence 15 (reproduced below) most effectively links the sentence to the rest of the paragraph?

<u>*Roth spurned*</u> *the art world and distrusted other artists, while managing to command their respect.*

(A) Because as a young man Roth spurned
(B) Since his time in Switzerland he was spurning
(C) By this time he had been spurning
(D) Despite his success, Roth spurned
(E) Nevertheless, by now he had spurned

35. Which sentence is best to add after sentence 15?

(A) His work, which sought to blur the line between art and life, influenced a generation of artists, including Andy Warhol.
(B) Roth's work encompassed drawing, painting, sculpture, collage, assemblage, music, poetry, art books, film, and video.
(C) Many American artists also used unconventional materials in their work.
(D) Ahead of his time, Roth could also be considered a post-modernist.
(E) Roth was born in 1930 in Hanover, Germany.

IF YOU FINISH BEFORE TIME IS CALLED, YOU MAY CHECK YOUR WORK ON THIS SECTION ONLY. DO NOT TURN TO ANY OTHER SECTION IN THE TEST.

SECTION 6

Time—25 Minutes
24 Questions

Directions: For each of the following questions, choose the best answer and darken the corresponding oval on the answer sheet.

Each sentence below has one or two blanks, each blank indicating that something has been omitted. Beneath the sentence are five words or sets of words labeled (A) through (E). Choose the word or set of words that, when inserted in the sentence, best fits the meaning of the sentence as a whole.

EXAMPLE:

Today's small, portable computers contrast markedly with the earliest electronic computers, which were ----.

(A) effective
(B) invented
(C) useful
(D) destructive
(E) enormous

1. Contrary to ---- about what it would be like if scientists predicted that the Earth would be hit by a large asteroid, subsequent calculations ---- that it would be unlikely to occur.

   (A) theories . . refuted
   (B) predictions . . challenged
   (C) speculations . . confirmed
   (D) disclaimers . . validated
   (E) doubts . . substantiated

2. The research in areas of human ---- and exploration suggests that these characteristics arise from both intrinsic motivations or drives to gain information and extrinsic explorative behavior.

   (A) orderliness
   (B) credulity
   (C) curiosity
   (D) shyness
   (E) morbidity

3. Judge Sanchez had a reputation for being ---- , presiding over his courtroom with fairness and impartiality.

   (A) equitable
   (B) immoderate
   (C) cumulative
   (D) unproductive
   (E) adulatory

4. Marisa felt like a fraud, for while she professed her ---- she knew she had ---- the unfortunate mistake.

   (A) profundity . . abhorred
   (B) enthusiasm . . condoned
   (C) innocence . . committed
   (D) immorality . . performed
   (E) repentance . . condemned

GO ON TO THE NEXT PAGE

5. Jack's essay was not ---- one, as it had been written hurriedly the night before from a careless ---- of information and research data.

   (A) a rambling . . collage
   (B) an ambiguous . . development
   (C) a coherent . . hodgepodge
   (D) an amorphous . . morass
   (E) an unintelligible . . harangue

6. In the 19th century, when few women were involved in political life and most were forced to remain in the home, the rebellious Constance Markievicz succeeded in ---- politics and ---- the domesticity planned for her.

   (A) obtaining . . succumbing to
   (B) escaping . . subverting
   (C) pursuing . . avoiding
   (D) ignoring . . observing
   (E) disavowing . . enjoying

7. The ---- of American baseball, its "seeming inviolability," was tainted in the late 1990s when investigators uncovered several unlawful drug-related abuses among players.

   (A) turpitude
   (B) sacrosanctity
   (C) perspicuity
   (D) verisimilitude
   (E) duplicity

8. The students wanted to create a new university radio show that celebrated innovation, creativity and diversity by providing an ---- of different types of music, combining progressive pop, jazz, reggae, classical and new music.

   (A) induction
   (B) amalgam
   (C) immersion
   (D) occlusion
   (E) estrangement

GO ON TO THE NEXT PAGE

Questions 9–10 are based on the following passage.

Although he never stood more than five feet, six inches tall, William Faulkner became something of a giant of American literature. More than simply a renowned Mississippi writer—he was born and wrote
(5) in that state—the Nobel Prize-winning novelist achieved fame throughout the world by using the details and peculiarities of his environment to create stunningly vivid settings for literary explorations of the temptations and passions that challenge us. And,
(10) given the fact that he never graduated from high school or received a college degree, it is apparent that Faulkner's remarkable skills as a writer came naturally to him.

9. In the context of the passage, the statement that Faulkner found fame by "using the details and peculiarities of his environment" (line 7) suggests that his

    (A) readers were able to identify fully with his descriptions of Mississippi life

    (B) writings accurately captured the stunning beauty of Mississippi

    (C) success can be partially attributed to the allure of the Mississippi landscape

    (D) depictions of Mississippi resonated well with his readership

    (E) descriptions of the Mississippi climate were uniquely accurate

10. In discussing Faulkner's lack of schooling, the author indicates his belief that Faulkner's writing abilities were

    (A) largely innate

    (B) slowly learned

    (C) always impressive

    (D) devoid of influences

    (E) underappreciated

GO ON TO THE NEXT PAGE

Questions 11–12 are based on the following passage.

Macular degeneration, a disturbance of the retina, is among the top causes of blindness in adults. The disease set upon me gradually, and only with the help of my microphone and speakers am I
(5) able today to get my message across at all. I am a computer programmer who, despite the best efforts of doctors, could not ward off the slow, blinding effects of the disease. Over the course of three quick years, the days became darker and
(10) darker. Yet the memory of the day I could no longer sit and type still jars me. Weeks later, the senses that never earned much of my attention— touch, smell, hearing—have risen to the challenge, and with the help of new tools I'm slowly learning
(15) how to do my job all over again.

11. The author's reference to "three quick years" (line 9) suggests that he

   (A) suffered from a particularly rare illness
   (B) viewed his doctors as unenergetic in their efforts to help him
   (C) found each day of his illness slow and plodding
   (D) perceives his vision as having declined rapidly
   (E) is likely to develop new sensory skills easily

12. The author discusses how some senses "never earned much" of his attention (line 12) in order to

   (A) indicate the irony of a computer programmer becoming blind
   (B) highlight the power of illness to refocus attention
   (C) lament the inability of doctors to ward off the disease
   (D) challenge the commonly-held belief that blind people cannot work
   (E) stress the importance of sensory perception to all mankind

GO ON TO THE NEXT PAGE

Questions 13–24 are based on the following passages.

The following passages discuss the ongoing debate in the music community whether disc jockeys (DJs), more specifically "turntablists," are actually musicians. Both passages were written in 2003 by professional turntablists.

Passage 1

I played guitar long before I bought my first pair of turntables, so I feel as equipped as anybody to offer an opinion on the debate. To begin with, it is very important to define what a DJ is because (5) it is an umbrella term for more than one thing. Normally, when I speak of a "DJ," I'm talking about turntablists, like myself, sometimes referred to as "scratchers." Innovative, often groundbreaking turntablists are often unfairly lumped together (10) in one broad category that includes dance club DJs, many of whom simply spin other performers' vinyl records with a minimum of alteration. Like a wedding DJ or a dance club DJ, a turntablist uses two or more turntables and mostly prerecorded (15) material by other artists, but that's essentially where the similarities end. But it is the stigma of using "material by other artists" that hangs over the head of every turntablist, and it brings us to the real crux of the debate: Is it possible to be a (20) musician if you do not create the actual music?

According to the dictionary, a musician is "a composer, conductor, or performer of music." A turntablist fits that description. I am undoubtedly a musician, and I take great offense at the (25) suggestion that I am not. My two turntables and mixer are the instruments with which I compose, conduct, and perform my music, unrehearsed for the thousands of people who come to hear me scratch every year. Like the guitar I picked up (30) when I was a teenager, the turntables are difficult to master; I have spent countless hours of my life experimenting, woodshedding the cutting, mixing, and beat-juggling necessary to be able to invoke the sounds that I want, when I want. Yes, I use (35) other performers' music as the base medium through which I experiment and create, but to say that a traditional musician is 100% original is not

exactly true. Even the most accomplished guitarists will employ licks and riffs in their playing (40) that they consciously or subconsciously picked up from others. Jimmy Page and Eric Clapton both "stole" blues musicians' songs and chord progressions and incorporated them as their own. Yet there is no debate over whether Clapton or Page (45) are really musicians.

In some ways, however, comparing scratch DJs with rock guitarists is a poor analogy. Turntablism is more like a new jazz. Like the bebop jazz musicians of the 40s and 50s who improvised around a (50) melody, scratchers reinterpret portions of a song to make it uniquely their own. The sounds produced are fresh and original and as distinctive from turntablist to turntablist as Mile Davis's trumpet or Charlie Parker's saxophone.

(55) Looking back at recent generations, both jazz and rock were not immediately accepted as valid music forms. The "Old Guard" music establishment did not immediately embrace the Beatles, yet somehow the legendary John Lennon and his (60) band mates still managed to sell a few albums. In the end, music comes down to 12 pitches, pure and simple. Anybody who has the skill and talent to manipulate those notes into something beautiful is a musician, regardless of the instrument.

Passage 2

(65) Like any endeavor that requires a certain level of skill, there are master turntablists and there are hacks. The quality of sound produced by a specific artist is a direct result of talent, ability, the material he or she works with, and the capacity to meld the (70) three into something worthwhile and listenable.

Ostensibly, at the heart of this debate is the fact that most DJs and turntablists use music created by others to compose their sound. But to me, this silly controversy exists simply because the true (75) definition of a musician is extremely vague and eternally arguable. From an academic point of view, there are those who argue that because a turntablist does not have the ability to alter the basic chord structure of the song they are using,

GO ON TO THE NEXT PAGE ⟶

(80) they are actually "distortionists" rather than musicians. But if being able to string together a couple of different chords is all that qualifies one as a "musician," strictly speaking, any one of us who has tinkered on the keys of a piano for a few min-
(85) utes can assign themselves the distinction. Without question there is a difference between being a true artist as opposed to a dabbler, but to the dabbler in question, what exactly is that difference? Whether you are a drummer, a sculptor, or a
(90) writer, in the end, it is nice to be able to express yourself in a manner that inspires others, but it is much more important to inspire yourself—even if you are just strumming the same two chords on your guitar over and over again. However, with all
(95) that said, in my decade of traveling the globe as a turntablist, I never considered myself a musician. I see myself more as a progressive artist, working on the fringe, but steadily moving closer to being realized by the kids who watch MTV.
(100) Though the criteria for what qualifies a musician or an artist is extremely vague, the truth is, one is no more culturally valid or important than the other. There are certainly accomplished musicians who are turntablists (some even press their
(105) own original material to spin), but to me, though turntablism deals directly with the creation of musical sounds, a turntablist is more like a painter than a guitar player or pianist. Like a painter, a turntablist needs a thorough understanding of the
(110) medium with which he or she is working, a good ear (rather than a painter's eye), and dedication to mastering the craft and the tools. The prerecorded music I work with is like the paint—though I did not physically create it, I can do with it whatever I
(115) want to achieve my desired effect. From those raw materials I create something more; I morph it into a beautiful piece distinctly my own. Am I a musician? Depends on whom you ask. Am I an artist in every sense of the word? No doubt.

13. The descriptions of the "thousands of people who come to hear me" (line 28) in Passage 1 and of "my decade of traveling the globe as a turntablist" (lines 95–96) in Passage 2 demonstrate that both performers

(A) are exorbitantly wealthy individuals
(B) have worked with each other in the past
(C) are more than just hobbyists
(D) have biases against traditional musicians
(E) spin and scratch their own songs

14. Both turntablists would probably agree that

(A) using prerecorded material of your own creation is better than using another artist's
(B) turntablism is an ephemeral art form that will not stand the test of time
(C) the debate about whether or not DJs and turntablists are musicians is personally meaningless
(D) turntablism will eventually become more accepted by the mainstream
(E) turntables are more difficult to master than the guitar

15. In line 32 in Passage 1, "woodshedding" most closely means

(A) sawing
(B) theorizing
(C) improvising
(D) spurning
(E) practicing

GO ON TO THE NEXT PAGE

16. Passage 2's author most probably would argue that the author's statement in lines 21–25 (According to …that I am not) in Passage 1 is

    (A) true, because a turntablist fits the dictionary description of a musician, and therefore it should not be open to debate

    (B) an overreaction, because the definition of a musician is very generalized and debatable

    (C) specious, because he admitted to using prerecorded music created by other artists

    (D) inaccurate, since turntablists are nothing more than "distortionists"

    (E) disappointing, because a painter has more integrity than a musician

17. In lines 34–35 (Yes, I use…really musicians) the author of Passage 1 offers an argument that is best defined as

    (A) reasonable

    (B) droll

    (C) simplistic

    (D) dishonest

    (E) irrational

18. From the author's comparison of a turntablist to a dance club DJ in lines 6–16 of Passage 1, it can be assumed that he

    (A) does not want the reader to confuse turntablists and dance club DJs with radio announcers

    (B) forgot to clarify that DJ stands for "disc jockey"

    (C) feels it is necessary to praise all types of DJs as musical innovators

    (D) does not consider most dance hall DJs to be his peers

    (E) does not believe it is possible for a wedding or dance club DJ to be talented

19. Passage 1's main purpose is to

    (A) describe different turntablist techniques

    (B) question the relevance of a debate

    (C) support one side of an argument

    (D) investigate an argument from a neutral position

    (E) dispute the opinion of a majority

20. The use of quotation marks around "stole" (line 42) in Passage 1, and "musician" (line 83) in Passage 2 both function to

    (A) imply that the authors want both words interpreted in their strictest sense

    (B) emphasize the importance of each word in their respective sentences

    (C) show that someone other the author is being quoted

    (D) clarify that both words have alternate meanings in music terminology

    (E) illustrate the looseness with which both authors employ the words.

21. Passage 2's author discusses the academic point of view in lines 76–85 (From an…distinction) mainly to

    (A) demonstrate that all music professors will never consider turntablists to be musicians

    (B) support the argument that she is an artist, not a musician

    (C) offer an example that illustrates the ease with which an argument on this subject can be attacked

    (D) present an irrefutable argument for those who do consider turntablists to be musicians

    (E) show how insulated most academic campuses are from the real world

GO ON TO THE NEXT PAGE

22. The attitude of the author of Passage 2 toward the "dabblers" (line 86–89) can best be characterized as

(A) neutral, because they have no bearing on her life either way

(B) negative, because they have nothing to offer as performers

(C) negative, because they mock the dedication of the master artists

(D) positive, because she believes a person trying to express himself is a good thing

(E) positive, because she believes they are actually the true artists

23. If the author of Passage 2 were to make a comparison similar to that in lines 47–54 of Passage 1, of a turntablist's sounds to "Mile Davis's trumpet or Charlie Parker's saxophone," she would most likely compare a turntablist's sounds to

(A) the neo-dada paintings of Robert Rauschenberg, who included "found" objects and images in his work that he did not create

(B) the expressionist paintings of Edvard Munch, who distorted reality in his art for emotional effect

(C) the music of Britney Spears, whose single "Baby One More Time" was MTV's most requested video ever

(D) the architecture of Bruce Graham, who designed the Sears Tower in Chicago

(E) the sound of the Beatles, which still influences young musicians to this day

24. Which of the following would best describe the author's tone in lines 112–119 ("The prerecorded music…No doubt") of Passage 2?

(A) assured

(B) perplexed

(C) overconfident

(D) acrimonious

(E) inquisitive

SECTION 7
Time—20 Minutes
16 Questions

Directions: For this section, solve each problem and decide which is the best of the choices given. Fill in the corresponding oval on the answer sheet. You may use any available space for scratchwork.

Notes:

(1) Calculator use is permitted.

(2) All numbers used are real numbers.

(3) Figures are provided for some problems. All figures are drawn to scale and lie in a plane UNLESS otherwise indicated.

(4) Unless otherwise specified, the domain of any function f is assumed to be the set of all real numbers x for which $f(x)$ is a real number.

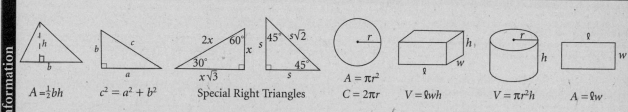

$A = \frac{1}{2}bh$ $c^2 = a^2 + b^2$ Special Right Triangles $A = \pi r^2$ $V = \ell wh$ $V = \pi r^2 h$ $A = \ell w$
$C = 2\pi r$

The sum of the degree measures of the angles in a triangle is 180.
The number of degrees of arc in a circle is 360.
A straight angle has a degree measure of 180.

1. If pencils cost $0.50 each and notebooks cost $3 each, which of the following represents the cost, in dollars, of p pencils and n notebooks?

   (A) $2pn$

   (B) $3.5pn$

   (C) $3.5(n + p)$

   (D) $3n + 0.50p$

   (E) $2(n + 0.50p)$

2. The average (arithmetic mean) of 7, 20, and x is 20. What is the value of x?

   (A) 20

   (B) 27

   (C) 32

   (D) 33

   (E) 40

3. Amanda, Ben, and Cindy made a total of 34 greeting cards. Ben made 4 times as many as Amanda, and Cindy made 3 times as many as Ben. How many greeting cards did Amanda make?

   (A) two

   (B) three

   (C) four

   (D) six

   (E) eight

4. If 0.05 percent of n is 5, what is 5 percent of n?

   (A) 900

   (B) 700

   (C) 500

   (D) 0.007

   (E) 0.005

GO ON TO THE NEXT PAGE

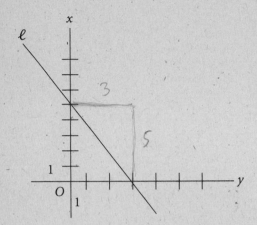

5. What is the equation of line ℓ in the figure above?

(A) $y = -\dfrac{5}{3}x + 3$

(B) $y = -\dfrac{5}{3}x + 5$

(C) $y = -\dfrac{3}{5}x + 5$

(D) $y = \dfrac{3}{5}x + 3$

(E) $y = \dfrac{3}{5}x + 5$

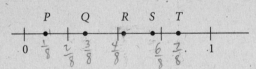

6. If the tick marks on the number line above are equally spaced, which of the lettered points P through T is between $\dfrac{1}{2}$ and $\dfrac{5}{8}$?

(A) P

(B) Q

(C) R

(D) S

(E) T

7. If $m^{-1}n = 2$, what does n equal in terms of m?

(A) $-2m$

(B) $\dfrac{1}{m}$

(C) $\dfrac{2}{m}$

(D) $2m$

(E) m^2

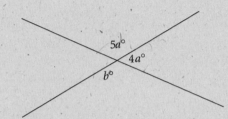

8. In the figure above, what is the value of b?

(A) 60

(B) 75

(C) 80

(D) 100

(E) 105

9. If $x^2 + x = 20$, which of the following is a possible value of $x^2 - x$?

(A) −30

(B) 20

(C) 30

(D) 40

(E) 450

GO ON TO THE NEXT PAGE

10. Megan began a one-way 5–mile bicycle trip by riding very quickly uphill for 2 miles. She rested for 10 minutes and then road slowly for the rest of the trip. Which of the following graphs could correctly represent the trip?

(A)
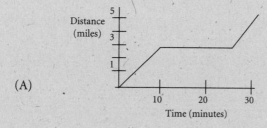

(D)
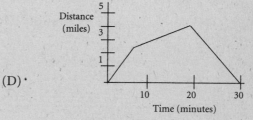

(B)
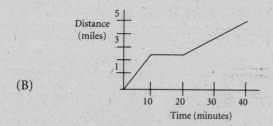

(E)
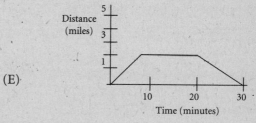

(C)
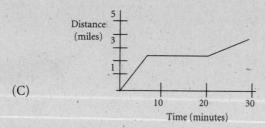

GO ON TO THE NEXT PAGE

11. There are 5 red, 5 green, 5 blue, and 5 yellow hats packaged in 20 identical, unmarked boxes, with 1 hat per box. What is the least number of boxes that must be selected in order to be sure that among the boxes selected 4 or more contain hats of the same color?

(A) 4
(B) 8
(C) 9
(D) 12
(E) 13

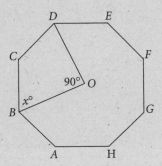

12. In the figure above, *ABCDEFGH* is a regular octagon with center *O*. What is the value of *x*?

(A) 90
(B) 82.5
(C) 67.5
(D) 57.5
(E) 45

13. Let the function *f* be defined by $f(t) = 6t$ for all numbers *t*. Which of the following is equivalent to $f(t - r)$?

(A) $\dfrac{t - r}{6}$

(B) $6t - r$

(C) $6t - 6r$

(D) $12(t - r)$

(E) $36tr$

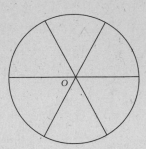

14. The circle above has an area of 16π and is divided into 6 congruent regions. What is the perimeter of one of these regions?

(A) $8 - 16\pi$

(B) $8 + \dfrac{4\pi}{9}$

(C) $8 + \dfrac{4\pi}{3}$

(D) $8 + 5\pi$

(E) $8 + 16\pi$

$$3x - 4y = 10$$
$$6x + wy = 16$$

15. For which of the following values of *w* will the system of equations above have <u>no</u> solutions?

(A) −8
(B) −4
(C)   0
(D)   4
(E)   8

GO ON TO THE NEXT PAGE

RESULTS OF A BOW & ARROW CONTEST

Number of shots	Number of people
1	5
2	6
3	7
4	8
5	4

16. In an archery contest, each person shot a bow & arrow at a target until the person missed the target. The table shows the results for 30 people who entered the contest. For example, 8 people hit the target on their first 3 tries and missed on their 4th shot. Based on information in the table, which of the following must be true?

    I. More than half the people hit the target on their first throw.

    II. For all of the shots attempted, more hit the target than missed it.

    III. No one hit the target 5 times.

(A) I only

(B) III only

(C) I and III only

(D) II and III only

(E) I, II, and III

IF YOU FINISH BEFORE TIME IS CALLED, YOU MAY CHECK YOUR WORK ON THIS SECTION ONLY. DO NOT TURN TO ANY OTHER SECTION IN THE TEST.   STOP

SECTION 8

Time—20 Minutes

19 Questions

Directions: For each of the following questions, choose the best answer and darken the corresponding oval on the answer sheet.

Each sentence below has one or two blanks, each blank indicating that something has been omitted. Beneath the sentence are five words or sets of words labeled (A) through (E). Choose the word or set of words that, when inserted in the sentence, best fits the meaning of the sentence as a whole.

EXAMPLE:

Today's small, portable computers contrast markedly with the earliest electronic computers, which were ----.

(A) effective
(B) invented
(C) useful
(D) destructive
(E) enormous

---

1. Although his leadership skills had been questioned, once the coach won his first championship everyone realized he was quite ---- managing his team.

   (A) remiss in
   (B) adept at
   (C) humorous about
   (D) hesitant about
   (E) contemptuous of

2. With the cave opening ---- by a dense wall of vines, the artifacts it contained remained concealed for centuries.

   (A) released
   (B) elevated
   (C) entangled
   (D) shrouded
   (E) attained

3. Although he usually felt comfortable speaking in front of audiences, this particular group was so large and intimidating that he suddenly found himself too ---- to ---- the topic before them.

   (A) impassioned .. analyze
   (B) timid .. discuss
   (C) cautious .. suppress
   (D) knowledgeable .. disregard
   (E) perceptive .. defend

4. Due to his ---- reputation, few were surprised when he joined the fight against ---- medical reforms.

   (A) modest .. acceptable
   (B) inescapable .. legitimate
   (C) insufficient .. overpowering
   (D) admirable .. unjust
   (E) unbelievable .. tolerable

GO ON TO THE NEXT PAGE

5. While fans faithful to the old ballpark considered its demolition ----, proponents of the new stadium found it quite ----.

   (A) momentous . . formidable
   (B) decisive . . unavoidable
   (C) unexpected . . ambiguous
   (D) advantageous . . beneficial
   (E) catastrophic . . constructive

6. The prosecutor was so frustrated by his lack of credible or convincing evidence that when describing the defendant during the trial he shamefully resorted to ----.

   (A) arbitration
   (B) narcissism
   (C) calumny
   (D) tenacity
   (E) solicitude

GO ON TO THE NEXT PAGE

Directions: The passages below are followed by questions based on their content; questions following a pair of related passages may also be based on the relationship between the paired passages. Answer the questions on the basis of what is <u>stated</u> or <u>implied</u> in the passages and in any introductory material that may be provided.

Questions 7–19 are based on the following passage.

The following passage is from a 1994 novel about a man who inadvertently rediscovers his long-lost daughter. The two main characters are Oscar and his daughter Celia.

Oscar stumbled his way through the darkness into the harsh light of the bathroom. The image reflected in the medicine cabinet mirror was that of an attractive middle-aged man, well over six
(5) feet tall with broad shoulders and a mop of black hair dappled with gray. His eyes were two different colors—his left was chocolate brown and his right was a deep ocean blue intertwined with a marbleized yellow and green—and they were set
(10) beneath a telling brow that more than once betrayed the true feelings hidden behind the steely demeanor of his strong jaw. Indeed, to the many eyes that admired him it was never hard to discern that Oscar perceived things in a manner so intense
(15) it often reflected in his every movement, like he was some kind of marionette in the hands of a clumsy puppeteer.

Oscar stooped close to the mirror and examined the faint lines on his face in the same meticulous
(20) manner he approached his art—proofreading each tiny crease on the cheeks and around his eyes and then the slightest documents near his mouth. Spawned from an excess of smiling in younger days that seemed a lifetime ago, in the landscape
(25) of Oscar's mind these wrinkles implode into deep crevices of a progressive doom. He snapped off the light and got dressed for his fierce daily run of over six miles; then he hit the street and disappeared into the darkness, where the race against
(30) his self started yet again.

Fifty-two years old, he cut swiftly through the evening. Each window he passed seemed to fall out of the darkness, like various portraits of the scenes inside. A portrait of a smiling wife in a blue
(35) space painted by the TV; another portrait of a young man readying himself for the promise of the evening; rooms peopled with old men comfortably relaxing in the materialization of their dreams that taunted Oscar and pushed him even
(40) further into the shadows.

In those shadows Oscar broke into a sprint. The streets darkened and were silenced by the breeze created by his speed. Though he was completely alone, he ran like a man being chased down and
(45) his pace did not flag until he neared the entrance to his building. He gathered his breath and walked back into the bright lobby towards the elevator, oblivious to the doorman's welcome as he entered.

At that same moment on the elevator, Celia
(50) Hargrove was leaning on her grandmother's wheelchair. As they descended toward the lobby, 18-year-old Celia reluctantly looked at her reflection in the elevator's mirrored wall, whispered to herself "*I am not cruel, only truthful*[1]," and sighed.
(55) Since she came to New York to spend the summer taking care of her grandmother, she had never felt more unsure and childish. The sophisticated manner of the women Celia enviously glimpsed on the city streets made her feel as if she'd be a child for-
(60) ever. She watched them hurrying across Broadway on their way to interesting places Celia could only imagine, or laughing with carmine mouths and fresh cigarettes in the dim backseats of taxicabs, on the inside of some joke to which Celia was not
(65) privy. They worked behind imposing store counters and breezy shop curtains, and held the hands of tall, handsome gentlemen as they leisurely strolled past, while Celia pushed her crabby old grandmother on her daily walks. Spending her
(70) days with the wizened old woman helped Celia to appreciate the gift of her own youth, yet every

GO ON TO THE NEXT PAGE

morning she awoke to find the disappointing
blessing of still feeling like a young girl.

Celia's mind shuffled through her young
thoughts and she quickly realized they'd forgotten
(75) something.

"Grammy, we've forgotten your medication
again, we'll have to go back up to get it."

"Oh I didn't forget. It makes me too tired, and
I'm tired enough as it is."

(80) "Well that's no excuse," said Celia, "We're going
back up."

The elevator doors parted and there Oscar
stood waiting for the two figures inside to exit.
When they did not, he found himself staring
(85) straight into the face of Celia. Oscar, was overcome with a feeling that he could not immediately
identify. Certainly, the young girl in front of him
was beautiful. Her long and shining black hair,
which she tucked behind her small ears, framed
(90) soulful eyes and lightly glossed lips that were
uncommonly large, and set perfectly in the
seraphic glow of her face. It was not Celia's
remarkable beauty, however, that disconcerted
Oscar. She had one blue and one brown eye
(95) almost identical to Oscar's eyes; it was like he was
looking into his own.

"Are you just going to stand there like an idiot,"
asked Grandma of Oscar, "or are you coming in?"

"I'm coming in," Oscar quietly replied as he
(100) entered the elevator.

Celia nervously fumbled through her purse and
put on her sunglasses.

"I hated them when I was your age," Oscar
timidly offered to Celia.

(105) "Hated what?"

"My eyes. I couldn't stand them," Oscar replied,
"But then one day I heard this famous quote about
beauty, and it changed my whole perspective."

The elevator doors opened before he could
(110) finish.

"This is my floor. I guess I'll have to keep you in
suspense until the next time we run into each
other."

[1.] *A line from Sylvia's Plath's poem "Mirror," which is written
from the point of view of a mirror.*

7. The best description of this passage would be

(A) a depiction of a chance encounter between a
long lost father and daughter

(B) a tearful reunion between a parent and child

(C) an illustration of how a father and daughter
can look very different

(D) the acquainting of the reader to one character
through the point of view of another

(E) a story of the conclusion of a parent's search
for his missing child

8. What does the description of Oscar in lines 6–12
("His eyes…jaw.") suggest about his character?

(A) he has an obsession with health and exercise

(B) he tries to hide his sensitive nature

(C) he is arrogant and abrasive

(D) he is not trustworthy

(E) he seems impenetrable

9. In reference to Oscar's "art" in lines 18–22, the
metaphorical use of the phrases "proofreading"
and "slightest documents" implies that Oscar is

(A) book editor

(B) an office clerk

(C) a novelist

(D) a lawyer

(E) a painter

10. The streets in the latter half of Oscar's run in the
fourth paragraph (In those shadows…building.)
can most closely be described as

(A) obstructed

(B) threatening

(C) teeming

(D) deadly

(E) clamorous

GO ON TO THE NEXT PAGE ⇨

11. Oscar's impressions while running in the third paragraph and Celia's observations of the "sophisticated" New York women in lines 57–60 both function primarily to

    (A) add a bit of humor to otherwise humorless passage

    (B) emphasize the contentedness of both characters

    (C) describe the different lifestyles of New York City residents

    (D) illustrate both characters' sense of being on the outside looking in

    (E) contrast Oscar's joyful personality to Celia's brooding personality.

12. In line 45, "flag" most closely means

    (A) to signal

    (B) to revive

    (C) to diminish

    (D) to identify

    (E) to fall down

13. The reference to Oscar being oblivious to the doorman in line 48 gives the impression that Oscar

    (A) could not hear the doorman's weak voice

    (B) has had an argument with the doorman

    (C) is not wearing his hearing aid

    (D) is completely lost in his own thoughts

    (E) is uncomfortable in social situations

14. Celia's quote of Sylvia Plath in line 54 reveals that she

    (A) believes herself to be unattractive

    (B) inherited a talent for writing from her father

    (C) is conceited about her good looks

    (D) has read all of Sylvia Plath's work

    (E) feels a connection with Sylvia Plath

15. The phrase "disappointing blessing" in lines 71–72 implies that Celia's urge to feel older was lessened by

    (A) her lack of any responsibilities

    (B) her religious beliefs

    (C) the promise of discovering her father

    (D) an understanding that youth is fleeting

    (E) the resentment of her grandmother

16. In the context of the passage, Oscar's first impression of Celia in lines 88–92 (Certainly... face.) functions to emphasize

    (A) Celia's insecurities about herself

    (B) Oscar's natural bias toward his daughter

    (C) Oscar's sensitive nature

    (D) the reason behind Celia's boastfulness

    (E) why first impressions are important

GO ON TO THE NEXT PAGE

17. Grandma's attitude towards Oscar in line 97–98 is best described as

    (A) sycophantic
    (B) tactful
    (C) feeble
    (D) diffident
    (E) brazen

18. Celia most probably put on her sunglasses because

    (A) she is sensitive to sunlight
    (B) she noticed Oscar's eyes
    (C) she wanted to Oscar to notice her
    (D) she did not want Oscar to recognize her
    (E) she started crying

19. Which of the following is most probably the quote about beauty which Oscar referred to in lines 107–109?

    (A) *Think of all the beauty still left around you and be happy* by Anne Frank
    (B) *Rarely do great beauty and great virtue dwell together* by Petrarch
    (C) *There is no excellent beauty that hath not some strangeness in the proportion* by Francis Bacon
    (D) *Beauty is a form of genius* by Oscar Wilde
    (E) *As we grow old … the beauty steals inward* by Ralph Waldo Emerson

IF YOU FINISH BEFORE TIME IS CALLED, YOU MAY CHECK YOUR WORK ON THIS SECTION ONLY. DO NOT TURN TO ANY OTHER SECTION IN THE TEST. | STOP

SECTION 9
Time—10 Minutes
14 Questions

Directions: For each question in this section, select the best answer from among the choices given and fill in the corresponding oval on the answer sheet.

The following sentences test correctness and effectiveness of expression. Part of each sentence or the entire sentence is underlined; beneath each sentence are five ways of phrasing the underlined material. Choice (A) repeats the original phrasing; the other four choices are different. If you think the original phrasing produces a better sentence than any of the alternatives, select choice (A); if not, select one of the other choices.

In making your selection, follow the requirements of standard written English; that is, pay attention to grammar, choice of words, sentence construction, and punctuation. Your selection should result in the most effective sentence—clear and precise, without awkwardness or ambiguity.

EXAMPLE: ANSWER:

Every apple in the baskets <u>are ripe and labeled according to the date it was picked</u>.   Ⓐ ● Ⓒ Ⓓ Ⓔ

(A) are ripe and labeled according to the date it was picked
(B) is ripe and labeled according to the date it was picked
(C) are ripe and labeled according to the date they were picked
(D) is ripe and labeled according to the date they were picked
(E) are ripe and labeled as to the date it was picked

---

1. To consider the idea of becoming a doctor and to think of it <u>that it is something that can be accomplished</u> while working full time is to underestimate the time and commitment required to complete medical school.

   (A) that it is something that can be accomplished
   (B) as something that can be accomplished
   (C) that it is an accomplishment one can do
   (D) as it was something that can be accomplished
   (E) as if it were like something to accomplish

2. <u>The development of modern democracy's present-day tenets</u> has required many sacrifices by generations of freedom-seeking individuals.

   (A) The development of modern democracy's present-day tenets
   (B) The present-day tenets of modern democracy have had development who
   (C) The way in which the present-day tenets of modern democracy get to be developed
   (D) Developing modern democracy and the present-day tenets of them
   (E) For modern democracy to develop their present-day tenets

GO ON TO THE NEXT PAGE ⟩

3. No lawyer can guarantee that he or she will win a case for a <u>client, an attorney who handles personal injury cases is no exception.</u>

    (A) client, an attorney who handles personal injury cases is no exception
    (B) client, and an attorney who handles personal injury cases is no exception
    (C) client; personal injury cases handled by attorneys are no exception
    (D) client; such a case as personal injury handled by an attorney is no exception
    (E) client, with those personal injury cases handled by attorneys being no exception

4. <u>Unlike most documentary filmmakers, Michael Moore actually appears in the movies he produces.</u>

    (A) Unlike most documentary filmmakers, Michael Moore actually appears in the movies he produces.
    (B) Unlike most documentary filmmakers, Michael Moore is different in that he actually appears in the movies he produces.
    (C) Unlike most documentary filmmakers, Michael Moore actually appears in the movies he produces and others do not.
    (D) Other documentary filmmakers do not, but Michael Moore's movies have him in them.
    (E) Different from most documentary filmmakers, appearances of Michael Moore are in the movies he produces.

5. One way Cameron raised his math grade was <u>because of doing the extra credit problems on his</u> final exam.

    (A) because of doing the extra credit problems on his
    (B) when he did the extra credit problems on his
    (C) through his doing of the extra credit problems on his
    (D) by its doing of the extra credit problems on his
    (E) by doing the extra credit problems on his

6. Having missed the application deadline, <u>the plan for Katy now was</u> to work for a semester, then reapply in February.

    (A) the plan for Katy now was
    (B) Katy's plan now was
    (C) Katy now devising the plan to
    (D) Katy nevertheless now devised the plan to
    (E) Katy now planned to

7. For the past few days, one of our teachers <u>were so absent-minded that we became concerned.</u>

    (A) were so absent-minded that we became concerned
    (B) were so absent-minded; that we became concerned
    (C) were so absent-minded that that we become concerned
    (D) was so absent-minded that we became concerned
    (E) was very absent-minded; so we becoming concerned

GO ON TO THE NEXT PAGE

8. Maria Montessori had a number of theories concerning how children learn, <u>which developed into</u> what is now known as the Montessori Method for education.

   (A) which developed into

   (B) so they were to be

   (C) with a result that they developed into

   (D) therefore developing into

   (E) consequently they would develop into

9. <u>Although the participation in extracurricular activities often results in students having less time to do homework</u>, the benefits of these activities outweigh their drawbacks.

   (A) Although the participation in extracurricular activities often results in students having less time to do homework

   (B) Although less time to do homework is often the result of students' participation in extracurricular activities

   (C) Students who participate in extracurricular activities often have less time for homework, but

   (D) Despite the fact of participating in extracurricular activities often resulting in less time for students to do their homework

   (E) In spite of the result of students having less time to do homework when they participate in extracurricular activities

10. The fundraising campaign continued for a <u>week; volunteers counted money every morning and night</u> with growing amazement.

    (A) week; volunteers counted money every morning and night

    (B) week, which meant volunteers counting money every morning and night

    (C) week; therefore, it meant that volunteers would count money every morning and night

    (D) week and therefore the volunteers would be counting money every morning and night

    (E) week; with volunteers counting money every morning and night

11. <u>Whereby the waiters sing as they serve the customers</u>, their tips are much higher than those of servers at other restaurants.

    (A) Whereby the waiters sing as they serve the customers

    (B) With the waiters and their singing as they serve the customers

    (C) In that there being singing by the waiters as they serve the customers

    (D) Because there is singing by the waiters as they serve the customers

    (E) Because the waiters sing as they serve the customers

12. The students found the members of the Irish theater troupe <u>equally as talented as their accents were</u> thick.

    (A) equally as talented as their accents were

    (B) equally talented and their accents

    (C) as talented and their accents

    (D) as talented as their accents were

    (E) as talented and their accents were

GO ON TO THE NEXT PAGE ▷

13. Although Vincent Van Gogh influenced countless artists after his death, during his lifetime, he failed to achieve fame for the art he <u>created nor profiting</u> from sales of his work.

    (A) created nor profiting

    (B) created nor did he profit

    (C) created nor to have profited

    (D) created or profited

    (E) created or to profit

14. The convenience and value of today's digital cameras <u>account for their popularity</u> with people.

    (A) account for their popularity

    (B) account for its popularity

    (C) accounts for its popularity

    (D) is why they are popular

    (E) are a reason for their popularity

Practice Test Five: **Answer Key**

SECTION 1

Essay

SECTION 2

1. A
2. B
3. E
4. E
5. B
6. D
7. D
8. A
9. B
10. A
11. E
12. C
13. E
14. D
15. B
16. B
17. C
18. D
19. E
20. C

SECTION 3

1. A
2. B
3. A
4. E
5. B
6. E
7. B
8. D
9. D
10. A
11. D
12. D
13. B
14. D
15. B
16. A
17. D
18. B
19. D
20. A
21. B
22. C
23. E
24. D

SECTION 4

1. A
2. D
3. D
4. B
5. E
6. C
7. C
8. C
9. 8.5
10. 5
11. 12
12. 4, 8, 12, or 16
13. 100
14. 16
15. 486
16. 103
17. 2
18. 9

SECTION 5

1. B
2. B
3. D
4. D
5. E
6. E
7. A
8. D
9. B
10. A
11. E
12. C
13. C
14. B
15. B
16. E
17. E
18. B
19. B
20. A
21. B
22. C
23. A
24. A
25. B
26. C
27. D
28. A
29. E
30. A
31. B
32. A
33. A
34. D
35. A

SECTION 6

1. C
2. C
3. A
4. C
5. C
6. C
7. B
8. B
9. D
10. A
11. D
12. B
13. C
14. D
15. E
16. B
17. A
18. D
19. C
20. E
21. C
22. D
23. A
24. A

SECTION 7

1. D
2. D
3. A
4. C
5. B
6. C
7. D
8. D
9. C
10. B
11. E
12. C
13. C
14. C
15. A
16. E

SECTION 8

1. B
2. D
3. B
4. D
5. E
6. C
7. A
8. B
9. C
10. B
11. D
12. C
13. D
14. A
15. D
16. A
17. E
18. B
19. C

SECTION 9

1. B
2. A
3. B
4. A
5. E
6. E
7. D
8. A
9. C
10. A
11. E
12. D
13. E
14. A

KAPLAN

Test Prep and Admissions

PRACTICE TEST FIVE

Critical Reading

	Number Right	Number Wrong	Raw Score
Section 3:	☐	− (.25 × ☐)	= ☐
Section 6:	☐	− (.25 × ☐)	= ☐
Section 8:	☐	− (.25 × ☐)	= ☐
	Critical Reading Raw Score	=	☐ (rounded up)

Writing

	Number Right	Number Wrong	Raw Score
Section 1:	☐ (ESSAY GRADE)	× 3.17	= ☐
Section 5:	☐	− (.25 × ☐)	= ☐
Section 9:	☐	− (.25 × ☐)	= ☐
	Writing Raw Score	=	☐ (rounded up)

Math

	Number Right	Number Wrong	Raw Score
Section 2:	☐	− (.25 × ☐)	= ☐
Section 4A: (QUESTIONS 1–8)	☐	− (.25 × ☐)	= ☐
Section 4B: (QUESTIONS 9–18)	☐	(no wrong answer penalty)	= ☐
Section 7:	☐	− (.25 × ☐)	= ☐
	Math Raw Score	=	☐ (rounded up)

Turn to page xiv to convert your raw score to a scaled score.

Answers and Explanations

SECTION 1

6 Score Essay

After the attacks on the World Trade Center and the Pentagon on September 11, 2001, my life and the lives of many people around the world changed. Although our lives were acted upon, and in many cases, destroyed by something we did not expect, we had a bigger say in how our lives were changed by it. This event showed me that we are changed by our own decisions in life.

My family was supposed to go on a vacation to Florida three months after September 11. However, my parents were worried that our family might not be safe on an airplane, so we cancelled our trip. We made the decision not to go and missed out on some fun and warmer weather, but we believed we were safer by not travelling. We did not go on the trip due to our own choice.

Another thing happened after September 11 that affected our family. My father, who used to work on Wall Street, lost his job, along with many others in his department. Losing his job meant my dad had to find something else so that he could keep paying the bills.

Although he had unemployment insurance for a number of months, he decided to check out the New York Teaching Fellows program. Now, four years later, my dad loves his job as a high school teacher. Losing his job happened to him without his consent, but in the way he handled this event, he found a more satisfying position than his job on Wall Street. My father's experiences showed me how to do the best you can with your circumstances.

Since the events of September 11, I have become more aware of how big or even small things can that are out of my control and can cause a change in my life. However, I have realized that although my life can be changed by outside events, I can use my decision-making power to make changes for myself.

6 Score Critique

All essays are evaluated on four basic criteria: Topic, Support, Organization, and Language. This essay begins with the author's interpretation of the topic, showing that the author understood the prompt. The introductory paragraph clearly states the author's opinion as well as a supporting example. The second and third paragraphs introduce personal examples that are developed throughout the essay. She fully develops these examples to support her opinion as she narrates a personal experience that illustrates her position on the assignment's question.

The organization of this essay is consistent and coherent, with transitional words and phrases (*yet, however, although, another, so, but, due to, since*) to link ideas and paragraphs. The essay's clear introduction leads logically into its body paragraphs, which in turn lead to a strong conclusion. The excellent support and organization of this essay show that the author spent enough time planning and that she followed her plan as she produced her essay.

Finally, the author's vocabulary and sentence structure are both sophisticated and varied, showing a high level of language ability and written expression. The absence of grammatical or spelling errors suggests that the author remembered to proofread her essay.

4 Score Essay

When I was ten years old, my mom had another baby. I was happy for her and yet I was upset that I was no longer the baby in the family. This event happened to me and I had very mixed feelings about getting a baby sister. Did I want a sister or a brother was not what mattered. She came home from the hospital and it seemed like everyone forgot about me, even my grandparents! I was really upset and I had to find some way to be happy. So, I guess that things change in life and so do we.

Before the baby was born, actually I was excited. I didn't think that anything bad would happen in the future to me as a result of the baby coming home to live with our family. But she needed a whole lot more attending than I had ever thought, and I was getting upset that my mom was too busy because of changing diapers and feeding the baby to pay attention to me. I complained that I never asked for a sister. They told to me I would be happy one day that I had a sister and friend.

My mother let me help take care of her and I was happier. It was fun to give her a bath. I even started giving her baby food after a few months. I felt more included and I had good feelings when my mom said I was a great big sister. She got older and could talk it was nice. I remember when we went on a family trip to visit my grandparents in Canada and had a good time playing with my sister. We went to the beach a lot and built sandcastles on Lake Michagin. We laughed and giggled alot.

So, my sister is older and at school, I help her with her homework and she really looks up to me. I show her how to play new things she has even shown me some tricks. Having a little sister is neat. I am trying to be a good example. I think this experience really helped me seeing that things in life changes a lot and so do people.

4 Score Critique

All essays are evaluated on four basic criteria: Topic, Support, Organization, and Language. The author begins this essay with a personal example to support her understanding of the prompt. However, she fails to take a clear position on the question in the assignment. By trying to support both sides of the issue, she fails to do a solid job of supporting either one.

The organization of this essay could be improved with transitional words or phrases between paragraphs to help the reader navigate the essay. Although the essay is structured appropriately, with a clear introduction and conclusion surrounding two body paragraphs, the ideas expressed are not strongly linked in a logical manner, suggesting that the author didn't spend enough time planning her essay before she began to write.

This writer could also improve her score by strengthening her grammar and usage skills. Her vocabulary is vague in places (*some, things*) and she uses *attending* where *attention* would be correct. There is some unclear pronoun usage (*they* in the second paragraph, *her* and *she* in the third paragraph), several spelling mistakes (alot instead of "a lot," *Michagin* instead of "Michigan"), and a few grammatical errors (*Did I want* instead of "Whether I wanted" in the first paragraph and *things in life changes* instead of "things in life change" in the final sentence. She also makes some fragment and run-on errors (a sentence beginning with *So* in the fourth paragraph, and run-ons in the third and fourth paragraphs. Although a few minor

grammar or usage errors will not hurt the score of a strong essay, this writer should leave time to proofread to correct any errors that detract from the logic and readability of her essay.

2 Score Essay

Things change but I don't have to change if I don't want to. I saw something the other night about how if you don't try in life you won't win. But what can you do when things happen that you have no control over? The show was called Fear Factor and it was about people having to have a lot of strenth and bravery to meet there goals. One guy actually ate the insects for food because there was nothing else. And I could not do it if he could, he would win and he did. The others were really disappointed and had to be eliminated. Thats what happens if you don't apply yourself to things.

The only way to really get what you want is to keep trying. Things can change but you don't have to change at all if people keep their eye on the ball. So no matter what the odds. You are still a good person for trying and you might even win in the end. My dad ran a marathon because he trained every day. It wasn't easy, but he did it every day, even though he had to think about bigger things outside him self like a job and his family to consider. I really admire him for it and started running too for awhile. You can make bigger changes for yourself than whats happening around you.

2 Score Critique

All essays are evaluated on four basic criteria: Topic, Support, Organization, and Language. This essay does address the prompt, but the supporting examples are weak and confusing. This makes the essay difficult to follow, since the reader doesn't know what point the writer is trying to make.

The writer provides two different examples in the two paragraphs, but neither fully supports his position related to the prompt. Similarly, the essay's organization is extremely weak, since the author doesn't provide a clear introduction, conclusion, or transitions between paragraphs. This writer needs to spend more time planning so he has an outline to follow while he's producing his essay.

Finally, the author's language is generic and repetitive (*nothing, happen, things, people*). In addition, his sentence structure is simplistic and occasionally incorrect, with two run-on sentences and two fragments, one beginning with the conjunction *and*, and the other with *so*. There are also some grammatical errors, including incorrect use of pronouns throughout (*there* instead of "their," *thats* instead of "that's") and spelling errors (*strenth* instead of "strength," *awhile* instead of "a while," *him self* instead of "himself"). To achieve a higher score on his SAT essay, this writer should leave enough time to proofread to correct any obvious mistakes.

SECTION 2

1.   A

Difficulty: Low

Strategic Advice: Remember that a perfect square can be the product of two negative numbers or two positive numbers.

Getting to the Answer:

$$x^2 - 49 = 0$$
$$x^2 = 49$$
$$x = 7$$
$$\text{or } x = -7$$

2.   B

Difficulty: Low

Strategic Advice: To find the area of a rectangle, multiply the width by the length. Be careful when translating from English into math.

Getting to the Answer:

Length (l) = 13 feet = 3 feet more than the width = $3 + w$

Width (w) = $l - 3 = 13 - 3 = 10$

Area: $l \times w$

$13 \times 10 = 130$ square feet

3.   E

Difficulty: Low

Strategic Advice: This is a two–step problem. Frist find a numerical value for s, then use that to find $3s$.

Getting to the Answer:

$$s = 3 \times 4 = 12$$
$$3 \times 12 = 36$$

4.   E

Difficulty: Low

Strategic Advice: Read each all of the answer choices before deciding, which is true.

Getting to the Answer:

(A) is false, because some integers in set T are negative. (B) is false, because every negative integer is not in set T. (C) is false, because *some* integers in set T are negative. (D) is false, because only *some* integers in set T are negative. (E) is true, there is a mix of positive and negative numbers in this set.

5.   B

Difficulty: Low

Strategic Advice: The measure of the perimeter is equal to the sum of the lengths of all three sides of a triangle.

Getting to the Answer:

If the length of one side is 4, then the sum of the length of the remaining sides is 12 (16 − 4).

Since both sides are equal each side is:
$$\frac{12}{2} = 6$$

Length of each of the other two sides: 6

6.   D

Difficulty: Medium

Strategic Advice: Use the information provided in the graph try to prove each answer choice wrong.

Getting to the Answer:

(A) is false; only 6 out of 14 students studied over 4 hours. (B) is false; none of the students studied 8 hours. (C) is false, 4 Juniors studied more than 2 hours. (D) is true, 2 Sophomores studied for more than 2 hours and 1 First–Year studied for more than 2 hours. (E) is false, Only 3 out of 14 students are First–Years.

7. D

Difficulty: Medium

Strategic Advice: Translate from English into math carefully. On Test Day, remember that terms like "the product of" or "the difference of" refer to the whole expression, not just the individual terms.

Getting to the Answer:

The product of z and $6 = (6z)$

Squaring of the product of z and 6: $(6z)^2$

The difference of z and 6: $(z-6)$

Squaring of the difference of z and 6: $(z-6)^2$

8. A

Difficulty: Medium

Strategic Advice: Determine how many whole pieces can be cut from the wire, then subtract that total length from the length of the original piece of wire.

Getting to the Answer:

6 feet $= 72$ inches

$$\begin{array}{r} 10 \\ 7\overline{)72} \\ -70 \\ \hline 2 \end{array}$$

2 inches of wire are left over.

9. B

Difficulty: Low

Strategic Advice: Since the equation is adding the absolute value of x and the absolute value of y it doesn't matter if the point is positive or negative.

Getting to the Answer:

A $(-1, 4)$ $|-1| + |4| = 5$

B $(-4, 2)$ $|-4| + |2| = 6$

B is the correct answer.

10. A

Difficulty: Medium

Strategic Advice: Find the possible values for n, then run those values through each of the Roman numeral tests. Eliminate any answer choice that does not contain a correct Roman numeral.

Getting to the Answer:

n could be either $\frac{3}{5}$, 4, or 8.

    I. False; $\frac{3}{5}$ is not an integer. Eliminate (C), (D), and (E).

   III. False; n cannot equal 5 since 5 is not present in both sets.

Only condition II is true, therefore the correct answer is (A).

11. E

Difficulty: Medium

Strategic Advice: "Directly proportional" means the values in ratio. Set the two proportions equal to one another and cross–multiply to solve for the missing variable.

Getting to the Answer:

$$\frac{y}{x} = \frac{30}{6}$$

$$\frac{30}{6} = \frac{y}{8}$$

$(30 * 8) \div 6 = 40$

12. C

Difficulty: Medium

Strategic Advice: Find the value of each term, then find the difference.

Getting to the Answer:

First find the value of the 35th term:

$5(35) + 2 = 177$

Next find the value of the 30th term:

$5(30) + 2 = 152$

Subtract to find the difference:

$177 - 152 = 25$

13. E

Difficulty: Medium

Strategic Advice: Use the formulae in the beginning of each section to help you get to the answer quickly. The formula for the volume of a right circular cylinder is $\pi r^2 h$. Since the question asks "closest volume," you can approximate a value for π.

Getting to the Answer:

First, find the area of the cylinder.

$V \pi r^2 h$

$= \pi(4)^2 (2) = 32\pi \approx 96$

Find the cube with the area closest to 96.

A: $2 \times 2 \times 2 = 8$

B: $3 \times 2 \times 2 = 12$

C: $4 \times 3 \times 2 = 24$

D: $3 \times 3 \times 3 = 27$

E: $3 \times 3 \times 4 = 36$

Cube E has area closest to 96.

14. D

Difficulty: Medium

Strategic Advice: Use Picking Numbers to help you get the correct answer quickly.

Getting to the Answer:

Try $n = -2$

$r = n^3 - 0.61 = (-2)^3 - 0.61 = -8 - 0.61 = -8.61$

$s = n^2 - 0.61 = (2)^2 - 0.61 = 4 - 0.61 = 3.39$

$t = (n - 0.61)^2 = (-2 - 0.61)^2 = (-2.61)^2 = 6.8121$

$-8.61 < 3.39 < 6.8121$

$r < s < t$

15. B

Difficulty: Medium

Strategic Advice: Divide each part of the ratio by the sum of the items in the ratio to determine the amount of the whole each part makes up.

Getting to the Answer:

If flour, sugar, and baking soda are mixed together in the ratio of 6:4:2. That means that flour makes up $\frac{6}{12}$ of the mix, sugar makes up $\frac{4}{12}$ of the mix, and baking soda makes up $\frac{2}{12}$ of the mix.

If sugar makes up $\frac{4}{12}$ of the mix, then for 6 pounds of mix

$\frac{4}{12} * 6 = \frac{24}{12} = 2$ pounds of sugar must be added.

16. B

Difficulty: Medium

Strategic Advice: Subtract the area of the oval from area of the rectangle to find the area of the unshaded region. Use the information given in the question to determine a numerical value for the area of the rectangle.

Getting to the Answer:

Area of the rectangle $= lw$

From the problem, $\frac{\pi lw}{5} = 8\pi$ so $\pi lw = 5(8\pi) = 40\pi$

$lw = \frac{40\pi}{\pi} = 40$

Area of the oval $= 8\pi$

Area of the unshaded region $= 40 - 8\pi \approx 14.867 \approx 15$

17. C

Difficulty: High

Strategic Advice: This question gives you two ways of figuring out the total number of markers in the class. Write the two equations, set them equal to each other, then use algebra and substitution to find the number of markers donated to the class.

Getting to the Answer:

If each student takes 2 markers, and 16 markers will be left, then the total number of markers can be represented by $m = 2s + 16$.

If 4 students do not take any markers, the rest of the students take 6 markers each, and no markers will be left, then the total number of markers can be represented by $m = 6(s - 4)$

$$2s + 16 = 6(s - 4)$$
$$2s + 16 = 6s - 24$$
$$16 = 4s - 24$$
$$40 = 4s$$
$$10 = s$$

$m = 2s + 16 = 2(10) + 16 = 20 + 16 = 36$

18. D

Difficulty: Medium

Strategic Advice: Notice that the shape inscribed in the triangle is a rectangle. Use the point on the line that is also a vertex of the rectangle to figure out an equation for the line in the form of $y = mx + b$.

Getting to the Answer:

The point on the line is (2,6) and from the question the slope is –3.

$$y = mx + b$$
$$6 = (-3)(2) + b$$
$$6 = -6 + b$$
$$12 = b$$

19. E

Difficulty: High

Strategic Advice: Picking numbers may not be the best strategy here, since you may have to pick up to five numbers to answer this question correctly. Remember that when dealing with division of exponents with the same base that you can subtract the exponent in the numerator by the exponent in the denominator to find the exponent the base is raised to.

Getting to the Answer:

$$r \& 1 = \frac{3^{r+1}}{3^{r-1}} = 3^{(r+1)-(r-1)} = 3^{r+1-r+1} = 3^2 = 9$$

It doesn't matter what the value of r is, $r \& 1$ will always equal 9.

20. C

Difficulty: Medium

Strategic Advice: Once Mary is assigned an office, there are less offices for Anne to be assigned to.

Getting to the Answer:

Probability Mary is assigned an office with an **X**: $\frac{2}{6} = \frac{1}{3}$

Probability Anne will be assigned an office with an **X** if Mary has been assigned and office with an **X**: $\frac{1}{5}$

The product of the two probabilities is the probability that both will be assigned an office with an **X**. $\frac{1}{3} * \frac{1}{5} = \frac{1}{15}$

SECTION 3

1. A

Difficulty: Low

What might you call something "intended to merely gain more information"? If all you really know is that Professor

Chang "intended to merely gain more information," and that this intention contrasted with the student feeling slighted, then he was probably just asking a question, a good prediction for the blank.

Choice (A) is great match for your prediction. In choice (B), a confession or admission of guilt would not necessarily be used to "gain more information." In choice (C), similarly, a dismissal would probably not be used to "gain more information." In choice (D), a condemnation could quite easily lead to someone feeling slighted. In choice (E), a *credo*, or statement of beliefs, would not necessarily be used to "gain more information."

2. B

Difficulty: Medium

"Despite" signals that the dog's appearance must contrast with how Stephanie spent her money. If all you know is that the appearance of Stephanie's dog contrasts with the amount of money she spent on his grooming, then her dog must appear neater than one would expect if very little money was spent on grooming, or messier than would be expected if lots of money were spent on grooming, so look for a choice that matches one of these sets of criteria.

In choice (A), one would expect, if *an enormous* amount of money had been spent on grooming, for the dog to look *orderly*. Choice (B) is a good fit for your prediction. In choice (C), the amount of money spent on grooming would not necessarily make a dog look more or less *annoyed*. In choice (D), similarly, the amount of money spent on grooming, *unrealistic* or otherwise, would not make a dog appear more or less *distracted*. In choice (E), once again, a well-groomed dog would not necessarily appear more or less *agitated*.

3. A

Difficulty: Medium

What would "an even more sophisticated machine" likely do to an invention that was once the most advanced on the market? If all you know is that there was a machine that "had been the most technologically advanced of its time," and that later "an even more sophisticated machine" came along, it is likely the newer machine replaced or succeeded the older one, both great predictions for the blank.

Choice (A) matches your prediction nicely. In choice (B), a "more sophisticated machine" would probably not increase or double an older one. In choice (C), while the "more sophisticated machine" could improve on the older one, it could not add to or actually increase it. In choice (D), the sentence never suggests that the "more sophisticated machine" waved the older one about. In choice (E), it does not make sense to say that the "more sophisticated machine" escaped or avoided the older one.

4.   E

Difficulty: Medium

What sort of arguments are "based on possibilities and speculation rather than proven certainties"?

If all you know about Jonas' arguments is that they were "based on possibilities and speculation rather than proven certainties," then you can really only conclude that he was known as a philosopher or dreamer, both great predictions for the blank.

In choice (A), the sentence does not indicate whether or not Jonas expected his arguments to be accepted without question, or that he devised a new religion or philosophy. In choice (B), one would not necessarily become known as a *consultant*, or paid advisor, because they "advanced arguments based on possibilities and speculation rather than proven certainties." In choice (C), similarly, one would not necessarily become known as a prodigy, or child-genius, simply for advancing "arguments based on possibilities and speculation rather than proven certainties." In choice (D), nothing in the sentence indicates Jonas was particularly concerned with material wealth or possessions. Choice (E) matches your prediction nicely.

5.   B

Difficulty: High

What aspect of a temple could be "violated by vandals' offensive graffiti"? The word "violated," which specifically refers to something sacred being treated disrespectfully, is important to note, as it suggests it was the sacredness of the temple, in particular, that was harmed by the vandals. Look for a word that means *sacred* or *holy*.

In choice (A), an immoral or wicked temple would probably not be "violated by the vandals' offensive graffiti". Choice (B) is a perfect match for your prediction. In choice (C), nothing in the sentence indicates the meaning of the temple was particularly clear or easily understood. In choice (D), graffiti or vandals could probably not effect a temple

appearing true or real. In (E), it would not make sense to refer to a temple as deceptive or dishonest, and even if it were, such qualities would not necessarily be "violated by vandals and offensive graffiti."

6.   E

Difficulty: Medium

Be sure the answer you choose is firmly supported by the passage, even if it's not stated. The author discusses the horse trainer to demonstrate that one type of animal—the horse—has *changing moods that trainers can perceive and adapt to*. Look for an answer that reflects this.

Choice (A) is extreme; nothing in the passage suggests that horses are more sensitive than other animals.

Choice (B) is out of scope; nothing in the passage indicates this. Choice (C) is out of scope; the passage does not discuss how *unique* a horse's emotional state is. Choice (D) is extreme; the passage does not compare the eagerness of horses to help with that of any other animal. Choice (E) is supported by the passage.

7.   B

Difficulty: High

Pay particular attention to Author 2's main point when thinking about how she would respond. Author 2 says there is no way to test for emotions, and so we cannot ever be sure what an animal is feeling. Author 2 would probably say that the trainers mentioned in Passage 1 are anthropomorphizing, not relying on scientific truths.

Choice (A) is extreme; Author 2 says that emotions cannot be scientifically quantified, not that they don't exist in animals. Choice (B) works well with your prediction. Choice (C) is out of scope; emotional relationships among animals are not discussed in either passage. Choice (D) is out of scope; Author 2 does not offer any alternative explanations. Choice (E) is out of scope; Author 2 does not address the requirements of animal training.

8.   D

Difficulty: Medium

If you aren't sure of a prediction, you can eliminate choices by working one passage at a time. Passage 1 says that animals have emotions and that it is useful for those who work with animals to take this into account. Passage 2 says that, since emotions cannot be scientifically measured, it is better not to take them into account. Look for a choice that matches this.

Choice (A) is out of scope; whom animals love is not addressed in either passage. Choice (B) is out of scope; Passage 1 does not compare animals to humans, and Passage 2 does not compare horses to *other animals*. Choice (C) is extreme; Passage 2 does not say that animals have *no* emotions, only that it is difficult to study them. Choice (D) works well with the prediction. Choice (E) is a misused detail; it is never stated in either passage that animals *anthropomorphize*.

9. D

Difficulty: Medium

When two passages appear to disagree on most points, any point of agreement will probably be something general and non-controversial.

The passages disagree on most things, but they do both talk about observing the *behavior* of animals. Look for an answer choice that reflects this.

Choice (A) is an opposite; Passage 2 says we can make no conclusion about this. Choice (B) is out of scope; neither passage compares horses to other animals. Choice (C) is a misused detail; only Passage 2 supports this. Choice (D) is compatible with both passages. Choice (E) is out of scope; neither passage addresses the issue of which animals are most *likely to express emotions*.

10. A

Difficulty: Medium

You should be predicting this for every passage in the course of taking notes. In this passage, the author depicts his intellectual journey to a deeper understanding of global conflicts, like the one that scarred his childhood. He goes on to describe how he *discovered a different way to analyze international conflicts*.

Choice (A) is correct; this matches the thrust of the prediction. Choice (B) is distortion; the author never mentions social justice. Choice (C) is out of scope; the author does not discuss this. Choice (D) is out of scope; while the author does expand his understanding, *well-rounded* is not an appropriate description of this development. Choice (E) is out of scope; the author did come to *view local populations as worthy of study*, but that is too narrow to be the purpose of the entire passage.

11. D

Difficulty: Medium

Knowledge of vocabulary can save time in finding correct answers.

The author states that his "introduction into the field of social history was fortuitous." When something is fortuitous, it represents a lucky accident. If you didn't know this, you still could find the correct answer here by reading further in the paragraph for context.

Choice (A) is out of scope; nothing in the passage suggests that the author's entry into the field was *difficult*. Choice (B) is out of scope; nothing in the passage suggests that the author's entry was confusing. Choice (C) is out of scope; nothing in the passage suggests that the author's entry was *unavoidable*. Choice (D) is correct; this matches the prediction. Choice (E) is out of scope; nothing in the passage suggests that the author's entry was *controversial*.

12. D

Difficulty: Low

Find the relevant detail, and reread the applicable text. Find the answer that restates that detail. In paragraph 2, the author discusses a professor who urged him to redirect his studies "from the global system to the local one. I...scoffed at the suggestion, for that type of study was the job of historians." So the author *considered that type of analysis the job of historians.*

Choice (A) is out of scope; the author never considers the professor's tenure. Choice (B) is out of scope; the author never discusses or defines *loftier goals*. Choice (C) is out of scope; the author does not discuss other *job offers*. Choice (D) is correct; this matches the text. Choice (E) is distortion; the author never makes a value judgment of the suggestion.

13. B

Difficulty: Medium

Be careful about answering a detail question from memory. You may fall for a tempting, but wrong, choice. From a general recollection of the passage or from your notes, you should know to look at the first paragraph. Near the end, the author writes, "I am still embarrassed by the fact that I went to school in order to contribute to world peace but found myself becoming a hawkish supporter of militarized solutions." Look for a match among the choices.

Choice (A) is a misused detail; the author escaped his country's civil war as a child, years before going to school. Choice (B) is correct; this matches the detail in the text. Choice (C) is an opposite; the author states that while this was the result, it was not the reason why he went to school. Choice (D) is distortion; the author eventually found this method superior to others, but it is not why he went to school. Choice (E) is distortion; this happened much later.

14. D

Difficulty: Medium

Gain context from the reference, and predict before peeking at the wrong choices. The sentence in question provides strong context: "By overlaying the two studies, I was eventually able to see how political motivations, calculations, and missteps affected groups and individuals who then fell into conflict." The author was able to understand more about the interplay between governments and the people, two groups the author states have been traditionally studied separately. Predict something like *combining*.

Choice (A) is distortion; this doesn't reflect the sense of combination that the author conveys. Choice (B) is out of scope; this doesn't make sense in context. Choice (C) is an opposite; the author is making best use of the studies rather than discarding them. Choice (D) is correct; this matches your prediction. Choice (E) is out of scope; this doesn't make sense in context.

15. B

Difficulty: Medium

Remember that a valid inference can never be more extreme than the facts upon which it is based. The author states that a knowledge of social history was helpful in understanding international conflict. Look for something in this vein.

Choice (A) is extreme; the author never goes so far as to say that global conflicts can *only* be examined through social history. Choice (B) is correct; the author states that he was able understand global conflict by studying social history. Thus, it must be true that social history provides important information on global conflict. Choice (C) is an opposite; the author never states that international conflicts have their basis in social history. Choice (D) is extreme; the author states that knowledge of social history helps to analyze global conflict, not that knowledge of social history

helps to avoid global conflict. Choice (E) is distortion; nothing in the passage indicates this.

16. A

Difficulty: Medium

Read the sentence in question and remember to make a prediction before looking at the choices. Notice that the author uses "catalyst" to refer to the previous sentence's discussion of bacteria that changed Earth into a thriving planet. So the author must be using this word to mean *agent of change*.

Choice (A) is correct; transforming a planet's atmosphere is certainly *significant*. Choice (B) is distortion; while the process would take time, suggesting *gradual* change, this is not the primary focus of the word in context. Choice (C) is out of scope; nothing in the passage indicates that the change would be *premature*. Choice (D) is an opposite; the paragraph indicates that the pace of change would be anything but *rapid*. Choice (E) is an opposite; clearly, the agent does facilitate change.

17. D

Difficulty: Medium

Vocab-in-context questions usually require you to find a synonym for a word as it is used in the text. Sometimes, as in this case, you will be asked to select a phrase most similar to the meaning the author intends for the word.

The author says, "warming stands as the first domino in terraforming Mars." Look at your notes and notice that, in the last paragraph, the author discusses successive events caused by that initial event. So the author must be using warming to represent *the initiating event for a succession of other events*.

Choice (A) is out of scope; this makes no sense within the context. Choice (B) is out of scope; this plays off another meaning of "domino." It makes no sense within the context, however. Choice (C) is out of scope; this does not make sense in context. Choice (D) is correct; this matches the thrust of the prediction. Choice (E) is an opposite; warming is the first step, not the culminating step.

18. B

Difficulty: Medium

As with all Inference questions, always keep in mind that a valid inference must be based on the facts in the passage.

Your first step should be to return to paragraph 3 and re-read what it says about Martian surface temperatures. This is discussed most fully in the first sentence: "Since Mars is about fifty percent farther from the Sun than is Earth and has only one percent as much atmospheric pressure, Martian surface temperatures average minus 81 degrees Fahrenheit." Look through the choices for references to Mars' distance from the Sun or atmospheric pressure.

Choice (A) is distortion; greenhouse gasses are discussed as a possible solution to the low temperatures, not as a cause of them. Choice (B) is correct; the sentence in question certainly indicates such a relationship. Choice (C) is out of scope; nothing in the paragraph supports this choice. Choice (D) is distortion; the paragraph states that the Martian atmosphere has one percent as much "atmospheric pressure" as Earth does. *Temperature* is irrelevant to this figure. Choice (E) is a misused detail; thickening of the Martian atmosphere is discussed in the sixth paragraph.

19. D

Difficulty: Medium

When asked about a detail, don't always try to answer from memory. Make sure you go back and re-read the relevant detail in order to find the correct answer.

Your notes should point you to paragraph 4, which discusses orbital mirrors. *Difficult to use* in the stem should alert you to look for drawbacks, which come after the word "Unfortunately" in line 53. The author says that, "unfortunately," each mirror would need to be "at least the size of West Virginia" to be any help, and that such a mirror would have to "weigh over 200,000 tons." Thus, the difficulty lies in size and weight. Look for this among the choices.

Choice (A) is an opposite; the paragraph states that NASA could do this. Choice (B) is a misused detail; this is a detail from the discussion about asteroids in paragraph 5. Choice Choice (C) is distortion; the paragraph states that the mirrors would melt portions of the polar ice caps, but it never states that the melting ice would flood Mars. Choice (D) is correct; this says that the mirrors are too massive, meaning they are too big and heavy. Choice (E) is a misused detail; this is a detail from the discussion of asteroids in paragraph 5.

20. A

Difficulty: Low

Do not mistake Function questions for Detail questions. Function questions require you to answer *why* the author includes the relevant information in the passage. The author writes that the mirrors would have to be at least as large as West Virginia to heat "even a small area" of Mars. Thus, he uses West Virginia to indicate the necessary size of the mirrors. Choice (A) is correct; this matches the prediction nicely. Choice (B) is out of scope; the comparison to West Virginia cannot indicate *orientation*. Choice (C) is distortion; the author mentions the "small" area of the Martian surface that would be heated. Choice (D) is distortion; it would be strange and surely unnecessary to use the outline of West Virginia as an indicator of shape. Choice (E) is out of scope; the reference is not focused on *orbital coordinates*.

21. B

Difficulty: Medium

Draw a conclusion based on the facts in the passage, and remember not to make huge leaps of logic. Your notes should direct you to paragraph 5, which is fairly long, making prediction difficult. Do a quick skim of the paragraph; then move through the choices eliminating clearly incorrect choices. Check those remaining against the passage.

Choice (A) is distortion; paragraph 5 says that, since objects closer to the Sun orbit faster than objects farther from the Sun, asteroids from farther orbits, near Pluto's, would have to be used. While we can infer that high speed somehow contributes to this difficulty, we cannot go so far as to infer that asteroids that orbit too fast are *not useful* for terraforming. Choice (B) works. The fifth paragraph states that it would be "too difficult" to move an asteroid near Mars, since objects closer to the Sun orbit faster than objects farther from the Sun. You can infer from this that faster-orbiting objects are hard to move. Choice (C) is extreme; the author never states that ammonia is *essential.* Choice (D) is distortion; the author references energy "equivalent" to that of a nuclear war, but not *nuclear elements.* Choice (E) is extreme; the paragraph never goes so far as to say that it would be *impossible* to land on an asteroid that orbits quickly.

22. C

Difficulty: High

Assess each statement independently, beginning with the one that appears most frequently. If the statement restates a detail mentioned in the passage, eliminate any answer choice that does not include that statement. If the statement contains a detail not mentioned in the passage, or distorts a detail from the passage, eliminate all answer choices that include that statement.

Rather than trying to predict all of the shared aspects, go directly to the statements and check them against the details the in the passage. Begin with either Statement I or Statement III, since they appear most frequently. Statement I is incorrect; it may seem tempting, but note that only the factory mentioned in the third method would actually *manufacture* greenhouse gasses. The other methods aim to release or create them naturally. Eliminate all answer choices containing this statement: (A), (D), (E). Statement II is also incorrect; only the factory construction mentioned in the third method seems to include a manned a mission to the planet. Eliminate all remaining answer choices containing Statement II: (B). Only (C) remains, so it should be correct, which it is.

Choice (A) is out of scope; see the discussion of Statement I above. Choice (B) is out of scope; see the discussion of Statement II above. Choice (C) is correct; all of the terraforming methods *aim to raise the surface temperature of Mars*. Choice (D) is distortion; see the discussion of Statement I above. Choice (E) is distortion; see the discussion of Statements I and II above.

23. E

Difficulty: High

"Strengthen" and "weaken" questions ask you to assess the links between the author's claims and the evidence given, and then either strengthen or weaken the argument. Strengthening requires you to find the answer choice that makes it more likely that the author's evidence leads to her claim. You should be looking to tighten the link between the claim mentioned here and the evidence for it. The claim is that Mars will oxygenate. The evidence for this claim is that plants will grow, absorbing carbon dioxide and releasing oxygen. You need to find an answer choice that increases the chances that plants will flourish on Mars.

Choice (A) is an opposite; this weakens the author's assertion. Choice (B) is out of scope; the length of time

does not matter. If plants will flourish in 900 years, then the argument is not weakened. Choice (C) is distortion; this answer choice does not strengthen the argument. Choice (D) is a misused detail; this fact alone does not strengthen the author's claim. Choice (E) is correct; this makes it more likely that plants will flourish on Mars.

24. D

Difficulty: Medium

Tone questions are very similar to questions about purpose. In fact, most of the time, characterizing the author's tone helps in selecting a purpose. Ask yourself, how does the author feel about this topic? What is her role in this discussion? We can answer with a few observations. First, the author is very knowledgeable and presents a fairly balanced evaluation of the idea of terraforming Mars. Second, the author seems supportive of the idea of terraforming Mars, but not to the extent that we might term her tone one of "advocacy." Look for something not too extreme, but indicating mild support for terraforming.

Choice (A) is extreme; one would not characterize the author as *passionate*. Choice (B) is an opposite; the author does not seem skeptical. In fact, she states on several occasions the viability of the plan to terraform Mars. Choice (C) is extreme; since this author is not even advocating, she certainly is not urgently entreating. Choice (D) is correct; this fits well. Choice (E) is distortion; this is too neutral.

SECTION 4

1. A

Difficulty: Low

Strategic Advice: On Test Day, you may find it helpful to redraw the figure in the question so that it looks like something you're more familiar with.

Getting to the Answer:

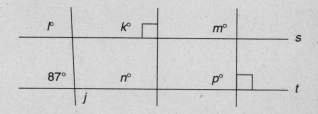

Parallel lines cut by a transversal form congruent opposite vertical angles, therefore $m\angle j = 87°$.

2. D

Difficulty: Low

Strategic Advice: Use the process of elimination to find the solution.

Getting to the Answer:

(A): Not divisible by 5

(B): Not divisible by 7

(C): Not divisible by 7

(D): Divisible by 5 and 7, but not divisible by 10.

(E): Not divisible by 7

3. D

Difficulty: Low

Strategic Advice: Pick numbers to get to the answer quickly. Just be sure to Pick numbers that follow the rules of the question; in other words, those that are found in the table.

Getting to the Answer:

Start with 0. Find out which answer choices yield −1 as your result.

(A): $0 - 1 = -1$.

(B): $0 + 1 = 1$. Eliminate B.

(C): $3(0) + 1 = 0 + 1 = 1$. Eliminate C.

(D): $3(0) - 1 = 0 - 1 = -1$.

(E): $1 - 3(0) = 1 - 0 = 1$. Eliminate E.

Now use 3 to find which answer choice yields 8.

(B): $3 + 1 = 4$. Eliminate B.

(D): $3(3) - 1 = 9 - 1 = 8$.

4. B

Difficulty: Low

Strategic Advice: Remember that a ray has one endpoint (starting point) and contains the given points and does not have a stopping point, whereas a segment starts at one point and ends at the other given point. Also keep in mind that intersection means the elements common to both sets.

Getting to the Answer:

The common area of ray *PT* and ray *SP* is segment *PS*.

5. E

Difficulty: Medium

Strategic Advice: First, find the total number of residents before determining the number of residents in a certain age group.

Getting to the Answer:

$r \times 0.15 = 9,000$

$r = 60,000$

10% are $20 - 29$, 15% are 20 and under

$60,000 \times 0.25 = 15,000$ residents are under 30

6. C

Difficulty: Medium

Strategic Advice: $f(x)$ is positive when the graph is above the *x*–axis.

Getting to the Answer:

Find the place where the graph is above the *x*–axis.

$1 < x < 7$

Also, $10 < x \le 14$

7. C

Difficulty: Medium

Strategic Advice: Note that Eduardo's average speed to school is twice that of the average speed coming from school, therefore, it takes twice as long to make trip home. So the trip to school takes $\frac{1}{3}$ of the total trip time.

Getting to the Answer:

$\frac{1}{3}$ of 3 hours = 1 hour. In one hour, going 60mph, Eduardo travels 60 miles. Since the mileage is the same on the return trip that means he travels for a total of 120 miles.

8. C

Difficulty: Medium

Strategic Advice: Find all possible solutions for the two equations, then determine which conditions can be met.

Getting to the Answer:

$$x^2 = 81$$

$$x = 9 \text{ or } x = -9$$

Roman numeral I is true. Eliminate (B).

$$2y^3 = 54$$

$$y = 3$$

II is false. Eliminate (D) and (E).

$$x + y = -6$$

$$-9 + 3 = -6$$

III is true. Eliminate (A).

9. 8.5

Difficulty: Low

Strategic Advice: Write an equation that represents what is being described in the problem.

Getting to the Answer:

$$\left(\frac{1}{2}n\right)(24) = 102$$

$$\frac{1}{2}n = 4.25$$

$$n = 8.5$$

10. 5

Difficulty: Low

Strategic Advice: When dealing with inequalities, use the same rules of algebra as you would with equations. Be sure to reverse the inequality sign in you multiply or divide by a negative number.

Getting to the Answer:

$$5x - 30 < 0$$

$$5x < 30$$

$$x < 6$$

x must be an integer less than 6, so the greatest integer solution is 5.

11. 12

Difficulty: Medium

Strategic Advice: Substitute the numbers given in the question and solve.

Getting to the Answer:

$$8 + \frac{(16)^2}{64} = 8 + \frac{256}{64} = 8 + 4 = 12$$

12. 4, 8, 12, or 16

Difficulty: Low

Strategic Advice: The sum of the measures of the interior angles in a triangle equals 180°. Pick numbers for g that follow the rules of the question.

Getting to the Answer:

$$g + 3g + h = 180$$

$$4g + h = 180$$

Pick $g = 41$.

$$4(41) + h = 180$$

$$164 + h = 180$$

$$h = 16$$

13. 100

Difficulty: Low

Strategic Advice: Find the total transportation expenses, then divide it by the total number of days.

Getting to the Answer:

$$80 + 70 + 105 = 255$$

$345 - 255 = 90$ total for transportation expenses

$\frac{90}{3} = 30$ per day for transportation

Expenses on Tuesday:

$30 + 70 = 100$ total expenses for Tuesday.

14. 16

Difficulty: Medium

Strategic Advice: Notice that $\triangle EFG$ is a 3–4–5 triangle. Use the 30–60–90–triangle rule to find the length of $\overline{DE}$.

Getting to the Answer:

Since $\triangle EFG$ is a 3–4–5 triangle, $\overline{EG} = 8$.

Now use the 30–60–90 triangle rules to find the length of $\overline{DE}$.

The hypotenuse is twice as long as the shortest side. Since the shortest side is 8, the measure of the hypotenuse is 16.

15. 486

Difficulty: Medium

Strategic Advice: Start with Saturday and work backwards to Monday to determine how much money Mr. Brown had to start with.

Getting to the Answer:

Sunday Morning: $2

Saturday Morning: $2 \times 3 = \$6$

Friday Morning: $6 \times 3 = \$18$

Thursday Morning: $18 \times 3 = \$54$

Wednesday Morning: $54 \times 3 = \$162$

Tuesday Morning: $162 \times 3 = \$486$

16. 103

Difficulty: Low

Strategic Advice: Median means "middle number." Divide the number of integers by 2 to find out how many integers are after the median, then add that number to the median.

Getting to the Answer:

$$
\begin{array}{r}
48 \\
2\overline{)97} \\
\underline{8} \\
17 \\
\underline{16} \\
1
\end{array}
$$

$55 + 48 = 103$

17. 2

Difficulty: Medium

Strategic Advice: Picking numbers will get you to the answer quickly. Start with a simple number that yields a remainder of 3 when you divide by 4.

Getting to the Answer:

$$
\begin{array}{r}
1 \\
4\overline{)7} \\
\underline{4} \\
3
\end{array}
$$

$22m = 22(7) = 154$

$$
\begin{array}{r}
19 \\
8\overline{)154} \\
\underline{8} \\
74 \\
\underline{72} \\
2
\end{array}
$$

18. 9

Difficulty: Medium

Strategic Advice: Since all of the points lie on the same line, the squares increase by the same ratio (the slope of the line). Figure out the value of the increase of the side of

the square, then set up a ratio with the complete sides of the squares.

Getting to the Answer:

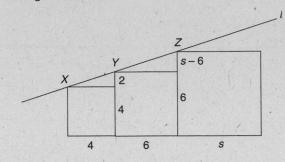

$\dfrac{2}{4} = \dfrac{s-6}{6}$

$(2)(6) = (4)(s-6)$

$12 = 4s - 24$

$36 = 4s$

$9 = s$

SECTION 5

1. B

Difficulty: Medium

A descriptive phrase or clause must be closely followed by the noun it is intended to modify. Since *Julie* is the one who was *shopping for a birthday present*, no noun or pronoun should appear between the descriptive clause and her name. Choice (B) puts *Julie* directly after the clause. Choice (C) is unnecessarily wordy, and the possessive *Julie's* is an adjective, not a noun. In choices (D) and (E), the *clearance sale* is doing the *shopping*; additionally, both introduce the passive voice unnecessarily.

2. B

Difficulty: Medium

Style errors may be difficult to spot; plug in answer choices methodically to see if a more concise version of the selection is included. While this is not technically a run-on sentence, combining the two clauses with *and* does not indicate how they relate, and the unnecessary subject pronoun in the second clause makes the sentence overly wordy. Choice (B) corrects both errors. Choice (C) includes a transition word (*thereby*) that is inappropriate in context.

Choice (D) is idiomatically incorrect; in this context, *agreed* must be followed by the infinitive ("to") verb form. Choice (E) is grammatically incorrect construction.

3. D

Difficulty: High

The gerund (*-ing*) verb form alone can never be the predicate (main) verb of a sentence. Choice (D) corrects the fragment error by changing the gerund to a verb phrase, *are using*. Choice (B) does not address the error. Choice (C) incorrectly introduces an additional subject (*they*). Choice (E) leaves the meaning of the second clause incomplete.

4. D

Difficulty: Medium

A verb must agree in number with its subject, which may not be the noun closest to it in the sentence. Here, the plural verb *were* does not agree with its singular subject *one*. (*Friends* is the object of the preposition *of.*) Both choices (D) and (E) correct the error, but choice (E) misuses the semicolon splice, which is only correct when used to combine two independent clauses. Choices (B) and (C) do not address the error.

5. E

Difficulty: Low

The shortest answer choice is frequently correct on the SAT, but make sure it is grammatically correct and does not change the meaning of the original selection. Choice (E) is concise without altering the meaning of the sentence. (B) is incorrect grammatical structure. Choice (C) uses a verb form that is incorrect in context. Choice (D) is also wordy and the pronoun *they* does not agree with its singular antecedent, *administration*.

6. E

Difficulty: Medium

When a sentence is making a comparison, make sure logical things are being compared. Here, here, hockey fans of the 1990s are being compared to the fans of the 1950s and 1960s. Both choices (D) and (E) correct the comparison, but choice (D) uses a preposition (*with*) that is incorrect in context. Choice (B) does not address the error. Choice (C) compares *hockey fans* to *hockey*.

7. A

Difficulty: High

Expect to see between five and eight Writing section sentences that contain no error. This sentence is correct as written. All of the other answer choices present illogical comparisons. Choice (B) compares *the inspiration of many female poets* to *Emily Dickinson*. Choices (C) and (D) compare *Emily Dickinson's poetry* to *many female poets*. Choice (E) compares *inspirations* to *many female poets*.

8. D

Difficulty: High

Whenever you see a comparison, make sure two logical things are being compared. As written, this sentence compares *the movement toward neo-classicism* to *either music or literature*. By adding the preposition *in,* choice (D) makes the comparison between *music or literature* and *architecture*. Choices (B) and (C) place the preposition incorrectly, violating parallel structure. Choice (E) repeats the preposition unnecessarily.

9. B

Difficulty: Medium

Be aware of words and phrases that mean essentially the same thing; the correct answer choice will eliminate such redundancies. Using *Because* and *the reason why* in the same sentence is redundant; choice (B) eliminates the redundancy without adding any new errors. Choices (C) and (D) are awkwardly constructed. (E) is unnecessarily wordy.

10. A

Difficulty: High

Some sentences with no errors have complex constructions. Be methodical in eliminating answer choices This sentence is correct as written. Choices (B) and (C) leave the meaning of the second clause incomplete. Choice (D) introduces the passive voice unnecessarily. Choice (E) creates a run-on sentence.

11. E

Difficulty: High

Two independent clauses must be joined by an appropriate conjunction or a semicolon in order to be grammatically correct. Choice (E) corrects this run-on sentence by joining the clauses with *and so*. Choice (B) is awkwardly constructed. Choices (C) and (D) do not address the error.

12. C

Difficulty: Low

Familiarize yourself with commonly used irregular verbs. The error here is in choice (C); "taken," not *took*, is correct with *had*. Choice (A) correctly uses *where* to indicate a location. Choice (B) is correct idiomatic usage. Choice (D) correctly uses the superlative since, presumably, Janet would have taken more than two *vacations*.

13. C

Difficulty: Low

The comparative form of an adjective is formed by adding either *-er* or *more*; using both is incorrect. "Richer," not *more richer* is the correct comparative form of "rich"; the error is in choice (C). Choice (A) is correct idiomatic usage. Choice (B) is an appropriate verb tense in context. Choice (D) agrees with its singular subject, *he*.

14. B

Difficulty: Low

There is is only correct with a singular object; "there are" is appropriate when the object is plural. Since *two guards* is plural, choice (B) should read "there are." Choices (A) and (D) are correct idiomatic usage. Choice (C) correctly uses the infinitive verb form.

15. B

Difficulty: Medium

When referring to people, the correct relative pronoun is "who." Since *athletes* are people, (B) should read "who." Choices (A) and (C) are idiomatically correct usage. Choice (D) is an appropriate verb tense in context.

16. E

Difficulty: High

Sentences that are correct as written are historically missed by more than half of all test takers. Be methodical in eliminating wrong answer choices. Choice (A) consists of a pronoun and a verb phrase, both of which are used appropriately. Choices (B) and (C) are idiomatically correct constructions. Choice (D) properly uses the comparative to refer to two items (*talent* and *hard work*).

17. E

Difficulty: Medium

Expect a total of between five and eight sentences in your SAT Writing sections to contain no error. Choice (A) is correct idiomatic usage. Choice (B) is appropriate use of the infinitive. The plural pronoun in choice (C) agrees with its plural antecedent *volunteers*. Choice (D) correctly uses the past perfect tense to describe an action that was completed prior to another stated action.

18. B

Difficulty: Medium

There is is only correct with a singular object; "there are" is appropriate when the object is plural. The error is in choice (B), which requires the plural *were* to agree with the object, *children*. Choice (A) appropriately relates the two clauses. Choice (C) is idiomatically correct usage. Choice (D) uses both the correct preposition and the correct pronoun in context.

19. B

Difficulty: Medium

Pronouns must agree in number with the nouns to which they refer. The error is in choice (B); the plural pronoun *these* is needed to agree with the plural antecedent *ads*. Choice (A) agrees with its singular subject, *department*. Choice (C) properly uses an adverb to modify *respond*. Choice (D) parallels the earlier phrase *to this*.

20. A

Difficulty: Medium

In general, correct SAT sentences use the simplest correct verb tense. The verb phrase in choice (A) is unnecessarily complicated; "have to prepare" would be both consistent and more concise. *Whereas*, in choice (B), correctly expresses the contrast between the two clauses. Choice (C) is appropriate use of the infinitive. Choice (D) is idiomatically correct usage.

21. B

Difficulty: Medium

A verb must agree with its subject noun, which may not be the noun closest to it in the sentence. The subject of the verb phrase in choice (B) is the plural *countries*, so "have signed" would be correct. Choices (A) and (D) are correct idiomatic usage. The verb in choice (C) agrees with the plural *treaties*.

22. C

Difficulty: Medium

Items in a series, list, or compound must be in parallel form. The first two verbs in this sentence are *familiarizes* and *teaches*; the verb in choice (C) should be parallel. Choice (A) is an appropriate preposition in context, choice (B) agrees with its singular subject *program*, and choice (D) is correct idiomatic usage.

23. A

Difficulty: High

A verb must agree with its subject noun, which may not be the verb closest to it in the sentence. Although *memos* is the noun closest to *indicate*, the verb's subject is actually the singular *analysis*; the error is in choice (A). (B) is correct use of the superlative, since the plan would presumably have more than two aspects. Choice (C) correctly uses the plural pronoun *those* to agree with the plural *aspects*. Choice (D) is correct idiomatic usage in context.

24. A

Difficulty: Medium

An idiom may be correctly constructed, but be incorrect for the context in which it is used. In this context, "Far from" would be the correct idiom in choice (A). The verb in choice (B) agrees with its singular subject, *Jason*; choice (C) correctly uses a plural verb phrase with *doctors*. Choice (D) is correct idiomatic usage.

25. B

Difficulty: High

Unless context makes it clear that more than one time period is referenced, verb tense usage should remain consistent within a sentence. The verb in choice (B) should be *has been*, in order to be consistent with *have been eating*. Choices (A) and (D) are correct idiomatic usage. Choice (C) uses the appropriate relative pronoun in context.

26. C

Difficulty: High

Some idiomatic expressions are only correct when constructed with a specific preposition. In this context, the

correct preposition with *consistent* is *with*; the error is in choice (C). Choice (A) uses the correct preposition in context. Choice (B) is appropriate use of the infinitive and choice (D) correctly uses the plural pronoun *those* to agree with its antecedent, *symptoms*.

27. D

Difficulty: High

The superlative is only correct when comparing three or more items; use the comparative when two items are references. Here, *the most unobstructed* is used to compare the views of two mountain ranges, *the Catskills and the Adirondacks*; "the more unobstructed" would be correct in choice (D). Choice (A) is a correctly used idiomatic phrase. Choice (B) properly relates the ideas in the two clauses. Choice (C) agrees with its plural subject *Adirondacks*.

28. A

Difficulty: High

Use the objective pronoun case after a preposition. In choices (A), "me" would be the correct pronoun to use as the object of the preposition. The verb in choice (B) agrees with its singular subject, *relationship*. Choice (C) correctly uses an adjective to modify a noun, and an adverb to modify the adjective. In choice (D), the plural pronoun *us* is correct for its plural antecedent *my roommate and I*.

29. E

Difficulty: Medium

Students often miss "correct as written" sentences; check each underlined segment in turn and choose choice (E) if you don't spot an error. Choices (A), (B), and (C) are all correct idiomatic usage. Choice (D) is an appropriate verb phrase in context.

30. A

Difficulty: Medium

Expect between five and eight sentences in the Writing sections to be correct as written. As written, this sentence contains no error. Choices (B) and (C) are sentence fragments. Choice (D) reverses the order of the events in the sentence, indicating that Roth had completed school before he cultivated his love of poetry and art. Choice (E) creates a run-on sentence.

31. B

Difficulty: Medium

In order to combine sentences, you must understand how the ideas in them are related. Choice (B) correctly links the ideas in the two sentences. Choice (A) simply joins the ideas without relating them in any way. Choices (C) and (D) incorrectly relate the new sentence to the remainder of the paragraph. Choice (E) incorrectly relates the ideas in the original sentence, creating a cause-and-effect relationship that is inappropriate in context.

32. A

Difficulty: Medium

Be wary of the pronoun "it" on the SAT; the testmaker frequently uses it without a clear antecedent. Choice (A) eliminates the ambiguity, and also makes the sentence active, rather than passive. Choices (B) and (D) fail to address the ambiguity error; choices (B), (C), (D), and (E) all remain in the passive voice. Additionally, *nevertheless* in choice (C) is inappropriate in context.

33. A

Difficulty: Medium

The gerund (-*ing*) verb form can never be the predicate (main) verb in a sentence. Choice (A) corrects the fragment by replacing the gerund with an appropriate predicate verb. None of the other choices addresses the error.

34. D

Difficulty: Medium

Your Reading Comprehension skills will be helpful for about half of all Improving Paragraphs questions. Since there is a contrast between the idea of someone being successful in a field and spurning others in that field, a contrast keyword is indicated here. Both choices (D) and (E) use contrast transition words, but the contrast in choice (E) is between Roth's suspicion and skepticism and his spurning the art word, which is inappropriate in context; the correct choice is choice (D). Choices (A) and (B) create a cause-and-effect relationship between the ideas that is inappropriate in context; additionally, Choice (A) creates a sentence fragment. Choice (C) does not properly relate the sentence to the rest of the paragraph.

35. A

Difficulty: Medium

Your Reading Comprehension skills will be helpful in about half of all Improving Paragraphs questions. Choice (A) is the best choice here, as it continues the paragraph's theme of Roth's relationship with other artists. The other answer choices provide details but are not encompassing statements appropriate in context for a final sentence at the end of a passage. Choices (B) and (E) contain information that would most logically be placed in the first paragraph. Choice (D) would make the most sense at the end of paragraph 2. Choice (C) is out-of-scope.

SECTION 6

1. C

Difficulty: Low

Start with the first blank. The hot word "contrary" indicates a contrast between the blanks. Note the words "subsequent calculations." Calculations are based on researched evidence, so look for a word that is contrary to studied calculations. The second blank must contain a word that refutes the prediction that an asteroid will hit earth. For the first blank, eliminate any answer choices that do not match the prediction "assumptions." This eliminates choices (D) and (E). Eliminate all choices for the second blank that are not synonymous with "verified." Thus, choices (A) and (B) can be eliminated.

Choice (C) is the credited answer.

2. C

Difficulty: Low

Locating the key hot words in this sentence will help you to form a prediction. "Research" in "...and exploration" arises from "drives to gain information" and "explorative behavior." Look for the answer choice that means "interest" or "desire to gain information."

In choice (A), humankind's desire to explore is not necessarily methodical or orderly. In choice (B), it is the desire to understand rather than "credulity" or the willingness to believe something that makes humans explore the unknown. Choice (C) is the correct answer. Choice (D) is the opposite of the prediction. Choice (E) does not match the prediction.

KAPLAN
Test Prep and Admissions

3.   A

Difficulty: Low

What type of reputation would a fair and impartial judge probably have? If all you know is that the judge presided over his courtroom with "fairness and impartiality," then he probably had a reputation for being fair and impartial, so look for a word that matches this definition, such as *evenhanded* or *just*.

Choice (A) is a perfect match for your prediction. In choice (B), a judge who was considered fair would probably not have a reputation for being *immoderate* or going beyond what is moral. In choice (C), one cannot really be *cumulative*, so this choice makes little sense here. In choice (D), being known as fair would not necessarily make someone *unproductive*. In choice (E), similarly, being considered impartial would not necessarily make one *adulatory*.

4.   C

Difficulty: Medium

If someone "felt like a fraud" or a liar, what might they have professed? The word "fraud" is the key word here; the sentence is describing something Marisa did involving an "unfortunate mistake" that made her feel like she had lied or misrepresented the truth, which suggests she did something bad. If Marisa had made an "unfortunate mistake," then to feel "like a fraud" she must have denied making the mistake or indicated she was blameless. *Blamelessness* and *made* are great fits for the blanks.

In choice (A), professing one's *profundity* or perceptiveness would not necessarily be a lie if one had actually expressed displeasure over a mistake. In choice (B), professing *enthusiasm* when one had actually *condoned* an "unfortunate mistake" would not necessarily be fraudulent. Choice (C) fits your prediction. In choice (D), professing one's *immorality* would not necessarily be a lie if one had *performed* a mistake. In choice (E), professing *repentance* or regret would be consistent with *condemning* a mistake.

5.   C

Difficulty: Medium

How might an essay "written hurriedly the night before" be flawed? Start with the second blank; something that had been "written hurriedly the night before" might be made up of a "careless" *assortment* or *mixture* of "information and research data." The words "as it had been" indicate that the

first blank is describing the result of this problem. If Jack's essay were written from a careless mixture of information, then it would probably "not" be very logical or articulate. *Assortment* and *articulate* make great predictions for the blanks.

In choice (A), if the essay were written from a "careless" *collage* of information, then it probably would have been *rambling*. In choice (B), if he had written the essay from a "careless" *development* of information, then it probably would have been *ambiguous*. Choice (C) your prediction perfectly matches. In choice (D), a careless *morass* of information would probably lead to an unstructured or *amorphous* essay. In choice (E), a *harangue* refers to a loud or angry speech, which, if his essay were based on such information, would not necessarily make it intelligible.

6.   C

Difficulty: Medium

The word "rebellious" is a big hint that Constance Markievicz was one of the "few women" involved in politics, who didn't remain at home. If Markievicz was "rebellious" then she was not like most women, who were not involved in political life and remained at home. Therefore Markievicz "succeeded in *participating in* politics and *escaping* or *avoiding* domesticity." As you're looking through the answer choices, note that the first blank is a verbal, and eliminate verbals that don't make sense preceding "politics."

In choice (A), it doesn't make sense for someone to "succeed in obtaining politics," and Markievicz certainly didn't "succumb to" domesticity. In choice (B), if Markievicz rebelled against the fact that women were not involved in political life, then she must have *participated in*, not *escaped* politics. Choice (C) matches your prediction. Choice (D) is exactly opposite to your prediction—Markievicz would have pursued, not ignored, politics, and avoided, not observed, domesticity. Choice (E) is also opposite to your prediction.

7.   B

Difficulty: Medium

What is another way of saying "inviolability"? If baseball's "seeming inviolability" was tainted, then its *honorability* or *hallowedness* was also tainted. Note that here you only need the first part of the sentence "the ...of American baseball, its 'seeming inviolability,'" because the quoted phrase describes the blank.

Choice (A) is the opposite of your prediction—*turpitude* refers to baseness or depravity, which is what the investigators uncovered, but not what was tainted. Choice (B) fits your prediction. Choice (C), *perspicuity,* refers to clearness and lucidity, which doesn't include the hallowed fervor or admiration of the word "inviolability." In choice (D), the question isn't baseball's seeming "truth" (or *verisimilitude*), but its seeming "inviolability" or *honorability*. Choice (E) is opposite to your prediction again—the investigators uncovered seeming *duplicity*, but *duplicity* wasn't tainted.

8. B

Difficulty: High

The students wanted to include a wide variety of music in their program. Focus on the combination of different types of music. The prediction should be "mixture," "array," or "combination."

In choice (A), The students were not *inducing* or *creating* the music; they were playing it. Choice (B) is the credited answer. In choice (C), someone can become "immersed" in music, but it is not possible to "provide an immersion" of music. Choice (D), *occlusion,* means "obstruction." Choice (E) means "alienation" and does not fit in the sentence.

9. D

Difficulty: High

Make sure you read the sentence in its entirety. What is Faulkner's "environment," and how does it relate to his writing? Although Inference questions ask you to evaluate conclusions not explicitly stated in the text, the correct choice will still be closely supported by evidence from the passage. If Faulkner lived and worked in Mississippi, and if he "achieved fame" by "using the details and peculiarities of his environment," then you can infer that Faulkner depicted Mississippi and that these depictions were effective or popular with his readers.

Choice (A) is extreme; the passage only states that Faulkner's fame resulted partly from his depictions of Mississippi, not that his readers could identify fully with life in this environment. Choice (B) is distortion; the passage describes the settings Faulkner created as "stunningly vivid," not necessarily beautiful. Choice (C) is out of scope; nothing in the passage refers specifically to the Mississippi landscape, and nowhere is the environment described as tempting or attractive. Choice (D) is a good match for your

prediction. Choice (E) is out of scope; the passage does not mention the climate in particular, nor does it suggest that Faulkner's descriptions were especially accurate.

10. A

Difficulty: Medium

Where in the passage is Faulkner's lack of schooling discussed? Re-read this portion of the text to refresh your memory. Use clues from the question stem to point you to the relevant portion of text. Remember, never answer a Detail question from memory! The question stem points you towards the last sentence of the passage, where Faulkner's lack of schooling is discussed. The author says it is "apparent" that Faulkner's skills "came naturally to him," suggesting that he believes Faulkner had an inborn talent for writing.

Choice (A) is a good match for your prediction. Choice (B) is out of scope; nothing in the passage refers to the speed with which Faulkner acquired his writing abilities. Choice (C) is extreme; although writing may have come "naturally" to Faulkner, this does not necessarily mean he was *always* an impressive writer. Choice (D) is distortion; while Faulkner had little formal schooling, the passage does not rule out other types of influences. Choice (E) is distortion; by describing Faulkner as "renowned" and saying that he "achieved fame," the author indicates that Faulkner's writing abilities were quite appreciated.

11. D

Difficulty: Low

Think about how the meaning of the sentence would be different without the word "quick." Notice how the author's phrasing conveys his impression of the passage of time, and try to find a choice that matches this impression. The author's vision deteriorated "Over the course of three quick years," until he found himself unable to work. This phrasing indicates that he feels like blindness gained on him rapidly, before he really had a chance to adjust to it. Look for a choice that captures this unexpectedly fast passage of time. Choice (A) is distortion; the passage says that macular degeneration "is among the top causes of blindness in adults," suggesting that the illness is not particularly rare. Choice (B) is distortion; the author states that his doctors gave his treatment their "best efforts." Choice (C) is an opposite; if the days were *slow and plodding* they would not have passed in "three quick years." Choice (D) is a good match for your prediction. Choice (E) is an irrelevant detail; the author does not connect the three years leading up to his blindness to his development of new sensory skills afterwards.

12. B

Difficulty: Medium

Think about what role the other senses are described as playing in the author's life. How are the other senses connected to re-learning his job? When a cited line implies that some sort of change has taken place, try to identify exactly what that change is. According to the passage, the author never used to pay much attention to touch, smell, and hearing, but when his sight deteriorated he realized that these senses could help him re-learn his job. Look for a choice that mentions this change in focus.

Choice (A) is out of scope; the author does not suggest that it is ironic that he has become blind. Choice (B) is a good match for your prediction. Choice (C) is distortion; the author only makes positive comments about the "best efforts" of doctors and does not mention other senses in order to lament doctors' inability to prevent blindness. Choice (D) is out of scope; the author does not discuss commonly held beliefs. Choice (E) is extreme; the passage focuses on one person's experience, not on issues of importance *to all mankind*.

13. C

Difficulty: Low

Ask yourself what role these references play. Note that they make the same point, so the correct choice will reflect something with which both authors would agree. These two descriptions function in their respective passages to illustrate that both turntablists are established professionals. Look for the choice that best sums this up.

Choice (A) is extreme; from the descriptions it would not be a stretch to assume that both performers are successful, but *exorbitantly wealthy* is far too extreme of a statement in the context of both passages to be the correct answer. Choice (B) is out of scope; it is not out of the realm of possibility that both turntablists have worked with each other in the past, but neither description makes this distinction. Choice (C) is a good match. Choice (D) is out of scope; neither author makes this distinction. Choice (E) is an opposite; both authors mention that they use prerecorded materials that they did not personally create.

14. D

Difficulty: Medium

You can eliminate any answer choice that contains an idea that even one of the authors would disagree with. In Passage 1, after the author compares his craft to jazz, he relates how both jazz and rock were not "immediately accepted" (line 56), and uses the Beatles as an example. In line 33, the author of Passage 2 views herself "as a progressive artist, working on the fringe, but steadily moving closer to being realized by the kids who watch MTV." Look for the explanation that best describes what is suggested by these examples.

Choice (A) is distortion; though Passage 2 mentions turntablists who "press their own original material" (line 40–41), neither author suggests it is *better* to do so. Choice (B) is an opposite; rather, all of the examples above suggest the contrary. Choice (C) is distortion; Passage 2's author may agree with this statement, however, the fact that the author of Passage 1 states that he "take(s) great offense to the suggestion" (line 24–25) that he is not a musician rules this choice out. Choice (D) should match your prediction well. Choice (E) is distortion; Both authors relate the skill and dedication required to be competent at the turntables; Passage 1 even directly compares learning the turntables to learning to play guitar, however neither author suggests that one instrument is more difficult to master than the other.

15. E

Difficulty: Low

Read for context and make a prediction before looking at the choices. Though this is a relatively obscure word, in context, it is not difficult to decipher its meaning. In line 32, the author relates how, like his guitar, the turntables were difficult to master. Then he goes on to tell how after countless hours of "woodshedding" different techniques for the turntables, he achieved that mastery. You could predict something like *refining* or *fine-tuning*.

Choice (A) is out of scope; this makes no sense in context. Choice (B) is out of scope; theorizing also makes no sense in context. One can only theorize on a subject after they have a solid grasp of it. Choice (C) is distortion; do not make the mistake of associating "experimenting" (line 31–32) with *improvising*. These words are not synonymous, and improvisation does not lead to mastery. Choice (D) is an opposite; it is impossible to master anything by rejecting it. Choice (E) is a match for your prediction.

16. B

Difficulty: Medium

When asked to infer what one author would say about another, begin by establishing the tone of the first author's passage. It can be inferred from the statement in lines 23–25 that the author of Passage 1 takes the debate seriously, for he "takes offense" that someone would suggest he is not a musician. The author of Passage 2, however, characterizes the debate over whether DJs and turntablists are actually musicians as "silly" because according to her, "the true definition of a musician is extremely vague and eternally arguable" (lines 74–76). In other words, she believes it's a pointless argument. Approach this question from her point of view, and look for the answer that would best describe how she would probably characterize the author's statement from Passage 1.

Choice (A) is an opposite; the author of Passage 2's statements regarding the definition of a musician as "vague" and "arguable" directly contradict this choice. Choice (B) matches your prediction. Choice (C) is distortion; though Passage 2's author does not consider herself a musician and also uses the music of others', she would probably not characterize the author's statements in Passage 1 as false because of her general indifference to the debate. Choice (D) is distortion; Passage 2's author says that some music professors consider turntablists "distortionists"; the author herself never makes this distinction. Choice (E) is an opposite; the Passage 2's author states that being a musician or artist is "no more culturally valid or important than the other."

17. A

Difficulty: Medium

Reread the sentence and make a prediction first; then look for a match among the choices. In these statements, the author presents an argument (some traditional music is not 100% original), and then proceeds to back it up with seemingly sound points about traditional musicians, invoking examples of Jimmy Page and Eric Clapton to help solidify his point of view. Look for the answer choice that best sums up what type of argument this argument could be classified as.

Choice (A) matches your prediction. Choice (B) is out of scope; the author's argument cannot be characterized as humorous. Choice (C) is out of scope; nothing in either passage indicates the author's argument is *simplistic*.

Choice (D) is an opposite; there is nothing offered in the passage to indicate that this is not true. Choice (E) is an opposite; the author offers a sound argument with solid points to back it up. It is hardly irrational.

18. D

Difficulty: Medium

When in doubt, remember that the correct answer choice will match up with the tone that the author has established in his passage. Your first big clue to answering this question is the author's statement that turntablists and other DJs are "unfairly lumped together." The second clue is the contrast between his descriptions of turntablists as "innovative" and "groundbreaking," and the dance club DJs, "who simply spin other performers' vinyl records." Look for the answer that best describes what these two clues express about the author's intentions for making the comparison.

Choice (A) is distortion; the author feels it is necessary to define the difference between turntablists and dance club DJs; radio announcers are never mentioned. Choice (B) is out of scope; there is nothing in the passage to suggest that the author purposely forgot to make this clarification. Choice (C) is distortion; the author only refers to turntablists as innovators. Choice (D) matches your prediction. Choice (E) is extreme; though the author does question the talents of dance club and wedding DJs, he never makes the extreme suggestion that it is not possible for them to possess talent.

19. C

Difficulty: Low

You should be predicting purpose on every passage you read. All you have to do then is look for the match. In the first sentence of the first passage, the author states that he is "as equipped as anybody to offer an opinion on the debate." In the second paragraph, the author reveals that opinion, which is that he, a turntablist, is "undoubtedly a musician." Using examples and comparisons, he uses the rest of the passage to support his stance on the subject. Look for the choice that best sums this up.

Choice (A) is distortion; the turntablist techniques of cutting, mixing, and beat juggling are mentioned in the passage, but they not are described in any way and serve only as supporting details. Choice (B) is distortion; this is the main purpose of the second passage. Choice (C) matches for your prediction. Choice (D) is an opposite; the author's position on the debate is clearly stated—he is not a neutral party. Choice (E) is distortion; in attempting to support his side of the argument, the author is indeed disputing the other; however, the passage never states that this opposing view is the more accepted of the two.

20. E

Difficulty: High

How does the author feel about the strict definitions of the words in question? Each author uses their respective word in quotation marks within the context of questioning their strict definitions. The author of Passage 1 puts *stole* in quotes as he is questioning originality in popular music; the author of Passage 2 puts *musician* in quotes while attempting to discount its strict definition. Think about why each author would choose to put quotes around those words in those particular situations, then look for choice that best reflects your prediction.

Choice (A) is an opposite; using the strictest definition of both words would weaken each author's argument. Choice (B) is distortion; certainly both words are important in their respective sentences, but the quotes cannot and do not emphasize that. Choice (C) is distortion; this is one of the basic uses of quotations marks, but they purpose is not served here. Choice (D) is out of scope; neither of these words have alternate meanings in music terminology; even if they did, the authors don't employ them here. Choice (E) matches your prediction.

21. C

Difficulty: Medium

Read the lines around the reference, if necessary, to establish context. One of the ways the author achieves the passage's overall purpose is by demonstrating that the actual definition of "musician" is too vague to be the basis of an argument. The discussion about the academic point view is an example of this; she offers it to the reader, and subsequently challenges it to prove her point. Look for the answer that best sums this up.

Choice (A) is extreme; to suggest that *all* music professors will *never* consider turntablists to be musicians is much too extreme to be a valid choice. Choice (B) is distortion; this choice makes no sense because in the discussion the author successfully weakens the academic argument. Choice (C) matches your prediction nicely. Choice (D) is an opposite; this discussion demonstrates that there is no irrefutable argument. Choice (E) is out of scope; this is never suggested in the passage.

22. D

Difficulty: Medium

Pinpointing the author's tone can help you a lot in questions such as this. The first thing you must ask yourself when approaching this type of question is whether the author's attitude was positive, negative, or neutral. Does the author say anything particularly disparaging about the dabblers? On the other hand, does she praise them? Could she care less? Here she defends them, stating that it is "more important to inspire yourself" than others. Knowing her attitude is positive, you can eliminate the three non-positive questions. Look to the surrounding context and choose your answer from the two "positive" choices.

Choice (A) is out of scope; it is always smart to double-check a neutral choice when you decide the author's attitude is positive or negative. The author, however, never makes the distinction presented in this choice. Choice (B) is an opposite; because you have determined the author's attitude is positive, eliminate this choice. Choice (C) is an opposite; this negative choice can be eliminated. Choice (D) matches your prediction. Choice (E) is distortion; this choice is actually too positive—in the passage, the author states that "without question there is a difference" between dabblers and true artists, not that the dabblers are the true artists.

23. A

Difficulty: High

Study the reference from the first passage to help you look for a similar setting in the second one. In Passage 2, the author states that a "turntablist is more like a painter than a guitar player or pianist," and says that the pre-recorded materials she works with are "the materials" from which she can "create something more" and "morph it into a beautiful piece distinctly (her) own." Using this information you should be able to narrow down your choices, and select the answer that would best make sense in hypothetical question.

Choice (A) is a great match for your prediction. Choice (B) is distortion; this is a tough choice, but ultimately choice (A) is better because the "found" objects and images mentioned compare well with the pre-recorded music turntablists use. Also, the "distorted reality" is very suggestive of the "distortionist" label in line 16. Choice (C) is distortion; the author does mention "being realized by the kids who watch MTV," (line 99) but this choice would make no sense within the context of her passage. Choice (D) is out of scope; neither author mentions *architecture*. Choice (E) is distortion; the author of Passage 1 invokes the Beatles; but again, a choice involving music is directly contradicted by the author's comments in Passage 2, and would make no sense in the context of her passage

24. A

Difficulty: Medium

If unsure, at least characterize the tone as positive, neutral or negative, which should then help narrow down the choices.

A good strategy for questions regarding an author's tone or attitude is to look for Keywords or phrases that are very suggestive of a particular choice. In the reference given, three important phrases can help lead to the answer: "I can do with it whatever I want," "a beautiful piece distinctly my own, " and, perhaps the most telling of all three clues, "No doubt." Look for the choice that best reflects the tone set by such phrases.

Choice (A) is a match for your prediction. Choice (B) is distortion; the author does ask the reader two questions in these five sentences, but she responds to her own questions with confident answers. She is not perplexed. Choice (C) is distortion; this choice is certainly enticing, but it is incorrect because though the author's tone is confident, there is nothing in the passage to indicate it is overly so. Choice (D) is out of scope; the author offers no harsh or caustic words or phrases that would signal this choice. Choice (E) is distortion; again, do not mistake the two questions in lines 117–119 for *inquisitiveness* on the part of the author, she just uses these as a device to help make her point.

SECTION 7

1. D

Difficulty: Low

Strategic Advice: Early questions are worth just as many points as late questions. Take your time in translating from English to math correctly.

Getting to the Answer:

Total cost of pencils: $0.50p$

Total cost of notebooks: $3n$

Sum of both: $3n + 0.50p$

2. D

Difficulty: Low

Strategic Advice: The arithmetic mean is defined by the sum of a set of numbers divided by the number of terms in the set of numbers.

Getting to the Answer:

$$\frac{7 + 20 + x}{3} = 20$$
$$7 + 20 + x = 60$$
$$x = 33$$

3. A

Difficulty: Medium

Strategic Advice: Define the other 2 variables in terms of one of the other variables.

Getting to the Answer:

$A + B + C = 34$

$B = 4A$

$C = 3B = 3(4A) = 12A$

$A + 4A + 12A = 34$

$17A = 34$

$A = 2$ greeting cards

4. C

Difficulty: Medium

Strategic Advice: When dealing with percent problems, remember that "of" means you will use multiplication.

Getting to the Answer:

0.05 percent of n is 5

$$\frac{0.05}{100} \times n = 5$$
$$0.0005 \times n = 5$$
$$n = \frac{5}{0.0005} = 10,000$$

5 percent of $n =$

$$\frac{5}{100} \times n =$$
$$0.05 \times n =$$

$0.05 \times n =$

$0.05 * 10,000 = 500$

5. B

Difficulty: Medium

Strategic Advice: Slope intercept form of a line is defined as $y = mx + b$, where m is the slope of the line and b is the y-intercept.

Getting to the Answer:

Slope: $-\dfrac{5}{3}$

y-intercept: 5

Equation of the line: $y = -\dfrac{5}{3}x + 5$

6. C

Difficulty: Medium

Strategic Advice: Divide the line into eighths, since the fractions in the question have 8 as their common denominator.

Getting to the Answer:

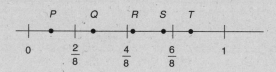

Tick mark to the left of R is $\dfrac{1}{2}$ or $\dfrac{4}{8}$

Tick mark to the right of S is $\dfrac{3}{4}$ or $\dfrac{6}{8}$

So, $\dfrac{5}{8}$ is between $\dfrac{4}{8}$ and $\dfrac{6}{8}$.

So, point R is in between $\dfrac{1}{2}$ and $\dfrac{5}{8}$.

7. D

Difficulty: Medium

Strategic Advice: A variable with a negative exponent is equal to 1 divided by that variable with a positive exponent.

Getting to the Answer:

$m^{-1}n = 2$

$\dfrac{n}{m} = 2$

$n = 2m$

8. D

Difficulty: Medium

Strategic Advice: Adjacent angles are supplementary, which equal 180° and vertical angles are congruent, which means they are equal to one another.

Getting to the Answer:

$5a + 4a = 180$

$9a = 180$

$a = 20$

$b = 5a$

$5 \times 20 = 100$

9. C

Difficulty: Medium

Strategic Advice: Factor to solve the first equation. Use those solutions to find the possible solutions to the second equation.

Getting to the Answer:

$x^2 + x = 20$

$x^2 + x - 20 = 0$

$(x + 5)(x - 4)$

$\quad -5 \quad\quad 4$

$x^2 - x$

$x = -5$

$(-5)^2 - (-5) = 25 + 5 = 30$

or

$x = 4$

$(4)^2 - 4 = 16 - 4 = 12$

The answer is (C).

10. B

Difficulty: Medium

Strategic Advice: The distance on the graph, except during the resting points, should always be increasing.

Getting to the Answer:

Find a graph that increases quickly until the two on the y-axis, then, is a horizontal line for 10 minutes on the x-axis, then slowly increases until the 5-mile mark on the y-axis.

The only graph that follows this pattern is (B).

11. E

Difficulty: Medium

If four hats need to be the same color, decide how many of each other color of hats could be chosen before having four of any color.

Getting to the Answer:

After 12 selections, it is possible to have chosen boxes containing 3 hats of each color, still not having 4 of any color. So on the 13th selection, you will have chosen the 4th hat of one of the colors.

12. C

Difficulty: Medium

Strategic Advice: To find the sum of the measures of the interior angles of a polygon use the equation $(n - 2) * 180$, where n is the total number of angles in the polygon. A regular polygon means that all of the interior angles and sides are equal.

Getting to the Answer:

Sum of the interior angles: $(8 - 2) \times 180 = 1080$

Measure of each interior angle: $\frac{1080}{8} = 135$

Angle C is 135°.

Measure of all the interior angles of polygon BCDO:
$(4 - 2) \times 180 = 360$

You know that the angle formed by the line and angle B is equal to the angle formed by the line and angle D because the length of both lines are equal since they both are from the origin of the polygon to an angle on the polygon.

$360 - 135 - 90 = 135 =$ measure of angle B and D.

$\frac{135}{2} = 67.5 =$ measure of angle B.

13. C

Difficulty: Medium

Strategic Advice: Use everything within the parenthesis to define x, not just the first term.

Getting to the Answer:

$f(t - r) = 6(t - r)$

$\qquad = 6t - 6r$

14. C

Difficulty: High

Strategic Advice: To find the measure of an arc of a circle divide the circumference of the circle by the fraction of the circle the arc covers.

Getting to the Answer:

The area of the circle is $\pi r^2 = 16\pi$, so the radius $= 4$; the diameter $= 8$.

Circumference of the circle: $d\pi = 8\pi$

Measure of the arc: $\frac{8\pi}{6} = \frac{4\pi}{3}$

Perimeter of the region: $2r +$ measure of the arc.

Perimeter of the region: $8 + \frac{4\pi}{3}$

15. A

Difficulty: High

Strategic Advice: Sometimes you may have to think about problems in a different way than how they're presented. In this problem, imagine that the equations given are equations of lines on a coordinate plane. Two equations have no common solutions when their lines are parallel, therefore put these two equations into slope–intercept form and make the slopes equal.

Getting to the Answer:

$3x - 4y = 10$

$\qquad -4y = -3x + 10$

$\qquad\quad y = \frac{3}{4}x - \frac{5}{2}$

$6x + wy = 16$

$\qquad\quad y = \frac{-6}{w}x + \frac{16}{w}$

$\qquad \frac{3}{4} = \frac{-6}{w}$

$\qquad 3w = -24$

$\qquad\quad w = -8$

16. E

Difficulty: High

Strategic Advice: To determine if the some of the conditions are true or false, you need to calculate how many total shots were taken and how many total shots were made.

Getting to the Answer:

    I. True because 25 out of 30 people hit the target on their first try. Eliminate (B) and (D).

    II. True, 89 shots were attempted, 59 shots were made. Eliminate (A) and (C).

    III. True, the most times a contestant hit the target in a row was 4.

SECTION 8

1. B

Difficulty: Low

How might wining the championship make the coach's "leadership skills" appear? If at first people "questioned," or doubted, the coach's leadership, then winning the championship would most likely make people realize he was quite *skilled* or *capable* of "managing his team." Look for a word that means *skilled*.

In choice (A), the coach's leadership would not appear *remiss* because he won the championship. Choice (B) is a perfect fit for your prediction. In choice (C), nothing in the sentence explores whether or not the coach was *humorous*. In choice (D), the fact that the coach won his first championship would not necessarily reveal he was *hesitant about* leading his team. In choice (E), if the coach had just won the championship, then he would most likely not be *contemptuous* or disapproving of running his team.

2. D

Difficulty: Low

If the cave's artifacts were concealed, how might the vine's have effected its opening? The sentence indicates that the artifacts were "concealed" as a direct result of the "dense wall of vines," so look for a word that describes how the vines *hid* the cave's opening.

In choice (A), *released* does not mean hidden. In choice (B), *elevating* something would not necessarily hide it. While choice (C) may be tempting considering that vines

could very well be *entangled*, such a description does not necessarily mean the opening would be hidden. Choice (D) is a good match for your prediction. In choice (E), a cave opening cannot really be *attained*, or acquired, by a wall of vines.

3. B

Difficulty: Medium

"Although" signals that "this particular group" made him feel quite differently than he "usually felt." If all you know about the sentence's subject is that he "usually felt comfortable speaking in front of audiences," then you know the blanks must be describing how he felt speaking in front of this particular group? As this group is described as "large and intimidating", it is likely the first blank indicates he felt too *uncomfortable* or *hesitant*, and that the second blank simply means to *speak*. Look for two words that refer to *hesitancy* and *speaking*.

In choice (A), the sentence only indicates he felt too uncomfortable, but not necessarily too emotional or *impassioned*, to speak before the group. Choice (B) is a great match for your prediction. In choice (C), feeling too *cautious* might have caused him to want to *suppress*, and not discuss, the topic. In choice (D), the sentence mentions nothing of how *knowledgeable* he is regarding the topic, only that he felt uncomfortable with this particular group. In choice (E), it is not that the subject feels too *perceptive*, but rather too intimidated, that has made him uncomfortable.

4. D

Difficulty: Medium

"Due to" signals that his reputation and his effort to join the fight must be consistent with one another. The words "few were surprised" indicate that the first blank *explains* the behavior referred to in the second blank, so look for two words that support one another, such as a poor reputation and a bad act, or a commendable reputation and a good act.

In choice (A), a *modest* reputation would not make it unsurprising that one might join a fight against *acceptable* reforms. In choice (B), again, an *inescapable* reputation is too vague a description to make it unsurprising that one might fight against any type of reforms, *legitimate* or otherwise. In choice (C), similarly, an *insufficient* reputation would probably not lead to anyone being particularly surprised by that person's actions. Choice (D) is a nice fit for your prediction. Choice (E) Once again, the word *unbelievable*, which does not distinguish between good or bad, is too vague for this sentence.

5. E

Difficulty: Medium

"While" indicates that the two blanks will contain words that contrast. The sentence establishes two groups of people: those "faithful to the old ballpark", and "proponents of the new stadium". As the sentence describes their respective opinions regarding the "demolition" of the old stadium, the first blank must describe a negative or unhappy reaction, while the second blank must describe a positive one. Contrasting words such as *appalling* and *productive* make a good prediction.

In choice (A), while *momentous*, meaning extremely important or crucial, could fit in the first blank, it would not make sense for the new stadium's proponents to consider the demolition of the old park *formidable*, or difficult to overcome. In choice (B), *unavoidable* fits nicely in the second blank, but the word *decisive* does not provide enough contrast here. In choice (C), *unexpected* and *ambiguous* essentially agree, rather than contrast, with one another. In choice (D), again, *advantageous* and *beneficial* basically mean the same thing. Choice (E) matches your prediction nicely.

6. C

Difficulty: High

If a prosecutor were short on effective evidence, what might he be compelled to do? The word "shamefully" indicates that the action described by the blank must be rather unfortunate, and given that a frustrating shortage of "credible or convincing evidence" is stressed, it is likely the blank describes an effort to *slander* or *falsify* information about the defendant. Look for a word that means to *slander* or *misrepresent*.

In choice (A), a "lack of credible or convincing evidence" would not necessarily cause one to enter into *arbitration*, which also cannot be referred to as a "shameful" act. In choice (B), nothing in the sentence suggests the prosecutor would have resorted to excessive self-admiration to help his cause. Choice (C) is a great match for your prediction. In choice (D), being "frustrated" by a "lack of credible or convincing evidence" would not necessarily cause one to

become more *tenacious* or firm in one's opinions. In choice (E), expressing *solicitude*, or concern, cannot really be considered a "shameful" act.

Questions 7–19

The following passage not only describes the events leading up to the moment the main character unknowingly encounters his long lost daughter, but it also provides insight into the similar personalities and insecurities of the two principal characters by displaying their initial reactions to each other.

7. A

Difficulty: Medium

What does the passage offer about both character's prior knowledge of each other? A global question requires that you look at the passage as a whole in order to arrive at the correct answer. What do the details supplied about both characters reveal about their meeting on the elevator? The passage depicts the thoughts and actions of a father and a daughter in the moments before they unknowingly meet for the first time on an elevator. What the passage does not offer or imply, however, is if either character is actively searching for the other, or when or how their relation is eventually revealed. Choose the answer that best describes these circumstances.

Choice (A) matches your prediction nicely; the passage offers nothing specific about their meeting other than it was a *chance encounter*. Choice (B) is out of scope; no tears were shed by either character. Choice (C) is distortion; though the circumstance's of both characters lives are different, they have the same color hair and distinctive eye coloring. Choice (D) is distortion; though the passage offers Oscar's first impression of Celia, this passage was written in the third person point of view of the author. Choice (E) is out of scope; nothing in the passage suggests that Oscar was searching for Celia or, for that matter, even knew she existed.

8. B

Difficulty: Medium

What does Oscar's "telling brow" actually reveal about his nature? In questions such as these, look for specific words that somehow relate to the descriptions offered by the author. The description of Oscar's "telling brow that more than once betrayed the true man hidden behind the steely demeanor of his strong jaw" suggests that Oscar tries to outwardly appear in a way contradictory to his inward nature. Look for the choice that best conveys what this reveals about Oscar's "true" personality and manner.

Choice (A) is a misused detail; while this may fit a later description of him in the passage, you are looking for what the specific line in question suggests about Oscar. Choice (B) is a good match for your prediction; the betrayal of a "true man hidden behind the steely demeanor" suggests that Oscar is actually a sensitive individual. Choice (C) is out of scope; nothing in the passage suggests that he is *arrogant* or *abrasive*. Choice (D) is distortion; this "betrayal" referred to in the passage does not imply that Oscar's nature is untrustworthy. Choice (E) is an opposite; the description reveals that Oscar tries to appear *impenetrable*, but his expressions betray him.

9. C
Difficulty: Low

What particular artistic career could be associated with the two metaphorical phrases? A simple inference question like this is not hard to decipher, just look at the text of the question and make try to make the most obvious connections. Essential to answering this question is to recognize that Oscar's "meticulous approach" to examining the wrinkles on his face is compared to his artistic endeavors, and the metaphorical phrases directly reference that comparison. Your prediction should reflect this connection to a specific art form.

Choice (A) is distortion; the editing of a book certainly deals with proofreading and documents, but it is not an art form. Choice (B) is distortion; an office clerk may also deal with proofreading and documents, but this is not an art form, either. Choice (C) should match your prediction; a novelist's art would entail proofreading and documents.

10. B
Difficulty: Medium

What word could best describe something that would cause a man to run like he "was being chased down?" Here, the key to this detail question is recognizing the tone of the specific situations the author presents. Since this question asks for a description of the streets, the words used by the author to help convey his description should lead you to

your answer. The author states that Oscar ran "in the shadows," and "the streets darkened and were silenced." Perhaps the most telling clue, however, was that although Oscar "was completely alone, he ran like a man being chased down." Look for the answer choice with the adjective that best reflects such descriptions.

Choice (A) is out of scope; there is no indication that the streets were *obstructed*. Choice (B) should match your prediction; the streets upon which Oscar ran are best described as *threatening*. Choice (C) is an opposite; the passage states that Oscar "was completely alone." Choice (D) is extreme; certainly the author's description of the streets conveyed some element of danger, but *deadly* is too extreme of an adjective to be correct. Choice (E) is an opposite; the passage states that "The streets…were silenced," which directly contradicts the assertion that they were noisy.

11. D
Difficulty: High

Oscar's impressions and Celia's observations, though of two totally separate scenes, convey something very similar about how both characters feel about themselves. What is it? Authors intentionally employ detail and description in their writing such as Oscar's impressions and Celia's observations to help establish elements of the character as well as compare and contrast them to other characters or situations in the passage. It is important to recognize that Oscar's impressions and Celia's observations share a common theme. This is illustrated by the fact that the seemingly positive images in line 39–40 "taunted Oscar and pushed him even further into the shadows," and Celia felt that the sophisticated women were "on the inside of some joke to which (she) was not privy." Use this to help predict what the author was trying to establish about both of the characters by using these examples.

Choice (A) is an opposite; in fact, Oscar's impressions and Celia's observations can be characterized as melancholy. Choice (B) is an opposite; Oscar's impressions and Celia's observations paint both characters as discontent. Choice (C) is distortion; Oscar's impressions and Celia's observations are descriptive of New York City life, but that is not their primary functions within the passage. Choice (D) is the correct choice; the descriptions in the passage convey the sense that both Oscar and Celia share a feeling of being *on the outside looking in*. Choice (E) is out of scope; you could characterize Celia's personality as *brooding*, however, Oscar's personality cannot be described as *joyful*.

12. C

Difficulty: Low

What does the description of Oscar's pace before it flags most likely indicate about the word's meaning? Often, vocabulary questions simply require switching each of the choices with the word in question to see which one makes the best sense in the surrounding context. "Flag" functions to indicate a change in Oscar's pace, but your answer needs to be more specific. In a straightforward vocabulary question such as this one, your best approach is to simply replace the word in question with each of the given choices to see which makes the most sense in context. Use this approach to help you arrive at your prediction.

Choice (A) is distortion; this is alternate definition of "flag" that makes no sense in context. Choice (B) is an opposite; Oscar was already running at top speed "like a man being chased down," it makes no sense that his pace would *revive* as he neared his apartment. Choice (C) is the best match; it fits perfectly in context. Choice (D) is distortion; this is another alternate definition of flag that makes no sense in context. Choice (E) is out of scope; nothing in the surrounding context indicates that Oscar fell down.

13. D

Difficulty: Low

Oscar did not ignore the door man, he was unaware of him. What does this tell you about his state of mind at the time? A strong vocabulary is important for inference questions as well. Often, knowing the definition of one tough word will be a big clue to your answer. Usually, when a person is oblivious to a person or a thing, it means that they are completely unaware of that person or thing's existence. Using what you have been given about Oscar's character in the passage, make a prediction that would best explain how Oscar could be unaware of the doorman.

Choice (A) is out of scope; there is nothing to suggest that the doorman has a weak voice. Choice (B) is distortion; this implies that Oscar was ignoring the doorman, not unaware of him. Choice (C) is out of scope; nothing in the passage suggests Oscar requires a hearing aid. Choice (D) is the best match for your prediction; the choice offers the best explanation for Oscar's obliviousness. Choice (E) is distortion; this choice also implies that Oscar was purposely

ignoring the doorman, which is contradicted by the use of the word "oblivious."

14. A

Difficulty: Medium

Why would a person be reluctant to look in a mirror? Often a question that references a specific detail from a passage can be answered not only from the detail in question, but surrounding details in context as well. The passage states that the poem from which Celia quoted was written from the point of the view of the mirror. Therefore, Celia was not referring to herself when she whispered the lines "*I am not cruel, only truthful,*" she was referring to the fact that a mirror does not lie. Taking this into account along with the added details that she looked at her reflection "reluctantly" and then "sighed" (line 52), look for the answer that contains the truth of what Celia saw in the mirror.

Choice (A) is correct; it makes sense that a person reluctant to look in the mirror probably doesn't like what they see. Choice (B) is a misused detail; it's possible Celia is a talented writer, but her ability to quote a line from a famous poem does not demonstrate that. Choice (C) is an opposite; a girl *conceited about her good looks* would not be reluctant to look in mirror. Choice (D) is extreme; one line from one Sylvia Plath poem does not indicate that Celia has read all of Plath's works. Choice (E) is out of scope; the quoting of one of Plath's lines does not necessarily mean Celia feels a connection with the poet.

15. D

Difficulty: High

What are some synonyms for the word "gift"? Authors often use phrases that seem contradictory to help describe a character's internal conflict. Celia The author characterized Celia's "feeling like a young girl" with the seemingly contradictory phrase "disappointing blessing" because of her internal contradiction: having an appreciation for "the gift of her own youth,"(line 71), while longing to be a more mature woman. The urge to feel older is the disappointment—look for the choice that best represents her appreciation of the blessing.

Choice (A) is an opposite; lines 55–56 states that Celia "came to New York to spend the summer taking care of her grandmother." Choice (B) is a misused detail; "blessing" does have some religious connotations, but they do not apply here. Choice (C) is distortion; it is not suggested in the passage that Celia was looking for her father. Choice (D) is the best match; Celia's urge to be older was lessened by her understanding getting older is inevitable. Choice (E) is distortion; there is no indication in the passage that the grandmother resents Celia's youth.

16. A

Difficulty: Medium

Celia is a beautiful girl who believes she is not. What might this tell you about Celia? When a passage presents characters with divergent points of view on the same situation, the differences often serve to highlight certain aspects of a character. Oscar's first impression of Celia was that she was a very beautiful girl, which directly contradicted her own impression of herself offered throughout the fifth passage. Look for choice that best describes what this revelation emphasizes about Celia.

Choice (A) is your best choice. Oscar's revelation of Celia's beauty emphasizes the insecurities she has about her looks. Choice (B) is distortion; Oscar sensed something strange about Celia, but he did not immediately know she was his daughter. Choice (C) is distortion; Oscar's ability to recognize physical beauty does particularly emphasize his sensitive nature. Choice (D) is an opposite; Nothing about Celia is boastful. Choice (E) is out of scope; this cliché makes no sense in the context of the passage

17. E

Difficulty: High

In contrast to Oscar and Celia's reserve, the author presents Grandma as loud and obnoxious. Think of some other words that would describe such an attitude. Essentially, this is a difficult vocabulary question that masquerades as a simple inference question. Your first approach should be to look for a match with a word that you understand before you attempt to decipher the words you do not. In the passage, Grandma's frankness is presented as a contrast to Oscar and Celia's reserve. This is most evident in line 97–98, where Grandma asked Oscar if he was "just going to stand there like an idiot," despite the fact she apparently did not know him. Look for the choice that contains the word that best describes this sort of attitude.

Choice (A) is out of scope; her attitude cannot be characterized as flattering or fawning. Choice (B) is an opposite; Grandma's attitude displayed an absence of tact. Choice (C) is an opposite; Grandma's attitude, though

perhaps a bit insolent, is certainly not weak. Choice (D) is an opposite; Grandma does not appear to lack self-confidence. Choice (E) fits best. Grandma's bold attitude borders on being contemptuous.

18. B

Difficulty: Medium

Why would Celia try to hide her eyes from Oscar? When reading a passage, having a good sense of a character's nature will help you to better understand the motives behind his actions. In terms of setting, you should be aware from earlier in the passage that it is the evening. It is likely that Celia put on her glasses to hide her eyes, which according to the passage, she did "nervously." Look for the choice that offers the best reason for why she would do this.

Choice (A) is an opposite; Oscar just returned from a run in the dark, so there could not be sunlight. Choice (B) is your best choice. Celia noticed Oscar's different eyes and did not want him to notice that hers were the same. Choice (C) is an opposite; Celia's insecure personality contradicts the choice. Choice (D) is distortion; this choice is too broad to be correct. True, Celia did not want Oscar to see her eyes, but the two characters had never seen each other before, so it would be impossible for Oscar to recognize her. Choice (E) is out of scope; the passage does not suggest that *she started crying*, nor was there a cause for her to cry.

19. C

Difficulty: High

How would you describe the specific quality of the characters' eyes that makes them beautiful? Questions that involve hypothetical reasoning are not as tough as they seem. Your best approach is to look for the choice that would seamlessly fit into the passage. As stated in the passage, Oscar and Celia both have eyes that are each a different color. In line 106 Oscar recognizes this shared trait and tells Celia that he "couldn't stand" his eyes when he was young, but a quote changed his "whole perspective." Therefore, the quote that best addresses the uniqueness of their eyes in a positive manner will be your answer.

Choice (A) is out of scope; this quote does not address the uniqueness of their eyes. Choice (B) is out of scope; this quote compares beauty and virtue. Choice (C) fits perfectly. It suggests that the uniqueness of their eyes—the *strangeness in the proportion*—is the very thing that makes them beautiful. Choice (D) is out of scope; the quote must address the characters' eyes, not their intellects. Choice (E) is distortion; this quote fits with a theme in the passage, but does fit its intended function within passage.

SECTION 9

1. B

Difficulty: High
Idioms require specific constructions to be correct; learn to recognize commonly tested ones. The construction *think of it* must be connected to what follows by *as*. Only choice (B) does so without introducing additional errors. (C) does not address the error. *It was* in choice (D) is incorrect with the idiom. Choice (E) introduces an inconsistent verb tense.

2. A

Difficulty: High
Use context clues to help you figure out unfamiliar words. Even if you weren't sure what *tenets* means, you could determine that this sentence is correct as written by checking the other answer choices for errors. Choice (B) uses the pronoun *who*, which is only correct when referring to people, to refer to *developments*. Choice (C) is unnecessarily wordy. Choices (D) and (E) use plural pronouns with a singular antecedent (*democracy*).

3. B

Difficulty: Medium
Although there are several ways to correct a run-on sentence, only one answer choice will do so without introducing additional errors. Choice (B) corrects the run-on error by adding the conjunction *and*. In choices (C), (D), and (E), the comparison is between *lawyer* and *personal injury cases.*

4. A

Difficulty: Medium
When an entire sentence is underlined, carefully examine the differences between the answer choices. This sentence is correct as written. The use of both *unlike* and *is different* in choice (B) is redundant, as are *unlike* and *do not* in choices (C). (D) and (E) are incorrect grammatical structure.

5. E

Difficulty: Medium
Look for the most concise way to express the ideas in the underlined selection. Choice (E) is concise without changing the meaning of the sentence or introducing any grammatical errors. Choices (B) and (C) are still unnecessarily wordy. (D) incorrectly uses *its* to refer to a person.

6. E

Difficulty: Medium
Although the passive voice will not always be incorrect on the SAT, check for an answer choice that makes the sentence active. Choice (E) makes Katy, rather than her plan, the subject of the sentence. Choice (B) is more concise, but still passive. Choice (C) creates a sentence fragment. Choice (D) is unnecessarily wordy.

7. D

Difficulty: Medium
A verb must agree in number with its subject, which may not be the noun closest to it in the sentence. Here, the plural teachers is the object of the preposition of, not the subject noun. One is the subject, so the correct verb form would be "was." Both choices (D) and (E) correct the verb, but choice (E) misuses the semicolon splice, which is only correct when used to join two independent clauses. Choices (B) and (C) do not address the error; additionally, choice (B) misuses the semicolon splice and choice (C) introduces an inconsistent verb tense.

8. A

Difficulty: Medium
Expect to see between five and eight sentences that contain no errors. This sentence is correct as written. Choices (B), (D), and (E) use transition words that alter the relationship between the clauses. Choice (C) is unnecessarily wordy.

9. C

Difficulty: Medium
Use of the passive voice will generally result in a sentence that is unnecessarily wordy. This sentence uses the passive voice and is overly wordy. Choice (C) is more concise without changing the meaning of the original sentence. Choices (B), (D), and (E) remain unnecessarily wordy.

10. A

Difficulty: Medium

When the underlined selection includes a semicolon, make sure both clauses are independent. This sentence contains no error. Choices (B), (C), and (D) create a cause-and-effect relationship between the clauses that is not present in the original; additionally, choice (C) uses the pronoun *it* without an antecedent and is unnecessarily wordy and choice (D) introduces an inconsistent verb tense. Choice (E) incorrectly uses a semicolon to join a subordinate clause to an independent one.

11. E

Difficulty: Medium

Make sure transition words properly relate the ideas within the sentence. Both (D) and (E) use *because* to create the appropriate relationship between the clauses, choice (D) is unnecessarily wordy. (B) is also overly wordy. Choice (C) is grammatically incorrect.

12. D

Difficulty: Medium

The construction of a comparison beginning with *as* is *as…as. Equally* is redundant in an *as…as* comparison. Choice (D) corrects the idiom; none of the other choices does so.

13. E

Difficulty: High

In sentences with multiple errors, make sure your answer choice addresses them all. Here, the object of the verb *failed* is the compound *to achieve…nor profiting.* There are two errors: the verbs are not parallel in form and *nor* would require *neither* to be correct in this context. Choice (E) corrects both errors. Choices (B), (C), and (D) all fail to correct the parallelism issue; choices (B) and (C) do not address the idiom error.

14. A

Difficulty: Medium

And is the only conjunction that creates a compound requiring the plural verb form. This sentence is correct as written, since the compound subject *convenience and value* requires the plural verb form *account.* Choice(B) uses a singular pronoun to refer to the plural *cameras.* Choice (C) uses a singular pronoun and the singular verb form, both of which are incorrect. Choice (D) uses the singular *is* with the plural compound subject. In choice (E), the singular *a reason* does not agree with the plural *convenience and value.*

SAT PRACTICE TEST SIX ANSWER SHEET

Remove (or photocopy) the answer sheet, and use it to complete the practice test.

How to Take the Practice Tests

Each Practice Test includes eight scored multiple-choice sections and one essay. Keep in mind that on the actual SAT, there will be an additional multiple-choice section—the experimental section—that will not contribute to your score.

Once you start a Practice Test, don't stop until you've gone through all nine sections. Remember, you can review any questions within a section, but you may not go back or forward a section.

Good luck!

Start with number 1 for each section. If a section has fewer questions than answer spaces, leave the extra spaces blank.

Section One
Section One is the writing section's essay component.
Lined pages on which you will write your essay can be found in that section.

Section Two

1. Ⓐ Ⓑ Ⓒ Ⓓ Ⓔ
2. Ⓐ Ⓑ Ⓒ Ⓓ Ⓔ
3. Ⓐ Ⓑ Ⓒ Ⓓ Ⓔ
4. Ⓐ Ⓑ Ⓒ Ⓓ Ⓔ
5. Ⓐ Ⓑ Ⓒ Ⓓ Ⓔ
6. Ⓐ Ⓑ Ⓒ Ⓓ Ⓔ
7. Ⓐ Ⓑ Ⓒ Ⓓ Ⓔ
8. Ⓐ Ⓑ Ⓒ Ⓓ Ⓔ

9. Ⓐ Ⓑ Ⓒ Ⓓ Ⓔ
10. Ⓐ Ⓑ Ⓒ Ⓓ Ⓔ
11. Ⓐ Ⓑ Ⓒ Ⓓ Ⓔ
12. Ⓐ Ⓑ Ⓒ Ⓓ Ⓔ
13. Ⓐ Ⓑ Ⓒ Ⓓ Ⓔ
14. Ⓐ Ⓑ Ⓒ Ⓓ Ⓔ
15. Ⓐ Ⓑ Ⓒ Ⓓ Ⓔ
16. Ⓐ Ⓑ Ⓒ Ⓓ Ⓔ

17. Ⓐ Ⓑ Ⓒ Ⓓ Ⓔ
18. Ⓐ Ⓑ Ⓒ Ⓓ Ⓔ
19. Ⓐ Ⓑ Ⓒ Ⓓ Ⓔ
20. Ⓐ Ⓑ Ⓒ Ⓓ Ⓔ
21. Ⓐ Ⓑ Ⓒ Ⓓ Ⓔ
22. Ⓐ Ⓑ Ⓒ Ⓓ Ⓔ
23. Ⓐ Ⓑ Ⓒ Ⓓ Ⓔ
24. Ⓐ Ⓑ Ⓒ Ⓓ Ⓔ

☐ # right in Section Two

☐ # wrong in Section Two

Section Three

1. Ⓐ Ⓑ Ⓒ Ⓓ Ⓔ
2. Ⓐ Ⓑ Ⓒ Ⓓ Ⓔ
3. Ⓐ Ⓑ Ⓒ Ⓓ Ⓔ
4. Ⓐ Ⓑ Ⓒ Ⓓ Ⓔ
5. Ⓐ Ⓑ Ⓒ Ⓓ Ⓔ
6. Ⓐ Ⓑ Ⓒ Ⓓ Ⓔ
7. Ⓐ Ⓑ Ⓒ Ⓓ Ⓔ
8. Ⓐ Ⓑ Ⓒ Ⓓ Ⓔ

9. Ⓐ Ⓑ Ⓒ Ⓓ Ⓔ
10. Ⓐ Ⓑ Ⓒ Ⓓ Ⓔ
11. Ⓐ Ⓑ Ⓒ Ⓓ Ⓔ
12. Ⓐ Ⓑ Ⓒ Ⓓ Ⓔ
13. Ⓐ Ⓑ Ⓒ Ⓓ Ⓔ
14. Ⓐ Ⓑ Ⓒ Ⓓ Ⓔ
15. Ⓐ Ⓑ Ⓒ Ⓓ Ⓔ
16. Ⓐ Ⓑ Ⓒ Ⓓ Ⓔ

17. Ⓐ Ⓑ Ⓒ Ⓓ Ⓔ
18. Ⓐ Ⓑ Ⓒ Ⓓ Ⓔ
19. Ⓐ Ⓑ Ⓒ Ⓓ Ⓔ
20. Ⓐ Ⓑ Ⓒ Ⓓ Ⓔ

☐ # right in Section Three

☐ # wrong in Section Three

Remove (or photocopy) this answer sheet, and use it to complete the practice test.

Start with number 1 for each section. If a section has fewer questions than answer spaces, leave the extra spaces blank.

Section Four

1. Ⓐ Ⓑ Ⓒ Ⓓ Ⓔ 10. Ⓐ Ⓑ Ⓒ Ⓓ Ⓔ 19. Ⓐ Ⓑ Ⓒ Ⓓ Ⓔ 28. Ⓐ Ⓑ Ⓒ Ⓓ Ⓔ
2. Ⓐ Ⓑ Ⓒ Ⓓ Ⓔ 11. Ⓐ Ⓑ Ⓒ Ⓓ Ⓔ 20. Ⓐ Ⓑ Ⓒ Ⓓ Ⓔ 29. Ⓐ Ⓑ Ⓒ Ⓓ Ⓔ
3. Ⓐ Ⓑ Ⓒ Ⓓ Ⓔ 12. Ⓐ Ⓑ Ⓒ Ⓓ Ⓔ 21. Ⓐ Ⓑ Ⓒ Ⓓ Ⓔ 30. Ⓐ Ⓑ Ⓒ Ⓓ Ⓔ
4. Ⓐ Ⓑ Ⓒ Ⓓ Ⓔ 13. Ⓐ Ⓑ Ⓒ Ⓓ Ⓔ 22. Ⓐ Ⓑ Ⓒ Ⓓ Ⓔ 31. Ⓐ Ⓑ Ⓒ Ⓓ Ⓔ

 # right in Section Four

5. Ⓐ Ⓑ Ⓒ Ⓓ Ⓔ 14. Ⓐ Ⓑ Ⓒ Ⓓ Ⓔ 23. Ⓐ Ⓑ Ⓒ Ⓓ Ⓔ 32. Ⓐ Ⓑ Ⓒ Ⓓ Ⓔ
6. Ⓐ Ⓑ Ⓒ Ⓓ Ⓔ 15. Ⓐ Ⓑ Ⓒ Ⓓ Ⓔ 24. Ⓐ Ⓑ Ⓒ Ⓓ Ⓔ 33. Ⓐ Ⓑ Ⓒ Ⓓ Ⓔ
7. Ⓐ Ⓑ Ⓒ Ⓓ Ⓔ 16. Ⓐ Ⓑ Ⓒ Ⓓ Ⓔ 25. Ⓐ Ⓑ Ⓒ Ⓓ Ⓔ 34 Ⓐ Ⓑ Ⓒ Ⓓ Ⓔ
8. Ⓐ Ⓑ Ⓒ Ⓓ Ⓔ 17. Ⓐ Ⓑ Ⓒ Ⓓ Ⓔ 26. Ⓐ Ⓑ Ⓒ Ⓓ Ⓔ 35. Ⓐ Ⓑ Ⓒ Ⓓ Ⓔ
9. Ⓐ Ⓑ Ⓒ Ⓓ Ⓔ 18. Ⓐ Ⓑ Ⓒ Ⓓ Ⓔ 27. Ⓐ Ⓑ Ⓒ Ⓓ Ⓔ

 # wrong in Section Four

Section Five

1. Ⓐ Ⓑ Ⓒ Ⓓ Ⓔ 9. Ⓐ Ⓑ Ⓒ Ⓓ Ⓔ 17. Ⓐ Ⓑ Ⓒ Ⓓ Ⓔ
2. Ⓐ Ⓑ Ⓒ Ⓓ Ⓔ 10. Ⓐ Ⓑ Ⓒ Ⓓ Ⓔ 18. Ⓐ Ⓑ Ⓒ Ⓓ Ⓔ
3. Ⓐ Ⓑ Ⓒ Ⓓ Ⓔ 11. Ⓐ Ⓑ Ⓒ Ⓓ Ⓔ 19. Ⓐ Ⓑ Ⓒ Ⓓ Ⓔ

 # right in Section Five

4. Ⓐ Ⓑ Ⓒ Ⓓ Ⓔ 12. Ⓐ Ⓑ Ⓒ Ⓓ Ⓔ 20. Ⓐ Ⓑ Ⓒ Ⓓ Ⓔ
5. Ⓐ Ⓑ Ⓒ Ⓓ Ⓔ 13. Ⓐ Ⓑ Ⓒ Ⓓ Ⓔ 21. Ⓐ Ⓑ Ⓒ Ⓓ Ⓔ
6. Ⓐ Ⓑ Ⓒ Ⓓ Ⓔ 14. Ⓐ Ⓑ Ⓒ Ⓓ Ⓔ 22. Ⓐ Ⓑ Ⓒ Ⓓ Ⓔ
7. Ⓐ Ⓑ Ⓒ Ⓓ Ⓔ 15. Ⓐ Ⓑ Ⓒ Ⓓ Ⓔ 23. Ⓐ Ⓑ Ⓒ Ⓓ Ⓔ
8. Ⓐ Ⓑ Ⓒ Ⓓ Ⓔ 16. Ⓐ Ⓑ Ⓒ Ⓓ Ⓔ 24. Ⓐ Ⓑ Ⓒ Ⓓ Ⓔ

 # wrong in Section Five

Remove (or photocopy) this answer sheet, and use it to complete the practice test.

Start with number 1 for each section. If a section has fewer questions than answer spaces, leave the extra spaces blank.

Section Six

1. Ⓐ Ⓑ Ⓒ Ⓓ Ⓔ
2. Ⓐ Ⓑ Ⓒ Ⓓ Ⓔ
3. Ⓐ Ⓑ Ⓒ Ⓓ Ⓔ
4. Ⓐ Ⓑ Ⓒ Ⓓ Ⓔ
5. Ⓐ Ⓑ Ⓒ Ⓓ Ⓔ
6. Ⓐ Ⓑ Ⓒ Ⓓ Ⓔ
7. Ⓐ Ⓑ Ⓒ Ⓓ Ⓔ
8. Ⓐ Ⓑ Ⓒ Ⓓ Ⓔ

9. Ⓐ Ⓑ Ⓒ Ⓓ Ⓔ
10. Ⓐ Ⓑ Ⓒ Ⓓ Ⓔ
11. Ⓐ Ⓑ Ⓒ Ⓓ Ⓔ
12. Ⓐ Ⓑ Ⓒ Ⓓ Ⓔ
13. Ⓐ Ⓑ Ⓒ Ⓓ Ⓔ
14. Ⓐ Ⓑ Ⓒ Ⓓ Ⓔ
15. Ⓐ Ⓑ Ⓒ Ⓓ Ⓔ
16. Ⓐ Ⓑ Ⓒ Ⓓ Ⓔ

17. Ⓐ Ⓑ Ⓒ Ⓓ Ⓔ
18. Ⓐ Ⓑ Ⓒ Ⓓ Ⓔ

☐ # right in Section Six

☐ # wrong in Section Six

If section 6 of your test book contains math questions that are not multiple choice, continue to item 9 below. Otherwise, continue to item 9 above.

9. 10. 11. 12. 13.

14. 15. 16. 17. 18.

Remove (or photocopy) this answer sheet, and use it to complete the practice test.

Start with number 1 for each section. If a section has fewer questions than answer spaces, leave the extra spaces blank.

Section Seven

1. Ⓐ Ⓑ Ⓒ Ⓓ Ⓔ　　9. Ⓐ Ⓑ Ⓒ Ⓓ Ⓔ　　17. Ⓐ Ⓑ Ⓒ Ⓓ Ⓔ
2. Ⓐ Ⓑ Ⓒ Ⓓ Ⓔ　　10. Ⓐ Ⓑ Ⓒ Ⓓ Ⓔ　　18. Ⓐ Ⓑ Ⓒ Ⓓ Ⓔ
3. Ⓐ Ⓑ Ⓒ Ⓓ Ⓔ　　11. Ⓐ Ⓑ Ⓒ Ⓓ Ⓔ　　19. Ⓐ Ⓑ Ⓒ Ⓓ Ⓔ
4. Ⓐ Ⓑ Ⓒ Ⓓ Ⓔ　　12. Ⓐ Ⓑ Ⓒ Ⓓ Ⓔ
5. Ⓐ Ⓑ Ⓒ Ⓓ Ⓔ　　13. Ⓐ Ⓑ Ⓒ Ⓓ Ⓔ
6. Ⓐ Ⓑ Ⓒ Ⓓ Ⓔ　　14. Ⓐ Ⓑ Ⓒ Ⓓ Ⓔ
7. Ⓐ Ⓑ Ⓒ Ⓓ Ⓔ　　15. Ⓐ Ⓑ Ⓒ Ⓓ Ⓔ
8. Ⓐ Ⓑ Ⓒ Ⓓ Ⓔ　　16. Ⓐ Ⓑ Ⓒ Ⓓ Ⓔ

☐ # right in Section Seven

☐ # wrong in Section Seven

Section Eight

1. Ⓐ Ⓑ Ⓒ Ⓓ Ⓔ　　9. Ⓐ Ⓑ Ⓒ Ⓓ Ⓔ
2. Ⓐ Ⓑ Ⓒ Ⓓ Ⓔ　　10. Ⓐ Ⓑ Ⓒ Ⓓ Ⓔ
3. Ⓐ Ⓑ Ⓒ Ⓓ Ⓔ　　11. Ⓐ Ⓑ Ⓒ Ⓓ Ⓔ
4. Ⓐ Ⓑ Ⓒ Ⓓ Ⓔ　　12. Ⓐ Ⓑ Ⓒ Ⓓ Ⓔ
5. Ⓐ Ⓑ Ⓒ Ⓓ Ⓔ　　13. Ⓐ Ⓑ Ⓒ Ⓓ Ⓔ
6. Ⓐ Ⓑ Ⓒ Ⓓ Ⓔ　　14. Ⓐ Ⓑ Ⓒ Ⓓ Ⓔ
7. Ⓐ Ⓑ Ⓒ Ⓓ Ⓔ　　15. Ⓐ Ⓑ Ⓒ Ⓓ Ⓔ
8. Ⓐ Ⓑ Ⓒ Ⓓ Ⓔ　　16. Ⓐ Ⓑ Ⓒ Ⓓ Ⓔ

☐ # right in Section Eight

☐ # wrong in Section Eight

Section Nine

1. Ⓐ Ⓑ Ⓒ Ⓓ Ⓔ　　9. Ⓐ Ⓑ Ⓒ Ⓓ Ⓔ
2. Ⓐ Ⓑ Ⓒ Ⓓ Ⓔ　　10. Ⓐ Ⓑ Ⓒ Ⓓ Ⓔ
3. Ⓐ Ⓑ Ⓒ Ⓓ Ⓔ　　11. Ⓐ Ⓑ Ⓒ Ⓓ Ⓔ
4. Ⓐ Ⓑ Ⓒ Ⓓ Ⓔ　　12. Ⓐ Ⓑ Ⓒ Ⓓ Ⓔ
5. Ⓐ Ⓑ Ⓒ Ⓓ Ⓔ　　13. Ⓐ Ⓑ Ⓒ Ⓓ Ⓔ
6. Ⓐ Ⓑ Ⓒ Ⓓ Ⓔ　　14. Ⓐ Ⓑ Ⓒ Ⓓ Ⓔ
7. Ⓐ Ⓑ Ⓒ Ⓓ Ⓔ
8. Ⓐ Ⓑ Ⓒ Ⓓ Ⓔ

☐ # right in Section Nine

☐ # wrong in Section Nine

Practice Test Six

SECTION 1
Time—25 Minutes
ESSAY

The essay gives you an opportunity to show how effectively you can develop and express ideas. You should, therefore, take care to develop your point of view, present your ideas logically and clearly, and use language precisely.

Your essay must be written in your Answer Grid Booklet—you will receive no other paper on which to write. You will have enough space if you write on every line, avoid wide margins, and keep your handwriting to a reasonable size. Remember that people who are not familiar with your handwriting will read what you write. Try to write or print so that what you are writing is legible to those readers.

You have twenty-five minutes to write an essay on the topic assigned below.

DO NOT WRITE ON ANOTHER TOPIC. AN OFF-TOPIC ESSAY WILL RECEIVE A SCORE OF ZERO.

Think carefully about the issue presented in the following excerpt and the assignment below.

> "Failure is impossible"
>
> *—Susan B. Anthony*

Assignment: Is it really impossible to fail? Are some failures simply unsuccessful attempts to accomplish what we set out to do, or do all failures ultimately provide some benefit, even if we can't see it right away? Plan and write an essay in which you develop your point of view on this issue. Support your position with reasoning and examples taken from your reading, studies, experience, or observations.

DO NOT WRITE YOUR ESSAY IN YOUR TEST BOOK.
You will receive credit only for what you write in your Answer Grid Booklet.

KAPLAN
Test Prep and Admissions

_____

_____

_____

_____

_____

_____

_____

_____

_____

_____

_____

_____

_____

_____

_____

_____

_____

_____

_____

IF YOU FINISH BEFORE TIME IS CALLED, YOU MAY CHECK YOUR WORK ON THIS SECTION ONLY. DO NOT TURN TO ANY OTHER SECTION IN THE TEST.   **STOP**

SECTION 2

Time—25 Minutes
24 Questions

Directions: For each of the following questions, choose the best answer and darken the corresponding oval on the answer sheet.

Each sentence below has one or two blanks, each blank indicating that something has been omitted. Beneath the sentence are five words or sets of words labeled (A) through (E). Choose the word or set of words that, when inserted in the sentence, <u>best</u> fits the meaning of the sentence as a whole.

EXAMPLE:

Today's small, portable computers contrast markedly with the earliest electronic computers, which were ---- .

(A) effective
(B) invented
(C) useful
(D) destructive
(E) enormous   Ⓐ Ⓑ Ⓒ Ⓓ ●

---

1. Many fishermen work tirelessly through the spring and summer months, ---- themselves to ---- the warmer temperatures and lack of inclement weather.

   (A) subjecting . . subsist on
   (B) encouraging . . compete for
   (C) tempting . . abstain from
   (D) forcing . . forage for
   (E) enabling . . benefit from

2. During the night, thunderstorms were ----, beginning and ending at almost regular intervals.

   (A) unmediated
   (B) spontaneous
   (C) periodic
   (D) incidental
   (E) endemic

3. Even though hostile protests and ---- marred the 1959 enrollment of Andrew Heidelberg at the all-white Norview High School, the aftermath of the decision to allow him to become Norview's first African American football player during his senior year was comparatively ----.

   (A) discord . . tranquil
   (B) pomp . . daunting
   (C) banality . . conventional
   (D) turmoil . . controversial
   (E) serenity . . opportune

4. The professor's remark was not intended as a criticism but as a ---- by which she sought further explanation.

   (A) query
   (B) confession
   (C) dismissal
   (D) condemnation
   (E) credo

5. Political figures who appear to be staunch supporters of the interests of the general public may not always be the ---- they purport to be, but rather ---- who favor selected groups that provide significant campaign benefactions.

   (A) demagogues . . mavericks
   (B) conservatives . . anarchists
   (C) populists . . elitists
   (D) moderates . . reactionaries
   (E) partisans . . snobs

GO ON TO THE NEXT PAGE

> **Directions:** The passages below are followed by questions based on their content; questions following a pair of related passages may also be based on the relationship between the paired passages. Answer the questions on the basis of what is <u>stated</u> or <u>implied</u> in the passages and in any introductory material that may be provided.

Questions 6–9 are based on the following passages.

Passage 1

With numerous economic indices reporting that consumer confidence is beginning to rebound strongly after a prolonged period of uncertainty, one would think the restaurant industry would
(5) feel encouraged. The fact is that consumer restaurant spending climbed steadily through even the worst of the recent economic downturns. While some of the industry's more cynical analysts attribute part of this growth to the ever-increasing
(10) laziness of the American public—an idea somewhat supported by a burgeoning community of new carryout restaurants—others point to the impressive creativity of restaurateurs who have formed lucrative relationships with some rather
(15) unconventional business partners like ballparks, airlines, and even department stores.

Passage 2

While eating out certainly has a positive effect on the nation's economy, often the effect is not so positive for consumers watching their waistlines
(20) or overall health. Not only do restaurant diners have less control over the nutritional content of their meals, but restaurant cooks, focused on enticing customers back, typically add more fats and salt to their recipes than a home cook would.
(25) Additionally, the portions many restaurants serve are oversized. As each year seems to find more and more consumers relying on restaurants for their daily food intake—some studies have pegged the share of households that cook at least twice a day
(30) at just over 30 percent—the nutritional value of restaurant food will become an increasingly important issue.

6. As used in Passage 1, the expression "some of the industry's more cynical analysts" (line 8) indicates that the author considers these analysts

(A) indefensibly critical
(B) overly optimistic
(C) fairly pessimistic
(D) rather inaccurate
(E) downright scornful

7. With the words "focused on enticing customers back" (lines 22–23), the author of Passage 2 implies that restaurant cooks

(A) lack all concern about the health of their customers
(B) believe healthy food is bad for the economy
(C) do not consider foods high in fat and salt unhealthy
(D) may sacrifice nutritional value to retain their clientele
(E) assume their customers are only concerned with taste

8. The author of Passage 2 suggests that the rise in consumer restaurant spending outlined in Passage 1 is

(A) inevitable
(B) unexpected
(C) potentially troubling
(D) crucial for the economy
(E) socially destructive

GO ON TO THE NEXT PAGE ⟩

9. Which of the following best describes a significant difference between the two approaches to the rise in consumer restaurant spending?

(A) Passage 1 examines this persistent growth; Passage 2, its human health implications.

(B) Passage 1 describes the creativity behind this growth; Passage 2, the moral repercussions.

(C) Passage 1 analyzes the disparity between the rise in consumer restaurant spending and the economy's decline; Passage 2 contradicts this analysis.

(D) Each passage explores a different reason behind the growing tendency to be health-conscious.

(E) Each passage takes a different perspective on the relationship between consumer confidence and the nation's economy.

GO ON TO THE NEXT PAGE

Questions 10–14 are based on the following passage.

This passage, about the formative years of the American media, was adapted from an essay on the relationship between newspapers and popular culture by Walter Fox.

Throughout American history, newspapers have played a crucial role in shaping our cultural life. The colonial press of the early 18th-century in America, although on the whole limited in circu-
(5) lation and dependent upon rather primitive technology, first established just how powerful newspapers could be as instruments of social change by moving the colonists to revolt against the British throne. Later, in the mid-1800s during
(10) a period known as the "penny press" era, the first newspapers designed for the "common man" came into print, constituting a journalistic revolution of sorts roughly comparable to President Andrew Jackson's political triumph for the American
(15) middle-class over the 40 years of government dominated by more aristocratic, upper-class elite. Yet, the formative significance of these periods in the constitution of the American press a side, it was the last few decades of the 19th-century that
(20) produced the most profound change in the relationship between the American press and its readership.

Whereas before, especially during slower news times, newspapers occupied a relatively
(25) ancillary position in American life, by 1900 such publications had become one of the primary determinants of public opinion. Although this transformation was undoubtedly fueled by the substantive social changes taking place throughout
(30) the nation, namely those of industrialization and the mass migrations that altered the American urban landscape, there were smaller technological breakthroughs in printing that also helped newspapers become more pervasive voices in society. In
(35) particular, by the turn of the 19th-century electronic printing presses were being used to churn out papers at previously unheard of costs. Additionally, newsprint prices fell dramatically and full-color printing techniques became cheap,
(40) allowing for striking visual images to adorn even the most mundane stories. But to look at these two areas of change, one social and the other technological, as separate catalysts is to miss the point; it was their union that created a massive newspa-
(45) per readership that has only grown over the past century.

Of particular significance during this period is the fact that this readership was not only enormous, but also largely composed of immigrants
(50) and former migrant farmers and laborers who had flocked to the growing cities by the hundreds of thousands only to hold a rather uncertain rung on the American economic ladder. This social positioning created a mass newspaper audience
(55) fervently reliant upon the relative immediacy of media reports to inform their constantly changing, unstable lives. The daily papers began to augment impressively comprehensive worldwide news coverage with more sensational, human-interest
(60) stories, a combination that proved to be particularly appealing for the new American urban culture. Thus, by the first decades of the 20th-century the American press was already the outspoken generator of American popular culture that it is
(65) today: a social position that would only be expanded with the advent of radio and television.

10. In line 18, "constitution" most nearly means

(A) disposition

(B) structuring

(C) design

(D) establishment

(E) temperament

GO ON TO THE NEXT PAGE

11. In the last sentence of the first paragraph, the author implies that the "last few decades of the 19th century" (line 19) were

    (A) a time when newspapers became the publication of choice for most Americans

    (B) a particularly formative time for the newly forged American urban culture

    (C) of greater historical significance than even President Jackson's victory over the political aristocracy

    (D) more important years for the newspaper industry than any other time period

    (E) even more intensely transformational for the press than earlier periods of great political change

12. In line 37, "unheard of" most nearly means

    (A) impossible

    (B) unthinkable

    (C) inappropriate

    (D) inconsistent

    (E) uncommon

13. In lines 41–43, "But to look...miss the point" suggests that these technological changes

    (A) made newspapers far more visually appealing to the average American

    (B) enabled the newspaper industry to exploit the growing urban workforce

    (C) allowed newspapers to reach a new, but financially limited, demographic

    (D) made newspapers so inexpensive that even rural communities could afford them

    (E) were a direct result of the growing trend towards urbanization

14. The discussion in lines 53–57 ("This social positioning...unstable lives") implies that newspapers were appealing to urban populations because they

    (A) were relatively affordable

    (B) could be read quickly and easily

    (C) covered very current events

    (D) contained sensational stories

    (E) focused on immigration and farming issues

GO ON TO THE NEXT PAGE

Questions 15–24 are based on the following passage.

The following passage is from a 2004 essay that discusses the decline in artistic awareness, appreciation, and taste in America.

While many of us express disdain at the declining condition of artistic awareness, let alone appreciation, in this country, we cannot honestly express surprise. This general decline in tastes has
(5) not escaped the commentary and analysis of cultural critics who have warned us that we may be turning into a nation of Philistines. These same critics have pointed to a pair of causes for this cultural decline. Perhaps, they note, the decline is due
(10) to the crumbling state of our educational system, or to the media's focus on pop culture and the general decline of taste this breeds. Nevertheless, this type of scholarly discussion about the roots of the decline, while relevant to sociological and cul-
(15) tural historical analysis, does nothing to solve the problem. Understanding the causes does not change the sad fact that the same country that gave the world film noir, jazz, and abstract expressionism now mostly concerns itself with teen
(20) movies and boy bands. We must use our understanding and analysis of the causes to address the problem of artistic decline in America.

Before we can begin a discussion of artistic decline, we must first define the word "art," an
(25) endeavor that has proven problematic, especially after the introduction of modern art forms during the twentieth century. Indeed, some may argue that the entire debate about artistic decline in this country is flawed due to our exclusion of modern
(30) forms of art such as pop music. Many claim that such discussion can be seen as snobby, even culturally imperious. Without entering the debate on the validity of the post-modern conception of art as an idea, the question of "what is art" must
(35) be addressed. But it should be addressed expeditiously. Far too much time has been spent arguing over whether a teen movie is more or less art than *Citizen Kane* is, or whether the music of a boy band is more or less art than are the works of
(40) Sondheim. To be fair, society should not adopt an exclusionary definition or attitude. Indeed, history has proven that today's pop music can be

tomorrow's great art in retrospect. Thus, we should accept all artistic endeavors as art.
(45) Individuals and critics should judge the quality of such endeavors. But this does not change the fact that today people are unaware of and uneducated about the classics, or even about recent movements in art apart from cinema, television, and
(50) pop music.

Think about a United States of America in which artistic education, and thus appreciation, flourishes, a place where parents read books on art and listen to classical music and opera as well as
(55) pop music. Children observe these adult activities and mimic them. Parents read to their children and educate them. These parents also give their children art books, classical recordings, and plays as gifts. These parents underwrite, with their tax
(60) dollars, public art, public broadcasting, and community art groups. In school, students receive an education in art history, classical music, and opera. This curriculum can also include pop culture such as the music videos, teen movies, and pop music
(65) students enjoy in their free time. In fact, a better education in art will better equip them to judge the artistic merit of these newer, more trendy art forms, or at least place these art forms in historical context and analyze them as an outgrowth of soci-
(70) etal and sociological trends—an important aspect of artistic knowledge that has been lost by the general public. When these children grow up, some may produce their own art, which would likely be higher in quality than the pop music and
(75) movies produced today. Imagine a land of such developed artistic production and taste! How can we achieve such a society?

Having noted that the proliferation of low quality art in pop culture can be addressed effectively
(80) by education, there remains one fundamental cause for the decline in artistic taste: the crumbling state of our educational system. The society dreamed of above can only be achieved by sustained efforts to improve the American educa-
(85) tional system. Unfortunately, with tightening budgets due to increased levels of government debt, often the first programs cut are those that provide art and music classes. Often these cuts are viewed as easy ones by the public since they do

GO ON TO THE NEXT PAGE

(90) not compromise the fundamentals supposedly
required for an adequate education: reading, writing, history, science, and math. However, what the
public often misses is that art, music, and culture
are inextricably tied to literary and historical
(95) developments that themselves stem from changes
in society and culture. A holistic approach to the
arts would both redefine their role in education
(thereby subsuming the argument of those who
want to focus on fundamentals) and improve the
(100) state of artistic education by teaching students in
an intertextual and multidisciplinary manner. The
first step in improving artistic awareness and taste
in this country will be not only to reinstate and
improve art, music, and other cultural classes but
(105) also to restructure the curriculum to provide a
more holistic education in which art, music, and
culture become a part of the fundamental education in history, literature, and society. This system
would require more funding, and most likely
(110) higher taxes. However, such a an investment
would pay dividends by ensuring a more educated
populace, one which is better equipped to analyze
its surroundings in an analytically balanced manner and one which appreciates all forms of human
(115) artistic endeavor.

15. According to the author, which endeavor has
proven problematic?

(A) improving the education system

(B) making art seem relevant

(C) defining the word "art"

(D) deciding what students should learn in school

(E) deciding whether or not to teach art

16. In the second paragraph of the passage (lines
36–40), the author suggests that too much time has
been spent

(A) debating the artistic merits of so-called
"classics"

(B) debating the artistic merits of modern works

(C) debating whether or not art education can be
improved

(D) debating whether or not historical perspective
should be used in art education

(E) comparing the artistic merits of different
works traditionally considered classics

17. The author mentions "film noir, jazz, and abstract
expressionism" (lines 18–19) chiefly in order to

(A) appeal to the reader's sense of nostalgia

(B) introduce a historical parallel

(C) examine the history of art

(D) remind the reader how tastes change over time

(E) suggest that current artistic works are inferior
to older ones

18. In line 32, "imperious" most nearly means

(A) imperative

(B) arbitrary

(C) regal

(D) urgent

(E) arrogant

19. In lines 51–59 ("Think about… gifts"), the
hypothetical United States described is noteworthy
because

(A) people have developed new interests

(B) parents share their interest in and enjoyment
of art

(C) children study art in school

(D) children and parents share many activities

(E) artistic knowledge is considered a valuable
skill

GO ON TO THE NEXT PAGE

20. The author includes the third paragraph (lines 51–77) primarily in order to

    (A) propose a vision of a utopian society

    (B) propose a vision of an artistically educated society

    (C) argue that pop culture leaves no lasting impact on society

    (D) observe that classic literature has great appeal for even reluctant students

    (E) indicate that contemporary and classical works are interchangeable

21. In lines 92–96 ("However...culture"), the education illustrated is best described as

    (A) elitist

    (B) philanthropic

    (C) eclectic

    (D) comprehensive

    (E) rudimentary

22. In lines 101–110, the author describes an education system that would be

    (A) more expensive than the current system

    (B) more celebrated than the current system

    (C) more controversial than the current system

    (D) more interesting than the current system

    (E) more likely to inspire than the current system

23. The main purpose of the passage is to

    (A) shift the focus of a debate from causes to effects

    (B) outline a debate and support one side

    (C) present a problem and suggest a solution

    (D) revive a discredited idea that might be able to solve a current problem

    (E) promote certain kinds of art

24. In the hypothetical United States the author discusses, why does the author imply that children will grow up to produce art that may be higher in quality than the pop music and movies produced today?

    (A) They would not want to disappoint their parents.

    (B) Society would not accept low quality art.

    (C) Their education would provide them with more artistic knowledge.

    (D) They would have more free time to experiment with their art.

    (E) Critics would judge the merits of the art more harshly.

SECTION 3
Time—25 Minutes
20 Questions

Directions: For this section, solve each problem and decide which is the best of the choices given. Fill in the corresponding oval on the answer sheet. You may use any available space for scratchwork.

Notes:

(1) Calculator use is permitted.

(2) All numbers used are real numbers.

(3) Figures are provided for some problems. All figures are drawn to scale and lie in a plane UNLESS otherwise indicated.

(4) Unless otherwise specified, the domain of any function f is assumed to be the set of all real numbers x for which $f(x)$ is a real number.

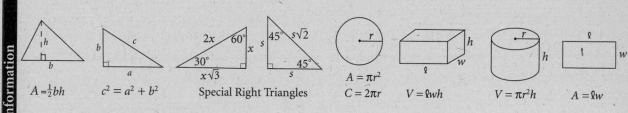

Information

$A = \frac{1}{2}bh$ $c^2 = a^2 + b^2$ Special Right Triangles $A = \pi r^2$ $C = 2\pi r$ $V = \ell wh$ $V = \pi r^2 h$ $A = \ell w$

The sum of the degree measures of the angles in a triangle is 180.
The number of degrees of arc in a circle is 360.
A straight angle has a degree measure of 180.

---

1. If $x^{\frac{1}{2}} = 3$, what is the value of x^2?

   (A) $\frac{1}{3}$

   (B) 6

   (C) 9

   (D) 12

   (E) 81

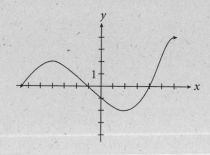

2. The figure above shows the graph of $g(x)$. What is the smallest value of $g(x)$ shown?

   (A) −2

   (B) 0

   (C) 2

   (D) 3

   (E) 5

GO ON TO THE NEXT PAGE

Movie Rentals for the Month of January

	New releases	Older titles	Total
Comedy	a	b	c
Drama	d	e	f
Total	g	h	i

3. In this table, each letter stands for the number of movies rented in January that fit the specified category. Which of the following expressions must be equal to i?

(A) $a + c$

(B) $c + h$

(C) $d + e$

(D) $d + e + f$

(E) $a + b + d + e$

4. If the length of one side of a triangle is 6 and the length of another side is 2, which of the following CANNOT be the length of the third side of the triangle?

(A) 5

(B) 6

(C) 7

(D) 7.5

(E) 8

**Number of Trees
in Beaumont City Parks**

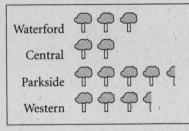

Waterford

Central

Parkside

Western

= 50 trees

5. In the pictograph above, the number of trees in each of four parks are shown. How many more trees are there in Parkside than Waterford?

(A) 50

(B) 75

(C) 100

(D) 125

(E) 150

6. If $5x - x = 2x + x - 5$, then $x =$

(A) -10

(B) -5

(C) -1

(D) 5

(E) 10

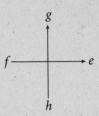

7. If the figure above represents the facts that $g > h$ and $e > f$, which of the following is true?

(A)

(B)

(C)

(D)

(E)

GO ON TO THE NEXT PAGE

8. If $y > 0$, what is 60 percent of $20y$?

(A) $1.2y$

(B) $10y$

(C) $12y$

(D) $15y$

(E) $120y$

9. If $q = \dfrac{5}{4}st$, what is the value of t when $s = 2$ and $q = 50$?

(A) 2.5

(B) 20

(C) 35

(D) 40

(E) 70

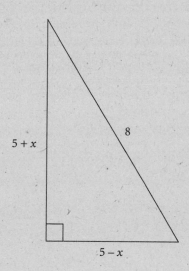

10. In the figure shown above, where $x < 5$, what is the value of $x^2 + 25$?

(A) 7

(B) 32

(C) 50

(D) 64

(E) 81

11. The measures of the angles of a triangle, in degrees, can be expressed by the ratio 4:5:6. What is the sum of the measures of the largest and smallest angles?

(A) 80

(B) 100

(C) 120

(D) 140

(E) 160

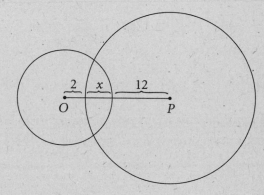

12. In the figure above, the radius of circle with center P is triple the radius of circle with center O. What is the value of x?

(A) 1

(B) 2

(C) 3

(D) 5

(E) 7

GO ON TO THE NEXT PAGE

Questions 13–14 refer to the following graph.

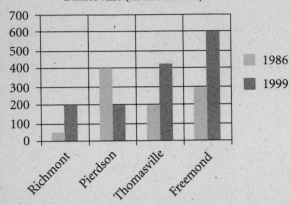

Population in Various Cities of
Baxterville (in thousands)

☐ 1986
■ 1999

13. Which of the following cities in Baxterville had a population in 1986 that was approximately $\frac{1}{2}$ that of its population in 1999?

    I. Richmont
   II. Pierdson
  III. Thomasville

(A) I only
(B) II only
(C) III only
(D) I and III only
(E) I, II, and III

14. From 1986 to 1999, the total population in the four cities increased by approximately what percent?

(A)   20%
(B)   50%
(C) 120%
(D) 140%
(E) 200%

15. At a certain company, some employees in the accounting department are also on the company bowling team, and none of the employees on the company bowling team are married. Which of the following statements must also be true?

(A) None of the employees in the accounting department are married.

(B) Some of the employees in the accounting department are married.

(C) Some of the employees in the accounting department are unmarried.

(D) More employees are on the bowling team than work in the accounting department.

(E) More employees work in the accounting department than are on the bowling team.

16. A class of 30 students had an average (arithmetic mean) of 92 points on a geography test out of a possible 100. If 10 of the students had a perfect score, what was the average score for the remaining students?

(A) 58
(B) 87
(C) 88
(D) 90
(E) 92

17. If a is a positive number, which of the following is equal to $a^2 \times a^{-2}$?

(A) 0
(B) 1
(C) a^{-4}
(D) a
(E) a^4

GO ON TO THE NEXT PAGE

18. In the diagram above, the diameter of circle O is 6. If the circle is cut in half, what is the total perimeter of the two pieces?

    (A) $3\pi + 3$
    (B) $6\pi + 6$
    (C) $6\pi + 12$
    (D) $12\pi + 6$
    (E) $12\pi + 12$

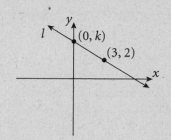

20. In the figure above, the slope of line l is $\dfrac{-1}{2}$. What is the value of k?

    (A) -6
    (B) $\dfrac{1}{2}$
    (C) $\dfrac{7}{2}$
    (D) 5
    (E) 8

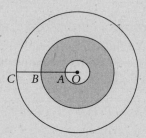

19. The diagram above shows three circles, all of which share a common origin O. If the lengths of segments $\overline{AB}$ and $\overline{BC}$ are both equal to the diameter of the smallest circle, what is the probability that a randomly selected point within the diagram will fall within the shaded region?

    (A) $\dfrac{8}{25}$

    (B) $\dfrac{9}{25}$

    (C) $\dfrac{1}{9}$

    (D) $\dfrac{5}{8}$

    (E) $\dfrac{8}{9}$

IF YOU FINISH BEFORE TIME IS CALLED, YOU MAY CHECK YOUR WORK ON THIS SECTION ONLY. DO NOT TURN TO ANY OTHER SECTION IN THE TEST.   STOP

SECTION 4

Time—25 Minutes
35 Questions

Directions: For each question in this section, select the best answer from among the choices given and fill in the corresponding oval on the answer sheet.

The following sentences test correctness and effectiveness of expression. Part of each sentence or the entire sentence is underlined; beneath each sentence are five ways of phrasing the underlined material. Choice (A) repeats the original phrasing; the other four choices are different. If you think the original phrasing produces a better sentence than any of the alternatives, select choice (A); if not, select one of the other choices.

In making your selection, follow the requirements of standard written English; that is, pay attention to grammar, choice of words, sentence construction, and punctuation. Your selection should result in the most effective sentence—clear and precise, without awkwardness or ambiguity.

EXAMPLE: ANSWER:

Every apple in the baskets <u>are ripe and labeled according to the date it was picked</u>.   Ⓐ ● Ⓒ Ⓓ Ⓔ

(A) are ripe and labeled according to the date it was picked
(B) is ripe and labeled according to the date it was picked
(C) are ripe and labeled according to the date they were picked
(D) is ripe and labeled according to the date they were picked
(E) are ripe and labeled as to the date it was picked

---

1. During the festivities to mark the centennial of the police station, <u>that was the time that the thieves robbed the bank</u>.

    (A) that was the time that the thieves robbed the bank
    (B) the bank was robbed by thieves
    (C) the thieves robbed the bank
    (D) the thieves used the time to rob the bank
    (E) was the time that the thieves robbing the bank happened

2. To address their financial woes, the vintners decided <u>to hold two tastings per year instead of one and they would increase</u> ticket prices by fifty percent.

    (A) to hold two tastings per year instead of one and they would increase
    (B) to hold two tastings per year instead of one and to increase
    (C) instead of one on holding two tastings per year and to increase
    (D) on holding two tastings per year instead of one for increasing
    (E) to holding two tastings per year instead of one, thus increasing

GO ON TO THE NEXT PAGE ⟩

3. Although most people think of Egyptian papyrus as the earliest paper, during the Han Dynasty, <u>the Chinese developing a process to create paper from individual plant fibers that</u> was much closer to techniques used in modern papermaking.

(A) the Chinese developing a process to create paper from individual plant fibers that

(B) the Chinese developing a process and creating paper from individual plant fibers that

(C) the Chinese developing a process to create paper from individual plant fibers, it

(D) the Chinese developed a process to create paper from individual plant fibers, it

(E) the Chinese developed a process to create paper from individual plant fibers that

4. During World War II, some of the brightest minds in America <u>was working in the New Mexico desert on a secret project that was</u> crucial to the Allied victory.

(A) was working in the New Mexico desert on a secret project that was

(B) were working in the New Mexico desert on a secret project; because it was

(C) was working in the New Mexico desert on a secret project; it was

(D) were working in the New Mexico desert on a secret project that was

(E) were working in the New Mexico desert on a secret project that were

5. Although the budget for the project had already been increased three times, <u>the contractors kept asking the committee for a greater amount of money</u> to complete the construction.

(A) the contractors kept asking the committee for a greater amount of money

(B) greater money was requested from the committee by the contractors

(C) the contractors kept asking that the committee give more money to them

(D) the amount of money asked for by the contractors from the committee kept increasing

(E) the contractors kept asking the committee for more money

6. There is more fresh water frozen in the polar ice caps <u>than</u> the rest of the world.

(A) than

(B) than where there is fresh water in

(C) than there is

(D) than fresh water of

(E) than there is in

7. <u>Like the well-known author Salman Rushdie, novelist Arundhati Roy has</u> been labeled a magical realist, even though she dislikes the term.

(A) Like the well-known author Salman Rushdie, novelist Arundhati Roy has

(B) Like the well-known magical realist author Salman Rushdie, the novelist Arundhati Roy has

(C) Similar to the well-known author Salman Rushdie, the novels of Arundhati Roy have

(D) The novels of Arundhati Roy, like the well-known author Salman Rushdie, have

(E) Arundhati Roy's novels, like those of the well-known author Salman Rushdie, have

GO ON TO THE NEXT PAGE

8. The coach chose Amanda to run the final lap of the relay, since her time was better than <u>either Gwen or Christine</u>.

   (A) either Gwen or Christine
   (B) either Gwen or else Christine
   (C) either Gwen or that of Christine
   (D) that of either Gwen or Christine
   (E) either that of Gwen or that of Christine

9. <u>Since many of the switches destroyed in the fire were custom-built is why</u> the train will be out of service for at least six months.

   (A) Since many of the switches destroyed in the fire were custom-built is why
   (B) Since many of the switches destroyed in the fire were custom-built,
   (C) Many of the switches destroyed in the fire were custom-built so therefore,
   (D) Because of many of the switches destroyed in the fire being custom-built,
   (E) The fact that many of the switches destroyed in the fire were custom-built is why

10. After the incident at Chernobyl, scientists detected radioactivity in the air <u>in Sweden, even though the accident had taken place more than 700 miles away</u>.

    (A) in Sweden, even though the accident had taken place more than 700 miles away
    (B) in Sweden, even though it was more than 700 miles away where the accident had taken place
    (C) in Sweden, even though where the accident had taken place was more than 700 miles away
    (D) in Sweden, more than 700 miles from there where the accident had taken place
    (E) in Sweden, the accident had taken place more than 700 miles away, however

11. Beethoven's Ninth Symphony is one of the most popular classical recordings available, <u>since this is the case, the CD is frequently backordered</u>.

    (A) since this is the case, the CD is frequently backordered
    (B) the CD is frequently backordered as a result of that
    (C) the CD is often unavailable because of that
    (D) the CD is frequently backordered for this reason
    (E) which means that the CD is frequently backordered

GO ON TO THE NEXT PAGE

Directions: The following sentences test your ability to recognize grammar and usage errors. Each sentence contains either a single error or no error at all. No sentence contains more than one error. The error, if there is one, is underlined and lettered. If the sentence contains an error, select the one underlined part that must be changed to make the sentence correct. If the sentence is correct, select choice (E). In choosing answers, follow the requirements of standard written English.

EXAMPLE:

<u>Whenever</u> one is driving late at night, <u>you</u> must take extra precautions <u>against</u>
  A   B   C

falling asleep <u>at the wheel</u>. <u>No error</u>
                 D   E

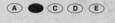

12. After graduation, Jeannette moved to San

    Francisco <u>where</u>, <u>like</u> her older sister, she <u>has began</u>
             A   B   C

    studying <u>for her graduate degree</u>. <u>No error</u>
            D   E

13. Drama has always been one of the <u>most popular</u>
                                     A

    courses at our school, <u>but</u> since Mr. Ferrier <u>began</u>
                       B   C

    teaching it, the classes are <u>more fuller</u> than ever.
                                D

    <u>No error</u>
      E

14. <u>Throughout</u> the parade, <u>there was</u> police
       A   B

    helicopters above the planned route, <u>both</u> to
                                 C

    protect against an attack from the air and

    <u>to monitor</u> activities on the ground. <u>No error</u>
       D   E

15. <u>According to</u> Italian coffee enthusiasts, espresso
       A

    machines <u>who</u> force water through ground coffee
             B

    <u>at less than</u> seven atmospheres of pressure <u>are</u>
       C   D

    unacceptable. <u>No error</u>
             E

16. <u>Although</u> we picture Earth with the Arctic
      A

    <u>on the top</u> and the Antarctic on the bottom, <u>our</u>
       B   C

    designations of north and south <u>are</u> really
                              D

    arbitrary. <u>No error</u>
          E

17. We don't expect as many <u>writers from</u> Great Britain
                             A

    and France <u>to attend</u> the conference <u>as have done</u>
              B   C

    so <u>in the past</u>. <u>No error</u>
        D   E

18. <u>Despite</u> aggressive recruiting, there <u>was</u>
      A   B

    <u>no more than</u> twelve women planning to apply
       C

    <u>to</u> the academy. <u>No error</u>
      D   E

19. The College Board <u>has added</u> a new section
                A

    <u>to the SAT</u>; <u>these</u> will help universities
       B   C

    <u>more accurately</u> assess a student's verbal
       D

    aptitude. <u>No error</u>
          E

GO ON TO THE NEXT PAGE ▷

20. Those paying by check <u>are having to wait</u> seven
                            A
    days to receive their tickets, <u>whereas</u> those paying
                                B
    <u>in cash</u> can pick theirs up <u>immediately</u>. <u>No error</u>
    C   D   E

21. Some of the world's greatest peacemakers,

    including Mahatma Gandhi <u>himself</u>, <u>has been</u>
                          A   B
    ineligible for the Nobel Peace Prize <u>because</u> the
                                    C
    award <u>is</u> not given posthumously. <u>No error</u>
         D   E

22. The fermentation of wine is a complicated

    chemical process that <u>requires</u> the vintner to add
                      A
    the correct amount of sugar and yeast <u>to keep</u> the
                                    B
    mixture at a constant temperature and

    <u>that he allows</u> the wine to age <u>properly</u>. <u>No error</u>
        C   D   E

23. Examination of survey results and financial records

    <u>reveal</u> that companies with <u>more stringent</u> safety
    A   B
    rules <u>in their factories</u> <u>pay</u> lower premiums for
             C   D
    workers' compensation insurance. <u>No error</u>
                                  E

24. Bill is the <u>captain on</u> the football team, <u>but</u> the
              A   B
    soccer coach <u>allows</u> his players to take turns
                 C
    <u>acting as</u> captain. <u>No error</u>
       D   E

25. <u>For the last</u> decade, American restaurants <u>were</u>
        A   B
    serving larger portions, a trend <u>which</u> nutritionists
                                C
    believe has contributed <u>to</u> an increase in obesity.
                          D
    <u>No error</u>
    E

26. <u>Despite</u> the <u>lack of</u> eye witness testimony, the
    A   B
    prosecutor <u>found</u> the circumstantial evidence
               C
    compelling enough to <u>charge Asher about</u> the
                              D
    robbery. <u>No error</u>
             E

27. When asked <u>which</u> baseball team was my favorite, I
             A
    <u>chose</u> the Yankees because <u>they</u> have the
    B   C
    <u>more impressive</u> history. <u>No error</u>
        D   E

28. Despite the harried pace of the office, my

    secretarial staff <u>and me</u> were able <u>to maintain</u> a
                    A   B
    calm demeanor <u>thanks to</u> <u>our</u> diligence and
                  C   D
    cooperation. <u>No error</u>
             E

29. <u>As</u> media liaison for the hospital, Wendy
    A
    demonstrated <u>a dedication</u> that was impressive <u>to</u>
                   B   C
    the chairman of the Board of Directors, who

    <u>had hired</u> her. <u>No error</u>
        D   E

GO ON TO THE NEXT PAGE ⇨

Directions: The following passage is an early draft of an essay. Some parts of the passage need to be rewritten.

Read the passage and select the best answer for each question that follows. Some questions are about particular sentences or parts of sentences and ask you to improve sentence structure or word choice. Other questions ask you to consider organization and development. In choosing answers, follow the conventions of standard written English.

Questions 30–35 are based on the following passage.

(1) Vaccination has become one of the most important and most widely used tools of modern medicine. (2) However, very few people know the history of vaccines and how they were developed. (3) Amazingly, the idea of vaccination goes back almost 300 years—a time when doctors still scoffed at the practice of washing their hands between patients—and found its inspiration in both traditional medicine and folklore. (4) The first vaccine was important in its own right, but it also provided the foundation for the many vaccines that have been developed since.

(5) In the early 18th century, Lady Mary Wortley Montagu traveled to Turkey with her family. (6) There, she observed a traditional practice called "variolation," a process by which uninfected patients were exposed to smallpox to infect them with a mild form of the disease. (7) Variolation, however, still posed a risk of a potentially fatal, full-scale smallpox infection. (8) Later in the 18th century, Edward Jenner began to examine a local legend. (9) It held that milkmaids who were exposed to cowpox became immune to the more dangerous smallpox. (10) The cowpox vaccine, by using a relatively safe, related virus, became the standard method of inoculating against smallpox.

(11) The cowpox vaccine developing from Jenner's work set the standard for vaccines—to find a "safe" virus that confers immunity without the risks of full-blown infection. (12) Later, the French scientist Louis Pasteur discovered that ineffective, outdated disease cultures could still confer immunity and could do so without causing infection. (13) He used this technique to develop a vaccine for rabies in 1885. (14) The technique of using "dead" viruses soon became an important method for developing new vaccines. (15) Vaccines using dead viruses include diphtheria, flu, and the oral polio vaccine.

30. Which of the following is the best version of the underlined portion of sentence 3 (reproduced below)?

Amazingly, <u>the idea of vaccination goes back almost 300 years</u>—a time when doctors still scoffed at the practice of washing their hands between patients—and found its inspiration in both traditional medicine and folklore.

(A) (As it is now)
(B) the idea of vaccination went back almost 300 years
(C) the idea of vaccination back almost 300 years
(D) for almost 300 years, the idea of vaccination had gone back
(E) the idea of vaccination going back almost 300 years

31. Which is the best version of the underlined portion of sentences 8 and 9 (reproduced below)?

Later in the 18th century, Edward Jenner began to examine <u>a local legend. It held that milkmaids</u> who were exposed to cowpox became immune to the more dangerous smallpox.

(A) a local legend, milkmaids
(B) a local legend and that milkmaids
(C) a local legend that although milkmaids
(D) a local legend that held that milkmaids
(E) a local legend that would hold that milkmaids

GO ON TO THE NEXT PAGE

32. What word should be inserted at the beginning of sentence 10 (reproduced below) to best connect it to the rest of the paragraph?

    The cowpox vaccine, by using a relatively safe, related virus, became the standard method of inoculating against smallpox.

    (A) However,
    (B) Furthermore,
    (C) Thus,
    (D) For example,
    (E) Because

33. Of the following, which is the best way to deal with sentence 11 (reproduced below)?

    The cowpox vaccine developing from Jenner's work set the standard for vaccines—to find a "safe" virus that confers immunity without the risks of full-blown infection.

    (A) Insert "In conclusion" at the beginning.
    (B) Change "confers" to "conferring."
    (C) Change "Jenner's" to "Edward Jenner's."
    (D) Change "developing" to "developed".
    (E) Insert "for example" at the end.

34. Which of the following is the best version of the underlined portion of sentences 14 and 15 (reproduced below)?

    The technique of using "dead" viruses soon became an important method for developing new vaccines. Vaccines using dead viruses include diphtheria, flu, and the oral polio vaccine.

    (A) The technique of using "dead" viruses soon became an important method for developing new vaccines and vaccines using dead viruses include

    (B) However, the technique of using "dead" viruses soon became an important method for developing new vaccines using dead viruses, including

    (C) Thus, an important method for developing new vaccines became the technique of using "dead" viruses, including

    (D) By using "dead" viruses, the technique that became important for developing new vaccines including

    (E) The technique of using "dead" viruses soon became an important method for developing new vaccines, including

35. Which sentence is best to add after sentence 15 to conclude the passage?

    (A) There is still much we have to learn about how vaccines became part of the modern medical system.

    (B) No doubt new vaccines will be developed in the future, using similar techniques.

    (C) We now know the institute named after Louis Pasteur has hosted eight Nobel Prize winners.

    (D) With the eradication of smallpox in 1980, the role of vaccines in preventing disease is likely to diminish.

    (E) Vaccine history is very interesting.

IF YOU FINISH BEFORE TIME IS CALLED, YOU MAY CHECK YOUR WORK ON THIS SECTION ONLY. DO NOT TURN TO ANY OTHER SECTION IN THE TEST.

SECTION 5

Time—25 Minutes
24 Questions

Directions: For each of the following questions, choose the best answer and darken the corresponding oval on the answer sheet.

Each sentence below has one or two blanks, each blank indicating that something has been omitted. Beneath the sentence are five words or sets of words labeled (A) through (E). Choose the word or set of words that, when inserted in the sentence, <u>best</u> fits the meaning of the sentence as a whole.

EXAMPLE:

Today's small, portable computers contrast markedly with the earliest electronic computers, which were ----.

(A) effective
(B) invented
(C) useful
(D) destructive
(E) enormous

---

1. The chief reminded his officers that every piece of evidence had to be carefully ---- to ensure nothing was lost and everything was readily ---- those who needed it.

   (A) praised .. scrutinized by
   (B) displayed .. comprehensible to
   (C) labeled .. accessible to
   (D) administered .. overlooked by
   (E) catalogued .. unobtainable to

2. In 1991, salsa outperformed ketchup by tens of millions of dollars in retail stores, ---- ketchup as the best-selling condiment in the United States.

   (A) supplanting
   (B) redoubling
   (C) augmenting
   (D) brandishing
   (E) evading

3. Because his senior status made him the most influential doctor in the hospital, his ---- seemed to make the entire facility more ---- in their patient care.

   (A) sagacity .. unscrupulous
   (B) leniency .. decorous
   (C) nonchalance .. tenacious
   (D) acrimony .. cheerful
   (E) ardor .. assiduous

4. Although Tom often looked ----, he actually dedicated ---- amount of time attempting to maintain a neat appearance.

   (A) orderly .. an enormous
   (B) disheveled .. an inordinate
   (C) annoyed .. an unfortunate
   (D) distracted .. an unrealistic
   (E) agitated .. a considerable

5. The Galapagos Islands sustain a ---- of life forms, an abundance that makes the area abound with life and activity.

   (A) melee
   (B) profusion
   (C) configuration
   (D) symmetry
   (E) dimension

GO ON TO THE NEXT PAGE

6. As a biologist, Henry is a talented ----; he enjoys going beyond specific facts and speculating about general principles.

(A) dogmatist
(B) consultant
(C) prodigy
(D) materialist
(E) theorist

7. Ephemeral wetlands are characterized by their tendency to completely dry out most summers, only to become ---- again the following fall, winter, or spring.

(A) inundated
(B) situated
(C) rejuvenated
(D) supplanted
(E) excavated

8. The committee rejected his thesis because it was based mainly on ---- rather than solid evidence and lacked ---- tested results.

(A) induction .. diminutively
(B) experimentation .. pragmatically
(C) intuition .. fiscally
(D) bombast .. theoretically
(E) conjecture .. empirically

GO ON TO THE NEXT PAGE

Directions: The passages below are followed by questions based on their content; questions following a pair of related passages may also be based on the relationship between the paired passages. Answer the questions on the basis of what is <u>stated</u> or <u>implied</u> in the passages and in any introductory material that may be provided.

Questions 9–10 are based on the following passage.

Having been born on Christmas Day—a coincidence that once inevitably left me feeling shortchanged on presents and the requisite center-of-attention distinction that usually accompanies
(5) a child's birthday—I now consider it a means to evade a birthday's inane pageantry. What degree of sincerity can a cake littered with candles really have if it is absolutely required that it be made, decorated, and given? And what if one's birthday
(10) is forgotten? Embarrassment and sadness usually ensue from such a mistake, hardly the ingredients for a day that is supposed to be enjoyed. So it is Christmas that provides my cover and supplies a powerful excuse for any lapses.

9. In line 2, "coincidence" most nearly refers to a

(A) concurrence of events

(B) shocking unlikelihood

(C) stroke of good luck

(D) twist of fate

(E) quirky happenstance

10. In line 13, "cover" is best understood as meaning

(A) armor

(B) diversion

(C) concealment

(D) canopy

(E) disguise

Questions 11–12 are based on the following passage.

The rarely-sighted three-toed sloth, long mistaken for a species of monkey, is one of the most unusual animals on earth. In fact, many characteristics of this tree-dwelling mammal seem to run
(5) counter to the instincts displayed by almost all wild animals. First, sloths are incredibly slow, tending to move no faster than six feet per minute, even when confronted by a predator. As a result, most sloths spend years in a single tree,
(10) making their way from branch to branch almost imperceptibly. Second, sloths spend almost their entire lives hanging upside down, even when eating, sleeping, mating, and—perhaps most remarkably—giving birth.

11. In lines 10–11, the author's description of sloths moving "almost imperceptibly" suggests that these animals

(A) move in ways that can be difficult to detect

(B) intentionally hide their movements

(C) rely upon stealth for survival

(D) are physically unable to move with any speed

(E) are essentially impossible to observe

12. According to the passage, the three-toed sloth's lack of speed and tendency to hang upside down are

(A) entirely unique evolutionary traits

(B) characteristics shared by some monkeys

(C) apparently contrary to the usual behavior of most wild animals

(D) detrimental to their eating, sleeping, and mating habits

(E) the most important causes of the sloth's vulnerability to predators

GO ON TO THE NEXT PAGE

Questions 13–24 are based on the following passages.

Both of the passages below are taken from articles on social science. Passage 1 is excerpted from an essay on language and intelligence. Passage 2 is taken from a news publication introducing readers to some of the ideas of social psychology.

Passage 1

At some point in your life, you have likely heard a character on TV or in a book say something along the lines of, "The thing that separates humans from the animals is…." You may have
(5) even heard such a sentiment completed in more than one way—some say it is our large brains, others our opposable thumbs, and still others claim it is our ability to use tools. While all of these attributes sound reasonable enough, none of
(10) them is truly unique to the human species—there are plenty of large mammals that have bigger brains than human beings, and we share our opposable thumbs and tool-using capabilities with several of our fellow primates. No, I would argue
(15) instead that the true thing that makes humans qualitatively different from other animals is our ability to use language.

Though there are people who claim that various phenomena from dolphin sounds to bird songs
(20) are "language," these arguments are typically confusions in terminology at best. There is no doubt that these noises serve to communicate ideas from animal to animal, but to most linguists the idea of language involves a means of communicating that
(25) is more complex, rule-based, and extensible—able to capture complicated ideas even with a relatively limited vocabulary.

Now, it seems reasonable to suppose that if human beings are several times more intelligent
(30) than these other creatures, our communications would be correspondingly more complex. However, I believe that the converse is actually the case—that the appearance of great intelligence in human beings is partly a product of our natural
(35) affinity for language. Language acquisition is not merely a function of our general reasoning capabilities; it is accomplished by particular and

unique regions of our brains during the first seven or so years of childhood. Anyone studying a
(40) second language knows how difficult it really is to achieve fluency in a foreign tongue using only our general cognitive abilities, after this "language acquisition device" has shut itself off.

As much as we'd like to believe it, language is
(45) not mankind's ingenious invention; it is our genetic birthright, and its acquisition is as instinctive and unconscious as salmon swimming upriver to spawn or geese flying south for the winter. Knowing this leads me to wonder: If other pri-
(50) mates or dolphins could speak as we do, enabling them to share ideas and pass on their accumulated knowledge rather than learning it anew with each successive generation, would they really be so different from us?

Passage 2

(55) Some of our nation's founding fathers would be appalled at the ease with which contemporary Americans accept the idea of political parties. Calling them "factions," these framers of the Constitution sincerely believed that parties were a
(60) threat to the creation of a true democracy. Although the bipartisan system has not yet brought our republic crashing down around our ears, we might indeed have cause to wonder how the party system arose in the first place. After all,
(65) there seems to be no essential connection between, say, two issues like taxation and capital punishment; nevertheless, most of the nation's voters huddle under one of the two all-encompassing ideological umbrellas held out by our two
(70) dominant political parties. Indeed, the endurance and tenacity of the two-party system might initially seem puzzling to the budding student of political science, but to those who have background in anthropology or social psychology it should come
(75) as no surprise.

After all, the human being is at heart a social animal; like dogs and gorillas, we are pack creatures, devoted by nature to mutual cooperation in order to increase the chances of survival for our
(80) entire group. Nowadays, we congregate in societies

GO ON TO THE NEXT PAGE ⟶

of millions and more, but in the beginning our
main social grouping was in tribes or clans of no
more than a few hundred individuals. Each tribe
had to compete for food, land, and other
(85) resources, making skirmishes between neighboring groups inevitable and frequent. The presence
of an outsider generally meant trouble, and thus
adherence to a common language and belief system both ensured the acceptance of the individual
(90) within his tribe and preserved the group's integrity,
helping it to remain united against external forces.
Conformity thus became an adaptation for survival; no individual wished to be cut off from the
group and left all alone to deal with the many dan-
(95) gers of the outside world.

In the modern day, of course, we live in much
larger societies that make many of the cultural values of our tribal ancestors obsolete. Nevertheless,
the desire for group acceptance still runs deep in
(100) our veins, and its results can be seen all the way
from nations and political parties to street gangs
and sports teams. Though our behavior is far
more complex than that of dogs and gorillas, the
principle is the same; we flock to those who share
(105) our tastes, interests, and beliefs because deep
down, we believe that they will protect us against
competing groups who may insult or even attack
us. Still, we humans have one advantage that other
social animals lack: the ability to reason and make
(110) discerning choices about the groups we join,
enabling us to form alliances that work for the
common good rather than simply struggling for
our own survival.

13. One technique employed by the author of Passage
    1 but not the author of Passage 2 is that of

    (A) addressing the reader directly
    (B) providing historical background
    (C) relating examples from the natural world
    (D) applying his argument to social issues
    (E) viciously attacking his opponents

14. In Passage 1, the phrase "While all of these
    attributes sound reasonable enough" (lines 8–9)
    implies that the author believes that

    (A) they are the defining characteristics of the
        human species
    (B) these adaptations are useful but not unique
    (C) such qualities are useless luxuries with no
        survival value
    (D) no single trait distinguishes human beings
        from animals
    (E) human beings would be helpless without
        them

15. In line 22, the word "serve" most nearly means

    (A) obey
    (B) help
    (C) deliver
    (D) provide
    (E) accumulate

16. The quotation marks in lines 42–43 most nearly
    serve to

    (A) express a tone of sarcasm
    (B) make reference to a distinguished source
    (C) draw extra attention to a crucial phrase
    (D) indicate the author's disagreement with the
        phrase
    (E) set apart an unusual bit of terminology

17. In Passage 1, the author's use of the word
    "birthright" (line 46) suggests that language is

    (A) inherited rather than earned
    (B) common rather than unique
    (C) deserved rather than desired
    (D) artificial rather than natural
    (E) cultural rather than universal

GO ON TO THE NEXT PAGE

18. The references to "linguists" (line 23, Passage 1) and "those who have background in anthropology" (lines 73–74, Passage 2) both provide examples of

    (A) uppity know-it-alls whose theories have little practical value

    (B) researchers whose theories are inspired but incorrect

    (C) fields of which the authors are members

    (D) academic authorities that bolster the authors' arguments

    (E) professionals who study human culture

19. In line 58, Passage 2's author uses quotation marks in order to

    (A) define a commonly misunderstood word

    (B) denote his distaste for the idea being expressed

    (C) poke fun at the folly of early Americans

    (D) refer to a particular document

    (E) introduce diction from a historical context

20. According to Passage 2, the "founding fathers" mentioned in line 55 would most likely be "appalled" at which of the following?

    (A) a candidate who refuses to take a stance on a particular issue

    (B) a citizen who always votes for the same political party regardless of its platform

    (C) a rebel who disagrees with one of the major values of his culture

    (D) a foreigner who attempts to spread his ideas in the United States

    (E) a political theorist who purports to have a solution to every problem the nation faces

21. The authors of both passages would likely support the idea that language is

    (A) the primary distinguishing factor of humanity

    (B) a tool for preserving cultural identity

    (C) common to many species across the globe

    (D) a useful adaptation for survival

    (E) an important topic for serious academic study

22. The author of Passage 1 would likely feel that in lines 108–110 ("Still...choices"), the author of Passage 2 is

    (A) making an unfair claim that humans can do things that other mammals cannot

    (B) successfully capturing the primary factor that separates people from the lower beasts

    (C) overestimating humans' intelligence and underestimating the power of communication

    (D) attributing moral value to something that is really just an adaptation for individual survival

    (E) forgetting to take useful teachings from the field of social psychology into account

GO ON TO THE NEXT PAGE

23. In Passage 2, the author's statement in lines 102–108 ("Though…attack us") mainly serves to

    (A) assert that a comparison between human beings and other mammals is a preposterous notion

    (B) suggest that dogs and gorillas would behave at least as intelligently as humans if they had language ability

    (C) imply that humans have stronger intellects than these animals but a weaker social structure

    (D) propose that we could learn much by applying rules from dog and gorilla societies to our own

    (E) acknowledge that he is only making an analogy, not stating an exact equivalence

24. How do the authors of the two passages differ in their basic beliefs about human reason and intelligence?

    (A) The author of Passage 1 believes human intelligence is overestimated due to our unique communication abilities, whereas the author of Passage 2 believes human intelligence is unique among all social animals.

    (B) The author of Passage 1 asserts that a human being's intelligence is largely verbal in nature, whereas the author of Passage 2 believes that it is comprised of many more components.

    (C) The author of Passage 1 assumes that intelligence is genetic and inborn, whereas the author of Passage 2 believes that it is significantly shaped by the society into which one is born.

    (D) The author of Passage 1 believes that humans have language ability because of their superior intelligence, whereas the author of Passage 2 argues that language and reason both developed due to social factors.

    (E) The author of Passage 1 believes that human reason is at the root of all of our moral failings, whereas the author of Passage 2 believes that it is our greater intelligence that has allowed human society to survive.

IF YOU FINISH BEFORE TIME IS CALLED, YOU MAY CHECK YOUR WORK ON THIS SECTION ONLY. DO NOT TURN TO ANY OTHER SECTION IN THE TEST.

STOP

SECTION 6

Time—25 Minutes

18 Questions

Directions: For this section, solve each problem and decide which is the best of the choices given. Fill in the corresponding oval on the answer sheet. You may use any available space for scratchwork.

Notes:

(1) Calculator use is permitted.

(2) All numbers used are real numbers.

(3) Figures are provided for some problems. All figures are drawn to scale and lie in a plane UNLESS otherwise indicated.

(4) Unless otherwise specified, the domain of any function f is assumed to be the set of all real numbers x for which $f(x)$ is a real number.

Information

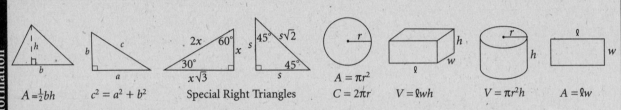

$A = \frac{1}{2}bh$ $c^2 = a^2 + b^2$ Special Right Triangles $A = \pi r^2$ $C = 2\pi r$ $V = \ell wh$ $V = \pi r^2 h$ $A = \ell w$

The sum of the degree measures of the angles in a triangle is 180.
The number of degrees of arc in a circle is 360.
A straight angle has a degree measure of 180.

1. If $f(x) = x^{-3} + x^3$, at which of the following values of x is $f(x)$ undefined?

(A) −3

(B) 0

(C) 1

(D) 2

(E) 3

2. Set A contains the letters A, E, I, O, and U. Set B contains the letters A, B, C, D, and E. What is the difference between the number of elements in the union of the two sets and the number of elements in their intersection?

(A) 4

(B) 6

(C) 7

(D) 8

(E) 10

Fruit 1 is an apple.   Fruit 5 is the same as fruit 2.
Fruit 2 is an orange.   Fruit 6 is a banana.
Fruit 3 is not an apple.   Fruit 7 is not a banana.
Fruit 4 is the same as fruit 1.

3. If a bag contains 20 pieces of fruit of three types (apples, oranges, bananas) and 7 pieces of fruit are chosen according to the rules above, which of the following must be true?

(A) One apple is drawn.

(B) One orange is drawn.

(C) Two apples are drawn.

(D) At least two bananas are drawn.

(E) At least two apples are drawn.

GO ON TO THE NEXT PAGE

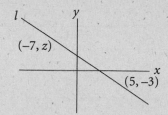

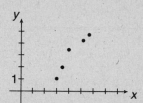

4. In the figure above, the slope of line l is $-\dfrac{5}{12}$.

   What is the value of z?

   (A) $\dfrac{1}{4}$

   (B) $\dfrac{1}{2}$

   (C) 1

   (D) 2

   (E) 4

5. The number of turtles in Mosquito Pond has doubled every three years since the pond was discovered. The number of turtles in the pond can be described as $n = (x)2^{\frac{t}{3}}$, where t is the number of years since the pond was discovered, n is the number of turtles in the pond at time t, and x is the number of turtles in the pond when it was discovered. If there were 160 turtles in Mosquito Pond nine years after it was discovered, then how many turtles lived in the pond the year it was discovered?

   (A) 2
   (B) 10
   (C) 20
   (D) 40
   (E) 160

6. If $c(x) = x^2 - 6$, how many times does the graph of $c(x)$ cross the x-axis?

   (A) 0
   (B) 1
   (C) 2
   (D) 3
   (E) 4

7. Which of the lines described by the following equations best fits these points?

   (A) $y = .3x - 3$
   (B) $y = .7x + 2$
   (C) $y = 1.3x - 3$
   (D) $y = 1.4x + 4$
   (E) $y = 4x - 3$

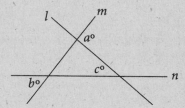

8. In the figure above, $c = 50$. What is the value of $a - b$?

   (A) 50
   (B) 65
   (C) 100
   (D) 130
   (E) 145

GO ON TO THE NEXT PAGE

Directions: For Student-Produced Response questions 9–18, use the grids at the bottom of the answer sheet page on which you have answered questions 1–8.

Each of the remaining 10 questions requires you to solve the problem and enter your answer by marking the ovals in the special grid, as shown in the example below. You may use any available space for scratch work.

Answer: 1.25 or $\frac{5}{4}$ or 5/4

Write answer in boxes.

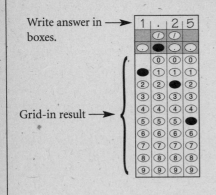

Grid-in result

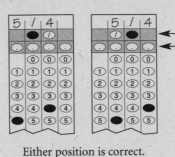

Fraction line
Decimal point

Either position is correct.

You may start your answers in any column, space permitting. Columns not needed should be left blank.

- It is recommended, though not required, that you write your answer in the boxes at the top of the columns. However, you will receive credit only for darkening the ovals correctly.

- Grid only one answer to a question, even though some problems have more than one correct answer.

- Darken no more than one oval in a column.

- No answers are negative.

- Mixed numbers cannot be gridded. For example: the number $1\frac{1}{4}$ must be gridded as 1.25 or 5/4.

(If | 1 | 1 | / | 4 | is gridded, it will be interpreted as $\frac{11}{4}$ not $1\frac{1}{4}$.)

- <u>Decimal Accuracy:</u> Decimal answers must be entered as accurately as possible. For example, if you obtain an answer such as 0.1666…, you should record the result as .166 or .167. **Less accurate values such as .16 or .17 are not acceptable.**

Acceptable ways to grid $\frac{1}{6}$ = .1666. . .

9. If $\frac{q}{2} = \frac{7}{10}$, what is the value of q?

SILLY YO–YO COMPANY'S APRIL SALES

	Small	Large	Total
Red		500	
Blue	1,000		
Total		3,200	5,000

10. Silly Yo-Yo Company sells only red and blue yo-yos, both of which are available in small and large sizes. On the basis of the information in the above table, how many red yo-yos were sold in April?

11. If m and n are two distinct prime numbers greater than 2, and $p = mn$, how many positive factors, including 1 and p, does p have?

12. The length and width of a rectangle are integers. If the area of the rectangle is 85, what is one possible value for the perimeter of the rectangle?

13. The population of Clarktown was 120 when the town was founded in 1900. Since then it has doubled every six years. The population of the town can be described by the equation $n = (120)2^{\frac{t}{6}}$, where n is the population and t is the number of years that have passed since 1900. In what year will the population of Clarktown be 7,680?

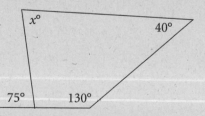

14. In the figure shown above, composed of four straight line segments, what is the value of x?

15. If $\frac{1}{10}(30x^3 + 20x^2 + 10x + 1) = ax^3 + bx^2 + cx + d$, for all values of x, where a, b, c, and d are all constants, what is the value of $a + b + c + d$?

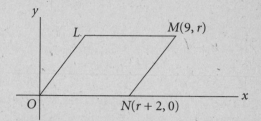

16. In the figure above, the area of parallelogram $LMNO$ is 24. What is the value of r?

17. For all positive integers c and d, let $c \, \mathfrak{R} \, d$ be defined as the remainder when c is divided by d. If $23 \, \mathfrak{R} \, w = 4$, what is the value of w?

18. The total cost of a car rental is the sum of

   (1) a basic fixed rental charge for the car and

   (2) an additional charge for every 25 miles traveled

   If the total cost to rent a car and drive it 50 miles is $200 and the total cost to rent a car and drive it 200 miles is $245, what is the total cost, in dollars to rent a car and travel 450 miles?

   (Disregard the $ sign when gridding your answer. If, for example, your answer is $1.37, grid 1.37)

IF YOU FINISH BEFORE TIME IS CALLED, YOU MAY CHECK YOUR WORK ON THIS SECTION ONLY. DO NOT TURN TO ANY OTHER SECTION IN THE TEST. | STOP

SECTION 7

Time—20 Minutes
19 Questions

Directions: For each of the following questions, choose the best answer and darken the corresponding oval on the answer sheet.

Each sentence below has one or two blanks, each blank indicating that something has been omitted. Beneath the sentence are five words or sets of words labeled (A) through (E). Choose the word or set of words that, when inserted in the sentence, best fits the meaning of the sentence as a whole.

EXAMPLE:

Today's small, portable computers contrast markedly with the earliest electronic computers, which were ----.

(A) effective
(B) invented
(C) useful
(D) destructive
(E) enormous

---

1. Before he could even hope to sell his faded, dirty furniture he had to have it ----.

   (A) requisitioned
   (B) enlarged
   (C) refurbished
   (D) demolished
   (E) relocated

2. His teacher deemed his absence from class ----; she had observed him playing vigorously with his friends throughout the day, without the slightest indication of illness.

   (A) indefensible
   (B) surreptitious
   (C) indefatigable
   (D) comprehensive
   (E) corrective

3. When the mysterious manuscript was originally discovered it was merely ----, but after years of fruitless research and more bewilderment it has become ----.

   (A) dignified . . mystifying
   (B) perplexing . . inexplicable
   (C) eccentric . . stolid
   (D) intriguing . . reasonable
   (E) logical . . questionable

4. Although he had vigorously ---- a career in journalism, Ricardo could not ---- the feeling that he lacked the initiative necessary to enter the newspaper business.

   (A) obtained . . succumb to
   (B) escaped . . subvert
   (C) pursued . . avoid
   (D) ignored . . observe
   (E) disavowed . . enjoy

GO ON TO THE NEXT PAGE

5. Tom nicknamed his dog ---- because she was known for chasing any dogs in the neighborhood that came near her, even puppies.

   (A) Bungler
   (B) Ruffian
   (C) Stickler
   (D) Daredevil
   (E) Naysayer

6. Xhosa funeral ceremonies may seem excessively ---- but the long, wailing ---- sung by friends and family members of the deceased provide a means of catharsis for the mourners.

   (A) tedious . . jingles
   (B) inchoate . . lullabies
   (C) lugubrious . . dirges
   (D) facetious . . ballads
   (E) sprightly . . eulogies

GO ON TO THE NEXT PAGE

Questions 7–19 are based on the following passage.

The following passage is an excerpt from a novel about a talk show host who is learning to deal with life after his program is cancelled.

The way late night talk show host Randolph Meyer learned of his long-running television program's demise was not at all how he pictured it would be. The foreboding phone call he imagined,
(5) from his producer or a network head, was instead replaced by a small, unforgiving headline in the morning's paper: *'Talk Night' Gets the Axe*.

He should have sensed something was wrong by the line of commiserative eyes that quietly fell
(10) upon him as he entered the diner, and the unusually gracious treatment by the normally curt waitress. Instead, he made the egotistical error of mistaking compassion for adulation. The unsettling gawks of strangers, which on previous mornings
(15) had imparted to him a confirmation of his success, were now prying daggers. Randolph's heart began to pound in his chest—not a good thing for a man his age. He paid for his breakfast and attempted to walk nonchalantly out of the estab-
(20) lishment, suppressing the urge to run to the tinted refuge of his car.

The canceling of the talk show came as a complete surprise to everyone but Randolph. Despite the show's decent ratings, he had a sense that the
(25) network had purposely neglected *Talk Night* since the hiring of its new president Abel Carver a year earlier. Armed with the latest buzzwords and a new "groundbreaking vision" for the sinking network, Carver introduced a strong course of action
(30) that Randolph quickly distilled into three words: *Style Over Substance*. To Randolph, that was a good description of Carver, as well.

"You gotta think outside the box," Carver would often tell Randolph, "It's the only way you can
(35) survive in this industry."

Randolph was a familiar fixture on late night television for three generations of Americans. He had managed to not only survive but to thrive in the industry for five decades prior to Abel Carver's
(40) tenure. Certainly "our old man" (Carver's pet name for Randolph) knew a thing or two about entertainment, and he was not about to change horses midstream. He thought about the legions of adoring (though he had to admit, graying) fans
(45) and the numerous Emmys, achievement awards, and other various accolades that filled an entire wall of his office. He then recalled his interviews and correspondences with some of the world's most powerful and intriguing figures, and dis-
(50) missed Carver with a lordly grunt.

True, Randolph's older and intellectual audience didn't fit Carver's target demographic, but CNS wasn't some cable theme channel; it was a genuine, one-of-a-kind network television institution,
(55) one of the first ever to broadcast over the country's airwaves. Networks like "Chrome" catered to the lowest common denominator, CNS did not. It all seemed a little backward to Randolph, anyway. By pandering to one specific segment of your
(60) audience, you completely ignore the others. The object was to attract as many viewers as possible; at least that was what Randolph always believed.

At this time of the day, Randolph's mobile phone would normally be ringing off the hook.
(65) Today, it was eerily silent. He stared at its shiny plastic housing and tried to will it to ring, to no avail. Who would be the first person to call? It should have been Carver, and he should have had the professional courtesy to personally break the
(70) news to him last night. Randolph, however, was not surprised by this selfishness and lack of professionalism. He never put much faith in those who demanded the respect of others rather than earning it.

GO ON TO THE NEXT PAGE ⇨

(75)   Given the circumstances, Randolph was surprisingly calm. He could not tell whether the initial
shock of the news had subsided or if he had yet to
grasp the true gravity of the situation. He had lost
his show. No matter how many times he repeated
(80) that sentence to himself it did not seem real.
Doubts were quickly filling Randolph's head.
Perhaps, as suggested by Carver, he should have
considered inviting more actors and pop stars on
the program instead of his usual stable of intellec-
(85) tuals and politicians. Maybe a new bandleader or
sidekick would indeed have breathed some new
life into the program.
     "No," Randolph reassured himself. "I'm glad I
stuck to my guns and didn't cave into Carver. I'd
(90) rather my show be cancelled than witness it turn
into a shadow of its former self." What he didn't
admit to himself, however, was that he couldn't
stomach the idea of Carver possibly being right.
Regardless of what Randolph thought of Abel
(95) Carver, CNS's ratings had measurably improved
since the young man was hired as the network's
president.
     Randolph often dreamed of having the time to
work on a novel, perhaps now he would finally get
(100) the chance. He would love to find another job in
TV, but he knew his hopes were probably slim; he
was fully aware of the paradox of his iconic
stature. He would forever be "Randolph Meyer,
legendary host of *Talk Night.*" Still, Randolph had
(105) been the host of *Talk Night* since he was a young
man, and the array of possibilities that now stood
before him sent a bittersweet shiver of excitement
throughout his entire being. He started his car and
decided to head to the studio to face the music. As
(110) quickly as his bubble of excitement inflated, however, it burst. Just as he pulled into the flow of
traffic, the ring of his cell phone flooded the car.

7. The narrator of the passage is

    (A) Randolph Meyer

    (B) Abel Carver

    (C) a colleague of Randolph and Abel

    (D) an onlooker with intimate knowledge of
         Randolph and his mindset

    (E) an onlooker who is not very familiar with
         Randolph

8. In line 25, the narrator's reference to *Talk Night* as
    being "purposely neglected" suggests Randolph
    believes that

    (A) he did not put enough effort into the show
         for it to remain successful

    (B) Carver wanted to get rid all of the network's
         talk shows

    (C) Carver planned on canceling the show from
         the beginning

    (D) he was the target of discrimination at the
         network

    (E) Carver's personal dislike for Randolph
         influenced his decision

9. In lines 45–47, the narrator catalogs Randolph's
    numerous accolades and achievements in order to

    (A) initially establish his current level of celebrity
         status

    (B) debunk Carver's statement that Randolph is
         too old to be a success

    (C) suggest that Randolph does not need advice
         on how to survive in television

    (D) offer justification for the canceling of *Talk
         Night*

    (E) illustrate the fruits of Carver's advice

GO ON TO THE NEXT PAGE ➤

10. Randolph's "lordly grunt," (line 50) is most likely a gesture of both

    (A) insecurity and dread
    (B) humor and sarcasm
    (C) megalomania and ignorance
    (D) doubt and anger
    (E) self-pride and reassurance

11. Randolph probably considers Carver's use of the term "think outside the box" (line 33) to be

    (A) helpful in brainstorming new ideas for the show
    (B) a needlessly ornate way to say "be creative"
    (C) an illustration of Carver's business background
    (D) a good description for Carver's own way of thinking
    (E) somewhat cryptic

12. According to the passage, Randolph thinks *Talk Night* was cancelled because

    (A) the show had poor ratings
    (B) CNS needed to change its image
    (C) his celebrity was not what it used to be
    (D) Carver's bandleader and sidekick were boring
    (E) he refused to conform it to Carver's "vision"

13. Taken in context, the phrase "some cable theme channel"(line 53) implies a network that

    (A) is revolutionary in its programming and content
    (B) is indistinguishable from many others
    (C) has a varied choice of programming subjects
    (D) has been around for quite some time
    (E) does not include talk shows as part of their programming

14. According to the passage, "Chrome" (line 56) is a channel that

    (A) attracts a high caliber of viewer
    (B) broadcasts shows that appeal to the brain instead of the senses.
    (C) specializes in mathematics and science programs
    (D) has extremely high ratings
    (E) appeals to a lowbrow viewer

15. Based on the passage, it can be presumed that a person "who demand(s) the respect of others rather than earning it" (lines 73–74) would

    (A) take responsibility for the consequences of his actions
    (B) treat everyone in the manner that they would like to be treated
    (C) be sensitive to those in subordinate positions
    (D) disregard the emotions of others to avoid personal discomfort
    (E) take the point of view of another in order to come to a decision

16. "Gravity" (line 78) most closely means

    (A) levity
    (B) attractiveness
    (C) seriousness
    (D) fairness
    (E) frivolousness

GO ON TO THE NEXT PAGE

17. The phrase "paradox of his iconic stature" (lines 102–103) is a reference to Randolph's knowledge that

    (A) he was on the brink of becoming an television icon

    (B) his image will be tarnished by the show's cancellation

    (C) he should have listened to Carver's suggestions

    (D) his great success on *Talk Night* will probably hinder his future endeavors in TV

    (E) he has not been praised for his work on *Talk Night*

18. The passage implies that Randolph's primary flaw is that

    (A) he is stubborn to a fault

    (B) he has the inability to trust anyone

    (C) despite his fame, he is very insecure

    (D) he is more concerned about *Talk Night*'s ratings than its content

    (E) he prefers style over substance

19. To Randolph, the prospect of life without *Talk Night* is

    (A) stupendous

    (B) frightening

    (C) depressing

    (D) incomprehensible

    (E) stimulating

IF YOU FINISH BEFORE TIME IS CALLED, YOU MAY CHECK YOUR WORK ON THIS SECTION ONLY. DO NOT TURN TO ANY OTHER SECTION IN THE TEST.

STOP

SECTION 8
Time—20 Minutes
16 Questions

Directions: For this section, solve each problem and decide which is the best of the choices given. Fill in the corresponding oval on the answer sheet. You may use any available space for scratchwork.

Notes:

(1) Calculator use is permitted.

(2) All numbers used are real numbers.

(3) Figures are provided for some problems. All figures are drawn to scale and lie in a plane UNLESS otherwise indicated.

(4) Unless otherwise specified, the domain of any function f is assumed to be the set of all real numbers x for which $f(x)$ is a real number.

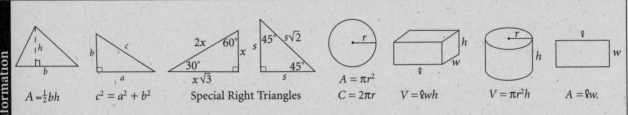

The sum of the degree measures of the angles in a triangle is 180.
The number of degrees of arc in a circle is 360.
A straight angle has a degree measure of 180.

1. If $(.0013)x = 0.013$, then $x =$

   (A) .01
   (B) .1
   (C) 1
   (D) 10
   (E) 100

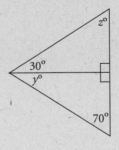

2. In the figure above, what is the value of $z + y$?

   (A) 80
   (B) 90
   (C) 100
   (D) 110
   (E) 120

GO ON TO THE NEXT PAGE

3. If t is 5 more than s, and s is 3 less than r, what is t when $r = 3$?

(A) −5

(B) −2

(C) 1

(D) 5

(E) 8

4. If $b > a > 0$, which of the following is less than $\dfrac{a}{b}$?

(A) 2

(B) $\dfrac{b}{a}$

(C) $\dfrac{1}{\frac{a}{b}}$

(D) $\dfrac{a}{2b}$

(E) $\dfrac{2a}{b}$

5. What is the y-intercept of the linear equation $3y - 33x = 12$?

(A) −4

(B) −2

(C) 0

(D) 3

(E) 4

6. If d is a positive odd integer, then $(d-1)(d-2)$ could equal which of the following?

(A) 12

(B) 13

(C) 14

(D) 15

(E) 16

7. Sam's locker combination consists of 3 two-digit numbers. The combination satisfies the three conditions below.

One number is even.

One number is a multiple of 3.

One number is the day of the month on which school started.

If each number satisfies exactly one of the conditions, which of the following could be the locker combination?

(A) 10–23–15

(B) 24–18–13

(C) 12–20–26

(D) 15–21–26

(E) 34–30–21

8. The percent increase from 6 to 16 is equal to the percent increase from 12 to what number?

(A) 16

(B) 22

(C) 23

(D) 32

(E) 36

GO ON TO THE NEXT PAGE

Questions 9–10 refer to the following graph.

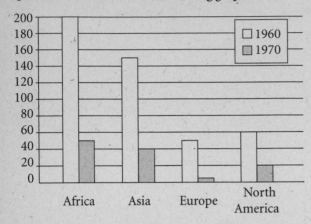

9. How many of the continents shown above had in 1970 less than one fifth of the number of smallpox cases they had in 1960?

(A) 0
(B) 1
(C) 2
(D) 3
(E) 4

10. From 1960 to 1970, the total number of smallpox cases in the four continents shown above decreased by what percentage?

(A) 20
(B) 25
(C) 40
(D) 55
(E) 75

11. If the average (arithmetic mean) of a, b, and c is p, which of the following is the average of a, b, c, and d?

(A) $\dfrac{3p + d}{4}$

(B) $\dfrac{3p + d}{3}$

(C) $\dfrac{p + d}{4}$

(D) $\dfrac{p + d}{2}$

(E) $\dfrac{3(p + d)}{4}$

12. A new airplane can travel at speeds up to 4680 miles per hour. Assuming that the airplane is traveling at top speed, how many miles can it travel in 10 seconds?

(A) 1.3
(B) 7.8
(C) 13
(D) 78
(E) 130

13. The least integer of a sum of consecutive integers is –33. If the sum is 34, how many integers are in the sum?

(A) 33
(B) 34
(C) 66
(D) 67
(E) 68

GO ON TO THE NEXT PAGE

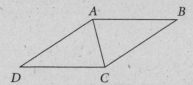

14. In the figure above, two identical isosceles triangles with side length of 13 are joined at their bases, which have a length of 10. What is the area of quadrilateral *ABCD*?

(A) 30

(B) 60

(C) 120

(D) 240

(E) 360

15. For $x \geq 1$, $\spadesuit x \spadesuit$ is defined as $\spadesuit x \spadesuit = \sqrt{(x-1)}$, which of the following is equal to $\spadesuit 37 \spadesuit - \spadesuit 5 \spadesuit$?

(A) 0

(B) $2\sqrt{2}$

(C) 4

(D) $4\sqrt{2}$

(E) $\sqrt{34}$

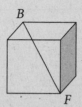

16. A square cube has a side length of 3. What is the length of a diagonal $\overline{BF}$ which cuts through the center of the cube?

(A) 3

(B) $3\sqrt{2}$

(C) $3\sqrt{3}$

(D) 18

(E) 27

IF YOU FINISH BEFORE TIME IS CALLED, YOU MAY CHECK YOUR WORK ON THIS SECTION ONLY. DO NOT TURN TO ANY OTHER SECTION IN THE TEST. STOP

SECTION 9

Time—10 Minutes
14 Questions

Directions: For each question in this section, select the best answer from among the choices given and fill in the corresponding oval on the answer sheet.

The following sentences test correctness and effectiveness of expression. Part of each sentence or the entire sentence is underlined; beneath each sentence are five ways of phrasing the underlined material. Choice (A) repeats the original phrasing; the other four choices are different. If you think the original phrasing produces a better sentence than any of the alternatives, select choice (A); if not, select one of the other choices.

In making your selection, follow the requirements of standard written English; that is, pay attention to grammar, choice of words, sentence construction, and punctuation. Your selection should result in the most effective sentence—clear and precise, without awkwardness or ambiguity.

EXAMPLE: ANSWER:

Every apple in the baskets <u>are ripe and labeled according to the date it was picked</u>.   Ⓐ ● Ⓒ Ⓓ Ⓔ

(A) are ripe and labeled according to the date it was picked
(B) is ripe and labeled according to the date it was picked
(C) are ripe and labeled according to the date they were picked
(D) is ripe and labeled according to the date they were picked
(E) are ripe and labeled as to the date it was picked

---

1. The Internet, on which many types of information can be found, can be <u>useful so that it</u> enables communication without costing a lot of money.

    (A) useful so that it
    (B) useful because it
    (C) useful, although it
    (D) useful in order that it
    (E) useful because they

2. In his speech, Mr. Smith <u>announced that he had</u> reason to expect that next year's revenues would be even stronger than this year's.

    (A) announced that he had
    (B) announced about having
    (C) made an announcement of having
    (D) gave an announcement that he had
    (E) had an announcement there about having

3. As weather conditions improve, the Department of Public Works <u>promising that it will be able to improve road conditions by</u> working overtime.

    (A) promising that it will be able to improve road conditions by
    (B) promising that it, able by improving road conditions and
    (C) promises that it will improve road conditions and
    (D) promises that it will be able to improve road conditions by
    (E) promises that improving road conditions by

GO ON TO THE NEXT PAGE ⟩

4. <u>For the most part, in the patterns of how a newborn sleeps, biology is the largest factor.</u>

(A) For the most part, in the patterns of how a newborn sleeps, biology is the largest factor.

(B) Generally, a newborn's sleep patterns are mostly biological ones.

(C) A newborn's sleep, as to patterns, are by and large biologically determined.

(D) A newborn's sleep patterns are largely biologically determined.

(E) Newborns mainly have their sleep patterns as a factor for biology.

5. Today, more and more women are becoming pediatricians, psychologists, psychiatrists, <u>and other medical specialties.</u>

(A) and other medical specialties

(B) and they work in other medical specialties

(C) and at work in other medical fields

(D) and specialists in other medical fields

(E) and in other medical specialties

6. Martial arts students may choose from among many levels of classes, <u>there is one which is</u> best for their particular skills.

(A) there is one which is

(B) of which there is one

(C) one of which is

(D) and one is

(E) one is

7. In the belief that a macrobiotic diet made him healthier, <u>Herbert will spend hours preparing his meals every day</u>.

(A) Herbert will spend hours preparing his meals every day

(B) Herbert spent hours preparing his meals every day

(C) hours of every day are spent on his meals by Herbert

(D) his meals occupied hours of every day for Herbert

(E) every day will find Herbert spending hours on his meals

8. <u>*Hamlet* and *Romeo and Juliet* are among Shakespeare's most frequently produced plays, as they actually involve very complex staging.</u>

(A) *Hamlet* and *Romeo and Juliet* are among Shakespeare's most frequently produced plays, as they actually involve very complex staging.

(B) Among Shakespeare's most frequently produced plays, very complex staging is actually involved with *Hamlet* and *Romeo and Juliet*.

(C) *Hamlet* and *Romeo and Juliet*, among Shakespeare's most frequently produced plays, actually involve very complex staging.

(D) *Hamlet* and *Romeo and Juliet* actually involve very complex staging, being among Shakespeare's most frequently produced plays.

(E) Actually, *Hamlet* and *Romeo and Juliet* involving very complex staging, they are among Shakespeare's most frequently produced plays.

GO ON TO THE NEXT PAGE

9. When someone picks up the phone, <u>you will be using</u> one of the greatest inventions of the modern age.

   (A) you will be using

   (B) it is using

   (C) you will use

   (D) he or she uses

   (E) it uses

10. Sent to Canada after the flu epidemic of the early 1900s, <u>his painting depicted Jonathan's first experience traveling by boat</u>.

    (A) his painting depicted Jonathan's first experience traveling by boat

    (B) Jonathan's first experience traveling by boat was the subject of his painting

    (C) the subject of his painting was Jonathan's first experience traveling by boat

    (D) Jonathan depicted his first experience traveling by boat in his painting

    (E) Jonathan, who had his first experience of traveling by boat, depicted this in his first painting

11. Jean Valentine's daughter said that <u>she had decided to write another book</u>, although no publication date was given.

    (A) she had decide to write another book

    (B) the decision was that her mother would write another book

    (C) her mother had decided to write another book

    (D) she decided that she will write another book

    (E) it was decided about her writing another book

12. <u>Although the principal has begun to hire new teachers for the high school</u>, she is nevertheless being held accountable for a shortage of staff.

    (A) Although the principal has begun to hire new teachers for the high school

    (B) Although beginning to hire, as principal, new teachers for the high school

    (C) The principal, beginning to hire the new teachers for the high school

    (D) The principal has begun to hire the new teachers for the high school, and

    (E) The principal, beginning to hire the new teachers for the high school, however

13. After I graduated from college, <u>many employment applications were filled out by me</u> before I finally got a job.

    (A) many employment applications were filled out by me

    (B) I filled out many employment applications

    (C) many employment applications being filled out by me

    (D) my having filled out many employment applications

    (E) many of the employment applications I filled out

14. <u>The bite pressure of wolves, harder than German shepherds,</u> is about 1,500 pounds per square inch.

    (A) The bite pressure of wolves, harder than German shepherds,

    (B) The bite pressure of wolves, which is harder than German shepherds,

    (C) Wolves' bite pressure, harder than those of German shepherds,

    (D) The bite pressure of wolves, harder than that of German shepherds,

    (E) Harder than German shepherds, the bite pressure of wolves

IF YOU FINISH BEFORE TIME IS CALLED, YOU MAY CHECK YOUR WORK ON THIS SECTION ONLY. DO NOT TURN TO ANY OTHER SECTION IN THE TEST.

THE ANSWER KEY APPEARS ON THE FOLLOWING PAGE.

Practice Test Six: **Answer Key**

SECTION 1

Essay

SECTION 2

1. E
2. C
3. A
4. A
5. C
6. C
7. D
8. C
9. A
10. D
11. E
12. B
13. C
14. C
15. C
16. B
17. E
18. E
19. B
20. B
21. D
22. A
23. C
24. C

SECTION 3

1. E
2. A
3. E
4. E
5. B
6. B
7. B
8. C
9. B
10. B
11. C
12. C
13. C
14. B
15. C
16. C
17. B
18. C
19. A
20. C

SECTION 4

1. C
2. B
3. E
4. D
5. E
6. E
7. A
8. D
9. B
10. A
11. E
12. C

13. D
14. B
15. B
16. E
17. E
18. B
19. C
20. A
21. B
22. C
23. A
24. A
25. B
26. D
27. D
28. A
29. E
30. A
31. D
32. C
33. D
34. E
35. B

SECTION 5

1. C
2. A
3. E
4. B
5. B
6. E
7. A
8. E
9. A
10. C
11. A

12. C
13. A
14. B
15. B
16. E
17. A
18. D
19. E
20. B
21. D
22. C
23. E
24. A

SECTION 6

1. B
2. B
3. E
4. D
5. C
6. C
7. C
8. A
9. 7/5
10. 1,300
11. 4
12. 44
13. 1936
14. 85
15. 6.1
16. 4
17. 19
18. 320

SECTION 7

1. C
2. A
3. B
4. C
5. B
6. C
7. D
8. C
9. C
10. E
11. B
12. E
13. B
14. E
15. D
16. C
17. D
18. A
19. E

SECTION 8

1. D
2. A
3. D
4. D
5. E
6. A
7. A
8. D
9. B
10. E
11. A
12. C
13. E

14. C
15. C
16. C

SECTION 9

1. B
2. A
3. D
4. D
5. D
6. C
7. B
8. C
9. D
10. D
11. C
12. A
13. B
14. D

PRACTICE TEST SIX

Critical Reading

	Number Right	Number Wrong	Raw Score
Section 2:	☐	− (.25 × ☐)	= ☐
Section 5:	☐	− (.25 × ☐)	= ☐
Section 7:	☐	− (.25 × ☐)	= ☐

Critical Reading Raw Score = ☐
(rounded up)

Writing

	Number Right	Number Wrong	Raw Score
Section 1:	☐ (ESSAY GRADE)	× 3.17	= ☐
Section 4:	☐	− (.25 × ☐)	= ☐
Section 9:	☐	− (.25 × ☐)	= ☐

Writing Raw Score = ☐
(rounded up)

Math

	Number Right	Number Wrong	Raw Score
Section 3:	☐	− (.25 × ☐)	= ☐
Section 6A: (QUESTIONS 1–8)	☐	− (.25 × ☐)	= ☐
Section 6B: (QUESTIONS 9–18)	☐	(no wrong answer penalty)	= ☐
Section 8:	☐	− (.25 × ☐)	= ☐

Math Raw Score = ☐
(rounded up)

Turn to page xiv to convert your raw score to a scaled score.

Answers and Explanations

SECTION 1

6 Score Essay

If I had been asked this question a month ago, I would have said "Of course, failure is possible." Whenever we embark on a project, we have a picture in our minds of what the "successful" result will be. And, if things don't turn out that way, we usually define the attempt as a failure. The answer seems obvious and simple, right?

Maybe not.

All my life, I have wanted to become a writer. For my birthday last year, my best friend gave me a book called *No Plot? No Problem*. The premise of this book is that you can write a novel in one month. I read the entire book, cover to cover, in one night, and was convinced there was no way I would not succeed. All you have to write is 1,667 words a day and, at the end of one month, you will have a novel approximately the length of *The Great Gatsby*. This didn't seem like an excessive amount of writing to me—I probably write than many words in e-mails to my friends every night, anyway.

For the first week I met, and even exceeded, my daily writing quota. My story, which was about a young girl who didn't get into any of her first-choice colleges and thought her life was over until she met the love of her life at a community college, was going very well. I had a large amount of interesting writing. F. Scott Fitzgerald, watch out!

Then, all of a sudden I hit the wall. A big wall. I couldn't think of 67 words to write, let alone 1,667. My story, which I had loved, became a symbol to me of the fact that I would probably never achieve my dream of writing professionally. I had "failed" to complete a novel in thirty days.

About six weeks ago, however, I saw an ad in the newspaper for a summer course at a college nearby. The course, which is called "Discovering Your Inner Writer," is being taught by members of the college's creative writing faculty, and is open to all ages. To apply, you had to submit five pages of original writing. I submitted the first five pages of my "failed" novel, and I got accepted into the class!

So, yes, I "failed" to complete my novel in the time frame I had set for myself. But this "failure" has resulted in my getting into a class that may benefit my future as a writer, even more than finishing that novel would have. My "failure" turned into a very exciting success! It is impossible to fail, I now know, because each and every event that happens has the possibility of opening a new and interesting door that you might not have even considered!

6 Score Critique

All essays are evaluated on four criteria: Topic, Support, Organization, and Language. This essay answers the question posed by the prompt, and does so in a very interesting way. The writer states that, had she been asked the question a month ago, her answer to the question would have been different. Clearly, her essay is going to let us know what happened to change her mind. This piques the reader's interest right away.

The support offered consists of only one anecdote, but it is extremely well developed. The writer takes us chronologically through her experience trying to write a novel, her initial feeling that she "failed," and how that failure turned into a success. She then sums up her message with a closing statement that wraps up the essay nicely. This indicates that she spent sufficient time on her plan before she began to produce her essay.

In addition, her sentence structure is varied and interesting. The language is strong with some good SAT-level vocabulary (*embark, premise, excessive, quota*), and there are no errors in grammar or usage. This indicates that the writer took time to proofread her work.

4 Score Essay

I think it is possible to fail if you do not take your failure and learn something from it. This way there is something touchable you can show from your "failure," and so you have not really failed because you have something to show. For example, if you failed English then, yes, that is a failure. But if you then go to Summer School and take English again, learn alot, and get a good grade, you haven't really failed, you just took a little longer to get there than most people.

If, however, you fail English and you decide "I just can't do this" and decide to drop out rather than even trying to fix your original failure then, yes, you failed. You failed because you didn't use that set back to better yourself, you just gave up.

Another example is on the television show "American Idol," where, even though there is only one winner at the end, a lot of the people who didn't win (i.e. failed) have turned that failure into success. Even William Hung, who was a terrible singer on the show, now has a commercial on for "Ask Jeeves." So this guy's failure at one thing resulted in success at another. No one would consider him a failure. His name is known all over the country.

Another example of a person turning around a failure is my brother Christopher, who takes Tai Kwon Do. He has taken it ever since he was five, and he has always passed every color belt the first time he took it. Then, two years ago, he dislocated his shoulder. He wasn't supposed to do his belt testing, but he did it anyway, and he didn't make it because his body hurt too much. He was upset that all of the kids who had been in his class since the beginning moved up a belt, but he stayed the same. For a while, he even quite Tai Kwon Do. But he missed it too much so he went back. He's in a class with new kids and he got his red belt ultimately. So you can't really call that a failure either. He just took more time then the others.

4 Score Critique

All essays are evaluated on four basic criteria: Topic, Support, Organization and Language. With better time management to allow for more development of examples, a less abrupt ending, and some proofreading, this essay might have received a 5, or even a 6.

This writer clearly understands the prompt and takes a position on the question presented in the first paragraph. He even presents three examples relevant to the prompt. However, none of his examples is sufficiently well-developed. The organization of the essay is adequate, indicating that the writer took some time to plan before beginning to produce his writing. There is also some use of fluid transitions between ideas, but they are basic and repetitive (*For example, Another example, Another example*). The essay also ends too abruptly; it seems that the writer ran out of time before he could formulate a concluding paragraph.

There are a number of sentence fragments and run-on sentences, some spelling errors (alot for "a lot," *quite* for "quit"), and some slang (*guy's, kids*). This writer needs to save time to proofread his work. Fixing basic spelling, grammar, and sentence structure errors is an easy way to bump your essay score up at least one point.

2 Score Essay

Susan B. Anthony said that "Failure is impossible" and I agree with it, very much so. Because you might fail at something, like getting a good SAT score, but you can take it again if that happens and study harder this time. The only real failure is stopping before you have accomplished what it is you set out to do.

This is exactly what happened to me when I tried out for cheerleading first semester my freshman year and I didn't make it. I was really really disappointed that I failed to make the squad, but I decided to improve my skills so I could show them I could do it. So I took gymnastics and went to a cheerleading camp over the summer. Sophomore year, I tried out again and this time I made it. Two of my best friends who tried out with me freshman year and also didn't make it didn't try out again. But to me, it's not like they failed. To me, they quit, not failed.

I guess what the Susan B. Anthony quotation means to me is that you can use your failures to spur you on to future success, or you can choose to just give up like my friends did. I choose not to give up, so for me, "Failure is impossible."

2 Score Critique

All essays are evaluated on four criteria: Topic, Support, Organization, and Language. This essay does address the prompt, but it is too brief and undeveloped to earn a higher score.

Only two examples are offered in support of the writer's position (an SAT score and the cheerleading squad), neither of which is adequately developed. Several more examples would be needed, unless the cheerleader story was explored in much greater detail.

This essay shows adequate organization, as far as it goes, indicating that the writer spent at least some time developing a plan before producing her essay. The first paragraph serves as an introduction, the second presents the example, and the third is a conclusion. However, the essay does little to develop the writer's ideas.

The vocabulary is unsophisticated, and the writer repeatedly uses the pronoun it without a clear antecedent. Her sentence structure is also shoddy. There are several sentence fragments, and some sentences use incorrect grammatical structure. Like all SAT-takers, this writer needs to save time to proofread her essay before turning it in.

SECTION 2

1.   E

Difficulty: Low

How might "warmer temperatures and lack of inclement weather" affect a fisherman?

If "many fishermen work tirelessly through the spring and summer months" because of the "warmer temperatures and lack of inclement weather" during this time, then they probably do so to allow themselves to gain something. *Allowing* and *gain from* make great predictions for the blanks.

In choice (A), a fisherman could not really *subsist*, or survive, on temperatures and a "lack of inclement weather." In choice (B), similarly, "warmer temperatures" and a "lack of inclement weather" cannot really be *competed for*. In choice (C), one cannot really *abstain from* or give up "warmer temperatures" and a "lack of inclement weather". In choice (D), one could not *forage* or look through objects for "warmer temperatures" and a "lack of inclement weather." Choice (E) matches your prediction nicely.

2.   C

Difficulty: Low

If the thunderstorms began and ended at regular intervals, what is a good word to describe them?

The modifying phrase "beginning and ending at almost regular intervals" describes the subject of the sentence, "thunderstorms." If thunderstorms started and stopped in this way, then they were recurring in a regular pattern.

In choice (A), if the thunderstorms were *unmediated*, then their coming and going was not interposed, or controlled, by some outside force, which may be true but has nothing to do with the modifying phrase. Choice (B) is the opposite of your prediction—the thunderstorms stopped and started in a regular pattern, not *spontaneously*. Choice (C) matches your prediction; *periodic* means a regular pattern. In choice (D) as in (B), a regular pattern cannot be *incidental*. Choice (E), *endemic,* describes something native or confined to a certain region, which is not stated in the sentence and has nothing to do with the modifying phrase.

3.   A

Difficulty: Medium

The sentence begins with the keywords "even though," so you automatically know that there is a contrast within the sentence. Consider each blank. The first blank must be another noun that would "mar the enrollment..." such as *hostility* or *fighting*. The second blank contrasts with the first, so it should have a positive tone. The aftermath of the decision "...was comparatively *calm*."

Choice (A) fits your prediction well. In choice (B), these two words are opposite in tone, but in the wrong order. In choice (C), *banality* suggests triviality, but if there were "hostile protests," the enrollment was clearly not seen as trivial. In choice (D), the two words are not sufficiently opposite in tone. In choice (E), the enrollment could not have had both "hostile protests" and *serenity*.

4.   A

Difficulty: Medium

If the remark was "not intended as a criticism," then what was it intended as?

The first part of the sentence sets up a contrast. The "remark" was "not intended as a criticism but as a...." Through the remark she wanted "further explanation," so the remark was probably more of a *question*.

Choice (A) matches your prediction. In choice (B), a professor's remark, or comment, on a student's work wouldn't be a *confession*. In choice (C), the word *dismissal* is too definite to want "further explanation." In choice (D), a *condemnation* is too similar to a criticism: it wouldn't make sense for the remark to be a *condemnation* but not a "criticism." In choice (E), *credo* is a deeply held belief, but if the professor seeks "further explanation," then she probably doesn't hold the belief.

5.   C

Difficulty: High

Note the contrast indicated by the word "but." The blanks will consist of two contradictory terms. Also, the words "appear to be" suggest that the first word will be in opposition to the word in the second blank.

Start with a prediction for the first blank. Someone who supports the people is in favor of public interests. The word in the second blank must mean someone who doesn't appeal to the general population but instead only to those who have money and who donated to the political campaign.

In choice (A), *demagogues* may work in the first blank because it refers to a person who wins support by appealing to popular feelings and prejudices. However, a "maverick" is an unorthodox or undisciplined person, not necessarily someone who favors selected groups of people. In choice (B), although politicians may be *conservatives* who are opposed to change, they are never *anarchists* who are in favor of abolishing the government. These words do

not match the contextual clues in the sentence. Choice (C) is the correct answer. Look at the root of the word *populists*; it refers to "people" or more generally to the population. A *populist* is someone who supports the general public. An *elitist* favors a selected group. In choice (D), these words do not match the predictions. A *moderate* is someone who does not hold extreme views and a *reactionary* is someone who is opposed to progress and reform. In choice (E), although *partisans* are people who are strong supporters or devotees to a particular cause—perhaps the rights of the general public—the word *snobs* is too extreme as it implies that a political figure would despise anyone who did not give money to support their campaign.

6.   C

Difficulty: Medium

Make sure you read the text surrounding the cited expression, since it can elaborate on or qualify the author's view.

Be aware of the author's overall tone. You can often eliminate incorrect choices because they are inconsistent with the tone of the text.

Notice that after the author uses the cited words, he acknowledges that this "cynical" characterization is "somewhat supported by a burgeoning community of new carryout restaurants." By adding this evidence, the author is clearly tempering the tone set by the cited words—the tone is negative, but not overly so.

Choice (A) is distortion; by including evidence that supports this critique, the author suggests that it perhaps has at least some merit. Choice (B) is an opposite; the phrase suggests that the analysts have a negative outlook, not a positive one. Choice (C) is a nice fit for your prediction. Choice (D) is distortion; again, by citing evidence that supports such cynicism, the author is agreeing on some level with the accuracy of these analysts. Choice (E) is extreme; nothing in the passage supports the use of such a strong description.

7.   D

Difficulty: High

What does the passage imply about the health implications of recipes with more fats and salt?

Make sure you set the cited words in context by evaluating them with the surrounding text in mind.

The cited sentence suggests that restaurants cooks are more concerned with retaining business than with the fat and salt content of their food. In other words, they want to keep their tables full, and to do so they may compromise the healthfulness of the food.

Choice (A) is extreme; the passage only implies that some cooks are *more* concerned with retaining customers than with health. Choice (B) is out of scope; the passage does not discuss cooks' beliefs about the economy. Choice (C) is out of scope; the passage does not discuss whether or not restaurant cooks consider foods higher in salt or fat "unhealthy," it only suggests that such recipes please customers. Choice (D) is a good match for your prediction. Choice (E) is extreme; the passage only suggests that customers are more likely to come back if the food is tasty, not necessarily that customers are *only* concerned with taste.

8. C

Difficulty: Medium

What is the author's tone in Passage 2? Look for a choice that matches this tone.

Although it can be easy to make your own assumptions when reading a passage, be sure to focus on the *author's* perspective when evaluating the choices.

Passage 1 outlines a rise in consumer restaurant spending even during bad economic times. In the first sentence of Passage 2, the author says that even though eating out is good for the economy, "often the effect is not so positive for consumers watching their waistlines or overall health." It would make sense, then, for the author of Passage 2 to be concerned if more people are spending money eating out. Notice the author's qualification, though: restaurant food *often* has less-than-ideal effects, but it doesn't necessarily have to be unhealthy if people are mindful of the nutritional content of restaurant foods.

Choice (A) is extreme; although the second author says that more and more people do in fact seem to be eating out, the passage does not suggest that a rise in restaurant spending is unavoidable. Choice (B) is out of scope; the author never explores whether or not the rise in restaurant spending was expected. Choice (C) is a good fit for your prediction. Choice (D) is extreme; the second author mentions that eating out "has a positive effect on the nation's economy," but it isn't necessarily crucial to the economy. Choice (E) is extreme; while the author expresses concern for the health of restaurant customers, the passage does not go so far as to suggest that a spending increase is "socially destructive."

9. A

Difficulty: Medium

What is the focus of each passage? Which passage is more directly concerned with the rise in spending itself?

Even when a question doesn't point you towards any particular portion of the text, make sure to find textual evidence that supports your answer choice.

The second sentence of Passage 1 states that this rise in spending occurred "through even the worst of the recent economic downturns." The passage then goes on to discuss possible reasons for the industry's growth even in a time of economic decline. Passage 2, on the other hand, focuses on the health effects of eating out. Look for a choice that captures this contrast.

Choice (A) nicely matches your prediction. Choice (B) is distortion; the first part is fine, but "moral repercussions" are not discussed in Passage 2. Choice (C) is distortion; again, this statement is true for Passage 1 but misrepresents Passage 2, which makes no mention of the economy's decline. Choice (D) is distortion; both passages mention a growing tendency to eat restaurant food, not a tendency to be health-conscious. Choice (E) is out of scope; Passage 2 does not discuss consumer confidence.

10. D

Difficulty: Low

Clues as to the meaning of a cited word can usually be found in the content immediately surrounding it. In this case, the earlier word "formative" is an important clue. If the author is stressing the "formative" significance of this period, then it must be a period when the American press is being founded or established.

(A) "Disposition" is the primary definition of the cited word and, because it refers to a person's tendencies or moods, it clearly doesn't fit the context. (B) "Structuring" is close, but too specific here as the structure or layout of the press industry is never described. (C) Again, "design" is too specific, as the context merely refers to the founding of the press, not its specific structure or appearance. Choice (D) is correct; "formative" marks the use of "constitution" as referring to the early stages of the American press. (E) "Temperament" is a primary definition of the cited word, but it is used to refer to a person, not an entire industry.

11. E

Difficulty: Medium

Inference questions require you to read between the lines and come to conclusions not explicitly stated in text, but the correct answer choice must still be firmly supported by evidence from the paragraph.

Notice that the author specifically refers to these decades as constituting the "most profound change," which implies that changes described earlier in the paragraph were *less* significant those of this particular period.

Choice (A) is out of scope; the paragraph describes newspapers as popular, but never specifically as the publication of choice. Choice (B) is distortion; the author is referring to the formative years of the American *press*, not necessarily urban culture. Choice (C) is out of scope; the paragraph never compares the *historical* significance of these events, only their significance in regards to the formation of the press. Choice (D) is distortion; the cited sentence only suggests that these years were more important than any preceding period, but not necessarily any periods that followed this time. Choice (E) is correct; this choice clearly states that these decades saw the American press' most significant moments of transformation, reflecting the statement made at the end of the first paragraph.

12. B

Difficulty: Low

Re-examining the details of the cited word's context is frequently helpful when considering the more general focus of the passage.

In this case, the author is essentially describing how the technological changes made newspaper production cheaper, as shown by references to newsprint prices falling "dramatically" and color techniques becoming "cheap." Given this focus, it seems that the cited word is describing costs that were so low that they would have been previously considered improbable or unimaginable.

Choice (A)'s *impossible* is tempting but, given the fact that prices actually did fall dramatically, it is too strong for this context. Choice (B) is correct; the costs of newspaper production had never been so low. Choice (C): while the cited word can be used to refer to something considered offensive or rude, this meaning doesn't match the context of the paragraph. Choice (D)'s *inconsistent* matches neither

the cited word nor its context. Choice (E)'s *uncommon* doesn't fit; the author is referring to prices that would have been considered unlikely, not infrequent.

13. C

Difficulty: High

Pay careful attention to the scope and focus of the context of the cited lines when predicting and ultimately choosing your answer.

The referenced content refers to two "areas of change", a direct reference to the focus of the preceding sentences on "industrialization and the mass migrations that altered the American urban landscape" and technological advancements, which the author describes as affecting the *finances* of the industry: "unheard of costs;" "prices fell dramatically;" "printing techniques also became cheap." In other words, the "union" of these two changes would be newspapers becoming accessible to this new demographic of migrants. Look for an answer choice that comes to a similar conclusion.

Choice (A) is out of scope; while the author mentions "striking" visual images, nothing suggests that this quality made newspapers more appealing to the *average* American. Choice (B) is distortion; the paragraph never suggests that newspapers exploited this demographic, only that the decreased costs allowed them to tap into this readership. Choice (C) is correct; if lowering production costs was connected to reaching this new readership, then it follows that this group was not able to afford newspapers before. Choice (D) is out of scope; the paragraph in question does not refer to a rural readership. Choice (E) is out of scope; the paragraph does not discuss a connection between these technological changes and urbanization.

14. C

Difficulty: Medium

Don't go out of your way to make an answer choice work; stick to the most immediate conclusions that can be drawn from the evidence found in the cited content.

In this case, if the newspapers were popular with a readership "fervently reliant upon the relative immediacy of media reports," then it can be concluded that these newspapers were popular because they fulfilled this particular need.

Choice (A) is an irrelevant detail; while this point is made earlier in the passage, it is not being made by this particular content. Choice (B) is out of scope; nothing in the paragraph describes these newspapers as "quickly and easily" readable. Choice (C) is correct; the inhabitants of urban America were living "constantly changing, unstable lives," making newspapers a vital source of information for news that could impact them in any number of ways. Choice (D) is an irrelevant detail; although this point is made later in the paragraph, the cited content does not refer to this characteristic. Choice (E) is out of scope; while the author indicates that this readership used the papers to "inform their constantly changing" lives, nothing suggests that these specific topics were focused on.

15. C

Difficulty: Medium

When asked about a detail, don't try to answer from memory. Make sure to find the relevant detail or details by checking your notes and then rereading the passage.

Your notes should list something like "a discussion of defining art" as the purpose of paragraph 2; if not, skim for the words "endeavor" and "problematic." Either way, you should find the first sentence of paragraph 2 mentioning: "Before we can begin a discussion of artistic decline, we must first define the word art, an endeavor that has proven problematic."

Choice (A) is distortion; the author discusses improving the education system in later paragraphs, but the author never characterizes this as a "problematic endeavor." Choice (B) is distortion; in later paragraphs, the author discusses how education can make art more relevant by linking it to historical and sociological developments, but the author never characterizes this as a "problematic endeavor." Choice (C) is correct; exactly as we predicted and exactly as the passage states. Choice (D) is distortion; in later paragraphs, the author discusses what students should learn in school, but the author never characterizes this as a "problematic endeavor." Choice (E) is distortion; in later paragraphs, the author discusses whether or not to teach art, but the author never characterizes this as a "problematic endeavor."

16. B

Difficulty: Medium

Use the relevant part of the passage as evidence from which to draw your own conclusion.

Since you are given the part of the passage from which you must draw the inference, skim paragraph 2 to find evidence of what the author characterizes as "too much time spent." In lines 36–40 the author says that, "far too much time has been spent arguing over whether a teen movie is more or less art than *Citizen Kane*, or whether a boy band is more or less art than Sondheim." Now examine the answer choices by comparing them to this information and eliminating those that do not necessarily have to be true based on it.

Choice (A) is an opposite; while the author discusses comparisons of "classics," the author does so in order to highlight the comparison of such classics to modern works, thereby judging the modern works' artistic merits. Choice (B) is correct; the author states, "Far too much time has been spent arguing over whether a teen movie is more or less art than *Citizen Kane* is, or whether the music of a boy band is more or less art than the works of Sondheim." Thus, the author implies that too much time has spent comparing modern works to more established works in order to judge the modern works' artistic merits. Choice (C) is a misused detail; the author mentions this in a later paragraph. Choice (D) is a misused detail; the author mentions this in a later paragraph. Choice (E) is distortion; the author never discusses comparisons of works traditionally considered classics to each other; the author discusses their comparison to newer works.

17. E

Difficulty: Medium

Function questions require you to determine the purpose of a component of the passage, such as a paragraph, or in this case a detail.

Your task is to determine why the author included this detail in the passage. Your notes should tell you that the author uses most of paragraph 1 to bemoan or lament the decline of artistic appreciation and awareness in America. Since the author thinks that it is "sad" that America concerns itself with "teen movies and boy bands" then the author must think that film noir, jazz, and abstract expressionism are better. Thus, he must be mentioning them in order to draw a comparison and suggest their superiority. Look for that in the answer choices.

Choice (A) is distortion; while the author does seem to be appealing to a sense of a lost golden age, the author uses that as part of the comparison to newer art to suggest its inferiority. Choice (B) is an opposite; far from making a historical parallel, this author suggests that newer works are inferior. Choice (C) is out of scope; the author never examines the history of art. Choice (D) is a misused detail; the author uses different details in a later paragraph to remind readers of this. Choice (E) is correct; just as we predicted.

18. E

Difficulty: Medium

Answer a Vocab-in-Context question as you would a sentence completion question. Remove the target word and then find the word in the answer choices that best fits in that blank given the context of the sentence.

The sentence in question states: "Many claim that our discussion can be seen as snobby, even culturally imperious." Since the author states that many people might think the discussion is "snobby" and then goes on to say "even culturally imperious" the author must be using imperious as a higher degree of the same meaning as snobby.

Choice (A) is out of scope; *imperative* is not a higher degree of snobbery. Choice (B) is an opposite; when something is *arbitrary*, it is not carefully chosen which means that it cannot relay the meaning of snobbery. Choice (C) is out of scope; *regal* simply means elegant in a royal way. While this may be associated with snobbery, it does not convey the same meaning. Choice (D) is out of scope; *urgent* is a dictionary meaning of imperious but it makes no sense in the context of the original sentence. Choice (E) is correct; *arrogant* can be used as a higher degree of snobbery. When placed into the original sentence, it replaces imperious perfectly.

19. B

Difficulty: High

As with all inference questions, always keep in mind that a valid inference must be true based on the relevant facts in the passage.

Reread the lines in question in order to find evidence of what distinguishes the author's hypothetical United States. Parents read to their children and educate them. These parents also give their children art books, classical recordings, and plays as gifts. Now evaluate each answer choice, choosing the one that must be true based on the author's statements.

Choice (A) is out of scope; the author's statements deal with a new interest in art, not new interests in general. Choice (B) is correct; the lines in question describe a country in which parents share their interests in and enjoyment of art with their children, so it must be true that this what the author finds distinguishing about this hypothetical country. Choice (C) is a misused detail; the author never mentions school in the piece of the paragraph mentioned by the question. Choice (D) is out of scope; the author's statements discuss sharing enthusiasm for art, not other activities. Choice (E) is distortion; in the referenced lines, the author never alludes to the value of artistic skill.

20. B

Difficulty: Low

Do not mistake function questions with detail questions. While both function and detail questions require you to find the relevant information in the passage, function questions require you to answer *why* the author includes the relevant information in the passage.

Your notes might indicate that in paragraph 3, the author advances a vision of an artistically educated society. If your notes do not indicate this, then simply revisit the paragraph by skimming it, and then evaluate what the author does in this paragraph. The author provides an example of a more artistically educated America. Thus, the author must have included the paragraph in order to propose or provide a vision of a more artistically educated society.

Choice (A) is distortion; the author merely provides a vision of a more artistically educated society, not a utopian one. Choice (B) is correct; exactly as we predicted. Choice (C) is out of scope; in the third paragraph, the author never examines whether pop culture leaves a lasting impact on society. Choice (D) is out of scope; the author never deals with classic literature and younger students. Choice (E) is distortion; while the author proposes studying both, the author never states that contemporary and classical works are interchangeable.

21. D

Difficulty: Medium

Inferences must be true given the facts in the passage. When asked to describe or characterize facts or a situation in the passage, choose the answer choice that must be characteristic of the facts or situation in the passage.

Use the line numbers to locate and reread the situation described by the author. The author states that since "art, music, and culture are inextricably tied to literary and historical developments which themselves stem from changes in society and culture" the educational system should focus on a more "holistic" approach that teaches "students in an intertextual and multi-disciplinary manner." Find the answer choice that must be characteristic of this education.

Choice (A) is distortion; the author describes an artistic education, not an elitist one. Choice (B) is distortion; the author describes an artistic education, not a charitable one. Choice (C) is an opposite; eclectic means mixed together from various elements. This might seem true, but eclectic implies a mismatching of items. The author argues that literature, art, and history are not mismatched at all. Choice (D) is correct; the author describes an education that takes an overarching view. "Comprehensive" characterizes this. Choice (E) is an opposite; rudimentary means basic; the education described by the author goes beyond the basics and fundamentals by contextualizing art within other developments in society, thus creating an overarching education.

22. A

Difficulty: Low

Use the relevant part of the passage as evidence from which to draw a conclusion. In lines 108–110, the author states that "this system would require more funding, and most likely higher taxes." Find the answer choice that must be true based on this information.

Choice (A) is correct; since the new system would require more funding and probably higher taxes, it must be true that the new system would be more expensive. Choice (B) is distortion; clearly, the author believes that the new system would be better, but the author's statements don't provide evidence that the new system would be more celebrated. Choice (C) is distortion; the passage never alludes to any controversy over the system. Choice (D) is distortion; the passage provides ample evidence that the new system will be more holistic, but not that the new system will be more interesting. Choice (E) is distortion; the passage provides no evidence that the system is more likely to inspire.

23. C

Difficulty: Medium

You need global answers to global questions, so keep your eye on the big picture when determining why an author writes a passage:

As you should have noted while reading the passage, the topic is the decline of artistic knowledge and appreciation in America. The author outlines causes for this decline then proposes a solution. Look for an answer choice that says something similar to this.

Choice (A) is distortion; in the first paragraph, the author does shift the focus of the debate from analyzing causes to proposing solutions, but the author does not attempt to shift the focus of the debate from causes to effects. Choice (B) is out of scope; the author never supports a side in a debate, the author proposes a solution. Choice (C) is correct; exactly as we predicted. Choice (D) is out of scope; the author never revives a discredited idea. Choice (E) is out of scope; the author does not promote certain types of art, the author promotes art education in general.

24. C

Difficulty: Medium

Since valid inferences must be true based on the information in the passage, they usually will not be profound. Valid inferences often merely combine two or more facts from the relevant part of the passage.

Paragraph 3 contains the discussion of the author's hypothetical United States. Skim the passage for any facts regarding the production of higher quality art. The paragraph states that "when these children grow up, some may produce their own art, perhaps art that is higher in quality than the pop music and movies produced today." In a preceding line, the paragraph states that, "a better education in art will better equip them to judge the artistic merit of these newer, more trendy art forms, or at least place these art forms in historical context and analyze them as an outgrowth of societal and sociological trends…." Now compare each answer choice to this information.

Choice (A) is distortion; the author never links parents to the production of better art. Choice (B) is extreme; the author presents a more artistically educated society, but the author never goes so far as to claim that this society would not accept lower quality art. Choice (C) is correct; the author presents children with better artistic educations, and then states that they would grow up to produce better art. Thus, their production of better art must stem from their artistic education. Choice (D) is distortion; the author never mentions free time. Choice (E) is distortion; the author never discusses how strictly critics would judge art in this hypothetical society.

SECTION 3

1. E

Difficulty: Low

Strategic Advice: Always read SAT questions carefully—this one asks for the value of x^2 and gives you the value of $x^{\frac{1}{2}}$. $x^{\frac{1}{2}}$ is the same as $\sqrt{x}$. You might find it easier to work with fractional exponents if you rewrite them as more familiar roots. Use the value of $x^{\frac{1}{2}}$ to find x, then square this to find x^2. Be careful not to stop too soon.

Getting to the Answer:

$$x^{\frac{1}{2}} = 3$$
$$(x^{\frac{1}{2}})^2 = x^1 = 9 \text{ or } x = 9 = 3^2$$
$$x^2 = 9^2 = 81$$

2. A

Difficulty: Low

Strategic Advice: The value of $g(x)$ at any point is the y-value of that point. What point on this graph is lowest? What is the y-value at that point?

Getting to the Answer:

The lowest point is $(2, -2)$. The y-value of that point is -2, choice (A).

3. E

Difficulty: Low

Strategic Advice: The key to this problem—as in many problems that deal with interpreting charts and tables—is really understanding what each value in the table represents.

Getting to the Answer:

The value of i must represent the total of all movies in the chart; you can think of it as either the sum of all comedies and dramas ($c + f$), or the sum of all new releases and older titles ($g + h$). Since neither of these expressions is given as an answer choice, the categories must be broken down further. Choice (E) expresses the sum of new comedies, old comedies, new dramas, and old dramas respectively, which is equivalent to i as well.

4. E

Difficulty: Medium

Strategic Advice: Here, if you remember the Triangle Inequality Theorem, you can score some easy points. The Triangle Inequality Theorem states that for any triangle, the measure of any side must be less than the sum of the other two sides, but greater than the difference of the other two sides.

Getting to the Answer:

Given the Triangle Inequality Theorem:

$$6 - 2 > x \text{ and } 6 + 2 < x$$
$$4 < x < 8$$

Of the answer choices, only (E) is outside this range.

5. B

Difficulty: Low

Strategic Advice: Make sure you look at the key before solving a graph or chart question.

Getting to the Answer:

There are 1.5 more tree–pictures for Parkside than Waterford. Since each picture equals 50 trees, then

$$1.5 \times 50 = 75$$

6. B

Difficulty: Medium

Strategic Advice: Remember to work carefully with simple algebra problems. If the algebra fails you, Backsolving would also be a great way to solve this problem.

Getting to the Answer:

$$5x - x = 2x + x - 5$$
$$4x = 3x - 5$$
$$x = -5$$

7. B

Difficulty: Low

Strategic Advice: Look for a pattern in the figure. What will help you figure out where the numbers need to go?

Getting to the Answer:

From the figure the larger numbers are on the side of the line with the arrow head. Look for this in your answer. Only (B) fits.

8. C

Difficulty: Medium

Strategic Advice: When solving percent problems, make sure you place the decimal point in the right place. You could also pick numbers if you get stuck.

Getting to the Answer:

$$0.60y \times 20y = 12y$$

9. B

Difficulty: Medium

Strategic Advice: When solving a question with multiple variables, plug in for the values you know and then solve as you would a single–variable equation.

Getting to the Answer:

$$50 = \frac{5}{4}(2)t$$
$$50 = \frac{10}{4}t$$
$$50 \div \frac{10}{4} = 50 \times \frac{4}{10} = 20$$
$$t = 20$$

10. B

Difficulty: Medium

Strategic Advice: The way to proceed here may not be immediately obvious, but when you're given a right triangle and some side lengths, it can never hurt to try applying the Pythagorean Theorem.

Getting to the Answer:

$$c^2 = a^2 + b^2$$
$$8^2 = (5 + x)^2 + (5 - x)^2$$
$$64 = (25 + 10x + x^2) + (25 - 10x + x^2)$$
$$64 = 2x^2 + 50$$
$$64 = 2(x^2 + 25)$$
$$32 = x^2 + 25$$

11. C

Difficulty: Medium

Strategic Advice: You know the ratio between the angles' measures, and you know that all three must sum to 180. Thus, all you have to do is find the factor to multiply with the numbers in the ratio in order to get the correct sum.

Getting to the Answer:

Ratio is 4:5:6, so express the measures of the angles as $4x$, $5x$, and $6x$.

$$4x + 5x + 6x = 180$$
$$15x = 180$$
$$x = 12$$

Angle measures, therefore, are

$$4(12) = 48, 5(12) = 60, 6(12) = 72.$$
$$72 + 48 = 120$$

12. C

Difficulty: Medium

Strategic Advice: This question is an arithmetic question disguised as a geometry question. Recognize that you can Backsolve here by using your answer choices, and you'll have the answer nailed down in no time!

Getting to the Answer:

x is the overlapping portion of the radii of the two circles, and we need to find a value for it that will make the radius of the P triple the radius of O. Start with choice C. If $x = 3$, then the radius of O would be 5 and the radius of P would be 15. $15 = 3 \times 5$, so (C) must be the correct choice.

13. C

Difficulty: Medium

Strategic Advice: Be sure to understand the chart given before trying to tackle the problem. In multiple choice problems like this, work through all the possibilities and eliminate choices as you go.

Getting to the Answer:

For Richmont, population increases from 50 to 200, which is definitely more than $\frac{1}{2}$. Eliminate (A), (D), and (E).

For Pierdson, population decreases, so eliminate (B).

For Thomasville, population increases from 200 to 400. Only III works.

14. B

Difficulty: Medium

Strategic Advice: To find percent increase, determine the difference between values and divide by original value.

Getting to the Answer:

Total Population in 1986 = 950

Total Population in 1999 = 1,425

$$\frac{1,425 - 950}{950} = 50\%$$

15. C

Difficulty: Medium

Strategic Advice: This problem can be solved through careful reasoning, but if you're still confused you can perform the logic-question equivalent of pick numbers— make up some imaginary characters to fit the situation and see which statement holds true.

Getting to the Answer:

Let Amanda, Ellen, Greg, and Max be in the accounting department. Some of these people, say Amanda and Greg, are on the bowling team. Since no one on the bowling team is married, Amanda and Greg are definitely unmarried. We don't know anything about whether Ellen and Max are married.

(A) is uncertain; it could be either true or false.

(B) is uncertain as well; you don't know enough about Ellen and Max.

(C) is necessarily true; you know Amanda and Greg are single.

(D) and (E) are uncertain; the question doesn't say anything about the number of employees in either group. Thus, (C) is the correct answer choice.

16. C

Difficulty: Medium

Strategic Advice: Use the formula for averages to find the missing pieces of an averages question.

Getting to the Answer: The average is the sum of the terms divided by the number of terms. So 10 students got 100, leaving 20 to get y scores each (we can assume each will have the same score) so we set up:

$$\frac{100(10) + 20y}{30} = 92$$

$$1,000 + 20y = 2,760$$

$$20y = 1,760$$

$$y = 88$$

17. B

Difficulty: Medium

Strategic Advice: Remember that a^{-2} is equal to $\frac{1}{a^2}$. If you have trouble simplifying the given expression, try picking a number for a to make the problem more concrete.

Getting to the Answer:

$$a^2 \times a^{-2} = a^2 \times \frac{1}{a^2} = \frac{a^2}{a^2} = 1$$

Or, say $a = 3$:

$$3^2 \times \frac{1}{3^2} = 9 \times \frac{1}{9} = \frac{9}{9} = 1$$

18. C

Difficulty: High

Strategic Advice: In order to visualize some geometry problems, it is necessary to draw the diagram split into its pieces. The perimeter of each semicircle is half of the perimeter (circumference) of the original circle plus the length of the straight edge.

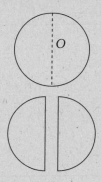

Getting to the Answer:

P of one semicircle $= \dfrac{1}{2}\pi d + 6$

$= \dfrac{1}{2}\pi(6) + 6$

$= 3\pi + 6$

P of two semicircles $= 2(3\pi + 6) = 6\pi + 12$

19. A

Difficulty: High

Strategic Advice: The probability that a randomly selected point will fall within the shaded area is equal to the ratio of the area that is shaded to the area of the entire figure. The area of the entire figure is equal to the area of the largest circle, and the area of the shaded area is equal to the area of the second circle minus the area of the smallest circle. To make the calculations easier, you can assume that the radius of the smallest circle equals 1, so its diameter is 2. Then the radius of the second circle is 3 and the radius of the largest circle is 5.

Getting to the Answer:

Shaded area:

$\pi(3^2) - \pi(1^2) = 9\pi - \pi = 8\pi$

Total area of figure: $\pi(5^2) = 25\pi$

Probability: $\dfrac{8\pi}{25\pi} = \dfrac{8}{25}$

20. C

Difficulty: High

Strategic Advice: Use the slope formula, $m = \dfrac{y_2 - y_1}{x_2 - x_1}$, with the two given points to get an equation involving k. Then solve for k. If you find yourself running out of time, you can easily narrow down the answer choices and make an

educated guess—you know that the slope of the line is negative, so k must be greater than 2, eliminating answer choices (A) and (B).

Getting to the Answer:

$\dfrac{2 - k}{3 - 0} = \dfrac{-1}{2}$

$\dfrac{2 - k}{3} = \dfrac{-1}{2}$

$4 - 2k = -3$

$7 = 2k$

$\dfrac{7}{2} = k$

SECTION 4

1. C

Difficulty: Low

Look for the most concise version of the selection that retains the meaning of the original sentence.

This sentence is awkward and unnecessarily wordy. (C) solves both of these problems without adding any additional errors. (B) introduces the passive voice unnecessarily. (D) and (E) are grammatically incorrect in structure.

2. B

Difficulty: Medium

In a compound predicate, both verbs must be in parallel form.

The verb phrase *would increase* should be *to increase* in order to parallel *to hold*; also, the pronoun *they* is unnecessary. (B) fixes both problems. (C) is awkwardly worded and fails to make the verbs parallel. (D) and (E) use transition words (*for* and *thus*) which are inappropriate in context.

3. E

Difficulty: Medium

The gerund (*-ing*) verb form can never be the predicate (main) verb in an independent clause.

As written, this sentence is a fragment, since neither of the clauses is independent. (E) corrects this without introducing other errors. (B) does not address the error. (C) is incorrect grammatical structure. (D) creates a run-on sentence.

4. D

Difficulty: Medium

A verb must agree with its subject noun, which may not be the noun closest to it in the sentence.

The subject of this sentence is *some*, which is grammatically plural, so the verb must also be in the plural form. (D) changes the singular *was* to the plural *were* without introducing any new errors. (B) and (E) correct the agreement error, but (B) misuses the semicolon splice, which is only correct when used to combine independent clauses, and (E) changes the verb in the second clause so it no longer agrees with its singular subject, *project*. (C) does not address the error.

5. E

Difficulty: Low

Although the shortest answer will not always be correct on the SAT, it's a good place to start, especially in wordiness questions.

A greater amount of is just a wordier way of saying "more;" (E) is concise while still maintaining the meaning of the original sentence. (B) changes the meaning of the sentence slightly (*greater money* is not the same thing as "more money"), and introduces the passive voice unnecessarily. (C) and (D) are still wordier than they need to be.

6. E

Difficulty: Medium

When a sentence contains a comparison, make sure that the elements presented can logically be compared.

As written, this sentence presents a comparison between *frozen water* and *the rest of the world*. Both (B) and (E) correct the comparison, but (B) is unnecessarily wordy. (C) is incorrect grammatical structure. (D) is incorrect idiomatic usage.

7. A

Difficulty: High

When all of the other answer choices are longer than the original, consider the possibility that the sentence is correct as written.

This sentence is correct as written. (B) is unnecessarily wordy. (C), (D), and (E) all compare Roy's novels to Rushdie rather than comparing Roy herself to Rushdie; additionally, all three say that Roy's *novels…have been labeled a magical realist.*

8. D

Difficulty: High

Comparisons must be structured so that logical things are compared.

Here, Amanda's *time* is being compared to *either Gwen or Christine*. (D) makes the comparison between the times of the three runners. (B) does not address the error. (C) compares the times of Amanda and Christine to Gwen, rather than her time. (E) is unnecessarily wordy.

9. B

Difficulty: Medium

Correct answer choices on the SAT will not contain redundancies.

Since and *is why* both set up a cause-and-effect relationship between clauses, so using both in the same sentence is redundant. (B) eliminates the redundancy. The other choices are all unnecessarily wordy.

10. A

Difficulty: High

Don't mistake formal or complex sentence structure for grammatical error.

This sentence is correct as written. (B) and (C) are awkward and unnecessarily wordy. (D) is incorrect grammatical structure. (E) creates a run-on sentence.

11. E

Difficulty: Medium

Although there are a number of ways to correct a run-on sentence, only one answer choice will do so without introducing any additional errors.

As written, this sentence is a run-on: two independent clauses joined by a comma splice. (E) corrects this by making the second clause subordinate. Neither (B), (C), nor (D) addresses the error.

12. C

Difficulty: Medium

Learn the correct forms of common irregular verbs; one or two SAT questions will most likely deal with this issue.

"Begun," not *began* is the proper form with *has*; the error is in (C). (A) uses *where* correctly. (On the SAT, "where" will only be correct when used to indicate a location or direction.) (B) and (E) are correct idiomatic usage in context.

13. D

Difficulty: Low

The comparative form of an adjective is formed by adding either the word "more" or the suffix "-er," but not both.

Fuller is the comparative form of the adjective "full;" adding *more* is incorrect. (A) correctly uses the superlative, since a school would have more than two courses. (B) appropriately expresses the contrast between the two clauses. (C) is an appropriate verb tense in context.

14. B

Difficulty: Medium

In a construction using *there*, the correct verb form is determined by the object that follows.

Since *police helicopters* is plural, (B) should read "there were." (A) is correct idiomatic usage in context. (C) properly sets up the idiom *both…and*. The infinitive in (D) correctly parallels *to protect*.

15. B

Difficulty: Medium

Who is only correct when referring to people; use "that" or "which" for other things, depending on the sentnce structure.

Espresso machines are things, not people, so *who* is incorrect in (B). (A) and (C) are correct idiomatic usage in context. (D) agrees with its plural subject, *espresso machines*.

16. E

Difficulty: Medium

Be methodical in eliminating wrong answer choices; this will help you to determine when a sentence has no error.

This sentence is correct as it is written. (A) correctly expresses the contrast between the two clauses. (B) is

correct idiomatic usage. (C) is the appropriate possessive pronoun with *we*. (D) agrees with its plural subject, *designations*.

17. E

Difficulty: High

Expect between five and eight Writing section sentences to be correct as written.

This sentence contains no error. (A) and (D) are correct idiomatic usage. (B) is appropriate use of the infinitive verb form. The verb in (C) agrees with the plural *writers*.

18. B

Difficulty: Low

Context will determine whether a singular or plural verb form should be used with *there*.

Since *twelve women* is plural, (B) should read "were." (A) correctly expresses the contrast between the two clauses. (C) is a correctly used idiomatic phrase. (D) is the appropriate preposition with *apply* in context.

19. C

Difficulty: Medium

A pronoun must agree in number with the noun it replaces.

In this sentence, *these* refers to *section*. Since *section* is singular; *it* would be the correct pronoun in (C). (A) agrees with its singular subject, *College Board*. (B) is idiomatically correct usage. (D) properly uses an adverbial phrase to modify the verb *assess*.

20. A

Difficulty: Low

Unless context requires a complex verb phrase, the correct answer will use the simplest correct verb tense.

(A) is unnecessarily wordy; "have to wait" would be correct here. (B) correctly expresses the contrast between the two clauses. (C) is correct idiomatic usage. (D) properly uses an adverb to modify the verb *pick…up*.

21. B

Difficulty: Medium

When used as a pronoun, "some" is considered grammatically plural.

Since the subject of this sentence is the pronoun *Some*, the verb in (B) should be "have been." (A) is correct idiomatic usage. (C) correctly establishes the cause-and-effect relationship between the two clauses. (D) agrees with its singular subject, *award*.

22. C

Difficulty: Medium

Items in a compound, series, or list must be parallel in form.

Since the first two verb forms in the series are infinitives, the third should be as well; (C) should read "to allow." (A) agrees with its singular subject *process*; (B) parallels the first infinitive (and, since only one underlined segment can be changed, must remain the same); (D) is proper use of an adverb, since *age* is used here as a verb.

23. A

Difficulty: High

The subject of a verb may not be the noun closest to it in the sentence.

The subject of the verb *reveal* here is the singular *Examination* (*survey results and financial records* is the compound object of the preposition *of*) so "reveals" would be correct in (A). (B) correctly uses an adverb (*more*) to modify an adjective (*stringent*). (C) is correct idiomatic usage. (D) agrees with its plural subject *companies*.

24. A

Difficulty: Medium

Many tested idioms involve the proper use of prepositions.

A person acts as the "captain of" a team; the error is in (A). (B) properly reflects the contrast between the two clauses. (C) agrees with its singular subject *coach*. (D) is correct idiomatic usage.

25. B

Difficulty: High

Make sure verb tenses properly express the time periods referred to.

For the last decade indicates an action that is still continuing, so the verb tenses should reflect this. *Has contributed* does so, but *were* does not; (B) should read "have been." (A) is correct idiomatic usage. (C) is an appropriate pronoun in context. (D) is the proper preposition with *contributed*.

26. D

Difficulty: Medium

Many idiomatic phrases require a specific preposition to be correct.

The preposition *about* is incorrect with the verb *charge*; "with" would be appropriate in this context. (A) appropriately expresses the contrast present in the two clauses. (B) is a properly used idiomatic phrase. (C) is an appropriate verb tense in context.

27. D

Difficulty: High

The comparative form is used to compare two things; the superlative must be used when comparing three or more.

Because there are more than two baseball teams to choose from, the superlative "most" would be correct in (D). (A) is an appropriate pronoun to refer to *team*. (B) is consistent verb tense usage. (C) correctly uses a plural pronoun to refer to *Yankees*.

28. A

Difficulty: Low

If a pronoun is part of a compound subject or object, read the sentence with just the pronoun to see if it makes sense. Since you wouldn't say "Me was able to maintain…" you know that the pronoun case here is wrong.

"And I," not *and me*, would be correct in (A). (B) is proper use of the infinitive verb form. (C) is correct idiomatic usage. (D) is the appropriate possessive pronoun in context.

29. E

Difficulty: Medium

Sentences with no errors frequently have complex or unusual structure.

This sentence is correct as written. (A), (B), and (C) are all correct usage in context. The past perfect in (D) is appropriate for an action completed prior to another stated past action.

30. A

Difficulty: Low

Complex sentence structure can make it difficult to determine verb tense agreement; cross out intervening phrases and clauses if it helps.

This sentence is correct as written. The past tense verb in (B) is idiomatically incorrect for the context in which it is used (*goes back* here is used to refer to time). (C) is incorrect grammatical structure. (D) and (E) use verb forms that are inconsistent with the other verb in the compound predicate, *found.*

31. D

Difficulty: Medium

Unlike Improving Sentences questions, Improving Paragraphs will not always repeat the original selection in choice (A). Read all IP answer choices carefully.

These sentences are not grammatically incorrect, so you're looking for an answer choice that improves their style.

(D) combines and relates the two sentences logically, without introducing any errors. (A) combines the sentences with just a comma, creating a run-on sentence. (B) is incorrect grammatical structure. (C) uses a contrast transition word (*although*) which is inappropriate in context. (E) introduces an inconsistent verb tense.

32. C

Difficulty: Medium

Context clues will help you determine the most appropriate transition word.

This question asks you to connect the final sentence of the second paragraph to the rest of the paragraph. The only choice that effectively makes this connection is (C). (A) indicates a contrast between ideas that is not present. (B) treats the sentence as if it were part of a progression. (D) incorrectly identifies the sentence as an illustration. (E) identifies the last sentence as a cause, rather than an effect; additionally, it creates a sentence fragment.

33. D

Difficulty: Medium

Make sure verb tenses accurately sequence the events they describe.

Paragraph 2 makes it clear that the development of the cowpox vaccine has already been completed, so *developing* is an inappropriate verb form. (D) corrects this. None of the other answer choices addresses the error.

34. E

Difficulty: Medium

If you don't spot a grammar or usage error, look for an answer choice that improves the selection's style.

Since both sentences deal with the use of "dead" viruses in vaccines, they can easily be combined. (E) does so without introducing any errors. (A) simply joins the two sentences with *and*; while not technically a grammatical error, this is not considered good SAT style. (B) uses a transition word that is inappropriate in context. The wording of (C) alters the meaning of the sentences. (D) creates a sentence fragment.

35. B

Difficulty: Medium

The last sentence in a passage should not introduce new or unrelated information.

The best choice here is (B), since it follows logically from paragraph 3's description of how vaccines are developed from "dead" viruses.

(A) might be a good introductory sentence for a new paragraph in a longer passage, but that's not what the question stem is asking for. (C) and (D) are outside the scope of this passage. (E) would make the most sense if placed somewhere in the first paragraph.

SECTION 5

1. C

Difficulty: Low

If the chief wanted ensure that "nothing was lost," what might he suggest be done to "every piece of evidence"?

The words "to ensure" indicate that the first blank supports or agrees with the second. And given that the first blank refers to something that would "ensure nothing was lost," a word like marked or tagged would make sense here. If carefully marking the evidence would "ensure nothing was lost," then it would also ensure that it was "readily" available for "those who needed it." *Marked* and *available* make great predictions for the blanks.

In choice (A) *praising* evidence would not necessarily "ensure nothing was lost," or that it could be "readily" *scrutinized by* "those who needed it." Choice (B) may be tempting, but simply *displaying* evidence would not necessary ensure that it was "readily" *comprehensible to* "those who needed it." Choice (C) is a good match for your prediction. In choice (D) *administering* something would not ensure that "nothing was lost," or that it could be "readily" *overlooked by* anyone. In choice (E) *catalogued* works perfectly in the first blank, but carefully listing or filing something would not make it "readily" *unobtainable to* "those who needed it."

2. A

Difficulty: Low

If salsa outperformed ketchup, then it was the most popular condiment.

If salsa "outperformed," or outsold, ketchup then it *beat* or *bested* ketchup as "the best-selling condiment." Note that the second clause modifies "salsa."

Choice (A) matches your prediction. In choice (B) "redoubling" means repeating or doubling, but it doesn't make sense for salsa to "repeat" ketchup. In choice (C) if salsa was "augmenting" ketchup, then it was adding to its sales, rather than beating its sales. In choice (D) "brandishing" means displaying ostentatiously, which doesn't make sense in context (how can salsa display something?). In choice (E) "evading" means escaping or avoiding, but salsa *bested* ketchup, it didn't avoid it.

3. E

Difficulty: Medium

"Because" signals the two blanks will agree with the doctor's "influential" status.

The words "seemed to make" indicate that the first blank will describe a quality that is consistent with the second blank. And if you know that he was the "most influential doctor in the hospital" and that the two blanks must agree with this reputation, then they must describe very *positive* qualities. The words "patient care" suggest the second blank is a positive word like *diligent* or *attentive*, suggesting the doctor influenced the facility in this way by being *dedicated* or *committed*. Dedicated and attentive make great predictions for the blanks.

In choice (A), remember, both words must describe positive qualities, and while *sagacity* is a positive word, *unscrupulous* or unprincipled is not. In choice (B), the two words must also be closely related, and *leniency* would probably not cause others to be *decorous*. In choice (C), a

nonchalant influence would not lead to *tenacious* behavior. In choice (D), these words contrast, as an *acrimonious* influence would probably lead to an unhappy environment. Choice (E) is a great match for your prediction.

4. B

Difficulty: Medium

The keyword "although" indicates a contrast.

"Although" immediately indicates a contrast between the way that "Tom often looked" and the fact that he "dedicated...time" to maintain a neat appearance. What could the contrast be? Tom probably "looked *messy* or *unkempt*" even though he dedicated *a huge* "amount of time" trying to maintain "a neat appearance."

In choice (A), if Tom looked "orderly" then it wouldn't be a surprise, or contrast, that he took a lot of time maintaining a neat appearance (and also he wouldn't be "attempting" to keep up such an appearance, he would actually be doing it). Choice (B) matches your prediction well. In choice (C), the fact that Tom tried to "maintain a neat appearance" doesn't contrast with him looking "annoyed." In choice (D), again, the fact that Tom tried to "maintain a neat appearance" doesn't contrast with him looking "distracted." In choice (E) as in (C) and (D), looking "agitated" doesn't contrast with trying to look "neat."

5. B

Difficulty: Medium

The second clause defines the first.

The second clause modifies the blank in the first clause, therefore defining, or explaining, the first clause. Therefore the blank is similar in meaning to "an abundance," the subject of the modifying clause. Look for a word such as *plenty* or *plethora*.

Choice (A) at first glance might seem correct, but the fact that the area "abounds with life and activity" doesn't necessarily mean that the mingling is tumultuous, as "melee" indicates. Choice (B) matches your prediction nicely. In choice (C), an "abundance" doesn't necessarily mean a specific organization, or "configuration." In choice (D) again, this is too specific: symmetry is a specific, balanced type of organization, which doesn't necessarily follow an "abundance" of life forms. In choice (E), "dimension" implies a measurement, or aspect, of something, but an aspect of life forms doesn't correspond to an "abundance."

6. E

Difficulty: Medium

If Henry goes "beyond specific facts" and speculates "about general principles," then what is he good at?

The key here is to be able to find a word that means "going beyond specific facts and speculating about general principals." Henry enjoys that and therefore is a talented *abstract thinker*.

In choice (A), a dogmatist is someone who expresses one specific dogma, or authoritative principle, and therefore probably doesn't "speculate" much. In choice (B), a consultant gives expert advice, but it doesn't necessarily involve "general principles." In choice (C), while Henry could be a "prodigy," or someone with exceptional talents or powers, the adjective has nothing to do with "specific facts" or "general principles." In choice (D), a "materialist" believes that worldly possessions constitute the greatest good in life—which is out of the scope of the sentence and particularly doesn't have much to do with biology. Choice (E) matches your prediction nicely.

7. A

Difficulty: High

What traits characterize wetlands? By nature they become flooded with water.

The hot words "only to become" indicate that although wetlands may "dry out" during the summer, they become the opposite of "dry" during the other seasons. A good prediction is "flooded" or "wet." It is not necessary to know the meaning of "ephemeral" to deduce the meaning of the word in the blank, but it is helpful to know that it means "fleeting" or "lasting only a short time."

Choice (A) is the credited answer; it means "flooded." In choice (B), the location of the wetlands does not shift and so they do not become "situated" or positioned elsewhere when the seasons change. In choice (C), although rainfall that returns with the wet seasons may "rejuvenate" or restore plant life, this is too charged a word to use. The sentence is discussing the state of the wetlands as being dry or wet; not the consequences of the environment receiving rainfall. In choice (D), if the wetlands dry out most summers, what would they be "supplanted" or replaced with during the other seasons? They become flooded with water, not replaced by something else. In choice (E), this word is in some ways the opposite of the prediction; rather than becoming filled with water, "excavated" means the

wetlands would be hollowed out or dug out.

8. E

Difficulty: High

The thesis was rejected because it lacked solid evidence. If it lacked significant results then was it based on guesses or facts? For the second blank, what kind of evidence is based on "tested results?"

A good prediction for the first blank is "guesses" or "theory" because a thesis is likely to be rejected if it is based on speculation. For the second blank, choose a word such as "observed" or "investigated."

In choice (A), *induction* or reasoning from examples is the opposite of the prediction. *Diminutively* or "tiny" is out of scope. In choice (B), *experimentation* can lead to solid conclusions. "Pragmatically" or "practically" would fit but eliminate based on the first blank. Eliminate choice (C) because of the second blank; the sentence does not discuss public revenue. In choice (D), *bombast* means that his language was too rhetorical or flowery. *Theoretically* or "speculatively" is the opposite of the prediction for the second blank. Choice (E) is the correct answer.

9. A

Difficulty: Medium

Common connotations of the word may not apply in every context, so you'll need to compare the tone or connotation of each choice with this particular passage.

Be aware that Vocab-in-Context questions usually test *secondary* meanings of words, rather than their most common meanings.

The opening sentence of the passage describes the combination of two events: Christmas Day and the narrator's birthday. Since the narrator never indicates that this union is particularly surprising, it is likely that the cited word is simply being used to refer to a simultaneous occurrence of two events.

Choice (A) is a good match for your prediction. Choice (B) is closer to the primary definition of "coincidence," and it is too strong to match the passage's context. Choice (C) also captures the primary definition of "coincidence," but it is not a good match for the text itself. Choice (D), fate is not mentioned in the passage. In choice (E), the word "quirky" suggests an unexpectedness that doesn't make sense in the context of this passage.

10. C

Difficulty: Medium

The correct answer must fit the context *and* express a meaning of the cited word. Watch out for choices that meet one of these criteria but not the other!

When a passage suggests that some sort of change has taken place, thinking about that change may help you identify the correct choice.

Make a connection back to the opening sentence, where the narrator suggests that his feelings about the timing of his birthday have changed. Although the coincidence caused him unhappiness as a child, he now feels that it enables him to "evade a birthday"s inane pageantry." This phrasing suggests that the author is using the word "cover" to say that Christmas is able to conceal his birthday, allowing him to avoid "pageantry" that may be insincere.

In choice (A), this definition does not make sense in the context. In choice (B), while this choice captures the author's meaning, it does not match the cited word. Choice (C) is a great match for your prediction. In choice (D), this is one definition of the word, but it does not fit the context of the passage. In choice (E), this definition is close, but it implies a change in one's appearance that makes no sense in this context.

11. A

Difficulty: Low

Remember that Inference questions do not ask you to stray far from the text when drawing a conclusion.

When evaluating the implications of an author's description, think about what particular aspects of the description are relevant in the context.

The author states that sloths move from branch to branch "almost imperceptibly," implying that their movements are so slow or gradual that they're difficult to notice or detect.

Choice (A) is a good fit for your prediction. Choice (B) is out of scope; the author does not indicate whether or not such slowness is intentional, only that sloths "tend" to move slowly. Choice (C) is out of scope; the author does not discuss whether or not sloths rely upon their slowness or stealth to survive. Choice (D) is distortion; the author never states that sloths are *unable* to move faster. Choice (E) is extreme; although the passage states that sloths are "rarely sighted," it does not go so far as to suggest that they are *impossible* to observe.

12. C

Difficulty: Medium

Pay careful attention to the structure of the passage. Since lack of speed and a tendency to hang upside down are presented as two separate points in the passage, be sure to identify what they are points *about*.

Rather than answering Detail questions from memory, always use the clues provided in the question to guide you through the text.

The author says that some of the sloth's characteristics "seem to run counter to the instincts displayed by almost all wild animals." Two such characteristics are discussed: lack of speed and a tendency to hang upside down. The correct choice will note that these are differences between sloths and almost all other wild animals.

Choice (A) is extreme; although the author suggests that these characteristics distinguish sloths from "almost all" other wild animals, this statement is too strong for the text. Choice (B) is distortion; the author never states why sloths were "long mistaken for a species of monkey." Choice (C) is a good match for your prediction. Choice (D) is an irrelevant detail; the passage says that sloths do these things upside down, but it does not suggests that this is detrimental to them. Choice (E) is out of scope; the passage does not describe sloths as vulnerable to predators.

13. A

Difficulty: Medium

This question doesn't refer to a specific part of the passage, but nevertheless you should make sure the answer choice you select is supported by the text.

Wrong answer choices will appear in Passage 2 only, both passages, or neither; only one answer choice makes an appearance in Passage 1 alone. Work through the choices to find it.

Choice (A) is a good choice; only Passage 1 uses the word "you" to speak to the reader directly. Choice (B) is an irrelevant detail; this example is found in Passage 2 but not Passage 1. Choice (C) is distortion; this example occurs in both passages. Choice (D) is an irrelevant detail; this example is found in Passage 2 but not Passage 1. Choice (E) is extreme; neither passage is guilty of a *vicious* attack; both are fairly calm.

14. B

Difficulty: Medium

Go back to the passage and read the quoted sentence and the one before it, for context. Although this is an Inference question, the correct choice should still stick close to the argument found in these sentences.

The clause following the quoted one finishes the thought by saying, "none of them is truly unique to the human species," so predict that the author believes such qualities are good to have, but they are not unique as some claim them to be.

Choice (A) is an opposite; in fact, the author is saying that these traits do not uniquely define human beings. Choice (B) is a good choice that matches your prediction closely. Choice (C) is distortion; the author is only arguing that other animals share these characteristics, not that they have *no survival value*. Choice (D) is an opposite; the following sentences go on to describe the author's belief that language use distinguishes humans from other animals. Choice (E) is out of scope; the author never discusses how well humans would cope without the adaptations they currently have.

15. B

Difficulty: Low

Go back to the original sentence, cross out the quoted word, and try to find another word or phrase that fills in the blank and preserves the author's original meaning. This should form the basis of your prediction.

The sentence is essentially saying that these noises function as, or at least assist in, communication; find the answer choice that agrees with this idea.

Choice (A) is out of scope; this is one definition of "serve," but it makes no sense in the context of the original sentence. Choice (B) is a good pick; the noises *help* animals to communicate. Choice (C) is out of scope; again, an alternate definition of "serve" that does not fit this context. Choice (D) is distortion; this is a bit closer to the correct meaning, but it still doesn't quite fit when plugged back into the original sentence. Choice (E) is out of scope; this choice makes no sense in the original context.

16. E

Difficulty: Medium

Go back to the sentence in question and reread it; make sure you understand the author's tone and know what the material within the quotation marks is before you make your prediction.

The phrase "language acquisition device" seems to be some sort of linguistic jargon, so predict that the author is using the quotation marks as an efficient way of introducing the term.

Choice (A) is out of scope; the author gives no indication of being sarcastic in this passage. Choice (B) is out of scope; the context makes clear that he is not directly quoting any particular source. Choice (C) is distortion; although the quotation marks do draw attention, nothing in the passage suggests that this phrase is particularly *crucial* to the author's argument. Choice (D) is distortion; nothing about the tone of the sentence suggests that the author disagrees with this piece of terminology. Choice (E) is a good match for your prediction.

17. A

Difficulty: Medium

Go back to the passage and read the entire sentence; it is always easier to make an accurate prediction about the author's meaning when you can place his words in the context of a broader argument.

The author here is contrasting the idea of language as an "ingenious invention" with the idea of it as a "genetic birthright," suggesting that it is a gift of our genes rather than a product of our labor and wit. Find the answer choice that best fits this paraphrase.

Choice (A) is a good match for the author's intended meaning. Choice (B) is an opposite; the author is in fact arguing that language is unique to the human species. Choice (C) is out of scope; the author never makes an argument that humans *deserve* language or discusses anyone *desiring* it. Choice (D) is an opposite; the actual argument is that language is a natural product of the way the human brain works. Choice (E) is an irrelevant detail; the reference to culture would be more appropriate for Passage 2, but it makes little sense even in that passage's context.

18. D

Difficulty: Medium

Go back to both of the sentences in question and examine how the references fit into the surrounding argument. Ask yourself what is common or similar between the two usages.

Both authors gently suggest that their general line of thought is supported by professional researchers in their respective fields; predict that both authors are using the examples to add academic weight to their reasoning.

Choice (A) is out of scope; there is no evidence that either passage takes a negative tone towards the researchers. Choice (B) is out of scope; again, there is no evidence that either author considers the academics to be *incorrect*. Choice (C) is out of scope; neither author claims to actually be a researcher in these fields. Choice (D) is a good match for your prediction. Choice (E) is distortion; this choice really only fits for the anthropologists, whereas linguists are devoted only to the systematic study of language itself.

19. E

Difficulty: Medium

Reread the sentence in question again and try to determine the author's tone towards his subject matter. In a question like this, a good grasp of the author's intended tone can be a big help in making an accurate prediction.

The author's tone appears to be fairly straightforward in giving the term the founding fathers used for political parties; predict that the author is simply mentioning a historical term.

Choice (A) is out of scope; the author never gives any indication that the word is *misunderstood*. Choice (B) is extreme; the author's tone is fairly neutral towards his subject matter. Choice (C) is extreme; again, the author's tone is not particularly negative. Choice (D) is out of scope; the tone is accurate, but the author never directly refers to a *particular document*. Choice (E) is a good fit for your prediction.

20. B

Difficulty: Medium

Although the answer choices do not contain content from the passage, you should still refer to the content mentioned in the question stem to help you figure out the main point of the question.

From the passage, some founding fathers would likely be "appalled" at Americans" easy acceptance of the two-party system. Look for an answer choice that provides an example of this idea.

- Choice (A) is out of scope; this example does not really apply to any of the passage's points. Choice (B) is a good fit

for your prediction. Choice (C) is an irrelevant detail; this might be applicable to the "tribal ancestors" mentioned later in the passage, but not the founding fathers. Choice (D) is an irrelevant detail; again, this might apply to other parts of the passage, but not the part concerning the framers of the Constitution. Choice (E) is out of scope; this does not really have anything to do with the passage.

21. D

Difficulty: Medium

This question does not refer to any part of a passage directly, but you should remember that language is discussed in the second passage only briefly. Your prediction should agree with both the language content in Passage 2 and the general assumptions of Passage 1.

Passage 2 mentions language as a way of identifying friendly members of one's own group; although this particular issue is not raised in Passage 1, you can make a more general prediction about the adaptative benefits of language.

Choice (A) is an irrelevant detail; this really only applies to the author of Passage 1. Choice (B) is an irrelevant detail; this could work for the author of Passage 2, but not Passage 1. Choice (C) is out of scope; this is not mentioned anywhere in Passage 2 and directly contradicts Passage 1. Choice (D) is a good generalization that matches your prediction well. Choice (E) is an irrelevant detail; the author of Passage 1 might agree with this, but it is not very relevant to anything in Passage 2.

22. C

Difficulty: High

In order to make an accurate prediction, you need a good grasp of the specific section cited for Passage 2 as well as the general claims of Passage 1. If you have highlighted or summarized each passage's main points, it should only take you a few seconds to refamiliarize yourself with the major arguments in Passage 1.

The author of Passage 2 is promoting the power of human intelligence, whereas the author of Passage 1 generally believes that our estimation of our own intelligence is inflated by the ease with which we communicate. Predict that the correct answer choice will take both of these viewpoints into account.

Choice (A) is distortion; the author of Passage 1 asserts himself that only humans are capable of language, so it is unlikely that he would consider a similar assertion *unfair*. Choice (B) is an opposite; the author of Passage 1 argues that language is actually the distinguishing factor between humans and other animals. Choice (C) is a good fit for your prediction. Choice (D) is out of scope; such an opinion is not within the bounds of the arguments in Passage 1, and it misinterprets the point being made in Passage 2. Choice (E) is an irrelevant detail; it is actually the author of Passage 2 who mentions social psychology, not the author of Passage 1.

23. E

Difficulty: High

Note the line numbers in question and reread the entire sentence, not just the quoted material, to get a good idea of the author's complete thought. Once you have his entire point in mind, it will be easier to assess the function of that one particular phrase.

Here, the author is making a comparison between humans and these other mammals, but he qualifies his statement by noting that human behavior is also more complex. Predict that the correct answer choice involves this compromise.

Choice (A) is an opposite; since the author is making this comparison himself, it seems unlikely that he would consider it *preposterous*. Choice (B) is an irrelevant detail; this sort of thinking is more in line with the author of Passage 1, not Passage 2. Choice (C) is distortion; the author of Passage 2 never asserts that the human social structure is *weaker* than other animals'. Choice (D) is out of scope; there is nothing in Passage 2 to suggest this. Choice (E) is the best match for your prediction.

24. A

Difficulty: High

This question relies on your knowledge of the main ideas in each passage, so if you have those written down already it will help you to briefly go over them before formulating a prediction. If you're having trouble making a decision, you can always skim the passages again to see if they seem to contradict a potential answer choice.

The first author tends to insist that human intelligence is partially an illusion arising from the effectiveness of our communication, while the second author assumes the more conventional belief that humans are far more intelligent than all other animals. Expect the correct answer

choice to hinge on this distinction.

Choice (A) is a good match for your prediction. Choice (B) is an irrelevant detail; this choice partially agrees with points in Passage 1 but these arguments are wholly irrelevant to the topics discussed in Passage 2. Choice (C) is out of scope; neither passage focuses on the relative influences of society and genetics on intelligence. Choice (D) is an opposite; this choice directly contradicts an argument made by the first author and distorts the arguments of the second author. Choice (E) is out of scope; neither passage is really concerned with humanity's moral failings or the survival of human society.

SECTION 6

1. B

Difficulty: Medium

Strategic Advice: Most people find it easier to work with negative exponents if they are written as fractions. Remember that a rational function is undefined when its denominator equals zero. Can any part of $f(x)$ be undefined?

Getting to the Answer:

$$f(x) = x^{-3} + x^3 = \frac{1}{x^3} + x^3$$

$\frac{1}{x^3}$ is undefined when $x^3 = 0$, that is, when $x = 0$.

Therefore, $f(x)$ is undefined when $x = 0$.

2. B

Difficulty: Medium

Strategic Advice: The union of two sets consists of all the elements that are in either or both sets. The intersection of two sets consists of the elements that the sets have in common. Don't forget that you're looking for the difference between the number of elements in the union and the intersection, not just the number of elements in the union or the intersection.

Getting to the Answer:

The union of these sets contains the letters A, E, I, O, U, B, C, and D. This is 8 elements.

The intersection contains the letters A and E. This is 2 elements.

$8 - 2 = 6$

3. E

Difficulty: Medium

Strategic Advice: For Logic problems, be sure to know the difference between what may be true and what must be true.

Getting to the Answer:

According to the list, Fruits 1 and 4 must be apples.

Fruit 7 may be an apple.

4. D

Difficulty: Medium

Strategic Advice: Use the slope formula to find the missing coordinate.

Getting to the Answer:

$$m = \frac{y_2 - y_1}{x_2 - x_1}$$

$$-\frac{5}{12} = \frac{z - (-3)}{-7 - 5}$$

$$-\frac{5}{12} = \frac{z + 3}{-12}$$

$$5 = z + 3$$

$$2 = z$$

5. C

Difficulty: Medium

Strategic Advice: Although this looks like a complicated problem, all you really have to do is plug the given information into the given equation and solve for x.

Getting to the Answer:

The problem states that there were 160 turtles in the pond nine years after it was discovered, so $n = 160$ and $t = 9$.

$$160 = (x)2^{\frac{9}{3}} = (x)2^3 = 8x$$

$$20 = x$$

So there were 20 turtles in the pond the year it was discovered.

6. C

Difficulty: Medium

Strategic Advice: The graph of $c(x)$ crosses the x-axis when $c(x)$ equals 0. You can either set $c(x)$ equal to zero and see how many values of x are solutions or just sketch the graph and observe the number of times it crosses the x-axis.

Getting to the Answer:

$$x^2 - 6 = 0$$

$$x^2 = 6$$

$$x = \pm \sqrt{6}, \text{ so the graph crosses the } x\text{-axis twice.}$$

7. C

Difficulty: Medium

Strategic Advice: See what information you can glean from the graph. What should the slope of the line be like? Where would the y-intercept be?

Getting to the Answer:

Because the position of the dots on the graph increases along the y-axis slightly faster than it increases along the x-axis, the slope of the graph must be slightly greater than 1. Although it is difficult to locate the y-intercept precisely, it must certainly be negative. Each of these pieces of information allows you to rule out some of the possible answers, leaving only one, $y = 1.3x - 3$.

8. A

Difficulty: High

Strategic Advice: What geometry fact can you use to get a, b, and c in the same equation? The fact that the interior angles of a triangle add up to 180 degrees. Figure out what each angle of the triangle is in terms of a, b, or c, then set up an equation and solve for $a - b$.

Getting to the Answer:

The three interior angles of the triangle are $180 - a$ (since a is supplementary to the interior angle), b (since b is vertical to the interior angle), and $c = 50$. Therefore:

$$180 - a + b + 50 = 180$$

$$-a + b = -50$$

$$a - b = 50$$

9. $\frac{7}{5}$

Difficulty: Low

Strategic Advice: Whenever you are given two fractions which are equal to each other, think of cross multiplying.

Getting to the Answer:

$10q = 14$

$q = \dfrac{14}{10} = \dfrac{7}{5}$

10. 1,300

Difficulty: Medium

Strategic Advice: Think about what you can deduce from the given information to fill in the blanks. You can choose any row or column with 2 of the 3 numbers present to start.

Getting to the Answer:

Total − large = small

$5,000 − 3,200 = 1,800$

Total small − blue small = red small

$1,800 − 1,000 = 800$

red small + red large = total red

$800 + 500 = 1,300$

11. 4

Difficulty: Medium

Strategic Advice: This type of problem is a good candidate for picking numbers.

Getting to the Answer:

Pick two prime numbers greater than two such as 3 and 5. Multiply them to get p or 15. Factoring 15 only gives us four factors (1, 3, 5, 15), so our answer is 4.

12. 44

Difficulty: Medium

Strategic Advice: Don't be afraid to draw a diagram if you are not given one. It usually helps make a complicated problem much simpler.

Getting to the Answer:

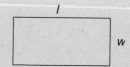

If l and w are integers, only 5 and 17 fit so that

$5 \times 17 = 85$

So the perimeter is

$5 + 5 + 17 + 17 = 44$

13. 1936

Difficulty: Medium

Strategic Advice: You are given an equation that describes the population of the town in terms of the years that have passed since 1900. Plug the given population into the equation for n, then solve for t. Remember that the question asks for the year the population will reach 7,680, not just t. If you have trouble working with this equation, you can also make a chart of the year and the population, doubling every six years until you reach 7,680. This is rather time-consuming.

Getting to the Answer:

$7,680 = (120)2^{\frac{t}{6}}$

$64 = 2^{\frac{t}{6}}$

$2^6 = 2^{\frac{t}{6}}$

$6 = \dfrac{t}{6}$

$36 = t$ (years since 1900)

$1900 + 36 = 1936$

14. 85

Difficulty: Medium

Strategic Advice: To solve this problem, you only need to remember two pieces of information—the number of degrees in a quadrilateral and the number of degrees in a straight line. Once you have these facts in mind, the solution is fairly straightforward.

Getting to the Answer:

The 75° angle and the unlabeled angle of the quadrilateral form a straight line, so their measures must sum to 180. Thus, the unlabeled angle must be

$180 − 75 = 105°$

The angles of a quadrilateral sum to 360°, so

$130 + 40 + 105 + x = 360$

$x = 360 − 130 − 40 − 105 = 85$

15. 6.1

Difficulty: Medium

Strategic Advice: Don't forget to use the distributive property when you have a sum of values multiplied by one number.

KAPLAN

Test Prep and Admissions

Getting to the Answer:

$\frac{1}{10}(30x^3 + 20x^2 + 10x + 1) = 3x^3 + 2x^2 + 1x + \frac{1}{10}$

so $a = 3, b = 2, c = 1, d = \frac{1}{10}$

Then, $3 + 2 + 1 + 0.1 = 6.1$

16. 4

Difficulty: Medium

Strategic Advice: Don't get confused if a diagram gives you too much information.

Getting to the Answer: The area of any quadrilateral is base times height, so use the coordinates to find the base and height.

$A = bh$

$b = r + 2$

$h = r$

Now substitute and solve:

$r(r + 2) = 24$

$r^2 + 2r = 24$

$r^2 + 2r - 24 = 0$

$(r + 6)(r - 4) = 0$

$r = -6$ or $r = 4$

Since r has to be positive according to the diagram, only 4 works.

17. 19

Difficulty: High

Strategic Advice: Don't let yourself get psyched out by the fact that a question is phrased to sound difficult and occurs late in a section. All this is asking is what number divides into 23 with a remainder of 4?

Getting to the Answer:

If the remainder is 4, that means w divides with no remainder into $23 - 4 = 19$. Only one number divides 19, itself. So $w = 19$. This makes sense, since $23 \div 19 = 1$ remainder 4.

18. 320

Difficulty: High

Strategic Advice: Take a complicated problem like this one

step at a time. Keep the ultimate end point in your head, and work towards it carefully.

Getting to the Answer:

From the problem we know that it costs an extra $45 to go 200 miles when compared to 50 miles. Thus, it costs $45 to travel an extra 150 miles and the additional charge is $15 for every 50 miles.

To travel 450 miles, one needs to go 400 miles more than in the first journey.

$\frac{400}{50} = 8$ and $8 \times \$15 = \$120$ and $\$200 + \$120 = \$320$

SECTION 7

1. C

Difficulty: Low

If you wanted to sell something that was "faded" and "dirty," what might you do to make it more attractive to potential buyers?

The words "Before he could even hope to sell" indicate that because the furniture was "faded" and "dirty," or essentially unattractive, it would be difficult to sell. Thus, the blank must describe an action that would eliminate those unattractive qualities, such as *restoration*.

In choice (A), *requisitioning*, or formally demanding something, would not necessarily make the furniture less faded and dirty. In choice (B), similarly, *enlarging* the furniture would not necessarily make it more attractive to a buyer. Choice (C) is a perfect match for your prediction. In choice (D), one could probably not sell furniture that had been *demolished*. While choice (E) may be tempting, *relocating* faded and dirty furniture would not necessarily make it easier to sell.

2. A

Difficulty: Low

If he had been "playing vigorously with his friends throughout the day," then most likely he was not too ill to attend class.

The words "without the slightest indication of illness" suggest the student said he missed class due to illness. If his teacher had seen him "playing vigorously with his friends throughout the day," then his absence would probably have seemed *inexcusable*, a good prediction for the blank.

Choice (A) is a good fit for your prediction. In choice (B), if the teacher was aware of his absence from class, then it could not have been done secretly. In choice (C), nothing in the sentence indicates that the student was frequently, or *indefatigably*, absent. In choice (D), an absence from class could not really be deemed all-inclusive. In choice (E), an absence from class would not have been seen as *correcting* anything because he had been playing with his friends all day.

3. B

Difficulty: Medium

The words "was merely" and "has become" signal that the second blank will build on or be stronger than the first.

The words "more bewilderment" are key here, as they indicate the first blank describes some degree of confusion. And if a manuscript was considered "mysterious" when it was originally discovered, then "years of fruitless research and more bewilderment" would not have made it any more understandable. Indeed, if the manuscript had been "merely" confusing at first, then after years of unsuccessful attempts to determine its meaning it would have seemed far more unexplainable. *Confusing* and *unexplainable* are great predictions for the blanks.

In choice (A), these words do not describe a characteristic that has become more pronounced over time, as something that is *dignified* would not necessarily become *mystifying* after years of unsuccessful research. Choice (B) is a great fit for your prediction. In choice (C), again, these words do not describe varying degrees of the same thing, as something that was *eccentric* or unconventional at first would not necessarily become emotionless after years of confusion. In choice (D), years of "fruitless research and more bewilderment" would not make something *intriguing* more *reasonable*. In choice (E), something mysterious would probably not be considered "merely logical."

4. C

Difficulty: Medium

"Although" signals the sentence will describe a contrast.

Start with the first blank; if whatever Ricardo did regarding a career in journalism was done "vigorously," or with great energy, then he must have been going after such a career. Moving on to the second blank, if his feelings here must

contrast with the actions described by the first blank, then he must have felt he did lack the "initiative necessary to enter the newspaper business." In other words, he "could not" have *prevented* himself from feeling this way, despite the initiative he'd shown. *Gone after* and *prevented* are good predictions for the blanks.

In choice (A), these words do not create the necessary contrast in the sentence. In choice (B), one cannot really undermine or *subvert* a feeling, and it doesn't make much sense to say Ricardo *escaped* a career in journalism. Choice (C) is a great fit for your prediction. In choice (D), again, these words create no contrast in the sentence, nor can one "vigorously" *ignore* something. In choice (E), once again, these words don't create a contrast, nor do they make much sense in the sentence.

5. B

Difficulty: Medium

The word "because" indicates that what follows provides a description of the nickname of Tom's dog. Thus, the behavior described will relate to the dog's nickname.

What kind of a dog would chase harmless puppies? The dog must be a "bully" or a "troublemaker." Look for a word that fits this prediction.

In choice (A), the dog does not necessarily make a mess of things. Choice (B) is the credited answer; "ruffians" are lawless, tough, violent hooligans. In choice (C), if the dog were described as being incessant or persistent this would work. In choice (D), if the dog were small and chased after larger dogs it would be daring, but all we are told is that the dog is aggressive. In choice (E), a "naysayer" is a person who has a negative or pessimistic view, or opposes or denies something. The word does have a negative connotation but it does not match the prediction.

6. C

Difficulty: High

It may be easier to eliminate based on the second blank. What type of a melancholy songs are sung at funerals?

The first blank must be negative because the "long, wailing" songs sung are not excessive but "cathartic." You don't need to know that "cathartic" means "emotional release" to figure out that a good prediction for the first blank would be "dismal" or "mournful."

Eliminate choice (A) based on the second blank; "jingles" are upbeat simple rhymes or ditties. In choice (B), "lullabies"

are soothing songs and not are not sung at funerals. For the first blank, the words "excessively inchoate" or "excessively undeveloped" contradict each other. Choice (C) is the credited answer. A *dirge* is a song of mourning and *lugubrious* means mournful. In choice (D), although a *ballad* is a song telling a story, eliminate based on "facetious" as this word means "intended to be amusing" and is the opposite of the prediction. In choice (E), *eulogy* is a piece of praise and may be spoken at a funeral, but *sprightly* or "lively or perky" does not match the prediction for the first blank.

Questions 7–19

This passage introduces us to Randolph Meyer, a TV talk show host whose program has just been cancelled. It describes the thoughts that run through his head shortly after he learns of the termination of his show. In these thoughts, where Meyer's struggles with a young network president are brought to light, a number of broader conflicts are addressed, such as the conflict between older and younger generations, traditional versus nontraditional thought, and the internal conflicts and doubts common to everyone. Through this description we are able to get a good sense of Randolph's true character and a better understanding of his plight.

7. D

Difficulty: Low

Do you normally refer to yourself by name when describing the personal events of your day?

In any question that asks you about a narrator, your first action should be to identify whether the passage was written in the first, second, or third person point of view. Recognizing this will help you to cut through the choices and get straight to the answer.

The consistent use of the pronoun "he" throughout this passage indicates that it was written in the third person; in other words, it was narrated by someone other than the characters referenced. Look for the choice that best describes who that someone might be.

Choice (A) is out of scope; it makes no sense that Randolph would refer to himself in the third person throughout the passage. Choice (B) is out of scope; this choice does not make sense, either. Carver would not constantly refer to

himself in third person. Choice (C) is distortion; sure it's possible that the narrator is a colleague of Randolph and Abel, but there is nothing in the passage to prove it. Choice (D) is the correct answer. The narrator's insight into Randolph and his thoughts indicates an *intimate knowledge* of the character. Choice (E) is an opposite; an observer who was not familiar with Randolph could not possibly have been able to describe the character and his thoughts so well.

8. C

Difficulty: Medium

According to the passage, when did Randolph feel this neglect started?

When you are asked to make an inference about a character's belief on a subject, your best approach is examine the passage's details that discuss his point of view.

In lines 24–27, the narrator states that the intentional neglect of the show was apparent to Randolph from the day Carver was hired. Select the choice that best explains what this suggests.

Choice (A) is an opposite; Randolph does not believe he is responsible for the cancellation. Choice (B) is extreme; the passage offers nothing to support this extreme statement. Choice (C) is a match. The fact Randolph sensed the network started to neglect his show soon after Carver was hired suggests that Carver wanted to cancel the show from his hiring. Choice (D) is distortion; the ageist reference in line 40 does suggest that Randolph felt like a target of discrimination, but it in the passage, it is the show that was being neglected, not Randolph. Choice (E) is out of scope; the passage does suggest that Carver disliked Randolph's show, but from that you cannot infer he disliked Randolph.

9. C

Difficulty: Medium

What do these accolades and achievements directly imply about Randolph's ability to survive in the television industry?

A good approach to any function question is to first identify how the example or examples in question are connected to other parts of the passage, and then determine for what purpose the author would include such an example.

After Carver offers Randolph advice on how to survive in the television industry in lines 33–35, the narrator states that Randolph had "managed to not only survive but to thrive in the industry for five decades prior to Abel Carver's tenure," and then illustrates this by describing some of his numerous achievements. Choose the answer that best defines the function of this description with the passage.

Choice (A) is distortion; Randolph's celebrity status was established in the opening paragraphs of the passage. Choice (B) is a misused detail; Carver calls Randolph "our old man," but he never states that he's *too old to be a success*. Choice (C) is the best answer. The examples of Randolph's achievements primarily function to suggest that perhaps *he does not need advice on how to survive in television*. Choice (D) is an opposite; in light of these achievements, it seems odd that the show was cancelled. Choice (E) is out of scope; most of the achievements were probably garnered long before Carver offered Randolph his advice.

10. E

Difficulty: High

Randolph's "lordly grunt" accompanies the dismissal of Carver's advice. What specific things does he use to justify the dismissal of this advice, and what do they reveal?

Questions that ask you to make inferences about what lies behind a character's motives require an understanding of the origin of those motives.

Synonyms of "lordly" include *dignified* and *noble*. In the passage Randolph expels this "lordly grunt" after dismissing Carver's advice and reminding himself of his achievements as an entertainer. At the same time, this gesture displays Randolph's confidence in himself and his choices, as well as pride in his achievements. Look for the choice that sums that up into two adjectives.

Choice (A) is out of scope; Randolph is actually self-assured to a fault, and a dignified grunt does not imply *dread* in any way. Choice (B) is out of scope; Randolph does not come off as humorous or sarcastic within context of the words in question or the passage as a whole. Choice (C) is extreme; these words are just a bit too strong to accurately convey the gesture. Choice (D) is out of scope; neither doubt nor anger is conveyed by this gesture. Choice (E) is your answer. Randolph's need to bask in his achievements after he dismisses Carver's advice indicates both a sense of pride and a desire to reassure himself of his actions.

11. B

Difficulty: Medium

Think about the way Randolph would describe Carver, then apply your deduction to this question.

Questions that ask you to deduce the way a character would think or act require that you have a solid understanding of the details you are given in the passage, so you can successfully employ them in your reasoning.

Buzzwords or catchphrases such as "think outside the box," are essentially just witty or imaginative ways of saying very ordinary things. The fact that in line 27 the narrator mentions Carver as one who employs buzzwords is significant because it ties directly into Randolph's assessment of Carver's plan for the network and Carver himself—*Style Over Substance*." Therefore, Randolph probably views the use of a catchphrase in the same light— flashy for sake of being flashy. Look for a choice that best fits with this deduction.

Choice (A) is out of scope; there is nothing in the passage to suggest this. Choice (B) fits. Randolph would most likely consider the use of a catchphrase as pointless. Choice (C) is out of scope; Carver's business background is never discussed in the passage. Choice (D) is an opposite; to "think outside the box" basically means to be creative. Randolph does not consider Carver to be creative. Choice (E) is out of scope; there's nothing *cryptic* about the use of a clichéd catchphrase.

12. E

Difficulty: Medium

What was the nature of the doubts that filled Randolph's head in lines 75–97?

No assumptions need to be made when answering detail questions; the answer is stated somewhere in the text.

As stated in the third paragraph, Randolph was not surprised that the show was canceled because when Carver was hired he introduced a new course of action to save the failing network, which included a "target demographic" (line 52) that *Talk Night*'s viewers did not fall into. In lines 82–87, it is revealed that Randolph refused to accept any of Carver's suggestions for the show, or in other words, he did not follow Carver's plan. Find the choice that best summarizes this.

Choice (A) is an opposite; line 24 states that the show had "decent" ratings. Choice (B) is an opposite; as detailed in lines 52–56, Randolph believes this to be untrue. Choice (C) is an opposite; Randolph has "iconic stature," lines 102–103. Choice (D) is distortion; though it might be assumed from the passage that this is true, it would only be *one* of the reasons for the cancellation, not *the* reason for it. Choice (E) matches. Randolph's doubts in line 28 reveal that he believes the show was cancelled because he did not take any of Carver's suggestions (i.e., conform to his vision).

13. B

Difficulty: Low

Why do you think the author does not offer a specific "cable theme channel" with which to compare to CNS?

Contrasting is a technique used by authors to illustrate what is different about two subjects. As such, one can draw assumptions about the unknown qualities of one subject that has been contrasted with another whose qualities are apparent or described.

In line 53, the narrator contrasts "some cable theme channel" with CNS, which he described as "a genuine, one-of-a-kind network television institution, one of the first ever to broadcast over the country"'s airwaves." This contrast suggests that CNS is unique; "some cable theme channel" is not. Look for the choice that expresses this.

Choice (A) is an opposite; in the context of the passage, the contrast suggests the opposite. Choice (B) is correct. By contrasting CNS with "some cable theme channel" the author suggests "some cable theme channel" is one of many similar, unremarkable channels. Choice (C) is an opposite; a "theme" channel implies that its programming has a singular theme, such as sports. Choice (D) is an opposite; if this were true, the contrast would make no sense because in terms of networks, CNS was "one of the first ever to broadcast over the country's airwaves." Choice (E) is out of scope; this is not suggested anywhere in the passage.

14. E

Difficulty: Medium

In context, "lowest common denominator" is used to denote an audience of shallow values and intellect.

A common way to emphasize or illustrate a positive or negative quality of a character or subject in a passage is to use a contrast or comparison.

At the heart of this question is Randolph's belief that *Talk*

Night's "older and intellectual audience" fits with CNS's reputation and history (line 51). To emphasize this, CNS is contrasted with "Chrome," which is described as a network that "catered to the lowest common denominator." Look for the choice that is best expressed by this contrast.

Choice (A) is an opposite; Randolph believes that CNS should attract a *high caliber of viewer*. Choice (B) is an opposite; this choice contradicts the contrast between CNS and "Chrome." Choice (C) is distortion; this choice assumes the literal interpretation of "lowest common denominator." Choice (D) is out of scope; this detail is mentioned or implied in the passage. Choice (E) is correct; the statement that "Chrome" caters to the lowest common denominator suggests that its programs appeal to *a lowbrow viewer*.

15. D

Difficulty: High

Do you think Carver's decision to cancel *Talk Night* was a difficult one?

Hypothetical questions ask you to make assumptions based on details in the passage. Recognizing what the specific details help to illustrate or emphasize will guide you in your reasoning.

In the context of the passage, the person who demands respect is Carver, whose "selfishness and lack of professionalism" (lines 71–72) did not surprise Randolph. Look for the choice that contains a scenario that would most likely be expected from a person in possession of these qualities.

Choice (A) is an opposite; Carver was the one who cancelled Randolph's show, yet he did not take responsibility for his actions by personally breaking the news to Randolph. Choice (B) is an opposite; by definition, selfishness is marked by a disregard for others. Choice (C) is an opposite; this contradicts the quality of being unprofessional. Choice (D) is the correct answer. Besides being a selfish, unprofessional act, Carver's decision to not call is a direct reflection of his disregard for Randolph's emotions. Choice (E) is an opposite; such an action would be entirely unselfish.

16. C

Difficulty: Medium

The "situation" mentioned in the passage is the cancellation of *Talk Night*. What one word would Randolph probably use to describe this situation?

Understanding a word's function in context is an important clue to deciphering its meaning.

In lines 75–76, the narrator states that Randolph was "surprisingly calm" and he was unsure whether he had grasped "the true gravity of the situation." Here, "gravity" is a descriptive noun that relates the state of the "situation," which is the cancellation of Randolph's show. Look for the word that makes the most sense in context if you replace it with gravity.

Choice (A) is an opposite; this is not a light-hearted situation. Choice (B) is distortion; this is a synonym for an alternate meaning of gravity that makes no sense in context. Choice (C) is the best choice; it makes sense that Randolph's calmness made him wonder if he hadn't quite grasped the seriousness of his show's cancellation. Choice (D) makes no sense in context. Choice (E) is an opposite; the idea that the cancellation was meaningless to Randolph is the opposite of what is implied in context.

17. D

Difficulty: High

The passage states in line 104 that Randolph will forever be known as the "legendary host of *Talk Night*." Will this help or hurt Randolph in the future?

Many times the answer to a question is found directly in the details in which it is surrounded.

A paradox is an apparent contradiction that is nevertheless true. To understand the paradox of Randolph's iconic stature (his fame) you must first look to the surrounding details to find an apparent contradiction. Prior to the statement about the paradox, the passage states that Randolph "would love to find another job in TV, but he knew his hopes were probably slim." This seems to make no sense; a big television star should not have a problem finding a job in television. However, the reason for the statement's truth is detailed in lines 103–104: Randolph would forever be "Randolph Meyer, legendary host of *Talk Night*." No matter what he may do in the future, he will always carry the stigma of being the host of *Talk Night*. Look for the choice that best expresses the implications of this truth.

Choice (A) is an opposite; this is directly contradicted by line 104 which states that Randolph was "legendary." Choice (B) is out of scope; nothing in the passage suggests that his image will be tarnished from the cancellation. Choice (C) is a misused detail; this is not a paradox. Choice (D) is correct. The paradox of his iconic stature is that his

great success on *Talk Night* will actually probably keep him from succeeding again on television. Choice (E) is an opposite; lines 45–47 state Randolph had "numerous Emmys, achievement awards, and other various accolades that filled an entire wall of his office."

18. A

Difficulty: Medium

How could Randolph have possibly saved his show?

The details of a character's actions, besides describing what the character does, also offer insight to his or her motives and personality.

The answer to this question lies in the second-to-last paragraph. As Randolph begins to doubt himself for refusing to take any of Carver's suggestions, he reassures himself by stating that "I'd rather my show be cancelled than witness it turn into a shadow of its former self" (lines 89–91). However, this is tempered with the narrator's revelation in the very next sentences that Randolph "couldn't stomach the idea of Carver possibly being right" and "CNS"s ratings had measurably improved" since the hiring of Carver. Look for the choice that best describes the flaw suggested by these details.

Choice (A) is your answer. Randolph's obstinate refusal to take any of Carver's suggestions, especially after it was revealed that Carver's methods were successful, show Randolph to be *stubborn to a fault*. Choice (B) is extreme; it can perhaps be inferred that Randolph had the inability to trust Carver, but to say he had trusted no one is too extreme to be correct. Choice (C) is an opposite; a person guilty of making an "egotistical error" of judgment (lines 89–91) would probably not be considered *insecure*. Choice (D) is an opposite; in line 12 Randolph states he'd rather see the show "cancelled than witness it turn into a shadow of its former self." Choice (E) is distortion; line 31 states this is a trait of Carver, not Randolph.

19. E

Difficulty: Low

How is Randolph's excitement described in line 107?

The tone of the correct answer choice should reflect the tone of the detail or details in question.

Lines 107–108 of the passage state that Randolph felt the cancellation of *Talk Night* presented him with possibilities that sent a "bittersweet shiver of excitement throughout his entire being." In other words, his excitement was tempered by the emotions associated with the loss of his show. Look for the choice that best expresses this feeling.

Choice (A) is a distortion. Randolph's excitement is bittersweet. This description is too positive to be correct. Choice (B) is out of scope; nothing in the passage suggests Randolph was frightened. Choice (C) is an opposite; the description is contradictory to Randolph's excitement. Choice (D) is an opposite; Randolph thinking about perhaps writing a novel illustrates that he can comprehend life without *Talk Night*. Choice (E) is correct. Of the choices, *stimulating* fits best because it manages to convey Randolph's excitement without being too positive or negative in tone.

SECTION 8

1. D

Difficulty: Low

Strategic Advice: Don't do excess math. All you need to know to solve this problem is how to get the decimal point to move.

Getting to the Answer:

$$(.0013)x = \frac{0.013}{.0013} = 10$$

2. A

Difficulty: Low

Strategic Advice: Whenever you are given two angles of a triangle, you can determine the third.

Getting to the Answer:

For the top half:

$$30° + 90° + z° = 180°$$
$$z° = 60°$$

For the bottom half:

$$70° + 90° + y° = 180°$$
$$y° = 20°$$
$$20 + 60 = 80$$

3. D

Difficulty: Low

Strategic Advice: Read the stem carefully to translate the sentence into the correct equations.

Getting to the Answer:

$$t = s + 5$$
$$s = r - 3$$

When $r = 3$,

$$s = 0$$

So,

$$t = 0 + 5$$
$$t = 5$$

4. D

Difficulty: Medium

Strategic Advice: A question involving variables in both the stem and answer choices is a perfect candidate for pick numbers.

Getting to the Answer:

Let $a = 2$ and $b = 3$. So, $\dfrac{a}{b} = \dfrac{2}{3}$

(A) $2 > \dfrac{3}{2}$

(B) $\dfrac{3}{2} > \dfrac{2}{3}$

(C) $\dfrac{1}{\frac{3}{2}} = \dfrac{2}{3}$

(D) $\dfrac{2}{6} < \dfrac{2}{3}$

(E) $\dfrac{4}{3} > \dfrac{2}{3}$

5. E

Difficulty: Low

Strategic Advice: The y-intercept of a linear equation is the value of the equation when $x = 0$. You could put this equation into slope-intercept form, but it is easier to just plug 0 in for x.

Getting to the Answer:

$3y - 33x = 12$, put in $x = 0$ to get

$$3y = 12$$

$$y = 4$$

6. A

Difficulty: Medium

Strategic Advice: Even though there are only variables in the question, pick numbers would still be a great strategy to try here.

Getting to the Answer:

Pick 7 for your positive odd integer.

$(d - 1)(d - 2) = (7 - 1)(7 - 2) = (6)(5) = 30$. Too large. Try a smaller number.

$(d - 1)(d - 2) = (5 - 1)(5 - 2) = (4)(3) = 12$.

7. A

Difficulty: Medium

Strategic Advice: Whenever you see underlined text in a question, it usually indicates very important information. Each number can only satisfy *exactly* one of each of the conditions. This type of problem is easiest if you look at the answer choices and use process of elimination. First eliminate the answer choices that have none or more than one even number. Then eliminate the answer choices that have none or more than one multiple of three.

Getting to the Answer:

Eliminate choices (B), (C), and (E) since they all have more than one even number.

Eliminate choice (D) because it has has two multiples of 3.

(A) has one even number (10), one odd multiple of 3 (15), and one number that satisfies neither of the other two requirements, so choice (A) is the correct choice.

8. D

Difficulty: Medium

Strategic Advice: Even though this question uses the word "percent", you are never asked to find the actual percent itself. Set this problem up as a ratio to get the answer more quickly.

Getting to the Answer:

$$\frac{16 - 6}{6} = \frac{x - 12}{12}$$

$$\frac{10}{6} = \frac{x - 12}{12}$$

$$120 = 6(x - 12)$$

$$120 = 6x - 72$$

$$192 = 6x$$

$$32 = x$$

9. B

Difficulty: Low

Strategic Advice: Questions involving graphs are usually relatively straightforward. The graph itself contains all the information you need. If you just figure out what you are being asked to find and then pull the necessary information out of the graph, you'll be well on your way to solving this question.

Getting to the Answer:

Let's look at the four continents. Africa went from 200,000 cases in 1960 to 50,000 cases in 1970, which is $\frac{1}{4}$ of the number in 1960. Asia went from 150,000 cases in 1960 to 40,000 cases in 1970, a little more than $\frac{1}{4}$ of the 1960 number. Europe went from 50,000 cases in 1960 to around 5,000 cases in 1970, $\frac{1}{10}$ of the 1960 number. And finally, North America went from 60,000 cases in 1960 to 20,000 in 1970, $\frac{1}{3}$ of the 1960 number. Therefore, only Europe had in 1970 less than $\frac{1}{5}$ of the cases they had in 1960, making the answer choice (B).

10. E

Difficulty: Medium

Strategic Advice: Before you dive into a question, you should always make sure you know exactly what you are trying to solve for. Remember the formula:

$$\text{percent change} = \frac{\text{(actual change)}}{\text{(original amount)}} \times 100\%$$

Getting to the Answer:

Total cases in 1960 (in thousands): $200 + 150 + 50 + 60 = 460$

Total cases in 1970 (in thousands): $50 + 40 + 5 + 20 = 115$

Actual change $= 460 - 115 = 345$

Percent change $= \frac{345}{460} \times 100\% = 0.75 \times 100\%$

11. A

Difficulty: High

Strategic Advice: The key to most average questions is to know how to use the average formula.

Getting to the Answer:

"The average (arithmetic mean) of $a, b,$ and c is p"

translates to $\frac{a+b+c}{3} = p$.

"The average of $a, b, c,$ and d" translates to

$\frac{a+b+c+d}{4} = ?$

Solve the first equation for $a + b + c$:

$a + b + c = 3p$

Now plug this into the second equation:

$\frac{a+b+c+d}{4} = \frac{3p+d}{4}$, which is (A).

12. C

Difficulty: Medium

Strategic Advice: When the SAT presents measurements in different units, convert everything to the same unit of measure and pay attention to the question that is asked.

Getting to the Answer: First, convert miles per hour to miles per minute: to do this, divide by 60.

$\frac{4680}{60} = 78$, so the plane can travel 78 miles per minute.

Ten seconds is one sixth of a minute, so divide 78 by 6 to find the number of miles the plane can travel in 10

seconds: $\frac{78}{6} = 13$.

13. E

Difficulty: High

Strategic Advice: The SAT will never expect you to compute large sums, even if they assume you know how to use a calculator. Always look for the shortcut.

Getting to the Answer:

The sum will stay negative as long as you keep adding negative numbers. When will it start going positive? When the positives cancel out the negatives. In other words, -33 will cancel out $+33$, -32 will cancel out $+32$, and so forth. All the consecutive integers from -33 to $+33$ (there's 67 of them—don't forget 0!) will add to zero, and then adding the next integer, 34, will make the sum 34. So there will be 68 consecutive integers, or (E).

14. C

Difficulty: High

Strategic Advice: When extra information is given in the question stem, fill in what you know and work from there.

Getting to the Answer:

Fill in the information for one triangle. One half of the triangle forms a 5:12:13 triangle. Thus, the height is 12 and the

area of one triangle $= \frac{1}{2} \times 12 \times 10 = 60$

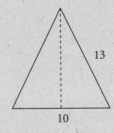

Since the parallelogram is made up of two triangles, the total area is $2 \times 60 = 24$

15. C

Difficulty: High

Strategic Advice: Don't get thrown off by complex equations and symbols you don't recognize. Once you get past the notation, this is a simple plug in problem.

Getting to the Answer:

$♠37♠ = \sqrt{37-1} = \sqrt{36} = 6$

$♠5♠ = \sqrt{(5-1)} = \sqrt{4} = 2$

$6 - 2 = 4$

16. C

Difficulty: High

Strategic Advice: Visualizing a 3–dimensional diagram can be difficult. Redraw this diagram if necessary. Be sure to label what you know as you work through the problem.

Getting to the Answer:

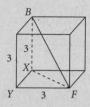

We're essentially trying to work out two Pythagorean Theorems, once for the $\overline{XF}$ base of the cube, and once again for $\overline{BF}$. Looking at the base of the cube, since $\overline{XY}$ and $\overline{YF}$ are both 3, the base forms a 45–45–90 right triangle with sides in the ratio of $x : x : x\sqrt{2}$. Therefore, the hypotenuse is $3\sqrt{2}$.

Now let's find $\overline{BF}$. This diagonal is a hypotenuse of a right triangle with legs of 3 and $3\sqrt{2}$, so let's apply the Pythagorean Theorem:

$$3^2 + (3\sqrt{2})^2 = \overline{BF}^2$$
$$9 + (9)(2) = \overline{BF}^2$$
$$9 + 18 = \overline{BF}^2$$
$$27 = \overline{BF}^2$$
$$\overline{BF} = \sqrt{27} = \sqrt{9}\sqrt{3} = 3\sqrt{3}$$

SECTION 9

1. B

Difficulty: Medium

Make sure that transition words and phrases correctly establish the relationship between the ideas they connect.

This sentence describes a cause (the Internet's enabling communication in a cost-effective way) and its effect (the Internet's usefulness). (B) correctly expresses this relationship. (A) and (D) reverse the cause and effect. (C) expresses a contrast that is inappropriate in context. In (E), the plural pronoun *they* does not agree with its singular antecedent, *the Internet*.

2. A

Difficulty: Medium

Being methodical about eliminating wrong answer choices will help you spot sentences that are correct as written.

This sentence contains no error. (B) is incorrect grammatical structure. (C), (D), and (E) are unnecessarily wordy.

3. D

Difficulty: Medium

The gerund (*-ing*) verb form can never be the main verb in a sentence.

This sentence is a fragment. (D) corrects it by replacing the gerund with a predicate verb form, *promises* (B) does not address the error. (C) is incorrect grammatical structure. (E) leaves the meaning of the sentence incomplete.

4. D

Difficulty: Medium

Look for the most concise choice that doesn't violate grammatical rules or the alter the sentence's original meaning. (D) expresses all of the meaning of the original sentence without introducing any additional errors. In (B), the use of both *Generally* and *mostly* is redundant. (C) is awkward and uses a plural verb, *are*, with a singular subject, *sleep*. (E) is idiomatically incorrect.

5. D

Difficulty: Medium

Items in a series or list must be presented in parallel form.

The women are becoming *specialists*, not *specialties*. (D) corrects the error; none of the other choices does so.

6. C

Difficulty: Medium

One way to correct a run-on sentence is to make one of the clauses subordinate. (C) corrects the run-on by making the second independent clause dependent. (B) is incorrect grammatical structure. (D) merely joins the clauses with *and*; while this is not technically a run-on, it is not considered good SAT style. (E) does not address the error.

7. B

Difficulty: Medium

Unless context makes it clear that the actions in a sentence take place at different times, verb tenses should remain consistent. (B) makes the verbs in the sentence consistently in the past tense. (C) introduces the passive voice unnecessarily. (D) is awkwardly constructed. (E) does not address the error.

8. C

Difficulty: High

Make sure transition words properly relate the ideas in the clauses they combine.

As written, this sentence tells us that *complex staging* is the reason that *Hamlet* and *Romeo and Juliet* are so frequently produced. (C) clarifies the relationship between these two ideas. In (B), *very complex staging* is *Among Shakespeare's most frequently produced plays*. (D) and (E) contain incorrect grammatical structure.

9. D

Difficulty: High

In a sentence with multiple errors, make sure your answer choice addresses them all.

You is the incorrect pronoun with *someone*, and the verb tenses here are inconsistent (D) corrects both errors. (B), (C), and (E) do not correct the pronoun error; (B) and (C) do not correct the verb tense inconsistency.

10. D

Difficulty: High

Make sure that any modifying phrases are correctly placed for the word(s) they are meant to modify.

As written, this sentence says that *his painting* was *Sent to Canada*. Both (D) and (E) correctly place *Jonathan* after the modifying phrase, but (E) is unnecessarily wordy. In (B), the introductory phrase modifies *experience*. In (C), it is *the subject* that was *Sent to Canada*.

11. C

Difficulty: Medium

A pronoun must have a clear, unambiguous antecedent.

As written, it is unclear whether *she* refers to *Jean Valentine* or her *daughter*. Both (B) and (C) clarify the pronoun's antecedent, but (B) is unnecessarily wordy. (D) and (E) do not address the error.

12. A

Difficulty: High

Expect to see between five and eight sentences that contain no errors.

This sentence is correct as written. (B), (C), (D), and (E) are grammatically incorrect. (D) fails to appropriately relate the ideas in the two clauses.

13. B

Difficulty: Low

Although the passive voice will not always be incorrect on the SAT, if a sentence can easily be made active, the correct answer choice will do so.

(B) makes the passive construction active. (C), (D), and (E) create sentence fragments.

14. D

Difficulty: High

When a sentence sets up a comparison, make sure logical things are being compared.

As written, this sentence compared *The bite pressure of wolves* to *German shepherds*. (D) corrects the comparison. (B) and (E) do not address the error. (C) uses a plural pronoun (*those*) to refer back to the singular noun *pressure*.

SAT PRACTICE TEST SEVEN ANSWER SHEET

Remove (or photocopy) the answer sheet, and use it to complete the practice test.

How to Take the Practice Tests

Each Practice Test includes eight scored multiple-choice sections and one essay. Keep in mind that on the actual SAT, there will be an additional multiple-choice section—the experimental section—that will not contribute to your score.

Once you start a Practice Test, don't stop until you've gone through all nine sections. Remember, you can review any questions within a section, but you may not go back or forward a section.

Good luck!

Start with number 1 for each section. If a section has fewer questions than answer spaces, leave the extra spaces blank.

Section One

Section One is the writing section's essay component.
Lined pages on which you will write your essay can be found in that section.

Section Two

1. Ⓐ Ⓑ Ⓒ Ⓓ Ⓔ
2. Ⓐ Ⓑ Ⓒ Ⓓ Ⓔ
3. Ⓐ Ⓑ Ⓒ Ⓓ Ⓔ
4. Ⓐ Ⓑ Ⓒ Ⓓ Ⓔ
5. Ⓐ Ⓑ Ⓒ Ⓓ Ⓔ
6. Ⓐ Ⓑ Ⓒ Ⓓ Ⓔ
7. Ⓐ Ⓑ Ⓒ Ⓓ Ⓔ
8. Ⓐ Ⓑ Ⓒ Ⓓ Ⓔ

9. Ⓐ Ⓑ Ⓒ Ⓓ Ⓔ
10. Ⓐ Ⓑ Ⓒ Ⓓ Ⓔ
11. Ⓐ Ⓑ Ⓒ Ⓓ Ⓔ
12. Ⓐ Ⓑ Ⓒ Ⓓ Ⓔ
13. Ⓐ Ⓑ Ⓒ Ⓓ Ⓔ
14. Ⓐ Ⓑ Ⓒ Ⓓ Ⓔ
15. Ⓐ Ⓑ Ⓒ Ⓓ Ⓔ
16. Ⓐ Ⓑ Ⓒ Ⓓ Ⓔ

17. Ⓐ Ⓑ Ⓒ Ⓓ Ⓔ
18. Ⓐ Ⓑ Ⓒ Ⓓ Ⓔ
19. Ⓐ Ⓑ Ⓒ Ⓓ Ⓔ
20. Ⓐ Ⓑ Ⓒ Ⓓ Ⓔ
21. Ⓐ Ⓑ Ⓒ Ⓓ Ⓔ
22. Ⓐ Ⓑ Ⓒ Ⓓ Ⓔ
23. Ⓐ Ⓑ Ⓒ Ⓓ Ⓔ
24. Ⓐ Ⓑ Ⓒ Ⓓ Ⓔ

☐ # right in Section Two

☐ # wrong in Section Two

Section Three

1. Ⓐ Ⓑ Ⓒ Ⓓ Ⓔ
2. Ⓐ Ⓑ Ⓒ Ⓓ Ⓔ
3. Ⓐ Ⓑ Ⓒ Ⓓ Ⓔ
4. Ⓐ Ⓑ Ⓒ Ⓓ Ⓔ
5. Ⓐ Ⓑ Ⓒ Ⓓ Ⓔ
6. Ⓐ Ⓑ Ⓒ Ⓓ Ⓔ
7. Ⓐ Ⓑ Ⓒ Ⓓ Ⓔ
8. Ⓐ Ⓑ Ⓒ Ⓓ Ⓔ

9. Ⓐ Ⓑ Ⓒ Ⓓ Ⓔ
10. Ⓐ Ⓑ Ⓒ Ⓓ Ⓔ
11. Ⓐ Ⓑ Ⓒ Ⓓ Ⓔ
12. Ⓐ Ⓑ Ⓒ Ⓓ Ⓔ
13. Ⓐ Ⓑ Ⓒ Ⓓ Ⓔ
14. Ⓐ Ⓑ Ⓒ Ⓓ Ⓔ
15. Ⓐ Ⓑ Ⓒ Ⓓ Ⓔ
16. Ⓐ Ⓑ Ⓒ Ⓓ Ⓔ

17. Ⓐ Ⓑ Ⓒ Ⓓ Ⓔ
18. Ⓐ Ⓑ Ⓒ Ⓓ Ⓔ
19. Ⓐ Ⓑ Ⓒ Ⓓ Ⓔ
20. Ⓐ Ⓑ Ⓒ Ⓓ Ⓔ

☐ # right in Section Three

☐ # wrong in Section Three

Section Four

1. Ⓐ Ⓑ Ⓒ Ⓓ Ⓔ   9. Ⓐ Ⓑ Ⓒ Ⓓ Ⓔ   17. Ⓐ Ⓑ Ⓒ Ⓓ Ⓔ
2. Ⓐ Ⓑ Ⓒ Ⓓ Ⓔ   10. Ⓐ Ⓑ Ⓒ Ⓓ Ⓔ   18. Ⓐ Ⓑ Ⓒ Ⓓ Ⓔ
3. Ⓐ Ⓑ Ⓒ Ⓓ Ⓔ   11. Ⓐ Ⓑ Ⓒ Ⓓ Ⓔ   19. Ⓐ Ⓑ Ⓒ Ⓓ Ⓔ
4. Ⓐ Ⓑ Ⓒ Ⓓ Ⓔ   12. Ⓐ Ⓑ Ⓒ Ⓓ Ⓔ   20. Ⓐ Ⓑ Ⓒ Ⓓ Ⓔ
5. Ⓐ Ⓑ Ⓒ Ⓓ Ⓔ   13. Ⓐ Ⓑ Ⓒ Ⓓ Ⓔ   21. Ⓐ Ⓑ Ⓒ Ⓓ Ⓔ
6. Ⓐ Ⓑ Ⓒ Ⓓ Ⓔ   14. Ⓐ Ⓑ Ⓒ Ⓓ Ⓔ   22. Ⓐ Ⓑ Ⓒ Ⓓ Ⓔ
7. Ⓐ Ⓑ Ⓒ Ⓓ Ⓔ   15. Ⓐ Ⓑ Ⓒ Ⓓ Ⓔ   23. Ⓐ Ⓑ Ⓒ Ⓓ Ⓔ
8. Ⓐ Ⓑ Ⓒ Ⓓ Ⓔ   16. Ⓐ Ⓑ Ⓒ Ⓓ Ⓔ   24. Ⓐ Ⓑ Ⓒ Ⓓ Ⓔ

right in Section Four

wrong in Section Four

Section Five

1. Ⓐ Ⓑ Ⓒ Ⓓ Ⓔ   9. Ⓐ Ⓑ Ⓒ Ⓓ Ⓔ   17. Ⓐ Ⓑ Ⓒ Ⓓ Ⓔ
2. Ⓐ Ⓑ Ⓒ Ⓓ Ⓔ   10. Ⓐ Ⓑ Ⓒ Ⓓ Ⓔ   18. Ⓐ Ⓑ Ⓒ Ⓓ Ⓔ
3. Ⓐ Ⓑ Ⓒ Ⓓ Ⓔ   11. Ⓐ Ⓑ Ⓒ Ⓓ Ⓔ
4. Ⓐ Ⓑ Ⓒ Ⓓ Ⓔ   12. Ⓐ Ⓑ Ⓒ Ⓓ Ⓔ
5. Ⓐ Ⓑ Ⓒ Ⓓ Ⓔ   13. Ⓐ Ⓑ Ⓒ Ⓓ Ⓔ
6. Ⓐ Ⓑ Ⓒ Ⓓ Ⓔ   14. Ⓐ Ⓑ Ⓒ Ⓓ Ⓔ
7. Ⓐ Ⓑ Ⓒ Ⓓ Ⓔ   15. Ⓐ Ⓑ Ⓒ Ⓓ Ⓔ
8. Ⓐ Ⓑ Ⓒ Ⓓ Ⓔ   16. Ⓐ Ⓑ Ⓒ Ⓓ Ⓔ

right in Section Five

wrong in Section Five

If section 5 of your test book contains math questions that are not multiple choice, continue to item 9 below. Otherwise, continue to item 9 above.

9.   10.   11.   12.   13.

14.   15.   16.   17.   18.

Remove (or photocopy) this answer sheet, and use it to complete the practice test.

Start with number 1 for each section. If a section has fewer questions than answer spaces, leave the extra spaces blank.

Section Six

1. Ⓐ Ⓑ Ⓒ Ⓓ Ⓔ	10. Ⓐ Ⓑ Ⓒ Ⓓ Ⓔ	19. Ⓐ Ⓑ Ⓒ Ⓓ Ⓔ	28. Ⓐ Ⓑ Ⓒ Ⓓ Ⓔ
2. Ⓐ Ⓑ Ⓒ Ⓓ Ⓔ	11. Ⓐ Ⓑ Ⓒ Ⓓ Ⓔ	20. Ⓐ Ⓑ Ⓒ Ⓓ Ⓔ	29. Ⓐ Ⓑ Ⓒ Ⓓ Ⓔ
3. Ⓐ Ⓑ Ⓒ Ⓓ Ⓔ	12. Ⓐ Ⓑ Ⓒ Ⓓ Ⓔ	21. Ⓐ Ⓑ Ⓒ Ⓓ Ⓔ	30. Ⓐ Ⓑ Ⓒ Ⓓ Ⓔ
4. Ⓐ Ⓑ Ⓒ Ⓓ Ⓔ	13. Ⓐ Ⓑ Ⓒ Ⓓ Ⓔ	22. Ⓐ Ⓑ Ⓒ Ⓓ Ⓔ	31. Ⓐ Ⓑ Ⓒ Ⓓ Ⓔ
5. Ⓐ Ⓑ Ⓒ Ⓓ Ⓔ	14. Ⓐ Ⓑ Ⓒ Ⓓ Ⓔ	23. Ⓐ Ⓑ Ⓒ Ⓓ Ⓔ	32. Ⓐ Ⓑ Ⓒ Ⓓ Ⓔ
6. Ⓐ Ⓑ Ⓒ Ⓓ Ⓔ	15. Ⓐ Ⓑ Ⓒ Ⓓ Ⓔ	24. Ⓐ Ⓑ Ⓒ Ⓓ Ⓔ	33. Ⓐ Ⓑ Ⓒ Ⓓ Ⓔ
7. Ⓐ Ⓑ Ⓒ Ⓓ Ⓔ	16. Ⓐ Ⓑ Ⓒ Ⓓ Ⓔ	25. Ⓐ Ⓑ Ⓒ Ⓓ Ⓔ	34 Ⓐ Ⓑ Ⓒ Ⓓ Ⓔ
8. Ⓐ Ⓑ Ⓒ Ⓓ Ⓔ	17. Ⓐ Ⓑ Ⓒ Ⓓ Ⓔ	26. Ⓐ Ⓑ Ⓒ Ⓓ Ⓔ	35. Ⓐ Ⓑ Ⓒ Ⓓ Ⓔ
9. Ⓐ Ⓑ Ⓒ Ⓓ Ⓔ	18. Ⓐ Ⓑ Ⓒ Ⓓ Ⓔ	27. Ⓐ Ⓑ Ⓒ Ⓓ Ⓔ	

☐ # right in Section Six

☐ # wrong in Section Six

Section Seven

1. Ⓐ Ⓑ Ⓒ Ⓓ Ⓔ	9. Ⓐ Ⓑ Ⓒ Ⓓ Ⓔ	17. Ⓐ Ⓑ Ⓒ Ⓓ Ⓔ
2. Ⓐ Ⓑ Ⓒ Ⓓ Ⓔ	10. Ⓐ Ⓑ Ⓒ Ⓓ Ⓔ	18. Ⓐ Ⓑ Ⓒ Ⓓ Ⓔ
3. Ⓐ Ⓑ Ⓒ Ⓓ Ⓔ	11. Ⓐ Ⓑ Ⓒ Ⓓ Ⓔ	19. Ⓐ Ⓑ Ⓒ Ⓓ Ⓔ
4. Ⓐ Ⓑ Ⓒ Ⓓ Ⓔ	12. Ⓐ Ⓑ Ⓒ Ⓓ Ⓔ	
5. Ⓐ Ⓑ Ⓒ Ⓓ Ⓔ	13. Ⓐ Ⓑ Ⓒ Ⓓ Ⓔ	
6. Ⓐ Ⓑ Ⓒ Ⓓ Ⓔ	14. Ⓐ Ⓑ Ⓒ Ⓓ Ⓔ	
7. Ⓐ Ⓑ Ⓒ Ⓓ Ⓔ	15. Ⓐ Ⓑ Ⓒ Ⓓ Ⓔ	
8. Ⓐ Ⓑ Ⓒ Ⓓ Ⓔ	16. Ⓐ Ⓑ Ⓒ Ⓓ Ⓔ	

☐ # right in Section Seven

☐ # wrong in Section Seven

Section Eight

1. Ⓐ Ⓑ Ⓒ Ⓓ Ⓔ	9. Ⓐ Ⓑ Ⓒ Ⓓ Ⓔ
2. Ⓐ Ⓑ Ⓒ Ⓓ Ⓔ	10. Ⓐ Ⓑ Ⓒ Ⓓ Ⓔ
3. Ⓐ Ⓑ Ⓒ Ⓓ Ⓔ	11. Ⓐ Ⓑ Ⓒ Ⓓ Ⓔ
4. Ⓐ Ⓑ Ⓒ Ⓓ Ⓔ	12. Ⓐ Ⓑ Ⓒ Ⓓ Ⓔ
5. Ⓐ Ⓑ Ⓒ Ⓓ Ⓔ	13. Ⓐ Ⓑ Ⓒ Ⓓ Ⓔ
6. Ⓐ Ⓑ Ⓒ Ⓓ Ⓔ	14. Ⓐ Ⓑ Ⓒ Ⓓ Ⓔ
7. Ⓐ Ⓑ Ⓒ Ⓓ Ⓔ	15. Ⓐ Ⓑ Ⓒ Ⓓ Ⓔ
8. Ⓐ Ⓑ Ⓒ Ⓓ Ⓔ	16. Ⓐ Ⓑ Ⓒ Ⓓ Ⓔ

☐ # right in Section Eight

☐ # wrong in Section Eight

Section Nine

1. Ⓐ Ⓑ Ⓒ Ⓓ Ⓔ	9. Ⓐ Ⓑ Ⓒ Ⓓ Ⓔ
2. Ⓐ Ⓑ Ⓒ Ⓓ Ⓔ	10. Ⓐ Ⓑ Ⓒ Ⓓ Ⓔ
3. Ⓐ Ⓑ Ⓒ Ⓓ Ⓔ	11. Ⓐ Ⓑ Ⓒ Ⓓ Ⓔ
4. Ⓐ Ⓑ Ⓒ Ⓓ Ⓔ	12. Ⓐ Ⓑ Ⓒ Ⓓ Ⓔ
5. Ⓐ Ⓑ Ⓒ Ⓓ Ⓔ	13. Ⓐ Ⓑ Ⓒ Ⓓ Ⓔ
6. Ⓐ Ⓑ Ⓒ Ⓓ Ⓔ	14. Ⓐ Ⓑ Ⓒ Ⓓ Ⓔ
7. Ⓐ Ⓑ Ⓒ Ⓓ Ⓔ	
8. Ⓐ Ⓑ Ⓒ Ⓓ Ⓔ	

☐ # right in Section Nine

☐ # wrong in Section Nine

Practice Test Seven

SECTION 1
Time—25 Minutes
ESSAY

The essay gives you an opportunity to show how effectively you can develop and express ideas. You should, therefore, take care to develop your point of view, present your ideas logically and clearly, and use language precisely.

Your essay must be written in your Answer Grid Booklet—you will receive no other paper on which to write. You will have enough space if you write on every line, avoid wide margins, and keep your handwriting to a reasonable size. Remember that people who are not familiar with your handwriting will read what you write. Try to write or print so that what you are writing is legible to those readers.

You have twenty-five minutes to write an essay on the topic assigned below.

DO NOT WRITE ON ANOTHER TOPIC. AN OFF-TOPIC ESSAY WILL RECEIVE A SCORE OF ZERO.

Think carefully about the issue presented in the following excerpt and the assignment below.

> "If you don't like something, change it. If you can't change it, change your attitude. Don't complain."
>
> —Maya Angelou

Assignment: Do you agree with Maya Angelou that it's pointless to complain? Plan and write an essay in which you develop your point of view on this issue. Support your position with reasoning and examples taken from your reading, studies, experience, or observations.

DO NOT WRITE YOUR ESSAY IN YOUR TEST BOOK.
You will receive credit only for what you write in your Answer Grid Booklet.

_____

_____

_____

_____

_____

_____

_____

_____

_____

_____

_____

_____

_____

_____

_____

_____

_____

_____

_____

_____

IF YOU FINISH BEFORE TIME IS CALLED, YOU MAY CHECK YOUR WORK ON THIS SECTION ONLY. DO NOT TURN TO ANY OTHER SECTION IN THE TEST.

STOP

KAPLAN
Test Prep and Admissions

SECTION 2

Time—25 Minutes
24 Questions

> **Directions:** For each of the following questions, choose the best answer and darken the corresponding oval on the answer sheet.

Each sentence below has one or two blanks, each blank indicating that something has been omitted. Beneath the sentence are five words or sets of words labeled (A) through (E). Choose the word or set of words that, when inserted in the sentence, <u>best</u> fits the meaning of the sentence as a whole.

EXAMPLE:

Today's small, portable computers contrast markedly with the earliest electronic computers, which were ----.

(A) effective
(B) invented
(C) useful
(D) destructive
(E) enormous

1. Recent fossil evidence suggests that carnivorous dinosaurs were ---- swimmers, but some paleontologists still think that these dinosaurs ---- the water.

   (A) swift . . entered
   (B) nervous . . loathed
   (C) accomplished . . feared
   (D) unskilled . . avoided
   (E) natural . . enjoyed

2. Cathedral windows are often ----, composed of thousands of pieces of luminous stained glass.

   (A) mysterious
   (B) intricate
   (C) sacred
   (D) descriptive
   (E) burnished

3. A Portuguese man-of-war moves over the sea ----, blown by the wind.

   (A) covertly
   (B) motionlessly
   (C) defiantly
   (D) passively
   (E) consistently

4. Her agent cultivated the actress's reputation for being ----, but in fact she was quite ---- in her private life and had many close friends.

   (A) reclusive . . gregarious
   (B) generous . . frugal
   (C) charming . . deranged
   (D) truculent . . admirable
   (E) eccentric . . garrulous

5. Though she earned her ---- as a muralist, the artist felt that she ---- more acclaim for her sculpture.

   (A) anonymity . . escaped
   (B) reputation . . deserved
   (C) fame . . deferred
   (D) distinction . . justified
   (E) notoriety . . publicized

GO ON TO THE NEXT PAGE

6. Whales that surface too quickly from deep dives may expire from decompression sickness, a sometimes ---- condition that also affects humans.

   (A) docile
   (B) succulent
   (C) mandatory
   (D) robust
   (E) lethal

7. The media seldom give those who seek careers in the public eye any ---- of the life-changing effects of the overwhelming ---- that often accompanies fame.

   (A) intimation . . adulation
   (B) euphemism . . aplomb
   (C) rhetoric . . acme
   (D) stasis . . euthanasia
   (E) mote . . abando

8. The Austrian ethologist Konrad Lorenz applied his studies of the instinctive behavior of fish in schools to the social dynamics of human ---- in groups.

   (A) fallibility
   (B) interaction
   (C) physiology
   (D) corruption
   (E) education

GO ON TO THE NEXT PAGE

Directions: The passages below are followed by questions based on their content; questions following a pair of related passages may also be based on the relationship between the paired passages. Answer the questions on the basis of what is <u>stated</u> or <u>implied</u> in the passages and in any introductory material that may be provided.

Questions 9–12 are based on the following passage.

Passage 1

If the most dire of the widespread global warming theories were accurate, the polar ice caps would currently be receding significantly. Recent studies, however, have demonstrated that the
(5) Arctic ice shelf is not only maintaining its mass, but also growing. In addition, satellite temperature readings, considered by many to be more reliable than surface temperatures taken by humans under varying conditions, indicate no global
(10) warming of the lower atmosphere. Environmental organizations have reported that Arctic Sea ice declined by 14 percent from 1978 to 1998. Yet a careful review of this research reveals that almost this entire drop occurred during a period of only
(15) one year, suggesting this temperature change was a result of an anomaly rather than a growing trend.

Passage 2

Following on the heels of convincing new evidence that the Arctic ice cap is rapidly melting— some studies, using satellite temperature readings,
(20) mark the decline at 20 percent over the past 20 years—efforts have begun to pass legislation that would reduce global warming pollution and curb climate change. Some of the proposed bills would require the manufacturing sector to restrict carbon
(25) dioxide emissions that, over the years, have contributed to a layer of pollution scientists believe traps a substantial portion of the sun's heat. It is significant that such discussions are taking place in the United States, the estimated producer of 25 per-
(30) cent of the world's carbon dioxide pollution.

9. The first sentence of Passage 1 functions primarily to

(A) explain why the ice caps could be affected by global warming

(B) introduce a theory the author later undermines

(C) state the author's central argument

(D) refute the seriousness of global warming concerns

(E) argue that global warming theories are inaccurate

10. In line 22, "curb" most nearly means

(A) to enclose

(B) to raise

(C) to control

(D) to line with stones

(E) to eliminate

11. The authors of both passages agree that

(A) global warming needs to be better controlled

(B) the evidence supporting global warming theories is questionable

(C) it is important to study a period of at least 20 years

(D) the polar ice caps are affected by global temperature changes

(E) satellite temperature readings are more accurate than surface readings

12. The author of Passage 1 argues that the research indicating the polar ice caps have declined by "20 percent over the past 20 years" cited in Paragraph 2 (lines 20–21) is

(A) inaccurate

(B) tainted

(C) debatable

(D) misleading

(E) unfortunate

GO ON TO THE NEXT PAGE

KAPLAN
Test Prep and Admissions

Questions 13–24 are based on the following passage.

In this excerpt from a novella, Eleanor faces a decision whether or not to end her 29-year marriage to Harold.

Even as she reached over to shut off the alarm clock, Eleanor knew that today was going to be unique. Suppressing a momentary surge of panic, she got out of bed and began doing the same

(5) things she had done every weekday morning for the past twenty-nine years. Putting on her slippers, she padded downstairs to start the coffee and prepare Harold's breakfast: orange juice, two eggs over easy, and two slices of toast, each cut in half

(10) and arranged in quarters around the edges of the plate. His doctor had warned Harold that eggs contained cholesterol that would clog his arteries, but Harold refused to change his diet. It was so like him, Eleanor reflected, as she dropped the

(15) slices of bread into the toaster. Above all else, Harold was a creature of habit. He wore the same two suits during the week, winter and summer, alternating day by day. As she reached into the refrigerator for the eggs and margarine (Harold's

(20) one concession to the doctor), Eleanor heard Harold turning on the shower in the upstairs bathroom. He would stay in the shower for exactly five minutes, because he always did, just as he always clipped his nails every Sunday night before

(25) going to bed. She dimly recalled that this methodical quality of Harold's had once been a source of great comfort to her. This morning that comfort seemed a million miles away.

Harold came downstairs just as Eleanor was

(30) transferring his eggs from the skillet to his plate. He had on the black suit today, which struck her as fitting. Black for mourning. Wordlessly, she set his plate on the table before him; wordlessly, he began to eat. For a couple of minutes, the only

(35) sounds in the kitchen—besides the ticking of the clock and the hum of the refrigerator—were of Harold eating, Harold sipping his juice, the clatter of his knife and fork against the stoneware. Eleanor leaned against the counter, staring at her

(40) coffee mug. Wisps of steam rose from it like spirits, each one vanishing almost as soon as it

became visible. She wished she were a wisp of steam, then realized suddenly that, to Harold, she probably was.

(45) Harold sopped up the last of the egg yolk with a piece of toast, and crammed the toast into his mouth. Still chewing, he rose from the table and left the kitchen without a word of thanks. As she heard him rummage in the front hall closet for his

(50) coat and hat, she resolved never to forget Harold's utter lack of courtesy and consideration. They were husband and wife, but they would never be friends.

"Bye," he said, returning to the kitchen. "I'll be

(55) home by dinnertime." He gave her a quick peck on the cheek, turned and headed out. Eleanor watched his retreating back, then waited for the sound of the front door closing behind him, the sound that would signal his departure from her

(60) life. It didn't come. Instead, suddenly, there he was again in the kitchen doorway, smiling.

"Did I forget to mention? I love you."

And then he was gone. Eleanor stood as if rooted to the spot, the blood drained from her face.

(65) Why, of all days, would he pick today to say that? She felt her resolve crumbling, and fought it. Was it wrong to want to make a fresh start? Didn't she deserve more than this loveless marriage? And it was loveless, despite what Harold had said.

(70) Clenching her fists, Eleanor forced herself to move, climbing the stairs and going into the bedroom. When she had showered and dressed, she went to her closet and opened the door. There stood her suitcase, packed for the last week, half-

(75) concealed by the dresses on their hangers. She stared at the suitcase as if mesmerized. It promised a new life of independence and self-worth, an end to this suffocating compromise. She picked it up, closed the closet door, took one last look at the

(80) bedroom, and headed downstairs.

At first it seemed to Eleanor that her departure, once begun, gained momentum with each passing second. By the time she closed the front door of the house and headed for her car, she felt like a bird

(85) taking wing. Yet, as she headed out of the driveway, Eleanor felt twenty-nine years of marriage drawing

GO ON TO THE NEXT PAGE ▷

her back, like gravity—invisible, inexorable. Her
foot drew away from the accelerator as if of its own
accord; tears welled in her eyes, obscuring her
(90) vision. She pulled the car over to the curb and sat
there, her thoughts in turmoil. Was she being too
hasty? Was there another solution? Perhaps all she
needed was a temporary respite, a little time and
distance to gain perspective. She glanced down at
(95) the road atlas on the seat beside her. New Mexico,
her intended destination, was two days' drive.
New Mexico, with its mountains and blue skies.
Perhaps the crystalline air there would clear her
mind. She put the car back into gear, and headed
(100) for the highway.

13. The manner in which Eleanor gets out of bed and
begins preparing Harold's breakfast suggests that
she is trying to

(A) repress her anger
(B) demonstrate her love for him
(C) offer him one last chance
(D) quell her apprehension
(E) understand his needs

14. The description of Harold's wardrobe
(lines 16–18) reveals which aspect of his character?

(A) attention to detail
(B) disdain for material possessions
(C) indifference to fashion
(D) adherence to routine
(E) pride in his appearance

15. The word "fitting" in line 32 means

(A) decorative
(B) timely
(C) apt
(D) useful
(E) likely

16. Eleanor probably imagines that she appears to
Harold as a wisp of steam because she thinks he

(A) has a fanciful imagination
(B) wishes she were not watching him eat
(C) prefers the company of other women
(D) habitually criticizes her cooking
(E) appears not to notice her presence

17. Eleanor decides that she and Harold "would never
be friends" (lines 52–53) because

(A) their backgrounds are so dissimilar
(B) Harold is too obsessed with his career
(C) she doesn't care about his feelings
(D) Harold behaves so thoughtlessly
(E) they have no interests in common

18. The reason Eleanor "felt her resolve crumbling"
(line 66) is probably because she

(A) had not expected Harold to express his
feelings
(B) decided to postpone leaving her marriage
(C) said nothing while Harold was eating breakfast
(D) had not realized the depth of her hostility
towards Harold
(E) had not yet eaten anything that morning

19. The "suffocating compromise" mentioned in
line 78 is probably a reference to

(A) men
(B) marriage
(C) divorce
(D) money
(E) retirement

GO ON TO THE NEXT PAGE →

20. Eleanor feels "like a bird taking wing" (lines 84-85) because

    (A) Harold has told Eleanor he loves her

    (B) she doesn't fear Harold any longer

    (C) she has finally begun her departure

    (D) she has always wanted to go to New Mexico

    (E) Harold doesn't know she's leaving him

21. The image of "gravity" (line 87) is used to emphasize Eleanor's

    (A) doubts about the value of marriage and family

    (B) emotional investment in her life with Harold

    (C) inability to communicate with Harold

    (D) lack of compassion for Harold

    (E) misgivings about what life after marriage will be like

22. The word "respite" (line 93) means

    (A) rest

    (B) strategy

    (C) journey

    (D) absence

    (E) therapy

23. At the end of the passage, as Eleanor leaves for New Mexico, her feelings about the future of her marriage are primarily

    (A) optimistic

    (B) pessimistic

    (C) frightened

    (D) resentful

    (E) unresolved

24. The purpose of this passage is to

    (A) describe the morning rituals of a couple that has been together for 29 years

    (B) show what a bad husband Harold was to Eleanor

    (C) tell how New Mexico is a fantastic place to go for peace and quiet

    (D) let the reader inside a woman's thought processes when deciding whether or not to end her marriage

    (E) compliment Eleanor on her bravery

SECTION 3
Time—25 Minutes
20 Questions

Directions: For this section, solve each problem and decide which is the best of the choices given. Fill in the corresponding oval on the answer sheet. You may use any available space for scratchwork.

Notes:

(1) Calculator use is permitted.

(2) All numbers used are real numbers.

(3) Figures are provided for some problems. All figures are drawn to scale and lie in a plane UNLESS otherwise indicated.

(4) Unless otherwise specified, the domain of any function f is assumed to be the set of all real numbers x for which $f(x)$ is a real number.

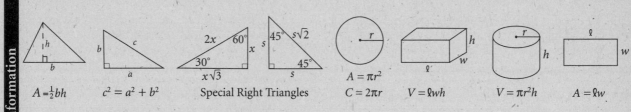

$A = \frac{1}{2}bh$ $c^2 = a^2 + b^2$ Special Right Triangles $C = 2\pi r$ $V = \ell wh$ $V = \pi r^2 h$ $A = \ell w$
$A = \pi r^2$

The sum of the degree measures of the angles in a triangle is 180.
The number of degrees of arc in a circle is 360.
A straight angle has a degree measure of 180.

Student	Regular Time (in seconds)
Paul	32.15
Grace	30.94
Logan	32.146
Charlene	33.815
Francisco	32.083

1. The chart above shows the results of a running race. If all the students started at the same time, who finished third?

(A) Paul

(B) Grace

(C) Logan

(D) Charlene

(E) Francisco

2. If $\dfrac{a^2}{2 \cdot 3} = 6 \times 49$, what is the value of a^2?

(A) 6^2

(B) 7^2

(C) 13^2

(D) 24^2

(E) 42^2

3. A certain pump can drain a full 375-gallon tank in 15 minutes. At this rate, how many more minutes would it take to drain a full 600-gallon tank?

(A) 9

(B) 15

(C) 18

(D) 24

(E) 25

GO ON TO THE NEXT PAGE

4. A gardener plants flowers in the following order: carnations, daffodils, larkspurs, tiger lilies, and zinnias. If the gardener planted 47 flowers, what kind of flower did he plant last?

(A) carnations

(B) daffodils

(C) larkspurs

(D) tiger lilies

(E) zinnias

5. Maja has the following scores on 7 quizzes in French class: 81, 76, 80, 84, 78, 91, 84. What was the median score of her French quizzes?

(A) 78

(B) 81

(C) 82

(D) 83

(E) 84

6. If $p < q$, $r < s$, and $r < q$, which of the following must be true?

    I. $p < s$
    II. $s < q$
    III. $r < p$

(A) None

(B) I only

(C) III only

(D) I and II

(E) II and III

DISTRIBUTION OF MONTHLY INCOME
FOR THE NEWTON FAMILY

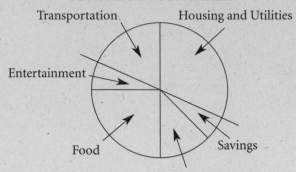

7. The circle graph above represents the distribution of the Newton family's monthly income. If the family's total income is $1,800 per month, approximately how much do they spend on housing and utilities per month?

(A) $300

(B) $450

(C) $600

(D) $750

(E) $900

8. If $x^2 + y = 0$, which of the following must be true?

(A) $x^2 = y$

(B) $xy = y$

(C) $x = \dfrac{y}{x}$

(D) $x^3 = y^2$

(E) $x^4 = y^2$

9. If the product of 3 positive integers is even, which of the following must be true?

(A) All of the integers are odd.

(B) All of the integers are even.

(C) Two of the integers are even and one is odd.

(D) At least one of the integers is odd.

(E) At least one of the integers is even.

GO ON TO THE NEXT PAGE

10. If *r* is a multiple of both 12 and 18, which of the following must be a factor of *r*?

    (A) 8
    (B) 24
    (C) 27
    (D) 30
    (E) 36

11. If $x > 0$, then $(4^x)(8^x) =$

    (A) 2^{9x}
    (B) 2^{8x}
    (C) 2^{6x}
    (D) 2^{5x}
    (E) 2^{4x}

12. The average (arithmetic mean) of six numbers is 6. If 3 is subtracted from each of four of the numbers, what is the new average?

    (A) $1\frac{1}{2}$
    (B) 2
    (C) 3
    (D) 4
    (E) $4\frac{1}{2}$

13. What is the perimeter of a triangle with vertices $(-1, 1)$, $(5, 1)$, and $(2, 5)$?

    (A) 16
    (B) 13
    (C) $6 + 2\sqrt{7}$
    (D) 11
    (E) $6 + 2\sqrt{5}$

14. How many different positive 2-digit integers are there such that the tens' digit is greater than 5 and the units' digit is odd?

    (A) 10
    (B) 12
    (C) 15
    (D) 20
    (E) 25

15. If *a* and *b* are positive integers, what is *a* percent of *b* percent of 200?

    (A) $\dfrac{ab}{100}$
    (B) $\dfrac{ab}{50}$
    (C) ab
    (D) $50ab$
    (E) $100ab$

16. Let the "tricate" of a number *x* be defined as one-third of the smallest multiple of 3 greater than *x*. If the tricate of *z* is 3, which of the following could be the value of *z*?

    (A) 2
    (B) 5
    (C) 7
    (D) 9
    (E) 11

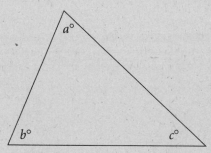

Note: Figure not drawn to scale

17. In the triangle above, $a + b = 80$, and $b + c = 140$. What is the value of *b*?

    (A) 40
    (B) 50
    (C) 80
    (D) 100
    (E) It cannot be determined from the information given.

GO ON TO THE NEXT PAGE

18. In the figure above, line RS passes through the origin. If the x-coordinate of point R is -6, what is the y-coordinate of R ?

(A) -9

(B) -6

(C) -4

(D) -3

(E) -2

19. A radio station emits a signal that can be received for 60 miles in all directions. If the intensity of the signal is strengthened so the reception increases by 40 miles in all directions, by approximately how many square miles is its region of reception increased?

(A) 6,300

(B) 10,000

(C) 10,300

(D) 20,000

(E) 31,400

20. Bill has to type a paper that is p pages long, in which each page contains w words. If Bill types an average of x words per minute, how many hours will it take him to finish the paper?

(A) $\dfrac{wp}{60x}$

(B) $\dfrac{wpx}{60}$

(C) $\dfrac{60wp}{x}$

(D) $\dfrac{wx}{60p}$

(E) $60wpx$

IF YOU FINISH BEFORE TIME IS CALLED, YOU MAY CHECK YOUR WORK ON THIS SECTION ONLY. DO NOT TURN TO ANY OTHER SECTION IN THE TEST.

STOP

SECTION 4

Time—25 Minutes
24 Questions

Directions: For each of the following questions, choose the best answer and darken the corresponding oval on the answer sheet.

Each sentence below has one or two blanks, each blank indicating that something has been omitted. Beneath the sentence are five words or sets of words labeled (A) through (E). Choose the word or set of words that, when inserted in the sentence, <u>best</u> fits the meaning of the sentence as a whole.

EXAMPLE:

Today's small, portable computers contrast markedly with the earliest electronic computers, which were ----.

(A) effective
(B) invented
(C) useful
(D) destructive
(E) enormous

---

1. Once he had intellectually ---- the difference between regional dialects, Fernando found himself speaking the language ----.

(A) rejected . . considerately
(B) grasped . . effortlessly
(C) mastered . . implicitly
(D) forgotten . . eloquently
(E) recognized . . ambiguously

2. The international news wire service ---- information ----, so that events are reported all over the world shortly after they happen.

(A) records . . accurately
(B) falsifies . . deliberately
(C) verifies . . painstakingly
(D) disseminates . . rapidly
(E) suppresses . . thoroughly

3. Lacking sacred scriptures or codified ----, Shinto is more properly regarded as a legacy of traditional religious practices and basic values than as a formal system of belief.

(A) followers
(B) boundaries
(C) dogma
(D) dispositions
(E) strata

4. We will face the idea of old age with ---- as long as we believe that it invariably brings poverty, isolation, and illness.

(A) regret
(B) apprehension
(C) enlightenment
(D) veneration
(E) reverence

5. As a playwright, Pinter is renowned for his mundane settings, his ---- yet poetic dialogue, and his aggressive, often mean-spirited characters.

(A) comprehensive
(B) lyrical
(C) colloquial
(D) ethereal
(E) affirmative

GO ON TO THE NEXT PAGE

Directions: The passages below are followed by questions based on their content; questions following a pair of related passages may also be based on the relationship between the paired passages. Answer the questions on the basis of what is <u>stated</u> or <u>implied</u> in the passages and in any introductory material that may be provided.

Questions 6–7 are based on the following passage.

Recently, I casually looked through a journal from my childhood. The pages were filled with ragged cartoons that seemed to have been drawn by someone else. Yet, as I flipped towards the end
(5) of the book, these awkward, almost unrecogniz- able creations from my past slowly began to come alive with familiarity. One page, covered in a mess of squares and stick figures depicting a billiards game, captured my attention. Suddenly I felt
(10) transported back to my grandparents' musty base- ment game room, even recalling my older broth- er's victorious taunts. I turned to the next page eagerly, now exhilarated by a sense of deep con- nection to this record of bygone years.

6. The author implies that initially he only "casually looked" (line 1) through the childhood journal because

(A) he could not remember the events it described

(B) he was not skilled at drawing

(C) he found its content unfamiliar

(D) he was not interested in his childhood

(E) he was embarrassed by his cartoons

7. The author's purpose in mentioning his brother's "victorious taunts" (line 12) is most likely to

(A) indicate that he had a strained relationship with his brother

(B) imply that this billiards game was particularly memorable

(C) criticize his brother's behavior

(D) suggest the journal recalled painful memories

(E) underscore the journal's ability to powerfully recall the past

Questions 8–9 are based on the following passage.

While the tarantula, the largest spider in the world, can easily intimidate with its impressive size, it actually poses no more danger to humans than a housefly. In fact, the tarantula's large size is
(5) rather ironic, for it constitutes a distinct disadvan- tage in the wild. Slow and conspicuous, the taran- tula is relatively easy prey for its most common predator, a black wasp—aptly called a tarantula hawk—that uses a tranquilizing sting to incapaci-
(10) tate its prey. Then, in a rather gruesome display of parasitic behavior, the tarantula hawk drags the paralyzed spider to a burrow, where it lays larva that slowly consume the still alive but helpless tarantula for months.

8. The author uses the term "ironic" in line 5 primarily in order to

(A) imply the tarantula is not as large as many assume

(B) underscore how tarantulas pose little threat to humans

(C) describe how the tarantula is more often prey than predator

(D) suggest the tarantula's vulnerability is incon- gruous with its appearance

(E) indicate the tarantula's vicious reputation is unwarranted

9. The author characterizes the tarantula as all of the following EXCEPT

(A) distinctive

(B) defenseless

(C) noticeable

(D) vulnerable

(E) impressive

GO ON TO THE NEXT PAGE

Questions 10–15 are based on the following passage.

There has been a great deal of scientific speculation about what caused the extinction of the dinosaurs. The following passage presents recent developments affecting this debate.

The question of why dinosaurs became extinct has puzzled paleontologists since the first dinosaur fossil was found almost two centuries ago. These great reptiles dominated the earth for
(5) almost 160 million years, but mysteriously died out approximately 65 million years ago. Various explanations for this disappearance have been offered, ranging from an epidemic to a sudden, catastrophic drop in temperature, but definitive
(10) proof has remained elusive.

In 1980, Luis Alvarez, winner of the Nobel Prize in Physics, suggested a novel explanation: cosmic extinction. According to Alvarez and his geologist son Walter, a huge meteor crashed into the earth's
(15) surface 65 million years ago, sending up a massive cloud of dust and rock particles. The cloud blocked out sunlight for a period of months or even years, disrupting plant photosynthesis and, by extension, the global food chain. The lack of vege-
(20) tation, coupled with a significant drop in tempera-ture, resulted in the extinction of the dinosaurs.

Alvarez based his theory on a curious piece of evidence: the presence of a thin layer of iridium that had recently been discovered in geologic sedi-
(25) ments laid down at approximately the time the dinosaurs died out. The metal iridium is rarely found on the earth's surface; Alvarez reasoned that it had either come up from the earth's core by vol-canic action, or been deposited from space,
(30) through the fall of one or more meteorites. He found the latter explanation more likely, given the even distribution of the iridium layer worldwide.

But paleontologists scoffed at the Alvarez extinc-tion theory. Neither Luis nor Walter Alvarez was a
(35) paleontologist, yet they claimed to have solved a mystery that had defied the efforts of paleontolo-gists for over a century. Professional hostility was also fueled by the somewhat abrasive style of the elder Alvarez. But the most important objection to
(40) the Alvarez theory was evidential. In order to cre-ate worldwide fallout on the scale suggested by Alvarez, the "doomsday" meteorite would have had

to be on the order of five miles in diameter; its impact would have formed a crater perhaps
(45) a hundred miles wide. Where was the crater?

Finally, a decade after the cosmic extinction theory was first proposed, the crater was found. Lying on the northern edge of Mexico's Yucatan Peninsula, the crater is 110 miles wide. Long
(50) buried under sediment, it had actually been dis-covered in 1981 by oil geologists, but datings of nearby rock samples taken at that time suggested that it was significantly older than 65 million years. New samples of melted rock from the crater
(55) itself were recently analyzed by an advanced dat-ing process, however, and were found to be 64.98 million years old. Many scientists now feel that, thanks to the Alvarez theory, the mystery of dinosaur extinction has finally been solved.

10. The word "elusive" in line 10 most nearly means

(A) evasive
(B) hard to understand
(C) difficult to find
(D) rare
(E) questionable

11. The author indicates that opponents of the Alvarez theory criticized both Luis and Walter Alvarez for

(A) publishing incomplete research
(B) being personally abrasive
(C) theorizing outside their own fields
(D) misinterpreting experimental data
(E) using improper investigative methods

12. The word "novel" is used in line 12 to mean

(A) original
(B) strange
(C) eccentric
(D) controversial
(E) fictitious

GO ON TO THE NEXT PAGE

13. In the second paragraph, the author mentions photosynthesis primarily in order to

   (A) refute the theory that an epidemic was responsible for dinosaur extinction

   (B) illustrate the importance of a clean atmosphere for life on earth

   (C) support the contention that dinosaurs were primarily plant-eaters

   (D) explain how the cloud of dust caused the extinction of dinosaurs

   (E) clarify how iridium was distributed evenly around the earth

14. According to the author, the discovery of a layer of iridium in geologic sediments (line 22–27) was considered unusual because

   (A) iridium had never been detected there before

   (B) the metal is normally quite scarce at the earth's surface

   (C) few volcanoes had been active during the era when the sediments were laid down

   (D) iridium had not previously been linked to worldwide fallout

   (E) nobody had previously thought to link iridium with dinosaur extinction

15. The Alvarez theory would most directly be strengthened by additional information concerning

   (A) the extraterrestrial origins of the Yucatan crater

   (B) the number of dinosaur species indigenous to the Yucatan area

   (C) the iridium content of the Yucatan crater

   (D) the discovery of a crater of similar age in the Southern Hemisphere

   (E) the volcanic forces responsible for burying the Yucatan crater

Questions 16–24 are based on the following passage.

Mention a rock garden to most people and, in response, they may ask you how to grow rocks, and why you would want to do so. Actually, a rock garden (also known as an alpine garden) contains
(5) not only rocks but also flowers that grow in mountainous regions. The flowers are planted in a bed of rocks, hence the name. Rock gardens are believed to have originated in China and Japan; they were introduced to the West in the seven-
(10) teenth century. The popularity of rock gardens has increased dramatically since then, and today there are numerous international rock garden societies with many thousands of members.

   One aspect of the appeal of rock gardens is that
(15) they provide gardeners the opportunity to culti-vate beautiful plants in growing conditions that are less than ideal. If the land is hilly, stony, or awkwardly-arranged, for example, a gardener would be unable to raise many traditional garden
(20) plants, since they could not survive such condi-tions. In contrast, alpine plants such as gentians, edelweiss, stonecrops, and saxifrages, as well as rockrose, columbine, phlox, and bluebell, not only survive but also thrive in these conditions because
(25) their native soils have characteristics similar to those of mountainous regions.

   In order to plant a rock garden, a gardener must start with the rocks, ensuring that they are arranged in a manner that is both beautiful and
(30) conducive to plant growth. If the ground is already rocky, the gardener need only rearrange the rocks into a growing area. In order to avoid uninspired placements that work against the beauty of the garden, the gardener should draw up plans of his
(35) or her rock garden before he or she begins the work. In addition, the rocks must be planted deeply into the soil—in some cases, half or more of a rock will be buried—so that they are stable and cannot be dislodged easily, which would upset
(40) the plants.

   Gardeners whose plot lacks a sufficient number or the proper kinds of rocks can buy them from local nurseries. Rocks native to a gardener's region

GO ON TO THE NEXT PAGE ⟫

work best and are usually readily available and
(45) inexpensive. Limestone is a good choice because
water and air are admitted into its pores. Some
sturdy alpine plants even have roots strong
enough to push through limestone's porous surface and become firmly established in the rock.
(50) Limestone is also characterized by nooks and
crannies that provide opportunities for the gardener to plant moss and lichens. The gardener
should look, too, for rocks that have interesting
and aesthetically-pleasing shapes and colors, since
(55) it is the juxtaposition of the rocks and plants, not
the beauty of the plants alone, that makes a rock
garden succeed. In this respect rock gardens differ
from traditional gardens, which focus on plants
and do not take the beauty of the medium in
(60) which flowers are planted into consideration.
     Once the rocks have been selected and put in
place, a gardener can plant the flowers. H. Lincoln
Foster, a famous American rock gardener, said that
the reason rock gardeners go through the trouble
(65) and heavy lifting required to create a rock bed is
that the plants that thrive in rock gardens "are
among…the easiest and most abundantly flowering garden plants." However, rock gardens do
require special care. Because plants in a rock gar-
(70) den are more exposed to the elements than are
those in a flat bed, they need more protection.
Nonetheless, rock garden devotees consider the
time it requires to care for and maintain their gardens well spent, since the flowers and the rocks
(75) together provide such beauty and delight.

16. The primary purpose of the passage is to

(A) encourage gardeners to abandon traditional
gardens in favor of rock gardens

(B) extol the artistic beauty of rock gardens

(C) provide general information about rock
gardens and alpine plants

(D) trace the history of rock gardens from their
origin in China and Japan

(E) compare alpine flowers to flowers grown in
flat bed gardens

17. According to the passage, why would someone with
an interest in gardening who does not live by grass
and fertile soil appreciate rock gardens?

(A) Rock gardens do not contain plant life—only
various forms of rocks.

(B) One can grow rock gardens in atypical
growing conditions.

(C) Rock gardens do not take a lot of work to
cultivate.

(D) A gardener does not need to buy anything to
start a rock garden of his own.

(E) Rock gardens are the most aesthetically
appealing plant forms that exist.

18. The author recommends limestone for rock
gardens for all of the following reasons EXCEPT

(A) it is porous

(B) it can hold moisture

(C) it has indentations in which to plant moss

(D) it is artistically shaped

(E) plant roots can become imbedded in it

GO ON TO THE NEXT PAGE

19. As used in line 32, the word "uninspired" means

    (A) plain
    (B) unplanned
    (C) artful
    (D) buried
    (E) alpine

20. According to the passage, rock garden plants require special care because

    I. the conditions in which they grow are less than ideal
    II. they are more exposed to the elements than are flat bed plants
    III. rock garden plants themselves are more delicate than flat bed plants

    (A) I only
    (B) II only
    (C) III only
    (D) I and II only
    (E) II and III only

21. In line 59, the word "medium" means

    (A) press
    (B) currency
    (C) climate
    (D) average
    (E) environment

22. The author uses H. Lincoln Foster's quotation in lines 66–68 to

    (A) emphasize the fact that rock garden plants need special care
    (B) explain what motivates gardeners to perform the work of creating rock gardens
    (C) instruct gardeners about how to arrange their plants in a pleasing way
    (D) describe the disadvantages of flat bed plants
    (E) remind gardeners that their plants need to be protected from the elements

23. According to the passage, the rocks in alpine gardens must be buried deeply because

    (A) this is the most aesthetically-pleasing placement
    (B) they are the first objects to be planted
    (C) firm placement is less disruptive to the plants
    (D) deep burial makes the rocks less secure
    (E) buried rocks are easier to maintain

24. It can be inferred from the passage that saxifrages

    (A) are not suitable for rock gardens
    (B) are not traditional garden plants
    (C) have roots that can burrow through limestone
    (D) are more beautiful in mountainous soils
    (E) will only survive in a rock garden

IF YOU FINISH BEFORE TIME IS CALLED, YOU MAY CHECK YOUR WORK ON THIS SECTION ONLY. DO NOT TURN TO ANY OTHER SECTION IN THE TEST.

SECTION 5

Time—25 Minutes
18 Questions

Directions: For this section, solve each problem and decide which is the best of the choices given. Fill in the corresponding oval on the answer sheet. You may use any available space for scratchwork.

Notes:

(1) Calculator use is permitted.

(2) All numbers used are real numbers.

(3) Figures are provided for some problems. All figures are drawn to scale and lie in a plane UNLESS otherwise indicated.

(4) Unless otherwise specified, the domain of any function f is assumed to be the set of all real numbers x for which $f(x)$ is a real number.

Information

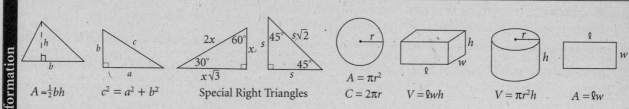

$A = \frac{1}{2}bh$ $c^2 = a^2 + b^2$ Special Right Triangles $A = \pi r^2$ $V = \ell wh$ $V = \pi r^2 h$ $A = \ell w$
$C = 2\pi r$

The sum of the degree measures of the angles in a triangle is 180.
The number of degrees of arc in a circle is 360.
A straight angle has a degree measure of 180.

---

1. If a, b, and c are positive numbers and $abc = b^2$, which of the following must equal b ?

    (A) ac

    (B) ab

    (C) bc

    (D) $\dfrac{a}{c}$

    (E) $\dfrac{c}{a}$

2. If $5a - b = 9$ and $3a + b = 15$, then $a + b =$

    (A) -3

    (B) 3

    (C) 5

    (D) 9

    (E) 12

GO ON TO THE NEXT PAGE

3. If $xyz \neq 0$, then $\dfrac{x^2y^3z^6}{x^6y^3z^2} =$

(A) xyz

(B) $\dfrac{z}{x}$

(C) $\dfrac{z^2}{x^2}$

(D) $\dfrac{z^3}{x^3}$

(E) $\dfrac{z^4}{x^4}$

4. If $0 < x + y$ and $y < 0$, which of the following statements must be true?

  I. $x < 0$
  II. $x < -y$
  III. $0 < x - y$

(A) I only

(B) II only

(C) III only

(D) I and II

(E) II and III

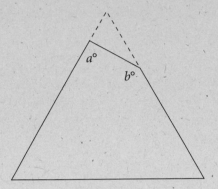

5. The figure above was formed by cutting off one corner of an equilateral triangle. What is the value of $a + b$?

(A) 60

(B) 90

(C) 120

(D) 180

(E) 240

6. A rectangular swimming pool has a volume of 8,640 cubic feet. If its length is 60 feet and its depth is 6 feet, what is the width of the pool in feet?

(A) 16

(B) 19

(C) 24

(D) 28

(E) 36

GO ON TO THE NEXT PAGE

7. If $f(x) = \dfrac{x+4}{x}$ and $g(x) = x^2 - 6$, what is the difference between $f(x)$ and $g(x)$ when $x = 2$?

    (A) 1
    (B) 2
    (C) 3
    (D) 5
    (E) 6

8. If $d(w) = \sqrt{w^2 + 1}$ for all real values of w, which of the following is NOT a possible value of $d(w)$?

    (A) 0
    (B) 1
    (C) 4.6
    (D) 7.25
    (E) 49

GO ON TO THE NEXT PAGE

Directions: For Student-Produced Response questions 9–18, use the grids at the bottom of the answer sheet page on which you have answered questions 1–8.

Each of the remaining 10 questions requires you to solve the problem and enter your answer by marking the ovals in the special grid, as shown in the example below. You may use any available space for scratch work.

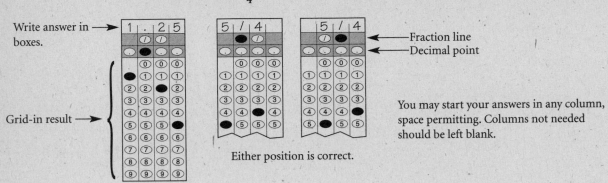

Answer: 1.25 or $\frac{5}{4}$ or 5/4

Write answer in boxes.

Grid-in result

Fraction line
Decimal point

Either position is correct.

You may start your answers in any column, space permitting. Columns not needed should be left blank.

- It is recommended, though not required, that you write your answer in the boxes at the top of the columns. However, you will receive credit only for darkening the ovals correctly.

- Grid only one answer to a question, even though some problems have more than one correct answer.

- Darken no more than one oval in a column.

- No answers are negative.

- Mixed numbers cannot be gridded. For example: the number $1\frac{1}{4}$ must be gridded as 1.25 or 5/4.

  (If $\boxed{1\,|\,1\,|\,/\,|\,4}$ is gridded, it will be interpreted as $\frac{11}{4}$ not $1\frac{1}{4}$.)

- **Decimal Accuracy:** Decimal answers must be entered as accurately as possible. For example, if you obtain an answer such as 0.1666..., you should record the result as .166 or .167. **Less accurate values such as .16 or .17 are not acceptable.**

Acceptable ways to grid $\frac{1}{6}$ = .1666...

GO ON TO THE NEXT PAGE

9. At an amusement park, each ride costs $1.50. However, a dozen ride tickets can be bought for $12.50 at the park entrance. How much money can be saved by buying a dozen tickets at once rather than buying each ticket separately? (Disregard the dollar sign when gridding your answer.)

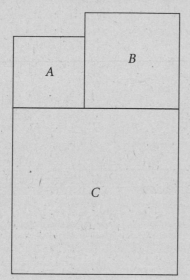

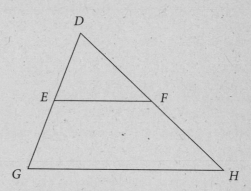

10. In the figure above, A, B, and C are squares. If the area of A is 9 and the area of B is 16, what is the area of C?

11. If $\frac{s}{t} - 4 = 5$ and $5rt + 2 = 6$, then $rs =$

12. If n is an integer such that $3n + 5$ is a prime number between 20 and 40, what is a possible value for n?

13. The ratio of boys to girls in a certain class is 3 to 4. If the total number of students in the class is greater than 20 and less than 30, what is a possible value for the total number of students in the class?

14. Clare has a collection of CDs she wants to store in a cubical box with edges of length 10 inches. If each CD has dimensions 5 inches by 5 inches by $\frac{1}{2}$ inch, what is the maximum number of CDs that can fit into the box?

15. In DGH above, $DE = EG$, $EF \parallel GH$, and the area of DGH is 30. What is the area of DEF?

16. If x is an integer between 300 and 400 that is divisible by 3, 6, and 9, what is one possible value of x?

17. Jill's pocket contains 3 quarters, 4 dimes, 2 nickels, and 6 pennies. If she takes out one coin at random, what is the probability that the coin is worth more than 5 cents?

18. Circle A has a circumference of 4π and circle B has a circumference of 8π. If the circles intersect at two points, what is a possible distance from the center of circle A to the center of circle B?

IF YOU FINISH BEFORE TIME IS CALLED, YOU MAY CHECK YOUR WORK ON THIS SECTION ONLY. DO NOT TURN TO ANY OTHER SECTION IN THE TEST.

STOP

SECTION 6

Time—25 Minutes
35 Questions

Directions: For each question in this section, select the best answer from among the choices given and fill in the corresponding oval on the answer sheet.

The following sentences test correctness and effectiveness of expression. Part of each sentence or the entire sentence is underlined; beneath each sentence are five ways of phrasing the underlined material. Choice (A) repeats the original phrasing; the other four choices are different. If you think the original phrasing produces a better sentence than any of the alternatives, select choice (A); if not, select one of the other choices.

In making your selection, follow the requirements of standard written English; that is, pay attention to grammar, choice of words, sentence construction, and punctuation. Your selection should result in the most effective sentence—clear and precise, without awkwardness or ambiguity.

EXAMPLE:

Every apple in the baskets <u>are ripe and labeled according to the date it was picked</u>.

ANSWER:

(A) are ripe and labeled according to the date it was picked
(B) is ripe and labeled according to the date it was picked
(C) are ripe and labeled according to the date they were picked
(D) is ripe and labeled according to the date they were picked
(E) are ripe and labeled as to the date it was picked

---

1. SAT subject tests are designed to evaluate your knowledge in <u>generally subjects, such as</u> social studies, science, math, and languages.

(A) generally subjects, such as
(B) general subjects, such as
(C) general subjects that are
(D) generally subjects and they are
(E) general subjects they are

2. <u>He never studied music formally, David is a success in the field.</u>

(A) He never studied music formally, David is a success in the field.
(B) He never studied music formally; so David is a success in the field.
(C) Because he never studied music formally David is a success in the field.
(D) Having never studied music formally, David is successful in its field.
(E) Although he never studied music formally, David is a success in the field.

GO ON TO THE NEXT PAGE

3. In *The Elements of Style*, William Strunk Jr. and E. B. White recommend writing in a natural tone, using figures of speech sparingly <u>and omitting needless words</u>.

  (A) and omitting needless words
  (B) and they should omit needless words
  (C) and you should omit needless words
  (D) and needlessly omitting words
  (E) and needless words should be omitted

4. The influence of Roman architecture is perhaps even more evident in the United States than <u>for either Europe or Asia</u>.

  (A) for either Europe or Asia
  (B) by either Europe or Asia
  (C) with either Europe or Asia
  (D) in either Europe or Asia
  (E) in either Europe or in Asia

5. The choreographer <u>Katherine Dunham having trained as an anthropologist, she studied</u> dance in Jamaica, Haiti, and Senegal.

  (A) Katherine Dunham having trained as an anthropologist, she studied
  (B) Katherine Dunham, who was also a trained anthropologist, studied
  (C) Katherine Dunham was a trained anthropologist and was also a student of
  (D) Katherine Dunham was a trained anthropologist and also participated in the study of
  (E) Katherine Dunham training as an anthropologist, she studied

6. <u>Weight training was begun by the girl to enhance</u> her strength and flexibility.

  (A) Weight training was begun by the girl to enhance
  (B) Weight training was begun by the girl for enhancing
  (C) Training with weights by the girl was begun in order to enhance
  (D) The girl began weight training to enhance
  (E) The girl had begun the exercise of weight training to enhance

7. One of the most common types of mistakes that inexperienced drivers make is failing to signal for a lane <u>change; another one that occurs</u> about as frequently is exceeding posted speed limits.

  (A) change; another one that occurs
  (B) change, another that occurs
  (C) change, the other, and it occurs
  (D) change; another one which is occurring
  (E) change and also occurring

8. In 1937, Pablo Picasso painted the stunning <u>*Guernica* and it conveys</u> his abhorrence of both war in general and the destruction of the Basque town of Guernica during the Spanish Civil War.

  (A) *Guernica* and it conveys
  (B) *Guernica* and being the conveyance of
  (C) *Guernica*, it conveys
  (D) *Guernica*, which conveys
  (E) *Guernica*, and conveys

GO ON TO THE NEXT PAGE

9. In an effort to prevent inadvertent violation of election rules, <u>the city has forbidden candidates from the posting of signs</u> at polling places.

    (A) the city has forbidden candidates from the posting of signs

    (B) the city has made forbidden the posting of signs by candidates

    (C) the city have forbidden candidates to post signs

    (D) the city has forbidden candidates from having posted signs

    (E) the city has forbidden candidates to post signs

10. Raised in a small, rural community, <u>it was only when I moved to a large metropolitan area that I realized how exciting city life could be</u>.

    (A) it was only when I moved to a large metropolitan area that I realized how exciting city life could be

    (B) when I moved to a large metropolitan area I realized how exciting city life could be

    (C) moving to a large metropolitan area made me realize how exciting city life could be

    (D) I did not realize how exciting city life could be until I moved to a large metropolitan area

    (E) exciting city life was unknown to me until I moved to a large metropolitan area

11. That singer's vocal power could be improved by increased lung capacity, greater range, <u>and working on better breath control</u> for demanding pieces.

    (A) and working on better breath control

    (B) and the development of better breath control

    (C) in addition the development of better breath control

    (D) and if he develops better breath control

    (E) and if he had better breath control

GO ON TO THE NEXT PAGE ▷

Directions: The following sentences test your ability to recognize grammar and usage errors. Each sentence contains either a single error or no error at all. No sentence contains more than one error. The error, if there is one, is underlined and lettered. If the sentence contains an error, select the one underlined part that must be changed to make the sentence correct. If the sentence is correct, select choice (E). In choosing answers, follow the requirements of standard written English.

EXAMPLE:

<u>Whenever</u> one is driving late at night, <u>you</u> must take extra precautions <u>against</u>
   A   B   C

falling asleep <u>at the wheel</u>. <u>No error</u>
           D   E

12. Two thousand years ago, the center <u>of</u> Europe <u>is</u>
                                   A   B

    Rome, <u>which</u> was renowned for its military power
           C

    <u>as well as</u> its sophisticated culture. <u>No error</u>
      D   E

13. <u>Some</u> people, <u>when faced</u> with the great suffering
    A   B

    throughout the world, <u>take</u> action and donate time,
                        C

    money, and effort to help others find some <u>relief of</u>
                                      D

    suffering. <u>No error</u>
             E

14. The sitcom, in contrast <u>to more sophisticated</u>
                          A

    forms of entertainment, <u>are</u> <u>consistently</u> more
                        B   C

    popular <u>with</u> all age groups. <u>No error</u>
          D   E

15. <u>Should</u> you have any <u>anxiety regarding</u> the test,
    A   B

    just remember <u>when</u> working carefully and
                  C

    methodically will make <u>it</u> more manageable.
                     D

    <u>No error</u>
      E

16. <u>Aided by</u> the graduate student, <u>the advanced</u>
    A   B

    economics class easily <u>mastered</u> statistical analysis
                     C

    <u>with the help of</u> computers. <u>No error</u>
        D   E

17. One <u>would have to be</u> <u>extremely</u> motivated,
           A   B

    focused, and industrious in order to be capable

    <u>to complete</u> medical school in <u>only</u> two years.
        C   D

    <u>No error</u>
      E

18. A Midwesterner <u>who</u> relocates to the urban
               A

    Northeast <u>may find</u> his new colleagues unsociable
            B

    <u>if they</u> pass him in the workplace <u>without hardly</u>
     C   D

    a word. <u>No error</u>
          E

19. Christopher Marlowe, though <u>immensely popular</u>
                              A

    during his own lifetime, is <u>not considering</u> as great
                         B

    a playwright as William Shakespeare, who

    <u>remained</u> <u>relatively obscure</u> throughout his own
      C   D

    career. <u>No error</u>
          E

GO ON TO THE NEXT PAGE

20. <u>Joyce Chen, whose</u> cookbook popularized dishes
       A
that might <u>otherwise</u> <u>have been</u> unknown in the
              B   C
United States, is most famous for culinary

techniques <u>she invented</u>. <u>No error</u>
              D   E

21. A pioneering scholar <u>of</u> anthropology, Ruth
                         A
Benedict <u>was also</u> a spokesperson <u>against</u> ethnic
          B   C
bigotry <u>which</u> recognized that cultures influence
         D
ideas about gender. <u>No error</u>
                      E

22. <u>Squandering</u> his inheritance, the prodigal <u>felt no</u>
      A   B
<u>regret about</u> wasting his <u>father's</u> hard-earned
   C   D
fortune. <u>No error</u>
          E

23. A shy but <u>incredible</u> intelligent young woman,
               A
Jane Eyre <u>finds</u> true love <u>despite</u> the limitations and
           B   C
judgment she was forced <u>to endure</u> as a poor
                          D
orphan. <u>No error</u>
         E

24. MIT, renowned for its <u>rigorously trained</u> scientists,
                           A
is designing <u>equipment for</u> the space program that
              B
<u>will be</u> better than <u>any other university</u>. <u>No error</u>
   C   D   E

25. Many people <u>believe</u> the arguments
                 A
<u>between my sister and I</u> <u>are more intense than</u>
         B   C
arguments <u>between most</u> family members.
            D

<u>No error</u>
 E

26. In the mid-twentieth century, much writing <u>about</u>
                                               A
intellect and language <u>were</u> widely influenced <u>by</u>
                        B   C
the <u>novels of</u> James Joyce. <u>No error</u>
     D   E

27. <u>That</u> his presentation on financial strategy was
     A
criticized <u>savagely</u> by his customers <u>who</u> watched it
            B   C
<u>came</u> as a shock to the analyst. <u>No error</u>
 D   E

28. A downfall in the economy could affect the ballet

season because programs <u>performed</u> in the new
                          A
symphony hall <u>cost</u> twice <u>as much</u> in overhead as
               B   C
<u>the old performance space</u>. <u>No error</u>
 D   E

29. Initially intended as a <u>comment on</u> <u>traditional</u>
                            A   B
politics, the strongly worded e-mail <u>exerted</u> great
                                      C
influence on the businesses <u>at its time</u>. <u>No error</u>
                             D   E

GO ON TO THE NEXT PAGE

Questions 30–35 are based on the following passage.

(1) In 1834, archeologists who studied the ancient Celtic civilization of 500 B.C.–500 A.D. had a great mystery on their hands. (2) They were excited to have discovered ten ruins of towns inhabited by the ancient Celts. (3) All of them contained an area in the center surrounded by a trench. (4) Trenches were often used as defenses, like a moat around a castle. (5) In this case they were not big enough to be an effective defense. (6) Therefore, the spaces must have had significance themselves. (7) People had all sorts of theories. (8) Maybe they were sports fields. (9) It was even suggested that these spaces were landing sites for space ships!

(10) Archeologists now believe that in fact Celts were preoccupied with the idea of sacred space. (11) Marked with a clear border, they were only used for religious rituals. (12) This theory explains other beliefs and practices associated with Celtic religion. (13) During holidays, priests would walk around the town three or nine times, making a symbolic border. (14) Ancient Celts also built temples on islands. (15) This makes sense because islands have a natural and obvious border. (16) They are land surrounded by water.

30. In the context of the first paragraph, which of the following is the best version of sentence 2 (reproduced below)?

    They were excited to have discovered ten ruins of towns inhabited by the ancient Celts.

    (A) They were excited to have discovered ten ruins of towns inhabited by the ancient Celts.

    (B) They are excited to have discovered ten ruins of towns inhabited by the ancient Celts.

    (C) Archeologists were excited to have discovered ten ruins of towns inhabited by the ancient Celts.

    (D) They were excited to have discovered ten ruins of towns that had been inhabited by the ancient Celts.

    (E) They were excited to have a discovery about ten ruins of towns inhabited by the ancient Celts.

31. To best connect sentence 5 to the rest of the first paragraph, which is the best word or phrase to insert at the beginning of sentence 5?

    (A) In fact,

    (B) However,

    (C) And,

    (D) Therefore,

    (E) But yet,

GO ON TO THE NEXT PAGE

32. Which of the following is the best way to combine sentences 7, 8, and 9 (reproduced below)?

    People had all sorts of theories. Maybe they were sports fields. It was even suggested that these spaces were the landing sites for space ships!

    (A) People had all sorts of theories that maybe they were sports fields or was even suggested that these spaces were the landing sites for space ships!

    (B) All sorts of theories were had that they were a sports field or a landing site for space ships was even suggested!

    (C) People had all sorts of theories, including that these spaces were sports fields or even landing sites for space ships!

    (D) That they were sports fields or even that these spaces were the landing sites for space ships were the theories that people had!

    (E) People had all sorts of theories like sports fields or even landing sites for space ships!

33. In the context of the first paragraph, which is the best version of the underlined portion of sentence 11 (reproduced below)?

    Marked with a clear border, they were only used for religious rituals.

    (A) they are only used for religious rituals

    (B) religious rituals happened only in them

    (C) Celts only used them for religious rituals

    (D) these areas were only used for religious rituals

    (E) they were only using for religious rituals

34. In context, which of the following is best to insert before "during holidays" in sentence 13?

    (A) Actually,

    (B) For example,

    (C) But,

    (D) In addition,

    (E) Among the beliefs and practices that are explained is,

35. Which of the following is the best way to combine sentences 14, 15, and 16 (reproduced below)?

    Ancient Celts also built temples on islands. This makes sense because islands have a natural and obvious border. They are land surrounded by water.

    (A) Ancient Celts, because they are land surrounded by water, also built temples on them and they have a natural and obvious border.

    (B) This makes sense because islands are land surrounded by water, have a natural and obvious border, and ancient Celts built temples on them.

    (C) Building temples on them, islands are land surrounded by water and this makes sense because they have a natural and obvious border.

    (D) Surrounded by water, ancient Celts built temples on islands and this makes sense because they have a natural and obvious border.

    (E) Ancient Celts also built temples on islands, which makes sense because islands, as land surrounded by water, have natural and obvious borders.

SECTION 7

Time—20 Minutes
19 Questions

Directions: For each of the following questions, choose the best answer and darken the corresponding oval on the answer sheet.

Each sentence below has one or two blanks, each blank indicating that something has been omitted. Beneath the sentence are five words or sets of words labeled (A) through (E). Choose the word or set of words that, when inserted in the sentence, <u>best</u> fits the meaning of the sentence as a whole.

EXAMPLE:

Today's small, portable computers contrast markedly with the earliest electronic computers, which were ----.

(A) effective
(B) invented
(C) useful
(D) destructive
(E) enormous

---

1. In response to the students' confused expressions, the teacher attempted to ---- the subject with a clear example.

    (A) extricate
    (B) evade
    (C) comprehend
    (D) elucidate
    (E) obfuscate

2. The ---- cat remained by the mouse hole all afternoon, watching for his meal.

    (A) apprehensive
    (B) emaciated
    (C) vigilant
    (D) prominent
    (E) indolent

3. Laura's excuse appeared credible at first, but further questioning and investigation revealed that it was completely ----.

    (A) valid
    (B) sardonic
    (C) righteous
    (D) fabricated
    (E) incredulous

4. The magnificent, ---- sets that depicted a futuristic city in Fritz Lang's epic film *Metropolis* are now widely regarded as an outstanding visual achievement.

    (A) prolific
    (B) modest
    (C) reticent
    (D) archaic
    (E) grandiose

5. As financial rewards grow and the desire to win at all costs is raised to a fever pitch, the baser elements of an athlete's personality can all too easily be ----.

    (A) intensified
    (B) qualified
    (C) submerged
    (D) reduced
    (E) rarefied

6. Though a hummingbird weighs less than one ounce, all species of hummingbirds are ---- eaters, maintaining very high body temperatures and ---- many times their weight in food each day.

    (A) voracious . . consuming
    (B) fastidious . . discarding
    (C) hasty . . locating
    (D) prolific . . producing
    (E) delicate . . storing

GO ON TO THE NEXT PAGE ▷

Directions: The passages below are followed by questions based on their content; questions following a pair of related passages may also be based on the relationship between the paired passages. Answer the questions on the basis of what is <u>stated</u> or <u>implied</u> in the passages and in any introductory material that may be provided.

Questions 7–19 are based on the following passages.

The following passages present two views of the genius of Leonardo da Vinci. Passage 1 emphasizes Leonardo's fundamentally artistic sensibility. Passage 2 offers a defense of his technological achievements.

Passage 1

What a marvelous and celestial creature was Leonardo da Vinci. As a scientist and engineer, his gifts were unparalleled. But his accomplishments in these capacities was hindered by the fact that he
(5) was, before all else, an artist. As one conversant with the perfection of art, and knowing the futility of trying to bring such perfection to the realm of practical application, Leonardo tended toward variability and inconstancy in his endeavors. His
(10) practice of moving compulsively from one project to the next, never bringing any of them to completion, stood in the way of his making any truly useful technical advances.

When Leonardo was asked to create a memorial
(15) for one of his patrons, he designed a bronze horse of such vast proportions that it proved utterly impractical—even impossible—to produce. Some historians maintain that Leonardo never had any intention of finishing this work in the first place.
(20) But it is more likely that he simply became so intoxicated by his grand artistic conception that he lost sight of the fact that the monument actually had to be cast. Similarly, when Leonardo was commissioned to paint the *Last Supper*, he left
(25) the head of Christ unfinished, feeling incapable of investing it with a sufficiently divine demeanor. Yet, as a work of art rather than science or engineering, it is still worthy of our greatest veneration, for Leonardo succeeded brilliantly in captur-
(30) ing the acute anxiety of the Apostles at the most dramatic moment of the Passion narrative.

Such mental restlessness, however, proved more problematic when applied to scientific matters.

When he turned his mind to the natural world,
(35) Leonardo would begin by inquiring into the properties of herbs and end up observing the motions of the heavens. In his technical studies and scientific experiments, he would generate an endless stream of models and drawings, designing complex and
(40) unbuildable machines to raise great weights, bore through mountains, or even empty harbors.

It is this enormous intellectual fertility that has suggested to many that Leonardo can and should be regarded as one of the originators of modern
(45) science. But Leonardo was not himself a true scientist. "Science" is not the hundred-odd principles or *pensieri** that have been pulled out of his *Codici*. Science is comprehensive and methodical thought. Granted, Leonardo always became fascinated by
(50) the intricacies of specific technical challenges. He possessed the artist's interest in detail, which explains his compulsion with observation and problem solving. However, such things alone do not constitute science, which requires the working
(55) out of a systematic body of knowledge—something Leonardo displayed little interest in doing.

* *pensieri*: (Italian) thoughts

Passage 2

As varied as Leonardo's interests were, analysis of his writings points to technology as his main concern. There is hardly a field of applied
(60) mechanics that Leonardo's searching mind did not touch upon in his notebooks. Yet some of his biographers have actually expressed regret that such a man, endowed with divine artistic genius, would "waste" precious years of his life on such a
(65) "lowly" pursuit as engineering.

To appreciate Leonardo's contribution to technology, one need only examine his analysis of the main problem of technology—the harnessing of energy to perform useful work. In Leonardo's

GO ON TO THE NEXT PAGE

(70) time, the main burden of human industry still rested on the muscles of humans and animals. But little attention was given to analyzing this primitive muscle power so that it could be brought to bear most effectively on the required tasks. Against *(75)* this background, Leonardo's approach to work was revolutionary. When he searched for the most efficient ways of using human muscle power, the force of every limb was analyzed and measured.

Consider Leonardo's painstaking building *(80)* approach to the construction of canals. After extensive analysis of the requirements for constructing a particular canal by hand, he concluded that the only reasonable solution was to mechanize the whole operation. Then he considered and *(85)* ultimately discarded numerous schemes to clear excavated material by wheeled vehicles. It was not that Leonardo underestimated wheeled vehicles. But he realized that a cart is useful only on level ground; on steep terrain the material's weight *(90)* would nullify the effort of the animal.

Having systematically rejected several solutions in this way, Leonardo began to examine the feasibility of excavation techniques incorporating a system of cranes. Power was again his main con- *(95)* cern. To activate a crane, the only transportable motor available at the time would have been a treadmill, a machine that converts muscle power into rotary motion. This is not to suggest that Leonardo invented the external treadmill. *(100)* However, it was Leonardo who first used the principle of the treadmill rationally and in accordance with sound engineering principles.

Because Leonardo's insights were sometimes so far beyond the standards of his time, their impor- *(105)* tance to the development of modern engineering is often underestimated. Many scholars, in fact, still regard his work merely as the isolated accomplishments of a remarkably prophetic dreamer, refusing to concede that Leonardo was one of our *(110)* earliest and most significant engineers.

7. The author of Passage 1 seems to regard the "perfection of art" (line 6) as

(A) a more valuable goal than scientific accomplishment

(B) achievable only with diligence and constant effort

(C) applicable to the solving of technical problems

(D) a model to which scientists should aspire

(E) unattainable in the fields of science and engineering

8. The word "variability" in line 9 most nearly means

(A) comprehensiveness

(B) changeability

(C) uncertainty

(D) confusion

(E) disorder

9. The author of Passage 1 considers the *Last Supper* ultimately successful as a work of art because it

(A) is much sought-after by collectors

(B) emphasizes the role of the Apostles in comforting Christ before his crucifixion

(C) captures the divinity of Christ on the eve of his death

(D) depicts a well-known moment in the history of Christianity

(E) conveys the anxiety felt by Christ's Apostles

GO ON TO THE NEXT PAGE

10. In line 34, the author most likely describes the way Leonardo "turned his mind to the natural world" in order to show that

(A) Leonardo's mind was constantly leaping from one topic to another

(B) elements of the natural world are all interconnected

(C) Leonardo's mind was preoccupied with scientific experiments

(D) Leonardo preferred artistic pursuits to scientific inquiry

(E) Leonardo tended to become distracted by his artistic projects

11. The author of Passage 1 is critical of Leonardo's "*pensieri*" (line 47) primarily because they

(A) are factually incorrect

(B) do not constitute a systematic body of thought

(C) contradict widely-accepted scientific principles

(D) were never thoroughly tested

(E) are based on intuition rather than observation

12. In the last paragraph of Passage 1, the author's attitude toward modern scientific investigation can best be characterized as

(A) sentimental

(B) disparaging

(C) respectful

(D) detached

(E) superficial

13. In lines 61–65, the author is critical of some of Leonardo's biographers primarily because they

(A) overestimate his artistic genius

(B) do not adequately recognize his technological contributions

(C) were careless in their analyses of his writings

(D) understate the importance of his artistic masterpieces

(E) ignore the value of science in relation to art and culture

14. The author of Passage 2 considers Leonardo's approach to work "revolutionary" (line 76) principally because he

(A) attempted to replace humans and animals with machines

(B) adapted traditional solutions to previously impossible tasks

(C) studied the mechanics of muscles with unprecedented thoroughness

(D) proposed technical solutions that most people regarded as impossible to achieve

(E) shifted the main burden of industry from human to animal power

15. In lines 84–90, the discussion of wheeled vehicles is presented in order to support the author's point about Leonardo's

(A) thoroughness in examining all possible solutions to a problem

(B) tendency to let his artistic genius interfere with his effectiveness as an engineer

(C) ability to arrive immediately at the best way of approaching a technical task

(D) harmful practice of moving from one idea to the next

(E) underestimation of traditional technology

GO ON TO THE NEXT PAGE

16. The word "concede" in line 109 of Passage 2 most nearly means

    (A) surrender
    (B) acknowledge
    (C) admit weakness
    (D) resign
    (E) sacrifice

17. Both passages suggest that which of the following is fundamental to scientific inquiry?

    (A) intuitive genius
    (B) familiarity with the perfections of art
    (C) an ability to combine knowledge from many different areas
    (D) meticulous observation and analysis
    (E) knowledge of the interconnectedness of all phenomena

18. The author of Passage 1 would probably regard the painstaking analysis of canal-building described in Passage 2 as an example of Leonardo's

    (A) revolutionary approach to work
    (B) ability to complete ambitious engineering projects
    (C) artistic fascination with details
    (D) predisposition to lose interest in specific problems
    (E) penchant for designing unbuildable machines

19. How would the author of Passage 2 respond to the implication in Passage 1 that Leonardo's insights did not result in "truly useful technical advances" (lines 12–13)?

    (A) Usefulness is not an appropriate criterion for judging solutions to technical problems.
    (B) Leonardo would have accomplished more had he not been distracted by his artistic endeavors.
    (C) Leonardo's invention of the external treadmill is one of countless useful advances he instigated.
    (D) Leonardo's ideas were so advanced that they often could not be put into practice in his time.
    (E) Leonardo's contributions to modern engineering have been deliberately ignored by many scholars.

SECTION 8

Time—20 Minutes
16 Questions

Directions: For this section, solve each problem and decide which is the best of the choices given. Fill in the corresponding oval on the answer sheet. You may use any available space for scratchwork.

Notes:

(1) Calculator use is permitted.

(2) All numbers used are real numbers.

(3) Figures are provided for some problems. All figures are drawn to scale and lie in a plane UNLESS otherwise indicated.

(4) Unless otherwise specified, the domain of any function f is assumed to be the set of all real numbers x for which $f(x)$ is a real number.

Information

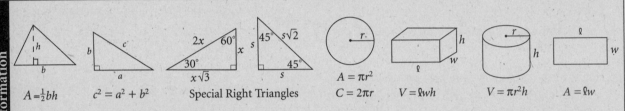

$A = \frac{1}{2}bh$ $c^2 = a^2 + b^2$ Special Right Triangles $A = \pi r^2$ $C = 2\pi r$ $V = \ell wh$ $V = \pi r^2 h$ $A = \ell w$

The sum of the degree measures of the angles in a triangle is 180.
The number of degrees of arc in a circle is 360.
A straight angle has a degree measure of 180.

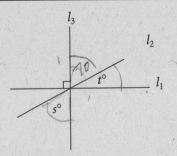

Note: Figure not drawn to scale

1. In the figure above, l_1, l_2, and l_3 intersect at one point. If $s = 70$, then $t =$

   (A) 80
   (B) 60
   (C) 50
   (D) 40
   (E) 20

2. A group of 48 employees is taking 11 cars to the annual company picnic. If each car will be occupied by 4 or 5 employees, what is the number of cars occupied by 5 employees?

   (A) 7
   (B) 6
   (C) 5
   (D) 4
   (E) 3

3. What is the value of x if $2x + 3x = 11$ and $2x - y = 7$?

   (A) 4
   (B) 6
   (C) 9
   (D) 11
   (E) 32

GO ON TO THE NEXT PAGE

4. $\frac{1}{3}$ of 60 is equal to what percent of 50?

(A) $16\frac{2}{3}\%$

(B) 20%

(C) $33\frac{1}{3}\%$

(D) 40%

(E) 60%

5. A television set costs $25 less than twice the cost of a radio. If the television and radio together cost $200, how much more does the television cost than the radio?

(A) $50

(B) $75

(C) $100

(D) $125

(E) $150

6. A ladder is placed against a building such that the top of the ladder forms an angle of 30° with the side of the building. If the ladder is 20 feet long, how far in feet is the bottom of the ladder from the base of the building?

(A) 5

(B) 10

(C) 15

(D) $20\sqrt{2}$

(E) $20\sqrt{3}$

7. A line segment joining two points on the circumference of a circle is 1 inch from the center of the circle at its closest point. If the circle has a 2-inch radius, what is the length of the line segment?

(A) 1

(B) $\sqrt{3}$

(C) 2

(D) $2\sqrt{3}$

(E) $4\sqrt{3}$

$$
\begin{array}{cc}
A & C \\
+A & +B \\
\hline
CB & 5 \\
\end{array}
$$

8. Each correctly worked addition problem above shows the sum of two 1-digit numbers. If the digits A, B, and C are nonzero, then $A =$

(A) 2

(B) 4

(C) 5

(D) 7

(E) 9

9. A frame 2 inches wide is placed around a rectangular picture with dimensions 8 inches by 12 inches. What is the area of the frame in square inches?

(A) 44

(B) 96

(C) 128

(D) 144

(E) 168

10. A coffee shop sold 35 cups of coffee. Of these, 15 contained sugar and 12 contained milk. If 13 cups contained neither milk nor sugar, how many cups must have contained both sugar and milk?

(A) 3

(B) 5

(C) 7

(D) 8

(E) 12

11. If $\dfrac{4}{\sqrt{r+4}} = 2$, what is the value of r?

(A) −4

(B) −2

(C) 0

(D) 2

(E) 4

GO ON TO THE NEXT PAGE

12. What is the y-intercept of the line that passes through the points $(1, 21)$ and $(4, 42)$?

    (A) 0
    (B) 7
    (C) 9
    (D) 14
    (E) 19

13. If $f(x) = x^{-3} + x^{3/2}$, what is the value of $f(3)$?

    (A) $\dfrac{1 + 3\sqrt{3}}{27}$

    (B) $\dfrac{1 + 3\sqrt{3}}{81}$

    (C) $\dfrac{1 + 81\sqrt{3}}{27}$

    (D) $1 + 27\sqrt{3}$

    (E) $27 + 81\sqrt{3}$

    r, s, t

14. In the sequence above, if each term after the first is x more than the previous term, what is the average of r, s, and t in terms of r and x?

    (A) $r + x$

    (B) $r + \dfrac{x}{3}$

    (C) $r + \dfrac{2x}{3}$

    (D) $\dfrac{r + x}{3}$

    (E) $3(r + x)$

Subtract 6 from x.
Divide this sum by 3.
Add 4 to this quotient.

15. Which of the following is the result obtained by performing the operations described above?

    (A) $\dfrac{x - 2}{3}$

    (B) $\dfrac{x + 2}{3}$

    (C) $\dfrac{x - 6}{3}$

    (D) $\dfrac{x + 6}{3}$

    (E) $\dfrac{6x + 4}{3}$

16. What is the least positive integer a for which $25a$ is the cube of an integer?

    (A) 1
    (B) 3
    (C) 5
    (D) 25
    (E) 125

IF YOU FINISH BEFORE TIME IS CALLED, YOU MAY CHECK YOUR WORK ON THIS SECTION ONLY. DO NOT TURN TO ANY OTHER SECTION IN THE TEST. STOP

KAPLAN
Test Prep and Admissions

SECTION 9

Time—10 Minutes
14 Questions

Directions: For each question in this section, select the best answer from among the choices given and fill in the corresponding oval on the answer sheet.

The following sentences test correctness and effectiveness of expression. Part of each sentence or the entire sentence is underlined; beneath each sentence are five ways of phrasing the underlined material. Choice (A) repeats the original phrasing; the other four choices are different. If you think the original phrasing produces a better sentence than any of the alternatives, select choice (A); if not, select one of the other choices.

In making your selection, follow the requirements of standard written English; that is, pay attention to grammar, choice of words, sentence construction, and punctuation. Your selection should result in the most effective sentence—clear and precise, without awkwardness or ambiguity.

EXAMPLE:

Every apple in the baskets <u>are ripe and labeled according to the date it was picked</u>.

ANSWER: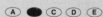

(A) are ripe and labeled according to the date it was picked
(B) is ripe and labeled according to the date it was picked
(C) are ripe and labeled according to the date they were picked
(D) is ripe and labeled according to the date they were picked
(E) are ripe and labeled as to the date it was picked

1. My roommate always complained of having too much homework, but in reality, <u>he had a lesser amount of homework to do than</u> other students.

   (A) he had a lesser amount of homework to do than
   (B) his homework was the least among
   (C) he was having less homework to do than
   (D) the amount of homework he had to do was the least of
   (E) he had less homework than

2. Children who grew up in the 1990s watched more television <u>than</u> the 1960s.

   (A) than
   (B) than did
   (C) than that of
   (D) than with the children in
   (E) than did children in

3. Although talent may be a crucial element on the road to fame, <u>it is difficult to succeed without a highly developed work ethic</u>.

   (A) it is difficult to succeed without a highly developed work ethic
   (B) being difficult to succeed without a highly developed work ethic
   (C) the difficulty in succeeding is when you don't have highly developed work ethic
   (D) without a highly developed work ethic, succeeding is difficult
   (E) it will be difficult to succeed without a highly developed work ethic

GO ON TO THE NEXT PAGE

Test Prep and Admissions

4. Nicolas believes that today's syrupy pop music is a musical form that <u>cannot endure long enough as a musical statement to affect or change the work of future musicians.</u>

(A) cannot endure long enough as a musical statement to affect or change the work of future musicians

(B) cannot endure long enough as a musical statement, for ages to come neither affecting or changing the work of future musicians

(C) is not a lasting musical statement that for ages to come will either affect or change the work of future musicians

(D) is not a lasting musical statement that will remain for ages affecting and changing the work of future musicians

(E) will not last long enough either to affect the work of future musicians

5. The Old City sections of modern <u>Stockholm, evocative</u> of the city's historical prosperity in that cobblestone, narrow streets, and lively shops abound.

(A) Stockholm, evocative

(B) Stockholm evoking

(C) Stockholm, evocations

(D) Stockholm are evocative

(E) Stockholm is evoking

6. The lawyer argued that although her client had indeed committed the crime of burglary, <u>the redemption is in his returning</u> the stolen items and expressing great remorse for his actions.

(A) the redemption is in his returning

(B) the redemption he has is in his returning

(C) her client had redeemed himself by returning

(D) her client was able to redeem himself when he returned

(E) redeeming himself in his return of

7. <u>Having led the league in combined scoring and rebounding statistics, the NBA named Kevin Garnett</u> as its Most Valuable Player for the 2003–2004 season.

(A) Having led the league in combined scoring and rebounding statistics, the NBA named Kevin Garnett

(B) The NBA, which chose Kevin Garnett for his combined scoring and rebounding statistics, named him

(C) Kevin Garnett's combined scoring and rebounding statistics led to his being named by the NBA

(D) Because of his leading the league in combined scoring and rebounding statistics, the NBA named Kevin Garnett

(E) Because he led the league in combined scoring and rebounding statistics, Kevin Garnett was named by the NBA

8. In the sixteenth century a group of Scottish nobles ended their traditional French <u>alliance, they joined forces</u> with the King of England in hopes of combining the two kingdoms.

(A) alliance, they joined forces

(B) alliance; they had joined forces

(C) alliance; they joined forces

(D) alliance, and so they would join forces

(E) alliance; in this way joining forces

9. The quarterback's lack of aim <u>had been exasperating to his team and he was</u> more accurate after several games.

(A) had been exasperating to his team and he was

(B) had been exasperating to his team; but he had been

(C) had been exasperating to his team, but he became more

(D) exasperated his team, however he became

(E) exasperated his team, while he was

GO ON TO THE NEXT PAGE ⟩

10. Saxophone playing must be enjoying <u>a surge in popularity, nearly 25 members</u> of our marching band play the sax.

   (A) a surge in popularity, nearly 25 members
   (B) a surge in popularity, although 25 members
   (C) a surge in popularity, and nearly 25 members
   (D) a surge in popularity; nearly 25 members
   (E) a surge in popularity, while nearly 25 members

11. The creation of low acid orange juice made it possible for people to enjoy juice that is healthy <u>as well as digests easily</u>.

   (A) as well as digests easily
   (B) and being digested as well
   (C) and also easily digests
   (D) and digests easily as well
   (E) as well as easily digestible

12. The method of printing fabric called *batik* originated in Southeast Asia; wax is applied to patterned areas, and <u>then boiled off after dyeing</u>.

   (A) then boiled off after dyeing
   (B) then, after dyeing, it is boiled off
   (C) later it is boiled off after dyeing
   (D) after which, dyers boil it off
   (E) then it is boiled off after its dyeing

13. <u>Some taxpayers knowingly violate IRS regulations when filing their tax returns, in other respects they are law-abiding citizens, however.</u>

   (A) Some taxpayers knowingly violate IRS regulations when filing their tax returns, in other respects they are law-abiding citizens, however.
   (B) Some taxpayers who are otherwise obedient citizens knowingly violate IRS regulations in their tax returns.
   (C) Some taxpayers violate IRS regulations knowingly and openly and are otherwise law-abiding citizens.
   (D) Although otherwise law-abiding citizens, some taxpayers, however, violate IRS regulations knowingly and openly.
   (E) Some taxpayers which violate IRS regulations knowingly and openly are in other respects law-abiding citizens.

14. <u>Underestimating their opponents' ability, the game was lost by the defending champions.</u>

   (A) Underestimating their opponents' ability, the game was lost by the defending champions.
   (B) The game was lost by the defending champions because of their underestimating their opponents' ability.
   (C) The defending champions, underestimating the ability of their opponents, and losing the game.
   (D) The defending champions lost the game because they underestimated their opponents' ability.
   (E) The game lost by the defending champions underestimating their opponents' ability.

IF YOU FINISH BEFORE TIME IS CALLED, YOU MAY CHECK YOUR WORK ON THIS SECTION ONLY. DO NOT TURN TO ANY OTHER SECTION IN THE TEST.

STOP

Practice Test Seven: **Answer Key**

SECTION 1

Essay

SECTION 2

1. C
2. B
3. D
4. A
5. B
6. E
7. A
8. B
9. B
10. C
11. D
12. D
13. D
14. D
15. C
16. E
17. D
18. A
19. B
20. C
21. B
22. A
23. E
24. D

SECTION 3

1. C
2. E
3. A
4. B
5. B
6. A
7. C
8. E
9. E
10. E
11. D
12. D
13. A
14. D
15. B
16. C
17. A
18. C
19. D
20. A

SECTION 4

1. B
2. D
3. C
4. B
5. C
6. C
7. E
8. D
9. B
10. C
11. C
12. A
13. D

14. B
15. C
16. C
17. B
18. D
19. A
20. B
21. E
22. B
23. C
24. B

SECTION 5

1. A
2. D
3. E
4. C
5. E
6. C
7. D
8. A
9. $5.50
10. 49
11. 36/5
12. 6 or 8
13. 21 or 28
14. 80
15. 7.5
16. 306, 324, 342, 360, 378, 396
17. 7/15
18. $2 < x < 6$

SECTION 6

1. B
2. E
3. A
4. D
5. B
6. E
7. A
8. D
9. E
10. D
11. B
12. B
13. D
14. B
15. C
16. E
17. C
18. D
19. B
20. E
21. D
22. E
23. A
24. D
25. B
26. B
27. E
28. D
29. D
30. D
31. B
32. C
33. D
34. B
35. E

SECTION 7

1. D
2. C
3. D
4. E
5. A
6. A
7. E
8. B
9. E
10. A
11. B
12. C
13. B
14. C
15. A
16. B
17. D
18. C
19. D

SECTION 8

1. E
2. D
3. A
4. D
5. A
6. B
7. D
8. D
9. B
10. B
11. C
12. D
13. C
14. A

15. D
16. C

SECTION 9

1. E
2. E
3. D
4. E
5. D
6. C
7. E
8. C
9. C
10. D
11. E
12. A
13. B
14. D

PRACTICE TEST SEVEN

Critical Reading

	Number Right	Number Wrong	Raw Score
Section 2:	☐	− (.25 × ☐)	= ☐
Section 4:	☐	− (.25 × ☐)	= ☐
Section 7:	☐	− (.25 × ☐)	= ☐
		Critical Reading Raw Score	= ☐

(rounded up)

Writing

	Number Right	Number Wrong	Raw Score
Section 1:	☐ (ESSAY GRADE)	× 3.17	= ☐
Section 6:	☐	− (.25 × ☐)	= ☐
Section 9:	☐	− (.25 × ☐)	= ☐
		Writing Raw Score	= ☐

(rounded up)

Math

	Number Right	Number Wrong	Raw Score
Section 3:	☐	− (.25 × ☐)	= ☐
Section 5A: (QUESTIONS 1–8)	☐	− (.25 × ☐)	= ☐
Section 5B: (QUESTIONS 9–18)	☐	(no wrong answer penalty)	= ☐
Section 8:	☐	− (.25 × ☐)	= ☐
		Math Raw Score	= ☐

(rounded up)

Turn to page xiv to convert your raw score to a scaled score.

Answers and Explanations

SECTION 1

Score 6 Essay

Nobody likes a whiner, the person who sits back and points out what is wrong with everything but does nothing to change things. However, complaining can be the first step toward making a change. Simply expressing dissatisfaction with a situation is a way of recognizing an injustice. One person's complaint can help others voice their frustration or anger, and this "complaining" can build to a movement for change. The inverse, accepting a bad situation and learning to live with it, can help perpetuate injustice. This is especially true for deeply rooted injustices—those that permeate an entire society. To the individual such injustice can seem impossible to change.

For example, an African American living in the South of the 1950s might have felt that segregation was something that was part of life. In response she might—believing that she could not change Southern society and being without the means to move to a less hostile place—have decided to change her attitude toward segregation. She might have decided to look for the positive side of this injustice, perhaps seeing how segregation helped build a strong African American community. While this sort of "grin-and-bear-it" attitude can help a person cope on a day-to-day basis, it demonstrates to the community that the unjust society works. The white Southerners who supported segregation could point to this sort of coping to prove that both communities, white and black, were happy living apart.

In the same situation, another African American might have decided not to look for the positive side of having to eat in separate restaurants, attend separate schools, and ride in the back of the bus. Instead, she might have complained to her relatives and friends about how unfair Southern society was. By simply complaining, this person would have been making a small protest against injustice. And, her friends and family might have agreed with her. This complaining has the potential to gather momentum and develop into something larger, something more than complaining.

The Civil Rights Movement was certainly not a movement of whiners. It was a movement of people committed to change. But, if most African Americans in the South had opted to change their attitude toward segregation rather than to complain about the injustice, the Civil Rights Movement might not have caught fire. Complaining is a way of recognizing injustice that can keep a person open to change. This unwillingness to adapt to injustice is the soil out of which all movements for change grow.

6 Score Critique

All essays are graded on four basic criteria: Topic, Support, Organization, and Language. The author sticks to the assignment, and the essay shows a thorough development of his stance on the topic. He explains his supporting example in detail, offers specific situations to back it up, and communicates his ideas in concise, persuasive language.

The essay is highly organized. The first paragraph introduces the writer's point of view—complaining does not have to be whining; often it can be the spark that brings about great change. The second paragraph introduces his main supporting example—the Civil Rights movement was one instance where "complaining" against unjust policies led to changing society as a whole. The following paragraphs offer colorful examples to back up his point, and his last paragraph wraps up his persuasion by wondering what might have happened had people not complained.

The writer's language and grammar is strong throughout. There is plentiful and meaningful variation in sentence structure, from short and simple sentences to longer complex sentences. Additionally, the essay is essentially error-free.

Score 4 Essay

The squeaky wheel gets the grease. This saying says if you complain you will get what you want. There is some truth in this saying, it is important to stick up for yourself and to complain if necessary. Last year, I worked as an sales clerk in a department store. I worked a few hours after school and one day on the weekend. I enjoyed the job because I am interested in fashion and retail. However, one of my coworkers took a dislike to me because she thought I had told everyone a secret of hers. She started to make problems for me at work. For example, she would steal my time card so I would not be able to punch back in after break. My time card would reappear at the end of the shift, and I would be reprimanded for not marking my hours properly. I was mad because I really hadn't told any secrets.

She would also make me look bad when I was with customers. For example, she would suggest that what I was telling them about the clothes was not true. I was very upset by my coworker's behavior but the manager was not easy to talk to and I was worried that it would seem that I could not handle my own problems. I knew I was good at my job. I thought I would seem like a baby to complain about this problem with my coworker.

However, one day my manager told me that if I made any more mistakes with my time card she would have to let me go. I was devastated because I took my job seriously. I finally decided to tell my manager about my problem with my coworker and she was very understanding. In fact she told me that she had decided to let my coworker go because she had been caught stealing merchandice from the store. As soon as my coworker was not working at the store, my manager could see that I had been telling the truth about my coworker. My manager later told me that I should have come to her much sooner with my problem instead of just putting up with the situation. I learned that sometimes it is important to complain and stick up for yourself instead of just putting up with a bad situation that you think you cannot change.

4 Score Critique

All essays are graded on four basic criteria: Topic, Support, Organization, and Language. The author sticks to the topic and includes a detailed example to support her point of view. The essay as a whole, however, is not entirely effective as a persuasive piece. The author merely recounts one story, from beginning to end, to tell her point of view. While her story does back up her stance on the topic, it goes on for too long and the essay becomes more about her personal account than responding to the prompt.

By telling the story of her work experience, the author provides good support that fulfills the assignment. However, the writer could have made her point of view clearer from the beginning, and then more concisely recounted the main details of her work story. She then could have given fuller detail about how the situation improved—the second half of the essay could have concentrated on how complaining changed things for the better. This would have been a stronger response to the prompt.

The essay exhibits organization, with a clear beginning, middle, and end. The language in the essay is somewhat unsophisticated, but only has minor errors in spelling, sentence structure, and grammar.

Score 2 Essay

My Mom always used to say to me "I don't like your attitude." She would say this when I was not doing what I was suposed to be doing or was doing something wrong. My mother taught me that your attitude is very important because you need to have a good attitude. If something is really horrible, you might want to complain. But alot of people have bad attitudes and their negative and complain alot. Complaining sometimes does people good, but usually doesn't do anybody any good. What you need to do is look at the situation and figure out how to make it better. This is having a good attitude. Once I did not get along with my teacher and I would tell my Mom that the teacher was picking on me and that I wanted to move classes. My mom told me that maybe it was something I was doing wrong and I should try harder to get along and I didn't know how to do this but I decided to try. When I started not thinking about my teacher not liking me but just doing my work and trying hard I started to do better and my teacher seemed to like me more. Then I started to like school and it ended up Mrs Carpenter was the best teacher I ever had.

Instead of complaining I tried to change things by having a good attitiude. Having a good attitude can turn a bad situation into something good if you are willing to try.

2 Score Critique

All essays are graded on four basic criteria: Topic, Support, Organization, and Language. The writer states a position on the topic in his first few sentences, but he doesn't state it strongly and clearly. Several times, he says that complaining does have benefits. When writing your essay, you want to make sure your readers know exactly what stance you're taking. The stance also seems to be more about attitude than complaining.

The writer tries to support his position through the use of a personal story about his teacher at school, but the story goes on too long. Shortening this example to tell his point, and then adding another relevant example, would have suited the author well.

The essay is presented in a good order, but is in need of a paragraph break. Essays should have a distinct introduction, a body, and a conclusion. The essay also has a good deal of spelling errors and grammar errors—there are a lot of run-on sentences and awkward sentences.

SECTION 2

1. C

Difficulty: Low

"But" indicates that there's a contrast between the two halves of the sentence. *Carnivorous* dinosaurs might have been good swimmers who hated the water, or they might have been bad swimmers who loved it. Only the word pair in choice (C), *accomplished . . feared,* reflects this sort of contrast. There's no contrast in the sentence when the words in choices (B), (D), and (E) are plugged into the blanks. And the sentence makes no sense when the words in choice (A), *swift . . entered,* are placed in the blanks.

2. B

Difficulty: Low

The clue in this sentence is the clause "composed of thousands of pieces of luminous stained glass," which reinforces the meaning of the word in the blank. Based on this clause, you can predict that this word must be something like "complex." So, the correct choice is (B), *intricate,* which is a synonym for complex.

3. D

Difficulty: Medium

The main clue in this sentence is the phrase "blown by the wind," which gives the impression of an unwilling or inactive type of movement. Choice (D), *passively,* means "not participating actively," and for the man-of-war to be moved by the wind, it would have to be passive. Since it's difficult to move motionlessly, (B)'s out, and none of the others mean anything like "inactively."

4. A

Difficulty: Medium

The pivotal signal here is the phrase "but in fact," which signals that the words that fit the two blanks will have opposite meanings. We have more information for the second blank, since we know that she "had many close friends," and the only word that fits here is *gregarious,* which means "outgoing or sociable." The first blank fits as well, as the opposite of gregarious is *reclusive.* The only other pair of opposites is (B), *generous* and *frugal,* but these don't have the necessary connection with the idea of having or lacking close friends.

5. B

Difficulty: Medium

For the first blank in this sentence, three different choices would fit: (B) *reputation,* (C) *fame,* or (E) *notoriety.* When you try the three possibilities in the second blank, though, only (B) works. She wouldn't want to *defer* or "put off" *acclaim,* and *publicize* acclaim doesn't work here either. However, it makes sense for the artist to *deserve,* or be worthy of, acclaim for her sculpture, so (B) is correct.

6. E

Difficulty: Medium

The second part of this sentence elaborates on decompression sickness, which the first part of the sentence says may cause whales' death. That context tells you that the sickness can be *lethal,* or fatal. Choice (A), *docile,* means teachable or obedient. *Succulent,* choice (B), means juicy or delectable, either literally or figuratively. Choice (C), *mandatory,* means required or compulsory. *Robust,* (D), means strong and/or healthy.

7. A

Difficulty: High

A good strategy for this question, which depends on context to identify the correct answer, is to try to fill in the blanks with a concept. The media gives information, so look for a first word that relates to information. Think about the kinds of things that can accompany fame to help you find an appropriate second word. An *intimation* is a suggestion or a hint, and *adulation* is excessive flattery or admiration. A *euphemism,* choice (B), is the substitution of a mild or vague term for one that might be offensive; and *aplomb* is self-confidence or poise. *Rhetoric*, choice (C), is effectiveness, art, or skill in speaking or writing; and acme means a high point or summit, usually figurative. *Stasis*, choice (D), is motionlessness or balance, often implying stagnation; and *euthanasia* is assisted suicide, sometimes called mercy-killing. A *mote*, choice (E), is a very small particle or speck; and the noun *abandon* is a total lack of inhibition, often resulting from abundant enthusiasm.

8. B

Difficulty: High

The key phrases here are "social dynamics" and "in groups." Although (E), *education*, may seem possible, *interaction* goes better with the idea of people relating to one another in a group setting.

9. B

Difficulty: Low

This type of function question asks you to identify the relationship between one sentence and the rest of the paragraph. The first sentence introduces a theory about global warming, and the rest of the paragraph works to disprove the theory. This matches (B). Choices (D) and (E) are out of scope.

10. C

Difficulty: Medium

In this question, the cited line describes the intended effects of the legislation that was a response to the melting Arctic ice cap. As this passage cites global warming as the cause of this melting, it would make sense that the legislation would work to limit or at least *control* such climate changes. Choice (B), *to raise*, is the opposite of *curb* as used in the paragraph. Choice (E), *to eliminate*, comes close to capturing the intended meaning of *curb*, but it is too extreme.

11. D

Difficulty: Low

This type of detail question essentially asks you to identify at least one area of common ground between two possibly conflicting arguments. While the authors disagree about the accuracy of global warming theories, a clear similarity is evident in the opening sentences of the two paragraphs. Although Passage 1 states that the polar ice caps are not melting and Passage 2 argues that they are receding, both

authors suggest that these caps would be affected by global temperature changes. Choice (C) is a misused detail—while both passages cite a period of 20 years, neither author suggests that it is "important" to study a period of this specific length.

12. D

Difficulty: Medium

Never try to answer detail questions from memory. Go back to the specific lines referenced by the question stem to find evidence to support your answer choice. The question is centered on the statements made by the author in Passage 1, so focus on the context surrounding the lines with the cited statistics. In particular, note that in the last sentence of the paragraph the author explores these statistics in more detail, stating that the ice decline actually came during "only one year," rather than 20. This statement suggests that this report is deceptive or misleading, which matches choice (D). Choice (A) is distortion. The author argues that the conclusions drawn from this report are deceptive, but not necessarily *inaccurate*. Choice (B) is incorrect because the author does not discuss whether this report is *intentionally* misleading. Nothing suggests that the author finds the conclusions *unfortunate*, (E).

13. D

Difficulty: Medium

This is the first question of the set, which means that the answer can most likely be found near the beginning of the passage. The author says in the second sentence that Eleanor is "suppressing a momentary surge of panic" as she gets out of bed; in other words, she is trying to *quell her apprehension*, (D).

14. D

Difficulty: Low

Always go back to the cited line and read the surrounding sentences to understand the context. Eleanor thinks of Harold's wardrobe when she reflects that "Harold was a creature of habit." Therefore, the author is using the description of the wardrobe to reveal Harold's *adherence to routine*, (D).

15. C

Difficulty: Medium

Avoid the temptation on vocabulary-in-context questions to select an answer from among the choices without going back and reading the sentence: It strikes Eleanor as "fitting" that Harold is wearing a black suit—"black for mourning" is appropriate to how she feels. In this context, fitting means *apt*, (C).

16. E

Difficulty: Medium

This question has no line reference, but since the questions in each set go through the passage in order, simply scan down the passage from the lines near the end of paragraph two tested in the previous question to find the reference to "wisps of steam." Eleanor thinks that, to Harold, she must be merely a wisp of steam. To find out why she thinks that, read the surrounding sentences. Harold ignores her, or *appears not to notice her presence*, (E), while he's eating breakfast.

17. D

Difficulty: Low

Read the sentence right before the cited sentence. Eleanor resolves "never to forget Harold's utter lack of courtesy and consideration." This is why "they would never be friends." The best paraphrase of "Harold's utter lack of courtesy and consideration" among the answer choices is (D), *Harold behaves so thoughtlessly*.

18. A

Difficulty: Medium

The sentences preceding the cited lines indicate that Eleanor "feels her resolve crumbling" because Harold has announced to her, as he is leaving, that he loves her. She certainly had *not expected Harold to express his feelings*, (A), and now he has thrown a temporary emotional wrench into her plans to leave him.

19. B

Difficulty: High

By packing up her suitcases, which "promise a new life of independence and self-worth," Eleanor is trying to bring an end to only one thing—her *marriage*. She views her marriage as "loveless" and as a "suffocating compromise."

20. C

Difficulty: Medium

Once again, it's important to read the sentences before and after the cited line. The author says that "it seemed to Eleanor that her departure, once begun, gained momentum with each passing second." This is what makes her feel "like a bird taking wing"—she has *finally begun her departure*, (C).

21. B

Difficulty: High

Eleanor feels "twenty-nine years of marriage drawing her back, like gravity" when she's pulling out of the driveway. In the following few sentences, she experiences grief and doubts about leaving Harold. Given this context, it's clear that the author uses the image of gravity to emphasize Eleanor's *emotional investment in her life with Harold*, (B).

22. A

Difficulty: Medium

In the context of the sentence in which "respite" appears, the word means "vacation" or *rest*, (A).

23. E

Difficulty: Medium

This question tests understanding of the tone of the end of the passage. Reading through the second half of the last paragraph, it seems that Eleanor is experiencing conflicting feelings: she wants to be free of her marriage but she also feels drawn back. As she drives away, she has not made the definite decision to leave her marriage forever. Her feelings are *unresolved*, (E).

24. D

Difficulty: Medium

This is a global question that deals with the passage as a whole. Remember that global questions do not ask you to analyze specific paragraphs, but rather how all the paragraphs fit together into one complete passage with a purpose. The beginning of the passage describes the morning rituals of Eleanor and Harold, (A), but the rest of the passage deals with a greater issue. Similarly, choice (C) only refers to a small portion of the passage. Choice (B) and (E) are matters of opinion, and this is not a persuasive piece, but a story. Choice (D) accurately describes the author's intent in writing the passage.

SECTION 3

1. C

Difficulty: Low

Strategic Advice: You're looking for the student who finished third, so number the students in order of their running time by comparing the decimal fractions.

Getting to the Answer: Grace had the shortest time, so she's in first place; Francisco with a time of 32.083 is in second place; and Logan with a time of 32.146 seconds is in third place.

2. E

Difficulty: Low

Strategic Advice: You must know how to calculate using powers to find the value of a^2.

Getting to the Answer: Clear the fraction by multiplying both sides by 6 to get rid of the denominator on the left:

$$6 \times \frac{a^2}{2 \cdot 3} = 6 \times (6 \times 49)$$
$$a^2 = 6^2 \times 49$$

Since $\quad 49 = 7^2,$
$$a^2 = 6^2 \times 7^2,$$
or $\quad a^2 = (6 \times 7)^2$. Therefore, $a^2 = 42^2$.

3. A

Difficulty: Low

Strategic Advice: You're given that a pump can drain a 375-gallon tank in 15 minutes. Therefore, the rate of the pump is $\frac{375 \text{ gallons}}{15 \text{ minutes}}$, or 25 gallons per minute.

Getting to the Answer: At this rate, the pump will drain a 600-gallon tank in $\frac{600}{25}$, or 24 minutes. So it will take $24 - 15$, or 9 more minutes to drain the 600-gallon tank.

4. B

Difficulty: Low

Strategic Advice: You're looking for the 47th flower in a repeating pattern. Since there are 5 different flowers in the pattern, the last flower in the pattern corresponds to a multiple of 5.

Getting to the Answer: The 5th, 10th, ... , and 45th flowers will be zinnias. But there will also be two remainders, and so the 46th will be the first flower in the pattern and the 47th will be the second flower, which is a daffodil.

5. B

Difficulty: Low

Strategic Advice: The median is the middle term in a group of terms arranged in numerical order.

Getting to the Answer: Arrange Maja's quiz scores from least to greatest: 76, 78, 80, 81, 84, 84, 91. So the middle term is 81, and choice (B) is correct.

6. A

Difficulty: Medium

Strategic Advice: Pay attention only to the exact information you're given.

Getting to the Answer: You're given that $p < q$ and $r < q$. However, this tells you nothing about the relationship between p and r; you only know that they're both less than q. So Statement III is not necessarily true, and you can eliminate choices (C) and (E). You're also given that $r < s$, but all this tells you is that q and s are greater than r; you can't determine the relationship between q and s. Therefore, Statement II is not necessarily true and choice (D) can be eliminated. Since s could be less than q, s could be less than p. So Statement I is not necessarily true, and choice (B) can be eliminated. Since none of the statements are necessarily true, choice (A) is correct.

7. C

Difficulty: Medium

Strategic Advice: Looking at the pie chart, you should see that Housing & Utilities represents about $\frac{1}{3}$ of the Newton's monthly expenses.

Getting to the Answer: Since their total monthly income is $1,800, the amount spent on Housing & Utilities is approximately $\frac{1}{3} \times \$1,800$, or $600.

8. E

Difficulty: Medium

Strategic Advice: You'll need to utilize the positive/negative laws and your knowledge about powers to solve this problem. Pick numbers for x and y.

Getting to the Answer: Let $x = 2$, so $x^2 = 4$. Therefore, y must equal -4 in order for the equation to remain true. So plug in 2 for x and -4 for y into each of the answer choices to see which one is true:

Choice (A):	Is	$(2)^2 = -4$?	No.	Eliminate.
Choice (B):	Is	$(2)(-4) = -4$?	No.	Eliminate.
Choice (C):	Is	$2 = -\dfrac{4}{2}$?	No.	Eliminate.
Choice (D):	Is	$(2)^3 = (-4)^2$?	No.	Eliminate.
Choice (E):	Is	$(2)^4 = (-4)^2$?	Yes.	

9. E

Difficulty: Medium

Strategic Advice: If the product of 3 positive integers is an even number, then at least one of the 3 integers must be even. Pick numbers to make this clearer.

Getting to the Answer:

$2 \times 3 \times 5 = 30$ Even

$7 \times 6 \times 9 = 378$ Even

$11 \times 13 \times 4 = 572$ Even

So choice (E) is correct.

10. E

Difficulty: Medium

Strategic Advice: You're given that r is a multiple of both 12 and 18. So list the first few multiples of each to find r:

Multiples of 12: 12, 24, 36, 48, 60

Multiples of 18: 18, 36, 54, 72, 90

Getting to the Answer: Since 36 is both a multiple of 12 and 18, r could equal 36. Scanning the answer choices, you should see that the only factor of 36 among the choices is 36 itself. So choice (E) is correct.

11. D

Difficulty: Medium

Strategic Advice: To be able to multiply 4^x and 8^x they must be expressed as powers with the same base. When you multiply powers with the same base, you add the exponents and keep the base.

Getting to the Answer: Since 4 and 8 are powers of 2, 4^x and 8^x can be written as powers of 2.

$$4 = 2^2, \text{ so } 4^x = (2^2)^x$$

When you raise a power to a power, you multiply the powers: so $(2^2)^x = 2^{2x}$.

And $8 = 2^3$, so $8^x = (2^3)^x = 2^{3x}$.

$$\text{So } (4^x)(8^x) = 2^{2x}\, 2^{3x} = 2^{2x+3x} = 2^{5x}.$$

12. D

Difficulty: Medium

Strategic Advice: Remember that

$$\text{average} = \frac{\text{Sum of terms}}{\text{Number of terms}}, \text{ in this case } 6 = \frac{\text{Sum of terms}}{6},$$

or Sum of terms $= 6 \times 6 = 36$.

Getting to the Answer: Now the sum of the terms is changed: 3 is subtracted from 4 of the numbers. The new sum of the terms will be 3×4, or 12 less than the original sum; that is, $36 - 12 = 24$. The new average is then

$$\frac{\text{New sum of terms}}{\text{Number of terms}} = \frac{24}{6} = 4.$$

13. A

Difficulty: Medium

Strategic Advice: For this coordinate geometry problem, the perimeter is the sum of the lengths of all the sides.

Getting to the Answer: First sketch the triangle. We have labeled the points A, B, and C.

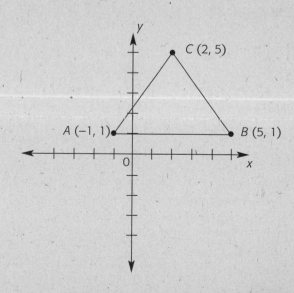

The length of AB is simply the difference in the x-coordinates, that is $5 - (-1) = 6$. Finding the lengths of BC and AC is trickier. Divide triangle BC into two right triangles by drawing a perpendicular line from C to side AB, as shown.

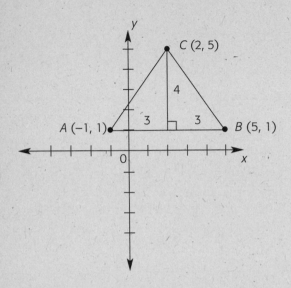

Now AC and BC are the hypotenuses of right triangles—you can find their length using the Pythagorean theorem.

$$(AC)^2 = 4^2 + 3^2 = 16 + 9 = 25.$$

So $AC = \sqrt{25} = 5$.

Similarly, $(BC)^2 = 4^2 + 3^2$, so $BC = 5$ also.

So the perimeter is $6 + 5 + 5 = 16$.

14. D

Difficulty: Medium

Strategic Advice: Simply count all the possibilities.

Getting to the Answer: If the numbers must have a tens' digit greater than 5, they must be 60 or greater. Since they are two digit numbers, they must be less than 100. Since the units' digit is odd, they must be odd. So you need to count all the odd numbers between 60 and 100. Well, there are 5 such numbers with a tens' digit of 6: 61, 63, 65, 67, and 69. Similarly there will be 5 more numbers with a tens' digit of 7, 5 more with a tens' digit of 8 and another 5 with a tens' digit of 9. That's $5 + 5 + 5 + 5$, or 20 such numbers.

15. B

Difficulty: Medium

Strategic Advice: In this percent word problem, since percent means hundredths, a percent $= \dfrac{a}{100}$ and b percent $= \dfrac{b}{100}$.

Getting to the Answer: So a percent of b percent of $200 =$

$$\frac{a}{100} \times \frac{b}{100} \times 200 = \frac{200ab}{10,000} = \frac{ab}{50}.$$

16. C

Difficulty: Medium

Strategic Advice: Read carefully.

Getting to the Answer: If the tricate of z is 3, that means that one third of the smallest multiple of 3 greater than z is 3. That is, the smallest multiple of 3 greater than z is $3 \times 3 = 9$. The smallest multiple of 3 greater than z will be 9 only if $6 < z < 9$. Answer choice (C) is the only number in this range so it must be correct.

17. A

Difficulty: High

Strategic Advice: The internal angles of any triangle sum to 180°, so $a + b + c = 180$.

Getting to the Answer: That gives you 3 different equations containing the 3 unknowns a, b and c — you can solve these for b. One way to do this is to combine the equations: $a + b = 80$ and $b + c = 140$.

Then:

$$a + b + b + c = 80 + 140$$
$$a + 2b + c = 220$$

Now subtract the third equation:

$$a + 2b + c - (a + b + c) = 220 - 180$$
$$a + 2b + c - a - b - c = 220 - 180$$
$$a - a + 2b - b + c - c = 40$$
$$b = 40$$

18. C

Difficulty: High

Strategic Advice: If you know the slope of RS you can find the y-coordinate of R using the slope formula. The slope of a line is the change in y-coordinates divided by the change in x-coordinates.

Getting to the Answer: Since the line also passes through the origin, (0,0), the slope of RS = the slope of

$$SO = \frac{6-0}{9-0} = \frac{6}{9} = \frac{2}{3}.$$ If the slope of RS is $\frac{2}{3}$ then

$$\frac{2}{3} = \frac{y\text{-coordinate of } R\text{-}6}{x\text{-coordinate of } R\text{-}9}$$

$$\frac{2}{3} = \frac{y\text{-coordinate of } R\text{-}6}{(-6)-9}$$

$$\frac{2}{3} = \frac{y\text{-coordinate of } R\text{-}6}{-15}$$

$$(-15)\frac{2}{3} = y\text{-coordinate of } R\text{-}6$$

$$-10 + 6 = y\text{-coordinate of } R$$

$$-4 = y\text{-coordinate of } R$$

19. D

Difficulty: High

Strategic Advice: Since the radio station can be received in all directions, its region of reception is a circle with the radio station at the center.

Getting to the Answer: Before the change, the signal could be received for 60 miles, so the area of reception was a circle with radius 60 miles. Now it can be received for 40 miles further, or for a total of 60 + 40, or 100 miles. The area is now a circle with radius 100 miles:

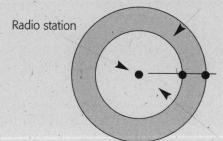

New region of recepction

Radio station

Old region of recepction

The increase is just the difference in these areas; that is, the shaded region on the above diagram.

$$\text{Increase} = \text{New area} - \text{Old area}$$
$$= \pi(100)^2 - \pi(60)^2$$
$$= 10,000\,\pi - 3,600\,\pi$$
$$= 6,400\,\pi$$

The value of π is a bit more than 3, so $6,400\,\pi$ is a bit more than $3 \times 6,400$, or just over 19,200. The only choice close to this is (D), 20,000.

20. A

Difficulty: High

Strategic Advice: The total number of words in the paper is the number of words per page times the number of pages; that is, wp.

Getting to the Answer: If Bill types at x words per minute, he can type wp words in $wp \div x$ minutes, or an average rate of $\frac{wp}{x}$ minutes. Now to convert from minutes to hours, simply divide by 60. So he takes $\frac{wp}{x} \div 60 = \frac{wp}{60x}$ hours to type the paper.

SECTION 4

1. B

Difficulty: Low

Start by filling in the second blank. (A), (C), and (E) can be rejected immediately; after all, it doesn't make sense to say that Fernando could speak a language *considerately*, *implicitly*, or *ambiguously*. But he could speak a language (B), *effortlessly* or (D), *eloquently*. Plugging the first word of choices (B) and (D) into the first blank eliminates (D), leaving choice (B). Forgetting the difference between dialects wouldn't make Fernando an accomplished linguist, but understanding the difference between them certainly might.

2. D

Difficulty: Low

The clause "so that events are reported all over the world shortly after they happen" provides a strong clue about what belongs in the blanks in the first part of the sentence. Since this clause conveys the notion that news spreads around the globe swiftly, the blanks must be filled by words like "transmitted" and "quickly." Only choice (D) contains these ideas. The word pairs in choices (C) and (E) completely contradict the second part of the sentence, and the word pairs in choices (A) and (B) don't relate logically to the rest of the sentence.

3. C

Difficulty: Medium

This sentence revolves around a contrast between Shinto and "a formal system of belief." So ask yourself, What does a formal system of belief have that Shinto does not? The only possibility is (C), *dogma*, which means "an established set of beliefs." The missing word must make sense following the adjective "codified," or "systematized." (C) does, but choices (A) and (B) clearly don't fit. Have you ever heard of "codified followers" or "codified boundaries"? Choices (D) and (E) are too vague to provide the necessary contrast between Shinto and a more formal system of belief.

4. B

Difficulty: Medium

The clues in this sentence are "poverty, isolation, and illness." If people believe that old age results in these bad things, then they are naturally going to be anxious about growing old, right? Therefore, we can predict that the blank must be filled by a word like "anxious." The only synonym for anxious among the choices is (B), *apprehension*. Choice (A) might have tempted you, but you can't *regret* something that hasn't happened yet. The words "we will face" show that the sentence is talking about old age as the future.

5. C

Difficulty: High

"Yet" indicates that there is a contrast in Pinter's dialogue. It is "poetic" but—we need a word that contrasts with "poetic." We can eliminate (B), (D), and (E). Choice (A) is tricky because poetry is usually brief, not *comprehensive*, "covering everything." But this word is usually used to describe a report, an exam, or an insurance policy, rather than dialogue in a play. Choice (C) is a better choice because *colloquial*, which means "characteristic of informal, familiar speech," contrasts nicely with "poetic," and fits the context of the sentence.

6. C

Difficulty: Medium

While it is important to note the change in the author's feelings that the paragraph describes—from an unemotional look at an old journal to eager anticipation of the next page—there are descriptions that more specifically explain

why the author, at first, only casually looked through the journal. In particular, the second sentence of the paragraph indicates that the drawings in the journal seemed to have been made "by someone else." The third sentence describes the drawings as "almost unrecognizable creations." This evidence suggests that at first the author was only casually interested because he found the journal's content *unfamiliar,* (C).

7. E

Difficulty: Medium

It is easy to become sidetracked by the quoted content and lose sight of its place within the paragraph as a whole. In this case, while the question specifically cites the author's mention of his brother's taunts, the author's purpose extends beyond that actual event towards the journal and childhood memories. In context, the memory is used as a strong example of the journal's effect on the author, (E). Choice (A) is out of scope; the paragraph is clearly not focused on the author's relationship with his brother.

8. D

Difficulty: High

The word *ironic* is used to describe the tarantula's large size. In the first two sentences the author suggests that the tarantula "can easily intimidate" with its size, but that, in the wild, this size is a "distinct disadvantage." This suggests that the author uses the cited word to underscore this contrast, or *incongruity*. Choice (A) is a distortion; the paragraph never suggests that the tarantula is actually smaller than many think. Choice (B) is an irrelevant detail. While the author makes this point, the context of the cited word doesn't suggest this purpose.

9. B

Difficulty: Medium

Match the one-word answer choices with specific evidence from the text, eliminating those choices that are directly supported by details in the paragraphs. Choice (B) is the only characterization the author does NOT use. The author describes the tarantula as "helpless" in one instance, but this characterization cannot be applied to tarantulas in general. Choice (A), *distinctive*, is supported by the author's description of the tarantula as "the largest spider in the world." Choice (C), *noticeable*, is a good synonym for "conspicuous," an adjective the author uses in the third sentence of the paragraph. Choice (D), *vulnerable.* is supported by the author's statement that the tarantula is "relatively easy prey" for the tarantula hawk. Choice (E), *impressive.* is used in the first sentence of the paragraph.

Questions 10–15

Here's a run-down of the passage. Paragraph 1: While scientists have various theories about the extinction, "definitive proof has remained elusive." Paragraph 2: Alvarez's idea is that it resulted from a meteor explosion that blocked sunlight and messed up the world food chain. Paragraph 3: Alvarez points to a global layer of iridium as evidence for his theory. Paragraph 4: Scientists' doubts about the Alvarez theory centered on the inability to find a big meteoric impact crater. Paragraph 5: A huge crater was recently found, convincing many scientists that Alvarez is right.

10. C
Difficulty: Medium

Always check back to the passage to see how a vocabulary word is used. Re-read paragraph 1 and you'll see that in this case, "elusive" refers to the fact that proof of how the dinosaurs died out is hard to find.

11. C
Difficulty: Medium

Neither Alvarez was a paleontologist; opponents of the Alvarez theory—who were paleontologists—criticized both Luis and Walter for theorizing about the field of paleontology. The other choices represent critiques that were leveled at only one Alvarez, or neither.

12. A
Difficulty: Low

Paragraph 1 tells you that various explanations for the disappearance of dinosaurs have been offered; paragraph 2 offers an *original*, or "novel," explanation (A).

13. D
Difficulty: Medium

The second paragraph explains the Alvarez theory of dinosaur extinction: a huge meteor crash created a cloud of dust, which disrupted plant photosynthesis. That disruption led to a lack of vegetation, which meant no food for dinosaurs to eat.

14. B
Difficulty: Medium

Read the sentence following the cited lines for your answer. The discovery of the layer of iridium was significant because iridium is rarely found on the earth's surface; Alvarez theorized that the presence of iridium meant that this metal either came from the earth's core, or from a meteorite.

15. C
Difficulty: High

Finding and correctly dating the Yucatan crater helped strengthen the Alvarez theory. Establishing that there was iridium in the crater would even further strengthen the theory; re-read paragraph 3 for evidence of this.

Questions 16–24

The overall aim of this passage is to provide information about rock gardens. The first paragraph mentions a common misconception from the name "rock garden" and goes on to explain what a rock garden is and where the idea originated. The second paragraph details one aspect of rock gardens' appeal: they can be planted in less-than-ideal conditions. The third and fourth paragraphs discuss how to set up a rock garden bed, focusing specifically on arranging and selecting appropriate rocks. The passage ends with a discussion of planting and caring for flowers in a rock garden.

16. C
Difficulty: Low

Thinking about the scope of a passage will help you identify the main idea. The passage is quite general, providing basic information about what rock gardens are, why gardeners like them, and how to create and maintain a rock garden. You can predict that the answer will have a similarly wide scope. Choice (C) is a nice match for your prediction. Choices (A) and (B) are examples of distortion. Although the passage mentions some advantages of rock gardens, the overall tone of the passage is informational rather than persuasive and although rock gardens are described as beautiful, overall the passage has a more broad focus. Choices (D) and (E) are misused details. The history of rock gardens is mentioned in the first paragraph, but the rest of the passage is not concerned with tracing this history; and although these types of flowers are compared in the passage, the comparison is not the author's main focus.

17. B

Difficulty: Low

Remember not to make generalizations or assumptions when answering Critical Reading questions. The author makes a point of saying that what makes rock gardens stand out is that they can grow beautiful plants in conditions that are less than ideal. This makes (B) a good choice. Choice (A) is incorrect because the author clearly states that rock gardens contain both plants and rocks. The rest of the passage also negates choices (C) and (D)—rock gardens may be able to grow in atypical places, but they do require work; and the author lists items a gardener might have to buy to grow a rock garden. Choice (E) is extreme—the author says that rock gardens are beautiful, but does not make a comparison to any other type of garden.

18. D

Difficulty: Low

Take the time to compare the choices to the text, rather than relying on your memory. Limestone is discussed in the fourth paragraph, so focus your attention here. The author says that limestone is a good choice because its pores admit water and air, because plant roots can become firmly established in it, and because its nooks and crannies provide a place for gardeners to plant moss and lichens. Look for a choice that does NOT mention any of these features. Choices (A), (B), (C), and (E) are all opposites. Choice (D) is the correct answer—while artistic shapes are discussed, the shape of limestone in particular is not mentioned in the passage.

19. A

Difficulty: Medium

Use your knowledge of prefixes and clues from the context to help you identify the meaning of the cited word. You can tell from the context that "uninspired placements" of rocks are a bad thing because they make the garden less beautiful. The author recommends advance planning to help avoid this problem. An arrangement *would* be inspired if it were exciting or stimulating, so you can infer that an *un*inspired arrangement is a dull one, or *plain*, (A).

20. B

Difficulty: Medium

Be sure to look specifically for reasons that rock garden plants require special care, since details mentioned for other reasons are not relevant to this question. The final paragraph mentions that rock gardens require special care. According to the passage, this is because rock garden plants need more protection, since they "are more exposed to the elements" than flat bed plants. Roman numeral II captures this reason. Less-than-ideal growing conditions are mentioned earlier in the passage, but you can eliminate Roman numeral I because the author does not connect this to the special care required by rock garden plants. Likewise, you can eliminate Roman numeral III because the plants themselves are not necessarily more delicate—they just require more protection because of their exposed position.

21. E

Difficulty: Medium

According to the passage, how does the planting of rock gardens differ from the planting of traditional gardens? The author is comparing rock gardens to traditional gardens, and one difference is that traditional gardens "focus on plants and do not take the beauty of the medium in which flowers are planted into consideration," whereas rock gardens do. Since you know that flowers are planted amongst rocks in rock gardens, you can infer that "medium" refers to the surrounding substance or *environment*, (E).

22. B

Difficulty: Medium

Looking at the phrase that introduces a quotation can provide clues about the quotation's function in the passage. The introductory clause in the sentence tells you that you're being given the *reason* that gardeners willingly undertake the hard work required to create rock beds. According to Foster, gardeners undertake this work because rock garden plants are so full of flowers and easy to care for. The author includes the quotation because it explains the gardeners' motivation, thus supporting the point that their time and effort is considered "well spent." Choices (A), (C), and (E) are misused details from other parts of the passage. Choice (D) is a distortion—although Foster implicitly suggests that rock garden plants may be better than other plants in some ways, this choice misrepresents the author's emphasis.

23. C

Difficulty: Medium

Take the time to check the choices against the text, avoiding those that mention details from other parts of the passage. You are told that deep burial is necessary so that the rocks "are stable and cannot be dislodged easily, which would upset the plants." Look for a choice that captures the fact that deeply buried rocks are more secure. Choice (C) is your best match. Choice (A) is distortion; the author is also concerned with the beauty of rock placement, but this is not the reason rocks must be buried deeply. Choice (B) is a misused detail; although the rocks must indeed be planted first, this is not the reason they must be buried deeply. Choice (D) is an opposite, and choice (E) is out of scope—the maintenance requirements of rocks are not discussed in this passage.

24. B

Difficulty: High

Use key words to identify when the author is making a comparison. Saxifrages are mentioned in a list of alpine plants that thrive in hilly, stony, or awkwardly-arranged growing conditions. The phrase "In contrast" tells you that this characteristic distinguishes alpine plants from "many traditional garden plants," which can't survive in such conditions. Choice (A) is an opposite; along with other plants in this list, saxifrages "not only survive but also thrive" in rock garden conditions. Choices (C) and (D) are misused details; burrowing roots are mentioned later in the passage, but the author does not say which specific plants have roots strong enough to burrow through limestone. You can infer that saxifrages originated in soils similar to those of mountainous regions, but it does not necessarily follow that the plants are more beautiful in mountainous soils. Choice (E) is extreme; saxifrages can thrive in rock gardens, but this is not necessarily the only place they can survive.

SECTION 5

1. A

Difficulty: Low

Strategic Advice: The best thing to do is isolate your variable.

Getting to the Answer: To solve in terms of b, divide both sides of the equation $abc = b^2$ by b:

$$\frac{abc}{b} = \frac{b^2}{b}$$
$$ac = b$$

2. D

Difficulty: Low

Strategic Advice: Try to eliminate one of your variables.

Getting to the Answer: Add the two equations to cancel out b:

$$5a - b = 9$$
$$3a + b = 15$$
$$8a = 24$$
$$a = 3$$

If $a = 3$, then $b = 15 - 3a = 15 - 9 = 6$.
So $a + b = 3 + 6 = 9$.

3. E

Difficulty: Low

Strategic Advice: Simplify this algebraic fraction by canceling common factors from the numerator and the denominator.

Getting to the Answer: x^2 means 2 factors of x; x^6 means 6 factors of x. Canceling, you're left with 4 factors of x, or x^4 in the denominator. The y's cancel out. Canceling the common factors of z, you're left with z^4 in the numerator. Combining the terms in the numerator and the denominator gives you $\frac{z^4}{x^4}$, choice (E).

4. C

Difficulty: Medium

Strategic Advice: Since you are asked which statements must be true, try to find a case where the conditions in the question hold, but the statement does not. If you can find such an example, you can discard any answer choice that includes that statement.

Getting to the Answer: Statement I: Let $x = 3$ and $y = -1$. Then $y < 0$ and $x + y > 0$, but x is not less than 0, so statement I is not always true. Discard answer choices (A) and (D).

Statement II: If $x = 3$ and $y = -1$, then $y < 0$ and $x + y > 0$, but x is not less than $-y$. So statement II is not always true. Discard answer choices (B) and (E).

There is no need to check statement III. Since answer choice (C) is the only one remaining, it must be correct.

5. E

Difficulty: Medium

Strategic Advice: Notice that a and b are 2 of the 4 angles in a quadrilateral.

Getting to the Answer: The sum of the measures of the interior angles of any quadrilateral always equals 360, so $a + b +$ the other two angles $= 360$. Note that the other two angles are also the base angles of an equilateral triangle, so each measures 60 degrees. So

$$a + b + 60 + 60 = 360;$$
$$a + b = 240.$$

6. C

Difficulty: Medium

Strategic Advice: The volume of a rectangular solid is given by the relationship

$$\text{Volume} = \text{length} \times \text{width} \times \text{height}$$

Getting to the Answer: In this case the height is equivalent to the given depth, so

$$8,640 = 60 \times 6 \times \text{width}$$
$$\frac{8,640}{60 \times 6} = \text{width}$$
$$24 = \text{width}$$

So the width of the swimming pool is 24 feet.

7. D

Difficulty: Medium

Strategic Advice: For this function question, first find the value of $f(2)$ and $g(2)$. Then find the difference between them. Be sure you've answered the right question before you fill in your answer—this question has lots of tempting places to stop before you've actually found what the question asks for.

Getting to the Answer:
$$f(2) = \frac{2 + 4}{2} = \frac{6}{2} = 3$$
$$g(2) = 2^2 - 6 = 4 - 6 = -2$$
$$3 - (-2) = 3 + 2 = 5$$

8. A

Difficulty: High

Strategic Advice: This question involves the range—that is, all possible values—of $d(w)$. Think about the limits of the function. Is there a number it must be smaller than? Is there a number it must be larger than?

Getting to the Answer:
$w^2 \geq 0$, since any number squared must be positive.
$$w^2 + 1 \geq 1$$
$$\sqrt{w^2 + 1} \geq 1$$

The only answer choice that is not greater than or equal to 1 is (A).

9. $5.50

Difficulty: Low

Strategic Advice: Be careful not to lose points on simple arithmetic questions.

Getting to the Answer: Buying 12 tickets separately costs 12 times $1.50, or $18. Buying a dozen tickets at once costs $12.50, so the difference in cost is $18 − $12.50, which equals $5.50.

10. 49

Difficulty: Low

Strategic Advice: Notice that a side of square C is made up of a side of square A and a side of square B. The area of a square is the square of the length of a side.

Getting to the Answer: Since the area of square A is 9, its side is 3; since the area of square B is 16, its side is 4. This makes a side of square C is equal to $3 + 4 = 7$, so its area is 49.

11. $\frac{36}{5}$

Difficulty: Medium

Strategic Advice: In this problem you need to work with a system of equations.

Getting to the Answer: You're asked for the value of *rs*, so solve for *t* in terms of *s* in the first equation and plug that into the second equation.

$$\frac{s}{t} - 4 = 5$$
$$s = 9t$$
$$\frac{s}{9} = t$$

Plug $\frac{s}{9}$ for *t* in the second equation:

$$5rt + 2 = 6$$
$$5r\left(\frac{s}{9}\right) + 2 = 6$$
$$\frac{5}{9}rs = 4$$
$$rs = 4 \times \frac{9}{5}$$
$$rs = \frac{36}{5}$$

12. 6 or 8

Difficulty: Medium

Strategic Advice: This can be solved by trial and error. Try different values of *n* until you find one that fits the given conditions.

Getting to the Answer: You want $3n + 5$ to be between 20 and 40. If $n = 6$, then $3n + 5 = 3(6) + 5 = 23$, which is a between 20 and 40. So 6 is a correct answer. Another correct answer is 8, since $3(8) + 5 = 29$, which is also a prime number between 20 and 40.

13. 21 or 28

Difficulty: Medium

Strategic Advice: This problem requires an understanding of how ratios work.

Getting to the Answer: Since the of boys to girls in the class is 3 to 4, the total number of students in the class must be a multiple of $3 + 4$, or 7. The multiples of 7 between 20 and 30 are 21 and 28. Either answer is correct.

14. 80

Difficulty: Medium

Strategic Advice: Find how many CDs she can fit in length, then in width, then in height.

Getting to the Answer: The box has dimensions 10 inches by 10 inches by 10 inches. Since each CD is 5 inches in length, she can fit $\frac{10}{5}$, or 2 rows of CDs along the length of the box. Each CD is 5 inches in width, so she can fit $\frac{10}{5}$, or

2 rows of CDs along the width of the box. Finally, each CD is $\frac{1}{2}$ inch deep, so she can fit $10 \div \frac{1}{2}$, or 20 rows of CDs along the depth of the box. 2 times 2 times 20 equals 80.

15. 7.5

Difficulty: Medium

Strategic Advice: Look for similar angles to help you determine values.

Getting to the Answer: Since *EF* is parallel to *GH*, angle *DEF* = angle *G* and angle *DFE* = angle *H*. Since angles *DEF* and *DFE* of $\triangle DEF$ are equal to angles *G* and *H*, respectively, of $\triangle DGH$, the triangles are similar. This tells you that corresponding sides of the two triangles are in proportion to one another. Since $DE = EG$, *DE*, a side of $\triangle DEF$, is half the length of *DG*, a corresponding side of $\triangle DGH$. So all the sides of $\triangle DGH$ are twice as long as the corresponding sides of $\triangle DEF$. Also, the height of *DGH* must be twice the corresponding height of *DEF*. Since the area of a triangle is $\frac{1}{2}bh$, the area of $\triangle DGH$ is four times the area of $\triangle DEF$. Since the area of $\triangle DGH$ is 30, the area of $\triangle DEF$ is 7.5.

16. 306, 324, 342, 360, 378, 396

Difficulty: Medium

Strategic Advice: You only need to find one number that fits the description and grid that in. Use the divisibility rules to help you find a correct answer.

Getting to the Answer: A number is divisible by 9 if the sum of its digits is divisible by 9. You don't need to check divisibility by 3, since a number that is divisible by 9 must be divisible by 3. A number is divisible by 6 if it's an even number divisible by 3. So you're looking for an even number between 300 and 400 that has digits which sum to a multiple of 9. With a little trial-and-error, you can find a number that works. For example, 306 works because it's an even number whose digits add up to 9.

Another approach is to multiply 3, 6, and 9. The result is 162, which is not between 300 and 400. However, if you multiply 162 by 2, you get 324, which is an acceptable answer.

17. $\frac{7}{15}$

Difficulty: Medium

Strategic Advice: Probability is

$$\frac{\text{Number of desired outcomes}}{\text{total of possible outcomes}}.$$

Getting to the Answer: The coins worth more than 5 cents are the quarters and dimes, so the number of desired outcomes is $3 + 4$, or 7. The total number of possible outcomes is the same as the total number of coins, which is $3 + 4 + 2 + 6$, or 15.

So the probability is $\frac{7}{15}$.

18. $2 < x < 6$

Difficulty: High

Strategic Advice: Draw some diagrams to solve this question.

Getting to the Answer: The circumference of a circle is $2\pi r$. Since the circumference of Circle A is 4π, its radius is 2; since the circumference of Circle B is 8π, its radius is 4. The circles intersect at two points, so they must overlap. If they were tangent (that is, touch at one point) with Circle A inside Circle B, the distance between their centers would be 2; if they were tangent with Circle A outside Circle B, the distance between their centers would be 6.

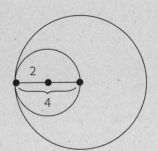

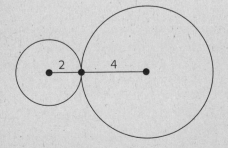

Since they are not tangent, the distance between their centers must fall between these extremes, and be greater than 2 but less than 6.

SECTION 6

1. B

Difficulty: Low

In this sentence, *subjects* is a noun, so it needs to be modified by the adjective *general*, not the adverb *generally*. Choices (C) and (E) correct the modifier, but they introduce new errors.

2. E

Difficulty: Medium

The original sentence is a comma splice—two complete ideas incorrectly joined by a comma. Only choice (E) presents an error-free sentence that shows the correct relationship between the two ideas. (B) and (C) show an illogical connection between the two ideas—David's success in the field should be contrasted with his lack of formal study. (D) is unnecessarily wordy.

3. A

Difficulty: Medium

To check for parallel structure, compare the simple verb forms in the list. Here, "writing," "using," and "omitting" are all consistent in the original sentence. Choices (B), (C), and (E) all violate the rules of parallel structure. By changing *needless* to *needlessly* and re-ordering the words, (D) alters the meaning of the sentence.

4. D

Difficulty: Medium

Choice (D) properly includes the preposition *in* to create a parallel between the objects being compared. Choices (A), (B), and (C) do not include the necessary preposition *in*. Choice (E) is unnecessarily wordy

5. B

Difficulty: High

As written, this is a run-on. Choice (B) is the most concise way to correct the sentence. Choices (C) and (D), while grammatically correct, are not as direct as choice (B).

6. D

Difficulty: Medium

When possible, replace the passive voice with the active voice. The *girl*, not *weight training*, is the doer of the action, so she should be the subject of the sentence. Choices (D) and (E) use the active voice, but only (D) is in the correct tense. Choice (E) uses the past perfect (*had begun*), which would only be correct if the action of beginning weight training preceded some other past action.

7. A

Difficulty: Medium

The sentence is correct as written; a semicolon connects two complete and closely related thoughts. Choice (B) creates a run-on sentence by joining the two sentences with a comma. Choices (C) and (E) fail to punctuate the sentence properly. Choice (D) uses the wrong verb tense and mistakenly uses *which* rather than *that*.

8. D

Difficulty: Low

As written, this is a run-on sentence. Only (D) correctly turns the second part of the sentence into a dependent clause: *Pablo Picasso painted…Guernica, which conveys his abhorrence…*. Choice (B) uses the awkward construction *being the conveyance of*. Choice (C) is a comma splice. Choice (E) incorrectly uses the present verb tense.

9. E

Difficulty: Medium

Choice (E) is the simplest way to express the meaning of the underlined portion. Choices (A) and (B) are both awkward and unnecessarily wordy. Choice (C) is more concise, but it presents an error in subject-verb agreement. The singular subject *city* needs a singular verb—*has*, not *have*. Choice (E) changes the tense and the meaning of the sentence.

10. D

Difficulty: High

The subject must be adjacent to the phrase modifying it. Choice (D) places the subject next to the introductory phrase modifying it. Choices (A), (B), (C), and (E) all fail to place the subject and its modifying phrase next to each other.

11. B

Difficulty: Medium

Items in a list must be parallel in form. The sentence lists three ways in which the singer could improve his vocal power. However, in the original sentence the first two items (*increased lung capacity* and *greater range*) are not parallel to the third item (*working on better breath control*). Only (B) corrects this without introducing another problem.

12. B

Difficulty: Low

Keep track of verb tenses. Choice (B) incorrectly uses the present tense of the verb to refer to the past. Choice (A) tests idiom and is correct. We say "center of." Choice (C) tests the difference between *which* and *that*. It introduces a clause of additional information, so *which* is correct. Choice (D) tests transition words.

13. D

Difficulty: Medium

Does *relief of suffering* sound right to you? The correct expression is "relief *from* suffering." Choice (A) is the correct use of *some*, and the verb forms in (B) and (C) are correct.

14. B

Difficulty: Low

This sentence has a descriptive phrase ("in contrast to more sophisticated forms of entertainment") separating the subject from the verb of the sentence. Cross out the phrase and figure out what the basic sentence is saying. The subject of this sentence is "The sitcom," which is singular. Therefore the verb should also be singular. The correct form should be "The sitcom…*is*…"

15. C

Difficulty: Medium

Although the phrase "remember when" is a correct form in some instances, notice that in this sentence, the future tense is used later on, so *when* creates an error in sentence structure. Instead, *that* is correct. Choices (A) and (B) raise various issues of verb tense, and Choice (D) raises the point that a pronoun must agree with the noun it replaces.

16. E

Difficulty: Medium

Predict what the answer choices are testing. Choice (A) tests idiom. We are aided *by* people. Choice (B) correctly uses an adjective to modify the noun *class*, Choice (C) tests verb tense and uses the past tense correctly, and Choice (D) tests preposition idioms. The phrase "with the help of" is correct here.

17. C

Difficulty: Medium

Some idiomatic expressions are only correct when constructed a certain way. *Capable to* is incorrect. The adjective *capable* requires the preposition *of*. Choice (C) contains the error.

18. D

Difficulty: Medium

Watch out for double negatives. *Not, no one, never,* and *nowhere* aren't the only negative words in English. There are also less obvious negatives: *without, scarcely, barely,* and *cannot but. Without hardly* is a double negative. The corrected sentence would read "with hardly a word" or "without so much as a word."

19. B

Difficulty: Low

There are a lot of subordinating phrases in this sentence. Cross them out and get to the main parts of the sentence. That will help you recognize the incorrect verb form of "not considering". Christopher Marlow is the subject of the sentence, but he is being compared to Shakespeare, so the verb form must express that comparison. As it is now, it seems as though Marlow himself is not considering something. For the sentence to be correct, the underlined portion needs to be "not considered."

20. E

Difficulty: Medium

The sentence is correct as written. Choice (A) tests the use of the possessive pronoun and is correct. Choice (B) tests adjective and adverb use. Choice (C) tests subject/verb agreement. The subject is plural so it is correct. Choice (D) tests pronoun use and is correct. So no error, (E).

21. D

Difficulty: High

This sentence tests your knowledge of relative pronouns. *Which* is used to refer to a thing, not a person. The antecedent of *which* is *Ruth Benedict*, so *who* is correct here, (D).

22. E

Difficulty: Low

This sentence contains no error, (E). The verb forms are correct, and the preposition *about* is used idiomatically with *regret.*

23. A

Difficulty: Medium

This is an example of using an adjective rather than an adverb to modify a verb. It is possible to argue that the sentence should read "A shy, but incredible, intelligent girl," but remember that an error in punctuation will never be the sole reason a choice is incorrect. Therefore, the proper form is *incredibly,* (A).

24. D

Difficulty: Medium

Choice (D) introduces an illogical comparison. The comparison is between *equipment*, not universities.

25. B

Difficulty: High

Choice (B) is incorrect. Prepositional phrases take the object form of pronouns, so *I* should be *me.*

26. B

Difficulty: Medium

The phrase *about intellect and language* masks the fact that the singular subject *writing* doesn't agree with the plural verb *were.* Choice (B) should read *was.*

27. E

Difficulty: High

The sentence could read "The analyst was shocked that his presentation…was criticized savagely by his customers." *Criticized savagely* could be *savagely criticized,* but either is correct. Therefore, although the sentence is unusual, there is no error.

KAPLAN
Test Prep and Admissions

28. D

Difficulty: High

This sentence presents an illogical comparison: The programs performed in the new symphony hall are compared to the old performance space. The correct sentence reads: "A downfall in the economy could affect the ballet season because programs performed in the new symphony hall cost twice as much as programs performed in the old performance space." The word *covered* correctly describes the programs. The verb *cost* agrees with *programs*. The phrase *as much* is idiomatically correct and introduces the comparison between the programs.

29. D

Difficulty: Medium

Businesses at its time is not correct in this case. The correct idiomatic phrase is *businesses of its time. Comment on* is idiomatically correct. The adjective *traditional* properly modifies the noun *politics*. The verb *exerted* is appropriately in the past tense.

30. D

Difficulty: High

The word *ruins* and the information in sentence 1 that the Celts lived from 500 B.C.–500 A.D. tell you that the ten towns are no longer inhabited. The original sentence implies that the archeologists found people living there. Only (D) fixes this error by changing the verb tense. Choice (B) creates a different verb tense error. The discovery was in 1834 so archeologists *were excited*. Choice (C) makes an unnecessary change. The subject of the previous sentence is *archeologists*, so it is clear that the pronoun *they* in sentence 2 refers to *archeologists*. Choice (E) would make the sentence incomplete by removing the main verb phrase *have discovered* and turning it into the noun *discovery*.

31. B

Difficulty: Medium

Sentence 5 presents information that contrasts with the sentence before it. Trenches are usually defensive, but in this case they are not. Only (B) and (E) provide contrast. Choice (E) is redundant and not idiomatically correct, so (B) is the best choice. Besides giving the wrong relationship, (C) would also create a fragment. Choice (A) would be redundant because *in fact* and *in this case* mean almost the

same thing. Choice (D) likewise establishes the wrong relationship.

32. C

Difficulty: Medium

Sentences 7 and 8 are choppy and should be connected to sentence 9. Choice (C) is a clear and grammatically correct sentence linking the three ideas. Choice (A) introduces a subject-verb agreement problem. The plural subject *people* does not agree with the singular verb *was*. Choice (B) is a run-on sentence. Choice (D) is in the passive voice , which makes the sentence awkward and puts emphasis in the wrong place. Choice (E) has an illogical comparison between *sports fields* and *landing sites* on the one hand, and *theories* on the other.

33. D

Difficulty: Medium

The sentence as it stands has an ambiguous pronoun: *they*. Choice (D) correctly substitutes *these areas* for the pronoun. In addition to not fixing the error, Choice (A) changes the verb tense to the present, which is incorrect. Choice (B) makes *marked with a clear border* refer to *religious rituals*, which is also not correct. Choice (C) similarly makes it sound like *Celts* were *marked with a clear border*. Choice (E) changes *used* to *using*, which makes the sentence a fragment.

34. B

Difficulty: Medium

Sentence 13 lacks a transition from sentence 12, which indicates that Celtic practices are explained by the new theory. Sentence 13 gives an example of a practice that is explained by the new theory. Choice (B) provides a good transition to an example. Choice (E) has the correct transition, but is wordy. Choices (A) and (C) indicate contrast, which is not present here. Choice (D) indicates continuing a list, which is not the situation here.

35. E

Difficulty: Medium

The correct answer should explain that ancient Celts built temples on islands because islands have a natural border; the revised sentence must also be grammatically correct. Choice (E) is the only sentence that works. Choice (A) uses the pronoun *they* ambiguously and doesn't clearly show the relationship between ideas. Choice (B) changes the relationship between the ideas, turning the sentences into a list. Choice (C) has a misplaced modifier. The islands did not build temples, the ancient Celts did. Choice (D) also has a misplaced modifier, using *surrounded by water* to modify *ancient Celts*.

SECTION 7

1. D

Difficulty: Medium

Don't give up when you see a few tough vocab words. Even if you don't know the answer right away, you can get closer by eliminating clearly wrong choices.

The students are "confused," so the teacher is trying to use an example. *Clarify* is a good prediction. Note, too, that you could eliminate two choices, even if you didn't know the meaning of *extricate*, *elucidate*, or *obfuscate*. A tough vocabulary word, but to *extricate* the subject makes no sense (A). The teacher is definitely not trying to *evade* the subject, (B). Choice (C) is tempting if you're in a hurry, but notice that it's the students, not the teacher, who need to *comprehend* the subject. Choice (D) is a great fit for your prediction. Choice (E) is the opposite of what you're looking for.

2. C

Difficulty: Medium

Your prediction is just a starting point. The answer may match the sentence perfectly but not be exactly what you predicted, so stay flexible. This is a very patient cat. In fact, *patient* is a pretty good prediction. An *apprehensive* cat might or might not wait all day. There's not a very strong connection. An *emaciated* cat would probably be pretty hungry, so it might wait all day. When you get to (C), however, you'll note that *emaciated* is not as strong a choice. *Vigilant* doesn't mean exactly the same thing as *patient*, your prediction, but *vigilant* is a great description of a cat that waits all afternoon for a mouse. A *prominent* cat doesn't make much sense. *Indolent* certainly doesn't describe a cat that waits all day for a mouse, (E).

3. D

Difficulty: Medium

As you get to the more difficult questions, watch out for tempting choices like (E). Make sure the word works when you read it in the sentence. This is a contrast sentence, and the blank contrasts with the word *credible*. In this context, that means *believable* or *valid*, so a good prediction might be *unbelievable*. *Valid* is the opposite of what you want. A *sardonic* excuse doesn't contrast with *credible*. Like (A), *righteous* is the opposite of your prediction (C). *Fabricated* fits well. Her excuse wasn't *credible*—it was actually completely made-up. Interesting, but watch out! *Incredulous* would describe people who don't believe the excuse, not the excuse itself.

4. E

Difficulty: High

For most Sentence Completions, either the vocab or the prediction is challenging, but not both. Here, it's not too difficult to make a prediction. The sets are "magnificent" and "an outstanding visual achievement," so the correct answer will be very positive. The artists who made the sets might be *prolific*, but the sets themselves can't be. If the sets were *modest*, they probably wouldn't be considered such a visual achievement (B). Like (A), this is something that could only apply to people. The sets couldn't be *reticent*. The sets should evoke the future, but *archaic* sets would do just the opposite. *Grandiose* fits perfectly. (You might recognize the word *grand*, even if you're not familiar with *grandiose*.)

5. A

Difficulty: High

In this example, we must assume that circumstances, such as the rise in rewards and the desire to win no matter what, could cause someone's personality to change in a negative way. In order to fill in the blank, we also need to know the word *base*, which means "morally low or mean-spirited." Therefore, for a negative change to occur, the base elements must be *intensified*, (A).

6. A

Difficulty: High

Start by filling in the first blank. Since the first part of the sentence contrasts a hummingbird's light weight with its appetite, you can predict that a word like "big" or "gluttonous"

must fill this blank. Only (A), *voracious*, matches this prediction. But just to be sure that (A) is correct, plug the second word of this choice into the second blank. It makes sense, doesn't it? Though hummingbirds weigh very little, they are *voracious* eaters with high body temperatures, *consuming* many times their weight in food each day.

Questions 7–19

The italicized Intro reveals the basic contrast between the two passages: Author #1 stresses Leonardo's "artistic sensibility," while Author #2 stresses his "technological achievements." Author #1 argues that Leonardo's artistic mentality interfered with his real accomplishments. He "tended toward variability and inconstancy in his endeavors," he was impractical and restless, and despite his extraordinary inventiveness, he was more of an artist than a true scientist. Author #2 has a diametrically opposite view, arguing that Leonardo was an engineering genius, that his approach to scientific problems was thoroughly systematic.

7.   E

Difficulty: High

The overall point of paragraph 1 is that Leonardo's accomplishments as a scientist and engineer were limited by the fact that he approached everything as an artist—he moved compulsively from one engineering project to the next because he realized that "the perfection of art" was not attainable in those fields.

8.   B

Difficulty: Medium

The author expands on Leonardo's "variability and inconstancy" at the end of the paragraph—we're told that Leonardo made a habit of "moving compulsively from one project to the next." So *variability* means *changeability*, (B).

9.   E

Difficulty: Low

The author's opinion of the *Last Supper* is expressed pretty clearly at the end of paragraph 2—despite its shortcomings, it is "worthy of our greatest veneration" because it "succeeded brilliantly in capturing the acute anxiety of the Apostles."

10.   A

Difficulty: Medium

Leonardo's approach to natural science is scatter-brained; he begins by "inquiring into the properties of herbs," and ends up "observing the motions of the heavens." So the author is describing it as an example of his "mental restlessness...when applied to scientific matters."

11.   B

Difficulty: High

The author's criticism of the "*pensieri*" is that while they reflect Leonardo's "compulsion with observation and problem-solving...such things alone do not constitute science, which requires the working out of a systematic body of knowledge."

12.   C

Difficulty: Medium

The author presents modern scientific investigation as "the working out of a systematic body of knowledge," implying throughout that Leonardo wasn't sufficiently disciplined in his work to pursue this. Essentially, the author's attitude towards science is *respectful*, (C).

13.   B

Difficulty: Medium

The author of Passage 2 is critical of Leonardo's biographers because they contradict her point of view. The author regards Leonardo as an engineer who made great contributions to technology, whereas biographers regard Leonardo's interest in engineering as a waste of time.

14.   C

Difficulty: Medium

Leonardo's approach to analyzing human muscle power was "revolutionary" because "little attention" had been given to this area before, (C).

15.   A

Difficulty: Low

The underlying point of paragraphs 2 and 3 in Passage 2 is that Leonardo was exhaustive in his approach to engineering problems. So wheeled vehicles are discussed to show that Leonardo was farsighted enough to realize that they weren't the solution to the problem of mechanizing canals.

16. B

Difficulty: Medium

The issue in the last paragraph is whether Leonardo was "one of our earliest and most significant engineers"—the author believes that he was, but the scholars refuse to *concede* this. Essentially, the author is suggesting that scholars are unwilling to admit this fact, so *concede* in this context means *acknowledge*.

17. D

Difficulty: Medium

The last sentence of Passage 1 defines science as "the working out of a systematic body of knowledge," suggesting that Leonardo wasn't interested in focusing his abilities. Passage 2 presents a contrasting picture of Leonardo, but suggests something very similar about the nature of scientific inquiry—we're told that Leonardo approached his engineering in a "painstaking" and "systematic" manner. So both authors would agree that *meticulous observation and analysis* is crucial to scientific inquiry.

18. C

Difficulty: Medium

The overall point of Passage 1 is that Leonardo's artistic temperament adversely affected his approach to science and engineering. We're told in the last paragraph that "he possessed an artist's interest in detail, which explains his compulsion with observation and problem-solving." Consequently, the author of Passage 1 would probably see Leonardo's painstaking work on canals in this light.

19. D

Difficulty: Medium

The last paragraph of Passage 2 explains why Leonardo's accomplishments as an engineer are so often overlooked. We're told that Leonardo's insights were often "far beyond the standards of his time." And so (D)—Leonardo was too *advanced*—would be the most appropriate response to the first author's criticism.

SECTION 8

1. E

Difficulty: Low

Strategic Advice: Remember that supplementary angles add up to 180°.

Getting to the Answer: Angle *s* has a vertical angle that must also equal 70 degrees. This 70-degree angle and angle *t* combine to form an angle which is supplementary to the right angle, since there are 180 degrees in a straight line. So $90 + 70 + t = 180, t = 20$.

2. D

Difficulty: Low

Strategic Advice: Try different combinations of people in each car.

Getting to the Answer: Let's try to put 4 employees in each car. Since there are 11 cars, 44 employees are seated. Now there are 4 employees left. Each of these 4 employees can sit in one of these cars. So now there are 7 cars with 4 employees in each car and 4 cars with 5 employees in each car. Choice (D) is correct.

3. A

Difficulty: Low

Strategic Advice: Try to reduce two variables to one variable.

Getting to the Answer: This is a problem in which you are working with a system of equations. Subtract the second equation from the first:

$$2x + 3y = 11$$
$$2x - y = 7$$
$$4y = 4$$
$$y = 1$$

Plugging this value for *y* back into the first equation, $2x + 3(1) = 11, 2x = 8, x = 4$.

4. D

Difficulty: Medium

Strategic Advice: This is a problem using common percent and fractional equivalents.

Getting to the Answer: Find $\frac{1}{3}$ of 60 and then figure what percent of 50 that number is. $\frac{1}{3} \times 60 = 20$. To find out what percent of 50 20 is, first find what fraction of 50 20 is. 20 is $\frac{20}{50}$ or $\frac{2}{5}$ of 50. To convert $\frac{2}{5}$ to a percent, multiply $\frac{2}{5}$ by 100%. $\frac{2}{5} \times 100\% = 40\%$.

5. A

Difficulty: Medium

Strategic Advice: Solve this linear equation by letting $r =$ the cost of the radio in dollars.

Getting to the Answer: A television set costs $25 less than twice the cost of the radio, or $2r - 25$. The two items total to $200, so $r + 2r - 25 = 200$, $3r = 225$, $r = 75$. So a radio costs $75 and a television set $125, making the cost of the television $125 - $75 = $50 more than a radio.

6. B

Difficulty: Medium

Strategic Advice: The key to this problem is drawing a diagram:

Getting to the Answer:

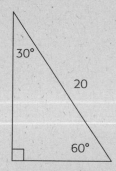

Since the top angle of the right triangle is 30 degrees, this is a 30-60-90 right triangle. You're asked to find the distance from the bottom of the ladder to the base of the building, which is the leg opposite the 30-degree angle and therefore half of the hypotenuse or $\frac{1}{2}$ of 20, which is 10.

7. D

Difficulty: Medium

Strategic Advice: Draw a diagram of the circle and the line segment to solve this problem.

Getting to the Answer:

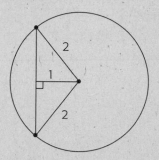

Notice that drawing in two radii gives you two right triangles, each with hypotenuse 2 and a leg of 1. Using the Pythagorean theorem, you can find that the length of the other leg is $\sqrt{3}$. Since each of these legs makes up half the line segment, the length of the line segment is $2\sqrt{3}$.

8. D

Difficulty: Medium

Strategic Advice: This problem tests your knowledge of number properties.

Getting to the Answer: The greatest possible sum of two single digits is 18, so from the first addition problem you can see that C must be 1. Looking at the second problem, $1 + B = 5$, so B must be 4. So $A + A = 14$ and $A = 7$.

9. B

Difficulty: Medium

Strategic Advice: Draw a diagram of the two rectangles according to the information you're given:

Getting to the Answer:

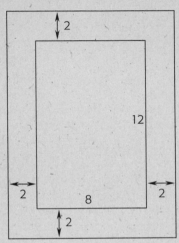

To find the area of the frame, you can subtract the area of the picture from the combined area of the frame and picture. Since the frame is 2 inches wide, the measurements of its outer edges are equal to those of the picture plus 4 inches. This makes its measurements 12 by 16. So the area of the frame and picture combined is 12 × 16 or 192 and the area of the picture is 8 × 12 or 96, making the area of the frame $192 - 96 = 96$.

10. B

Difficulty: Medium

Strategic Advice: Avoid confusion by breaking this word problem down step by step.

Getting to the Answer: Since 35 cups of coffee were sold and 13 contained neither milk nor sugar, then $35 - 13 = 22$ contained either milk, sugar, or both. You know that 15 contained sugar and 12 contained milk; this totals 27. But there are only 22 cups of coffee, so $27 - 22 = 5$ must contain both milk and sugar.

11. C

Difficulty: Medium

Strategic Advice: You could square both sides of this equation immediately to remove the square root, or you could simplify it a little first. Backsolving also works well on this type of problem.

Getting to the Answer:

$$\frac{4}{\sqrt{r+4}} = 2$$

$$4 = 2\sqrt{r+4}$$
$$2 = \sqrt{r+4}$$
$$4 = r + 4$$
$$0 = r$$

12. D

Difficulty: Medium

Strategic Advice: To solve this problem, first set up an equation for the line from the given points. You might try sketching the line to estimate the y-intercept, but this is a difficult line to sketch accurately.

Getting to the Answer: To find an equation for the line, start by finding its slope, using the formula $\frac{y_2 - y_1}{x_2 - x_1}$. Then plug one of the given points into the equation $y = mx + b$, where m is the slope and b is the y-intercept, and solve for b.

Slope: $\frac{42 - 21}{4 - 1} = \frac{21}{3} = 7$

y-intercept:

$$21 = 7(1) + b$$
$$21 - 7 = b$$
$$14 = b$$

13. C

Difficulty: Medium

Strategic Advice: Most people find it easier to work with negative exponents if they are written as fractions. Note that the answer choices may not be in the same form as your original answer, so be prepared to simplify.

Getting to the Answer:

$$f(3) = 3^{-3} + 3^{\frac{3}{2}}$$
$$= \frac{1}{3^3} + \sqrt{3^3}$$
$$= \frac{1}{27} + \sqrt{27}$$
$$= \frac{1}{27} + 3\sqrt{3}$$
$$= \frac{1}{27} + \frac{27(3\sqrt{3})}{27}$$
$$= \frac{1 + 81\sqrt{3}}{27}$$

14. A

Difficulty: Medium

Strategic Advice: This is a type of problem in which you are solving for one variable in terms of another. If each term is x more than the previous term, then each term must equal x plus the previous term. In other words, $s = r + x$ and $t = s + x$.

Getting to the Answer: Combining those 2 equations gives you

$t = (r + x) + x = r + 2x$. The average of r, s and t is $\frac{r + s + t}{3}$. Substituting $r + x$ for s and $r + 2x$ for t gives you

$$\frac{r + s + t}{3} = \frac{r + (r + x) + (r + 2)}{3} = \frac{3r + 3x}{2} = \frac{3(r + x)}{3} = r + x,$$

answer choice (A).

15. D

Difficulty: Medium

Strategic Advice: You use different mental skills, such as mechanical, conceptual, or creative, in different questions. Ask yourself what particular skill(s) a question appears to test; doing so will help you bring the proper kind of focus to a question. This question, for example, almost exclusively challenges your ability to translate from English into math.

Getting to the Answer:

Follow directions:

"Subtract 6 from x" means $x - 6$.

"Divide this sum by 3" means $\frac{x - 6}{3}$.

"Add 4 to this quotient" means $\frac{x - 6}{3} + 4$.

Then merely simplify:

$$\frac{x - 6}{3} + \frac{12}{3} = \frac{x + 6}{3}$$

16. C

Difficulty: High

Strategic Advice: This question is so brief, yet so potentially challenging. The best way to approach it is to distinguish the separate ideas that it brings into play.

Getting to the Answer:

Begin by thinking about cubes of integers.

$$1^3 = 1$$
$$2^3 = 8$$
$$3^3 = 27$$

… and so on. $25a$ is such a cube. So what you're really asked here is, how much farther must you continue the list of cubes before you get to a number that 25 goes into?

Is 25 a factor of 4^3, or 64? No.

Is 25 a factor of 5^3, or 125? Yes. 25 goes into 125 five times, so the minimum number a can be is 5.

SECTION 9

1. E

Difficulty: Low

Look for the most concise answer that does not introduce any additional errors.

As written, this sentence is awkward and unnecessarily wordy; Choice (E) corrects this. Choices (B) and (D) use incorrect grammatical structure; additionally, (D) is even wordier than the original. Choice (C) introduces a verb tense that is inappropriate in context.

2. E

Difficulty: Medium

Make sure that comparisons are structured to compare logical things. Here, *children* are being compared to *the 1960s*. Choice (E) makes the comparison between children in the two eras. Choice (B) does not address the error. Choice (C) uses a singular pronoun, *that*, to refer to the plural *children*. Choice (D) is idiomatically incorrect usage in context.

3. D

Difficulty: High

Pronouns are frequently used without antecedents in everyday speech, but such usage will be incorrect on the SAT. In this sentence, the pronoun *it* has no antecedent. Choice (D) eliminates the ambiguous pronoun without introducing any additional errors. Choice (B) has no independent clause, so it is a sentence fragment. Choice (C) is incorrect grammatical structure. Choice (E) does not address the error.

4. E

Difficulty: High

Eliminate redundant words to make sentences more concise. As written, this sentence is unnecessarily wordy, and *musical statement* is unnecessary, since *musical form* is already used in the first part of the sentence, and *affect* and *change* mean essentially the same thing. Choice (E) eliminates the redundant words and does not introduce additional errors. None of the other answer choices address the redundancies; additionally, (B) fails to correctly complete the comparative structure *neither...nor*. Choices (C) and (D) are wordy and awkward.

5. D

Difficulty: Low

As written, this is a sentence fragment. Choices (D) and (E) add a verb, but (E) introduces an error in subject-verb agreement. The plural subject *sections* doesn't agree with the singular verb *is*.

6. C

Difficulty: Medium

The clause *the redemption is in his returning* is non-idiomatic and awkward in itself. Moreover, the lawyer argued two things: that her client had committed the crime, and that the client had redeemed himself by returning the items. These two clauses must be parallel in form. The first uses the past perfect *had...committed* and the subject *her client*. The underlined portion should do the same. Choice (C) uses *her client* and the past perfect *had redeemed*. Also, *returning the stolen items* is parallel to *expressing great remorse*, so (C) fits back into the original sentence.

7. E

Difficulty: Medium

The original sentence has a modification error. *Kevin Garnett led the league in combined scoring and rebounding statistics*...but the subject directly following the introductory phrase is *the NBA*, which indicates that the *NBA* led the league. Only (E) correctly places *Kevin Garnett* directly after the introductory phrase. Choices (B) and (C) remove the introductory phrase altogether, which fixes the modification problem, but the choices unnecessarily eliminate the fact that Garnett's *combined scoring and rebounding statistics* led the league.

8. C

Difficulty: Medium

The sentence is a run-on with a comma splice joining two independent clauses. Choice (C) correctly combines two independent clauses with a semicolon. Choice (B) uses a semicolon, but illogically switches to the past perfect tense. Choice (D) illogically uses *would join* instead of the simple past tense. Choice (E) creates a sentence fragment by joining an independent and dependent clause with a semicolon.

9. C

Difficulty: Medium

This sentence uses the conjunction *and* instead of appropriately indicating contrast. Choice (C) shows the correct sequence of events, *he became* more accurate after his lack of aim *had been exasperating*, with the appropriate contrast indicated by *but*. Choices (B) and (E) lose the logical sequence of tenses. Choice (D) is a run-on, requiring a semicolon before *however*.

10. D

Difficulty: Medium

Choice (D) correctly combines the two independent clauses with a semicolon. Choices (B) and (E) use contrasting transition words that are illogical in context. Choice (C) merely adds *and*, which does not logically connect the two ideas.

11. E

Difficulty: High

The verb *digests* should parallel the adjective *healthy*. Choice (E) corrects the parallel with the adjective *digestible*. None of the other answer choices are parallel. Choice (B) uses the verb *being digested*, which also changes the meaning. Choices (C) and (D) keep the original verb form.

12. A

Difficulty: Medium

The original sentence is the simplest and best version.

13. B

Difficulty: High

(B) corrects the error in the run-on sentence. Choice (C) uses the conjunction *and* instead of indicating a contrast with *but*. Choice (D) unnecessarily includes the word *however*; contrast is already indicated by *although*. Choice (E) uses *which* in place of *who*.

14. D

Difficulty: Medium

When possible, change the passive voice to the active voice. Only (D) uses the active voice in a complete sentence. Choices (A) and (B) use the passive voice. Choices (C) and (E) are sentence fragments.

SAT PRACTICE TEST EIGHT ANSWER SHEET

Remove (or photocopy) the answer sheet, and use it to complete the practice test.

How to Take the Practice Tests

Each Practice Test includes eight scored multiple-choice sections and one essay. Keep in mind that on the actual SAT, there will be an additional multiple-choice section—the experimental section—that will not contribute to your score.

Once you start a Practice Test, don't stop until you've gone through all nine sections. Remember, you can review any questions within a section, but you may not go back or forward a section.

Good luck!

Start with number 1 for each section. If a section has fewer questions than answer spaces, leave the extra spaces blank.

Section One

Section One is the writing section's essay component.
Lined pages on which you will write your essay can be found in that section.

Section Two

1. Ⓐ Ⓑ Ⓒ Ⓓ Ⓔ
2. Ⓐ Ⓑ Ⓒ Ⓓ Ⓔ
3. Ⓐ Ⓑ Ⓒ Ⓓ Ⓔ
4. Ⓐ Ⓑ Ⓒ Ⓓ Ⓔ
5. Ⓐ Ⓑ Ⓒ Ⓓ Ⓔ
6. Ⓐ Ⓑ Ⓒ Ⓓ Ⓔ
7. Ⓐ Ⓑ Ⓒ Ⓓ Ⓔ
8. Ⓐ Ⓑ Ⓒ Ⓓ Ⓔ

9. Ⓐ Ⓑ Ⓒ Ⓓ Ⓔ
10. Ⓐ Ⓑ Ⓒ Ⓓ Ⓔ
11. Ⓐ Ⓑ Ⓒ Ⓓ Ⓔ
12. Ⓐ Ⓑ Ⓒ Ⓓ Ⓔ
13. Ⓐ Ⓑ Ⓒ Ⓓ Ⓔ
14. Ⓐ Ⓑ Ⓒ Ⓓ Ⓔ
15. Ⓐ Ⓑ Ⓒ Ⓓ Ⓔ
16. Ⓐ Ⓑ Ⓒ Ⓓ Ⓔ

17. Ⓐ Ⓑ Ⓒ Ⓓ Ⓔ
18. Ⓐ Ⓑ Ⓒ Ⓓ Ⓔ
19. Ⓐ Ⓑ Ⓒ Ⓓ Ⓔ
20. Ⓐ Ⓑ Ⓒ Ⓓ Ⓔ

right in Section Two

wrong in Section Two

Section Three

1. Ⓐ Ⓑ Ⓒ Ⓓ Ⓔ
2. Ⓐ Ⓑ Ⓒ Ⓓ Ⓔ
3. Ⓐ Ⓑ Ⓒ Ⓓ Ⓔ
4. Ⓐ Ⓑ Ⓒ Ⓓ Ⓔ
5. Ⓐ Ⓑ Ⓒ Ⓓ Ⓔ
6. Ⓐ Ⓑ Ⓒ Ⓓ Ⓔ
7. Ⓐ Ⓑ Ⓒ Ⓓ Ⓔ
8. Ⓐ Ⓑ Ⓒ Ⓓ Ⓔ

9. Ⓐ Ⓑ Ⓒ Ⓓ Ⓔ
10. Ⓐ Ⓑ Ⓒ Ⓓ Ⓔ
11. Ⓐ Ⓑ Ⓒ Ⓓ Ⓔ
12. Ⓐ Ⓑ Ⓒ Ⓓ Ⓔ
13. Ⓐ Ⓑ Ⓒ Ⓓ Ⓔ
14. Ⓐ Ⓑ Ⓒ Ⓓ Ⓔ
15. Ⓐ Ⓑ Ⓒ Ⓓ Ⓔ
16. Ⓐ Ⓑ Ⓒ Ⓓ Ⓔ

17. Ⓐ Ⓑ Ⓒ Ⓓ Ⓔ
18. Ⓐ Ⓑ Ⓒ Ⓓ Ⓔ
19. Ⓐ Ⓑ Ⓒ Ⓓ Ⓔ
20. Ⓐ Ⓑ Ⓒ Ⓓ Ⓔ
21. Ⓐ Ⓑ Ⓒ Ⓓ Ⓔ
22. Ⓐ Ⓑ Ⓒ Ⓓ Ⓔ
23. Ⓐ Ⓑ Ⓒ Ⓓ Ⓔ
24. Ⓐ Ⓑ Ⓒ Ⓓ Ⓔ

right in Section Three

wrong in Section Three

Remove (or photocopy) this answer sheet, and use it to complete the practice test.

Start with number 1 for each section. If a section has fewer questions than answer spaces, leave the extra spaces blank.

Section Four

1. Ⓐ Ⓑ Ⓒ Ⓓ Ⓔ   9. Ⓐ Ⓑ Ⓒ Ⓓ Ⓔ   17. Ⓐ Ⓑ Ⓒ Ⓓ Ⓔ
2. Ⓐ Ⓑ Ⓒ Ⓓ Ⓔ   10. Ⓐ Ⓑ Ⓒ Ⓓ Ⓔ   18. Ⓐ Ⓑ Ⓒ Ⓓ Ⓔ
3. Ⓐ Ⓑ Ⓒ Ⓓ Ⓔ   11. Ⓐ Ⓑ Ⓒ Ⓓ Ⓔ
4. Ⓐ Ⓑ Ⓒ Ⓓ Ⓔ   12. Ⓐ Ⓑ Ⓒ Ⓓ Ⓔ
5. Ⓐ Ⓑ Ⓒ Ⓓ Ⓔ   13. Ⓐ Ⓑ Ⓒ Ⓓ Ⓔ
6. Ⓐ Ⓑ Ⓒ Ⓓ Ⓔ   14. Ⓐ Ⓑ Ⓒ Ⓓ Ⓔ
7. Ⓐ Ⓑ Ⓒ Ⓓ Ⓔ   15. Ⓐ Ⓑ Ⓒ Ⓓ Ⓔ
8. Ⓐ Ⓑ Ⓒ Ⓓ Ⓔ   16. Ⓐ Ⓑ Ⓒ Ⓓ Ⓔ

right in Section Four

wrong in Section Four

If section 5 of your test book contains math questions that are not multiple choice, continue to item 9 below. Otherwise, continue to item 9 above.

9.   10.   11.   12.   13.

14.   15.   16.   17.   18.

Section Five

1. Ⓐ Ⓑ Ⓒ Ⓓ Ⓔ   10. Ⓐ Ⓑ Ⓒ Ⓓ Ⓔ   19. Ⓐ Ⓑ Ⓒ Ⓓ Ⓔ   28. Ⓐ Ⓑ Ⓒ Ⓓ Ⓔ
2. Ⓐ Ⓑ Ⓒ Ⓓ Ⓔ   11. Ⓐ Ⓑ Ⓒ Ⓓ Ⓔ   20. Ⓐ Ⓑ Ⓒ Ⓓ Ⓔ   29. Ⓐ Ⓑ Ⓒ Ⓓ Ⓔ
3. Ⓐ Ⓑ Ⓒ Ⓓ Ⓔ   12. Ⓐ Ⓑ Ⓒ Ⓓ Ⓔ   21. Ⓐ Ⓑ Ⓒ Ⓓ Ⓔ   30. Ⓐ Ⓑ Ⓒ Ⓓ Ⓔ
4. Ⓐ Ⓑ Ⓒ Ⓓ Ⓔ   13. Ⓐ Ⓑ Ⓒ Ⓓ Ⓔ   22. Ⓐ Ⓑ Ⓒ Ⓓ Ⓔ   31. Ⓐ Ⓑ Ⓒ Ⓓ Ⓔ
5. Ⓐ Ⓑ Ⓒ Ⓓ Ⓔ   14. Ⓐ Ⓑ Ⓒ Ⓓ Ⓔ   23. Ⓐ Ⓑ Ⓒ Ⓓ Ⓔ   32. Ⓐ Ⓑ Ⓒ Ⓓ Ⓔ
6. Ⓐ Ⓑ Ⓒ Ⓓ Ⓔ   15. Ⓐ Ⓑ Ⓒ Ⓓ Ⓔ   24. Ⓐ Ⓑ Ⓒ Ⓓ Ⓔ   33. Ⓐ Ⓑ Ⓒ Ⓓ Ⓔ
7. Ⓐ Ⓑ Ⓒ Ⓓ Ⓔ   16. Ⓐ Ⓑ Ⓒ Ⓓ Ⓔ   25. Ⓐ Ⓑ Ⓒ Ⓓ Ⓔ   34 Ⓐ Ⓑ Ⓒ Ⓓ Ⓔ
8. Ⓐ Ⓑ Ⓒ Ⓓ Ⓔ   17. Ⓐ Ⓑ Ⓒ Ⓓ Ⓔ   26. Ⓐ Ⓑ Ⓒ Ⓓ Ⓔ   35. Ⓐ Ⓑ Ⓒ Ⓓ Ⓔ
9. Ⓐ Ⓑ Ⓒ Ⓓ Ⓔ   18. Ⓐ Ⓑ Ⓒ Ⓓ Ⓔ   27. Ⓐ Ⓑ Ⓒ Ⓓ Ⓔ

right in Section Five

wrong in Section Five

Remove (or photocopy) this answer sheet, and use it to complete the practice test.

Start with number 1 for each section. If a section has fewer questions than answer spaces, leave the extra spaces blank.

Section Six

1. Ⓐ Ⓑ Ⓒ Ⓓ Ⓔ
2. Ⓐ Ⓑ Ⓒ Ⓓ Ⓔ
3. Ⓐ Ⓑ Ⓒ Ⓓ Ⓔ
4. Ⓐ Ⓑ Ⓒ Ⓓ Ⓔ
5. Ⓐ Ⓑ Ⓒ Ⓓ Ⓔ
6. Ⓐ Ⓑ Ⓒ Ⓓ Ⓔ
7. Ⓐ Ⓑ Ⓒ Ⓓ Ⓔ
8. Ⓐ Ⓑ Ⓒ Ⓓ Ⓔ

9. Ⓐ Ⓑ Ⓒ Ⓓ Ⓔ
10. Ⓐ Ⓑ Ⓒ Ⓓ Ⓔ
11. Ⓐ Ⓑ Ⓒ Ⓓ Ⓔ
12. Ⓐ Ⓑ Ⓒ Ⓓ Ⓔ
13. Ⓐ Ⓑ Ⓒ Ⓓ Ⓔ
14. Ⓐ Ⓑ Ⓒ Ⓓ Ⓔ
15. Ⓐ Ⓑ Ⓒ Ⓓ Ⓔ
16. Ⓐ Ⓑ Ⓒ Ⓓ Ⓔ

17. Ⓐ Ⓑ Ⓒ Ⓓ Ⓔ
18. Ⓐ Ⓑ Ⓒ Ⓓ Ⓔ
19. Ⓐ Ⓑ Ⓒ Ⓓ Ⓔ
20. Ⓐ Ⓑ Ⓒ Ⓓ Ⓔ
21. Ⓐ Ⓑ Ⓒ Ⓓ Ⓔ
22. Ⓐ Ⓑ Ⓒ Ⓓ Ⓔ
23. Ⓐ Ⓑ Ⓒ Ⓓ Ⓔ
24. Ⓐ Ⓑ Ⓒ Ⓓ Ⓔ

☐ # right in Section Six

☐ # wrong in Section Six

Section Seven

1. Ⓐ Ⓑ Ⓒ Ⓓ Ⓔ
2. Ⓐ Ⓑ Ⓒ Ⓓ Ⓔ
3. Ⓐ Ⓑ Ⓒ Ⓓ Ⓔ
4. Ⓐ Ⓑ Ⓒ Ⓓ Ⓔ
5. Ⓐ Ⓑ Ⓒ Ⓓ Ⓔ
6. Ⓐ Ⓑ Ⓒ Ⓓ Ⓔ
7. Ⓐ Ⓑ Ⓒ Ⓓ Ⓔ
8. Ⓐ Ⓑ Ⓒ Ⓓ Ⓔ

9. Ⓐ Ⓑ Ⓒ Ⓓ Ⓔ
10. Ⓐ Ⓑ Ⓒ Ⓓ Ⓔ
11. Ⓐ Ⓑ Ⓒ Ⓓ Ⓔ
12. Ⓐ Ⓑ Ⓒ Ⓓ Ⓔ
13. Ⓐ Ⓑ Ⓒ Ⓓ Ⓔ
14. Ⓐ Ⓑ Ⓒ Ⓓ Ⓔ
15. Ⓐ Ⓑ Ⓒ Ⓓ Ⓔ
16. Ⓐ Ⓑ Ⓒ Ⓓ Ⓔ

☐ # right in Section Seven

☐ # wrong in Section Seven

Section Eight

1. Ⓐ Ⓑ Ⓒ Ⓓ Ⓔ
2. Ⓐ Ⓑ Ⓒ Ⓓ Ⓔ
3. Ⓐ Ⓑ Ⓒ Ⓓ Ⓔ
4. Ⓐ Ⓑ Ⓒ Ⓓ Ⓔ
5. Ⓐ Ⓑ Ⓒ Ⓓ Ⓔ
6. Ⓐ Ⓑ Ⓒ Ⓓ Ⓔ
7. Ⓐ Ⓑ Ⓒ Ⓓ Ⓔ
8. Ⓐ Ⓑ Ⓒ Ⓓ Ⓔ

9. Ⓐ Ⓑ Ⓒ Ⓓ Ⓔ
10. Ⓐ Ⓑ Ⓒ Ⓓ Ⓔ
11. Ⓐ Ⓑ Ⓒ Ⓓ Ⓔ
12. Ⓐ Ⓑ Ⓒ Ⓓ Ⓔ
13. Ⓐ Ⓑ Ⓒ Ⓓ Ⓔ
14. Ⓐ Ⓑ Ⓒ Ⓓ Ⓔ
15. Ⓐ Ⓑ Ⓒ Ⓓ Ⓔ
16. Ⓐ Ⓑ Ⓒ Ⓓ Ⓔ

17. Ⓐ Ⓑ Ⓒ Ⓓ Ⓔ
18. Ⓐ Ⓑ Ⓒ Ⓓ Ⓔ
19. Ⓐ Ⓑ Ⓒ Ⓓ Ⓔ

☐ # right in Section Eight

☐ # wrong in Section Eight

Section Nine

1. Ⓐ Ⓑ Ⓒ Ⓓ Ⓔ
2. Ⓐ Ⓑ Ⓒ Ⓓ Ⓔ
3. Ⓐ Ⓑ Ⓒ Ⓓ Ⓔ
4. Ⓐ Ⓑ Ⓒ Ⓓ Ⓔ
5. Ⓐ Ⓑ Ⓒ Ⓓ Ⓔ
6. Ⓐ Ⓑ Ⓒ Ⓓ Ⓔ
7. Ⓐ Ⓑ Ⓒ Ⓓ Ⓔ
8. Ⓐ Ⓑ Ⓒ Ⓓ Ⓔ

9. Ⓐ Ⓑ Ⓒ Ⓓ Ⓔ
10. Ⓐ Ⓑ Ⓒ Ⓓ Ⓔ
11. Ⓐ Ⓑ Ⓒ Ⓓ Ⓔ
12. Ⓐ Ⓑ Ⓒ Ⓓ Ⓔ
13. Ⓐ Ⓑ Ⓒ Ⓓ Ⓔ
14. Ⓐ Ⓑ Ⓒ Ⓓ Ⓔ

☐ # right in Section Nine

☐ # wrong in Section Nine

Practice Test Eight

SECTION 1
Time—25 Minutes
ESSAY

The essay gives you an opportunity to show how effectively you can develop and express ideas. You should, therefore, take care to develop your point of view, present your ideas logically and clearly, and use language precisely.

Your essay must be written in your Answer Grid Booklet—you will receive no other paper on which to write. You will have enough space if you write on every line, avoid wide margins, and keep your handwriting to a reasonable size. Remember that people who are not familiar with your handwriting will read what you write. Try to write or print so that what you are writing is legible to those readers.

You have twenty-five minutes to write an essay on the topic assigned below.

DO NOT WRITE ON ANOTHER TOPIC. AN OFF-TOPIC ESSAY WILL RECEIVE A SCORE OF ZERO.

Think carefully about the issue presented in the following excerpt and the assignment below.

> "During a biology class on metamorphosis, a teacher showed her class a series of pictures. The first was of a caterpillar. The next was of the caterpillar forming a chrysalis. The last was of a beautiful monarch butterfly emerging from its cocoon. One student was so impressed by this that he wrote in his notebook: "beautiful things can come from unpromising beginnings."
>
> –Jen Defulimakis, *Collected Writings*

Assignment: Do you think that people are capable of finding happiness or are they always searching for something beyond what they have? Plan and write an essay in which you develop your point of view on this issue. Support your position with reasoning and examples taken from your reading, studies, experience, or observations.

DO NOT WRITE YOUR ESSAY IN YOUR TEST BOOK.
You will receive credit only for what you write in your Answer Grid Booklet.

_____

_____

_____

_____

_____

_____

_____

_____

_____

_____

_____

_____

_____

_____

_____

_____

_____

_____

_____

_____

_____

IF YOU FINISH BEFORE TIME IS CALLED, YOU MAY CHECK YOUR WORK ON THIS SECTION ONLY. DO NOT TURN TO ANY OTHER SECTION IN THE TEST.

SECTION 2

Time—25 Minutes

20 Questions

Directions: For this section, solve each problem and decide which is the best of the choices given. Fill in the corresponding oval on the answer sheet. You may use any available space for scratchwork.

Notes:

(1) Calculator use is permitted.

(2) All numbers used are real numbers.

(3) Figures are provided for some problems. All figures are drawn to scale and lie in a plane UNLESS otherwise indicated.

(4) Unless otherwise specified, the domain of any function f is assumed to be the set of all real numbers x for which $f(x)$ is a real number.

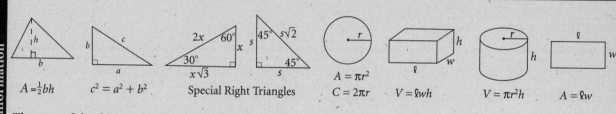

$A = \frac{1}{2}bh$ $c^2 = a^2 + b^2$ Special Right Triangles $A = \pi r^2$ $V = \ell wh$ $V = \pi r^2 h$ $A = \ell w$

$C = 2\pi r$

The sum of the degree measures of the angles in a triangle is 180.

The number of degrees of arc in a circle is 360.

A straight angle has a degree measure of 180.

1. If $5x + 3 = 21$, then $5x + 10 =$

(A) 28

(B) 30

(C) 32

(D) 34

(E) 36

2. In the figure above, AB and CD intersect at point X. If EX bisects angle BXD, what is the degree measure of angle CXB?

(A)   60

(B)   90

(C) 100

(D) 110

(E) 120

GO ON TO THE NEXT PAGE

3. If $a - 2b = 10$, $b - 3c = 5$, and $c = 1$, what is the value of a?

(A) −4
(B) 10
(C) 18
(D) 26
(E) 36

4. John has more money than Billy but less than Sean. If j, b, and s represent the amounts of money of John, Billy, and Sean, respectively, which of the following is true?

(A) $b < j < s$
(B) $s < j < b$
(C) $j < s < b$
(D) $j < b < s$
(E) $b < s < j$

5. A "complex prime" is any integer greater than 1 that has exactly three positive integer factors–itself, its square root, and 1. Of the following, which is a complex prime?

(A) 169
(B) 144
(C) 81
(D) 64
(E) 37

6. The perimeter of square A is 4 times the perimeter of square B. If the perimeter of square B is given to be 18, then what is the length of a single side of square A?

(A) 4.5
(B) 18
(C) 22
(D) 48
(E) 72

7. C, D, and E are points on a line, in that order. If the length of segment CE is 30, and the length of segment CD is twice the length of DE, what is the length of segment CD?

(A) 10
(B) 15
(C) 20
(D) 25
(E) 30

8. If a is an odd negative number and b is a positive even number, which of the following must be even and positive?

(A) $a + b$
(B) $-ab$
(C) ab
(D) $\dfrac{b}{a}$
(E) $b - a$

9. The Suzukis are having a picnic at their house where they will serve pasta salad to all of the guests. One pound of pasta salad either serves 6 adults or 10 children. If the Suzukis have 34 guests, 10 of whom are children, how many pounds of pasta salad will they need to serve all of the guests?

(A) 3
(B) 4
(C) 5
(D) 6
(E) 7

10. $(-3a^2b^6)^3 =$

(A) $9a^5b^9$
(B) $-9a^5b^9$
(C) $9a^6b^{18}$
(D) $27a^6b^{18}$
(E) $-27a^6b^{18}$

GO ON TO THE NEXT PAGE

11. If the sum of three numbers is 27, what is the average (arithmetic mean) of the three numbers?

    (A) 0
    (B) 9
    (C) 12
    (D) 16
    (E) 18

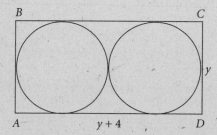

12. In the figure above, two circles with the same area are inscribed in rectangle *ABCD*. If the area of the rectangle is 32, what is the area of one of the circles?

    (A) 4π
    (B) 5π
    (C) 6π
    (D) 8π
    (E) 10π

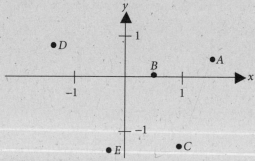

13. Which of the following points has coordinates (x, y) such that $x - y < 0$?

    (A) *A*
    (B) *B*
    (C) *C*
    (D) *D*
    (E) *E*

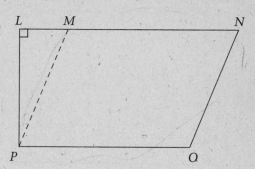

Note: Figure not drawn to scale

14. If $LP = 12$ and the length of each side of parallelogram *MNOP* is 13, as shown in the figure above, what is the area of *LNOP*?

    (A) 162
    (B) 186
    (C) 199
    (D) 216
    (E) 229

15. When the average (arithmetic mean) of a list of prices is multiplied by the number of prices, the result is *n*. What does *n* represent?

    (A) the average of the prices
    (B) the number of prices
    (C) half of the number of prices
    (D) the sum of the prices
    (E) half of the sum of the prices

GO ON TO THE NEXT PAGE

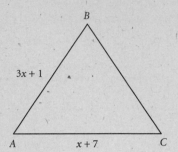

16. In the figure above, what is the perimeter of equilateral triangle ABC?

(A) 3

(B) 9

(C) 10

(D) 15

(E) 30

17. A box of crayons contains only red, green, and blue crayons. The probability of randomly selecting a red crayon from the box is $\frac{2}{5}$, and the probability of randomly selecting a blue crayon is $\frac{1}{4}$. Which of the following could be the total number of crayons in the box?

(A) 12

(B) 16

(C) 20

(D) 25

(E) 32

18. What was the initial amount of water in a barrel, in liters, if there are now x liters, y liters were lost, and 6 liters were added?

(A) $x + y - 6$

(B) $y - x + 6$

(C) $x + y + 6$

(D) $y - x - 6$

(E) $x - y + 6$

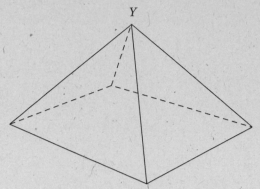

Note: Figure not drawn to scale

19. The square pyramid shown above has a height of 12 feet and the length of each edge of the base is 16 feet. What is the length of YZ, in feet?

(A) $2\sqrt{5}$

(B) $2\sqrt{7}$

(C) $4\sqrt{13}$

(D) $4\sqrt{17}$

(E) 20

20. After the first term, each term in a sequence is 4 greater than $\frac{1}{4}$ of the preceding term. If n is the first term of the sequence and $n \neq 0$, what is the ratio of the second term to the first term?

(A) $\dfrac{n + 16}{4}$

(B) $\dfrac{n + 4}{4}$

(C) $\dfrac{n + 16}{4n}$

(D) $\dfrac{n + 4}{4n}$

(E) $\dfrac{16 - n}{4}$

IF YOU FINISH BEFORE TIME IS CALLED, YOU MAY CHECK YOUR WORK ON THIS SECTION ONLY. DO NOT TURN TO ANY OTHER SECTION IN THE TEST. **STOP**

SECTION 3

Time—25 Minutes
24 Questions

> **Directions:** For each of the following questions, choose the best answer and darken the corresponding oval on the answer sheet.

Each sentence below has one or two blanks, each blank indicating that something has been omitted. Beneath the sentence are five words or sets of words labeled (A) through (E). Choose the word or set of words that, when inserted in the sentence, <u>best</u> fits the meaning of the sentence as a whole.

EXAMPLE:

Today's small, portable computers contrast markedly with the earliest electronic computers, which were ----.

(A) effective
(B) invented
(C) useful
(D) destructive
(E) enormous

1. In the ---- atmosphere of the basement, the stacks of old newspapers turned yellow and ----, emitting an odor that reached all the way to the first floor.

    (A) underground .. outdated
    (B) dank .. musty
    (C) cool .. useless
    (D) shadowy .. wrinkled
    (E) cluttered .. faded

2. Once a ---- population center, the city gradually lost residents to the factory towns of the North.

    (A) bustling
    (B) manufactured
    (C) rural
    (D) seedy
    (E) deserted

3. In the summertime, ---- rains often ---- the hillside slopes, causing landslides and washing away people's precarious houses.

    (A) torrential .. deluge
    (B) gentle .. purge
    (C) treacherous .. sustain
    (D) liberal .. desecrate
    (E) fecund .. bolster

4. Those who reject psychological theory and point to its scientific ---- must consider that it contains a substantial amount of truth, based not on ----, but on clinical observations.

    (A) inadequacies .. assumptions
    (B) foundations .. data
    (C) basics .. speculation
    (D) strengths .. experience
    (E) deficiencies .. evidence

5. That she found the film ---- was a surprise, given her usual ---- towards dramatic stories.

    (A) predictable .. spontaneity
    (B) poignant .. impassivity
    (C) irrelevant .. animosity
    (D) anachronistic .. perspicacity
    (E) affected .. originality

GO ON TO THE NEXT PAGE

6. The fullest edition of the letters of H.P. Lovecraft consists of five volumes; however, only a small fraction of Lovecraft's ---- correspondence has ever been published.

(A) laconic
(B) unknown
(C) voluminous
(D) verbal
(E) popular

7. Describing Linda as an exemplary pupil, the principal lauded her academic achievements and urged the other students to ---- her performance.

(A) elucidate
(B) mollify
(C) emulate
(D) castigate
(E) reflect

8. Nearly all epiphytic ferns are ---- tropical rain forests; while they do not require soil, they cannot survive without constant moisture.

(A) uprooted to
(B) steeped in
(C) inimical to
(D) decorative in
(E) endemic to

GO ON TO THE NEXT PAGE

Directions: The passages below are followed by questions based on their content; questions following a pair of related passages may also be based on the relationship between the paired passages. Answer the questions on the basis of what is <u>stated</u> or <u>implied</u> in the passages and in any introductory material that may be provided.

Questions 9–12 are based on the following passages.

Passage 1

As scores of newly released scientific studies bolster the already sound body of evidence indicating that the behavior, concentration, and even intelligence of grade school students are inextrica-
(5) bly linked to the nutrients they take in, the food being served in school cafeterias is coming under closer scrutiny. The results of these examinations are, in many cases, revealing rather deplorable eating conditions. According to some experts,
(10) many school systems are not even coming close to supporting the unique nutritional needs of growing children, a problem that seems to stem less from budgetary constraints and more from general dietary ignorance.

Passage 2

(15) With parental organizations and government health officials becoming increasingly critical of the nutritional value of the cafeteria foods being offered by school systems, school administrators are finding themselves pressed into a tight spot by
(20) two opposing forces. On the one hand, parents and health experts want schools to provide lunch options that contain the vegetables and minerals required by growing bodies; conversely, schools complain that they must compete, from an eco-
(25) nomic standpoint, with fast-food restaurant chains that can better attract the appetites of teenagers. While parents may be loathe to the idea of such establishments influencing the dietary decisions of school boards, an unprofitable cafete-
(30) ria can quickly become a significant budgetary drain.

9. As used in line 2, "sound" most nearly means

(A) complete
(B) flawless
(C) thorough
(D) good
(E) wholesome

10. In the last sentence of Passage 2 (lines 27–31) the author implies that

(A) many school cafeterias are unprofitable
(B) school boards are often forced to make difficult decisions
(C) most students are simply uninterested in eating health foods
(D) mimicking fast-food restaurants is often profitable for cafeterias
(E) school boards are usually unconcerned with the nutritional value of cafeteria food

GO ON TO THE NEXT PAGE

11. The authors of both passages agree that

   (A) the eating conditions in many schools are unacceptable

   (B) offering nutritional food choices is a growing concern

   (C) parental organizations and school boards often disagree

   (D) good nutrition is closely linked to success in school

   (E) cafeteria lunch options are becoming increasingly unhealthy

12. Which statement best describes how the authors of the two passages differ in their views on school cafeteria food?

   (A) The author of Passage 1 suggests that schools are largely unaware of the nutritional needs of children, whereas the author of Passage 2 implies it is a challenge to attract students to healthier foods.

   (B) The author of Passage 1 criticizes the lunch options offered by many schools, whereas the author of Passage 2 expresses sympathy for the tough decisions school boards are forced to make.

   (C) The author of Passage 1 praises the increased scrutiny of cafeteria food options, whereas Passage 2 suggests parental organizations and health officials have exaggerated the problem.

   (D) The author of Passage 1 argues that schools must be made more aware of the nutritional needs of children, whereas Passage 2 implies a cafeteria must be profitable to survive.

   (E) The author of Passage 1 relies upon evidence from scientific studies, whereas the author of Passage 2 focuses on data obtained by government health officials.

GO ON TO THE NEXT PAGE ⟩

Questions 13–18 are based on the following passage.

*The author of this passage is a scientist who studies
leatherbacks, an ancient species of sea turtles.*

Of the deep-diving animals, the champions have
always been assumed to be the marine mammals:
the great whales and earless seals. Weddell seals
have been recorded diving to nearly 2,000 feet, ele-
(5) phant seals to nearly 4,000 feet, and sperm whales
to more than 7,000 feet. Our recent investigations,
however, suggest that an ancient species of reptile,
the leatherback sea turtle, may also rank among
the ocean's greatest air-breathing divers. While
(10) measuring the dives of leatherbacks near the U.S.
Virgin Islands, my wife, Karen, and I recorded a
650-pound female that sounded to more than
3,330 feet and remained submerged for some thir-
ty-seven minutes. Unfortunately, this unexpected
(15) behavior continued beyond the range of our
recording instruments; we estimate that she
reached a maximum depth of about 4,265 feet.
Leatherbacks are such consummate swimmers
that they rarely stop moving, a behavior that has
(20) made it impossible to keep them in captivity. They
adjust poorly to the confines of a tank and usually
swim persistently against the walls until the tank
breaks or they seriously harm themselves.
Researchers have therefore been developing
(25) methods of studying them at sea. We use the time-
depth recorder, an instrument capable of recording dive depth, dive duration, ascent and descent
rates, and surface times. During the 1984 and
1985 nesting seasons, we attached recorders to ten
(30) female leatherbacks that had just laid eggs. As a
result, we were able to monitor their behavior
when they returned to the sea. To our astonish-
ment, we found that the turtles were diving almost
continuously, day and night, averaging ten min-
(35) utes per dive and five dives per hour. A typical
dive was far from gradual; both descent and ascent
were almost vertical. Upon returning to the
surface, the turtles gulped a quick breath and
immediately headed straight down again.
(40)   Why the incessant diving? At first we were
baffled, but we soon realized that the turtles were

probably following their main food source, jellyfish. In tropical waters, jellyfish are most common
at great depths, in a biological zone called the
(45) deep scattering layer. This zone consists of a horizontal layer of zooplankton that hovers below
1,800 feet during the day and migrates to the surface at night. Despite years of research, scientists
cannot agree on why organisms collect in these
(50) deep, dense layers. However, we do know that they
migrate to the surface at night to feed on phytoplankton, then gradually retreat from daylight,
maintaining themselves within a gloomy zone that
receives less than one percent of the surface illu-
(55) mination.
A leatherback's dives seem to follow the movements of the deep scattering layer. As dusk
approaches, the turtle executes shallower and shallower dives. As dawn approaches dives become
(60) increasingly deep, probably reflecting the pursuit
of jellyfish as the invertebrates retreat from the
light of dawn.
These are inferences, of course, since we have
not been able to directly observe leatherbacks
(65) feeding, but we have collected some additional
circumstantial evidence. During the 1985 nesting
season, we weighed turtles each time they came
ashore to nest (females come ashore to lay separate clutches of eggs as many as eleven times each
(70) nesting season). The results seem to corroborate
the hypothesis that females feed between bouts of
nesting. Overall body-weight loss for most individuals was negligible, despite an average of 120
pounds of egg production. Indeed, two of the
(75) turtles gained weight as the season progressed.

GO ON TO THE NEXT PAGE

13. In lines 32–39, the author most likely describes a specific behavior of the leatherbacks in order to

   (A) show how impressive the diving activity of the leatherbacks is
   (B) correct a common belief about the movement of the deep scattering layer
   (C) explain how leatherback breeding is carried out
   (D) suggest that the behavior of leatherbacks is unpredictable
   (E) give the reader an insight into the life of a marine biologist

14. The word "gradual" in line 36 most nearly means

   (A) continuous
   (B) slow
   (C) sloping
   (D) progressive
   (E) deliberate

15. The question at the beginning of the third paragraph serves to

   (A) point out an area in which further research is required
   (B) introduce a new topic for discussion
   (C) show that the data from the time-depth recorder has limitations
   (D) suggest that the turtles studied were behaving in a novel way
   (E) emphasize the importance of asking questions in science

16. Which of the following best explains why turtles "execute shallower and shallower dives" (lines 58–59) as dusk approaches?

   (A) The turtles cannot locate their prey as the light dims in deeper waters.
   (B) The turtles stay at the surface to feed on phytoplankton at night.
   (C) The turtles' prey comes closer to the surface at night to feed.
   (D) The number of available jellyfish declines as night approaches.
   (E) Turtles come ashore to nest more often at night than in the daytime.

17. The author uses "circumstantial evidence" (line 66) to suggest that

   (A) female leatherbacks prefer phytoplankton as their main food source
   (B) leatherbacks execute deeper dives than other sea turtles
   (C) the turtles come ashore repeatedly during each nesting season
   (D) female leatherbacks are better divers than male leatherbacks
   (E) female leatherbacks find most of their food in the deep scattering layer

18. The author's primary objective is to

   (A) speculate about the nesting patterns of leatherbacks
   (B) dispute misconceptions about the feeding activity of leatherbacks
   (C) describe the use of the time-depth recorder
   (D) encourage others to pursue studies of leatherbacks
   (E) offer his own findings about the behavior of leatherbacks

GO ON TO THE NEXT PAGE

Questions 19–24 are based on the following passage.

In this excerpt from a short story, Marc realizes that he has offended his friends by bragging about a dangerous practical joke.

"I'm sorry," said Camilla, a little louder this time. Her face was flushed and she was shaking her head as if she'd just lost patience with an infant. Marc watched her push her half-empty
(5) plate towards the center of the table and run a hand through her hair with a sweeping motion. He groaned inwardly. I can't believe I've offended her again. The cafeteria was beginning to empty now, leaving isolated pockets of students hunched
(10) over cups of coffee in the long lanes of sunlight streaming through the windows. Camilla's voice had risen, and it had a camaraderie about it, as if she was sharing a joke. "I've gotta say," she was saying, "you could try showing some considera-
(15) tion for other people for a change."

Nobody was laughing, though. A line seemed to have been crossed. Camilla's words hung oddly in the air for a few seconds and the talk at a neighboring table swelled briefly to fill the void. Marc
(20) felt a momentary impulse to get angry, and suppressed it. Why was she always overreacting to things he said? He liked her a lot, but you had to watch your mouth in her company. Part of the price Camilla paid for being intelligent was that
(25) there were certain things she cared strongly about. Problem was, part of the price of caring strongly about things was a tendency to get emotional when it wasn't warranted. Often the most innocuous remark would set her off. There were always
(30) these minefields in the conversation. One minute you'd be strolling along admiring the view, and the next, you'd have tripped her wire and the whole landscape would have changed. Marc couldn't understand this; he came from a long line
(35) of rationalists, and people who couldn't voice a disagreement without getting upset made him uncomfortable. He put his fork down and looked around.

Pete, Jose, Karen, and Camilla. People seemed to
(40) have lost interest in their food. The two guys had stopped rocking on the backs of their chairs and were sitting poised in mid-air, looking at each other. Karen, who was directly opposite, was just staring into her cup of coffee. Karen was his clos-
(45) est friend. But looking at her now, he could see that she was disappointed, as if the coffee was turning bitter in her mouth. He'd touched a nerve with her too. Marc's neck was burning unaccountably. He and Karen had spent whole summers in
(50) her backyard, hanging out under her chestnut tree, dissecting each other's private lives. He'd never dated her, but Marc couldn't think of a single woman who knew him better. He used to justify the relationship to his father on the grounds
(55) that Karen would save him the expense of seeing an analyst when he got older. He looked at her. She ought to know him well enough not to judge him on the basis of one misjudged statement. And yet, sitting four feet away on the other side of the
(60) table, she'd never looked so distant.

Without knowing exactly what he'd done, Marc realized that he'd really done it now, and he felt the silence incriminating him. "Now wait just a minute. Hold on there," he said, producing a laugh
(65) from somewhere. Marc was the statesman of the class. People joked about how much money he was going to make coming out of law school. But he was groping for his words now, his eyes flickering over the countertop as if the words he was
(70) looking for were visible there.

19. In line 28, "warranted" most nearly means

(A) guaranteed

(B) intended

(C) arrested

(D) justified

(E) expected

20. In lines 29–33, the analogy to walking in a minefield is used to emphasize

    (A) Marc's fear of offending other people
    (B) Camilla's discomfort at upsetting others
    (C) the unpredictability of Camilla's reactions
    (D) the close understanding between Marc and Camilla
    (E) Marc's annoyance at Camilla's behavior

21. In line 51, "dissecting" most nearly means

    (A) confessing
    (B) analyzing
    (C) criticizing
    (D) inventing
    (E) cutting

22. The summers Marc has spent with Karen (lines 49–54) are probably mentioned in order to

    (A) point out that Marc has few close women friends
    (B) indicate the longstanding nature of their friendship
    (C) suggest that Marc resents having to seek his father's approval
    (D) show that Marc has overcome many obstacles in his private life
    (E) underline Marc's regret at not having pursued their relationship further

23. In line 62, Marc feels that he has "really done it now" because

    (A) he has lost his ability to express himself
    (B) he has overestimated Karen's loyalty to him
    (C) he seems to have offended his closest friend
    (D) he has interrupted the flow of the conversation
    (E) he will have to explain the situation to his father

24. In line 65, Marc's reputation as "the statesman of the class" is most likely mentioned in order to indicate that

    (A) he is noted for his diplomacy
    (B) many people resent his success
    (C) he is generally an articulate speaker
    (D) he is a popular student on campus
    (E) his ambitions are not realistic

KAPLAN
Test Prep and Admissions

SECTION 4

Time—25 Minutes

18 Questions

Directions: For this section, solve each problem and decide which is the best of the choices given. Fill in the corresponding oval on the answer sheet. You may use any available space for scratchwork.

Notes:

(1) Calculator use is permitted.

(2) All numbers used are real numbers.

(3) Figures are provided for some problems. All figures are drawn to scale and lie in a plane UNLESS otherwise indicated.

(4) Unless otherwise specified, the domain of any function f is assumed to be the set of all real numbers x for which $f(x)$ is a real number.

Information

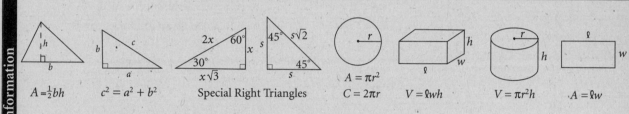

$A = \frac{1}{2}bh$ $c^2 = a^2 + b^2$ Special Right Triangles $A = \pi r^2$ $C = 2\pi r$ $V = \ell w h$ $V = \pi r^2 h$ $A = \ell w$

The sum of the degree measures of the angles in a triangle is 180.

The number of degrees of arc in a circle is 360.

A straight angle has a degree measure of 180.

1. Which of the following is an equation equivalent to the statement "12 less than the product of 3 and b is 9"?

(A) $3(b - 12) = 9$

(B) $12 - 3b = 9$

(C) $3b - 12 = 9$

(D) $12b - 3 = 9$

(E) $12 + 3b = 9$

2. If $\sqrt{x} = 3$ then $x^2 - 1 =$

(A) 2

(B) 8

(C) 80

(D) 81

(E) 82

GO ON TO THE NEXT PAGE

Test Prep and Admissions

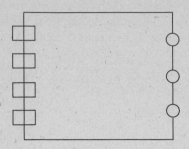

3. The figure above is the aerial view of an open parking lot where the rectangles represent the entrances and the circles represent the exits. What is the total number of ways a driver can enter and exit the parking lot?

(A) 3
(B) 4
(C) 7
(D) 10
(E) 12

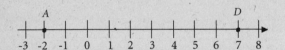

4. In the number line above, if segment AD is divided into 3 equal parts by points B and C, which of the following is a possible coordinate for point C?

(A) 0
(B) 2
(C) 3
(D) 4
(E) 5

5. Tariq has $10 and wants to buy 21 oranges at $0.30 each and 12 apples at $0.50 each. If there is no sales tax, how much more money does he need?

(A) $2.00
(B) $2.30
(C) $2.60
(D) $12.00
(E) $12.30

C	D
−1	−4
1	2
3	8
5	14

6. Which of the following equations satisfies the relationship between C and D in the table above?

(A) $D = C - 3$
(B) $D = 2C$
(C) $D = 2C + 2$
(D) $D = 3C - 1$
(E) $D = 3C + 1$

GO ON TO THE NEXT PAGE >

7. Kyanna used three pieces of ribbon, each 8 inches long, to make each hair bow for her craft project. Kyanna had a 200–foot spool of ribbon when she started. If no ribbon was wasted, which of the following represents the number of <u>feet</u> of ribbon that was left on the roll after she made g hair bows? (12 inches = 1 foot)

(A) $200 - 8g$

(B) $200 - 2g$

(C) $200 - g$

(D) $200 - \dfrac{1}{2}g$

(E) $200 - \dfrac{1}{4}g$

8. The center of a circle is at the origin of a rectangular coordinate plane. If the points $(-3, 0)$, $(0, 3)$, and $(3, 0)$ are on the circumference of the circle, what is the probability that a randomly selected point from within the circle will fall within the triangle formed by those three points?

(A) $\dfrac{1}{4}$

(B) $\dfrac{1}{\pi}$

(C) $\dfrac{1}{3}$

(D) $\dfrac{\pi}{4}$

(E) $\dfrac{\pi}{3}$

GO ON TO THE NEXT PAGE

KAPLAN

Test Prep and Admissions

Directions: For Student-Produced Response questions 9–18, use the grids at the bottom of the answer sheet page on which you have answered questions 1–8.

Each of the remaining 10 questions requires you to solve the problem and enter your answer by marking the ovals in the special grid, as shown in the example below. You may use any available space for scratch work.

Answer: 1.25 or $\frac{5}{4}$ or 5/4

Write answer in → boxes.

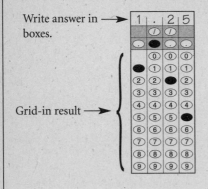

Grid-in result →

Fraction line
Decimal point

Either position is correct.

You may start your answers in any column, space permitting. Columns not needed should be left blank.

- It is recommended, though not required, that you write your answer in the boxes at the top of the columns. However, you will receive credit only for darkening the ovals correctly.

- Grid only one answer to a question, even though some problems have more than one correct answer.

- Darken no more than one oval in a column.

- No answers are negative.

- Mixed numbers cannot be gridded. For example: the number $1\frac{1}{4}$ must be gridded as 1.25 or 5/4.

(If ⟨1 1 / 4⟩ is gridded, it will be interpreted as $\frac{11}{4}$ not $1\frac{1}{4}$.)

- <u>Decimal Accuracy:</u> Decimal answers must be entered as accurately as possible. For example, if you obtain an answer such as 0.1666..., you should record the result as .166 or .167. **Less accurate values such as .16 or .17 are not acceptable.**

Acceptable ways to grid $\frac{1}{6}$ = .1666...

GO ON TO THE NEXT PAGE

KAPLAN
Test Prep and Admissions

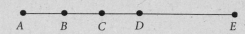

9. In the figure above, *D* is the midpoint of *AE*, and
    AB = *BC* = *CD*. If *AE* = 3, what is the length of *AB*?

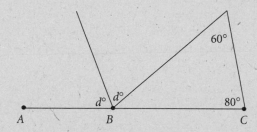

Note: Figure not drawn to scale

10. In the figure above, if *ABC* is a straight line, what is
    the value of *d*?

11. If $x = \left(2 - \dfrac{1}{3}\right) + \left(\dfrac{1}{3} - \dfrac{1}{5}\right) + \left(\dfrac{1}{5} - \dfrac{1}{7}\right) + \left(\dfrac{1}{7} - \dfrac{1}{9}\right)$
    what is the value of *x*?

12. If $a > 0$, $b > \dfrac{3}{4}$, and $2a + b = 1$, what is one possible
    value for *a*?

13. The area of a circle is less than 36π but greater than
    25π. If the diameter of this circle is an integer, what
    is the radius of this circle?

14. If $\dfrac{(x + y)}{(x - y)} = 7$, what is the value of $\dfrac{x}{y}$?

15. In a recent union poll, 80 percent of the 1,500
    union members voted. Of the voting members, 40
    percent answered "yes" to a certain yes–no
    proposal and 125 employees did not respond to
    that particular proposal. How many employees
    answered "no" to this proposal?

16. The total cost of a special occasion cake at a
    particular bakery is the sum of

    (1) a basic fixed charge for baking and
        decorating the cake
    (2) an additional charge for each layer of cake
        that is desired.

    If the total cost of a 3-layer cake is $62.50 and the
    total cost of a 6-layer cake is $85.00, what is the
    total cost, in dollars, of a 7-layer cake?

    (Disregard the $ sign when gridding your answer.
    If, for example, your answer is $23.50, grid 23.50)

17. If increasing 45 by *P* percent yields the same result
    as decreasing 75 by *P* percent, what is the value of *P*?

18. A man is laying tiles in his bathroom. He uses five
    colors of tile: red, blue, yellow, green, and pink, and
    lays them down in pairs of different colored tiles. If
    he uses each possible color pair (regardless of
    order, so red-blue is the same as blue-red) exactly 3
    times, how many total tiles are there in his
    bathroom?

IF YOU FINISH BEFORE TIME IS CALLED, YOU MAY CHECK YOUR WORK ON
THIS SECTION ONLY. DO NOT TURN TO ANY OTHER SECTION IN THE TEST.

SECTION 5
Time—25 Minutes
35 Questions

Directions: For each question in this section, select the best answer from among the choices given and fill in the corresponding oval on the answer sheet.

The following sentences test correctness and effectiveness of expression. Part of each sentence or the entire sentence is underlined; beneath each sentence are five ways of phrasing the underlined material. Choice (A) repeats the original phrasing; the other four choices are different. If you think the original phrasing produces a better sentence than any of the alternatives, select choice (A); if not, select one of the other choices.

In making your selection, follow the requirements of standard written English; that is, pay attention to grammar, choice of words, sentence construction, and punctuation. Your selection should result in the most effective sentence—clear and precise, without awkwardness or ambiguity.

EXAMPLE:

Every apple in the baskets <u>are ripe and labeled according to the date it was picked</u>.

ANSWER:

(A) are ripe and labeled according to the date it was picked
(B) is ripe and labeled according to the date it was picked
(C) are ripe and labeled according to the date they were picked
(D) is ripe and labeled according to the date they were picked
(E) are ripe and labeled as to the date it was picked

---

1. Mary Cassatt was <u>an artist and she painted many beautiful pictures</u> of mothers and children.

   (A) an artist and she painted many beautiful pictures
   (B) an artist, she painted many beautiful pictures
   (C) an artist which painted many beautiful pictures
   (D) an artist who painted many beautiful pictures
   (E) an artist by whom many beautiful pictures were painted

2. Urban sprawl spreads development over large amounts of land, puts long distances between homes and job centers, <u>and makes people more dependent</u> on cars.

   (A) and makes people more dependent
   (B) and people become more dependent
   (C) also making people more dependent
   (D) and there is more dependence of people
   (E) making people more dependent

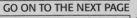

3. Despite the Preservation Society's efforts to save the old mill, the overwhelming majority of city council members <u>voted for destructing it</u>.

   (A) voted for destructing it
   (B) voted to destroy it
   (C) voted with its destruction
   (D) voted for the destruction of it
   (E) voted so that it would be destroyed

4. Jumping over fantastic obstacles in the video game, <u>right before the player a dragon roared</u>.

   (A) right before the player a dragon roared
   (B) a dragon, right before the player, roared
   (C) there was a dragon roaring right before the player
   (D) the player saw right before him a dragon was roaring
   (E) the player saw a dragon roaring right before him

5. Dr. Maisell argued that although many medical schools have excelled at training future diagnosticians, <u>the failure is in their not educating</u> students in the psychology of illness.

   (A) the failure is in their not educating
   (B) the failure they have is in their not educating
   (C) they failed not to educate
   (D) they have failed to educate
   (E) failing in their education of

6. Charles Dickens wrote <u>novels and they capture</u> the society of Victorian England at its best and worst.

   (A) novels and they capture
   (B) novels, being the capture of
   (C) novels, they capture
   (D) novels that capture
   (E) novels, and capturing in them

7. The young pianist's beautiful melodic line and <u>tone is remarkably like</u> her mother's violin playing, in which warmth, imagination, and speedy fingering are elegantly combined.

   (A) tone is remarkably like
   (B) tone, remarkably like
   (C) tone, remarkable and like
   (D) tone are remarkably like
   (E) tone remarkable similar to

8. <u>The unique culture of Cork is primarily founded by</u> its great musical and lyrical traditions.

   (A) The unique culture of Cork is primarily founded by
   (B) The unique culture of Cork is primarily founding upon
   (C) The primary culture of Cork, which is unique, comes from
   (D) Cork's unique culture comes primarily by
   (E) Cork has a unique culture founded primarily on

GO ON TO THE NEXT PAGE

9. <u>Having an exceptionally beautiful mountain range and heavy winter snowfall, the International Olympic Committee chose Salt Lake City</u> as the site of the 2002 Winter Olympics.

(A) Having an exceptionally beautiful mountain range and heavy winter snowfall, the International Olympic Committee chose Salt Lake City

(B) The Olympic Committee which was choosing Salt Lake City for its exceptionally beautiful mountain range and heavy winter snowfall saw it

(C) Salt Lake City's exceptionally beautiful mountain range and heavy winter snowfall were the reasons for its being the choice of the International Olympic Committee

(D) Because it has an exceptionally beautiful mountain range and heavy winter snowfall, Salt Lake City was chosen by the International Olympic Committee

(E) Based on its exceptionally beautiful mountain range and heavy winter snowfall, the Olympic Committee chose Salt Lake City

10. The others in my horseback riding class are very <u>accomplished; they win</u> ribbons in every competition they enter.

(A) accomplished; they win

(B) accomplished; which allows them to win

(C) accomplished, they have been winners

(D) accomplished, and so they would win

(E) accomplished, by winning

11. <u>The school's music department was once close to cutting its program in half, it is</u> now a well-funded, thriving part of the school.

(A) The school's music department was once close to cutting its program in half, it is

(B) The school's music department that once was close to cutting its program in half, it is

(C) The school's music department, because it was once close to cutting its program in half, is

(D) The school's music department was once close to cutting its program in half, and it is

(E) The school's music department, once close to cutting its program in half, is

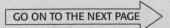
GO ON TO THE NEXT PAGE

Directions: The following sentences test your ability to recognize grammar and usage errors. Each sentence contains either a single error or no error at all. No sentence contains more than one error. The error, if there is one, is underlined and lettered. If the sentence contains an error, select the one underlined part that must be changed to make the sentence correct. If the sentence is correct, select choice (E). In choosing answers, follow the requirements of standard written English.

EXAMPLE:

<u>Whenever</u> one is driving late at night, <u>you</u> must take extra precautions <u>against</u>
  A   B   C

falling asleep <u>at the wheel</u>. <u>No error</u>
          D   E

---

12. All of the children <u>waiting</u> for the school bus <u>seen</u>
                    A   B

    the crossing guard <u>walking out</u> into the street
                          C

    <u>to stop traffic</u>. <u>No error</u>
        D   E

13. We had been gardening for <u>no more for</u> one hour
                             A

    <u>when it</u> became <u>apparent that</u> our supply of
      B   C

    fertilizer would not be <u>sufficient</u> for the whole
                           D

    garden. <u>No error</u>
          E

14. The FBI <u>maintains</u> strict <u>requirements for</u> citizens
          A   B

    <u>who are</u> <u>interested in</u> joining the Bureau. <u>No error</u>
      C   D   E

15. Everything about the case <u>are</u> strange and
                    A

    suspicious, <u>as</u> there was no sign of forced entry,
          B

    nothing of great value <u>was stolen</u> and the only
                    C

    finger prints <u>around the house</u> were the owners'.
               D

    <u>No error</u>
      E

16. <u>While</u> many children <u>claim hearing</u> Santa's
    A   B

    reindeer on the roof, no one has proved that

    <u>such a person</u> <u>truly</u> exists. <u>No error</u>
      C   D   E

17. Concert-goers at the stadium <u>who waited</u> hours for
                          A

    the entrance of their favorite music group <u>includes</u>
                                B

    <u>more than</u> one hundred fans from European
      C

    countries <u>who</u> traveled long distances for the show.
            D

    <u>No error</u>
      E

18. <u>It</u> did not occur to the interviewer <u>to ask</u> either the
    A   B

    job applicant <u>nor</u> his reference <u>whether</u> the
            C   D

    applicant had completed the project he initiated.

    <u>No error</u>
      E

GO ON TO THE NEXT PAGE ⟹

19. <u>Just as</u> some companies <u>flounder</u> in an economic
      A   B
    downturn, so others <u>seem</u> to thrive in <u>them</u>.
                 C   D
    <u>No error</u>
      E

20. It has been shown that chimps are <u>a great deal</u> like
                             A
    humans, <u>because</u> we <u>cannot</u> expect <u>to converse</u>
          B   C   D
    with them, or any other animal, as we do with one

    another. <u>No error</u>
           E

21. Lazy and disorganized, Bob is <u>known as</u>
                        A
    <u>one of those</u> people <u>that</u> always arrive to class
      B   C
    <u>long after</u> it has started. <u>No error</u>
      D   E

22. <u>In the long run</u>, <u>having</u> a president and a governor
        A   B
    of opposing parties may actually help, <u>not hinder</u>
                               C
    <u>his</u> ability to succeed. <u>No error</u>
    D   E

23. Inside the football stadium, Susan <u>liked watching</u>
                            A
    the home team's pre-game warm-ups, <u>which she</u>
                            B
    considered <u>more interesting</u> <u>than the visiting team</u>.
         C   D
    <u>No error</u>
      E

24. <u>Extremely similar</u> reforms <u>were proposed</u> by the
        A   B
    men <u>appointed to</u> the Ministry of Finance because
          C
    both men consulted <u>by</u> the same experts. <u>No error</u>
                 D   E

25. From their <u>study of</u> the stars, ancient mariners
             A
    could navigate <u>confidently</u> without
                 B
    <u>dependence upon</u> the hi-tech devices <u>in use</u> today.
        C   D
    <u>No error</u>
      E

26. <u>While</u> the effect of disease-causing agents on
      A
    cigarette smokers <u>has been known</u> for years, only
                  B
    recently <u>has</u> the damaging effects of cigarette
            C
    smoke on second-hand smokers <u>become</u>
                          D
    recognized. <u>No error</u>
             E

27. The director <u>wanted Delia to</u> portray her character
               A
    with <u>most conviction</u>, so he suggested
         B
    <u>that she remember</u> an actual experience that
         C
    <u>had saddened</u> her. <u>No error</u>
      D   E

GO ON TO THE NEXT PAGE ⟩

28. The chef <u>herself</u> is carrying out the grand finale
                      A
    <u>of the celebration,</u> an extraordinary cake
                 B
    <u>that is smothered</u> in strawberries and <u>was topped</u>
                 C   D
    with eighteen sputtering candles. <u>No error</u>
                                              E

29. The mail-order firms <u>recruit</u> salespeople through
                                 A
    the internet, creating a network through which
    they will attempt <u>at contacting</u> <u>those</u> homeowners
                            B   C
    who might buy <u>their</u> products. <u>No error</u>
                        D   E

Directions: The following passage is an early draft of an essay. Some parts of the passage need to be rewritten.

Read the passage and select the best answer for each question that follows. Some questions are about particular sentences or parts of sentences and ask you to improve sentence structure or word choice. Other questions ask you to consider organization and development. In choosing answers, follow the conventions of standard written English.

Questions 30–35 are based on the following passage.

(1) Although all people process information in a variety of manners, most people have one method they prefer. (2) Some people are visual learners. (3) They process information best by seeing the information displayed either textually or graphically. (4) For these types of students, a teacher should write the main points or key terms on the board as she lectures. (5) Other students rely much more on oral processing. (6) These students are auditory learners. (7) They prefer to hear information presented and they particularly enjoy discussing the information. (8) These methods solidify the information in their minds. (9) Other learners, although this is a much smaller group, are kinesthetic learners. (10) Kinesthetic means movement. (11) These learners like to do hands-on activities. (12) They prefer the basics of the information be presented in bulleted precise form. (13) Then, they actually learn about the material by working with it.

30. The teacher explains to the student author of this passage that the assignment was to demonstrate the student's ability to use complex sentences. How could sentences 5, 6, and 7 be best merged into a complex sentence?

(A) Other students rely much more on oral processing, are auditory learners, and prefer to hear information presented and discussing it.

(B) Other students rely much more on oral processing; they are auditory learning; they prefer to hear information presented and they particularly enjoy discussing the information.

(C) Other students are auditory learners who rely much more on oral processing and who prefer to hear the information presented and to discuss it.

(D) Auditory learners prefer to hear information and to discuss it.

(E) Some students are auditory and they prefer hearing and discussing information

31. The main idea of this passage is

(A) students process information in various ways

(B) there are three primary strategies for teaching students

(C) visual learners are more numerous than auditory or kinesthetic learners

(D) learners employ a variety of information-seeking strategies

(E) teachers should employ all three methods when teaching students

GO ON TO THE NEXT PAGE

32. The word *textually* in the passage means:

   (A) in tabular form

   (B) written

   (C) contextually

   (D) within the information being presented

   (E) allowing for written or oral format

33. A student who has strong auditory skills would probably enjoy which of the following activities the most?

   (A) reading a map

   (B) creating a mural

   (C) debating two sides of an issue

   (D) reading about the parts of the ear

   (E) caring for the classroom parrot

34. This is the introductory paragraph for a five-paragraph essay. What would be the best way to structure the remaining paragraphs?

   (A) have two paragraphs about strategies to employ each type and two paragraphs about skills each employs

   (B) have three paragraphs in the body containing further information (one for visual, one for auditory, and one for kinesthetic) and a concluding paragraph summarizing the information

   (C) divide this paragraph between Sentences 4 and 5; Sentence 5 would begin the second paragraph; the third paragraph would include information about the brain and its processor; paragraphs 4 and 5 would compare the brain to the types

   (D) have four paragraphs in the body, one for boys as visual learners, one for girls as visual learners, then one for boys vs. girls as auditory learners, and one for boys vs. girls as kinesthetic learners

   (E) have three paragraphs in the body containing information about advantages of each type in the second paragraph, disadvantages of each type in the third paragraph, and comparison of the two in the fourth paragraph

35. A phrase that could be used to strengthen sentence 1 in the passage would be:

   (A) *plethora of ways* instead of *variety of manners*

   (B) *variety of ways* instead of *variety of manners*

   (C) *variety of methods* instead of *variety of manners*

   (D) *different manners* instead of *variety of manners*

   (E) *number of manners* instead of *variety of manners*

IF YOU FINISH BEFORE TIME IS CALLED, YOU MAY CHECK YOUR WORK ON THIS SECTION ONLY. DO NOT TURN TO ANY OTHER SECTION IN THE TEST.

STOP

SECTION 6
Time—25 Minutes
24 Questions

Directions: For each of the following questions, choose the best answer and darken the corresponding oval on the answer sheet.

Each sentence below has one or two blanks, each blank indicating that something has been omitted. Beneath the sentence are five words or sets of words labeled (A) through (E). Choose the word or set of words that, when inserted in the sentence, <u>best</u> fits the meaning of the sentence as a whole.

EXAMPLE:

Today's small, portable computers contrast markedly with the earliest electronic computers, which were ----.

(A) effective
(B) invented
(C) useful
(D) destructive
(E) enormous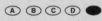

1. She found her work so ---- that she lost herself in it and was completely ---- the noise surrounding her.

   (A) inspiring . . annoyed by
   (B) complex . . involved in
   (C) absorbing . . oblivious to
   (D) exhausting . . taken with
   (E) repetitive . . afraid of

2. The graceful curves of the old colonial-era buildings that dominated the old part of the city contrasted sharply with the modern, ---- subway stations and made the latter appear almost anachronistic.

   (A) rectilinear
   (B) grimy
   (C) festive
   (D) gigantic
   (E) efficient

3. In contrast to their widespread image as ---- carnivores, many species of piranha are vegetarian.

   (A) nomadic
   (B) lugubrious
   (C) voracious
   (D) covetous
   (E) exotic

4. Although both plants control soil erosion, kudzu disrupts the local ecology by displacing native flora, while vetiver has no ---- effects.

   (A) foreseeable
   (B) adverse
   (C) domestic
   (D) permanent
   (E) advantageous

5. The world of Heinrich Boll's early novels is one of impersonal malice, thinly camouflaged with patriotic and other ---- clichés, in which relief is provided only by occasional ---- of genuine human emotion.

   (A) pragmatic . . absences
   (B) ideological . . manifestations
   (C) conceptual . . lapses
   (D) ephemeral . . loss
   (E) scholarly . . vestiges

GO ON TO THE NEXT PAGE

Directions: The passages below are followed by questions based on their content; questions following a pair of related passages may also be based on the relationship between the paired passages. Answer the questions on the basis of what is <u>stated</u> or <u>implied</u> in the passages and in any introductory material that may be provided.

Questions 6–7 are based on the following passage.

By the time it finally roused me, I somehow knew my alarm clock had been beeping for a while. Outside my window, the sky was still dark, faintly illuminated by the stars, a moon shrouded
(5) by clouds, and a faded orange horizon that signaled the city was also just beginning to wake. After a cold shower cleared my drowsy mind of the confusion left by convoluted dreams and hours of sleep, I remembered why I was not
(10) still sleeping. I had taken on a paper route. The realization seemed to hit me like a blow to my stomach, inciting a dull pain of regret that only deepened with the understanding that my every morning would begin just as jarringly as this one.

6. In the first sentence, the author mentions his alarm clock in order to make which point?

(A) He had conscientiously prepared for his paper route.

(B) He was used to waking up early in the morning.

(C) He was lucky to have set the alarm or he would not have awakened in time.

(D) He was so deeply asleep that the alarm could not immediately wake him.

(E) He was not looking forward to waking up so early every morning.

7. In lines 9–10, the words "I remembered why I was not still sleeping" suggest that the author was

(A) disoriented by his early awakening

(B) entirely unenthusiastic about his paper route

(C) a rather forgetful individual

(D) unconcerned with the responsibilities of his paper route

(E) somewhat confused about the details of his new job

Questions 8–9 are based on the following passage.

While he is called the father of the montage—a widely-used cinematic technique that involves a rapid succession of different shots, often superimposed—Russian director Sergei Eisenstein's influ-
(5) ence on the modern movie is considerably more profound than this simple characterization suggests. His seven films, though not a particularly large body of work, contained a clarity and sharpness of composition that made the depth of his
(10) plots and the powerful complexity of his juxtaposed images remarkably accessible to most viewers. In this way, Eisenstein essentially demonstrated to the notoriously pretentious cinematic establishment of his day that the average viewer
(15) could not only consume abstract expressions through film, but that they could enjoy doing so.

8. The author refers to Eisenstein as the "father of the montage" (line 1) in order to

(A) underscore his immense contribution to film

(B) suggest his impact has been underappreciated

(C) explain how his films were so powerful

(D) celebrate his place in cinematic history

(E) imply his influence has been exaggerated

9. The author gives all of the following as reasons why Eisenstein's films were important EXCEPT for their ability to

(A) lucidly communicate complexity

(B) superimpose contrasting shots

(C) entertain with abstraction

(D) empower the average viewer

(E) challenge the cinematic establishment's perceptions

GO ON TO THE NEXT PAGE

Questions 10–18 are based on the following passage.

In the following passage, the author explores some contrasts in the way that Arabs and Americans relate to each other spatially.

In spite of over two thousand years of contact, Westerners and Arabs still do not understand each other. Americans visiting the Middle East are immediately struck by two conflicting sensations.
(5) In public they are compressed and overwhelmed by smells, crowding, and high noise levels; in Arab homes Americans are apt to rattle around, feeling somewhat exposed and inadequate because there is too much space.
(10)   Proxemics, the study of people's responses to spatial relationships, can shed a lot of light on these misunderstandings. One of my earliest discoveries in the field of intercultural communication was that the position of the bodies of people
(15) in conversation varies from culture to culture. It used to puzzle me that a special Arab friend seemed unable to walk and talk at the same time. After years in the United States, he could not bring himself to stroll along, facing forward while
(20) talking. Our progress would always be arrested while he edged ahead, cutting slightly in front of me and turning sideways so we could see each other. Once in this position, he would stop. His behavior was explained when I learned that for
(25) the Arabs, to view another person peripherally is regarded as impolite. In Arab culture, you are expected to be involved when interacting with friends.
This emphasis on involvement and participa-
(30) tion also expresses itself in Arab cities, where the notion of privacy in a public place is a foreign concept. Business transactions in the bazaar, for example, are not just conducted between buyer and seller, but are participated in by everyone.
(35) Anyone who is standing around may join in. If a grownup sees a boy breaking a window, he must stop him even if he doesn't know him. If two men are fighting, the crowd must intervene. On a political level, when a government such as ours fails
(40) to intervene when trouble is brewing, this is

construed as taking sides. But given the fact that few people in the world today are even remotely aware of the cultural mold that forms their thoughts, it is normal for Arabs to view our
(45) behavior as though it stemmed from their own hidden set of assumptions.
In the home, the Arab dream is for lots of space, which unfortunately many Arabs cannot afford. Yet when an Arab has space, it is very different
(50) from what one finds in most American homes. Spaces inside Arab upper-middle-class homes are tremendous by our standards. They avoid partitions because Arabs do not like to be alone. The form of the home is such as to hold the family
(55) together inside a single protective shell, creating an environment where personalities are intermingled and take nourishment from each other like the roots and soil. If one is not with people and actively involved in some way, one is deprived of
(60) life. An old Arab saying reflects this value: "Paradise without people should not be entered because it is Hell." For this reason, Arabs in the United States often feel socially and sensorially deprived and long to be back where there is
(65) human warmth and contact.
Since there is no physical privacy as we know it in the Arab family, not even a word for privacy, one could expect that the Arabs might use some other means to be alone. Their way to be alone is
(70) to stop talking. Like the English, an Arab who shuts himself off in this way is not indicating that anything is wrong or that he is withdrawing, only that he wants to be alone with his thoughts or does not want to be intruded upon. One subject I
(75) interviewed said that her father would come and go for days at a time without saying a word, and no one in the family thought anything of it. Yet for this very reason, an Arab exchange student visiting a Kansas farm failed to pick up the cue that
(80) his American hosts were mad at him when they gave him the "silent treatment." He only discovered something was wrong when they took him to town and tried forcibly to put him on a bus to Washington, D.C., the headquarters of the
(85) exchange program responsible for his presence in the United States.

GO ON TO THE NEXT PAGE ⇒

10. According to the passage, the "two conflicting sensations" that Americans experience in the Middle East (lines 3–9) are

    (A) understanding and confusion

    (B) involvement and participation

    (C) friendliness and hostility

    (D) crowding and spaciousness

    (E) silence and noise

11. The author most likely describes the behavior of his Arab friend (lines 15–23) in order to

    (A) cite an incident which led to a breakthrough in his research

    (B) support the idea that Americans and Arabs cannot communicate with each other

    (C) demonstrate that Arabs respond differently to spatial relationships

    (D) emphasize the difficulty of learning the customs of other countries

    (E) point out the impersonal nature of American cities

12. The author's friend was most likely "unable to walk and talk at the same time" (line 17) because

    (A) he was fascinated by American cities

    (B) his command of spoken English was poor

    (C) he was not familiar with Western customs

    (D) he was unaccustomed to talking in public

    (E) he did not wish to seem rude

13. The word "arrested" is used in line 20 to mean

    (A) apprehended

    (B) delayed

    (C) anticipated

    (D) accelerated

    (E) annoyed

14. In lines 37–38, the custom of intervening when two men fight is presented as an example of the Arabs'

    (A) compassion for strangers

    (B) desire to appear polite

    (C) respect for law and order

    (D) dislike of personal conflict

    (E) emphasis on public participation

15. The author most likely regards the Arab's attitude towards government policy (lines 38–41) as

    (A) an effective strategy for resolving international disputes

    (B) a typical Western misunderstanding of Arab culture

    (C) an overly simplistic approach to the complexities of foreign policy

    (D) an understandable reaction given how little most people know about other cultures

    (E) a symptom of the problems involved in Middle Eastern politics

16. According to paragraph 4, the most crucial difference between American homes and Arab homes lies in the

    (A) average cost of house

    (B) size of house available

    (C) number of occupants housed

    (D) use of space inside the house

    (E) area of land surrounding the house

GO ON TO THE NEXT PAGE

17. Judging from the discussion in paragraph 5, silence in Arab culture is often a way to

   (A) resolve arguments between relatives
   (B) indicate displeasure with guests
   (C) express unhappiness within families
   (D) communicate involvement with friends
   (E) obtain a psychological form of privacy

18. The author uses the story about the Arab exchange student (lines 78–86) primarily to illustrate that

   (A) Arabs visiting the United States often experience homesickness
   (B) ignoring other people is rarely an effective form of punishment
   (C) silence is not considered unusual in Arab households
   (D) Arab and American cultures share a similar sense of humor
   (E) it is difficult to recognize anger in foreign cultures

GO ON TO THE NEXT PAGE

Questions 19–24 are taken from the following passage.

When I accepted a volunteer position as a social worker at a domestic violence shelter in a developing nation, I imagined the position for which my university experience had prepared me. I envi-
(5) sioned conducting intake interviews and traipsing around from organization to organization seeking the legal, psychological, and financial support that the women would need to rebuild their lives. When I arrived, I felt as if I already had months of
(10) experience, experience garnered in the hypothetical situations I had invented and subsequently resolved single-handedly and seamlessly. I felt thoroughly prepared to tackle head-on the situation I assumed was waiting for me.
(15) I arrived full of zeal, knocking at the shelter's door. Within moments, my reality made a sharp break from that which I had anticipated. The coordinator explained that the shelter's need for financial self-sufficiency had become obvious and
(20) acute. To address this, the center was planning to open a bakery. I immediately enthused about the project, making many references to the small enterprise case studies I had researched at the university. In response to my impassioned reply, the
(25) coordinator declared me in charge of the bakery and left in order to "get out of my way." At that moment, I was as prepared to bake bread as I was to run for political office. The bigger problem, however, was that I was completely unfamiliar
(30) with the for-profit business models necessary to run the bakery. I was out of my depth in a foreign river with only my coordinator's confidence to keep me afloat.
They say that necessity is the mother of inven-
(35) tion. I soon found that it is also the mother of initiative. I began finding recipes and appropriating the expertise of friends. With their help making bread, balancing books, printing pamphlets and making contacts, the bakery was soon running
(40) smoothly and successfully. After a short time it became a significant source of income for the house.

In addition to funds, baking bread provided a natural environment in which to work with and
(45) get to know the women of the shelter. Kneading dough side by side, I shared in the camaraderie of the kitchen, treated to stories about their children and the towns and jobs they had had to leave behind to ensure their safety. Baking helped me
(50) develop strong relationships with the women and advanced my understanding of their situations. It also improved the women's self-esteem. Their ability to master a new skill gave them confidence in themselves, and the fact that the bakery con-
(55) tributed to the upkeep of the house gave the women, many of them newly single, a sense of pride and the conviction that they had the capability to support themselves.
Baking gave me the opportunity to work in a
(60) capacity I had not at all anticipated, but one that proved very successful. I became a more sensitive and skillful social worker, capable of making a mean seven-grain loaf. Learning to bake gave me as much newfound self-confidence as it gave the
(65) women, and I found that sometimes quality social work can be as simple as kneading dough.

19. The primary purpose of the passage is to show how the author

(A) was shocked by the discrepancy between her earlier ideas about her work and the reality she faced

(B) discovered a talent her overly-focused mind had never allowed her to explore

(C) broadened how she defined the scope of her work

(D) developed her abilities to orchestrate a for-profit business enterprise

(E) was abroad in a developing country when she encountered and overcame a challenging situation

GO ON TO THE NEXT PAGE

KAPLAN
Test Prep and Admissions

20. The statement that the author arrived "full of zeal" (line 15) indicates that she was

    (A) anxious and insecure
    (B) eager and interested
    (C) confident but uninformed
    (D) cheerful but exhausted
    (E) enthusiastic but incompetent

21. The author was initially enthusiastic about the idea of the bakery because she

    (A) considered it from a theoretical point of view
    (B) hoped to obtain a leadership position in the bakery
    (C) wanted to demonstrate her baking knowledge to her new coordinator
    (D) believed it would be a good way to build the women's self-esteem
    (E) was a strong proponent of self-sufficiency projects for non-profit organizations

22. The comparison in lines 26–28 ("At that moment...political office") demonstrates the author's belief that

    (A) the bakery would never be a success
    (B) social workers should not be involved in either baking or politics
    (C) it was unfair of the coordinator to ask the author to run the bakery
    (D) similar skills were involved in both baking and politics
    (E) she was unqualified for a job baking bread

23. Lines 28–31 ("The bigger...bakery") suggest that the author believed that

    (A) learning the necessary business practices would be a more daunting challenge than learning to bake bread
    (B) good business practices are more important to running a successful bakery than is the quality of the bread
    (C) her coordinator's confidence in for-profit business models was misplaced
    (D) for-profit business models are significantly more complex than the non-profit models with which she was familiar
    (E) her coordinator would be unwilling to help her

24. The last sentence ("Learning...dough") indicates that the author

    (A) lacked self-confidence just as much as the women with whom she worked
    (B) found that performing social work is surprisingly easy with no education
    (C) underestimated her own ability to learn new skills
    (D) discovered that social work is more effective when it includes tactile activities
    (E) derived a benefit from her work while helping others

IF YOU FINISH BEFORE TIME IS CALLED, YOU MAY CHECK YOUR WORK ON THIS SECTION ONLY. DO NOT TURN TO ANY OTHER SECTION IN THE TEST. STOP

SECTION 7

Time—20 Minutes

16 Questions

Directions: For this section, solve each problem and decide which is the best of the choices given. Fill in the corresponding oval on the answer sheet. You may use any available space for scratchwork.

Notes:

(1) Calculator use is permitted.

(2) All numbers used are real numbers.

(3) Figures are provided for some problems. All figures are drawn to scale and lie in a plane UNLESS otherwise indicated.

(4) Unless otherwise specified, the domain of any function f is assumed to be the set of all real numbers x for which $f(x)$ is a real number.

Information

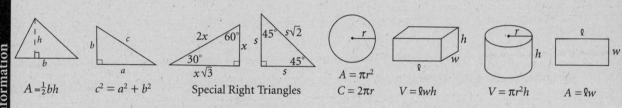

$A = \frac{1}{2}bh$ $\qquad$ $c^2 = a^2 + b^2$ $\qquad$ Special Right Triangles $\qquad$ $A = \pi r^2$ $\qquad$ $C = 2\pi r$ $\qquad$ $V = \ell wh$ $\qquad$ $V = \pi r^2 h$ $\qquad$ $A = \ell w$

The sum of the degree measures of the angles in a triangle is 180.
The number of degrees of arc in a circle is 360.
A straight angle has a degree measure of 180.

---

1. A certain car needs 15 gallons to travel 300 miles. At this rate, how many gallons are needed to travel 500 miles?

   (A) 16
   (B) 20
   (C) 25
   (D) 30
   (E) 35

2. If $8 \times 27 \times 64 = r^3$, what is the value of r?

   (A) 6
   (B) 12
   (C) 18
   (D) 24
   (E) 32

3. If $a^2 - 16 = b^2$, and $2a = 10$, which of the following could be a value for b?

   (A) −1
   (B) 0
   (C) 1
   (D) 2
   (E) 3

GO ON TO THE NEXT PAGE

3, 8, 13, 18, 23, 28, 33, 38

4. If from the sequence of numbers above, a new sequence is created by increasing each odd-valued term by 3 and decreasing each even-valued term by 2, the sum of the terms of this new sequence is how much greater than the sum of the terms of the original sequence?

(A) 4
(B) 6
(C) 8
(D) 10
(E) 12

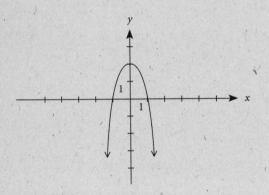

5. Which of the following equations best describes the curve in the figure above?

(A) $y = x^2 - 2$
(B) $y = x^2 + 2$
(C) $y = -x^2$
(D) $y = 1 - x^2$
(E) $y = 2 - x^2$

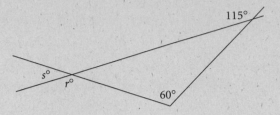

Note: Figure not drawn to scale.

6. In the figure above, what is the value of $r - s$?

(A) 50
(B) 55
(C) 60
(D) 65
(E) 70

7. At a certain company, the annual Winter Party is always held on the second Friday of December. What is the latest possible date for the party?

(A) December 14
(B) December 15
(C) December 18
(D) December 20
(E) December 22

8. If the perimeter of equilateral triangle E equals the perimeter of square S, what is the ratio of the length of a side of square S to the length of a side of triangle E?

(A) 1:1
(B) 2:3
(C) 3:4
(D) 4:3
(E) 2:1

GO ON TO THE NEXT PAGE

Population of City X, 1980–1988
(in hundred thousands)

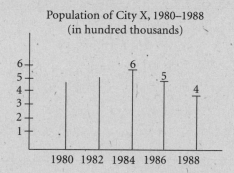

9. In the graph above, if the percent decrease from the 1986 population to the 1988 population was the same as the percent decrease from the 1988 population to the 1990 population, what was the 1990 population in City X?

(A) 350,000
(B) 320,000
(C) 300,000
(D) 280,000
(E) 250,000

10. Hillary buys a television on a twelve-month installment plan. If each of her first three installments is twice as much as each of her nine remaining installments, and her total payment is $600, how much is her first installment?

(A) $20
(B) $35
(C) $40
(D) $65
(E) $80

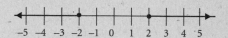

11. Which of the following inequalities best describes the indicated values on the number line above?

(A) $|x - 2| \leq 2$
(B) $|x - 2| \geq 2$
(C) $|x| \leq 2$
(D) $|x| \geq 2$
(E) $|x + 2| \geq 2$

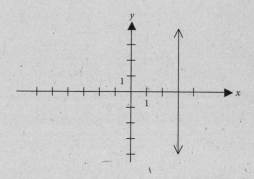

12. Which of the following equations describes a line perpendicular to the line shown in the diagram above?

(A) $y = x$
(B) $y = x - 3$
(C) $y = x + 3$
(D) $y = 3$
(E) $x = 3$

GO ON TO THE NEXT PAGE

KAPLAN
Test Prep and Admissions

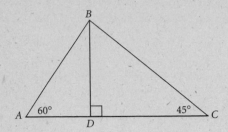

13. In the figure above, if $AB = 8$, what is the area of triangle BCD?

(A) 8
(B) 16
(C) 24
(D) 20
(E) 48

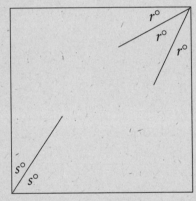

Note: Figure not drawn to scale

14. In the square above, what is the value of $s - r$?

(A) 15
(B) 20
(C) 25
(D) 30
(E) 45

15. When the sum of the odd integers from 5 to 27, inclusive, is subtracted from the sum of the even integers from 8 to 30, inclusive, the result is

(A) 1
(B) 3
(C) 27
(D) 30
(E) 36

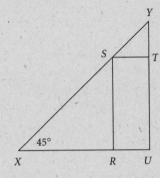

16. In the figure above, if rectangle $RSTU$ has a perimeter of 12, what is the area of triangle XYU?

(A) 12
(B) 15
(C) 18
(D) 21
(E) 24

IF YOU FINISH BEFORE TIME IS CALLED, YOU MAY CHECK YOUR WORK ON THIS SECTION ONLY. DO NOT TURN TO ANY OTHER SECTION IN THE TEST.

STOP

Test Prep and Admissions

SECTION 8
Time—20 Minutes
19 Questions

Directions: For each of the following questions, choose the best answer and darken the corresponding oval on the answer sheet.

Each sentence below has one or two blanks, each blank indicating that something has been omitted. Beneath the sentence are five words or sets of words labeled (A) through (E). Choose the word or set of words that, when inserted in the sentence, <u>best</u> fits the meaning of the sentence as a whole.

EXAMPLE:

Today's small, portable computers contrast markedly with the earliest electronic computers, which were ----.

(A) effective
(B) invented
(C) useful
(D) destructive
(E) enormous

1. While the federal government promised to ---- its tax forms, many taxpayers still find them so ---- that they have to seek professional assistance.

(A) mystify . . infuriating
(B) shorten . . expensive
(C) replace . . comprehensible
(D) simplify . . bewildering
(E) rewrite . . familiar

2. The ---- hooves of the horses, the blaring of the trumpets, and the beating of drums combined to create a ---- on medieval battlefields.

(A) thundering . . cacophony
(B) running . . danger
(C) furious . . horror
(D) thrashing . . situation
(E) plodding . . calm

3. Although the long-term effects of the council's measures could be ---- , no one can deny that the city is now enjoying an increase in tourism.

(A) stated
(B) compared
(C) discussed
(D) inquired
(E) debated

4. In order to maintain the ---- for which he was well known, the manager refused a tempting offer to ignore ---- in the corporation's accounting practices.

(A) geniality . . irregularities
(B) integrity . . improprieties
(C) dishonesty . . policies
(D) cordiality . . inconsistencies
(E) frankness . . rules

GO ON TO THE NEXT PAGE

5. Though the politician's inauguration was a generally ---- occasion, it was not without moments of ---- , including a few jokes during her acceptance speech.

(A) grim . . cleverness
(B) exciting . . curiosity
(C) mirthful . . humor
(D) solemn . . levity
(E) sober . . gravity

6. We usually imagine the French aristocracy to have lived a life of ---- , but there is new evidence that many of its members were forced by exigencies to be quite frugal.

(A) thrift
(B) malice
(C) prudence
(D) opulence
(E) beneficence

GO ON TO THE NEXT PAGE

Directions: The passages below are followed by questions based on their content; questions following a pair of related passages may also be based on the relationship between the paired passages. Answer the questions on the basis of what is <u>stated</u> or <u>implied</u> in the passages and in any introductory material that may be provided.

Questions 7–19 are based on the following passages.

Passage 1

Writing is among the most mysterious of human activities. Every writer can testify that the Muses* once invoked by the poets are a reality. Unless he is writing mechanically, the writer does
(5) not experience his writing as an act of creation; he experiences it as an act of discovery: it comes or happens or is given to him, and when it does, he recognizes it at once for his own. It is not within the power of his will to summon it forth if it
(10) refuses to come; nor is he capable of resisting it for long when it starts to demand release.

The key to unlocking the floodgates, I believe, is a key in that it is musical: it is finding the tone of voice, the only tone of voice, in which the particu-
(15) lar piece of writing will permit itself to be written. Once this key is found, the author will enter a state of bliss such as exists nowhere else on earth. He will sit at his typewriter and watch, in delight and amazement, as sentences mysteriously shape
(20) themselves into rhythms he knows to be right, and paragraphs begin to shape themselves into an organically coherent pattern that miraculously corresponds only better, much better to the dim vision which had driven him to his desk in the
(25) first place.

Finished, he will be exhausted and exhilarated, all anxieties gone; he will feel that everything in the world makes sense after all, that there is an order to things, and that he himself is part of that
(30) order. At root, it is the writer's search for order that gives successful writing the quality of organic imagination, and which exists not only in poems and stories, but in any form of writing, however humble or trivial.

(35) Writing always involves someone sitting with an implement and an inchoate idea before a blank sheet of paper and in terror at the answering blankness of his or her own mind. Consequently,

if one is speaking of the experience of being a
(40) writer, the only meaningful distinction is between writers who are willing to accept the risks of suffering entailed by the effort to tap their own inner potentialities of organic coherence, and those who are unable or unwilling to take such
(45) risks.

* Muses: supernatural powers believed by the ancient poets to be the source of artistic inspiration.

Passage 2

Personally, I find writing a very difficult process indeed, a task requiring enormous discipline. The only way I can ensure a consistent output is to approach writing as if it were a job like any other,
(50) and turn in a forty-hour week. Essentially, you could say that I've chosen to adopt a professional attitude to writing, rather than an artistic one. There are a great many young writers around who believe the popular myth that great novels are
(55) written by strokes of divine inspiration, rather than hard work. Unfortunately, experience has taught me not only that this isn't necessarily true, but also that there are a host of dangerous mis- conceptions that go along with it. The problem is
(60) that in our society today, whether we're thinking about the creative process, the role of the artist, or indeed the nature of art itself, we're still laboring under fanciful notions inherited from the Romantic movement in the nineteenth century.
(65) Since Coleridge wrote on the power of the imagi- nation, there has been this belief that the creation of art is unlike every other form of human pro- ductivity. Since great art is by definition extraordi- nary, people assume that it must be produced by a
(70) solitary genius, a Wordsworth, in a state of mysti- cal insight into the nature of things.

The reality, at least as far as writing novels is concerned, is that the creative process is often a lot more like breaking rocks to look for gold: hard
(75) labor with no guaranteed reward. I wouldn't deny

GO ON TO THE NEXT PAGE

for a minute that it takes a special talent to write
anything approaching literary merit. To an extent,
writers are born rather than made; it's an imaginative response to narrative, a sensitivity towards
(80) language, and a curiosity about human nature
that drives people to write in the first place. But I
think it's very important that young people who
aspire to write realize that there are years of experience behind the first few pages of a great novel.

(85)   For me, learning to write was a long and hard
apprenticeship. I had a library wall of books to
read before I understood what kind of novels I
wanted to write, and an enormous amount of
bruising self-questioning to undertake. Today,
(90) there's such a strong emphasis placed on novelty
and originality in the publishing world that
virtues such as craft and maturity of vision are
often overlooked. In the long term, however, I
think it's the work that strikes the balance between
(100) the literary tradition and the individual talent that
stands the test of time, and this is the attitude I try
to bring to my work.

7. In line 4, the word "mechanically" most nearly
    means

    (A) awkwardly
    (B) efficiently
    (C) unimaginatively
    (D) eloquently
    (E) technically

8. In context, the phrase "unlocking the floodgates"
    (line 12) suggests that creative writing

    (A) is a skill that almost anyone can acquire
    (B) can be an overwhelmingly difficult process
    (C) derives its power from depicting dramatic
        events
    (D) requires a rigid sense of structure and form
    (E) is in part beyond the writer's conscious
        control

9. In lines 16–25 the author attempts to convey the
    creative writer's sense of

    (A) frustration at the unpredictability of writing
    (B) regret at not having planned a project
        completely
    (C) wonder at the seemingly magical process of
        creation
    (D) gratitude at discovering an unsuspected talent
    (E) pride in the fruits of his or her hard labors

10. In line 23, "dim" means

    (A) vague
    (B) ignorant
    (C) pessimistic
    (D) dark
    (E) simple-minded

11. In lines 30–34, the author refers to forms of writing
    other than poems and stories in order to

    (A) suggest that all forms of writing are born out
        of a search for order
    (B) underline the difficulty of moving from one
        genre of writing to another
    (C) dispel some misconceptions about the
        superiority of literature to nonfiction
    (D) portray the frustration of writing in obscurity
    (E) indicate the differences between literature
        and other forms of writing

12. The author of Passage 2 adopts a "professional
    attitude to writing" (lines 51–52) in order to

    (A) stay competitive with younger writers
    (B) maintain a high level of productivity
    (C) compensate for his lack of inspiration
    (D) reserve time for other important activities
    (E) avoid the arrogant attitudes of self-styled
        "artists"

GO ON TO THE NEXT PAGE

13. In line 63, the word "fanciful" most nearly means

    (A) atypical

    (B) elaborate

    (C) mysterious

    (D) unrealistic

    (E) attractive

14. The author suggests that Coleridge's writings on the power of imagination

    (A) emphasized the role of maturity in an artist

    (B) propagated erroneous ideas about artistic creativity

    (C) exaggerated the importance of the arts

    (D) ignored the long years required to develop writing skills

    (E) exalted the value of experience over natural talent

15. The author of Passage 2 most likely considers the analogy to "breaking rocks to look for gold" (line 74) appropriate because writing

    (A) demands unusual talent

    (B) resembles a form of punishment

    (C) often appears futile to others

    (D) sometimes results in frustration

    (E) can be very profitable

16. The statement that "writers are born rather than made" (line 78) suggests that

    (A) the most talented writers create without apparent effort

    (B) many writers labor for years before they are recognized

    (C) creative writing should be encouraged at an early age

    (D) innate abilities play an important role in determining who will become a writer

    (E) most writers are heavily influenced by their childhood experiences

17. In the last paragraph of Passage 2, the author is critical of the publishing world primarily because of its

    (A) overvaluing of innovation

    (B) championing of work that is merely competent

    (C) neglect of older writers

    (D) refusal to take chances on experimental works

    (E) emphasis on work that is likely to sell well

18. The author of Passage 2 would most likely react to the description of the writing process presented in Passage 1 by pointing out that it

    (A) does not reflect the hard work that writing involves

    (B) puts too much emphasis on the musicality of words

    (C) fails to explain whether writers are born or made

    (D) emphasizes novelty at the expense of craft

    (E) implies that the structure of a work is not important

19. Judging from the last paragraphs of each passage, the two authors would probably agree that good writing requires a substantial amount of

    (A) life experience

    (B) inspiration

    (C) background reading

    (D) maturity

    (E) emotional pain

IF YOU FINISH BEFORE TIME IS CALLED, YOU MAY CHECK YOUR WORK ON THIS SECTION ONLY. DO NOT TURN TO ANY OTHER SECTION IN THE TEST. **STOP**

SECTION 9

Time—10 Minutes
14 Questions

Directions: For each question in this section, select the best answer from among the choices given and fill in the corresponding oval on the answer sheet.

The following sentences test correctness and effectiveness of expression. Part of each sentence or the entire sentence is underlined; beneath each sentence are five ways of phrasing the underlined material. Choice (A) repeats the original phrasing; the other four choices are different. If you think the original phrasing produces a better sentence than any of the alternatives, select choice (A); if not, select one of the other choices.

In making your selection, follow the requirements of standard written English; that is, pay attention to grammar, choice of words, sentence construction, and punctuation. Your selection should result in the most effective sentence—clear and precise, without awkwardness or ambiguity.

EXAMPLE:

Every apple in the baskets <u>are ripe and labeled according to the date it was picked</u>.

ANSWER:
(A) ● (C) (D) (E)

(A) are ripe and labeled according to the date it was picked
(B) is ripe and labeled according to the date it was picked
(C) are ripe and labeled according to the date they were picked
(D) is ripe and labeled according to the date they were picked
(E) are ripe and labeled as to the date it was picked

---

1. <u>Because differing study habits cause many roommate disputes is the reason why</u> the Student Housing Board discussed the issue at the beginning of the term.

   (A) Because differing study habits cause many roommate disputes is the reason why

   (B) Because differing study habits cause many roommate disputes,

   (C) Differing study habits cause many roommate disputes and are the reason for why

   (D) As a result of differing study habits causing many roommate disputes,

   (E) The fact that differing study habits are the cause of many roommate disputes is why

2. Students cannot do what they please in the <u>classroom because what any of them does would have an effect on other students' work</u>.

   (A) classroom because what any of them does would have an effect on other students' work

   (B) classroom because it has an effect on the work of other students

   (C) classroom because what they do affects the work of other students

   (D) classroom, and the reason is the effect our actions have on the work of other students

   (E) classroom, our actions having an effect on the work of other students

GO ON TO THE NEXT PAGE

Test Prep and Admissions

3. The design of the interior lobby of the <u>Empire State Building was particularly grand for the time period, importing</u> marble for the ceiling from France, Italy, Belgium and Germany.

   (A) Empire State Building was particularly grand for the time period, importing

   (B) Empire State Building had a particularly grand design for the time period, importing

   (C) Empire State Building, which was particularly grand for the time period, required imported

   (D) Empire State Building, being particularly grand for the time period, imported

   (E) Empire State Building, particularly grand for the time period, imported

4. Although the dancers were nervous at the beginning of their performance, <u>having shown remarkable ease as the performance</u> progressed.

   (A) having shown remarkable ease as the performance

   (B) once they showed remarkable ease when the performance had been

   (C) but showing remarkable ease as the performance

   (D) they showed remarkable ease as the performance

   (E) but they showed remarkable ease when the performance

5. <u>Although a few studies have shown that</u> a disproportionate number of artistic people are left-handed, the connection between left-handedness and creativity remains highly debated.

   (A) Although a few studies have shown that

   (B) A few studies have shown that

   (C) Therefore, a few studies have shown

   (D) Where a few studies have shown that

   (E) Conversely, a few studies have shown

6. The marathon runner's early burst of speed <u>had been exciting to some, she was</u> slower after several miles.

   (A) had been exciting to some, she was

   (B) had been exciting to some; however, she was

   (C) had been exciting to some; and she had been

   (D) excited some, while she was

   (E) excited some, but she is

7. Galileo begged Rome's indulgence for his support of a Copernican system, <u>through which the Earth circled the sun instead of occupied a central position in the universe</u>.

   (A) through which the Earth circled the sun instead of occupied a central position in the universe

   (B) in which the Earth circled the sun instead of occupying a central position in the universe

   (C) that had the Earth circling the sun instead of its occupation in a central position in the universe

   (D) which the Earth was circling the sun instead of the central position in the universe it occupied

   (E) that the Earth circled the sun instead of a central position in the universe

8. The use of laser surgery has made it possible for doctors to be not only less obtrusive <u>but also more accurate</u>.

   (A) but also more accurate

   (B) but also being accurate

   (C) but also accurately

   (D) and being accurate as well

   (E) and accurately as well

GO ON TO THE NEXT PAGE

9. <u>The success of that new restaurant is generally credited for its chef.</u>

   (A) The success of that new restaurant is generally credited for its chef.

   (B) The success of that new restaurant has been generally accredited to its chef.

   (C) The chef of that new restaurant generally receives credit for its success.

   (D) The chef of that new restaurant had with its success been credited.

   (E) That was the new restaurant for which its chef was the cause of success.

10. Costing much less than imported coffee, <u>a third of Fiji's coffee supply now comes from locally grown coffee.</u>

   (A) a third of Fiji's coffee supply now comes from locally grown coffee

   (B) of Fiji's supply of coffee, a third now comes from locally grown coffee

   (C) Fiji now supplies a third of its total coffee from locally grown coffee

   (D) locally grown coffee now provides a third of Fiji's coffee supply

   (E) Fiji's coffee supply from locally grown coffee produces about a third of it

11. The nondisclosure agreement protects the company's trade secrets, <u>but signing it is required of all new employees.</u>

   (A) but signing it is required of all new employees

   (B) therefore the signing of it is required of all new employees

   (C) signing it is required of all new employees

   (D) and they require all new employees to sign it

   (E) so all new employees are required to sign it

12. The annual income of the average African citizen is 211 <u>dollars, the average American's income is</u> almost 27,591 dollars.

   (A) dollars, the average American's income is

   (B) dollars however, the average American's income is

   (C) dollars, yet the average American's income is

   (D) dollars; whereas the average American's income is

   (E) dollars; but the average American's income is

13. The current global competition in education has required students to have longer days to learn as much as possible, <u>this situation causing parents to miss</u> their own carefree school days.

   (A) this situation causing parents to miss

   (B) which is the cause of parents missing

   (C) this causing parents' missing of

   (D) a situation causing parents to miss

   (E) and with it parents' miss from

14. In France, school reformers noted that teachers had reported dissatisfaction <u>last year, even before the controversial Fillon reforms were drafted.</u>

   (A) last year, even before the controversial Fillon reforms were drafted

   (B) last year, but that was before the controversial Fillon reforms were even drafted

   (C) last year, the controversial Fillon reforms were not even drafted at that time

   (D) last year, without the controversial Fillon reforms having even been drafted

   (E) last year, this being before the controversial Fillon reforms were even drafted

IF YOU FINISH BEFORE TIME IS CALLED, YOU MAY CHECK YOUR WORK ON THIS SECTION ONLY. DO NOT TURN TO ANY OTHER SECTION IN THE TEST.  STOP

THE ANSWER KEY APPEARS ON THE FOLLOWING PAGE.

Practice Test Eight: **Answer Key**

SECTION 1

Essay

SECTION 2

1. A
2. E
3. D
4. A
5. A
6. B
7. C
8. B
9. C
10. E
11. B
12. A
13. D
14. B
15. D
16. E
17. C
18. A
19. D
20. C

SECTION 3

1. B
2. A
3. A
4. A
5. B
6. C
7. C
8. E
9. C
10. D
11. B
12. A
13. A
14. C
15. B
16. C
17. E
18. E
19. D
20. C
21. B
22. B
23. C
24. C

SECTION 4

1. C
2. C
3. E
4. D
5. B
6. D
7. B
8. B

9. 1/2 or .5
10. 70
11. 17/9, 1.88, or 1.89
12. $0 < a < 1/8$
13. 11/2 or 5.5
14. 4/3 or 1.33
15. 595
16. 92.50
17. 25
18. 60

SECTION 5

1. D
2. A
3. B
4. E
5. D
6. D
7. D
8. E
9. D
10. A
11. E
12. B
13. A
14. E
15. A
16. B
17. B
18. C
19. D
20. B
21. C
22. D
23. D
24. D
25. E

26. C
27. B
28. D
29. B
30. D
31. D
32. C
33. C
34. D
35. E

SECTION 6

1. C
2. A
3. C
4. B
5. B
6. D
7. A
8. B
9. D
10. D
11. C
12. E
13. B
14. E
15. D
16. D
17. E
18. C
19. C
20. B
21. A
22. E
23. A
24. E

SECTION 7

1. C
2. D
3. E
4. A
5. E
6. E
7. A
8. C
9. B
10. E
11. D
12. D
13. C
14. A
15. E
16. C

SECTION 8

1. D
2. A
3. E
4. B
5. D
6. D
7. C
8. E
9. C
10. A
11. A
12. B
13. D
14. B
15. D
16. D
17. A
18. A
19. E

SECTION 9

1. B
2. C
3. C
4. D
5. A
6. B
7. B
8. A
9. C
10. D
11. E
12. C
13. D
14. A

PRACTICE TEST EIGHT

Critical Reading

	Number Right	Number Wrong	Raw Score

Section 3: ☐ − (.25 × ☐) = ☐

Section 6: ☐ − (.25 × ☐) = ☐

Section 8: ☐ − (.25 × ☐) = ☐

Critical Reading Raw Score = ☐

(rounded up)

Writing

	Number Right	Number Wrong	Raw Score

Section 1: ☐ (ESSAY GRADE) × 3.17 = ☐

Section 5: ☐ − (.25 × ☐) = ☐

Section 9: ☐ − (.25 × ☐) = ☐

Writing Raw Score = ☐

(rounded up)

Math

	Number Right	Number Wrong	Raw Score

Section 2: ☐ − (.25 × ☐) = ☐

Section 4A: ☐ − (.25 × ☐) = ☐
(QUESTIONS 1–8)

Section 4B: ☐ (no wrong answer penalty) = ☐
(QUESTIONS 9–18)

Section 7: ☐ − (.25 × ☐) = ☐

Math Raw Score = ☐

(rounded up)

Turn to page xiv to convert your raw score to a scaled score.

Answers and Explanations

SECTION 1

6 Score Essay

When I look at Jared, my adopted brother, I remember the first time I met him. I think about the beginning of our relationship, which was pretty bad, and how it led to the great relationship we have today. The development of the love between Jared and me is a great example of an unpromising beginning that led to powerful positive results.

Jared was a foster child for most of his life. For various reasons, like alcoholism and drug abuse, his mother and father couldn't take care of him and his two brothers. Since he was small, he had been bounced from foster home to foster home, and it had obviously exacted a toll from him. He wasn't very friendly with anyone, and it was apparent that he didn't trust anyone. Because his home life was never stable, Jared hadn't done well in school over the years. He was a young teenager on the edge of disaster.

All of that started to turn around when Jared came to live with us. My parents decided to become foster parents because they love children and want to help them when they're in trouble. They have four kids of their own, but they said they have more love to share. Jared was the first foster child they welcomed into our home. He was angry a lot of the time, walking around with a scowl on his face. I am closest to him in age, so my parents wanted us to be buddies. I wasn't eager to make the effort, but one day my father explained that a lot of Jared's unhappiness stemmed from his unstable family situation. Jared hadn't grown up with parents who were there for him—he had grown up moving from one stranger's home to the next. Once I realized that, I decided to try harder to befriend Jared. Little by little, Jared and I connected and became friends. I don't want to give the impression that this was fast or easy. It wasn't. But we did it.

Today Jared and I hang out a lot. Even though he's a year older than I, he is in some of the same classes as I am

because he has to make up some subjects he missed. We are also both on the basketball team. I really love being with Jared and I love him. We are now more than friends; we are brothers. Our unpromising beginning has ended up in a relationship that makes us both better, happier people.

6 Score Critique

All essays are graded on four basic criteria: Topic, Support, Organization, and Language. The author sticks to the assignment, and the essay shows a thorough development of his ideas. He explains the situation from its unpromising beginning to its positive conclusion, using specific details throughout.

The essay is highly organized. The first paragraph introduces the writer's idea—his relationship with Jared is great now although it wasn't always; the second describes the relationship to the point where it began to change; the last explains the current relationship between the writer and Jared.

The writer's language is strong, particularly with words such as "exacted" and "scowl." There is plentiful and meaningful variation in sentence structure, from short and simple sentences to longer complex sentences. Additionally, the essay is essentially error-free.

4 Score Essay

Many experiences that don't start out well get better and end up being really positive. This is what happened when I first went to sleep-away camp a few years ago. A lot of kids I know go to sleep-away camp from the time their very little. I didn't go until I was 14 which is pretty old. At first, I thought the two weeks of camp would be miserable, but by the end of the session it had turned into a wonderful and memorable time.

When I got to camp a lot of the girls in my group knew each other from last year, and some even were there since they were eight or nine years old. A few saw each other over the winter. I was the only one there without a friend. I thought, "Oh boy this isn't going to be fun." I imagined myself spending the whole time alone, being bored and lonely. While everyone around me would be laughing or talking with a great friend.

I'm glad to say that this didn't turn out to be the case. After only a few days I got friendly with the two other girls in my bunk. They let me hang out with them and their other friends. Before I knew it I was having a really great time. I've even stayed friends with some of the people I met that summer. And I went back to the camp the next year.

In conclusion, this was a good example of when "beautiful things can come from unpromising beginnings."

4 Score Critique

All essays are graded on four basic criteria: Topic, Support, Organization, and Language. The author sticks to the topic extremely well and includes sufficient support for her ideas, particularly in the early part of the essay. The end of the essay, however, does not sustain the quality of the beginning. In particular, the conclusion is weak. The author merely quotes from the assignment to conclude the essay. While citing a few words from the statement won't lose you points, in itself it doesn't add anything to the essay.

By telling the story of her camping experience in light of the topic, the author provides the support that she needs to fulfill the assignment. However, the writer could have given fuller detail about how the situation improved. The second half of the essay relies on generalities like "I was having a really great time" instead of providing the concrete details that would be found in a 5 or 6 essay.

The essay exhibits tight organization, with a clear beginning, middle, and end. The language in the essay is generally unsophisticated, and the sentence structure lacks variety. There are also a few noticeable errors in sentence structure, including omitted commas and sentence fragments.

2 Score Essay

I think there are many times that one can point at when something starts out horrible and then gets ok or even great. I have certinly had this happen. I felt that way the first day of high school. I thought it would be horrible. But its turned out to be an ok time with some good friends and even some good teachers.

In literature I think of the Wizard of Oz. Dorothy and Toto are lost and a lot of bad things happen but they wind up getting back to Kansas. They also make friends as they go on the yelow brick road. These are the cowardly lion, the tinman and scarecrow. This is an example of when good things happen even though you don't think their going to.

When a person feels that something isn't happening the way he or she wants it too it is a good idea for him/her to keep going because you never know how it will turn out. It could turn out very good.

2 Score Critique

All essays are graded on four basic criteria: Topic, Support, Organization, and Language. The writer states a position on the topic in her first sentence, but she doesn't entirely succeed in developing this position. The essay is all over the place. She uses the first-person "I," then switches the second-person "you," and finally to the impersonal, "a person." She was unable to find her voice.

The writer tries to support her position through the use of a personal story about the beginning of high school and *The Wizard of Oz*, but doesn't develop either point.

The essay has some basic organization, with a separate paragraph for *The Wizard of Oz* example. However, the essay lacks a clear introduction, and movement from idea to idea is choppy.

The language of the essay is generally substandard. The essay is riddled with grammatical and structural errors. Here are a few things that you can learn from this writer's mistakes: Avoid slang or colloquial words like "ok." Know the difference between and proper use of "its" and "it's" and "there," "their," and "they're." Avoid the use of "he or she" and "him/her." Instead, pick one and stick with it throughout the essay.

SECTION 2

1. A

Difficulty: Low

Strategic Advice: The important thing to remember here is that when solving an algebraic equation, you have to do the same thing to both sides of the equation. You're given an equation with $5x + 3$ on the left side of the equal sign and the question asks about $5x + 10$. To make $5x + 3$ look like $5x + 10$, just add 7. But since you've added 7 to the left side of the equation, you have to add 7 to the right side of the equation also. Adding 7 to the right side of the equation gives you $21 + 7$, or 28, answer choice (A).

Getting to the Answer:

A more mathematical way of expressing what you just did is to write it out like this:

$5x$	$+$	3	$=$	21
	$+$	$+7$		$+7$
$5x$	$+$	10	$=$	28

2. E

Difficulty: Medium

You have to know a few facts about geometry and lines and angles. The word "bisects" means "cuts in half." So, if line *EX* bisects angle *BXD*, it cuts angle *BXD* into two equal halves. The diagram shows that angle *BXE* is 30°, and since it is half of angle *BXD*, angle *BXD* must equal 60°.

Now that you've found the degree measure of angle *BXD*, find the degree measure of angle *CXB*. Angles *CXB* and *BXD* are supplementary angles because they form line segment *CXD*. So angle *CXB* plus angle *BXD* equals 180°. Since angle *BXD* is 60°, angle *CXB* equals 180° − 60° or 120°.

You can eliminate two answer choices by just eyeballing the figure. Assume that the angle measurement is about what it looks like. You should know what a 90-degree angle looks like — the corner of a piece of paper. Angle *CXB* in the figure is clearly greater than 90°, so choices (A) and (B) can be eliminated. So you could guess among answer choices (C), (D), and (E).

3. D

Difficulty: Low

Strategic Advice: Early questions like this one are not trying to trick you or test your ability to think critically, but rather just to be careful in your calculations. Remember this, and you can rack up easy points on Test Day.

Getting to the Answer:

$$b - 3c = 5$$
$$b - 3(1) = 5$$
$$b = 8$$
$$a - 2b = 10$$
$$a - 2(8) = 10$$
$$a - 16 = 10$$
$$a = 26$$

4. A

Difficulty: Low

Strategic Advice: As with many word problems, this question tests your ability to translate words into a formula. Once you write this formula, the answer should be clear.

Getting to the Answer:

John has more money than Billy, so $b < j$. John has less money than Sean, so $j < s$. Combining these two together gives us $b < j < s$, so the correct choice is (A).

5. A

Difficulty: Medium

Strategic Advice: If you carefully apply the conditions in the question to the answer choices, you should have no problem with this one.

Getting to the Answer:

We know we are looking for a number that has only 3 factors, so let's see which one of the answer choices has only 3 factors. Choice (A), 169, has just 3 factors: 1, 13, and 169. Choices (B), (C), and (D) have many more than 3 factors, and choice (E), 37, has just 2 factors, since it is a prime number. Thus, (A) is the correct choice.

6. B

Difficulty: Low

Strategic Advice: Make sure you read the question carefully here. In early problems, it's easy to leap to conclusions about what the question is asking; make sure you realize you're finding the length of a single side, not the entire perimeter of square A.

Getting to the Answer:

Perimeter of $A = 4$(perimeter of B) $= 4(18) = 72$

One side of $B =$ (perimeter of B) $\div 4 = 72 \div 4 = 18$

7. C

Difficulty: Medium

Strategic Advice: You should always be sure that you know what you're solving for before you dive into a question; this can save you a lot of time in the end.

Getting to the Answer:

CD and DE make up CE. If $CE = 30$ and CD is twice the length of DE, then $CD = 20$ and $DE = 10$. We are solving for CD, however, so the answer is choice (C).

8. B

Difficulty: Medium

Whenever you see questions dealing with properties of odd or even numbers you should always approach it the same way—by picking numbers. Remember that what is true for one odd or even number is generally true for all of them. So pick the most simple odd or even numbers for your variables and just see what happens.

Here you're told not only that a is an odd number but also that it's negative, so just pick a negative odd number for a. -1 would be a good choice. Since b is positive as well as even, 2 would be a good choice for b. Now all you have to do is plug those values into the answer choices. (Just don't forget the rules of multiplying and dividing by negative numbers.)

(A) $(-1) + 2 = 1$

(B) $-(-1)(2) = 2$

(C) $(-1)(2) = -2$

(D) $\dfrac{2}{-1} = -2$

(E) $2 - (-1) = 2 + 1 = 3$

The only one which is even and positive is answer choice (B).

9. C

Difficulty: Medium

Strategic Advice: Like with many word problems, Backsolving, or plugging your answers back into the question stem, is a good strategy to use here.

Getting to the Answer:

Start with choice (C). If 5 pounds of pasta salad are needed, it would be enough to feed either 30 adults or 50 children or some combination of the two. Since there are 10 children at the party, they would need 1 pound of pasta salad, and the remaining 4 pounds for the adults. Since there are $34 - 10 = 24$ adults at the party, and each pound of pasta salad feeds 6 adults, the remaining 4 pounds will feed $4 \times 6 = 24$ adults, making (C) the correct choice.

10. E

Difficulty: Medium

Strategic Advice: Careful application of the rules of exponents will yield results here and on Test Day.

Getting to the Answer:

$(-3a^2b^6)^3 = (-3)^3 (a^2)^3 (b^6)^3 = -27 \, a^{2\times3}b^{6\times3} = -27a^6b^{18}$

11. B

Difficulty: Medium

Strategic Advice: Remember the major three-part formula:

$$average = \frac{sum\ of\ terms}{number\ of\ terms}$$

Getting to the Answer:

$$sum = 27$$
$$number\ of\ terms = 3$$
$$So,\ average = \frac{27}{3} = 9$$

12. A

Difficulty: High

Strategic Advice: Here you've got a rectangle with sides y and $y + 4$ and area 32. Let's forget about the circles for a minute. This means that $y(y + 4) = 32$. You can make this into the quadratic equation $y^2 + 4y - 32 = 0$ and solve for y, but it's much easier to just try to guess the value of y. What 2 numbers have 32 as their product where one is 4 greater than the other?

Getting to the Answer:

The numbers 8 and 4 should come to mind. Then $y = 4$, the width of the rectangle is 4, and the length is 8. Now to the circles. You have to notice something important here — the diameter of each circle is the same length as the width of the rectangle. If you draw a vertical diameter in either circle you'll see that. So what's the length of the diameter? That's right, 4. So the radius is half of that, or 2, and the area is $\pi \times 2^2$, or 4π, choice (A).

This is also a good eyeballing problem. If the rectangle has an area of 32, then half the rectangle has an area of 16. The area of either circle looks like it's less than half the area of the rectangle, or less than 16. Which answer choices are less than 16? If you remember that π is a little more than 3, then you'll know that only choices (A) and (B) are less than 16, so you can narrow it down to two answer choices and guess.

13. D

Difficulty: Medium

Strategic Advice: Here you have to know something about coordinate geometry. The easiest way to do this question is to estimate values for the x- and y-coordinates of each point.

Getting to the Answer:

Look at point A. It looks like the x-coordinate of A is about $1\frac{1}{2}$. It also looks like the y-coordinate of point A is about $\frac{1}{2}$. Is $x - y < 0$ in this case? No, because $1\frac{1}{2} - \frac{1}{2} = 1$, so choice (A) is out. Since point B is sitting right on the x-axis, its y-coordinate is 0. Its x-coordinate looks like it's about $\frac{1}{2}$, and $\frac{1}{2} - 0 = \frac{1}{2}$, so (B) is out also. Point C looks like the point $(1, -1\frac{1}{4})$, so $x - y$ is $1 - (-1\frac{1}{4})$, which is positive. Eliminate (C). (D) is $(-1\frac{1}{2}, \frac{1}{2})$ so $x - y$ is $-1\frac{1}{2} - \frac{1}{2}$ which is negative, so choice (D) is correct.

You might have wanted to approach this a little more theoretically. Under what conditions would the expression $x - y$ be negative? If x is a positive number, or 0, then $x - y$ would be negative if y were greater than x. Are there any points which meet those requirements? No, because although points A, B, and C all have positive x-coordinates, they also all have y-coordinates which are smaller than their respective x-coordinates. What about when x is negative? If x is negative and y is positive, then $x - y$ must be negative, so all you have to do is find a point where x is negative (to the left of the y-axis) and y is positive (above the x-axis) and you've found the answer, again choice (D).

14. B

Difficulty: High

Strategic Advice: If a diagram in a question contains unfamiliar shapes, try altering the diagram to make it contain more familiar ones.

Getting to the Answer:

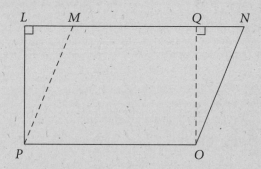

By adding point Q and drawing in line OQ, you can make the diagram look much friendlier. If we ignore MP, the diagram now consists of rectangle $LQOP$ and triangle NOQ; summing the areas of these two figures will give us the area of $LNOP$. We know that $LP = 12$ and $OP = 13$, so the area of $LQOP = 12 \times 13$, or 156. Since $LP = 12$, OQ must also equal 12. If $NO = 13$, NOQ must be a 5-12-13 triangle and $QN = 5$. The area of a triangle $= \frac{1}{2}bh$, so the area of $NOQ = \frac{1}{2}(5)(12) = 30$, so the area of $LNOP = 156 + 30 = 186$.

15. D

Difficulty: Medium

Strategic Advice: Often, later questions will take a simple concept and disguise it as a more difficult question.

Getting to the Answer:

This question is really just a rearrangement of the average formula. Since we are dealing with prices in this question, the average formula is:

$$\frac{\text{Sum of the prices}}{\text{number of prices}} = \text{average of the prices.}$$

If we multiply both sides of the formula by the number of prices, we get that the sum of the prices = average of the prices × number of prices, the quantity quoted in the question. Thus, (D) is the correct choice.

16. E

Difficulty: Medium

Strategic Advice: Equilateral means "equal in length." So an equilateral triangle is a triangle whose 3 sides are all equal in length. So if the expressions $3x + 1$ and $x + 7$ represent sides of an equilateral triangle, they must be equal.

Getting to the Answer:

Use this to set up an algebraic equation: $3x + 1 = x + 7$, which can be solved for x. The result is $x = 3$, and all you have to do is plug that into either expression. That will tell you that the length of a side of this equilateral triangle is 10, so the perimeter, which is the sum of the length of the sides, is equal to $10 + 10 + 10$, or 30, choice (E).

17. C

Difficulty: Medium

Strategic Advice: Since we have a word problem with numbers in the answer choices, Backsolving might be a good strategy to try here.

Getting to the Answer:

Since we are dealing with crayons, we know that the number of crayons of each color will have to be an integer. Starting with choice (C), $20 \times \frac{2}{5} = 8$, which is a whole number, and $20 \times \frac{1}{4} = 5$, also a whole number, so 20 is a possible value for the number of crayons, and (C) is the correct choice.

18. A

Difficulty: High

Strategic Advice: Picking numbers is always a good choice for a question with multiple variables in the question stem and answer choices.

Getting to the Answer:

Let's have $x = 8$ and $y = 7$. We know that the initial amount + 6 liters − 7 liters must equal 8 liters, i.e. the initial amount decreased by 1 liter to become 8 liters, so the initial amount of water must have been 9 liters. Now we just have to substitute x and y into the answer choices to see which one gives us 9 liters.

(A) $8 + 7 - 6 = 9$, so (A) is the correct choice.

19. D

Difficulty: High

Strategic Advice: Anytime you are given a diagram that does not show all the information given in the question, it's usually a good idea to draw that information into the diagram.

Getting to the Answer:

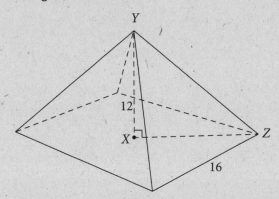

In the diagram above, we have drawn in the height of the pyramid and labeled the known lengths. We can find YZ by recognizing that it is the hypotenuse of the right triangle XYZ as labeled in the diagram above. If we can find the lengths of the other two sides, we can use the Pythagorean Theorem to find YZ. We already know that $XY = 12$, and XZ is equal to half of the diagonal of the square base. To find the length of this diagonal, we know that it is the hypotenuse of another right triangle whose legs are sides of the base. Therefore, since the length of both legs is 16, we know this is a 45-45-90 triangle, making the length of the diagonal $16\sqrt{2}$. Therefore, $XZ = 8\sqrt{2}$. Using the Pythagorean Theorem:

$$(YZ)^2 = 12^2 + (8\sqrt{2})^2$$
$$(YZ)^2 = 144 + 128$$
$$YZ = \sqrt{272}$$
$$YZ = 4\sqrt{17}$$

20. C

Difficulty: High

Strategic Advice: If you can see through the difficult wording of this question and realize that you can pick numbers here, the question will become much easier.

Getting to the Answer:

Let's pick 4 for n. Then, the second term of our series becomes $\frac{4}{4} + 4$, or 5. Therefore, the ratio of the second term to the first term is 5:4, or $\frac{5}{4}$. Now, just substitute n into the answer choices and see which one equals $\frac{5}{4}$.

(A) $\frac{(4 + 16)}{4} = 5$, so (A) is incorrect.

(B) $\frac{(4 + 4)}{4} = 2$, so (B) is incorrect

(C) $\frac{(4 + 16)}{4(4)} = \frac{5}{4}$, so (C) is the correct choice.

Checking (D) and (E) will confirm this.

SECTION 3

1. B

Difficulty: Low

The second blank is defined by the phrase "emitting an odor"; a good prediction might be "moldy" or "rank." Choice (B), *dank .. musty,* is the only choice that has a word matching the prediction for the second blank. *Dank*, which means "unpleasantly moist," fits in the first blank, so choice (B) is the correct choice for this question.

2. A

Difficulty: Low

The clue here is "once," which tells you that there is a contrast between the past and present populations of the city. Since the city has lost residents, you can predict that it used to be more densely populated. The word in the blank will be something like "busy" or "lively." *Bustling* is the word that comes closest. *Manufactured* and *rural* don't make any sense when they're plugged in, and whether the city was *seedy* or not is irrelevant. *Seedy* means "disreputable or squalid." This has nothing to do with population density. *Deserted* is the opposite of what you need in the blank.

3. A

Difficulty: Medium

Predictions can be made for both of the blanks based on the information that the rains caused landslides and washed away people's houses. The first blank has to be something like "overwhelming," because *gentle* rains could not cause so much damage. Likewise, the second blank will be "inundate" or "flood." Choice (A), *torrential… deluge,* has the necessary words—*torrential* means "like a tumultuous outpouring." *Purge* means "to make free of something unwanted." Choice (C) is wrong because although the rains are *treacherous*, they certainly do not *sustain* the hillside slopes. *Desecrate* means "to profane or violate the sanctity of." To be *fecund* is to be fertile, and when you *bolster* something you "reinforce or support" it.

4. A

Difficulty: Medium

Since those who reject psychological theory are going to concentrate on its scientific "shortcomings," you can use the first-blank words of the choices to narrow the possibilities down to (A), *inadequacies*, and (E), *deficiencies*. Now for the second blank: the phrase "not on—, but on clinical observations" indicates that the blank contrasts with clinical observation. You could predict a word like "theories," and you find that *assumptions* comes close, whereas *evidence* is the opposite of what's needed. Choice (A) is the correct answer.

5. B

Difficulty: Medium

The sentence sets up a contrast between the woman's opinion of the film and how she usually feels about such "dramatic stories." You don't know what either of these (her opinion or her general attitude) is, exactly; you just know that the two have to be roughly the opposite of each other. Be careful, though. This doesn't mean that all you need are two opposite words for the blanks. *Predictable .. spontaneity* are rough opposites, but *spontaneity* doesn't fit in the sentence. How can someone have spontaneity towards dramatic stories? The words in choice (B), *poignant .. impassivity,* work the best. *Poignant* means "touching" and *impassivity* is "being unresponsive emotionally." Clearly it would be a surprise that a woman who normally has no emotional response to dramatic stories found a film *poignant.* Choice (C) is wrong because it wouldn't be surprising that someone with *animosity,* or "ill will," towards dramatic stories would find the film *irrelevant. Anachronistic* means "chronologically out of place," while *perspicacity* means "shrewdness." *Affected* describes something that is faked in order to impress people, for example, a foreign accent.

6. C

Difficulty: Medium

To fill the blank, you need an adjective that describes Lovecraft's correspondence. The first half of the sentence (before the semicolon) indicates that Lovecraft wrote five volumes of letters, which is quite a bit, so you can predict that the blank will be a word like "abundant or extensive." *Voluminous,* which means "capable of filling several volumes," fits perfectly. *Laconic,* which means using a minimum of words," has the opposite meaning of the predicted word. There is no indication in the sentence that Lovecraft's correspondence is *unknown* or *popular;* and *verbal* is out because you wouldn't need to specify that a bunch of letters contained words.

7. C

Difficulty: Hard

This question tests vocabulary. It's fairly easy to see that the principal would want other students to "imitate" Lisa's performance, but finding the choice to match this prediction may be more difficult. The choice that means "to imitate" is *emulate,* (C). *Elucidate* means "to illustrate or clarify;" *mollify* means "to soothe or calm;" *castigate* means "to chastise or reprimand." One cannot *reflect* a performance, so (E) is wrong.

8. E

Difficulty: Hard

There's no reason to get worried as soon as you see words in the sentence you don't understand, like "epiphytic" in this one. Usually you can either figure out what the word means or you don't need to know what it means, as with "epiphytic." What you do need to see is that the semicolon signals that the two halves of the sentence are related in meaning. If "epiphytic" ferns can't survive without constant moisture, then they can only live in tropical rain forests, which have a lot of moisture. You can predict something like "only found in" for the blank. *Endemic to,* which means

"restricted to a region," matches the prediction. This is a tough word, but that's to be expected, since we're at the end of the set. *Steeped in* means "plunged into a liquid." Tea bags are steeped in hot water to make tea. *Inimical to* means "hostile to."

Questions 9–12

These two short paired passages present different views on the issue of school cafeteria food. The first passage focuses on the failure of school food to meet the nutritional needs of children. The second passage discusses this failure, but also describes how financial pressures influence school cafeteria offerings.

9. C

Difficulty: Medium

As the cited word is used to describe a "body of evidence" that continues to grow, and has been "bolstered" by new studies, the adjective *thorough* is the best fit. While *complete* and *flawless* come close to matching the context, the fact that the body of evidence is growing stronger indicates that it is not yet *complete* or *flawless.*

10. D

Difficulty: Medium

The referenced sentence makes two statements: that parents may not want fast-food restaurants influencing what their children eat, and that an unprofitable cafeteria can be a financial burden. By bringing these two statements together in a single sentence, the author implies that it is fast-food-like lunch options that can make a cafeteria profitables, (D). The passage never discusses the profitability of cafeterias in general, so (A) is out. Choice (B) is distortion. The passage only suggests that school boards must sometimes go against the will of the parents, not necessarily that such decisions are "difficult." Choice (C) is also distortion. The passage only suggests that fast-food can "better attract the appetites of teenagers," not that *most* students are uninterested in healthy foods. Choice (E) is extreme. While the passage suggests that school boards sometimes must pick profitability over nutrition, it doesn't go so far as to suggest that they are unconcerned with nutrition.

11. B

Difficulty: High

Because it is easy to make your own assumptions when reading through the passages, make sure to go back and re-examine the text. When you have found specific evidence, you can be sure of your answer choice. Although both passages discuss different aspects of the food problem in schools, the two authors agree that offering nutritional food choices is a growing concern. Choices (A) and (D) refer to Passage I only. Only Passage 2 refers to school boards and parental organizations, (C). And neither passage suggests that the nutritional value of school food is declining (E); they only indicate that concern is growing.

12. A

Difficulty: Medium

In this case, the view of the author of Passage 1 is made clear in the last sentence, which states that the school food problem is most likely the result of "general dietary ignorance." Passage 2's viewpoint is also expressed towards the end of the paragraph, which mentions that students are attracted to fast-food, and that while parents might not approve of such an influence, schools need to make their food attractive for the cafeteria to be profitable. Choice (A) nicely matches the viewpoints of the two authors. Choice (B) is extreme. While this statement accurately represents Passage 1, the author of Passage 2 does not go so far as to express *sympathy* for school boards. Choice (C) is a distortion; nothing in Passage 2 indicates that the author finds parental or governmental concerns *exaggerated*. Choice (D) is also a distortion of Passage 2, which only indicates that a cafeteria could be a financial burden if it is not profitable, not necessarily that it could not *survive*. Choice (E) distorts both passages. Passage 1 only briefly cites scientific studies, and Passage 2 never mentions government data.

Questions 13–18

The overall sense of the passage is that the author, a scientist who is fascinated by the deep-diving of leatherback turtles, is reporting what he and his wife have learned about the turtles' behavior. He tells of recording—at least, partially—the dive of a female leatherback in the first paragraph. In the second paragraph, the author discusses the difficulty of studying leatherbacks: they can't be kept in captivity. An instrument known as the time-depth recorder has been designed to measure turtle-diving at sea. Using this instrument, the author found that female leatherbacks dive almost continuously. Why do the turtles dive? This is the question the author attempts to answer in the final three paragraphs. It seems that the turtles are following the movements of a group of organisms known as the deep scattering layer; this is where jellyfish, the turtles' food source, are. The author has two main pieces of evidence for this hypothesis: 1) the turtles' pattern of diving seems to match the movement of the deep scattering layer, and 2) turtles do not lose weight between bouts of nesting.

13. A

Difficulty: Low

The "specific behavior" that the author describes in the cited lines is the continuous diving of the turtles. The author at this point is relating how astonished he and his wife were when they first recorded the turtles' diving. He is conveying a sense of *how impressive the diving activity of the leatherbacks is*, (A). The author has not yet talked about the deep scattering layer, so (B) is out. *Leatherback breeding* is never even mentioned in the passage. Choice (D) is wrong because the author is not suggesting that the turtles' behavior is *unpredictable*. It may be unexpected and astonishing because the scientists didn't know much about the turtles, but that doesn't mean the turtles behave unpredictably. Finally, you may get an *insight into the life of a marine biologist* from this part of the passage, but the author's purpose is to describe the leatherbacks, not his lifestyle.

14. C

Difficulty: Medium

Several of the choices are possible definitions of "gradual." Remember that with all Vocabulary-in-Context questions, you need to check how the word is used in the context of the passage. Approach this question in the same way as you would a Sentence Completion. Put a blank in the sentence in place of "gradual," and you see that the word in the blank has to have a meaning opposite of "vertical." In other words, "gradual" and "vertical" have opposite meanings here. The only word among the possible answers that has a meaning opposite of "vertical" is *sloping,* (C).

15. B

Difficulty: Medium

The question "Why the incessant diving?" serves to lead the reader into a discussion of the author's attempts to explain the turtles' diving behavior. The author is using the device of asking a question and then answering it in order to *introduce a new topic for discussion,* (B). Although the turtles' diving may be an area requiring *further research*, the author does not pose the question to make this point. Nor is he making a statement about the *limitations* of the time-depth recorder; you already know from the previous paragraph what the instrument can and cannot do. There is no suggestion here that the turtles were *behaving in a novel way*. How would the researchers know if the behavior were novel or not? This was the first time they ever monitored the turtles. Finally, (E) is far too broad to be the right answer—watch out for this common kind of wrong answer type.

16. C

Difficulty: Hard

Read the lines surrounding lines 51–57. The deep scattering layer "migrates to the surface at night to feed on phytoplankton, then gradually retreats from daylight…A leatherback's dives seem to follow the movements of the deep scattering layer." The reason turtles make shallower dives as dusk approaches is that their food source is getting closer to the surface, (C). Clearly turtles can locate their prey at night, so (A) is out. Choice (B) can be eliminated because turtles feed on jellyfish, not phytoplankton. Choices (D) and (E) may seem to be reasonable choices, but they don't work in the context of the passage.

17. E

Difficulty: Medium

You can answer this question without reading all of the final paragraph. The author says that they "have not been able to directly observe leatherbacks feeding, but we have collected some additional circumstantial evidence." It stands to reason, then, that the additional evidence will support what the author has been claiming in the previous two paragraphs, that *female leatherbacks find most of their food in the deep scattering layer*, choice (E). Choices (A), (B), and (D) have little to do with the information in the passage. Choice (C) may have been distracting because the author does mention that *female leatherbacks come ashore repeatedly during each nesting season*, but this is not the circumstantial evidence the author uses, nor is it what the author is trying to prove.

18. E

Difficulty: Medium

The correct answer to this Big Picture question should jump right out at you now that you've done the other questions and re-read quite a bit of the passage in the process. The author doesn't say much about leatherbacks' *nesting patterns* or about *misconceptions* concerning the leatherback's feeding activity choice (B). His description of the time-depth recorder is a detail, not his primary objective. Choice (D) is wrong because the author never encourages others to study leatherbacks. Instead, he is *offer[ing] his own findings about the behavior of leatherbacks,* choice (E). A shortcut to answering this question would have been to take a look at the verbs in the answer choices first. Does the author *dispute* anything or *encourage* in the passage? No, so these two choices could have been eliminated right away, leaving you with only three to examine more closely.

Questions 19–24

With this fiction passage, you really needed to read the introduction (something you should always do, in any case). If you didn't, you wouldn't have had any idea what caused the extremely uncomfortable situation to arise between Marc and his friends, and you'd be confused throughout the passage because the author never specifically mentions what has upset Camilla and Karen. The first paragraph centers on Camilla's reaction to Marc's bragging and Marc's realization that he has offended her once again. In the second paragraph, the author airs Marc's opinion on Camilla's tendency to "overreact." She gets "emotional when it isn't warranted," from Marc's point of view, as a consequence of her intelligence and the fact that she cares strongly about certain things. Marc's attention and thoughts turn to Karen in the third paragraph when he sees that he has offended her also, even though they've been friends for a long time. The final paragraph depicts Marc's initial, awkward attempts to smooth the situation over.

19. D

Difficulty: Medium

Marc thinks that Camilla has a tendency to get emotional when it isn't "warranted." You get a clue about what "not warranted" means in the next sentence: "the most innocuous remark would set her off." In other words, she has no good reason, in Mark's eyes, to get so upset; she tends to get emotional when it isn't *justified*, (D). It may be true that Camilla gets upset when she doesn't *intend* to, or when Marc doesn't *expect* it, but these are not possible meanings of the word "warranted."

20. C

Difficulty: Low

Marc compares having a conversation with Camilla to walking in a minefield: "one minute you'd be strolling along admiring the view, and the next, you'd have tripped her wire…" This analogy emphasizes *the unpredictability of Camilla's reactions*, (C). The author never mentions *Marc's fear of offending other people*, *Camilla's discomfort at upsetting others* or *the close understanding between Marc and Camilla*. As for (E), Marc may be annoyed at Camilla's behavior—the author says he suppresses a momentary impulse to get angry—but this doesn't have anything to do with the minefield analogy.

21. B

Difficulty: Medium

Choices (B), (C), and (E) are all possible meanings of the word "dissecting," so you have to go back to the passage to find the meaning of the word in context. Karen and Marc had spent whole summers "dissecting each other's private lives." So *analyzing* is the right meaning of dissecting here; *criticizing* has too sharp a connotation, and *cutting* is too literal (remember to watch out for the most common meaning of the word—usually it's not the correct choice).

22. B

Difficulty: Low

In the line immediately following the description of Marc's summers with Karen, the author says that "Marc couldn't think of a single woman who knew him better." The summers spent with Karen show the *long-standing nature of their friendship*, (B). This choice should have stood out because it's the only one that fits in the context of the third paragraph, which is all about the fact that Marc has also

offended Karen, even though they've been friends for a long time. Nowhere does the author mention that Marc has *few close women friends*, that *Marc has to overcome many obstacles in his private life*, or that Marc regrets *not having pursued* a relationship with Karen further. Choice (C) is based on a misinterpretation of the line that says "Marc used to justify the relationship to his father…" This does not mean that Marc had to seek his father's approval; "justify" means "rationalize" here.

23. C

Difficulty: Low

Marc's feeling that he'd "really done it now" comes right on the heels of his realization that he has offended Karen, his closest friend, in addition to upsetting Camilla. Reading a few lines up from the phrase quoted in the question stem makes this clear. Marc doesn't feel that he's "really done it now" because he's lost the ability to talk—it's the other way around. Choice (B) is wrong because there is no reason to think that Karen is not loyal to him. She is simply annoyed at him right now. Choices (D) and (E) can be eliminated quickly because they don't make sense in the context of the passage.

24. C

Difficulty: Medium

The author says that Marc was the "statesman of the class…people joked about how much money he was going to make…" However, Marc is "groping for his words now…" You can make the inference that the author talks about Marc being the statesman of the class in order to show that he is *generally an articulate speaker*, but he's floundering now. It's true that being the statesman means that Marc is also probably *noted for his diplomacy* and is *a popular student on campus*. These do not, however, touch upon the contrast the author is making between Marc's usual articulate self and his current awkwardness. There is no evidence in the passage that people resent Marc's success or that his *ambitions are not realistic*.

SECTION 4

1. C

Difficulty: Low

Strategic Advice: This is a translation problem, so you have to take the words a few at a time and find the equivalent algebraic equation.

Getting to the Answer:

Start with the words "12 less than." What if you were asked, "What is 12 less than 20?" That's easy, right? 12 less than 20 is just 20 minus 12. So 12 less than the product of something is going to look like something minus 12. The next part of the phrase is "the product of 3 and b." You should know that a product is the result of multiplying two numbers together. So the product of 3 and b is just 3 times b, or $3b$. Therefore 12 less than the product of 3 and b is just 12 less than $3b$, or $3b - 12$. The next word, "is," means equals, so we have "$3b - 12 =$." What does it equal? 9, of course, so the entire equation is $3b - 12 = 9$, choice (C). You might have been tempted by choice (A), which is similar, but notice that in (A) the 12 is being subtracted from b, not from the product of anything.

2. C

Difficulty: Low

Strategic Advice: Don't rush when working with simple variable problems.

Getting to the Answer:

If $\sqrt{x} = 3$, then $x = 9$. Plug $x = 9$ into the expression $x^2 - 1$, which gives you $81 - 1 = 80$.

3. E

Difficulty: Low

Strategic Advice: For each of the 4 entrances, there are 3 exits. To find the number of combinations possible, multiply the number of entrances by the number of exits:

Getting to the Answer:

$4 \times 3 = 12$.

4. D

Difficulty: Low

Strategic Advice: Since A is at -2 and D is at 7, AD has a length of 9 and B and C must be three units away from the endpoints.

Getting to the Answer:

The coordinates of B and C must be $-2 + 3 = 1$ and $7 - 3 = 4$. You aren't told which point goes where, but only one answer choice, (D), contains one of these values.

5. B

Difficulty: Low

Strategic Advice: First find out how much Tariq's purchase will cost.

Getting to the Answer:

21 oranges at 30 cents each will cost $21 \times \$0.30 = \$6.30$. 12 apples at 50 cents each will cost $12 \times \$0.50 = \$6.00$. The total purchase would cost $\$6.30 + \$6.00$, or $\$12.30$. Since Tariq only has $10, he needs $\$12.30 - \$10.00$, or $\$2.30$ more.

6. D

Difficulty: Medium

Strategic Advice: The fastest way to do this problem is to plug the values of C and D listed in the chart into each of the answer choices.

Getting to the Answer:

Start with choice (A). Plugging in -1 and -4 works, as $-4 = -1 - 3$, but does $2 = 1 - 3$? No, so move on to the next one. Since $-4 \neq 2(-1)$, (B) can be eliminated. $-4 \neq 2(-1) + 2$, so (C) can be eliminated as well. Look at (D):

Does $-4 = 3(-1) - 1$?   Yes.

Does $2 = 3(1) - 1$?   Yes.

Does $8 = (3)(3) - 1$?   Yes.

Does $14 = 3(5) - 1$?   Yes.

Since all the pairs work for choice (D), that's the answer. Just for practice, look at (E). Plugging in the first pair of values gives you $-4 = 3(-1) + 1$. Is this true? No, because $3(-1) + 1 = -2$.

7. B

Difficulty: Medium

Strategic Advice: Don't let the difference between inches and feet confuse you here. Stay focused on the using feet for your answer.

Getting to the Answer:

For each hair bow, 3 pieces of 8 inch long ribbon are used, so that is 24 inches or 2 feet of ribbon. She made g hair bows, so the total amount of ribbon she used was $2g$. So if the spool has 200 feet of ribbon, we can say that she used $200 - 2g$ feet of ribbon.

8. B

Difficulty: High

Strategic Advice: If a geometry question does not provide a diagram, sketch your own. Important things to notice about this problem are the radius of the circle and the base and height of the triangle.

Getting to the Answer:

To find the probability that a randomly selected point from within the circle will fall within the triangle, find the area of the triangle and divide it by the area of the circle.

radius: 3

base: 6

height: 3

Area of triangle: $\frac{1}{2}(6)(3) = 9$

Area of circle: $\pi(3^2) = 9\pi$

Probability: $\frac{9}{9\pi} = \frac{1}{\pi}$

9. $\frac{1}{2}$ or .5

Difficulty: Medium

Strategic Advice: You're given that the whole line segment, AE, is 3. Since D is the midpoint of AE, D must cut AE in half. That means that AD is $1\frac{1}{2}$ and DE is $1\frac{1}{2}$. AD is made up of three small line segments, all of which are equal in length. That means that each one must measure one-third of $1\frac{1}{2}$, which is $\frac{1}{2}$. So AB has length $\frac{1}{2}$, and you can put $\frac{1}{2}$ or .5 into your grid.

10. 70

Difficulty: Medium

Strategic Advice: If you notice that there is a triangle on the right side of the figure with 2 labeled angles from that triangle, you can probably solve this one.

Getting to the Answer:

The 2 labeled angles are 60° and 80°, so the third angle of the triangle must be $180 - 60 - 80 = 40°$. The 40° angle and the two angles labeled $d°$ make up a straight line, so $40 + d + d = 180$. That means that $40 + 2d = 180$, $2d = 140$, and $d = 70$, so grid in the number 70.

11. $\frac{17}{9}$, 1.88, or 1.89

Difficulty: Medium

Strategic Advice: Here you could do a lot of arithmetic and get the right answer, but you should have noticed a shortcut. Since this is a long string of numbers which are being added and subtracted together, you don't really need the parentheses.

Getting to the Answer:

You can add or subtract these fractions in any order. Notice that at one point you are adding $\frac{1}{3}$ and at another point subtracting $\frac{1}{3}$. Plus $\frac{1}{3}$ minus $\frac{1}{3}$ is just 0. The same is true of $\frac{1}{5}$ and $\frac{1}{7}$ so you can just cross out the terms $-\frac{1}{3}$, $+\frac{1}{3}$, $-\frac{1}{5}$, $+\frac{1}{5}$, $-\frac{1}{7}$, and $+\frac{1}{7}$. That leaves you with $x = 2 - \frac{1}{9} = \frac{18}{9} - \frac{1}{9} = \frac{17}{9}$, so grid in $\frac{17}{9}$. (Not $1\frac{8}{9}$. You can't grid in mixed numbers.)

12. $0 < a < \dfrac{1}{8}$

Difficulty: Medium

Strategic Advice: This one requires some thought. If $2a + b = 1$, what kind of numbers could the variables a and b represent? Could they be negative? No, because you're given the algebraic inequalities $a > 0$ and that $b > \dfrac{3}{4}$. Since a and b are both positive, and $2a$ and b sum to 1, a and b must both be fractions between 0 and 1. What possible values could they represent?

Getting to the Answer:

Well, suppose b were equal to $\dfrac{3}{4}$. Then $2a$ would have to equal $\dfrac{1}{4}$ since $\dfrac{1}{4} + \dfrac{3}{4} = 1$. You're given that b is greater than $\dfrac{3}{4}$, so $2a$ must be less than $\dfrac{1}{4}$ in order for $2a$ and b to sum to 1. If $2a$ is less than $\dfrac{1}{4}$, then a is less than $\dfrac{1}{8}$. a is also a positive number, so any value for a that is greater than 0 and less than $\dfrac{3}{4}$ is correct.

You could also have picked numbers. Since b plus some positive number sum to 1, b must be less than 1, but you're given that $b > \dfrac{3}{4}$. So pick a number for b that is between $\dfrac{3}{4}$ and 1, such as $\dfrac{7}{8}$. If $b = \dfrac{7}{8}$, then $2a + \dfrac{7}{8} = 1$, $2a = \dfrac{1}{8}$, and $a = \dfrac{1}{16}$, which is greater than 0 and therefore meets the only other requirement you're given for a.

13. $\dfrac{11}{2}$ or 5.5

Difficulty: Medium

Strategic Advice: If the area of a circle is 36π its radius is 6, and if the area of a circle is 25π its radius is 5. Therefore if a circle's area is less than 36π but greater than 25π, its radius must be less than 6 but greater than 5.

Getting to the Answer:
Since the diameter of a circle is twice the radius, the diameter is less than 12 but greater than 10. There is only one integer that is less than 12 and more than 10, so the diameter must be 11. The radius of the circle must be $\dfrac{11}{2}$, or 5.5.

14. $\dfrac{4}{3}$ or 1.33

Difficulty: Medium

Strategic Advice: This one seems confusing, since you're given the value of $x + y$ over $x - y$ and asked to find $\dfrac{x}{y}$. The way to do it is to just try and solve the algebraic equation like you normally would, but try to solve it for $\dfrac{x}{y}$ rather than for x or for y.

Getting to the Answer:

Since you're given the value of a fraction, first multiply both sides of the equation by $x - y$ to get rid of the denominator. That gives you $x + y = 7(x - y)$. Is there any way of getting rid of the x's and y's and getting just $\dfrac{x}{y}$? Try dividing both sides by y:

$x + y = 7(x - y)$	Divide both sides by y.
$\dfrac{x}{y} + 1 = \dfrac{7}{y}(x - y)$	Multiply out.
$\dfrac{x}{y} + 1 = \dfrac{7x}{y} - 7$	Add 7 to both sides.
$\dfrac{x}{y} + 8 = \dfrac{7x}{y}$	Subtract $\dfrac{x}{y}$ from both sides.
$8 = \dfrac{6x}{y}$	Divide both sides by 6.
$\dfrac{8}{6} = \dfrac{x}{y}$	Reduce the fraction.
$\dfrac{4}{3} = \dfrac{x}{y}$	That's the answer!

So put $\dfrac{4}{3}$ in your grid. (And even though $\dfrac{4}{3}$ is the same as $1\dfrac{1}{3}$, don't be tempted to put $1\dfrac{1}{3}$ into the grid, since you can't grid in mixed numbers.)

15. 595

Difficulty: Medium

Strategic Advice: Problems like this are tricky because there are so many steps to take before you find the answer. Always make sure the answer is what the question is asking for before you stop working.

Getting to the Answer:

Number of voters = 80%(total union members)

$(.80)(1,500) = 1,200$

Number of voters who answered yes: = 40%(number who voted)

$(.40)(1,200) = 480$

Number of voters who didn't answer yes: =

number who voted − number who voted yes

$1,200 − 480 = 720$

Number of voters who answered no: =

numer who didn't answer yes − number who didn't respond

$720 − 125 = 595$

16. 92.50

Difficulty: Medium

Strategic Advice: Find the difference in costs between the 3-layer cake and the 6-layer cake, then use that difference to find the additional cost per layer.

Getting to the Answer:

$85.00 − 62.50 = 22.50$

$22.50 ÷ 3 = 7.50 = $ cost per layer

So, the cost for a 7-layer cake would be the cost of a 6-layer cake plus an additional layer:

$85.00 + 7.50 = 92.50$

17. 25

Difficulty: Medium

Strategic Advice: This is an example of a percent increase and/or decrease problem. Increasing 45 by P percent means adding P percent of 45 to 45, so increasing 45 by P percent results in $45 + (P\% \text{ of } 45)$ or $45 + \frac{P}{100} \times 45$,

which equals $45 + \frac{45P}{100}$. Decreasing 75 by P percent means taking P percent of 75 away from 75, so decreasing 75 by P percent results in $75 − (P\% \text{ of } 75)$ or $75 − \frac{P}{100} \times 75$ which equals $75 − \frac{75P}{100}$

Getting to the Answer:

Increasing 45 by P percent gives the same result as decreasing 75 by P percent, so you have the equation = $45 + \frac{45P}{100} = 75 − \frac{75P}{100}$. Now solve this equation for P. Subtracting 45 from both sides results in $\frac{45P}{100} = 30 − \frac{75P}{100}$.

Adding $\frac{75P}{100}$ to both sides gives you $\frac{120P}{100} = 30$. Multiplying both sides by $\frac{100}{120}$ results in $P = \frac{100}{120} \times 30 = \frac{100 \times 30}{120}$.

Canceling a factor of 30 from the top and bottom gives you

$\frac{100}{4}$ which equals 25. So $P = 25$.

18. 60

Difficulty: High

Strategic Advice: For these logic problems, try making a diagram if you are confused. Visualizing what are you are dealing with will often help to bring about the solution.

Getting to the Answer:

Solving this problem comes mainly from understanding it. The man uses five different tile colors, let's call them R, B, Y, G and P for short. We can make a diagram of all of the two-color combinations involved:

RB RY RG RP

BY BG BP

YG YP

GP

We see that there are $4 + 3 + 2 + 1 = 10$ possible tile pairings. If each is used exactly 3 times, we have $10 \times 3 = 30$ pairs, and since each pair contains 2 tiles, there are a total of $30 \times 2 = 60$ tiles used.

SECTION 5

1. D

Difficulty: Low

As written, this is a run-on sentence. Choice (D) is concise and uses the correct relative pronoun, which will be *who* in context. Choice (B) is also a run-on sentence. Choice (C) eliminates the run-on, but incorrectly uses the relative pronoun *which* to refer to Mary Cassatt, a person. Choice (E) is overly wordy and makes unnecessary use of the passive voice.

2. A

Difficulty: Medium

Each item in the list begins with a verb—*spreads, puts, makes*. This is an example of parallel structure, and the sentence is correct as written. All the other choices violate parallelism in one way or another.

3. B

Difficulty: Hard

In addition to being somewhat wordy, the underlined portion of the original sentence incorrectly uses the *-ing* form of the verb *destruct*, which specifically refers to intentionally destroying a missile or rocket after it has been launched. This makes no sense in the context of the sentence, which is about an old building. The word that is needed here is *destroy,* (B). All of the other choices are somewhat awkward or wordy revisions.

4. E

Difficulty: Medium

There is a modification problem in the original sentence. The subject *the player* should directly follow the introductory phrase that describes her. Only (D) and (E) lead with the subject, but (D) awkwardly places *right before him* in between the subject and the dragon and needlessly adds the past tense *was*. Choices (B) and (C) do not correct the modification error.

5. D

Difficulty: Medium

Parts of sentences that express similar thoughts should be written in similar ways. The sentence says that *medical schools have excelled at*…In order to make this parallel,

you need to change the underlined part of the sentence to *they have failed to* (D). (B) creates an awkward, wordy, unidiomatic sentence. (C) introduces a double negative with *failed not*. (E) creates a sentence fragment.

6. D

Difficulty: Low

This sentence is a run-on that is unnecessarily wordy and awkward. Choice (D) corrects the run-on by making the second clause dependent, and it is the most concise. Be wary of the *being* construction, as used in choice (B). It is rarely correct. Choice (C) creates a run-on. Choice (E) introduces multiple errors, including the incorrect use of a comma and the incorrect verb tense.

7. D

Difficulty: Medium

The compound subject "melodic line and tone" requires a plural verb, not the singular verb *is*. Only (D) corrects this error in agreement. The other choices result in a sentence fragment.

8. E

Difficulty: Medium

The original sentence has two problems—the use of the passive voice and an idiomatic error. The correct expression here is *founded on*, not *founded by*. Choice (E) addresses both problems. Choice (B) incorrectly uses an *-ing* verb. Choice (C) is unnecessarily wordy. And *primarily by* in (D) is idiomatically incorrect.

9. D

Difficulty: Medium

In the original sentence, the modifier is misplaced so that it seems that the Olympic Committee, not Salt Lake City, has the beautiful mountain range and heavy snowfall. Choice (D) changes the sentence to a cause/effect structure and corrects the modification error. This sentence uses the passive voice, but it is the best revision available. In (B), the verb tense is incorrect. Although technically correct, (C) is wordy and awkward, particularly with the construction "reasons for its being the choice of…" Choice (E) repeats the modification error of the original sentence.

10. A

Difficulty: Low

This sentence correctly uses a semicolon to connect two independent clauses. Choice (B) makes the second clause independent, so the semicolon is incorrect. Choices (C) and (D) create run-on sentences; (D) has an additional verb tense error. Choice (E) makes *winning ribbons* the cause and *being accomplished* the effect, rather than the other way around.

11. E

Difficulty: Medium

The original sentence is a run-on. Choice (E) makes the second clause a descriptive phrase, creating a much more concise sentence. The intervening phrase *once close to cutting its program in half* correctly modifies the *department*, and the verb *is* agrees with the subject *department*. Choice (B) adds *that*, which makes the first clause dependent, but uses the pronoun *it* in the second clause, creating a sentence structure error. Choice (C) changes the meaning by adding causality (*because it was once close to…*), which isn't logical (because the department almost cut its program it half, it is now thriving?). Choice (D) incorrectly adds the conjunction *and*. This conjunction can connect two independent clauses, but *and* indicates similarity, and these clauses actually contrast.

12. B

Difficulty: Low

The action took place in the past, and should use the simple past tense *saw* instead of the past participle of the verb (*seen*). The verbs *waiting* and *walking* are in the correct form, and the phrase *to stop traffic* is idiomatically correct.

13. A

Difficulty: Low

The phrase *no more for* is idiomatically incorrect. Instead, it should read "no more than."

14. E

Difficulty: Low

The sentence is correct as written. The verb *maintains* agrees with the singular subject *FBI* and is correctly in the present tense. The prepositions *for* and *in* correctly follow *maintains* and *interested*, respectively. The pronoun *who* clearly refers to *citizens*.

15. A

Difficulty: Low

The word *Everything* is singular despite the fact that it refers to a collection of many things, so the verb that follows it must be singular as well. The sentence should read "Everything about the case *is* strange and suspicious…" Choice (B) is concerned with transitions, (C) tests verb tense understanding, and (D) deals with creating proper prepositional phrases.

16. B

Difficulty: High

The phrase *claim hearing* is not idiomatically correct. Choice (B) should read "claim to have heard." The contrasting transition word *while* is used appropriately, as is the adverb *truly,* (D). The phrase *such a person* is idiomatically correct.

17. B

Difficulty: Medium

The action of this sentence takes place in the past, as indicated by the verbs *waited* and *traveled*. Therefore, *includes* should also be in the past tense; it should be *included*.

18. C

Difficulty: Medium

The construction *either…or* requires *or*, not *nor*.

19. D

Difficulty: Medium

A pronoun should have, and agree in number with, a clear antecedent. If, in context, it's unclear what the pronoun references, a revision is needed. In this sentence, the plural pronoun *them* incorrectly refers back to the singular noun *economic downturn*. Choice (A) is correct idiomatic use. Choices (B) and (C) are consistent, both presenting tense verbs.

20. B

Difficulty: Hard

The two parts of the sentence do not have a cause-and-effect relationship, so the word *because* is incorrect here. A conjunction like *but* should be used to show the contrast between the two ideas.

21. C

Difficulty: Hard

Don't use *that* to refer to a person; use *who* or *whom*. In this sentence, the proper form is *who*. Choices (A), (B), and (D) all test your knowledge of idiomatic phrases.

22. D

Difficulty: Medium

Like all other pronouns, possessive pronouns must have clear antecedents with which they agree in number. In this sentence, it is unclear who *he* is. Choices (A) and (C) are correct idiomatic usage. Choice (B) is appropriate use of the gerund.

23. D

Difficulty: Medium

Susan compares the home team's warm-ups to the visiting team, which is an illogical comparison. She should compare the warm-ups of both teams. Choice (D) is your answer. The phrase *liked watching*, choice (A), is correctly in the past tense. The phrase *which she* uses the correct relative pronoun, and the phrase *more interesting* works because two things are compared.

24. D

Difficulty: Low

Choice (D) uses the wrong preposition. It should be *with*, not *by*. Choice (A) correctly has an adverb modifying an adjective. Choice (B) tests verb tense, and past tense is consistent with the rest of the sentence. Choice (C) tests idiom. People are appointed to positions.

25. E

Difficulty:

This sentence has no error. Choices (A), (C), and (D) all raise various idiomatic expressions, and (B) tests your knowledge of modifying verbs with adverbs rather than adjectives.

26. C

Difficulty: High

Reversing the word order can help you find the error. Does it make sense to say, "The damaging effects of cigarette smoking *has* become recognized"? No. The plural subject *effects* takes the plural verb *have*, not the singular *has*, (C).

27. B

Difficulty: Medium

In (B), the comparative *most* should be *more*. Only two things are compared: Delia's actual performance and the performance the director wanted. In (A), the verb and subject agree, and *want…to* is the correct idiom. Choice (C) is idiomatically correct. In choice (D), the past perfect tense of *sadden* is correctly used to describe an event that had happened already in Delia's life.

28. D

Difficulty: Low

In (A), the word *herself* is used to emphasize the importance of the chef's gesture. In (B), the prepositional phrase correctly describes the grand finale. In (C), the word *that* is used correctly and the present verb tense is correct. Choice (D), however, is a past tense verb, incorrect in this present tense sentence. Every verb in a sentence should agree in tense, unless one refers clearly to a different time from the rest of the action in that sentence.

29. B

Difficulty: High

Some idioms require a particular verb tense in their construction. When used in this context, *attempt* should be followed by the infinitive verb form; *attempt at contacting* should be *attempt to contact*. (A) agrees with its plural subject *firms*. (C) agrees with the plural noun it modifies, *homeowners*. (D) is also correctly plural, since it refers to *mail-order firms*.

30. C

Difficulty: Medium

Choice (C) is a complex sentence (containing at least one independent clause and one dependent clause). It also includes the main components included in the original sentences. Choice (A) is not correct because it is not a complex sentence. It is actually a simple sentence with a compound verb. Choice (B) is not correct because, while it is a complex sentence, it contains awkward wording. Choice (D) actually conveys most of the information in the original three sentences, but it is not a complex sentences. Choice (E) is a compound sentence.

31. A

Difficulty: Hard

This passage is about the three ways students process information. This is a straight comprehension question. Choice (B) is not correct because it is not about strategies. The next paragraph might indeed be about that, but this paragraph simply introduces the processing methods. Choice (C) gives a specific accurate detail but it is not the overall main idea of the passage. Choice (D) is accurate, but not the best answer. The passage is about processing, not seeking. Choice (E) is also accurate, but does not describe the main idea presented in the passage.

32. B

Difficulty: Medium

The word *textually* simply refers to words *written in text*. Choice (A) is not correct because *in tabular form* means being presented *in a table*. Choice (C) is not correct because it refers to the words surrounding the information, not simply the idea of being written in words.

Choice (D) is another way of saying *contextually*, not *textually*. Choice (E) is not accurate because *textually* does not include *oral* formats.

33. C

Difficulty: Medium

This is a comprehension question. Based on sentence 7, auditory students would enjoy a debate (discussing the information) more so than the other options listed (reading, creating a mural, nurturance).

34. B

Difficulty: Low

This is the classic format of a five-paragraph essay (tell what you're going to tell them, tell them, tell them what you told them). The introduction introduced the three types. The body would expound upon them. The conclusion should summarize. Choice (A) is not correct because it does not embrace the idea that this was the introduction. It does not include a conclusion either. The suggestion in (C) would make the paragraphs poorly organized. Choices (D) and (E) do not include conclusions.

35. B

Difficulty: Medium

This simple phrase does improve the clarity. Choice (A) is too flowery. Choice (C) includes redundancy. Choice (D) is not as clear as *variety of ways*. Choice (E) still uses *manners*, which is not as clear as *ways*.

SECTION 6

1. C

Difficulty: Low

The important idea in this sentence is that the woman "lost herself in her work," which means it must have been *inspiring, complex,* or *absorbing*, not *exhausting* or *repetitive*. If she were really involved in her work, she would have been ignorant of the noise around her. This rules out (A) and (B); if the work were *inspiring* or *complex*, she wouldn't be *annoyed by* or *involved in* the noise. Choice (C) works: her work was so *absorbing* that she was completely oblivious to the noise.

2. A

Difficulty: Medium

This sentence has quite a bit of verbiage that you can ignore. The important thing to see is that there is a contrast between the "modern, ---- subway stations" and the "graceful curves" of the old buildings. The word in the blank, therefore, has to be something like "rectangular." Choice (A), *rectilinear,* which means "characterized by straight lines," is the only one of the choices that provides the necessary contrast.

3. C

Difficulty: Medium

"In contrast to" signals that there is a difference between the piranhas' image and the reality that many species of piranha are vegetarian. The word in the blank has to emphasize the piranha's image as a carnivore. Choice (C), *voracious*, or "greedy, ravenous, having a huge appetite," works best. *Nomadic* means "moving from place to place"; *lugubrious* means "mournful"; *covetous* means "eagerly desiring something belonging to someone else." Choice (E) might have been tempting, but the fact that piranhas seem *exotic* has nothing to do with their diet.

4.   B

Difficulty: Medium

The structural clue "while" alerts you that vetiver does not have a disruptive impact on the local ecology like kudzu does. A good prediction for the blank would then be "negative," because vetiver has "no negative effects." The only good match for this prediction among the choices is (B), *adverse*, which means "unfavorable." Vetiver clearly has *foreseeable* and *advantageous* effects because it controls soil erosion, so these choices are wrong. Choice (C), *domestic*, doesn't make sense in the sentence. Since you don't know whether kudzu's impact on the ecology is permanent, (D) doesn't fit either.

5.   B

Difficulty: Hard

Narrowing your focus helps with this sentence. Look at the phrase "patriotic and other ---- clichés." The first blank has to be a word for a category that "patriotic" falls into, such as *ideological,* choice (B). For the second blank, you can infer that in an impersonal world, relief will come from occasional "displays" of emotion. Choice (B), *ideological .. manifestations*, has what you need to fill the blanks. *Pragmatic*, (A), which means "practical," doesn't work in the first blank, and *absences* is the opposite of what we want in the second blank. *Ephemeral* means "lasting a very short time," while *vestiges* means "trace or marks left by something."

Questions 6–7

In this short Reading Comprehension passage, the author describes waking up in the early hours of the morning to start his first morning working a paper route. Before even beginning the route, the author regrets having taken on the job.

6.   D

Difficulty: Medium

The reasoning behind the author's use of a particular word or phrase can usually be found in the content that surrounds the word or phrase. In this case, the author not only mentions his alarm clock, but also points out that it "had been beeping for a while" by the time he was finally awakened by it. In other words, it had not awakened him easily. Because the author highlights these particular details,

and because the entire paragraph focuses on how painfully early the author was required to get up, it is likely the clock was mentioned to emphasize this point. Choice (A) is out of scope; just the fact that the author set his alarm does not necessarily indicate that he was thoroughly prepared for the paper route. Choice (B) is an opposite answer; the author seems to be totally unaccustomed to waking this early. Choice (C) draws on too many assumptions that are not supported by the actual details presented in the paragraph. And (E) is an irrelevant detail. While the author certainly makes this point in the paragraph, the mention of his alarm clock does not in itself do so.

7.   A

Difficulty: Medium

While inference questions ask you come to conclusions that are not actually stated in the text, you must still find detailed support in the paragraph for whatever answer choice you make. All that you can safely assume from the cited words is that the author, in his first waking moments, forgot all about his paper route. Because the paragraph emphasizes the earliness, it can be inferred that the unusual time created the author's confusion. Choice (B) is too extreme. While the author mentions "regret" over his decision to take on the paper route, it cannot be inferred that these momentary feelings reflect his *entire* opinion of his new job. Nothing in the short passage supports (C); such a general characterization of the author's personality cannot be accurately inferred from the details of this one morning. Similarly, nothing in the paragraph indicates that the author forgot about the paper route because he was "unconcerned" with the responsibilities of his new job, so (D) is incorrect. And though the author sleepily forgot about why he was awake, nothing indicates that he was confused about the specifics of the paper route, (E).

Questions 8–9

This short passage explains how the director Sergei Eisenstein influenced modern movies. He is most widely known for his use of the montage, but Eisenstein was also successful in making complex and abstract expressions accessible to the general viewing public.

8. B

Difficulty: Medium

A phrase or word can have one meaning when it is isolated from the text, as it is in the question stem, and quite another in the context of the passage. In this case, the cited words come in a sentence that not only attributes the invention of the popular montage technique to Eisenstein, but that also refers to this attribution as a "simple characterization." The correct answer must capture the idea that Eisenstein was *more* than just the creator of the montage. Choice (B) does this. Choice (A) is distortion. While the sentence as a whole underscores Eisenstein's "immense contribution to film," this reference is described as one that has served to *minimize* this influence. Choice (D) similarly distorts information from the passage. The paragraph as a whole certainly celebrates Eisenstein's important place in cinematic history, but this particular reference is used to describe how his contribution has been oversimplified. Choice (E) is an opposite answer; the cited words are used to suggest Eisenstein's influence has been somewhat minimized, not *exaggerated*.

9. D

Difficulty: Medium

Be careful on "EXCEPT" questions. All four of the wrong answers will be contained in the passage, and the correct answer will be the exception. Because the entire paragraph describes the importance of Eisenstein's films, begin by eliminating those answer choices clearly supported by evidence in the text. Choice (A) is supported by the second sentence, where the author describes Eisenstein's work as capable of clearly conveying complex images and deep plots. Choice (B) is supported by the opening sentence, where the author describes Eisenstein's use of the montage. Choice (C) is supported by the concluding sentence of the paragraph, where the author asserts that Eisenstein's audiences "could enjoy" his abstract expressions. Choice (E) is supported by the final sentence of the paragraph. This leaves (D) as the correct answer. While the author mentions that Eisenstein's films were "powerful" for the "average viewer," and that they demonstrated most viewers were capable of appreciating far more than the establishment gave them credit for, nowhere is it stated that these works made the viewers themselves more confident or powerful.

Questions 10–18

The author of this passage is interested, as the introduction alerts you, in how Arabs and Americans respond differently to spatial relationships. After introducing his subject, known as the study of proxemics, the author goes on to consider various examples of the differences between Arabs and Americans. In the second paragraph he shows how Arabs and Americans have different expectations regarding body position during a conversation. Arabs expect "involvement" when interacting with friends. This notion of involvement extends to public domains, according to the third paragraph; involvement and even intervention is expected on levels ranging from business transactions to government.

The differences are not limited to public places, as the author establishes in the last two paragraphs. Arabs arrange their homes to get large open spaces, thus creating "an environment where personalities are intermingled." They feel socially and sensorially deprived in America. This does not mean, however, that Arabs cannot attain privacy in their own homes; they do so merely by not talking. Since not talking has a completely different meaning in America, awkward situations—such as that of the Arab exchange student in Kansas—can arise out of miscommunication between members of the two cultures.

10. D

Difficulty: Low

The first question is fairly straightforward. Reading the lines directly below the phrase "two conflicting sensations" will clue you in to what sensations the author has in mind. Americans feel "compressed and overwhelmed" in public in the Middle East and "exposed" in the wide open spaces of the Arab home. Choice (D), *crowding and spaciousness*, sums up the sensations well. Choice (A) is wrong because Americans may experience *confusion* in the Middle East but the author doesn't say there is any *understanding*. *Involvement and participation* are not conflicting, nor is there any evidence to suggest that Americans feel either of the two in the Middle East. The author does not mention *friendliness and hostility*. Choice (E) may have been tempting because Americans do experience high noise levels in Arab public places, but the author doesn't talk about *silence* in the first paragraph.

11. C

Difficulty: Medium

The author uses the example of the difficulty of walking and talking with his Arab friend to highlight the difference in "position of the bodies of people in conversation from culture to culture." In other words, the author is *demonstrat[ing] that Arabs respond differently from Americans to spatial relationships,* (C). The incident with his Arab friend was not a breakthrough in his research (A), but one of his "earliest discoveries." Choice (B) is out because the author and his friend are certainly communicating with each other; the friend is merely having difficulty doing so while walking alongside the author. Although it took the author a little while to understand his friend's behavior, he does not mention this to emphasize that it is difficult to learn foreign customs (D)—the scope of (D) is far too broad (a typical wrong answer type). Finally, (E) can be eliminated because the author never mentions *American cities* in the passage.

12. E

Difficulty: High

The work you do in answering one question may help you answer another. If you had reread the second paragraph in order to answer the last question, you should have been able to pick out the correct answer here. The author's Arab friend was "unable to walk and talk at the same time" because, as the author learns, "to view another person peripherally is regarded as impolite." He doesn't *wish to seem rude*, (E). Perhaps the most tempting wrong choice was (C); it's wrong because the fact that the author's friend follows his own customs and not Western customs does not necessarily mean that he is not familiar with Western customs. There is no evidence for (A), (B), and (D) in the second paragraph or anywhere else in the passage.

13. B

Difficulty: Medium

Beware of the obvious choice, *apprehended*, which is the most common use of the word *arrested. Arrested* has a completely different meaning as it is used in the passage. From the context of the passage, it is clear that the Arab is stopping, or *delaying*, the progress of the two of them walking together by insisting on facing the author while they talk.

14. E

Difficulty: Medium

The example of intervening when two men fight is presented in the third paragraph, where the previous question also came from. Since the author is discussing the Arabs' *emphasis on public participation* in this paragraph as a whole, (E) should have jumped right out. Choices (A), (B), (C), and (D) are all reasonable-sounding answers that don't reflect the context of the passage, which just goes to show that you should always go back to check the context before picking an answer.

15. D

Difficulty: Medium

The Arab attitude toward government policy is that when a government does not intervene "when trouble is brewing," this is the same thing as taking sides. The answer to this question lies in the next sentence: it is normal for Arabs to see the actions of other governments this way because they don't understand the "cultural mold" of their own thoughts. Choice (D) is the best paraphrase of this idea. The author does not make the judgment that not taking sides is *an effective strategy,* or that the Arab approach is *simplistic,* (C). Choice (B) has things backwards: the author is talking about how Arabs misunderstand the actions of Western governments, not the other way around. Finally, (E) is out because it is too broad and sweeping (remember that wrong answer type?); the author isn't making any global statement about Middle Eastern politics.

16. D

Difficulty: Low

You don't have to go very far in paragraph 4 to realize that the word "space" keeps appearing again and again. This is indeed what the author is talking about here: the use of space inside Arab homes and how different it is from what you find in American homes. If you had a good grasp of the Big Picture, perhaps you didn't even need to re-read the paragraph, for you would know that the use of space inside of the Arab home was its general topic. All of the other choices are things that the author never mentions at all.

17. E

Difficulty: Medium

A few lines into the fifth paragraph, the author says that the Arabs' "way to be alone is to stop talking." Silence doesn't mean that "anything is wrong or that [the Arab] is withdrawing, only that he wants to be alone with his thoughts…" The best paraphrase of this among the answer choices is (E); silence is a way for Arabs to *obtain a psychological form of privacy*. The dangerous choices to be avoided are *indicate displeasure with guests* and *express unhappiness within families*, both of which are ways that silence can be used in American culture. Choice (B) especially may have been tempting because of the author's story at the end of the passage. Always be sure to read the question stem carefully.

18. C

Difficulty: Low

In the author's story, the Arab exchange student does not realize that his hosts are mad at him because silence does not mean the same thing to him as it does to them. As you know from the fifth paragraph, *silence is not considered unusual in Arab households,* (C). Although it may be true that *Arabs visiting the U.S. often experience homesickness* and that *ignoring other people is rarely an effective punishment*, the author doesn't tell his story to make either of these points. *Sense of humor* isn't discussed in the passage at all, so (D) is out. Finally, the story does show that it can be *difficult to recognize anger in foreign cultures*, but once again, this isn't what the author is trying to illustrate.

Questions 19–24

19. C

Difficulty: Low

Look for the main change the author undergoes. The passage begins with a description of what the author envisioned doing in her work at the shelter: "conducting intake interviews and traipsing around from organization to organization seeking the legal, psychological, and financial support that the women would need." At the end of the passage, she relates how her unanticipated baking endeavor made her "a more sensitive and skillful social worker." Look for a choice that expresses her changed view of social work. Choice (C) works well, because the author came to see

social work as being more diverse than she originally envisioned. Choice (A) is extreme; although the author's "reality" did differ from what she expected, the passage does not focus on her shock, but rather on how she responded to it. Choice (B) is out of scope; the passage does not address the author's psychological constraints. Choices (D) and (E) are misused details; though the bakery was for-profit, business abilities are not the focus of the passage and the fact that the author was abroad in a *developing country* is not emphasized in the passage.

20. B

Difficulty: Medium

The paragraph preceding the citation indicates that the author had spent a significant amount of time imagining her work and felt "thoroughly prepared." It is thus likely that she arrived at the shelter with a positive, confident attitude—she was eager and interested, choice (B). Choices (A) and (D) are opposites. Choice (C) is a misused detail; although she was uninformed about the actual content of her job, the author does not express this until later in the paragraph.

Choice (E) is distortion; the author was not incompetent, only unprepared to run the bakery.

21. A

Difficulty: High

The author's enthusiasm at the beginning of the second paragraph contrasts with her shock a few sentences later, when she discovers she will be in charge of the bakery. Her references to the "case studies" she researched reveal that she was initially enthusiastic about the *concept* of the bakery, not necessarily about her practical involvement in it. Choice (A) matches your prediction nicely. Choice (B) is the opposite; initially, the author felt "out of her depth" at being put in charge of the bakery. Choices (C) and (D) are distortion; initially the author had little knowledge of baking and the author only later found that the bakery "improved the women's self-esteem." Choice (E) is out of scope; the passage does not address the author's beliefs about such projects in general.

22. E

Difficulty: Low

The author believed that starting the bakery presented a "problem," and she never mentions any political experience or ambitions. We can infer that the author feels she is equally unsuited to perform either activity, choice (E). Choice (A) is extreme; the fact that the author feels "unprepared" does not mean she thinks the bakery will *never* work. Choice (B) is distortion; though the author did not expect the bakery to be part of her job, this doesn't mean she believes it should not be. Choices (C) and (D) are out of scope; the author's feelings about her coordinator are not discussed and no connection is made between the skills necessary for politics and those needed for baking bread.

23. A

Difficulty: Medium

Just before the cited sentence, the author relates one problem: she was unprepared to bake bread. In the cited sentence, the author relates a second problem: she was "completely unfamiliar with" for-profit business models. This second problem, she suggests, was the "bigger" one that might pose more of a challenge. Choice (A) is a good match. Choice (B) is distortion; the author is discussing her own comparative lack of preparation for each activity, not the relative importance of each. Choices (C) and (D) are misused details; the coordinator's confidence is mentioned in the *next* sentence, and the author does not express a belief that confidence in for-profit business models is misplaced. Also, the fact that the coordinator "left" the author does not mean she was unwilling to help, only that she did not. Choice (D) is out of scope; the passage does not compare the relative complexity of for-profit and non-profit business models.

24. E

Difficulty: High

The author makes two points in this sentence: baking improved her self-confidence as well as that of the shelter residents, and simple activities can be helpful in social work. Look for a choice that picks up on one or both of these ideas. Choice (E) is a good match. Choices (A) and (B) are distortion; the women's self-confidence and the author's rose together, but this does not mean that their self-confidence levels were initially equal. Also, although social work can be "as simple as kneading dough," this does not necessarily mean it is an easy profession for those who (unlike the author) have no education. Choices (C) and (D) are out of scope; the author's prior expectations about learning new skills are not discussed and baking is the only hands-on activity discussed.

SECTION 7

1. C

Difficulty: Medium

Strategic Advice: If a car needs 15 gallons of gas to travel 300 miles, it will need a lot more to travel 500 miles, certainly more than 16, so one thing you can do here is eliminate choice (A). Call the number of gallons you need to go 500 miles x.

Getting to the Answer:

To solve, the best thing to do is set up a proportion:

$$\frac{15 \text{ Gallon}}{300 \text{ Miles}} = \frac{x \text{ Gallons}}{500 \text{ Miles}}$$

$$\frac{15}{300} = \frac{x}{500}$$

$$300x = (15)(500)$$

$$x = 25$$

2. D

Difficulty: Medium

Strategic Advice: This problem tests your knowledge of powers and is certainly solvable by multiplying $8 \times 27 \times 64$ on your calculator and then finding the cube root of the result, but it's just as easy to do on paper.

Getting to the Answer:

8 is 2^3, 27 is 3^3, and 64 is 4^3. The equation can be rewritten as $2^3 \times 3^3 \times 4^3 = r^3$. If you remember all the rules of exponents, you'll know that $2^3 \times 3^3 \times 4^3$ can be rewritten as $(2 \times 3 \times 4)^3$. Even if you didn't remember that, you could figure it out by just multiplying out and shifting terms around:

$$2^3 \times 3^3 \times 4^3 = 2 \times 2 \times 2 \times 3 \times 3 \times 3 \times 4 \times 4 \times 4$$
$$= 2 \times 3 \times 4 \times 2 \times 3 \times 4 \times 2 \times 3 \times 4$$
$$= (2 \times 3 \times 4)^3$$

$2 \times 3 \times 4$ is 24,

$$\text{so } 24^3 = r^3$$

and $r = 24$, choice (D).

3. E

Difficulty: Medium

Strategic Advice: Here you're working with a system of equations, one of which has 2 variables and one which has 1 variable. A good way to solve this substitution.

Getting to the Answer:

If $2a = 10$, then dividing both sides by 2 gives you $a = 5$. If $a = 5$, then $a^2 - 16 = b^2$ can be written $5^2 - 16 = b^2$, or $25 - 16 = b^2$, or $9 = b^2$. If b^2 is 9, then b must be 3 or -3, and choice (E), 3, could be a value for b.

4. A

Difficulty: Medium

Strategic Advice: The sequence that you're given has 8 numbers, 4 of which are odd and 4 of which are even. You want to know how the sum of those numbers would change if the individual numbers changed by various amounts. You don't need to start adding up the numbers in the sequence—you're only concerned with how the sum would change, not what its value is.

Getting to the Answer:

There are 4 odd numbers in the sequence. The question tells you that each odd-valued term will be increased by 3. Then the sum will increase by 4×3, or 12. If each even-valued term is decreased by 2, that's the same as decreasing 4 of the terms by 2 each, or the entire sequence by 4×2, or 8. So the sum of the sequence will increase by 12 and decrease by 8. That's like adding 12 and then subtracting 8, which is the same as adding 4, choice (A).

5. E

Difficulty: Medium

Strategic Advice: If you're not sure what the various transformations of $y = x^2$ presented in the answer choices look like, you can try plugging in a few points from the graph to see which equation works. (1, 1) is a good point to test.

Getting to the Answer:

$$y = 1, x = 1$$
$$1 = 2 - (1^2)$$
$$1 = 2 - 1$$
$$1 = 1$$

Only choice (E) passes through this point.

6. E

Difficulty: Medium

Strategic Advice: You've got a bunch of lines and angles here, with a triangle in the middle. One of the interior angles of the triangle is 60°. The other 2 interior angles of the triangle are unknown, but the one on the right and the angle marked 115° make up a straight line, or 180°. That means the interior angle on the right measures 180° − 115°, or 65°. The 3 interior angles of a triangle add up to 180°, so the third interior angle of the triangle, the one on the left, must measure 180 − 60 − 65, or 55°.

Getting to the Answer:

That 55° interior angle of the triangle is on the same side of the straight line as the angle labeled $r°$, so r must be 180 − 55, or 125°. The 55° angle and the angle labeled $s°$ are vertical angles, so they are equal and $s = 55$. Therefore, $r - s = 125 - 55$, or 70, answer choice (E).

7. A

Difficulty: Medium

Strategic Advice: The date of the second Friday in December depends on what day the first of the month falls on. If the first of the month is a Friday, then the 8th of the month is also a Friday, since $1 + 7$ is 8. If the first of the month is a Tuesday, then the first Friday is the 4th, and the second Friday is the 11th.

Getting to the Answer:

If you try putting the first of the month on each of the days of the week, you'll find that the latest possible date for the first Friday occurs when the first of the month falls on a Saturday. In that case, the first Friday falls on the 7th, and the second Friday falls on the 14th, choice (A).

8. C

Difficulty: High

Strategic Advice: You want to find the ratio of the length of a side of the square to the length of a side of the triangle. You're told that the square and the triangle have equal perimeters. The perimeter of any polygon is the sum of the lengths of its sides. In an equilateral triangle, all three sides have the same length. Call the length of each side of the equilateral triangle t. Then the perimeter of equilateral triangle E is $3t$. In a square, all four sides have the same length. Call the length of each side of the square s. Then the perimeter of square S is $4s$.

Getting to the Answer:

The perimeter of the triangle and the square are equal, so $3t = 4s$. Since you want the ratio of the length of a side of the square to the length of a side of the triangle, solve the equation $3t = 4s$ for $\frac{s}{t}$. Dividing both sides of $3t = 4s$ by t results in $3 = \frac{4s}{t}$. Dividing both sides by 4 gives you $\frac{3}{4} = \frac{s}{t}$. So $\frac{s}{t} = \frac{3}{4}$ and the ratio is 3:4.

9. B

Difficulty: High

Strategic Advice: For this question you have to know not only how to read graphs, but also how to find a percent decrease.

The population in 1986 is 500,000, since the bar above 1986 reaches to 5 on the graph and the graph is in units of 100,000. The population in 1988 is 400,000. What's the percent decrease in population if it goes from 500,000 to 400,000? It's just $\frac{500,000 - 400,000}{500,000} \times 100\% = \frac{100,000}{500,000} \times 100\% = \times 100\% = 20\%$.

Getting to the Answer:

If the percent decrease in population from 1988 to 1990 is the same as the percent decrease from 1986 to 1988, then from 1988 to 1990 the population also decreased by 20%. 20% of the 1988 population was 20% of 400,000, or 80,000, so the 1990 population was $400,000 - 80,000 = 320,000$, answer choice (B).

10. E

Difficulty: Medium

Strategic Advice: Let's call Hillary's first installment x dollars. Then each of the second and third installments was also x dollars and each of her remaining nine installments was $\frac{1}{2}$ of x dollars, or $\frac{x}{2}$ dollars. Since her total payment was 600

dollars and this total was made up of 3 payments of x dollars each and 9 payments of $\frac{x}{2}$ dollars each, you can set up an equation and solve it for x.

Getting to the Answer:

$$3x + \frac{9x}{2} = 600$$

$$\frac{6x}{2} + \frac{9x}{2} = 600$$

$$\frac{15x}{2} = 600$$

$$x = \frac{2}{15}(600) = 2(40) = 80$$

Her first installment was 80 dollars.

11. D

Difficulty: Medium

Strategic Advice: You could try sketching each answer choice on a number line to see which one produces the given values. This could be somewhat time-consuming, however, so you might instead want to think about the absolute value the difference between two numbers.

Getting to the Answer:

For example, $|x - 2| < 2$ indicates that the difference between x and 2 is less than 2, and therefore that x is between 0 and 4. In this question, $|x| \geq 2$ produces the given pattern. The difference between x and 0 is greater than or equal to 2, so the selected values on the number line are less than or equal to -2 and greater than or equal to 2.

12. D

Difficulty: Medium

Strategic Advice: The line in the diagram is a vertical line, so a line perpendicular to that line will be horizontal. If you're not sure which of the answer choices represents a horizontal line, you can sketch a few points to see what each line looks like.

Getting to the Answer:

$y = 3$ is a horizontal line.

13. C

Difficulty: High

Strategic Advice: The figure shows two small triangles joined together to form a larger triangle. Since the only side you know the measure of is *AB*, it's probably a good idea to start by just looking at the triangle *ABD* and the angles of this triangle. Angle *BDC* is a right angle, and since angles *BDC* and *BDA* lie on a straight line, *BDA* must also be a right angle. You're given that angle *DAB* is 60°. Therefore, angle *ABD* must be 30° and you have a 30-60-90 right triangle. Remember that the lengths of the sides of a 30-60-90 right triangle are always in the ratio $1:\sqrt{3}:2$ *AB* is the hypotenuse, or longest side of triangle *ABD*, so it must correspond to the "2" in the $1:\sqrt{3}:2$ ratio.

Getting to the Answer:

Since $8 = 4 \times 2$, the other two sides must be 4×1, or 4, and $4 \times \sqrt{3}$, which can just be written $4\sqrt{3}$. Which side is which? The smallest side must be opposite the smallest angle, so the side with length 4 must be *AD*, which is opposite the 30° angle, and the remaining side, *BD* must measure $4\sqrt{3}$.

Now work with the other small triangle. You were given that angle *BDC* is 90° and that angle *BCD* is 45°, so angle *DBC* must also be 45°, which makes triangle *BCD* a 45-45-90 right triangle. You just figured out that *BD* measures $4\sqrt{3}$. Remember the Pythagorean ratio for 45-45-90 triangles, $1:1:\sqrt{2}$. Even if you didn't remember that one, you could probably figure out that sides *BD* and *DC* must be equal in length since they are both opposite 45° angles. So if *BD* measures $4\sqrt{3}$, then *DC* also measures $4\sqrt{3}$. The area of a right triangle is just $\frac{1}{2}$ (leg$_1$)(leg$_2$), or $\frac{1}{2} \times 16 \times 3$, or 24, choice (C).

You also could have eyeballed it. Since it's given that *AB* is 8, you could use the edge of your answer grid as a ruler to compare the lengths of *AB* and *DC*. You'd find that *DC* is a little bit shorter than *AB*, probably somewhere around 7. Compare *AB* with *BD* and notice that *BD* is also a little bit shorter than *AB*, and again guess 7 for the length of *BD*. Since *DC* is around 7 and *BD* is around 7, the area of *BCD* is around $\frac{1}{2} \times 7 \times 7$, or $\frac{1}{2} \times 49$, or $24\frac{1}{2}$, which is closest to 24, choice (C).

14. A

Difficulty: Medium

Strategic Advice: Because the figure in the problem is a square, you know that each angle of the quadrilateral measures 90 degrees. Therefore, when a corner is divided into 2 equal angles, the measure of each of those new angles is $90 \div 2$, or 45 degrees, so $s = 45$.

Getting to the Answer:

When a corner is divided into 3 equal angles, those new angles measure $90 \div 3$, or 30 degrees, so $r = 30$. The question asks for the value of $s - r$, so subtract 30 from 45, leaving 15.

15. E

Difficulty: High

Strategic Advice: Don't add up all these numbers on your calculator. There is so much calculation involved here that there must be an easier way to do the problem. Look at the sets of numbers. There are 12 elements in each set. For each element in the odd set there is a corresponding element in the even set which is 3 greater. That is 5 and 8, 7 and 10, and so on up to 27 and 30. So every element in the even set is three greater than a corresponding element in the odd set; the result of subtracting the odds from the evens will be the number of elements in the sets times 3.

Getting to the Answer:

That is, $12 \times 3 = 36$.

16. C

Difficulty: High

This is a tricky multiple figures problem. You've got a rectangle in the middle of a triangle. The only thing you know about the rectangle is that its perimeter is 12. What do you know about the triangle? One angle is a right angle and another angle is labeled 45°, so the third angle, *XYU*, must also be 45°.

Getting to the Answer:

Since *RSTU* is a rectangle, all its interior angles are right angles. Two of its interior angles, *SRU* and *STU*, lie on straight lines. That means that angles *SRX* and *STY* are also right angles. Now you have 2 small right triangles next to the rectangle. Each of these right angles has an angle that measures 45°, so the third angle in each of these triangles must also measure 45°. Now you know the measurement of every angle in the figure and can label all of them appropriately. Since *RSTU* is a rectangle, let's call line segments *ST* and *RU* l, for length. Notice that line segment *ST* is not only a side of the rectangle, but also a leg of triangle *YST*. Since *YST* is a 45-45-90, or isosceles right triangle, its legs must also be equal in length. So if *ST* is l, then *YT* is l also. If *ST* and *RU* represent the length of the rectangle, then *SR* and *TU* must represent the width of the rectangle, so you can call those 2 line segments *w*. Since *SR* is one leg of isosceles right triangle *SXR*, then *XR* must also have length *w*. Now you know the relationship between all the line segments.

Back to the perimeter. The perimeter of *RSTU* is 12, so $2(w + l) = 12$. That means that $w + l = 6$. Notice that the sides of the larger triangle, *XU* and *YU*, are also equal to $w + l$. *XU* is made up of *XR* and *RU*, which have lengths *w* and l, respectively, and *YU* is made up of *YT*, or l, and *TU*, or *w*. Since each of the legs of triangle *XYU* have length $w + l$, and $w + l = 6$, the legs of triangle *XYU* each have length 6. The area of a right triangle is $\frac{1}{2}$ the product of the lengths of the legs, or $\frac{1}{2} \times 6 \times 6$, or 18, answer choice (C).

SECTION 8

1.   D

Difficulty: Medium

The word "while" indicates that the two missing words must be opposite, or nearly opposite, in meaning. The government probably promised to make the forms easier to use, or to *simplify* them. The second blank should contrast with that, so *bewildering*, (D), is a good prediction.

The words in choice (A) don't show a contrast between the blanks. In choice (B), *shorten* works pretty well for the first blank, but *expensive* doesn't contrast with that. Be careful here; it's the taxes, not the tax forms, that people might find *expensive*. For choices (C) and (E), if the forms were *comprehensible* or *familiar*, people wouldn't need professional help.

2.   A

Difficulty: Medium

Be sure that your choice captures the full meaning of the sentence—here, several of the choices make some sense, but don't involve sounds. The sentence begins with a list of sounds. For the first blank, *loud* is a good prediction. The second blank needs to sum up this noise, so look for something that means *big noise*. Choice (A) works perfectly. In choice (B), *running* doesn't describe a sound, and *danger* doesn't fit either. (Why would trumpets and drums be dangerous?) In choice (C), a battlefield might be a *horror*, but this term doesn't capture the sounds described. In choice (D), *situation* doesn't describe the sounds, and is too neutral to fit here. Finally, for choice (E), it seems unlikely that you would find many *plodding* horses in a battle, and *calm* is the opposite of your prediction for the second blank.

3.   E

Difficulty: Medium

The sentence sets up a contrast between the short- and long-term effects of some measures. The short-term effects are positive, but the long-term effects are uncertain. Look for a choice that captures this idea. *Debated* fits well—it conveys that people don't know what the long-term effects will be, and that those effects might differ from the positive, short-term effects. In choices (A) and (C), the words bear no reflection to the increase in tourism. Choice (B) does not make sense here—*compared* with what? Similarly, with choice (D), you could say that the council *inquired into the effects*, but *inquired* by itself doesn't fit here.

4.   B

Difficulty: Medium

If you didn't know the word *improprieties*, you could probably still eliminate the four wrong answer choices. It looks like the corporation wanted the manager to ignore some shady accounting policies, so *illegal actions* is a good prediction for the second blank. The manager refused to ignore this, so he must have been maintaining his *honesty*, or (B). That makes choice (C) the opposite of the word you're looking for. In choice (A), *irregularities* fits well in the second blank, but *geniality* would not make him ignore those irregularities. *Cordiality* would not make someone ignore inconsistencies in accounting, and if the manager ignored accounting *rules*, that wouldn't indicate *frankness*. In fact, it would indicate the opposite.

5. D

Difficulty: High

The second blank must have something to do with the "few jokes," so *humor* is a good prediction. The word "though" indicates contrast, so the first blank might be *serious*. Choice (D) is a good match. In choice (A), *cleverness* and *grim* both work fine by themselves, but they don't contrast one another, so they don't work. In choice (B), it seems unlikely that the inauguration would be particularly *exciting*, but, even if it were, the word *curiosity* doesn't provide the contrast that the sentence demands. In choice (C), *humor* is great for the second blank, but *mirthful* doesn't give the contrast you need. Similarly, in choice (E), *sober* works fine, but jokes wouldn't provide *gravity*.

6. D

Difficulty: High

The aristocracy was actually "frugal," so the first blank should contrast with frugality. Choices (B) and (E) do not do this. *Luxury* and *excess* are both good predictions, making choice (D) a good match. Choices (A) and (C) are the opposite of what you're looking for.

Questions 7–19

The author of Passage 1 believes that the writer experiences his writing as an "act of discovery" that is not in his power to control. When the writer finds the proper tone of voice for his writing, he enters some sort of magical state in which "sentences mysteriously shape themselves" right before his eyes. After he is finished, he will feel "that there is an order to things, and that he himself is part of that order." The author of Passage 2, on the other hand, approaches his writing "as if it were a job like any other." He ascribes "dangerous" notions like that of the author of Passage 1 to the influence of the nineteenth-century Romantic movement. Writing to him is "hard labor with no guaranteed reward." Although being a good writer takes talent, it also requires a lot of difficult learning and, for him at least, "an enormous amount of bruising self-questioning."

7. C

Difficulty: Low

The author of Passage 1 says that unless a writer is "writing mechanically," he experiences his writing as an act of

discovery. "Mechanically" is used here in the sense of *unimaginatively,* (C). None of the other choices works in the context of the sentence.

8. E

Difficulty: Low

Reading a few lines up from the reference to "unlocking the floodgates," you find the author asserting that creative writing is "not within the power of [the writer's] will to summon forth" or to resist. When he talks about how to "unlock the floodgates," then, he is suggesting that creative writing is *in part beyond the writer's conscious control,* (E). The author of Passage 1 never says that *almost anyone* can be a writer, that writing derives its power from depicting dramatic events, or that it requires a rigid sense of structure and form. He does suggest that writing can be very difficult, (B), but not until the end of the passage.

9. C

Difficulty: Medium

The author describes his vision of what happens when the writer finds the right tone of voice for his writing: he sits and watches as sentences and paragraphs mysteriously form themselves, etc. What is being conveyed here is the writer's sense of *wonder at the seemingly magical process of creation,* (C). You probably could have picked out (C) without going back to the passage, simply by eliminating the other choices. The author of Passage 1 never talks about *frustration at the unpredictability of writing* or about *discovering an unsuspected talent*. A writer is driven by a "dim vision" and does not seem to need to *plan a project*. Writing is *hard labor* to the author of Passage 2, not the author of Passage 1.

10. A

Difficulty: Medium

Look at the context in which "dim" appears. The author is poetically describing what happens during creative writing: "…paragraphs begin to shape themselves into an organically coherent pattern that corresponds only better, much better to the dim vision which had driven him to his desk in the first place." Cutting through the flowery language, you see that the writer only has a vague idea of what he wants to write when he sits down, but things get much clearer once he starts to write. "Dim" is used in the sense of *vague,* (A).

11. A

Difficulty: Low

Re-reading the sentence at the end of the third paragraph in Passage 1 should be enough to enable you to pick out the right choice. It is the writer's search for order, according to the author, "…which exists not only in poems and stories, but in any form of writing, however humble or trivial." Choice (A) paraphrases this nicely. The other choices may seem to be plausible general reasons for referring to different forms of writing, but they don't work in the context of Passage 1.

12. B

Difficulty: Medium

As with the previous question, all of the choices here seem like plausible reasons for adopting a "professional attitude to writing." Only one can fit what the author actually says, though, which is that the only way he can "ensure a consistent output is to approach writing as if it were a job like any other." He wants to *maintain a high level of productivity,* (B).

13. D

Difficulty: Medium

The author of Passage 2 attacks the "dangerous misconceptions" that many people have about the creative process of writing. The problem, he states, is that we still believe the "fanciful notions" of the Romantic movement. "Fanciful" clearly has a negative connotation here, which makes *unrealistic* the best choice.

14. B

Difficulty: High

As we saw in the last question, the author of Passage 2 launches an attack on the Romantics and their fanciful notions about artistic creativity. His main target is Coleridge, whose work led to the belief "that the creation of art is unlike every other form of human productivity"—an idea the author doesn't agree with at all. The author is suggesting, therefore, that Coleridge's writings *propagated erroneous ideas about artistic creativity,* (B). The author himself, not Coleridge, emphasizes the *role of maturity in an artist,* so (A) is out. Choice (C) is wrong because the author thinks that Coleridge spread false ideas about art, not that Coleridge *exaggerated the importance of the arts.* Furthermore, there is no suggestion in the passage that Coleridge ignored how long it takes to learn writing skills or that he exalted experience over talent.

15. D

Difficulty: Medium

The author of Passage 2 compares writing to "breaking rocks to look for gold" in emphasizing that writing is hard work with no guaranteed reward. Looking through the answer choices, the one that echoes this sentiment most reasonably is (D). The author does think that writing requires *unusual talent,* but that has nothing to do with his analogy. Choice (B) is far too extreme, while (C) is out because the author is not considering here what other people think of writers. Nor is he concentrating on the possible rewards of writing, (E), although such rewards do, no doubt, exist.

16. D

Difficulty: High

When he says that "writers are born rather than made," the author means that some people feel compelled to write by their "response to narrative…sensitivity towards language, and…curiosity about human nature." These are *innate abilities* that *play an important role in determining who will become a writer* (D). Choice (A) contradicts the author's continual stress on writing as hard labor. Choice (B) is reasonable, but does not explain the author's statement. Choices (C) and (E) both contradict the idea that writers are born, not made; if childhood experiences make someone a writer, then a writer would be made, not born.

17. A

Difficulty: Medium

Several of the choices here look good, especially (E), until you re-read the last paragraph of Passage 2. The author criticizes the publishing world for overlooking "craft and maturity of vision" in favor of "novelty and originality." Choice (A) is therefore the right answer. None of the other choices, plausible as it may seem to be, is mentioned by the author in his criticism of the publishing world.

18. A

Difficulty: Medium

The second paragraph of Passage 1 has been the subject of several questions so far. It's the description of creative writing as a kind of blissful mystical experience in which sentences and paragraphs form before the writer's eyes. Look through the choices to see which one jumps out—you know enough at this point to predict what Passage 2's author would say. He would see this description of the writing process as overly romantic, and point out that it *does not reflect the hard work that writing involves,* (A). The author of Passage 2 doesn't give an opinion about the *musicality of words* or the *structure of a work*. His idea that writers are *born, not made* is not his main concern; the true nature of writing is. As for (D), this criticism simply doesn't apply to the description of the writing process in Passage 1.

19. E

Difficulty: High

The author of Passage 1 spends his last paragraph discussing the terror that a writer faces staring a blank page, and the fact that a writer has to be willing to risk suffering in the process of writing. The author of Passage 2 talks about the "enormous amount of bruising self-questioning" he had to undertake before he started to write. Judging from this, the two authors would agree that writing entails a lot of *emotional pain,* (E). The author of Passage 2, but not the author of Passage 1, stresses the importance of *life experience, background reading* and *maturity*. Only the author of Passage 1 emphasizes the importance of *inspiration*.

SECTION 9

1. B

Difficulty: Medium

Look for the most concise answer choice that does not introduce any additional grammatical errors. As written, this sentence is unnecessarily wordy. Choice (B) is concise and contains to errors. Choices (C), (D), and (E) are still overly wordy.

2. C

Difficulty: High

Make sure that verb tenses properly express the sequence of events in a sentence. As written, this sentence is unnecessarily wordy, and the verb phrase *would have* is inappropriate in context. Choice (C) corrects both errors. In (B), the pronoun *it* does not have a clear antecedent. Choice (D) is overly wordy, and the first person pronoun *our* is inconsistent with *Students*. Choice (E) also incorrectly uses *our*.

3. C

Difficulty: Medium

Did *the design of the interior lobby* import the marble? Of course not. This sentence contains a modifying phrase without any clear subject for the phrase to modify. Choice (C) fixes this error by adding the verb *required*, as the *design* clearly *required* imported marble. Choice (B) doesn't address the modification problem. Choices (D) and (E) change *importing* to the past tense verb *imported*, and may sound more concise, but they still indicate that the *design* imported the marble.

4. D

Difficulty: Low

The verb form *having shown* incorrectly indicates that the second clause happened before the first. Choice (D) corrects this and makes the second clause independent. Choice (B) incorrectly uses the past perfect *had been*. Choice (C) doesn't correct the fragment. Choice (E) redundantly uses the contrast transition word *but.* The relationship between the clauses has already been established with *Although* at the beginning of the sentence.

5. A

Difficulty: Medium

This sentence might sound odd, but it is grammatically correct. The transition word *Although* correctly sets up a contrast between the two clauses: many artists are left-handed, but a biological explanation for creativity is debatable. Choice (B) removes the transition word altogether, which creates a run-on sentence with a comma splice. Choice (C) illogically adds the causal word *therefore*. Choice (D) incorrectly uses the word *where*, which indicates a continued idea, not a contrast. Choice (E) starts with the word *conversely*, which would only be correct if it were preceded by a contrasting idea.

6. B

Difficulty: Medium

As written, this is a run-on created by a comma splice. Choice (B) shows the correct sequence of events (*she was slower* after her early speed *had been exciting*), and the clauses are appropriately connected by a semicolon and the contrasting word *however*. Choice (C) incorrectly joins two independent clauses with a semicolon and the coordinating conjunction *and*. It also loses the logical sequence of tenses. Choices (D) and (E) lose the logical sequence of tenses.

7. B
Difficulty: Medium

There are two problems in the original sentence: the preposition *through* is idiomatically incorrect, and *occupied* should be *occupying*. Choice (B) corrects both errors, using the idiomatically correct *in*. Choice (C) creates an awkward sentence structure and unnecessarily turns the verb *occupying* into the noun *occupation*. Choice (D) creates problems in sentence structure and meaning. It is unclear what the pronoun *it* refers to, the Earth or the sun. Choice (E), though the shortest answer, changes the meaning of the sentence, suggesting that the Earth circled, not occupied, a central position in the universe.

8. A
Difficulty: Medium

The sentence is correct as written. The two adjectives *obtrusive* and *accurate* are in parallel form. Choice (B) is wordy and creates an error in parallelism. Choices (C) and (E) incorrectly use the adverb *accurately*. Choice (D) is also not parallel.

9. C
Difficulty: Medium

The original sentence, in addition to using the passive voice, has an idiomatic error. The restaurant's success should be credited *to*, not *for*, the chef. Choice (C) changes the sentence to the active voice and is idiomatically correct with *receives credit for*. Choice (B) incorrectly uses *accredited* instead of *credited*. Choice (D) unnecessarily changes the verb tense, making for an awkward sentence. Choice (E) continues the use of the passive voice.

10. D
Difficulty: High

The opening phrase *Costing much less than imported coffee* modifies *locally grown coffee*, so *locally grown coffee* needs to immediately follow that phrase. Only (D) fixes the error.

11. E
Difficulty: Medium

The two clauses in this sentence don't contrast each other, so the conjunction *but* in the original sentence is incorrect. Choice (E) is the best revision, using the conjunction *so* to show the correct relationship between the clauses and switching the object to the subject to make a more clear and concise sentence. Choice (B) is awkward, using the preposition *of* twice. Choice (C) creates a comma splice. The pronoun *they* in (D) is ambiguous—it is not at all clear to whom *they* refers.

12. C
Difficulty: High

As written, the sentence is a run-on. You need a conjunction and the correct punctuation to connect the two clauses. Choice (C) correctly uses a comma and the coordinating conjunction *yet* to clearly express the contrasting relationship between the two clauses. Choice (B) is a run-on. Choice (D) incorrectly uses a semicolon instead of a comma. Choice (E) incorrectly uses a semicolon and *but*, a coordinating conjunction that should be used with a comma.

13. D
Difficulty: High

Look for the clearest grammatically correct answer choice. As written, this sentence is awkward. The clause after the comma is meant to elaborate on the information provided in the first clause; (D) is the clearest version. Choices (B) and (C) are not as clear as (D). Choice (E) uses grammatically incorrect structure.

14. A
Difficulty: Medium

Don't mistake complex or formal sentence structure for a grammatical error. This sentence is correct as written. Choices (B) and (E) are unnecessarily wordy. Choice (C) creates a run-on sentence. Choice (D) introduces the passive voice unnecessarily.

SAT PRACTICE TEST NINE ANSWER SHEET

Remove (or photocopy) the answer sheet, and use it to complete the practice test.

How to Take the Practice Tests

Each Practice Test includes eight scored multiple-choice sections and one essay. Keep in mind that on the actual SAT, there will be an additional multiple-choice section—the experimental section—that will not contribute to your score.

Once you start a Practice Test, don't stop until you've gone through all nine sections. Remember, you can review any questions within a section, but you may not go back or forward a section.

Good luck!

Start with number 1 for each section. If a section has fewer questions than answer spaces, leave the extra spaces blank.

Section One

Section One is the writing section's essay component.
Lined pages on which you will write your essay can be found in that section.

Section Two

1. Ⓐ Ⓑ Ⓒ Ⓓ Ⓔ
2. Ⓐ Ⓑ Ⓒ Ⓓ Ⓔ
3. Ⓐ Ⓑ Ⓒ Ⓓ Ⓔ
4. Ⓐ Ⓑ Ⓒ Ⓓ Ⓔ
5. Ⓐ Ⓑ Ⓒ Ⓓ Ⓔ
6. Ⓐ Ⓑ Ⓒ Ⓓ Ⓔ
7. Ⓐ Ⓑ Ⓒ Ⓓ Ⓔ
8. Ⓐ Ⓑ Ⓒ Ⓓ Ⓔ

9. Ⓐ Ⓑ Ⓒ Ⓓ Ⓔ
10. Ⓐ Ⓑ Ⓒ Ⓓ Ⓔ
11. Ⓐ Ⓑ Ⓒ Ⓓ Ⓔ
12. Ⓐ Ⓑ Ⓒ Ⓓ Ⓔ
13. Ⓐ Ⓑ Ⓒ Ⓓ Ⓔ
14. Ⓐ Ⓑ Ⓒ Ⓓ Ⓔ
15. Ⓐ Ⓑ Ⓒ Ⓓ Ⓔ
16. Ⓐ Ⓑ Ⓒ Ⓓ Ⓔ

17. Ⓐ Ⓑ Ⓒ Ⓓ Ⓔ
18. Ⓐ Ⓑ Ⓒ Ⓓ Ⓔ
19. Ⓐ Ⓑ Ⓒ Ⓓ Ⓔ
20. Ⓐ Ⓑ Ⓒ Ⓓ Ⓔ

right in Section Two

wrong in Section Two

Section Three

1. Ⓐ Ⓑ Ⓒ Ⓓ Ⓔ
2. Ⓐ Ⓑ Ⓒ Ⓓ Ⓔ
3. Ⓐ Ⓑ Ⓒ Ⓓ Ⓔ
4. Ⓐ Ⓑ Ⓒ Ⓓ Ⓔ
5. Ⓐ Ⓑ Ⓒ Ⓓ Ⓔ
6. Ⓐ Ⓑ Ⓒ Ⓓ Ⓔ
7. Ⓐ Ⓑ Ⓒ Ⓓ Ⓔ
8. Ⓐ Ⓑ Ⓒ Ⓓ Ⓔ

9. Ⓐ Ⓑ Ⓒ Ⓓ Ⓔ
10. Ⓐ Ⓑ Ⓒ Ⓓ Ⓔ
11. Ⓐ Ⓑ Ⓒ Ⓓ Ⓔ
12. Ⓐ Ⓑ Ⓒ Ⓓ Ⓔ
13. Ⓐ Ⓑ Ⓒ Ⓓ Ⓔ
14. Ⓐ Ⓑ Ⓒ Ⓓ Ⓔ
15. Ⓐ Ⓑ Ⓒ Ⓓ Ⓔ
16. Ⓐ Ⓑ Ⓒ Ⓓ Ⓔ

17. Ⓐ Ⓑ Ⓒ Ⓓ Ⓔ
18. Ⓐ Ⓑ Ⓒ Ⓓ Ⓔ
19. Ⓐ Ⓑ Ⓒ Ⓓ Ⓔ
20. Ⓐ Ⓑ Ⓒ Ⓓ Ⓔ
21. Ⓐ Ⓑ Ⓒ Ⓓ Ⓔ
22. Ⓐ Ⓑ Ⓒ Ⓓ Ⓔ
23. Ⓐ Ⓑ Ⓒ Ⓓ Ⓔ
24. Ⓐ Ⓑ Ⓒ Ⓓ Ⓔ

right in Section Three

wrong in Section Three

Section Four

1. Ⓐ Ⓑ Ⓒ Ⓓ Ⓔ 10. Ⓐ Ⓑ Ⓒ Ⓓ Ⓔ 19. Ⓐ Ⓑ Ⓒ Ⓓ Ⓔ 28. Ⓐ Ⓑ Ⓒ Ⓓ Ⓔ
2. Ⓐ Ⓑ Ⓒ Ⓓ Ⓔ 11. Ⓐ Ⓑ Ⓒ Ⓓ Ⓔ 20. Ⓐ Ⓑ Ⓒ Ⓓ Ⓔ 29. Ⓐ Ⓑ Ⓒ Ⓓ Ⓔ
3. Ⓐ Ⓑ Ⓒ Ⓓ Ⓔ 12. Ⓐ Ⓑ Ⓒ Ⓓ Ⓔ 21. Ⓐ Ⓑ Ⓒ Ⓓ Ⓔ 30. Ⓐ Ⓑ Ⓒ Ⓓ Ⓔ
4. Ⓐ Ⓑ Ⓒ Ⓓ Ⓔ 13. Ⓐ Ⓑ Ⓒ Ⓓ Ⓔ 22. Ⓐ Ⓑ Ⓒ Ⓓ Ⓔ 31. Ⓐ Ⓑ Ⓒ Ⓓ Ⓔ
5. Ⓐ Ⓑ Ⓒ Ⓓ Ⓔ 14. Ⓐ Ⓑ Ⓒ Ⓓ Ⓔ 23. Ⓐ Ⓑ Ⓒ Ⓓ Ⓔ 32. Ⓐ Ⓑ Ⓒ Ⓓ Ⓔ
6. Ⓐ Ⓑ Ⓒ Ⓓ Ⓔ 15. Ⓐ Ⓑ Ⓒ Ⓓ Ⓔ 24. Ⓐ Ⓑ Ⓒ Ⓓ Ⓔ 33. Ⓐ Ⓑ Ⓒ Ⓓ Ⓔ
7. Ⓐ Ⓑ Ⓒ Ⓓ Ⓔ 16. Ⓐ Ⓑ Ⓒ Ⓓ Ⓔ 25. Ⓐ Ⓑ Ⓒ Ⓓ Ⓔ 34 Ⓐ Ⓑ Ⓒ Ⓓ Ⓔ
8. Ⓐ Ⓑ Ⓒ Ⓓ Ⓔ 17. Ⓐ Ⓑ Ⓒ Ⓓ Ⓔ 26. Ⓐ Ⓑ Ⓒ Ⓓ Ⓔ 35. Ⓐ Ⓑ Ⓒ Ⓓ Ⓔ
9. Ⓐ Ⓑ Ⓒ Ⓓ Ⓔ 18. Ⓐ Ⓑ Ⓒ Ⓓ Ⓔ 27. Ⓐ Ⓑ Ⓒ Ⓓ Ⓔ

☐ # right in Section Four

☐ # wrong in Section Four

Section Five

1. Ⓐ Ⓑ Ⓒ Ⓓ Ⓔ 9. Ⓐ Ⓑ Ⓒ Ⓓ Ⓔ 17. Ⓐ Ⓑ Ⓒ Ⓓ Ⓔ
2. Ⓐ Ⓑ Ⓒ Ⓓ Ⓔ 10. Ⓐ Ⓑ Ⓒ Ⓓ Ⓔ 18. Ⓐ Ⓑ Ⓒ Ⓓ Ⓔ
3. Ⓐ Ⓑ Ⓒ Ⓓ Ⓔ 11. Ⓐ Ⓑ Ⓒ Ⓓ Ⓔ
4. Ⓐ Ⓑ Ⓒ Ⓓ Ⓔ 12. Ⓐ Ⓑ Ⓒ Ⓓ Ⓔ
5. Ⓐ Ⓑ Ⓒ Ⓓ Ⓔ 13. Ⓐ Ⓑ Ⓒ Ⓓ Ⓔ
6. Ⓐ Ⓑ Ⓒ Ⓓ Ⓔ 14. Ⓐ Ⓑ Ⓒ Ⓓ Ⓔ
7. Ⓐ Ⓑ Ⓒ Ⓓ Ⓔ 15. Ⓐ Ⓑ Ⓒ Ⓓ Ⓔ
8. Ⓐ Ⓑ Ⓒ Ⓓ Ⓔ 16. Ⓐ Ⓑ Ⓒ Ⓓ Ⓔ

☐ # right in Section Five

☐ # wrong in Section Five

If section 5 of your test book contains math questions that are not multiple choice, continue to item 9 below. Otherwise, continue to item 9 above.

9. 10. 11. 12. 13.

14. 15. 16. 17. 18.

Remove (or photocopy) this answer sheet, and use it to complete the practice test.

Start with number 1 for each section. If a section has fewer questions than answer spaces, leave the extra spaces blank.

Section Six

1. Ⓐ Ⓑ Ⓒ Ⓓ Ⓔ	9. Ⓐ Ⓑ Ⓒ Ⓓ Ⓔ	17. Ⓐ Ⓑ Ⓒ Ⓓ Ⓔ
2. Ⓐ Ⓑ Ⓒ Ⓓ Ⓔ	10. Ⓐ Ⓑ Ⓒ Ⓓ Ⓔ	18. Ⓐ Ⓑ Ⓒ Ⓓ Ⓔ
3. Ⓐ Ⓑ Ⓒ Ⓓ Ⓔ	11. Ⓐ Ⓑ Ⓒ Ⓓ Ⓔ	19. Ⓐ Ⓑ Ⓒ Ⓓ Ⓔ
4. Ⓐ Ⓑ Ⓒ Ⓓ Ⓔ	12. Ⓐ Ⓑ Ⓒ Ⓓ Ⓔ	20. Ⓐ Ⓑ Ⓒ Ⓓ Ⓔ
5. Ⓐ Ⓑ Ⓒ Ⓓ Ⓔ	13. Ⓐ Ⓑ Ⓒ Ⓓ Ⓔ	21. Ⓐ Ⓑ Ⓒ Ⓓ Ⓔ
6. Ⓐ Ⓑ Ⓒ Ⓓ Ⓔ	14. Ⓐ Ⓑ Ⓒ Ⓓ Ⓔ	22. Ⓐ Ⓑ Ⓒ Ⓓ Ⓔ
7. Ⓐ Ⓑ Ⓒ Ⓓ Ⓔ	15. Ⓐ Ⓑ Ⓒ Ⓓ Ⓔ	23. Ⓐ Ⓑ Ⓒ Ⓓ Ⓔ
8. Ⓐ Ⓑ Ⓒ Ⓓ Ⓔ	16. Ⓐ Ⓑ Ⓒ Ⓓ Ⓔ	24. Ⓐ Ⓑ Ⓒ Ⓓ Ⓔ

☐ # right in Section Six

☐ # wrong in Section Six

Section Seven

1. Ⓐ Ⓑ Ⓒ Ⓓ Ⓔ	9. Ⓐ Ⓑ Ⓒ Ⓓ Ⓔ
2. Ⓐ Ⓑ Ⓒ Ⓓ Ⓔ	10. Ⓐ Ⓑ Ⓒ Ⓓ Ⓔ
3. Ⓐ Ⓑ Ⓒ Ⓓ Ⓔ	11. Ⓐ Ⓑ Ⓒ Ⓓ Ⓔ
4. Ⓐ Ⓑ Ⓒ Ⓓ Ⓔ	12. Ⓐ Ⓑ Ⓒ Ⓓ Ⓔ
5. Ⓐ Ⓑ Ⓒ Ⓓ Ⓔ	13. Ⓐ Ⓑ Ⓒ Ⓓ Ⓔ
6. Ⓐ Ⓑ Ⓒ Ⓓ Ⓔ	14. Ⓐ Ⓑ Ⓒ Ⓓ Ⓔ
7. Ⓐ Ⓑ Ⓒ Ⓓ Ⓔ	15. Ⓐ Ⓑ Ⓒ Ⓓ Ⓔ
8. Ⓐ Ⓑ Ⓒ Ⓓ Ⓔ	16. Ⓐ Ⓑ Ⓒ Ⓓ Ⓔ

☐ # right in Section Seven

☐ # wrong in Section Seven

Section Eight

1. Ⓐ Ⓑ Ⓒ Ⓓ Ⓔ	9. Ⓐ Ⓑ Ⓒ Ⓓ Ⓔ	17. Ⓐ Ⓑ Ⓒ Ⓓ Ⓔ
2. Ⓐ Ⓑ Ⓒ Ⓓ Ⓔ	10. Ⓐ Ⓑ Ⓒ Ⓓ Ⓔ	18. Ⓐ Ⓑ Ⓒ Ⓓ Ⓔ
3. Ⓐ Ⓑ Ⓒ Ⓓ Ⓔ	11. Ⓐ Ⓑ Ⓒ Ⓓ Ⓔ	19. Ⓐ Ⓑ Ⓒ Ⓓ Ⓔ
4. Ⓐ Ⓑ Ⓒ Ⓓ Ⓔ	12. Ⓐ Ⓑ Ⓒ Ⓓ Ⓔ	
5. Ⓐ Ⓑ Ⓒ Ⓓ Ⓔ	13. Ⓐ Ⓑ Ⓒ Ⓓ Ⓔ	
6. Ⓐ Ⓑ Ⓒ Ⓓ Ⓔ	14. Ⓐ Ⓑ Ⓒ Ⓓ Ⓔ	
7. Ⓐ Ⓑ Ⓒ Ⓓ Ⓔ	15. Ⓐ Ⓑ Ⓒ Ⓓ Ⓔ	
8. Ⓐ Ⓑ Ⓒ Ⓓ Ⓔ	16. Ⓐ Ⓑ Ⓒ Ⓓ Ⓔ	

☐ # right in Section Eight

☐ # wrong in Section Eight

Section Nine

1. Ⓐ Ⓑ Ⓒ Ⓓ Ⓔ	9. Ⓐ Ⓑ Ⓒ Ⓓ Ⓔ
2. Ⓐ Ⓑ Ⓒ Ⓓ Ⓔ	10. Ⓐ Ⓑ Ⓒ Ⓓ Ⓔ
3. Ⓐ Ⓑ Ⓒ Ⓓ Ⓔ	11. Ⓐ Ⓑ Ⓒ Ⓓ Ⓔ
4. Ⓐ Ⓑ Ⓒ Ⓓ Ⓔ	12. Ⓐ Ⓑ Ⓒ Ⓓ Ⓔ
5. Ⓐ Ⓑ Ⓒ Ⓓ Ⓔ	13. Ⓐ Ⓑ Ⓒ Ⓓ Ⓔ
6. Ⓐ Ⓑ Ⓒ Ⓓ Ⓔ	14. Ⓐ Ⓑ Ⓒ Ⓓ Ⓔ
7. Ⓐ Ⓑ Ⓒ Ⓓ Ⓔ	
8. Ⓐ Ⓑ Ⓒ Ⓓ Ⓔ	

☐ # right in Section Nine

☐ # wrong in Section Nine

Practice Test Nine

SECTION 1
Time—25 Minutes

Essay

The essay gives you an opportunity to show how effectively you can develop and express ideas. You should, therefore, take care to develop your point of view, present your ideas logically and clearly, and use language precisely.

Your essay must be written in your Answer Grid Booklet—you will receive no other paper on which to write. You will have enough space if you write on every line, avoid wide margins, and keep your handwriting to a reasonable size. Remember that people who are not familiar with your handwriting will read what you write. Try to write or print so that what you are writing is legible to those readers.

You have twenty-five minutes to write an essay on the topic assigned below.

DO NOT WRITE ON ANOTHER TOPIC. AN OFF-TOPIC ESSAY WILL RECEIVE A SCORE OF ZERO.

Think carefully about the issue presented in the following excerpt and the assignment below.

> "If you would thoroughly know anything, teach it to others. One who ceases to learn cannot adequately teach."
>
> —Tryon Edwards, *Dictionary of Thoughts*

Assignment: Do you think that teaching something to another person can help you to learn or master a subject or process? Plan and write an essay in which you develop your point of view on this issue. Support your position with reasoning and examples taken from your reading, studies, experience, or observations.

DO NOT WRITE YOUR ESSAY IN YOUR TEST BOOK.
You will receive credit only for what you write in your Answer Grid Booklet.

KAPLAN
Test Prep and Admissions

SECTION 2

Time—25 Minutes

20 Questions

Directions: For this section, solve each problem and decide which is the best of the choices given. Fill in the corresponding oval on the answer sheet. You may use any available space for scratchwork.

Notes:

(1) Calculator use is permitted.

(2) All numbers used are real numbers.

(3) Figures are provided for some problems. All figures are drawn to scale and lie in a plane UNLESS otherwise indicated.

(4) Unless otherwise specified, the domain of any function f is assumed to be the set of all real numbers x for which $f(x)$ is a real number.

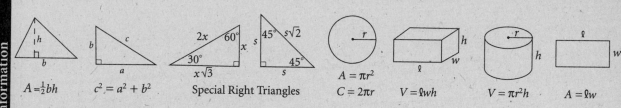

$A = \frac{1}{2}bh \qquad c^2 = a^2 + b^2 \qquad$ Special Right Triangles $\qquad A = \pi r^2 \qquad V = \ell w h \qquad V = \pi r^2 h \qquad A = \ell w$

$C = 2\pi r$

The sum of the degree measures of the angles in a triangle is 180.

The number of degrees of arc in a circle is 360.

A straight angle has a degree measure of 180.

1. A caterer has 120 slices of bread, 75 slices of ham, and 75 slices of cheese. If she needs to make sandwiches each consisting of 2 slices of bread, 1 slice of ham, and 1 slice of cheese, what is the greatest number of sandwiches she can make?

   (A) 60
   (B) 65
   (C) 75
   (D) 90
   (E) 120

2. If $x = 1$ and $y = -1$, then $x^2 + 2xy + y^2 =$

   (A) −1
   (B)   0
   (C)   1
   (D)   2
   (E)   4

GO ON TO THE NEXT PAGE

3. In the figure above, 6 gears are placed next to each other such that if one gear turns, all the gears turn. If gear A is turned clockwise, how many of the 6 gears will turn counterclockwise?

(A) 1
(B) 2
(C) 3
(D) 4
(E) 5

Questions 4 and 5 refer to the following graphs.

EMPLOYEES BY DEPARTMENT AT COMPANY X
100% = 800 employees

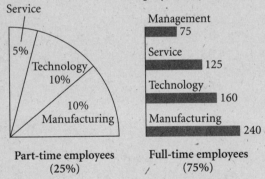

Part-time employees
(25%)

Full-time employees
(75%)

4. According to the graphs above, the total number of full-time employees is how many more than the total number of part-time employees at Company X?

(A) 100
(B) 200
(C) 300
(D) 400
(E) 500

5. What percent of all employees at Company X work in the manufacturing department?

(A) 40%
(B) 37.5%
(C) 35%
(D) 30%
(E) 25%

6. If Maurice has $80.00, and he spends $32.45 on clothes and gives $27.55 to his sister, what fraction of the original $80.00 does Maurice have left?

(A) $\frac{1}{5}$

(B) $\frac{1}{4}$

(C) $\frac{3}{10}$

(D) $\frac{1}{2}$

(E) $\frac{3}{5}$

7. If $x^2 - 4x - 12 = 0$, what is the value of $2x^2 - 8x$?

(A) 0
(B) 4
(C) 12
(D) 16
(E) 24

8. A "factor-rich" integer is defined as one for which the sum of its positive factors, not including itself, is greater than itself. Which of the following is a "factor-rich" integer?

(A) 6
(B) 8
(C) 9
(D) 10
(E) 12

GO ON TO THE NEXT PAGE

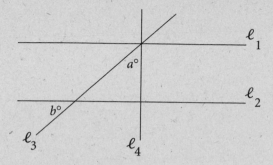

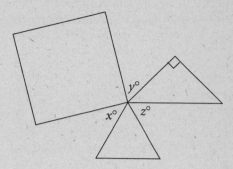

Note: Figure not drawn to scale.

9. In the figure above, if ℓ_1 is parallel to ℓ_2 and ℓ_4 is perpendicular to ℓ_2, which of the following must be true?

    I. $\ell_1 \perp \ell_4$
    II. $a = b$
    III. $a + b = 90$

    (A) I only

    (B) II only

    (C) I and II only

    (D) I and III only

    (E) II and III only

10. A bicyclist riding at 12 miles an hour for 2 hours travels twice the distance a hiker travels walking at 4 miles an hour for how many hours?

    (A) 2

    (B) 3

    (C) 4

    (D) 5

    (E) 6

11. Which of the following conditions would make $2a - 2b < 0$?

    (A) $a = b$

    (B) $a > 0$

    (C) $b > 0$

    (D) $a < b$

    (E) $a > b$

12. In the figure above, a square, an isosceles right triangle, and an equilateral triangle share the common point D. What is the value of $x + y + z$?

    (A) 165

    (B) 170

    (C) 175

    (D) 185

    (E) 195

13. If a and b are integers and $2a + 5b = 15$, which of the following CANNOT be a value of b?

    (A) −1

    (B) 1

    (C) 2

    (D) 3

    (E) 5

14. If $-1 < y < 0$, which of the following is the greatest?

    (A) y^2

    (B) $1 - y$

    (C) $1 + y$

    (D) $2y$

    (E) $\dfrac{1}{y + 2}$

GO ON TO THE NEXT PAGE

15. If set A is {3, 5, 7, 11, 19} and set B consists of all the even numbers between 1 and 11, how many elements are in the union of the two sets?

(A) 0
(B) 10
(C) 11
(D) 19
(E) 30

16. A certain company employs 25 women and 25 men. Some employees drive to work and the rest take public transportation. If 29 employees drive to work, and exactly 6 men take public transportation, how many women drive to work?

(A) 6
(B) 8
(C) 10
(D) 11
(E) 13

17. Jackie wants to place some photographs into her photo album and discovers that pages 10 through 25, including 10 and 25, are unfilled. If she can place 4 photographs on each unfilled page, what is the total number of photographs she can place on these pages?

(A) 68
(B) 64
(C) 60
(D) 16
(E) 15

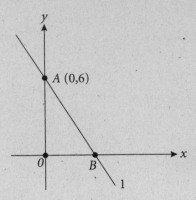

18. In the figure above, if the slope of line l is $-\frac{3}{2}$, what is the area of triangle AOB?

(A) 24
(B) 18
(C) 16
(D) 14
(E) 12

NOON TEMPERATURE READING IN CITY X in Degrees Fahrenheit	
Monday	67
Tuesday	71
Wednesday	72
Thursday	73
Friday	76

19. The noon temperature for each of the first five days of a given week is recorded in the table above. If the median noon temperature for the whole week was 73 degrees Fahrenheit, which of the following could have been the respective noon temperatures, in degrees Fahrenheit, for Saturday and Sunday of the same week?

(A) 68 and 72
(B) 69 and 71
(C) 70 and 77
(D) 72 and 74
(E) 74 and 77

GO ON TO THE NEXT PAGE ⇨

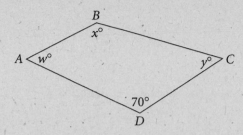

Note: Figure not drawn to scale.

20. In quadrilateral ABCD above, if $x < 45$, which of the following describes all the possible values and only the values for $w + y$?

(A) $115 < w + y < 360$

(B) $115 < w + y < 290$

(C) $185 < w + y < 360$

(D) $245 < w + y < 290$

(E) $245 < w + y < 360$

SECTION 3
Time—25 Minutes
24 Questions

Directions: For each of the following questions, choose the best answer and darken the corresponding oval on the answer sheet.

Each sentence below has one or two blanks, each blank indicating that something has been omitted. Beneath the sentence are five words or sets of words labeled (A) through (E). Choose the word or set of words that, when inserted in the sentence, best fits the meaning of the sentence as a whole.

EXAMPLE:

Today's small, portable computers contrast markedly with the earliest electronic computers, which were ----.

(A) effective
(B) invented
(C) useful
(D) destructive
(E) enormous

---

1. The British social philosopher Thomas Malthus predicted that population growth would eventually ---- world food production, resulting in massive famine and political unrest.

   (A) pressure
   (B) forbid
   (C) resist
   (D) surpass
   (E) confront

2. While ---- a belief in intellectual discussion, Dr. Brown brooked no deviation from his ideas and cut off anyone who did not ---- .

   (A) regretting . . agree
   (B) admitting . . debate
   (C) professing . . concur
   (D) avowing . . question
   (E) abandoning . . protest

3. Employers often find that even if wage increases can be ---- over a particular period of serious economic difficulties, dissatisfaction is built up and demands are merely ----, not canceled.

   (A) abolished . . satisfied
   (B) realized . . increased
   (C) overturned . . redressed
   (D) requested . . relinquished
   (E) moderated . . postponed

4. Though the Greek author Thucydides used psychological insight rather than documented information to ---- speeches to historical figures, he is still considered an impartial and ---- historian.

   (A) dictate . . endless
   (B) transmit . . illustrious
   (C) disseminate . . relevant
   (D) attribute . . accurate
   (E) promote . . inventive

GO ON TO THE NEXT PAGE

5. Readers previously ---- by the complexity and ---- of Joyce's *Ulysses* will find Gilbert's study of the novel a helpful introduction.

   (A) charmed . . obscurity
   (B) rejected . . length
   (C) inhibited . . intelligibility
   (D) daunted . . allusiveness
   (E) enlightened . . transparency

6. Aware that the pace of construction had slowed, but unwilling to risk ---- the wrath of their superiors, the project managers continued to ---- that the highway extension would be completed on schedule.

   (A) comprehending . . prove
   (B) divulging . . argue
   (C) incurring . . maintain
   (D) predicting . . assert
   (E) detecting . . believe

7. Though she earned her ---- as a muralist, the artist felt that she ---- more acclaim for her sculpture.

   (A) anonymity . . escaped
   (B) reputation . . deserved
   (C) fame . . deferred
   (D) distinction . . justified
   (E) notoriety . . publicized

8. As a young man, Thomas Merton underwent a religious conversion, gradually changing from ---- to a devout Roman Catholic.

   (A) an archetype
   (B) a bibliophile
   (C) a martinet
   (D) an aesthete
   (E) an agnostic

GO ON TO THE NEXT PAGE

Directions: The passages below are followed by questions based on their content; questions following a pair of related passages may also be based on the relationship between the paired passages. Answer the questions on the basis of what is <u>stated</u> or <u>implied</u> in the passages and in any introductory material that may be provided.

Questions 9–10 are based on the following passage.

The librarian raised his brow as he found the evidence in my bag. I stood before him, a college student who refused to shave, sporting a black beret and dark glasses. I wanted to follow my
(5) parents' example; they had fought the Communists in Russia by running an underground museum. None of this mattered to my accuser. He simply removed the book from my bag and reminded me in his purple air that "one does not take books
(10) from the Bodleian Library at the University of Oxford—not even Her Majesty the Queen possesses borrowing privileges." I walked away, but not before proclaiming, "This library is an evil institution like the Soviet Union, and I am
(15) attempting to liberate information!"

9. It can be inferred from the passage that the author believes that the Bodleian Library

    (A) has rules similar to the Soviet Union's

    (B) confines information

    (C) is aligned with Communists

    (D) should be open to the public

    (E) should retain its policy on borrowing privileges

10. The description of the librarian as having a "purple air" (line 9) suggests that

    (A) the librarian was arrogant in his attitude toward the author

    (B) the author thought the librarian was intimidating

    (C) the librarian was intent on humiliating the author

    (D) the librarian was irate

    (E) the librarian associated himself with the royal family

Questions 11–12 refer to the passage below.

Although not quite as famously endemic of the Everglades as the American crocodile, the far more endearing manatee is perhaps more symbolic of the unique wildlife found in this vast tropical
(5) swamp. In particular, the manatees found in the Florida Everglades, though occasionally observed in unprotected waterways in the northern regions of the state, are rarely found anywhere else in the country. This manatee concentration in southern
(10) Florida is not surprising, given the fact that swimming in water even a single degree colder than 68° Fahrenheit can be fatal to these bulbous, slow, and exceedingly fragile creatures.

11. The author's characterization of the manatee as "more symbolic" (line 3) of the Everglades than the crocodile suggests that

    (A) the manatee is actually more famous than the American crocodile

    (B) the manatee has more endearing qualities than the American crocodile

    (C) the American crocodile is less endemic of the Everglades than many assume

    (D) the Everglades are a better habitat for manatees than American crocodiles

    (E) the Everglades are not necessarily the American crocodile's primary habitat

12. The author describes the manatee as all of the following EXCEPT

    (A) capable of invoking affection

    (B) native to the Florida Everglades

    (C) rather bloated looking

    (D) representative of the Everglades

    (E) living a tenuous existence

GO ON TO THE NEXT PAGE

Questions 13–24 are based on the following passage.

The following passage was excerpted from an essay in an academic journal on the origins of art.

Most of human prehistory has left behind no convincing trace of art at all. Perhaps our remote ancestors painted their bodies, but if that was the first art, it wouldn't have survived for us to know (5) about. The first preserved art developed more or less simultaneously in Europe, Africa, and Australia, with some further recent discoveries of old art in Asia and the Americas as well. Early art itself assumed many forms, ranging from wood- and (10) bone-carving, engraving, bas relief, and three-dimensional sculpture to painting and music. Best known to modern Europeans are the cave paintings of so-called Cro-Magnon people in France and Spain, living in the era termed the Paleolithic (15) (from about 40,000 to 10,000 years ago). Those cave paintings rivet our attention not only because they include great art by any standard, but also because of the obvious questions that flash out. What sort of people were those painters? What (20) motivated them to paint and why did they do it in caves?

Upon entering the larger caves in France, the answer seems obvious. The long, high, silent corridors of Gargas and Rouffignac fill the viewer with (25) awe, while the riot of colored stalactites and stalagmites in Cougnac stuns us with its beauty. Probably Cro-Magnon spelunkers* explored for the same reasons. In that respect, as in so many others, they were like modern humans, whereas (30) their predecessors, the Neanderthals—like modern apes—rarely penetrated the caves beyond the zone of sunlight. We think of cave art as made by "cavemen," a term that immediately evokes images of hairy brutes, partly draped in animal furs. In fact, (35) the Cro-Magnons lived far from caves, as well as within them; we think of them as cavemen only because the garbage they left in caves is more likely to have been preserved than other artifacts. From their garbage, burials, and art, we know that

(40) they had needles, buttons, sewn clothing, and parkas and were probably as warmly dressed as modern Eskimos. They marked their caves with trail signs termed claviforms, which warned Cro-Magnon tourists to stay on the right hand side of (45) wide passages, to look for art in concealed niches, and to avoid bumping their heads in places with low ceilings. Their footprints are still on the cave floor, their handprints and marks of their scaffolding still on the cave walls. Visiting some of the (50) sites, you get the vivid sense that the artists had walked off the job only yesterday.

Like modern art, Cro-Magnon art varies widely in quality, even within the same cave chamber. Some of it impresses us as great, some as amateur-(55) ish. Professional artists visiting the caves often point out the sophisticated techniques by which some Cro-Magnon artists succeeded in conveying a sense of scale, motion, and perspective. Exquisite pieces such as the clay bison and the carved (60) wrestling ibex from Tuc d'Audoubert achieve their expressiveness with an economy of line and shape. Especially notable is the obviously intentional exploitation of irregular cave surfaces to transform some cave paintings into three-dimensional (65) compositions. Most of the larger cave paintings depict animals rather than people. Archeologists used to believe that the paintings were of the animal species most often hunted. We now realize that although the most frequently painted animals (70) —horses and bison—were indeed hunted, they account for a much higher proportion of painted animals than of the hunter's bag. Today's art provides the answer to this puzzle; the animals we prefer to depict aren't the ones that we most often (75) eat, use, or encounter.

But why did the Cro-Magnons create cave art in the first place? Archeologists used to debate various functional interpretations: that the paintings represented mindless copies of nature by savage (80) people, or magical rites to ensure success at hunting or depictions of myths, and so on. Such unitary theories fell into disfavor as anthropologists began to ask contemporary aboriginal Australians and bushmen why they create their own rock art.

GO ON TO THE NEXT PAGE ▷

(85) The reasons turned out to be ones that any future art historian would be very unlikely to deduce.

The same image—for example, a fish painted by aboriginal Australians—proves to have been painted for different reasons on different occasions. *(90)* Some fish paintings serve to mark a tribal territory, others tell a story ("I caught this big fish"), still others spring from the traces of shamans. It shouldn't surprise us that the Cro-Magnons' motives may have been equally diverse, given all *(95)* the evidence for their modern mentality.

   * spelunker: modern term for an amateur cave explorer

13. In line 3, the author most likely mentions body-painting in order to suggest that

   (A) the use of paint began earlier than is commonly believed

   (B) the earliest forms of art are probably lost to our knowledge

   (C) art served many different functions in prehistoric society

   (D) cave paintings were not the most common form of prehistoric art

   (E) prehistoric hunters used body art as a form of hunting magic

14. According to the author, the Cro-Magnon cave paintings "rivet our attention" (line 16) because they

   (A) provide insight into the origins of modern art

   (B) raise questions about when the first art was created

   (C) stimulate curiosity about the people who created them

   (D) depict people and animals that we know nothing about

   (E) cast doubt on common assumptions about our remote ancestors

15. In lines 23–28, the author suggests that Cro-Magnon people painted in caves because caves

   (A) accommodated even the largest paintings

   (B) provided inspiring settings for their work

   (C) sheltered the paintings from the elements

   (D) offered the privacy that painters needed

   (E) protected the paintings from human damage

16. The word "riot" in line 25 can best be taken to mean

   (A) profusion

   (B) disorder

   (C) brawl

   (D) interaction

   (E) violence

17. According to the author, the term "cavemen" (lines 32–33) evokes a misleading image of Cro-Magnon people as

   (A) less advanced than the Neanderthals

   (B) more dependent on animals than is normally assumed

   (C) incapable of building their own dwellings

   (D) more primitive than they actually were

   (E) capable of great brutality toward animals

18. It can be inferred from lines 36–38 that more Cro-Magnon artifacts have been found in caves than elsewhere primarily because

   (A) the majority of Cro-Magnon people lived in caves

   (B) artifacts in other locations are more likely to have decayed

   (C) trail signs led archeologists to many cave sites

   (D) archeologists are more likely to study cave sites

   (E) Cro-Magnon people used caves as storehouses

GO ON TO THE NEXT PAGE

19. In line 62, "notable" most nearly means

(A) infamous

(B) conspicuous

(C) important

(D) glaring

(E) remarkable

20. The phrase "they account for…hunter's bag" (lines 70–72) suggests that the animals most often depicted in cave paintings

(A) were not hunted by Cro-Magnon people

(B) played an important role in hunting rituals

(C) represented important figures in Cro-Magnon mythology

(D) were not the ones most often hunted by Cro-Magnons

(E) were misleadingly shown surrounded by human hunters

21. Which best captures the meaning of the phrase "functional interpretations" in line 78?

(A) definitions

(B) analogies

(C) philosophies

(D) explanations

(E) techniques

22. According to paragraph 4, the theories mentioned in lines 78–82 "fell into disfavor" when scientists discovered that

(A) the Cro-Magnons were more advanced than the Neanderthals

(B) the rock art produced today serves several different functions

(C) many painted images were used by the Cro-Magnons as trail signs

(D) Cro-Magnon paintings were identical to the work of present-day Australian aborigines

(E) images of animals were associated with hunting rituals

23. The author's main goal in describing Cro-Magnon art and artifacts is to show that the Cro-Magnon people of France and Spain were

(A) more advanced than their contemporaries in other places

(B) dependent on hunting far more than on agriculture

(C) not the same people who are commonly called "cavemen"

(D) artistically more sophisticated than many later civilizations

(E) surprisingly similar in many ways to modern humans

24. The primary purpose of this passage is to

(A) compare the artistic motives of the Cro-Magnons to that of aboriginal Australians and bushmen

(B) teach about the eating and hunting habits of the Cro-Magnons as opposed to current man

(C) detail the history of the Cro-Magnons

(D) compliment the skilled artistic work of the Cro-Magnons

(E) explore an early form of art and what it says about its creators

IF YOU FINISH BEFORE TIME IS CALLED, YOU MAY CHECK YOUR WORK ON THIS SECTION ONLY. DO NOT TURN TO ANY OTHER SECTION IN THE TEST. **STOP**

SECTION 4

Time—25 Minutes
35 Questions

Directions: For each question in this section, select the best answer from among the choices given and fill in the corresponding oval on the answer sheet.

The following sentences test correctness and effectiveness of expression. Part of each sentence or the entire sentence is underlined; beneath each sentence are five ways of phrasing the underlined material. Choice (A) repeats the original phrasing; the other four choices are different. If you think the original phrasing produces a better sentence than any of the alternatives, select choice (A); if not, select one of the other choices.

In making your selection, follow the requirements of standard written English; that is, pay attention to grammar, choice of words, sentence construction, and punctuation. Your selection should result in the most effective sentence—clear and precise, without awkwardness or ambiguity.

EXAMPLE:

ANSWER:

Every apple in the baskets <u>are ripe and labeled according to the date it was picked</u>.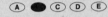

(A) are ripe and labeled according to the date it was picked
(B) is ripe and labeled according to the date it was picked
(C) are ripe and labeled according to the date they were picked
(D) is ripe and labeled according to the date they were picked
(E) are ripe and labeled as to the date it was picked

1. My father worked his way through <u>law school attending classes in the day</u> and waiting tables at a restaurant at night.

   (A) law school attending classes in the day
   (B) law school; attending classes all day
   (C) law school, he attended classes in the day
   (D) law school, attending classes in the day
   (E) law school, having attended classes in the day

2. Although my alarm clock did not go off, <u>causing me to arrive no more</u> than ten minutes late.

   (A) causing me to arrive no more
   (B) and yet I arrived no more
   (C) it did not cause me to arrive more
   (D) and it did not cause me to arrive more
   (E) yet causing me to arrive no more

3. <u>The magazine, once close to losing all its assets, is</u> now a thriving and popular enterprise.

   (A) The magazine, once close to losing all its assets, is
   (B) The magazine was once close to losing all its assets, it is
   (C) The magazine that once having been close to losing all its assets is
   (D) The magazine, because it was once close to losing all its assets, is
   (E) The magazine was once close to losing all its assets, and it is

GO ON TO THE NEXT PAGE

4. Celia was skeptical at the beginning of the lecture, <u>having shown great interest once the professor's talk gathered</u> some steam.

   (A) having shown great interest once the professor's talk gathered

   (B) but showing great interest once the professor's talk gathered

   (C) however she showed great interest once the professor's talk gathered

   (D) but she showed great interest once the professor's talk gathered

   (E) once she showed great interest when the professor's talk gathered

5. A White House internship pays little, <u>but one that does provide</u> valuable experience.

   (A) but one that does provide

   (B) but that does provide

   (C) but it does provide

   (D) however providing

   (E) however that does provide

6. High-speed digital cable, once considered too expensive for widespread <u>home computer use, it is now priced</u> to compete with standard dial-up services.

   (A) home computer use, it is now priced

   (B) home computer use, is now priced

   (C) home computer use, and now priced

   (D) home computer use, since being priced

   (E) home computer use, when it was priced

7. Punctuality is considered a very important trait <u>in the United States, in other cultures, it is not unusual for people to arrive</u> as much as an hour late for a scheduled appointment.

   (A) in the United States, in other cultures, it is not unusual for people to arrive

   (B) in the United States, but in other cultures, it is not unusual for people to arrive

   (C) in the United States, so in other cultures, it is not unusual for people to arrive

   (D) in the United States, it is not unusual for people in other cultures to arrive

   (E) in the United States, in other cultures, it is not unusually for people to arrive

8. The United States Department of Education subsidizes <u>educational loans they will deliver the funds directly to your school to pay your tuition</u>.

   (A) educational loans they will deliver the funds directly to your school to pay your tuition

   (B) educational loans; they will deliver the funds directly to your school to pay your tuition

   (C) funds delivered directly to your school to pay your tuition in the form of educational loans

   (D) educational loans and that can be delivered directly to your school to pay your tuition

   (E) educational loans, to your school is where the funds to pay your tuition will be directly delivered

GO ON TO THE NEXT PAGE

9. For some college students, <u>the ability to sleep late in the morning seems more important</u> than taking the classes required for graduation.

(A) the ability to sleep late in the morning seems more important

(B) having the ability to sleep late in the morning seems more important

(C) there seems to be more importance in sleeping late in the morning

(D) more importance is seemingly placed on sleeping late

(E) sleeping late in the morning seems more important

10. Standing on a chair and shouting to be heard over the crowd, <u>the speech was given by a man we had never seen before</u>.

(A) the speech was given by a man we had never seen before

(B) the speech has been given by a man we had never seen before

(C) that was the speech the man we had never seen before gave

(D) a man we had never seen before has given the speech

(E) a man we had never seen before gave the speech

11. <u>The collapse of that company was brought about by its irresponsible executives.</u>

(A) The collapse of that company was brought about by its irresponsible executives.

(B) The executives of that company brought irresponsibly about its collapse.

(C) The irresponsible executives of that company had brought about their collapse.

(D) The irresponsible executives of that company brought about its collapse.

(E) That was the company its irresponsible executives caused to collapse.

GO ON TO THE NEXT PAGE >

Directions: The following sentences test your ability to recognize grammar and usage errors. Each sentence contains either a single error or no error at all. No sentence contains more than one error. The error, if there is one, is underlined and lettered. If the sentence contains an error, select the one underlined part that must be changed to make the sentence correct. If the sentence is correct, select choice (E). In choosing answers, follow the requirements of standard written English.

EXAMPLE:

Whenever one is driving late at night, you must take extra precautions against
  A   B   C

falling asleep at the wheel. No error
            D   E

Ⓐ ● Ⓒ Ⓓ Ⓔ

12. The primary difference among the two positions
                         A
    advertised is that one is exciting and the other
            B C
    is boring. No error
      D   E

13. In 1492 Columbus sailed the ocean blue and

    thought that he had discovered a new world, but
      A   B
    the indigenous people of North America

    will be discovering America long before Columbus
      C   D
    was even born. No error
           E

14. The quarterback, after his terrible failure to throw
                             A
    a complete pass, went about complete shamefaced
                B   C
    and was available to only a few of his teammates.
                 D
    No error
      E

15. This week, the company started Hawaiian Shirt
                    A
    Day in an attempt by creating a higher amount
                B
    of employee spirit in the office. No error
      C   D   E

16. Arthur Miller's morality allows him to write plays
                               A
    that arise from and expresses the repercussions that
      B   C
    modern life has had on Americans. No error
          D   E

17. Local hotels have been almost totally destroyed
             A   B
    by the earthquake, so lodging is difficult to find.
               C   D
    No error
      E

18. The seasonal fruits are such a popular gift item that
                  A
    it has become necessary to find ways of hastening
      B   C
    the development of its trees. No error
          D   E

19. Cost/benefit analysis is the approved basis on
                  A
    which to determine which project to implement,
        B
    replacing more political criteria. No error
      C   D   E

GO ON TO THE NEXT PAGE ⟶

20. Among the great moments in 20th century

    history, the toppling of the Berlin Wall

    <u>are</u> <u>probably seen</u> <u>by Germans</u> as one of the
    A   B   C

    <u>most felicitous</u>. <u>No error</u>
        D   E

21. <u>While</u> some people <u>have</u> dogs because they want
      A   B

    companionship, others <u>want</u> them to protect <u>them</u>.
                C   D

    <u>No error</u>
      E

22. <u>Inevitably</u>, the economies of agricultural nations
      A

    will not affect the world economy, <u>so, until</u> prices
                     B

    of agricultural products are as high as <u>technology</u>,
                     C

    some nations <u>will grow</u> slowly. <u>No error</u>
            D   E

23. <u>Eventually</u>, the company's new <u>practice of</u> reducing
      A   B

    the production quality of many products may

    decrease, <u>not increase</u>, <u>their</u> gross profit. <u>No error</u>
          C   D   E

24. If he <u>had started</u> <u>before Friday</u>, he might have
         A   B

    succeeded <u>in completing</u> the <u>remarkably</u> difficult
            C   D

    assignment before it was due. <u>No error</u>
                   E

25. <u>In many ways,</u> James Joyce, Samuel Beckett, and
      A

    Seamus Deane used similar aspects of Ireland in

    their novels, <u>but</u> Beckett <u>was</u> the <u>more abstract</u> in
            B   C   D

    his interpretations. <u>No error</u>
               E

26. José Limón, <u>assuredly</u> one of the today's most
            A

    <u>inventive</u> modern dance choreographers, <u>brought</u>
      B   C

    to the stage a new <u>approach to</u> movement and
                 D

    musicality. <u>No error</u>
           E

27. The FBI <u>maintains</u> strict <u>requirements for</u> citizens
           A   B

    <u>who are</u> <u>interested in</u> joining the Bureau. <u>No error</u>
      C   D   E

28. Everything about the case <u>are</u> strange and
                  A

    suspicious, <u>as</u> there was no sign of forced entry,
           B

    nothing of great value <u>was stolen</u>, and the only
                 C

    finger prints <u>around the house</u> were the owners'.
              D

    <u>No error</u>
      E

29. Concerned <u>about</u> the playoff game <u>on</u> Saturday,
           A   B

    each of the team members <u>spent</u> most of the week
               C

    practicing <u>their</u> plays. <u>No error</u>
         D   E

GO ON TO THE NEXT PAGE

KAPLAN
Test Prep and Admissions

Directions: The following passage is an early draft of an essay. Some parts of the passage need to be rewritten.

Read the passage and select the best answer for each question that follows. Some questions are about particular sentences or parts of sentences and ask you to improve sentence structure or word choice. Other questions ask you to consider organization and development. In choosing answers, follow the conventions of standard written English.

Questions 30–35 are based on the following passage.

(1) Today's rock climbing is the closest humans have ever come to free, rapid, non-mechanical ascent and descent of rock faces. (2) Nearly everyone numbers a famous climber among their heroes, with young people revering Spiderman, while adults admire those who conquered Mount Everest. (3) Anyone who has tried to scale a schoolyard wall or even scrambled over a high fence has experienced it.

(4) In its infancy, rock climbing was too perilous for any but the most daring. (5) Recent improvements in gear, techniques, and training, have virtually removed danger from the sport. (6) Sport climbers, for example, wear special rubber-soled shoes that enable them to cling to the rock.

(7) When I climb, I wear a harness and am connected by a rope to another harnessed person. (8) This person, or belay, can use the rope to stop my fall.

(9) After I reach the summit, sometimes hundreds of feet above ground, it is time to rappel down. (10) When you alight, you can feel as if you are falling, but you can choose just how quickly you will go. (11) Although I may gather speed, I never feel out of control. (12) It is a simple matter for my belay or me to slow or stop my descent.

(13) Cliff rappels, like hopping off a bunkbed or— for those who never had to share a room—like jumping off a chain-link fence just before the bottom.

30. Which of the following is the best version of the underlined portion of sentence 2 (reproduced below)?

Nearly everyone numbers a famous climber among their <u>heroes, with young people revering</u> Spiderman, while adults admire those who conquered Mount Everest.

(A) (As it is now)
(B) heroes, and young people revere
(C) heroes; young people revere
(D) heroes; young people have revered
(E) heroes. Young people revered

31. In context, what is the best way to revise sentence 3 (reproduced below)?

Anyone who has tried to scale a schoolyard wall or even scrambled over a high fence has experienced it.

(A) Insert "Unfortunately" at the beginning.
(B) Change "has tried" to "tries."
(C) Change "schoolyard wall" to "wall without noticeable features."
(D) Change "has" to "have."
(E) Change "it" to "the exhilaration of climbing."

32. In context, which of the following is best to insert after "training" in sentence 5?

(A) however,
(B) then,
(C) consequently,
(D) nonetheless,
(E) in fact,

GO ON TO THE NEXT PAGE

33. Where is the best place to insert the following sentence?

    Safe climbing also involves reliance on the skill and alertness of other people.

    (A) after sentence 4
    (B) after sentence 5
    (C) before sentence 7
    (D) before sentence 9
    (E) before sentence 12

34. In context, which is the best version of sentence 10 (reproduced below)?

    When you alight, you can feel as if you are falling, but you can choose just how quickly you will go.

    (A) (As it is now)

    (B) When I alight, I may feel as if I am falling, but I can choose just how quickly I will go.

    (C) When I alighted, I felt almost as if I had been falling, but I chose just how quickly to fall.

    (D) Once you alight, you can feel as if you are falling, but you can choose the speed at which you will go.

    (E) A jump like this one feels almost like falling, but it is possible for one to choose just how quickly to go.

35. In context, which one of the following is the best way to phrase the underlined portion of sentence 13 (reproduced below)?

    Cliff rappels, like hopping off a bunk bed or—for those who never had to share a room—like jumping off a chain-link fence just before the bottom.

    (A) Cliff rappels, like hopping off a bunk bed

    (B) Rappelling down a cliff, like hopping off

    (C) Rappelling down a cliff is like hopping off a bunk bed

    (D) Lastly, to rappel is like hopping off a bunk bed

    (E) Hopping off a bunk bed is like rappelling

SECTION 5

Time—25 Minutes

18 Questions

Directions: For this section, solve each problem and decide which is the best of the choices given. Fill in the corresponding oval on the answer sheet. You may use any available space for scratchwork.

Notes:

(1) Calculator use is permitted.

(2) All numbers used are real numbers.

(3) Figures are provided for some problems. All figures are drawn to scale and lie in a plane UNLESS otherwise indicated.

(4) Unless otherwise specified, the domain of any function f is assumed to be the set of all real numbers x for which $f(x)$ is a real number.

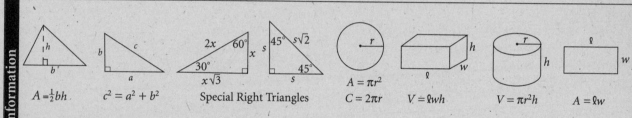

$A = \frac{1}{2}bh$ $c^2 = a^2 + b^2$ Special Right Triangles $A = \pi r^2$ $C = 2\pi r$ $V = \ell wh$ $V = \pi r^2 h$ $A = \ell w$

The sum of the degree measures of the angles in a triangle is 180.
The number of degrees of arc in a circle is 360.
A straight angle has a degree measure of 180.

1. If $4(x + 5) = 24$, then what is the value of x?

   (A) 1
   (B) $\frac{19}{4}$
   (C) 6
   (D) $\frac{29}{4}$
   (E) 19

2. At a dinner ceremony, each guest is given the choice of 4 different appetizers and 7 entrees. How many different combinations are there of one appetizer and one entree?

   (A) 3
   (B) 11
   (C) 14
   (D) 22
   (E) 28

GO ON TO THE NEXT PAGE

3. If $x + 2y = 14$, $y = z + 2$, and $z = 4$, then what is the value of x?

   (A) 2
   (B) 4
   (C) 6
   (D) 8
   (E) 10

4. If $\dfrac{x + y}{x}$, and y is a positive integer, what is the value of x?

   (A) $-y$
   (B) 0
   (C) y
   (D) y^2
   (E) $\dfrac{1}{y}$

5. Laurel is taller than Nick but shorter than Vince. If we let the letters l, n, and v represent the heights of Laurel, Nick, and Vince, in that order, which of these is true?

   (A) $l < n < v$
   (B) $l < v < n$
   (C) $n < l < v$
   (D) $n < v < l$
   (E) $v < l < n$

6. The difference between m and the square of n is equal to the square root of the sum of m and n.

   Which of the following expressions is the same as the statement above?

   (A) $m - \sqrt{n} = (m + n)^2$
   (B) $m - n^2 = \sqrt{m + n}$
   (C) $m - n^2 = \sqrt{m} + \sqrt{n}$
   (D) $m - \sqrt{n} = m^2 + n^2$
   (E) $m^2 - n^2 = \sqrt{m + n}$

7. In the sequence 7, 14, 28, x, 112,... what is the value of x?

   (A) 35
   (B) 56
   (C) 63
   (D) 75
   (E) 91

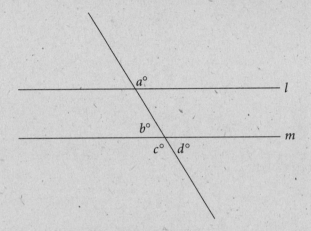

Note: Figure not drawn to scale.

8. In the figure above, lines l and m are parallel and $a = 110$. Which of the following is equal to the sum of b, c, and d?

   (A) 250
   (B) 260
   (C) 270
   (D) 280
   (E) 290

GO ON TO THE NEXT PAGE

Directions: For Student-Produced Response questions 9–18, use the grids at the bottom of the answer sheet page on which you have answered questions 1–8.

Each of the remaining 3 questions requires you to solve the problem and enter your answer by marking the ovals in the special grid, as shown in the example below. You may use any available space for scratch work.

Answer: 1.25 or $\frac{5}{4}$ or 5/4

Write answer in boxes.

Grid-in result →

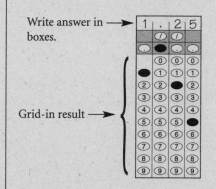
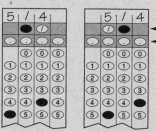

Fraction line
Decimal point

You may start your answers in any column, space permitting. Columns not needed should be left blank.

Either position is correct.

- It is recommended, though not required, that you write your answer in the boxes at the top of the columns. However, you will receive credit only for darkening the ovals correctly.

- Grid only one answer to a question, even though some problems have more than one correct answer.

- Darken no more than one oval in a column.

- No answers are negative.

- Mixed numbers cannot be gridded. For example: the number $1\frac{1}{4}$ must be gridded as 1.25 or 5/4.

(If `1 1 / 4` is gridded, it will be interpreted as $\frac{11}{4}$ not $1\frac{1}{4}$.)

- Decimal Accuracy: Decimal answers must be entered as accurately as possible. For example, if you obtain an answer such as 0.1666..., you should record the result as .166 or .167. **Less accurate values such as .16 or .17 are not acceptable.**

Acceptable ways to grid $\frac{1}{6}$ = .1666...

GO ON TO THE NEXT PAGE ➤

9. If $ab = 6$, $c - b = 5$, and $2c = 16$, what is the value of $a + b + c$?

10. If exactly 50 out of the 400 seniors at a college are majoring in economics, what percent of the seniors are NOT majoring in economics? (Disregard the % sign when gridding in your answer.)

11. Five pens cost as much as 2 notebooks. If the cost of one notebook and one pen is $1.75, what is the cost, in dollars, of 1 notebook? (Disregard the $ sign when gridding in your answer.)

12. On a certain test, the highest score possible is 100 and the lowest is 0. If the average of four tests is 86, what is the lowest possible score of the four exams?

13. If v is a three-digit number less than 250 that has a remainder of 2 when divided by 3, 4, or 5, what is a possible value for v?

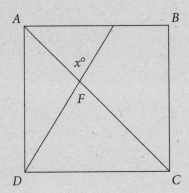

14. In square $ABCD$ above, if the measure of angle ADF is 36 degrees, what is the value of x?

15. On a number line, what is the coordinate of point X if the distance from X to $\frac{1}{4}$ is the same as the distance from X to $\frac{1}{6}$?

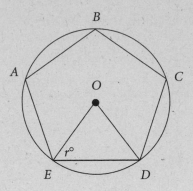

16. In the figure above, polygon $ABCDE$ has equal sides and is inscribed in circle O. If O is the center of the circle, what is the value of r?

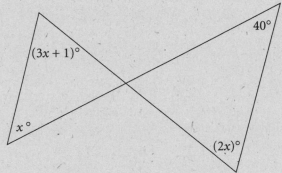

Note: Figure not drawn to scale

17. In the figure above, what is the value of x?

18. In an 8 by 8 checkerboard with 64 unit squares, what is the ratio of all the unit squares that are completely surrounded by other unit squares to all the unit squares on the border?

IF YOU FINISH BEFORE TIME IS CALLED, YOU MAY CHECK YOUR WORK ON THIS SECTION ONLY. DO NOT TURN TO ANY OTHER SECTION IN THE TEST. **STOP**

SECTION 6

Time—25 Minutes
24 Questions

Directions: For each of the following questions, choose the best answer and darken the corresponding oval on the answer sheet.

Each sentence below has one or two blanks, each blank indicating that something has been omitted. Beneath the sentence are five words or sets of words labeled (A) through (E). Choose the word or set of words that, when inserted in the sentence, <u>best</u> fits the meaning of the sentence as a whole.

EXAMPLE:

Today's small, portable computers contrast markedly with the earliest electronic computers, which were ----.

(A) effective
(B) invented
(C) useful
(D) destructive
(E) enormous   Ⓐ Ⓑ Ⓒ Ⓓ ●

1. Until his defeat by the newcomer, the veteran boxer won most of his bouts by knockouts and had achieved an ---- series of wins.

   (A) inconsequential
   (B) exaggerated
   (C) able-bodied
   (D) unbroken
   (E) observable

2. Photographer Edward Weston's work was akin to alchemy, his camera lens magically transforming ----, everyday items such as vegetables into objects of ---- beauty.

   (A) inexpensive . . tawdry
   (B) mundane . . resplendent
   (C) small . . enormous
   (D) decorative . . functional
   (E) artificial . . natural

3. The spokesperson for the group said that the issues raised by the controversy have ---- that go far beyond the matter presently under discussion.

   (A) expectations
   (B) ramifications
   (C) proponents
   (D) inferences
   (E) critics

4. Prime Minister Neville Chamberlain of Great Britain adopted a ---- approach to Hitler, even accepting Germany's annexation of Austria.

   (A) hasty
   (B) precarious
   (C) haughty
   (D) conciliatory
   (E) dependent

5. Many who were ---- enough to witness Sir Michael Redgrave's performance in the role of Uncle Vanya assert that it was the ---- of his career.

   (A) close . . scourge
   (B) astute . . encore
   (C) fortunate . . pinnacle
   (D) hapless . . height
   (E) lucky . . nadir

GO ON TO THE NEXT PAGE

Directions: The passages below are followed by questions based on their content; questions following a pair of related passages may also be based on the relationship between the paired passages. Answer the questions on the basis of what is <u>stated</u> or <u>implied</u> in the passages and in any introductory material that may be provided.

Questions 6–9 are based on the following passages.

Passage 1

As more and more antibiotics are prescribed by doctors for their patients every year—a trend many in the medical industry consider a direct result of increasingly and often unrealistically
(5) demanding practitioner schedules—a growing number of Americans are proving dangerously resistant to antibiotic treatments. Public health officials have been warning the medical industry for decades about this very problem; their reports
(10) have documented how such widespread use of antibiotics can encourage the proliferation of harmful antibiotic-resistant bacteria. Yet, as enormous and notoriously stingy health management organizations, or HMOs, began swallowing up
(15) more private medical practices, patient turnover seemed to take precedent over patient care.

Passage 2

Although the case can be made that most antibiotic-resistant medical problems stem from excessive human use of such medications, there is
(20) a growing body of evidence that suggests the medications used by farmers to treat their livestock can have a significant effect on these problems as well. Roughly 30 years ago, farmers found themselves trying to keep pace economically by invest-
(25) ing in ever-larger herds. Animal antibiotics became a cost-effective solution to the increased risk of disease that these larger herds were open to. Today, however, convincing studies show that the antibiotic-resistant bacteria created by such
(30) treatments can transfer from animal to consumer, thus contributing to the growing antibiotic-resistance problem among humans.

6. In the last sentence of Passage 1 (lines 12–16), the author implies that

(A) antibiotic treatments are relatively easy and cheap to prescribe

(B) HMOs are oblivious to antibiotic-resistance problems

(C) only large HMOs can afford antibiotic treatments

(D) HMOs have demonstrated little concern for patient care

(E) private medical practices are more careful than large HMOs

7. In line 27, "open" most nearly means

(A) unobstructed

(B) free

(C) vulnerable

(D) receptive

(E) accessible

8. The author of Passage 2 would most likely characterize the arguments made by the author of Passage 1 as

(A) overly critical

(B) inappropriate

(C) misinformed

(D) limited

(E) insightful

GO ON TO THE NEXT PAGE

9. The authors of both passages agree that antibiotic-resistance problems

    (A) are more prevalent today than they were in the past

    (B) are caused by the over prescription of antibiotics

    (C) have been well documented for decades

    (D) have only recently become serious

    (E) could be devastating to the health of many

Questions 10–15 are based on the following passage.

The following is an excerpt from a magazine article on our changing use of leisure time.

Twenty years ago Staffan Linder, a Swedish economist, wrote a book arguing that higher wages did not necessarily mean an increase in well-being. Linder observed that with increased
(5) productivity came the possibility of shorter work hours and a wider availability of consumer goods. People had a choice: more "leisure" time or more consumption. Only the wealthy could have both. If the average person wanted to indulge in expen-
(10) sive recreation like skiing or sailing, it would be necessary to work more—to trade free time for overtime or a second job. Whether because of the effectiveness of advertising or from simple acquis-itiveness, most people chose consumption over
(15) time. According to U.S. News and World Report, in 1989 Americans spent more than $13 billion on sports clothing; put another way, more than a billion hours of potential leisure time were exchanged for leisure wear—for increasingly elab-
(20) orate running shoes, certified hiking shorts, and monogrammed warm-up suits. In 1989, to pay for these indulgences, more workers than ever before recorded—6.2 percent—held more than two jobs.

There is no contradiction between the surveys
(25) that indicate a loss of free time, and the claim that the weekend dominates our leisure. Longer work hours and more overtime cut mainly into weekday leisure. So do longer commutes, driving the kids,

and Friday-night shopping. The weekend—or
(30) what's left of it after Saturday household chores—is when we have time to relax. But the weekend has imposed a rigid schedule on our free time, which can result in a sense of urgency ("soon it will be Monday") that is at odds with relaxation.
(35) The freedom to do anything has become the obli-gation to do something, and the list of dutiful recreations includes strenuous disciplines intend-ed for self-improvement, competitive sports, and skill-testing pastimes. Recreations like tennis and
(40) sailing are hardly new, but before the arrival of the weekend they were for most people mostly sea-sonal activities. Once a year, when vacations came around, tennis rackets were removed from the back of the cupboard, swimwear was taken out of
(45) mothballs, or skis were dusted off. The accent was less on technique than on having a good time.

Today, however, the availability of free time has changed this casual attitude. The very frequency of weekend recreations allows continual participa-
(50) tion and improvement, which encourages the development of proficiency and skill. The desire to do something well, whether it is sailing a boat or building a boat, reflects a need that was previously met in the workplace. Competence was shown on
(55) the job—holidays were for messing around. Now the situation is reversed. Technology has removed craft from most occupations. Hence an unexpect-ed development in the history of leisure: for many people weekend free time has become not a chance
(60) to escape work but a chance to create work that is more meaningful—to work at recreation—in order to realize the personal satisfaction that the workplace no longer offers.

GO ON TO THE NEXT PAGE ⟩

10. The author most likely mentions skiing and sailing in line 10 primarily in order to

(A) indicate that some sports are inaccessible for the average person

(B) point out that some recreations are unnecessarily expensive

(C) show how certain recreations involve a sacrifice in leisure time

(D) dispel some misconceptions about the cost of leisure activities

(E) emphasize the importance of choosing recreations that are affordable

11. The author mentions "the effectiveness of advertising" in line 13 in order to

(A) condemn the naivety of the average consumer

(B) suggest an explanation for today's high expenditure on recreation

(C) criticize the powerful influence of the media

(D) indicate why certain brands of sports clothing are so popular

(E) question the statistical accuracy of newspaper studies

12. The word "indulgences" in line 22 most nearly means

(A) rewards

(B) luxuries

(C) whims

(D) expenses

(E) favors

13. The author's description of people taking swimwear "out of mothballs" (line 45) conveys a sense of

(A) relief that annual vacations are more exciting today

(B) resentment at the amount of time consumed by household chores

(C) despair in the passing of traditional customs

(D) irony at the infrequency of seasonal recreations

(E) disappointment at the lack of enthusiasm for swimming

14. The "casual attitude" described in line 48 was primarily a result of a

(A) belief in enjoying recreation

(B) restriction on working overtime

(C) skepticism about self-improvement

(D) shortage of training facilities

(E) resistance towards buying sports equipment

15. The author's conclusion at the end of the passage would be most directly supported by additional information concerning

(A) which occupations still require a level of expertise and knowledge

(B) how different people employ skills in their leisure activities

(C) how many people regularly participate in sailing today

(D) what role advertising plays in the promotion of sports accessories

(E) which technologies have removed the craft from leisure activities

GO ON TO THE NEXT PAGE

Questions 16–22 are based on the following passage.

The following is adapted from a history of astronomy textbook.

Dark matter is the undetected matter that some astronomers believe makes up the missing mass of the universe. Astronomers once believed that interstellar spaces were largely empty and quite
(5) transparent. The advent of photography, however, showed a complicated structure of star clouds and rifts and holes where there were few or no stars. As research continued, it was accepted that these were clouds of obscuring material now known as
(10) dark matter.

Astronomers initially were reluctant to accept that the bright and dark nebulae within the Milky Way might be an indication of a substrate of gas and dust in interstellar space. The consequence of
(15) an absorbing dust, which dims the light of distant stars and complicates the determination of their distances and intrinsic brightnesses, was a very serious obstacle for researchers.

Astronomers were finally convinced of the pres-
(20) ence of dark matter by the patient work of Robert J. Trumpler. He grouped hundreds of open star clusters into types according to their structures and shapes. Once grouped, the relative distance of the various clusters within one type could then
(25) be measured by two methods. First, the Main Sequence stars of, for example, spectral type F had the same absolute magnitude in all the clusters. Therefore, the greater the difference in the observed apparent magnitudes of such stars in any two
(30) clusters, the greater the difference in the distances of the two clusters. This is often referred to as the "fainter means more distant" method. For the "smaller means more distant" method, used for clusters of the same intrinsic size, the angular
(35) diameter of a cluster on the sky was used as a measure of its distance.

Trumpler's two methods did not give compatible results: the distances given by the apparent magnitude method were greater than those given
(40) by the angular diameters, thus showing that the starlight had been dimmed in its passage to the Earth. The presence of a general absorption at all wavelengths was thus proven.

Trumpler then investigated the selective absorp-
(45) tion phenomenon. If interstellar dust particles are about the same size as the wavelength of light, then the star would appear to be redder than its spectral type would suggest. (The setting sun appears red for just this reason.) This phenome-
(50) non increases the measured "colored index" of the star by an amount that is called the "color excess." It was difficult to measure the quantities exactly on photographs, but photoelectric methods used after 1950 could measure stellar magnitudes; color
(55) excess then became a powerful method for correct- ing for the effects of the interstellar dust. Trumpler thus concluded that an absorption was taking place in the Milky Way.

16. This passage is primarily concerned with

(A) dark matter in interstellar space
(B) the advent of photography in astronomy
(C) star clouds and rifts and holes in space
(D) empty space between stars
(E) astronomy

17. In line 4, "interstellar" most nearly means

(A) in the universe
(B) between the Earth and the Sun
(C) star clouds
(D) where there are no stars
(E) empty and transparent

GO ON TO THE NEXT PAGE

18. The consequence of dark matter in the Milky Way was serious to astronomers because

(A) they were reluctant to accept a more general substrate of gas and dust

(B) they believed that the spaces between stars were largely empty

(C) it would complicate the determination of distances of stars

(D) they would be forced to admit they were wrong about interstellar space

(E) dark matter could not be transparent

19. In line 17, "intrinsic" most nearly means

(A) the appearance to the naked eye

(B) complicating the determination of a star's distance

(C) belonging to the essential nature of the star

(D) the appearance to an astronomer

(E) the brightness of a star

20. The author's statement that the presence of dark matter "was a very serious obstacle for researchers" (lines 17–18) suggests that

(A) dark matter would have detrimental effects on the Milky Way

(B) photography would replace the need for astronomers

(C) astronomers would replace researchers in the scientific arena

(D) dark matter would change the course of astronomical thinking

(E) dark matter would make it easier to determine a star's distance

21. According to the passage, the presence of a general absorption at all wavelengths is evidenced by the discovery that

(A) the distances given by the apparent magnitude method are always less than those given by the angular diameters

(B) the distances given by the apparent magnitude method were greater than those given by angular diameters

(C) dust particles are about the same size as the wavelength of light

(D) fainter means more distant

(E) smaller means more distant

22. Why does the setting sun appear red?

(A) the phenomenon of elective adsorption

(B) color excess

(C) the phenomenon of selective absorption

(D) interstellar dust

(E) dark matter

GO ON TO THE NEXT PAGE

Questions 23–24 are based on the following passage.

Ralph Waldo Emerson's groundbreaking career was born as the young 19th-century writer and philosopher traveled down a misdirected career path to the ministry. Likely pressed by his father,
(5) a Boston church leader of some renown, Emerson enrolled in divinity school after he completed his undergraduate studies. It did not take long, however, for disillusionment to settle in. Emerson grew restless amidst what he perceived as the
(10) stiflingly rigid modes of thinking of his church, a mismatch that, in retrospect, is not difficult to imagine. Indeed, Emerson based his influential philosophy of Transcendentalism on extremely creative sources and concepts, far afield from the
(15) church tradition.

23. The author uses the words "in retrospect" (line 11) to emphasize that Emerson

(A) became known for innovative thought

(B) came to be critical of all rigid modes of thought

(C) was a particularly secular man

(D) later renounced his father's influence

(E) regretted his enrollment in divinity school

24. The author's reference to "stiflingly rigid modes of thinking" (line 10) suggests that

(A) Emerson found divinity school uninspiring

(B) Emerson was known for being rebellious

(C) Emerson chose the wrong divinity school

(D) Emerson was unwilling to be forced into his beliefs

(E) divinity schools are notoriously strict

IF YOU FINISH BEFORE TIME IS CALLED, YOU MAY CHECK YOUR WORK ON THIS SECTION ONLY. DO NOT TURN TO ANY OTHER SECTION IN THE TEST. **STOP**

SECTION 7

Time—20 Minutes

16 Questions

Directions: For this section, solve each problem and decide which is the best of the choices given. Fill in the corresponding oval on the answer sheet. You may use any available space for scratchwork.

Notes:

(1) Calculator use is permitted.

(2) All numbers used are real numbers.

(3) Figures are provided for some problems. All figures are drawn to scale and lie in a plane UNLESS otherwise indicated.

(4) Unless otherwise specified, the domain of any function f is assumed to be the set of all real numbers x for which $f(x)$ is a real number.

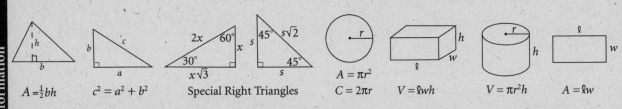

$A = \frac{1}{2}bh$ $c^2 = a^2 + b^2$ Special Right Triangles $A = \pi r^2$ $V = \ell wh$ $V = \pi r^2 h$ $A = \ell w$
$C = 2\pi r$

The sum of the degree measures of the angles in a triangle is 180.
The number of degrees of arc in a circle is 360.
A straight angle has a degree measure of 180.

1. If Thomas went shopping with $15 and ended up with a debt of $5, how much money did he spend?

(A) $5
(B) $10
(C) $15
(D) $20
(E) $25

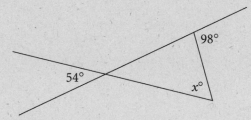

2. In the figure above, what is the value of x?

(A) 24
(B) 28
(C) 36
(D) 44
(E) 48

GO ON TO THE NEXT PAGE

3. There are a total of 256 people at a party. If after every 5 minutes, half of the people present leave, how many people will still remain after 20 minutes?

(A) 128
(B) 80
(C) 64
(D) 32
(E) 16

4. If $\overline{x}$ is defined by $\overline{x} = 5x - \dfrac{x}{2}$, then $\overline{8} =$

(A) 36
(B) 38
(C) 40
(D) 45
(E) 48

5. If $0.4x + 2 = 5.6$, what is the value of x?

(A) 0.9
(B) 1.4
(C) 9
(D) 14
(E) 90

6. If a rectangle of perimeter 12 has a width that is 2 less than its length, what is its area?

(A) 6
(B) 8
(C) 10
(D) 20
(E) 35

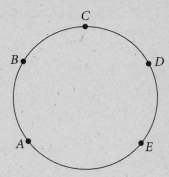

7. In the figure above, if points A, B, C, D, and E are on the circumference of a circle, what is the total number of different line segments that can be drawn to connect all possible pairs of the points shown?

(A) six
(B) eight
(C) ten
(D) fifteen
(E) twenty

8. In a recent survey, 80% of the people polled were registered voters and 75% of the registered voters voted in the last election. What fraction of all those surveyed were registered voters that did not vote in the last election?

(A) $\dfrac{1}{10}$

(B) $\dfrac{1}{5}$

(C) $\dfrac{1}{4}$

(D) $\dfrac{4}{5}$

(E) $\dfrac{4}{8}$

GO ON TO THE NEXT PAGE

KAPLAN

Test Prep and Admissions

9. If a solution of iodine and alcohol contains 4 ounces of iodine and 16 ounces of alcohol, how many ounces of alcohol should evaporate so that the ratio of iodine to the solution is 2 to 3?

(A) 6
(B) 7
(C) 8
(D) 10
(E) 14

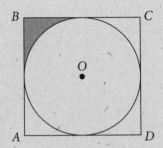

Note: Figure not drawn to scale.

10. In the figure above, circle O is inscribed in square $ABCD$. If the circumference of circle O is 4π, what is the area of the shaded region?

(A) $\pi - 2$
(B) $4 - \pi$
(C) $4 + \pi$
(D) $16 - 4\pi$
(E) $16 + 4\pi$

11. Lines m and n are parallel. If lines m and n are cut by three different transversals, what is the least number of points of intersection that can occur among the five lines?

(A) three
(B) four
(C) five
(D) six
(E) eight

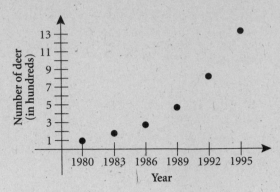

12. A biologist surveyed the deer population in Smith Park every three years. The figure above shows her results. If d is the number of deer present in the park and t is the number of years since the study began in 1980, which of the following equations best represents the deer population of Smith Park?

(A) $d = 100 + 2t$
(B) $d = 100 + 200\,t$
(C) $d = 100 + 20\,t^2$
(D) $d = (100)2^{\frac{t}{4}}$
(E) $d = (100)2^{\,t}$

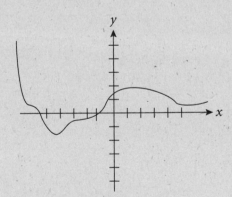

13. The figure above shows the graph of $r(x)$. At what value(s) of x does $r(x)$ equal 0?

(A) -5 only
(B) -1 only
(C) 1 only
(D) 1 and 5
(E) -5 and -1

GO ON TO THE NEXT PAGE

14. If $g^{\frac{2}{3}} > 4$, which of the following must be true?

(A) $g > 8$

(B) $g > 2$

(C) $g < 2$

(D) $g < 8$

(E) none of the above

15. In a standard coordinate plane, if Q is the point $(1, 5)$, R is the point $(1, 1)$, and S is the point $(4, 1)$, what is the value of QS?

(A) 3

(B) 4

(C) 5

(D) 6

(E) 7

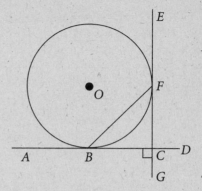

16. In the figure above, AD is tangent to the circle at point B and EG is tangent to the circle at point F. $BF = 2$. What is the area of the circle?

(A) 2π

(B) 3π

(C) 4π

(D) $4\pi\sqrt{2}$

(D) 8π

SECTION 8

Time—20 Minutes
19 Questions

Directions: For each of the following questions, choose the best answer and darken the corresponding oval on the answer sheet.

Each sentence below has one or two blanks, each blank indicating that something has been omitted. Beneath the sentence are five words or sets of words labeled (A) through (E). Choose the word or set of words that, when inserted in the sentence, best fits the meaning of the sentence as a whole.

EXAMPLE:

Today's small, portable computers contrast markedly with the earliest electronic computers, which were ----.

(A) effective
(B) invented
(C) useful
(D) destructive
(E) enormous   Ⓐ Ⓑ Ⓒ Ⓓ ●

1. Except for life stages when they may function as "loners," wolves act as ---- animals, generally living in packs with strong bonds and clear hierarchies.

   (A) carnivorous
   (B) fearsome
   (C) social
   (D) singular
   (E) wild

2. Psychologists disagree about whether multiple personality is ---- disease or a shield behind which some criminals hide in order to ---- prosecution.

   (A) a fallacious . . forestall
   (B) an authentic . . ensure
   (C) a genuine . . evade
   (D) an invalid . . elude
   (E) a diagnosable . . guarantee

3. Despite its stated goals of fostering productivity and hard work, the company promotes many unproductive and ---- employees.

   (A) creative
   (B) discontented
   (C) independent
   (D) lackadaisical
   (E) meritorious

4. Many ecologists believe that a recent forest fire which ---- a vast, remote section of Indonesia was the most severe ---- disaster the earth has suffered in centuries.

   (A) destroyed . . inflammable
   (B) devastated . . environmental
   (C) precipitated . . natural
   (D) singed . . intangible
   (E) burned . . scientific

GO ON TO THE NEXT PAGE

5. The city has ---- its program for recycling waste in an effort to reduce the amount of garbage that must be ---- or dumped in landfills.

   (A) improved . . produced
   (B) restricted . . amassed
   (C) adapted . . rescued
   (D) expanded . . burned
   (E) abolished . . buried

6. Bluegrass, a direct ---- of old-time string-band music of the late 1920s, is ---- by its more syncopated rhythm and its higher-pitched strident vocals.

   (A) descendant . . distinguished
   (B) variety . . disciplined
   (C) outgrowth . . illustrated
   (D) compromise . . characterized
   (E) expression . . safeguarded

Directions: The passages below are followed by questions based on their content; questions following a pair of related passages may also be based on the relationship between the paired passages. Answer the questions on the basis of what is <u>stated</u> or <u>implied</u> in the passages and in any introductory material that may be provided.

Questions 7–19 are based on the following passages.

Passage 1

Surgeons can perform phenomenal feats. They replace clogged coronary arteries with blood vessels from the leg. They reconnect capillaries, tendons, and nerves to reattach severed fingers. They even

(5) refashion parts of intestines to create new bladders. But surgeons find it difficult to reconstruct complicated bones like the jawbone or those of the inner ear. And only rarely can they replace large bones lost to disease or injury.

(10) The challenge stems from the nature of bones. Unlike other types of tissue, bones with one normal shape cannot be reworked into other shapes. Nor can doctors move large bones from one part of the body to another without severely disabling

(15) a person. Existing treatments for bone defects are all short-term and limited. Surgeons can replace some diseased joints with plastic or metal implants, but artificial hips or knees steadily loosen and must be reconstructed every few years.

(20) Fortunately, surgeons are beginning to overcome these obstacles by creating bone substitutes from, of all things, muscle. The idea of making bones from muscle is not all that strange. Muscle, bone, fat, blood vessels, and bone marrow all

(25) develop in human embryos from the same loosely organized tissue.

In 1987 scientists isolated a bone-inducing protein called osteogenin from cows. Osteogenin can make undifferentiated human tissue produce

(30) cartilage and bone. But few surgeons have used osteogenin because it is hard to control. If sprinkled directly onto a defect, for instance, the entire area might stiffen to bone if a tiny bit fell on surrounding blood vessels and nerves.

(35) More recently, plastic surgeons have circumvented that snag by prefabricating bones away from the immediate site of a defect. Flaps of animal thigh muscles are taken and placed in osteogenin-

coated silicone rubber molds of the desired shape.

(40) The molds are implanted in the same animal's abdomen to provide a suitable biologic environment for transforming muscle into bone. Within weeks, the molds yield tiny, perfectly detailed bone segments.

(45) So far, surgeons have made bones from muscles in small animals, but have not yet tried the process in humans. For one thing, osteogenin is available only in small amounts. Secondly, the safety and effectiveness of the process must first be tested on

(50) larger animals.

Passage 2

We have entered a new era in medicine. In scarcely more than a generation, artificial organs have evolved from temporary substitutes to long-functioning devices. Millions of people live with

(55) cardiac pacemakers, arterial grafts, hip-joint prostheses, middle-ear implants, and intraocular lenses. Eventually, artificial organs will allow ordinary, healthy people to live longer—or, more appropriately, to die young at a ripe age. So far, though,

(60) even the best substitutes lag far behind their natural counterparts. But the obstacles to better implants are not purely technical. Because such devices require human testing, their development poses a challenge to our cultural and ethical values.

(65) Although many patients volunteer for tests of unproven medical devices, such altruism—and the medical progress it engenders—is hampered by medical ethicists and others who call for more restrictions on human testing. While people favor-

(70) ing restrictions are well-intentioned, their standards are inappropriate.

The only way to gain the information needed for refining artificial organs is through experiments on people. Research using animals will not

(75) suffice. The mechanics of bone joints, for example, differs markedly from species to species. The

GO ON TO THE NEXT PAGE ⟶

replacement of wrists, knees, and finger joints poses complex engineering problems because of the heavy mechanical loads involved and the range (80) of motion required. Since there is no generally accepted large-animal model for the human bones and joints that orthopedic devices are designed to replace, human evaluation is essential.

In developing each new implant, the experience (85) gained from human testing becomes the critical bottleneck in the experimental process. In the case of artificial heart devices, engineering design is not currently the main obstacle. Heart implants can sustain patients for weeks while they await (90) transplants. These results are achieved with a variety of devices. But in other cases, the same devices can fail to keep patients alive. It appears that success depends less on the particular model used than on the patient's age, overall health, and (95) the quality of postoperative care.

Clearly, what is lacking today in coronary care are not new devices or techniques but simply more experience. How much blood should be pumped, and for how long? How can the natural heart be (100) weaned from mechanical assistance? When do the risks outweigh the benefits of further surgical assistance? There is little justification for developing new designs until such questions are adequately answered, and they can be answered only in human (105) subjects.

7. The author of Passage 1 expects that future experiments concerned with making bone from muscle will

(A) encounter no serious problems

(B) be limited mostly to smaller animals

(C) be hindered by surgeons opposed to the process

(D) face enormous technical obstacles

(E) involve larger animals and perhaps humans

8. In Passage 1, the author indicates all of the following about osteogenin EXCEPT

(A) current supplies are limited

(B) tests of its effectiveness have been limited

(C) its application can be easily controlled

(D) its safety for human use is undetermined

(E) some surgeons hesitate to use it

9. In line 37, "immediate" means

(A) near

(B) instant

(C) next in line

(D) directly understood

(E) current

10. The last paragraph in Passage 1 contains

(A) a review of current knowledge

(B) a qualification of an earlier remark

(C) a challenge to a contradictory view

(D) a summary of previous ideas

(E) a demand for an alternative approach

11. In Passage 2, the author intends the phrase "to die young at a ripe age" (line 59) to mean

(A) dying prematurely from an illness or accident

(B) dying young of an illness prevalent among older people

(C) extending one's life despite being ill

(D) maintaining a healthier body into old age

(E) living much longer than the average lifespan

12. The author's comments about medical ethicists in paragraph 2 of Passage 2 are best described as

(A) embarrassed

(B) deferential

(C) disapproving

(D) amused

(E) sarcastic

GO ON TO THE NEXT PAGE

13. In line 70, "standards" most nearly means

   (A) slogans
   (B) measurements
   (C) examples
   (D) banners
   (E) principles

14. In line 85, "critical" most nearly means

   (A) decisive
   (B) aggressive
   (C) skeptical
   (D) perceptive
   (E) fault-finding

15. The author of Passage 2 uses the example of artificial heart devices primarily to

   (A) show that important knowledge about coronary care is lacking
   (B) praise scientists' ability to fight coronary disease
   (C) counter lingering doubts about the safety and value of artificial implants
   (D) demonstrate an urgent need for better engineered heart devices
   (E) point out several new treatments now available to heart patients

16. The questions in lines 98–102 serve to

   (A) illustrate the value of new models of artificial hearts
   (B) refute the arguments of those opposed to the use of artificial implants
   (C) show that scientists' understanding of coronary disease is inadequate
   (D) suggest the author's own skepticism about using human subjects
   (E) indicate areas of research that have attracted wide publicity

17. Which statement about both authors is true?

   (A) Both cite the views of those with whom they disagree.
   (B) Both cite the limited capacity of surgeons to treat some problems.
   (C) Both demand an increase in the use of humans in medical tests.
   (D) Both mention cultural values as barriers to scientific research.
   (E) Both advocate a more rapid development of new implant procedures.

18. What obstacle to the wider use of osteogenin for making bones would the author of Passage 2 probably stress?

   (A) Osteogenin is likely to remain scarce and expensive.
   (B) Data about the effects of osteogenin on people may be difficult to obtain.
   (C) The bones and joints of large animals are very different than those of small animals.
   (D) Osteogenin is hard to use during surgery.
   (E) Artificial bones are inferior in quality to their natural counterparts.

19. The purpose of the last paragraph of Passage 2 is similar to that of Passage 1 in its emphasis of the need to

   (A) develop new and improved devices for human implantation
   (B) focus primarily on medical experiments with larger animals
   (C) proceed immediately to medical experiments using humans
   (D) gather information that is relevant to the treatment of human patients
   (E) curb the growing use of animals in testing

SECTION 9
Time—10 Minutes
14 Questions

Directions: For each question in this section, select the best answer from among the choices given and fill in the corresponding oval on the answer sheet.

The following sentences test correctness and effectiveness of expression. Part of each sentence or the entire sentence is underlined; beneath each sentence are five ways of phrasing the underlined material. Choice (A) repeats the original phrasing; the other four choices are different. If you think the original phrasing produces a better sentence than any of the alternatives, select choice (A); if not, select one of the other choices.

In making your selection, follow the requirements of standard written English; that is, pay attention to grammar, choice of words, sentence construction, and punctuation. Your selection should result in the most effective sentence—clear and precise, without awkwardness or ambiguity.

EXAMPLE: ANSWER:

Every apple in the baskets <u>are ripe and labeled according to the date it was picked</u>.   (A) ● (C) (D) (E)

(A) are ripe and labeled according to the date it was picked
(B) is ripe and labeled according to the date it was picked
(C) are ripe and labeled according to the date they were picked
(D) is ripe and labeled according to the date they were picked
(E) are ripe and labeled as to the date it was picked

---

1. In the Stone Age, hunters wore shoes insulated with hay, moss, and rare bear fats, <u>since such is the case, only a few pairs of similar design exist today</u>.

   (A) since such is the case, only a few pairs of similar design exist today
   (B) and only a few pairs of similar design exist today because of that
   (C) no more than a few pairs of similar design exist today as a result
   (D) the number of pairs of similar design today is only a few for this reason
   (E) and so only a few pairs of a similar design exist today

2. Chemical-filled sunblocks, which are used often by tourists in tropical areas, can be <u>detrimental so that they</u> can harm fragile coral reefs.

   (A) detrimental so that they
   (B) detrimental because they
   (C) detrimental, although they
   (D) detrimental in order that they
   (E) detrimental because it

GO ON TO THE NEXT PAGE

3. Each of the reporters <u>were tracking the lead individually, but neither thought to call the other, so them collaborating</u> was never possible.

(A) were tracking the lead individually, but neither thought to call the other, so them collaborating

(B) was tracking the lead individually, but neither thought to call the other, so the collaborating of them

(C) were tracking the lead individually, but neither thought to call the other, so collaboration

(D) were tracking the lead individually, but neither thought to call the other, so the collaborating of them

(E) was tracking the lead individually, but neither thought to call the other, so collaboration

4. Sergio liked studying <u>marketing, of which he found the sports publicity classes especially interesting</u>.

(A) marketing, of which he found the sports publicity classes especially interesting

(B) marketing; he found the sports publicity classes especially interesting

(C) marketing, and it was especially the sports publicity classes that were of interest

(D) marketing; the interesting sports publicity classes especially

(E) marketing, especially interesting to him were the sports publicity classes

5. Despite the medical convention scheduled for this weekend, <u>calling only four or five hotels</u> before I found one with rooms available.

(A) calling only four or five hotels

(B) and yet I called only four or five hotels

(C) I called only four or five hotels

(D) but calling only four or five hotels

(E) yet calling only four or five hotels

6. Walking home through the deserted woods, <u>right behind us a dog barked</u>.

(A) right behind us a dog barked

(B) there was a dog barking right behind us

(C) a dog barked right behind us

(D) we heard a dog bark right behind us

(E) we hear right behind us a dog barking

7. Before their trip to Latin America, the group <u>practiced continuous for learning</u> Spanish.

(A) practiced continuous for learning

(B) practiced continuously to learn

(C) practiced to learn continuously

(D) practiced continuously for learning

(E) practiced continuous to learn

8. To be a good waiter, you should keep your clothes clean <u>and your walk should be a graceful one</u>.

(A) and your walk should be a graceful one

(B) while your walk is a graceful one

(C) and your walk being graceful

(D) with walking gracefully

(E) and walk gracefully

9. Yoga is one of the oldest forms of exercise, <u>it was practiced</u> for hundreds of years by Eastern yogis before the more modern yoga class entered sports clubs around the world.

(A) it was practiced

(B) practiced

(C) though it was practiced

(D) thus practiced

(E) and practiced

GO ON TO THE NEXT PAGE

10. *Sesame Street* teaches children reading skills in a way that is entertaining <u>as well as informs</u>.

   (A) as well as informs

   (B) and being informative as well

   (C) as well as informative

   (D) and informs as well

   (E) as well as information

11. Eating foods rich in carbohydrates before a race is common among marathon runners, all <u>of them need</u> reliable energy sources for peak performance.

   (A) of them need

   (B) of them are needing

   (C) which need

   (D) of whom need

   (E) need

12. <u>Renee Fleming is a world-renowned opera singer, she is admired especially for her vocal range, and she</u> will perform in the most important concert of her career within the next month.

   (A) Renee Fleming is a world-renowned opera singer, she is admired especially for her vocal range, and she

   (B) Renee Fleming is a world-renowned opera singer who is admired especially for her vocal range, and

   (C) Renee Fleming, a world-renowned opera singer whose vocal range being admired especially,

   (D) Renee Fleming, a world-renowned opera singer, the vocal range of which is admired especially

   (E) Renee Fleming, a world-renowned opera singer admired especially for her vocal range,

13. <u>Published by the International Organization for Standardization, many businesses use their voluntary standardization guidelines to facilitate communication.</u>

   (A) Published by the International Organization for Standardization, many businesses use their voluntary standardization guidelines to facilitate communication.

   (B) Published by the International Organization for Standardization, many businesses use their voluntary standardization guidelines for the facilitation of communication.

   (C) Many businesses use, to facilitate communication, the voluntary standardization guidelines which are published by the International Organization for Standardization.

   (D) To facilitate communication, many businesses use the voluntary standardization guidelines published by the International Organization for Standardization.

   (E) Many businesses use the voluntary standardization guidelines to facilitate communication that are published by the International Organization for Standardization.

GO ON TO THE NEXT PAGE

14. <u>While the patronage system was an artist's sole means of support, they had a prevalent idea that a portrait should be flattering and not depicting flaws.</u>

   (A) While the patronage system was an artist's sole means of support, they had a prevalent idea that a portrait should be flattering and not depicting flaws.

   (B) The idea that prevailed about a portrait during the patronage system was that it should flatter a sitter not depicting any of his flaws.

   (C) The idea that a portrait should flatter a sitter and not depict any of his flaws prevailed as long as the patronage system was an artist's sole means of support.

   (D) Prevalent as an idea as long as the patronage system was an artist's sole means of support was for a portrait to flatter a sitter and not depict any of his flaws.

   (E) Prevalent as long as the patronage system was an artist's sole means of support they had the idea that a portrait would flatter a sitter and not depict any of his flaws.

THE ANSWER KEY APPEARS ON THE FOLLOWING PAGE.

Practice Test Nine: **Answer Key**

SECTION 1

Essay

SECTION 2

1. A
2. B
3. C
4. D
5. A
6. B
7. E
8. E
9. D
10. B
11. D
12. A
13. C
14. B
15. B
16. C
17. B
18. E
19. E
20. D

SECTION 3

1. D
2. C
3. E
4. D
5. D
6. C
7. B
8. E
9. B
10. A
11. E
12. B
13. B
14. C
15. B
16. A
17. D
18. B
19. E
20. D
21. D
22. B
23. E
24. E

SECTION 4

1. D
2. C
3. A
4. D
5. C
6. B
7. B
8. B
9. E
10. E
11. D

12. A
13. C
14. C
15. B
16. C
17. E
18. D
19. E
20. A
21. D
22. C
23. D
24. E
25. D
26. E
27. E
28. A
29. D
30. C
31. E
32. A
33. C
34. B
35. C

SECTION 5

1. A
2. E
3. A
4. A
5. C
6. B
7. B
8. A
9. 13
10. 87.5
11. 1.25
12. 44

13. 122,182, or 242
14. 81
15. 5/24
16. 54
17. 19.5
18. 9/7

SECTION 6

1. D
2. B
3. B
4. D
5. C
6. A
7. C
8. D
9. A
10. C
11. B
12. B
13. D
14. A
15. B
16. A
17. A
18. C
19. C
20. D
21. B
22. D
23. A
24. D

SECTION 7

1. D
2. D
3. E
4. A
5. C
6. B
7. C
8. B
9. E
10. B
11. B
12. D
13. E
14. E
15. C
16. A

SECTION 8

1. C
2. C
3. D
4. B
5. D
6. A
7. E
8. C
9. A
10. A
11. D
12. C
13. E
14. A
15. A
16. C
17. B
18 B
19. D

SECTION 9

1. E
2. B
3. E
4. B
5. C
6. D
7. B
8. E
9. B
10. C
11. D
12. E
13. D
14. C

PRACTICE TEST NINE

Critical Reading

	Number Right	Number Wrong	Raw Score
Section 3:	☐	− (.25 × ☐) =	☐
Section 6:	☐	− (.25 × ☐) =	☐
Section 8:	☐	− (.25 × ☐) =	☐
	Critical Reading Raw Score	=	☐
			(rounded up)

Writing

	Number Right	Number Wrong	Raw Score
Section 1:	☐ (ESSAY GRADE)	× 3.17 =	☐
Section 4:	☐	− (.25 × ☐) =	☐
Section 9:	☐	− (.25 × ☐) =	☐
	Writing Raw Score	=	☐
			(rounded up)

Math

	Number Right	Number Wrong	Raw Score
Section 2:	☐	− (.25 × ☐) =	☐
Section 5A: (QUESTIONS 1–8)	☐	− (.25 × ☐) =	☐
Section 5B: (QUESTIONS 9–18)	☐	(no wrong answer penalty) =	☐
Section 7:	☐	− (.25 × ☐) =	☐
	Math Raw Score	=	☐
			(rounded up)

Turn to page xiv to convert your raw score to a scaled score.

Answers and Explanations

SECTION 1

6 Score Essay

Many of us are familiar with the expression, "Those who can, do. Those who can't, teach." However, this phrase neglects the essential role of teachers. To teach a subject, you have to know the subject and figure out how to pass on that knowledge to others, and this process improves your own mastery of the subject that you teach. Thus, teaching a subject does enhance your knowledge of that subject, as I discovered from personal experience.

One of my favorite subjects in high school has always been English. I love words and writing. My freshman English teacher noticed my enthusiasm, so she recruited me to work in an after-school program as a tutor for middle school students who needed to improve their writing before getting to high school. At first, I was nervous about taking on this responsibility. After all, I didn't really know how I managed to write well or why I liked doing it so much. But my teacher convinced me to join the program, and I soon realized how teaching someone else to write could improve my own writing.

My seventh-grade student had a wonderful imagination, but she couldn't put her ideas together on paper in a way that made sense. She was very frustrated by low grades on her creative essays, and after reading one of her compositions, I could understand both her frustration and her teacher's low evaluation. This student's problem was primarily a result of poor narrative flow. Her ideas were wonderfully interesting, but she jumped from one topic to another so quickly that it was very difficult to understand what she was trying to say. As she and I discussed her essays, I had to find ways to explain to her what was missing and how to improve her writing. I was obligated to put into words certain parts of the writing process that I hadn't really thought about before. As we continued our meetings, I realized that not only was I learning from her but that my own writing was also improving. My advice to my student led me to re-evaluate and refine my compositions. If I hadn't had the opportunity to teach this student, I would not have gained this knowledge and insight about my own writing.

Truly, then, my personal experience shows that teaching a subject to someone else can help you to more thoroughly know the subject in question. In this life, we all have certain skills. When we choose to share these skills with others, we become teachers and increase our own understanding and mastery of the skill we pass on.

6 Score Critique

All essays are evaluated on four basic criteria: Topic, Support, Organization, and Language. This essay begins strongly with an introduction that explains the author's interpretation of the prompt and clearly announces her opinion. The introduction transitions smoothly into the first body paragraph, which introduces the author's example, based on her personal experience. This paragraph moves smoothly into the next, which further develops and supports the author's single example. Finally, the concluding paragraph neatly wraps up the author's argument. This author clearly took time to plan her essay, resulting in a coherent and consistent essay that is well organized and offers sufficient support for her thesis.

The author's use of specific details, particularly in the third paragraph, makes the essay outstanding. In addition, the author uses varied sentence structure and language to express her ideas. She includes numerous keywords and phrases ("however," "thus," "One," "At first," "After all," "but") to help guide her reader as she develops her essay. The author's attention to detail, as evidenced by a lack of grammatical or spelling errors, also indicates that she allowed herself sufficient time to proofread her essay at the end.

4 Score Essay

It's interesting to claim you can learn more about a subject if you teach it. In a way, this makes alot of sense, since you would have to explain the subject to your students, which would make you think more about the subject or do additional research to supplement your teaching. However, I think this idea only applies to certain situations. An example of when it doesn't work is the movie *Mona Lisa Smile*. An example of when it does work is my experience coaching a youth soccer team.

In *Mona Lisa Smile* Julia Roberts plays an art teacher at Wellesley College. All of her students are girls from wealthy families. These students don't want to learn anything that isn't in their textbooks but Julia Roberts forces them to look at different types of art and to look at classic art in different ways so they start to appreciate other perspectives and styles. The students definitely learn more about art but Julia Roberts doesn't learn anything knew about this subject.

On the other hand I know that I have learned alot about soccer from coaching a team of elementary school kids. When I started I already knew the basic rules and strategies but I didn't know how to teach this to the kids on my team. It's pretty difficult to figure out how to explain the game to kids in a way that they'd understand, and I had to learn more about soccer and the league rules to be a good coach. I definitely know that I learned alot from this experience about soccer and about teaching and working with kids.

So their are times when teaching something can help you learn or master that subject or skill especially when its the first time that you're teaching. However, if you're an experienced teacher, you're more of an authority or expert on the subject already, so you really won't add to your own knowledge just by teaching to others.

4 Score Critique

All essays are evaluated on four basic criteria: Topic, Support, Organization, and Language. The author begins this essay with a rather vague statement, but then quickly moves on to state his opinion of the prompt, indicating to the reader that his essay will provide two opposing examples. Both examples are fairly well developed and supported in the subsequent paragraphs, showing that the author took time to plan his essay and list his examples before he began to write.

The essay is well organized, with clear transitions between paragraphs and frequent keywords and phrases ("However," "An example," "but," "On the other hand," "So"). However, several sentences lack appropriate punctuation, resulting in run-ons and somewhat unclear sentences (third and fourth sentences of paragraph two, second sentence of paragraph three, first sentence of paragraph four). These sentence structure errors, along with several usage errors, prevent the essay from scoring any higher than a 4. The author uses "alot" instead of "a lot" three times in the first and third paragraphs; "knew" instead of "new" in the second paragraph; "their" instead of "there" and "its" instead of "it's" in the fourth paragraph. To improve this aspect of his writing, the author should plan time for proofreading.

2 Score Essay

How can you teach something to someone if you don't already know how to do it? That's just not possible. You need to learn something from a teacher before you can try teaching it to someone else so thinking you could learn something by trying to teach it just doesn't make no sense.

Like algebra. Most high school students like me have to take this math class sometime during high school. If we already knew how to do algebra why would we have to take it? But we don't know so we need a math teacher to teach it to us. That's how we learn it. It's not possible for me to learn algebra by teaching it to my friends if I've never took the class.

Teaching and learning are like flip sides of the same coin so you can't have both happening at the same time. Teachers help you learn a subject and I guess learning could help you to teach that subject later but you can't learn it by teaching because you have to know it already to teach it to someone else. So no, teaching something to another person doesn't really help you learn it.

2 Score Critique

All essays are evaluated on four basic criteria: Topic, Support, Organization, and Language. This essay launches immediately into the topic, showing that the author has understood the prompt. Although the author doesn't digress from the topic, the remainder of the essay lacks organization and support. The essay includes a single example in the second paragraph, which is not sufficient to persuade the reader of the author's opinion as stated in the first paragraph. Additionally, the author uses circular logic that obscures his meaning. This writer needs to invest more time brainstorming relevant examples and planning his essay.

Another weak part of this essay is the lack of clear organization and structure. The author includes no transition words or phrases between paragraphs and uses few keywords to help the reader navigate the essay. To improve this aspect of his essay, the writer should plan his essay before beginning to write.

Finally, the language is redundant and the sentences lack variety of structure. Several run-on sentences or fragments result from a lack of appropriate punctuation (last sentence of the first paragraph, first and third sentences of the second paragraph, first and second sentences of the third paragraph).

Finally, the author has failed to correct some grammatical errors, such as "just doesn't make no sense" instead of "just doesn't make sense" in the first paragraph and "took" instead of "taken" in the second paragraph.

SECTION 2

1. A

Difficulty: Low

Strategic Advice: We've got a lot of food, and we're making some skimpy sandwiches with only one slice of ham and one slice of cheese in each one. If there are 75 slices of ham and 75 slices of cheese, then we should be able to make 75 sandwiches, right? Certainly you can't make more than 75 sandwiches, so choices (D) and (E) can be eliminated. The question is: Is there enough bread to make 75 sandwiches?

Getting to the Answer: There are 120 slices of bread, and each sandwich gets 2 slices of bread, so there is enough bread for only 60 sandwiches. So the caterer can only make 60 sandwiches. The correct answer is (A).

2. B

Difficulty: Low

Strategic Advice: This is a fairly straightforward algebra question. To solve, simply plug the given values for x and y into the equation.

Getting to the Answer: You're given the expression $x^2 + 2xy + y^2$. Since x is 1 and y is -1, this expression becomes

$$x^2 + 2xy + y^2 = (1)^2 + 2(1)(-1) + (-1)^2$$
$$= 1 + (2)(-1) + 1$$
$$= 1 + (-2) + 1$$
$$= 1 - 2 + 1$$
$$= 0$$

Be careful here with the operations involving negative numbers. Remember that when you square -1, or any other negative number, you get a positive number, and that adding a negative number is the same as subtracting a positive number.

There's a shortcut here that you may have noticed. The expression $x^2 + 2xy + y^2$ is equivalent to $(x + y)^2$. Since $x + y = 1 + (-1) = 1 - 1 = 0$, $(x + y)^2$ is also equal to 0.

3. C

Difficulty: Low

Strategic Advice: If you look at the drawing, and think about how gears work, you'll see that the teeth of each gear pushes the gear next to it to make it go around. Let's call the gears A, B, C, etc. from left to right.

Getting to the Answer: If gear A is turned clockwise, then its teeth will push the teeth on the left side of gear B down. This will make gear B turn counterclockwise. Since gear B is turning counterclockwise, the teeth will be moving up when they are on the right side, touching gear C. That will push the teeth on the left side of gear C up, and make gear C turn clockwise. Do you see the pattern now? This will make D turn counterclockwise, E turn clockwise, and finally F turn counterclockwise. Since A, C, and E will turn clockwise and B, D, and F will turn counterclockwise, 3 gears will turn counterclockwise, choice (C).

Questions 4–5:

Whenever you have a graph question, it's a good idea to spend at least a few seconds examining the graph before you begin. Here you have what looks like part of a pie chart and a bar graph, both describing the employees at Company X. From the note under the title you know that there are 800 employees, and from the notes under the graph you know that 75% of them work full-time and 25% of them work part-time. Notice that the full-time employees are represented by the bar graph, which gives the number of full-time employees in each department, whereas the part-time employees are represented by the pie chart, which gives the numbers of part-time employees as a percentage of the total number of employees.

4. D

Difficulty: Medium

Strategic Advice: In this percent word problem, you already know from your examination of the graphs that 75% of the employees work full-time, 25% work part-time, and that there are 800 employees in all. That means that there are 75% × 800 = 600 full-time employees and 25% × 800 = 200 part-time employees.

Getting to the Answer: Since 600 is 400 more than 200, the number of full-timers is 400 more than the number of part-timers, and the correct answer is (D).

You could also have done this by finding the difference of the percents first. Since 75% are full-time and 25% are part-time, the difference between them is just $75\% - 25\% = 50\%$, since they are percents of the same whole. 50% of 800 is 400, again choice (D).

5.   A

Difficulty: Medium

Strategic Advice: Now you have to figure out what percent of the employees work in the manufacturing department. What makes this hard is that there are 2 kinds of employees—part-time and full-time—and 2 kinds of graphs that represent them. You'll have to figure out the number of part-timers in manufacturing and the number of full-timers in manufacturing separately, then add those 2 amounts together, and then figure out what percent of the total that number represents.

Getting to the Answer: First, find the number of full-time employees in manufacturing. That's easy—you can just read that off the bar graph, which tells you that there are 240 full-time employees in manufacturing. Now for the part-timers. The pie wedge that says "manufacturing" also says "10%." But 10% of what? Be careful here—it's not 10% of the total number of part-timers; it's 10% of the total number of workers, or 10% of 800, which is 80. So there are 80 part-timers and 240 full-timers in manufacturing, for a total of 320 workers in manufacturing. Since there are 800 workers total, the percent is just $\frac{320}{800}$, or $\frac{40}{100}$ or 40%, answer choice (A).

6.   B

Difficulty: Low

Strategic Advice: Be careful when you translate English to math.

Getting to the Answer: Maurice starts out with $80. He spends $32.45 on clothes, so after he buys the clothes he has $80 - $32.45 = $47.55 left. Then he gives $27.55 to his sister, so he has $47.55 - $27.55 = $20 left. You need to find what fraction of the original $80 he still has, or what fraction of $80 the $20 he has left is. That fraction is just $\frac{20}{80}$ or $\frac{1}{4}$, choice (B).

7.   E

Difficulty: Medium

Strategic Advice: In this question you don't have to solve for x, so if you did a lot of work, solved for x, and then plugged one or both of the values back into the expression $2x^2 - 8x$, you did a lot of unnecessary work. If you're given an algebra problem that you're not solving for the value of one variable, you should always look carefully at the expression you're solving for. Can you see any similarities between the expression you're solving for and the information you're given?

Getting to the Answer: In this problem, you should have noticed that $2x^2 - 8x$ looks very similar to $x^2 - 4x$. In fact, you can *factor out* a 2: $2x^2 - 8x = 2(x^2 - 4x)$. So, if $x^2 - 4x - 12 = 0$, then $x^2 - 4x = 12$, and $2x^2 - 8x = 2(x^2 - 4x) = 2(12)$ or 24, answer choice (E).

8.   E

Difficulty: Medium

Strategic Advice: Don't be scared by the term "factor-rich." It's just a made-up expression that is defined by concepts that you already know. The question tells you that all it means for a number to be factor-rich is that when you add up all the *factors* of the number except for the number itself, that sum is greater than the number. All you have to do is go through the answer choices and add up the factors of each one except for the number itself.

Getting to the Answer: The factors of 6 are 1, 2, 3, and 6; adding all of them except 6 gives us $1 + 2 + 3 = 6$. The result is not greater than 6, so 6 is not factor-rich. For choice (B) you add $1 + 2 + 4 = 7$, which is not greater than 8. Choice (C) is 9, so you add $1 + 3 = 4$. No good. The factors of 10 are 1, 2, 5, and 10, and $1 + 2 + 5 = 8$, so 10 is not factor-rich either. Since you're left with only one answer choice, (E), it must be correct, but just to check add up $1 + 2 + 3 + 4 + 6 = 16$, which is indeed greater than 12, so choice (E) is correct.

9.   D

Difficulty: Medium

Strategic Advice: In this question you have 2 parallel lines, ℓ_1 and ℓ_2, and 2 lines which cross both of them, ℓ_3 and ℓ_4. Forget about ℓ_3 for a minute, and look what happens where ℓ_4 crosses ℓ_1 and ℓ_2.

Getting to the Answer: Since ℓ_4 is perpendicular to ℓ_2, all the angles that are formed where those 2 lines cross are right angles. And, since ℓ_1 is parallel to ℓ_2, the angles that are formed where ℓ_4 and ℓ_1 meet are also right angles. That means that ℓ_1 and ℓ_4 must also be perpendicular to each other, which means that statement I is true. That means you can eliminate answer choices (B) and (E).

ℓ_3 also crosses the two parallel lines and together with ℓ_4 creates a triangle in between them. Since all the angles formed where ℓ_2 and ℓ_4 meet are right angles, the triangle is a right triangle. One of the other angles of the triangle measures $a°$, but what about the third angle of the triangle? Well, that angle is formed by the same lines that form the angle labeled $b°$, so that angle inside the triangle must also measure $b°$. Since the 3 angles inside the triangle measure $a°$, $b°$, and 90°, and the sum of the angles in a triangle is always 180°, $a + b + 90 = 180$, which means that $a + b = 90$, so statement III is true. Now you can eliminate answer choices (A) and (C), and since choice (D) is the only one left, it must be correct.

Notice that you didn't even have to deal with statement II once you figured out that statements I and III were true. This often happens in Roman Numeral questions. Just for the record, though, statement II is not necessarily true. You know that $a + b = 90$, so if $a = b$ then a and b are each 45. However, although that's how a and b look in the figure, there's no information there that would indicate that. b could just as easily be a 46°, a 43°, or a 50° angle, so statement II is false.

10. B

Difficulty: Medium

Strategic Advice: Take this question one step at a time.

Getting to the Answer: A bicyclist riding at 12 miles an hour for 2 hours travels twice as far as a hiker. How far does the bicyclist travel? That's easy, 12 miles an hour for 2 hours is just 12×2 or 24 miles. If the bicyclist travels twice as far as the hiker, and the bicyclist travels 24 miles, the hiker must travel 12 miles, since 24 is twice 12. The hiker walks at 4 miles an hour for a total of 12 miles. Since $4 \times 3 = 12$, the hiker must walk for 3 hours at 4 miles an hour to go a total of 12 miles, so the correct answer choice is (B).

11. D

Difficulty: Medium

Strategic Advice: Remember, solving inequalities is the same as solving equations with one exception—if you multiply or divide by a negative number you have to change the direction of the inequality sign. You can solve this one pretty easily.

Getting to the Answer: Start by adding $2b$ to each side, and then divide by 2:

$2a - 2b < 0$
$\quad 2a < 2b$
$\quad\;\; a < b$

This tells you that $2a - 2b$ is less than 0 when, and only when, a is less than b, so the correct answer is choice (D).

12. A

Difficulty: High

Strategic Advice: This question is nowhere near as complicated as it seems. You're given that the figure shows a square, an isosceles right triangle, and an equilateral triangle, and you have to find the total measure of the angles in between them. The first thing to do is to think about what you know about the angles in squares and triangles. You probably remember that each angle of a square measures 90°, each angle of an equilateral triangle measures 60°, and that the 2 angles other than the right angle in an isosceles right triangle each measure 45°. That means that the angle in between the $x°$ and the $y°$ angle measures 90°, the angle in between the $y°$ and the $z°$ angle measures 45°, and the angle in between the $z°$ and the $x°$ angle measures 60°. Another thing that you should remember is that all the angles around a point add up to 360°.

Getting to the Answer: There are 6 angles around point D, the one in the square, the two in the 2 triangles, and the three measuring $x°$, $y°$, and $z°$. So, $x + y + z + 90 + 45 + 60 = 360$, and $x + y + z = 165$, choice (A).

13. C

Difficulty: Medium

Strategic Advice: Here you're given that a and b are *integers*, but you don't know whether they are positive or negative, so there are a lot of possible values of a and b that fit the equation $2a + 5b = 15$. One way to solve this one is to backsolve—to try each answer choice.

Getting to the Answer: Plug in the given value for b and see if the equation works. If you start with choice (C), which is a good idea when backsolving, you're in luck here. If b were equal to 2, the equation $2a + 5b = 15$ would be $2a + 10 = 15$, or $2a = 5$, or $a = 2.5$. But you're given that a is an integer, so a cannot possibly be 2.5, so $b = 2$ doesn't work and choice (C) is correct.

You might have noticed that in the equation $2a + 5b = 15$ you have an even number, $2a$, plus another number, $5b$, being equal to an odd number, 15. An even number plus an even number equals an even number, and an even number plus an odd number equals an odd number, so the expression $5b$ must be an odd number. If $5b$ is an odd number, then b must be an odd number (since odd $\times$ odd = odd and odd $\times$ even = even). Therefore the correct answer choice is the one even number, again choice (C).

14. B

Difficulty: Medium

Strategic Advice: Since you're given that y is between -1 and 0, why not pick an appropriate number for y and plug it into each answer choice?

Getting to the Answer: Try $y = -\frac{1}{2}$. Then choice (A) is $y^2 = \left(-\frac{1}{2}\right)^2 = \frac{1}{4}$;

(B) is $1 - y = 1 - \frac{1}{2} = 1\frac{1}{2}$;

(C) is $1 + y = 1 + \left(-\frac{1}{2}\right) = \frac{1}{2}$;

(D) is $2y = 2\left(-\frac{1}{2}\right) = -1$; and

(E) is $\frac{1}{y + 2} = \frac{1}{\left(-\frac{1}{2}\right) + 2} = \frac{1}{\frac{3}{2}} = \frac{2}{3}$.

Choice (B) is the greatest.

15. B

Difficulty: Medium

Strategic Advice: The union of two sets consists of all the elements that appear in either set.

Getting to the Answer: Set A contains 5 elements. Set B contains 5 elements, none of which are in set A. Their union contains $5 + 5 = 10$ elements.

16. C

Difficulty: Medium

Strategic Advice: A good way to solve this question is by making yourself a little table.

Getting to the Answer: Each employee is described by two different things. Each one is a woman or a man and each one either drives to work or takes public transportation. So make this table:

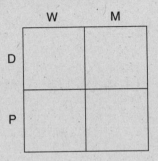

In this table, each box will contain the number of employees having the two appropriate attributes. For example, the box in the lower right-hand corner is the number of men who take public transportation. You can also put numbers in the margins. For example, you can put the number of women in the company below the box in the lower left-hand corner. Now begin to put numbers in the table from the information in the question. The question tells you that there are 25 women and 25 men, and that 29 employees drive to work. Each of these three pieces of information describes only one attribute of the employees, so these numbers will go in the appropriate margins. We're told that 6 men take public transportation. This describes both attributes, so put a 6 in the lower right-hand box. Now your table should look like this:

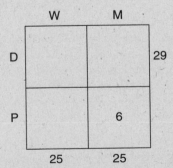

What you want to find is the number of women who drive to work, which is the number that must go in the upper left-hand box. So fill in information in the table, hoping that you can work your way to the upper left-hand box. You know that there are a total of 25 men in the company and that 6 men drive to work. This means that the remaining 25 – 6 or 19 men take public transportation. So put a 19 in the upper right-hand box. Now you're going to be able to find the number of women who drive to work. Since 29 employees drive to work and 19 men drive to work, 29 – 19 or 10 women drive to work. If you also put a 10 in the upper left-hand box, your table should look like this:

	W	M	
D	10	19	29
P		6	
	25	25	

So 10 women drive to work.

17. B

Difficulty: Medium

Strategic Advice: Careful here! If you said to yourself: "This is simple, pages 10–25 are empty, that's 25 – 10 = 15 pages at 4 photos a page, that's 60 photos all together…" then you fell into a trap! Never pick an obvious answer on a hard problem.

Getting to the Answer: The catch here is that page 10 is empty, too, and if you count from 10 to 25 while including both 10 and 25 you'll see that there is a total of 16 empty pages, not 15. Since $16 \times 4 = 64$, the correct answer is (B). In general, if a and b are integers and $a < b$, the number of integers from a through b inclusive (meaning that you're including a and b) is $b - a + 1$.

18. E

Difficulty: High

Strategic Advice: If the slope of a line is $-\frac{3}{2}$, that means every time the y-coordinate decreases by 3, the x-coordinate increases by 2. So, if the y-coordinate goes

from 6 to 0, as it does if you travel along line l from point A to point B, it decreases by 6, or 2×3. Therefore the x-coordinate must increase by 2×2, or 4.

Getting to the Answer: Since the x-coordinate of A is 0, the x-coordinate of B must be 4, so point B's coordinates are (4, 0). That means that the length of OB is 4. Since the length of OA is 6, the *area* of the triangle is $\frac{1}{2} \times 4 \times 6 = 12$, choice (E).

19. E

Difficulty: High

Strategic Advice: In this question you're given that 73 is the *median* of a group of 7 numbers (one for each day of the week). That means that 3 numbers must be less than 73 and 3 numbers must be greater than 73. 67, 71, and 72, the temperatures for Monday, Tuesday, and Wednesday, respectively, are each less than 73. The other 3 temperatures must be greater than 73.

Getting to the Answer: The Friday temperature is 76, and among the answer choices the only values for Saturday and Sunday which are both greater than 73 are 74 and 77, choice (E).

20. D

Difficulty: High

Strategic Advice: One important thing to remember about quadrilaterals is that the sum of the interior angles is 360°.

Getting to the Answer: That means that $w + x + y + 70 = 360$, and therefore $w + x + y = 290$. x must be a positive, but it can be a number very close to 0. If x actually were 0 then $w + y$ would be 290. If x were very slightly larger than 0, $w + y$ would be very slightly smaller than 290. So, 290 must be the upper bound of the range of values that $w + y$ could have, so the correct answer must be choice (B) or choice (D). If x were equal to 45, then $w + 45 + y$ would be 290, and $w + y$ would be 245. However, x can't equal 45, but its largest possible value could be a number very slightly smaller than 45. That means that $w + y$ would equal a number very slightly larger than 245. So, 245 must be the lower bound of the range of values that $w + y$ could have. That means that the correct answer must be choice (D).

SECTION 3

1. D

Difficulty: Low

This is about the philosopher Thomas Malthus's predictions about population growth—kind of an intimidating subject if you haven't read much philosophy. But don't worry. This sentence is pretty simple once you take it apart and look for clues. The biggest clue is the word *famine*. You're told that population growth does something to food production, resulting in famine. Well, you know that when many people are hungry and there's not enough food to go around, famine happens. Or, to put it in terms of the sentence, population growth would exceed food production, resulting in massive famine. The answer choice that best matches this prediction is choice (D), *surpass*.

2. C

Difficulty: Low

The key to this sentence is that Dr. Brown "brooked no deviation from his ideas." In other words, he wouldn't put up with anyone who disagreed, which through the use of "while" is contrasted with his supposed belief in discussing issues. Hence, choice (C): Brown *professes* or claims to have such a belief, but he interrupts anyone who doesn't *concur*, or agree. Choice (A) makes no sense: there's no contrast between *regretting* a belief in discussion and cutting off those who don't agree with you. Choices (B), (D), and (E) may be a bit confusing. They're just the opposite of what's needed in the second blank. Since Brown doesn't tolerate disagreement, he probably would not cut off anyone who did not choice (B), *debate*, choice (D), *question*, or choice (E), *protest*.

3. E

Difficulty: Medium

Here you may find it easier to fill in the second blank first, because it contains the catchy phrase "merely ----, not canceled." Look for clichéd phrases like this on sentence completions—they can help you get the answer fast. What probably pops into your head when you read "merely ----, not canceled" is "merely put off, not canceled." That's logical. What you need in this second blank is something that means the employees have put off their demands for now, but will bring them up again in the future. So choice (E), *postponed*, is correct. Choice (E)'s first word works as

well: it makes sense that employers would try to *moderate* wage increases during serious economic difficulties.

4. D

Difficulty: Medium

Here you're looking for words that fit with the phrases " ---- speeches to historical figures" and "an impartial and ---- historian." The only choice that fits is (D). Though Thucydides used psychological insight rather than documented information to *attribute* speeches to historical figures, he is still considered an impartial and *accurate* historian. Choice (A) doesn't work, because historians are never referred to as *endless*. Choices (B), (C), and (E) don't work because the first word in each choice—(B), *transmit* ("to send"); (C), *disseminate* ("to distribute"); (E), *promote* ("to advance")—doesn't fit with the phrase "speeches to historical figures." Thucydides is an author. He's describing historical figures in his writing, not writing speeches for them.

5. D

Difficulty: Medium

When you're working on Sentence Completions, look for clues that aren't immediately obvious. For instance, notice *complexity* here. *Complexity* might not have jumped out at you, but it's key to figuring out both blanks. Whatever goes in the first blank has to describe how readers would react to a novel's complexity. Would they be (A), *charmed,* by its complexity? Probably not. They probably wouldn't be (B), *rejected,* by its complexity either. (C), *inhibited*; (D), *daunted;* or (E), *enlightened;* are possible, but only (D) fits in the second blank. In (D), it makes sense to say that readers who are *daunted*, or intimidated, by the *allusiveness*, or symbolic quality, of Joyce's novel would find Gilbert's study a helpful introduction. Don't be intimidated by hard words like allusiveness. If you don't know the vocabulary, you can still use logic to rule out most of the wrong choices.

6. C

Difficulty: Medium

Wrath means "anger." In the first blank here, you can predict that the project managers were unwilling to risk arousing the anger of their superiors, or bosses. Choice (C) is correct—*incurring* means bringing down on oneself, becoming liable or subject to. Choice (C)'s second word, *maintain*, also works. Maintain here isn't being used to mean "to keep in repair," as in "maintain a car." It's being used in its secondary meaning: "to assert or declare." Watch out for secondary meanings like these on the SAT.

7. B

Difficulty: Medium

For the first blank in this sentence, three different choices would fit: (B), *reputation*, (C), *fame*, or (E), *notoriety*. When you try the three possibilities in the second blank, though, only (B) works. She wouldn't want to (C), *defer*, or "put off" *acclaim*, and (E), *publicize* acclaim doesn't work here either. However, it makes sense for the artist to deserve, or be worthy of, acclaim for her sculpture, so (B) is right.

8. E

Difficulty: High

The word in the blank has to have something to do with religion. Choice (E) is the only choice that does. An *agnostic* is someone who is uncertain about the existence of God. In choice (A), an *archetype* is an original pattern or model. In choice (B), a *bibliophile* is a book-lover or book collector. In choice (C), a *martinet* is a strict disciplinarian, one who rigidly follows rules. In choice (D), an *aesthete* is someone who appreciates and cares about beauty or beautiful art. The vocabulary is pretty hard here. As always, if you can rule out one clearly wrong choice, it's worth your while to guess rather than skip the question.

Questions 9–10

In this short narrative passage, the author recounts the experience of being caught attempting to take a book out of the Bodleian Library, a research institution that does not lend books to anyone.

9. B

Difficulty: Low

In the last sentence, the author says that he is "liberating information." This makes choice (B) the most reasonable inference. If the author believes he is "liberating information," then he must believe it was confined to start with. Choice (A) may have been tempting, but the author never alludes to any similarity between Soviet and Bodleian rules. He only says that the two institutions are evil. Similarly,

choice (C) is out because the author never implies any alliance between the Bodleian and Communists. While the author does believe that the Bodleian confines information, he never indicates an opinion about opening the library to the public, choice (D). Choice (E) contradicts the author's behavior in the passage; he disagrees with the library's lending policy.

10. A

Difficulty: Medium

Reread the sentence and notice that the author uses "purple air" to describe the librarian's condescending, or *arrogant*, (A), attitude. Nothing suggests that the author thought the librarian was *intimidating*, choice (B). On the contrary—the author doesn't hesitate to protest the librarian's actions. Choice (C) is too extreme. The librarian is arrogant and unkind, but his purpose is to keep the book in the library, not to *humiliate* the author. Choice (D) contradicts the earlier description of the librarian "simply" removing the book from the author's bag. He wouldn't "simply" remove it if he were irate. Nothing supports choice (E). The color purple is associated with royalty, and the librarian says that even the Queen cannot borrow books from the library, but these two facts don't add up to the librarian actually associating himself with royalty.

Questions 11–12

This short passage provides information about the manatee, a creature found primarily in the Florida Everglades.

11. E

Difficulty: Medium

In the case of this inference question, it is important to understand the particular meaning of the word "symbolic" as it is used in the paragraph. Note that here "symbolic" refers to how the manatee better represents the "unique wildlife found in" the Everglades. The word "unique" indicates that the manatee is really only found in the Everglades, suggesting that the same cannot be said of the American crocodile, choice (E). The fact that the manatee may be more "symbolic" than the crocodile does not necessarily indicate that the manatee is *more famous*, so choice (A) is out. Choice (B) is an irrelevant detail. While the author makes this point, the manatee's endearing nature is not connected in the paragraph with its ability to symbolize the Everglades. The paragraph does not explore what most people assume about the American crocodile, choice (C), or indicate which animal is better suited to the Everglades habitat, choice (D).

12. B
Difficulty: Medium

You need to be careful here—you're looking for the *wrong* answer. Eliminate those answers that are clearly supported by the text. The author describes the manatees as "endearing," so they are *capable of invoking affection,* choice (A). In the last sentence, he calls them "bulbous," which is close to *bloated,* choice (C). The author thinks of the manatees as "symbolic," or *representative of the Everglades,* choice (D). Finally, the manatees are "fragile," needing a specific water temperature to survive. This matches, choice (E). Only choice (B), then, is not mentioned in the passage.

Questions 13–24

There are some disconcerting place-names and scientific terms in this passage, but you don't need to know any of them to get the points the author makes about some of the earliest preserved art—cave paintings. The first paragraph ends with a few questions: what sort of people were the cave painters? Why did they paint at all, and specifically why in caves? These questions outline the rest of the passage for you. Keep this in mind if you ever encounter a passage with a similar format—it gives you a handle on the material.

13. B
Difficulty: Low

If you figure out what big points the author makes in the lines you're referred to, you'll probably have no trouble understanding why the author mentions body-painting (or whatever specific detail a question asks about). To do this, you usually have to read a line or two around the line reference you've been given. These lines tell us that if prehistoric humans made art, they haven't left us any trace of it. Body-painting is mentioned as an example of the kind of art they may have made, but which we can't have any evidence of choice (B). None of the other choices matches the point the author makes in these lines. The author is not

making a point about when people began using paint, choice (A). Choices (C), (D), and (E) bring up things not discussed until later in the passage.

14. C
Difficulty: Low

Again, go back to the passage and read around the line reference. The author says the paintings "rivet our attention" because they are "great art," and because they raise questions about the people who painted them. Now check the answer choices. Choice (B) probably jumped out, because it starts, *raise questions about*.... But read carefully! The rest of the choice doesn't make sense. Choice (C), although not as eye-catching, is correct. Choice (A) is from left-field. We do know some things about the people and animals depicted in cave paintings, so choice (D) is wrong. Finally, the point is that the paintings raise questions, not that they *cast doubt,* so choice (E) is out.

15. B
Difficulty: Medium

Don't let strange words throw you—in this or any question. Even if you don't know where "Gargas and Rouffignac" are, or what stalactites or stalagmites are, the point is in plain English: they "fill us with awe" and "stun us with their beauty." The author speculates that the cave painters must have felt the same way. This should lead you to choice (B). The other choices provide reasons that might sound sensible, but they don't come from the passage. Don't choose an answer just because it makes sense to you; be sure there's evidence in the passage.

16. A
Difficulty: Medium

Assuming you've already gone to the line where "riot" is used (as you should do with all vocabulary-in-context questions), which choices can you eliminate? Certainly choices (C), *brawl,* and (E), *violence,* since the word is used to describe something of great beauty. The most common definitions of a word are usually wrong, so you can also eliminate choice (B). That leaves choices (A) and (D). Only choice (A), *profusion,* makes sense in context.

17. D

Difficulty: Medium

In the quoted lines, the author says the term "cavemen" evokes an image of "hairy brutes," but then says that the Cro-Mags actually had "needles, buttons, parkas, and trail signs" in their caves. In other words, they're misrepresented as stupid brutes, when in fact they were quite sophisticated. Choice (D) sums this up, and is correct. Choice (A) is too specific—the author's not comparing Cro-Mags with Neanderthals. She is talking about the contrast between the popular image of Cro-Mags and the reality of their existence. Choices (B) and (E) are not discussed—don't go making huge inferences! Choice (C) refers to a nearby detail but misses the bigger point.

18. B

Difficulty: Low

This question asks you to make a not-too-subtle inference. The passage says, "garbage left in caves is more likely to have been preserved than other artifacts," which is almost the same as saying that *artifacts in other locations are more likely to have decayed*. Choice (B) is correct: it makes common sense, and it matches what's in the passage. Choice (A) is out because the author actually says that Cro-Mags lived both in caves and far from them; she says nothing about the *majority* of them. Archaeologists found trail signs inside caves, not outside them, choice (C). The author says nothing about what sites archaeologists are more likely to study—choice (D) infers too much. Choice (E) is never mentioned.

19. E

Difficulty: Medium

Never skip a Vocabulary-in-Context question—they're less time-consuming than the other question types. What's going on in the lines around the word "notable"? The author's describing some specific examples of cave art, and she then says that some "especially notable" works were done on irregular wall surfaces in order to suggest three-dimensionality. The best substitute for "notable" in that sentence is *remarkable*, choice (E). Two choices, (A) and (D), are negative-sounding and easy to eliminate. *Conspicuous*, (B), and *important*, (C), are much trickier, but they don't fit the sentence as well as choice (E). Be sure to check every choice before you make your move. The best answer may be hiding in choice (E).

20. D

Difficulty: Medium

In this question, you have to make a mild interpretation—but remember, don't go overboard. Read a line or two before the one you're referred to. The phrases "used to believe" and "we now realize" indicate a contrast. What did archaeologists formerly believe? That the paintings were of the animals most often hunted by Cro-Magnons. So now, scientists must've found out that animals in cave paintings were *not* the most hunted, choice (D). A too-quick reading of these lines might've led you to (A). But the author says, "the most frequently painted animals were indeed hunted," so choice (A) is out. If you picked choices (B), (C), or (E), you're focusing too narrowly on the quoted phrase itself. Remember to read a line or two around it, to properly understand the context.

21. D

Difficulty: Medium

This question is easier than it looks—it's basically just a vocabulary-in-context question, asking about a term rather than a single word. If you read a little before and after the quoted line, you find that "functional interpretations" simply means *explanations*, choice (D)—explanations (mostly wrong ones) of why Cro-Magnons created cave art.

22. B

Difficulty: Medium

You probably read the "theories" this question refers to while answering question 21, so just go back and find out why these theories "fell into disfavor." The following lines say that they became unpopular when anthropologists began asking contemporary native Australians why they create their rock art. The reasons are diverse, choice (B). Choice (D) goes too far: the author doesn't say the Cro-Magnon paintings were *identical* to present-day aboriginal paintings. *Neanderthals*, (A), and *trail-signs*, (C), are not discussed in paragraph 4. And choice (E) makes no sense.

23. E

Difficulty: High

A big picture question. Unlike the questions you've been dealing with, this one doesn't give you a line reference. You need an answer that represents the whole passage. Does

KAPLAN
Test Prep and Admissions

choice (A) do this? No, Cro-Magnon *contemporaries* are never discussed. Does choice (B)? No, *agriculture* isn't discussed. As for choice (C), the author's point isn't that Cro-Magnons weren't cavemen, but that they differed from our image of cavemen. Anyway, this isn't the author's main point. Neither is choice (D)—the author never claims Cro-Magnons were *artistically more sophisticated than later civilizations*. Choice (E) is best: at points throughout the passage (paragraphs 2, 3, and 4), the author likens Cro-Magnons to modern people.

24. E

Difficulty: High

This is another big picture question that asks you to consider the passage as a whole. Be careful not to choose an answer simply because you have seen it stated somewhere in the passage—the question is asking the author's primary purpose in writing the *entire* essay. Choices (A) and (B) can be found in places, but do not summarize the main idea. Choice (C) is somewhat true—the passage does give some history of the Cro-Magnons, but the passage was not written to talk about history. Nor was it written to (D), *compliment the artistic work of the Cro-Magnons*. The author does mention that many of the works were impressive, but the passage is not a review of their work. The best choice is then choice (E); the passage as a whole explores the cave art of the Cro-Magnons, and begins to describe what this art says about the people and their history.

SECTION 4

1. D

Difficulty: Medium

The phrase *attending classes in the day and waiting tables at a restaurant at night* is additional information describing how the father worked his way through law school, so it should be set off from the rest of the sentence with a comma. Choice (B) incorrectly uses a semicolon—the second part of the sentence is not an independent clause. Choice (C) creates a comma splice. Choice (E) fixes the sentence structure error, but it unnecessarily changes the verb tense.

2. C

Difficulty: Low

As written, this sentence is a fragment. Choice (C) makes it a complete sentence without changing the meaning. The *yet* in choices (B) and (E) is unnecessary, as contrast has already been set up with *Although* at the beginning of the sentence. Choice (D) does not address the problem of the sentence fragment.

3. A

Difficulty: Medium

This sentence is correct as written. Choice (B) is a run-on sentence. Choice (C) is a mess. Choice (D) introduces a cause/effect that is not present in the original sentence. Choice (E) is not as concise as the original sentence.

4. D

Difficulty: Medium

As written, the sentence doesn't show the correct sequence of events or the correct transition between ideas. The verb form *having shown* incorrectly indicates that the second clause happened before the first. Choice (D) corrects this by using the simple past tense. It also correctly adds the contrasting conjunction *but*, which along with a comma can connect two independent clauses. Choice (B) incorrectly uses the gerund *showing*. Choice (C) creates a comma splice with the transition *however*. For this version of the sentence to be correct, the comma would have to be replaced with a semicolon. Choice (E) illogically uses the word *once*.

5. C

Difficulty: Medium

As written, the second clause is missing a subject. Choice (C) properly uses *it* to refer back to the noun *internship*, creating two independent clauses correctly joined by a comma and the coordinating conjunction *but*. Choices (B) and (E) incorrectly use *that* as a conjunction; choice (D) uses an improper verb form.

6. B

Difficulty: Low

The pronoun *it* is unnecessary in the original version, and choice (B) eliminates the redundancy without introducing any new errors. Choices (C), (D), and (E) create a sentence fragment, making everything after the subject one long description without a main verb.

7. B

Difficulty: Medium

A sentence with two subjects and two predicate (main) verbs is a run-on. Context and the relationship between the two ideas will indicate how the error should be addressed. Here, the two thoughts are contrasting in nature, so a contrast transition word should be used to combine them. Choice (B) does this with *but*. Choice (C) incorrectly implies a cause-and-effect relationship between the two ideas. Choice (D) simply rewords the selection without addressing the error. Choice (E) incorrectly uses the adverb *unusually*.

8.   B

Difficulty: Medium

As it is, this sentence is a run-on. Choice (B) correctly uses a semicolon to separate these two complete but related thoughts. Choice (C) is wordy and awkwardly constructed. Choice (D) uses the pronoun *that* without a clear antecedent. Choice (E) is also awkward and makes unnecessary use of the passive voice.

9.   E

Difficulty: High

Although more than one version is grammatically correct, choice (E) is the most concise and direct version of the sentence. All of the other choices are unnecessarily wordy or awkward.

10. E

Difficulty: Medium

In the original sentence, a speech is standing on a chair and shouting. Modifying phrases need to be next to the thing or person they modify. Choice (E) fixes both the modification and passive voice problems by putting *a man* rather than *the speech* directly after the modifying clause. Choice (D) addresses the errors, but it also introduces an incorrect verb tense.

11. D

Difficulty: Medium

When you can, change the passive voice to the active voice. The *irresponsible executives* are the doers of the action in the sentence, so they should be the subject. Choices (B), (C), and (D) address the issue of voice, but

only choice (D) does so without introducing new errors. Choice (B) creates an awkward sentence with the verb phrase *brought irresponsibly about.* Choice (C) introduces a new verb tense and changes the meaning of the original sentence. By referring to *their collapse*, the sentence makes it sound as if the executives themselves, not the company, collapsed.

12. A

Difficulty: High

The sentence only compares two things, so the correct word is between, not *among,* choice (A).

13. C

Difficulty: Low

The sentence makes it clear that the indigenous people of North America were in America *before* Columbus, so the correct verb form should be past tense, not future tense. The correct form is *discovered* or even *had discovered*.

14. C

Difficulty: Medium

The phrase *complete shamefaced* incorrectly has an adjective (*complete*) modifying another adjective (*shamefaced*). An adverb is used to modify an adjective, so the phrase should read *completely shamefaced*.

15. B

Difficulty: Low

To be idiomatically correct, the phrase *by creating,* choice (B) should read *to create.* The verb *started,* (A), is correctly in the present tense. The phrases in choices (C) and (D) use the correct prepositions.

16. C

Difficulty: Low

The plural subject *plays* doesn't agree with the singular verb *expresses.* Choice (C) should be *express.* The infinitive verb *to write,* choice (A) is correct. The phrases in choices (B) and (D) are in the correct tense and idiomatically correct.

17. E

Difficulty: Medium

Though it uses the passive voice, this sentence is grammatically correct as written.

18. D

Difficulty: Medium

The singular pronoun *its* incorrectly refers to the plural subject *fruits*. Note that the subject is *fruits*, not *item*. *Its* should be *their*.

19. E

Difficulty: Medium

This is a complex sentence, but it is correct as written.

20. A

Difficulty: Medium

The subject *toppling* is singular, and so (A) should be the singular *is*. The phrases in choices (B), (C), and (D) are all idiomatically correct.

21. D

Difficulty: Medium

This sentence has an ambiguous pronoun. As written, it is unclear to whom the *them* in the sentence refers. Does *them* mean the others, the people who have dogs for companionship, or dogs themselves? Just because you understand what the sentence *intends* to say doesn't mean that what is written actually expresses that intention.

22. C

Difficulty: High

Comparisons should be in parallel form. Choice (C) is incorrect because *technology* is compared to *prices of agricultural products*. To be correct, choice (C) should be *prices of technological products*.

23. D

Difficulty: High

The phrase *not increase their gross profit* refers to the company's gross profit. There is only *one* company, so the possessive pronoun should be *its* instead of *their*.

24. E

Difficulty: Medium

The sentence is correct as written. The verb *had started,* choice (A), is in the correct tense because it happened before *he might have succeeded.* The phrase *before Friday,* choice (B), is idiomatically correct. The word *succeeded*

takes the correct preposition *in,* choice (C), and the adverb *remarkably,* choice (D), correctly modifies the adjective *difficult.*

25. D

Difficulty: High

More than two people are being compared. Choice (D) should read *most abstract* rather than *more abstract*. The phrase *in many ways,* choice (A) is idiomatically correct. The transition word *but,* choice (B) sets up the contrast and the verb *was,* choice (C) is correctly in the past tense.

26. E

Difficulty: Medium

Remember that several sentences, like this one, will be correct as written.

27. E

Difficulty: Medium

The sentence is correct as written. The verb *maintains,* choice (A) agrees with the singular subject *FBI* and is correctly in the present tense. The prepositions *for,* (B), and *in,* (D), correctly, follow *maintains* and *interested,* respectively. The pronoun *who,* choice (C), clearly refers to *citizens*.

28. A

Difficulty: Low

The word *Everything* is singular despite the fact that it refers to a collection of many things, so the verb that follows it must be singular as well. The sentence should read *Everything about the case* is *strange and suspicious*…choice (B) is concerned with transitions, choice (C), tests verb tense understanding and choice (D) deals with creating proper prepositional phrases.

29. D

Difficulty: Medium

Always make sure that pronouns agree in number and gender with the noun or pronoun to which they're referring. The pronoun *their* which is plural is referring to the pronoun *each,* which is singular. If you were correcting this sentence, you would have to replace *their* with *his* or *her*. Notice that the plural noun, *members* is *not* the subject of the verb, but is placed in the sentence to distract the unprepared test taker.

Choice (A), *about,* is one of the prepositions that can be used with *concerned.* Choice (B), the preposition *on* is used correctly. Choice (C), the past tense verb correctly expresses the time indicated in the sentence.

30. C

Difficulty: Medium

The original sentence has two problems: incorrect punctuation and verb tense. A semicolon is used to link two independent, closely related clauses. In addition, the verb tense of *revering* must match *admire.* Only choice (C) addresses both issues. *Admire* is present tense. Choices (D) and (E) are both past tense. Choice (B) uses an illogical conjunction.

31. E

Difficulty: Medium

In the original sentence, the pronoun *it* isn't clearly defined. You need to explain what the person experienced. Choice (E) is the only choice that clarifies this issue. Choice (A) introduces an unnecessary modifier with an incorrect relationship to the rest of the sentence. The verbs in the sentence are both in the correct tense; choices (B) and (D) suggest improper changes. Choice (C) is grammatically correct, but it is overly wordy and fails to clarify what *it* refers to.

32. A

Difficulty: Medium

Sentence 4 introduces the concept of danger. Sentence 5 presents items that have reduced the risks of rock climbing. You need a transition between those items and reduced danger in the second clause. The contrasting transition *however,* choice (A), is the only choice that works. Choice (B) represents time, not contrast. Choice (C) shows cause-and-effect, which misrepresents the relationship between the items. Choice (D) indicates contrast, but sounds awkward. The use of *in fact* in choice (E) incorrectly implies continuation and gives unwarranted emphasis.

33. C

Difficulty: Medium

The second paragraph talks about safety gear, with a specific example in Sentence 6. Sentence 7 begins the next paragraph with a reference to a piece of safety gear, and

then adds the importance of another person. A sentence about others' roles in rock climbing safety would smooth the transition. Choice (C) is the right place to introduce other people into the safety equation. Choices (A) and (B) present the information too soon; the following sentences don't support the supplied information. In contrast, choices (D) and (E) provide the information after the introduction of other people.

34. B

Difficulty: Medium

Point-of-view (first person, second person, etc.) should not shift back and forth in a paragraph. Sentences 9 and 11 are written in the first person, while sentence 10 is in the second person. In this question, you are only offered the opportunity to fix sentence 10, so it should be in first person like the sentences that surround it. Only choice (B) puts the sentence in first person and in the correct verb tense. Choice (A) offers no correction. Choice (C) presents the correct point of view, but introduces a new error by switching to past tense. Choice (D) remains in the second person. Choice (E) incorrectly changes the point of view to the third person, using the pronoun *one.*

35. C

Difficulty: Medium

As written, sentence 13 is a fragment. Choices (A) and (B) offer no correction. The use of *lastly* in choice (D) places the sentence in a non-existent series, while choice (E) reverses the comparisons. Only choice (C) correctly offers a verb and maintains the parallel structure.

SECTION 5

1. A

Difficulty: Low

Strategic Advice: This is an early algebra problem and one of the easier questions you'll see in this section.

Getting to the Answer:

$4(x + 5) = 24$

Divide both sides by 4: $x + 5 = 6$

Subtract 5 from both sides: $x = 1$

2. E

Difficulty: Low

Strategic Advice: With combination problems, the trick is to multiply the components together. This should make sense—just think that for each of the 7 entrees, there are 4 appetizer choices, so you need to multiply 7 times 4.

Getting to the Answer:

$7(4) = 28$

3. A

Difficulty: Low

Strategic Advice: This is just a substitution problem; the only catch is that it has two steps. Since you have a numerical value for z, plug that in first, and then you'll have a numerical value for y to plug into the first equation.

Getting to the Answer:

$y = z + 2$
$y = 4 + 2$
$y = 6$

Then, substitute 6 for y:

$x + 2y = 14$
$x + 2(6) = 14$
$x + 12 = 14$
$x = 2$

4. A

Difficulty: Medium

Strategic Advice: If a fraction equals zero, then its numerator equals zero. (If the denominator of a fraction equals zero, then that fraction is undefined.)

Getting to the Answer:

$\frac{x+y}{x} = 0$
$x + y = 0$
$x = -y$

5. C

Difficulty: Low

Strategic Advice: Don't let yourself get confused by word problems with lots of variables.

Getting to the Answer:

Laurel is taller than Nick: $n < l$

Laurel is shorter than Vince: $l < v$

So, $n < l < v$.

6. B

Difficulty: Medium

Strategic Advice: This question purely tests your ability to translate English into math.

Getting to the Answer:

"square of n" $= n^2$

"difference between m and the square of n" $= m - n^2$

"sum of m and n" $= m + n$

"square root of the sum of m and n" $= \sqrt{m + n}$

Now equate the two sides of the sentence:

$m - n^2 = \sqrt{m + n}$

7. B

Difficulty: Low

Strategic Advice: Look for a pattern in the sequence. Except for the first term, each term in this sequence is the result of doubling the previous term:

Getting to the Answer: $28 \times 2 = 56$ and $56 \times 2 = 112$.

8. A

Difficulty: Medium

Strategic Advice: Remember the rules for parallel lines and transversals. All acute angles are equal, and all obtuse angles are equal. If a is 110, then the corresponding angle below it has the same measure. If you also remember that the measure of a straight line is 180°, you're in good shape.

Getting to the Answer:

$110 + d = 180$
$d = 70$
$b + c = 180$ (because the two angles form a straight line)
$b + c + d = 180 + 70 = 250$

9. 13

Difficulty: Low

Strategic Advice: In this problem, in which you solve three equations with three variables, it's a good idea to start working with the simplest one. The 3rd equation only has one variable in it, so start with that one.

Getting to the Answer: If $2c = 16$, then $c = 8$. Now that you have a value for c, the next logical step is to plug that value into any other equation that has c in it. The second equation is $c - b = 5$, so that becomes $8 - b = 5$. That means that b is 3. Plugging $b = 3$ into the first equation gives you $3a = 6$, which means that $a = 2$. Now you know that a is 2, b is 3, and c is 8, so $a + b + c = 2 + 3 + 8 = 13$, so grid that in.

10. 87.5

Difficulty: Medium

Strategic Advice: In this percent word problem, if 50 out of 400 seniors are majoring in economics, then $400 - 50$ or 350 seniors are not majoring in economics. Since Percent × Whole = Part, then $pecent = \dfrac{part}{whole}$. 350 is the part and 400 is the whole, so the percent you're looking for is just $\dfrac{350}{400}$.

Getting to the Answer: Dividing both numbers by 4 gives you $\dfrac{87.5}{100}$, which is 87.5%, so just grid in 87.5.

11. 1.25

Difficulty: Medium

Strategic Advice: This is another problem in which you solve two equations with two variables. Another way of saying that 5 pens cost as much as 2 notebooks is the equation $5P = 2N$. That's just translating from words to math, by using N to represent the cost of a notebook and P to represent the cost of a pen.

Getting to the Answer:

If one notebook plus one pen cost $1.75, then $N + P = \$1.75$. If you take the first equation and solve for P, you get $P = \dfrac{2N}{5}$. You can plug that into the second equation to get $N + \dfrac{2N}{5} = \$1.75$, or $\dfrac{7N}{5} = \$1.75$. Solving for N gives you $N = \dfrac{5}{7} \times (1.75) = \$1.25$, so put 1.25 in the grid.

12. 44

Difficulty: Medium

Strategic Advice: The 4 scores you're given here average to 86, and you can use this average to find the unknown score. That means that the sum of the 4 scores divided by 4 is 86, and so the sum of the scores is 4×86, or 344. That's just another way of stating the average formula:

if average $= \dfrac{\text{Sum of the terms}}{\text{Number of terms}}$,

then sum of the terms = average × number of terms. If you have 4 scores that add up to a particular number, and you want 1 score to be as low as possible, you have to make the other 3 scores as high as possible.

Getting to the Answer: The highest possible value for any one score is 100, so the lowest score occurs when the other 3 scores are each 100, and $100 + 100 + 100 +$ the lowest score = 344. A little bit of arithmetic will tell you that the lowest score must be 44, which is what you should put into the grid.

13. 122, 182, or 242

Difficulty: Medium

Strategic Advice: Here you're told that v leaves a remainder of 2 when it's divided by 3, 4, or 5. This means that $v - 2$ is a multiple of 3, 4, and 5. Since 3, 4, and 5 have no common factors greater than 1, $v - 2$ must be a multiple of $3 \times 4 \times 5 = 60$.

Getting to the Answer: So v is 2 more than a multiple of 60. Keep in mind that v is a three-digit number less than 250. So v can't be $2 + 60$ or 62. But v could be $2 + 2(60) = 122$, v could be $2 + 3(60) = 182$, and v could be $2 + 4(60) = 242$. Notice that $2 + 5(60) = 302$ is greater than 250. So v can't be 302, or 2 more than any larger multiple of 60. So v could only be 122, 182, or 242.

14. 81

Difficulty: Medium

Strategic Advice: Since you're given that angle ADF is 36°, the first thing to do is to label that angle 36° in the diagram. Do you see any other angles that you know the measure of?

Getting to the Answer: Since $ABCD$ is a square, the corner angles are all 90°, and since AC is a diagonal, it cuts those corner angles in half. Therefore angles DAF, FAB, BCF, and DCF are all 45° angles. If you write all that on the diagram, you should notice that you now know the measure of 2 out of the 3 angles of triangle ADF. Since angle ADF is 36° and angle DAF is 45°, angle AFD must be $180° - 36° - 45° = 99°$. Since AFD and the angle measuring $x°$ lie on a straight line, x must be $180 - 99 = 81$. Grid in an 81.

15. $\frac{5}{24}$

Difficulty: Medium

Strategic Advice: You probably want to start this question by drawing a number line.

Getting to the Answer:

Put $\frac{1}{6}$ and $\frac{1}{4}$ on your number line, with $\frac{1}{6}$ to the left of $\frac{1}{4}$ since it is smaller:

What point is the same distance from $\frac{1}{6}$ as it is from $\frac{1}{4}$? Certainly it's the point that is halfway in between $\frac{1}{6}$ and $\frac{1}{4}$, so that must be where point X is. The distance from point X to either $\frac{1}{6}$ or $\frac{1}{4}$ is half the distance from $\frac{1}{6}$ to $\frac{1}{4}$. The distance from $\frac{1}{6}$ to $\frac{1}{4}$ is just the difference of the 2 numbers, or $\frac{1}{4} - \frac{1}{6}$. However, you can't subtract $\frac{1}{6}$ from $\frac{1}{4}$ because they are fractions with different denominators. You can find a common denominator, like 12. $\frac{1}{4} = \frac{3}{12}$ and $\frac{1}{6} = \frac{2}{12}$, so the difference between $\frac{1}{6}$ and $\frac{1}{4}$ (and therefore the distance between them on the number line) is $\frac{3}{12} - \frac{2}{12} = \frac{1}{12}$. The distance from X to $\frac{1}{6}$ is half of $\frac{1}{12}$, or $\frac{1}{2} \bullet \frac{1}{12} = \frac{1}{24}$, so put everything in terms of 24ths. $\frac{1}{6} = \frac{2}{12} = \frac{1}{24}$ and $\frac{1}{4} = \frac{3}{12} = \frac{6}{24}$. If you put this on the number line, it becomes clear what X is since X is halfway between $\frac{4}{24}$ and $\frac{6}{24}$:

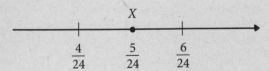

The coordinate of X must therefore be $\frac{5}{24}$, so put that into the grid.

16. 54

Difficulty: Medium

Strategic Advice: The polygon *ABCDE* is clearly a five-sided polygon, which is called a pentagon. *OE* and *OD* are radii of the circle, and if you draw lines from *O* to *A*, *B*, and *C*, those lines will also be radii of the circle. If you do that you'll see that since the sides of the pentagon are equal, all those radii divide the pentagon into 5 identical triangles. Therefore those radii divide the circle into 5 equal pieces. That means that each of the central angles formed by those radii measures $\frac{1}{5}$ of the whole circle, or $\frac{1}{5} \times 360° = 72°$.

Getting to the Answer: So, angle *DOE* measures 72°. Since 2 of the sides of triangle *OED* are radii of the circle and therefore equal in length, the triangle is isosceles. That means that angles *OED* and *ODE* are equal, so they both measure $r°$. So, $r° + r° + 72° = 180°$, which means that $r = 54$.

17. 19.5

Difficulty: High

Strategic Advice: The figure shows 2 triangles that are formed by 2 lines that cross each other plus 2 additional lines. Each triangle has an unlabeled angle, both of which are formed where the two longer lines cross. That means that the 2 unlabeled angles are vertical angles, so they must be equal to each other. Label each of those 2 angles $y°$. Then the triangle on the left has angles measuring $y°$, $x°$, and $(3x + 1)°$, and the triangle on the right has angles measuring $y°$, $(2x)°$, and 40°. The sum of the angles of any triangle is 180°, so $y + x + (3x + 1) = 180$, and $y + 2x + 40 = 180$. That gives you two equations and two unknowns, so you should be able to solve for both x and y.

Getting to the Answer: There are a number of different ways to do so, but the easiest is to just forget the 180 and set the sums of the angles equal to each other:

$$y + x + (3x + 1) = y + 2x + 40$$
$$y + 4x + 1 = y + 2x + 40$$
$$4x + 1 = 2x + 40$$
$$2x + 1 = 40$$
$$2x = 39$$
$$x = 19.5$$

So just put 19.5 into the grid.

18. $\frac{9}{7}$

Difficulty: High

Strategic Advice: If you draw yourself an 8 by 8 checkerboard, you'll see that the only unit squares that are not completely surrounded by other unit squares are the unit squares on the border. Also, the unit squares that are completely surrounded by other unit squares make up a bigger square, which is 6 by 6. That is, there are 6 unit squares along each dimension of this larger 6 by 6 square.

Getting to the Answer: So the number of unit squares that are completely surrounded by other squares is 6 × 6 or 36. There are 8 × 8 or 64 squares on the checkerboard. So the number of unit squares that are not completely surrounded by other squares, which is also the number of unit squares on the border, is 64 − 36 = 28. The ratio of the number of unit squares that are completely surrounded by other squares to the number of unit squares on the border is $\frac{36}{28}$. Dividing the numerator and denominator by 4, you find that the ratio is $\frac{9}{7}$.

SECTION 6

1. D

Difficulty: Low

Since the veteran boxer won most of his bouts by knockouts, you can assume that he was pretty successful. Choice (D), *unbroken,* is the only choice that describes his series of wins in a way that suggests success; an *unbroken* series of victories would be a winning streak with no losses. Choices (A) and (B) are both contradicted by the rest of the sentence. Choice (C), *able-bodied,* may seem to fit in a sentence about a boxer, but what's an *able-bodied* series of wins? This choice sounds odd when you plug it in. Only choice (D) makes sense.

2. B

Difficulty: Medium

Look for context clues. The first major clue in the sentence is "everyday." You're looking for a word with a similar meaning for the first blank. In the second, you need something to describe what the objects were transformed into, a word to contrast with "everyday." That takes you to choice (B). *Mundane* is almost a synonym for "everyday." The second

word in choice (B), *resplendent,* or extraordinary, is a good contrast, and fits when plugged into the sentence. Choices (C) and (E) can be eliminated because their first words don't work. Everyday things like vegetables aren't *small* or *artificial.* In choice (A), *inexpensive,* might seem to fit with the idea of "everyday items such as vegetables." But (A)'s second word, *tawdry,* or cheap and gaudy, makes no sense. In choice (D), vegetables might be *decorative,* but *functional* doesn't provide the contrast we're looking for.

3. B

Difficulty: Medium

Here, you know that the issues "go far beyond" the immediate controversy referred to in the sentence. So you can predict they have "implications" or "consequences" beyond the matter presently under discussion. The best match for this prediction is choice (B), *ramifications. Ramifications* are resulting developments or consequences. Choice (C), *proponents,* are advocates or supporters. Choice (D), *inferences,* are conclusions.

4. D

Difficulty: Medium

The phrase "even accepting" in the second part of the sentence implies that Chamberlain's approach to German aggression was not a particularly tough or militant one, especially since he tolerated Germany's annexation of Austria. Therefore, it's likely that Chamberlain adopted a non-aggressive, accepting approach to Hitler. The choice that comes closest to this prediction is choice (D), *conciliatory,* meaning "tending to pacify or accommodate." Choice (B), *precarious,* means "uncertain or dangerous," and choice (C), *haughty,* means "arrogant, snobby, huffy." Choice (A), *hasty,* means fast.

5. C

Difficulty: High

Although we don't know what kind of performance Redgrave gave, we can infer that it was either good or bad. If it was good, we can predict people who were lucky enough to see the performance say it was the height of his career. Basically, we want two positive words if Redgrave did a good job, or two negative words if he bombed. The only choice showing this relationship is choice (C): those fortunate enough to witness Redgrave's performance say it was the *pinnacle*, or height, of his career. Choice (A) *scourge* means "something that annoys or destroys." Choice (B) *astute* means shrewd or perceptive. Choice (D) *hapless* means "unlucky." Choice (E), *nadir,* means "the lowest point."

Questions 6–9

Both passages address the issue of diseases that are becoming resistant to treatment with antibiotics. The first passage indicates that antibiotic overuse among people has led to this problem. The second passage indicates that increased antibiotic use in livestock has also contributed to the problem.

6. A

Difficulty: Medium

Notice that in the cited lines the author connects high antibiotic usage with the growth of HMOs, which are described as "notoriously stingy" and more concerned about "patient turnover" than "patient care." This evidence suggests that the author is implying that antibiotics are over prescribed by HMOs because they are relatively inexpensive and don't take a lot of time to prescribe, choice (A). The paragraph does not explore whether or not HMOs are aware of antibiotic-resistance problems, so choice (B) is out of scope. Choice (C) is an opposite answer. The sentence suggests that such treatments are popular because they are cheap. Choice (D) is wrong because the paragraph doesn't go so far as to suggest that HMOs are unconcerned about their patients. Finally, choice (E) is out because the author only implies that private practices do not prescribe as many antibiotics as HMOs, not necessarily that they are more *careful*.

7. C

Difficulty: Low

By going back to the referenced sentence, you can see that the author uses "open" to describe a risky situation that involves disease. In other words, the larger herds were more *vulnerable* to disease choice (C). Choices (A), *unobstructed*, (B), *free*, and (E), *accessible* are all primary definitions of "open", but they do not work within the context of the passage. Choice (D), *receptive,* is close, but it mistakenly suggests that the herd would welcome disease.

8. D

Difficulty: Medium

In this case, the intersection comes most clearly in the opening sentence of Passage 2. Here the author says that arguments attributing antibiotic-resistant problems to "excessive human use of such medications" ignore the fact that animal medications also play a role. This is the exact focus of Passage 1, so the author of Passage 2 would consider the argument made by the author of Passage 1 to be rather inadequate or *limited,* choice (D). The author of Passage 2 clearly thinks this is an important issue, so it is unlikely that he would find the author of Passage 1 to be *overly critical*. Choice (B) is a distortion; while the author of Passage 2 states that the first author's perspective "ignores" important information, he clearly indicates that such a "case can be made." Choice (C) is also a distortion. The second author only asserts that the first has not given enough weight to the impact of animal medications, not necessarily that the first author is unaware of this impact. Finally, choice (E) is wrong because the second author clearly believes the first author is overlooking important information.

9. A

Difficulty: High

Ignore the first author's views on HMOs and the second author's description of how bacteria can transfer from animals to humans. Instead, focus on how each author describes the antibiotic-resistance problem itself. Passage 1 refers to "a growing number of Americans" that suffer from this problem, while Passage 2 describes how the effect of animal medications began "roughly 30 years ago." This convergence of information indicates that both authors agree the problem is worse today than it was in the past, choice (A). Only Passage 1 cites over-prescription as a definitive cause of the problem or specifically mentions a history of documentation, so choices (B) and (C) are out. Choice (D) comes close to capturing the area of commonality between the two paragraphs, but neither author really suggests that the problem was not serious in the past, only that it is more *widespread* today. Choice (E) is too extreme. While both authors describe the problem as serious, neither suggests it is a devastating threat.

Questions 10–15

This is a not-too-difficult social science passage that only has a few big ideas. If you felt confused at any point, it would've been worthwhile to check the questions. They clarify things and are fairly straightforward. Your first reading should've given you these ideas: Paragraph 1 says that people have less free time now than they used to, because people are choosing to work overtime to be able to afford expensive leisure-time activities. Paragraph 2 says that although people have less free time during the week, on weekends they feel compelled to participate in strenuous, skill-testing activities. Paragraph 3 explains that this is because technology has removed "craft" from most professions, so people try to prove their competency by mastering demanding leisure activities.

10. C

Difficulty: Medium

Go back and read a few lines around the quoted line to see the context in which "skiing and sailing" are mentioned. The author's point is that if you want to go skiing or sailing in your free time, unless you are rich, you'll have to spend some of that "free time" working to be able to afford those expensive pastimes. That makes choice (C) correct. The point is not that expensive sports are *inaccessible* for the average person, choice (A), but that they require a sacrifice of time. The author is not commenting on the cost of sports like skiing and sailing, choice (D), or whether they are *unnecessarily expensive,* choice (B). Choice (E) is out because the author is not giving out advice about what type of recreation to choose.

11. B

Difficulty: Medium

Don't over-interpret the passage with a question like this one—the answer is fairly straightforward. For example, choices (C), (D), and (E) give way too much information for what is found in the text. The author simply says that either because advertising is very effective, or because people just want to own stuff, they choose to work more hours. So the "effectiveness of advertising" is one possible reason why people spend so much on recreation, choice (B). Choice (A) sounds much too extreme—the author never *condemns* the average consumer for anything.

12. B

Difficulty: Low

After reading a line or two around the word "indulgences," it should be clear that the author uses that word to refer to items like "elaborate running shoes" and "monogrammed warm-up suits." These clearly are not choice (E), *favors.* There's nothing in the context to support the idea that they are choice (A), *rewards;* they certainly are not *expenses,* choice (D), and while choice (C), *whims,* comes close, choice (B), *luxuries,* is the better answer.

13. D

Difficulty: Medium

The author's point in lines 39–46 is that until recently, many leisure activities could only be pursued once a year. The example of taking swimwear out of mothballs illustrates this point ironically—people swam so infrequently, they had to put their swimwear in long-term storage, choice (D). Choice (A) is wrong because the author expresses no particular opinion about annual vacations today. *Household chores,* choice (B), is a distortion of the idea of "digging equipment out and dusting it off." Choice (C) is out because *despair* is too strong a word—watch out for these kinds of wrong choices—and because taking out swimwear hardly fits the description of a *traditional custom.* Finally, there was no *lack of enthusiasm for swimming* in the past—it was just enjoyed in a different way than it is now, choice (E).

14. A

Difficulty: High

The "casual attitude" is described at the end of paragraph 2. It is the emphasis on "having a good time" during recreation, rather than focusing on "technique." Choices (C) and (D) jump out as wrong, because they're never discussed. Choice (E) is also off-base; people never had *a resistance towards buying sports equipment.* You can scan paragraph 1 to be sure, but there was never a *restriction on working overtime,* so choice (B) is out. That leaves choice (A), which may not seem like a very precise answer, but by process of elimination it has to be correct. Remember not to argue with what you're given—choose the best answer, and move on.

15. B

Difficulty: Medium

Scan the end of paragraph 3 to identify "the author's conclusion." That's where the author argues that people "work at recreation" because technology has taken the craft out of their jobs. Now check the choices. Choice (B) should jump out as correct—describing the skills that people employ in their leisure time would support the idea that people are doing "meaningful work" on the weekends. Information about jobs that still *require a level of expertise,* (A), would weaken the author's point. Information about choices (C) and (D) wouldn't affect the author's conclusion—these choices refer to earlier points. Choice (E) may have been tempting—but information about technologies in the workplace would not support the author's conclusion as directly as information about the skills now involved in leisure activities—choice (B).

16. A

Difficulty: Low

The thesis, or main idea, is generally introduced in the first paragraph. Notice that "dark matter" is introduced immediately, and see that its discovery is more clearly defined within the first paragraph.

Choice (A) is a good match. Choice (B) is a misused detail; photography did indeed aid in the discovery of dark matter, but this is not the focus of the passage. Choice (C) is a misused detail; dark matter does present itself as *star clouds and rifts and holes*, but there is a better term—dark matter—which is discussed at length. Choice (D) is an opposite; the passage explains that astronomers discovered that the space between stars is filled with dark matter, and therefore is not empty. Choice (E) is out of scope; dark matter is a topic within astronomy, but the passage does not cover the entire field of astronomy.

17. A

Difficulty: Low

What spaces are being discussed in this passage? The passage is concerned with dark matter in the universe. Determine where the spaces are that are under consideration.

Choice (A) is a good match for your prediction; Trumpler researched occurrences of light in the Milky Way, not only the dark space between the stars. Choice (B) is distortion; although there is interstellar space between the Earth and the Sun, the article is concerned with more than that distance. Choice (C) is a misused detail; star clouds are present in interstellar space. Choice (D) is a misused detail; dark matter is present where there are no stars, but interstellar applies to the universe as a whole, stars and all. Choice (E) is a misused detail; interstellar applies to the arena in which empty and transparent space was once believed to exist.

18. C

Difficulty: Medium

The key word to this question is "consequence." The second paragraph introduces the reader to the reluctance astronomers held toward the theory of dark matter. The second sentence continues with "The consequence…." The consequence of this dark matter is that it "would dim the light…and further complicate the determination of their distances…."

Choice (A) is a misused detail; astronomers were indeed reluctant; however, reluctance was not a consequence of dark matter. Choice (B) is a misused detail; again, astronomers did originally believe that the spaces between stars were empty, but this does not define the consequence of dark matter. Choice (C) is a good match for your prediction; this finding of dark matter would establish decades of previous research inaccurate. Choice (D) is extreme; the passage does not state that astronomers were embarrassed to admit they were wrong. Choice (E) is distortion; indeed, the problem for astronomers was that dark matter was not transparent; however, this does not explain the consequence of such a discovery.

19. C

Difficulty: Medium

Astronomers are concerned with determining distances and the brightness of stars. Which aspect of a star's brightness would a researcher be interested in? Astronomers are concerned with obtaining/observing the true nature of a star. The paragraph describes how the discovery of dark matter obscures this true, or intrinsic, brightness.

Choice (A) is an opposite; a star's appearance to the naked eye is easily obtained. It is the true brightness of the star that is complicated by the presence of dark matter. Choice (B) is a misused detail; "intrinsic" is not used to describe the complication of determining a star's distance. Choice (C) is a good match for you prediction. Choice (D) is extreme; "intrinsic" is used to describe an attribute of the star's brightness, not the astronomer's perception. Choice (E) is distortion; the passage asserts that "intrinsic" describes brightness, but this does not define the term.

20. D

Difficulty: High

The sentence is concerned with the consequence of "an absorbing dust," which would be "a very serious obstacle to researchers." What consequence does the sentence describe? Reread the sentence to determine the seriousness of the discovery of dark matter. Note that it "complicates the determination" of a star's distance and true brightness, which is the goal of an astronomer.

Choice (A) is extreme; the passage does not state that dark matter is detrimental to the Milky Way. Choice (B) is distortion; the advent of photography aided astronomers in their discovery of dark matter. Choice (C) is extreme; astronomers and researchers are synonymous in this passage. Choice (D) is a good match for your prediction; the presence of dark matter would create a paradigm shift, and develop the need to redefine current astronomical thinking. Choice (E) is an opposite; dark matter would make it more difficult to determine a star's distance.

21. B

Difficulty: Medium

Line 42–43 state "The presence of a general absorption at all wavelengths was thus proven." What does "thus" imply? Read the preceding sentence to determine that the distances given by the apparent magnitude method were greater than those given by the angular diameters.

Choice (A) is extreme; the distances were greater. Choice (B) is a good match for your prediction; the fourth paragraph explains the relationship between apparent magnitude and angular diameter and how the discrepancy between the two prove the presence of general a absorption. Choice (C) is a misused detail; dust particles and light wavelengths are discussed in the following paragraph, and are used as a detail regarding the red appearance of light. Choice (D) is a misused detail; "fainter means more distant" was a method employed by Trumpler, not the outcome of his research. Choice (E) is a misused detail; likewise, "smaller means more distant" was a method employed by Trumpler, not the outcome of his research.

22. D

Difficulty: High

The statement regarding the setting sun refers to the reason, which is mentioned in the preceding sentence. Reread the sentence before the example of the setting sun, which is used to illustrate the point.

Choice (A) is extreme; *elective adsorption* is never mentioned in this passage. Choice (B) is a misused detail; color excess is the amount of increase of the color index, which is used to determine selective absorption. Choice (C) is a misused detail; interstellar dust and color excess was key in Trumpler's investigation of selective absorption. Choice (D) is a good match for your prediction. Choice (E) is distortion; absorption of dark matter is the theme of the passage, but is not a detailed enough reason for the redness of the setting sun.

23. A

Difficulty: Medium

Go back to the passage and reread the cited sentence. The passage indicates that "in retrospect," the mismatch between Emerson and the "stiflingly rigid" church is "not difficult to imagine. The author's words serve to emphasize how different, or *innovative*, Emerson's philosophy was in comparison to church tradition, choice (A). Choice (B) makes too much of a leap. While Emerson did chafe at the modes of thinking in his church, nothing in the paragraph indicates he criticized *all* rigid modes of thinking. The paragraph does not describe Emerson's personal level of religious devotion, so choice (C) isn't a reasonable answer. Choice (D) is out because the paragraph only notes that Emerson felt disillusioned about the divinity school his father may have pressed him to join. It never indicates that he renounced, or rejected, his father. Finally, the paragraph does not explore whether or not Emerson wished he had never enrolled in divinity school, so choice (E) is incorrect.

24. D

Difficulty: Low

The passage indicates that in divinity school Emerson became disillusioned and restless, finding the teachings of the school stifling and rigid. This characterization suggests that he found these modes of thinking unpleasant, likely because they could not be changed or because he felt compelled to adopt them unquestioned, choice (D). Choice (A) isn't a reasonable inference. Emerson rejected the philosophies of his divinity school, but this does not mean that he was uninspired by the experience; it is certainly possible to be inspired by negative influences. While Emerson is described as "creative," he is never referred to as *rebellious,* choice (B). Nothing in the paragraph suggests that another divinity school would have been better suited for Emerson, so choice (C) can't be the answer. Choice (E) makes a generalization about divinity school.

SECTION 7

1. D

Difficulty: Low

Strategic Advice: If Thomas wound up in debt, it means that he spent more money than he actually had—a situation that you're all familiar with. So, the correct answer must be greater than the amount of money he had, which was $15, so eliminate choices (A), (B), and (C).

Getting to the Answer:

If he has a debt of $5, then he must have spent all the money he had, or $15, and then borrowed another $5 and spent that also. So he spent a total of $15 + $5, or $20, choice (D).

2. D

Difficulty: Medium

Strategic Advice: Here, the angle marked $x°$ is in a triangle with 2 other unknown angles. However, one of those unknown angles of the triangle, the one just above the $x°$ angle, lies on a straight line with an angle measuring 98°. Therefore that angle must measure $180° - 98° = 82°$. The third angle in the triangle is opposite a 54° angle that is formed by the intersection of 2 straight lines. So the third angle of the triangle must also measure 54°.

Getting to the Answer:

The 3 angles of a triangle add up to 180°, so $54° + 82° + x° = 180°$, and $x = 44$, choice (D).

3. E

Difficulty: Medium

Strategic Advice: Since something happens every 5 minutes at this party, look at each five-minute interval.

Getting to the Answer:

At first there are 256 people. After 5 minutes half of them leave. That means that 128 people leave and 128 people are left after 5 minutes. 5 minutes after that, or 10 minutes after it started, half the remaining people leave. That means that half of 128, or 64, people leave and 64 are left after 10 minutes. 15 minutes after it started, half the remaining 64, or 32, people leave and 32 people are left. 20 minutes after it started, half of 32, or 16, people leave, and so finally only 16 people are left to eat all those ham and cheese sandwiches from section 2. Answer choice (E) is correct.

4. A

Difficulty: Medium

Strategic Advice: Remember, in a symbolism problem you shouldn't worry that there's a strange symbol you've never seen before. It's just a made-up symbol that is always defined by mathematical concepts that you've seen before. Here, an x with a circle around it just means to plug x into an equation.

Getting to the Answer:

If $\textcircled{x} = 5x - \frac{x}{2}$, then $\textcircled{8} = 5(8) - \frac{8}{2}$, or $40 - 4$, which is 36, answer choice (A).

5. C

Difficulty: Medium

Strategic Advice: This question involves solving an algebraic equation and working with decimals, so if you had trouble with it, you might need to review one or both of those topics. All you have to do to solve this problem is work with the equation step by step until you get x alone on one side:

Getting to the Answer:

$0.4x + 2 = 5.6$	Subtract 2 from both sides.
$0.4x = 3.6$	Multiply both sides by 10 to get rid of the decimals.
$4x = 36$	Divide by 4.
$x = 9$	And you've found x, answer choice (C).

6. B

Difficulty: Medium

Strategic Advice: If a rectangle has a perimeter of 12, then $2(W + L) = 12$, where W is the width of the rectangle and L is its length.

Getting to the Answer: If $2(W + L) = 12$, then $W + L = 6$. If the width is 2 less than the length, then $W = L - 2$. You can plug $L - 2$ for W into the equation $W + L = 6$, so $W + L = 6$ becomes $(L - 2) + L = 6$, and so $2L - 2 = 6$, $2L = 8$, and $L = 4$. If the length is 4, then the width, which is 2 less, must be 2. The *area* of a rectangle with length 4 and width 2 is $4 \times 2 = 8$, answer choice (B).

7. C

Difficulty: Medium

Strategic Advice: The easiest way to do this one is to just draw lines from each point and then add up the number of line segments drawn.

Getting to the Answer: From point A, draw one line to each of points B, C, D, and E. From point B, you already have a line to point A, so just draw a line to each of points C, D, and E. From point C you have already drawn lines to A and B, so draw in a line to point D and one to point E, and finally draw a line from point D to point E. (You've drawn a star inside a pentagon—very artistic!) Can you see any point that is unconnected to any other point? No, so just add up the number of lines you've already drawn—there are $4 + 3 + 2 + 1$ or 10 of them, answer choice (C).

8. B

Difficulty: High

Strategic Advice: Whenever you have a percent word problem that doesn't give you a definite amount and asks you a question like "What fraction of the total…?", you should pick a number for the total.

Getting to the Answer: Since you're dealing with percents here, and will be *converting the percents to fractions*, a good number for the total is 100. So, say that 100 people were polled. 80% of the 100 people were registered voters, so 80 people were registered voters. 75% of the registered voters voted in the last election, so $75\% \times 80$, or 60 people voted in the last election. If 60 of the 80 registered voters actually voted in the last election then $80 - 60 = 20$ of the registered voters didn't vote in the last election. The fraction of the people surveyed who were registered but didn't vote is $\frac{20}{100}$, or $\frac{1}{5}$, answer choice (B).

9. E

Difficulty: High

Strategic Advice: Mixture problems are very tricky. The important thing to look for in a mixture problem is this: which quantities stay the same and which quantities change? Here the alcohol is evaporating but the iodine is not. Therefore, the quantity of iodine will be unchanged.

Getting to the Answer: So, start with 4 ounces of iodine and 16 ounces of alcohol, and end with 4 ounces of iodine and an unknown quantity of alcohol, which you can call x ounces. That means that in the end the whole solution has a total of $4 + x$ ounces, since the solution is made up of only iodine and alcohol. The final quantities of iodine and total solution are in the ratio of 2 to 3. That means that the *ratio* of 4 to $4 + x$ is equal to the ratio of 2 to 3, or $\frac{4}{4 + x} = \frac{2}{3}$, which is just an *algebraic equation* that can be easily solved:

$$\frac{4}{4 + x} = \frac{2}{3} \qquad \text{Cross-multiply.}$$

$2(4 + x) = 4 \times 3 \qquad$ Multiply out the left side.

$\qquad 8 + 2x = 12 \qquad$ Subtract 8.

$\qquad\qquad 2x = 4 \qquad$ Divide both sides by 2.

$\qquad\qquad x = 2 \qquad$ That's the amount of alcohol left.

If there are 2 ounces of alcohol left after starting with 16 ounces, then $16 - 2 = 14$ ounces must have evaporated, so the correct answer is 14, choice (E).

10. B

Difficulty: High

Strategic Advice: The shaded region is one of four equal pieces left when the circle is subtracted from the square. So to find the area of the shaded region you must subtract the area of the circle from the area of the square and then take $\frac{1}{4}$ of this difference. You must first find the area of the circle and the area of the square. To find the area of the circle, you must know its radius.

Getting to the Answer: You're told that the circumference of the circle is 4π. You also know that the circumference C of a circle is related to its radius r by the formula $C = 2\pi r$. So here, $4\pi = 2\pi r$ and $r = 2$. The area of the circle is πr^2 which equals $\pi(2)^2$ or 4π. To find the area of the square, you must know the length of its side. If you draw in the diameter of the circle whose endpoints are the point where the circle touches side *BC* of the square and the point where the circle touches side *AD* of the square, you'll see that the side of the square is equal in length to the diameter of the circle. The radius of the circle is 2, so its diameter, which is twice the radius, is 2×2 or 4. Since the side of the square is 4, its area is its side squared or 4^2, which is 16. The area of the square is 16 and the area of the circle is 4π, so the area outside the circle and inside the square is $16 - 4\pi$. So the area of the shaded region is $\dfrac{16 - 4\pi}{4} = 4 - \pi$.

11. B

Difficulty: Medium

Strategic Advice: Drawing a diagram is the key to solving this problem.

Getting to the Answer:

Draw two *parallel lines*, *m* and *n*; now draw three different *transversals* through them, trying to form the least number of points of intersection.

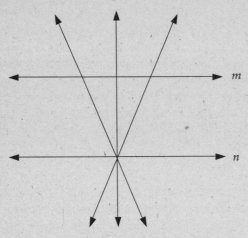

From the diagram above, you can see that the number is 4, since the three transversals can pass through the first parallel line at different points, yet pass through a common point on the second parallel line.

12. D

Difficulty: Medium

Strategic Advice: Think about the graph of each answer choice. If several look similar, or if you're not sure what an

equation should look like when graphed, try plugging in the information given in the figure above.

Getting to the Answer: For instance, you could use the information for the year 1992. This is $1992 - 1980 = 12$ years after the study began, so $t = 12$. From the graph, $d = 800$. Plug these numbers into each equation to see which one is true. $(100)2^{\frac{12}{4}} = (100)2^3 = (100)8 = 800$, so (D) is correct.

13. E

Difficulty: Medium

Strategic Advice: Remember, the value of $r(x)$ is shown by the *y*-value of each point.

Getting to the Answer: When $r(x) = 0$, the graph touches the *x*-axis. This graph touches the *x*-axis at $x = -5$ and $x = -1$.

14. E

Difficulty: High

Strategic Advice: Inequalities work just like equations, with the exception that if you multiply or divide by a negative number, you must change the direction of the sign. Remember that either a positive or a negative number will produce a positive number when squared. You could also approach this problem by trying to think of numbers that fulfill the given inequality but fall outside the range of each answer, or numbers within each range that do not fulfill each inequality.

Getting to the Answer:
$$a^{\frac{b}{c}} = \sqrt[c]{a^b}$$
$$g^{\frac{2}{3}} = \sqrt[3]{g^2}$$
$$\sqrt[3]{g^2} > 4$$
$$(\sqrt[3]{g^2})^3 > (4)^3$$
$$g^2 > 64$$
$$g > 8 \text{ or } g < -8$$

15. C

Difficulty: High

Strategic Advice: This problem can be solved by using the distance formula, $\sqrt{(x_1 - x_2)^2 + (y_1 - y_2)^2}$, or by considering the properties of right triangles. If you sketch a quick diagram of the given points, you will notice that they form a right triangle with side lengths of 3 and 4. You can then use the Pythagorean Theorem ($a^2 + b^2 = c^2$) or your knowledge of common right triangles to find QS, the hypotenuse.

Getting to the Answer:

$$\sqrt{(4-1)^2 + (1-5)^2}$$
$$= \sqrt{3^2 + (-4)^2}$$
$$= \sqrt{9 + 16}$$
$$= \sqrt{25}$$
$$= 5$$

or $3^2 + 4^2 = 9 + 16 = 25 = c^2$

$5 = c$

16. A

Difficulty: High

Strategic Advice: This question asks for the area of a circle. To find the area, you'll need to know the radius. Look for parts of the figure that equal the radius of the circle. How can you find the length of those parts of the figure?

Getting to the Answer: Since $\overline{AD}$ is tangent to the circle at point B and $\overline{EG}$ is tangent to the circle at point F, line segments $\overline{BC}$ and $\overline{CF}$ form two sides of a square whose other two sides are $\overline{BO}$ and $\overline{FO}$. Therefore, $\overline{BC}$ and $\overline{CF}$ are the same length as the radius of the circle. To find the length of one of these line segments, notice that $\triangle BCF$ is a 45-45-90 triangle, and that the ratio between its sides is therefore $x : x : x\sqrt{2}$. Since $BF = 2$, $BC = \dfrac{2}{\sqrt{2}} = \sqrt{2}$. The following diagram summarizes this information:

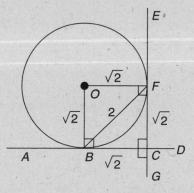

Since the radius of the circle is $\sqrt{2}$, its area is $\pi(\sqrt{2})^2 = 2\pi$.

SECTION 8

1. C

Difficulty: Low

The phrase "generally living in packs with strong bonds and clear *hierarchies*" virtually defines the missing word. Animals like wolves that live in such groups are *social* animals, in contrast to the "lone wolf" stereotype alluded to in the sentence's opening phrase, choice (C). While wolves are, choice (A), *carnivorous*, or meat-eating, the topic of the sentence is their social habits, not their eating habits. The words *wild,* choice (E), and *singular,* choice (D), both miss the sentence's point—that wolves live in packs. *Fearsome,* (B), can have two nearly opposite meanings: "frightening" or "timid."

2. C

Difficulty: Medium

The sentence sets up a contrast between two differing views of multiple personality, either it's a ---- disease or it's a shield that some criminals use to ---- prosecution. Since it's a safe bet that criminals don't want to be prosecuted, or tried for their crimes, the second blank should be filled by a word like escape. To provide the necessary contrast, the first word must be something like genuine. *Genuine .. evade* is the best match for this prediction. *Authentic* ("genuine") and *diagnosable* ("capable of having its cause determined") might fit in the first blank, but the second words in choices (B) and (E)—*ensure* and *guarantee,* respectively—contrast sharply with our prediction for the second blank. In choices (A) and (D), the second words are possibilities, but the first words don't fit. In choice (A), *forestall* means "prevent," but *fallacious* means "false," just the opposite of what's needed in the first blank. Likewise, in choice (D), *elude,* fits the second blank, but *invalid* ("not legitimate") doesn't work in the first blank.

3. D

Difficulty: Medium

The sentence sets up a contrast between the company's goal of "*fostering* ("encouraging") productivity and hard work" and the fact that it promotes "…unproductive and ---- employees." "Unproductive" obviously contrasts with productivity, so it's logical to assume that the correct answer should be something that contrasts with hard work—perhaps something like "lazy." *Lackadaisical,* which means "indifferent, lazy, or apathetic," comes closest to this prediction. The workers may well be *discontented*, choice (B), but *discontented* doesn't complete the sentence's implied contrast with hard work. *Meritorious*, in choice (E), means "deserving of praise or reward."

4. B

Difficulty: Medium

For the first blank, it's fairly easy to reason that a large forest fire would burn or destroy a large area or section. But that prediction only helps eliminate choice (C), *precipitated*, which means "caused" or "established." Because the sentence is about a forest fire, and because it starts off talking about what many ecologists believe, *environmental* makes sense in the second blank, and *devastated* ("reduced to ruins") makes sense in the first, choice (B). *Inflammable,* choice (A), means "easily set on fire." The forest might have been *inflammable*, but the disaster couldn't have been. *Singed*, or "slightly burned," in choice (D), may have been tempting in a sentence about a forest fire, but choice (D)'s second word, *intangible*, doesn't work; it means "incapable of being felt, touched, or defined." As for choice (E), *burned* would work, but ecologists would more likely be concerned with an environmental disaster than with a scientific one.

5. D

Difficulty: Medium

It's easier to fill the second blank first for this question, because the word in the blank must be consistent with "or dumped." Only choices (D), *burned,* or (E), *buried,* would be consistent with *dumped*. And choice (E) doesn't work; if the program were *abolished*, then we can assume that the amount of garbage wouldn't be reduced.

6. A

Difficulty: Medium

Here we see that bluegrass could be a *descendant,* (A), a *variety,* (B), or an *outgrowth,* (C). However, neither *disciplined* nor *illustrated* works in the second blank. Bluegrass has a different rhythm and differently-pitched vocals, so it must be *distinguished*, or set apart from, old-time string band music.

Questions 7–19

Although these two passages discuss issues in medical research, don't be intimidated by the subject matter. Read through the passages once to get a general feel for them. The question stems will direct you back to the specific sentences you'll need to understand to get the answers. Also, read through Passage 1 and do the questions that refer to it, and then read through Passage 2 and do the rest of the questions.

Passage 1 talks about the difficulty of reconstructing or replacing certain bones in humans. A recent advance has been the creation of bone substitutes from muscle using the protein osteogenin. While osteogenin can't be used directly on a defect, it can be used to prefabricate bones in molds implanted in an animal's abdomen. The process hasn't been tried in humans, though, because osteogenin is scarce, and because it has to be tested on larger animals first.

Passage 2 has a distinctly different tone. The author is not objective and impartial; he's taking a stand on an issue: he argues that testing on humans is necessary in order to make improvements in artificial organs. Using animals, he says, isn't good enough: there are no good animal models for human bones and joints. Moreover, testing on humans gives doctors crucial experience. The author concludes that there's no point in developing new designs for artificial organs until present ones have been evaluated on people.

7. E

Difficulty: Medium

The stem contains no line reference, but the only place the author talks about future experiments in making bone from muscle is the last paragraph. She says there that surgeons "have not yet tried the process in humans" and that it "must first be tested on larger animals." The author expects, therefore, that future experiments will "involve larger animals and perhaps humans," choice (E). There's no evidence that future experiments will *encounter no serious problems,* choice (A), that they will *be hindered by surgeons,* choice (C), or that they *face enormous technical obstacles,* choice (D). And despite the fact that all experiments have so far been *limited to smaller animals* choice, (B), it's clear that this isn't what the author expects in the future.

8. C

Difficulty: Medium

Here's an example of the all/EXCEPT question type. Information about osteogenin is spread over the last three paragraphs, so scan through the choices to see if one jumps out before you start digging through the passage. Choice (C), *its application can be easily controlled*, should strike you as false because the author says in paragraph 4 that osteogenin is hard to control—it might turn an entire area to bone if sprinkled on a defect. If you didn't spot choice (C), you had to confirm the other choices. *Current supplies* [of osteogenin] *are limited,* choice (A), is indicated in paragraph 6. This is also where the author says that *tests of its effectiveness have been limited,* choice (B), to small animals, and that osteogenin's *safety for human use is undetermined,* choice (D). The fact that *some surgeons hesitate to use it,* choice (E), because it's hard to control is stated in paragraph 4.

9. A

Difficulty: Medium

As with many Vocabulary-in-Context questions, all of the choices are actual definitions of the cited word, "immediate." However, only one makes sense in the context of the sentence: "plastic surgeons have circumvented that snag by prefabricating bones away from the *immediate* site of a defect." Here, "immediate" describes the physical site and nearby area of a defect. Only choice (A), *near,* fits. Choice (B), *instant,* and choice (E), *current,* refer to time, so they don't make sense in context. Neither the *next in line* site of a defect nor the *directly understood* site of a defect makes sense, so choices (C) and (D) are also incorrect.

10. A

Difficulty: Medium

You've already had to go back and read through the last paragraph a couple of times by now, so glance through the choices. *A review of current knowledge,* choice (A), looks good right away, because the author points out in the last paragraph how far surgeons have gone in experimenting with and learning about the new process. There's no *qualification of an earlier remark,* choice (B). Choice (C) is out because the author never mentions, no less challenges, a contradictory view. The final paragraph presents new facts and ideas rather than a *summary of previous ideas,* choice (D). As for choice (E), the author's call for testing on larger animals is a demand

not *for an alternative approach* but for a guarantee of safety and effectiveness before the process is tried on people.

11. D

Difficulty: Medium

The phrase "to die young at a ripe age" doesn't make much sense until you understand its context. The author is discussing the eventual benefits of artificial organs: ordinary people can live longer or, even better, they can die young at a ripe age. "Dying young at a ripe age" does not mean *living longer,* choice (E). Nor does it mean *dying prematurely,* choice (A), *dying young of an illness,* choice (B), or *extending one's life despite being ill,* choice (C)—none of these is a positive thing. The author's talking about the benefits of artificial organs. "Dying young at a ripe age" means dying at a normal old age after having enjoyed a relatively young body during your life; in other words, it means *maintaining a healthier body into old age,* choice (D).

12. C

Difficulty: Low

In paragraph 2 of Passage 2, the author accuses medical ethicists of hampering the activities of human volunteers. He declares that the ethicists are "well-intentioned" but *their standards are inappropriate.* Clearly, the author is *disapproving,* choice (C), of them. None of the other words comes close to describing the author's attitude.

13. E

Difficulty: Medium

Looking down through the choices, you can see that the only one that can be eliminated right away is *slogans,* choice (A), which is not a synonym for standards. To pick the right one, go back and locate "standards" in its context. The author says that the "standards," or *principles,* choice (E), of the medical ethicists are inappropriate. *Measurements,* choice (B), *examples,* choice (C), and *banners,* choice (D), don't make sense in the context of the sentence.

14. A

Difficulty: Medium

Here's another Vocabulary-in-Context question. Checking the sentence, "critical" is used to mean *decisive,* choice (A): the author is stating that the need to use humans leads to a *decisive,* or very significant, "bottleneck in the experimental process." Critical isn't used to mean *aggressive,* choice (B), *skeptical,* choice (C), *perceptive,* choice (D), or *fault-finding,* choice (E).

15. A

Difficulty: Medium

The author discusses the use of artificial heart devices in paragraph 4. The design of the devices is not a problem, he says; rather, it's the lack of experience researchers have had using them with human subjects. He points out that heart devices may work in one patient and not in another, depending on age, health, and the quality of postoperative care. He repeats his point at the beginning of the next paragraph: what's lacking in coronary care is simply more experience, choice (A). The author doesn't *praise scientists' ability to fight coronary disease,* choice (B); he's saying it could be much better if human testing were done. The author never mentions any *lingering doubts* about artificial heart implants, choice (C). Choice (D) contradicts the passage directly: the author says that "engineering design is not currently the main obstacle." Finally, choice (E) is wrong because the author never discusses *several new treatments now available to heart patients.*

16. C

Difficulty: Low

The author poses the questions in the last paragraph in order to identify information that scientists still lack. He's showing that their knowledge of coronary disease is incomplete, choice (C)—that's why human testing is so essential. He's not illustrating the value of any new devices, choice (A)—he's opposed at present to new devices. Nobody else's arguments are being refuted here, choice (B). Choice (D) turns the author's ideas around: he supports human testing. As for choice (E), the "wide publicity" of the research misses the point. The point is simple: these are questions that need to be answered.

17. B

Difficulty: Low

The answer here has to be fairly general, because the connection between the two passages is indirect. Take the answer choices one by one and evaluate each one using evidence from the passages. For example, choice (A) is wrong because the author of Passage 1 doesn't disagree

with anyone or cite any views different from hers. Choice (B), though, is accurate: the author of Passage 1 talks about the difficulty surgeons have in reconstructing and replacing bones, and the author of Passage 2 laments surgeons' lack of experience in using artificial organs. Choices (C) and (D) are wrong because only the author of Passage 2 demands an increase in the number of human subjects or mentions cultural values as a barrier to research. As for choice (E), neither author advocates a more rapid development of new implant procedures.

18. B

Difficulty: Medium

Passage 2 is devoted to arguing for the testing of artificial organs on humans; the author believes that restrictions on human testing are a major obstacle to improved devices. Before checking the choices, predict what the author of Passage 2 might say about the wider use of osteogenin. No doubt he'd say that gaining experience with the use of osteogenin on humans would be difficult—exactly what choice (B) says. Choices (A) and (D) cite valid obstacles to the wider use of osteogenin, but they're wrong because there's no reason to think that the author of Passage 2 would stress them. Choices (C) and (E) are out because they aren't obstacles to the use of osteogenin at all.

19. D

Difficulty: Medium

The last paragraph of Passage 1 states that the process of bone prefabrication has not yet been tried on humans—that it needs to be tested on large animals first. The last paragraph of Passage 2 features questions about coronary care that can only be answered through human testing. In other words, both authors are stressing the need to *gather information that's relevant to the treatment of human patients,* choice (D). Choice (A) is out because neither author sees the need to *develop new and improved devices for human implantation.* The author of Passage 1 suggests that experiments should next be carried out on larger animals, which rules out choice (C), while the author of Passage 2 wants testing on humans, which eliminates choice (B). As for choice (E), neither author advocates *curbing the growing use of animals in testing.*

SECTION 9

1. E

Difficulty: Medium

Fix awkward sentences by eliminating unnecessary words. As written, this sentence is awkward and unnecessarily wordy. (E) is concise and contains no errors. In (B), the antecedent for the pronoun *that* is unclear. (C) and (D) create run-on sentences.

2. B

Difficulty: Medium

Look for the most concise answer that correctly expresses the relationship between ideas. As written, this sentence is unnecessarily wordy, and *so that* does not correctly express the relationship between the ideas. (The *sun block* is the cause of the *harm*.) Choice (B) correctly expresses this with the transition word *because*. Choices (C) and (D) also use transition words that are inappropriate in context. The pronoun *it* in choice (E) does not agree with the plural antecedent *sunblocks*.

3. E

Difficulty: High

Words like *each*, *one of*, and *every* are grammatically singular. This question refers to *each of the reporters*, but uses *were*, the plural form of the verb. Also, *them collaborating* is grammatically incorrect. Choice (E) addresses these problems by changing *were* to *was* and uses the noun *collaboration*. Choice (B) fixes the verb problem, but not the incorrect pronoun. Choices (C) and (D) do not address the subject-verb error.

4. B

Difficulty: High

Look for sentence logic as well as sentence style; to what is *which* referring here? The phrase *of which* implies a selection from multiple choices, but the pronoun's only antecedent is the singular *marketing*. Choice (B) eliminates the pronoun altogether and joins the two independent clauses with a semicolon splice. The pronoun *it* in choice (C) does not have a clear antecedent; this sentence is also unnecessarily wordy. Choice (D) misuses the semicolon splice which is only correct between two independent clauses. Choice (E) is a run-on sentence.

5. C

Difficulty: Low

As written, this is a sentence fragment. Choice (C) corrects this and does not introduce any additional errors. In choices (B) and (E), *yet* is redundant with *despite*. Choice (D) also uses a redundant conjunction (*but*), and fails to correct the fragment.

6. D

Difficulty: Medium

A correctly structured sentence will clearly show what a modifying word or phrase describes. When the meaning is unclear, the sentence needs to be revised. As written, it is the dog, not *us*, that was walking home. Choice (D) correctly places the pronoun *we* after the modifying phrase. Choice (E) corrects the modification error but is awkward.

7. B

Difficulty: Medium

There are two main problems. The adjective *continuous* incorrectly modifies the verb *practice*; it should be the adverb *continuously*. Second, the phrase *for learning* is idiomatically incorrect. Only choice (B) addresses both problems. Choice (C) changes the meaning because the adverb *continuously* modifies *to learn* instead of *practiced*. Choice (D) retains the idiomatic error, and choice (E) does not use the adverb.

8. E

Difficulty: Low

The sentence as it stands is unnecessarily wordy. Choice (B) perpetuates this error. Choice (C) creates a fragment. Choice (D) is an incorrect prepositional phrase. Only choice (E) fixes the error without introducing a new one.

9. B

Difficulty: High

This is a run-on sentence: two independent clauses connected with a comma splice. You can turn the second clause into a descriptive phrase by removing *it was*. Choice (B) makes that change. Choice (C) incorrectly adds the contrasting transition word *though* and choice (D) the causal word *thus*. Choice (E) incorrectly uses *and*, which creates a sentence that is grammatically correct but illogical.

10. C

Difficulty: Medium

Make sure that items being compared are presented in the same form. Here, *entertaining* is a participle (verb form used as an adjective), but *informs* is a verb. To correctly complete the parallel construction, you need another adjective. Both choices (B) and (C) correctly replace *informs* with *informative*, but choice (B) uses an incorrect verb form. Choice (D) simply rewords the selection, and choice (E) incorrectly replaces the verb with a noun (*information*).

11. D

Difficulty: High

Don't just focus on the few words that are underlined. The entire sentence is a run-on with a comma splice. To make the second clause dependent, choice (D) uses *whom* to create a clause that correctly modifies *marathon runners*. The objective case is correct because *whom* is the object of the preposition. Choice (B) is still a run-on and only substitutes *are needing* for the simple present used in the original sentence. Choice (C) incorrectly uses *which* to refer to people instead of *whom*. Choice (E) is also still a run-on.

12. E

Difficulty: Medium

This sentence is long and rambling, a sentence type that the SAT frowns upon. Look for the relationship among the several ideas. What is subordinate? What is modifying or causal? The main action is that Renee Fleming will perform in the most important concert of her career. Everything else provides description of Fleming. Choice (E) puts all the information in the proper place. Choice (B) clarifies that the first two ideas are descriptions of Fleming, but does not make these descriptions subordinate to her important concert. Choice (C) awkwardly uses the participial phrase *being admired especially*. Choice (D) uses the relative pronoun *which* to refer to a person.

13. D

Difficulty: High

A modifying word or phrase must clearly relate to the word or phrase it is meant to describe. As written, it sounds as if the businesses, and not the guidelines, are published by the International Organization for Standardization. Choice (D) corrects this error in the most concise way. Choice (B) makes the sentence wordier and does not address the error. Choices (C) and (E) are awkwardly constructed.

14. C

Difficulty: High

The original sentence has the ambiguous pronoun *they*—it doesn't clearly to refer to anyone. Choice (B) is an awkward rephrasing and ends by breaking the parallel structure *should flatter…and not depict.* Choice (D) is awkward and non-idiomatic (*Prevalent as an idea…was for a portrait to flatter*). Choice (E) also contains the ambiguous *they.*

SAT PRACTICE TEST TEN ANSWER SHEET

Remove (or photocopy) the answer sheet, and use it to complete the practice test.

How to Take the Practice Tests

Each Practice Test includes eight scored multiple-choice sections and one essay. Keep in mind that on the actual SAT, there will be an additional multiple-choice section—the experimental section—that will not contribute to your score.

Once you start a Practice Test, don't stop until you've gone through all nine sections. Remember, you can review any questions within a section, but you may not go back or forward a section.

Good luck!

Start with number 1 for each section. If a section has fewer questions than answer spaces, leave the extra spaces blank.

Section One

Section One is the writing section's essay component.
Lined pages on which you will write your essay can be found in that section.

Section Two

1. Ⓐ Ⓑ Ⓒ Ⓓ Ⓔ	9. Ⓐ Ⓑ Ⓒ Ⓓ Ⓔ	17. Ⓐ Ⓑ Ⓒ Ⓓ Ⓔ	
2. Ⓐ Ⓑ Ⓒ Ⓓ Ⓔ	10. Ⓐ Ⓑ Ⓒ Ⓓ Ⓔ	18. Ⓐ Ⓑ Ⓒ Ⓓ Ⓔ	
3. Ⓐ Ⓑ Ⓒ Ⓓ Ⓔ	11. Ⓐ Ⓑ Ⓒ Ⓓ Ⓔ	19. Ⓐ Ⓑ Ⓒ Ⓓ Ⓔ	# right in Section Two
4. Ⓐ Ⓑ Ⓒ Ⓓ Ⓔ	12. Ⓐ Ⓑ Ⓒ Ⓓ Ⓔ	20. Ⓐ Ⓑ Ⓒ Ⓓ Ⓔ	
5. Ⓐ Ⓑ Ⓒ Ⓓ Ⓔ	13. Ⓐ Ⓑ Ⓒ Ⓓ Ⓔ		
6. Ⓐ Ⓑ Ⓒ Ⓓ Ⓔ	14. Ⓐ Ⓑ Ⓒ Ⓓ Ⓔ		
7. Ⓐ Ⓑ Ⓒ Ⓓ Ⓔ	15. Ⓐ Ⓑ Ⓒ Ⓓ Ⓔ		# wrong in Section Two
8. Ⓐ Ⓑ Ⓒ Ⓓ Ⓔ	16. Ⓐ Ⓑ Ⓒ Ⓓ Ⓔ		

Section Three

1. Ⓐ Ⓑ Ⓒ Ⓓ Ⓔ	10. Ⓐ Ⓑ Ⓒ Ⓓ Ⓔ	19. Ⓐ Ⓑ Ⓒ Ⓓ Ⓔ	28. Ⓐ Ⓑ Ⓒ Ⓓ Ⓔ	
2. Ⓐ Ⓑ Ⓒ Ⓓ Ⓔ	11. Ⓐ Ⓑ Ⓒ Ⓓ Ⓔ	20. Ⓐ Ⓑ Ⓒ Ⓓ Ⓔ	29. Ⓐ Ⓑ Ⓒ Ⓓ Ⓔ	
3. Ⓐ Ⓑ Ⓒ Ⓓ Ⓔ	12. Ⓐ Ⓑ Ⓒ Ⓓ Ⓔ	21. Ⓐ Ⓑ Ⓒ Ⓓ Ⓔ	30. Ⓐ Ⓑ Ⓒ Ⓓ Ⓔ	# right in Section Three
4. Ⓐ Ⓑ Ⓒ Ⓓ Ⓔ	13. Ⓐ Ⓑ Ⓒ Ⓓ Ⓔ	22. Ⓐ Ⓑ Ⓒ Ⓓ Ⓔ	31. Ⓐ Ⓑ Ⓒ Ⓓ Ⓔ	
5. Ⓐ Ⓑ Ⓒ Ⓓ Ⓔ	14. Ⓐ Ⓑ Ⓒ Ⓓ Ⓔ	23. Ⓐ Ⓑ Ⓒ Ⓓ Ⓔ	32. Ⓐ Ⓑ Ⓒ Ⓓ Ⓔ	
6. Ⓐ Ⓑ Ⓒ Ⓓ Ⓔ	15. Ⓐ Ⓑ Ⓒ Ⓓ Ⓔ	24. Ⓐ Ⓑ Ⓒ Ⓓ Ⓔ	33. Ⓐ Ⓑ Ⓒ Ⓓ Ⓔ	
7. Ⓐ Ⓑ Ⓒ Ⓓ Ⓔ	16. Ⓐ Ⓑ Ⓒ Ⓓ Ⓔ	25. Ⓐ Ⓑ Ⓒ Ⓓ Ⓔ	34 Ⓐ Ⓑ Ⓒ Ⓓ Ⓔ	# wrong in Section Three
8. Ⓐ Ⓑ Ⓒ Ⓓ Ⓔ	17. Ⓐ Ⓑ Ⓒ Ⓓ Ⓔ	26. Ⓐ Ⓑ Ⓒ Ⓓ Ⓔ	35. Ⓐ Ⓑ Ⓒ Ⓓ Ⓔ	
9. Ⓐ Ⓑ Ⓒ Ⓓ Ⓔ	18. Ⓐ Ⓑ Ⓒ Ⓓ Ⓔ	27. Ⓐ Ⓑ Ⓒ Ⓓ Ⓔ		

Remove (or photocopy) this answer sheet, and use it to complete the practice test.

Start with number 1 for each section. If a section has fewer questions than answer spaces, leave the extra spaces blank.

Section Four

1. Ⓐ Ⓑ Ⓒ Ⓓ Ⓔ   9. Ⓐ Ⓑ Ⓒ Ⓓ Ⓔ   17. Ⓐ Ⓑ Ⓒ Ⓓ Ⓔ
2. Ⓐ Ⓑ Ⓒ Ⓓ Ⓔ   10. Ⓐ Ⓑ Ⓒ Ⓓ Ⓔ   18. Ⓐ Ⓑ Ⓒ Ⓓ Ⓔ
3. Ⓐ Ⓑ Ⓒ Ⓓ Ⓔ   11. Ⓐ Ⓑ Ⓒ Ⓓ Ⓔ   19. Ⓐ Ⓑ Ⓒ Ⓓ Ⓔ
4. Ⓐ Ⓑ Ⓒ Ⓓ Ⓔ   12. Ⓐ Ⓑ Ⓒ Ⓓ Ⓔ   20. Ⓐ Ⓑ Ⓒ Ⓓ Ⓔ
5. Ⓐ Ⓑ Ⓒ Ⓓ Ⓔ   13. Ⓐ Ⓑ Ⓒ Ⓓ Ⓔ   21. Ⓐ Ⓑ Ⓒ Ⓓ Ⓔ
6. Ⓐ Ⓑ Ⓒ Ⓓ Ⓔ   14. Ⓐ Ⓑ Ⓒ Ⓓ Ⓔ   22. Ⓐ Ⓑ Ⓒ Ⓓ Ⓔ
7. Ⓐ Ⓑ Ⓒ Ⓓ Ⓔ   15. Ⓐ Ⓑ Ⓒ Ⓓ Ⓔ   23. Ⓐ Ⓑ Ⓒ Ⓓ Ⓔ
8. Ⓐ Ⓑ Ⓒ Ⓓ Ⓔ   16. Ⓐ Ⓑ Ⓒ Ⓓ Ⓔ   24. Ⓐ Ⓑ Ⓒ Ⓓ Ⓔ

☐ # right in Section Four

☐ # wrong in Section Four

Section Five

1. Ⓐ Ⓑ Ⓒ Ⓓ Ⓔ   →9. Ⓐ Ⓑ Ⓒ Ⓓ Ⓔ   17. Ⓐ Ⓑ Ⓒ Ⓓ Ⓔ
2. Ⓐ Ⓑ Ⓒ Ⓓ Ⓔ   10. Ⓐ Ⓑ Ⓒ Ⓓ Ⓔ   18. Ⓐ Ⓑ Ⓒ Ⓓ Ⓔ
3. Ⓐ Ⓑ Ⓒ Ⓓ Ⓔ   11. Ⓐ Ⓑ Ⓒ Ⓓ Ⓔ
4. Ⓐ Ⓑ Ⓒ Ⓓ Ⓔ   12. Ⓐ Ⓑ Ⓒ Ⓓ Ⓔ
5. Ⓐ Ⓑ Ⓒ Ⓓ Ⓔ   13. Ⓐ Ⓑ Ⓒ Ⓓ Ⓔ
6. Ⓐ Ⓑ Ⓒ Ⓓ Ⓔ   14. Ⓐ Ⓑ Ⓒ Ⓓ Ⓔ
7. Ⓐ Ⓑ Ⓒ Ⓓ Ⓔ   15. Ⓐ Ⓑ Ⓒ Ⓓ Ⓔ
8. Ⓐ Ⓑ Ⓒ Ⓓ Ⓔ   16. Ⓐ Ⓑ Ⓒ Ⓓ Ⓔ

☐ # right in Section Five

☐ # wrong in Section Five

If section 5 of your test book contains math questions that are not multiple choice, continue to item 9 below. Otherwise, continue to item 9 above.

9. 10. 11. 12. 13.

14. 15. 16. 17. 18.

Remove (or photocopy) this answer sheet, and use it to complete the practice test.

Start with number 1 for each section. If a section has fewer questions than answer spaces, leave the extra spaces blank.

Section Six

1. Ⓐ Ⓑ Ⓒ Ⓓ Ⓔ   9. Ⓐ Ⓑ Ⓒ Ⓓ Ⓔ   17. Ⓐ Ⓑ Ⓒ Ⓓ Ⓔ
2. Ⓐ Ⓑ Ⓒ Ⓓ Ⓔ   10. Ⓐ Ⓑ Ⓒ Ⓓ Ⓔ   18. Ⓐ Ⓑ Ⓒ Ⓓ Ⓔ
3. Ⓐ Ⓑ Ⓒ Ⓓ Ⓔ   11. Ⓐ Ⓑ Ⓒ Ⓓ Ⓔ   19. Ⓐ Ⓑ Ⓒ Ⓓ Ⓔ
4. Ⓐ Ⓑ Ⓒ Ⓓ Ⓔ   12. Ⓐ Ⓑ Ⓒ Ⓓ Ⓔ   20. Ⓐ Ⓑ Ⓒ Ⓓ Ⓔ
5. Ⓐ Ⓑ Ⓒ Ⓓ Ⓔ   13. Ⓐ Ⓑ Ⓒ Ⓓ Ⓔ   21. Ⓐ Ⓑ Ⓒ Ⓓ Ⓔ
6. Ⓐ Ⓑ Ⓒ Ⓓ Ⓔ   14. Ⓐ Ⓑ Ⓒ Ⓓ Ⓔ   22. Ⓐ Ⓑ Ⓒ Ⓓ Ⓔ
7. Ⓐ Ⓑ Ⓒ Ⓓ Ⓔ   15. Ⓐ Ⓑ Ⓒ Ⓓ Ⓔ   23. Ⓐ Ⓑ Ⓒ Ⓓ Ⓔ
8. Ⓐ Ⓑ Ⓒ Ⓓ Ⓔ   16. Ⓐ Ⓑ Ⓒ Ⓓ Ⓔ   24. Ⓐ Ⓑ Ⓒ Ⓓ Ⓔ

☐ # right in Section six

☐ # wrong in Section Six

Section Seven

1. Ⓐ Ⓑ Ⓒ Ⓓ Ⓔ   9. Ⓐ Ⓑ Ⓒ Ⓓ Ⓔ
2. Ⓐ Ⓑ Ⓒ Ⓓ Ⓔ   10. Ⓐ Ⓑ Ⓒ Ⓓ Ⓔ
3. Ⓐ Ⓑ Ⓒ Ⓓ Ⓔ   11. Ⓐ Ⓑ Ⓒ Ⓓ Ⓔ
4. Ⓐ Ⓑ Ⓒ Ⓓ Ⓔ   12. Ⓐ Ⓑ Ⓒ Ⓓ Ⓔ
5. Ⓐ Ⓑ Ⓒ Ⓓ Ⓔ   13. Ⓐ Ⓑ Ⓒ Ⓓ Ⓔ
6. Ⓐ Ⓑ Ⓒ Ⓓ Ⓔ   14. Ⓐ Ⓑ Ⓒ Ⓓ Ⓔ
7. Ⓐ Ⓑ Ⓒ Ⓓ Ⓔ   15. Ⓐ Ⓑ Ⓒ Ⓓ Ⓔ
8. Ⓐ Ⓑ Ⓒ Ⓓ Ⓔ   16. Ⓐ Ⓑ Ⓒ Ⓓ Ⓔ

☐ # right in Section Seven

☐ # wrong in Section Seven

Section Eight

1. Ⓐ Ⓑ Ⓒ Ⓓ Ⓔ   9. Ⓐ Ⓑ Ⓒ Ⓓ Ⓔ   17. Ⓐ Ⓑ Ⓒ Ⓓ Ⓔ
2. Ⓐ Ⓑ Ⓒ Ⓓ Ⓔ   10. Ⓐ Ⓑ Ⓒ Ⓓ Ⓔ   18. Ⓐ Ⓑ Ⓒ Ⓓ Ⓔ
3. Ⓐ Ⓑ Ⓒ Ⓓ Ⓔ   11. Ⓐ Ⓑ Ⓒ Ⓓ Ⓔ   19. Ⓐ Ⓑ Ⓒ Ⓓ Ⓔ
4. Ⓐ Ⓑ Ⓒ Ⓓ Ⓔ   12. Ⓐ Ⓑ Ⓒ Ⓓ Ⓔ
5. Ⓐ Ⓑ Ⓒ Ⓓ Ⓔ   13. Ⓐ Ⓑ Ⓒ Ⓓ Ⓔ
6. Ⓐ Ⓑ Ⓒ Ⓓ Ⓔ   14. Ⓐ Ⓑ Ⓒ Ⓓ Ⓔ
7. Ⓐ Ⓑ Ⓒ Ⓓ Ⓔ   15. Ⓐ Ⓑ Ⓒ Ⓓ Ⓔ
8. Ⓐ Ⓑ Ⓒ Ⓓ Ⓔ   16. Ⓐ Ⓑ Ⓒ Ⓓ Ⓔ

☐ # right in Section Eight

☐ # wrong in Section Eight

Section Nine

1. Ⓐ Ⓑ Ⓒ Ⓓ Ⓔ   9. Ⓐ Ⓑ Ⓒ Ⓓ Ⓔ
2. Ⓐ Ⓑ Ⓒ Ⓓ Ⓔ   10. Ⓐ Ⓑ Ⓒ Ⓓ Ⓔ
3. Ⓐ Ⓑ Ⓒ Ⓓ Ⓔ   11. Ⓐ Ⓑ Ⓒ Ⓓ Ⓔ
4. Ⓐ Ⓑ Ⓒ Ⓓ Ⓔ   12. Ⓐ Ⓑ Ⓒ Ⓓ Ⓔ
5. Ⓐ Ⓑ Ⓒ Ⓓ Ⓔ   13. Ⓐ Ⓑ Ⓒ Ⓓ Ⓔ
6. Ⓐ Ⓑ Ⓒ Ⓓ Ⓔ   14. Ⓐ Ⓑ Ⓒ Ⓓ Ⓔ
7. Ⓐ Ⓑ Ⓒ Ⓓ Ⓔ
8. Ⓐ Ⓑ Ⓒ Ⓓ Ⓔ

☐ # right in Section Nine

☐ # wrong in Section Nine

Practice Test Ten

SECTION 1
Time—25 Minutes
ESSAY

The essay gives you an opportunity to show how effectively you can develop and express ideas. You should, therefore, take care to develop your point of view, present your ideas logically and clearly, and use language precisely.

Your essay must be written in your Answer Grid Booklet—you will receive no other paper on which to write. You will have enough space if you write on every line, avoid wide margins, and keep your handwriting to a reasonable size. Remember that people who are not familiar with your handwriting will read what you write. Try to write or print so that what you are writing is legible to those readers.

You have twenty-five minutes to write an essay on the topic assigned below.

DO NOT WRITE ON ANOTHER TOPIC. AN OFF-TOPIC ESSAY WILL RECEIVE A SCORE OF ZERO.

Think carefully about the issue presented in the following excerpt and the assignment below.

> "When I examine myself and my methods of thought, I come close to the conclusion that the gift of fantasy has meant more to me than my talent for absorbing positive knowledge."
>
> > –Albert Einstein
>
> "There is nothing more dreadful than imagination without taste."
>
> > –Johann Wolfgang von Goethe

Assignment: Do you believe that fantasy or imagination is more important than knowledge? Plan and write an essay in which you develop your point of view on this issue. Support your position with reasoning and examples taken from your reading, studies, experience, or observations.

DO NOT WRITE YOUR ESSAY IN YOUR TEST BOOK.
You will receive credit only for what you write in your Answer Grid Booklet.

SECTION 2
Time—25 Minutes
20 Questions

Directions: For this section, solve each problem and decide which is the best of the choices given. Fill in the corresponding oval on the answer sheet. You may use any available space for scratchwork.

Notes:

(1) Calculator use is permitted.

(2) All numbers used are real numbers.

(3) Figures are provided for some problems. All figures are drawn to scale and lie in a plane UNLESS otherwise indicated.

(4) Unless otherwise specified, the domain of any function f is assumed to be the set of all real numbers x for which $f(x)$ is a real number.

Information

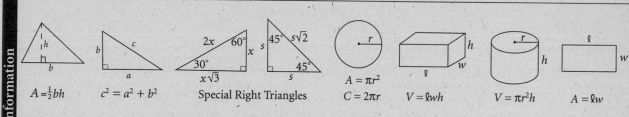

$A = \frac{1}{2}bh$ $c^2 = a^2 + b^2$ Special Right Triangles $A = \pi r^2$ $C = 2\pi r$ $V = \ell wh$ $V = \pi r^2 h$ $A = \ell w$

The sum of the degree measures of the angles in a triangle is 180.
The number of degrees of arc in a circle is 360.
A straight angle has a degree measure of 180.

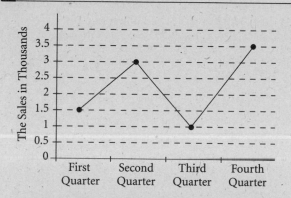

1. What is the percent increase from the third quarter to the fourth quarter for the tire sales represented in the chart above?

(A) 2.5

(B) 40

(C) 71.5

(D) 100

(E) 250

2. Jeweler A can set an average round-cut diamond in 20 minutes. Jeweler B requires 15 minutes to set the same type of diamond. In 8 hours, how many more diamonds can be set by Jeweler B than by Jeweler A?

(A) 40

(B) 24

(C) 16

(D) 8

(E) 1

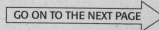
GO ON TO THE NEXT PAGE

KAPLAN
Test Prep and Admissions

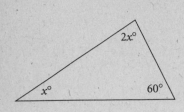

Figure 1   Figure 2

3. Based on the information in Figure 1 above, what is the value of y in Figure 2?

(A)   4

(B)   10

(C)   20

(D)   30

(E)   120

4. The force needed to stretch a spring varies directly with the distance the spring is stretched from its equilibrium position. If 50 pounds of force stretch a spring 8 inches from equilibrium, how much, in inches, will the spring be stretched by a force of 75 pounds?

(A)   10

(B)   12

(C)   33

(D)   248

(E)   468.75

5. If $x^{\frac{y}{2}} = 64$, where x and y are positive integers and $x > y$, what is the value of $x + y$?

(A)   4

(B)   7

(C)   8

(D)   10

(E)   12

6. If $n > 0$, what is the value of $3^{\frac{n}{2}} + 3^{\frac{n}{2}} + 3^{\frac{n}{2}}$?

(A) $\frac{3}{2}(3^{\frac{n}{2}})$

(B) $3^{\frac{n}{6}}$

(C) $3^{\frac{n}{2}+1}$

(D) $3^{\frac{3n}{2}}$

(E) $9^{\frac{n}{2}}$

7. If $f(x) = 3x - 8$ and $g(x) = \sqrt{2x^2 + 7}$, what is the value of $f(g(3))$?

(A)   1

(B)   3

(C)   5

(D)   7

(E)   9

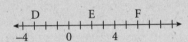

8. On the number line above, each of the letters D, E, and F corresponds to a different number. Which of those letters could correspond to the value of x if $|3 - x| > 5$?

(A)   D only

(B)   E only

(C)   F only

(D)   D or F

(E)   D, E, or F

GO ON TO THE NEXT PAGE

9. If $-1 < N < 1$ and $N \neq 0$, which of the following statements is always true?

    I. $N < 2N$
    II. $N^2 < N$
    III. $N^2 < \dfrac{1}{N^2}$

(A) I only
(B) II only
(C) III only
(D) I and III
(E) II and III

10. If X is the set of positive multiples of 2 and Y is the set of positive multiples of 3, then the intersection of X and Y is:

(A) the set of all positive integers
(B) the set of all positive real numbers
(C) the set of positive multiples of 3
(D) the set of positive multiples of 5
(E) the set of positive multiples of 6

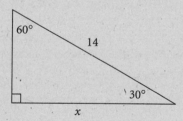

11. What is the value of x in the figure above?

(A) 7
(B) $7\sqrt{3}$
(C) $14\sqrt{3}$
(D) 28
(E) $28\sqrt{3}$

12. On a certain test, a class of 12 students has an average (arithmetic mean) score of 80. A second class of 18 students has an average score of 85. What is the average score of the combined classes?

(A) 82
(B) 82.5
(C) 83
(D) 84
(E) 84.5

13. The sum of two consecutive positive integers is never divisible by

(A) 2
(B) 3
(C) 5
(D) 7
(E) 211

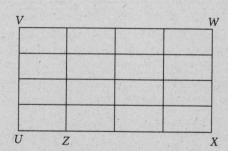

14. In the figure above, rectangle $UVWX$ is divided into 16 identical rectangles, four to a column and four to a row, as shown above. The ratio of the length to the width of each rectangle is 2 to 1. If rectangle $UVWX$ has an area of 72 square units, what is the length of UZ?

(A) 1.5
(B) 2
(C) 3
(D) 4
(E) 12

GO ON TO THE NEXT PAGE

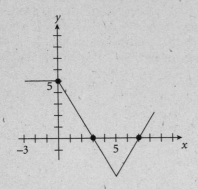

15. The graph of $f(x)$ is shown above. For what values of x does $f(x)$ have a negative slope?

(A) $x > 0$

(B) $x > 3$

(C) $x > 5$

(D) $0 < x < 5$

(E) $3 < x < 7$

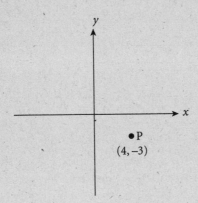

16. In the figure above, a line is to be drawn through point P so that it has a slope of 0. Through which of the following points must the line pass?

(A) $(0, 0)$

(B) $(-4, 3)$

(C) $(-4, -3)$

(D) $(-3, 4)$

(E) $(4, 3)$

17. If a, b, and x are positive integers, and $a \diagdown b$ with x on top is defined as the number of different triangles with sides of lengths a, b, and x, what is the value of $2 \diagdown 7$ with x on top?

(A) 2

(B) 3

(C) 4

(D) 5

(E) 6

18. In the standard x, y-coordinate plane, the center of circle O is the origin. If circle O has an area of 25π, each of the following points lies on the circumference of the circle EXCEPT

(A) $(5, 0)$

(B) $(4, -4)$

(C) $(3, 4)$

(D) $(-3, 4)$

(E) $(-4, 3)$

19. If m and n are positive integers and $2m + 3n = 15$, what is the sum of all possible values of m?

(A) 2

(B) 3

(C) 5

(D) 6

(E) 9

GO ON TO THE NEXT PAGE

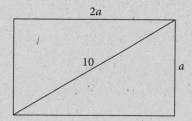

20. The figure above is a rectangle. What is the value of *a*?

(A) $\sqrt{5}$

(B) $\dfrac{10}{3}$

(C) $\dfrac{10\sqrt{3}}{3}$

(D) $2\sqrt{5}$

(E) $10\sqrt{5}$

SECTION 3
Time—25 Minutes
35 Questions

Directions: For each question in this section, select the best answer from among the choices given and fill in the corresponding oval on the answer sheet.

The following sentences test correctness and effectiveness of expression. Part of each sentence or the entire sentence is underlined; beneath each sentence are five ways of phrasing the underlined material. Choice (A) repeats the original phrasing; the other four choices are different. If you think the original phrasing produces a better sentence than any of the alternatives, select choice (A); if not, select one of the other choices.

In making your selection, follow the requirements of standard written English; that is, pay attention to grammar, choice of words, sentence construction, and punctuation. Your selection should result in the most effective sentence—clear and precise, without awkwardness or ambiguity.

EXAMPLE: ANSWER:

Every apple in the baskets <u>are ripe and labeled according to the date it was picked</u>.   Ⓐ ● Ⓒ Ⓓ Ⓔ

(A) are ripe and labeled according to the date it was picked
(B) is ripe and labeled according to the date it was picked
(C) are ripe and labeled according to the date they were picked
(D) is ripe and labeled according to the date they were picked
(E) are ripe and labeled as to the date it was picked

---

1. Community meetings were <u>most effectively at eradicating crime</u> in our neighborhood because the adults and young people learned to trust one another.

   (A) most effectively at eradicating crime
   (B) effectively at eradicating crime
   (C) most effective at eradicating crime
   (D) most effectively, eradicating crime
   (E) most effective eradicated crime

2. First, the spark plugs fire in the automobile engine, igniting a series of gasoline explosions, <u>and after that there are these pistons that are driven up and down inside the engine</u>.

   (A) and after that there are these pistons that are driven up and down inside the engine
   (B) and then pistons drive the engine up and down
   (C) and then there are pistons who are driven up and down inside the engine
   (D) which causes pistons to be driven up and down inside the engine
   (E) which after that there are these pistons that are driven up and down inside the engine

GO ON TO THE NEXT PAGE

3. Mahatma Gandhi, one of India's most highly respected leaders, <u>were convinced that the practice</u> of peaceful resistance, or *Satyagraha*, was the only viable means of protest.

   (A) were convinced that the practice

   (B) were convicted whenever the practice

   (C) were practically convinced that the idea

   (D) was convinced that the practice

   (E) was convinced by the practice

4. The Baja peninsula is a stretch of barren desert <u>in my Mexican guidebook</u> bordered on both sides by stunning beaches.

   (A) in my Mexican guidebook

   (B) from my Mexican guidebook

   (C) that, according to my guidebook about Mexico, is

   (D) that I read about in my guidebook about Mexico

   (E) in our enormous guidebook about Mexico

5. Five-year-old <u>Maria shaked her head vigorously from side to side</u>, indicating emphatically that she did not want to go to the dentist.

   (A) Maria shaked her head vigorously from side to side

   (B) Maria shaked her head vigorously sideways

   (C) Maria shook her head vigorously from side to side

   (D) Maria shook her head vigorously on both sides

   (E) Maria vigorously shook around her head

6. Government agencies have developed an early warning system <u>which system also warns people about the strength of the storm that the warning is about</u> so that residents know how to prepare.

   (A) which system also warns people about the strength of the storm that the warning is about

   (B) that also rates the strength of the approaching storm

   (C) that is a system that also warns people about the strength of the storm that is approaching

   (D) which is a system that also rates the approaching storm that the warning is about

   (E) which is a system that also warns people about the strength of the storm that is being warned about

7. <u>Poetry throughout the ages have always been</u> a spoken art form, and many poets are celebrating the current resurgence of community poetry slams.

   (A) Poetry throughout the ages have always been

   (B) Poetry throughout the ages has always been

   (C) Poetry throughout the ages always having been

   (D) Poems throughout the ages has always been

   (E) Poems throughout the ages will have been

8. The weather along the Irish coast broke clear and unusually calm on Saturday, so we were astonished to observe, as we walked several miles along the shore, that <u>there was not a single ship on site</u>.

   (A) there was not a single ship on site

   (B) there was not a single ship in sight

   (C) there is not a single ship on site

   (D) the single ship was on the site

   (E) there was not a solitary ship on site

GO ON TO THE NEXT PAGE ▷

9. <u>Julia felt well when she remembered</u> the thrill of defeating her traditional tennis rival Katie O'Mara in the annual Lakeview summer tournament.

   (A) Julia felt well when she remembered
   (B) Julia felt more well when she remembered
   (C) Julia felt good when she remembered
   (D) Julia remembered feeling good at
   (E) Julia felt well because she remembered

10. That night, <u>one of the keynote speakers argue persuasively</u> that the growing influence of exit polls on public opinion and politics was inherently dangerous.

    (A) one of the keynote speakers argue persuasively
    (B) the keynote speakers argue persuasively
    (C) one of the keynote speakers argues persuasively
    (D) one of the keynote speakers persuaded
    (E) one of the keynote speakers argued persuasively

11. Among the accomplishments of President James Knox Polk are <u>the creation of an independent treasury, establishing lower tariffs, and purchasing</u> the Oregon territory.

    (A) the creation of an independent treasury, establishing lower tariffs, and purchasing
    (B) the creating of an independent treasury, the establishment lower tariffs, and purchasing
    (C) the creation of an independent treasury, the establishment of lower tariffs, and the purchase of
    (D) creating an independent treasury, establishing lower tariffs, and the purchase of
    (E) creation of an independent treasury, establishing lower tariffs, and purchasing

GO ON TO THE NEXT PAGE

Directions: The following sentences test your ability to recognize grammar and usage errors. Each sentence contains either a single error or no error at all. No sentence contains more than one error. The error, if there is one, is underlined and lettered. If the sentence contains an error, select the one underlined part that must be changed to make the sentence correct. If the sentence is correct, select choice (E). In choosing answers, follow the requirements of standard written English.

EXAMPLE:

<u>Whenever</u> one is driving late at night, <u>you</u> must take extra precautions <u>against</u>
  A   B   C

falling asleep <u>at the wheel</u>. <u>No error</u>
          D   E

Ⓐ ● Ⓒ Ⓓ Ⓔ

12. <u>Because</u> the previous night's storm <u>had downed</u>
    A   B
several trees along the road, <u>it appeared unlikely</u>
                                   C
that many students <u>would</u> arrive on time for the
                      D
assembly. <u>No error</u>
        E

13. As the curtain rose <u>to reveal</u> the <u>darkened</u> stage, the
                A   B
audience could <u>distinguished</u> the
          C
<u>shadowy movements</u> of seven dancers. <u>No error</u>
       D   E

14. The director <u>wanted Delia to</u> portray her character
                 A
with <u>most conviction</u>, so he suggested
        B
<u>that she remember</u> an actual experience that
       C
<u>had saddened</u> her. <u>No error</u>
    D   E

15. The chef <u>herself</u> is carrying out the grand finale
        A
<u>of the celebration,</u> an extraordinary cake
    B
<u>that is smothered</u> in strawberries and <u>was topped</u>
    C   D
with eighteen sputtering candles. <u>No error</u>
                           E

16. <u>Filing</u> bankruptcy, while <u>it may ultimately be</u> the
    A   B
only solution <u>for some failing</u> businesses,
               C
<u>is hardly never</u> the first choice. <u>No error</u>
    D   E

17. In Jungian analysis, dreams are <u>thought to be</u>
                               A
<u>windows into</u> the <u>unconscious</u> desires and conflicts
   B   C
of <u>the person which</u> undergoes analysis. <u>No error</u>
       D   E

18. Although during the past year many parents
<u>have asked about</u> our reasons for including a
    A
writing sample on the test, <u>never before</u> <u>has</u> the
                       B   C
qualifications of the test makers been <u>so widely</u>
                                  D
challenged. <u>No error</u>
        E

19. If one <u>is interested</u> in <u>understanding</u> <u>even more</u>
       A   B   C
about the history of democracy in the ancient
world, <u>they should</u> consider taking our course in
        D
ancient civilizations. <u>No error</u>
             E

GO ON TO THE NEXT PAGE ➡

20. It is hilarious <u>when</u> my sister pulls on <u>her black wig</u>
           A   B
and <u>performs</u> her <u>imitation of Elvis Presley</u> singing
       C   D
"Blue Suede Shoes." <u>No error</u>
               E

21. Shakespeare's tragedy *Richard II* <u>about a king</u> who
                                 A
<u>was</u> an <u>ineffectual ruler</u> <u>because he had</u> the
 B   C   D
temperament of a poet. <u>No error</u>
                  E

22. The spokesman for the university <u>indicated that</u>
                               A
this year a <u>significantly lower</u> percentage <u>of their</u>
          B   C
student enrollment resulted directly <u>from</u> its mass
                          D
mailings sponsored annually by the alumni
association. <u>No error</u>
        E

23. Unlike Florence, <u>which lays</u> in the northern regions
             A
of the Italian peninsula, Sicily <u>was once</u> settled by
                           B
the Greeks and <u>therefore</u> <u>boasts</u> many ancient
           C   D
Greek temples and theaters. <u>No error</u>
                    E

24. We spent <u>a most enjoyable</u> afternoon lounging on
          A
the grass, <u>watching for exceptional</u> shaped
           B
<u>cumulus clouds</u>, and naming shapes <u>that they</u>
   C   D
brought to mind. <u>No error</u>
           E

25. Many of that doctor's patients claim
<u>having suffered</u> whiplash injuries, <u>but</u> none of
    A   B
them have proved <u>such an injury</u> was <u>actually</u>
                C   D
incurred. <u>No error</u>
       E

26. The measure of good toys for children under the
age of five is that, <u>no matter</u> how <u>reckless</u> they
                A   B
<u>are used</u>, they are not capable <u>of injuring</u> the child
  C   D
using them. <u>No error</u>
        E

27. The first American <u>protest on</u> African slavery, the
              A
1688 Germantown Quaker declaration <u>exerted</u>
                          B
tremendous influence <u>on both</u> the Pennsylvania
              C
religious communities and the abolition
movement <u>of its</u> time. <u>No error</u>
       D   E

28. The panel of judges <u>scoring</u> the Olympic gymnasts
              A
<u>found</u> the quality of the floor programs <u>were</u>
 B   C
generally excellent but <u>somewhat</u> uneven. <u>No error</u>
               D   E

29. The gopher is now <u>such a</u> nuisance to local
             A
homeowners that it <u>has become</u> absolutely
              B
necessary <u>to find ways</u> of controlling the direction
       C
<u>of their</u> tunneling. <u>No error</u>
  D   E

GO ON TO THE NEXT PAGE ▷

Directions: The following passage is an early draft of an essay. Some parts of the passage need to be rewritten.

Read the passage and select the best answer for each question that follows. Some questions are about particular sentences or parts of sentences and ask you to improve sentence structure or word choice. Other questions ask you to consider organization and development. In choosing answers, follow the conventions of standard written English.

Questions 30–35 are based on the following passage.

(1) When I visited England last year, I wanted to attend a football match (football in England is what is called soccer in the United States). (2) My mother wouldn't let me. (3) She tells me, "The fans are much too violent." (4) I really wanted to go so I did some research on English fans' violence.

(5) Through my research I realized that my mother would never let me go to a game. (6) But beyond that, I felt sad that hooliganism was such a reality in England. (7) They cause riots, and innocent football fans are sometimes injured by them when football-related fights get out of control. (8) England had tried all sorts of remedies to stop the violence. (9) They couldn't stop hooliganism from increasing. (10) The English tried creating lists of people banned from stadiums. (11) At international matches some known hooligans weren't even allowed into the country. (12) Some say that the older generation of hooligans was teaching the younger. (13) It is just human nature and crowd mentality. (14) But there was an argument that rang even more true for me: poverty was an underlying cause. (15) Economic data indicating that the football teams with the highest rate of violence were situated in the poorest areas.

30. In context, which is the best version of the underlined portion of sentence 3 (reproduced below)?

    She tells me, "The fans are much too violent."

    (A) (As it is now)
    (B) My mother tells me,
    (C) This was because she tells me,
    (D) She told me,
    (E) She suggested:

31. In context, which is the best version of the underlined portion of sentence 7 (reproduced below)?

    They cause riots, and innocent football fans are sometimes injured by them when football-related fights get out of control.

    (A) (As it is now)
    (B) They caused riots and innocent football fans were sometimes injured by them
    (C) Causing riots and injuring innocent football fans, the hooligans caused problems
    (D) The hooligans cause riots and sometimes injure innocent football fans
    (E) Innocent football fans sometimes cause riots and are injured

32. In context, which is the best version of the underlined portions of sentences 8 and 9 (reproduced below)?

    England had tried all sorts of remedies to stop the violence. They couldn't stop hooliganism from increasing.

    (A) England had tried all sorts of remedies for stopping the violence. They couldn't stop
    (B) England had tried all sorts of remedies to stop the violence and it couldn't stop
    (C) England had tried all sorts of remedies to stop the violence, but it couldn't stop
    (D) Although England had tried all sorts of remedies to stop the violence, they also stopped
    (E) It seems that England tried all sorts of remedies, but it couldn't stop the violence and

GO ON TO THE NEXT PAGE

33. In context, which of the following words are the most logical to insert at the beginning of sentence 13 (reproduced below)?

    It is just human nature and crowd mentality.

    (A) I see that
    (B) They say that
    (C) Others say that
    (D) However,
    (E) As a result,

34. In context, which is the best version of the underlined portion of sentence 15 (reproduced below)?

    Economic data indicating that the football teams with the highest rate of violence were situated in the poorest areas.

    (A) (As it is now)
    (B) seeming to indicate that the football teams
    (C) are indicating that the football teams
    (D) indicated that the football teams
    (E) had been indicating that the football teams

35. Where is the best place to insert the following sentence?

    Instead of just punishing acts of hooliganism, England should attack poverty, the source.

    (A) after sentence 5
    (B) after sentence 7
    (C) after sentence 10
    (D) after sentence 13
    (E) after sentence 15

SECTION 4
Time—25 Minutes
24 Questions

Directions: For each of the following questions, choose the best answer and darken the corresponding oval on the answer sheet.

Each sentence below has one or two blanks, each blank indicating that something has been omitted. Beneath the sentence are five words or sets of words labeled (A) through (E). Choose the word or set of words that, when inserted in the sentence, <u>best</u> fits the meaning of the sentence as a whole.

EXAMPLE:

Today's small, portable computers contrast markedly with the earliest electronic computers, which were ----.

(A) effective
(B) invented
(C) useful
(D) destructive
(E) enormous

1. The cat demonstrated her astonishing ---- by leaping from the low porch step to the top of the five-foot fence.

    (A) balance
    (B) awkwardness
    (C) agility
    (D) height
    (E) curiosity

2. Although the news he reported was ----, the anchorman remained calm, keeping his fear from his expression.

    (A) confusing
    (B) unexpected
    (C) anxious
    (D) exciting
    (E) dreadful

3. While the federal government promised to ---- its tax forms, many taxpayers still find them so ---- that they have to seek professional assistance.

    (A) mystify . . infuriating
    (B) shorten . . expensive
    (C) replace . . comprehensible
    (D) simplify . . bewildering
    (E) rewrite . . familiar

4. The ---- hooves of the horses, the blaring of the trumpets, and the beating of drums combined to create a ---- on medieval battlefields.

    (A) thundering . . cacophony
    (B) running . . danger
    (C) furious . . horror
    (D) thrashing . . situation
    (E) plodding . . calm

5. Although the long-term effects of the council's measures could be ----, no one can deny that the city is now enjoying an increase in tourism.

    (A) stated
    (B) compared
    (C) discussed
    (D) inquired
    (E) debated

GO ON TO THE NEXT PAGE

6. In order to maintain the ---- for which he was well known, the manager refused a tempting offer to ignore ---- in the corporation's accounting practices.

    (A) geniality . . irregularities
    (B) integrity . . improprieties
    (C) dishonesty . . policies
    (D) cordiality . . inconsistencies
    (E) frankness . . rules

7. Though the politician's inauguration was a generally ---- occasion, it was not without moments of ----, including a few jokes during her acceptance speech.

    (A) grim . . cleverness
    (B) exciting . . curiosity
    (C) mirthful . . humor
    (D) solemn . . levity
    (E) sober . . gravity

8. We usually imagine the French aristocracy to have lived a life of ----, but there is new evidence that many of its members were forced by exigencies to be quite frugal.

    (A) thrift
    (B) malice
    (C) prudence
    (D) opulence
    (E) beneficence

GO ON TO THE NEXT PAGE

> **Directions:** The passages below are followed by questions based on their content; questions following a pair of related passages may also be based on the relationship between the paired passages. Answer the questions on the basis of what is <u>stated</u> or <u>implied</u> in the passages and in any introductory material that may be provided.

Questions 9–10 are based on the following passage.

San Francisco's cable cars get their name from the long, heavy cable that runs beneath the streets along which the cars travel. This cable system resembles a giant laundry clothesline with a pulley
(5) at each end. Electricity turns the wheels of the pulleys, which in turn make the cable move. Under its floor, each car has a powerful claw that grips the cable when the car is ready to move, and releases the cable when the car needs to stop. The
(10) cars themselves are not powered and don't gener-ate any locomotion. Instead, they simply cling to the cable, which pulls them up and down San Francisco's steep hills.

9. The author includes the image of a laundry clothesline in order to

(A) amuse the reader

(B) provide helpful visual imagery

(C) compare the everyday importance of cable cars and laundry

(D) show the extreme simplicity of the cable's mechanism

(E) stress that clotheslines also work on a pulley system

10. Which of the following questions is answered by the passage?

(A) What provides the energy to turn the wheels of a common laundry clothesline?

(B) How is the pulley system used to steer the cars from one street to another?

(C) How long has the cable car system been in use?

(D) Which component of the cable car system provides the force for movement?

(E) What special challenges for the cable cars are presented by San Francisco's steep hills?

Question 11–12 are based on the following passage.

Though the detective story began with the work of Edgar Allan Poe and Emile Gaboriau, Arthur Conan Doyle must be credited with creating the most popular detective in the history of the genre.
(5) Sherlock Holmes first appeared in the novel *A Study in Scarlet* (1887). His sharp wits, keen eyes, and compelling personality made him an overnight sensation. In fact, when Doyle pushed Holmes over a cliff to his death in an 1893 story,
(10) readers were so outraged that the writer was forced to resurrect his hero. Doyle's blueprint of an all-knowing protagonist, tantalizing clues, and a tidy, moralistic conclusion has since become the foundation of an entire literary tradition.

11. According to the passage, Doyle is unlike Poe and Gaboriau in that Doyle

(A) invented the detective story genre

(B) created the most popular fictional detective

(C) used tantalizing clues in his stories

(D) created a compelling protagonist

(E) wrote popular novels

12. The description of the "blueprint" (line 11) serves to convey

(A) the care with which Doyle's stories were crafted

(B) that Doyle's stories are quite enjoyable

(C) that Doyle's work was too formulaic

(D) the extent to which Doyle was influenced by Poe and Gaboriau

(E) that the Holmes stories served as a precedent for the detective genre

GO ON TO THE NEXT PAGE

Questions 13–24 are based on the following passage.

The following passage is adapted from an art history website that details the careers of American artists.

Winslow Homer stands alone among American painters of the late 1800s. He had little academic training, remained largely untouched by the innovations of the French Impressionists of his era,
(5) and associated little with other artists. Despite—or perhaps because of—his refusal to follow the prescribed path to artistic success, he earned a comfortable living as a painter, and even before his death was revered by many as one of the fathers of
(10) American painting.

Homer was born in Boston in 1836 and grew up in the Massachusetts countryside. Before he reached his teens, he had decided to become an artist. He took the first step towards that goal in
(15) 1854 by accepting an apprenticeship at a printing company, where he designed advertisements and sheet-music covers. By 1859, he had moved to New York and was working as an illustrator for *Harper's Weekly*, a successful periodical. A few
(20) courses at a New York art school during his stay in the city would constitute the entirety of his formal training—a highly unorthodox foundation for a painting career in Homer's time.

In order to appreciate Homer's independence, it's
(25) instructive to consider the importance of critical acceptance to most painters in the nineteenth century. Then, displaying paintings in major annual exhibitions was the primary means for young painters to show their work to the public and crit-
(30) ics. In order to be included in these exhibitions, paintings had to be submitted to juries, panels of painters who were usually older and quite conservative. The juries awarded prizes to the canvases they liked, decided which of the submitted paint-
(35) ings to include in the exhibits, and chose where to display the works. Judges would often "punish" young painters whose work did not please them by rejecting their canvases or hanging them in the darkest corners of the rooms. This system made
(40) younger painters dependent on older ones; a young painter clearly had a strong incentive to paint in a way that would please conservative critics and colleagues. Homer, however, neither sought

nor gained recognition in this stuffy world of aca-
(45) demic painting, charting instead his own course.

When the American Civil War broke out, *Harper's* made Homer an artist-correspondent, and his war paintings, such as *Prisoners at the Front* (1866), garnered him a national reputation. Like Civil War
(50) photographer Matthew Brady, Homer portrayed the profound isolation of those in battle and the dignity and courage of individual soldiers, rather than the then-prevalent sensational action scenes that glossed over the realities of war. After the war, Homer made
(55) his permanent residence at his family home in Prout's Neck, Maine, far from the art world of New York City. Aside from a few trips to Europe, he remained in Maine and painted busily for the rest of his life. Homer's subject matter was indigenously
(60) American—American seascapes, American workers, and unsentimental American scenes in all their natural power and dignity. This was a major contribution to the arts in America, challenging the widely held belief that the only art worthy of a drawing-
(65) room or museum wall was must be European, or at least reflect European subjects and styles.

Though many art critics paid little attention to Homer during his lifetime, the art-buying public and the younger generation of American painters
(70) greatly admired his work. He supported himself comfortably on the sales of his oils and watercolors, and younger painters like John Sloan and George Luks embraced his realistic style and devotion to American subjects. Thus, despite his dissociation
(75) from the professional art world, Homer had a great influence on the future of American painting.

The Fog Warning (1885) offers a good example of Homer in his prime. It depicts a fisherman alone in his boat, pitted against the elements of the sea and
(80) the approaching storm, reliant in his own intelligence and strength. It is for these powerful, severe images of nature, particularly of the sea, that Homer is best known. Robert Henri, a respected American painter and disciple of Homer, described the power
(85) of these images: "Look at a Homer seascape. There is order in it and grand formation. It produces on your mind the whole vastness of the sea, a vastness as impressive and uncontrollable as the sea itself."

GO ON TO THE NEXT PAGE ▷

13. The primary purpose of the passage is to

(A) describe the major works of Winslow Homer

(B) chronicle the most important events in Winslow Homer's life

(C) describe and analyze Winslow Homer's career

(D) illustrate the influence that Winslow Homer had on succeeding generations of painters

(E) compare and contrast Winslow Homer's work with that of popular European artists of his era

14. The phrase "stands alone" in line 1 establishes that Homer was

(A) ordinary

(B) talented

(C) aloof

(D) shy

(E) unique

15. The author most likely regards Homer's "refusal to follow the prescribed path to artistic success" (lines 6–7) as

(A) evidence that Homer did not value economic success

(B) an indication that Homer believed himself to be more talented than were his contemporaries

(C) a reason that Homer was ashamed of his lack of formal training

(D) a contributing factor to Homer's eventual success

(E) a rejection of European subjects and styles

16. Which of the following was NOT a characteristic of the nineteenth-century jury system for selecting and displaying paintings as described in the passage?

(A) Young painters were subjected to the judgments of older painters.

(B) The art-viewing public was unlikely to see works that the judges disliked.

(C) Young painters were encouraged to please painters of the previous generation.

(D) It left Homer with no means to present his work to the public.

(E) Judges could show disapproval without rejecting a painting.

17. The author would be most likely to agree that Homer's work and that of nineteenth-century European artists differ primarily in the

(A) subject matter and style of the works

(B) level of talent among the painters

(C) setting in which the works were completed

(D) critical acclaim the works received

(E) the artistic merit of the works

18. As used in lines 53–54, "glossed over" most nearly means

(A) polished

(B) shined

(C) avoided

(D) highlighted

(E) questioned

GO ON TO THE NEXT PAGE

19. The author most likely notes the separation of Homer's Maine residence from New York City in order to

    (A) underscore Homer's inability to obtain the approval of New York art juries

    (B) illustrate Homer's independence from the art establishment of his time

    (C) cite a probable influence on the subject matter Homer chose for his work

    (D) create an atmosphere of rugged isolationism

    (E) highlight a critical detail in the chronology of Homer's career

20. The description of *The Fog Warning* serves primarily to

    (A) support the assertion that Homer was in his prime when he painted this picture

    (B) familiarize the reader with the most important of Homer's works

    (C) explain critic's rejection of Homer's original subject matter

    (D) provide a description of the rigors of maritime life

    (E) help illustrate why Homer is considered a great artist

21. The word "embraced" in line 73 most nearly means

    (A) shunned

    (B) accepted

    (C) surrounded

    (D) grasped

    (E) denied

22. The author most likely includes a quotation from Robert Henri (lines 85–88) in order to

    (A) support the assertion that Homer influenced young American painters

    (B) embellish the description of Homer's seascapes

    (C) emphasize the self-reliance of the subject of the painting

    (D) establish that Henri was a perceptive art critic

    (E) illustrate the differences between Homer's work and that of contemporary European painters

23. The author would most likely agree that Homer succeeded as an artist primarily because

    (A) his work at *Harper's Weekly* elevated him to national prominence

    (B) he was not formally trained

    (C) people responded to his original style and American themes

    (D) a younger generation of painters considered him highly influential

    (E) those who refuse to follow established paths are more likely to succeed

24. Based on the passage, Winslow Homer's personality could best be described as

    (A) independent and confident

    (B) assertive and inquisitive

    (C) ambitious and calculating

    (D) cautious and autonomous

    (E) self-sufficient and sociable

IF YOU FINISH BEFORE TIME IS CALLED, YOU MAY CHECK YOUR WORK ON THIS SECTION ONLY. DO NOT TURN TO ANY OTHER SECTION IN THE TEST.

KAPLAN
Test Prep and Admissions

SECTION 5

Time—25 Minutes

18 Questions

Directions: For this section, solve each problem and decide which is the best of the choices given. Fill in the corresponding oval on the answer sheet. You may use any available space for scratchwork.

Notes:

(1) Calculator use is permitted.

(2) All numbers used are real numbers.

(3) Figures are provided for some problems. All figures are drawn to scale and lie in a plane UNLESS otherwise indicated.

(4) Unless otherwise specified, the domain of any function f is assumed to be the set of all real numbers x for which $f(x)$ is a real number.

Information

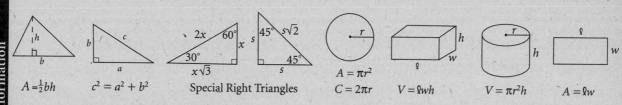

$A = \frac{1}{2}bh$ $c^2 = a^2 + b^2$ Special Right Triangles $A = \pi r^2$ $V = \ell wh$ $V = \pi r^2 h$ $A = \ell w$

$C = 2\pi r$

The sum of the degree measures of the angles in a triangle is 180.

The number of degrees of arc in a circle is 360.

A straight angle has a degree measure of 180.

1. If $\frac{2x}{3} = \frac{4}{5}$ then $x =$

   (A) $\frac{2}{5}$

   (B) $\frac{5}{12}$

   (C) $\frac{5}{6}$

   (D) $\frac{6}{5}$

   (E) $\frac{12}{5}$

2. Which of the following groups contains three fractions that are equal?

   (A) $\frac{1}{3}, \frac{1}{6}, \frac{1}{9}$

   (B) $\frac{2}{5}, \frac{10}{25}, \frac{12}{30}$

   (C) $\frac{1}{2}, \frac{2}{4}, \frac{4}{6}$

   (D) $\frac{2}{3}, \frac{2}{6}, \frac{2}{9}$

   (E) $\frac{3}{4}, \frac{10}{12}, \frac{75}{100}$

GO ON TO THE NEXT PAGE

KAPLAN

Test Prep and Admissions

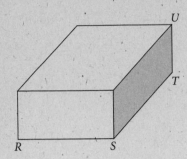

3. In the rectangular solid above, $RS = 8$, $ST = 12$, and $UT = \frac{1}{3} ST$. What is the volume of the solid?

(A) 384
(B) 240
(C) 96
(D) 32
(E) 24

4. If $m^2 + 7 = 29$, then $m^2 - 7 =$

(A) 15
(B) 22
(C) 71
(D) 78
(E) 484

5. If 125 percent of x is 150, what is x percent of 75?

(A) 70
(B) 90
(C) 120
(D) 150
(E) 185

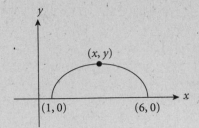

6. In the figure above, what is the x-coordinate of the point on the semicircle that is the farthest from the x-axis?

(A) 2.5
(B) 3.5
(C) 4
(D) 4.25
(E) 4.5

7. If $a = \dfrac{12b^4}{c}$, what happens to the value of a when both b and c are tripled?

(A) a is multiplied by 27
(B) a is multiplied by 12
(C) a is multiplied by 9
(D) a is tripled
(E) a is unchanged

8. If $n < 3 < \dfrac{1}{n}$, then n could be which of the following?

(A) 5
(B) 1
(C) $\dfrac{1}{3}$
(D) $\dfrac{1}{5}$
(E) $-\dfrac{1}{5}$

GO ON TO THE NEXT PAGE

Directions: For Student-Produced Response questions 9–18, use the grids at the bottom of the answer sheet page on which you have answered questions 1–8.

Each of the remaining 10 questions requires you to solve the problem and enter your answer by marking the ovals in the special grid, as shown in the example below. You may use any available space for scratch work.

Answer: 1.25 or $\frac{5}{4}$ or 5/4

Write answer in → boxes.

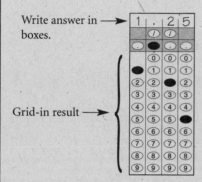

Grid-in result →

Either position is correct.

Fraction line
Decimal point

You may start your answers in any column, space permitting. Columns not needed should be left blank.

- It is recommended, though not required, that you write your answer in the boxes at the top of the columns. However, you will receive credit only for darkening the ovals correctly.

- Grid only one answer to a question, even though some problems have more than one correct answer.

- Darken no more than one oval in a column.

- No answers are negative.

- Mixed numbers cannot be gridded. For example: the number $1\frac{1}{4}$ must be gridded as 1.25 or 5/4.

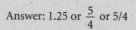
(If is gridded, it will be interpreted as $\frac{11}{4}$ not $1\frac{1}{4}$.)

- **Decimal Accuracy:** Decimal answers must be entered as accurately as possible. For example, if you obtain an answer such as 0.1666..., you should record the result as .166 or .167. **Less accurate values such as .16 or .17 are not acceptable.**

Acceptable ways to grid $\frac{1}{6}$ = .1666...

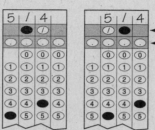

GO ON TO THE NEXT PAGE

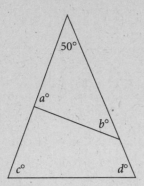

9. In the figure above, what is the value of
   $a + b + c + d$?

10. If an object travels at a speed of 3 feet per second,
    how many feet does it travel in half an hour?

11. How many square units is the area of an isosceles
    right triangle whose hypotenuse has a length of
    $8\sqrt{2}$ units?

12. The ratio of 1.5 to 18 is the same as the ratio of x
    to 2.4. What is the value of x?

13. If $a > 0$ and $a^b a^3 = a^{\frac{10}{3}}$, what is the value of b?

14. What is the least possible integer value for which
    40 percent of that integer is greater than 2.8?

15. $-2, -1, 0, 1, 2, 1, 0, -1, -2, -1, 0, 1$

    The first ten terms of a sequence are shown above.
    What is the sum of the first 88 terms?

16. If $x > 5$ and $\dfrac{14}{\sqrt{x-5}} = 7$ what is the value of x?

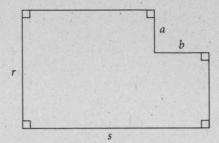

17. If $r + s$ in the figure above is 13, what is the
    perimeter of the figure?

18. If $x > 0$ and $y > 0$, x^3 is half of x^2, and y^3 is one
    third of y^2, what is the value of $x + y$?

SECTION 6

Time—25 Minutes
24 Questions

> **Directions:** For each of the following questions, choose the best answer and darken the corresponding oval on the answer sheet.

Each sentence below has one or two blanks, each blank indicating that something has been omitted. Beneath the sentence are five words or sets of words labeled (A) through (E). Choose the word or set of words that, when inserted in the sentence, <u>best</u> fits the meaning of the sentence as a whole.

EXAMPLE:

Today's small, portable computers contrast markedly with the earliest electronic computers, which were ----.

(A) effective
(B) invented
(C) useful
(D) destructive
(E) enormous

1. The novelist shocked his editor by ---- the book on which he had been working for seven years and starting over.

   (A) abridging
   (B) supplemented
   (C) abandoning
   (D) truncating
   (E) praising

2. The new film is so ---- that the public is polarized into a group of people who are angered by it and those who applaud the director's courage.

   (A) mundane
   (B) creative
   (C) controversial
   (D) pertinent
   (E) daunting

3. The highway commission initially felt that the new road would be ---- and was surprised to find it ---- to the city's transportation needs.

   (A) redundant . . irrelevant
   (B) unnecessary . . vital
   (C) inappropriate . . unsuited
   (D) dangerous . . attributable
   (E) scenic . . damaging

4. The salesman advised his frugal customer to buy the small gas grill, since it was the most ---- model.

   (A) tasteful
   (B) secure
   (C) costly
   (D) manageable
   (E) economical

5. The film critic ---- the movie, saying that the script lacked structure and the characters were laughably shallow.

   (A) derided
   (B) remembered
   (C) belied
   (D) praised
   (E) ignored

GO ON TO THE NEXT PAGE

Directions: The passages below are followed by questions based on their content; questions following a pair of related passages may also be based on the relationship between the paired passages. Answer the questions on the basis of what is <u>stated</u> or <u>implied</u> in the passages and in any introductory material that may be provided.

Questions 6–9 are based on the following passages.

Passage 1

Marvin Freeman's groundbreaking new study of the plays of Henrik Ibsen will alter the course of Ibsen scholarship forever. Previously, scholars limited the areas of their studies to a particular phase
(5) of Ibsen's career, since a different scholarly approach seemed to fit each of the phases. Freeman has instead taken on the entirety of Ibsen's work. Happily, this breadth of scholarship does not diminish the depth with which Freeman
(10) explores each work. The career of Ibsen is now liberated from arbitrary divisions and stands before us as a complete picture. It will be years before we can appreciate fully the service that Freeman has rendered.

Passage 2

(15)   In his new tome on the plays of Henrik Ibsen, Marvin Freeman presumes to consider all of the 26 plays, a period of writing that spanned some 50 years. This experiment, while yielding some interesting observations, does not serve as a useful
(20) scholarly model. Over the course of Ibsen's career, the playwright's approach evolved so drastically that it is impossible to fully consider all of his works in the confines of a single study. Freeman is forced to simplify where complexity would be
(25) more apt. While Freeman exhibits tremendous dedication to his subject, this devotion ultimately cannot save the project from its own ambition.

6. In the Passage 1, the "arbitrary divisions" in line 11 refer to

(A) the unsuccessful scholarly approaches that have been applied to Ibsen's work

(B) the breaks that Ibsen took between writing his plays

(C) a rift that Freeman has created among Ibsen scholars

(D) distinctions between various phases of Ibsen's career

(E) Freeman's dissatisfaction with previous Ibsen scholarship

7. The last sentence of Passage 1 functions primarily to

(A) imply that the book is very difficult to read

(B) highlight the lasting importance of the book

(C) celebrate Freeman's triumph over obstacles

(D) argue that additional scholarship will clarify Freeman's intent

(E) paraphrase the closing argument of Freeman's book

GO ON TO THE NEXT PAGE

8. The author of Passage 2 implies that Freeman's attempt to write about Ibsen's entire career in a single book is

   (A) overwhelming but not idealistic
   (B) feasible but not sufficient
   (C) admirable but not successful
   (D) viable but not important
   (E) desirable but not achievable

9. The author of Passage 2 would most likely regard the approach of the scholars mentioned in lines 3–6 as

   (A) of appropriate scope
   (B) inferior to that of Freeman
   (C) of lasting importance to future generations
   (D) unsuitable for Ibsen's career
   (E) difficult to assess

GO ON TO THE NEXT PAGE

Questions 10–20 are based on the following passage.

The following is adapted from an article written for family caretakers of sufferers from dementia, a group of diseases that affect some elderly people.

Historically, a variety of terms have been used to describe the symptoms of forgetfulness and loss of reasoning ability that occur as people age. These include organic brain syndrome, hardening
(5) of the arteries, chronic brain syndrome, Alzheimer's Disease, and senility. Increasingly however, the medical profession has grouped these diseases under a single name—dementia. Derived from Latin roots meaning *away* and *mind*, demen-
(10) tia refers to a loss or impairment of mental powers. Some of the diseases that fall under the heading of dementia are treatable, while others are not. (Thyroid disease, for example, may cause symptoms of dementia that can be reversed with the
(15) proper medication.) The symptoms of dementia can be divided broadly into those that affect memory and those that affect thoughts and feelings, though the division is not an entirely neat one. Both types of symptoms can influence behav-
(20) ior. A deeper understanding of the causes and effects of dementia is vital for those who care for its sufferers, and, where possible, for the sufferers themselves.

Many people are surprised to learn that severe
(25) memory loss in older adults is not part of the normal aging process. In fact, a vast majority of the people who survive into their eighties and nineties never experience significant memory loss or other symptoms of dementia. Fifteen percent of older
(30) adults suffer from milder impairments as the result of dementia, and only five percent suffer from a severe intellectual impairment. It's also important to note that not all areas of memory are affected equally by dementia. Research shows
(35) that the mind stores and processes fact-based memories differently from memories of emotions, and that dementia can damage one kind of memory without damaging the other. Furthermore, highly-developed social skills are often retained
(40) longer than are insight and judgment, making early-stage dementia difficult to diagnose. Short-term memory is usually affected earlier than long-term

memory, a seemingly paradoxical situation in which dementia sufferers vividly recall childhood
(45) memories but are unable to remember that morning's breakfast menu. This is especially frustrating, since the sufferers often feel otherwise mentally fit. Eventually, however, severe memory loss becomes debilitating and sabotages sufferers as
(50) they attempt even routine tasks.

While memory loss by itself can lead to anxiety and depression, these feelings are often instead directly caused by biochemical changes that result from dementia. Patients often feel inexplicably
(55) lost, vulnerable, and helpless. Biochemical changes can also lead to suspicion or even full-blown paranoia, alienating caretakers and loved ones. These feelings of paranoia sometimes lead sufferers to hide valuables from imagined dangers, only to
(60) then forget the hiding places, a problem familiar to many caregivers. It's especially important to identify paranoia and depression that is biochemical in nature rather than that caused by frustration and memory loss, since biochemical paranoia
(65) and depression can often be at least partially relieved by medication.

Because the symptoms of dementia are so dramatic and distressing, both for the sufferer and those around him or her, people who care for peo-
(70) ple with dementia need to be especially patient, with both the sufferer and themselves. This is particularly true when the caregiver is a loved one. When the sufferer is the victim of irrational paranoid delusions, for example, the caregiver should
(75) understand these delusions are symptoms of the illness. Confronting the patient about this irrationality will only worsen the situation. Instead, it's often more helpful to deflect the situation by involving the patient in a pleasant, absorbing task.
(80) Caregivers also need to monitor their own behavior and feelings. They are under extreme stress and should avail themselves of family and professional support networks.

GO ON TO THE NEXT PAGE ⇒

10. The primary purpose of the passage is to

(A) argue for the classification of many diseases as forms of dementia

(B) explore how memory loss affects behavior

(C) explain the causes of dementing illness

(D) educate caretakers about the effects of dementia

(E) summarize the history of mental illness

11. As used in the passage, the word "neat" (line 18) most nearly means

(A) natural

(B) uncluttered

(C) distinct

(D) genuine

(E) favorable

12. According to the author, severe memory loss in elderly adults is

(A) unlikely to affect behavior

(B) often the result of anxiety and depression

(C) likely to leave social skills intact indefinitely

(D) the leading cause of dementia

(E) less common than is often believed

13. Based on lines 38–41 ("Furthermore … dementia,"), the author would most likely agree that it is often difficult to diagnose early-stage dementia because

(A) the speech and actions of patients appear to be normal

(B) patients retain much of their insight and judgment

(C) medication is of little help in such cases

(D) fact-based memories are stored differently than emotional memories

(E) social skills are difficult to quantify scientifically

14. The author cites "that morning's breakfast menu" (lines 45–46) as an example of

(A) a frustrating experience

(B) a short-term memory

(C) a social skill

(D) a mundane task

(E) a fact-based memory

15. The author notes that it is especially important to diagnose the cause of paranoia and anxiety in dementia sufferers because

(A) caregivers need to take advantage of support networks

(B) medical treatment may be helpful

(C) anxiety is more common than paranoia

(D) such an understanding will alleviate the symptoms

(E) diagnosis will prevent the misplacing of valuables

16. According to the author, anxiety and depression in dementia sufferers can be caused by both

(A) memory loss and biochemistry

(B) suspicion and paranoia

(C) short-term and long-term memory

(D) mundane tasks and social skills

(E) family and professional support networks

17. The word "absorbing" in line 79 means

(A) engrossing

(B) porous

(C) dry

(D) irrelevant

(E) demanding

GO ON TO THE NEXT PAGE

18. The author notes that "Caregivers also need to monitor their own behavior and feelings" (lines 80–81) in order to detect

   (A) depression and anxiety caused by biochemical changes
   (B) the effectiveness of medication taken by sufferers of dementia
   (C) threats to their own health and well being
   (D) the importance of family and professional support networks
   (E) pleasant tasks to engage dementia sufferers

19. According to the passage, a patient with dementing illness may suffer from all of the following EXCEPT

   (A) anxiety and depression
   (B) inability to perform simple tasks
   (C) irrational suspicion
   (D) memory loss
   (E) side-effects from medication

20. Which of the following best describes the author's tone in the last paragraph?

   (A) confrontational
   (B) distressed
   (C) lighthearted
   (D) sympathetic
   (E) indifferent

GO ON TO THE NEXT PAGE

Questions 21–24 are based on the following passages.

Passage 1

The recently legislated "do-not-call" registry aimed at blocking telemarketers' access to private households has been an exceedingly popular move by the federal government. For many Americans
(5) who are growing increasingly frustrated with unsolicited marketing calls interrupting dinnertime or Sunday morning snoozes, the new list of roughly 50 million names has provided some relief. For those who once filled the estimated 2 million tele-
(10) services industry jobs that will be lost, however, this reprieve will likely go unappreciated. As a result of this conflict, the list has been taken into the courts, where the federal commission charged with overseeing the registry will square off against
(15) the lawsuits of nearly 5,000 telemarketing-reliant companies.

Passage 2

The newly drafted "do-not-call" legislation, while popular among millions of American consumers, has appropriately set-off a free speech
(20) debate in the federal court system. Proponents of the bill, which allows individuals to register their phone numbers as unavailable to telemarketers, argue that the new directive is simply a long overdue step to protect consumers from unsolicited
(25) marketing intrusions into their private lives. The reality, however, is undeniably more complicated than this slant suggests. The argument can certainly be made that the registry unduly discriminates against certain marketing tools and, subsequently,
(30) the products they promote. It is impossible to determine that one intrusion, say, a highway billboard, is less severe than another.

21. The teleservices workers mentioned in Passage 1 would most likely consider the "do-not-call" registry

(A) a necessary restriction
(B) a divisive force
(C) unlawful legislation
(D) a temporary nuisance
(E) a destruction of their livelihood

22. In line 27, "slant" most nearly means

(A) decline
(B) influence
(C) distortion
(D) opinion
(E) deviation

23. Which aspect of the "do-not-call" legislation is discussed in Passage 2, but not in Passage 1?

(A) its popularity
(B) its fairness
(C) its subjectivity
(D) its conflict with free speech
(E) its impact on employment

24. Which of the following is a focus that is shared by the two passages?

(A) the costs of the registry for consumers
(B) the registry's enormous impact on telemarketers
(C) the great societal need the legislation has filled
(D) the role courts will play in the registry's composition
(E) the potential drawbacks of the legislation

SECTION 7

Time—20 Minutes

16 Questions

Directions: For this section, solve each problem and decide which is the best of the choices given. Fill in the corresponding oval on the answer sheet. You may use any available space for scratchwork.

Notes:

(1) Calculator use is permitted.

(2) All numbers used are real numbers.

(3) Figures are provided for some problems. All figures are drawn to scale and lie in a plane UNLESS otherwise indicated.

(4) Unless otherwise specified, the domain of any function f is assumed to be the set of all real numbers x for which $f(x)$ is a real number.

Information

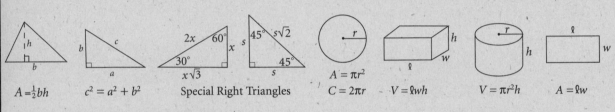

$A = \frac{1}{2}bh$ $c^2 = a^2 + b^2$ Special Right Triangles $A = \pi r^2$ $C = 2\pi r$ $V = \ell w h$ $V = \pi r^2 h$ $A = \ell w$

The sum of the degree measures of the angles in a triangle is 180.

The number of degrees of arc in a circle is 360.

A straight angle has a degree measure of 180.

---

1. What is the fewest number of 3s that can be multiplied together to yield a number greater than 100?

    (A) 4

    (B) 5

    (C) 11

    (D) 33

    (E) 34

$$P \qquad Q \qquad R$$

2. If P, Q, and R on the number line above represent consecutive odd integers, which of the following is NOT true?

    (A) $P + Q$ is an even integer.

    (B) $P + Q + R$ is an odd integer.

    (C) $R - P$ is an even integer.

    (D) $\dfrac{P + Q}{2}$ is an even integer.

    (E) $\dfrac{P + R}{2}$ is an even integer.

GO ON TO THE NEXT PAGE

3. Six lines intersect at one point, to form 12 equal angles that are non-overlapping. What is the measure, in degrees, of one of these angles?

   (A) 15
   (B) 20
   (C) 30
   (D) 45
   (E) 60

4. If $m = \left| \dfrac{1}{x} \right|$ and $n = \dfrac{1}{y}$, what is the value of $m + n$ when $x = -2$ and $y = -3$?

   (A) $-\dfrac{5}{6}$
   (B) $-\dfrac{1}{6}$
   (C) 0
   (D) $\dfrac{1}{6}$
   (E) $\dfrac{5}{6}$

5. If $p = 2$, what is $2q(7 - 6p)$ in terms of q?

   (A) $-10q$
   (B) $10q$
   (C) $14q - 12$
   (D) $28 - 6q$
   (E) $36q$

6. If 50 percent of 40 percent of a number is 22.8, what is the number?

   (A) 25.3
   (B) 45.6
   (C) 57
   (D) 85.5
   (E) 114

7. If $(2x^2 + 5x - 3)(4x - 1) = ax^3 + bx^2 + cx + d$ for all values of x, what is the value of b?

   (A) -22
   (B) -18
   (C) -17
   (D) 18
   (E) 22

8. Let $<a, b>$ be defined as the set of all integers between, but not including, a and b. For example, $<-3, 3> = \{-2, -1, 0, 1, 2\}$. Which of the following does NOT have the same number of elements as the intersection of $<-4, 4>$ and $<0, 7>$?

   (A) $<-2, 2>$
   (B) $<-1, 4>$
   (C) $<-3, 1>$
   (D) $<3, 7>$
   (E) $<1, 5>$

9. In a certain country, the ratio of people over 50 to people under 50 is 3 to 5. What percent of the population is under 50?

   (A) 30
   (B) 37.5
   (C) 50
   (D) 60
   (E) 62.5

GO ON TO THE NEXT PAGE

10. If a "sump" number is defined as one in which the sum of the digits of the number is greater than the product of the digits of the same number, which of the following is a "sump" number?

    (A) 123
    (B) 234
    (C) 332
    (D) 411
    (E) 521

11. If the average (arithmetic mean) of 14 consecutive integers is 20.5, what is the average of the first seven integers?

    (A) 10.25
    (B) 14.5
    (C) 17
    (D) 18.25
    (E) 19

12. If $12 = r^y$, then $12r =$

    (A) r^{y+1}
    (B) r^{y+2}
    (C) r^{y+12}
    (D) r^{12y}
    (E) r^{2y}

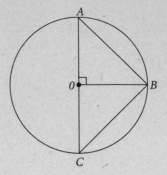

13. In the figure above, O is the center of the circle. If $AB = 6\sqrt{2}$, what is the area of $\triangle ABC$?

    (A) $36\sqrt{2}$
    (B) 36
    (C) $72\sqrt{2}$
    (D) 72
    (E) $24\sqrt{2}$

14. If a, b, and c are all integers greater than 1 and $ab = 14$ and $bc = 21$, which of the following must be true?

    (A) $c > a > b$
    (B) $b > c > a$
    (C) $b > a > c$
    (D) $a > c > b$
    (E) $a > b > c$

GO ON TO THE NEXT PAGE

15. Ahmed rolled an eight-sided polygon six times. Each face of the polygon has a number from 1–8 painted on it. No two numbers are repeated. Each roll yields one number face up.

The first roll yields an even number.

The second roll yields an odd number.

The third roll yields the number 5.

The fourth roll yields a number smaller than 4.

The fifth roll yields the same number as the fourth roll.

The sixth roll yields a number smaller than the fifth roll.

Which of the following must be true?

(A) Ahmed could have rolled a 5 three times.

(B) Ahmed could have rolled a 2 more frequently than he could have rolled any other numbers.

(C) Ahmed rolled more odd numbers than even numbers.

(D) Ahmed rolled a 3 at least once.

(E) Ahmed rolled a 1 on four rolls

16. The average (arithmetic mean) of two numbers is equal to twice the positive difference between the two numbers. If the larger number is 35, what is the smaller number?

(A) 3

(B) 9

(C) 15

(D) 21

(E) 27

IF YOU FINISH BEFORE TIME IS CALLED, YOU MAY CHECK YOUR WORK ON THIS SECTION ONLY. DO NOT TURN TO ANY OTHER SECTION IN THE TEST. STOP

SECTION 8

Time—20 Minutes
19 Questions

Directions: For each of the following questions, choose the best answer and darken the corresponding oval on the answer sheet.

Each sentence below has one or two blanks, each blank indicating that something has been omitted. Beneath the sentence are five words or sets of words labeled (A) through (E). Choose the word or set of words that, when inserted in the sentence, <u>best</u> fits the meaning of the sentence as a whole.

EXAMPLE:

Today's small, portable computers contrast markedly with the earliest electronic computers, which were ----.

(A) effective
(B) invented
(C) useful
(D) destructive
(E) enormous

---

1. Whenever she felt tired after work, a brisk walk along the beach amid the ---- sea air never failed to ---- her fatigue and leave her re-energized.

(A) humid . . hasten
(B) salty . . exacerbate
(C) bracing . . alleviate
(D) damp . . reprove
(E) chilly . . aggravate

2. "Old Nick" is one of several ---- people use when they want to refer indirectly to the Devil.

(A) euphemisms
(B) banalities
(C) arguments
(D) apostrophes
(E) eulogies

3. Because its bookkeepers altered some figures and completely fabricated others, the company's financial records were entirely ----.

(A) cursory
(B) disseminated
(C) singular
(D) concealed
(E) spurious

4. When the children won the baseball game, their parents were so ---- that ---- reaction spread through the stands.

(A) perplexed . . a spirited
(B) enraged . . a distressing
(C) dejected . . a raucous
(D) elated . . an exuberant
(E) thrilled . . a scornful

5. Once he had intellectually ---- the difference between regional dialects, Fernando found himself speaking the language ----.

(A) rejected . . considerately
(B) grasped . . effortlessly
(C) mastered . . implicitly
(D) forgotten . . eloquently
(E) recognized . . ambiguously

6. Advocates of free speech argue that in order to ---- the right of Americans to express their opinions, no citizen who expresses unpopular sentiments should be ----.

(A) maximize . . divulged
(B) ensure . . ostracized
(C) diminish . . inhibited
(D) elucidate . . restricted
(E) embellish . . praised

GO ON TO THE NEXT PAGE

Directions: The passages below are followed by questions based on their content; questions following a pair of related passages may also be based on the relationship between the paired passages. Answer the questions on the basis of what is <u>stated</u> or <u>implied</u> in the passages and in any introductory material that may be provided.

Questions 7–19 are based on the following passages.

The following passages concern the novel Moby Dick *by American author Herman Melville (1819–1891), which tells the story of the hunt by Captain Ahab for the whale named Moby Dick. Passage 1 is adapted from a 1852 review from a literary magazine, and Passage 2 is by a modern literary critic.*

Passage 1

In *Moby Dick*, Mr. Melville is evidently trying to ascertain how far the public will consent to be imposed upon. He is gauging, at once, our gulli-
bility and our patience. Having written one or two

(5) passable extravagancies, he has considered himself privileged to produce as many more as he pleases, increasingly exaggerated and increasingly dull. In vanity, in caricature, in efforts at literary innovation—generally as clumsy as they are ineffectual—

(10) and in low attempts at humor, each one of his vol-
umes has been an advance among its predecessors. Mr. Melville never writes naturally. His sentiment is forced, his wit is forced, and his enthusiasm is forced. And in his attempts to display to the

(15) utmost extent his powers of "fine writing," he has succeeded, we think, beyond his most optimistic expectations.

The work is an ill-compounded mixture of romance and matter-of-fact. The idea of a con-

(20) nected and collected story has obviously visited and abandoned its writer again and again in the course of composition. The style of his tale is in places disfigured by mad (rather than bad) English; and its conclusion is hastily, weakly, and

(25) obscurely written. The result is, at all events, a strange book—neither so compelling as to be entertaining, nor so instructively complete as to take place among documents on the subject of the Great Whale, his capabilities, his home, and his

(30) capture. Our author must be henceforth num-
bered in the company of those writers who occasionally tantalize us with indications of talent, while they constantly summon us to endure monstrosities, carelessness, and bad taste.

(35) The truth is, Mr. Melville has survived his reputa-
tion. If he had been contented with writing one or two books, he might have been famous, but his vanity has destroyed all his chances for immortality, or even of a good name with his own generation.

(40) For, in sober truth, Mr. Melville's vanity is immeasurable. He will either be first among the book-making tribe, or he will be nowhere. He will center all attention upon himself, or he will abandon the field of literature at once. From this mor-

(45) bid self-esteem, coupled with a most unbounded love of fame, spring all Mr. Melville's efforts, all his rhetorical contortions, all his declamatory abuse of society, all his inflated sentiment, and all his insinuating licentiousness.

Passage 2

(50) Many readers have dismissed Herman Melville's epic novel *Moby Dick* as "a treatise on whaling" because it contains so many chapters that explore the intricacies of the whaling trade in the mid-
nineteenth century. Such passages make no direct

(55) mention of the events that make up the novel's plot, and instead provide a wealth of factual infor-
mation on topics such as undersea plant life and the anatomy of great whales. Such critics feel that alternating such discursive material with the narra-

(60) tive detracts from the compelling account of the hunt for Moby Dick, the eponymous white whale. However, these critics fail to realize that Melville is slyly, if paradoxically, advancing the plot through these admittedly dry passages of purely factual data.

(65) The whale Moby Dick is—unsurprisingly, given the book's title—pivotal to the plot. The story concentrates on the pursuit of the whale by

GO ON TO THE NEXT PAGE

Captain Ahab, a master whaler who has long been obsessed with his prey. In order to portray the
(70) hunt as a titanic struggle, Melville needed to paint a detailed portrait of the whale—a worthy rival for the ruthless and skilled Ahab. How could Melville create such a sense of personality and agency for a mute animal? How could he make the
(75) character of Moby Dick as compelling and fully-realized as Ahab?

Melville met these challenges by educating the reader. Melville had served on a whaling ship himself, and had also read much of the most current
(80) scientific information available about the creatures. Drawing on this deep understanding, Melville interspersed a number of instructional chapters throughout the book which conveyed a sense of the intelligence and majesty of these ani-
(85) mals. As with any literary portrait, Melville also saw the need to create a palpable sense of the place the character inhabited. Several chapters describe the climate and environment of the whale's underwater world, including an entire
(90) chapter on the plants to be found on the ocean floor. Just as Melville's contemporary Charles Dickens created vivid portrayals of London to cast a sense of light and shade on his characters, so did Melville describe the sea in order to more fully
(95) reveal the character of Moby Dick.

Melville set before himself not only the task of describing whales and their environments, but also of describing whaling and the culture of its practitioners. At its core, *Moby Dick* is the chroni-
(100) cle of a man's obsession. In order to paint a convincing picture of Ahab's fixation, Melville needed the reader to appreciate the tremendous financial and psychic prize such an enormous and unusual whale would represent to a master whaler such as
(105) Ahab. Melville also takes considerable pains to clearly portray the techniques and culture of whaling; several chapters are devoted entirely to describing the process of hunting and killing a whale. Although these chapters don't advance the
(110) plot directly, they help the reader appreciate the foolishness and bravery of a crew aboard a small ship, armed with only a few harpoons, attempting

to bring down a creature as gigantic and powerful as Moby Dick.

7. The phrase "an advance among its predecessors" (lines 11) indicates that the author of Passage 1 believes that

(A) Melville's works have steadily decreased in quality

(B) Melville's literary innovations were based on the work of others

(C) *Moby Dick* is the finest novel that Melville wrote

(D) Melville was a talented, innovative writer

(E) the descriptive passages about whaling detract from the novel's plot

8. The author of Passage 1 most likely uses quotation marks around the phrase "fine writing" (line 15) in order to convey

(A) the high esteem that he has for *Moby Dick*

(B) his contempt for Melville's writing style

(C) that the words were first written by another critic

(D) the success of Melville's literary ambitions

(E) that Melville used the term to refer to his own writing

9. The discussion of "a connected and collected story" (lines 19–20) in Passage 1 implies that

(A) Melville mixed a narrative plotline with instructional material to help readers appreciate the characters

(B) *Moby Dick* has more literary merit than Melville's previous work.

(C) more of the novel is devoted to instructive rather than entertaining material

(D) the author believes that the novel lacks a continuous plotline

(E) Melville had moments of inspiration separated by periods of doubt

GO ON TO THE NEXT PAGE ⟩

10. The author of Passage 1 notes that *Moby Dick* is "a strange book" (line 26) because

    (A) whaling is an unusual subject
    (B) Melville's writing style is forced rather than natural
    (C) it fails to be effective as either a novel or an informational work
    (D) one of the main characters is an animal
    (E) the ending of the book is not well constructed

11. The author of Passage 1 would most likely agree that

    (A) the discussion of the whale's environment contributes positively to the novel
    (B) Melville's greatness stems from his ambition to be considered among the finest novelists
    (C) it's unwise to write novels with instructional elements
    (D) readers who criticize the non-fiction elements of *Moby Dick* fail to appreciate the importance of the factual information
    (E) Melville's earlier works were of higher quality than *Moby Dick*

12. As used in line 64, "dry" most nearly means

    (A) dehydrated
    (B) ironic
    (C) tedious
    (D) fascinating
    (E) accurate

13. The questions at the end of the second paragraph of Passage 2 ("How could Melville…as Ahab?" lines 73–76) serve to

    (A) cast doubt on the success of Melville's narrative techniques
    (B) echo the questions asked by the novel's characters
    (C) imply that Melville's characters are not believable
    (D) define a problem addressed by Melville
    (E) illustrate an unusual approach to the form of the novel

14. According to the author of Passage 2, Melville's description of the underwater environment and Dickens's portrayal of London are similar in that both

    (A) create a dark, mysterious aura
    (B) serve to educate the reader
    (C) are unusual narrative techniques
    (D) detract from the plot of each author's novels
    (E) help to illuminate each author's characters

15. As used in line 105, the phrase "takes considerable pains" most nearly means

    (A) makes a deliberate effort
    (B) undergoes unpleasant experiences
    (C) unsuccessfully attempts
    (D) makes it possible
    (E) wisely endeavors

GO ON TO THE NEXT PAGE

16. The author of Passage 2 would most likely react to the description of *Moby Dick* as "an ill-compounded mixture" (line 18) in Passage 1 by asserting that

   (A) Melville failed to fully integrate the fictional and instructional elements in the novel

   (B) the description of ocean plant life creates a sense of place for the character of the whale

   (C) the nonfiction passages in the novel help the reader fully appreciate the story

   (D) Melville's vanity prompted him to attempt such an ambitious novel

   (E) many readers find the information about whales and whaling fascinating

17. The authors of both passages agree that the techniques used by Melville in *Moby Dick*

   (A) are highly effective

   (B) are similar to those of Charles Dickens

   (C) create a vivid sense of place

   (D) combine fictional and informational elements

   (E) are bolder than those of his previous works

18. The author of Passage 1 would most likely regard the "critics" mentioned in lines 58–61 as

   (A) correct

   (B) impatient

   (C) unsophisticated

   (D) misguided

   (E) ambitious

19. Which statement best describes how the authors of the two passages differ in their views on Melville's writing?

   (A) The author of Passage 1 views it as excellent, while the author of Passage 2 has a more moderate view.

   (B) The author of Passage 1 criticizes it as vain and tedious, while the author of Passage 2 describes it as innovative and admirable.

   (C) The author of Passage 1 feels that it is flawed but noteworthy, while the author of Passage 2 offers unqualified praise.

   (D) The author of Passage 1 describes it as declining in quality, while the author of Passage 2 feels that it improved steadily over the course of Melville's career.

   (E) The author of Passage 1 feels that it contains narrative and informational elements, while the author of Passage 2 describes it as purely narrative.

SECTION 9
Time—10 Minutes
14 Questions

Directions: For each question in this section, select the best answer from among the choices given and fill in the corresponding oval on the answer sheet.

The following sentences test correctness and effectiveness of expression. Part of each sentence or the entire sentence is underlined; beneath each sentence are five ways of phrasing the underlined material. Choice (A) repeats the original phrasing; the other four choices are different. If you think the original phrasing produces a better sentence than any of the alternatives, select choice (A); if not, select one of the other choices.

In making your selection, follow the requirements of standard written English; that is, pay attention to grammar, choice of words, sentence construction, and punctuation. Your selection should result in the most effective sentence—clear and precise, without awkwardness or ambiguity.

EXAMPLE: ANSWER:

Every apple in the baskets <u>are ripe and labeled according to the date it was picked</u>.   Ⓐ ● Ⓒ Ⓓ Ⓔ

(A) are ripe and labeled according to the date it was picked
(B) is ripe and labeled according to the date it was picked
(C) are ripe and labeled according to the date they were picked
(D) is ripe and labeled according to the date they were picked
(E) are ripe and labeled as to the date it was picked

1. The economic recession was already <u>crippling and lasted three years, which duration made it appear</u> completely disastrous.

    (A) crippling and lasted three years, which duration made it appear
    (B) crippling, and because of lasting three years, it made it appear
    (C) crippling and lasted the duration of three years to make it appear
    (D) crippling, and its lasting three years made it appear
    (E) crippling and, by lasting three years, making it appear

2. The problem of bias in <u>journalism, often exacerbated in some countries because</u> the government controls the media.

    (A) journalism, often exacerbated in some countries because
    (B) journalism, often exacerbated in some countries and
    (C) journalism, often exacerbated in some countries when
    (D) journalism is often exacerbated in some countries where
    (E) journalism is often exacerbated in some countries so

GO ON TO THE NEXT PAGE

3. Although a significant percentage of Americans are overweight, some people have difficulty gaining weight <u>permanently and keeping it on</u>.

   (A) permanently and keeping it on
   (B) permanent and have it stay on
   (C) and have it be on permanently
   (D) and make it permanent
   (E) and keeping it on permanently

4. I love to cheer at <u>sporting events, of which I enjoy basketball games the most</u>.

   (A) sporting events, of which I enjoy basketball games the most
   (B) sporting events; I enjoy basketball games the most
   (C) sporting events; enjoying basketball games the most
   (D) sporting events; it is basketball games that I enjoy the most
   (E) sporting events, what I enjoy the most are basketball games

5. Three women in the booth of the Swan Diner <u>were angrily discussing the terms of the lease and arguing about</u> the level of commitment expected from each of them.

   (A) were angrily discussing the terms of the lease and arguing about
   (B) were angrily discussing the terms of the lease, but they argued about
   (C) discussing angrily the terms of the lease, and arguing for
   (D) was angrily discussing the terms of the lease, and arguing about
   (E) were angrily discussing the terms of the lease, and argued about

6. Unlike a root canal, which is the preferred method for saving a diseased tooth, <u>chewing problems can result from an extraction</u>.

   (A) chewing problems can result from an extraction
   (B) problems with chewing can result from an extraction
   (C) an extraction is resulting in chewing problems
   (D) an extraction can result in chewing problems
   (E) an extraction resulting in chewing problems

7. <u>Although they had been only the most casual acquaintances at school</u>, Jack was as glad to see Penny in this unfamiliar city as he would have been to see his best friend.

   (A) Although they had been only the most casual acquaintances at school
   (B) Since they had been only the most casual acquaintances at school
   (C) They had been only the most casual acquaintances at school
   (D) Although they had been only the most casually acquainted at school
   (E) Although they have been only the most casual acquaintances at school

8. For days, one of the Olympic favorites <u>were swimming so slowly that her coaches thought she was</u> hurt.

   (A) were swimming so slowly that her coaches thought she was
   (B) was swimming so slowly that her coaches thought something were
   (C) were swimming so slowly; so her coaches thought something has been
   (D) was swimming so slowly that her coaches thought she was
   (E) was swimming so slowly; so her coaches thought of it as

GO ON TO THE NEXT PAGE ▷

9. At the start of Salman Rushdie's novel *Midnight's Children*, a boy is born at the exact moment that India attains independence and <u>becoming intimately connected to the fate of the country</u>.

   (A) becoming intimately connected to the fate of the country

   (B) becomes intimately connected to the fate of the country

   (C) intimately connected to the fate of the country

   (D) being intimately connected to the fate of the country

   (E) the country, a fate he is intimately connected to

10. <u>One often discovering quotes in fiction often that are</u> noteworthy for their novelty or their cleverness, or both.

    (A) One often discovering quotes in fiction often that are

    (B) One often discovers quotes in fiction that are

    (C) One often discovers quotes in fiction that you find

    (D) Often one notices quotes in fiction; they are

    (E) Often one notices quote in fiction in which they are

11. Buying good shoes, training daily, and, above all, <u>the competition in numerous races are</u> the keys to becoming a world class runner.

    (A) the competition in numerous races are

    (B) the competing of numerous races are

    (C) to compete in numerous races is

    (D) competing in numerous races is

    (E) competing in numerous races are

12. <u>Although only</u> half the size of an ant, the gallfly can be cataloged and studied in the same way as any larger creature.

    (A) Although only

    (B) Whereas only

    (C) Despite a size

    (D) While its size is

    (E) Since it is

13. While studying at the University of Michigan, <u>that was when Arthur Miller developed a profound passion for writing</u>.

    (A) that was when Arthur Miller developed a profound passion for writing

    (B) Arthur Miller developed a profound passion for writing

    (C) then the development of Arthur Miller's profound passion for writing took place

    (D) Arthur Miller's profound passion for writing was developed

    (E) a profound love for drama developed in Arthur Miller

14. The teenagers promised <u>to return to their homes and they would eat</u> a healthy dinner and talk with their parents.

    (A) to return to their homes and they would eat

    (B) to return to their homes to eat

    (C) to returning to their homes, thereby eating

    (D) with returning to their homes for the eating of

    (E) on the return to their homes for the eating of

IF YOU FINISH BEFORE TIME IS CALLED, YOU MAY CHECK YOUR WORK ON THIS SECTION ONLY. DO NOT TURN TO ANY OTHER SECTION IN THE TEST. STOP

Practice Test Ten: **Answer Key**

SECTION 1

Essay

SECTION 2

1. E
2. D
3. B
4. B
5. E
6. C
7. D
8. A
9. C
10. E
11. B
12. C
13. A
14. C
15. D
16. C
17. E
18. B
19. E
20. D

SECTION 3

1. C
2. D
3. D
4. C
5. C
6. B
7. B
8. B
9. C
10. E
11. C
12. E
13. C
14. B
15. D
16. D
17. D
18. C
19. D
20. E
21. A
22. C
23. A
24. B
25. A
26. B
27. A
28. C
29. D
30. D
31. D
32. C
33. C
34. D
35. E

SECTION 4

1. C
2. E
3. D
4. A
5. E
6. B
7. D
8. D
9. B
10. D
11. B
12. E
13. C
14. E
15. D
16. D
17. A
18. C
19. B
20. E
21. B
22. B
23. C
24. A

SECTION FIVE

1. D
2. B
3. A
4. A
5. B
6. B
7. A
8. D
9. 260

10. 5,400
11. 32
12. 1/5 or .2
13. 1/3 or .333
14. 8
15. 0
16. 9
17. 26
18. 5/6 or .833

SECTION 6

1. C
2. C
3. B
4. E
5. A
6. D
7. B
8. C
9. A
10. D
11. C
12. E
13. A
14. B
15. B
16. A
17. A
18. C
19. E
20. D
21. E
22. D
23. D
24. E

SECTION 7

1. B
2. E
3. C
4. D
5. A
6. E
7. D
8. B
9. E
10. D
11. C
12. A
13. B
14. B
15. B
16. D

SECTION 8

1. C
2. A
3. E
4. D
5. B
6. B
7. A
8. B
9. D
10. C
11. E
12. C
13. D
14. E
15. A
16. C
17. D

18. A
19. B

SECTION 9

1. D
2. D
3. E
4. B
5. A
6. D
7. A
8. D
9. B
10. B
11. E
12. A
13. B
14. B

PRACTICE TEST TEN

Critical Reading

	Number Right	Number Wrong	Raw Score

Section 4: $\boxed{}$ $-$ $\left(.25 \times \boxed{}\right)$ $=$ $\boxed{}$

Section 6: $\boxed{}$ $-$ $\left(.25 \times \boxed{}\right)$ $=$ $\boxed{}$

Section 8: $\boxed{}$ $-$ $\left(.25 \times \boxed{}\right)$ $=$ $\boxed{}$

Critical Reading Raw Score $=$ $\boxed{}$

(rounded up)

Writing

	Number Right	Number Wrong	Raw Score

Section 1: $\boxed{}$ (ESSAY GRADE) $\times$ 3.17 $=$ $\boxed{}$

Section 3: $\boxed{}$ $-$ $\left(.25 \times \boxed{}\right)$ $=$ $\boxed{}$

Section 9: $\boxed{}$ $-$ $\left(.25 \times \boxed{}\right)$ $=$ $\boxed{}$

Writing Raw Score $=$ $\boxed{}$

(rounded up)

Math

	Number Right	Number Wrong	Raw Score

Section 2: $\boxed{}$ $-$ $\left(.25 \times \boxed{}\right)$ $=$ $\boxed{}$

Section 5A:
(QUESTIONS 1–8) $\boxed{}$ $-$ $\left(.25 \times \boxed{}\right)$ $=$ $\boxed{}$

Section 5B:
(QUESTIONS 9–18) $\boxed{}$ $\left(\text{no wrong answer penalty}\right)$ $=$ $\boxed{}$

Section 7: $\boxed{}$ $-$ $\left(.25 \times \boxed{}\right)$ $=$ $\boxed{}$

Math Raw Score $=$ $\boxed{}$

(rounded up)

Turn to page xiv to convert your raw score to a scaled score.

Answers and Explanations

SECTION 1

6 Score Essay

In my opinion, it may be hard to know whether the imagination or facts is most important, because we need them both. Without facts, scientists and inventors would have nothing to think about. But then again, being able to see things in your mind seems crucial to making new discoveries and inventing new products.

To conduct even a basic experiment requires an imagination. Scientists begin with what they know. Then they have to imagine a result so they can state a hypothesis or theory. Then, if experimenting can't prove the theory, the scientist has to combine the same facts or new ones and use his or her imagination again to make another educated guess.

In 2003, a robot was invented that could be controlled by a monkey's mind. Someone had to imagine the robot and to believe it was possible to build it. I believe that many people must have also been imagining this machine for a long time. For example, paraplegics might have dreamt of a useful invention like this. Some lazy people who have no handicaps might also fantasize about a machine that makes it so they never have to lift a finger.

Most inventive people are always using their imaginations. The man who invented the microwave oven was doing radar research, testing a new vacuum tube and noticed that the candy bar in his pocket melted. So he put a few popcorn kernels near the tube and they popped. Art Fry invented the post-it because he was irritated when his bookmark kept falling out of his hymnal at church. He worked with adhesives, and suddenly realized one of them would make a removable but secure bookmark.

I think most inventions are a result of facts and imagination. Perhaps that's what an imagination is, to combine facts in a unique and surprising way. In this way the imagination and information are partners in discovery.

6 Score Critique

The essay is scored based on four basic criteria: Topic, Support, Organization, and Language. This essay does well on all counts, so it has earned a 6.

This essay demonstrates an especially strong grasp of the writing assignment, earning high points for topic, support, and organization. The author states a thesis in paragraph 1, and then provides several specific, relevant examples of how the imagination and facts are used together by both scientists and inventors.

The writing stays on track, using the writer's previous knowledge to discuss the topic comfortably. The writer uses key phrases such as *in my opinion*, *but then again*, *I believe that*, and *for example*, to link connected ideas. Vocabulary is strong (*crucial, hypothesis,* and *fantasize,* for example). The closing paragraph sums up the writer's opinion, and although it could use a few supporting details, nevertheless leaves the reader with a summary understanding. This oversight doesn't affect the generally high quality of the essay.

4 Score Essay

I think that for most people imagination is the most important thing. We all love superheroes, because they have superhuman traits that we can imagine ourselves having as well. In novels, normal people solve problems by using their imaginations. And the ideas a person thinks of that no one else thinks of, is what makes them the person that they are.

And anyway, people are always using their imaginations. Politicians need to have a vision for a better future. Then, advertisers try to get us to use our imaginations so we buy products we didn't even want. Then, this morning in geometry, our teacher asks us to use our imaginations to see the shapes of an equation. Then, in science, I always have to imagine black holes in outer space. In history, I have to imagine important places and things that happened. If I didn't use my imagination, I couldn't understand these facts.

The more I think about it, the more I realize that imagination is much more important to me than facts and information and anyway I like to use my imagination to reach my goals. When I have a problem, I usually solve it by imagining my way out. When I have a goal, such as winning the track competition, I always begin training by imagining myself winning. Then I can do the work I need to do. And anyway, if I was thinking only about facts, I would never even try.

4 Score Critique

The essay is scored based on four basic criteria: Topic, Support, Organization, and Language. This author attempted with some success to fulfill the assignment, but several of the references to literature and to the author's own experience are undeveloped and confused. Although you can guess what the author meant, there is not a clear explanation of why superheroes are interesting. In the final paragraph, the author begins to explain an example from his or her own life, but doesn't fully develop it with convincing details.

The essay has a moderately strong beginning, but the ending introduces new ideas rather than summing up the main ideas, so the reader does not have a good sense of completion. The language and vocabulary in the essay could be improved. Phrases like *and anyway* distract the reader from meaning. In the second paragraph, the verb *asks* is the wrong tense, and the use of *then* is repetitive.

Overall, the essay looks like the writer began seriously thinking about the idea in the final paragraph. It would have been a better essay if the writer had spent a few minutes thinking and outlining ideas before beginning to write. Then one or two main ideas could have been better developed.

2 Score Essay

My neighbor did something different that nobody did before and it was the start of a new idea. He learned to be a cook at a restaurant but in the town where we lived, nobody cooked anything but regular American food. He was from India. They are from India so my neighbor got this new idea to cook Indian food. So the first thing he did was make some stuff at home and we are his neighbors. We got to eat lots of new kinds of food. Some of it was not so good and we didn't like it and so, he wouldn't make it no more. And my sister came home late that night because she had missed the bus.

But some was good and then, he started a catering business. He would go to people's houses and make them the food. Everybody started to like it more and he got bigger and bigger and then he had more money and he opened up a restaurant of his own.

Our neighbor got a lot happier after he thought of his new idea and then he wanted to move back to India for awhile so he could learn more, but his family didn't really want to go. His daughter is in my class and she is good at math.

2 Score Critique

The essay is scored based on four basic criteria: Topic, Support, Organization, and Language. In this essay, the author addresses the general idea of using the imagination but does not present a point of view and tells a story that has very little logical organization. Many of the sentences are too long and have grammatical problems (*he wouldn't make it no more* and *Some was good*.) The essay lacks a thesis statement and a closing summary and in general does not answer the assignment. The writer could use this story to write an acceptable essay, if each paragraph expressed ideas related to one another and related to the comparative importance of imagination and fact.

SECTION 2

1. E

Difficulty: Low

Strategic Advice: Questions like this one ask you to interpret information in a graph. First, make sure you know what quantities are plotted on each axis. Then, review the question. This question asks you to find a percent increase, not simply an increase.

Getting to the Answer:

$$\frac{3.5 - 1}{1} = 2.5 = 250\%$$

2. D

Difficulty: Low

Strategic Advice: Don't jump ahead of yourself on questions like these. Use ratios to analyze Jeweler A and Jeweler B separately. Then, compare the two.

Getting to the Answer:

Jeweler A

$$\frac{3}{\text{hr}} \times 8 \text{ hour} = 24$$

Jeweler B

$$\frac{4}{\text{hr}} \times 8 \text{ hour} = 32$$

$$32 - 24 = 8$$

3. B

Difficulty: Medium

Strategic Advice: Questions with more than one figure require you to transfer information from one figure to the next. Analyze Figure 1 alone to solve for x. Then insert the value of x into Figure 2.

Getting to the Answer:

Figure 1:

$$180° - 60° = 3x$$
$$40° = x$$

Figure 2:

$$4y = x$$
$$4y = 40°$$
$$y = 10°$$

4. B

Difficulty: Low

Strategic Advice: The phrase, "varies directly," means that this problem can be solved by setting up a ratio. When dealing with a ratio question, be sure to compare like quantities. For example, set up a proportion with the number of pounds in the numerator of each fraction and the number of inches in the denominator of each fraction. That way you will solve for the correct values on Test Day.

Getting to the Answer:

$$\frac{50}{8} = \frac{75}{x}$$
$$50x = 600$$
$$x = 12$$

5. E

Difficulty: Medium

Strategic Advice: Don't be intimidated when exponents are fractions. Think about how you can make the equation true. Work backwards to solve for the missing variables.

Getting to the Answer:

$8^2 = 64$, so $x = 8$.

So $\frac{y}{2}, y = 4$.

$$8 + 4 = 12$$

6. C

Difficulty: Medium

Strategic Advice: Questions such as this will be your pay off on Test Day for having absorbed certain facts during your preparation—such as how to add terms with like exponents. (This question is also a great one for picking numbers. The easiest number to try is $n = 2$, which narrows the choices down to choices (C) and (E). Choosing $n = 4$ gets you to choice (C) right away.)

Getting to the Answer:

$$3^{\frac{n}{2}} + 3^{\frac{n}{2}} + 3^{\frac{n}{2}} = 3\left(3^{\frac{n}{2}}\right)$$
$$= 3^1 \times 3^{\frac{n}{2}}$$
$$= 3^{\frac{n}{2} + 1}$$

7. D

Difficulty: Medium

Strategic Advice: Many test takers are intimidated by functions such as this one. The trick is to take your time and fill in the variables as you can. In this case, start inside the parentheses and find $g(x)$ when x is 3. Then use this value to solve for $f(x)$ when $x = g(3)$.

Getting to the Answer:

$$g(3) = \sqrt{2(3)^2 + 7}$$
$$\sqrt{18 + 7} = \sqrt{25} = 5$$

$$f(5) = 3(5) - 8 = 15 - 8 = 7$$

8. A

Difficulty: Medium

Strategic Advice: On Test Day, be sure to analyze the information in any number lines, graphs, or diagrams before you begin. In this question, you can figure out the values of the letters. You can then try each value in the inequality described in the question.

Getting to the Answer:

$D = -3$

$|3 - (-3)| = 6$; $6 > 5$? Yes

$E = 2$

$|3 - 2| = 1$; $1 > 5$? No

$F = 6$

$|3 - 6| = 3$; $3 > 5$? No

9. C

Difficulty: Medium

Strategic Advice: This question raises two important insights for Test Day. One is value of picking numbers. The other is to pay attention to qualifying words such as *always* and *never*.

Getting to the Answer:

Try $-.5$ for N:

I $N < 2N$

    $-.5 < 2(-.5)$

    $-.5 < -1$

    No

II $N^2 < N$

    $(-.5)^2 < -.5$

    $.25 < -.5$

    No

III $N^2 < \dfrac{1}{N^2}$

    $(-.5)^2 < \dfrac{1}{(-.5)^2}$

    $.25 < 4$

    Yes

10. E

Difficulty: Medium

Strategic Advice: It's always a great idea to read a question and then ask yourself, "OK, what essentially is being asked of me here?" In this case, the issue boils down to realizing that the only numbers that are multiples of both 2 and 3 are multiples of 6—the product of 2 and 3.

Getting to the Answer:

$X = \{2, 4, 6, 8, 10, 12, 14, 16, 18, \ldots\}$

$Y = \{3, 6, 9, 12, 15, 18, \ldots\}$

$X \cap Y = \{6, 12, 18, \ldots\}$

11. B

Difficulty: Medium

Strategic Advice: This type of question will earn you quick points on Test Day if you can work nimbly with the rules of right triangles during your preparation. (Those rules, by the way, will be provided to you on Test Day.) The ratio of side lengths for a 30-60-90 triangle is $1:\sqrt{3}:2$.

Getting to the Answer:

The measure of the side opposite 30 is 7—half the hypotenuse. The measure of the side opposite 60 is therefore $7\sqrt{3}$.

12. C

Difficulty: Medium

Strategic Advice: Some questions seem daunting on first read, but are much less so on reflection. This one, for example, really just tests whether you know the average formula:

$$\text{average} = \frac{\text{sum of terms}}{\text{number of terms}}$$

Getting to the Answer:

$$? = \frac{12(80) + 18(85)}{30}$$

$$? = \frac{960 + 1530}{30} = \frac{2490}{30} = 83$$

13. A

Difficulty: Medium

Strategic Advice: The trick to questions such as this one is to recognize the relationship between the terms. If one integer is even, the next consecutive integer must be odd (and vice versa).

Getting to the Answer:

Odd + even = odd

Even + odd = odd

An odd number is not divisible by 2.

14. C

Difficulty: Medium

Strategic Advice: The wording of the question makes the content sound more complex than it really is. Take your time and label the figure with the information you know. Once you do so, you will find the question boils down to simple algebra.

Getting to the Answer:

Call the width of $UVWX$ w and the length $2w$:

$2w(w) = 72$

$2w^2 = 72$

$w^2 = 36$

$w = 6 = UV$

$UX = 12$

$UZ = \dfrac{12}{4} = 3$

15. D

Difficulty: Medium

Strategic Advice: The problem almost solves itself if you recall that a slope is negative when it slants downward.

Getting to the Answer:

The slope is negative when the height of the line is decreasing, between the y axis and $x = 5$.

16. C

Difficulty: Medium

Strategic Advice: Perhaps the best beginning you can make with a question is to sharply define its key issue or issues. In this case, that issue is the properties of a line whose slope is zero.

Getting to the Answer:

A line with a slope of zero is horizontal. A horizontal line that passes through $(4, -3)$ has infinitely many points, every one of which has a y-coordinate of -3.

17. E

Difficulty: High

Strategic Advice: Don't let complex-looking symbol questions daunt you. They merely give you some rule that you'll be asked to work with later in the question. In this case, the symbol should make you think, "How many triangles could exist with integer side measures a, b, and x?" This question, in turn, should conjure in your mind the Triangle Inequality Theorem, which requires that in any triangle, the measure of any side be less than the sum of, and greater than the difference between, the two other sides.

Getting to the Answer:

$7 - 2 < x < 7 + 2$

$5 < x < 9$

$x = 6, 7, 8$

18. B

Difficulty: High

Strategic Advice: Think of questions as puzzles, the parts of which you must piece together quickly. How could the facts

that a circle is centered at the origin and has area 25π relate to the identification of points on the circumference of the circle? If its area is 25π its radius is 5, which is also the hypotenuse of an infinite number of right triangles whose side lengths are the absolute values of the x- and y-coordinates of the points named in the choices. Once you realize this—and you might realize it more easily if you draw out the situation described here—answering the question is as easy as applying the Pythagorean Theorem to the choices.

Getting to the Answer:

(A) $5^2 + 0^2 = 25$? Yes.

(B) $4^2 + (-4)^2 = 25$? No.

(C) $3^2 + 4^2 = 25$? Yes.

(D) $(-3)^2 + 4^2 = 25$? Yes.

(E) $(-4)^2 + 3^2 = 25$? Yes.

19. E

Difficulty: High

Strategic Advice: SAT Math doesn't throw words around casually; the question stem mentions that m and n are *positive* and that they're *integers*. These data limit the possible values of m and n more severely than you might have imagined.

Getting to the Answer:

If m is 1, $3n$ is not an integer.

If m is 2, $3n$ is not an integer.

If m is 3, $3n$ *is* an integer—n is 3.

If m is 4, $3n$ is not an integer.

If m is 5, $3n$ is not an integer.

If m is 6, $3n$ *is* an integer—n is 1.

If m is 7, $3n$ is not an integer.

If m is 8, you've exceeded a sum of 15.

So m can be 3 or 6, and the sum of 3 and 6 is 9.

20. D

Difficulty: High

Strategic Advice: A question can that appears this late in the game can be of high difficulty for one of three reasons: it is conceptually very sophisticated; it is mechanically complex; it is both mechanically and conceptually hard. Identifying *how* a question is hard can help you by focusing on the skills needed to tackle it successfully. In this case, nothing conceptually advanced is happening; you're just called upon to employ the Pythagorean Theorem using some variables instead of numbers only.

Getting to the Answer:

$$a^2 + (2a)^2 = 10^2$$
$$a^2 + 4a^2 = 100$$
$$5a^2 = 100$$
$$a^2 = 20$$
$$a = \sqrt{20} = 2\sqrt{5}$$

SECTION 3

1. C

Difficulty: Low

The error here is the misuse of an adverb *effectively* for an adjective *effective*. Choice (C) corrects the error without introducing a new one. Choice (B) drops the superlative for no reason. Choices (D) and (E) don't correct the error.

2. D

Difficulty: High

The underlined segment is unnecessarily wordy. Choice (D) succinctly and clearly expresses the action. Choice (B) is tempting because it is so short, but while the shortest answer is frequently correct, this one has the pistons driving the engine. Choice (C) incorrectly uses *who* in reference to an object. Choice (E) is also unnecessarily wordy.

3. D

Difficulty: Medium

When a subject and verb are separated by a clause, it may be more difficult to recognize a subject-verb agreement problem. Choice (D) is the correct answer, as the singular verb form *was* agrees with the singular subject *Mahatma Gandhi*. Choice (B) changes the meaning of the sentence, confusing *convicted* with *convinced*. Choice (C) doesn't correct the error, and changes the meaning by introducing the word *practically*. Choice (E) uses the wrong preposition, changing the meaning of the phrase.

4. C

Difficulty: Medium

The problem is that the underlined prepositional phrase implies that the stretch of desert is actually inside the book. First, determine what was meant, then decide what words will convey the meaning. Choice (C) is the correct answer. Choices (B) and (E) do not address the problem. Choice (D) changes the problem; now beaches border the guidebook.

5. C

Difficulty: Low

Make sure you know the past tenses of commonly tested irregular verbs. This sentence contains an irregular verb *shake;* its past tense is *shook* not *shaked*. Choice (C) is the right answer. Choice (B) doesn't correct the error, and changes the meaning of the sentence. Choices (D) and (E) are idiomatically incorrect.

6. B

Difficulty: High

The meaning of the sentence is confused by the clumsiness of the modifying phrase. Choice (B) clarifies the meaning. Choice (C) rearranges a few words but is also wordy (for example repeating the verb *warn* unnecessarily). Choice (D) reduces some, but not all, of the wordiness. Choice (E) is even wordier than the original.

7. B

Difficulty: Medium

Subject and verb should always agree in number, and verbs should be in the simplest tense that conveys the intended meaning. The plural verb *have been* does not agree with the singular subject, *poetry*. Choice (C) makes the first clause, which was independent, a fragment without a verb. Choice (D) uses an acceptable alternative subject, but there is no need for this change, and with a new plural subject we still have a problem with subject-verb agreement. Choice (E) illogically uses a future perfect form.

8. B

Difficulty: Medium

The writer used the phrase *on site* when what is meant is *in sight*. Since the speaker walks several miles along the shore, it is clear that no particular *site* is intended. Choice (B)

contains the correct idiomatic expression. The verb change in choice (C) adds another problem. Choice (D) changes the meaning of the phrase. Choice (E) changes the adjective, for no reason.

9. C

Difficulty: High

Some adjectives and adverbs are easy to confuse. The underlined phrase uses the adverb *well* in place of the adjective *good* to describe how Julia felt. As an adjective, *well* relates to health, not happiness. Therefore, choice (C) is the best revision. Choices (B) and (E), while adding an adjective and changing the preposition respectively, do not revise the original mistake. Choice (D) incorrectly changes the meaning of the sentence.

10. E

Difficulty: High

In the underlined passage the subject and verb do not agree, and the words *That night* tell us that the verb should be in the past tense. Choice (E) corrects both errors. Choice (B) changes the meaning of the phrase. Choice (C) corrects the agreement problem, but not the tense. Choice (D) does not work with the rest of the sentence.

11. C

Difficulty: High

Here you encounter another case of similar elements not being expressed in similar form. The sentence talks about *the creation…establishing…and purchasing*. In order to make this list parallel you need to replace the two gerunds with nouns, or the noun with a gerund. Look among the choices for either of these two options. Choice (C) changes everything to nouns—*the creation…the establishment…and the purchase*. All the other choices maintain the incorrect mix of nouns and gerunds.

12. E

Difficulty: High

In the opening clause, the underlined word *because* is used correctly, and the verb tense *had downed* is also correct. The phrase *it appeared unlikely,* choice (C), shows correct subject-verb agreement and it also makes sense within the context of the sentence. Choice (D) also shows the correct usage of the auxiliary verb *would,* so there is no error in the sentence.

13. C

Difficulty: Medium

Choice (C) is the past tense form of the verb *distinguish* which cannot be used with the auxiliary verb *could,* and therefore, choice (C) is the correct answer. Choice (A) is a prepositional phrase in which both the preposition and the verb tense are correct. Choice (B) is the adjective *darkened,* an appropriate descriptive word for a stage. Choice (D) includes an adjective and a noun which are both correct in relation to each other and within the sentence.

14. B

Difficulty: Low

In choice (B), the comparative *most* should be *more.* Only two things are compared: Delia's actual performance and the performance the director wanted. In choice (A), the verb and subject agree, and *want…to* is the correct idiom. Choice (C) is idiomatically correct. In choice (D), the past perfect tense of *sadden* is correctly used to describe an event that had happened already in Delia's life.

15. D

Difficulty: Medium

In choice (A), the word *herself* is used to emphasize the importance of the chef's gesture. In choice (B), the prepositional phrase correctly describes the grand finale. In choice (C), the word *that* is used correctly and the present verb tense is correct. Choice (D), however, is a past tense verb, incorrect in this present tense sentence. Every verb in a sentence should agree in tense, unless one refers clearly to a different time from the rest of the action in that sentence.

16. D

Difficulty: Low

Choice (A) is in correct form for the subject of the sentence. Choice (B) is idiomatically correct, with an adverb modifying the verb. In choice (C), *for* is the correct preposition, and two appropriate adjectives describe *business.* In choice (D), *hardly never* is a double negative. Some people may speak this way, but it is an error in diction, or choice of language.

17. D

Difficulty: High

Choice (A) is the correct verb tense and number, and *thought to be* is the correct idiom. Choice (B) is the correct number, matching *dreams*. Choice (C) is an adjective modifying the noun *desires*. Choice (D) incorrectly uses the relative pronoun *which* instead of *who* when referring to *the person*, so choice (D) is the right answer.

18. C

Difficulty: Medium

The error in this sentence is the singular verb *has* in choice (C), because the subject *qualifications* is plural. Since *qualifications* is not underlined, the only way to correct this error is by changing the verb: *have the qualifications*... The perfect verb form is correct in choice (A) because it refers to actions the happened over the past year. Choice (B) is an idiomatically correct word choice. Choice (D) is correctly an adverb, modifying the verb *challenged*.

19. D

Difficulty: Low

The pronoun *they* does not agree with the pronoun *one* already used in the sentence. Since *one* is not underlined, this can be corrected only by replacing *they should* with *one should*. Choice (A) is correctly in the present tense, and choices (B) and (C) are idiomatically correct word choices.

20. E

Difficulty: Medium

Choice (A) is a correct use of *when* to indicate time. Choice (B) contains a possessive pronoun and adjective that appropriately describe the noun *wig*. The verb *performs* in choice (C) agrees with the subject *sister* and also with the previous present tense verbs (*is* and *pulls*). Choice (D) is idiomatically correct.

21. A

Difficulty: Medium

A complete sentence requires both a subject and a verb. Choice (A) is missing the crucial verb *is*, which should be placed between Richard II and the word *about*. Therefore, choice (A) is the right answer. Choice (B) is a verb in agreement with its subject *who*. Choice (C) contains an adjective correctly modifying the noun *ruler*. Choice (D) is

introduced by an appropriate transition word, uses the pronoun *he* correctly to refer to Richard, and uses a verb with the correct tense and number.

22. C

Difficulty: Medium

There is a problem with the plural pronoun *their* being used to refer to a particular university. If you were uncertain about whether using *their* to refer to the university was an error, seeing the singular *its* later in the sentence should have helped you decide.

23. A

Difficulty: Medium

Writers may confuse words that are similar in spelling, such as the verbs *raise* and *rise* and *lay* and *lie.* Make sure you understand the differences. In choice (A), though *which* is correctly used, the word *lays* is the wrong word. The writer should have used *lies,* which refers to the location of Florence. Choice (B) is the correct verb tense and number. Choice (C) correctly uses the transition word *therefore.* Choice (D) is the correct verb tense and agrees with the subject, *Sicily.*

24. B

Difficulty: High

Choice (A) uses the superlative *most* correctly, and the adjective *enjoyable* appropriately describes the afternoon. In choice (B), the word *exceptional* is not the correct form. Because the word modifies the adjective *shaped,* it should be the adverb *exceptionally.* In choice (C), both the adjective and noun are correct. In choice (D), *that* is the correct relative pronoun, and *they* refers unambiguously to the clouds.

25. A

Difficulty: Medium

The problem lies in choice (A): *claim having suffered* is not idiomatic in standard written English. It should be *claim to have suffered* or *claim that they have suffered.* The other choices are all correct. The word *but* provides a link between the two major parts of the sentence and contrasts the ideas they present. The phrase *such a condition* and the adverb *actually* are also correct, although other phrases and adverbs could be equally correct.

26. B

Difficulty: Low

Although the passive is always questionable on the SAT, it is NOT always wrong. The error here is that *reckless* modifies the passive verb *are used*, but it is an adjective. It should be changed to the adverb *recklessly*. Choices (A) and (D) are idiomatically correct word choices. Choice (C) is an appropriate use of the passive voice, and is properly plural to agree with the subject (*toys*).

27. A

Difficulty: Medium

As soon as you see a clear error in the sentence, STOP searching for others. Answer and move on; there will be only one error in each sentence. The phrase *protest on* is incorrect American usage: One might protest *for* or *against* something. Choice (B) is proper use of the past tense, choice (C) correctly introduces the two parallel elements *community* and *movement*, and *of its,* (D), is the correct preposition.

28. C

Difficulty: High

The error is in choice (C): the verb *were* is plural, but the subject *quality* is singular. The correct verb is *was*.

29. D

Difficulty: Medium

Note that the test maker gave you a hint: The verb *is* following *gopher* is singular. The error is in choice (D): The pronoun *their* in the phrase *of their* should be *it* because it refers to the singular noun *gopher*. Choices (A) and (C) are idiomatically correct word choices. Choice (B) is correctly in the perfect past tense.

30. D

The author is telling a story about what happened last year, so the mother's action should be in the past tense choice (D). Choices (B) and (C) don't address the tense issue. Choice (B) unnecessarily substitutes *my mother* for *she*, and choice (C) incorrectly uses the causal word *because*.

31. D

Sentence 7 introduces the ambiguous pronoun *they* and uses the passive voice. Choice (D) correctly substitutes *the*

hooligans for *they* and uses the present tense. Choice (B) doesn't address the pronoun problem. Choice (C) is redundant and uses the past tense. Choice (E) substitutes the football fans, instead of the hooligans, for *they*.

32. C

The two sentences here contain a contrast, so they should be connected with a conjunction or transition that indicates contrast. Choice (C) does this with the conjunction *but*; it also changes the plural *they* to the singular *it* to agree with the singular *England*. Choice (B) uses the incorrect transition word *and*. Choice (D) is opposite to the author's meaning. Choice (E) adds a questioning tone not in the original with *it seems,* in addition to being wordy.

33. C

The correct answer should clarify the relationship between sentence 12 and sentence 13. Sentence 12 offers one explanation offered by *Some*. Sentence 13 is another possibility, offered by others, and choice (C) indicates that. Choice (A) is incorrect because there is no indication this is the author's opinion. Choice (B) introduces the ambiguous pronoun *they*. Choices (D) and (E) set up incorrect relationships: contrasting and causal, respectively.

34. D

The original sentence 15 is a fragment. Choice (D) uses the past tense *indicated*, turning the fragment into a sentence that works within the context of the passage. Choice (B) is still a fragment. Choices (C) and (E) use incorrect verb tenses.

35. E

The sentence offers a conclusion based on the economic data in sentence 15, so it should conclude the passage. Choice (A) would interrupt the idea in sentences 5 and 6 of how the author feels. Choice (B) would interrupt the idea in sentences 8 and 9 that England can't stop the increase of hooliganism. Choice (C) sounds right at first, but it's too early—poverty isn't mentioned again until sentence 14. Choice (D) is incorrect because the next sentence begins with the contrasting transition word *but;* however, the inserted sentence and sentence 14 do not contrast.

SECTION 4

1.   C

Difficulty: Low

Don't fall for commonly paired words, like *cat* and *curiosity*. Look for something that describes the impressive leap of this cat.

In choice (A), *balance* might help the cat stay on top of the fence, but it wouldn't help her jump up there. Choice (B) is an opposite; an astonishing leap does not reveal *awkwardness*. Choice (C) is a good match. In choice (D), the fence, not the cat, is tall. In choice (E), well, a cat might show *curiosity*, but the leap doesn't reveal this.

2.   E

Difficulty: Low

Use word charge to quickly determine whether you are looking for a positive or a negative word. The anchorman felt fear, so the news must have been pretty *frightening*.

Choice (A) doesn't address the anchor's "fear." In choice (B), something could be *unexpected* without being frightening. In choice (C), the newscaster might be *anxious*, but the news itself cannot be. Looking at choice (D), like choice (B), this word lacks the negative charge of your prediction. Choice (E) fits well.

3.   D

Difficulty: Medium

The word "while" indicates that the two missing words must be opposite, or nearly opposite, in meaning. The government probably promised to make the forms easier to use, or to *simplify* them. The second blank should contrast with that, so *complicated* is a good prediction.

In choice (A), these words don't show a contrast between the blanks. In choice (B), *shorten* works pretty well for the first blank, but *expensive* doesn't contrast with that. Be careful here; it's the taxes themselves, not the tax forms, that people might find *expensive*. In choice (C), If the forms were *comprehensible*, people wouldn't need professional help. Choice (D) is a good match. In choice (E), if the forms were *familiar*, taxpayers would not to seek help.

4.   A

Difficulty: Medium

Be sure that your choice captures the full meaning of the sentence—here, several of the choices make some sense, but don't involve sounds. The sentence begins with a list of sounds. For the first blank, *loud* is a good prediction. The second blank needs to sum up this noise, so look for something that means *big noise*.

In choice (A), *thundering* is a great match for the sound of the horses, and *cacophony* perfectly captures the noise of the battlefield. In choice (B), *running* doesn't describe a sound, and *danger* doesn't fit either. (Why would trumpets and drums be dangerous?) In choice (C), a battlefield might be a *horror*, but this term doesn't capture the sounds described. In choice (D), *situation* doesn't describe the sounds, and is too neutral to fit here. In choice (E), it seems unlikely that you would find many *plodding* horses in a battle, and *calm* is the opposite of your prediction for the second blank.

5.   E

Difficulty: Medium

The sentence sets up a contrast between the short- and long-term effects of some measures. The short-term effects are positive, but the long-term effects are uncertain. Look for a choice that captures this idea.

In choice (A), simply *stating* the long-term effects wouldn't contrast the short-term benefits. (You don't know if the long-term effects will be good or bad.) In choice (B), *compared* with what? This choice doesn't make sense here. In choice (C), like (A), *discussed* bears no relation to the increase in tourism. In choice (D), you could say that the council *inquired into the effects*, but *inquired* by itself doesn't fit here. Choice (E) is correct; *debated* fits well. It conveys that people don't know what the long-term effects will be, and that those effects might differ from the positive, short-term effects.

6.   B

Difficulty: Medium

If you didn't know the word *improprieties*, you could probably still eliminate the four wrong answer choices. It looks like the corporation wanted the manager to ignore some shady accounting policies, so *illegal actions* is a good prediction for the second blank. The manager refused to ignore this, so he must have been maintaining his *honesty*.

In choice (A), *irregularities* fits well in the second blank, but *geniality* would not make him ignore those irregularities. Choice (B) fits your prediction well. In choice (C), *dishonesty* is the opposite of the word you're looking for. In choice (D), *cordiality* would not make someone ignore inconsistencies in accounting. In choice (E), if the manager ignored accounting *rules*, that wouldn't indicate *frankness*. In fact, it would indicate the opposite.

7. D

Difficulty: High

The second blank must have something to do with the "few jokes," so *humor* is a good prediction. The word "though" indicates contrast, so the first blank might be *serious*.

In choice (A), *cleverness* and *grim* both work okay by themselves, but they don't contrast one another, so they don't work in the sentence. In choice (B), it seems unlikely that the inauguration would be particularly *exciting*, but, even if it were, the word *curiosity* doesn't provide the contrast that the sentence demands. In choice (C), *humor* is great for the second blank, but *mirthful* doesn't give the contrast you need. Choice (D) is a good match. In choice (E), *sober* works fine, but jokes wouldn't provide *gravity*.

8. D

Difficulty: High

Often, you can ignore a few tough words that don't affect your prediction, like the word "exigencies" in this sentence. The aristocracy was actually "frugal," so the first blank should contrast with frugality. *Luxury* and *excess* are both good predictions.

Choice (A) is the opposite of what you're looking for. Choice (B) doesn't contrast with "frugal." Choice (C), like (A), is the opposite of your prediction. Choice (D) is a good match. In (E), *beneficence* doesn't contrast with "frugal."

9. B

Difficulty: Low

Beware of answers like choice (D); don't make assumptions about the author's point of view that aren't warranted by the passage. The author is describing how the cable cars work, and uses the image of a laundry line because it's likely to be familiar to most readers.

Choice (A) is out of scope; although you may find the image amusing, the author's purpose is to inform, not amuse. Choice (B) is a good match. Choice (C) is out of scope; the paragraph doesn't discuss laundry. Choice (D) is distortion; the author never indicates that the mechanism is simple, although you might think it so from the description. Choice (E) is out of scope; the passage is not about clotheslines.

10. D

Difficulty: Medium

Read Detail questions carefully. Choices like (A) begin just fine, then "veer off course." Don't waste your time trying to make a prediction for a question like this, jump right into the answers.

Choice (A) is out of scope; the laundry line is mentioned only briefly, and the author doesn't say much about how it works. Choice (B) is out of scope; the author describes what makes the cars start and stop, but never mentions steering. Choice (C) is out of scope; the paragraph provides no historical context. Choice (D) is discussed. The moving cable provides the force, and the cars simply hang on. Choice (E) is out of scope; the hills are mentioned in passing in the last sentence, but no special challenges are mentioned.

11. B

Difficulty: Low

The author writes that the detective story began with Poe and Gaboriau, but Doyle "must be credited with creating the most popular detective."

Choice (A) is an opposite; Poe and Gaboriau invented the genre, not Doyle. Choice (B) is a good match. Choice (C) is a misused detail; you don't know that Poe and Gaboriau did not also use tantalizing clues. Choice (D) is a misused detail; Poe and Gaboriau might also have created compelling protagonists. Choice (E) is a misused detail; the novels of Poe and Gaboriau may have also been popular.

12. E

Difficulty: Medium

Remember that the correct answer must directly answer the question. A choice can fit with an author's point of view and still be wrong. The author writes that this "blueprint…has since become the foundation of an entire literary tradition." Search for an answer choice that refers to Doyle's influence on later writers of detective fiction.

Test Prep and Admissions

Choice (A) is out of scope; the author never states that Doyle's stories were unusually well-crafted. Choice (B) is distortion; the author would likely agree with this statement, but this answer choice leaves out the sense that Doyle influenced other writers. Choice (C) is out of scope; although Doyle's work might have been somewhat formulaic, the word *too* doesn't fit with the author's positive point of view. Choice (D) is out of scope; the author never discusses the extent to which Doyle was influenced by the inventors of the detective story. Choice (E) is a good match.

Questions 13–24

This fairly straightforward Humanities passage discusses the career of American painter Winslow Homer. Paragraph 1 introduces the topic and main idea of the passage—Homer was a successful and influential artist who didn't follow a traditional path. In paragraph 2 you learn a little about Homer's early life, including the fact that he received little formal training. Paragraph 3 describes the nineteenth-century painting jury system in which young painters were judged by conservative older judges. Homer didn't participate in this system. In paragraph 4, you learn that Homer found success with his Civil War paintings in *Harper's* magazine. He then moved to Maine where he painted American subjects. Paragraph 5 states that Homer found little critical acceptance in his own lifetime, but heavily influenced future generations of painters. The final paragraph describes *The Fog Warning*, and cites it as an example of Homer's greatness.

13. C
Difficulty: Low

Each paragraph in a passage of this length should relate to and support the main idea of the passage as a whole: The passage talks about Homer's career, from his development as a young painter in New York, though his war-time work at *Harper's*, to his eventual success as a painter of scenes of American nature. The passage also gives some context for the career: a description of the art jury system and a description of a typical Homer painting.

Choice (A) is out of scope; only *The Fog Warning* is described in any detail. Choice (B) is out of scope; few specific events are described. Choice (C) is a good match. Choice (D) is out of scope; succeeding generations of

painters are mentioned only in paragraph 5. Choice (E) is out of scope; European artists are mentioned only in a single paragraph.

14. E
Difficulty: Medium

Many wrong choices fit well with a word or phrase, but don't fit with the sentence or passage as a whole. After the phrase in question, the author lists many characteristics of Homer's life and career that were very unusual for his time, so *unusual* is a good prediction.

Choice (A) is the opposite of your prediction. In choice (B), although the author would agree that Homer was *talented*, the phrase "stands alone" doesn't convey this. After all, there must be other painters that the author would consider *talented*. In choice (C), someone who "stands alone" might be *aloof*, but this has a somewhat negative connotation that is not in keeping with the tone of the rest of the passage. In choice (D), a *shy* person might "stand alone," but the author never indicates that this is the case with Homer. Choice (E) matches your prediction and fits well as the opening of the paragraph and the passage.

15. D
Difficulty: Medium

Search for phrases where the author offers an opinion, like the phrase "or perhaps because of" in this passage. The author says that "despite—or perhaps because of" this rejection, Homer found success. So rejection didn't hold him back and may in fact have helped him.

Choice (A) is an opposite; the author says that Homer sold lots of paintings and did well for himself economically. Choice (B) is out of scope; though Homer must have been very confident, there's no reason to believe that he didn't respect the talent of other painters. Choice (C) is an opposite; because the author portrays Homer as independent, it seems unlikely the artist would be ashamed of his unusual career path. Choice (D) is a good match. Choice (E) is extreme; although Homer did reject European styles and subjects, that is not the extent of Homer's unusual career path. Another unusual aspect was his lack of extensive formal training.

16. D

Difficulty: High

Mark up your test book! For questions like this one, cross out the answer choices that describe details that *do* appear. Go back to the third paragraph and eliminate all the choices that *do* appear. The leftover choice is the correct answer.

Choice (A) is an opposite; the juries that judged paintings were made up of "usually older" painters. Choice (B) is an opposite; the exhibitions were "the primary means for young painters to show their works." Choice (C) is an opposite; "young painters had a strong incentive to paint pictures that would please conservative critics." Choice (D) was *not* a characteristic, since Homer presented his work through *Harper's* and later sold many paintings. Choice (E) is an opposite; juries could hang canvases "in the darkest corners of the rooms."

17. A

Difficulty: Low

In paragraph 4, the author writes that Homer's work represented a major change from the idea that American paintings should reflect "European subjects and styles." Therefore, the subjects and styles of Homer's paintings must have been different from those of European painters.

Choice (A) matches your prediction. Choice (B) is extreme; although the passage indicates that Homer was very talented, there's no reason to believe that the author wouldn't also describe the Europeans as talented. Choice (C) is out of scope; the author never mentions where European painters did their painting. Choice (D) is out of scope; although Homer didn't receive critical acclaim in his lifetime, there's no reason to believe that this didn't also happen to many European artists. Choice (E) is out of scope; the author is fond of Homer's works, but some of the European works must possess artistic merit.

18. C

Difficulty: Medium

This sentence relates what Homer *didn't* do, so don't fall for a choice that describes what he *did* do, like choice (E). The author states that Homer portrayed the isolation of soldiers. His work was honest and didn't "gloss over the realities of war." In other words, he didn't *ignore* those aspects.

Choice (A) is a common meaning for "gloss," but it doesn't fit here. In choice (B), again, this has to do with the sense of "gloss" as shiny; it doesn't work in the sentence. Choice (C) is a good match. Choice (D) is the opposite of your prediction. In choice (E), you could argue that Homer *questioned* the wisdom of war through his striking images, but the question is about what he *didn't* do, since he didn't "gloss over the realities of war."

19. B

Difficulty: Low

Function questions often concentrate on words or phrases that emphasis a major point of the passage. The author makes a big point of Homer's independence from the established art world, and the phrase "far from the art world of New York City" helps to illustrate that independence.

Choice (A) is distortion; the passage states that Homer didn't even seek recognition from the world of academic painting, so the author wouldn't agree that Homer was unable "to obtain the approval of New York art juries." Choice (B) is a good match. Choice (C) is out of scope; the author never mentions the specific sources of Homer's inspiration. Choice (D) is out of scope; this choice describes the atmosphere of Homer's paintings, not the passage itself. Choice (E) is extreme; the distance from Maine to New York doesn't qualify as a "critical detail," and the author isn't attempting to give a complete chronology.

20. E

Difficulty: Medium

To find the function of an example, ask "What does this illustrate? If I were the author, why would I include an example?" The passage as a whole is about Homer's career. In order to fully appreciate Homer, the reader needs to get some sense of what his paintings are like. The description of *The Fog Warning* helps convey this.

Choice (A) is distortion; the description of the painting is intended to shed light on Homer's entire career, not argue for the importance of a single period in that career. Choice (B) is extreme; the author never states that this painting is the *most* important one. Choice (C) is an opposite; the author seems to believe that the painting is excellent, so the description would hardly explain why critics didn't like it. Choice (D) is out of scope; the passage is about Homer, not the quality of life at sea. Choice (E) is a good match.

21. B

Difficulty: Medium

Be careful not to get caught up in definitions of the word that may be correct, but not correct in this particular context, like choices (C) and (D). This is not referring to a physical embrace. Choice (B) works best—the painters eagerly accepted his new style. Choices (A) and (E) are opposites.

22. B

Difficulty: Medium

Paragraph 6 describes *The Fog Warning*; the Henri quotation helps to complete this description.

Choice (A) is a misused detail; although Henri is described as a "disciple," the passage as a whole is describing Homer's work itself, not the influence of that work. Choice (B) is a good match. Choice (C) is a misused detail; the author mentions the self-reliance of the fisherman, but Henri speaks only of the power of the sea. Choice (D) is out of scope; the author never mentions Henri's ability as an art critic. Choice (E) is out of scope; no specifics are given about European paintings, so Henri's quote cannot contrast Homer's work with European painting.

23. C

Difficulty: Medium

Even when you can't make a specific prediction, take a moment to consider the author's point of view before you dive into the answer choices. The author is obviously fond of Homer and emphasizes that the artist's work was unlike what other people were doing at the time. Look for a choice that fits in with this idea and the rest of the passage.

Choice (A) is distortion; the author mentions Homer's success at *Harper's*, but doesn't imply that this is the *primary* reason for his success. In addition, this choice doesn't address the quality of Homer's work. Choice (B) is a misused detail; Homer was not formally trained, but the author never implies that this fact was the *primary* cause of Homer's popularity. Also, like (A), this choices doesn't discuss Homer's paintings. Choice (C) fits well with the ideas expressed in the passage. Choice (D) is a misused detail; the author would agree with this statement, but Homer's influence is not the reason for his popularity. Choice (E) is out of scope; the author writes only about Homer, and doesn't imply that his success illustrates any general principle.

24. A

Difficulty: High

Homer's personality is never directly addressed in the passage; each answer choice should be weighed against his actions to decide which is correct. Although Homer's personality is not mentioned directly, you know that he made his own way in the art world, so look for a choice that alludes to this sense of independence.

In (A), *independent* is your prediction exactly, and *confident* also seems like a good description of someone who did not seek the approval of art critics. Choice (B) is out of scope; there's no evidence that Homer was particularly *inquisitive*. Choice (C) is out of scope; there's no evidence that Homer was *calculating*, and the negative tone of the term doesn't fit with this pro-Homer passage. Choice (D) is an opposite; Homer seems far too strong willed to be described as *cautious*. Choice (E) is out of scope; Homer is not portrayed as particularly *sociable*.

SECTION 5

1. D

Difficulty: Low

Strategic Advice: This type of question does not test your ability to interpret information as much as it tests your ability to be careful in your calculations.

Getting to the Answer:

Cross multiply:

$$10x = 12$$
$$x = \frac{12}{10}$$
$$x = \frac{6}{5}$$

2. B

Difficulty: Low

Strategic Advice: Define an issue in its simplest terms. Here, for example, ask yourself, "In which choice does every fraction reduce to the same thing?"

Getting to the Answer:

Once you see that every fraction in (B) equals $\frac{2}{5}$ there's no need to check the remaining choices—though if doing so would make you feel more secure about your answer, check quickly.

3. A

Difficulty: Low

Strategic Advice: Many test takers are intimidated by three-dimensional shapes. But in many cases, these questions break down to simple arithmetic once you label all of the information you know.

Getting to the Answer:

$$\overline{UT} = \frac{1}{3}(\overline{ST}) = \frac{1}{3}(12) = 4$$

$$V = lwh = 8 \times 12 \times 4 = 384$$

4. A

Difficulty: Low

Strategic Advice: On Test Day, you can save time and stress if you avoid unnecessary calculations. In this question, for example, you don't need to calculate a square root. You can also save time if you review the answer choices. The difference $m^2 - 7$ must be less than $m^2 + 7$, so you can quickly eliminate (C), (D), and (E).

Getting to the Answer:

$$m^2 + 7 = 29$$
$$m^2 = 22$$
$$m^2 - 7 = 22 - 7 = 15$$

5. B

Difficulty: Medium

Strategic Advice: Like many questions on the SAT, this one requires you to translate from English into math. Once translated, this question becomes straightforward arithmetic.

Getting to the Answer:

$$1.25x = 150$$
$$x = 120$$

Expressed as a percent, 120 is 1.2.

$$1.2(75) = 90$$

6. B

Difficulty: Medium

Strategic Advice: Questions such as this entail mechanical calculation based on abstract reasoning. Do the latter first; then the mechanical calculation quickly but carefully.

Getting to the Answer:

The point on the semicircle farthest from the x-axis is the topmost point of the semicircle—the point directly above the center of the semicircle. If the diameter of the circle is 5, it's radius is 2.5. So 1 (the point on the x-axis at which the semicircle starts) plus 2.5 is 3.5.

7. A

Difficulty: High

Strategic Advice: You can manage this question by using algebra or by picking numbers.

Getting to the Answer:

Imagine that $b = 1$ and that $c = 1$. Then $a = 12$. Triple b and c and then $\frac{12b^4}{c} = \frac{12(3)^4}{3} = \frac{(12)(81)}{3} = 324$, which is 12×27.

8. D

Difficulty: High

Strategic Advice: Use the numbers provided in the choices as hints about the kinds of numbers you should have in mind.

Getting to the Answer:

$5 < 3 < \frac{1}{5}$? No.

$1 < 3 < 1$? No.

$\frac{1}{3} < 3 < 3$? No.

$\frac{1}{5} < 3 < 5$? Yes.

$-\frac{1}{5} < 3 < -5$? No.

9. 260

Difficulty: Low

Strategic Advice: Expect the first Grid-in, like the first few Multiple Choice questions, to test your mechanical ability or your understanding of basic facts such as, in this case, that without respect to the particular shape a triangle takes, the sum of its angles must be 180 degrees.

Getting to the Answer:

Small triangle:

$$a + b = 180° - 50°$$
$$a + b = 130°$$

Large triangle:

$$c + d = 180° - 50°$$
$$c + d = 130°$$
$$130° + 130° = 260°$$

10. 5,400

Difficulty: Low

Strategic Advice: Sometimes part of the challenge of questions involving units of measurement is making such units—in this case, seconds and hours—consistent.

Getting to the Answer:

$$\frac{3 \text{ ft}}{S} \times \frac{60 \text{ S}}{1 \text{ min}} \times \frac{30 \text{ min}}{1 \text{ half hour}} = \frac{5,400 \text{ ft}}{\text{half hour}}$$

11. 32

Difficulty: Low

Strategic Advice: Invest time developing your skills with 45-45-90 right triangles (and 30-60-90s as well). Even though the ratios of the sides are provided on test day, you'll move more deftly through questions if you've practiced beforehand.

Getting to the Answer:

Leg : leg : hypotenuse in a 45-45-90 is $1:1:\sqrt{2}$. If the hypotenuse is $8\sqrt{2}$, each leg is 8. Because the legs are also the base and height, the area of the triangle in question is $\left(\frac{1}{2}\right)(8)(8) = 32$.

12. $\frac{1}{5}$ or .2

Difficulty: Medium

Strategic Advice: Don't let the decimals throw you. Proportions always work the same way, without respect to the kinds of numbers they relate.

Getting to the Answer:

$$\frac{1.5}{18} = \frac{x}{2.4}$$
$$18x = (1.5)(2.4)$$
$$x = 0.2$$

13. $\frac{1}{3}$ or .333

Difficulty: Medium

Strategic Advice: Fractional exponents are subject to the same rules as any other kind of exponent, so if you know those rules-and you should make knowing them a priority-you'll slice through questions like this one quickly and efficiently.

Getting to the Answer:

$$a^b a^3 = a^{b+3}$$
$$b + 3 = \frac{10}{3}$$
$$b = \frac{10}{3} - 3 = \frac{1}{3}$$

14. 8

Difficulty: Medium

Strategic Advice: On Test Day, look for clues that tell you how to solve the problem. The words greater than in this question suggest that you are solving an inequality.

Getting to the Answer:

$$.40x > 2.8$$
$$x > \frac{2.8}{.40}$$
$$x > 7$$

15. 0

Difficulty: High

Strategic Advice: Look for a pattern.

Getting to the Answer:

The terms repeat in groups of 8, and the sum of every such group is zero. The 88th term will be the last of 11 repetitions of this cycle.

16. 9

Difficulty: High

Strategic Advice: Questions with square roots can be intimidating. However, they are solved like any other type of algebra question. Treat the square root as a single quantity until you isolate it on one side of the equation. Then square both sides to get rid of the square root.

Getting to the Answer:

$$\frac{14}{\sqrt{x-5}} = 7$$

$$\frac{14}{7} = 7\sqrt{x-5}$$

$$2^2 = (\sqrt{x-5})^2$$

$$4 = x - 5$$

$$9 = x$$

17. 26

Difficulty: High

Strategic Advice: This question challenges you to rearrange in clever and creative ways the information you are given in the question stem. Also, remember that you're solving for perimeter, not area.

Getting to the Answer:

$$\begin{aligned} P &= 2r + 2s \\ &= 2(r + s) \\ &= 2(13) = 26 \end{aligned}$$

18. $\frac{5}{6}$ or .833

Difficulty: High

Strategic Advice: One way to make a question very daunting to most test takers is to present data in relatively complex form. Use algebra to manipulate the situation by rendering complicated-looking relationships into simple terms.

Getting to the Answer:

$$x^3 = \frac{1}{2}x^2$$

Divide both sides by x^2:

$$x = \frac{1}{2}$$

$$y^3 = \frac{1}{3}y^2$$

Divide both sides by y^2.

$$y = \frac{1}{3}$$

$$x + y = \frac{1}{2} + \frac{1}{3} = \frac{3+2}{6} = \frac{5}{6}$$

SECTION 6

1. C

Difficulty: Low

The key here is the phrase "starting over," so *abandoning* and *throwing away* are good predictions.

In choice (A), he wouldn't need to start over after *abridging* the book. In choice (B), he wouldn't need to start over after *supplementing* the book. Choice (C) works. In choice (D), he wouldn't need to start over after *truncating*, or shortening, the book. In choice (E), he wouldn't need to start over after *praising* the book.

2. C

Difficulty: Low

Watch out for straightforward definition sentences: these can provide easy points. This movie polarizes people—some people are angered by it and others think it's courageous. In other words, it's *controversial*.

In choice (A), people wouldn't get so worked up about a *mundane* movie. In choice (B), a *creative* film wouldn't necessarily make people angry. Choice (C) is perfect. In choice (D), a *pertinent* film wouldn't necessarily be courageous. In choice (E), a *daunting* film wouldn't necessarily anger people.

3. B

Difficulty: Low

Some sentences are too ambiguous to allow you to make a specific prediction. Since the commission was surprised, the blanks must contrast each other. Beyond that, it's difficult to make a prediction.

In choice (A), these words both have a negative tone, and don't provide the contrast that you're looking for. Choice (B) makes sense. "The commission thought the road would be *unnecessary* and was surprised to find it *vital*." In choice (C), either one of these words could describe a road, but the word pair doesn't provide the contrast you need. In choice (D), there's no contrast between *dangerous* and *attributable*. In choice (E), this one might be tempting, but it doesn't make much sense to say that a road is "*damaging* to the city's transportation needs." What would it mean to be *damaging* to needs?

4. E

Difficulty: Medium

A knowledge of vocabulary can make the difference between a right and wrong answer on Sentence Completions. The clue here is the vocabulary word *frugal* which means thrifty. If the customer is thrifty she will want a grill that doesn't cost much: one that is *inexpensive*.

In choice (A), *tasteful* doesn't fit with "frugal." In choice (B), a "frugal" person might or might not want a *secure* model—you can't tell from the sentence. In choice (C), this is the opposite of what you're looking for. In choice (D), a small grill might be the most *manageable* model, but that concern doesn't follow from the word "frugal." Choice (E) is a good match.

5. A

Difficulty: Medium

Remember to guess when you can narrow down your choices. Here, you can eliminate choices (B), (D), and (E). The critic said "the script lacked structure and the characters were shallow." Clearly the critic did not like this movie, so your prediction for the blank is something like *disapproved of.*

Choice (A) is a good match. Choice (B) doesn't follow from the critic's description of the movie. In choice (C), it doesn't make sense to say the critic *belied* the movie. In choice (D), the critic certainly didn't *praise* the movie. In choice (E), since the critic made comments, you can't say that he *ignored* the movie.

6. D

Difficulty: Medium

Several questions test your ability to understand references from a word or phrase to another part of the passage. What are the divisions that Freeman has left behind? "Previously, scholars limited themselves to a particular phase of Ibsen's career." Freeman doesn't do this, so the divisions are between the phases of Ibsen's writing.

Choice (A) is extreme; the author wouldn't describe previous scholarship as "unsuccessful." Choice (B) is out of scope; there is no discussion of Ibsen himself taking breaks. Choice (C) is out of scope; the author doesn't mention any result that has followed from Freeman's book. Choice (D) matches your prediction. Choice (E) is out of scope; the "arbitrary divisions" refer to the previous scholarship, not Freeman's reaction to that scholarship.

7. B

Difficulty: Medium

Let the author's tone help you quickly eliminate wrong choices. Considering this author's positive attitude towards Freeman's book, the sentence must be high praise. The author is pointing out that this book will be important for a long time.

Choice (A) is an opposite; this negative tone doesn't fit at all. Choice (B) is a good match. Choice (C) is out of scope; the author doesn't discuss obstacles that Freeman faced. Choice (D) is an opposite; the author never states that Freeman's work is unclear. Choice (E) is out of scope; the author makes no attempt to paraphrase Freeman.

8. C

Difficulty: High

Author 2 does find some nice things to say about Freeman's book: "This experiment, while yielding some interesting observations, does not serve as a useful scholarly model." But, his overall opinion is that the book lacks depth—too much simplification.

Choice (A) is an opposite; *overwhelming* is ok, but *not idealistic* is the opposite of the author's viewpoint. The author does think Freeman's project is too idealistic. Choice (B) is an opposite; *feasible* means possible or attainable, just the opposite of author 2's view. Choice (C) is correct; author 2 says that Freeman "exhibits tremendous dedication" so *admirable* fits well. The author also thinks Freeman's project is too ambitious, in other words, *not successful.* Choice (D) is an opposite; author 2 thinks that the attempt is *not viable.* In choice (E), the author never indicates that a work covering Ibsen's entire career is *desirable.*

9. A

Difficulty: Medium

When a question involves several different viewpoints, take a moment to get everything straight before you attack the answer choices. Before Freeman, scholars concentrated on a particular phase of Ibsen's career. These are the scholars mentioned in Passage 1. Since author 2 feels that Freeman tried to cover too much, he probably feels that scholars before Freeman took the right approach.

Choice (A) is a good match. Choice (B) is an opposite; this is the opinion of author 1, not author 2. Choice (C) is a misused detail; author 1 describes the scholarship of

Freeman in this way, but author 2 never speculates about the future. Choice (D) is an opposite; author 2 feels that the scholars' approach is more appropriate than Freeman's. Choice (E) is out of scope; there's no reason to believe that author 2 finds the scholars' work *difficult to* assess.

Questions 10–20

This Natural Science passage discusses the effects of dementia. (Note how much is *not* discussed, such as the history and causes of dementia.) In paragraph 1, the author states that the effects of dementia can be divided into those that affect memory and those that affect thoughts and feelings (paragraphs 2 and 3 discuss these aspects separately). The last sentence of paragraph 1 indicates that the primary audience for the passage is the caregivers for sufferers of dementia. Paragraph 2 discusses the effects of dementia on memory. Specifically, you learn that memory loss doesn't happen to everyone, and that short-term memory and judgment are affected differently than long-tem memory and social skills. Paragraph 3 discusses feelings of anxiety and depression that are caused by biochemical effects of dementia. Paragraph 4 concludes by advocating an approach that caregivers should adopt.

10. D

Difficulty: Medium

The words *primary purpose* tell you that you need an answer that addresses all the ideas in the passage, not just a detail.

The passage discusses the effects of dementia on its sufferers. The author discusses memory loss, behavior problems, and paranoia, among other symptoms. The primary audience is caregivers for dementia sufferers. Look for a choice that reflects this approach to the subject.

Choice (A) is out of scope; the author is presenting information, not arguing for a certain viewpoint. Choice (B) is distortion; tempting, but this leaves out the discussion of biochemical changes. Choice (C) is distortion; the author does not address the causes of dementia. Choice (D) is good match. Choice (E) is out of scope; this is way too broad to be correct. The author focuses on one aspect of mental illness—dementia.

11. C

Difficulty: Low

Even low-difficulty vocab-in-context questions will contain inappropriate, more common meanings of words to act as distracting wrong answer choices. The author says that the symptoms of dementia can be divided into two categories, but that the division is not particularly "neat." In other words, some symptoms don't fit perfectly into either category or seem to fit in both. A good prediction might be *separate*.

In choice (A), the author doesn't indicate that the division is not *natural*. In choice (B), you wouldn't describe a division as *uncluttered* or cluttered. Choice (C) is a good match. In choice (D), this indicates that the author doesn't feel the distinction is valid, which doesn't fit. In choice (E), the author doesn't indicate that the division is particularly *favorable* or unfavorable.

12. E

Difficulty: Low

You can back up the correct answer to a detail question with specific information from the passage. Memory loss comes up often in the passage, so it's difficult to make a prediction here. Read each choice carefully to see which one fits the passage.

Choice (A) is an opposite; in paragraph 1, the author says that severe memory loss often affects behavior. Choice (B) is distortion; this reverses the cause-effect relationship: in paragraph 3, the author says that memory loss can cause depression. Choice (C) is extreme; in paragraph 2, the author says that social skills are often retained longer than judgment, but this doesn't mean that social skills will never be affected by memory loss. Choice (D) is distortion; memory loss is a *result*, not a *cause*, of dementia. Choice (E) is correct; this echoes the first sentence of paragraph 2.

13. A

Difficulty: High

Some inference questions are very similar to function questions, and require you to understand the reason that an author includes a detail or example. Why would it be difficult to spot dementia in patients whose social skills are still intact? Well, when people talk to the patients, the patients seem healthy, since they still act normally.

Choice (A) is it. Choice (B) is an opposite; the passage states that insight and judgment deteriorate *before* social skills. Choice (C) is out of scope; there is no discussion of the effects of medication in this paragraph. Choice (D) is a misused detail; this doesn't explain why a patient's intact social skills would make it difficult to diagnose dementia in the patient. Choice (E) is out of scope; the author never discusses scientific quantifying.

14. B

Difficulty: Medium

Whenever the question stem addresses a specific sentence in the passage, reread the sentence carefully. The author writes that short-term memory goes before long-term, and the breakfast menu is an example of a short-term memory that is lost.

Choice (A) is distortion; forgetting the menu might be frustrating, but the breakfast itself is not frustrating. Choice (B) is a good match. Choice (C) is a misused detail; social skills are mentioned in the paragraph, but don't have much to do with breakfast. Choice (D) is a misused detail; while the author later says later in the passage that dementia sufferers have problems with mundane tasks, the breakfast menu isn't a task. Choice (E) is a misused detail; fact-based memories are mentioned in the paragraph, but they are not the subject of the sentence referred to in this question.

15. B

Difficulty: Low

Some questions just require you to understand what's right on the page. When you go back to the passage, you read that "biochemical paranoia and depression can often be partially relieved by medication." So, it's important to know the cause because the disease may be treatable.

Choice (A) is a misused detail; this reference occurs much later in the passage. Choice (B) is a good match. Choice (C) is out of scope; the author doesn't describe either symptom as more common. Choice (D) is distortion; the understanding alone is not sufficient. It's the medication that provides relief. Choice (E) is a misused detail; the author never implies a connection between misplaced valuables and medication.

16. A

Difficulty: High

Detail questions can almost always be answered by finding a specific phrase or sentence in the passage. Use your Roadmap to find the discussion of depression and anxiety in the first sentence of paragraph 3: "While memory loss by itself can lead to anxiety and depression, these feelings are

often instead directly caused by biochemical changes that result from dementia." So both memory loss and biochemical changes can cause anxiety and depression.

Choice (A) is perfect. Choice (B) is distortion; the author actually states that suspicion and paranoia can be the *result* of anxiety and depression, not the cause. Choice (C) is a misused detail; these are discussed in relation to memory loss, not anxiety and depression. Choice (D) is a misused detail; the author mentions that the *inability* to perform mundane tasks can cause frustration, not the tasks themselves. The author never states that social skills themselves cause anxiety and depression. Choice (E) is a misused detail; these are mentioned as resources for caregivers, not causes of depression.

17. A

Difficulty: Low

Trust your prediction; don't be distracted by choices that make some sense but don't capture the full meaning of the sentence. Caretakers should distract patients by giving them something "absorbing" to do. A good prediction would be *distracting*.

Choice (A) fits. Choice (B) is related to another meaning of absorbing but makes no sense here. Choice (C) is also related to another sense of absorbing, but is not correct in this sentence. In choice (D), the task may or may not be *irrelevant*. The important thing is that it is distracting. Choice (E) like (D), may or may not be true and doesn't match your prediction.

18. C

Difficulty: Low

Inference questions test whether you understand a point that the author implies, but doesn't state directly. After the quoted phrase, the author writes "They are under extreme stress, and should avail themselves of family and professional support networks." So, being a caretaker is stressful, and caretakers should make sure that they are not suffering from that stress.

Choice (A) is distortion; they might suffer from depression and anxiety, but it would be caused by environment and stress, not biochemical changes. Choice (B) is out of scope; the passage never encourages caretakers to watch for the effects of medication. Choice (C) is a good match. Choice (D) is distortion; the networks are important because of the stress of being a caretaker, but it doesn't make sense to say that caretakers will *detect the importance* by observing themselves. Choice (E) is a misused detail; this is a remedy for dementia sufferers. It's not something that caretakers will detect by observing their own behavior.

19. E

Difficulty: Medium

Although each detail appears somewhere in the passage, you may remember that a detail was mentioned without needing to look it up. Dive in and eliminate everything that appears in the passage.

Choice (A) is true. This appears in paragraph 3. Choice (B) is true. This appears in paragraph 2. Choice (C) is true. This appears in paragraphs 3. Choice (D) is true. This is discussed in depth in paragraph 2. Choice (E) is never mentioned, so it's the correct answer.

20. D

Difficulty: Low

For tone questions, don't forget to make a general prediction before attacking the choices. The author recommends understanding for both the patient and caregiver. In fact, *understanding* is a good prediction.

Choice (A) is an opposite; the author is highly sympathetic, not *confrontational*. Choice (B) is extreme; the author is concerned, not *distressed*. (The intended reader might be distressed, but the author's tone is soothing.) Choice (C) is an opposite; the author considers this topic to be a very serious one. Choice (D) is a good fit. Choice (E) is an opposite; the author is extremely sympathetic, the opposite of *indifferent*.

Questions 21–24

These two short paired passages both focus on the conflict arising from the recent "do-not-call" legislation, which allows individuals to block calls from telemarketers. The first passage is informative about both sides of the conflict, while the second passage suggests that the new legislation is an infringement on free speech.

21. E

Difficulty: Medium

According to Passage 1, the new registry will eliminate an estimated two million jobs for teleservices workers. Given

this context, and the wording "this reprieve will likely go unappreciated," it is likely that these workers would consider the registry the cause of their job loss, choice (E). Choice (A) is an opposite answer; the words "this reprieve will likely go unappreciated" suggest the workers would not consider this bill "necessary." The paragraph does not discuss whether or not the bill could create infighting or divisions within any particular group, so choice (B) is incorrect. Choice (C) is distortion. The paragraph only mentions that "telemarketing-reliant companies," not the workers themselves, asserted the list is unlawful. And nothing in the passage indicates that the "do-not-call" legislation would be temporary, so choice (D) is out.

22. D

Difficulty: Medium

A good strategy for answering vocab-in-context questions is to place the answer choices into the context of the passage to see which one makes the most sense. In this case, the cited word *slant* clearly describes a statement made in the previous sentence, so start there. It describes what "proponents of the bill…argue," suggesting that *slant* refers to a biased statement, or opinion, choice (D). Choice (A), *decline*, is a primary definition of *slant*, but it makes no sense in the context of the passage. Similarly, choices (B) and (E) do not fit the passage's context. While choice (C), *distortion*, comes closer to capturing the author's intended meaning, its meaning is too negative to fit within the context of the passage.

23. D

Difficulty: Low

Only Passage 2 raises the issue of free speech, choice (D). Both passages touch on the popularity of the legislation choice (A), and the legal conflicts arising from it, choice (D). Neither passage really explores the fairness of the bill, choice (B). Only Passage 1 explores the bill's impact on employment.

24. E

Difficulty: Medium

This global question asks you to identify how the focus of each paragraph is similar. Choice (E) is the best expression of how the passages are similar. Both focus on drawbacks— Passage 1 details the job loss, and Passage 2 explores the larger free speech issues. Neither passage explores the potential costs of the registry for consumers, so choice (A)

is out. Only Passage 1 really focuses on the bill's impact on telemarketers themselves, so choice (B) can't be the answer. Choice (C) is wrong because neither passage explores any larger societal need that the bill could fill. And choice (D) is wrong because the passages only explore the actual legality of the bill, not how the courts could shape its composition.

SECTION 7

1. B

Difficulty: Low

Strategic Advice: It's never a bad idea to ask yourself as you read a question, "Exactly what does this mean?" In particular, a key insight in this question stem is the realization that "number of 3s that can be multiplied" is a way of describing powers of 3.

Getting to the Answer:

$3^1 > 100$? No, 3 is not more than 100.

$3^2 > 100$? No, 9 is not more than 100.

$3^3 > 100$? No, 27 is not more than 100.

$3^4 > 100$? No, 81 is not more than 100.

$3^5 > 100$? Yes, 81 times 3 will be more than 100.

2. E

Difficulty: Low

Strategic Advice: Because this question touches upon the area of arithmetic known as number properties, it's ripe for picking numbers.

Getting to the Answer:

Say $P = 1$, $Q = 3$, and $R = 5$.

$1 + 3 = 4$, which is even, so (A) is true.

$1 + 3 + 5 = 9$, which is odd, so (B) is true.

$5 - 1 = 4$, which is even, so (C) is true.

$\dfrac{1 + 3}{2} = 2$, which is even, so (D) is true.

$\dfrac{1 + 5}{2} = 3$, which is odd, so (E) is not true.

3. C

Difficulty: Low

Strategic Advice: Draw out what's described in the stem; you'll then quickly see what's at issue in getting to the solution.

Getting to the Answer:

The 12 angles form a circle. The total number of degrees in a circle is 360°.

$360° \div 12 = 30°$

4. D

Difficulty: Medium

Strategic Advice: Some questions aren't conceptually complex; instead, they test your ability to work meticulously. So do so—but also move quickly.

Getting to the Answer:

$$m = \left|\frac{1}{-2}\right| = \frac{1}{2}$$

$$n = -\frac{1}{3}$$

$$m + n = \frac{1}{2} + \left(-\frac{1}{3}\right) = \frac{1}{2} - \frac{1}{3} = \frac{3}{6} - \frac{2}{6} = \frac{1}{6}$$

5. A

Difficulty: Medium

Strategic Advice: This is merely a dressed-up substitution question. Replace p with 2; then simplify the expression.

Getting to the Answer:

$$2q(7 - 6[2]) = 2q(7 - 12) = 2q(-5) = -10q$$

6. E

Difficulty: Medium

Strategic Advice: Know the major translations between English and math. "Of" signifies multiplication, for example.

Getting to the Answer:

$$(.50)(.40)x = 22.8$$

$$.20x = 22.8$$

$$x = \frac{22.8}{.20} = 114$$

7.   D

Difficulty: Medium

Strategic Advice: Early on in the test, you will probably encounter some questions, like this one, that test your ability to make accurate calculations. Write quickly but carefully, to ensure that you can keep track of the terms you use.

Getting to the Answer:

Multiply each term in $(2x^2 + 5x - 3)$ by each term in $(4x - 1)$:

$2x^2(4x - 1) + 5x(4x - 1) - 3(4x - 1)$

$8x^3 - 2x^2 + 20x^2 - 5x - 12x + 3$

b is the coefficient of x^2

$b = -2 + 20 = 18$

8.   B

Difficulty: Medium

Strategic Advice: Define and keep your eye on exactly what's asked of you. In this question, don't stop when you find the intersection of the two sets; you need the number of elements in the intersection, not the specific elements themselves.

Getting to the Answer:

$<-4, 4> = \{-3, -2, -1, 0, 1, 2, 3\}$

$<0, 7> = \{1, 2, 3, 4, 5, 6\}$

Intersection $= \{1, 2, 3\}$

That's three elements.

(A) $-1, 0$ 1 (3 elements) (B) 0, 1, 2, 3 (4 elements) (C) $-2, -1, 0$ (3 elements) (D) 4, 5, 6 (3 elements) (E) 2, 3, 4 (3 elements)

9.   E

Difficulty: Medium

Strategic Advice: Recognize the difference between part-to-part and part-to-whole ratios, and be able to toggle between one type and the other; on Test Day, at least one question will hinge on your ability to do so.

Getting to the Answer:

$\dfrac{\text{over } 50}{\text{under } 50} = \dfrac{3}{5}$

total $= 3 + 5 = 8$ parts

under $50 = \dfrac{5}{8} = 62.5$

10. D

Difficulty: Medium

Strategic Advice: Don't be thrown by a strange word (what's a "sump," anyway?) or symbols in SAT questions. Focus on the relationships or operations the question describes.

Getting to the Answer:

In order to be a "sump" number, the sum of a number's digits is greater than their product.

(A) Is the sum $(1 + 2 + 3 = 6)$ greater than the product $(1 \times 2 \times 3 = 6)$? No.

(B) Is the sum $(2 + 3 + 4 = 9)$ greater than the product $(2 \times 3 \times 4 = 24)$? No.

(C) Is the sum $(3 + 3 + 2 = 8)$ greater than the product $(3 \times 3 \times 2 = 18)$? No.

(D) Is the sum $(4 + 1 + 1 = 6)$ greater than the product $(4 \times 1 \times 1 = 4)$? Yes.

(E) Is the sum $(5 + 2 + 1 = 8)$ greater than the product $(5 \times 2 \times 1 = 10)$? No.

11. C

Difficulty: Medium

Strategic Advice: The average (arithmetic mean) of a set of consecutive integers equals the mean of the set.

Getting to the Answer:

If 20.5 is the average of the set, it is also the median. So the set contains the seven consecutive integers starting at 21 and increasing, and also the seven consecutive integers starting at 20 and decreasing: 20, 19, 18, 17, 16, 15, 14. The average of this latter group is also its median: 17.

12. A

Difficulty: High

Strategic Advice: You're given 12 and asked for $12r$—which means you want to multiply 12 by r. But remember that if you multiply the 12 on the left side of the equation by r, you must do the same to the r^y on the right side.

Getting to the Answer:

$12 = r^y$

$12r = rr^y$

$12r = r^1 r^y$

$12r = r^{y+1}$

13. B

Difficulty: High

Strategic Advice: The key to multiple figures is to pass information from one figure to the next. Notice, for example, that the legs of the right triangles are also radii of the circle.

Getting to the Answer:

Since OA and OB are both radii, they have equal lengths. This means $\triangle AOB$ and $\triangle OBC$ are 45-45-90 triangles, in which the ratio of leg to leg to hypotenuse is $1:1:\sqrt{2}$. So if AB—a chord of the circle and the hypotenuse of the 45-45-90 has length $6\sqrt{2}$, the radius of the circle is 6.

$$\triangle ABC = \frac{1}{2}(b)(h)$$

$$\triangle ABC = \frac{1}{2}(12)(6)$$

$$\triangle ABC = 36$$

14. B

Difficulty: Medium

Strategic Advice: If time is short, some very quick and simple algebraic manipulation can bring you down to a 50-50 guess on this question. If $ab = 14$ and $bc = 21$, then $b = \frac{14}{a} = \frac{21}{c}$. If $\frac{14}{a} = \frac{21}{c}$, $\frac{a}{c} = \frac{14}{21} = \frac{2}{3}$, so c must be more than a, leaving only (A) and (B) as possibilities.

Getting to the Answer:

Given that your range is integers greater than one, if ab is 14, either a is 2 and b is 7, or vice versa. And if bc is 21, either c is 3 and b is 7, or vice versa. Because b and 7 are the only common elements in both equations, b must be 7. Because a and c are in the ratio of 2 to 3, a must be 2 itself and c must be 3 itself.

15. B

Difficulty: High

Strategic Advice: Don't let a long list of instructions intimidate you.

Go through the list item-by-item and, for each roll, write down the possible outcomes.

Getting to the Answer:

On the first roll, Ahmed could have rolled a 2, 4, 6, or 8.

On the second roll, Ahmed could have rolled a 1, 3, 5, or 7.

On the third roll, Ahmed rolled a 5.

On the fourth roll, Ahmed rolled a 2 or 3.

On the fifth roll, Ahmed rolled a 2 or 3 (the same as the previous roll).

On the sixth roll, Ahmed rolled a 1 or 2.

You might have thought that Ahmed could have rolled a 1 on the fourth and fifth rolls since 1 is smaller than 4. However, since his sixth roll had to be smaller than the fifth, he could not have rolled 1 on the fourth or fifth rolls since that would contradict the information given about the sixth roll.

Must (A) be true? No, he could have rolled a 5 only twice.

Must (B) be true? Yes, he could have rolled a 2 four times, the most of any possibility. The next most frequent roll is 3, which could occur three times.

Must (C) be true? No, the majority of the rolls could be either even or odd.

Must (D) be true? No, he *may* roll a 3, but does not necessarily do so.

Must (E) be true? No, it's possible for Ahmed to roll a 1 only twice.

16. D

Difficulty: High

Strategic Advice: There are a lot of facts thrown at you in this problem, so go through the information and organize it into math equations.

Getting to the Answer:

The question refers to two numbers, the larger of which is 35.

The average formula is $\frac{\text{sum of numbers}}{\text{quantity of numbers}}$. Therefore, the average of the two numbers in this problem is $= \frac{35 + x}{2}$, where x is the smaller of the two numbers.

The average of the two numbers is equal to twice the positive difference between the numbers: $2(35 - x)$.

$\frac{35 + x}{2} = 2(35 - x)$. (How do you know that the difference is $(35 - x)$ and not $(x - 35)$? Because the problem refers to the positive difference, and because 35 is the larger of the two numbers, $(x - 35)$ would be negative.)

$$\frac{35 + x}{2} = 2(35 - x)$$

$$35 + x = 4(35 - x)$$

$$35 + x = 140 - 4x$$

$$35 + 5x = 140$$

$$5x = 105$$

$$x = 21$$

SECTION 8

1. C

Difficulty: Low

This woman relieves her after-work exhaustion by walking along the beach. Thus the implied adjective in the first blank, describing the sea air, will reinforce this idea. In the second blank, we need a synonym for "relieve." Thus, choice (C): the *bracing*, or invigorating, sea air always manages to alleviate her fatigue. The other choices make no sense. The sea air might be *humid*, *salty*, *damp*, or *chilly*, but those qualities wouldn't hasten, *exacerbate* (worsen), reprove (scold), or aggravate the woman's exhaustion.

2. A

Difficulty: Medium

The word in the blank will describe terms that refer indirectly to some thing or idea. The right answer is choice (A)—*euphemisms* are polite, inoffensive or less explicit terms that are used to name an unpleasant, frightening or offensive reality. "Passed away" is an example of a euphemism. People say "passed away" instead of "died." *Banalities* are things that are commonplace or worn-out. *Apostrophes* are marks used to indicate the omission of one or more letters in a word, as in the word "can't." *Eulogies* are formal speeches of praise. At a funeral, speakers might deliver eulogies about the person that died.

3. E

Difficulty: Medium

A good vocabulary will help you figure out this one. The bookkeepers altered some financial records and completely fabricated others, so you need a word like "altered," "falsified," or "fake" for the blank. *Spurious* means "false, lacking authenticity," so it's a good match.

4. D

Difficulty: Medium

Since the kids won, their parents must have been pretty *happy*, and the reaction was probably *joyous*. Choice (D) fits both blanks well. The parents wouldn't be *perplexed* that their children won. (Unless they thought the team was really lousy!)

They wouldn't be *enraged* or *dejected* (depressed) at the team's victory. And their reaction wouldn't be *scornful*, or negative.

5. B

Difficulty: Medium

Start by filling in the second blank. Choices (A), (C), and (E) can be rejected immediately; after all, it doesn't make sense to say that Fernando could speak a language *considerately*, *implicitly*, or *ambiguously*. But he could speak a language *effortlessly* or *eloquently*. Plugging the first word of choices (B) and (D) into the first blank eliminates choice (D), leaving choice (B). Forgetting the difference between dialects wouldn't make Fernando an accomplished linguist, but understanding the difference between them certainly might.

6. B

Difficulty: High

Since the sentence deals with "advocates of free speech," you can predict that they want to protect the right to express opinions. So a good prediction for the first blank would be *guarantee*. What would they feel about citizens who express unpopular sentiments? They would want these citizens to have the right to speak freely: they wouldn't want them to be *censored*. The advocates would not want to *diminish* freedom. Choice (B) fits best. In choice (A), it doesn't make sense to say that a person is *divulged*, or revealed. You could say that their *name* is divulged, but that's not what appears in the sentence. *Restricted* works pretty well for the second blank, but it's doesn't make sense to say that not restricting people will *elucidate*, or explain freedom. And doesn't make sense to say that freedom is *embellished*, or decorated.

Questions 7–19

Passage 1

This is a very challenging passage. Because it was written a long time ago, the style is old-fashioned and a lot of the vocabulary is difficult. Remember, though, that you don't need to understand every word to do well on the questions for a passage. In fact, you can often skip an entire sentence and still do just fine.

In paragraph 1, the author indicates that he's not at all fond of *Moby Dick*. He says that it seems like Melville is testing the reader's patience, and that this book is more "exaggerated" and "dull" than Melville's previous works. Paragraph 2 notes that the book is a strange blend of story and fact, and the writer feels that the book doesn't work as either. In paragraph 3, the author writes that the first couple of Melville's books were okay, but, in his subsequent works, he has gone downhill. Melville should have stopped while he was ahead, but he ruined his reputation with *Moby Dick*.

Passage 2

This passage is modern and a little easier to handle. Paragraph 1 cites the opinions of critics (like author 1) who feel that *Moby Dick* has too much information unrelated to the plot. Author 2 disagrees, and the rest of the passage describes why. Paragraph 2 notes that Melville needed the reader to consider the whale to be a worthy rival for Ahab. This was a challenge, since the whale can't speak. In paragraph 3, the author notes that Melville chose to educate the reader in order to illuminate the character of the whale. Consequently, the book has lots of information about whales and the sea. Paragraph 4 notes that there is also plenty of information about the process of whaling—hunting and killing whales. The author feels that this information gives the reader a better picture of Ahab's obsession.

7.   A

Difficulty: High

Be careful with questions that ask about a term or phrase that the author uses sarcastically. This appears in the first paragraph, where author 1 states that each of Melville's works has gotten worse. They have "advanced" only in negative qualities such as "vanity" and being "clumsy" and "ineffective." So, the author is using the term sarcastically.

Choice (A) matches your prediction. Choice (B) is out-of-scope; there is no mention of other authors anywhere in the passage. Choice (C) is an opposite; this is tempting if you didn't read paragraph 1 carefully. Choice (D) is distortion; author 1 says that the novel was an advance in efforts at innovation, but he means it in a negative way. The innovation was clumsy and ineffective. Choice (E) is a misused detail; the author would agree with this, but it doesn't come up until paragraph 2.

8.   B

Difficulty: Medium

Especially on tough passages, you can often get several questions right just based on the author's tone. Since the author hates *Moby Dick* so much, the quotes around "fine writing" are used to show that he doesn't really believe it to be fine at all.

Choice (A) is an opposite; even if you don't understand much of the passage, it should be clear that the author doesn't hold the novel in high esteem. Choice (B) is a good match. Choice (C) is out of scope; the author doesn't mention any other critics. Choice (D) is distortion; tempting, but the author is using the word "success" sarcastically. Melville was successful only in showing that his writing was poor. Even if you didn't fully understand this sentence, you could eliminate it because it is far too positive. Choice (E) is out of scope; there is no indication that Melville actually used the term "fine writing" himself.

9.   D

Difficulty: Medium

The author believes that the book is "an ill-compounded mixture" of a novel and an instructional work. So, when he says that "the idea of a connected and collected story has obviously visited and abandoned its writer again and again," he is implying that the plot appears and disappears as you read the book, since it's interrupted by the factual sections.

Choice (A) is distortion; this is the opinion of author 2, but it's much too positive for author 1. Choice (B) is an opposite; in paragraph 1, the author makes exactly the opposite claim. Choice (C) is out of scope; the author says that the novel is a strange blend of both kinds of material, but doesn't describe one as more prevalent. Choice (D) is a good match. Choice (E) is distortion; this interpretation is too literal. Also, since the author describes Melville as vain and over-confident, it seems unlikely author 1 would attribute *periods of doubt* to Melville.

KAPLAN
Test Prep and Admissions

10. C

Difficulty: Medium

Some sentences from Reading Comp passages are constructed much like Sentence Completions. A word is immediately followed by a phrase that provides a definition. Right after the quoted phrase, you read "neither so compelling as to be entertaining, nor so instructively complete as to take place among documents on the subject of the Great Whale," In other words, the book doesn't work as a novel or an instructional document.

Choice (A) is out of scope; the author never says that whaling is an unusual subject for a book. Choice (B) is a misused detail; the author does say this in paragraph 1, but not in paragraph 2, where the "strange book" reference occurs. Choice (C) is a good match. Choice (D) is out of scope; this is mentioned in Passage 2, but not in Passage 1. Choice (E) is a misused detail; the author does say this, but it's not mentioned in the sentence that explains why he considers *Moby Dick* a strange book.

11. E

Difficulty: High

Treat Inference questions about tone like global questions—consider the entire passage. Look for a choice that captures the writer's highly critical tone.

Choice (A) is an opposite; this is the opinion of author 2, not author 1. Choice (B) is distortion; the author does note that Melville was ambitious, but would not agree with the word *greatness*. Choice (C) is extreme; the author doesn't like *Moby Dick*, but that doesn't mean it's *always* a bad idea to include instructional elements. Choice (D) is distortion; this is the thesis of Passage 2, not Passage 1. Choice (E) is supported in two places. In paragraph 1, the author notes that Melville's novels are getting worse, and in paragraph 3, he writes that Melville should have stopped while he was ahead.

12. C

Difficulty: Low

The word "admittedly" indicates that the author feels that, though the passages are important, the author knows that they are a little "dry" or *boring*.

Choice (A) is a common meaning of dry, but it makes no sense here. In choice (B), the context doesn't suggest that the passages are *ironic*. Choice (C) is a good match. Choice

(D) is the opposite of what you're looking for. Choice (E) doesn't make sense after the word "admittedly."

13. D

Difficulty: Low

In paragraph 2, the author illustrates the importance of making the whale a well-developed character, and the questions at the end of paragraph help to describe the problems involved in this task.

Choice (A) is an opposite; the author feels that Melville's techniques are highly effective. Choice (B) is distortion; these are questions asked by author 2, not by Melville's characters. Choice (C) is an opposite; this choice is too negative in tone to fit with the passage. Choice (D) is a good match. Choice (E) is distortion; this is tempting, but be careful. The questions at the end of paragraph 2 show a problem. It's Melville's solution to that problem that forms *an unusual approach to the form of the novel*.

14. E

Difficulty: Medium

The passage notes that Dickens described London in order to "create a sense of light and shade on his characters," and Melville described the sea "in order to more fully reveal the character of Moby Dick." So, both authors described places in order to add to the descriptions of their characters.

Choice (A) is out of scope; the author doesn't describe London or the underwater environment as *dark* or *mysterious*. Choice (B) is a misused detail; this is true of Melville, but the author never indicates that this is true of Dickens. Choice (C) is distortion; although some of Melville's techniques may be unusual, the author never says this about Dickens's work. Choice (D) is an opposite; the author feels that it adds to each author's novel in a positive way. Choice (E) is a good match.

15. A

Difficulty: Low

Melville devoted several chapters to "describing the process of hunting and killing a whale," so a good prediction would be that he *worked hard* to "clearly portray the techniques and culture of whaling."

Choice (A) is a good match. In choice (B), the word "pains" might make this a tempting choice, but it doesn't fit in the sentence. In choice (C), the author feels that the attempts to describe whaling were successful. In choice (D), he doesn't just make it possible, he actually does the describing. In choice (E), the author would agree that Melville was wise to describe whaling, but this doesn't follow from the phrase "takes considerable pains."

16. C

Difficulty: Medium

As the questions shift to focus on both passages, be especially careful to keep straight the viewpoints of the two authors. Author 1 feels that *Moby Dick* was unsuccessful both as a novel and as an information work. In paragraph 2 of Passage 2, author 2 argues against exactly this point. He says that critics who dismiss *Moby Dick* as a treatise on whaling "fail to realize that Melville is…advancing the plot." In other words, critics like author 1 just don't get it.

Choice (A) is an opposite; this is the opinion of author 1, not author 2. Choice (B) is a misused detail; this addresses only the issue of the descriptions of ocean plant life and not the bigger issue of the many parts of *Moby Dick* that convey information about whales and whaling. Choice (C) is a good match. Choice (D) is an opposite; again, this is the view of author 1, not author 2. Choice (E) is an opposite; author 2 says that the information is important, but "dry."

17. D

Difficulty: Low

Open-ended questions like this one often yield best to elimination rather than a prediction. The authors don't agree about much, so go through the answer choices and eliminate anything that applies only to one of the authors.

Choice (A) is an opposite; this applies only to author 2. Choice (B) is a misused detail; this is only mentioned in passage 2. Choice (C) is an opposite; only author 2 discusses sense of place. Choice (D) is correct; this is discussed in paragraph 2 of Passage 1 and is the main focus of Passage 2. Choice (E) is a misused detail; only Passage 1 discussed Melville's previous works.

18. A

Difficulty: Low

Note that this question asks about the reaction of author 1 to the critics cited in Passage 2. It's *not* asking about his reaction to author 2. The "critics" feel that *Moby Dick* is a

"treatise on whaling" and "that alternating such discursive material with the narrative detracts" from the work. Author 1 would agree with this, since he also feels that the book doesn't have a continuous narrative.

Choice (A) is correct; author 1 would agree with the critics. Choice (B) is an opposite; author 1 doesn't feel that readers should be more patient with Melville. Choice (C) is an opposite; author 2 might agree with this assessment, but author 1 would not. Choice (D) is an opposite; author 1 thinks that the critics are right on track. Choice (E) is distortion; author 1 says that it's Melville who is too *ambitious*, not his readers.

19. B

Difficulty: Low

Sum up the positions of each author in your mind. Author 1 feels that Melville is lousy, while author 2 thinks Melville is great.

Choice (A) is an opposite; author 1 would definitely deny that Melville is excellent. Choice (B) is perfect. Choice (C) is distortion; author 1 doesn't seem to find the work particularly noteworthy. Choice (D) is out of scope; *Moby Dick* is the only Melville work that author 2 discusses, so you there's no evidence that this is an improvement over other works. Choice (E) is an opposite; author 1 states that *Moby Dick* is a blend of a plotline and other, non-fictional elements.

SECTION 9

1. D

Difficulty: High

Look for the most concise answer choice that does not introduce additional errors.

As written, this sentence is awkward and unnecessarily wordy. Only choice (D) corrects these errors without introducing additional issues. Choice (B) is still wordy and the repeated use of the pronoun *it* makes it unclear. Choice (C) is also wordy, and introduces a cause-and-effect relationship between the clauses which is incorrect in context. Choice (E) creates a sentence fragment.

2. D

Difficulty: Medium

A sentence must have a subject and a verb in an independent clause and express a complete thought.

As written, this sentence is a fragment. Choice (D) corrects the error by adding the verb *is*. Choices (B) and (C) do not address the error. Choice (E) reverses the cause-and-effect relationship between the clauses.

3. E

Difficulty: High

Items in a series, list, or compound must be parallel in structure.

As written, the adverb *permanently* destroys the parallel structure of *gaining…and keeping.* Choice (E) corrects the error. The verb forms in choices (B), (C), and (D) are not parallel; additionally, choice (B) uses the adjective *permanent* to modify the verb form *gaining,* and the pronoun *it* in choice (D) is ambiguous in context.

4. B

Difficulty: Medium

Some sentences in this section will test your knowledge of word choice.

The prepositional phrase *of which* is incorrectly used here; choice (B) eliminates the phrase and combines the two independent clauses with a semicolon splice. Choice (C) misuses the semicolon splice, which is only correct when used to connect two independent clauses. In choice (D), the pronoun *it* has no antecedent. Choice (E) is a run-on sentence.

5. A

Difficulty: Medium

If you think there are no errors in a sentence, there's a good chance (about 15%, in fact) that you're right.

Choice (B) uses a conjunction that is inappropriate in the context of the sentence. Choice (C) removes the predicate (main) verb, creating a sentence fragment. Choice (D) uses *was,* which is incorrect with the plural subject women. Choice (E) violates the parallel structure of the two verbs.

6. D

Difficulty: Medium

Make sure that modifying phrases are properly placed for what they are meant to modify.

An extraction, rather than *chewing problems*, is what is *Unlike a root canal.* Choices (C), (D), and (E) makes this change, but choice (C) introduces an inappropriate verb tense, and choice (E) is a sentence fragment. In (B), the opening phrase is modifying *problems.*

7. A

Difficulty: Medium

"Correct as written" sentences require a little more work; be methodical in checking the answer choices for errors.

Choice (B) creates an inappropriate cause-and-effect relationship between the clauses. Choice (C) creates a run-on sentence, since both clauses are independent and they are joined only by a comma splice. Choice (D) is incorrect grammatical structure. Choice (E) introduces an incorrect verb tense.

8. D

Difficulty: Medium

The subject of a verb may not be the noun closest to it in the sentence.

Even though *favorites* is the closest noun to the verb *were,* its subject is actually the singular pronoun *one* (*favorites* is the object of the preposition *of*). Choice (D) corrects this error by changing *were* to *was.* Choice (B) corrects the error, but incorrectly uses the plural verb *were* with the subject *something.* Choice (C) does not address the error, introduces an inconsistent verb tense, and incorrectly uses the semicolon splice. Choice (E) corrects the original error, but uses the pronoun *it* without a clear antecedent and misuses the semicolon splice.

9. B

Difficulty: Medium

Items in a list, series, or compound must be parallel in form.

The simple predicate of this sentence is the compound verb *is born…and becoming.* Choice (B) makes the second verb parallel to the first. Choices (C) and (E) are incorrect grammatical structure and change the meaning of the original selection. Choice (D) leaves the meaning of the second clause incomplete.

10. B

Difficulty: Low

The gerund (*-ing*) verb can not be used as the main verb of a sentence.

As written, this is a sentence fragment, and the repetition of *often* is redundant. Choice (B) corrects both errors. Since the sentence starts out using the third person pronoun *one*, switching to the second person *you*, as choice (C) suggests, is incorrect. Choice (D) creates a run-on sentence. In (E), it is unclear to what *they* is referring.

11. E

Difficulty: Medium

Items in a list must be in parallel form.

This sentence violates the rules of parallel structure. The first two items in the list are gerund (*-ing*) verb forms: *buying* and *training*. Therefore, the third item should be in the same form. Both choices (D) and (E) correct this error, but the singular verb *is* in (D) is incorrect with a compound subject. The preposition *of* in (B) is idiomatically incorrect in context. Choice (C) does not address the error, and also uses the singular verb form incorrectly.

12. A

Difficulty: Medium

Be methodical in eliminating answer choices, but if you don't find an error don't be afraid to choose choice (A).

This sentence contains no error. The transition *Whereas* in choice (B) is inappropriate in context. Choices (C) and (D) use *size* redundantly. The transition word *Since* in choice (E) expresses cause and effect, which is inappropriate in this context.

13. B

Difficulty: Low

Choose the most concise answer choice that does not violate any grammar rules.

As written, the underlined phrase is overly wordy. Choice (B) eliminates the unnecessarily transition words and is grammatically correct. Choice (C) is even wordier than the original selection. Choices (D) and (E) unnecessarily introduce the passive voice.

14. B

Difficulty: Low

If you don't spot a grammatical error, look for errors in style.

As written, this sentence is unnecessarily wordy. Although the shortest answer will not always be correct for Wordiness questions, that is the case here; choice (B) is the appropriate choice. Choices (C) and (E) use grammatically incorrect structure. Choice (D) is incorrect idiomatic usage.

SAT PRACTICE TEST ELEVEN ANSWER SHEET

Remove (or photocopy) the answer sheet, and use it to complete the practice test.

How to Take the Practice Tests

Each Practice Test includes eight scored multiple-choice sections and one essay. Keep in mind that on the actual SAT, there will be an additional multiple-choice section—the experimental section—that will not contribute to your score.

Once you start a Practice Test, don't stop until you've gone through all nine sections. Remember, you can review any questions within a section, but you may not go back or forward a section.

Good luck!

Start with number 1 for each section. If a section has fewer questions than answer spaces, leave the extra spaces blank.

Section One

Section One is the writing section's essay component.
Lined pages on which you will write your essay can be found in that section.

Section Two

1. Ⓐ Ⓑ Ⓒ Ⓓ Ⓔ
2. Ⓐ Ⓑ Ⓒ Ⓓ Ⓔ
3. Ⓐ Ⓑ Ⓒ Ⓓ Ⓔ
4. Ⓐ Ⓑ Ⓒ Ⓓ Ⓔ
5. Ⓐ Ⓑ Ⓒ Ⓓ Ⓔ
6. Ⓐ Ⓑ Ⓒ Ⓓ Ⓔ
7. Ⓐ Ⓑ Ⓒ Ⓓ Ⓔ
8. Ⓐ Ⓑ Ⓒ Ⓓ Ⓔ

9. Ⓐ Ⓑ Ⓒ Ⓓ Ⓔ
10. Ⓐ Ⓑ Ⓒ Ⓓ Ⓔ
11. Ⓐ Ⓑ Ⓒ Ⓓ Ⓔ
12. Ⓐ Ⓑ Ⓒ Ⓓ Ⓔ
13. Ⓐ Ⓑ Ⓒ Ⓓ Ⓔ
14. Ⓐ Ⓑ Ⓒ Ⓓ Ⓔ
15. Ⓐ Ⓑ Ⓒ Ⓓ Ⓔ
16. Ⓐ Ⓑ Ⓒ Ⓓ Ⓔ

17. Ⓐ Ⓑ Ⓒ Ⓓ Ⓔ
18. Ⓐ Ⓑ Ⓒ Ⓓ Ⓔ
19. Ⓐ Ⓑ Ⓒ Ⓓ Ⓔ
20. Ⓐ Ⓑ Ⓒ Ⓓ Ⓔ
21. Ⓐ Ⓑ Ⓒ Ⓓ Ⓔ
22. Ⓐ Ⓑ Ⓒ Ⓓ Ⓔ
23. Ⓐ Ⓑ Ⓒ Ⓓ Ⓔ
24. Ⓐ Ⓑ Ⓒ Ⓓ Ⓔ

☐ # right in Section Two

☐ # wrong in Section Two

Section Three

1. Ⓐ Ⓑ Ⓒ Ⓓ Ⓔ
2. Ⓐ Ⓑ Ⓒ Ⓓ Ⓔ
3. Ⓐ Ⓑ Ⓒ Ⓓ Ⓔ
4. Ⓐ Ⓑ Ⓒ Ⓓ Ⓔ
5. Ⓐ Ⓑ Ⓒ Ⓓ Ⓔ
6. Ⓐ Ⓑ Ⓒ Ⓓ Ⓔ
7. Ⓐ Ⓑ Ⓒ Ⓓ Ⓔ
8. Ⓐ Ⓑ Ⓒ Ⓓ Ⓔ

9. Ⓐ Ⓑ Ⓒ Ⓓ Ⓔ
10. Ⓐ Ⓑ Ⓒ Ⓓ Ⓔ
11. Ⓐ Ⓑ Ⓒ Ⓓ Ⓔ
12. Ⓐ Ⓑ Ⓒ Ⓓ Ⓔ
13. Ⓐ Ⓑ Ⓒ Ⓓ Ⓔ
14. Ⓐ Ⓑ Ⓒ Ⓓ Ⓔ
15. Ⓐ Ⓑ Ⓒ Ⓓ Ⓔ
16. Ⓐ Ⓑ Ⓒ Ⓓ Ⓔ

17. Ⓐ Ⓑ Ⓒ Ⓓ Ⓔ
18. Ⓐ Ⓑ Ⓒ Ⓓ Ⓔ
19. Ⓐ Ⓑ Ⓒ Ⓓ Ⓔ
20. Ⓐ Ⓑ Ⓒ Ⓓ Ⓔ

☐ # right in Section Three

☐ # wrong in Section Three

Remove (or photocopy) this answer sheet, and use it to complete the practice test.

Start with number 1 for each section. If a section has fewer questions than answer spaces, leave the extra spaces blank.

Section Four

1. Ⓐ Ⓑ Ⓒ Ⓓ Ⓔ	10. Ⓐ Ⓑ Ⓒ Ⓓ Ⓔ	19. Ⓐ Ⓑ Ⓒ Ⓓ Ⓔ	28. Ⓐ Ⓑ Ⓒ Ⓓ Ⓔ
2. Ⓐ Ⓑ Ⓒ Ⓓ Ⓔ	11. Ⓐ Ⓑ Ⓒ Ⓓ Ⓔ	20. Ⓐ Ⓑ Ⓒ Ⓓ Ⓔ	29. Ⓐ Ⓑ Ⓒ Ⓓ Ⓔ
3. Ⓐ Ⓑ Ⓒ Ⓓ Ⓔ	12. Ⓐ Ⓑ Ⓒ Ⓓ Ⓔ	21. Ⓐ Ⓑ Ⓒ Ⓓ Ⓔ	30. Ⓐ Ⓑ Ⓒ Ⓓ Ⓔ
4. Ⓐ Ⓑ Ⓒ Ⓓ Ⓔ	13. Ⓐ Ⓑ Ⓒ Ⓓ Ⓔ	22. Ⓐ Ⓑ Ⓒ Ⓓ Ⓔ	31. Ⓐ Ⓑ Ⓒ Ⓓ Ⓔ
5. Ⓐ Ⓑ Ⓒ Ⓓ Ⓔ	14. Ⓐ Ⓑ Ⓒ Ⓓ Ⓔ	23. Ⓐ Ⓑ Ⓒ Ⓓ Ⓔ	32. Ⓐ Ⓑ Ⓒ Ⓓ Ⓔ
6. Ⓐ Ⓑ Ⓒ Ⓓ Ⓔ	15. Ⓐ Ⓑ Ⓒ Ⓓ Ⓔ	24. Ⓐ Ⓑ Ⓒ Ⓓ Ⓔ	33. Ⓐ Ⓑ Ⓒ Ⓓ Ⓔ
7. Ⓐ Ⓑ Ⓒ Ⓓ Ⓔ	16. Ⓐ Ⓑ Ⓒ Ⓓ Ⓔ	25. Ⓐ Ⓑ Ⓒ Ⓓ Ⓔ	34 Ⓐ Ⓑ Ⓒ Ⓓ Ⓔ
8. Ⓐ Ⓑ Ⓒ Ⓓ Ⓔ	17. Ⓐ Ⓑ Ⓒ Ⓓ Ⓔ	26. Ⓐ Ⓑ Ⓒ Ⓓ Ⓔ	35. Ⓐ Ⓑ Ⓒ Ⓓ Ⓔ
9. Ⓐ Ⓑ Ⓒ Ⓓ Ⓔ	18. Ⓐ Ⓑ Ⓒ Ⓓ Ⓔ	27. Ⓐ Ⓑ Ⓒ Ⓓ Ⓔ	

right in Section Four

wrong in Section Four

Section Five

1. Ⓐ Ⓑ Ⓒ Ⓓ Ⓔ	9. Ⓐ Ⓑ Ⓒ Ⓓ Ⓔ	17. Ⓐ Ⓑ Ⓒ Ⓓ Ⓔ
2. Ⓐ Ⓑ Ⓒ Ⓓ Ⓔ	10. Ⓐ Ⓑ Ⓒ Ⓓ Ⓔ	18. Ⓐ Ⓑ Ⓒ Ⓓ Ⓔ
3. Ⓐ Ⓑ Ⓒ Ⓓ Ⓔ	11. Ⓐ Ⓑ Ⓒ Ⓓ Ⓔ	19. Ⓐ Ⓑ Ⓒ Ⓓ Ⓔ
4. Ⓐ Ⓑ Ⓒ Ⓓ Ⓔ	12. Ⓐ Ⓑ Ⓒ Ⓓ Ⓔ	20. Ⓐ Ⓑ Ⓒ Ⓓ Ⓔ
5. Ⓐ Ⓑ Ⓒ Ⓓ Ⓔ	13. Ⓐ Ⓑ Ⓒ Ⓓ Ⓔ	21. Ⓐ Ⓑ Ⓒ Ⓓ Ⓔ
6. Ⓐ Ⓑ Ⓒ Ⓓ Ⓔ	14. Ⓐ Ⓑ Ⓒ Ⓓ Ⓔ	22. Ⓐ Ⓑ Ⓒ Ⓓ Ⓔ
7. Ⓐ Ⓑ Ⓒ Ⓓ Ⓔ	15. Ⓐ Ⓑ Ⓒ Ⓓ Ⓔ	23. Ⓐ Ⓑ Ⓒ Ⓓ Ⓔ
8. Ⓐ Ⓑ Ⓒ Ⓓ Ⓔ	16. Ⓐ Ⓑ Ⓒ Ⓓ Ⓔ	24. Ⓐ Ⓑ Ⓒ Ⓓ Ⓔ

right in Section Five

wrong in Section Five

Remove (or photocopy) this answer sheet, and use it to complete the practice test.

Start with number 1 for each section. If a section has fewer questions than answer spaces, leave the extra spaces blank.

Section Six

1. Ⓐ Ⓑ Ⓒ Ⓓ Ⓔ   9. Ⓐ Ⓑ Ⓒ Ⓓ Ⓔ   17. Ⓐ Ⓑ Ⓒ Ⓓ Ⓔ
2. Ⓐ Ⓑ Ⓒ Ⓓ Ⓔ   10. Ⓐ Ⓑ Ⓒ Ⓓ Ⓔ   18. Ⓐ Ⓑ Ⓒ Ⓓ Ⓔ
3. Ⓐ Ⓑ Ⓒ Ⓓ Ⓔ   11. Ⓐ Ⓑ Ⓒ Ⓓ Ⓔ
4. Ⓐ Ⓑ Ⓒ Ⓓ Ⓔ   12. Ⓐ Ⓑ Ⓒ Ⓓ Ⓔ
5. Ⓐ Ⓑ Ⓒ Ⓓ Ⓔ   13. Ⓐ Ⓑ Ⓒ Ⓓ Ⓔ
6. Ⓐ Ⓑ Ⓒ Ⓓ Ⓔ   14. Ⓐ Ⓑ Ⓒ Ⓓ Ⓔ
7. Ⓐ Ⓑ Ⓒ Ⓓ Ⓔ   15. Ⓐ Ⓑ Ⓒ Ⓓ Ⓔ
8. Ⓐ Ⓑ Ⓒ Ⓓ Ⓔ   16. Ⓐ Ⓑ Ⓒ Ⓓ Ⓔ

right in Section Six

wrong in Section Six

If section 6 of your test book contains math questions that are not multiple choice, continue to item 9 below. Otherwise, continue to item 9 above.

9.   10.   11.   12.   13.

14.   15.   16.   17.   18.

Section Seven

1. Ⓐ Ⓑ Ⓒ Ⓓ Ⓔ   9. Ⓐ Ⓑ Ⓒ Ⓓ Ⓔ   17. Ⓐ Ⓑ Ⓒ Ⓓ Ⓔ
2. Ⓐ Ⓑ Ⓒ Ⓓ Ⓔ   10. Ⓐ Ⓑ Ⓒ Ⓓ Ⓔ   18. Ⓐ Ⓑ Ⓒ Ⓓ Ⓔ
3. Ⓐ Ⓑ Ⓒ Ⓓ Ⓔ   11. Ⓐ Ⓑ Ⓒ Ⓓ Ⓔ   19. Ⓐ Ⓑ Ⓒ Ⓓ Ⓔ
4. Ⓐ Ⓑ Ⓒ Ⓓ Ⓔ   12. Ⓐ Ⓑ Ⓒ Ⓓ Ⓔ
5. Ⓐ Ⓑ Ⓒ Ⓓ Ⓔ   13. Ⓐ Ⓑ Ⓒ Ⓓ Ⓔ
6. Ⓐ Ⓑ Ⓒ Ⓓ Ⓔ   14. Ⓐ Ⓑ Ⓒ Ⓓ Ⓔ
7. Ⓐ Ⓑ Ⓒ Ⓓ Ⓔ   15. Ⓐ Ⓑ Ⓒ Ⓓ Ⓔ
8. Ⓐ Ⓑ Ⓒ Ⓓ Ⓔ   16. Ⓐ Ⓑ Ⓒ Ⓓ Ⓔ

right in Section Seven

wrong in Section Seven

Remove (or photocopy) this answer sheet, and use it to complete the practice test.

Start with number 1 for each section. If a section has fewer questions than answer spaces, leave the extra spaces blank.

Section Eight

1. Ⓐ Ⓑ Ⓒ Ⓓ Ⓔ   9. Ⓐ Ⓑ Ⓒ Ⓓ Ⓔ
2. Ⓐ Ⓑ Ⓒ Ⓓ Ⓔ   10. Ⓐ Ⓑ Ⓒ Ⓓ Ⓔ
3. Ⓐ Ⓑ Ⓒ Ⓓ Ⓔ   11. Ⓐ Ⓑ Ⓒ Ⓓ Ⓔ
4. Ⓐ Ⓑ Ⓒ Ⓓ Ⓔ   12. Ⓐ Ⓑ Ⓒ Ⓓ Ⓔ
5. Ⓐ Ⓑ Ⓒ Ⓓ Ⓔ   13. Ⓐ Ⓑ Ⓒ Ⓓ Ⓔ
6. Ⓐ Ⓑ Ⓒ Ⓓ Ⓔ   14. Ⓐ Ⓑ Ⓒ Ⓓ Ⓔ
7. Ⓐ Ⓑ Ⓒ Ⓓ Ⓔ   15. Ⓐ Ⓑ Ⓒ Ⓓ Ⓔ
8. Ⓐ Ⓑ Ⓒ Ⓓ Ⓔ   16. Ⓐ Ⓑ Ⓒ Ⓓ Ⓔ

☐ # right in Section Eight

☐ # wrong in Section Eight

Section Nine

1. Ⓐ Ⓑ Ⓒ Ⓓ Ⓔ   9. Ⓐ Ⓑ Ⓒ Ⓓ Ⓔ
2. Ⓐ Ⓑ Ⓒ Ⓓ Ⓔ   10. Ⓐ Ⓑ Ⓒ Ⓓ Ⓔ
3. Ⓐ Ⓑ Ⓒ Ⓓ Ⓔ   11. Ⓐ Ⓑ Ⓒ Ⓓ Ⓔ
4. Ⓐ Ⓑ Ⓒ Ⓓ Ⓔ   12. Ⓐ Ⓑ Ⓒ Ⓓ Ⓔ
5. Ⓐ Ⓑ Ⓒ Ⓓ Ⓔ   13. Ⓐ Ⓑ Ⓒ Ⓓ Ⓔ
6. Ⓐ Ⓑ Ⓒ Ⓓ Ⓔ   14. Ⓐ Ⓑ Ⓒ Ⓓ Ⓔ
7. Ⓐ Ⓑ Ⓒ Ⓓ Ⓔ
8. Ⓐ Ⓑ Ⓒ Ⓓ Ⓔ

☐ # right in Section Nine

☐ # wrong in Section Nine

Practice Test Eleven

SECTION 1
Time—25 Minutes
ESSAY

The essay gives you an opportunity to show how effectively you can develop and express ideas. You should, therefore, take care to develop your point of view, present your ideas logically and clearly, and use language precisely.

Your essay must be written in your Answer Grid Booklet—you will receive no other paper on which to write. You will have enough space if you write on every line, avoid wide margins, and keep your handwriting to a reasonable size. Remember that people who are not familiar with your handwriting will read what you write. Try to write or print so that what you are writing is legible to those readers.

You have twenty-five minutes to write an essay on the topic assigned below.

DO NOT WRITE ON ANOTHER TOPIC. AN OFF-TOPIC ESSAY WILL RECEIVE A SCORE OF ZERO.

Think carefully about the issue presented in the following excerpt and the assignment below.

> "When you reach an obstacle, turn it into an opportunity. You have the choice. You can overcome and be a winner, or you can allow it to overcome you, and be a loser. It is far better to be exhausted from success than to be rested from failure."
>
> –Mary Kay Ash

Assignment: What is your view of the idea that every obstacle can be turned into an opportunity? In an essay, support your position by discussing an example (or examples) from literature, the arts, science and technology, current events, or your own experience or observation.

DO NOT WRITE YOUR ESSAY IN YOUR TEST BOOK.
You will receive credit only for what you write in your Answer Grid Booklet.

_____

_____

_____

_____

_____

_____

_____

_____

_____

_____

_____

_____

_____

_____

_____

_____

_____

_____

IF YOU FINISH BEFORE TIME IS CALLED, YOU MAY CHECK YOUR WORK ON
THIS SECTION ONLY. DO NOT TURN TO ANY OTHER SECTION IN THE TEST.

SECTION 2

Time—25 Minutes
24 Questions

Directions: For each of the following questions, choose the best answer and darken the corresponding oval on the answer sheet.

Each sentence below has one or two blanks, each blank indicating that something has been omitted. Beneath the sentence are five words or sets of words labeled (A) through (E). Choose the word or set of words that, when inserted in the sentence, <u>best</u> fits the meaning of the sentence as a whole.

EXAMPLE:

Today's small, portable computers contrast markedly with the earliest electronic computers, which were ----.

(A) effective
(B) invented
(C) useful
(D) destructive
(E) enormous   Ⓐ Ⓑ Ⓒ Ⓓ ⬤

---

1. Once an independent nation, Catalonia is now a region of Spain; nevertheless, it ---- a sense of ---- because it continues to have its own language and culture.

   (A) surrenders . . rebellion
   (B) retains . . autonomy
   (C) experiences . . privilege
   (D) boasts . . arrogance
   (E) suffers . . neglect

2. Finding her old dolls and toys in the attic evoked ---- in the old woman as she fondly remembered her childhood.

   (A) gratitude
   (B) determination
   (C) regret
   (D) melancholy
   (E) nostalgia

3. The two giant pandas at the National Zoo in Washington, DC are closely ----: scientists record their hormone levels daily, and 24-hour video cameras constantly ---- their activities.

   (A) praised . . record
   (B) monitored . . document
   (C) criticized . . report
   (D) evaluated . . approve
   (E) questioned . . verify

4. Though Benjamin Franklin's presence at salons and dinner parties in France may have appeared ---- in a time of war, he had a serious purpose; he ingratiated himself with the French court and gained its ---- for the American cause of independence from England.

   (A) disrespectful . . compliments
   (B) frivolous . . support
   (C) irrelevant . . approval
   (D) extravagant . . permission
   (E) rebellious . . respect

GO ON TO THE NEXT PAGE

5. In response to the students' confused expressions, the teacher attempted to ---- the subject with a clear example.

   (A) extricate
   (B) evade
   (C) comprehend
   (D) elucidate
   (E) obfuscate

6. The ---- cat remained by the mouse hole all afternoon, watching for his meal.

   (A) apprehensive
   (B) emaciated
   (C) vigilant
   (D) prominent
   (E) indolent

7. Laura's excuse appeared credible at first, but further questioning and investigation revealed that it was completely ----.

   (A) valid
   (B) sardonic
   (C) righteous
   (D) fabricated
   (E) incredulous

8. The magnificent, ---- sets that depicted a futuristic city in Fritz Lang's epic film *Metropolis* are now widely regarded as an outstanding visual achievement.

   (A) prolific
   (B) modest
   (C) reticent
   (D) archaic
   (E) grandiose

GO ON TO THE NEXT PAGE

Questions 9–13 are based on the following passage.

The following is adapted from an encyclopedia of wartime technology.

Flexible personal body armor made from interlocking iron or steel rings existed as long ago as
the ancient Roman era. Used primarily as protection for elite, heavy cavalry troops, various forms
(5) of so-called chain mail armor—either as a complete garment or combined with other forms of
protection—were relatively rare and expensive at
that time, and less practical than the *lorica segmentata*. This was an iron cuirass* favored by the
(10) Roman infantry made from segmented steel plates
hung on a leather harness.
For centuries after the fall of imperial Rome, the
craft of fashioning mail armor fell into disuse.
However, it then reemerged in the medieval peri-
(15) od with such vigor that, by the fourteenth century,
entire armies could feasibly be outfitted with practical and effective linked metal armor suits. The
type of armor historians often call chain mail—
usually called simply mail by its contemporaries—
(20) had many advantages for the individual fighting
man in the age of steel weapons. It combined the
flexibility and suppleness of cloth with the
impact-absorbing mass and cut resistance of rigid
metal plates. Edged weapons, no matter how
(25) sharp, were incapable of slashing or sawing
through a well-fashioned mail suit. Moreover,
when struck with a blunt object, the links trans-
fered the force through the mass of the garment,
absorbing a significant amount of shock impact
(30) and inhibiting its transfer to the soft human tissues underneath.
The process of manufacturing a mail shirt was
enormously labor-intensive in pre-industrial
times. Each of the thousands of individual links
(35) that made up a full suit, or harness, had to be
individually cut from a coil of hand-drawn wire.
The ends of the links were flattened and drilled
with tiny holes, and the links were then looped

into the garment and riveted closed. By varying
(40) the pattern of interlocking links, a master mailer
was able to grow or shrink the metal garment, and
to "knit" sleeves, mittens, hoods, and other complex forms. Eventually the ascendancy of
improved stabbing and piercing weapons acceler-
(45) ated the obsolescence of linked mail armor, and
the need for greater protection spurred the development of armor made with cleverly articulated
rigid steel plates instead. Today only a few examples of medieval linked metal armor suits remain.

*cuirass: a piece of protective armor which protects the upper body

9. Which of the following can be inferred about
ancient Roman armor from the passage?

(A) The *lorica segmentata* fell into disuse and
then had a resurgence in the medieval period.

(B) Ancient Roman linked-mail armor was less
effective than the armor made in the fourteenth century.

(C) The improved stabbing and piercing weapons
used by Rome's military opponents made
flexible mail armor impractical for Roman
troops.

(D) Armor made from segmented steel plates was
unsuitable for wear by cavalry troops.

(E) The *lorica segmentata* was a more practical
form of protection for the infantry than flexible mail armor.

10. As used in line 13, "fashioning" most nearly means

(A) creating
(B) purchasing
(C) dressing
(D) locating
(E) sewing

GO ON TO THE NEXT PAGE

11. Which of the following statements is best supported by the passage?

    (A) The use of mail armor declined steeply because of a lack of an adequate network of skilled craftsmen to create the armor.

    (B) Flexible linked-metal armor represented a practical solution to a technological need in a particular historical era.

    (C) The availability of practical mail armor was limited mainly to the fourteenth century.

    (D) Linked-metal armor was of such limited usefulness that it quickly became obsolete when the superior technology of articulated metal plates became widespread.

    (E) The unique characteristics of flexible linked-metal armor make it a useful technology for applications today.

12. According to the passage, all of the following were steps in the process of creating a medieval mail harness EXCEPT

    (A) flattening and drilling holes in the ends of each link

    (B) varying the pattern of interlocking links to form contours

    (C) cutting the individual links from a coil of wire

    (D) suspending the completed mail suit from a leather harness

    (E) riveting the cut ends of the metal links shut

13. The function of the first sentence of the third paragraph ("The process...times") can best be described as

    (A) countering an argument made earlier in the passage

    (B) stating the central thesis of the passage

    (C) providing evidence for a hypothesis that follows

    (D) explaining a paradox described in the previous paragraph

    (E) advancing an assertion which is subsequently reinforced with details

GO ON TO THE NEXT PAGE

Questions 14–24 are based on the following passage.

In this passage, the author describes a man's contemplation of his childhood on a farm that his family has recently sold.

Yesterday there was a forest of corn here. Thomas remembered racing through it blindly, his forearms raised to protect his face from the rough leaves. Playing in the corn was one of his pastimes,
(5) a pastime of any boy who lived on a farm that planted it. He would run until he was out of breath, gasping and disoriented by the spears of green towering over his head. It's easy to become lost in a corn field, to walk in endless circles. It's
(10) easier still, by picking a row of corn and following it out, to leave. Leaving the corn was easy.

For eighty years the family had grown corn on its hundred-acre plot. In his grandfather's day, even in his father's, wheat and timothy were also
(15) sown to help feed cattle and pigs. While there had been no animals on the land in Thomas's time, Thomas's father spoke at length about those days, when he himself had been a child. Back then, Thomas's father had dedicated every one of his
(20) free hours to taking care of the farm: grinding chop, cleaning up after the animals, mending fences, and performing innumerable other taxing chores. Later, it was just corn, sold to some big company out East that his father said paid them a
(25) little less every year. It wasn't about the money though; his father would have made do with just enough to keep things going. His concern was family and tradition, the agricultural way of life.

During harvest, Thomas would ride on the
(30) enormous thresher with his father. In the cabin, above the green sea parting before them, he would listen as his father explained the significance of a life dedicated to agriculture. As Thomas nibbled on a lunch packed by his mother, his father
(35) expounded upon his philosophy that a man must not be separated from the land that provides for him, that the land was sacrosanct. He would say, time and again, "A man isn't a man without land to call his own."
(40) He was not an uneducated man, Thomas's father. He had completed high school and probably could have gone to college if he wanted, but he

was a man of the earth, and his spirit was tied to the soil. Agriculture was not his profession; it was
(45) his passion, one that he tried to seed in the hearts of his three boys. Thomas's two older brothers had little time for farm work, however. What chores they were not forced to do went undone or were done by Thomas; their energies were focused on
(50) cars, dating, and dance halls.

Even at a young age, Thomas was able to see in his father's eyes the older man's secret despair. The land that had been in his family for three generations was not valued by the fourth. Not even little
(55) Tommy, who always rode in the cabin with him and helped out as much as he was able, would stay and tend the fields. The world had grown too large, and there were too many distractions to lure young men from their homes. Boys these days did
(60) not realize they had a home until it was too late.

Sitting on the hood of his jeep, Thomas gazed out over dozens of acres of orange survey stakes that covered what was once his family's farm. The house, barn, and silos were all gone, replaced by construc-
(65) tion trailers and heavy equipment. The town that lay just five miles up the road had grown into a city, consuming land like a hungry beast. Thomas's father had been the last farmer left in the county, holding out long after the farm became unprof-
(70) itable. He farmed after his sons left and his wife died; he farmed until his last breath, on principle.

Now a highway and several shopping malls were going to take his place, Thomas thought. His brothers both said it was inevitable, that progress
(75) cannot be halted. They argued that if the family did not sell the land, the city would claim eminent domain and take it from them for a fraction of what they could get by selling it. Thomas did not feel he had any right to disagree. After all, he had
(80) chosen to leave the farm as well, to pursue his education. Though he didn't stand in their way, and though his profit from the lucrative sale was equal to his brothers', Thomas was sure he felt something that they could not. The money didn't
(85) matter much to him; he had enough to get by. It was something about the land. Now that he had finally found his way back to it, he was losing it. He was losing his home.

GO ON TO THE NEXT PAGE

14. The opening sentence primarily serves to introduce a sense of

    (A) urgency
    (B) immediacy
    (C) accurate recollection
    (D) purposeful contemplation
    (E) passing time

15. In line 7, the word "spears" most nearly means

    (A) spires
    (B) structures
    (C) weapons
    (D) shoots
    (E) thorns

16. The final sentence of the first paragraph most clearly conveys

    (A) a foreshadowing of developments that are described later in the passage
    (B) the ease with which one can avoid getting lost in a cornfield
    (C) the simplicity of Thomas's childhood
    (D) the importance of corn to Thomas's father
    (E) the joy Thomas took as a boy in wandering the cornfields

17. In line 22, the word "taxing" most nearly means

    (A) monetary
    (B) expensive
    (C) rejuvenating
    (D) tiring
    (E) unskilled

18. Which of the following terms would Thomas most likely use to describe his father?

    (A) aristocratic
    (B) naive
    (C) autonomous
    (D) cosmopolitan
    (E) dogmatic

19. Based on the passage, a thresher (line 30) is most likely used to

    (A) mend fences
    (B) harvest crops
    (C) construct shopping malls
    (D) plant seeds
    (E) survey land

20. Thomas's father's statement in lines 38–39 ("a man...own") primarily shows the father to be

    (A) discouraged because he is getting less money for his corn each year
    (B) overwhelmed by the number of tedious chores he must complete each day
    (C) convinced that his life as a farmer is worth-while
    (D) pleased that his youngest son is with him as he threshes the corn
    (E) grateful that he is making enough money to support his family

21. The most likely cause of the "secret despair" (line 52) that Thomas sees in his father's eyes is the father's

    (A) disappointment that Thomas didn't help as much as he could have with the farm chores
    (B) worry about his sons' preoccupation with cars, dating, and dancing
    (C) regret that he didn't attend college even though he could have done so
    (D) unhappiness with his marriage
    (E) sadness that his sons would not care for the family farm in the same way that he had

GO ON TO THE NEXT PAGE

22. The description in lines 46–50 of Thomas's brother's interests ("Thomas's. . .dance halls") highlights

    (A) the difference between the brothers as young men and as adults

    (B) reasons that Thomas performed the brothers' neglected chores

    (C) the considerable conflict between the brothers and their father

    (D) the brothers' desire to profit from the sale of the farm

    (E) the dichotomy between the brothers' values and those of their father

23. An important function of the sixth paragraph is to

    (A) establish that the narrative to this point has been a flashback

    (B) contrast Thomas's current life with his past life

    (C) show that the timeline of the story has been in reverse chronological order

    (D) summarize the plot

    (E) foreshadow Thomas's future

24. The last sentence of the passage ("He. . .home") suggests that Thomas feels

    (A) regretful nostalgia

    (B) excited anticipation

    (C) righteous anger

    (D) overwhelming despair

    (E) unaccustomed relief

IF YOU FINISH BEFORE TIME IS CALLED, YOU MAY CHECK YOUR WORK ON THIS SECTION ONLY. DO NOT TURN TO ANY OTHER SECTION IN THE TEST.

STOP

SECTION 3
Time—25 Minutes
20 Questions

Directions: For this section, solve each problem and decide which is the best of the choices given. Fill in the corresponding oval on the answer sheet. You may use any available space for scratchwork.

Notes:

(1) Calculator use is permitted.

(2) All numbers used are real numbers.

(3) Figures are provided for some problems. All figures are drawn to scale and lie in a plane UNLESS otherwise indicated.

(4) Unless otherwise specified, the domain of any function f is assumed to be the set of all real numbers x for which $f(x)$ is a real number.

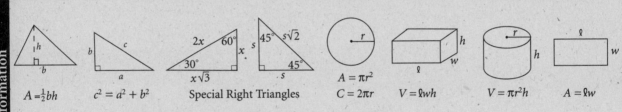

$A = \frac{1}{2}bh$ $c^2 = a^2 + b^2$ Special Right Triangles $C = 2\pi r$ $V = \ell wh$ $V = \pi r^2 h$ $A = \ell w$

The sum of the degree measures of the angles in a triangle is 180.
The number of degrees of arc in a circle is 360.
A straight angle has a degree measure of 180.

1. If $a^3 - b = a^3 - 5$, then $b =$

   (A) -5
   (B) $-\sqrt[3]{5}$
   (C) $\sqrt[3]{5}$
   (D) 5
   (E) 15

2. A certain pie is made by baking the crust for 7 to 10 minutes, adding the filling, and baking the entire pie for another 15 to 18 minutes. What are the minimum and maximum total baking times for this pie?

   (A) 7 minutes and 10 minutes
   (B) 10 minutes and 18 minutes
   (C) 15 minutes and 18 minutes
   (D) 22 minutes and 25 minutes
   (E) 22 minutes and 28 minutes

3. If $\frac{q}{r} = 4$, $\frac{q}{s} = 6$, and $s = 2$, what is the value of r?

   (A) 2
   (B) 3
   (C) 5
   (D) 6
   (E) 12

4. Between which two digits of the number 987654 should a decimal point be placed so that the value of the resulting number is equal to 9.87654×10^4?

   (A) 9 and 8
   (B) 8 and 7
   (C) 7 and 6
   (D) 6 and 5
   (E) 5 and 4

GO ON TO THE NEXT PAGE

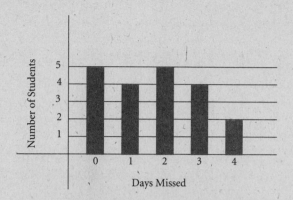

Days Missed

5. The bar graph above shows the number of days of class that 20 students missed. What is the average (arithmetic mean) number of days that each student missed?

(A) 1

(B) 1.5

(C) 1.7

(D) 2

(E) 2.3

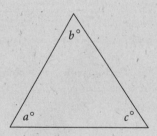

Note: Figure not drawn to scale.

6. In the figure above, if $b = 2a$ and $c = 3a$, what is the value of a?

(A) 20

(B) 30

(C) 45

(D) 50

(E) 60

7. After 4 apples were added to a sack, there were 3 times as many apples in the sack as before. How many apples were in the sack before the addition?

(A) 0

(B) 1

(C) 2

(D) 3

(E) 4

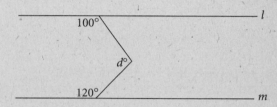

8. In the figure above, lines l and m are parallel. What is the value of d?

(A) 100

(B) 110

(C) 120

(D) 130

(E) 140

9. The value of $x + 6$ is how much greater than the value of $x - 2$?

(A) 4

(B) 6

(C) 8

(D) $x + 4$

(E) $x + 8$

GO ON TO THE NEXT PAGE

10. If $a < b < c < 0$, which of the following must be true?

    I $a - b < c$
   II $-a > -c$
  III $a + b < b + c$

(A) I only
(B) III only
(C) I and II only
(D) II and III only
(E) I, II, and III

11. Jo spends 25 percent of her monthly income on food, 30 percent on rent, 20 percent on insurance, and 10 percent on entertainment and miscellaneous expenses. Of her remaining income, she gives half to charity and saves the rest. If Jo saves 75 dollars every month, what is her total monthly income?

(A) $1,000
(B) $1,500
(C) $1,600
(D) $2,500
(E) $5,000

12. Which of the following equations represents the statement "When the square of q is subtracted from the square root of the sum of r and s, the result is equal to the square of the sum of t and r"?

(A) $(r + s)^2 - q^2 = (t + r)^2$
(B) $(r + s)^2 + q^2 = (t - r)^2$
(C) $\sqrt{r + s} - q^2 = (t + r)^2$
(D) $q^2 - \sqrt{r + s} = (t - r)^2$
(E) $q^2 - \sqrt{(r + s)^2} = (t + r)^2$

13. Line l has a slope of 1 and contains the point $(1, 2)$. Which of the following points is also on line l?

(A) $(1, 1)$
(B) $(2, 2)$
(C) $(1, 3)$
(D) $(0, 2)$
(E) $(2, 3)$

14. For all real numbers x and y, let ♣ be defined by $x ♣ y = x^2 - y$. What is the value of $4 ♣ (3 ♣ 2)$?

(A) 1
(B) 9
(C) 15
(D) 24
(E) 40

15. If q and r are prime numbers, which of the following CANNOT be a prime number?

(A) $q + r$
(B) $q - r$
(C) qr
(D) $qr + 1$
(E) $qr + 2$

16. If the lengths of two sides of a triangle are 9 and 15, which of the following CANNOT be the length of the third side?

(A) 5
(B) 9
(C) 10
(D) 15
(E) 20

GO ON TO THE NEXT PAGE

17. If a and b are positive integers and the ratio of $a + 2$ to $b + 2$ is the same as the ratio of $a + 4$ to $b + 4$, which of the following must be true?

    I. $a = b$
    II. $a = 2$
    III. $b = 2a$

  (A) None
  (B) I only
  (C) II only
  (D) III only
  (E) II and III only

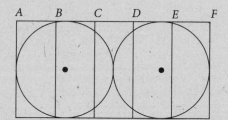

18. The figure above shows two circles of equal size. Each circle is tangent to the other circle at one point and tangent to the large rectangle at three points. The vertical line segments that intersect the large rectangle at points A through F divide the large rectangle into five smaller rectangles of equal size. If the length of line segment AB is 2, what is the radius of each circle?

  (A) 2
  (B) 2.25
  (C) 2.5
  (D) 3
  (E) 5

19. For any positive odd integer k, how many even integers are greater than zero and less than k?

  (A) $k - 1$

  (B) $\dfrac{k}{2}$

  (C) $\dfrac{2}{k}$

  (D) $\dfrac{k-1}{2}$

  (E) $\dfrac{2}{k-1}$

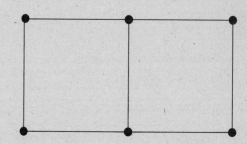

20. In the figure above, a one-foot by two-foot lattice is constructed from 7 one-foot pipes and 6 connectors of two types: 4 L connectors, each of which joins 2 pipes, and 2 T connectors, each of which joins 3 pipes. Which of the following gives the correct number of each type of connector that would be used to make a one-foot by five-foot lattice in the same way?

  (A) 4 L, 5 T
  (B) 4 L, 8 T
  (C) 4 L, 10 T
  (D) 20 L, 8 T
  (E) 20 L, 10 T

SECTION 4
Time—25 Minutes
35 Questions

Directions: For each question in this section, select the best answer from among the choices given and fill in the corresponding oval on the answer sheet.

The following sentences test correctness and effectiveness of expression. Part of each sentence or the entire sentence is underlined; beneath each sentence are five ways of phrasing the underlined material. Choice (A) repeats the original phrasing; the other four choices are different. If you think the original phrasing produces a better sentence than any of the alternatives, select choice (A); if not, select one of the other choices.

In making your selection, follow the requirements of standard written English; that is, pay attention to grammar, choice of words, sentence construction, and punctuation. Your selection should result in the most effective sentence—clear and precise, without awkwardness or ambiguity.

EXAMPLE: ANSWER:

Every apple in the baskets <u>are ripe and labeled according to the date it was picked</u>.   Ⓐ ● Ⓒ Ⓓ Ⓔ

(A) are ripe and labeled according to the date it was picked
(B) is ripe and labeled according to the date it was picked
(C) are ripe and labeled according to the date they were picked
(D) is ripe and labeled according to the date they were picked
(E) are ripe and labeled as to the date it was picked

---

1. Hearing that the test results exceeded state mandates, <u>a party was thrown by the math teacher</u> for the students.

   (A) a party was thrown by the math teacher
   (B) a party was thrown
   (C) the math teacher was thrown a party
   (D) the math teacher threw a party
   (E) the math teacher had thrown a party

2. Many students prefer social studies over <u>science classes, another one of the preferences is that students prefer English</u> over foreign-language classes.

   (A) science classes, another one of the preferences is that students prefer English
   (B) science classes, which is also a preference for English
   (C) science classes; another student preference is for English
   (D) science classes; another preference is that students prefer English
   (E) science classes; students prefer English

GO ON TO THE NEXT PAGE ▷

3. Joe Smith wrote the biography but refused <u>to be credit as the author nor in any other capacity</u> for the commercial success of the book.

   (A) to be credit as the author nor in any other capacity

   (B) to be credit as the author or

   (C) to be credited as the author nor in any other capacity

   (D) to be credited as the author or

   (E) to neither be credited as the author nor

4. George Balanchine was <u>almost as skillful a dancer as he was at choreography.</u>

   (A) almost as skillful a dancer as he was at choreography

   (B) almost as skillful at dance as he was a choreographer

   (C) almost skillful as a dancer and a choreographer

   (D) almost as skillful a dancer as at choreography

   (E) almost as skillful a dancer as he was a choreographer

5. Staring out over the ocean, <u>the waves gave the sailor a sense of stability.</u>

   (A) the waves gave the sailor a sense of stability

   (B) the sailor gave a sense of stability to the waves

   (C) the sailor felt a sense of stability from the waves

   (D) waving gave the sailor a sense of stability

   (E) the waves gave a sense of stability to the sailor

6. <u>Many football players vent their anger on the playing field, daily in their lives they are calm though.</u>

   (A) Many football players vent their anger on the playing field, daily in their lives they are calm though.

   (B) Many football players vent their anger on the playing field, though in their daily lives they are calmer than that.

   (C) Many football players are angrier on the playing field than daily.

   (D) Many football players vent their anger on the playing field though in their daily lives they are calm.

   (E) Many football players vent their anger on the playing field, though calm in their daily lives.

7. Certain constellations have a particular meaning for those people <u>which have a belief in astrology.</u>

   (A) which have a belief in astrology

   (B) who believe in astrology

   (C) whom believe in astrology

   (D) that believe in astrology

   (E) who believe in horoscopes

8. <u>Relying on its news, CNN is a television station many people watch.</u>

   (A) Relying on its news, CNN is a television station many people watch.

   (B) Relying on its news, the television station CNN is the one many people watch.

   (C) A television station watched by many people relying on its news is CNN.

   (D) Relying on its news, many people watch the television station CNN.

   (E) Many people, relying on CNN, and watching it.

GO ON TO THE NEXT PAGE

KAPLAN
Test Prep and Admissions

9. The technique of Impressionism is perhaps best seen <u>in either Monet's or Renoir's</u> work.

   (A) in either Monet's or Renoir's

   (B) either in Monet's or in Renoir's

   (C) either Monet's or Renoir's

   (D) within Monet's or Renoir's

   (E) in Monet's or Renoir's

10. Tom hated to watch <u>golf, of which he found the length particularly boring</u>.

   (A) golf, of which he found the length particularly boring

   (B) golf; he found the length particularly boring

   (C) golf, which he found particularly boring

   (D) golf, to which he found the length particularly boring

   (E) golf; which he found particularly boring in length

11. The government <u>imposed sanctions on a renegade nation last month after they violated</u> the terms of a worldwide arms-control agreement.

   (A) imposed sanctions on a renegade nation last month after they violated

   (B) imposed sanctions on a renegade nation last month after it was violating

   (C) has imposed sanctions on a renegade nation last month after they violated

   (D) imposed sanctions on a renegade nation last month after that nation violated

   (E) imposed sanctions on a nation of renegades last month after they violated

GO ON TO THE NEXT PAGE

Directions: The following sentences test your ability to recognize grammar and usage errors. Each sentence contains either a single error or no error at all. No sentence contains more than one error. The error, if there is one, is underlined and lettered. If the sentence contains an error, select the one underlined part that must be changed to make the sentence correct. If the sentence is correct, select choice (E). In choosing answers, follow the requirements of standard written English.

EXAMPLE:

<u>Whenever</u> one is driving late at night, <u>you</u> must take extra precautions <u>against</u>
   A   B   C

falling asleep <u>at the wheel</u>. <u>No error</u>
            D   E

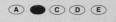

---

12. <u>That</u> his presentation on financial strategy was
   A
criticized <u>savagely</u> by his customers <u>who</u> watched it
           B   C
<u>came</u> as a shock to the analyst. <u>No error</u>
 D   E

13. A downfall in the economy could affect the ballet

season because programs <u>performed</u> in the new
                          A

symphony hall <u>cost</u> twice <u>as much</u> in overhead as
              B   C
<u>the old performance space</u>. <u>No error</u>
          D   E

14. The other students and <u>her</u> <u>distinctly</u> felt taken
                    A   B
<u>advantage of</u> when tested <u>on facts</u> not learned in
   C   D
class. <u>No error</u>
     E

15. The <u>other</u> cyclists and <u>me</u> <u>immediately</u> started
       A   B   C
pedaling when we heard the whistle <u>blown</u> by the
                           D
race organizer. <u>No error</u>
            E

16. <u>Although</u> the amount of money in the bank
    A
accounts <u>keep</u> dwindling, the account holders
          B
<u>claim that</u> their finances <u>are improving</u>. <u>No error</u>
   C   D   E

17. To compare a new investment opportunity <u>to one's</u>
                                         A
previous stock losses <u>is a more</u> advantageous
                    B
strategy <u>than</u> <u>attempting</u> to turn a profit without
          C   D
referring back to them. <u>No error</u>
                   E

18. <u>Like</u> that of many braggarts, <u>the businessman's</u>
    A   B
success sounded <u>impressive</u> but in fact was not
                C
because he had done no work <u>to attain</u> it. <u>No error</u>
                       D   E

19. Permanent <u>loss of</u> eyesight if <u>they stare</u> <u>too long</u> at
            A   B   C
the sun <u>is a common</u> problem during eclipses.
         D
<u>No error</u>
 E

GO ON TO THE NEXT PAGE

20. The bidders <u>for</u> the museum-restored, newly
        A
    framed painting <u>clearly</u> wanted <u>to purchase</u> <u>artistic</u>
          B   C   D
    recognized work for their collections. <u>No error</u>
                                  E

21. No one <u>dares</u> to contradict the high school
         A
    principal, <u>for</u> she has the authority <u>to detract</u> from
           B   C
    a student's grade point average <u>for any</u> reason.
                            D
    <u>No error</u>
      E

22. The store manager <u>telephoned</u> the warehouse
               A
    manager <u>after</u> <u>he failed</u> <u>to deliver</u> the products on
         B   C   D
    the correct day. <u>No error</u>
               E

23. The doctors <u>researching</u> diseases <u>affecting the</u> liver
             A   B
    <u>find</u> that the consumption of alcohol was <u>generally</u>
     C   D
    an indicator of susceptibility to the disease.

    <u>No error</u>
      E

24. The scientist <u>conducting</u> the experiment in the rain
             A
    forest was less interested in why the particular

    species was prevalent <u>than in</u> whether <u>they have</u>
                  B   C
    <u>violently</u> taken over another species' habitat.
      D
    <u>No error</u>
      E

25. Voters in the school-board election <u>who chose</u> the
                          A
    candidate on the ballot <u>includes</u> <u>at least</u> twenty
                   B   C
    <u>whose</u> votes were influenced by the candidate's
     D
    delicious cookies. <u>No error</u>
                E

26. During the debate, Jack <u>attended closely</u> to the
                    A
    Independent Party candidate's economic plan,

    <u>which Jack</u> thought was <u>better structured</u>
        B   C
    <u>than the other candidate.</u> <u>No error</u>
        D   E

27. Edward Villella's talent enables him <u>to stage</u> ballets
                          A
    <u>that develop from</u> <u>and incorporate</u> the feeling that
         B   C
    George Balanchine <u>intended.</u> <u>No error</u>
              D   E

28. Many people claim <u>to have seen</u> UFOs, <u>but</u> not one
                A   B
    <u>have</u> proved that <u>such an object</u> exists. <u>No error</u>
      C   D   E

29. This year, the company <u>announces</u> Take Your
                 A
    Daughter to Work Day in an effort <u>to build</u> the
                        B
    morale <u>of employees</u> in the head office
         C
    <u>during the recession.</u> <u>No error</u>
        D   E

GO ON TO THE NEXT PAGE ⇨

Directions: The following passage is an early draft of an essay. Some parts of the passage need to be rewritten.

Read the passage and select the best answer for each question that follows. Some questions are about particular sentences or parts of sentences and ask you to improve sentence structure or word choice. Other questions ask you to consider organization and development. In choosing answers, follow the conventions of standard written English.

Questions 30–35 are based on the following passage.

(1) At the bowling alley, a large wooden placard declared "Brookfield Alley's Best Bowler of the Year." (2) When asked whose picture was placed below it, the owner said they always placed the picture of the person who scored the highest score in a single game during the previous year. (3) When asked who "they" was, he answered, "The owner of the bowling alley." (4) When asked who that was, the answer was "Me." (5) So, basically, I determined, the owner of the bowling alley chose the bowler of the year.

(6) My brother, Bill, had his picture there one year. (7) However, I am a better bowler than my brother. (8) He had a lucky game. (9) Now, don't get me wrong. (10) Bill is a good bowler. (11) That high game was a 269. (12) That is a good score in anyone's book. (13) But, it was a fluke. (14) Bill got lucky. (15) He bowled a bunch of strikes in a row. (16) He got on a roll. (17) His success seemed to breed more success in each succeeding frame. (18) He kept on getting them. (19) He messed up in the 7th frame, but then pulled out a spare. (20) On the next frame, he got a strike again. (21) The owner started watching. (22) The game got verified. (23) Bill became the "Bowler of the Year."

(24) For Christmas that year, my parents had the clipping from the newspaper framed. (25) I cringed when I saw that. (26) Bill was not the "Bowler of the Year." (27) He wasn't even the bowler of that night. (28) We had bowled three games. (29) I had won the first two games handily. (30) But, then Bill had his streak of luck. (31) And, like I said before, the owner noticed. (32) So, good ole Bill became bowler of the year. (33) Baloney!

30. Based on the first paragraph, is the use of the word *they* in sentence 2 accurately used and why?

(A) It is used accurately because it is a report of the owner's words when he answered a question.

(B) It is used inaccurately because the author of the text has turned the owner of the bowling alley into a *they*.

(C) It is not used accurately because one should never use a pronoun without its antecedent in the sentence.

(D) It is used correctly because *they* refers to the author and his brother.

(E) It should be *them*.

31. If one wanted to combine sentence 11 and sentence 12, which would be the best way to do so?

(A) That high game was a 269; and that is a high score in anyone's book.

(B) That high score was a 296, and that was a high score for anyone's book.

(C) That high game was a 269, and that is a high score in anyone's book.

(D) Because 269 is a high score in anyone's book, that was a high game.

(E) That high game was a 269, but that was a high score in anyone's book.

GO ON TO THE NEXT PAGE

32. According to the passage, the award of the best bowler of the year assumes that

    (A) bowlers come in all shapes, sizes, and ages, but that it is the number of points overall that matter

    (B) top performance in a single game is the best measure of a bowler

    (C) bowlers' averages may fluctuate but the top score is the true measure of their growth

    (D) the top bowler usually also has the top average for the year

    (E) bowling is a team sport with individual contribution

33. The tone of this passage could best be described as

    (A) business
    (B) informational
    (C) persuasive
    (D) sarcastic
    (E) expository

34. In which type of publication would this passage most likely appear?

    (A) a news story
    (B) a factual magazine article
    (C) an anthology of narrative poetry
    (D) a memoir
    (E) a college advice guide

35. If you were asked to combine sentences 14 and 15 into a single sentence, which would be the best choice?

    (A) Bill got lucky; and, he bowled a bunch of strikes in a row.

    (B) Lucky Bill, he bowled a bunch of strikes in a row.

    (C) He bowled a bunch of strikes in a row because he was lucky.

    (D) Bill got lucky and bowled a bunch of strikes in a row.

    (E) Bill's luck caused him to bowl a bunch of strikes in a row.

IF YOU FINISH BEFORE TIME IS CALLED, YOU MAY CHECK YOUR WORK ON THIS SECTION ONLY. DO NOT TURN TO ANY OTHER SECTION IN THE TEST. **STOP**

SECTION 5
Time—25 Minutes
24 Questions

Directions: For each of the following questions, choose the best answer and darken the corresponding oval on the answer sheet.

Each sentence below has one or two blanks, each blank indicating that something has been omitted. Beneath the sentence are five words or sets of words labeled (A) through (E). Choose the word or set of words that, when inserted in the sentence, <u>best</u> fits the meaning of the sentence as a whole.

EXAMPLE:

Today's small, portable computers contrast markedly with the earliest electronic computers, which were ----.

(A) effective
(B) invented
(C) useful
(D) destructive
(E) enormous

1. Because he was usually so ----, Mr. Harris shocked his students with his violent reaction to their minor misbehavior in class.

   (A) knowledgeable
   (B) articulate
   (C) trustworthy
   (D) insistent
   (E) tranquil

2. Because Phillis Wheatley exposed the injustices of slavery in her poems, some of which were written as early as the 1760s, she is believed to be in the ---- of American abolitionists.

   (A) vanguard
   (B) service
   (C) rear
   (D) favor
   (E) realm

3. The earth hosts a ---- of insects—a number so large that it is easy to imagine the planet's surface as a heaving mass of tiny life.

   (A) dearth
   (B) rehash
   (C) profusion
   (D) moderation
   (E) jumble

4. The observation that a significant percentage of the population did not ---- the Black Plague has led scientists to study the descendants of the survivors in hopes of discovering a gene that provided ----.

   (A) fear .. immortality
   (B) recognize .. health
   (C) struggle with .. strength
   (D) contract .. immunity
   (E) believe in .. responsibility

5. Although Susan B. Anthony and Elizabeth Cady Stanton came from ---- backgrounds, they overcame their differences in a ---- effort to secure for women the right to vote.

   (A) conventional .. failed
   (B) diverse .. joint
   (C) discordant .. beleaguered
   (D) dignified .. frivolous
   (E) similar .. united

GO ON TO THE NEXT PAGE

Directions: The passages below are followed by questions based on their content; questions following a pair of related passages may also be based on the relationship between the paired passages. Answer the questions on the basis of what is <u>stated</u> or <u>implied</u> in the passages and in any introductory material that may be provided.

Questions 6–7 are based on the following passage.

Ever since the movie *Jaws*, sharks have been feared and reviled as menaces of the sea. Can you picture, then, a shark swimming close to the surface of the ocean, its mouth wide open, looking
(5) for all the world like it's "catching rays"? The basking shark, named for its propensity to bask (or laze about) in the sun, does just that. Don't be fooled, though; like all sharks, the basking shark can be dangerous to human beings. In fact, there
(10) are reports of harpooned basking sharks attacking the boat in which the harpooner is riding. In addition, the basking shark's skin contains dermal denticles that have seriously wounded divers and scientists who have come in contact with the
(15) sharks.

6. The second sentence ("Can...rays") is meant to convey

(A) a comical picture of an animal that is usually regarded as menacing

(B) that sharks are not dangerous, despite their portrayal in *Jaws*

(C) an in-depth look at the habits of the basking shark

(D) the reason why basking sharks have attacked boats

(E) why sharks are menaces of the sea

7. A "dermal denticle" (lines 12–13) is most likely

(A) one of the basking shark's teeth

(B) a dangerous part of the basking shark's skin

(C) something that protects the basking shark from the sun

(D) a conduit for the basking shark's food

(E) the only way a basking shark can defend itself

Questions 8–9 are based on the following passage.

While some playwrights are known for writing essays defending their own work or criticizing the work of competing writers, Arthur Miller's essays are simply about theater. While we may discover
(5) politics and favoritism when we comb through Miller's essays looking for such things, in doing so, we may risk missing the point of the works— Miller wants only for us to benefit from his years of experience. Even his earliest essays read as vir-
(10) tual how-to manuals for new playwrights and directors. These works ring with clarity and forthrightness, and are filled with thoughtful and often provocative opinions. These essays teach us what the theater is, what it might be, and how to make
(15) it so.

8. In lines 9–10, "virtual" most nearly means

(A) organic

(B) electronic

(C) moral

(D) near

(E) cybernetic

9. The author of the passage suggests that Miller's essays differ from other playwrights' essays in that

(A) Miller's essays are more recent than those of other playwrights

(B) Miller wrote more essays than most other playwrights

(C) Miller's essays have had more influence than anyone else's

(D) Miller's essays are not self-serving

(E) Miller wrote essays about American theater

GO ON TO THE NEXT PAGE

Questions 10–15 are based on the following passage.

In 1838, at the age of twenty, Frederick Douglass escaped from slavery. He became a journalist and powerful speaker for the abolition movement, and, in 1845, published his autobiographical Narrative of the Life of Frederick Douglass, an American Slave. *The passage below is excerpted from that work.*

I lived in Master Hugh's family for about seven years. During this time, I succeeded in learning to read and write. In accomplishing this, I was compelled to resort to various stratagems. I had no
(5) regular teacher. My mistress, who had kindly begun to instruct me, had finally taken the advice of her husband and not only ceased to instruct but had set herself against my being instructed by anyone else.
(10) The plan I adopted was that of making friends of all the little white boys whom I met in the street. As many of these as I could, I converted into teachers. With their aid, I finally succeeded in learning to read. When I was sent on errands, I
(15) always took my book with me, and by doing my errand quickly I found time to get a lesson before my return. I used to carry bread with me, which was always in the house and to which I was always welcome. This bread I used to bestow upon the
(20) hungry urchins, who in return would give me that more valuable bread of knowledge. I am strongly tempted to give the names of two or three of those boys, but prudence forbids—not that it would injure me, but it might embarrass them; for it is
(25) almost an unpardonable offense to teach slaves to read in this Christian country. It is enough to say that the fellows lived on Philpot Street, very near Durgin and Bailey's shipyard.
I was now about twelve years old, and the
(30) thought of being a slave for life began to bear heavily upon my heart. Just about this time, I got hold of a book entitled *The Columbian Orator*, where I met with one of Sheridan's* mighty speeches on behalf of Catholic emancipation.
(35) These were choice documents to me. They gave tongue to interesting thoughts of my own, which had died away for want of utterance. The moral which I gained from the dialogue between master and slave was the power of truth over the

(40) conscience of even a slaveholder. What I got from Sheridan was a bold denunciation of slavery and a powerful vindication of human rights. The reading of these documents enabled me to utter my thoughts and to meet the arguments brought
(45) forward to sustain slavery.
But while they relieved me of one difficulty, they brought on another even more painful. The more I read, the more I was led to abhor my enslavers. I could regard them in no other light
(50) than as a band of successful robbers, who had left their homes, and gone to Africa, and stolen us from our homes, and in a strange land reduced us to slavery. As I read and contemplated the subject, behold! that very discontentment which Master
(55) Hugh had predicted would follow my learning to read had come. Learning to read had given me a view of my condition, without the remedy. The idea of freedom had roused my soul to eternal wakefulness. It was heard in every sound, and seen
(60) in every thing. It was ever present to torment me with a sense of my wretched condition.

Richard Sheridan (1751–1816): an English writer and politician, was famous for his speeches calling for full citizenship for Roman Catholics and the abolition of slavery in the British Empire.

10. The primary focus of the passage is on the

(A) interaction between Douglass and various childhood friends

(B) difficult relationship between Douglass and his master and mistress

(C) ways in which learning to read influenced Douglass's attitude towards slavery

(D) the importance of literature in civil rights movements

(E) powerful impact of Sheridan's political speeches

GO ON TO THE NEXT PAGE

11. According to paragraph 1, Douglass was "compelled to resort to various stratagems" (lines 3–4) because his mistress

    (A) persisted in ignoring her husband's advice

    (B) was alarmed at his growing opposition to slavery

    (C) realized that educating slaves was against the law

    (D) was frustrated by the lack of progress in his reading lessons

    (E) was opposed to his learning to read

12. In line 21, the reference to "the bread of knowledge" is used to emphasize

    (A) the urgent need for food among the poor

    (B) the generosity of the Hugh family towards Douglass

    (C) the relationship between wealth and education

    (D) the importance Douglass attached to his lessons

    (E) the availability of bread in Douglass's area

13. In line 30, "bear" most likely means

    (A) carry

    (B) weigh

    (C) experience

    (D) suffer

    (E) endure

14. In line 50, the author most likely describes slaveowners as "a band of successful robbers" in order to

    (A) dispel some misconceptions about the legitimacy of slavery

    (B) portray the emotional trials involved in acquiring knowledge

    (C) suggest the unpopularity of slaveowners amongst human rights advocates

    (D) emphasize his increasing anger against the system of slavery

    (E) indicate the accuracy of his master's predictions

15. In lines 58–59, the phrase "eternal wakefulness" suggests that Douglass

    (A) was unable to determine the causes of his unhappiness

    (B) approached life with a renewed sense of optimism

    (C) searched constantly for a plan to make his way to freedom

    (D) was preoccupied by an awareness of his enslaved condition

    (E) devoted most of his time to researching his African origins

GO ON TO THE NEXT PAGE

Questions 16–22 are based on the following passage.

The following is adapted from a medical reference guide regarding the heart and cardiovascular system.

The heart is responsible for moving blood to all of the body's tissues through a 60,000-mile net-work of vessels. The pumping of the heart relies on an intricate system of muscle (myocardium),
(5) valves, coronary vessels, the conduction (electri-cal) system, arteries and veins, and the sac around the heart (pericardium).

The human heart is divided into four chambers, the walls of which are made of the myocardium,
(10) the muscle that contracts rhythmically under the stimulation of electrical currents. The myocardi-um is composed of individual muscle cells called myocytes, which work together to contract and relax the heart chambers in the correct sequence
(15) to pump blood to the lungs and the body. The heart is able to pump blood in a coordinated manner because of the arrangement of the cells and the electrical messages that pass easily between the cells. This cardiovascular pump oper-
(20) ates by squeezing blood out of its chambers (con-traction) and then expanding to allow blood in (relaxation). The action is similar to squeezing water out of a soft plastic bottle while holding it under water and then releasing the grasp so that
(25) water is sucked back into the bottle as it re-expands.

The right side of the heart, which is composed of the right atrium and right ventricle, is responsi-ble for pulmonary circulation. That is, it pumps
(30) blood through the lungs, where it receives oxygen and rids itself of carbon dioxide. The left side of the heart, composed of the left atrium and left ventricle, receives the newly oxygenated blood and pumps it through the body where it delivers oxy-
(35) gen and picks up carbon dioxide (waste). Blood must circle from the right side of the heart and through the lungs before being delivered to the left side and throughout the body.

"Used blood" returns to the right side of the
(40) heart via two large veins—the superior vena cava (from the head and arms) and the inferior vena cava (from the legs and abdomen). Blood from the right heart is dark bluish red because it is

deoxygenated, or lacks oxygen. The blood from
(45) the left heart is oxygenated, and therefore is bright red. Blood from the left heart is delivered to the body through the aorta, the largest blood vessel in the body.

Because the heart never rests while it supplies
(50) blood to the rest of the body, it actually works harder than any other muscle in the body and needs a much richer blood supply than other muscles. Although the heart makes up less than 1% of a person's body weight, it requires 4%–5%
(55) of its blood.

16. The passage is primarily concerned with

(A) pulmonary circulation
(B) the structure and function of the heart
(C) blood supply to the heart
(D) contraction and relaxation of the heart
(E) the cardiovascular system

17. Myocytes are muscle cells responsible for

(A) opening and closing the heart valves
(B) providing oxygen to the blood
(C) allowing the heart to rest
(D) contracting and relaxing the heart chambers
(E) circulating blood from the left side of the heart to the right side

18. "Relaxation" (line 22) most nearly means

(A) resting
(B) squeezing blood out of its chambers
(C) pumping
(D) releasing the grasp
(E) expanding to allow blood in

GO ON TO THE NEXT PAGE

19. Pulmonary circulation is

   (A) the right heart chamber

   (B) the pumping of blood through the lungs, where it is oxygenated

   (C) the pumping of blood through the aorta, which delivers it to the body

   (D) the left heart chamber

   (E) through the coronary blood vessels

20. In line 33, "oxygenated" most nearly means

   (A) supplied with oxygen

   (B) in need of oxygen

   (C) supplied with oxygen and carbon dioxide

   (D) bright red

   (E) dark bluish red

21. The author's use of quotation marks around "used blood" (line 39) implies

   (A) the blood is now waste

   (B) the blood is bright red

   (C) the blood is deoxygenated, and is now waste

   (D) the blood has circulated throughout the body

   (E) the blood must return to the left side of the heart

22. According to the passage, the heart requires how much of one's blood supply?

   (A) less than 1%

   (B) the same amount of blood as the body's other organs

   (C) 4%–5%

   (D) a richer supply

   (E) 1%

Questions 23–24 are based on the following passage.

Though I never found any hard evidence to prove the age-old story of a huge great white shark who wandered up the Hudson to attack a young girl swimming a creek, I did learn that it
(5) was not out of the realm of possibility. But if the attack did indeed occur, a bull shark more likely was the guilty party. Unlike their equally ferocious cousins the great white and tiger sharks, bull sharks can survive in bodies of water with lower
(10) levels of salinity than the ocean, and are known to frequent rivers such as the Amazon and Mississippi in search of prey.

23. As used in line 1, "hard" most closely means

   (A) hearsay

   (B) confidential

   (C) brutal

   (D) factual

   (E) theoretical

24. A tiger shark probably did not attack the girl because

   (A) it is not as dangerous as a great white or bull shark

   (B) is too small to inflict serious damage

   (C) tiger sharks have never been spotted in the Mississippi

   (D) the story is not true

   (E) they cannot adapt to river water

IF YOU FINISH BEFORE TIME IS CALLED, YOU MAY CHECK YOUR WORK ON THIS SECTION ONLY. DO NOT TURN TO ANY OTHER SECTION IN THE TEST.  STOP

SECTION 6

Time—25 Minutes

18 Questions

Directions: For this section, solve each problem and decide which is the best of the choices given. Fill in the corresponding oval on the answer sheet. You may use any available space for scratchwork.

Notes:

(1) Calculator use is permitted.

(2) All numbers used are real numbers.

(3) Figures are provided for some problems. All figures are drawn to scale and lie in a plane UNLESS otherwise indicated.

(4) Unless otherwise specified, the domain of any function f is assumed to be the set of all real numbers x for which $f(x)$ is a real number.

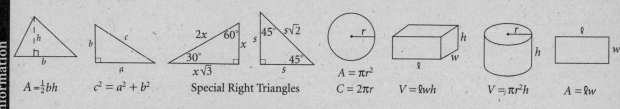

$A = \frac{1}{2}bh$ $\quad$ $c^2 = a^2 + b^2$ $\quad$ Special Right Triangles $\quad$ $A = \pi r^2$ $\quad$ $V = \ell wh$ $\quad$ $V = \pi r^2 h$ $\quad$ $A = \ell w$

$C = 2\pi r$

The sum of the degree measures of the angles in a triangle is 180.

The number of degrees of arc in a circle is 360.

A straight angle has a degree measure of 180.

1. If $\dfrac{5}{d} = \dfrac{3}{2}$, then $2d =$

   (A) $1\dfrac{2}{3}$

   (B) $3\dfrac{1}{3}$

   (C) $6\dfrac{2}{3}$

   (D) $7\dfrac{1}{2}$

   (E) 15

2. If every digit of a whole number is either a 1 or a 7, the number must be

   (A) prime

   (B) odd

   (C) even

   (D) divisible by 7

   (E) divisible by 11

3. If $9\sqrt{x} + 7 = 16$, $x =$

   (A) 1

   (B) 3

   (C) 5

   (D) 8

   (E) 9

4. In the equation $y = kx$, $x = 4$ when $y = 6$ and k is a constant. What is the value of y when $x = 16$?

   (A) 1

   (B) 2

   (C) 10

   (D) 14

   (E) 24

GO ON TO THE NEXT PAGE

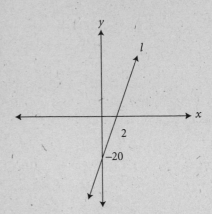

Note: Figure not drawn to scale.

5. Which of the following is the equation of line l in the graph above?

(A) $y = 10x - 20$
(B) $y = x^2 - 20$
(C) $y = 2x + 20$
(D) $y = 2x^2 - 10x$
(E) $y = x + 10$

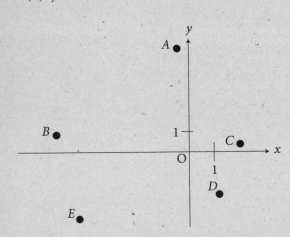

6. In the figure above, for which point is the product of the point's x-coordinate and y-coordinate the greatest?

(A) A
(B) B
(C) C
(D) D
(E) E

7. If $a = 9c^2 + 4$ and $b = 7 + 3c$, what is a in terms of b?

(A) $2b^2 - 7b + 49$
(B) $b^2 - 14b + 49$
(C) $b^2 + 14b + 49$
(D) $b^2 - 14b + 53$
(E) $b^2 + 14b + 53$

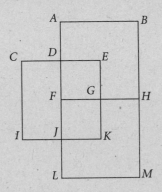

8. In the figure above, three identical squares overlap so that two smaller identical squares, $DEGF$ and $FGKJ$, are formed. If the area of square $ABHF$ is 100 square units, what is the area of figure $ABMLJICD$, in square units?

(A) 150
(B) 200
(C) 250
(D) 300
(E) 350

GO ON TO THE NEXT PAGE

Directions: For Student-Produced Response questions 9–18, use the grids at the bottom of the answer sheet page on which you have answered questions 1–8.

Each of the remaining 10 questions requires you to solve the problem and enter your answer by marking the ovals in the special grid, as shown in the example below. You may use any available space for scratch work.

Answer: 1.25 or $\frac{5}{4}$ or 5/4

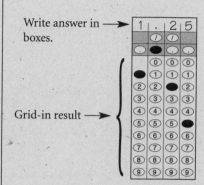

Write answer in boxes.

Grid-in result

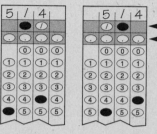

Fraction line
Decimal point

Either position is correct.

You may start your answers in any column, space permitting. Columns not needed should be left blank.

- It is recommended, though not required, that you write your answer in the boxes at the top of the columns. However, you will receive credit only for darkening the ovals correctly.

- Grid only one answer to a question, even though some problems have more than one correct answer.

- Darken no more than one oval in a column.

- No answers are negative.

- Mixed numbers cannot be gridded. For example: the number $1\frac{1}{4}$ must be gridded as 1.25 or 5/4.

(If ⏐1⏐1⏐/⏐4⏐ is gridded, it will be interpreted as $\frac{11}{4}$ not $1\frac{1}{4}$.)

- Decimal Accuracy: Decimal answers must be entered as accurately as possible. For example, if you obtain an answer such as 0.1666..., you should record the result as .166 or .167. **Less accurate values such as .16 or .17 are not acceptable.**

Acceptable ways to grid $\frac{1}{6}$ = .1666...

GO ON TO THE NEXT PAGE

9. If $d + 2h = 8$ and $4d = 10$, what is the value of h?

10. A certain book club charges $35.00 per year, plus $4.50 for every book ordered through the club. There are no other charges. If Mr. Jones was charged $62.00 in one year of membership in the book club, how many books did he order?

11. Points A, B, C, and D lie on a line in that order. B is the midpoint of segment AC and C is the midpoint of segment AD. If the length of segment AD is 16 centimeters, what is the length of segment BD in centimeters?

$$
\begin{array}{r}
AA \\
\times\, AA \\
\hline
ABA \\
\end{array}
$$

12. In the above equation, A and B represent distinct digits in a correctly solved multiplication problem. What is one possible value of $A + B$?

13. A restaurant has 25 entrées and 40 side dishes. If Mary wants to order one entrée and one side dish, how many different combinations of entrée and side dish could she order?

14. The last Friday of a 31-day month could be at most how many days after the first Monday of that same month?

15. For every positive integer n, $n! = n \times (n-1) \times (n-2)$.

For example, $4! = 4 \times 3 \times 2 \times 1 = 24$. What is the value of? $\dfrac{29!}{27!}$

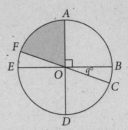

16. In the figure above, AD, BE, and CF are all diameters of the circle. If the shaded area is equal to $\dfrac{1}{6}$ the area of the circle, what is the value of q?

17. If the median of the values of $3x$, $5x$, and $\dfrac{1}{2}x$ is 18, then what is the value of x?

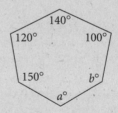

Note: Figure not drawn to scale.

18. In the figure above, what is the sum of a and b?

SECTION 7
Time—20 Minutes
19 Questions

Directions: For each of the following questions, choose the best answer and darken the corresponding oval on the answer sheet.

Each sentence below has one or two blanks, each blank indicating that something has been omitted. Beneath the sentence are five words or sets of words labeled (A) through (E). Choose the word or set of words that, when inserted in the sentence, best fits the meaning of the sentence as a whole.

EXAMPLE:

Today's small, portable computers contrast markedly with the earliest electronic computers, which were ----.

(A) effective
(B) invented
(C) useful
(D) destructive
(E) enormous   Ⓐ Ⓑ Ⓒ Ⓓ ●

1. While the federal government promised to ---- its tax forms, many taxpayers still find them so ---- that they have to seek professional assistance.

   (A) mystify . . infuriating
   (B) shorten . . expensive
   (C) replace . . comprehensible
   (D) simplify . . bewildering
   (E) rewrite . . familiar

2. The ---- hooves of the horses, the blaring of the trumpets, and the beating of drums combined to create a ---- on medieval battlefields.

   (A) thundering . . cacophony
   (B) running . . danger
   (C) furious . . horror
   (D) thrashing . . situation
   (E) plodding . . calm

3. Although the long-term effects of the council's measures could be ----, no one can deny that the city is now enjoying an increase in tourism.

   (A) stated
   (B) compared
   (C) discussed
   (D) inquired
   (E) debated

4. In order to maintain the ---- for which he was well known, the manager refused a tempting offer to ignore ---- in the corporation's accounting practices.

   (A) geniality . . irregularities
   (B) integrity . . improprieties
   (C) dishonesty . . policies
   (D) cordiality . . inconsistencies
   (E) frankness . . rules

5. Lee's ---- response to the teacher's inquiry earned her an unpleasant trip to the principal's office

   (A) reactionary
   (B) inveterate
   (C) pecuniary
   (D) flippant
   (E) lax

6. Gertrude Stein championed many ---- artists of her time because she appreciated the new and experimental nature of their art.

   (A) avant-garde
   (B) competitive
   (C) impugned
   (D) dilatory
   (E) mannered

GO ON TO THE NEXT PAGE ⇒

Directions: The passages below are followed by questions based on their content; questions following a pair of related passages may also be based on the relationship between the paired passages. Answer the questions on the basis of what is <u>stated</u> or <u>implied</u> in the passages and in any introductory material that may be provided.

Question 7–19 are based on the following passages.

The following adaptations from recent scholarly articles offer different perspectives on the harsh conditions faced by nineteenth century female factory workers in the urban centers of the United States. Both passages reflect the oppressive working environment created by the Waltham-Lowell system of organization in textile factories.

The Waltham-Lowell system, a business philosophy and manufacturing strategy, was named for its creator and the Massachusetts town in which it was first implemented in 1815. As a manufactur-
(5) ing system, it combined the various stages of the textile manufacturing process under one roof, while as a business system, it detailed a set of comprehensive rules and regulations for workers. To implement the Waltham-Lowell system, factory
(10) owners preferred to employ female workers—often called factory girls—because women would work for lower wages and were then considered easier to control than men.

Many of the system's regulations, including a
(15) requirement that the women live in company-owned boarding houses, had been created primarily to assure families that their daughters would not be corrupted by factory life. Ironically, however, many of the women employed were actually
(20) forced to leave their families' homes, even when those families lived within easy commuting distance of the factories, and even when the women were married. Needless to say, living away from home and among strangers was a stressful and
(25) disorienting experience for many.

The extremely poor living conditions of the boarding houses created further problems. Most factory houses were overcrowded, dirty, and infested with vermin. These conditions, combined
(30) with shared beds and poor ventilation, allowed diseases to spread and caused health problems for many of the workers. However, it's important for modern researchers to note that American factories were not alone in maintaining boarding

(35) houses for workers. In fact, conditions in company-run American boarding houses were actually uniformly superior to those in Europe, where conditions were even more cramped and the ethics of the owners more base.
(40) While these living conditions were regrettable, some economists have advanced that the managers of the textile factories had little choice. The American textile market of the last century was extremely competitive, since the supply of textiles
(45) created by the nation's numerous domestic factories far exceeded consumer demand. Furthermore, foreign competitors, including English and Indian factories, began selling excess textile products in America at the beginning of the 1800s.
(50) Compounding the problem, foreign textile factories could often afford to sell their products in the American market for less than domestic manufacturers, because foreign factories set their wages far below what Americans found tolerable. American
(55) factories were thus constantly facing the risk of bankruptcy, and many managers felt that taking measures to preserve the health, comfort, and safety of their factory workers would have been financial suicide.

Passage 2
(60) Widely utilized in the mid-nineteenth century, the Waltham-Lowell system encompassed a set of atrocious working rules that created a dismal environment for workers in textile factories. Many factory practices had ill effects on the health of
(65) workers, the majority of whom were young women. Loud machines running all day long in a small space affected the hearing of the workers, while poor ventilation filled the air with cotton lint and toxins from the whale-oil lamps used to
(70) light the factories.

Problems were not limited to purely environmental factors. Workers also lived in constant fear of the factories' agents—supervisors who would punish them severely for any time spent not work-

GO ON TO THE NEXT PAGE ▷

(75) ing. In fact, agents could fire workers almost at
whim because of the seemingly endless supply of
labor willing to replace the young women on the
factory floor. The workers were usually not
permitted to speak while operating the machines
(80) because the agents feared that talking would distract
the women from their work and slow production.
Not surprisingly, breaks were also infrequent, or
absent altogether—even bathroom breaks were
strongly discouraged. Ironically given these condi-
(85) tions, workers were expected to be neatly dressed
in clean clothes at all times in case someone of
note came to visit the mill. As a result, much of
what little free time the young women had was
spent washing or mending clothes.
(90)   Some aspects of the Waltham-Lowell system
were not only degrading but downright dangerous. The factory management's obsession with
keeping workers at their tasks extended to keeping
all factory doors locked during working hours. As
(95) a result, emergency evacuations were difficult or
impossible. In 1911, a fire broke out in New York
City's Triangle Shirtwaist Factory, and many workers died. Though one might hope that such a
tragedy would have finally brought about changes,
(100) the factory owners were actually acquitted of
criminal charges, and required to pay damages of
only seventy-five dollars to each of 23 victims'
families that sued. Sadly, the practice of locking
factory doors remained common for several years.
(105)   Though some charge that the Waltham-Lowell
system was a result of economic necessity, we
must realize that the factory managers who implemented this system made deliberate decisions to
increase profits at the expense of their workers,
(110) and that these workers—even those who fell ill or
died—were treated by factory managers as objects
to be replaced. Owners should instead have
replaced the reprehensible Waltham-Lowell system
with another: that of common decency, to be
(115) respected above the baser "ideals" of nineteenth-
century capitalism.

7. The attitude of the author of Passage 1 toward the
factory workers who endured harsh conditions is
best described as

(A) reserved sympathy

(B) complete disinterest

(C) ironic contempt

(D) spirited befuddlement

(E) unreserved appreciation

8. The word "base" as used in line 39 most nearly
means

(A) elevated

(B) immoral

(C) absent

(D) harmful

(E) foundational

9. According to Passage 1, the primary reason that
factories required factory workers to live in
boarding houses was to

(A) placate the fears of the workers' families

(B) ensure that the girls were not corrupted by
city life

(C) prevent disease among factory girls

(D) restrict the social activities of female factory
workers

(E) separate girls from their families

10. "Advanced" as used in line 41 most closely means

(A) proceeded

(B) argued

(C) denied

(D) progressed

(E) concealed

GO ON TO THE NEXT PAGE

11. Which of the following, if true, would most weaken the assertion in Passage 1 about the necessity of subjecting factory girls to unsafe conditions?

(A) Textile factories in France were financially successful even though they refused to make factory girls endure harsh conditions.

(B) The Waltham-Lowell system actually produced a smaller increase in profit than did the competing Bennington system.

(C) The estimated costs of increasing worker safety and health in the nineteenth century to acceptable levels would have been more than the total profits of factories in that era.

(D) Many twentieth-century factories treated factory workers with care and dignity and still had higher profits than nineteenth-century factories.

(E) An early nineteenth-century workers' rights activist approached all American and foreign factories with a plan to improve working conditions while maintaining profits, but this plan was rejected by all factories.

12. In the second paragraph of Passage 2, the description of the conditions imposed by factory agents serves to

(A) argue that American factory conditions were superior to those in Europe

(B) illustrate the role of factory agents in creating the poor working conditions discussed

(C) argue that such conditions were immoral by modern standards

(D) explain why factory agents were responsible for the 1911 fire

(E) illustrate the economic necessity of the harsh conditions

13. In the context of Passage 2, the reference to the Triangle Shirtwaist Factory fire in lines 96–105 serves to

(A) illustrate the prevalence of fires in factories that used the Waltham-Lowell system

(B) elicit unwarranted sympathy for the victims of a tragic factory accident

(C) demonstrate the dangerous conditions created by the uncaring attitude of factory owners toward their workers

(D) exemplify the extent to which factories tried to protect the safety of female workers

(E) illustrate the negligent behavior common among factory workers in New York City

14. According to Passage 2, the "tragedy" mentioned in line 99

(A) claimed 23 victims

(B) led to imprisonment for those responsible

(C) remained common for several years

(D) resulted from the whale-oil lamps used to light the factories

(E) failed to bring about immediate reform in working conditions

15. Which of the following most accurately describes the organization of the final paragraph of Passage 2?

(A) Evidence is questioned but ultimately accepted, leading to the main conclusion.

(B) An assertion is made and then supported with statistical evidence.

(C) A view is mentioned, then argued against.

(D) A widely held view is dismissed, and a new view is defended with historical evidence.

(E) Past circumstances are described in both moral and economic terms, resulting in a contradiction.

GO ON TO THE NEXT PAGE ⇒

16. The passages differ in their evaluations of factory owners in that Passage 1 claims that

(A) market conditions partially excuse the poor work environment created by factory owners

(B) factory owners compensated society for their reprehensible actions in the factory through philanthropic work

(C) the use of the Waltham-Lowell system enabled American factories to compete with European and Indian factories

(D) factory regulations caused many health problems for workers

(E) the Waltham-Lowell system was superior to previous factory organization schemes

17. Which of the following is an aspect of the Waltham-Lowell System emphasized in Passage 2, but not in Passage 1?

(A) the difficult conditions in factory boarding houses

(B) the role of agents in factory life

(C) health hazards faced by factory girls

(D) the demands of the families of factory girls

(E) the role of safety supervisors on the factory floor

18. Both passages mention which of the following aspects of nineteenth-century factory life?

(A) the extensive demands of factory agents

(B) the health problems caused by factory life under the Waltham-Lowell system

(C) the demand that workers dress neatly

(D) the superiority of working conditions in actories outside of New York State

(E) the generosity of factory owners toward workers

19. The author of Passage 1 would most likely agree with which of the following statements about the "economic necessities" (line 106) cited by the author of Passage 2?

(A) Such necessities cannot excuse the inhumane treatment of factory workers.

(B) The results of these necessities were likely more drastic in the United States than overseas.

(C) These economic necessities resulted from the pressures created by the demands of the families of factory workers.

(D) The necessities forced unfortunate compromises that could not easily be avoided.

(E) These conditions were solely a result of pressure from European and Indian competitors.

SECTION 8
Time—20 Minutes
16 Questions

Directions: For this section, solve each problem and decide which is the best of the choices given. Fill in the corresponding oval on the answer sheet. You may use any available space for scratchwork.

Notes:

(1) Calculator use is permitted.

(2) All numbers used are real numbers.

(3) Figures are provided for some problems. All figures are drawn to scale and lie in a plane UNLESS otherwise indicated.

(4) Unless otherwise specified, the domain of any function f is assumed to be the set of all real numbers x for which $f(x)$ is a real number.

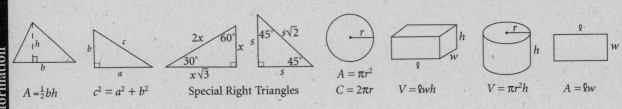

$A = \frac{1}{2}bh$ $c^2 = a^2 + b^2$ Special Right Triangles $A = \pi r^2$ $V = \ell wh$ $V = \pi r^2 h$ $A = \ell w$
$C = 2\pi r$

The sum of the degree measures of the angles in a triangle is 180.
The number of degrees of arc in a circle is 360.
A straight angle has a degree measure of 180.

1. If $7d < 4r$ and $4r < 8p$, which of the following must be true?

   (A) $7d < 8p$
   (B) $8p < 7d$
   (C) $p < d$
   (D) $r = 2p$
   (E) $2r = p$

Location	Number of Boxes	Number of Toys in Each Box
Basement	4	10
Garage	2	6
Attic	5	7

2. The chart above shows the location of all the toys stored at Joe's house. According to the chart, what is the total number of toys at Joe's house?

   (A) 23
   (B) 40
   (C) 57
   (D) 87
   (E) 123

GO ON TO THE NEXT PAGE

3. If the average (arithmetic mean) of 8 numbers is greater than 10 and less than 12, which of the following could be the sum of the 8 numbers?

    (A) 70
    (B) 80
    (C) 90
    (D) 100
    (E) 110

4. The Earth makes one complete rotation about its axis every 24 hours. Assuming it rotates at a constant rate, through how many degrees would Goannaville, Australia rotate from 1:00 p.m. on January 2 to 4:00 p.m. on January 3?

    (A) 202°
    (B) 250°
    (C) 350°
    (D) 363°
    (E) 405°

5. If S is the set of all numbers between −3.5 and 3.5, inclusive, T is the set of all prime numbers, and U is the set of all positive integers, then the intersection of S, T, and U contains how many elements?

    (A) 0
    (B) 1
    (C) 2
    (D) 3
    (E) More than 3

6. Which of the following expressions must be positive for all values of a and b?

    (A) $a + b$
    (B) $a^2 - b^2 + 10$
    (C) $a^2 + b^2 + 1$
    (D) $a^3 + b^3 + 16$
    (E) $a^4 + b^2 + a^2$

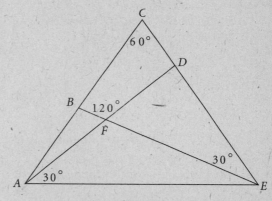

Note: Figure not drawn to scale.

7. In the equilatral triangle ACE above, AD and BE are line segments. Which of the following is NOT a right triangle?

    (A) ABF
    (B) ACD
    (C) ADE
    (D) AFE
    (E) BCE

8. The initial number of elements in a certain set is p, where $p > 0$. If the number of elements in the set doubles every hour, which of the following represents the total number of elements in the set after exactly 24 hours?

    (A) $24p$
    (B) $48p$
    (C) $2p^{24}$
    (D) $(2p)^{24}$
    (E) $(2^{24})p$

GO ON TO THE NEXT PAGE

9. The absolute value of a certain integer is greater than 3 and less than 6. Which of the following could NOT be 2 less than the integer?

    (A) −7
    (B) −6
    (C) 2
    (D) 3
    (E) 4

Questions 10–12 refer to the following sequence of steps.

    1 Choose a number between .5 and .99.

    2 Multiply the number from the previous step by 20.

    3 Determine the largest integer less than or equal to the number obtained from the previous step.

    4 Subtract 4 from the number obtained from the previous step.

    5 Write down the resulting number.

10. If .62 is the number chosen in step 1, what is the number written in step 5?

    (A) 6.2
    (B) 8
    (C) 9
    (D) 16
    (E) 62

11. Which of the following could be a number written in step 5 after steps 1 through 4 have been performed?

    (A) 0
    (B) 5
    (C) 7.4
    (D) 14
    (E) 17

12. Which, if any, of the following changes could be made to the sequence of steps without changing the number written in step 5?

    (A) remove step 2
    (B) remove step 3
    (C) replace step 3 with step 4 and vice versa
    (D) replace step 2 with step 4 and vice versa
    (E) none of the above

13. If $w = 3^3$, which of the following expressions is equal to 3^8?

    (A) $5w$
    (B) w^5
    (C) $8w$
    (D) $8w^2$
    (E) $9w^2$

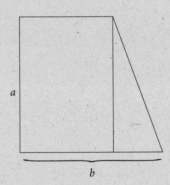

14. The figure above is formed from a square and a right triangle. What is its area?

    (A) $\dfrac{a(a + b)}{2}$
    (B) $\dfrac{a^2 + b^2}{2}$
    (C) $\dfrac{a(b - a)}{2}$
    (D) $a^2 + b^2$
    (E) $\dfrac{a^2 + ab}{2}$

GO ON TO THE NEXT PAGE

15. A certain brand of soup contains 10 percent tomato paste by volume. Which of the following expressions represents the percent of tomato paste by volume in a mixture of *s* cups of soup and *w* cups of water?

(A) $\dfrac{10s}{w}\%$

(B) $\dfrac{10}{s+w}\%$

(C) $\dfrac{s+w}{10}\%$

(D) $\dfrac{10s}{s+w}\%$

(E) $\dfrac{s}{10(s+w)}\%$

16. How many integers are there that are greater than 30, less than 40, and have exactly two factors (excluding the number itself and 1), which are both prime?

(A) two
(B) three
(C) four
(D) five
(E) six

IF YOU FINISH BEFORE TIME IS CALLED, YOU MAY CHECK YOUR WORK ON THIS SECTION ONLY. DO NOT TURN TO ANY OTHER SECTION IN THE TEST.

STOP

KAPLAN
Test Prep and Admissions

SECTION 9

Time—10 Minutes

14 Questions

Directions: For each question in this section, select the best answer from among the choices given and fill in the corresponding oval on the answer sheet.

The following sentences test correctness and effectiveness of expression. Part of each sentence or the entire sentence is underlined; beneath each sentence are five ways of phrasing the underlined material. Choice (A) repeats the original phrasing; the other four choices are different. If you think the original phrasing produces a better sentence than any of the alternatives, select choice (A); if not, select one of the other choices.

In making your selection, follow the requirements of standard written English; that is, pay attention to grammar, choice of words, sentence construction, and punctuation. Your selection should result in the most effective sentence—clear and precise, without awkwardness or ambiguity.

EXAMPLE: ANSWER:

Every apple in the baskets <u>are ripe and labeled according to the date it was picked</u>.   Ⓐ ● Ⓒ Ⓓ Ⓔ

(A) are ripe and labeled according to the date it was picked
(B) is ripe and labeled according to the date it was picked
(C) are ripe and labeled according to the date they were picked
(D) is ripe and labeled according to the date they were picked
(E) are ripe and labeled as to the date it was picked

---

1. The state of New Jersey, <u>is one of the smallest states in the union, being also</u> the most densely populated.

    (A) is one of the smallest states in the union, being also
    (B) although one of the smallest states in the union, is
    (C) being one of the smallest states in the union makes it
    (D) which is one of the smallest states in the union, although it is
    (E) whose size is the smallest in the union, makes it

2. Just as Ernest Hemingway created many novels about Paris and E.M. Forrester several about India, <u>so John Steinbeck produced numerous writings about America</u>.

    (A) so John Steinbeck produced numerous writings about America
    (B) John Steinbeck produces writings about America, and numerously
    (C) John Steinbeck's contribution is to produce writings about America in a numerous amount
    (D) and so then, for John Steinbeck, numerous writings about America are produced
    (E) and like them John Steinbeck produced numerous writings about America

GO ON TO THE NEXT PAGE

3. James obtained a French visa two years ago, <u>and he has been living in France ever since</u>.

   (A) and he has been living in France ever since

   (B) since that time he has lived there

   (C) where ever since he lives

   (D) he has been living in France since then

   (E) and since then is living there

4. Observers of democratic elections have said that their role is at once thrilling because of its importance <u>but its limitations are still an aggravation</u>.

   (A) but its limitations are still an aggravation

   (B) although it is aggravatingly limited

   (C) and it is aggravating in its limitations

   (D) while being so limited as to aggravate them

   (E) and aggravating because of its limitations

5. Before registering a motor vehicle in our state, <u>the applicants' cars must be checked by their mechanics</u>.

   (A) the applicants' cars must be checked by their mechanics

   (B) applicants must have their cars checked by their mechanics

   (C) their mechanics must check the car of each applicant

   (D) the cars of applicants must be checked by their mechanics

   (E) a check of each one's car must be done by their mechanics

6. <u>If we compare the population of China with America over time, we see that the Chinese population are</u> increasing.

   (A) If we compare the population of China with America over time, we see that the population of China are

   (B) Comparing the population of China with America, we see that the population of China is

   (C) In comparison with America, the population of China is

   (D) To compare the population of China with America is to show that they are

   (E) A comparison over time of the populations of China and America shows that the population of China is

7. Singer and songwriter Bob Dylan became a great lyricist because he knew that <u>if you presented political ideas in song it</u> could have a deeper impact on listeners than any personal thoughts.

   (A) if you presented political ideas in song it

   (B) with the ideas of politics presented in song they

   (C) ideas which were presented politically in song

   (D) by presenting political ideas in song

   (E) presenting political ideas in song

8. <u>Before being widely collected for its</u> artistic drawings and interesting stories, comic books were purchased cheaply by little boys across America.

   (A) Before being widely collected for its

   (B) Until having been widely collected for its

   (C) Up to them being widely collected for their

   (D) Before they were widely collected for their

   (E) Until they have been widely collected for their

GO ON TO THE NEXT PAGE

9. Satisfying even the pickiest of eaters, <u>the effect of Donald's exotic spices is to make bland foods delicious</u>.

   (A) the effect of Donald's exotic spices is to make bland foods delicious

   (B) Donald makes bland foods delicious with his exotic spices

   (C) the effect of the exotic spices, used by Donald, is to make bland foods delicious

   (D) Donald has had the effect of making bland foods delicious with exotic spices

   (E) exotic spices, used by Donald, have effect in making bland foods delicious

10. Some parents <u>believe not only that excessive television viewing wastes</u> their children's time, but also that it lowers their attention spans.

   (A) believe not only that excessive television viewing wastes

   (B) believe that excessive television viewing could be wasteful of

   (C) are believing that excessive television viewing not only wastes

   (D) have believed that excessive television viewing wastes not only

   (E) believe that excessive television viewing not only by itself can waste

11. Elodie became popular at school when she won her classmates over with her sense of <u>humor, and they were made to laugh</u>.

   (A) humor, and they were made to laugh

   (B) humor and making them laugh

   (C) humor with the result being them laughing

   (D) humor in where they laugh

   (E) humor and made them laugh

12. The integrity of journalism <u>rests on honest reporting, respect for news sources, and it requires balanced stories</u>.

   (A) rests on honest reporting, respect for news sources, and it requires balanced stories

   (B) rests on honest reporting, respect for news sources, and balanced stories

   (C) rest on reporting that is honest, treatment of news sources that is respectful, and stories of a balanced nature

   (D) rests on reporting that is honest, being respectful of news sources, and requires balanced stories

   (E) rest on honest reporting, respect for news sources, and the requirements of balanced stories

13. Used as either playthings or modes of transportation, <u>scooters, they are increasingly trendy on city streets</u>.

   (A) scooters, they are increasingly trendy on city streets

   (B) their trend on city streets has increased

   (C) they have become more trendy on city streets

   (D) scooters are increasingly trendy on city streets

   (E) scooters, they are trendy on city streets

14. <u>The Internet startup, often using unorthodox methods, quickly made their</u> service the most popular on the market.

   (A) The Internet startup, often using unorthodox methods, quickly made their

   (B) The Internet startup was often unorthodox in its methods for quickly making its

   (C) Using methods that were often unorthodox, the Internet startup , in quickly making its

   (D) Unorthodox methods were often used by the Internet startup while it was quickly making its

   (E) Often using unorthodox methods, the Internet startup quickly made its

IF YOU FINISH BEFORE TIME IS CALLED, YOU MAY CHECK YOUR WORK ON THIS SECTION ONLY. DO NOT TURN TO ANY OTHER SECTION IN THE TEST.

THE ANSWER KEY APPEARS ON THE FOLLOWING PAGE.

Practice Test Eleven: **Answer Key**

SECTION 1

Essay

SECTION 2

1. B
2. E
3. B
4. B
5. D
6. C
7. D
8. E
9. E
10. A
11. B
12. D
13. E
14. B
15. D
16. A
17. D
18. C
19. B
20. C
21. E
22. E
23. A
24. A

SECTION 3

1. D
2. E
3. B
4. E
5. C
6. B
7. C
8. E
9. C
10. D
11. A
12. C
13. E
14. B
15. C
16. A
17. B
18. C
19. D
20. B

SECTION 4

1. D
2. C
3. D
4. E
5. C
6. D
7. B
8. D
9. A
10. B
11. D
12. E
13. D

14. A
15. B
16. B
17. D
18. E
19. B
20. D
21. C
22. C
23. C
24. C
25. B
26. D
27. E
28. C
29. A
30. D
31. B
32. C
33. D
34. B
35. E

SECTION 5

1. E
2. A
3. C
4. D
5. B
6. A
7. B
8. D
9. D
10. C
11. E
12. D

13. B
14. D
15. D
16. B
17. D
18. E
19. B
20. A
21. D
22. C
23. D
24. E

SECTION 6

1. C
2. B
3. A
4. E
5. A
6. E
7. D
8. C
9. 2.75 or 11/4
10. 6
11. 12
12. 3
13. 1,000
14. 25
15. 812
16. 30
17. 6
18. 210

SECTION 7

1. D
2. A
3. E
4. B
5. D
6. A
7. A
8. B
9. A
10. B
11. E
12. B
13. C
14. E
15. C
16. A
17. B
18. B
19. D

SECTION 8

1. A
2. D
3. C
4. E
5. C
6. C
7. D
8. E
9. E
10. B
11. D
12. C
13. E
14. A

15. D
16. D

SECTION 9

1. B
2. A
3. A
4. E
5. B
6. E
7. E
8. D
9. B
10. A
11. E
12. B
13. D
14. E

PRACTICE TEST ELEVEN

Critical Reading

	Number Right	Number Wrong	Raw Score
Section 2:	☐	− (.25 × ☐)	= ☐
Section 5:	☐	− (.25 × ☐)	= ☐
Section 7:	☐	− (.25 × ☐)	= ☐

Critical Reading Raw Score = ☐
(rounded up)

Writing

	Number Right	Number Wrong	Raw Score
Section 1:	☐ (ESSAY GRADE)	× 3:17	= ☐
Section 4:	☐	− (.25 × ☐)	= ☐
Section 9:	☐	− (.25 × ☐)	= ☐

Writing Raw Score = ☐
(rounded up)

Math

	Number Right	Number Wrong	Raw Score
Section 3:	☐	− (.25 × ☐)	= ☐
Section 6A: (QUESTIONS 1–8)	☐	− (.25 × ☐)	= ☐
Section 6B: (QUESTIONS 9–18)	☐	(no wrong answer penalty)	= ☐
Section 8:	☐	− (.25 × ☐)	= ☐

Math Raw Score = ☐
(rounded up)

Turn to page xiv to convert your raw score to a scaled score.

Answers and Explanations

SECTION 1

6 Score Essay

Every obstacle can be turned into an opportunity, if one has the right attitude or perspective. People with this attitude are buoyant, not easily discouraged, and welcome challenges and adversity. One personal example took place in sixth grade, when I broke my hand by falling off my bicycle. The doctor had to put it into a cast.

The cast was a real obstacle. It was on my right hand, the one I write with. It looked like homework would be impossible! But I learned to type with one hand, and I did my English and social studies work on the typewriter. My mom helped me by writing out my math homework based on answers I gave her. The experience sure helped my typing! It also made me learn the value of work, and gave me a chance to really learn to appreciate my mother.

In addition, having the cast was an excuse to improve my basketball game. I was a decent player, but most comfortable with my right hand. But with the cast on I was forced to practice dribbling with my left hand, and now I can go either way.

Finally, there was one other unexpected benefit. In art class, I was never very good. But one day, with my hand still in the cast, I tried drawing with my left hand. To my surprise, I was much better at it than before! The cast is long gone, but I still draw left-handed and am really quite good at it. Maybe I'd never have known about this ability if I hadn't made my obstacle into my opportunity.

6 Score Critique

The essay is scored based on four basic criteria: Topic, Support, Organization, and Language. This essay demonstrates an especially strong grasp of the writing assignment, earning especially high points for Topic, Support, and Organization. The author states a thesis in paragraph 1, provides several specific, relevant examples of how the obstacle was turned to good effect in paragraph 2, and concludes with a final, highlighted example. These are discussed in a clear and convincing way.

Vocabulary is also strong ("buoyant," for example), and the essay has a good grasp on strong grammar and sentence structure.

4 Score Essay

To say that every obstacle can be turned into an opportunity is to be an optimist. Some people just always look on the bright side, and are able to overcome there obstacles.

Dorothy in the *Wizard of Oz* is stranded by the tornado and can't go home. So instead of just sitting there, she takes the opportunity to make friends with Scarecrow and others, and to rid the world of wicked witches. Her optimism wins her the right to go back to Kansas.

In the real world, Marie Curie was told women couldn't be scientists. But she was optimistic and persevered and discovered radium. Now there are more women scientists than ever.

Ophelia in *Hamlet* however, is not an optimist. She and Hamlet fall in love but then he pushes her away. She doesn't understand why and kills herself.

I like to think I'm an optimist too. If somebody tells me I can't do something, I just try harder until I can. Take field hockey: I went out as a freshman and barely made the team, but worked and worked and this year was a starter on the varsity. We came in second in the league. Life is like that if you look on the bright side. Don't get discouraged. Every cloud has a silver lining. So if you are an optimist, every obstacle is an opportunity.

4 Score Critique

The essay is scored based on four basic criteria: Topic, Support, Organization, and Language. This author attempted with some success to fulfill the assignment. She gives some relevant examples from literature and history that work well with the prompt. But her examples are a bit underdeveloped and confused. The essay is too short to develop its ideas well. The author should explain more how the obstacles she mentions became opportunities for the individuals in question. Also, she could have left out the example about Ophelia, which does not really fit in well with the essay.

The essay also relies a bit too much on clichés ("look on the bright side" and "more than ever"). Note the effective parallelism in the first sentence, though.

Overall, it seems as if EITHER the writer had a hard time coming up with ideas, and rushed to write the essay in the last few minutes; OR ELSE the writer had three ideas but couldn't choose among them. It would have been a better essay if the writer had selected one of these and developed it well, instead of trying to write about all three.

2 Score Essay

I don't agree with this statement, that we can turn every obstacle into an opportunity. Some obstacles are just the way they are and there's nothing you can do about it. Like if I wanted to be a NBA basketball player. In the NBA you have to be tall as a tree, and I'm the shortest person in the whole school. Back in elementary school too. So I'm never going to opportunity to play the NBA. There is nothing I can do about that.

And if you die young like from leukemia, that obstacle doesn't give you the opportunity to do anything with your life. There is nothing you could have done.

So it depends on the obstacle. The quote should have said MANY obstacles or SOME obstacle. It just depends.

2 Score Critique

The essay is scored based on four basic criteria: Topic, Support, Organization, and Language. While the author does present a point of view clearly, this essay is deficient in both development and presentation. It's perfectly acceptable for the author to disagree with the stimulus statement, but she provides hardly any support for that position. The ideas presented are extremely thin, and there's no logical organization to them. Finally, this essay's prose leaves out words ("So I'm never going to opportunity…"), is too colloquial ("Like if I wanted to be…"), and seriously violates the rules of standard written English ("Back in elementary school too.").

SECTION 2

1. B

Difficulty: Low

Don't settle for a choice that kind of works, like (C). Make sure it captures the entire meaning of your prediction. Catalonia is not an independent nation anymore, but it continues to have its own language and culture. So a good prediction might be "*keeps* a sense of *independence*." Choice (B) is a perfect match. In choice (A), if Catalonia were *surrendering*, the word "nevertheless" wouldn't make sense. Choice (C) is not out of the question, since the people of Catalonia might feel *privileged*, but it doesn't have much to do with the issue of independence. Choice (D) is too extreme—there's nothing to indicate that the people of Catalonia are *arrogant*. Choice (E) is the opposite of what you're looking for. If the people have their own language and culture, they probably don't feel *neglected*.

2. E

Difficulty: Low

This is another definition sentence. The woman "fondly remembered her childhood," so look for a choice that fits this definition. Choice (E) is a perfect fit. In choice (A), she might feel *gratitude*, but that doesn't mean fondly remembering something. There's not much support for choice (B) in the sentence. What would she be *determined* about? For choices (C) and (D), *regret* and *melancholy* are too negative; she's "fondly" remembering.

3. B

Difficulty: Low

In order to predict what goes in the first blank, look at the explanation following the colon. The scientific records and video cameras suggest that *watched* or *observed* would work for both the first and second blanks. Both *monitored* and *document* fit your prediction. For choice (A), *record* is great, but *praised* doesn't work here—cameras can't praise the pandas. In choice In choice (C), *criticized* is too negative—you're looking for neutral words. In choice (D), *evaluated* isn't bad, but how could a camera *approve* activities? In choice (E), anyone who *questioned* the pandas would be in for a very one-sided conversation.

4.   B

Difficulty: Medium

Sometimes the correct answer to a two-blank Sentence Completion hinges on just one of the blanks. Four of the five answer choices here have OK choices for the second blank, so the question hinges on finding a word that contrasts with "serious." The keyword "though" signals that the first blank will contrast with "serious." *Trivial* and *playful* are good predictions. In the second half of the sentence, you might predict that Franklin gained the *support* of the French.

In choice (A), *disrespectful* looks possible for the first blank, but the second word doesn't quite work—why would a government give its *compliments* to a cause? In choice (B), *frivolous*, or thoughtless, is a fine match for the first blank, and *support* is what you predicted for the second blank. In choice (C), *irrelevant* doesn't contrast very clearly with "serious"; its tone is not sufficiently negative. In choice (D), *extravagant*, or excessive, kind of works for the first blank, but it doesn't make sense that one government would need to get the *permission* of another government. In choice (E), *rebellious* is not a very good match for your prediction—it doesn't contrast with "serious."

5.   D

Difficulty: Medium

Don't give up when you see a few tough vocab words. Even if you don't know the answer right away, you can get closer by eliminating clearly wrong choices. The students are "confused," so the teacher is trying to use an example. *Clarify* is a good prediction. Note, too, that you could eliminate two choices, even if you didn't know the meaning of *extricate*, *elucidate*, or *obfuscate*.

In choice (A), to *extricate* the subject, which means to free him, makes no sense. In choice (B), the teacher is definitely not trying to *evade* the subject. Choice (C) is tempting if you're in a hurry, but notice that it's the students, not the teacher, who need to *comprehend* the subject. Choice (D) is a great fit for your prediction, as *elucidate* means to explain, make clear. Choice (E) is the opposite of what you're looking for, since *obfuscate* means to confuse or to conceal.

6.   C

Difficulty: Medium

This is a very patient cat. In fact, *patient* is a pretty good prediction.

In choice (A), an *apprehensive* cat might or might not wait all day. There's not a very strong connection. In choice (B), an *emaciated*, or skeletal and starved, cat would probably be pretty hungry, so it might wait all day. When you get to (C), however, you'll note that *emaciated* is not as strong a choice. *Vigilant*, or watchful, doesn't mean exactly the same thing as *patient*, your prediction, but *vigilant* is a great description of a cat that waits all afternoon for a mouse. In choice (D), a *prominent* cat? That doesn't make much sense. In choice (E), *indolent* means lazy, and certainly doesn't describe a cat that waits all day for a mouse.

7.   D

Difficulty: Medium

As you get to the more difficult questions, watch out for tempting choices like (E). Make sure the word works when you read it in the sentence. This is a contrast sentence, and the blank contrasts with the word *credible*. In this context, that means believable or valid, so a good prediction might be *unbelievable*.

In choice (A), *valid* means true, and is the opposite of what you want. In choice (B), a *sardonic*, or sarcastic, excuse doesn't contrast with *credible*. Choice (C), like (A), *righteous*, or upright and moral, is the opposite of your prediction. In choice (D), *fabricated* fits well. Her excuse wasn't *credible*—it was actually completely made-up. Choice (E) is interesting, but watch out! *Incredulous* would describe people who don't believe the excuse, not the excuse itself.

8.   E

Difficulty: High

The sets are "magnificent" and "an outstanding visual achievement," so the correct answer will be very positive.

In choice (A), the artists who made the sets might be *prolific*, or abundant and creative, but the sets themselves can't be. In choice (B), if the sets were *modest*, they probably wouldn't be considered such a visual achievement. In choice (C), like (A), this is something that could only apply to people. The sets couldn't be *reticent*, or unwilling to talk. In choice (D), the sets should evoke the future, but *archaic* sets are very old-fashioned, and would do just the opposite. In choice (E), *grandiose* fits perfectly. (You might recognize the word grand, even if you're not familiar with *grandiose*).

Questions 9–13

The passage explores the rise and fall of chain mail armor. In paragraph 1, you learn that chain mail existed in ancient Rome, but was used only by cavalry, and was secondary to the *lorica segmentata*. In paragraph 2, the author describes the increasing popularity of chain mail starting in the fourteenth century, as well some reasons for this increase. Finally, paragraph 3 describes the laborious process of creating the chain mail, and notes that improved weapons caused chain mail to gradually fall out of favor.

9. E
Difficulty: High

When you go back to the first paragraph, you read that although chain mail did exist in the Roman era, it was used primarily by the cavalry. The infantry preferred something called *lorica segmentata*. Look for a choice that sums this up.

Choice (A) is misuse of detail; no, it was chain mail that had a resurgence in the medieval period. Choice (B) is out of scope; this one may be tempting, since you know that mail was more *popular* in the fourteenth century, but you don't actually know that it was more *effective*. Maybe the increase in its popularity was due to some other cause. Choice (C) is misuse of detail; mail fell out of use due to improved stabbing weapons, but not until after the fourteenth century. Choice (D) is extreme; steel plates are mentioned in the discussion of the *lorica segmentata*, and the author also notes that primarily cavalry troops used chain mail. There's no real evidence, however, that steel plates weren't practical for cavalry or that no cavalry troops used steel plates. Choice (E) suits the facts you noted in your prediction.

10. A
Difficulty: Low

Although "fashion" often refers to fancy clothing, it's used here to mean that the craftsmen made chain mail armor, so *making* is a fine prediction.

Choice (A) fits your prediction. In choice (B), the art of *purchasing* chain mail? That doesn't work. Choice (C) might be a distracter based on the more common meaning of "fashion." In choice (D), *locating* chain mail is not an art. Choice (E) also seems to refer to the more common meaning of "fashion"—*sewing* isn't the right word to use with thick, heavy armor.

11. B
Difficulty: Medium

Of course you can't make a prediction on such an open-ended question, so spend your time carefully sorting through the answer choices. Eliminate anything that's contradicted by the passage or anything not directly stated or implied.

Choice (A) is an opposite; there seem to have been plenty of craftsmen. The problem was that different weapons made the mail obsolete. Choice (B) is true. Starting in the fourteenth century, mail became popular because it offered superior protection. Choice (C) is out of scope; although the mail became popular starting in the fourteenth century, you don't know that it was limited to that time. It may have continued to be available into the fifteenth century or for even longer. Choice (D) is extreme; although mail was eventually replaced, there's no evidence that this was an immediate transition. Also, the author certainly wouldn't describe chain mail as *of limited usefulness*. Choice (E) is out of scope; the author never discusses modern uses of chain mail.

12. D
Difficulty: Low

"EXCEPT" questions require you to eliminate the four true choices in order to identify the one false one. That false choice is the correct answer. Compare each answer choice against the process described in paragraph 3.

Choice (A) is true. This appears in the third sentence. Choice (B) is true. This appears in the third sentence. Choice (C) is true. This appears in the second sentence. Choice (D) is false. This refers to the *lorica segmentata* in the first paragraph, not to chain mail. Choice (E) is true. This appears in the second sentence.

13. E
Difficulty: Medium

For Function questions about a single sentence, the key is usually to identify the role of that sentence in its paragraph.

The sentence in question says that it was very hard to make chain mail, and much of the third paragraph then describes what this process was.

Choice (A) is out of scope; the author never advances a particular opinion or argument, and certainly never counters an argument. Choice (B) is extreme; although it's important that it was difficult to make chain mail, this idea is only one aspect of the entire topic. It's not the central thesis. Choice (C) is an opposite; actually, the sentence is itself an assertion, and the information that follows provides the evidence. Choice (D) is out of scope; there's no paradox anywhere in the passage. Choice (E) matches your prediction pretty well.

Questions 14–24

Paragraph 1 establishes the location and characterizes Thomas's feelings about growing up on a farm. Paragraph 2 gives a bit of the history of the farm and Thomas's family's experience with it, while in paragraph 3, Thomas's relationship with his father is explored. In paragraph 4, you learn more about Thomas's family, especially his father. Paragraph 5 provides you with the root of the conflict in the story: despite his father's efforts, the farm would not survive another generation in the family. In paragraph 6, you learn that Thomas is an adult, looking over the farm (now a construction site) one last time, while a flood of associated thoughts and feelings wash over him. Paragraph 7 conveys the conclusion that Thomas reaches: like his father, Thomas has discovered a personal investment in, and a connection to, the land, and he will miss it.

As is true in many narrative passages, it is important here to monitor the feelings of the main character (in this case, Thomas) and what those feelings tell you. Without being aware of the emotional undercurrent of Thomas's thoughts, you could overlook the realization he reaches at the end of the story, and its relationship to the various moments he contemplates in the narrative.

14. B

Difficulty: High

Function questions sometimes require you to go beyond what appears on the page and speculate about the author's motivation in writing something.

Once you understand that the first part of the passage takes place at various times in the main character's past, you can infer that "yesterday" does not literally mean the day before today, but is used metaphorically to indicate a compression of time, as in the phrase "it felt like it was just yesterday."

Choice (A) is distortion; *urgency* implies a sense of pressure and, perhaps, danger. There is no particular

urgency in observing an empty field. Choice (B) matches the sense of "just yesterday" you predicted. Choice (C) is distortion; Thomas may be recollecting accurately, but the author isn't writing the sentence in order to convey this—after all, Thomas's powers of recollection are never referred to in the passage. Choice (D) is distortion; although Thomas is *contemplating* in a very general way, it doesn't seem very *purposeful*. That is, he's not contemplating in order to accomplish something. Choice (E) is distortion; there is a strong sense of the passage of time in the story as a whole, but the first sentence alone does not convey this.

15. D

Difficulty: Medium

Always be suspicious of the everyday, primary meanings of words in Vocab-in-Context questions. The paragraph describes Thomas as a young boy running through a forest of corn. The sentence in which "spears" is found describes the corn as towering and green. So, you are looking for a word that fits in with this general description of the corn.

Choice (A) fits with the word "towers," with no relation to corn. Choice (B) is a little too vague, since *structures* doesn't convey that the corn stalks were tall and thin. Choice (C) is the primary meaning of "spears," but not the correct one in this context. Choice (D) is a good fit with the word "spears," and with the general description of the corn. Choice (E), like (C), sounds too dangerous to fit.

16. A

Difficulty: High

Some Function questions can't be answered without considering the passage as a whole.

Why would the author repeat the idea "leaving the corn was easy"? It may not make much sense when you first read it, but by the time you finish the passage, you see that the entire story is about Thomas leaving life on the farm. So the author is giving you a hint ahead of time.

Choice (A) is a good match. Choice (B) may convey this, but the author probably also has some other, more important, meaning in mind. Otherwise it probably wouldn't be the subject of a question. In choice (C), the author never indicates that Thomas's life was particularly simple. Also, it's hard to see how a sentence about cornfields could convey this. Choice (D) is a theme of the passage, but it's not discussed in the first paragraph. In choice (E), Thomas did seem to enjoy himself, but the idea that it's easy to leave a cornfield doesn't have a very direct relationship to this.

17. D

Difficulty: Medium

Vocabulary-in-Context questions send you back to the passage; read the sentences before and after the sentence in which the word appears. All of the chores listed look pretty tough, so look for a word that means something like *tiring*.

Choice (A) is related to a common meaning of "taxing," but not appropriate here. Choice (B) is, again, related to a more common meaning of "taxing." Choice (C) is an opposite; these chores sound anything but *rejuvenating*. Choice (D) is your exact answer. In choice (E), all of these chores sound like skills one would need to learn.

18. C

Difficulty: High

The answer to this question will come from the passage as a whole, not from one particular sentence or word.

Throughout the passage you are given clues, from both Thomas's father's words and actions, about what the father believes: a person should work hard and own land. In other words, the father is *self-reliant*.

Choice (A) is an opposite; in the fourth paragraph, we read that Thomas's father is "a man of the earth." This is the opposite of *aristocratic*. Choice (B) is an opposite; Thomas's father seems quite wise. Choice (C) is a good match. Choice (D) is an opposite; again, "man of the earth" doesn't seems very compatible with this choice. Choice (E) is distortion; while Thomas's father seems to have had strong opinions, the passage doesn't suggest that he was inflexible.

19. B

Difficulty: Medium

Wrong answer choices on questions like this one will almost certainly contain details from the wrong part of the passage.

In the sentence in question, you learn that Thomas and his father would ride the enormous thresher during harvest time.

Choice (A) is a misused detail; mending fences is mentioned in the second, not the third, paragraph. Choice (B) makes sense. Choice (C) is a misused detail; shopping

malls are mentioned in the final paragraph, not paragraph 3. Choice (D) is distortion; planting seeds would happen at the beginning, not the end, of a growing cycle. Choice (E) is a misused detail; surveying land is mentioned in paragraph 6, not paragraph 3.

20. C

Difficulty: Medium

Inference questions require you to put information together and draw a conclusion. The quote indicates that Thomas's father feels strongly about the need to own land—so strongly, in fact, that he defines manhood by whether or not a man has land of his own.

Choice (A) is a misused detail; while it's true that the corn is fetching lower prices each year, there's no indication that the father is discouraged by this fact. Choice (B) is an opposite; the father seems like he enjoys the farm work—in any case, we certainly can't infer that he is discouraged by the amount of work he needs to do. Choice (C) fits nicely with the summary above. Choice (D) is out of scope; Thomas's father may indeed be pleased that Thomas is with him, but the passage doesn't say so, and the quote doesn't refer to this. Choice (E) is out of scope; again, this may or may not be true—the passage does not discuss the topic.

21. E

Difficulty: Medium

Remember that inferences on the SAT follow very directly from the evidence. You shouldn't do too much work to make a choice fit. Immediately following the line about Thomas's father's "secret despair," you read, "The land that had been in his family for three generations was not valued by the fourth." From that, you can infer that the father is sad that the farm will not be cared for by Thomas and his brothers.

Choice (A) is an opposite; in the fifth paragraph, the author states that "little Tommy helped out as much as he was able." Choice (B) is distortion; although Thomas's brothers did have these interests, we don't know that the father was worried about them. Choice (C) is distortion; while the author says that Thomas's father could probably have gone to college, you don't know that he regrets not having done so. Choice (D) is out of scope; we don't hear anything about the marriage. Choice (E) is a good paraphrase of your prediction.

22. E

Difficulty: Medium

Questions like this one are particularly susceptible to elimination strategies.

The paragraph in which this sentence appears emphasizes that the father knew his sons did not share his own interest in farm work. Instead, the brothers were into having a good time.

Choice (A) is a misused detail; we don't hear about the brothers as adults until the end of the passage, and then, their interests don't necessarily contrast with those of their youth. Choice (B) is a misused detail; actually, you are never given reasons for why Thomas performed his brothers' chores—you are only told that he sometimes did so. Choice (C) is distortion; although the brothers and father didn't share the same values, there's no mention of actual conflict between them. Maybe they just agreed to disagree. Choice (D) is distortion; this doesn't appear until the final paragraph. In choice (E), there is indeed a division between the values of the brothers and the father. If you didn't know the word, you could instead eliminate the other four choices.

23. A

Difficulty: High

As always with function questions, answer the question "Why?"

The author goes to some trouble in paragraph 6 to show that the farm is now gone, and that many things have changed. Everything in the first five paragraphs happened in the past.

Choice (A) reflects the shift in time described above. Choice (B) is distortion; you don't learn much about Thomas's present life in the sixth paragraph, so it doesn't make sense to say the author is contrasting the past and present of Thomas's life. Choice (C) is an opposite; reverse chronology would be from the present to the past, but this story goes from the past to the present. Choice (D) is out of scope; if paragraph six were a summary of the plot, then it would contain references to the action that took place in the prior paragraphs. Choice (E) is out of scope; there's no indication in this paragraph of what lies ahead for Thomas.

24. A

Difficulty: Medium

Inference questions require you to put information together and draw a conclusion.

By the end of the passage it's clear that Thomas is more in sympathy with his father's feelings about the farm than he had perhaps realized, and certainly more than his brothers are. He feels he's losing his home, and he's sad about that; he wishes that it were still his home.

In choice (A), both *nostalgia* and *regretful* fit well. Choice (B) is an opposite; Thomas seems a bit melancholy, the opposite of this choice. Choice (C) is out of scope; there's nothing in Thomas's thoughts or behavior that indicates anger. Choice (D) is extreme; while Thomas may be a bit sad, this is way too extreme. Choice (E) is out of scope; nothing in the passage suggests *relief*.

SECTION 3

1. D

Difficulty: Low

Strategic Advice: Be sure not to do more work than you need: to find b, you do not need to solve for a.

Getting to the Answer:

$$a^3 - b = a^3 - 5$$
$$-b = -5$$
$$b = 5$$

2. E

Difficulty: Low

Strategic Advice: You can find the minimum baking time for this pie by adding the minimum baking time for the crust (7 minutes) to the minimum baking time for the entire pie (15 minutes). Similarly, you can add the maximum baking time for the crust (10 minutes) to the maximum baking time for the entire pie (18 minutes) to find the maximum possible baking time.

Getting to the Answer:

$7 + 15 = 22$ minutes

$10 + 18 = 28$ minutes

3. B

Difficulty: Medium

Strategic Advice: Sometimes the first piece of information you need to answer a question is the last piece of information provided in the question stem.

Getting to the Answer:

$$\frac{q}{s} = 6$$

$$\frac{q}{2} = 6$$

$$q = 12$$

$$\frac{q}{r} = 4$$

$$\frac{12}{r} = 4$$

$$12 = 4r$$

$$3 = r$$

4. E

Difficulty: Low

Strategic Advice: If part of a problem seems complicated, try to rewrite it in a simpler way. In this case, 9.87654×10^4 can be written much more simply.

Getting to the Answer:

$9.87654 \times 10^4 = 98765.4$

5. C

Difficulty: Medium

Strategic Advice: To find the average of a set of numbers, divide the sum of the numbers by the number of numbers. This is a very important formula.

Getting to the Answer:

$$\frac{0(5) + 1(4) + 2(5) + 3(4) + 4(2)}{20}$$

$$= \frac{0 + 4 + 10 + 12 + 8}{20} = \frac{34}{20} = 1.7$$

6. B

Difficulty: Medium

Strategic Advice: This problem involves two concepts that appear very frequently on the SAT. First, the sum of the interior angles of any triangle is 180 degrees. Second, all the variables in the problem can be written in terms of one variable, in this case a.

Getting to the Answer:

$$a + b + c = 180$$

$$a + 2a + 3a = 180$$

$$6a = 180$$

$$a = 30$$

7. C

Difficulty: Medium

Strategic Advice: This problem revolves around translating from English to math. You'll need to choose a variable to represent the number of apples in the sack before the addition (for instance, x), then set up an equation using the information in the first sentence, and finally solve that equation for x.

Getting to the Answer:

$$x + 4 = 3x$$

$$4 = 2x$$

$$2 = x$$

8. E

Difficulty: Medium

Strategic Advice: In many geometry problems, you'll need to draw your own figure or (as in this case) add something to a given figure to help you solve a problem. You'll also need to remember that the sum of the internal angles of a triangle and the sum of the angles along a straight line are both 180 degrees.

Getting to the Answer:

First, sketch a line perpendicular to *l* and *m*. By definition, this creates two right triangles:

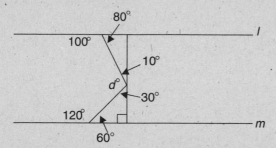

The three angles along the new line add up to 180 degrees:

$10 + d + 30 = 180$

$d + 40 = 180$

$d = 140$

9. C

Difficulty: Medium

Strategic Advice: Always read the question carefully. This question doesn't ask for the value of *x* or the sum of $x + 6$ and $x - 2$. Instead, it asks for the difference between the two expressions. Although the algebraic method is shown below, picking numbers is also a good way to solve this problem.

Getting to the Answer:

$(x + 6) - (x - 2) = 6 - (-2) = 8$

10. D

Difficulty: Medium

Strategic Advice: This problem asks about the properties of negative numbers. If you forget any of the rules of number properties, picking numbers can help you rule out incorrect answers.

Getting to the Answer:

   I. $a - b < c$ is not necessarily true. For instance, if a, b, and c were $-3, -2$, and -1, then this inequality would be $-3 - (-2) = -1 < -1$.

Since a number cannot be less than itself, statement I is not true. Eliminate (A), (C), and (E).

   II. $a < c$, so $-a > -c$. Eliminate (B). The answer must be (D), but for the sake of practice, go on to consider the third statement.

  III. $a < c$, so $a + b < b + c$.

11. A

Difficulty Medium

Strategic Advice: To solve this question, you must translate English into math and understand percents. Each of the percentages given in the first sentence of this problem is a percent of Jo's monthly income, which you might call *J* while setting up your equation. Since Jo gives half her remaining income to charity and saves the rest, the amount of income that remains after she has spent everything listed in the first sentence is twice the amount she saves.

Getting to the Answer:

$.25J + .3J + .1J + .2J + 150 = J$

$.85J + 150 = J$

$150 = .15J$

$1,000 = J$

12. C

Difficulty: Medium

Strategic Advice: This problem tests your ability to read carefully more than your ability to do math. Be sure to pay attention to which variables are subtracted from which, and don't be fooled by answers that look similar to the correct answer. You may find it helpful to write out your answer before looking at the answer choices so that plausible but incorrect answers will not distract you.

Getting to the Answer:

$\sqrt{r + s} - q^2 = (t + r)^2$

13. E

Difficulty: Medium

Strategic Advice: Don't do more work than you have to! Remember that the slope of a line represents the change in the value of the *y*-coordinate over the change in the value of the *x*-coordinate. If the slope of the line is 1, that means that for every unit of change in *y*, there is a corresponding unit of change in *x*.

Getting to the Answer:

From the point $(1, 2)$, you can move one unit up and one unit to the right (that is, along a slope of 1) to reach the point $(2, 3)$. No other choice satisfies this condition.

14. B

Difficulty: Medium

Strategic Advice: Don't worry when you see an odd symbol like the one in this problem: the operation defined by the symbol will always be given in the problem. All you need to do is plug the given numbers into the given equation and solve it carefully. Be sure to work all parts of the problem in the correct order.

Getting to the Answer:

$$(3 \clubsuit 2) = 3^2 - 2 = 9 - 2 = 7$$
$$4 \clubsuit (3 \clubsuit 2) = 4 \clubsuit 7 = 4^2 - 7 = 16 - 7 = 9$$

15. C

Difficulty: Medium

Strategic Advice: A prime number is a number whose only distinct factors are itself and 1. (The number 1 itself is not prime.) If you get stuck on a problem like this, pick numbers.

Getting to the Answer:

The number qr will have q and r as factors, so it cannot be prime. All other answer choices can be prime if q and r are prime numbers.

16. A

Difficulty: Medium

Strategic Advice: This question hinges on the Triangle Inequality Theorem: the length of each side of a triangle must be greater than the difference between the other two sides and less than the sum of the other two sides. Therefore, the third side of this triangle must be greater than the difference between, and less than the sum of, 9 and 15.

Getting to the Answer:

$15 - 9 = 6$

$15 + 9 = 24$

$6 < \text{length of third side} < 24$

17. B

Difficulty: Medium

Strategic Advice: The easiest way to solve this problem is to express the given ratios as an equation and simplify it. You'll then clearly see which of the statements must be true and which ones are merely special cases.

Getting to the Answer:

$$\frac{a+2}{b+2} = \frac{a+4}{b+4}$$
$$(a+2)(b+4) = (a+4)(b+2)$$
$$ab + 2b + 4a + 8 = ab + 4b + 2a + 8$$
$$2b + 4a = 4b + 2a$$
$$b + 2a = 2b + a$$
$$a = b$$

(Note that statement II can be true, but is not necessarily true, and that statement III is true only if a and b are both 0.)

18. C

Difficulty: Medium

Strategic Advice: This problem is much less complicated than it seems to be at first glance. Notice that line segment AF is the same length as the diameter of the circle on the left plus the diameter of the circle on the right. Since the vertical line segments along line AF divide the large rectangle into 5 equal smaller rectangles, they also divide line AF into 5 equal pieces.

Getting to the Answer:

$AB = 2$, so $AF = 2(5) = 10$

$\dfrac{10}{2} = 5$ (the diameter of each circle)

$\dfrac{5}{2} = 2.5$ (the radius of each circle)

19. D

Difficulty: High

Strategic Advice: If you get stuck on a problem like this one, picking numbers can be very helpful. Try picking a small positive odd number for k, then counting the number of even integers between it and 1.

Getting to the Answer:

There are $k - 1$ integers less than k and greater than zero. Half of them, or $\dfrac{k-1}{2}$, are even.

20. B

Difficulty: High

Strategic Advice: The easiest way to do this problem is to sketch a one-foot by five-foot lattice and count the connectors of each type. You could also consider the question logically: each vertical pipe will be connected to two or four horizontal pipes. The vertical pipes on the ends of the lattice will be connected to two horizontal pipes each, using two *L* connectors. Each other vertical pipe will be connected to four horizontal pipes using two *T* connectors. A one-foot by five-foot lattice would require six vertical pipes, of which two would have two *L* connectors each. The other four would have two *T* connectors each.

Getting to the Answer:

L connectors: $2(2) = 4$

T connectors: $4(2) = 8$

SECTION 4

1. D

Difficulty: Medium

The sentence contains a modification error, eliminating choice (A). The introductory phrase cannot modify the noun that immediately follows it, *party*—a party doesn't hear things, a person does—in this case, the math teacher. The underlined portion also uses the passive voice, which is rarely part of the credited choice in the SAT.

(B) does not correct the error, and loses part of the meaning of the sentence. (C) distorts the meaning of the sentence. (D) and (E) correct the modification error, but (E) uses the past perfect (*had thrown*), which would only be correct if the sentence referred to some other past action that it preceded. So (D) is correct.

2. C

Difficulty: Medium

One of the main problems in this sentence is the comma splice: the incorrect use of a comma to connect two complete sentences. So (A) and (B) are incorrect.

(C) correctly uses the semicolon and makes the two sentences parallel. If split into two sentences, this could read: *Many students prefer social studies over science classes. Another student preference is for English over foreign language classes.* (B) doesn't correct the run-on sentence. (D) corrects this problem but doesn't fix the wordiness or make the sentences parallel. (E) corrects the run-on sentence but eliminates any connection between the two ideas.

3. D

Difficulty: High

The question is difficult because the sentence contains two problems. First, *to be credit* is an incorrect form of the past tense. It should read *to be credited*. Second, "nor" is not correct usage here. Since the first part of the statement ("refused to be credit…") isn't expressed in the negative the correct connector is "or."

(C) and (D) correct the first problem but only (D) eliminates the *nor*. (E) adds *neither* so that the sentence includes *neither* and *nor,* but here the *neither* forms a double negative: *refused to neither be credited*…this is incorrect. Only (D) works.

4. E

Difficulty: Low

The sentence compares two things: Balanchine's skill as a dancer and his skill as a choreographer. The structure of the comparison must be parallel.

(C) and (E) fix this problem—*dancer* and *choreographer* are parallel structures. (C), however, changes the meaning of the sentence. Balanchine was not *almost skillful*. He was almost as skillful a dancer as he was a choreographer. (E) is correct. (B) and (D) do not correct the parallelism problem.

5. C

Difficulty: Medium

The introductory phrase should be followed by the noun that it modifies. Remember to check modification whenever you see an introductory phrase on Improving Sentences questions.

Who stares out over the ocean? The sailor. (B) and (C) both use the correct noun. However, (B) states that the sailor gave stability to the waves. This doesn't make sense. (C) is the only answer with the correct noun that makes sense. *The sailor felt a sense of stability from the waves.*

6. D

Difficulty: Medium

This sentence is a run-on, containing two independent sentences joined by a comma. Since none of the answer choices correct this by adding a semicolon, look for an answer that inserts an appropriate conjunction between the sentences, or that makes one of the independent clauses a subordinate clause.

(B), (D), and (E) all insert an appropriate conjunction *though* that shows the relationship between the two ideas. Only (D) corrects the style problems of *daily in their lives they are calm though*. (B) adds to the style problems by adding *than that*. (E) eliminates the parallelism between the two sentences. (C) omits the idea that they are calm in their daily lives, only stating that they are not as angry. Only (D) is correct.

7. B

Difficulty: Medium

The sentence uses the pronoun *which* to refer to people.

(B) and (E) use the correct pronoun *who* to refer to people, but only (B) keeps the idea of the original sentence. (E) introduces horoscopes instead of astrology. (C) uses *whom* instead of *who*. (D) uses *that* to refer to people.

8. D

Difficulty: Medium

Check to see if the introductory phrase modifies the correct noun. It is intended to modify *many people* (many people rely on the news), but *CNN* immediately follows it.

(C) and (D) place the correct noun directly after the introductory phrase, but (C) is inappropriately reversed, needlessly wordy, and awkward. Only (D) has the correct arrangement of words. (B) substitutes the wrong noun as modifier. CNN doesn't rely on its news; many people do. (E) is a sentence fragment; it contains no verb.

9. A

Difficulty: Medium

The sentence is correct as written. Don't forget answer choice (A). It is correct about as often as any other choice.

Note the word pair *either* and *or*. (A) gives the correct usage. (B) is correct but unnecessarily complicates the sentence. (C) eliminates *in*. (D) and (E) eliminate *either* from the word pair.

10. B

Difficulty: Medium

The relative pronoun *which* is misused here. Tom finds the length of golf particularly boring, not golf itself.

Instead of joining the two ideas clumsily, (B) makes each idea independent and links them with a semicolon. (C) and (E)

change the meaning. Tom finds the length of golf particularly boring, not golf itself. (D) adds the preposition *to*, which does not correct the usage problem.

11. D

Difficulty: Medium

Take a look at the pronouns here. *They* has an incorrect antecedent; it should refer to the nation, but then it would have to be the singular, *it*. However, if you replace *they* with *it*, another problem arises—an unclear antecedent. Does *it* refer to the nation or the government? You have to make that distinction in your choice. Only (D) does this, by replacing the pronoun with the noun *nation*. (B) is incorrect because it replaces *they* with *it*, and *violated* with *was violating*. You can eliminate (C) because it changes *imposed* to *has imposed*, and maintains the incorrect pronoun, *they*. (E) changes the meaning of the sentence—*a renegade nation* becomes *a nation of renegades*.

12. E

Difficulty: High

If the relative pronoun clause confuses you, reverse the order.

The sentence could read *The analyst was shocked that his presentation…was criticized savagely by his customers. Criticized savagely* could be *savagely criticized* but either is correct. Therefore, although the sentence is unusual, there is no error.

13. D

Difficulty: Medium

When two things are being compared (i.e., something is twice as much as something else), check to make sure that the comparison is logical.

This sentence presents an illogical comparison: The *programs performed in the new symphony hall* are compared to *the old performance space*. The correct sentence reads: *A downfall in the economy could affect the ballet season because programs performed in the new symphony hall cost twice as much as programs performed in the old performance space*.

The word *performed*, (A), correctly describes the programs. The verb *cost*, (B), agrees with programs. The phrase *as much*, (C), is idiomatically correct and introduces the comparison between the programs.

14. A

Difficulty: Medium

Although the sentence might sound strange, look for the obvious error.

Is the pronoun *her* correct? Would you say "her felt taken advantage of"? No. The pronoun *her* is part of the subject of the sentence, so it should be *she*.

The adverb *distinctly*, (B), correctly modifies the verb *felt* (*felt distinctly* is also a correct phrasing and might sound better to you). The prepositions *of*, (C), and *on*, (D), are correctly used.

15. B

Difficulty: Low

Pronouns are often misused in spoken English; so even if they sound correct, check to be sure.

Try the sentence without *the other cyclists*. Would you say "me immediately started pedaling"? No. The pronoun *me* is part of the subject of the sentence, so it should be "I." The word *other*, (A), shows that *me* is part of the group. The adverb *immediately*, (C), correctly modifies the verb *started*. *Blown* correctly modifies *whistle*.

16. B

Difficulty: Low

When you see a word like *amount*, remember that even though it refers to a number of things, it is singular.

The subject *amount* is singular, and so the verb should be *keeps*. *Although*, (A), connects the two parts of the sentence. *Claim*, (C), is plural, agreeing with *account holders*. *Are improving* is the correct use of the progressive verb form.

17. D

Difficulty: High

Note that this sentence presents a comparison; look to see whether the comparison is logical.

Comparisons require parallel structure; here, since the first thing being compared is *to compare*, the second should be "to attempt" (rather than *attempting*). The preposition *to*, (A), is correctly placed after the verb *compare*. The verb *is*, (B), agrees with the subject *to compare* (even though the word closest to the verb is the plural noun *losses*). *Than*, (C), completes the idiom *is more than*.

18. E

Difficulty: High

Don't forget that (E) is the correct answer choice just as many times as the other answer choices are.

Take the sentence choice by choice. The modifying phrase *like that of many braggarts*, (A), correctly refers to and modifies *the businessman's success*, (B). The adjective *impressive*, (C), correctly refers to the success. The expression *had done no work to attain it*, (D), is good, idiomatic English.

19. B

Difficulty: Medium

When you see a pronoun in a sentence, look to see if it clearly refers to something.

The pronoun *they* doesn't clearly refer to anything in the sentence. A noun is needed to clarify this. A correct version of the sentence might read: *Permanent loss of eyesight if viewers stare too long at the sun is a common problem during eclipses.* The preposition *of*, (A), is correct idiomatically in *permanent loss of*. The phrases *too long*, (C), and *is a common problem*, (D), are both correctly used.

20. D

Difficulty: Medium

Don't get bogged down by the subject matter; look for common grammar problems.

Here, an adjective, *artistic*, modifies a verb, *recognized*. To correct this, the adverb *artistically* should modify *recognized*. The preposition *for*, (A), correctly precedes *the museum-restored*. The adverb *clearly*, (B), correctly modifies *wanted*, and the infinitive *to purchase*, (C), is idiomatically correct with the verb *wanted*.

21. C

Difficulty: High

Don't forget that sometimes the SAT tests knowledge of vocabulary words.

The word *detract* (which means *to disparage* or *to pull down from*) is incorrectly used here. A correct word could be *subtract*. As you build your vocabulary, pay close attention to similar words, such as "detract" and "subtract." The SAT often tests the subtle differences. The verb *dares*,

(A), agrees with *no one* and is in the present tense just like the rest of the sentence. The conjunction *for* (B), logically, connects the two parts of the sentence. The phrase *for any reason* in (D) is good, standard English.

22. C

Difficulty: High

Look to see whether the pronoun clearly refers to someone.

The pronoun *he* could refer to the store manager or the warehouse manager. Even though it would make more sense that the warehouse manager makes the deliveries, we can't be sure. To make the sentence unambiguous, we could repeat the title in the correct position. The infrequently used verb *telephoned* (A), is correct and appropriately in the past tense. The preposition *after*, (B), is correct, and *to deliver* is the correct form to follow the verb *failed*.

23. C

Difficulty: High

When there are phrases or clauses between the subject and verb, check for agreement.

This is a tricky question. The verbs *find* and *was* are in different tenses. The sentence is in the past tense—the doctors have already found this out—so *find* should become *found*. *Researching*, (A), and *affecting*, (B), are standard written English. The adverb *generally* correctly modifies *was*.

24. C

Difficulty: High

This is a complicated sentence. Look to see if pronouns clearly refer to something specific.

The pronoun *they* actually refers to a *particular species* that is singular (even though species ends in an "s"; this one is tricky). So *they* should be replaced by *it* and the verb should be the singular *has* instead of *have*. The word *conducting*, (A), is properly used. *Than in*, (B), correctly parallels the idea that begins with *less interested in*. The adverb *violently*, (D), correctly modifies the verb *taken over*.

25. B

Difficulty: Medium

Note that there is an intervening phrase between the subject and the verb; is there still agreement?

The plural subject *voters* does not agree with the singular verb *includes*. *Includes* should be changed to *include*. The

expression *who chose*, (A), is correctly in the past tense; *at least*, (C), is good, idiomatic English; and *whose*, (D), is a correct relative pronoun referring to the voters.

26. D

Difficulty: Medium

Jack, the subject of the sentence, is making a comparison. Is it logical?

Jack improperly compares the Independent Party candidate's economic plan with the other candidate, instead of with the other candidate's plan. The verb *attended*, (A), is properly in the past tense and the adverb *closely* correctly follows. The expression *which Jack*, (B), is correct standard written English, and *better structured*, (C), correctly sets up the comparison between the two plans.

27. E

Difficulty: High

Don't let the fact that you may not have heard of Villella or Balanchine distract you from the grammar.

There is no error. The expressions *to stage*, (A), *that develop from*, (B), and *and incorporate*, (C), are standard written English. *Intended* is in the appropriate tense, as George Balanchine intended the ballets to have such feeling before Edward Villella staged them.

28. C

Difficulty: Low

This sentence includes four verbs, so check their tense agreement.

The subject *not one* is singular, but the verb *have* is plural; it should be *has*. This is tricky because *not one* does refer to the *many people*, but only one of the many people, so it is singular. *To have seen*, (A), is idiomatic in good, standard English. *But*, (B), provides a logical link between the two contrasting parts of the sentence. The expression *such an object* is correct.

29. A

Difficulty: Medium

Look at the sequence of events and determine whether the tenses are appropriate.

Announces is incorrectly in the present tense, as the announcement took place in the past. It should read *announced*. *To build the morale*, (B), is good, idiomatic English. *Of employees,* (C), and *during the recession,* (D), both appropriately use prepositions.

30. A

Difficulty: Medium

The owner obviously used the word *they* so it should be written as it were in this sentence. Later, the owner clarifies that *they* actually refers to the *owner of the bowling alley.* Choice (B) is not correct because it was not the author who did the identification of the owner as a *they.* Choice (C) is not correct because one may use a pronoun in a sentence with its antecedent being in a previous sentence. Choice (D) is not correct because *they* does not refer to the author and his brother. Choice (E) is not correct because *them* would be the objective case and the *they* in sentence 2 is subjective case.

31. C

Difficulty: High

These two sentences can be combined with a simple conjunction. Choice (A) is incorrect because it includes both a semi-colon and a conjunction. Choice (B) changes the meaning by using *score* in place of *game,* and by using the preposition *for.* While Choice (D) is a complex sentence, it does not convey the correct meaning here. The use of the conjunction *but* changes the meaning.

32. B

Difficulty: Medium

This comprehension question indicates that the person who has the best game of the year is named the best bowler. Choice (A) is not correct because overall points don't matter.

There is no indication of *growth* in the passage so (C) is not correct. The passage does not address averages so (D) is not correct. Choice (E) is not correct because the passage does not include any reference to the fact that bowling can be a team sport.

33. C

Difficulty: Medium

This passage was written to persuade. It appears the author wants to change the mind of the reader. There is no indication that the passage is about business, so (A) is not

correct. Choices (B) and (E) are not correct because the passage is not written to convey information (such as in an encyclopedia). Choice (D) is not correct because, in sarcasm, the writer says the opposite of what he means. This author is very straightforward in saying what he means.

34. D

Difficulty: Medium

The tone of this passage indicates that the writer is writing a first-person account. He is also writing about memories he has. This makes it a memoir. Choices (A) and (B) are not correct because the tone of the passage is not factual. Choice (C) is not correct because the format is not poetry. There is nothing about college in the passage so (E) is not correct.

35. D

Difficulty: High

This sentence uses the subject *Bill* and gives it a compound verb *got* and *bowled* that works well. Choice (A) is not correct because one does not use a semi-colon with a conjunction. Choices (B) and (C) are both grammatically correct, but they do not convey the idea that he *got* lucky. Choice (E) is not as strong as (D) in the way it expresses the sentiment.

SECTION 5

1. E

Difficulty: Low

Since the first few questions in a section are usually the easiest, be sure to avoid careless mistakes and get those points. The students were shocked at Mr. Harris's outburst, so he must usually be pretty *calm.* Choice (E) is a good match.

As for the rest of the choices, the word in the blank isn't what surprised the students.

2. A

Difficulty: Low

Remember that only one choice can be correct. If several choices have the same meaning, none of them can be correct. The poems were written a long time ago, so Wheatley must have been something of a *pioneer* in the movement. Choice (A) works best. In choice (B), her actions were indeed in the *service* of the cause of abolitionists, but this choice ignores the part of the sentence that says she wrote these poems a long time ago. Choice (C) is the opposite of what you're looking for. She was in the front, not the *rear*. Choice (D), like (B), makes sense with the first half of the sentence, but it ignores the fact that her poems were written so long ago. In choice (E), "the *realm* of the abolitionist" might mean she is part of the movement, but then this would have the same meaning as (B), and perhaps (D). They can't all be right!

3. C

Difficulty: Medium

Your prediction doesn't have to be fancy. It should just give you an idea of what you're looking for.

Apparently there are a whole lot of insects. In fact, *a lot* is a pretty good prediction.

Choice (A) is the opposite of what you're looking for. Choice (B) makes almost no sense in the sentence: "A *rehash* of insects"? Choice (C) is perfect. Choice (D) is not as much an opposite as (A), but still very different from your prediction. Choice (E) doesn't create the impression that insects cover the entire earth's surface, as the question suggests.

4. D

Difficulty: Medium

As you go through the choices, you might keep a choice like (C), even though it feels a little funny, until you find a better choice, like (D).

The Black Plague was an epidemic disease, so the percentage of the population being discussed must have either contracted the disease or not. Unless the scientists are truly evil, they are probably looking for people who didn't get the disease. So *contracted* is a good prediction for the first blank (remember, it is preceded by the word "not"), while *protection* fits well in the second one.

In choice (A), *fear* almost makes sense, but respectable scientists aren't going to be looking for *immortality*. In choice (B), if some people didn't *recognize* the plague, then their descendants wouldn't be of any help in the search for *health*. Choice (C) is tempting, but *struggle with* the plague doesn't quite match your prediction. When you get to (D), you should recognize it as a much better match. In choice (E), why wouldn't people *believe in* the plague? Also, why would a gene lead to *responsibility*?

5. B

Difficulty: Medium

The correct answer isn't necessarily the one with the most challenging vocabulary.

The women had differences, so they probably came from *different* backgrounds. Since they overcame these differences, they must have made a *combined*, or perhaps a *successful*, effort.

Choice (A), *failed* definitely doesn't match your prediction for the second blank. Choice (B) matches your predictions for both blanks. In choice (C), the words are tough, but neither one fits your predictions. In choice (D), a campaign to earn women the right to vote certainly wouldn't be considered *frivolous*. In choice (E), the second blank fits well, but the first is the opposite of what you're looking for.

6. A

Difficulty: Low

Remember that the author of a passage writes every sentence for a reason. In a question like this one, put yourself in the author's shoes and ask, "If I were writing this passage, why would I write this sentence"?

The image of a deadly shark catching rays is pretty funny, so look for something that sums this up.

Choice (A) fits your prediction well. Choice (B) is an opposite; the end of the paragraph points out that these sharks are pretty dangerous, so the author wouldn't agree with this sentiment. Choice (C) is extreme; the sentence is much too short to be considered in-depth. Choice (D) is out of scope; boat attacks are mentioned, but the author never gives any reasons. Choice (E) is extreme; *menace* is a negatively charged word, and the rest of the passage doesn't have this negative tone.

7.   B

Difficulty: Medium

Even when a Detail question doesn't provide a line reference, you probably still need to go back to the passage for information.

The author says that basking sharks can be dangerous to people, and, as an example, notes that divers and scientists have been hurt by the denticles in the sharks' skin. Look for a choice that makes sense in that context.

Choice (A) is distortion; the word "denticle" may make you think of teeth, but the passage says that denticles are contained in the shark's skin, not its mouth. Choice (B) fits what you found in the passage. Choice (C) is distortion; protection, yes, but nothing in the passage indicates that the shark needs protection from the sun. Choice (D) is out of scope; there's no support for this in the passage—there's no mention of food anywhere. Choice (E) is distortion; the denticles are *one* way for the shark to protect itself, but not necessarily the only way (Those teeth have to be good for something).

8.   D

Difficulty: Low

For Vocab-in-Context questions, be aware of multiple definitions.

Virtual is a word we hear all the time today in phrases such as "virtual reality." Don't rely on that for context. The passage says that the essays are a lot like manuals—they are *almost* manuals.

In choice (A), *organic* manuals makes no sense. Choice (B) is the "virtual reality" trap. His essays may or may not be in *electronic* format, there's no telling. In choice (C), this is a play on one of the definitions of *virtue*, but it doesn't fit here. Choice (D) is a reasonable match to your prediction. Choice (E) is another "virtual reality" trap.

9.   D

Difficulty: Medium

"Suggests" tells us that this is an Inference question. Keep the author's overall tone in mind when you research the question.

The relevant part of the paragraph is the very beginning. Other playwrights write about themselves or cut the other guy down. Miller doesn't do that. That must be the difference the question is asking about.

Choice (A) is out of scope; we do not learn anything about time frame. Choice (B) is out of scope; the passage does not mention quantity. Choice (C) is out of scope; although the author of this passage might wish that Miller is the most influential essayist, there is no indication that this is actually true. Choice (D) matches the prediction nicely. Choice (E) is distortion; yes, this may be true, but it could also be true of other playwright-essayists.

Questions 10–15

The introduction tells you that this is an excerpt from an autobiography. Your first read-through should've given you a general idea of the main points: Douglass learned to read and write through his own resourcefulness; he was influenced greatly by a specific piece of writing; and the more he read, the more tormented he became by his conviction that freedom was rightfully his.

10.   C

Difficulty: Medium

Remember that with Global questions you need to find a choice that covers the main points of the passage without being too broad or too narrow. In this case, (A) is much too narrow. Douglass mentions that he made friends with some white boys only to let the reader know how he learned to read. How learning to read influenced his ideas about slavery, (C), is the primary focus of the passage—it's the idea everything in the passage relates to. Choice (D) is out of-scope. It blows up the book that influenced Douglass into "literature," and the discussion of slavery into "civil rights movements." It doesn't mention Douglass, reading, or slavery at all. If you have trouble with a Global question, you can either do the other questions first, which might clarify the main idea for you, or eliminate any too-broad or too-narrow choices and guess.

11.   E

Difficulty: Low

Don't be put off by the vocabulary in this (or any) question stem. Use the information you're given—the line reference—to figure it out. What does Douglass say about his mistress in paragraph 1? Simply that she started to teach him to read and write, but then (influenced by her husband) stopped, and wouldn't let anyone else teach him either. That's what choice (E) says. Choice (A) is wrong because we found in paragraph 1 that Douglass's mistress finally took her husband's advice—not that she "persisted in ignoring it." Choice (B) is wrong because there is no mention of Douglass's opposition to slavery in paragraph 1—if you chose (B), you're inferring too much. The same goes for choices (C) and (D).

12. D

Difficulty: Medium

With a question about an analogy, you don't want to be too literal. In the lines you're referred to, Douglass describes how he gave bread to hungry boys in exchange for lessons—"the bread of knowledge." Since he says this kind of "bread" is "more valuable" than actual food, it must've been very important to him, as (D) has it. If you chose (B), you're focusing too much on details and losing sight of the main points. Choice (E) distorts a small fact (the availability of bread) into an improbable inference. Choice (C) takes the word "valuable" to mean financially valuable, but Douglass means knowledge is valuable in other ways.

13. B

Difficulty: Medium

"Bear" has a number of different definitions, so you must go back to the context to figure out the answer. You should do this with all Vocabulary-in-Context questions. Choice (B) makes the most sense. Choice (D) might've tempted you, since Douglass is "suffering" at the thought of being a slave for life. But it's the situation that implies suffering, not the word "bear."

14. D

Difficulty: High

This question's a little harder than most, so if you had trouble with it, you should've come back to it, or eliminated choices and guessed. Remember, all questions are worth the same, so don't lose time on any single one. In this case, a good approach is to figure out the point of the paragraph, and then find an answer that makes sense. What's Douglass's main point there? He says that the more he read, the more he realized that slavery was a large-scale form of robbery, which increased his outrage. So Douglass describes slaveowners as "robbers" to emphasize that as his knowledge increased, so did his anger, (D). Choice (A) is tricky. The description of slaveowners as "robbers" may indicate that Douglass's misconceptions about the

legitimacy of slavery had been dispelled, but it's not Douglass's goal here to do that for others. Choices (B) and (C) don't make much sense in this context. Choice (E) is wrong because it's not Douglass's goal to prove his master's predictions.

15. D

Difficulty: Medium

Read the lines you're referred to, and a line or two more, to understand the context in which the phrase "eternal wakefulness" is used. Douglass says that he "saw" and "heard" freedom everywhere—that the idea of freedom tormented him, since he was supposed to be a slave for life. "Eternal wakefulness" refers to the way his soul had been affected by the idea of freedom. Now check the choices to see which one fits with these ideas. Choice (D) matches, and is the right answer. Choice (A) is out because Douglass knows all too well the causes of his unhappiness. Choice (B) is wrong because it's too positive—it doesn't capture the "torment" Douglass discusses. Choice (C) might be the next step he takes, but he doesn't mention his "plans" for freedom in this excerpt. Finally, Douglass says nothing about "researching his African origins" anywhere in the passage.

16. B

Difficulty: Low

The main idea, or thesis, is generally stated in the opening paragraph. Notice that the author states the function of the heart and lists the mechanical attributes of the heart in the opening paragraph.

Choice (A) is a misused detail; pulmonary circulation is briefly discussed, but the passage contains more information about the heart other than pulmonary circulation. Choice (B) is a good match; this answer best reflects the thesis stated in the opening paragraph. Choice (C) is out of scope; although the heart's need for more blood compared with other organs is mentioned, this is not the primary concern of the passage. Choice (D) is a misused detail; the second paragraph is concerned with the pumping of the heart; however, the other paragraphs explore other functions and aspects of the heart. Choice (E) is out of scope; although the author mentions the cardiovascular system in the opening sentence, the passage focuses on the heart.

17. D

Difficulty: Medium

The question tells the reader that myocytes are muscle cells. Look for a section of the passage that discusses a muscle in the heart. The passage explains that the myocardium is composed of cells called myocytes, which work together to contract and expand the heart chambers.

Choice (A) is out of scope; the function of heart valves is not discussed in detail in this passage. Choice (B) is distortion; although the myocytes of the myocardium are responsible for pumping the blood to the lungs, they are not responsible for oxygenation. Choice (C) is extreme; the heart never rests. Choice (D) is a good match; myocytes compose the myocardium, which contracts and relaxes the heart chambers. Choice (E) is distortion; blood must always be pumped through the right side of the heart first before passing to the left side.

18. E

Difficulty: Medium

"Contraction" and "relaxation" are both states of the heart pumping cycle, which are defined in this sentence. Because "relaxation" is set in parentheses, the definition/context precedes it.

Choice (A) is distortion; the final paragraph states that the heart never *rests*. Choice (B) is an opposite; contraction is the process of *squeezing blood* from the heart's chambers. Choice (C) is distortion; relaxation is a part of the *pumping* process, but this does not define the term. Choice (D) is a misused detail; the plastic bottle simile is used to illustrate the *pumping* process, but it does not define the term "relaxation." Choice (E) is a good match for your prediction; the definition of relaxation in this context is stated prior to the parentheses: "expanding to allow blood in."

19. B

Difficulty: Medium

Pulmonary circulation is mentioned in line 29. Read the following sentence for context.

The author's use of "That is," establishes that pulmonary circulation is about to be defined. In this case, the pumping of blood through the lungs and oxygenation compose the process of pulmonary circulation.

Choice (A) is a misused detail; pulmonary circulation begins in the right heart chamber, but the circuit is also composed of the lungs. Choice (B) is a good match for your prediction. Choice (C) is an opposite; blood is pumped through the left side of the heart and the aorta following pulmonary circulation. Choice (D) is extreme; the left heart chamber is not involved in pulmonary circulation. Choice (E) is extreme; coronary blood vessels are mentioned in the opening paragraph, but the passage does not discuss their use.

20. A

Difficulty: Medium

Line 33 is provided; re-read the sentences before and after line 33 to further ascertain the context of the word "oxygenated." Line 33 mentions the blood is "newly" oxygenated; line 30 says that the blood "receives oxygen" in the lungs.

Choice (A) is a good match for your prediction; pulmonary circulation supplies oxygen to the blood. Choice (B) is an opposite; "deoxygenated" is when the blood is in need of oxygen. Choice (C) is a misused detail; blood returning to the heart from the body is supplied with carbon dioxide, but it is in need of oxygen. Choice (D) is distortion; although oxygenated blood is indeed bright red, the context in line 33 does not state this. Choice (E) is an opposite; deoxygenated blood is dark bluish red.

21. D

Difficulty: High

What does blood deliver to the body, as it pertains to this passage? "Used blood" is returned to the right side of the heart. Because the body has taken the oxygen it needs from the blood, it is returned to the heart.

Choice (A) is extreme; the passage never asserts that blood is considered waste. Choice (B) is an opposite; the deoxygenated blood is dark bluish red. Choice (C) is a misused detail; although the blood is indeed deoxygenated, it is not waste, but instead will be passed through the right heart and lungs to be oxygenated. Choice (D) is a good match for your prediction; blood delivers nutrients to the organs and tissues of the body; once it circulates, it is "used" and must return to the heart to be oxygenated and circulated again. Choice (E) is an opposite; deoxygenated blood returning from the body must return to the right side of the heart in order to be oxygenated.

22. C

Difficulty: Low

The heart's mass and blood needs in proportion to the body are mentioned. The sentence begins with the word "Although," which sets the heart's mass (1%) apart from its blood requirements (4%–5%).

Choice (A) is a misused detail; the heart compromises less than 1% of the body's weight. Choice (B) is extreme; this is the opposite of what the paragraph is explaining. Choice (C) is a good match for your prediction. Choice (D) is a misused detail; the heart does need a richer supply, but the question asks how much. Choice (E) is a misused detail; as with (A), the heart comprises 1% or less of a person's body weight.

23. D

Difficulty: Low

What is needed to verify something as a truth? The author states that she was unable to prove the truth of the shark story because of a lack of a specific type of evidence. What choice best describes the type of evidence she needed?

Choice (A) is distortion; the shark story itself is *hearsay*, the author wants to back it up with solid evidence. Choice (B) is an irrelevant detail; *confidential* makes no sense in context. Choice (C) is distortion; *brutal* is synonymous with "hard" when it used to describe toughness or insensitivity; it makes no sense as applied in this context. Choice (D) should match your prediction. Choice (E) is an opposite; the information the author presents about bull sharks could be considered *theoretical* evidence because she proves *in theory* it could have happened.

24. E

Difficulty: Low

What is it about the bull shark that makes it different from the two other types of sharks mentioned in the passage? In the passage, the author states that "Unlike … the great white and tiger sharks, bull sharks can survive in bodies of water with lower levels of salinity than the ocean." Look for the answer that best rephrases this detail to fit the question.

Choice (A) is distortion; the passage states that tiger sharks are "equally ferocious" as great whites and bull sharks. Choice (B) is out of scope; a tiger shark's size is never mention in the passage. Choice (C) is an irrelevant detail; the girl was supposedly attacked in the Hudson River. Choice (D) is distortion; the information about the bull

shark proves that the events in the story could have happened. Choice (E) is a good match for your prediction.

SECTION 6

1. C

Difficulty: Low

Strategic Advice: Sometimes even questions of low difficulty contain traps for the unwary. Here, notice that you're asked, not for d, but for $2d$.

Getting to the Answer:

$$3d = 10$$
$$d = \frac{10}{3}$$
$$2d = \frac{20}{3} = 6\frac{2}{3}$$

2. B

Difficulty: Low

Strategic Advice: Notice how much or how little a question constrains the range of numbers you're dealing with. In this case, when you think of a number that satisfies the requirements of the question stem, do you notice how *un*constrained you are? All these numbers work: 1, 7, 17, 71, 111, 777, etc.

Getting to the Answer:

The number 1 rules out every choice but the answer.

3. A

Difficulty: Low

Strategic Advice: If you're unsure of how to handle problems with square roots of variables, Backsolve or use your given answers. But as you'll see below, the algebraic solution isn't prohibitively complicated.

Getting to the Answer:

$$9\sqrt{x} = 9$$
$$\sqrt{x} = \frac{9}{9} = 1$$
$$x = 1$$

4. E

Difficulty: Medium

Strategic Advice: Break complex processes down into separate steps. Here, first determine k; then use that value to find y.

Getting to the Answer:

Use $x = 4$ when $y = 6$ to solve for k:

$6 = k(4)$

$k = \dfrac{3}{2}$

Use $k = \dfrac{3}{2}$ and $x = 16$ to solve for y:

$y = \dfrac{3}{2}(16)$

$y = 24$

5. A

Difficulty: Medium

Strategic Advice: When you are unsure of how to write the equation of a line, remember that the answer choices are right in front of you. Pick points off of the graph and then plug them into the given equations.

Getting to the Answer:

Use the point (2,0) to test out the given equations:

$y = 10x - 20$

$0 = 10(2) - 20$

$0 = 20 - 20$

$0 = 0$

Choice (A) works.

6. E

Difficulty: Medium

Strategic Advice: This problem may look a little intimidating, but what it really tests is your knowledge of positive and negative numbers. Notice that the products of the x- and y-coordinates of the points in quadrants I and III (the upper right and lower left) are positive. On the other hand, notice that the products of the x- and y-coordinates of the points in quadrants II and IV are negative, because in II and IV one coordinate is positive and the other negative. Positive numbers are larger than negative numbers, so either (C) or (E) is correct.

Getting to the Answer:

Point E is much farther from the origin than point C, so the product of its coordinates is larger in E than in C.

7. D

Difficulty: High

Strategic Advice: This problem asks for a in terms of b. You're given a in terms of c, so to get a in terms of b, you need to find c in terms of b. Then plug this expression into a for c.

Getting to the Answer:

Finding c in terms of b:

$b = 7 + 3c$

$b - 7 = 3c$

$\dfrac{b - 7}{3} = c$

Finding a in terms of b:

$a = 9c^2 + 4$

$a = 9(\dfrac{b - 7}{3})^2 + 4$

$a = 9(\dfrac{b^2 - 14b + 49}{9}) + 4$

$a = b^2 - 14b + 49 + 4$

$a = b^2 - 14b + 53$

8. C

Difficulty: High

Strategic Advice: There are several ways to approach this problem. For instance, you could begin by finding the length of the sides of the large squares, then dividing the figure into areas based on that length and calculating the area of each zone. This is a perfectly good way to solve the problem, but it will most likely take more time than the method described below, which relies on adding a few lines to the original diagram.

Getting to the Answer:

You're given that the large squares are identical, and also that $DEGF$ and $FGKJ$ are identical. E and K must therefore the centers of the $ABHF$ and $FHML$, respectively. So each large square in the figure can be divided into four smaller, identical squares as shown here:

The area of a large square is 100 square units, so the area of a small square is $\dfrac{100}{4} = 25$ units. The figure is made up of 10 small squares, so its total area is 250 square units.

9. 2.75 or $\frac{11}{4}$

Difficulty: Medium

Strategic Advice: Many SAT questions require multiple steps. In this case, first find the value of d from the second equation; then use that in the first equation to find the value of h.

Getting to the Answer:

$$4d = 10$$

$$d = \frac{10}{4} = \frac{5}{2}$$

$$d + 2h = 8$$

$$\frac{5}{2} + 2h = 8$$

$$2h = \frac{16}{2} - \frac{5}{2} = \frac{11}{2}$$

$$h = \frac{11}{4}$$

10. 6

Difficulty: Low

Strategic Advice: First, subtract the fixed cost from the total amount Mr. Jones was charged to find the amount he spent on books. Then divide this by the cost of one book to find the number of books he ordered.

Getting to the Answer:

$$62 - 35 = 27$$

$$\frac{27}{4.50} = 6$$

11. 12

Difficulty: Medium

Strategic Advice: Sketching a diagram will often help you visualize geometry problems. Think about the relationship between the lengths of the different line segments in this problem.

Getting to the Answer:

Since C is the midpoint of segment AD, which is 16 cm long, segments AC and CD must each be 8 cm long. B is the midpoint of AC, so AB and BC are each 4 cm long. Segment BD is $4 + 8 = 12$ cm long.

12. 3

Difficulty: Medium

Strategic Advice: This particular problem can easily be solved by trial and error. Since the digits of number AA are the same, there re only 9 possible numbers to try.

Getting to the Answer:

$$\begin{array}{r} 11 \\ \times 11 \\ \hline 121 \end{array}$$

$$1 + 2 = 3$$

13. 1,000

Difficulty: Medium

Strategic Advice: This question deals with finding the number of possible combinations of two objects. No matter which entrée Mary selects, she could order any of the 40 side dishes.

Getting to the Answer:

$$25 \times 40 = 1,000$$

14. 25

Difficulty: Medium

Strategic Advice: One approach to this problem would be to draw a calendar, placing the first of the month on Monday and counting the days between that and the last Friday. While this technique doesn't take too long on this particular problem, it can be cumbersome when dealing with larger numbers. A faster approach is shown below.

Getting to the Answer:

The last Friday in the month is four days after the last Monday. The last Monday in the month is some multiple of seven days after the first Monday. Therefore, the last Friday is $7n + 4$ days after the first Monday, where n is an integer. The largest possible value of $7n + 4$ that is less than 31 is 25.

15. 812

Difficulty: Medium

Strategic Advice: Although you could find the value of 29! and the value of 27!, this would be extremely time-consuming. Many SAT problems can be done in both a time-consuming manner and a faster way. Try to find parts of the problem that cancel out to save yourself time and effort.

$$\frac{29!}{27!} = \frac{29 \times 28 \times 27!}{27!} = 29 \times 28 = 812$$

16. 30

Difficulty: Medium

Strategic Advice: Many of the more difficult geometry questions on the SAT can be simplified by noticing relationships between different parts of the diagram. In this case, knowing the relationship between the area of the shaded sector and the area of the circle as a whole gives us the measure of the angle between *AD* and *CF*. This in turn gives us the measure of *q*.

Since the shaded area $\frac{1}{6}$ the area of the circle, the angle between *AD* and *CF* is $\frac{1}{6}$ of 360 degrees, or 60 degrees.

The angles along *CF* add up to 180 degrees, so $60 + 90 + q = 180$ and $q = 30$.

17. 6

Difficulty: Medium

Strategic Advice: The median of a set of numbers is the number in the middle when the numbers are arranged in increasing order.

Getting to the Answer:

These numbers should be in the order $\frac{1}{2}x$, $3x$, and $5x$. The median is $3x$.

$3x = 18$

$x = 6$

18. 210

Difficulty: Medium

Strategic Advice: You probably already know that the interior angles of a triangle add up to 180 degrees and that the angles around a given point add up to 360 degrees. You

can use these two pieces of information to find the sum of the interior angles of any convex multi-sided figure. You can also memorize the formula derived from the approach outlined below, which is $180n - 360 =$ sum of interior angles, where n is the number of sides. Once you have found the sum of the interior angles of this figure, you need only subtract the known angles to find the sum of *a* and *b*.

Getting to the Answer:

First, divide the figure into a number of triangles which meet at a central point:

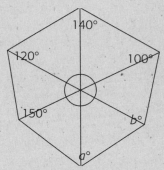

The sum of the interior angles of each triangle is 180 degrees. The angles around the central point (marked by the small circle) add up to 360 degrees. Therefore, the total sum of the interior angles of the six-sided polygon is

$$180(6) - 360 = 720.$$

$$720 - (150 + 120 + 140 + 100) = 210$$

SECTION 7

1. D

Difficulty: Low

The word *while* indicates that the two missing words must be opposite, or nearly opposite, in meaning. The government probably promised to make the forms easier to use, or to *simplify* them. The second blank should contrast with that, so *complicated* is a good prediction. Choice (D) is a good match for both blanks.

Choice (A) doesn't show the necessary contrast between the blanks. Infuriating means "angering, frustrating." In (B), *shorten* works pretty well for the first blank, but *expensive* doesn't contrast with that. Be careful here; it's the taxes themselves, not the tax forms, that people might find expensive. Eliminate (C); if the forms were *comprehensible*, people wouldn't need professional help. Similarly, if the forms were *familiar* (E), taxpayers would not to seek help.

2. A

Difficulty: Low

Be sure that your choice captures the full meaning of the sentence—here, several of the choices make some sense, but don't involve sounds. The sentence begins with a list of sounds. For the first blank, "loud" is a good prediction. The second blank needs to sum up this noise, so look for something that means "big noise." In (A), thundering is a great match for the sound of the horses, and cacophony, which means "dissonance, unpleasant noise," perfectly captures the noise of the battlefield.

In (B), running doesn't describe a sound, and danger doesn't fit either. Why would trumpets and drums be dangerous? Choice (C) has a similar problem. A battlefield might be a horror, but this term doesn't capture the sounds described. In (D), situation doesn't describe the sounds. And (E) is wrong because it seems unlikely that you would find many plodding horses in a battle, and calm is the opposite of your prediction for the second blank.

3. E

Difficulty: Low

Trust your ear. If a choice doesn't sound right, eliminate it. The sentence sets up a contrast between the short- and long-term effects of some measures. The short-term effects are positive, but the long-term effects are uncertain. Choice (E) captures this idea. Debated conveys that people don't know what the long-term effects will be, and that those effects might differ from the positive, short-term effects.

Simply *stating,* (A), or *discussing,* (C), the long-term effects wouldn't contrast the short-term benefits. Choice (B), *compared,* doesn't make sense here. You could say that the council *inquired,* (D), into the effects, but inquired by itself doesn't fit here.

4. B

Difficulty: Medium

If you didn't know the word *improprieties*, which means "improper actions, infractions," you could probably still eliminate the four wrong answer choices. It looks like the corporation wanted the manager to ignore some shady accounting policies, so *illegal actions* is a good prediction

for the second blank. The manager refused to ignore this, so he must have been maintaining his *honesty*. Choice (B) fits your prediction well.

In (A), *irregularities* fits well in the second blank, but *geniality*, which means "friendliness," would not make the manager ignore those irregularities. In (C), *dishonesty* is the opposite of the word you're looking for. Like geniality, (D), *cordiality*, or "polite friendliness," would not make someone ignore inconsistencies in accounting. Finally, (E) is an opposite answer. If the manager ignored accounting rules, that wouldn't indicate *frankness*, or "directness."

5. D

Difficulty: High

To answer this question using context, ask yourself what kind of response might warrant a chat with the principal. In (D), *flippant* means disrespectful lightheartedness, with "disrespectful," of course, being the pertinent connotation. Choice (B), *inveterate*, means firmly established, usually with regard to attitude or habit. *Pecuniary*, answer (C), refers to money; and *reactionary*, (A), means extremely conservative, especially in politics. Answer choice (E), *lax*, means loose or slack, often in the figurative sense of lacking in rigor or strictness.

6. A

Difficulty: High

Straight definition-style questions can still be challenging if the word being defined in tough. What kind of artists create "new and experimental" art? A good prediction is *experimental* or *creative*. Choice (A) fits perfectly. In (B), artists might be *competitive*, but this doesn't match the rest of the sentence. In (C) and (D) the words are challenging but don't have anything to do with the rest of the sentence, as *impugned* means to attack verbally or to call into question and *dilatory* means slow or lazy. In (E), artists might be *mannered*, but this doesn't match the second half of the sentence.

Questions 7–19

Passage 1

The first paragraph of Passage 1 introduces the Waltham-Lowell system. It is described as a system of factory organization and rules implemented in the nineteenth

Questions 7–19

Passage 1

The first paragraph of Passage 1 introduces the Waltham-Lowell system. It is described as a system of factory organization and rules implemented in the nineteenth century to increase profits. Then, you learn that, for economic reasons, women were preferred as factory workers. The second paragraph discusses the requirement that factory girls live in company boarding houses. The adverse consequences of this rule are described, but it is also pointed out that one of the reasons for this rule was to placate the girls' families. The third paragraph describes another problem with the boarding house regulation: health issues related to overcrowding and unsanitary conditions. The final paragraph concludes the passage with a partial justification of the Waltham-Lowell system and the factory leadership. The author argues that economic demands, including the threat of bankruptcy, made the poor conditions in American factories necessary.

Passage 2

The first paragraph of Passage 2 describes the Waltham-Lowell system as mandating atrocious factory conditions. The health risks of the system are detailed. The second paragraph then describes factory agents as supervisors who enforced regulations and often fired workers with little provocation. The third paragraph describes the practice of locking factory doors to keep workers inside the building. This led to a tragic accident at a factory in New York City, but the owners of the factory were not punished significantly. The final paragraph makes clear the author's opinion that the working conditions of the factories were inexcusable, regardless of economic conditions.

7.   A

Difficulty: Low

In questions about the author's attitude, beware of extreme answer choices. The answer is often quite moderate.

From the description of boarding-house life in the third paragraph, you know that the author feels sorry for the women. But the last paragraph suggests that the author also feels the conditions were perhaps necessary in order for the factories to be economically successful. Look for something that sums up these mixed feelings.

In choice (A), *sympathy* fits well, and *reserved* conveys the sense that the author feels the conditions were necessary. Choice (B) is an opposite; the author is sympathetic, not *disinterested*. Choice (C) is an opposite; again, the author is sympathetic, not *contemptuous*. Choice (D) is out of scope; the author doesn't seem at all confused, so *befuddlement* doesn't fit. Choice (E) is extreme; the author might be appreciative of the workers, but *unreserved* is too extreme, and doesn't fit the mixed feelings of your prediction.

8.   B

Difficulty: Medium

Treat a challenging Vocab-in-Context like a Sentence Completion problem.

In the sentence in question, the author says that European boarding houses were even worse than their American counterparts. So even if you've never seen the word *base* used in this way, you know that it must be negative since it applies to the European boarding-house owners. Look for a negative word that could describe ethics, and keep in mind other meanings for the word *base*, like the base of a mountain.

In choice (A), in this context, this word indicates that something is highly moral, the opposite of what you're looking for. In choice (B), *immoral* ethics sounds good. Choice (C) is a tempting meaning, but *absent* doesn't seem to match any of the other, more familiar meanings of *base*. Choice (D) is tempting, but it's the actions that were *harmful*, not the ethics that motivated the actions. Choice (E) matches *base*, but doesn't fit in the sentence.

9.   A

Difficulty: Medium

"According to Passage 1" tells you that this will ask about a specific detail. Don't try to answer from memory.

This detail appears in the second paragraph. Check out lines 16–18: "Primarily to assure families that their daughters would not be corrupted by factory life."

Choice (A) is a good match. Choice (B) is distortion; the passage discusses *factory* life, not *city* life. Choice (C) is a misused detail; the boarding houses spread—rather than prevented—disease. Choice (D) is out of scope; the social activities of the workers are never discussed. Choice (E) is distortion; this was indeed an effect, as shown in the second sentence of the second paragraph, but it's not the reason that factory owners instituted the policy.

10. B

Difficulty: Low

The correct answer in a Vocab-in-Context question won't just work in a particular sentence—it will also make the sentence work in the entire passage.

Since "the economists advanced" an idea, *advanced* must be something that you can do with an idea. The final paragraph presents this idea, and the author seems to regard the idea as reasonable, so look for something that says the economists stated the idea.

Choice (A) is the typical meaning of *advanced*—but it doesn't fit here. When you read choice (B) back, it makes perfect sense. Choice (C), the word makes sense in the sentence, but then the sentence doesn't work with the rest of the paragraph. The author wouldn't talk about a group *denying* an idea that hasn't even been stated yet. In choice (D), can you *progress* an idea? That doesn't make much sense. In choice (E), like (C), sounds OK in the sentence, but that sentence then doesn't make sense in the paragraph as a whole.

11. E

Difficulty: High

For Reasoning questions, summarize the author's argument in your own words before looking at the answer choices.

The author thinks that factory owners had no choice because they would have lost money and gone out of business if they had instituted better working conditions. Look for an answer choice that would weaken this argument.

Choice (A) is out of scope; tempting, but no. Conditions in France don't necessarily have anything to do with conditions in America. Maybe it's easier to run a factory in France for some reason that just doesn't apply in America. Choice (B) is out of scope; maybe this Bennington system is even crueler to workers. We don't know anything about this Bennington system, so this fact doesn't weaken the argument. Choice (C) is an opposite; this doesn't weaken the argument—it strengthens it. It just proves that it would have been a poor business strategy to improve working conditions. Choice (D) is out of scope; maybe twentieth-century factories had technologies or other advantages not available to nineteenth-century factories. Since the situations are not the same, the improved twentieth-century conditions don't weaken the argument that poor conditions were necessary in the nineteenth century. Choice (E) fits. If

factory owners had a way to improve conditions without lowering profits, then this weakens the author's argument that poor conditions were necessary.

12. B

Difficulty: Medium

In paired passages, it's extremely important to keep the authors straight. Don't fall for choices that mix up the authors' points of view.

What part does this paragraph play in the passage as a whole? The author feels that the system created poor working conditions, and the second paragraph explains the part of agents in this process.

Choice (A) is a misused detail; this comes from the author of Passage 1, not Passage 2. Choice (B) matches your prediction. Choice (C) is a misused detail; the author speaks of the immorality of the system in the final, but not in the second, paragraph. Choice (D) is a misused detail; the fire isn't mentioned until the third paragraph. Choice (E) is a misused detail; again, this comes from Passage 1, not Passage 2.

13. C

Difficulty: Low

Read each answer choice carefully, and don't get caught in a trap: for example, (E) is wrong because of a single word.

The third paragraph, which describes the fire, says that "the Waltham-Lowell system…[was] downright dangerous." So, look for something that says the factory owners created dangerous conditions.

Choice (A) is out of scope; the author only mentions a single fire, and doesn't suggest that such events happened often. Choice (B) is distortion; the author feels the accident was a tragedy, so sympathy wouldn't be *unwarranted*. Choice (C) matches your prediction. Choice (D) is an opposite; the author feels that factory owners didn't do enough to protect workers. Choice (E) is distortion; it's the factory owners, not the workers, who were negligent.

14. E

Difficulty: Medium

On Detail questions, watch out for answer choices that bring in irrelevant information from other parts of the passage.

Reread the sentence in which the word appears. The author notes that one would hope that the tragedy would bring about change, but that nothing much happened to the factory owners, and that factories continued to lock their doors for several years.

Choice (A) is distortion; the passage mentions 23 families, not 23 victims. There might have been victims whose families did not sue. Choice (B) is an opposite; the next-to-last sentence in the third paragraph states that the owners were acquitted of criminal charges, so they *didn't* go to jail. Choice (C) is distortion; the practice of locking doors remained common, but we don't know that tragedies of this sort remained common, since we don't know if fires continued to happen frequently. Choice (D) is a misused detail; the whale-oil lamps in the first paragraph created pollution, not fires. Choice (E) matches the last two sentences of the paragraph.

15. C

Difficulty: Medium

If you're asked about the structure of a paragraph, go back and quickly reread each sentence to figure out what's going on.

Author 2 mentions the view also held by author 1—that factory owners had to create poor working conditions in order to make money and stay in business. Author 2 then goes on to disagree, and proposes that a system "of common decency" should have been used instead.

In choice (A), no evidence is introduced in the final paragraph. In choice (B), no statistical evidence is introduced in the final paragraph. Choice (C) matches your prediction. In choice (D), we don't know how widely held any of the views discussed are, and no historical evidence is presented in the final paragraph. In choice (E), the author doesn't feel say that there is a contradiction. To the author, the choice is clear: the factory owners were in the wrong.

16. A

Difficulty: Low

With paired passages, you will almost always see a question that asks you to pinpoint an issue or issues on which the two authors disagree.

Both authors agree that the working conditions were bad, but they disagree in their final paragraphs. Author 1 states that the conditions were necessary in order for factories to stay in business, while author 2 states that the conditions were unacceptable and that another system should have been implemented.

In choice (A), here, the phrase *market conditions* means the economic situation, so this matches your prediction. Choice (B) is out of scope; neither author mentions philanthropy. Choice (C) is an opposite; both authors seem to agree that the system made American textile mills more competitive. Choice (D) is an opposite; the authors agree that health problems arose from the system. Choice (E) is out of scope; neither author mentions previous systems.

17. B

Difficulty: Low

When asked about the differences between two authors, watch out for opposite answer choices.

Both passages talk about poor conditions, but Passage 1 deals more with boarding houses, while Passage 2 deals with working conditions in the factories.

Choice (A) is an opposite; boarding houses are discussed in Passage 1, not Passage 2. Choice (B) is correct; this appears in the second paragraph of Passage 2, but never appears in Passage 1. Choice (C) is an opposite; this is discussed by both authors. Choice (D) is an opposite; this appears in Passage 1, but not Passage 2. Choice (E) is out of scope; safety supervisors are not mentioned in either paragraph.

18. B

Difficulty: Low

Remember to consult your outline if you need to find a detail quickly.

There are too many possibilities here to make a prediction, so get your outline of the passages ready and eliminate anything that doesn't appear in both passages.

Choice (A) is an opposite; this is mentioned in Passage 2, but not Passage 1. In choice (B), the final paragraph of Passage 2 and the third paragraph of Passage 1 both mention that health problems were caused by factory conditions. Choice (C) is an opposite; this is mentioned in Passage 1, but not Passage 2. Choice (D) is out of scope; this is not mentioned in either passage. Choice (E) is an opposite; both authors stress that factory owners were anything but generous.

19. D

Difficulty: High

Paired passage Inference questions hinge directly on your ability to keep straight the viewpoints of the two authors.

Author 2 is using the phrase "economic necessities" with some irony. She doesn't believe that these conditions were really necessary. Author 1, however, feels that economic conditions did in fact force the factory owners to create poor working conditions. Since the question asks about author 1, this is the viewpoint you are looking for.

Choice (A) is an opposite; this choice presents the viewpoint of the wrong author. Choice (B) is an opposite; actually, Passage 1 states that conditions boarding houses in the United States were better than those overseas. Choice (C) is a misused detail; the boarding houses were seen as a response to workers' families, but the economic conditions had a different cause (overseas competition). Choice (D) is a good match. Choice (E) is extreme; this choice is tempting, but *solely* is a bit too strong. We don't know that overseas competition is definitely the *only* cause.

SECTION 8

1. A

Difficulty: Low

Strategic Advice: Don't do more work than you have to. This problem does not require you to find *d*, *r*, or *p*, even in terms of each other.

Getting to the Answer:

$7d < 4r < 8p$.

Therefore, $7d < 8p$.

2. D

Difficulty: Low

Strategic Advice: Be sure to understand the information in the chart. One column gives the number of boxes in each location, while the other gives the number of toys in each box, not the total number of toys in that location.

Getting to the Answer:

$4(10) + 2(6) + 5(7) = 40 + 12 + 35 = 87$

3. C

Difficulty: Medium

Strategic Advice: Remember that the average of a set of numbers is equal to their sum divided by the number of numbers in the set. Therefore, the sum of a set of numbers equals their average times the number of numbers in the set.

Getting to the Answer:

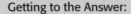

$10(8) = 80$, so the sum must be greater than 80.

$12(8) = 96$, so the sum must be less than 96.

4. E

Difficulty: Medium

Strategic Advice: Since the Earth makes a complete rotation about its axis in 24 hours, any point on its surface must rotate through 360° in that time.

Getting to the Answer:

Goannaville rotates 360° in the 24 hours from 1:00 p.m. January 2 to 1:00 p.m. January 3. In the three hours between 1:00 p.m. and 4:00 p.m. on January 3, it rotates $\frac{3}{24}(360°) = 45°$ more.

$360° + 45° = 405°$

5. C

Difficulty: Low

Strategic Advice: Sets are a topic new to the 2005 SAT. While questions about sets are more likely to be of low or medium rather than high difficulty, they will, at any difficulty level, assume that you're familiar with some of the basic terminology of sets. With that in mind, begin to absorb a few facts. The things in a set are called elements or members. The union of sets is the set of elements in one or more of the sets being united. Think of the union set as what you get when you merge sets. The symbol for union set is ∪. The intersection of sets is the set of common elements of the sets being intersected. Think of the intersection as the overlap of sets. The symbol for the intersection of sets is ∩.

Getting to the Answer:

To be in $S∩T∩U$—that is, the intersection of S, T, and U—a number would have to be: between −3 and 3, inclusive; prime; and positive. Given the sets in question, the only such numbers are 2 and 3. Remember that 1 is not prime; test takers who forget that fact wrongly choose (D).

6. C

Difficulty: Medium

Strategic Advice: Both *a* and *b* can be positive, negative, or equal to zero. The square of a negative or a positive number will be positive. Zero is neither positive nor negative.

Getting to the Answer:

$a + b$ can be ruled out because a or b (or both) could be negative or zero.

$a^2 - b^2 + 10$ can be ruled out because b^2 could be greater than $a^2 + 10$.

$a^2 + b^2 + 1$ is correct. a^2, b^2, and 1 are all positive, so their sum must be positive.

$a^3 + b^3 + 16$ can be ruled out because a or b could be negative, and the cube of a negative number is negative.

$a^4 + b^2 + a^2$ can be ruled out because a and b could both equal zero.

7. D

Difficulty: Medium

Strategic Advice: Do not assume that the measurements of the angles in this figure resemble the way the figure is drawn. Any figure on the SAT that is not drawn to scale is drawn in such a way as to be deliberately misleading. To find the angles, you will need to use three pieces of information: the sum of the interior angles of a triangle is 180°, the sum of the angles along a straight line is 180°, and vertical angles—angles pointed toward each other—are equal. Using this information, you can find the measure of every angle in the diagram, as shown below. Any triangle with a 90° angle is a right triangle.

Getting to the Answer:

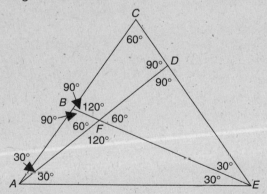

8. E

Difficulty: Medium

Strategic Advice: Questions about exponential growth can be quite challenging to most test takers. You'll be the exception if you come to think about such questions in commonsense terms. To double is simply to multiply by

two. The question calls for this doubling to occur 24 times. The mathematical way of expressing "doubling to occur 24 times" is 2^{24}.

Getting to the Answer:

The answer is the total growth that occurs, times the original population. Again, total growth is 2^{24}. The original population is p.

9. E

Difficulty: Medium

Strategic Advice: When you come upon absolute value questions, one great immediate reaction is to think, "Every positive number is the absolute value of two numbers: the number itself, and the negative of the number."

Getting to the Answer:

Call the integer n. If the absolute value of n is between 3 and 6, n must be -5, -4, 4, or 5. Two less than each of these would be choices (A), (B), (C), and (D), respectively.

10. B

Difficulty: Medium

Strategic Advice: This problem tests your ability to read instructions and perform calculations carefully. Follow each step of the procedure in order and avoid careless errors to find the answer.

Getting to the Answer:

$.62(20) = 12.4$

The largest integer less than 12.4 is 12

$12 - 4 = 8$

11. D

Difficulty: Medium

Strategic Advice: Follow the steps for the smallest and largest numbers that can be selected in step 1 to find the smallest and largest numbers than can be written in step 5. This range includes all possible numbers you can write down in step 5. And numbers outside that range, therefore, are not correct.

Getting to the Answer:

Lower bound:

$.5(20) = 10$

10 is the largest integer less than or equal to 10

$10 - 4 = 6$

Upper bound:

$.99(20) = 19.8$

19 is the largest integer less than or equal to 19.8

$19 - 4 = 15$

Therefore, the only numbers that could be written in step 5 are the integers between 10 and 15. 0 and 5 are too small, 7.4 is not an integer, and 17 is too large.

12. C

Difficulty: Medium

Strategic Advice: Think about what is happening at each step. What kind of change does each step make to the number? It may be helpful to try picking a few sample numbers to see what happens.

Getting to the Answer:

It does not matter whether you find the greatest integer less than or equal to the number and then subtract 4 or you subtract four from the number and then find the greatest lower integer. Either order produces the same number in step 5.

13. E

Difficulty: Medium

Strategic Advice: Remember the rules of multiplying exponents and raising numbers with exponents to powers. Plug 3^3 into each answer choice and see which one equals 3^8.

Getting to the Answer:

$9(3^3)^2 = 9(3^{3 \times 2}) = 9(3^6) = 3^2(3^6) = 3^{2+6} = 3^8$

14. A

To find the area, add the dimensions of the square and the triangle. First re-label the diagram as follows:

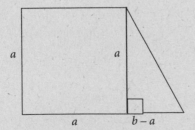

The area of a square is the length of a side squared, so the area of this square is a^2. The area of this right triangle is $\frac{1}{2}(\text{leg}_1 \times \text{leg}_2) = \frac{1}{2}(a)(b - a) = \frac{ab}{2} - \frac{a^2}{2}$. So the combined area is:

$$a^2 + \frac{ab}{2} - \frac{a^2}{2} = \frac{2a^2}{2} - \frac{a^2}{2} + \frac{ab}{2}$$

$$= \frac{a^2}{2} + \frac{ab}{2}$$

$$= \frac{a^2 + ab}{2}$$

$$= \frac{a(a + b)}{2}$$

15. D

Difficulty: High

Strategic Advice: The percent of tomato paste in the mixture will be the amount of tomato paste in the soup divided by the total amount of soup and water in the mixture. It can be confusing to work a complex problem like this one using variables, so if you're not sure about your answer you might want to try picking numbers instead.

Getting to the Answer:

The amount of tomato paste in s cups of soup is 10 percent of s, or $10\% \times s$. The total amount of soup and water is $s + w$.

Therefore, the percent of tomato paste in the mixture is $\frac{10s}{s + w}\%$.

16. D

Difficulty: High

Strategic Advice: There's no real shortcut to this problem; you just need to list the numbers from 31 to 39 and examine their factors to see which numbers have only two prime factors.

Getting to the Answer:

31 and 37 are prime themselves, so they have only one prime factor.

32 and 36 have too many factors; factors of 32 are 2, 4, 8, and 16, while factors of 36 are 2, 3, 4, 6, 9, 12, and 18.

33, 34, 35, 38, and 39 all have two factors that are both prime; $33 = 11(3)$, $34 = 17(2)$, $35 = 7(5)$, $38 = 19(2)$, and $39 = 13(3)$.

SECTION 9

1. B

Difficulty: Low

Transition words must express the correct relationship between ideas.

As written, this sentence does not use an appropriate transition to express the contrast between ideas. (B) corrects this with the transition word *although.* (C) and (E) express a cause-and-effect relationship between the clauses that is inappropriate in context. (D) is a sentence fragment.

2. A

Difficulty: High

Don't mistake complex or formal sentence structure for grammatical error. Eliminate answer choices methodically if you don't spot an error, but remember—between five and eight Writing section questions will be correct as written.

This sentence is correct as written. (B) and (E) fail to correctly complete the idiom *just as…so.* (C) and (D) introduce verb tenses that are incorrect in context.

3. A

Difficulty: Medium

Be methodical in eliminating answer choices, but if you don't spot an error, don't be afraid to choose (A).

This sentence is correct as written; the two independent clauses are properly combined by the conjunction *and.* (B) and (D) are run-on sentences. (C) and (E) introduce verb tenses that are incorrect in context.

4. E

Difficulty: High

Some idiomatic and comparative structures require parallel structure.

The idiomatic phrase *at once* must be completed with the conjunction *and,* and the items combined must be in parallel form. (E) corrects both errors. (B) and (D) do not address either error. (C) corrects the idiom, but not the parallelism.

5. B

Difficulty: High

Make sure modifying phrases are correctly placed before the noun are meant to modify.

As written, this sentence states that *the…cars* are *registering a motor vehicle.* Additionally, the sentence is unnecessarily in the passive voice. (B) corrects both errors by placing the correct noun, *applicants,* directly after the modifying phrase. In (C), *mechanics* are the ones *registering a motor vehicle.* (D) does not address either error. (E) is still in the passive voice and it is unclear what the opening phrase is meant to modify.

6. E

Difficulty: High

Make sure you select an answer choice that addresses all of the sentence's errors.

This sentence contains two errors: *the population of China* is compared to *America* and the plural verb *are* does not agree with the singular subject *population.* (E) corrects both errors. (B) does not address the comparison error, and the pronoun *we* in (B) has no antecedent. (C) and (D) do not address the comparison error.

7. E

Difficulty: Medium

Pronouns must always have clear antecedents.

The pronouns *it* and *you* do not have clear antecedents. (E) corrects this error by eliminating both pronouns. (B) and (C) are unnecessarily wordy; additionally, the pronoun *they* in (B) does not have a clear antecedent. (D) is incorrect grammatical structure.

8. D

Difficulty: Medium

The antecedent of a pronoun may appear after it in the sentence.

The singular pronoun *its* does not agree with its plural antecedent, *comic books.* (D) corrects this error with the pronouns *they* and *their.* (B) and (E) change the meaning of the sentence by replacing *Before* with *Until;* additionally, (B) fails to address the pronoun agreement error and both introduce inappropriate verb tenses in context. (C) is incorrect grammatical structure and the pronoun *them* is the wrong case in context.

9. B

Difficulty: Medium

Make sure modifying phrases are correctly placed for the nouns they are meant to modify.

As written, the opening clause modfies *effect*. Both (B) and (D) correctly place *Donald* directly after the clause; however, (D) introduces an inconsistent verb tense. (C) does not address the error. (E) is incorrect grammatical structure.

10. A

Difficulty: Medium

You will encounter between five and eight questions that are correct as written on the SAT.

This sentence is correct as written. The verb *believe* agrees with the subject *parents* and the idiom *not only…but also* is used correctly. (B) and (E) do not use the proper construction of the idiom *not only…but also*; additionally, (E) is unnecessarily wordy. (C) uses the incorrect verb phrase *are believing*. (D) incorrectly changes the verbs to the past tense *have believed*.

11. E

Difficulty: Medium

While the passive voice will not always be incorrect on the SAT, check to see if passive sentences can easily be made active.

Were made to laugh (A) is a passive verb construction; (E) makes it active without changing the meaning or introducing additional errors. (B) leaves the meaning of the second clause incomplete. (C) is unnecessarily wordy. (D) is incorrect grammatical structure.

12. B

Difficulty: Low

Items in a series, list, or compound must be parallel in structure.

As written, this sentence violates the rules of parallel structure. (B) makes the third item in the series parallel to the first two. (C) and (E) incorrectly use the plural verb form *rest* with the singular noun *integrity.* (D) does not address the error.

13. D

Difficulty: Low

Look for the most concise answer choice that does not introduce any additional errors.

The pronoun *they* is incorrect here; the subject of this sentence is *scooters.* (D) corrects this without introducing additional errors. The pronoun *their* in (B) and *they* in (C) are used without antecedents. (E) makes the sentence more concise, but does not address the original error, and loses some of the meaning of the original sentence.

14. E

Difficulty: Medium

A pronouns must agree with its antecedent, which may not be the noun closest to it in the sentence.

The antecedent for the plural pronoun *their* is actually the singular *startup;* the plural *methods,* although closer to the pronoun in the sentence, is part of a separate descriptive phrase. Although all of the choices correct this error, only (E) does so concisely and without introducing any new errors. (B) and (D) are unnecessarily wordy; (D) also uses the passive voice unnecessarily. (C) creates a sentence fragment.

SAT PRACTICE TEST TWELVE ANSWER SHEET

Remove (or photocopy) the answer sheet and use it to complete the practice test.

How to Take the Practice Tests

Each Practice Test includes eight scored multiple-choice sections and one essay. Keep in mind that on the actual SAT, there will be an additional multiple-choice section—the experimental section—that will not contribute to your score.

Once you start a Practice Test, don't stop until you've gone through all nine sections. Remember, you can review any questions within a section, but you may not go back or forward a section.

Good luck!

Start with number 1 for each section. If a section has fewer questions than answer spaces, leave the extra spaces blank.

Section One

Section One is the writing section's essay component.
Lined pages on which you will write your essay can be found in that section.

Section Two

1. Ⓐ Ⓑ Ⓒ Ⓓ Ⓔ   9. Ⓐ Ⓑ Ⓒ Ⓓ Ⓔ   17. Ⓐ Ⓑ Ⓒ Ⓓ Ⓔ
2. Ⓐ Ⓑ Ⓒ Ⓓ Ⓔ   10. Ⓐ Ⓑ Ⓒ Ⓓ Ⓔ   18. Ⓐ Ⓑ Ⓒ Ⓓ Ⓔ
3. Ⓐ Ⓑ Ⓒ Ⓓ Ⓔ   11. Ⓐ Ⓑ Ⓒ Ⓓ Ⓔ   19. Ⓐ Ⓑ Ⓒ Ⓓ Ⓔ
4. Ⓐ Ⓑ Ⓒ Ⓓ Ⓔ   12. Ⓐ Ⓑ Ⓒ Ⓓ Ⓔ   20. Ⓐ Ⓑ Ⓒ Ⓓ Ⓔ
5. Ⓐ Ⓑ Ⓒ Ⓓ Ⓔ   13. Ⓐ Ⓑ Ⓒ Ⓓ Ⓔ   21. Ⓐ Ⓑ Ⓒ Ⓓ Ⓔ
6. Ⓐ Ⓑ Ⓒ Ⓓ Ⓔ   14. Ⓐ Ⓑ Ⓒ Ⓓ Ⓔ   22. Ⓐ Ⓑ Ⓒ Ⓓ Ⓔ
7. Ⓐ Ⓑ Ⓒ Ⓓ Ⓔ   15. Ⓐ Ⓑ Ⓒ Ⓓ Ⓔ   23. Ⓐ Ⓑ Ⓒ Ⓓ Ⓔ
8. Ⓐ Ⓑ Ⓒ Ⓓ Ⓔ   16. Ⓐ Ⓑ Ⓒ Ⓓ Ⓔ   24. Ⓐ Ⓑ Ⓒ Ⓓ Ⓔ

☐ # right in Section Two

☐ # wrong in Section Two

Section Three

1. Ⓐ Ⓑ Ⓒ Ⓓ Ⓔ   9. Ⓐ Ⓑ Ⓒ Ⓓ Ⓔ   17. Ⓐ Ⓑ Ⓒ Ⓓ Ⓔ
2. Ⓐ Ⓑ Ⓒ Ⓓ Ⓔ   10. Ⓐ Ⓑ Ⓒ Ⓓ Ⓔ   18. Ⓐ Ⓑ Ⓒ Ⓓ Ⓔ
3. Ⓐ Ⓑ Ⓒ Ⓓ Ⓔ   11. Ⓐ Ⓑ Ⓒ Ⓓ Ⓔ   19. Ⓐ Ⓑ Ⓒ Ⓓ Ⓔ
4. Ⓐ Ⓑ Ⓒ Ⓓ Ⓔ   12. Ⓐ Ⓑ Ⓒ Ⓓ Ⓔ   20. Ⓐ Ⓑ Ⓒ Ⓓ Ⓔ
5. Ⓐ Ⓑ Ⓒ Ⓓ Ⓔ   13. Ⓐ Ⓑ Ⓒ Ⓓ Ⓔ
6. Ⓐ Ⓑ Ⓒ Ⓓ Ⓔ   14. Ⓐ Ⓑ Ⓒ Ⓓ Ⓔ
7. Ⓐ Ⓑ Ⓒ Ⓓ Ⓔ   15. Ⓐ Ⓑ Ⓒ Ⓓ Ⓔ
8. Ⓐ Ⓑ Ⓒ Ⓓ Ⓔ   16. Ⓐ Ⓑ Ⓒ Ⓓ Ⓔ

☐ # right in Section Three

☐ # wrong in Section Three

Remove (or photocopy) this answer sheet and use it to complete the practice test.

Start with number 1 for each section. If a section has fewer questions than answer spaces, leave the extra spaces blank.

Section Four

1. Ⓐ Ⓑ Ⓒ Ⓓ Ⓔ 9. Ⓐ Ⓑ Ⓒ Ⓓ Ⓔ 17. Ⓐ Ⓑ Ⓒ Ⓓ Ⓔ
2. Ⓐ Ⓑ Ⓒ Ⓓ Ⓔ 10. Ⓐ Ⓑ Ⓒ Ⓓ Ⓔ 18. Ⓐ Ⓑ Ⓒ Ⓓ Ⓔ
3. Ⓐ Ⓑ Ⓒ Ⓓ Ⓔ 11. Ⓐ Ⓑ Ⓒ Ⓓ Ⓔ 19. Ⓐ Ⓑ Ⓒ Ⓓ Ⓔ
4. Ⓐ Ⓑ Ⓒ Ⓓ Ⓔ 12. Ⓐ Ⓑ Ⓒ Ⓓ Ⓔ 20. Ⓐ Ⓑ Ⓒ Ⓓ Ⓔ
5. Ⓐ Ⓑ Ⓒ Ⓓ Ⓔ 13. Ⓐ Ⓑ Ⓒ Ⓓ Ⓔ 21. Ⓐ Ⓑ Ⓒ Ⓓ Ⓔ
6. Ⓐ Ⓑ Ⓒ Ⓓ Ⓔ 14. Ⓐ Ⓑ Ⓒ Ⓓ Ⓔ 22. Ⓐ Ⓑ Ⓒ Ⓓ Ⓔ
7. Ⓐ Ⓑ Ⓒ Ⓓ Ⓔ 15. Ⓐ Ⓑ Ⓒ Ⓓ Ⓔ 23. Ⓐ Ⓑ Ⓒ Ⓓ Ⓔ
8. Ⓐ Ⓑ Ⓒ Ⓓ Ⓔ 16. Ⓐ Ⓑ Ⓒ Ⓓ Ⓔ 24. Ⓐ Ⓑ Ⓒ Ⓓ Ⓔ

☐ # right in Section Four

☐ # wrong in Section Four

Section Five

1. Ⓐ Ⓑ Ⓒ Ⓓ Ⓔ 9. Ⓐ Ⓑ Ⓒ Ⓓ Ⓔ 17. Ⓐ Ⓑ Ⓒ Ⓓ Ⓔ
2. Ⓐ Ⓑ Ⓒ Ⓓ Ⓔ 10. Ⓐ Ⓑ Ⓒ Ⓓ Ⓔ 18. Ⓐ Ⓑ Ⓒ Ⓓ Ⓔ
3. Ⓐ Ⓑ Ⓒ Ⓓ Ⓔ 11. Ⓐ Ⓑ Ⓒ Ⓓ Ⓔ
4. Ⓐ Ⓑ Ⓒ Ⓓ Ⓔ 12. Ⓐ Ⓑ Ⓒ Ⓓ Ⓔ
5. Ⓐ Ⓑ Ⓒ Ⓓ Ⓔ 13. Ⓐ Ⓑ Ⓒ Ⓓ Ⓔ
6. Ⓐ Ⓑ Ⓒ Ⓓ Ⓔ 14. Ⓐ Ⓑ Ⓒ Ⓓ Ⓔ
7. Ⓐ Ⓑ Ⓒ Ⓓ Ⓔ 15. Ⓐ Ⓑ Ⓒ Ⓓ Ⓔ
8. Ⓐ Ⓑ Ⓒ Ⓓ Ⓔ 16. Ⓐ Ⓑ Ⓒ Ⓓ Ⓔ

☐ # right in Section Five

☐ # wrong in Section Five

If section 5 of your test book contains math questions that are not multiple choice, continue to item 9 below. Otherwise, continue to item 9 above.

9. 10. 11. 12. 13.

14. 15. 16. 17. 18.

Remove (or photocopy) this answer sheet and use it to complete the practice test.
Start with number 1 for each section. If a section has fewer questions than answer spaces, leave the extra spaces blank.

Section Six

1. Ⓐ Ⓑ Ⓒ Ⓓ Ⓔ	10. Ⓐ Ⓑ Ⓒ Ⓓ Ⓔ	19. Ⓐ Ⓑ Ⓒ Ⓓ Ⓔ	28. Ⓐ Ⓑ Ⓒ Ⓓ Ⓔ
2. Ⓐ Ⓑ Ⓒ Ⓓ Ⓔ	11. Ⓐ Ⓑ Ⓒ Ⓓ Ⓔ	20. Ⓐ Ⓑ Ⓒ Ⓓ Ⓔ	29. Ⓐ Ⓑ Ⓒ Ⓓ Ⓔ
3. Ⓐ Ⓑ Ⓒ Ⓓ Ⓔ	12. Ⓐ Ⓑ Ⓒ Ⓓ Ⓔ	21. Ⓐ Ⓑ Ⓒ Ⓓ Ⓔ	30. Ⓐ Ⓑ Ⓒ Ⓓ Ⓔ
4. Ⓐ Ⓑ Ⓒ Ⓓ Ⓔ	13. Ⓐ Ⓑ Ⓒ Ⓓ Ⓔ	22. Ⓐ Ⓑ Ⓒ Ⓓ Ⓔ	31. Ⓐ Ⓑ Ⓒ Ⓓ Ⓔ
5. Ⓐ Ⓑ Ⓒ Ⓓ Ⓔ	14. Ⓐ Ⓑ Ⓒ Ⓓ Ⓔ	23. Ⓐ Ⓑ Ⓒ Ⓓ Ⓔ	32. Ⓐ Ⓑ Ⓒ Ⓓ Ⓔ
6. Ⓐ Ⓑ Ⓒ Ⓓ Ⓔ	15. Ⓐ Ⓑ Ⓒ Ⓓ Ⓔ	24. Ⓐ Ⓑ Ⓒ Ⓓ Ⓔ	33. Ⓐ Ⓑ Ⓒ Ⓓ Ⓔ
7. Ⓐ Ⓑ Ⓒ Ⓓ Ⓔ	16. Ⓐ Ⓑ Ⓒ Ⓓ Ⓔ	25. Ⓐ Ⓑ Ⓒ Ⓓ Ⓔ	34 Ⓐ Ⓑ Ⓒ Ⓓ Ⓔ
8. Ⓐ Ⓑ Ⓒ Ⓓ Ⓔ	17. Ⓐ Ⓑ Ⓒ Ⓓ Ⓔ	26. Ⓐ Ⓑ Ⓒ Ⓓ Ⓔ	35. Ⓐ Ⓑ Ⓒ Ⓓ Ⓔ

☐ # right in Section Six

☐ # wrong in Section Six

Section Seven

1. Ⓐ Ⓑ Ⓒ Ⓓ Ⓔ	9. Ⓐ Ⓑ Ⓒ Ⓓ Ⓔ	17. Ⓐ Ⓑ Ⓒ Ⓓ Ⓔ
2. Ⓐ Ⓑ Ⓒ Ⓓ Ⓔ	10. Ⓐ Ⓑ Ⓒ Ⓓ Ⓔ	18. Ⓐ Ⓑ Ⓒ Ⓓ Ⓔ
3. Ⓐ Ⓑ Ⓒ Ⓓ Ⓔ	11. Ⓐ Ⓑ Ⓒ Ⓓ Ⓔ	19. Ⓐ Ⓑ Ⓒ Ⓓ Ⓔ
4. Ⓐ Ⓑ Ⓒ Ⓓ Ⓔ	12. Ⓐ Ⓑ Ⓒ Ⓓ Ⓔ	
5. Ⓐ Ⓑ Ⓒ Ⓓ Ⓔ	13. Ⓐ Ⓑ Ⓒ Ⓓ Ⓔ	
6. Ⓐ Ⓑ Ⓒ Ⓓ Ⓔ	14. Ⓐ Ⓑ Ⓒ Ⓓ Ⓔ	
7. Ⓐ Ⓑ Ⓒ Ⓓ Ⓔ	15. Ⓐ Ⓑ Ⓒ Ⓓ Ⓔ	
8. Ⓐ Ⓑ Ⓒ Ⓓ Ⓔ	16. Ⓐ Ⓑ Ⓒ Ⓓ Ⓔ	

☐ # right in Section Seven

☐ # wrong in Section Seven

Section Eight

1. Ⓐ Ⓑ Ⓒ Ⓓ Ⓔ	9. Ⓐ Ⓑ Ⓒ Ⓓ Ⓔ
2. Ⓐ Ⓑ Ⓒ Ⓓ Ⓔ	10. Ⓐ Ⓑ Ⓒ Ⓓ Ⓔ
3. Ⓐ Ⓑ Ⓒ Ⓓ Ⓔ	11. Ⓐ Ⓑ Ⓒ Ⓓ Ⓔ
4. Ⓐ Ⓑ Ⓒ Ⓓ Ⓔ	12. Ⓐ Ⓑ Ⓒ Ⓓ Ⓔ
5. Ⓐ Ⓑ Ⓒ Ⓓ Ⓔ	13. Ⓐ Ⓑ Ⓒ Ⓓ Ⓔ
6. Ⓐ Ⓑ Ⓒ Ⓓ Ⓔ	14. Ⓐ Ⓑ Ⓒ Ⓓ Ⓔ
7. Ⓐ Ⓑ Ⓒ Ⓓ Ⓔ	15. Ⓐ Ⓑ Ⓒ Ⓓ Ⓔ
8. Ⓐ Ⓑ Ⓒ Ⓓ Ⓔ	16. Ⓐ Ⓑ Ⓒ Ⓓ Ⓔ

☐ # right in Section Eight

☐ # wrong in Section Eight

Section Nine

1. Ⓐ Ⓑ Ⓒ Ⓓ Ⓔ	9. Ⓐ Ⓑ Ⓒ Ⓓ Ⓔ
2. Ⓐ Ⓑ Ⓒ Ⓓ Ⓔ	10. Ⓐ Ⓑ Ⓒ Ⓓ Ⓔ
3. Ⓐ Ⓑ Ⓒ Ⓓ Ⓔ	11. Ⓐ Ⓑ Ⓒ Ⓓ Ⓔ
4. Ⓐ Ⓑ Ⓒ Ⓓ Ⓔ	12. Ⓐ Ⓑ Ⓒ Ⓓ Ⓔ
5. Ⓐ Ⓑ Ⓒ Ⓓ Ⓔ	13. Ⓐ Ⓑ Ⓒ Ⓓ Ⓔ
6. Ⓐ Ⓑ Ⓒ Ⓓ Ⓔ	14. Ⓐ Ⓑ Ⓒ Ⓓ Ⓔ
7. Ⓐ Ⓑ Ⓒ Ⓓ Ⓔ	
8. Ⓐ Ⓑ Ⓒ Ⓓ Ⓔ	

☐ # right in Section Nine

☐ # wrong in Section Nine

Practice Test Twelve

SECTION 1
Time—25 Minutes
ESSAY

The essay gives you an opportunity to show how effectively you can develop and express ideas. You should, therefore, take care to develop your point of view, present your ideas logically and clearly, and use language precisely.

Your essay must be written in your Answer Grid Booklet—you will receive no other paper on which to write. You will have enough space if you write on every line, avoid wide margins, and keep your handwriting to a reasonable size. Remember that people who are not familiar with your handwriting will read what you write. Try to write or print so that what you are writing is legible to those readers.

You have twenty-five minutes to write an essay on the topic assigned below.

DO NOT WRITE ON ANOTHER TOPIC. AN OFF-TOPIC ESSAY WILL RECEIVE A SCORE OF ZERO.

Think carefully about the issue presented in the following excerpt and the assignment below.

> "In seeking truth you have to get both sides of a story."
> —Walter Cronkite

Assignment: Do you agree with Walter Cronkite that it's necessary to see both sides of an issue in order to discover the truth? Plan and write an essay in which you develop your point of view on this issue. Support your position with reasoning and examples taken from your reading, studies, experience, or observations.

DO NOT WRITE YOUR ESSAY IN YOUR TEST BOOK.
You will receive credit only for what you write in your Answer Grid Booklet.

_____
_____
_____
_____
_____
_____
_____
_____
_____
_____
_____
_____
_____
_____
_____
_____
_____
_____

IF YOU FINISH BEFORE TIME IS CALLED, YOU MAY CHECK YOUR WORK ON THIS SECTION ONLY. DO NOT TURN TO ANY OTHER SECTION IN THE TEST.

SECTION 2

Time—25 Minutes

24 Questions

Directions: For each of the following questions, choose the best answer and darken the corresponding oval on the answer sheet.

Each sentence below has one or two blanks, each blank indicating that something has been omitted. Beneath the sentence are five words or sets of words labeled (A) through (E). Choose the word or set of words that, when inserted in the sentence, <u>best</u> fits the meaning of the sentence as a whole.

EXAMPLE:

Today's small, portable computers contrast markedly with the earliest electronic computers, which were ----.

(A) effective

(B) invented

(C) useful

(D) destructive

(E) enormous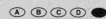

---

1. Renowned buildings such as "Fallingwater" and the eminent Solomon R. Guggenheim Museum in New York City ---- Frank Lloyd Wright as one of the most ---- architects of the 20th century.

   (A) buoyed . . irrelevant

   (B) established . . prominent

   (C) surrendered . . prolific

   (D) decried . . cynical

   (E) categorized . . mundane

2. Although the class was told by their math teacher that the exercises in the chapter review were ---- , the students knew that some questions on the exam would be the same as those found in the review.

   (A) pivotal

   (B) ritualistic

   (C) salient

   (D) supplementary

   (E) solemn

3. Instead of being ---- by her oppressive boss and unfortunate working conditions, the young professional found ---- in the workplace by exhibiting her talents to higher executives and moving up the corporate ladder.

   (A) discouraged . . reconciliation

   (B) defeated . . prosperity

   (C) elevated . . happiness

   (D) aided . . opportunity

   (E) delayed . . unity

4. Many towns bordering two different countries have a heterogeneous population and can boast of a ---- of different foods that incorporate a ---- of various ingredients.

   (A) multiplicity . . variety

   (B) proliferation . . moderation

   (C) ambivalence . . focus

   (D) dearth . . depletion

   (E) abridgment . . imitation

GO ON TO THE NEXT PAGE

5. Despite his apparent ---- lifestyle, the old man was known to drink to excess when visited by friends.

   (A) temperate
   (B) laconic
   (C) duplicitous
   (D) aesthetic
   (E) voluble

6. Nostradamus gained a reputation for ---- as he accurately predicted events such as wars complete with descriptions of vehicles that were not invented until long after his death.

   (A) prescience
   (B) sincerity
   (C) avarice
   (D) complicity
   (E) mendacity

7. The ---- reputation of the publishing world was ---- in 1989 when investigators at Pompano Press discovered that one of the firm's editors was accepting books for publication not because of the merits of the books, but because he was bribed by their authors.

   (A) sterling . . enhanced
   (B) sacrosanct . . sullied
   (C) irreproachable . . facilitated
   (D) deficient . . compromised
   (E) auspicious . . coveted

8. Although the political candidate was ---- by her admirers, she ---- her campaign before the first debate was held.

   (A) supported . . abandoned
   (B) lauded . . illuminated
   (C) denounced . . criticized
   (D) disdained . . subverted
   (E) bolstered . . retaliated

9. Lee's ---- response to the teacher's inquiry earned her an unpleasant trip to the principal's office.

   (A) flippant
   (B) inveterate
   (C) pecuniary
   (D) reactionary
   (E) lax

GO ON TO THE NEXT PAGE ⟩

Directions: The passages below are followed by questions based on their content; questions following a pair of related passages may also be based on the relationship between the paired passages. Answer the questions on the basis of what is <u>stated</u> or <u>implied</u> in the passages and in any introductory material that may be provided.

Questions 10–11 are based on the following passage.

What plagues both political parties in the United States today is their need to win over the voting public at any cost. Since the average American voter has only an acquaintance with the
(5) crucial issues of the day and an even narrower grasp of the ways in which policy can address them, politicians are forced to mount often-vicious attacks on their competitors to capture the interest of the electorate. Rather than elect the
(10) best candidates for the task at hand, the American voter, election after election, chooses what appears to be the lesser of multiple evils, electing, in effect, the best worst candidate for the job.

10. The "plague" (line 1) on both political parties could be best described as their

    (A) reliance on polls to determine the feelings of the voting public

    (B) willingness to attack their closest competitors

    (C) need to appeal to an ill-informed electorate

    (D) lack of concern for the views of most voters

    (E) refusal to appeal to lower-income families

11. The word "acquaintance" in line 4 most nearly means

    (A) polite relationship

    (B) superficial familiarity

    (C) fraught discussion

    (D) complex dialogue

    (E) nuanced exchange

Questions 12–13 are based on the following passage

Translating poetry from one language to another involves ingenuity and creativity, as well as technical skill. Some people think translators should be as faithful as possible to the original
(5) author's wording, but I believe the spirit of the original should be preserved, even if this means using a bit of creative license when it comes to the actual words. Recently I read two different translations of "Tonight I Can Write," by Pablo Neruda.
(10) The first translation was quite literal, while the second took more liberty with Neruda's words but preserved the tone and flow of the original. I found the first translation dry and static, while the rhythm of the second translation was delightful.

12. The phrase "even if this means using a bit of creative license when it comes to the actual words" (lines 6–8) serves to

    (A) accentuate the contrast between ingenuity and creativity

    (B) imply that the spirit of a translation is totally unrelated to the actual words used in that translation

    (C) provide a definition of the expression "poetic license"

    (D) draw a parallel between dry, static translations and translations in which the tone and flow of the original is preserved

    (E) acknowledge that preserving the spirit of the original may be incompatible with remaining as faithful as possible to the author's wording

GO ON TO THE NEXT PAGE

13. The author of the passage demonstrates which attitude toward the view that translators should be as faithful as possible to the original poet's wording?

(A) respectful disagreement

(B) puzzled appreciation

(C) guarded curiosity

(D) firm concurrence

(E) complete disparagement

Questions 14–24 are based on the following passage.

This passage is excerpted from a historian's account of the development of European classical music.

During the first half of the nineteenth century, the political and social currents in Europe in the aftermath of the French Revolution brought with them significant developments in the world of
(5) music. Patronage of the arts was no longer considered the exclusive province of the aristocracy. The increasingly prosperous middle class swelled the ranks of audiences at public concerts and music festivals. New opera houses were built to accom-
(10) modate the demand, and these in turn enabled musicians to reach a larger public. Furthermore, the elevated status of the middle-class increased the participation of women in the musical field, which had traditionally been associated with men.
(15) Bourgeois families encouraged their daughters to take advantage of the new-found leisure time by studying voice or piano, since this would improve their marriage possibilities and thus be an asset in the family's climb to social acceptance. Singing in
(20) particular became a focus of the woman's education, stemming from the traditional notion that a mother's singing was beneficial in nurturing a child. So many women became involved in amateur musical activities, in fact, that all the busi-
(25) nesses that served music—piano-building, music publishing and music journalism—burgeoned.

Society was only beginning to enlarge its concept of appropriate musical education and activities for women, however. Female musical profes-
(30) sionals were still very uncommon. Even the most competent could be forbidden by husbands and fathers to appear in public, to publish music under their own names, or to accept fees for their teaching if the men feared that these activities
(35) would have a negative impact on the family's social status. The advice and support of a man was still a necessity in the musical career of a woman, no matter how talented she was.

GO ON TO THE NEXT PAGE ⇨

The prevailing negative opinions that continued
(40) to constrain women musicians, especially composers, during this century can be traced back to
the previous one. Many prominent eighteenth-
century writers believed that women did not
possess the intellectual and emotional capacity to
(45) learn or to create as artists. The influential social
and educational philosopher Jean-Jacques
Rousseau, for example, asserted that "women, in
general, possess no artistic sensibility... nor
genius." Furthermore, it was held to be unneces-
(50) sary and even dangerous for women to acquire
extensive musical knowledge, as such knowledge
could only detract from the business of being a
wife and mother. Johann Campe's opinion of
female composers was representative of this view:
(55) "Among a hundred praiseworthy female composers hardly one can be found who fulfills simultaneously all the duties of a reasonable and good
wife, an attentive and efficient housekeeper, and a
concerned mother."
(60)   Most nineteenth-century men and women
seemed to agree with these sentiments. Women
who performed publicly or attempted creative
work therefore suffered not only societal censure
but internal conflicts about the propriety and sen-
(65) sibility of their own aspirations. Even the great
Clara Schumann, who was exceptional in that she
was encouraged both by her husband and by the
musical public to compose, entertained doubts
about her creative ability. In 1839 she wrote, "I
(70) once believed that I possessed creative talent, but I
have given up this idea; a woman must not desire
to compose." Standard views on proper feminine
behavior were so firmly entrenched that this
mother of eight could not recognize the signifi-
(75) cance of her own accomplishments.
Schumann was in fact a trail-blazer—one of the
very first female composers to construct a large-
scale orchestral work. In the early nineteenth century, the "art song" was considered to be the "safe,"
(80) appropriate genre for women composers. The art
song was a type of chamber music and as such fit
comfortably into a domestic environment—the
woman's domain. Women composers also gravitated to the art song as a medium for musical
(85) expression because its composition did not

require the intensive training (often denied to
women musicians) that the more intricate sonata
or symphony did. Schumann defied convention,
however, when she composed the "masculine"
(90) orchestral piece Piano Concerto in A Minor.
Although not among those considered her finest, the
work demonstrated to the women musicians who
followed Schumann that female musical creativity
could slip loose from the bonds of society.

14. The primary purpose of the passage is to

   (A) highlight the achievements of a woman com-
       poser in the nineteenth century
   (B) investigate why women were held to be inca-
       pable of artistic creation
   (C) discuss the obstacles confronting women
       musicians in the nineteenth century
   (D) criticize nineteenth-century men for stifling
       the musical talent of women
   (E) compare the status of nineteenth-century
       women musicians to their predecessors

15. It can be inferred from the passage that the overall
    effect of the "political and social currents in
    Europe" (lines 1–5) was to

   (A) lower music to the rank of popular culture
   (B) establish the equality of women to men
   (C) break down barriers between the middle and
       the upper class
   (D) improve the economy of European countries
   (E) dampen the interest in music among the
       upper classes

GO ON TO THE NEXT PAGE

16. The first paragraph of the passage suggests that for the majority of bourgeois women, their increased participation in music in the nineteenth century was

   (A) consistent with their traditional roles in the family

   (B) burdensome since they were now obliged to become involved

   (C) ground-breaking in that women had not become professional musicians before

   (D) discouraged by men because playing as an amateur was socially inappropriate

   (E) justified, considering that women had shown talent equal to men's in music

17. The statement that the "advice and support of a man was still a necessity" (lines 36–37) for a woman musician, no matter how talented she was, suggests primarily that women musicians

   (A) were more emotionally fragile than their male counterparts

   (B) accepted the fact that they had little experience in making decisions

   (C) were as critical of themselves as the men in the family were of them

   (D) generally conformed to accepted norms of behavior

   (E) did not need ability so long as they were well connected

18. In the third paragraph (lines 39–59), the author presents evidence to show that

   (A) the perception of women in society can be altered

   (B) women had an indirect influence on eighteenth-century philosophy

   (C) nineteenth-century beliefs about women were long-standing and firmly rooted

   (D) chauvinism was even more rampant in the eighteenth than in later centuries

   (E) the role of great intellectuals is to point out society's faults

19. In line 48, "sensibility" most nearly means

   (A) aptitude

   (B) direction

   (C) thoughtfulness

   (D) practicality

   (E) knowledge

20. The quotation from Campe (lines 55–59) suggests that he thought women

   (A) did not have the ability to compose

   (B) had too many domestic responsibilities

   (C) could balance the demands of home and career

   (D) ought to concentrate their efforts in a single area

   (E) should not neglect domestic duties in favor of music

21. The fourth paragraph (lines 60–75) suggests that one reason women musicians suffered internal conflicts about performing and composing was the

   (A) level of intensity required in order to succeed

   (B) potential disapproval from other women

   (C) supportive opinions of their contemporaries

   (D) fierce competition from male colleagues

   (E) lack of confidence exhibited by their idols

22. The author most likely includes the example of Clara Schumann (lines 65–69) in order to

   (A) illustrate the typical achievements of nineteenth-century women musicians

   (B) prove that nineteenth-century women did compose music

   (C) show what nineteenth-century women had to overcome to be creative musicians

   (D) show that it was a woman who developed orchestral works as a genre

   (E) suggest that women musicians were justified in neglecting their families

GO ON TO THE NEXT PAGE

23. If Schumann was a trail-blazing composer, why, according to the author, did she write in 1839 that she no longer thought she had creative talent?

    (A) She was compelled by her husband to do so in order to preserve the family's social status.

    (B) She was not receiving the praise that she once had.

    (C) She had not produced anything of significance by that time.

    (D) She had been influenced by society's view of women.

    (E) She felt she had exhausted her talent in the creation of *Piano Concerto in A Minor.*

24. The description of the art song in lines 80–83 primarily serves to

    (A) support the claim that Schumann's work was unconventional

    (B) introduce a new point of view into the discussion

    (C) provide an example of Schumann's orchestral innovation

    (D) criticize women composers for putting up with discrimination

    (E) suggest that creative inspiration should come from one's environment

SECTION 3

Time—25 Minutes
20 Questions

Directions: For this section, solve each problem and decide which is the best of the choices given. Fill in the corresponding oval on the answer sheet. You may use any available space for scratchwork.

Notes:

(1) Calculator use is permitted.

(2) All numbers used are real numbers.

(3) Figures are provided for some problems. All figures are drawn to scale and lie in a plane UNLESS otherwise indicated.

(4) Unless otherwise specified, the domain of any function f is assumed to be the set of all real numbers x for which $f(x)$ is a real number.

Information

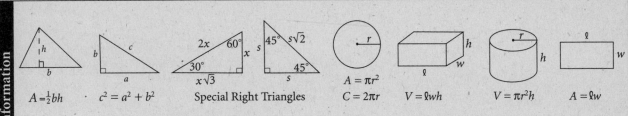

$A = \frac{1}{2}bh$ $c^2 = a^2 + b^2$ Special Right Triangles $A = \pi r^2$ $V = \ell wh$ $V = \pi r^2 h$ $A = \ell w$
$C = 2\pi r$

The sum of the degree measures of the angles in a triangle is 180.
The number of degrees of arc in a circle is 360.
A straight angle has a degree measure of 180.

1. If an object travels at 5 feet per minute, how many feet does it travel in 2 seconds?

   (A) 120

   (B) 10

   (C) $\frac{2}{5}$

   (D) $\frac{1}{6}$

   (E) $\frac{1}{12}$

2. On a certain test, if a student answers 80 to 90 percent of the questions correctly, he will receive a letter grade of B. If there are 40 questions on the test, what is the minimum number of questions the student can answer correctly to receive a grade of B?

   (A) 24

   (B) 28

   (C) 32

   (D) 33

   (E) 36

GO ON TO THE NEXT PAGE

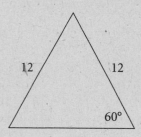

3. What is the perimeter of the triangle above?

   (A) 24
   (B) 28
   (C) 30
   (D) 36
   (E) 40

4. Of the following numbers, which is <u>least</u>?

   (A) $2 + \dfrac{1}{2}$

   (B) $2 - \dfrac{1}{2}$

   (C) $\dfrac{1}{2} - 2$

   (D) $2 \times \dfrac{1}{2}$

   (E) $2 \div \dfrac{1}{2}$

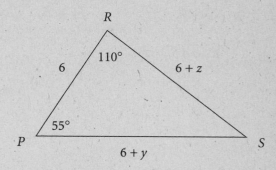

5. In $\triangle PRS$ above, which of the following must be true?

   (A) $y < z$
   (B) $y > z$
   (C) $y = z$
   (D) $y = 6$
   (E) $y > 6$

6. If $x \wedge y$ is defined by the expression $(x - y)^x + (x + y)^y$, what is the value of $4 \wedge 2$?

   (A) 52
   (B) 44
   (C) 28
   (D) 20
   (E) 16

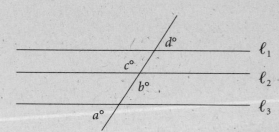

7. In the figure above, ℓ_1 is parallel to ℓ_2 and ℓ_2 is parallel to ℓ_3. What is the value of $a + b + c + d$?

   (A) 180
   (B) 270
   (C) 360
   (D) 450
   (E) It cannot be determined from the information given.

GO ON TO THE NEXT PAGE ➡

8. After 6 new cars entered the parking lot and 2 cars left the parking lot, there were 2 times as many cars as before. How many cars were parked in the parking lot before the changes?

(A) 2
(B) 4
(C) 6
(D) 8
(E) 10

9. In a certain triangle, the measure of the largest angle is 40 degrees more than the measure of the middle-sized angle. If the measure of the smallest angle is 20 degrees, what is the degree measure of the largest angle?

(A) 60
(B) 80
(C) 100
(D) 120
(E) 160

10. If d is a positive odd integer, then $(d-1)(d-2)$ could equal which of the following?

(A) 12
(B) 13
(C) 14
(D) 15
(E) 16

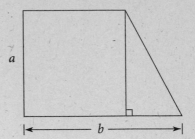

11. The figure above is formed from a square and a right triangle. What is its area?

(A) $\dfrac{a(a+b)}{2}$

(B) $\dfrac{a^2 + b^2}{2}$

(C) $\dfrac{a(b-2)}{2}$

(D) $a^2 + b^2$

(E) $a^2 + \dfrac{ab}{2}$

12. If the sum of 4 numbers is between 53 and 57, then the average (arithmetic mean) of the 4 numbers could be which of the following?

(A) $11\dfrac{1}{2}$

(B) 12

(C) $12\dfrac{1}{2}$

(D) 13

(E) 14

GO ON TO THE NEXT PAGE

13. A rectangular box is 24 inches long, 10 inches wide, and 15 inches high. If exactly 60 smaller identical rectangular boxes can be stored perfectly in this larger box, which of the following could be the dimensions, in inches, of these smaller boxes?

(A) 2 by 5 by 6

(B) 3 by 4 by 6

(C) 3 by 5 by 6

(D) 4 by 5 by 6

(E) 5 by 6 by 12

Questions 14–15 refer to the following diagram.

EDUCATION / CAREER PLANS FOR
CENTERVILLE HIGH SCHOOL GRADUATES

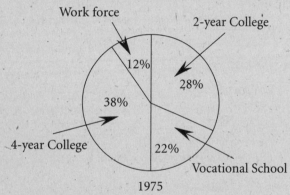

1975

Total number of graduates: 600

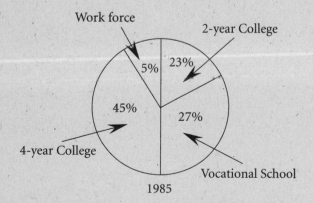

1985

Total number of graduates: 700

14. In 1975, how many graduates from Centerville High School chose either to enter the work force or to continue their education at a vocational school?

(A) 204

(B) 168

(C) 132

(D) 72

(E) 34

15. How many more graduates went on to a four-year college in 1985 than in 1975?

(A) 42

(B) 49

(C) 60

(D) 87

(E) 154

16. If the sum of the consecutive integers from −15 to x, inclusive, is 51, what is the value of x?

(A) 15

(B) 16

(C) 18

(D) 53

(E) 66

17. When 20 is divided by the positive integer x, the remainder is 2. For how many different values of x is this true?

(A) one

(B) two

(C) three

(D) four

(E) five

GO ON TO THE NEXT PAGE

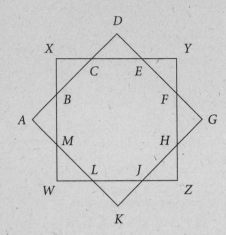

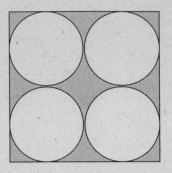

18. In the figure above, two squares *ADGK* and *WXYZ* overlap such that $AB = BC = CD$ and all the triangles are isosceles. If the area of square *ADGK* is 9, what is the area of the entire figure?

(A) 10

(B) $10\frac{1}{4}$

(C) $10 + \sqrt{2}$

(D) 14

(E) $10 + 4\sqrt{2}$

19. Let $\_g\_$ be defined as $\_g\_ = 2g^2 - 2$ for all values of g. If $\_x\_ = x^2$, what is the value of of x ?

(A) −2

(B) 1

(C) $\sqrt{2}$

(D) 2

(E) $2\sqrt{2}$

20. Each of the circles in the figure above has a radius of 2. If a point on the figure is chosen at random, what is the probability that point is in the shaded area?

(A) $\dfrac{1}{16\pi}$

(B) $\dfrac{1}{4\pi}$

(C) $\dfrac{\pi - 1}{4}$

(D) $\dfrac{4 - \pi}{4}$

(E) $\dfrac{1}{64 - 16\pi}$

IF YOU FINISH BEFORE TIME IS CALLED, YOU MAY CHECK YOUR WORK ON THIS SECTION ONLY. DO NOT TURN TO ANY OTHER SECTION IN THE TEST.

STOP

SECTION 4

Time—25 Minutes
24 Questions

Directions: For each of the following questions, choose the best answer and darken the corresponding oval on the answer sheet.

Each sentence below has one or two blanks, each blank indicating that something has been omitted. Beneath the sentence are five words or sets of words labeled (A) through (E). Choose the word or set of words that, when inserted in the sentence, best fits the meaning of the sentence as a whole.

EXAMPLE:

Today's small, portable computers contrast markedly with the earliest electronic computers, which were ----.

(A) effective
(B) invented
(C) useful
(D) destructive
(E) enormous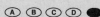

1. Leonardo da Vinci was a ---- artist; he was a painter, sculptor, draftsman, architect, and inventor.

   (A) demonstrative
   (B) nebulous
   (C) meticulous
   (D) versatile
   (E) metaphoric

2. Jamal found the movie stubs lying on the counter to be ---- evidence that his friends had gone to the cinema without him; it was unquestionable that they had seen *Spiderman*.

   (A) immaterial
   (B) potential
   (C) incriminating
   (D) nominal
   (E) indisputable

3. When training for a marathon, runners prepare themselves for a challenge that is both ---- and mentally ---- .

   (A) illusory . . taxing
   (B) exaggerated . . balanced
   (C) physically . . demanding
   (D) appealing . . indulgent
   (E) strenuous . . dubious

4. Healthy lifestyle choices such as exercising regularly and maintaining a nutritious diet can promote ---- yet are often ---- by the busy lives people today lead.

   (A) extinction . . enhanced
   (B) longevity . . hampered
   (C) behavior . . belied
   (D) morality . . bolstered
   (E) reproduction . . confirmed

5. The detectives knew they had to act punctiliously because any mistakes, even the slightest ---- , would compromise the stake out.

   (A) query
   (B) gibe
   (C) gaffe
   (D) tryst
   (E) tribute

GO ON TO THE NEXT PAGE

Directions: The passages below are followed by questions based on their content; questions following a pair of related passages may also be based on the relationship between the paired passages. Answer the questions on the basis of what is <u>stated</u> or <u>implied</u> in the passages and in any introductory material that may be provided.

Questions 6–9 are based on the following passages

Passage 1

When commercial fish farming—a technique that essentially applies the breeding structures used for raising animals on land to the ocean—was first introduced, it was seen as a creative alternative to
(5) the depletion of the world's large finfish and shell-fish populations through conventional harvesting methods. New research, however, is beginning to reign in this initial enthusiasm. About 29 million tons of large finfish were farmed in 1997; no doubt
(10) a significant contribution to the world's fish supplies. Yet the cost of this production was roughly 10 million tons of smaller wild fish used as feed, an amount that, if perpetuated, could soon virtually wipe out both the world's supply of small fish and
(15) the potential of fish farming.

Passage 2

Our seemingly insatiable appetite for seafood delicacies like smoked salmon, king prawns, and grilled sea bass has inevitably contributed to a sharp reduction in ocean fish populations. As a
(20) growing number of commercial boats found themselves frequently returning to shore with empty nets, it became clear that supply was starting to run significantly short of an ever-increasing demand. But then came a potential solution in the
(25) form of a tried and true method of food production: farming. Today, while traditional ocean fisheries remain in decline, commercial fish farming is booming—and presently premium fish remain on menus across the world. Through ingenuity and
(30) flexible thinking, a seemingly doomed resource was made more sustainable.

6. The first sentence of Passage 1 indicates that fish farming was initially considered to be

(A) a complicated technique

(B) an innovative method

(C) a simple improvement on a successful process

(D) environmentally safe

(E) not yet practical

7. The word "sharp" in line 19 of Passage 2 most nearly means

(A) piercing

(B) intense

(C) abrupt

(D) appreciable

(E) clear

8. Both passages raise which of the following questions regarding commercial fish farming?

(A) Will fish farming ultimately help or harm wild fish populations?

(B) Is commercial fish farming a sustainable means of food production?

(C) What will happen when wild fish supplies are fully depleted?

(D) Can commercial fish farming meet the growing demand for premium fish?

(E) How can fish farming techniques be made more environmentally kind?

GO ON TO THE NEXT PAGE

9. The passages differ in their evaluations of commercial fish farming in that Passage 1 focuses on

(A) the relationship between farmed and wild fish populations, whereas Passage 2 addresses the discrepancy between fish supplies and demand

(B) statistics to make an argument, whereas Passage 2 relies more on general predictions

(C) the results of various research studies, whereas Passage 2 relies primarily on data obtained from fisheries

(D) the application of land-based farming techniques to the ocean, whereas Passage 2 considers fish farming as a more unique method

(E) finfish and shellfish populations, whereas Passage 2 addresses fish populations in general

Questions 10–15 are based on the following passage

Gwendolyn Brooks (1917–2000) was a Pulitzer-Prize-winning poet. The following essay discusses her relationship to the Harlem Renaissance, a black literary and artistic movement based in Harlem in the 1920s and early 1930s.

When Gwendolyn Brooks published her first collection of poetry, *A Street In Bronzeville,* in 1945 most reviewers recognized Brooks's versatility and craft as a poet. Yet, while noting her stylis-
(5) tic successes, few of her contemporaries discussed the critical question of Brooks's relationship to the Harlem Renaissance. How had she addressed herself, as a poet, to the literary movement's assertion of the folk and African culture, and to its promo-
(10) tion of the arts as the agent to define racial integrity?
The New Negro poets of the Harlem Renaissance expressed a deep pride in being black; they found reasons for this pride in ethnic identity and her-
(15) itage; and they shared a common faith in the fine arts as a means of defining and reinforcing racial pride. But in the literal expression of this impulse, the poets were either romantics or realists; quite often within the same poem, both. The realistic
(20) impulse, as defined best in the poems of McKay's *Harlem Shadows* (1922), was a sober reflection upon Blacks as second-class citizens, segregated

from the mainstream of American socioeconomic life, and largely unable to realize the wealth and
(25) opportunity that America promised. The romantic impulse, on the other hand, as defined in the poems of Sterling Brown's *Southern Road* (1932), often found these unrealized dreams in the collective strength and will of the folk masses.
(30) In comparing the poems in *A Street In Bronzeville* with various poems from the Renaissance, it becomes apparent that Brooks brings many unique contributions to bear on this tradition. The first clue that *A Street In Bronzeville*
(35) was, at its time of publication, unlike any other book of poems by a black American is its insistent emphasis on demystifying romantic love between black men and women. During the Renaissance, ethnic or racial pride was often focused with
(40) romantic idealization of the black woman. A casual streetwalker in Langston Hughes's poem "When Sue Wears Red," for example, is magically transformed into an Egyptian Queen. In *A Street In Bronzeville*, this romantic impulse runs headlong
(45) into the biting ironies of racial discrimination. There are poems in which Hughes, McKay, and Brown recognize the realistic underside of urban life for black women. But for Brooks, unlike the Renaissance poets, the victimization of poor black
(50) women becomes not simply a minor chord but a predominant theme.
Brooks's relationship with the Harlem Renaissance poets, as *A Street In Bronzeville* ably demonstrates, was hardly imitative. As one of the
(55) important links with the black poetic tradition of the 1920s and 1930s, she enlarged the element of realism that was an important part of the Renaissance world view. Although her poetry is often conditioned by the optimism that was also a
(60) legacy of the period, Brooks rejects outright their romantic prescriptions for the lives of black women. And in this regard, she serves as a vital link with the black Arts Movement of the 1960s, the subsequent flowering of black women as poets
(65) and social activists, and the rise of black feminist aesthetics in the 1970s.

GO ON TO THE NEXT PAGE ⟩

10. The passage indicates that the critical response to the initial publication of Gwendolyn Brooks's *A Street In Bronzeville* was one of

   (A) interest in her revival of ethnic pride

   (B) appreciation of her technical accomplishment as a poet

   (C) intense debate over her relationship to the Harlem Renaissance

   (D) acclaim for her contribution to the feminist movement

   (E) concern that her realistic approach was derivative

11. The question in lines 7–11 chiefly serves to

   (A) illustrate how critical opinions can change over time

   (B) summarize the points raised by contemporary critics

   (C) introduce a more general discussion of visual art

   (D) outline the issues that the author proposes to discuss

   (E) urge the reader to revise his or her opinion on the subject

12. The author suggests that one issue the Harlem Renaissance poets were united over was

   (A) the stylistic achievement of Brooks's first poems

   (B) the power of dreams to lead people out of adversity

   (C) the role of the arts in expressing cultural pride

   (D) the insensitivity of the movement's critics

   (E) the need to portray women's lives more accurately

13. The poem "When Sue Wears Red" (lines 40–43) is mentioned primarily as an example of

   (A) a growing awareness of urban discrimination

   (B) the romanticized portrayal of black women

   (C) the versatility and craft of Brooks's poetry

   (D) the role of the imagination in the creative process

   (E) a change in attitudes toward romantic love

14. In line 59, "conditioned" means

   (A) enlightened

   (B) paralleled

   (C) conveyed

   (D) influenced

   (E) distorted

15. The primary focus of the passage is on the

   (A) unprecedented attempts by Brooks to address social problems in her work

   (B) contrasting styles that evolved during the Harlem Renaissance

   (C) innovative contributions Brooks brought to a literary tradition

   (D) different ways in which poets have dealt with prejudice as a theme

   (E) ways in which Brooks's poetry influenced subsequent feminist writers

GO ON TO THE NEXT PAGE

Questions 16–17 are based on the following passage.

The Hubble Heritage Project, a team of
astronomers who assemble and publish many of
the NASA Hubble Space Telescope's pictures,
recently celebrated the five-year anniversary of the
(5) Project by releasing an image of the Sombrero, a
massive galaxy situated 28 million light-years from
Earth on the southern edge of Virgo. Named the
Sombrero because it resembles the broad-
brimmed Mexican hat, the galaxy has a halo of
(10) stars that contains approximately 2,000 star clusters, ten times the number that compose the Milky
Way. To create one of the largest Hubble composite images ever produced, the Heritage team took
six pictures of the Sombrero, then pieced them
(15) together to create the final mosaic.

16. According to the passage, the image of the
Sombrero galaxy

(A) is the first of its kind

(B) was released to illustrate the capacity of the
Hubble telescope

(C) is ten times larger than available images of
the Milky Way

(D) is made up of several smaller images

(E) was a cause for celebration in the scientific
community

17. All of the following statements about the Sombrero
are true, EXCEPT

(A) it is 28 million light-years from Earth

(B) it has more star clusters than the Milky Way

(C) it resembles a Mexican hat

(D) it is a huge galaxy

(E) it was discovered approximately five years ago

Questions 18–24 are based on the passage below.

This passage, adapted from the arts column of a prominent national newspaper, discusses the art movement known as Impressionism, which developed primarily in France in the second half of the 1800s.

Though he would one day be considered a innovator and founding father of the artistic movement known as Impressionism, Claude Monet (1840–1926) began his career as a fairly
(5) traditional representational artist. His painting gradually changed, however, as he became interested in light and how it affects perception—an interest that led him to attempt to paint light itself rather than the objects off of which light reflected.
(10) Monet also rejected the tradition of painting in a dedicated studio, and left the confines of his dusty room to paint outside. Many of his friends and fellow artists, including Pisarro, Renoir, and Cezanne, were also interested in working alfresco
(15) and joined him in painting outdoors. This group, the core of the movement that would later be classified as Impressionism, made it a common practice to paint the same scene many times in a day to explore the changes in the light, using small
(20) patches of color rather than the large brush strokes and blended color that had characterized artistic technique until that time. The Impressionists were thus attempting to evoke a mood rather than document a specific scene or
(25) event, as had been the aim of earlier painters.

This move away from representation was also effected by a technological development, as photography became more affordable and popular. Before the development of photography, painting
(30) was the primary means of documenting the marriages, births, and business successes of the wealthy. Photographers soon took over much of this role because photographs were faster, more accurate, and less expensive than paintings. This
(35) freed the Impressionists to find new roles for their medium and encouraged the public to think about painting in a new way. It was no longer just a means of recording significant events; it now reflected an artist's unique vision of a scene or
(40) moment.

Today, Impressionism enjoys a privileged position with many art historians and critics, although this was certainly not always the case. As the movement was developing, most critics were at
(45) best uninterested and often appalled by the work. Even the name of the movement was originally a derisive critique. A critic who, like most of his colleagues, prized realism in paintings, declared the movement "Impressionism" after the name of the
(50) painting *Impression: A Sunrise*, by Monet. The critic considered the Impressionists' works unfinished—only an impression, rather than a complete painting. It is safe to say that such a critic would be in the minority today, however.
(55) Impressionist paintings are now some of the most prized works in the art world. Museums and individuals pay huge sums to add these works to their collections, and the reproductions of the artworks are among the most popular fine art posters sold.

18. The primary purpose of the passage is to

   (A) condemn the critics who prevented the Impressionists from exhibiting their work
   (B) contrast Monet's work with that of Pisarro, Renoir, and Cezanne
   (C) describe the primary characteristics of Monet's paintings
   (D) explain the origins of Impressionism and Monet's role in the movement
   (E) argue that photography is a better medium than painting for representing events

19. According to the passage, the Impressionists did all of the following EXCEPT

   (A) paint the same scene at different times of the day
   (B) paint the light reflected by objects
   (C) use small areas of color rather than large, blended areas
   (D) receive acclaim from their contemporaries
   (E) reconsider the role of painting in society

GO ON TO THE NEXT PAGE →

20. In line 20, the author most likely mentions "patches of color" to describe

    (A) the light that the Impressionists encountered when they worked outdoors

    (B) a shortcoming of traditional paintings

    (C) a distinguishing characteristic of modern painters

    (D) an innovative technique used by Impressionist painters

    (E) an artistic feature present in paintings but lacking in photography

21. The discussion of photography (lines 26–40) serves as

    (A) a contrast to the discussion of traditional painting

    (B) the most important context in which to understand Impressionism

    (C) a description of an innovation that affected the development of Impressionism

    (D) a clarification of the public's dislike of Impressionism

    (E) a demonstration of its similarities to painting

22. The author of the passage would most likely describe the medium of photography as

    (A) expensive

    (B) precise

    (C) false

    (D) inconsistent

    (E) prestigious

23. The "critic" mentioned in line 51 would most likely agree that

    (A) Impressionist paintings are inferior because they fail to clearly represent their subjects

    (B) Impressionism now enjoys a much more prestigious place in the art world than it once did

    (C) Monet's *Impression: A Sunrise* was a highly influential work

    (D) the use of photography to document important events freed painters to explore other roles

    (E) Impressionist paintings are now rightly recognized by the public as important works

24. In line 56 "prized" most nearly means

    (A) awarded

    (B) discovered

    (C) valued

    (D) decorated

    (E) sought

IF YOU FINISH BEFORE TIME IS CALLED, YOU MAY CHECK YOUR WORK ON THIS SECTION ONLY. DO NOT TURN TO ANY OTHER SECTION IN THE TEST.   STOP

SECTION 5
Time—25 Minutes
18 Questions

Directions: For this section, solve each problem and decide which is the best of the choices given. Fill in the corresponding oval on the answer sheet. You may use any available space for scratchwork.

Notes:

(1) Calculator use is permitted.

(2) All numbers used are real numbers.

(3) Figures are provided for some problems. All figures are drawn to scale and lie in a plane UNLESS otherwise indicated.

(4) Unless otherwise specified, the domain of any function f is assumed to be the set of all real numbers x for which $f(x)$ is a real number.

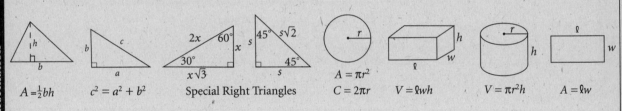

$A = \frac{1}{2}bh$ $c^2 = a^2 + b^2$ Special Right Triangles $A = \pi r^2$ $V = \ell wh$ $V = \pi r^2 h$ $A = \ell w$
$C = 2\pi r$

The sum of the degree measures of the angles in a triangle is 180.
The number of degrees of arc in a circle is 360.
A straight angle has a degree measure of 180.

1. What is the hundredths' digit in the number 123,456.789 ?

   (A) 1
   (B) 4
   (C) 5
   (D) 8
   (E) 9

2. If the average (arithmetic mean) of 6 numbers is greater than 30 and less than 60, which of the following could be the sum of the 6 numbers?

   (A) 100
   (B) 180
   (C) 250
   (D) 360
   (E) 420

GO ON TO THE NEXT PAGE

3. Raphael just bought a piece of furniture from a store that sells only sofas and chairs. Which of the following must be true?

   (A) The piece of furniture is a sofa.

   (B) The piece of furniture is a chair.

   (C) The piece of furniture is not a leather sofa.

   (D) The piece of furniture is not a wooden chair.

   (E) The piece of furniture is not a wooden table.

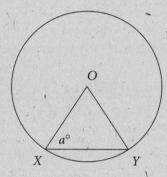

Note: Figure not drawn to scale

4. In the figure above, points X and Y lie on circle O. If $\angle XOY = 72°$, what is the value of a ?

   (A) 21

   (B) 36

   (C) 54

   (D) 72

   (E) 108

   Subtract 4 from y.
   Divide this sum by 2.
   Add 4 to this quotient.

5. Which of the following is the result obtained by performing the operations described above?

   (A) $\dfrac{y-2}{4}$

   (B) $\dfrac{y+2}{4}$

   (C) $\dfrac{y-4}{2}$

   (D) $\dfrac{y+4}{2}$

   (E) $\dfrac{4y+4}{2}$

6. There are a total of 20 marbles in a bag containing only red marbles, blue marbles, and yellow marbles. If a marble is selected at random, the probability of getting a red marble is $\dfrac{2}{5}$ and the probability of getting a blue marble is $\dfrac{1}{2}$. How many yellow marbles are in the bag?

   (A) 1

   (B) 2

   (C) 4

   (D) 8

   (E) 10

7. At a certain restaurant, there are 25 tables and each table has either 2 or 4 chairs. If there is a total of 86 chairs accompanying the 25 tables, how many tables have exactly 4 chairs?

   (A) 9

   (B) 12

   (C) 15

   (D) 18

   (E) 21

8. How many three-digit integers less than 400 are there such that the sum of the hundreds' and units' digits is equal to the square of the tens' digit?

   (A) four

   (B) five

   (C) six

   (D) seven

   (E) eight

GO ON TO THE NEXT PAGE

Directions: For Student-Produced Response questions 9–18, use the grids at the bottom of the answer sheet page on which you have answered questions 1–8.

Each of the remaining 10 questions requires you to solve the problem and enter your answer by marking the ovals in the special grid, as shown in the example below. You may use any available space for scratch work.

Answer: 1.25 or $\frac{5}{4}$ or 5/4

Write answer in boxes.

Grid-in result

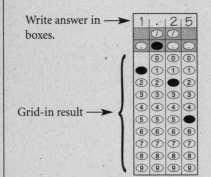

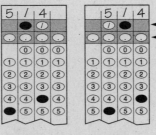

Fraction line
Decimal point

Either position is correct.

You may start your answers in any column, space permitting. Columns not needed should be left blank.

· It is recommended, though not required, that you write your answer in the boxes at the top of the columns. However, you will receive credit only for darkening the ovals correctly.

· Grid only one answer to a question, even though some problems have more than one correct answer.

· Darken no more than one oval in a column.

· No answers are negative.

· Mixed numbers cannot be gridded. For example: the number $1\frac{1}{4}$ must be gridded as 1.25 or 5/4.

· **Decimal Accuracy:** Decimal answers must be entered as accurately as possible. For example, if you obtain an answer such as 0.1666…, you should record the result as .166 or .167. **Less accurate values such as .16 or .17 are not acceptable.**

Acceptable ways to grid $\frac{1}{6}$ = .1666…

(If ☐1☐1☐/☐4☐ is gridded, it will be interpreted as $\frac{11}{4}$ not $1\frac{1}{4}$.)

GO ON TO THE NEXT PAGE

9. If $-6x + 8 = -2x - 7$, what is the value of x?

10. If x is $\frac{1}{4}$ of y, y is $\frac{2}{5}$ of z, and $z > 0$, then x is what fraction of z?

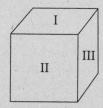

11. In the rectangular solid above, if the areas of top face I, front face II, and right face III are 24, 2, and 3 respectively, what is the volume of the rectangular solid?

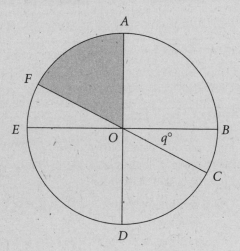

12. In the figure above, AD, BE, and CF are all diameters of the circle. If the shaded area is equal

to $\frac{1}{6}$ the area of the circle, what is the value of q?

13. Lucy drove from her house to a friend's house at an average speed of 40 miles per hour. She returned home along the same route at an average speed of 60 miles per hour. If her total driving time was 1 hour, how many total miles did Lucy drive?

14. Grid in a three-digit number which is the product of three consecutive even numbers.

15. The average (arithmetic mean) of 10 exam grades is 87. If the highest and lowest grades are removed from the set, the average of the remaining 8 exam grades is 90. What is the average of the 2 exam grades that were removed?

16. If $a > 0$, $b > \frac{3}{4}$, and $2a + b = 1$, what is one possible value for a?

17. In the xy-coordinate plane, the graph of $x = y^2 + 2$ intersects the line l at $(3, a)$ and $(11, b)$. What is the greatest possible slope of l?

18. Circle A has a circumference of 4π and circle B has a circumference of 8π. If the circles intersect at two points, what is a possible distance from the center of circle A to the center of circle B?

SECTION 6

Time—25 Minutes

35 Questions

1. At the beginning of the 21st century, one reason bars in New York City became cleaner than <u>before, the smoking of cigarettes prohibited throughout the city's indoor establishments</u>.

   (A) before, the smoking of cigarettes prohibited throughout the city's indoor establishments

   (B) before, throughout the city's indoor establishments, the smoking of cigarettes was prohibited

   (C) before, there was a prevention throughout the city's indoor establishments of smoking cigarettes

   (D) before, they prevented cigarette smoking throughout the city's indoor establishments

   (E) before was that cigarette smoking was prohibited in the city's indoor establishments

2. Many movie theaters have morning "mom and baby" movie <u>screenings, which offer benefits to both the parents and</u> the cinemas.

   (A) screenings, which offer benefits to both the parents and

   (B) screenings, which offers benefits to both the parents and

   (C) screenings, which offer both benefits to the parents plus

   (D) screenings; it offers benefits both to the parents as well as

   (E) screenings; this offers benefits to both the parents and

GO ON TO THE NEXT PAGE ▷

3. One of the most famous admirers of Pete Townsend, <u>Eddie Vedder, is the singer for Pearl Jam, performing</u> Townsend's songs in concert.

(A) Eddie Vedder, is the singer for Pearl Jam, performing

(B) Eddie Vedder who sings for Pearl Jam and performed

(C) Eddie Vedder sings for Pearl Jam who performs

(D) Eddie Vedder, the singer for Pearl Jam, performs

(E) the singer, Eddie Vedder, performs for Pearl Jam

4. <u>For the most part, in the ability of how a child speaks a foreign language, early instruction is the main determinant.</u>

(A) For the most part, in the ability of how a child speaks a foreign language, early instruction is the main determinant.

(B) Generally, a child's ability and speech in a foreign language is mostly from early instruction.

(C) A child's ability, as to speaking in a foreign language, is by and large determined by early instruction.

(D) A child's ability to speak a foreign language is largely dependant on early instruction.

(E) Children mainly have early instruction as a determinant for speaking a foreign language.

5. As their work load gets heavier, first year law students <u>trying to keep up with their assignments by</u> drinking a lot of coffee.

(A) trying to keep up with their assignments by

(B) trying to keep up with their assignments and

(C) tried to keep up with their assignments by

(D) try to keep up with their assignments by

(E) trying keeping up with their assignments by

6. In his interview, Mr. Wead <u>announced that he had</u> many tape recordings of the President.

(A) announced that he had

(B) announced about having

(C) made an announcement of having

(D) gave an announcement that he had

(E) had an announcement about having

7. <u>Unlike Soviet leaders who preceded him, Mikhail Gorbachev</u> did not prohibit foreign literature or films.

(A) Unlike Soviet leaders who preceded him, Mikhail Gorbachev

(B) Unlike the prohibitions of Soviet leaders who preceded him, Mikhail Gorbachev

(C) Under Mikhail Gorbachev's leadership, unlike Soviet leaders who preceded him,

(D) Different from the Soviet leaders who preceded him, Mikhail Gorbachev's laws

(E) Mikhail Gorbachev, differently from Soviet leaders who preceded him,

8. The extraordinary stature of the California redwood trees is perhaps even more apparent in their weight than <u>either their height or age</u>.

(A) either their height or age

(B) either their height or in their age

(C) either in their height or age

(D) in either their height or age

(E) in either their height or in their age

GO ON TO THE NEXT PAGE

9. Underground "samizdat" newspapers in the Soviet Union <u>delivering international information to citizens waiting</u> for a new free press.

   (A) delivering international information to citizens waiting

   (B) delivering international information to citizens and wait

   (C) delivering international information and giving it to citizens, they waited

   (D) delivered international information to citizens waiting

   (E) delivered international information to citizens, who were meanwhile waiting

10. Out-of-state students usually do not end up receiving as much financial aid as local students <u>do, this being why so many students</u> choose to attend college in their home state.

    (A) do, this being why so many students

    (B) do, this is why so many students

    (C) do; this fact explains why so many students

    (D) do; this fact explaining the reason for why so many students

    (E) do; explaining why so many students

11. Sixty years ago, women were more likely to become teachers, secretaries, or homemakers <u>than other work</u>.

    (A) than other work

    (B) than working in other fields

    (C) than at work in other fields

    (D) than workers in other fields

    (E) than in other lines of work

GO ON TO THE NEXT PAGE

Directions: The following sentences test your ability to recognize grammar and usage errors. Each sentence contains either a single error or no error at all. No sentence contains more than one error. The error, if there is one, is underlined and lettered. If the sentence contains an error, select the one underlined part that must be changed to make the sentence correct. If the sentence is correct, select choice (E). In choosing answers, follow the requirements of standard written English.

EXAMPLE:

<u>Whenever</u> one is driving late at night, <u>you</u> must take extra precautions <u>against</u>
  A   B   C

falling asleep <u>at the wheel.</u> <u>No error</u>
           D   E

12. <u>When</u> we counted the growth rings in the <u>ancient</u>
   A   B
redwood stumps, we <u>found</u> that the life of each of
                     C
these <u>trees spanned</u> many centuries of history.
           D
<u>No error</u>
  E

13. <u>Even though</u> the old teapot was the most <u>careful</u>
     A   B
crafted ceramic Mr. Pfent had <u>ever made</u>, it could
                              C
not prevent water <u>from</u> seeping through the
                     D
bottom. <u>No error</u>
         E

14. <u>Although</u> the circus had <u>totally</u> eliminated its
    A   B
popular animal acts, its acrobatic teams

<u>had improved</u> greatly, <u>and it kept</u> the audiences
   C   D
interested. <u>No error</u>
           E

15. Only after weeks <u>of deliberation</u> could the jury
                A
<u>decide that</u> Ms. Fixel, a <u>prominent</u> businesswoman
    B   C
respected <u>of everyone</u>, was innocent of insider
           D
trading. <u>No error</u>
     E

16. <u>Because</u> binary stars revolve around each other
   A
and block one another's light, often <u>it seems</u> <u>to be</u>
                            B   C
a single star <u>when viewed</u> through a telescope.
             D
<u>No error</u>
  E

17. Liam <u>wakes up</u> early <u>on weekdays, he</u> trains <u>with</u>
      A   B   C
the track team before school <u>begins</u>. <u>No error</u>
                       D   E

18. J.S. Bach was not <u>an average</u> Baroque composer,
                 A
simply <u>producing</u> pieces of music at the request
       B
<u>of his patron</u>, but rather an artist who transcended
   C
his position and deserves the awe <u>with which</u> he is
                              D
regarded today. <u>No error</u>
              E

19. <u>Of</u> all the dresses <u>in the shop</u>, the pale satin gown
   A   B
<u>seemed</u> the <u>more dramatic</u> to Alicia. <u>No error</u>
   C   D   E

GO ON TO THE NEXT PAGE

20. <u>To become</u> an Olympic gymnastics all-around gold
       A
    medal winner like Carly Patterson, one <u>has to be</u> so
                                                B
    versatile that <u>you</u> <u>can compete</u> well in all four
                    C   D
    events. <u>No error</u>
             E

21. The heart <u>is fundamentally</u> a powerful and
                    A
    <u>very persistent</u> pump <u>that</u> distributes blood
          B   C
    <u>throughout</u> our bodies. <u>No error</u>
          D   E

22. Peter the Great <u>totally</u> changed <u>the landscape of</u>
                        A   B
    St. Petersburg <u>and it had been</u> a swamp <u>unused</u> by
                        C   D
    previous tsars. <u>No error</u>
                     E

23. When we are children we often <u>become attached</u> to
                                       A
    a specific item, <u>like</u> a teddy bear or a blanket, that
                      B
    stays with <u>you</u> <u>through</u> our adult years. <u>No error</u>
                C   D   E

24. Riparian habitats <u>that</u> <u>form around</u> any river,
                        A   B
    stream, or lake <u>supports</u> abundant wildlife
                      C
    <u>such as birds</u>, rodents, reptiles, and amphibians.
          D
    <u>No error</u>
       E

25. <u>Many</u> writers <u>agree</u> that the endurance required of
       A   B
    a novelist, <u>comparable to</u> that <u>required of</u> a
                    C   D
    marathon runner. <u>No error</u>
                      E

26. A batik <u>artist employing</u> the wax-resist process
                 A
    paints <u>complicated</u> designs on fabric with hot wax
                B
    and then <u>submerging</u> the fabric in dyes of the
                  C
    <u>brightest</u> colors. <u>No error</u>
         D   E

27. The roadrunner is an uncommon bird <u>who</u>
                                          A
    <u>requires</u> a dry habitat with open ground for
       B
    running <u>so</u> it can capture its <u>preferred</u> prey of
             C   D
    lizards or snakes. <u>No error</u>
                        E

28. Every time Glenn returns to his apartment, he <u>has</u>
                                                    A
    to walk through the courtyard, then up four flights
    of stairs, and then <u>walks down the hallway</u> <u>before</u>
                              B   C
    he <u>arrives</u> at his door. <u>No error</u>
          D   E

29. <u>Although</u> some writers <u>argue having</u> writers block
       A   B
    is a chemical problem in the brain, no scientist has
    shown that <u>such a malady</u> <u>in fact</u> occurs. <u>No error</u>
                    C   D   E

GO ON TO THE NEXT PAGE

Questions 30–35 are based on the following passage.

(1) Today's technology includes miracle medicines. (2) It also boasts excellent transportation. (3) Also, many methods of communication have improved people's lives. (4) However, I believe that there is a negative side to the impact of progress. (5) Hunter-gatherer tribes and small ethnic groups lose their territories and they have a hard time holding on to their unique and ancient cultures and one sign of this is the gradual disappearance of languages.

(6) In America, hundreds of Native American languages are kept alive by just a handful of people and, in places like Cameroon, and Papua New Guinea, some languages are spoken by only two or three people. (7) I am concerned about this issue, because many of the customs and traditional ideas of a culture are imbedded in its language. (8) The folktales, jokes, and songs of a culture are in its native tongue, as are the special names of places that give fascinating hints about history.

(9) It's impossible to rely on native speakers to save their own languages. (10) This is because younger people often become bilingual and eventually found it easier to communicate in the new language. (11) In some places, such as Ireland, the native language Gaelic is taught to schoolchildren. (12) However, learning a language in school is very different from using it in daily life. (13) In areas of Galway, where Gaelic is still used, the language is alive and evolving. (14) Some linguists and anthropologists are working to record people who speak endangered languages and they are also working as well at times to translate these languages before they disappear forever.

30. Which of the following is the best way to combine sentences (1), (2), and (3) reproduced below?

Today's technology includes miracle medicines. It also boasts excellent transportation. Also, many methods of communication have improved people's lives.

(A) Today's technology includes miracle medicines while it also boasts excellent transportation and also many methods of communication that have improved people's lives.

(B) Today's technology includes miracle medicines, excellent transportation, and many methods of communication that have improved people's lives.

(C) Today's technology, including miracle medicines, excellent transportation, and many methods of communication that have improved people's lives.

(D) People's lives have been improved by today's technology, these include miracle medicines, excellent transportation, and many methods of communication.

(E) Miracle medicines, excellent transportation, and many methods of communication are among today's technology that has improved people's lives.

GO ON TO THE NEXT PAGE

31. Of the following, which is the best version of sentence 5 (reproduced below)?

    Hunter-gatherer tribes and small ethnic groups lose their territories and they have a hard time holding on to their unique and ancient cultures and one sign of this is the gradual disappearance of languages.

    (A) (As it is now)

    (B) Hunter-gatherer tribes and small ethnic groups lose their territories, but they have a hard time holding on to their unique and ancient culture, so one sign of this is the gradual disappearance of languages.

    (C) Hunter-gatherer tribes and small ethnic groups lose their territories, have a hard time holding on to their unique and ancient cultures, and one sign of this is the gradual disappearance of languages.

    (D) Hunter-gatherer tribes and small ethnic groups lose their territories and have a hard time holding on to their unique and ancient cultures; one sign of this is the gradual disappearance of languages.

    (E) Hunter-gatherer tribes and small ethnic groups lose their territories; and have a hard time holding on to their unique and ancient cultures, one sign of this being the gradual disappearance of languages.

32. Which of the following phrases, if inserted at the beginning of sentence 8, would best tie it to the rest of the paragraph?

    (A) For example,

    (B) In fact,

    (C) On the other hand,

    (D) Although

    (E) Because

33. What is the best way to deal with sentence 10 (reproduced below)?

    This is because younger people often become bilingual and eventually found it easier to communicate in the new language.

    (A) Leave it as it is.

    (B) Change "This" to "That."

    (C) Replace the comma with a semicolon.

    (D) Replace "found" with "find."

    (E) Replace "in the new language" with "in a new language."

34. Of the following, which is the best version of sentence 14 (reproduced below)?

    Some linguists and anthropologists are working to record people who speak endangered languages and they are also working as well at times to translate these languages before they disappear forever.

    (A) (As it is now.)

    (B) Some linguists and anthropologists are working to record people who speak endangered languages; they are also working as well at times to translate these languages before they disappear forever.

    (C) Some linguists and anthropologists are working to record people who speak endangered languages and to translate these languages before they disappear forever.

    (D) Some linguists and anthropologists who are working to record people who speak endangered languages and also to translate these languages before they disappear forever.

    (E) Some linguists and anthropologists are working to record people who speak endangered languages and they also work as well at times translating these languages before they disappear forever.

GO ON TO THE NEXT PAGE

KAPLAN
Test Prep and Admissions

35. Including a paragraph on which of the following would most strengthen the writer's argument?

   (A) examples of arguments against preserving languages

   (B) additional stories about people who are the last speakers of a language

   (C) arguments against the use of technology in recording and translation

   (D) further statements about the writer's opinions

   (E) specific examples of cultural ideas that are imbedded in language

IF YOU FINISH BEFORE TIME IS CALLED, YOU MAY CHECK YOUR WORK ON THIS SECTION ONLY. DO NOT TURN TO ANY OTHER SECTION IN THE TEST.

STOP

Test Prep and Admissions

SECTION 7

Time—20 Minutes
19 Questions

Directions: For each of the following questions, choose the best answer and darken the corresponding oval on the answer sheet.

Each sentence below has one or two blanks, each blank indicating that something has been omitted. Beneath the sentence are five words or sets of words labeled (A) through (E). Choose the word or set of words that, when inserted in the sentence, best fits the meaning of the sentence as a whole.

EXAMPLE:

Today's small, portable computers contrast markedly with the earliest electronic computers, which were ----.

(A) effective
(B) invented
(C) useful
(D) destructive
(E) enormous   Ⓐ Ⓑ Ⓒ Ⓓ ●

---

1. ---- two doses of the Hepatitis A vaccine over a period of six to twelve months is ---- providing protection from the disease for ten years.

   (A) Constraining . . required for
   (B) Distributing . . unsuccessful in
   (C) Reconstituting . . instrumental in
   (D) Administering . . effective in
   (E) Disseminating . . unverified for

2. After all of the passengers were safely aboard lifeboats, the crew of the King Cruiser made every attempt to ---- what scuba diving equipment they could off of the ---- diveboat before it sank.

   (A) qualify . . obsolete
   (B) salvage . . floundering
   (C) exacerbate . . defunct
   (D) revitalize . . prosperous
   (E) commandeer . . lucrative

3. Despite the markings that ranked the trail as moderately difficult, the hikers found the trek to be challenging as the path was ---- ; it meandered ceaselessly around the riverbank for miles.

   (A) panoramic
   (B) precipitous
   (C) serpentine
   (D) circumcribed
   (E) retrograde

GO ON TO THE NEXT PAGE ⇒

4. Staging Shakespeare's plays in modern dress can often lead to compelling theater, even though critics interested only in historical accuracy find it ----

(A) credible
(B) anachronistic
(C) implacable
(D) timeless
(E) imaginative

5. Her physician determined that her headaches were ---- by caffeine, so Liz decided to ---- coffee and other caffeinated beverages.

(A) induced . . renounce
(B) alleviated . . subtract
(C) created . . destroy
(D) exacerbated . . promote
(E) enhanced . . neglect

6. After the accident Jidapa's friends found that her behavior had changed drastically; once sprightly and friendly, she now seemed disheartened and unaffable, the ---- of her former self.

(A) remnant
(B) antithesis
(C) consequence
(D) extremity
(E) mainstay

GO ON TO THE NEXT PAGE

Directions: The passages below are followed by questions based on their content; questions following a pair of related passages may also be based on the relationship between the paired passages. Answer the questions on the basis of what is <u>stated</u> or <u>implied</u> in the passages and in any introductory material that may be provided.

Questions 7–19 are based on the following passage

The following passages discuss the future of the Internet and the conflicting ideas surrounding its direction and usefulness. Both passages were written in 2005 by Silicon Valley executives.

Passage 1

The Internet boom of the late 1990s created much of the necessary infrastructure and awareness to advance the Internet not only as a form of technology but also as a public and consumer
(5) product. Nevertheless, though new dot-com companies rapidly expanded and marketed their products during the late 1990s, the dot-coms failed to attract significant numbers of consumers or, consequently, much in the way of profits. As an end
(10) result, most of the dot-coms of the late 1990s failed. Today, however, due to two key changes in the market, dot-com companies, along with their niche in the economy, are poised to return stronger than ever.

(15) The first factor that indicates a dot-com resurgence is the proliferation of broadband Internet service in the United States. The financial boom that the dot-coms precipitated and experienced during the late 1990s proved unsustainable largely
(20) due to the lack of demand for dot-com services, specifically online retailing—known as "e-tailing." This lack of demand was not a result of consumer preference, but rather of the consumer's lack of access. The number of Americans who possessed
(25) access to the Internet remained low even during the late 1990s. Furthermore, even those with access had slower dial-up access, which precluded them from fully exploiting the conveniences developed by the dot-coms. Today, though, many more
(30) households have broadband, which continues to penetrate the market rapidly.

The second factor that indicates a dot-com resurgence is the entry of traditional, established companies into the market. During the late 1990s,
(35) new dot-com companies attempted to provide traditional services like grocery and apparel retailing. The existing, traditional economy, known as the "brick-and-mortar" economy for its reliance on physical locations consumers could visit, did not
(40) previously interact with the "new economy." Today, existing powerhouse companies have established Internet sites that catalogue all of the goods and services they sell. Such companies already bear the costs and revenues of traditional retail-
(45) ing. They do not need to build infrastructure such as warehouses, inventories, a labor force and delivery mechanisms as the dot-coms once needed to do. These companies have few barriers to entry to the online marketplace as they need only establish
(50) a website that lists their products.

Given the favorable conditions that have emerged in the online marketplace, it would be safe to assume that as more and more consumers gain Internet access, the online marketplace will
(55) continue to grow. This will set the stage for the revolution that the Internet inaugurated. Soon, we will see how truly life-changing this technology can be.

Passage 2

The Internet will undoubtedly revolutionize life
(60) in the twenty-first century, but not through its current prevailing use. A revolution in human life and relations began with the advent of the microcomputer. The revolution continued through the networking of the world's computers. However,
(65) this network, the Internet, has been grossly misused. The most powerful communication and data tool ever developed currently functions as nothing more than an electronic catalogue site for retailers.

While corporations, universities and govern-
(70) ment entities have utilized the Internet for administrative and operational purposes, the most

GO ON TO THE NEXT PAGE ⟶

important uses of the Internet have not yet been
implemented. Greater even than the dreams of the
builders of the library of Alexandria is the
(75) Internet's potential as a repository of human
knowledge. Imagine a world similar to that often
portrayed in science fiction movies, in which a
character merely queries a computer about any
fact or procedure and receives an answer. This is
(80) the world the Internet is creating.

    Universities, governments, corporations and
society at large should cooperate in mounting an
effort to begin depositing information on computers and servers. University, government and
(85) private libraries should begin scanning their hold-
ings in order to make all of the volumes in print
available online. Museums, galleries and collectors
should begin taking and digitizing photos of their
collections. Media outlets should begin scanning
(90) their news archives and digitizing all news footage.
Television networks and film companies should
digitize their content. Imagine the wealth of
knowledge that would be available electronically!

    Collecting all of the knowledge in the world
(95) would be useless without a way to find a particular piece. The creation of the library of Alexandria
first necessitated a method for organizing information. In response, librarians created alphabeti-
zation and indexing. This allowed the library to
(100) store increasingly large numbers of volumes and
amounts of information. Similarly, before we can
realize the Internet's potential to store humanity's
knowledge, we must first create search engines
capable of indexing the hard drives of every com-
(105) puter on earth.

    These schemes should not cause panic among
media content creators and literary publishers.
"Available" content does not mean free content.
Content providers can charge fees for the access
(110) and licensing of online content and information.
Just as consumers pay to buy books and visit
museums, they can pay to read books and browse
collections online. Such fee structures already exist
for cable television and pay-per-view media.
(115)   Sadly, so long as American corporations and
consumers treat the Internet as a retail tool, we
will never realize the full potential of the information superhighway.

7. The author of the first passage offers two
   arguments that can best be characterized as

   (A) emotional
   (B) redundant
   (C) political
   (D) allegorical
   (E) pragmatic

8. "Exploiting" (line 28) primarily represents
   an action that is

   (A) unjust
   (B) heroic
   (C) political
   (D) productive
   (E) irrelevant

9. Which of the following best summarizes the "second
   factor" mentioned by the author of Passage 1?

   (A) New dot-coms take over previously failed
      e-tailing endeavors.
   (B) An established department store chain starts
      e-tailing its goods on the Internet.
   (C) Dot-coms that survived during the 1990s return
      to profitability due to broadband proliferation.
   (D) Dot-coms index information, data and media
      and make it available for a fee.
   (E) Brick-and-mortar companies replace dot-
      coms and take over their market space.

10. The primary purpose of Passage 1 is to

   (A) refute arguments that state that the Internet
      economy is dead
   (B) describe the current state of the Internet
      economy
   (C) predict which types of dot-coms will succeed
      in the future
   (D) explain why dot-coms failed
   (E) argue why dot-coms will return to
      prominence

GO ON TO THE NEXT PAGE ⟩

11. The last two sentences of Passage 1 convey

   (A) promise
   (B) loyalty
   (C) adoration
   (D) dissonance
   (E) doubt

12. In Passage 2, lines 66–68 ("The most powerful...
   site for retailers") convey a tone that can be best
   described as

   (A) frivolous
   (B) ambivalent
   (C) apologetic
   (D) hopeful
   (E) ironic

13. The author of Passage 2 reveals an attitude toward
   "the Internet's potential as a repository of human
   knowledge" that is best described as

   (A) neutral, because it will have very little impact
   on everyday life
   (B) negative, because it can take money away
   from content owners
   (C) positive, because it can facilitate the storage
   and exchange of information
   (D) positive, because it can be used to facilitate
   the exchange of goods and services
   (E) negative, because it can be used to hold and
   provide private information

14. The author of Passage 2 mentions "science fiction
   movies" (line 77) primarily in order to

   (A) offer an example of the wrong way to develop
   the Internet
   (B) illustrate the outlandish nature of most
   Internet predictions
   (C) foreshadow how powerful the Internet can be
   (D) cite an example of how the Internet is used
   today
   (E) allude to the dangers of widespread Internet
   usage

15. The author of Passage 2 would most likely argue
   that the situation discussed by the author of
   Passage 1 in lines 11–14 ("due to two key
   changes...stronger than ever") is

   (A) unlikely due to technological constraints
   (B) probable but undesirable
   (C) an advancement over the current uses of the
   Internet
   (D) a less than ideal use of the Internet's strengths
   (E) an obstacle to further development of the
   Internet

16. The authors of both passages would likely agree that

   (A) the Internet can significantly impact society
   (B) the Internet's primary use should be
   information storage and exchange
   (C) the Internet's future is primarily as
   a marketplace
   (D) entry by traditional companies will reshape
   the Internet
   (E) broadband proliferation will fuel Internet
   growth

GO ON TO THE NEXT PAGE ⇒

17. The last paragraphs of both passages primarily serve to

  (A) present a final piece of evidence in order to establish the author's credibility

  (B) make predictions based on the passage's arguments

  (C) warn the reader of the consequences referenced in the passage

  (D) present an alternative viewpoint and refute it

  (E) leave the reader with a rhetorical question based on the passage's argument

18. The author of Passage 1 would probably respond to the plan by the author of Passage 2 to digitize media by stating that

  (A) non-commercial applications for the Internet are destined for failure

  (B) it will fail without the entry of "brick-and-mortar" companies

  (C) there are too many barriers for entry

  (D) dot-coms cannot provide traditional services

  (E) proliferation of broadband access would help implement it

19. The reference to "online marketplace" (line 49) in Passage 1 and "fee structures" (line 113) in Passage 2 both serve to note that the two authors believe that

  (A) the Internet can generate revenue

  (B) the Internet should not be free

  (C) broadband access should carry fees

  (D) intellectual property must be protected

  (E) the Internet will fail without business backing

IF YOU FINISH BEFORE TIME IS CALLED, YOU MAY CHECK YOUR WORK ON THIS SECTION ONLY. DO NOT TURN TO ANY OTHER SECTION IN THE TEST.   STOP

SECTION 8

Time—20 Minutes

16 Questions

Directions: For this section, solve each problem and decide which is the best of the choices given. Fill in the corresponding oval on the answer sheet. You may use any available space for scratchwork.

Notes:

(1) Calculator use is permitted.

(2) All numbers used are real numbers.

(3) Figures are provided for some problems. All figures are drawn to scale and lie in a plane UNLESS otherwise indicated.

(4) Unless otherwise specified, the domain of any function f is assumed to be the set of all real numbers x for which $f(x)$ is a real number.

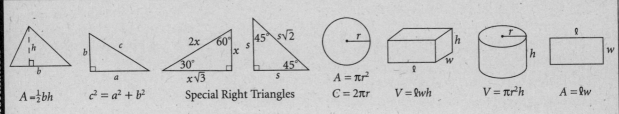

$A = \frac{1}{2}bh$ $c^2 = a^2 + b^2$ Special Right Triangles $A = \pi r^2$ $V = \ell wh$ $V = \pi r^2 h$ $A = \ell w$
$C = 2\pi r$

The sum of the degree measures of the angles in a triangle is 180.
The number of degrees of arc in a circle is 360.
A straight angle has a degree measure of 180.

1. If $4x + 2 = 26$, then $4x + 8 =$

    (A) 32
    (B) 34
    (C) 36
    (D) 38
    (E) 40

2. If $y > 0$, what is 60 percent of $20y$?

    (A) 1.2y
    (B) 10y
    (C) 12y
    (D) 15y
    (E) 120y

GO ON TO THE NEXT PAGE

3. All of the following are equal to $9x^2$ EXCEPT:

   (A) $x^2 + 8x^2$

   (B) $4x + 5x$

   (C) $(9x)(x)$

   (D) $(3x)(3x)$

   (E) $(-3x)(-3x)$

4. If $r(b) = \dfrac{(b^2 - 7)}{(b + 7)}$, what is the value of $r(7)$?

   (A) 0

   (B) 3

   (C) 4

   (D) 7

   (E) 12

5. For which of the following sets of numbers is the average (arithmetic mean) greater than the median?

   (A) $\{-2, -1, 0, 1, 2\}$

   (B) $\{-2, -1, 0, 1, 3\}$

   (C) $\{-2, 0, 0, 0, 2\}$

   (D) $\{-3, -1, 0, 1, 2\}$

   (E) $\{-3, -1, 0, 1, 3\}$

6. 40 percent of 210 is the same as $33\dfrac{1}{3}$ percent of what number?

   (A) 840

   (B) 280

   (C) 252

   (D) 175

   (E)   84

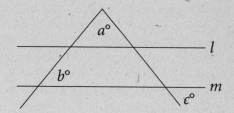

7. In the figure above, if $l \parallel m$ and $c = 50$, what must a be in terms of b?

   (A) b

   (B) $-b$

   (C) $130 + b$

   (D) $130 - b$

   (E) $180 - b$

8. If x and y are different positive integers and $3x + y = 17$, the difference between the largest possible value of y and the smallest possible value of y is

   (A) 16

   (B) 13

   (C) 12

   (D)   4

   (E)   3

9. If 70 percent of x is 2,100, then what is 40 percent of x?

   (A) 3,000

   (B) 2,020

   (C) 1,800

   (D) 1,470

   (E) 1,200

GO ON TO THE NEXT PAGE

10. At 2 P.M. in Littleville, New York, it is 7 P.M. in Williamshire, England. A satellite orbiting the Earth is visible in Littleville at 7 A.M. (Littleville time) but does not cross the sky over Williamshire until 6 P.M. (Williamshire time). A second satellite is seen over Williamshire at noon (Williamshire time) and takes the same amount of time to become visible in Littleville. When, in Littleville time, does the second satellite become visible?

(A) 11 A.M.

(B) 1 P.M.

(C) 5 P.M.

(D) 6 P.M.

(E) 11 P.M.

11. Some clay is shaped into a sphere with a radius of 2 inches. If more clay is added to the original sphere so that the radius is increased by 4 inches, then the volume of the new sphere is how many times greater than the volume of the original sphere?

(A) 3

(B) 8

(C) 27

(D) 64

(E) 208

12. If $g(t) = t^2 - 4$, then the graph of $g(t)$ crosses the x-axis when t equals

(A) -2 only

(B) 0 only

(C) 2 only

(D) -2 and 2 only

(E) $-2, 0,$ and 2

13. If $2^{2x-3} = 8$, then what is the value of x ?

(A) 0

(B) 1

(C) 2

(D) 3

(E) 4

14. The populations of two species of bacteria in a petri dish vary inversely. If there are 1000 bacteria of species A when there are 500 bacteria of species B, how many bacteria of species B are there when there are 2,000 bacteria of species A ?

(A) 250

(B) 500

(C) 750

(D) 1,000

(E) 2,000

15. If $a = 3(2c^2 + 3c + 4)$ and $b = -c + 4$, what is a in terms of b ?

(A) $6b^2 - 48b + 96$

(B) $6b^2 - 57b + 132$

(C) $6b^2 - 57b + 144$

(D) $6b^2 - 9b - 132$

(E) $6b^2 - 9b + 144$

GO ON TO THE NEXT PAGE

16. In a certain pet store, every third goldfish has long fins, and every fourth goldfish has a long tail. If a fish is selected at random from a tank of 120 fish, what is the probability that the fish will have long fins <u>and</u> a long tail?

   (A) $\dfrac{1}{12}$

   (B) $\dfrac{1}{7}$

   (C) $\dfrac{2}{7}$

   (D) $\dfrac{7}{12}$

   (E) $\dfrac{12}{7}$

Test Prep and Admissions

SECTION 9
Time—10 Minutes
14 Questions

1. Undergraduate students may choose from many different major fields of <u>study, there is one which is</u> best for their personal interests.

   (A) study, there is one which is
   (B) study, of which there is one
   (C) study, one of which is
   (D) study, and one of them is
   (E) one is

2. In the belief that foreign news programs aided him in learning languages, <u>James will spend an hour watching them every day</u>.

   (A) James will spend an hour watching them every day
   (B) James spent an hour watching them every day
   (C) an hour of every day are spent watching them by James
   (D) they occupied an hour of every day for James
   (E) every day will find James spending an hour on watching them

3. <u>Chocolate is among Switzerland's most popular exports, as it was actually invented by the Aztecs.</u>

   (A) Chocolate is among Switzerland's most popular exports, as it was actually invented by the Aztecs.
   (B) Among Switzerland's most popular exports, the Aztecs is actually invented chocolate.
   (C) Chocolate, which is among Switzerland's most popular exports, was actually invented by the Aztecs.
   (D) Chocolate was actually invented by the Aztecs, being among Switzerland's most popular exports.
   (E) Actually, chocolate being invented by the Aztecs, it is among Switzerland's most popular exports.

GO ON TO THE NEXT PAGE

4. When someone listens to a current pop or rock song, <u>you hear</u> music influenced by decades of musicians and genres including gospel and country.

   (A) you hear

   (B) it hears

   (C) you will hear

   (D) he or she hears

   (E) they hear

5. Born and raised on the coast of California, <u>the Beach Boys' hit songs celebrate life in the sun and surf</u>.

   (A) the Beach Boys' hit songs celebrate life in the sun and surf

   (B) the Beach Boys celebrate life in the sun and surf in their hit songs

   (C) a celebration of life in the sun and surf is in the Beach Boys' hit songs

   (D) life in the sun and surf is celebrated in the Beach Boys' hit songs

   (E) the Beach Boys, who celebrate life in the sun and surf in their hit songs

6. Professor Schonle's son told the magazine that <u>he had decided not to accept the new position</u>, even though the current chairman has already resigned.

   (A) he had decided not to accept the new position

   (B) the decision was that his father would not accept the new position

   (C) his father had decided not to accept the new position

   (D) he decided that he will not accept to be placed in the new position

   (E) it was decided about his not accepting the chairman's position

7. <u>Although the college has begun to decrease the size of its classes</u>, it is still receiving hundreds of protest letters.

   (A) Although the college has begun to decrease the size of its classes

   (B) Although beginning to decrease, as the college, the size of its classes

   (C) The college, beginning to decrease the size of its classes

   (D) The college has begun to decrease the size of its classes, and

   (E) The college, beginning to decrease the size of its classes, however

8. When we meet new people, we make <u>assumptions about them and then those assumptions are reconsidered</u> as we get to know them better.

   (A) assumptions about them and then those assumptions are reconsidered

   (B) assumptions about them and then reconsider those assumptions

   (C) assumptions about them, reconsidering those assumptions then

   (D) assumptions about them, we reconsider those assumptions

   (E) assumptions about them and then they are reconsidered by us

9. <u>The songs of Ray Charles, often more energetic than his contemporaries,</u> became popular because they blended disparate musical genres.

   (A) The songs of Ray Charles, often more energetic than his contemporaries,

   (B) The songs of Ray Charles, which are often more energetic and than his contemporaries,

   (C) The songs of Ray Charles, often fuller of energy than those of his contemporaries,

   (D) The songs of Ray Charles, often more energetic than those of his contemporaries,

   (E) Often being more energetic than his contemporaries, the songs of Ray Charles

GO ON TO THE NEXT PAGE ⇨

10. Writer Upton Sinclair fought to improve public health in America by <u>revealing the unsanitary practices of the meat industry, he successfully influenced politicians to require higher standards for these companies</u>.

   (A) revealing the unsanitary practices of the meat industry, he successfully influenced politicians to require higher standards for these companies

   (B) revealing the unsanitary practices of the meat industry and successfully influencing politicians to require higher standards for these companies

   (C) his revealing the unsanitary practices of the meat industry and successful influence over politicians to require higher standards for these companies

   (D) revealing the unsanitary practices of the meat industry, although successfully influencing politicians to require higher standards for these companies

   (E) revealing the unsanitary practices of the meat industry for whom he was successful in influencing politicians to require higher standards

11. One of the benefits of our new insurance plan is <u>that every family is allowed to choose their own</u> health care providers.

   (A) that every family is allowed to choose their own

   (B) that every family is allowed to choose its own

   (C) that every family being allowed to choose their own

   (D) how families are allowed choosing each their own

   (E) how the choices of families are made on their own

12. Discovering a wide spectrum of cultural events in a rural town is not as easy as <u>it is</u> in a college town.

   (A) it is

   (B) is that

   (C) for those

   (D) for that

   (E) are those

13. Bias in the media, <u>already apparent due to the influence of large conglomerates, threaten</u> to become even more serious when journalists are afraid to write articles that contradict their editors' opinions.

   (A) already apparent due to the influence of large conglomerates, threaten

   (B) already apparent due to the influence of large conglomerates, threatens

   (C) already more apparent due to large conglomerates, threatens

   (D) having been made apparent by the influence of large conglomerates, threaten

   (E) after having been made apparent by large conglomerates, threaten

14. As a student at Highland Park High School, <u>L.J. Smith became a serious competitor in various sports, which ultimately led to</u> a high paying NFL career.

   (A) L.J. Smith became a serious competitor in various sports, which ultimately led to

   (B) L.J. Smith's competition in various sports became both serious and it ultimately led him to

   (C) where L.J. Smith became a serious competitor in various sports, ultimately leading him to

   (D) L.J. Smith became a serious competitor in various sports, having led him ultimately to

   (E) where he became a serious competitor in various sports, L.J. Smith, as a result, ultimately went on to

IF YOU FINISH BEFORE TIME IS CALLED, YOU MAY CHECK YOUR WORK ON THIS SECTION ONLY. DO NOT TURN TO ANY OTHER SECTION IN THE TEST.

THE ANSWER KEY APPEARS ON THE FOLLOWING PAGE.

Practice Test Twelve: **Answer Key**

SECTION 1

Essay

SECTION 2

1. B
2. D
3. B
4. A
5. A
6. A
7. B
8. A
9. A
10. B
11. E
12. A
13. B
14. C
15. C
16. A
17. D
18. C
19. A
20. E
21. B
22. C
23. D
24. A

SECTION 3

1. D
2. C
3. D
4. C
5. B
6. A
7. C
8. B
9. C
10. A
11. A
12. E
13. A
14. A
15. D
16. C
17. D
18. A
19. C
20. D

SECTION 4

1. D
2. E
3. C
4. B
5. C
6. B
7. D
8. B
9. A
10. B
11. D
12. C
13. B

14. D
15. C
16. D
17. E
18. D
19. D
20. D
21. C
22. B
23. A
24. C

SECTION 5

1. D
2. C
3. E
4. C
5. D
6. B
7. D
8. D
9. 15/4 or 3.75
10. 1/10 or .1
11. 12
12. 30
13. 48
14. 192, 480 or 960
15. 75
16. $0 < a < 1/8$
17. .5 or 1/2
18. 6

SECTION 6

1. E
2. A
3. D
4. D
5. D
6. A
7. A
8. D
9. D
10. C
11. D
12. E
13. B
14. D
15. D
16. B
17. B
18. E
19. D
20. C
21. E
22. C
23. C
24. C
25. C
26. C
27. A
28. B
29. B
30. B
31. D
32. A
33. D
34. C
35. E

SECTION 7

1. D
2. B
3. C
4. B
5. A
6. B
7. E
8. D
9. B
10. E
11. A
12. E
13. C
14. C
15. D
16. A
17. B
18. E
19. A

SECTION 8

1. A
2. C
3. B
4. B
5. B
6. C
7. D
8. C
9. E
10. B
11. C
12. D
13. D
14. A

15. C
16. A

SECTION 9

1. C
2. C
3. C
4. D
5. B
6. C
7. A
8. B
9. D
10. B
11. B
12. A
13. B
14. A

PRACTICE TEST TWELVE

Critical Reading

	Number Right	Number Wrong	Raw Score
Section 2:	□	− (.25 × □)	= □
Section 4:	□	− (.25 × □)	= □
Section 7:	□	− (.25 × □)	= □
	Critical Reading Raw Score	=	□
			(rounded up)

Writing

	Number Right	Number Wrong	Raw Score
Section 1:	□ (ESSAY GRADE)	× 3.17	= □
Section 6:	□	− (.25 × □)	= □
Section 9:	□	− (.25 × □)	= □
	Writing Raw Score	=	□
			(rounded up)

Math

	Number Right	Number Wrong	Raw Score
Section 3:	□	− (.25 × □)	= □
Section 5A: (QUESTIONS 1 0)	□	− (.25 × □)	= □
Section 5B: (QUESTIONS 9–18)	□	(no wrong answer penalty)	= □
Section 8:	□	− (.25 × □)	= □
	Math Raw Score	=	□
			(rounded up)

Turn to page xiv to convert your raw score to a scaled score.

Answers and Explanations

SECTION 1

6 Score Essay

Seeking both sides of the story is the foundation of our legal system. It takes both prosecution and defense to discover the truth in a courtroom. I volunteer as a prosecuting attorney for the mock court in my town. The mock court is part of the family court and we try juvenile cases with the help of local attorneys. In my work with the mock court I have discovered how important it is to get both sides of the story.

This fall I worked on a case prosecuting "Jack" who had been arrested for spray painting the wall of a local elementary school. The evidence in the case seemed overwhelming. The police caught Jack with a can of spray paint at the school; the paint was on his shoes; and he had already done community service for damaging a park bench. I felt very confident of my case going into the courtroom, and I became even more convinced of Jack's guilt when saw how he acted in the court. He seemed hostile and uncooperative.

However, the defense made a case that Jack had not done the actual spray painting. The defense attorney asserted that Jack had been at the school with some older boys who ran when the police arrived, leaving Jack and the empty can of paint. According to Jack's testimony, he had not run with the others because he knew that if he was caught leaving the scene he would be in even more trouble, especially as he already had a record with the police. I was very surprised when the defense was able to produce two witnesses who backed-up Jack's story. He was cleared of all charges.

This case taught me how easy it is to be prejudiced by one set of facts. With just one side of the story, the evidence the police gathered and my own impression of Jack, I was completely convinced that he was guilty. Had it been up to me, I would have sentenced him without a second thought. However, through the process of the trial I heard Jack's version of the events. With the new evidence, I was forced to reevaluate my impression of Jack. Behavior that I had initially interpreted as hostility, I came to see as fear and anxiety.

In our legal system, the prosecution and defense each represent one side of the story, and it is their job to tell that story as convincingly as they can. However, the judge or the jury listens to both sides in order to determine the truth of the case. The court is built around the principle of hearing both sides of a story, but it is not the only place where this idea applies. In journalism, personal arguments, and any situation in which it is necessary to make a judgment, a person who only has one set of facts can easily be led astray by prejudice and preconceived notions. It is always important to gather all the facts before deciding on the truth of the matter.

6 Score Critique

All essays are evaluated on four basic criteria: Topic, Support, Organization, and Language. This essay begins strongly with an introduction that leads well into the writer's single but extremely well-developed example. Providing background, she announces her stand on the prompt and provides her thesis for the essay. The introduction transitions smoothly into the first body paragraph, which describes the author's example, based on her personal experience. This paragraph moves smoothly into the next, which further develops and supports the author's single example. Finally, the concluding paragraph neatly wraps up the author's argument. This author clearly took time to plan her essay, resulting in a coherent and consistent essay that is well organized and offers sufficient support for her thesis.

The author's use of specific details in her narrative about Jack's case makes the essay outstanding. In addition, the author uses varied sentence structure and language to express her ideas. She includes keywords like "however" to demonstrate how her point of view changed by having both sides of the story. The author's attention to detail, as evidenced by a lack of grammatical or spelling errors, also indicates that she allowed herself sufficient time to proofread her essay at the end.

4 Score Essay

When you want to know the truth, it is important to get both sides of the story. This is especially true in journalism. Every good reporter knows that you cannot rely on just one source. I work as a reporter on my school paper and I have learned to always get both sides of the story.

I was decided to write a story about recycling in our town for the "Local Happenings" column. I interviewed the head of the recycling plant for my story. I was really pleased that I had gotten an interview with the head of all the recycling in the town. He took me around the recycling plant and showed me all about how materials are recycled and answered my questions about how the program is working in our town. I worked all weekend on a long article. When I turned in my article the advisor for the paper told me I had to do more work. At first I thought she was being unfair, but she explained that you can't just rely on one person for a story, unless it was an interview.

She helped me set up interviews with a garbage collector, and also suggested I interview people from different neighborhoods to see how they felt about the new recycling program. I discovered that the garbage collector had some very negative things to say about the program. He thought it has been badly introduced so people did not know how to sort their garbage which made his job more difficult. Some people thought the program was great and other people thought it was a waste of time.

I ended up writing a much better article, and I learned a lot more about recycling in my town by getting both sides of the story.

4 Score Critique

All essays are evaluated on four basic criteria: Topic, Support, Organization, and Language. The author states his opinion of the prompt immediately, indicating to the reader that his essay will provide an example from his own experience on the school newspaper. The example is fairly well developed and supported in the subsequent paragraphs, showing that the author took time to plan his essay and list his ideas before he began to write.

The essay is well organized, except for the conclusion, which is short and seems hastily added. The word choice and sentence structure is not remarkable, with generic language and frequent use of sentences starting with "I." Errors like "I was decided" and "the program is working" in the second paragraph detract from the essay and indicate that proofreading would have helped this writer's score.

2 Score Essay

In the story the Gift of the Magi the man sells his watch so he can buy his wife combs for her hair but his wife sold her hair to buy her husband a chain for his watch. This story shows that sometimes it is good not have both sides of the story. If the man knew that his wife was going to sell her hair he would never have brought her the combs. And if his wife knowed that he was going to sell his watch she would never have bought him his watchchain. Then they never would have known how generous they were. This is the moral of the story. When I first read the story I thought it was meant to be sad. Because neither of them could enjoy there new presents. But when we studied the story I learned that is actually a happy story because they realize that they would part with there most important thing to make their husband or wife happy.

Both the husband and his wife were trying to suprise the other person, and the suprize was the most important part. If they had knew what the other person was doing they would not have been able to surpize them. Sometimes it is good not know everything because that takes all the mystery out of life and makes it impossible to have something really special happen like in the story the Gift of the Magi.

2 Score Critique

All essays are evaluated on four basic criteria: Topic, Support, Organization, and Language. This essay launches immediately into an example, and does show that the author has understood the prompt. However, although the author doesn't digress from the topic, the remainder of the essay lacks organization and support. The essay includes a single example in its two paragraphs, but the development of his topic is poorly executed. The author includes few transition words or phrases between paragraphs and uses few keywords to help the reader navigate the essay. To improve this aspect of his essay, the writer should plan his essay before beginning to write.

The language is redundant and the sentences lack variety of structure. Several run-on sentences or fragments result from a lack of appropriate punctuation. Finally, the author has failed to correct some spelling errors, such as "surprize" in the second paragraph.

SECTION 2

1. B

Difficulty: Low

The hot words "renowned" and "eminent" indicate that the blanks will both be positive.

Start with the second blank. The architect of well-known, famous buildings must have been "well-known" and "acclaimed" himself. The prediction for the first blank must support Wright's becoming so distinguished; a word such as "proved" works.

In choice (A), although *buoyed* works in the first blank, *irrelevant* or *inappropriate* is the opposite of the prediction for the second blank. Choice (B) is the credited answer. Read the answer choice back in. In choice (C), *surrendered* has a negative connotation and it is a bit extreme; buildings cannot *surrender* or (give up) a person as being either a good, bad, or *prolific* (productive) architect. In choice (D), both words are negative; the predictions show they must be positive. *Decried* means to disparage or put down and a person who is *cynical* believes that people's motives are usually bad or selfish. The word *cynical* is out of the scope or idea of the sentence. In choice (E), *categorized* is not the best choice for the first blank and "mundane" or "ordinary" does not fit as it is the opposite of the prediction.

2. D

Difficulty: Low

The hot word "although" suggests a contrast between the word in the blank and the fact that questions in the book are likely to appear on the exam.

The chapter review is either required or not required. Given that the questions on the exam will be required to be answered, and taking into consideration the contrast between the word "required" and the word in the blank, a good prediction would be that the chapter review exercises are "not required" or "additional" questions.

Choice (A) can be eliminated because it is the opposite of the prediction. Only if the word "although" were eliminated and the word "and" was inserted after the blank would this word fit into the context of the sentence. If the students knew that these questions were to be found on the exam, then doing the review may have already become *ritualistic* but the teacher would not use this word denoting "routine" to encourage the class to do extra studying. The teacher

would not announce the *optional* questions as being *salient* or noticeable. Choice (D) is the correct answer. In choice (E), this word means "serious," but relates to demeanor or attitude, not to how the students are to treat the additional questions.

3. B

Difficulty: Medium

She made the best of a lousy situation. The key word is "instead." Instead of letting her boss get her down, the young professional found something positive in the workplace that helped her move up. For the second blank you're looking for a word with a positive charge.

Looking at (A), *discouraged* would work, but it wouldn't make sense that she would have found *reconciliation* when nothing in the sentence implies she was feeling sorry for anything. Choice (B) works. Instead of being *defeated*, or beaten, she rose above the difficulty and found *prosperity*. As for choice (C), people aren't generally *elevated* by oppressive things. In choice (D) again, oppressive things rarely *aid* in anything. Lastly, in choice (E), even if she was *delayed* by her oppressive boss, how would finding *unity* in the workplace help her be upwardly mobile?

4. A

Difficulty: Medium

Start with the first blank. Towns that consist of a "heterogeneous population," or one that is made up of various sorts of people, tend to have food that reflects the many different tastes of the inhabitants. If you didn't know the meaning of "heterogeneous" you could figure out that "towns bordering two different countries" would offer an array of foods. For the second blank, the word must be synonymous with the word in the first blank.

Start with a prediction for the first blank. A word such as "variety" or "diversity" would work. The second blank should support the first with a word such as a "range" of various ingredients.

Choice (A) is the credited answer. In choice (B), the first choice can be eliminated because the sentence says nothing about the size of the population growing. A growing population would imply an increasing amount of different foods would come to exist; however, nothing about growth is mentioned. The second choice is the opposite of the prediction. In choice (C), the first choice is out of scope; the town wouldn't have "mixed feelings towards" different foods. The second choice doesn't match the prediction. In choice (D), both blanks do not work. *Dearth* or "scarcity" is the opposite of the prediction, and nothing is said about a reduction of ingredients available caused by using them. In choice (E), the first blank does not fit because nothing is said about either the population or the amount of food increasing or decreasing. The second blank does not work; towns would not boast of artificial ingredients.

5. A

Difficulty: Medium

The hot words "despite" and "apparent" clue you in to the fact that his lifestyle was not what the word in the blank describes. What word describes someone who does not "drink to excess?" A good prediction would be someone who leads an "abstinent" or "self-restrained" lifestyle.

Choice (A) is the correct answer. *Temperate* means "disciplined" or "self-restrained." In choice (B) *laconic* means "brief" or "concise." The fact that the man is old and has therefore lived a long life is not what is being contrasted by the hot words and the word in the blank. In choice (C), *duplicitous* means "deceitful;" who was the old man deceiving? He would only be deceptive if he were trying to hide his drinking habits. In choice (D), this word can mean either "artistic" or "tasteful." Whether or not his lifestyle was *aesthetic* is not related to his drinking habits. Someone can drink alcohol and still be regarded as being "tasteful." As for choice (E), the man being talkative or not has nothing to do with drinking.

6. A

Difficulty: Medium

Focus on the hot word "predicted." He became known for what if he was able to foresee future events? The prediction should be a word that means Nostradamus had a knowledge of events before they occurred, such as "foresight." Eliminate all answer choices that do not match this prediction.

Choice (A) is the credited answer. As for choice (B), Nostradamus became known for his predictions, not for honesty or *sincerity*. Looking at choice (C), this word is out of scope; nothing is said about Nostradamus being greedy. As for choice (D), be careful; *complicity* does not mean "complicated;" it means involvement as an accomplice in a crime. Finally, in choice (E), because his predictions were accurate, Nostradamus was not being untruthful.

7. B

Difficulty: High

The publishers were up to no good, so this news must have hurt their reputation—in fact, "hurt" is a great prediction for the second blank. Since their reputation was hurt, it must have been pretty "good" to begin with, another solid prediction. Choice (B) is a great match for both blanks. Choices (A) and (C) are great matches for the first prediction, but the second words are opposites of your prediction. In choice (D), if the reputation was *deficient*, then it wouldn't have been changed by the news of shady business practices. In choice (E), you might not be sure if the first word fits, but the second one makes no sense. If a reputation is *coveted*, or desired, then it has to be coveted by someone, and no such person is mentioned in the sentence.

8. A

Difficulty: High

You know that "admirers" are people who feel positively toward their candidate, so "admired" is a good prediction for the first blank. For the second blank, look for something that would contrast with having supporters, like "messed up" or "cancelled." Choice (A) works well for both blanks. In choice (B), the first blank is a great fit, but it doesn't make much sense to say that she *illuminated* her campaign. In choices (C) and (D), she wouldn't be *denounced* or *disdained* by her supporters, both very negative actions. In choice (E), *bolstered*, or strengthened, is a pretty good fit, but it doesn't make sense to *retaliate*, or get revenge, on a campaign.

9. A

Difficulty: High

To answer this question using context, ask yourself what kind of response might warrant a chat with the principal. *Flippant* means disrespectful lightheartedness, with *disrespectful*, of course, being the pertinent connotation. Answer choice (B), *inveterate,* means firmly established, usually with regard to attitude or habit. *Pecuniary,* answer choice (C), refers to money; and *reactionary*, choice (D), means extremely conservative, especially in politics. Answer choice (E), *lax*, means loose or slack, often in the figurative sense of lacking in rigor or strictness.

10. B

Difficulty: Low

The phrase "an even narrower grasp" in describing the voting public's understanding of policy suggests that "acquaintance" gives a negative evaluation of the voting public's political awareness. Choice (B) matches the negative tone. Choices (A), (D), and (E) are too positive. Eliminate choice (C) because the public is, in the author's estimation, not engaged in any sort of discussion with the crucial issues, *fraught* or otherwise.

11. E

Difficulty: Medium

When you see the words "even if," you can expect some qualification or drawback to follow. In the context of the sentence as a whole, you see that the qualification is associated with preserving the spirit of the original rather than being as faithful as possible to the author's wording. Choices (A) and (D) are both distortions, and the phrase *totally unrelated* makes choice (B) extreme.

12. A

Difficulty: Medium

For questions about an author's attitude, first look for words and phrases indicating whether his or her attitude is positive or negative. Once you have narrowed down the choices, think about which answer reflects the tone of the passage most accurately. The phrase "Some people think" suggests that the author may not agree. This prediction is reinforced by the following phrase "but I believe," which contrasts the view of "some people" with the author's own view. Only choice (A) expresses disagreement and is consistent with the author's overall tone in the passage. Choices (B) and (C) are both distortions; nothing in the passage indicates *puzzlement* or *curiosity* about the view. Choice (E) is too negative. The author disagrees but does not express scorn or disdain for the view.

13. B

Difficulty: Medium

Making a strong prediction is your best ally here.

Author 1 is insecure because her emotional health is regarded as "uncool" by her friends; Jessie in Passage 2 is described as insecure about who she is and her battle with bipolar disorder. Look for an answer that says they are *insecure about their respective states of emotional health.*

Choice (A) is a misused detail; Author 1 may feel this, but there is no evidence to support that Jessie does. Choice (B) matches your prediction. Choice (C) is a misused detail; while Jessie may use deceptive manipulation, she is not

particularly successful since the narrator is aware of it. And Author 1 does not attempt to practice deception. Choice (D) is an opposite; Jessie in Passage 2 is manipulative, which is nearly the opposite of being *genuine*. Choice (E) is out of scope; while this may be true of the narrator in Passage 1, there is nothing to support that this is true of Jessie in Passage 2.

Questions 14–24

This passage is about the societal prejudices women musicians had to overcome in the nineteenth century.

The introduction describes music's nineteenth century shift from a male-dominated, aristocratic activity to one that encompassed the rising middle class. The second paragraph tells us that while women were encouraged to pursue music—to better lure potential husbands—the support of a man was still necessary for a woman to forge a musical career. The misogynist views of seventeenth century philosophers Rousseau and Campe, who believed women inferior and better suited to raising children, are then discussed. In the fourth paragraph, we learn that the views of these philosophers were widely held by both men and women; even Clara Schumann, the best-known woman composer of her day, had doubts about her musical abilities. The final paragraph describes Schumann's musical accomplishments.

14. C

Difficulty: Low

With the exception of the first paragraph, which serves as the introduction, the entire passage is about the societal prejudice that women musicians had to overcome in the nineteenth century. Choice (C) is correct.

Choice (A) focuses too narrowly on the end of the passage. Choice (B) is wrong because the author never explores the reasons women were ever held to be incapable of artistic creativity. Nor is the author out to choice (D), criticize nineteenth-century men; she always maintains a historian's distance from her subject. Choice (E) is wrong because the status of women before the nineteenth century is discussed in only one paragraph.

15. C

Difficulty: Medium

According to the first paragraph, the new political and social currents in Europe led to increased involvement of the middle class in the arts, which was formerly the exclusive province of the aristocracy. Also, the author says the middle class began to enjoy elevated status. Choice (C) captures these ideas. Choice (A) is wrong because the point is not that music was lowered; it's that the middle class was elevated. We can see from the information in the passage that choice (B) is inaccurate. Choice (D) exaggerates a detail at the end of the first paragraph concerning the growth of the music industry. Choice (E) is a false inference based on the first paragraph; the aristocrats may well have continued to be interested in music.

16. A

Difficulty: Medium

Choice (A) is the correct answer because 1) women were allowed to become involved in music in order to enhance the family's social status through marriage (a traditional role), and 2) singing was especially encouraged because it fit in with the traditional conception of the mother.

There is no evidence at all in the passage to support choice (B). Choice (C) is wrong because the increased participation of bourgeois women was in amateur, not professional, music. Choice (D) directly contradicts what we're told in the first paragraph. Choice (E) is wrong because the author never explicitly says that women's increased participation in music was justified by their show of talent.

17. D

Difficulty: Low

The point of the entire second paragraph is that women musicians in the nineteenth century were still subject to the authority of the men. Due to societal standards and beliefs, women could not pursue a musical career without the permission and support of the men. In other words, women musicians were not allowed to act independently choice (D). None of the other choices is supported by the passage at all.

18. C

Difficulty: Medium

The third paragraph is devoted to a discussion of eighteenth-century beliefs concerning women as artists—beliefs that held sway in the nineteenth century as well. The author is demonstrating that "nineteenth-century beliefs about women were long-standing and firmly rooted" choice (C).

Choice (A) is wrong because the third paragraph really shows how the perception of women did not change from the eighteenth to the nineteenth centuries. Choice (B) is not supported by anything in the third paragraph. Choice (D) is out because it doesn't seem that chauvinism was any worse in the eighteenth century than in the nineteenth—it was about the same. Choice (E) is wrong because the philosophers in the third paragraph aren't pointing out any faults in society.

19. A

Difficulty: Medium

Look to the previous sentence ("…writers believed that women did not possess the intellectual and emotional *capacity* to learn or create as artists") to understand what Rousseau means by "women…possess no artistic sensibility." "Aptitude" is the right synonym for "capacity" and therefore the right synonym for "sensibility" as well, since "capacity" and "sensibility" mean the same thing here.

20. E

Difficulty: Medium

Campe's view is presented to show that people thought it was more important for women to be wives and mothers than to be composers. Campe criticizes women composers on the basis that they have neglected their domestic duties. Choice (E) is therefore the correct answer.

Campe never suggests that women cannot compose, and he certainly doesn't think they have too many domestic responsibilities, so choices (A) and (B) are out. Choice (C) contradicts Campe. Choice (D) is wrong because Campe would never advocate women concentrating exclusively on music.

21. B

Difficulty: Medium

According to the fourth paragraph, nineteenth century men *and* women agreed with the ideas of the eighteenth-century philosophers. Therefore, one source of the "societal censure" and "internal conflicts" that women musicians suffered must have been "disapproval from other women," choice (B).

The author never says women had a problem with intensity choice (A) or competition from men choice (D). Choice (C) is clearly wrong because women did not receive many supportive opinions. Choice (E) is a distortion of information in the paragraph: Schumann is cited as an example of a great woman musician with internal conflicts caused by society; she is not the reason other women had internal conflicts.

22. C

Difficulty: High

The author brings up the example of Schumann in order to show that even the most accomplished woman musician could be led by societal beliefs to doubt her own ability. In Schumann, the reader can see just how great the obstacles were for women who wanted to be creative musicians choice (C).

Schumann's achievements were far from typical, so choice (A) can be eliminated. Choice (B) is wrong because there is never any question that there were at least some nineteenth-century women who composed music. Choice (D) is a distortion of the last paragraph's point that Schumann was one of the first female composers to compose an orchestral work. Choice (E) isn't supported by anything in the passage.

23. D

Difficulty: Low

Choice (D) is correct because it paraphrases the last sentence of the fourth paragraph.

There is no evidence in the passage to support any of the other choices.

24. A

Difficulty: Low

The author describes the art song—the genre considered appropriate for women and the type of music that women composers gravitated to out of necessity—in order to

emphasize just how much Schumann "defied convention" in composing an orchestral piece. Choice (A) is correct.

No new point of view is ever introduced into the passage, so choice (B) is incorrect. Choice (C) is wrong because the art song is not a type of orchestral work. Choice (D) is out because the author never criticizes nineteenth-century women at all. Choice (E) simply misconstrues the point the author makes by describing the art song.

SECTION 3

1. D

Difficulty: Low

Strategic Advice: Sometimes the biggest challenge of a question is not its math but its English: notice here that you're given data in both minutes and seconds. Avoid trap choices (such as (B) in this case) by making these units of measurement consistent.

Getting to the Answer:

$$\frac{5 \text{ ft.}}{60 \text{ sec}} = \frac{?}{2}$$
$$60? = 10$$
$$? = \frac{10}{60} = \frac{1}{6}$$

2. C

Difficulty: Low

Remember that questions involving ranges of possible values often require you to use either or both extreme values—a minimums or maximum to answer correctly. Here, for example, you need only 80% of 40.

Getting to the Answer:

$$.80(40) - 32$$

3. D

Difficulty: Low

Focus how one piece of data leads to another. If two sides are equal, the two angles opposite are equal. Then only 60 degrees remains for the top angle—which means that the triangle is equilateral: all three sides and all three angles are equal.

Getting to the Answer:

$$12 + 12 + 12 = 36$$

4. C

Difficulty: Low

Strategic Advice: Often, and especially early in a section, questions test not so much your ability to conceptualize advanced math concepts as your ability to quickly and carefully perform basic operations. Practice such questions (like this one), and on Test Day you'll move through them with speed and meticulousness. Notice, by the way, that this is one of those very rare questions in which the logic of the question itself prevents the test maker from presenting the choices in size order, as they are normally presented.

Getting to the Answer:

(A) $2 + \frac{1}{2} = 2\frac{1}{2}$

(B) $2 - \frac{1}{2} = 1\frac{1}{2}$

(C) $\frac{1}{2} - 2 = -1\frac{1}{2}$

(D) $2 \times \frac{1}{2} = 1$

(E) $2 \div \frac{1}{2} = 4$

5. B

Difficulty: Medium

Strategic Advice: The side opposite a larger angle is the larger side. Find the missing angle, then use the relationships between the angles to find the relationships between the sides.

Getting to the Answer:

$$\angle S = 180 - (110 + 55) = 15$$

$\overline{PS}$ is the longest side because it is opposite the 110° angle. $\overline{RS}$ is shorter than $\overline{PS}$ but longer than $\overline{PR}$. Therefore, $6 + y > 6 + z > 6$. You can simplify this inequality to $y > z > 0$.

(E) This may or may not be true. Eliminate.

(D) This may or may not be true. Eliminate.

(C) Not possible. Eliminate.

(B) Correct.

(A) Not possible. Eliminate

6. A

Difficulty: Medium

Strategic Advice: Don't let the $\wedge$ scare you. Just plug the values into the equation.

Getting to the Answer:

$x = 4$ and $y = 2$

$(x - y)^x + (x + y)^y$

$(4 - 2)^4 + (4 + 2)^2$

$(2)^4 + (6)^2$

7. C

Difficulty: Medium

When a transversal crosses parallel lines, all acute angles are equal and all obtuse angles are equal. So the angle to the right of c is equal to d, and the angle to the left of b is equal to a, as shown:

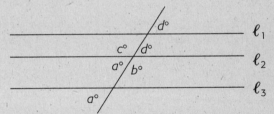

Since c and d make up a straight line, $c + d = 180$.
Since a and b make up a straight line, $a + b = 180$.
So $a + b + c + d = 180 + 180 = 360$.

8. B

Difficulty: Medium

Strategic Advice: This is a great problem to practice your English to math translation skills with. Translate each part of the word problem into an equation and then solve.

Getting to the Answer:

$$x + 6 - 2 = 2x$$
$$4 = x$$

9. C

Difficulty: Medium

Strategic Advice: Sketching a figure may help you organize the information quickly.

Getting to the Answer:

The question asks for the measure of the largest angle, so set that equal to x. The measure of the middle-sized angle is 40 degrees less than the degree measure of the largest angle, or $x - 40$. The measure of the smallest angle is 20 degrees. The sum of the measures of the three interior angles of any triangle is 180 degrees.

$$x + (x - 40) + 20 = 180.$$
$$x + x - 40 + 20 = 180$$
$$2x - 20 = 180$$
$$2x = 200$$
$$x = 100$$

10. A

Difficulty: Medium

Strategic Advice: Even though there are only variables in the question, picking numbers would still be a great strategy to try here.

Getting to the Answer:

Pick 7 for your positive odd integer.

$$(d - 1)(d - 2) = (7 - 1)(7 - 2) = (6)(5) = 30.$$

Too large. Try a smaller number.

$$(d - 1)(d - 2) = (5 - 1)(5 - 2) = (4)(3) = 12.$$

11. A

Difficulty: Medium

Strategic Advice: To find the area, add the dimensions of the square and the triangle. First re-label the diagram as follows:

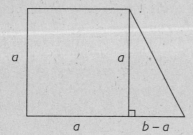

Getting to the Answer:

The area of a square is the length of a side squared, so the area of this square is a^2. The area of this right triangle is

$$\frac{1}{2}(\text{leg}_1 \times \text{leg}_2) = \frac{1}{2}(a)(b - a) = \frac{ab}{2} - \frac{a^2}{2}.$$

So the combined area is:

$$a^2 + \frac{ab}{2} - \frac{a^2}{2} = \frac{2a^2}{2} - \frac{a^2}{2} + \frac{ab}{2}$$
$$= \frac{a^2}{2} + \frac{ab}{2}$$
$$= \frac{a^2 + ab}{2}$$
$$= \frac{a(a + b)}{2}$$

12. E

Difficulty: Medium

Strategic Advice: Getting comfortable with the average formula means points on Test Day.

Getting to the Answer:

$$\text{average} = \frac{(\text{sum of numbers})}{(\text{quantity of numbers})}$$

You know that the sum of four numbers is between 53 and 57. Therefore, the average of this group is between $\frac{53}{4} = 13\frac{1}{4}$ and $\frac{57}{4} = 14\frac{1}{4}$. Only one answer choice fits in this range: (E) 14.

13. A

Difficulty: Medium

Strategic Advice: Don't let questions about volume intimidate you. You already know how to calculate area: it's length × width. To find volume, simply add another dimension: length × width × depth.

Getting to the Answer:

There are boxes of two sizes in this problem. The larger box is 24 inches long, 10 inches wide, and 15 inches high. Its volume is:

24 in. × 10 in. × 15 in. = 3,600 cubic inches

You know that there are 60 identical smaller boxes that fit perfectly into the larger box's volume. What is the volume of each of these? Divide the large box's volume by the number of smaller boxes to find your answer.

$$\frac{(3,600 \text{ cu. in.})}{60} = 60 \text{ cu. in.}$$

Check the dimensions in each answer choice to see which results in a volume of 60 cu. in.

(A) 2 × 5 × 6 = 60. That's your answer.

(B) 3 × 4 × 6 = 72

(C) 3 × 5 × 6 = 90

(D) 4 × 5 × 6 = 120

(E) 5 × 6 × 12 = 360

14. A

Difficulty: Medium

Strategic Advice: The first graph deals with 1975. From it you can see that, of the 600 graduates, 12% chose to enter the work force and 22% chose to go to vocational school. Adding the percents gives you 12% + 22% = 34%.

Getting to the Answer: 34% of $600 = \frac{34}{100} \times 600 = 204$. So 204 graduates chose either to enter the work force or go to vocational school.

15. D

Difficulty: Medium

Strategic Advice: First find how many graduates went on to a four-year college in 1985. Looking at the second graph, you can see that 45% of the 700 graduates went to a four-year college;

that is $\frac{45}{100} \times 700 = 315$ graduates. In 1975, 38% of the 600 graduates went to a four-year college; that is $\frac{38}{100} \times 600 = 228$ graduates.

Getting to the Answer: The difference is

$315 - 228 = 87$ graduates.

16. C

Difficulty: High

Strategic Advice: Don't let problems like this slow you down. If you can't figure it out at first glance mark it to come back to if you have time at the end.

Getting to the Answer: Since we are adding the integers together, the negative integers will negate the value of the positive integers up through 15. So we start with 16 to find numbers that will total 51. We only need to add 16 + 17 + 18 to get 51, so our answer is 18.

17. D

Difficulty: High

Strategic Advice: If the remainder is 2, what number does x always divide into?

Getting to the Answer: 20 divided by x has a remainder of 2, so x divides by (or is a factor of) $20 - 2 = 18$.

The factors of 18 are: 1, 2, 3, 6, 9, and 18.

But if you divide 20 by 1 or 2, there's no remainder. Cross these off the list, and that leaves 3, 6, 9, and 18, so the answer is (D).

18. A

Difficulty: High

Strategic Advice: Add the information in the question stem to the diagram. What can you infer from the area of $ADGK$? What does it mean that the triangles are isosceles?

Getting to the Answer: Since the area of square $ADGK$ is 9, each side of the square is 3 units long. Since $AB = BC = CD$, $AB = BC = CD = 1$. Each of the triangles is right isosceles triangle, so the ratio between the sides of each triangle is $x : x : x\sqrt{2}$. Add this information to the diagram:

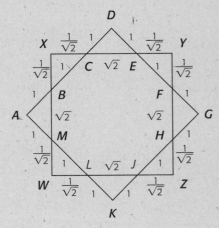

As you can see, the total area of the figure is the area of square $ADGK$ plus the area of the four triangles with legs of $\frac{1}{\sqrt{2}}$.

Each of these triangles has an area of $\frac{1}{2}\left(\frac{1}{\sqrt{2}}\right)\left(\frac{1}{\sqrt{2}}\right) = \frac{1}{4}$, so the total area of the figure is $9 + 4\left(\frac{1}{4}\right) = 10$.

19. C

Difficulty: High

Strategic Advice: Don't let tough algebra problems intimidate you. Often, getting the problem set up is the most difficult part. Then solving the problem goes quickly.

Getting to the Answer: $\_x\_ = 2x^2 - 2$ and $\_x\_ = x^2$, so set them equal to each other,

$$2x^2 - 2 = x^2$$
$$2x^2 = x^2 + 2$$
$$x^2 = 2$$
$$x = \pm\sqrt{2}$$

20. D

Difficulty: High

Strategic Advice: A great beginning to a question like this one is to map out a path that will get you to the answer. By comparing the area of the entire *square* to the *areas of the circles* inside, you can find the requested probability. (Since the figure is drawn to scale, you could also eyeball to eliminate (A) and (B), which are too small.)

Getting to the Answer:

$$\text{probability} = \frac{\text{desired outcomes}}{\text{possible outcomes}}$$

$$= \frac{\text{area}_{\text{square minus circles}}}{\text{area}_{\text{square}}}$$

$$= \frac{8^2 - 4(\pi[2]^2)}{8^2}$$

$$= \frac{64 - 16\pi}{64}$$

$$= \frac{16(4 - \pi)}{64}$$

$$= \frac{4 - \pi}{4}$$

SECTION 4

1. D

Difficulty: Low

Look for the hot words that describe what kind of an artist da Vinci was. There are many of them for a reason!

An artist who is proficient in many types of art forms is able to do many different things. Therefore, the prediction could be "adaptable" or maybe "talented."

Although artists tend to be *demonstrative* or uninhibited or unreserved, the sentence does not describe the emotional aspect of da Vinci's work. Choice (B) does not match the prediction. Nothing is said to indicate that he was unique or obscure. As for choice (C), the details of his artwork are not discussed here so there is no way of knowing if da Vinci was *meticulous*; that is, careful or thorough. Choice (D) is the credited answer. It means adaptable or flexible and matches the prediction. There is no indication whether his artwork was *metaphoric*, or more straightforward and literal.

2. E

Difficulty: Low

Look for the hotwords that define the blank. The semicolon serves as a structural clue that what follows relates to what was said before it. If it was "unquestionable" that his friends had seen *Spiderman*, then the evidence was undeniable, uncontestable, or certain. Look for an answer choice that matches this prediction. It may be helpful to break the answer choices apart by looking at their prefixes and suffixes.

Choice (A) is the opposite of the prediction; it means "not important." Choice (B) is too weak; it suggests that the movie stubs are possible evidence that his friends had gone to the movies without him. Possible is not as certain as "no denying." Jamal's friends were not necessarily proven guilty, choice (C). They had seen a movie and did not do anything that suggests they had participated in a crime or a malevolent act. Choice (D) is the opposite of the prediction; nominal means very small or insignificant. Choice (E) is the credited answer. Break the word apart if you are unsure of its meaning; *indisputable* means not disputable or not questionable.

3. C

Difficulty: Low

What type of a challenge is a marathon? Easy or difficult? In what ways other than mentally are marathons difficult? At least one of the blanks must describe why marathons are challenging. Think of a prediction for the second blank. Marathons are mentally "draining" or "strenuous." For the first blank, decide in what way marathons are primarily taxing; they are a challenge of fitness and bodily training.

In choice (A), although *taxing* (difficult) works in the second blank, eliminate this answer choice based on the first blank. The challenge is not illusory (imagined). In choice (B), neither word fits. The challenge of running a very long race is not *exaggerated* and describing a physical event as being mentally *balanced* does not make sense. Choice (C) is the correct answer. As for choice (D), some runners may see the challenge as *appealing* or interesting, but the process of preparing for a strenuous race is not indulgent. Lastly in choice (E), *strenuous* works in the first blank but mentally *dubious* does not work.

4. B

Difficulty: Medium

Note the contrast word "yet." The first word will be positive and the second word will be negative. What is "promoted" by "healthy lifestyle choices?" The first blank describes the benefits of healthy choices and must contain a positive word. A good prediction is "increased health" or "longer lifespan." The second blank must challenge this remark because busy lives reduce the time people have to exercise and eat right. For the second blank your prediction should be "prevented" or "challenged."

In choice (A), both words are the opposite of the predictions. Choice (B) is the credited answer. Choice (C), *behavior,* is too general of a term. The blank is referring to the results of healthy behaviors, such as an increased lifespan. Although belied has a negative connotation, healthy lifestyles are not necessarily contradicted, but rather challenged by busy lives. Choice (D), *morality* is positive but out of scope and *bolstered* (supported) is the opposite of the prediction. Eliminate choice (E) based on the second blank; it is the opposite of the prediction. *Reproduction* may be enhanced by healthy choices but this isn't what the sentence is discussing.

5. C

Difficulty: High

You don't need to know the meaning of the word "punctiliously" to make a prediction for the word in the blank. What action would "compromise" a stake out?

What words describe a type of mistake? The blank could read "blunder." Eliminate any answer choices that don't match this prediction.

You can eliminate choice (A) because the sentence is not refering to a possible dispute between the detectives. Choice (B), *gibe,* means "jeer" or "laugh at" and does not match the prediction. Choice (C) is the credited answer. A *tryst,* choice (D), is a pact made between lovers and has nothing to do with detectives working on a case. A *tribute,* choice (E), cannot compromise a stake out.

6. B

Difficulty: Low

The first sentence refers to fish farming as a "creative alternative," which matches nicely with choice (B) an *innovative method.* Eliminate choice (A) because the author does not discuss whether or not the technique is

complicated. The environmental impact and practicality of fish farming aren't discussed at all in the first sentence, so both choices (D) and (E) are incorrect.

7. D

Difficulty: High

While you may know various meanings of the cited word, it is important to go back and refamiliarize yourself with its specific use in the text. Here, "sharp" is used to describe the reduction in ocean fish populations due to fishing; later in the passage the author states that such supplies were "starting to run *significantly* short." Given this context, choice (D), *appreciable,* is the correct definition. Choice (A), *piercing,* is a primary definition of "sharp;" primary meanings are often incorrect on vocabulary-in-context questions.

8. B

Difficulty: Medium

While it's unlikely that the passages will lay out the questions that are raised by their content, look at the text to find issues that are essentially left unresolved or words that suggest uncertainty. Passage 1 cites "new research" that questions fish farming and suggests in its final sentence some uncertainty over the lasting "potential of fish farming." Passage 2 also refers to fish farming as a "potential solution" that could make wild fish populations "more sustainable." In both instances, the passages are at the very least questioning the long-term effectiveness of fish farming. Choices (A) and (E) are incorrect because they are only addressed in Passage 1. Only Passage 2 addresses choice (D), and neither passage speculates about a world without wild fish, choice (C).

9. A

Difficulty: Medium

The final sentence of Passage 1 indicates that this author is primarily concerned with how fish farming is affecting wild fish populations. Likewise, the second-to-last sentence of Passage 2 refers to how "premium fish remain on menus" and the sustainability of fish as a resource. Choice (A) expresses the different focuses of the passages. Passage 2 makes no predictions, so choice (B) is incorrect. Choice (C) is a distortion; Passage 2 only briefly refers to fisheries. Choices (D) and (E) are also distortions. Choice (D) doesn't capture the focus of either passage, and choice (E) incorrectly describes Passage 2 as focusing on fish in general, not premium fish.

Questions 10–15

Paragraph 1 states that Brooks' relationship with the earlier poets of the Renaissance was overlooked. Paragraph 2 explains that there were two basic impulses in poetry during the Harlem Renaissance, a romantic and a realistic one. Paragraph 3 says that Brooks's poetry in the 1940s reflected a more realistic view of the problems of poor black women. Paragraph 4 emphasizes Brooks' realism and notes her influence on black artists of the 1960s and 1970s.

10. B

Difficulty: Low

The critics' initial response to *A Street in Bronzeville* is discussed in the first two sentences. These lines tell you that critics praised Brooks's "craft" and "stylistic successes." This should lead you to choice (B), which is a good paraphrase of these comments.

11. D

Difficulty: Low

The question you're referred to ends the first paragraph. That means it will probably be answered or discussed in the rest of the passage. So the purpose it serves is to introduce the rest of the passage. The only answer choices whose first words sound possible are choices (C) and (D). After reading the rest of choices (C) and (D), you'll find that choice (D) best describes the passage.

12. C

Difficulty: Low

This question asks about a detail covered in the passage, but it doesn't give you a line reference. Since questions 10 and 11 covered paragraph 1, you should start looking in paragraph 2. The paragraph's first sentence tells you that the Renaissance poets were proud of their cultural heritage, and believed that the arts were a good place to express that pride.

13. B

Difficulty: Medium

The preceding lines tell you exactly what the poem is exemplifying: The tendency to romanticize black women.

14. D

Difficulty: Low

Another Vocabulary-in-Context question. As always, be sure to check the context. You're sent to the final paragraph where the author discusses influences on Brooks's poetry. The sentence "conditioned" appears in says that although Brooks rejected the romanticizing aspect of Renaissance, she was "conditioned" by its optimism. The word "although" indicates a contrast: if she rejected one thing, she must have accepted, or been *influenced*, by another.

15. C

Difficulty: High

With "primary focus" questions you need to find an answer choice that sums up the passage without being too broad or too narrow. For example, choice (D) is too broad (it doesn't even mention Brooks!) and choice (E) is too narrow (this is only mentioned at the end of the last paragraph). Choice (C) has the right focus—Brooks—and covers the discussion of her relation to the "literary tradition" of the Harlem Renaissance.

16. D

Difficulty: Low

Look through the short passage to see where the images of the Sombrero are discussed. You'll notice that the author describes it as a "composite," "pieced together," and a "mosaic." You can infer that the final image was made up of many pieces.

Choice (A) is out of scope; the author never mentions this. Choice (B) is a distortion; the author says the image was released to celebrate the anniversary of the Hubble Heritage Project, not to prove what the Hubble can do. Choice (C) is out of scope; the comparison in the passage is to the Milky Way itself, not to *images* of the Milky Way. Choice (D) matches your prediction. Choice (E) is a distortion; the author doesn't mention the rest of the *scientific community*.

17. E

Difficulty: Medium

With "EXCEPT" questions, eliminate all answers that are included in the passage. Sometimes the right answer will be a choice that could be true, but is not supported by the passage. Verify each of the statements against the information in the passage.

Choice (A) is true; this is a direct quote from the passage. Choice (B) is true; the passage says it has "ten times" the star clusters that the Milky Way has. Choice (C) is true; another direct quote from the passage. Choice (D) is true; the passage describes it as "massive." As for choice (E), the Hubble Heritage Project is five years old, but the passage doesn't mention when the Sombrero was discovered.

Questions 18–24

The passage traces the development of Impressionism, noting especially the contributions of Claude Monet. Paragraph 1 describes the gradual development of Impressionism under Monet and his colleagues. The author concentrates on the artistic goals and techniques of the artists. Paragraph 2 explores how the development of photography helped create a new role for painting—a role embraced by the Impressionists. Paragraph 3 explores the critical reception of the Impressionists. Their contemporaries disparaged their works, but these paintings today "are some of the most prized works in the art world."

18. D

Difficulty: Medium

A quick scan at the first word of each answer choice can often help you rule out several choices. With answer choices like these, look at the beginning verbs. Think first of the tone of the passage, which in this case is pretty neutral—the author gives a brief history of Impressionism with a focus on Claude Monet. Eliminate all verbs that are not in keeping with that tone.

Choice (A) is extreme; the word *condemn* is too negative. Choice (B) is out of scope; the author doesn't talk about the other painters enough for the word *contrast* to work here. Choice (C) is a distortion; the word *describe* sounds good, but this choice is too specific. The author doesn't talk too much about the paintings themselves, and this choice leaves out the bigger picture of Impressionism in general. Choice (D) explains the overall purpose pretty well. Choice (E) is a distortion; the author never really *argues* for anything here. The purpose is simply to describe or explain.

19. D

Difficulty: Medium

In "EXCEPT" questions you're looking for four *true* statements and one *false* one; the *false* one is the correct answer to the question. Hunt for each of these details in the passage.

Choice (A):"This group…made it a common practice among them to paint the same scene many times in a day…." Choice (B): "…an interest that led him to attempt to paint light itself rather than the objects off of which light reflected." Choice (C): "…using small patches of color rather than the large brush strokes and blended color…" Choice (D): This is the opposite of what happened, as described in paragraph 3. People didn't like the paintings at first. Choice (E): "This freed the Impressionists to find new roles for their medium and encouraged the public to think about painting in a new way."

20. D

Difficulty: Medium

In Function questions, be sure to consider the role of a detail in both the paragraph and the passage as a whole. At the end of paragraph 1, where this phrase occurs, the author mentions that the Impressionists used a technique—patches of colors—to capture the light. This is different, she states, from the large brush strokes and blended color that characterized painting technique to this time.

Choice (A) is distortion; while it's true that the Impressionists painted outdoors, the author never offers a description of the light they encountered there. Choice (B) is extreme; the author says that the Impressionists were innovators, but never implies that the old paintings were inferior. Choice (C) is extreme; you don't know from the passage that *all* modern painters used this technique—you only know that the Impressionists did. Choice (D) is a good fit. Choice (E) is out of scope; this comes from the wrong part of the passage—it's from paragraph 2.

21. C

Difficulty: Medium

With function questions, be sure to answer, "Why?" The author mentions photography in paragraph 2. She says that photography took over some of painting's traditional documentary role, so painters began to think about painting in a new way.

Choice (A) is an opposite; photography filled some of the same needs as traditional painting but the author is not contrasting the two media. Choice (B) is extreme; it is an influencing factor, but not necessarily the most important one. Choice (C) matches your prediction. Choice (D) is out of scope; the description of the critical and public reception of Impressionism occurs in paragraph 3, while the discussion of photography takes place in paragraph 2. Choice (E) is out of scope; the author does mention that photography and painting can fill some of the same roles (documentation), but a comparison of the two media is not the author's purpose.

22. B

Difficulty: Low

Even though the author uses several adjectives to describe photography, you need only one. According to the author, photographs took over much of the documentary role that paintings held previously because photography is faster, more accurate, and less expensive. So, you need a word that means either *faster*, *more accurate* or *less expensive*.

Choice (A) is an opposite; the author says that photography is less expensive than painting. Choice (B), *precise*, is a pretty close synonym for *accurate*, so this is a good fit. Choice (C) is an opposite; the author says that photography is accurate, so this doesn't fit. Choice (D) is out of scope; there's nothing in the passage to indicate that photography is particularly *consistent* (or inconsistent, for that matter.) Choice (E) is out of scope; the author never addresses the *prestige* of photography.

23. A

Difficulty: High

The author writes that "such a critic would be in the minority today." What does she mean by "such a critic"? The previous sentence says that a critic considered the Impressionist painting to be incomplete, so look for an opinion that fits with this outlook.

Choice (A) fits well with the critic described in the passage. Choice (B) is distortion; this is the opinion of the author, not the critic. Choice (C) is out of scope; the critic described didn't much like the painting, and might or might not describe it as *influential*. Choice (D) is a distortion; although the author would certainly agree with this, you don't know the critic's opinion on the subject. Choice (E) is an opposite; the critic doesn't like the paintings, so the word *rightly* makes this a statement that the critic would disagree with.

24. C

Difficulty: Low

Critics and the public are now very fond of the Impressionists, so the word "prized" here means *valued*.

Choice (A) might be tempting, since prizes are *awarded*, but the passage doesn't indicate that awards are given to the paintings. The paintings are well-known, so it doesn't make sense to say they are *discovered*, choice (B). Choice (C) is perfect. Like choice (A), choice (D) is related to the sense of giving out prizes or awards, and doesn't fit here. The paintings are highly sought after, but this isn't conveyed by the word "prized", choice (E).

SECTION 5

1. D

Difficulty: Low

The hundredths' digit is the second digit after the decimal point, which in this case is 8.

2. C

Difficulty: Medium

Strategic Advice: Work carefully using the average formula and this problem should earn you quick points:

$$\text{average} = \frac{\text{sum of terms}}{\text{number of terms}}$$

Getting to the Answer:

Set up the inequality:

$$30 < \frac{x + y + z + a + b + c}{6} < 60$$

Multiply all terms by 6:

$$180 < x + y + z + a + b + c < 360$$

Only choice (C) falls between 180 and 360.

3. E

Difficulty: Low

Strategic Advice: Pay attention to whether a question asks for what could be true, must be false, or, in this case, must be true.

Getting to the Answer:

(A) could be true

(B) could be true

(C) could be true

(D) could be true

(E) must be true

4. C

Difficulty: Medium

Strategic Advice: When presented with a circle, identify the radii of the circle. This will help you draw relationships between the sides and angles of any triangles inscribed in a circle. Remember that the sum of the interior angles of a triangle is 180°.

Getting to the Answer:

Since $\overline{XO}$ and $\overline{OY}$ are radii and therefore equal,

$$m\angle a = m\angle OYX.$$

$$180 - 72 = 108$$

$$m\angle a = \frac{108}{2} = 54$$

5. D

Difficulty: Medium

Strategic Advice: You use different mental skills, such as mechanical, conceptual, or creative, in different questions. Ask yourself what particular skill(s) a question appears to test; doing so will help you bring the proper kind of focus to a question. This question, for example, almost exclusively challenges your ability to translate from English into math.

Getting to the Answer:

Follow directions:

"Subtract 4 from y" means $y - 4$.

"Divide this sum by 2" means $\frac{y-4}{2}$.

"Add 4 to this quotient" means $\frac{y-4}{2} + 4$.

Then merely simplify:

$$\frac{y-4}{2} + \frac{8}{2} = \frac{y+4}{2}$$

6. B

Difficulty: Medium

Strategic Advice: As you read a question, ask yourself, "What could I do with this piece of data?" In this case, if you know that 20 is the total number of marbles, then when you read that "the probability of getting a red marble is $\frac{2}{5}$," you should think, "From this I could figure out the quantity of red." And so on with blues. Once you've done this, what your left with will be the number of yellows—the answer.

Getting to the Answer:

$$\frac{2}{5}(20) = 8 \text{ red}$$

$$\frac{1}{2}(20) = 10 \text{ blue}$$

$$8 + 10 = 18 \text{ red marbles and blue marbles}$$

20 total marbles − 18 red and blue marbles
$$= 2 \text{ yellow marbles}$$

7. D

Difficulty: Medium

Strategic Advice: The best way to do this problem is to use common sense. If there were 4 chairs at all 25 tables, there would be 100 total seats. If there were 1 table with 2 chairs and 24 with 4 chairs, there would be $(24 \times 4) + 2 = 96 + 2 = 98$ chairs. Therefore, for every 1 table with 2 chairs, you lose 2 chairs from the sum.

Getting to the Answer: The total of 86 chairs in the restaurant is 14 less than the 100-chair maximum. $14 \div 2 = 7$, so there are 7 tables with 2 chairs and 18 tables with 4. Double-check this by computing $(18 \times 4) + (7 \times 2) = 72 + 14 = 86$.

Another way to do this problem is to plug the answer choices into the following equation:

$$4t + 2(25 - t) = 86$$

Start with choice (C) since it's in the middle:

$$4(15) + 2(25 - 15) = 60 + 20 = 80$$

That's too few chairs. You have to try a bigger choice. Try (D):

$$4(18) + 2(25 - 18) = 72 + 14 = 86$$

It works! Either way you approach this problem, the answer is (D).

8. D

Difficulty: High

Strategic Advice: The first thing you need to do is find what the tens' digit can be. You are given that the sum of the other two digits must equal the square of the tens' digit and that the hundreds' digit must be 3, 2, or 1.

Getting to the Answer: Therefore, the greatest possible sum of the hundreds' and tens' digits is 3 + 9, or 12. The square of the tens' digit must be 12 or less, and the only perfect squares less than 12 are 0, 1, 4, and 9. Since there is no way the hundreds' digit can equal 0, you can eliminate

0 as an option. The tens' digit can either be $\sqrt{1} = 1$, $\sqrt{4} = 2$, or $\sqrt{9} = 3$. Now count the combinations of numbers between 100 and 400 in which the sum of the hundreds' digit and the units' digit equals 1, 4, or 9. The easiest way to do this is to list the possibilities:

110   123   222   321   138   237   336

There are 7 possibilities, choice (D).

9. $\frac{15}{4}$ **or 3.75**

Difficulty: Low

Strategic Advice: This is a pretty straightforward algebra problem that involves solving for one variable. Work carefully to avoid any mathematical errors.

Getting to the Answer:

$$-6x + 8 = -2x - 7$$
$$-4x = -15$$
$$x = \frac{15}{4}$$

10. $\frac{1}{10}$ **or .1**

Difficulty: Medium

Strategic Advice: You can either solve this problem algebraically, or pick numbers, starting with z.

Getting to the Answer:
$$x = \frac{1}{4}y = \frac{1}{4}\left(\frac{2}{5}z\right) = \frac{2}{20}z = \frac{1}{10}z$$

11. 12

Difficulty: Medium

Strategic Advice: Here you have a figure that is not drawn to scale, so eyeballing won't help much. The area of the top of the solid is much greater than the areas of the sides, so the solid probably doesn't look much like the figure anyway. Don't let the figure mislead you.

Getting to the Answer:

You know that volume is length × width × height, so label the edges accordingly. Assume that the vertical lines represent the height of the solid and label all the vertical lines h. You can also assume that the horizontal lines represent the width and label them w, and the diagonal lines are the length, so label them l. So the area of face I is wl, the area of face II is hw, and the area of face III is lh. This means that you can write down 3 algebraic equations; $w = 24$, $hw = 2$, and $lh = 3$. Now you have 3 equations

and 3 unknowns, and you should be able to solve. It's not obvious how to solve, however, so you'll have to play around with these equations. Adding or subtracting them doesn't get you very far, but if you multiply any 2 of them together something interesting happens. For example, if you multiply the first 2 equations together you get a new equation, $wl \times hw = 24 \times 2$, or $w^2 lh = 48$. Notice that the left side of the new equation is w^2 times lh, which is also w^2 times the left side of the third equation. So, if you divide the new equation by the third equation you get $\frac{w^2 lh}{lh} = \frac{48}{3}$, or $w^2 = 16$. That means that w must be 4, so l is 6 and h is $\frac{1}{2}$, and the volume is $4 \times 6 \times \frac{1}{2}$, or 12.

12. 30

Difficulty: Medium

Strategic Advice: Many of the more difficult geometry questions on the SAT can be simplified by noticing relationships between different parts of the diagram. In this case, knowing the relationship between the area of the shaded sector and the area of the circle as a whole gives us the measure of the angle between AD and CF. This in turn gives us the measure of q.

Getting to the Answer:

Since the shaded area is $\frac{1}{6}$ the area of the circle, the angle between AD and CF is of 360 degrees, or 60 degrees. The angles along CF add up to 180 degrees, so

$60 + 90 + q = 180$ and $q = 30$.

13. 48

Difficulty: Medium

Strategic Advice: Making a table is always an excellent way to approach rate questions.

Getting to the Answer:

Let d be the distance to/from the friend's house, and solve for the time using $t = \frac{d}{r}$:

	Rate	Time	Distance
To friend's	40	$\frac{d}{40}$	d
From friend's	60	$\frac{d}{60}$	d
Overall		$\frac{d}{40} + \frac{d}{60}$	$2d$

Now solve for d using the fact that the overall time was 1 hour:

$$\frac{d}{40} + \frac{d}{60} = 1$$

$$\frac{3d}{120} + \frac{2d}{120} = 1$$

$$\frac{5d}{120} = 1$$

$$d = 1\left(\frac{120}{5}\right) = 24 \text{ (this is the distance each way).}$$

We're interested in the total distance of $2(24) = 48$.

14. 192, 480, or 960

Difficulty: Medium

Strategic Advice: The best way to do this problem is to use trial and error. Just choose three consecutive even integers and see if their product is a 3-digit number. Start with 2, 4, and 6 and go from there.

Getting to the Answer:

$$2 \times 4 \times 6 = 48$$

That doesn't work, so now try 4, 6, and 8:

$$4 \times 6 \times 8 = 192$$

That combination works, so grid in 192. Other possible combinations are $6 \times 8 \times 10 = 480$ and

$$8 \times 10 \times 12 = 960.$$

15. 75

Difficulty: High

Strategic Advice: Since you're starting off with a group of 10 numbers and then removing 2 of them, the highest and the lowest, express the sum of the 10 numbers as the sum of the highest number, the lowest number, and the other 8 numbers. The sum of the 10 numbers is equal to the highest number + the lowest number + the sum of the other 8 numbers.

Getting to the Answer

If you call the highest number h, the lowest number l, and the sum of the other 8 numbers S, you can express the sum of the 10 numbers as $h + 1 + S$. Then the average of

the 10 numbers is $\frac{h + 1 + S}{10}$, which you're given is 87. The average of the eight numbers is just $\frac{S}{8}$, and you're given that that's 90. You want to know the average of the 2 grades that were removed, or $\frac{h + 1}{2}$. If $\frac{S}{8} = 90$ then $S = 90 \times 8 = 720$. And if $\frac{h + 1 + S}{10} = 87$, then $h + 1 + S = 87 \times 10 = 870$. But you know that $S = 720$, so $h + 1 + 720 = 870$, and $h + 1 = 150$. Then the average of h and l is $\frac{150}{2}$, or 75.

16. $0 < a < \frac{1}{8}$

Difficulty: Medium

Strategic Advice: This one requires some thought.

If $2a + b = 1$, what kind of numbers could the variables a and b represent? Could they be negative? No, because you're given the algebraic inequalities $a > 0$ and that $b > \frac{3}{4}$. Since a and b are both positive, and $2a$ and b sum to 1, a and b must both be fractions between 0 and 1. What possible values could they represent?

Getting to the Answer

Well, suppose b were equal to $\frac{3}{4}$. Then $2a$ would have to equal $\frac{1}{4}$ since $\frac{1}{4} + \frac{3}{4} = 1$. You're given that b is greater than $\frac{3}{4}$, so $2a$ must be less than $\frac{1}{4}$ in order for $2a$ and b to sum to 1. If $2a$ is less than $\frac{1}{4}$, then a is less than $\frac{1}{8}$. a is also a positive number, so any value for a that is greater than 0 and less than $\frac{1}{8}$ is correct.

You could also have picked numbers. Since b plus some positive number sum to 1, b must be less than 1, but you're given that $b > \frac{3}{4}$. So pick a number for b that is between $\frac{3}{4}$ and 1, such as $\frac{7}{8}$. If $b = \frac{7}{8}$, then $2a + \frac{7}{8} = 1$, $2a = \frac{1}{8}$, and $a = \frac{1}{16}$, which is greater than 0 and therefore meets the only other requirement you're given for a.

17. .5 or $\frac{1}{2}$

Difficulty: High

Strategic Advice: You may not have talked about equations that look like this in your math class, but try plugging in points to draw a sketch $-x = 3$ and $x = 11$ are good ones to start with, since these are the ones relevant to the problem.

Getting to the Answer:

If you plug in $x = 3$:
$$3 = y^2 + 2$$
$$1 = y^2$$
$$y = \pm 1$$

This means that $(3, 1)$ and $(3, -1)$ are both on the curve.

Next, try $x = 11$:
$$11 = y^2 + 2$$
$$9 = y^2$$
$$y = \pm 3$$

This means that $(11, 3)$ and $(11, -3)$ are both on the curve.

At this point, you could plot the four points and figure out how to get the largest slope possible.

18.   6

Difficulty:

Strategic Advice: Draw some diagrams to solve this question.

Getting to the Answer:

The circumference of a circle is $2\pi r$. Since the circumference of Circle A is 4π, its radius is 2; since the circumference of Circle B is 8π, its radius is 4. The circles intersect at two points, so they must overlap. If they were tangent (that is, touch at one point) with Circle A inside Circle B, the distance between their centers would be 2; if they were tangent with Circle A outside Circle B, the distance between their centers would be 6.

SECTION 6

1.   E

Difficulty: High

Even a sentence with multiple verbs and verb forms can be a fragment; look for a subject and predicate verb in an independent clause.

As written, this sentence is a fragment, since none of its clauses are independent. There is no main verb following the subject *bars.* Choice (E) corrects this error without introducing any new ones. Choices (B) and (C) are

unnecessarily wordy and fail to relate the two clauses. The pronoun *they* in choice (D) has no clear antecedent.

2.   A

Difficulty: High

If you don't spot an error, don't be afraid to select choice (A).

This sentence is correct as written. The verb *offer* is in agreement with the plural subject *movie screenings* and the idiom *both…and* is used correctly. Choices (B), (D), and (E) all incorrectly change the plural verb *offer* to the singular *offers*; additionally, the singular pronouns *it* in choice (D) and *this* in choice (E) do not agree with the plural *screenings.* Choice (C) is incorrect grammatical structure.

3.   D

Difficulty: High

If you don't spot a grammar or usage error, look for an error in style. As written, this sentence is unnecessarily wordy. Choice (D) makes the sentence more concise without introducing any grammatical errors. Choice (B) is a sentence fragment. Choices (C) and (E) are incorrect grammatical structure.

4.   D

Difficulty: Medium

Not all long selections denote wordiness issues, but always check for a more concise version of the sentence.

As written, this sentence is overly wordy. Choice (D) is concise and doesn't lose any of the meaning of the original sentence. Choices (B), (C), and (E) are all still awkward and wordy.

5.   D

Difficulty: Medium

The gerund (*-ing*) verb cannot be the main verb of a sentence.

As written, this sentence is a fragment. Choice (D) corrects this error. Choices (B) and (E) do not correct the fragment error. Choice (C) introduces an inconsistent verb tense.

6.   A

Difficulty: Low

If you don't spot an error, don't be afraid to select choice (A).

This sentence is correct as written. The preposition *about* in choice (B) is idiomatically incorrect with *announced.* Choices (C), (D), and (E) are awkward and unnecessarily wordy.

7. A

Difficulty: High

Expect between five and eight sentences on the SAT to be correct as written.

The sentence is correct as written. Choice (B) illogically suggests that *Mikhail Gorbachev* is a *prohibition.* Choice (C) compares *Gorbachev's leadership* to other *Soviet leaders.* Choice (D) compares *Soviet leaders* to *Gorbachev's laws.* Choice (E) is incorrect grammatical structure.

8. D

Difficulty: High

Comparative idioms require that the items compared be in parallel structure.

The idiom intended here is *more apparent in...than in...;* the items compared must also be parallel. Choice (D) makes both changes. The preposition *in* is placed incorrectly in choices (B) and (C). Choice (E) is unnecessarily wordy.

9. D

Difficulty: Low

Even a sentence with multiple verbs can be a fragment; look for a subject and predicate verb in an independent clause.

As written, this sentence is a fragment because the gerund (*-ing*) verb form can never be used as the main verb of a sentence. Choice (D) corrects this error. Choice (B) does not address the error. Choice (C) is incorrect grammatical structure. Choice (E) is unnecessarily wordy.

10. C

Difficulty: High

Pronouns on the SAT must have clear and unambiguous antecedents.

This sentence has two problems. The verb *being* in the sentence's second clause leaves the clause's meaning incomplete. Also, the pronoun *this* does not have a clear antecedent. Choice (C) corrects both errors. Choice (B) does not address the ambiguity error and is also a run-on sentence. Choice (D) is unnecessarily wordy and misuses the semicolon splice by using it to combine an independent and a subordinate clause. Choice (E) also misuses the semicolon splice.

11. D

Difficulty: Medium

Make sure comparisons are structured to compare logical things.

Here, *teachers, secretaries, or homemakers* are compared to *work.* Choice (D) corrects this error by using the parallel noun *workers.* Choice (B) compares *teachers, secretaries, or homemakers* to *working.* Choices (C) and (E) violate the rules of parallel structure

12. E

Difficulty: Medium

A high percentage of test takers fail to recognize "correct as written" sentences; learn to check each choice methodically.

Choice (A) is an appropriate use of *When,* which will only be correct on the SAT when referring to time. Choice (B) correctly uses an adjective to modify the noun *stumps.* Choices (C) and (D) both use the correct verb tense in context

13. B

Difficulty: Low

Adverbs modify verbs, adjectives, and other adverbs, while adjectives modify nouns.

In choice (B), the adjective *careful* is used to modify the verb *crafted;* "carefully" would be the correct form here. Choice (A) is an appropriate idiomatic phrase. Choice (C) is an appropriate verb tense in context; choice (D) is the appropriate preposition in context

14. D

Difficulty: Medium

In a sentence with multiple nouns, make sure any pronouns agree in number with the appropriate antecedents.

In choice (D), the singular pronoun *it* does not agree with its plural antecedent *teams;* "they" would be appropriate here. Choice (A) establishes the contrasting relationship between the sentence's two clauses. Choice (B) correctly uses an adverb to modify the verb *eliminated.* Choice (C) is the correct tense, since the action it describes occurred prior to another completed action (*kept*).

15. D

Difficulty: Medium

Most idiom questions on the SAT will involve the proper use of prepositions.

In this context, *respected* required the preposition "by"; the error is in choice (D). Choice (A) uses the preposition *of* correctly. Choice (B) is the appropriate verb form with the auxiliary verb *could,* and *that* is correctly used as a conjunction.

16. B

Difficulty: Medium

In choice (B), the singular pronoun *it* is used to refer to the plural noun *binary stars.* Choice (A) is an appropriate conjunction, showing the causal relationship between the two clauses of the sentence. Choice (D) is idiomatically correct use of *when* to refer to a time.

17. B

Difficulty: Low

Two independent clauses combined with a comma splice create a run-on sentence.

As written, the sentence is a run-on. Replacing the comma in choice (B) with a semicolon, or inserting "because" before *he* would correct the error. The verb in choice (A) agrees with its singular subject. Choice (C) is an appropriate preposition in context. Choice (D) is the correct verb form with *school.*

18. E

Difficulty: High

Don't let formal or complex sentence structure trip you up. Check each answer choice in turn, and select choice (E) if the sentence is correct as written.

This is a complicated sentence with a number of clauses, but it is constructed correctly. Choice (A) correctly uses an article and an adjective to modify a noun. Choices (B), (C), and (D) are all correct idiomatic usage.

19. D

Difficulty: Medium

Use the comparative form when comparing two items; the superlative is correct when comparing three or more things.

Since the sentence refers to *all the dresses in the shop*, "most dramatic" would be correct in choice (D). Choices (A) and

(B) are correct idiomatic usage. Choice (C) is an appropriate verb tense in context.

20. C

Difficulty: Medium

Pronouns must be used consistently throughout a sentence.

Because this sentence starts with the pronoun *one, one* should be used throughout. Therefore, choice (C) is incorrect. Choice (A) is proper use of the infinitive. The verbs in choices (B) and (D) are in agreement with their subjects and in the proper tenses in context.

21. E

Difficulty: High

Expect to see between five and eight Writing sentences with no error.

After carefully checking each of the underlined words and phrases, you should see that they are all correct in this sentence. Choice (A) agrees with its singular subject *heart*, and properly uses an adverb to modify a verb. Choice (B) uses an adverb to modify an adjective and an adjective to modify a noun. Choice (C) is an appropriate transition in context and choice (D) is a correctly used preposition.

22. C

Difficulty: Medium

Two independent clauses simply joined by a conjunction make a run-on sentence.

The error is in choice (C). Choice (A) properly uses an adverb to modify the verb *changed*. Choice (B) is idiomatically correct. Choice (D) is in the appropriate verb form.

23. C

Difficulty: High

When a sentence uses a pronoun like *you* or *we*, its usage must be consistent.

This sentence starts off using the first person pronoun *we*, then switches to the second person *you*; choice (C) should be "us." Choice (A) agrees with its plural subject; choice (B) and choice (D) are both idiomatically correct in context.

24. C

Difficulty: Medium

A noun serving as the object of a preposition cannot be the subject of a verb.

The subject of *supports* is the plural *habitats*; choice (C) should be *support*. Choice (A) uses the correct relative pronoun in context. The verb in choice (B) agrees in number with its pronoun subject *that* (referring to *habitats*). Choice (D) is correct idiomatic usage.

25. C

Difficulty: Medium

A sentence can have multiple nouns and verbs and still be a fragment.

As written, this sentence is a fragment, since it has no independent clause. Changing choice (C) to *is comparable to* would correct the error. Choice (A) properly uses an adjective to modify a noun. Choice (B) agrees with its plural subject *writers*. Choice (D) is idiomatically correct usage.

26. C

Difficulty: Medium

In a compound verb, all verb forms must be parallel.

The simple predicate of this sentence is *paints… and… submerging.* Choice (C) should read *submerges.* Choice (A) properly use the participle *employing* to modify *artist.* Choices (B) and (D) correctly uses adjectives to modify the nouns *designs* and *colors,* respectively.

27. A

Difficulty: Medium

The relative pronoun *who* is only correct when used to refer to people.

That would be the correct relative pronoun in choice (A). The verb in choice (B) agrees with its singular subject *bird.* Choice (C) is an appropriate use of *so* as a conjunction. Choice (D) properly uses *preferred* to modify *prey.*

28. B

Difficulty: Medium

Items in a list or a series must have parallel structure.

Here, there are three items listed in a series: *through the courtyard, up four flights of stairs,* and *walks down the hallway.* The third item is not parallel to the other two; choice (B) contains the error. Choices (A) and (D) agree with their singular subjects. Choice (C) is the correct preposition on context.

29. B

Difficulty: Medium

The phrase *argue having* is not idiomatically correct.

Choice (B) should read *argue that having* (or simply *argue that*). The contrasting transition word *although,* choice (A), is used appropriately as is the adverb *in fact,* choice (D). The phrase *such a malady* is idiomatically correct.

30. B

Difficulty: Medium

In order to combine sentences, you must first understand how the ideas in these sentences relate to one another. Each of these sentences refers to an aspect of "Today's technology," so a sentence with "Today's technology" as its subject and the various aspects listed in a series is the simplest and most concise way to combine them. Choice (B) does this without introducing any errors. Choice (A) simply strings the sentences together without relating them in any way. Choice (C) lacks a predicate (main) verb, and so is a fragment. Choice (D) is a run-on sentence, and the pronoun *these* has no logical plural antecedent. Choice (E) is incorrect grammatical structure.

31. D

Difficulty: Medium

There are several ways to correct a run-on sentence, but only one answer choice will do so without introducing any additional errors. As written, this sentence consists of three independent clauses, combined with the conjunction "and." Since the first two clauses have the same subject, the first "and" and the subject pronoun "they" can be eliminated, combining the first two clauses into one clause with a compound verb ("lose…and have"). Since the third clause introduces the topic of the next paragraph, joining that clause to the new one with a semicolon splice is the best option. Choice (D) does this without introducing any new errors. The transition words in choice (B) do not properly relate the ideas contained in the three clauses. Choice (C) is somewhat more concise than the original, but doesn't relate the clauses as well as choice (D). Choice (E) misuses the semicolon splice, which is only correct when used to combine two independent clauses.

32. A

Difficulty: Low

This question type requires you to determine how sentence 8 relates to the rest of the paragraph. Sentence 7 discusses "the customs and traditional ideas of a culture" that "are imbedded in its language." Sentence 8 gives three examples of these customs and ideas. Choice (A) correctly relates the two sentences. Choices (B), (C), (D), and (E) do not properly relate sentences 7 and 8. Additionally, choices (D) and (E) create sentence fragments by making it into a dependent clause.

33. D

Difficulty: Low

Unless a sentence clearly references more than one time frame, verb tenses should remain consistent. Choice (D) corrects the sentence's inconsistent verb tense usage. Choices (B) and (E) do not address the error. Choice (C) misuses the semicolon splice, which is only correct when used to combine two independent clauses.

34. C

Difficulty: High

Eliminating redundant phrases will reduce wordiness. Using both "also" and "as well as" is redundant, and since both clauses have the same subject, "they are…working…at times" is unnecessary as well. Choice (C) reduces the wordiness without introducing any additional errors. Choice (B) replaces the conjunction "and" with a semicolon splice, which is not incorrect, but does not significantly reduce the wordiness. Choice (D) creates a sentence fragments made up of two subordinate clauses. Choice (E) is somewhat shorter than the original, but not as concise as choice (C).

35. E

Difficulty: High

Use your Reading Comprehension skills to answer "strengthen argument" questions. Although the writer indicates that the preservation of cultural ideas is one of the most important reasons for working to preserve endangered languages, she does not provide any specific examples. Choice (E) would significantly strengthen her argument. Choice (A) would weaken the writer's argument. Choice (B) would be interesting, but would not add anything to the writer's argument. Choice (C) is out of scope; the argument concerns the necessity, not the methodology, of preserving

these languages. More examples of the writer's opinion, as choice (D) suggests, would not strengthen her argument.

SECTION 7

1. D

Difficulty: Low

Pick out the hot words: "—ing *doses* of a *vaccine* is—in *providing protection*."

Start with the first blank. Vaccines can either be given or not given. If your prediction for the first blank is "giving," then the second blank should be positive in order to support this answer choice. A good prediction for the second blank would then be "successful" at providing protection.

Choice (A), is the opposite of the prediction. Choice (B), *unsuccessful in*, is the opposite of the prediction for the second blank. Choice (C), *reconstituting*, or *restoring*, doses of the vaccine does not fit. Vaccines are not *restored* (although they may sometimes have to be readministered). Choice (D) is the credited answer. As to choice (E), both choices do not work; giving someone a dose of vaccine is not the same as *disseminating* or spreading it widely. *Unverified for* is the opposite of the prediction.

2. B

Difficulty: Low

If a boat is sinking, what condition is it in? Regarding the first blank, the crew would be attempting to do what with the equipment that would otherwise be lost? Using the hot words to form a prediction for the blanks, the crew would be trying to "save" what equipment they could off of the "struggling" boat.

Choice (A), *qualifying*, or preparing, the equipment is not the same as recovering it. Although the boat may have been *obsolete* or outdated, this does not describe the manner in which it sank or even why it sank. Choice (B) is the correct answer. In choice (C), the boat was *defunct* (no longer functioning) but the crew would not be *exacerbating* the equipment or making it worse. As to choice (D), these words do not match the predictions; the crew would not try to *revitalize* equipment and a sinking diveboat is certainly not *prosperous*. In choice (E), the first choice is too extreme. *Commandeer* means more along the lines of "seizing" or "confiscating" and suggests taking against the will of someone else. *Lucrative* does not work in the second blank as it means "profitable."

3. C

Difficulty: Medium

Look for structural clues. The colon indicates that what follows it describes what goes in the blank; look for the hotwords that come after the punctuation mark.

If the path "meandered…for miles" then it must have "winded" and "twisted" around the riverbank.

Choice (A) is out of scope; the hiking trail may have afforded "panoramic" (scenic) views but this is not mentioned in the sentence. Sentence completion questions will never ask you for information that is not presented in the question stem. As to choice (B), there is no indication that the trail was *precipitous* or *steep*. Choice (C) is the credited answer. The trail did not necessarily *circumscribe* the river (follow it in a circular path); the sentence describes a river, not a pond. If you did not know the meaning of this word, break it apart; circles by nature are round, so to *circumscribe* something means to go around it. There is no indication that the path twisted back on itself or went backwards, choice (E).

4. B

Difficulty: Medium

There are a lot of clues to put together here. The sentence mentions "Shakespeare's plays in modern dress." Some critics don't seem to like this, however ("even though"), because they are interested in historical accuracy. They must think the modern dress is out of place, so a good prediction is *inappropriate*. Choice (B) fits perfectly. Although choice (C) has the negative charge you're looking for, its meaning doesn't fit with the critics' concerns. Choice (A) is close to the opposite of what you're looking for. In choice (D), *timeless* means belonging to no particular time, but the modern dress and Shakespeare belong to specific, distinct time periods. Finally, choice (E) is too positive, since the critics don't like the productions.

5. A

Difficulty: High

The sentence is somewhat ambiguous. Perhaps the headaches were relieved by caffeine, in which case Liz would decide to drink more coffee. Or, maybe the

headaches are caused by caffeine, in which case Liz would decide to quit drinking coffee.

Choice (A) makes sense; if caffeine were giving her headaches, she would want to *renounce*, or give up, coffee. For choices (B) and (C), It doesn't make sense to *subtract* or to *destroy* coffee. In choice (D), if caffeine were making her headaches worse, Liz wouldn't want to *promote* coffee. Finally, for choice (E), *enhanced* wouldn't be used with something negative like headaches. Also, Liz could neglect to drink coffee, but simply *neglecting* coffee doesn't make much sense.

6. B

Difficulty: High

Note the hot words "changed drastically" followed by the example of her change in behavior from "sprightly and friendly" to "disheartened and unaffable." Jidapa seemed to be the "opposite" of her former self. Check the answer choices to see if they match this prediction.

In choice (A), the sentence does not suggest that she became less of a certain way; she changed from behaving one way to acting quite the opposite. Choice (B) is the correct answer. As to choice (C), her change in behavior was a result of the accident but the sentence is comparing Jidapa to her former self and is not discussing the reasons for her change. "The extremity of her former self" does not make sense choice (D). Read back answer choices into the sentence to make sure that they fit. Even if the word were "extreme," the sentence does not suggest that she became an extreme version of her former self (i.e. more friendly or more sprightly). In choice (E), this word does not fit; her behavior couldn't change to become "mainstay" or the "chief support" of herself.

Questions 7–19

Passages 1 and 2 look at the role of the Internet in the 21st century. Passage 1 examines potential developments in Internet commerce and a new beginning for the dot.com; Passage 2 examines the information dissemination potential of the internet.

7. E

Difficulty: Medium

When asked to describe or characterize an author's argument in one word, make sure to characterize the author's tone and pick the answer choice that matches. The author of the first passage uses arguments based on fact, experience, and logic. Find the word that describes them in that way.

Choice (A) is an opposite; the author employs reason, not emotion. Choice (B) is distortion; each argument makes a distinct point. Choice (C) is out of scope; politics never enters the discussion in the first passage. Choice (D) is also out of scope; allegory employs representational characters or situations to portray themes and arguments. This author does not use such a tactic. Choice (E) is correct; this choice suggests an argument based on facts, experience, and logic, in line with the prediction.

8. D

Difficulty: Medium

Some vocab-in-context questions function similarly to Inference questions in that they require you to infer the sense or meaning that the author seeks to communicate through a word or phrase. The author states that many users "had slower dial-up access, which precluded them from fully exploiting the conveniences developed by the dot-coms." The exploitation to which the author refers is an exploitation of a good or service. You should predict that in this context, "exploiting" must refer to use and enjoyment.

Choice (A) is distortion; this refers to the most common use of the word, but it makes no sense within the context. Choice (B) is out of scope; this refers to the noun "exploit," which refers to a heroic or successful act. Choice (C) is out of scope; politics never enters the discussion in the first passage. Choice (D) is correct; this matches the prediction. Choice (E) is out of scope; this doesn't make sense in context.

9. B

Difficulty: High

Don't eliminate an answer choice in an inference question simply because it seems too obvious. Valid inferences often seem obvious, since they must be true based on the information in question. Either your notes or a skimming of the passage for the words "second factor" should point you to the third paragraph of Passage 1. The author states, "The second factor that indicates a dot-com resurgence is the entry of traditional, established companies into the market." He explains that in the 1990s dot-coms tried to provide traditional services and retailing, but now "brick-and-mortar"

companies are using the Internet to sell their own catalogue of goods. Use this as your prediction.

Choice (A) is an opposite; the author states that traditional, "brick-and-mortar" companies will enter "e-tailing" in some of the places where dot-coms failed. Choice (B) is correct; this is an example of what the author calls "brick-and-mortar" companies getting involved in the Internet. Choice (C) is a misused detail; this is the author's first factor. Choice (D) is a misused detail; this is an argument by the author of Passage 2. Choice (E) is extreme; the author states that traditional companies will enter the market, but never states that they will replace dot-coms and take over the market.

10. E

Difficulty: Medium

Characterize the author's tone then vertically scan the first word of each answer choice and eliminate any that do not match. Fully read only the remaining answer choices to find the correct one. Your reading of the passage and your notes should indicate that the author certainly conveys an opinion in this passage, so a vertical scan should immediately eliminate choices (B) and (D) since *describe* and *explain* are too neutral. Further, your reading of the passage and your notes should lead you to predict that the author argues or advocates that the dot-com industry will return. At this point, you should eliminate choice (A) since this author argues for his own opinion, not against someone else's. Now fully read the remaining choices (C) and (E) and select the one that best matches your prediction.

Choice (A) is an opposite; this author argues for his or her own opinion, not against another's. Choice (B) is out of scope; in the first paragraph, the author describes the current state of the Internet economy only as an introduction to the overall purpose. Choice (C) is out of scope; this author does predict which types of dot-coms will succeed in the future, but this is a supporting detail for the second part of the argument, not the overall purpose of the passage. Choice (D) is also out of scope; this author does explain why dot-coms failed in the first paragraph, but the author uses this explanation as an introduction to the overall purpose. Choice (E) is correct; this matches the author's tone and purpose.

11. A

Difficulty: Medium

Some Inference questions are similar to vocab-in-context questions in that they require you to infer what the author's words mean or convey. Reread the sentences in question. Ask yourself, what attitude does the author communicate? The author's prediction, that "we will see how truly life-changing" the Internet resurgence will be, is one of confidence, hope and promise. Now find the word that best expresses this hopeful attitude.

Choice (A) is correct; *promise* conveys the confidence and hope that the author communicates. Choice (B) is distortion; this doesn't make sense in context. Choice (C) is a distortion; the author may find the Internet worthy of praise for what it can do, but the sentences in question do not convey something like *adoration*. Choice (D) is an opposite; *dissonance* means inconsistency between beliefs and actions—the author never exhibits such inconsistency. Choice (E) is also opposite; the author never expresses *doubt* about the Internet. Furthermore, since the author's attitude is positive, you can quickly eliminate this negative word.

12. E

Difficulty: Medium

Some inference questions ask you to interpret what the author means to convey in a certain phrase. As with all such questions, remember not to go too far beyond what follows directly from the information in the passage. In the reference given, the author notes the innate power of the Internet while lamenting its commercial use. Look for an answer choice that conveys the incongruity between the author's characterization of the Internet's power and its actual use.

Choice (A) is an opposite; *frivolous* conveys a lack of seriousness, but this author's tone is very serious. Choice (B) is also an opposite; *ambivalent* conveys uncertainty and fluctuation, while this author conveys a definite and pronounced opinion. Choice (C) is distortion; the author may find the state of the Internet lamentable, but the author never apologizes for it. Choice (D) is an opposite; the lines in question convey frustration and lament. Choice (E) is correct; irony is a situation of incongruity between the actual result and an expected result.

13. C

Difficulty: Medium

When an inference question asks you to describe an author's attitude, first characterize whether the attitude is positive, negative or neutral; then eliminate choices that do not match the predicted tone. First read the statement in question. The author states that the "Internet's potential as a repository of human knowledge" is "greater even than the dreams of the builders of the library of Alexandria." He foresees a world where anyone can query a computer for the answer to a question. The author clearly holds high hopes for an Internet that can hold a plethora of information. Use this as your prediction.

Choice (A) is distortion; the author's attitude is positive, not neutral. Choice (B) is an opposite; this is too negative in tone. Choice (C) is correct; this perfectly characterizes the author's attitude. Choice (D) is a misused detail; this characterizes the attitude conveyed in the first passage. Choice (E) is an opposite; the author's attitude is positive, not negative.

14. C

Difficulty: Medium

Always contextualize the detail in question by assessing its function within the broader function of the paragraph. Go back to the cited sentence and ask yourself why the author references science fiction movies. The entire paragraph discusses the potential of the Internet. In fact, the very next sentence states, "this is the world the Internet is creating." Thus, the detail about science fiction movies must discuss what the Internet can become. Find that in the answer choices.

Choice (A) is an opposite; the author looks forward to this path of development for the Internet. Choice (B) is distortion; *outlandish* implies that the author's vision would be unattainable. This doesn't match the context. Choice (C) is correct; this matches the thrust of the passage. Choice (D) is distortion; the author cites an example of how the Internet can be used in the future, which, according to the author, is different from its use today. Choice (E) is also distortion; the author encourages greater—and more beneficial—use of the Internet.

15. D

Difficulty: Medium

Questions like these require you to characterize a difference between the two authors' points of view. Many wrong answer choices contain an issue mentioned in only one of the passages. If you made good notes, reviewing them alone might be enough to answer this question. While both authors believe in the future growth potential of the Internet, the first author is concerned with its financial impact and the second author is concerned with its impact on human knowledge. Thus, when the first author discusses a resurgence in the Internet economy, you should note that the second author would find this less important than the uses he champions.

Choice (A) is opposite; the author of Passage 2 holds high technological hopes for the Internet. Choice (B) is extreme; the author of Passage 2 disapproves of the Internet's use as *solely* a retailing device, but he doesn't state that Internet retailing itself is *undesirable*. Choice (C) is an opposite; the author of Passage 2 finds such uses relatively unimportant. Choice (D) is correct; the author of Passage 2 finds retail uses less important than informational ones. Choice (E) is distortion; the author of Passage 2 never mentions whether or not the situation would be an obstacle for the Internet.

16. A

Difficulty: Low

Questions like these require you to characterize the key similarity between the two authors' points of view. Remember that the wrong choices might mention something the authors disagree on, or an issue only referenced in one of the passages. Assess each answer choice, one-by-one, checking your notes to find the locations in each passage that discuss relevant material. Eliminate the ones that are not necessarily true based on both passages.

Choice (A) is correct; though the authors differ on how the Internet can impact society, both believe that it can do so. Choice (B) is a misused detail; only Passage 2 suggests this. Choice (C) is a misused detail; only Passage 1 suggests this. Choice (D) is a misused detail; this is a detail from Passage 1 only. Lastly, choice (E) is also a misused detail; this is a detail from Passage 1 only.

17. B

Difficulty: Medium

Good notes will always help you to know the purpose of any paragraph. Your notes, or a quick rereading of the short final paragraphs of each passage, should indicate the generality that both make predictions based on the facts and arguments in the passage. Find that in the answer choices.

Choice (A) is out of scope; neither author presents new evidence in the final paragraph. Choice (B) is correct; this should match what's in your notes. Choice (C) is out of scope; neither author uses the last paragraph to *warn the reader*. Choice (D) is out of scope; neither author presents an *alternative viewpoint* in his final paragraph. Choice (E) is also out of scope; neither author poses a *rhetorical question* in the final paragraph.

18. E

Difficulty: Medium

To answer how an author might respond, research her purpose and tone. Check both of your sets of notes. The author of Passage 2 wants to digitize media and states that businesses can profit from the digitization. The author of Passage 1 never addresses this issue, but does state that the reason for the failure of the Internet economy was the lack of access to broadband. Find the answer choice that reflects these sentiments.

Choice (A) is extreme; the author of Passage 1 states that the Internet economy stalled due to technological and business factors, but he implies nothing this extreme. Choice (B) is distortion; the author of Passage 1 states that the entry of "brick-and-mortar" companies will aid retailing on the Internet. The author never links this scenario to media digitization. Choice (C) is distortion; the author of Passage 1 states that "brick-and-mortar" companies face fewer barriers to entry into the Internet marketplace than do dot-coms. Choice (D) is extreme; the author of Passage 1 states that "brick-and-mortar" companies face fewer barriers to entry into the Internet marketplace than do dot-coms, not that *dot-coms cannot provide traditional services*. Choice (E) is correct; the author of Passage 1 states that the reason for the failure of the Internet economy was the lack of access to broadband. Thus, according to this author, broadband is a useful tool for business applications using the Internet.

19. A

Difficulty: Medium

Questions like these require you to characterize how or why details in the passage show similarity between the two authors' points of view. The author of Passage 1 discusses the Internet solely as a business, or business tool. The author of Passage 2 discusses the Internet's impact on human knowledge. The second author also states that business can generate revenue while furthering global information storage and exchange. You can link that to the first author's idea that the Internet holds financial promise; both details indicate that the Internet can make money, even though the authors disagree on the primary uses.

Choice (A) is correct; this matches the ideas behind these details. Choice (B) is out of scope; neither author discusses whether the Internet itself should be free, and both suggest ways to generate revenue from it. Choice (C) is out of scope; only the author of Passage 1 discusses broadband access. Regardless, neither author discusses broadband fees. Choice (D) is out of scope; although the author of Passage 2 discusses digitizing media and other content, neither author discusses how to deal with *intellectual property* issues. Choice (E) is extreme; while both authors discuss revenue and business to some extent, neither one goes so far as to suggest this.

SECTION 8

1. A

Difficulty: Low

Strategic Advice: Algebra problems that appear to be straightforward may be just that: straightforward. So don't make them more difficult than they are. Focus on carefully working through the necessary steps until you have your answer.

Getting to the Answer:

$$4x + 2 = 26$$
$$4x = 24$$
$$x = 6$$

Plug 6 in for x in the expression $4x + 8$:

$$4(6) + 8 = 24 + 8 = 32$$

2. C

Difficulty: Medium

Strategic Advice: Set up a proportion.

Getting to the Answer:

$$\frac{60}{100} = \frac{x}{20y}$$

Then, cross-multiply to find your missing y-value: $60 \times 20y = 100 \times x$

$$1{,}200y = 100x$$
$$\frac{1{,}200y}{100} = 12y$$

3. B

Difficulty: Low

Strategic Advice: Check each choice, one at a time.

Getting to the Answer:

(A) $x^2 + 8x^2$, equals $9x^2$

(B), however, doesn't: to *add* $4x$ and $5x$, you add just the coefficients and keep the variable part the same.

So, $4x + 5x = 9x$. Choices (C), (D) and (E) are each equal to $9x^2$.

4. B

Difficulty: Medium

Strategic Advice: Remember to follow the order of operations and work carefully, and you should have no trouble with this function problem and others like it.

Getting to the Answer:

$$\frac{(7^2 - 7)}{(7 + 7)} = \frac{(49 - 7)}{(7 + 7)} = \frac{42}{14} = 3$$

5. B

Difficulty: Medium

Strategic Advice: Questions such as this one reward test takers who resist the impulse the rush into calculation and, instead, step back and think about the sorts of numbers they're dealing with. Notice that in each choice, the median is zero. The question then boils down to which choice has an average greater than zero.

Getting to the Answer:

No calculations are necessary to determine that in (A), (C), and (E), the average is zero. (A) is a set of evenly spaced numbers—in such a situation the median and the average are equal. (C) and (E) are merely variations on this theme: in each case, the middle three numbers are evenly spaced, and the numbers on either end of the set are equally spaced from the median. The effect of this arrangement is that, again, the median equals the average. You're left with (B) and (D). In which case would the average be pulled higher than the median? The 3 in (B) pulls the average of that set slightly above the median, while the −3 in (D) pulls the average of that set slightly below the median.

6. C

Difficulty: Medium

Strategic Advice: Questions such as this one assess your ability to perform multi-step operations. Move quickly but carefully, and pay attention to where you're going.

Getting to the Answer:

$$0.4(210) = 84$$

$$84 = 33\tfrac{1}{3}\%(?)$$

$$84 = \dfrac{\frac{100}{3}}{100}(?)$$

$$? = (84)\left(\dfrac{100}{\frac{100}{3}} \right) = (84)(3) = 252$$

7. D

Difficulty: Medium

Strategic Advice: You'll need to bring your knowledge of the properties of triangles and parallel lines into play if you want to solve this question.

Getting to the Answer:

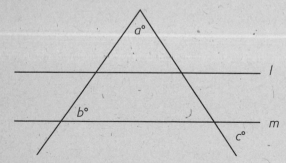

If $c = 50$, the angle vertical to it also equals 50.
The angles of a triangle must add up to 180, so

$$a + b + 50 = 180, \text{ and}$$

$$a + b = 130.$$

Solve for a and you find that $a = 130 - b$, choice (D).

8. C

Difficulty: Medium

Strategic Advice: Questions involving minimum and maximum values can seem intimidating on first glance, but often, as in this case, boil down to a few simple scenarios.

Getting to the Answer:

First try the possible scenarios:

$$3x + y = 17$$
$$3(1) + (14) = 17$$
$$3(2) + (11) = 17$$
$$3(3) + (8) = 17$$
$$3(4) + (5) = 17$$
$$3(5) + (2) = 17$$

Now find the range of y: $14 - 2 = 12$

9. E

Difficulty: Medium

Strategic Advice: If you forget your percent formulas, this is also an excellent problem for an educated guess. You know that 40 percent of something is substantially less than 70 percent of the same thing, so the best answer is probably either choice (D) or (E).

Getting to the Answer:

$$percent = \dfrac{part}{whole} \times 100$$

Call the unknown whole x.

$$70 = 100\left(\dfrac{2,100}{x}\right)$$

$$70x = 100(2,100)$$

$$x = \dfrac{100(2,100)}{70}$$

$$x = 3,000$$

$$percent = \dfrac{part}{whole} \times 100$$

Call the unknown part y.

$$40 = \dfrac{y}{3,000} \times 100$$

$$40 = \dfrac{100y}{3,000}$$

$$40 = \dfrac{1}{30}y$$

$$y = 1,200$$

10. B

Difficulty: Medium

Strategic Advice: The time difference between Littleville and Williamshire is 5 hours, with Williamshire time being 5 hours later than Littleville time.

Getting to the Answer:

If the first satellite reaches Williamshire at 6 P.M., then it is 1 P.M. in Littleville, so the trip took 6 hours. If the second satellite is in Williamshire at noon and also takes 6 hours, then it reaches Littleville at 6 P.M. Williamshire time, or 1 P.M. Littleville time.

11. C

Difficulty: Medium

Strategic Advice: The volume V of a sphere is related to its radius r by the equation $V = \frac{4}{3}\pi r^3$. The original sphere had a radius of 2 inches. The new sphere has a radius of $2 + 4 = 6$ inches. To find how many times greater the volume of the new sphere is, divide the volume of the new sphere by the volume of the old sphere.

Getting to the Answer:

Since volume $= \frac{4}{3}\pi r^3$, this equals

$$\frac{\frac{4}{3}\pi 6^3}{\frac{4}{3}\pi 2^3}$$

$$= \frac{6^3}{2^3}$$

$$= \frac{216}{8}$$

6 cubed is 216, and 2 cubed is 8. Reducing the fraction makes it equal to 27.

12. D

Difficulty: Medium

Strategic Advice: The graph of a function crosses the x-axis when the value of the function equals zero. Find the values of t at which $g(t) = 0$ by solving the equation $t^2 - 4 = 0$. You could also backsolve this problem, plugging each possible value of t into the function to see which ones give a value of 0.

Getting to the Answer:

$$t^2 - 4 = 0$$
$$(t - 2)(t + 2) = 0$$
$$t = 2 \text{ or } -2$$

13. D

Difficulty: Medium

Strategic Advice: When working with exponents, convert the values to the same base. Then you can concentrate solely on the exponents. If you have trouble working with exponents, you can Backsolve.

Getting to the Answer:

$$2^{2x - 3} = 8$$
$$2^{2x - 3} = 2^3$$

Now set the exponents equal to each other:

$$2x - 3 = 3$$
$$2x = 6$$
$$x = 3$$

14. A

Difficulty: Medium

Strategic Advice: Since the populations vary inversely, they can be described by the equation $B = \frac{k}{A}$, where k is a constant. Use the given values of A and B (the population of each species) to find k, then use k to calculate the population of species B.

Getting to the Answer:

$$500 = \frac{k}{1000}$$
$$500,000 = k$$
$$B = \frac{500,000}{2,000} = \frac{500}{2} = 250$$

15. C

Difficulty: High

Strategic Advice: In a substitution problem like this, look for the common term that will help you express one equation in terms of another. Substitute carefully!

Getting to the Answer:

Start with the smallest equation. Express it in terms of c.

$$b = -c + 4$$
$$-b + 4 = c$$

Substitute this into the other equation:

$$a = 3(2c^2 + 3c + 4)$$
$$a = 3[2(-b + 4)^2 + 3(-b + 4) + 4]$$
$$a = 3[2(b^2 - 8b + 16) + -3b + 12 + 4]$$
$$a = 3[2b^2 - 16b + 32 + -3b + 12 + 4]$$
$$a = 3[2b^2 - 16b + 32 + -3b + 16]$$
$$a = 3[2b^2 - 19b + 48]$$
$$a = 6b^2 - 57b + 144$$

16. A

Difficulty: Medium

Strategic Advice: This problem deals with the probability that the fish has <u>both</u> characteristics, so multiply the probability of having long fins $\left(\frac{1}{3}\right)$ by the probability of having a long tail $\left(\frac{1}{4}\right)$. Even if you're not sure how to find this probability, you can reason that it is less likely for the fish to have both characteristics than to have just one characteristic or the other. Therefore, the probability of the fish having both characteristics must be less than $\frac{1}{4}$ (the probability that it has a long tail). This eliminates all but (A) and (B). You can use this kind of logic to narrow your choices down and increase your chance of guessing correctly on many problems.

Getting to the Answer:

$$\frac{1}{3} \times \frac{1}{4} = \frac{1}{12}$$

SECTION 9

1. C

Difficulty: Medium

One way to correct a run-on sentence is to make one of the independent clauses subordinate.

As written, this sentence is a run-on. Choice (C) corrects this by making the second clause subordinate. Choices (B) and (D) correct the error, but are unnecessarily wordy. Choice (E) does not address the error.

2. B

Difficulty: High

Unless context makes it clear that more than one time frame is referred to, verb tenses within a sentence should remain consistent.

The first clause of the sentence is in the past tense, so the underlined verb should be also. Choice (B) makes the correction. Choice (C) introduces the passive voice unnecessarily, and the plural verb *are* does not agree with the singular noun *hour*. Choice (D) fails to make it clear whether *they* refers to *programs* or *languages*. Choice (E) is unnecessarily wordy.

3. C

Difficulty: Medium

Make sure transition words properly relate the ideas in the sentence.

Here, the transition word *as* suggests a cause-and-effect relationship between the clauses that is inappropriate in the context. Choice (C) logically relates the clauses. In choice (B), *the Aztecs* are what is *among Switzerland's most popular exports.* Choice (D) does not address the error. Choice (E) uses incorrect grammatical structure.

4. D

Difficulty: Medium

Pronouns uses should remain consistent within a sentence.

This sentence starts out using the third person pronoun *someone,* the switches to the second person pronoun *you.* Choice (D) corrects this error with the third person pronouns *he* and *she.* The pronoun *it* in choice (B) is incorrect when referring to people. Choice (C) does not address the pronoun error. Choice (E) incorrectly uses a plural pronoun with a singular antecedent.

5. B

Difficulty: High

A possessive noun functions as an adjective within a sentence.

As written, this sentence says that it was *hit songs*, not the Beach Boys themselves, that were *born and raised on the coast of California*. Choices (B) and (E) correctly place *the Beach Boys* directly after the clause; however, choice (E) creates a sentence fragment. In choice (C), the opening phrase modifies *celebration*; in choice (D), it modifies *life*.

6. C

Difficulty: Medium

Ambiguous pronouns will always be wrong on the SAT; pronouns must refer to clear and specific antecedents.

As written, this sentence does not make it clear whether the pronoun *he* is meant to *Professor Schonle* or his *son*. Choice (C) eliminates the ambiguous pronoun. Choice (B) eliminates the ambiguous pronoun, but makes the sentence unnecessarily wordy. Choice (D) does not address the error. The pronoun *his* in choice (E) is ambiguous, and the sentence uses incorrect grammatical structure.

7. A

Difficulty: Medium

Expect to see between five and eight sentences on the SAT that do not have any errors.

This sentence is correct as written. Choice (B) is awkwardly worded. Choice (C) uses grammatically incorrect structure. Choices (D) and (E) fail to properly relate the ideas in the two clauses.

8. B

Difficulty: High

Unnecessary use of the passive voice will make a sentence overly wordy.

As written, this sentence uses the passive voice unnecessarily. Choice (B) puts the sentence in the active voice without introducing any additional errors. Choices (C) and (D) are in the active voice, but choice (C) uses incorrect grammatical structure and choice (D) creates a run-on sentence. Choice (E) does not address the passive error, and uses the pronoun *they* without an antecedent.

9. D

Difficulty: High

Make sure items in a comparative structure are can logically be compared.

As written, the sentence is comparing Ray Charles' *songs* to *his contemporaries*. Both choices (C) and (D) correct the comparison error, but *fuller or energy* in choice (C) is idiomatically incorrect. Choices (B) and (E) do not address the comparison error.

10. B

Difficulty: Medium

One way to correct a run-on sentence is to make one of the independent clauses subordinate.

As written, this is a run-on sentence because two independent clauses cannot be joined simply by a comma. Choice (B) corrects this by making the second clause subordinate and using an appropriate conjunction *and*. Choice (C) is awkward and needlessly wordy. Choice (D) uses a contrast transition word that is inappropriate in this context. Choice (E) distorts the meaning of the sentence.

11. B

Difficulty: High

Nouns like "family," "committee," and "team," even though they refer to multiple people, are considered grammatically singular.

The plural pronoun *their* does not agree with the singular antecedent *family*. Choice (B) corrects this error without introducing any new ones. Choice (C) creates a sentence fragment because a gerund (-*ing*) verb cannot be used as the main verb of a sentence. Choice (D) is awkward, and *are allowed choosing* is idiomatically incorrect; "allowed" in this context must be followed by the infinitive form of the verb. Choice (E) changes the meaning of the original selection.

12. A

Difficulty: High

If you don't spot an error, don't be afraid to select choice (A).

This sentence is correct as written. The pronoun *it* and the singular verb *is* are correct with the antecedent *discovering* which, in this context, is used as a noun and is grammatically singular. *That* in choices (B) and (D), and *those* in choices (C) and (E) do not have clear antecedents; additionally, choice (E) incorrectly uses a plural verb form.

13. B

Difficulty: Medium

A verb must agree with its subject noun, which may not be the noun closest to it in the sentence.

The subject of the sentence is singular (*bias*), so the plural verb *threaten* is incorrect. Choices (B) and (C) both correct this error; however, choice (C) changes the meaning of the original selection. Choices (D) and (E) do not address the error.

14. A

Difficulty: Medium

Expect between five and eight sentences on the SAT to be correct as written.

This sentence is correct as written. An appropriate transition word (*which*) is used, and the sentence is complete and concise. Choices (B) and (E) make the sentence unnecessarily wordy; additionally, choice (B) fails to use parallel structure in the items joined by the conjunction phrase *both…and.* Choice (C) is a sentence fragment. Choice (D) is incorrect grammatical structure.

NOTES

NOTES

NOTES

NOTES

NOTES

NOTES

How Did We Do? Grade Us.

Thank you for choosing a Kaplan book. Your comments and suggestions are very useful to us. Please answer the following questions to assist us in our continued development of high-quality resources to meet your needs. Or go online and complete our interactive survey form at **kaplansurveys.com/books**.

The title of the Kaplan book I read was: _____

My name is: _____

My address is: _____

_____

My e-mail address is: _____

What overall grade would you give this book?   (A) (B) (C) (D) (F)

How relevant was the information to your goals?   (A) (B) (C) (D) (F)

How comprehensive was the information in this book?   (A) (B) (C) (D) (F)

How accurate was the information in this book?   (A) (B) (C) (D) (F)

How easy was the book to use?   (A) (B) (C) (D) (F)

How appealing was the book's design?   (A) (B) (C) (D) (F)

What were the book's strong points? _____

How could this book be improved? _____

Is there anything that we left out that you wanted to know more about?

Would you recommend this book to others?   ☐ YES   ☐ NO

Other comments: _____

_____

_____

Do we have permission to quote you?   ☐ YES   ☐ NO

Thank you for your help.
Please tear out this page and mail it to:

Managing Editor
Kaplan, Inc.
1440 Broadway, 8th floor
New York, NY 10018

Thanks!

KAPLAN

Test Prep and Admissions

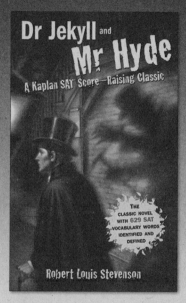
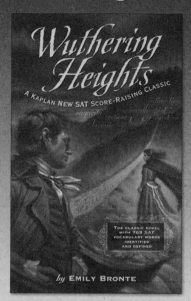
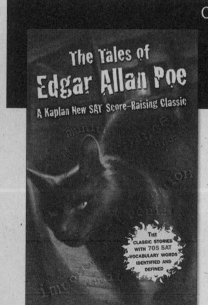